Jiangsu & Anhui
Pages 208–243

Shanghai
Pages 188–207

Zhejiang & Jiangxi
Pages 244–263

Hunan & Hubei
Pages 264–279

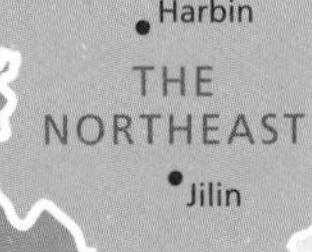

Fujian
Pages 290–299

Guangdong & Hainan
Pages 300–311

Hong Kong & Macau
Pages 312–343

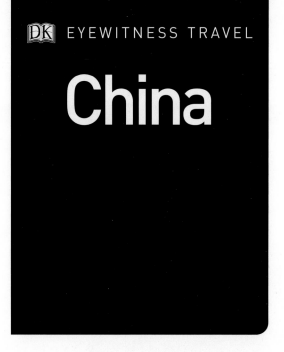

DK EYEWITNESS TRAVEL

China

DK EYEWITNESS TRAVEL
China

Project Editors Hugh Thompson, Kathryn Lane
Project Art Editor Gadi Farfour
Editor Vandana Mohindra
Designers Mathew Kurien, Maite Lantaron, Pallavi Narain, Rebecca Milner
Picture Researcher Ellen Root
Research Assistant Monica Yue Hua Ma
Map Co-ordinators Uma Bhattacharya, Casper Morris
DTP Designer Jason Little

Main Contributors
Donald Bedford, Deh-Ta Hsiung, Christopher Knowles, David Leffman, Simon Lewis, Peter Neville-Hadley, Andrew Stone

Consultants
Christopher Knowles, Peter Neville-Hadley

Photographers
Demetrio Carrasco, Ian Cumming, Eddie Gerald, Nigel Hicks, Colin Sinclair, Chris Stowers, Linda Whitwham

Illustrators
Richard Bonson, Stephen Conlin, Gary Cross, Richard Draper, Kevin Goold, Paul Guest, Claire Littlejohn, John Mullany, Chris Orr, Arun Pottirayil

Printed in Malaysia
First American Edition, 2005

18 19 20 21 10 9 8 7 6 5 4 3 2 1

Published in the United States by DK Publishing, 345 Hudson Street, New York, New York 10014
A Penguin Random House Company

Reprinted with revisions 2008, 2010, 2012, 2014, 2016, 2018

Published in the UK by Dorling Kindersley Limited.

A catalog record of this book is available from the Library of Congress.

ISSN 1542-1554
ISBN 978-1-4654-6910-6

Floors are referred to throughout in accordance with American usage; ie the "first floor" is at ground floor level.

Introducing China

Beijing & the North

Central China

The South

The Dragon Screen, Palace Museum, Beijing

The information in this DK Eyewitness Travel Guide is checked regularly.

Every effort has been made to ensure that this book is as up-to-date as possible at the time of going to press. Some details, however, such as telephone numbers, opening hours, prices, gallery hanging arrangements and travel information are liable to change. The publishers cannot accept responsibility for any consequences arising from the use of this book, nor for any material on third party websites, and cannot guarantee that any website address in this book will be a suitable source of travel information. We value the views and suggestions of our readers very highly. Please write to: Publisher, DK Eyewitness Travel Guides, Dorling Kindersley, 80 Strand, London, WC2R 0RL, UK, or email: travelguides@dk.com.

◀ **Title page** The Great Wall meandering through mountainous terrain **Front cover image** The Great Wall of China **Back cover image** Karst hills along the Li River, Yangshuo, near Guilin

Contents

San Ta pagodas, Dali, Yunnan

Fengxian Si, the largest of the Buddhist Longmen Grottoes, Henan

HOW TO USE THIS GUIDE

This Eyewitness Travel Guide helps you to get the most from your visit to China, providing expert recommendations as well as detailed practical information. The opening chapter, *Introducing China*, maps the country and sets it in its historical and cultural context. Each of the seven regional sections is divided into area chapters that cover from one to three provinces each. Here you will find descriptions of the most important sights with maps, pictures, and illustrations. Hotel and restaurant recommendations can be found in *Travelers' Needs*. The *Survival Guide* contains practical information on everything from transportation to personal safety.

1 At a Glance
A map-based feature introduces each of the seven regional sections, giving an illustrated overview of the area. The map indicates major cities and sights.

Getting Around gives a brief description of long-distance transportation in the region.

Locator maps show the color-coded chapter divisions within the section.

2 Regional Feature
Each regional introduction highlights aspects of the area's culture, history, geography, and cuisine. Fascinating features are sprinkled throughout the area chapters as well.

3 Chapter Introduction
Each chapter is coded a different color. For easy reference, all sights in the area are numbered and plotted on a map. The black bullet numbers also indicate the order in which the sights are covered in the chapter.

A map shows cities, passenger rail routes, and all major roads.

4 Town Map

Within each chapter, important towns and cities are described in detail, and numerous sights recommended. A Visitors' Checklist gives practical information and a handy map locates the main sights and transportation hubs.

Visitors' Checklist provides the address, opening times, transport information, and more.

A sight list corresponds to the bullets on the map.

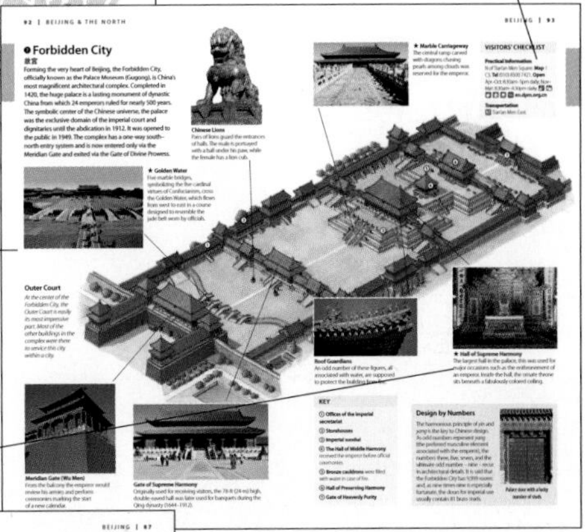

5 Major Sights

Historic buildings are intricately illustrated; museums have color-coded floor plans to help locate the best exhibits; and natural parks have maps with walking routes.

Stars indicate the features that no visitor should miss.

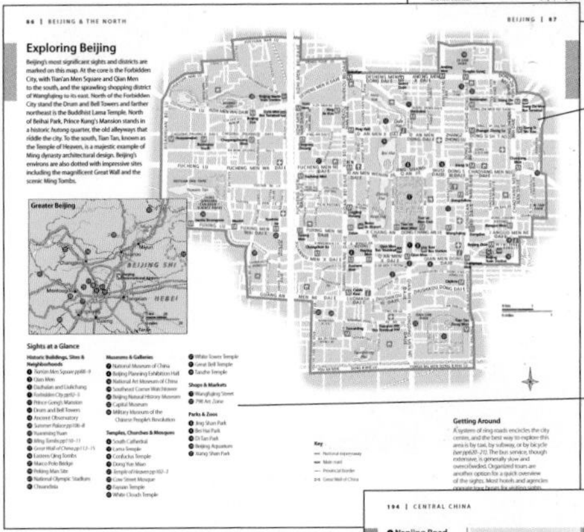

6 Major City Map

Beijing, Hong Kong, and Shanghai each have their own chapters with introductory maps – sights are plotted with numbered bullets. Hong Kong and Beijing have detailed *Street Finder* maps as well.

Bulleted sights are listed in alphabetical order.

Each chapter has color-coded thumb tabs. See the inside front cover for a map showing all chapters.

7 Detailed Information

A description is given for each main sight, along with practical information and it's name in Chinese characters. The entries appear in the same order as the numbering on the map at the beginning of the chapter.

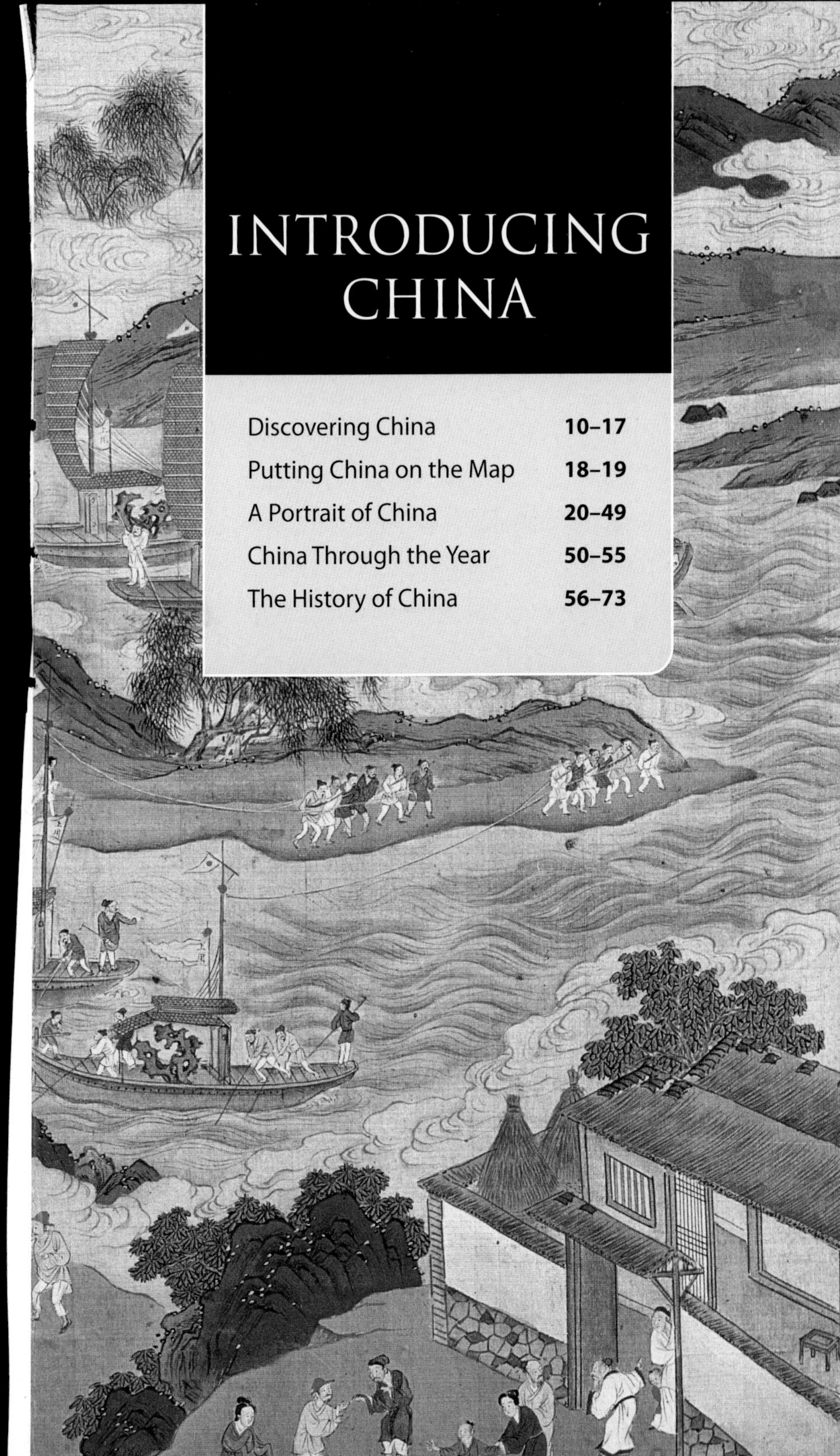

INTRODUCING CHINA

DISCOVERING CHINA

The following itineraries have been designed to take in as many of China's highlights as possible, while minimizing long-distance travel. First are three two-day tours of the country's most iconic cities: Beijing, Shanghai, and Hong Kong. The itineraries can be followed individually or combined to form a week-long tour. Extra suggestions are provided for those who wish to extend their stay to ten days. Next come two seven-day tours, covering two beautiful areas of southwest China. These can be combined to make a fascinating two-week journey across the region. Finally, there is a two-week itinerary that traces the ancient Silk Road from Xi'an to Kashgar. Pick, combine, and follow your favorite itineraries, or simply dip in and out and be inspired.

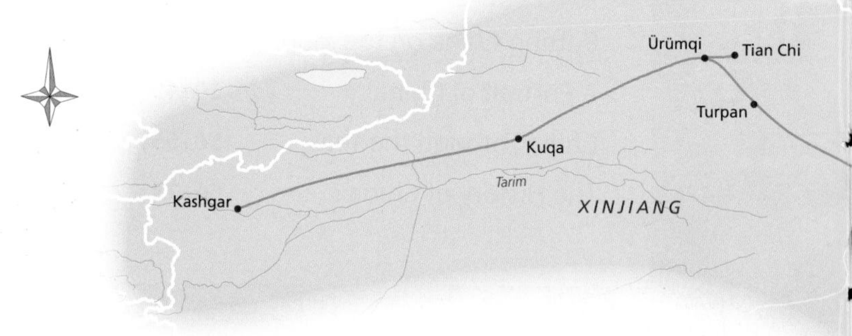

0 kilometers 300

0 miles 300

Key

- A Week in Guangxi and Yunnan
- A Week in Sichuan and Chongqing
- Two Weeks on the Silk Road

Two Weeks on the Silk Road

- Discover China's ancient imperial capital, **Xi'an**, see the **Terracotta Army**, and explore the **Muslim Quarter**.
- Visit the Buddhist caves at **Dunhuang** and **Maiji Shan**, their centuries-old art preserved by their inaccessibility.
- Gaze west across the desert from **Jiayuguan Fort**, the last outpost along the Great Wall; do not miss **Xuanbi Changcheng**, a restored section of wall nearby.
- Relax under shady grape vines in **Turpan**, and explore the atmospheric ruins of **Jiaohe** and **Gaochang** nearby.
- Fill up on lamb kebabs, hand-pulled noodles and fruit at **Ürümqi**'s street markets.
- Explore the Grand Mosque in **Kuqa**.
- Wander through fabled **Kashgar**'s old town, and rub shoulders with shoppers from across Central Asia at the huge Sunday market.

A Week in Guangxi & Yunnan

- Float down **Guilin**'s Li River through scenery that has inspired poets and painters for centuries.
- Stroll among limestone karst peaks outside **Yangshuo** and browse the town's bustling night market.
- Sip locally grown tea by the side of **Kunming**'s Green Lake, and explore the city's colonial past.
- Marvel at the weird and wonderful rock formations in Yunnan's **Stone Forest**.
- Travel along the old Burma Road to historic **Dali**, home of the Bai people.
- Lose yourself in the cobbled streets of **Lijiang Old Town**, a UNESCO World Heritage Site.
- Explore the villages in the **Lijiang** valley and take a cable car to the snow-capped summit of **Yulong Xue Shan**.

◀ Detail of a *History of the Emperors of China*, a series of 17th-century silk paintings

Dafo, Leshan
This giant Tang-dynasty Buddha statue was sculpted out of the rock face over a 90-year period, completed in 803 AD, making it one of the oldest and largest Buddha statues in China.

A Week in Sichuan and Chongqing

- Get close to giant pandas at Chengdu's **Panda Breeding Center**, and discover the mysterious remains of a 3,000-year-old civilization at the **Sanxingdui Museum**.
- Visit the beautiful old village of **Huanglongxi**, and marvel at the 230-ft (71-m) high **Buddha statue at Leshan**.
- Relax at a historic teahouse in **Zigong**, a salt-mining town for over two millennia, and discover the fascinating **Dazu** grottoes.
- Watch the frenetic activity at Chongqing's **Chaotian Men** docks and try the spicy local cuisine.
- Cruise slowly down the mighty Yangzi River through the stunning scenery of the **Three Gorges**, stopping at fascinating sights en route.

Dunhuang
Jiayuguan
GANSU
QINGHAI
NINGXIA
Lanzhou
Huang
Xiahe
Maiji Shan
Terracotta Army
Xi'an
HENAN
SHAANXI
Jiuzhaigou
Huanglong
HUBEI
SICHUAN
CHONGQING
Three Gorges Dam
Yangzi
Yichang
Chengdu
Huanglongxi
Yangzi
Mekong
Dazu
Emei Shan
Leshan
Chongqing
Zigong
Shangri-La
Yangzi
Changsha
Tiger Leaping Gorge
Yulong Xue Shan
GUIZHOU
HUNAN
Baisha
Lijiang
Guiyang
Longsheng
Dali
Kunming
Guilin
Stone Forest
Yangshuo
YUNNAN
Hongshui
Li
GUANGXI
Guangzhou
Xi
Yuan
Mekong

The Imperial Vault at Tian Tan, or the Temple of Heaven

Two Days in Beijing

***China's capital, Beijing is home to many fascinating sights, from the Forbidden City to the vibrant street life of the city's* hutongs.**

- **Arriving** Beijing Capital, 18 miles (30 km) northeast of central Beijing, is the main airport. Trains run frequently to the city, 6am–10pm daily.
- **Moving on** Shanghai takes 2 hours 30 minutes by plane, or 5 hours by express train.

Day 1

Morning Start in the heart of the city at **Qian Men** *(p90)*, on the southern edge of **Tian'an Men Square** *(pp88–9)*. Stroll around the square, stopping at **Mao's Mausoleum** *(p88)* to file past his glass casket. Continue north and enter the confines of the **Forbidden City** *(pp92–5)*. Allow at least 2 hours to explore this, the former imperial palace and China's most impressive architectural complex.

Afternoon Climb Coal Hill in **Jing Shan Park** *(p96)* for magnificent views, then walk north to the traditional Beijing courtyard houses around **Qian Hai** and **Hou Hai** *(see map, p87)* and explore this fascinating area. In the evening, relax in a lakeside bar or restaurant, or catch the Beijing Opera performance at **Prince Gong's Mansion** *(p96)*.

Day 2

Morning Head out to the **Summer Palace** *(pp106–8)* on the city's northwest outskirts. This former imperial retreat is beautifully landscaped; palaces and pavilions dot a wooded hillside that overlooks a series of pretty lakes. Climb up Longevity Hill, soak up the scenery from the Long Corridor, and – if you visit in the summer – take a boat out onto Kunming Lake.

Afternoon Back in the city, head to the **Temple of Heaven** *(pp102–3)*, one of China's largest temple complexes, then go shopping at **Hong Qiao Market** *(p118)*. For eating out, pick a restaurant in **Taikoo Li** *(p118)*.

To extend your trip...
Visit the **Great Wall** *(p114)*. Head to Badaling, the most popular section, 44 miles (70 km) away, or to less touristy Mutianyu, 56 miles (90 km) northeast of the city center.

Two Days in Shanghai

Catch glimpses of China's past and future in this exciting, cosmopolitan city.

- **Arriving** Shanghai has two airports: Pudong, 28 miles (45 km) from the Bund, and Hongqiao, 9 miles (15 km) away. Both are served by the metro,Pudong is also linked to the city by Maglev train.
- **Moving on** The flight from Shanghai to Hong Kong takes 2 hours 30 minutes.

Day 1

Morning Begin on **Jinmao Tower**'s 88th-floor observation deck *(p195)*, with its fantastic views. Walk south along the **Huangpu River** *(p201)*, then take a ferry across to the Jinlingdong Lu Pier. A short walk through the old city leads to the **Yu Gardens and Bazaar** *(pp198–9)* and its classical Chinese garden.

Afternoon Browse the shops of **Nanjing Road** *(p194)* and explore the **Bund** *(pp192–3)*, its grandiose buildings a reminder of Shanghai's fascinating past. End the day at a bar or restaurant on the Bund, overlooking Pudong's dramatic skyline.

Day 2

Morning Wander through **People's Park** *(p194)*, a green space where locals gather each day to exercise, gossip, or relax. Spend the rest of the morning at the excellent **Shanghai Museum** *(pp196–7)*. Allow at least 2 hours

The zigzag bridge leading to the delightful Huxinting Teahouse at Yu Gardens, Shanghai

to see the main exhibits, which include ceramics and classical Chinese furniture

Afternoon Stroll east from Shaanxi Road South metro station through the **French Concession** *(p200)*, either along Huaihai Dong Road, with its shops, or negotiating the villa-lined streets to the south. Stop at the leafy French-style **Fuxing Park** *(p200)* and the nearby **Sun Yat-Sen Memorial Residence** *(p200)*. End the day with dinner in fashionable **Xintiandi** *(p207)*.

To extend your trip...
Take the high-speed train to **Hangzhou** *(pp246–9)* and spend two days exploring West Lake and the tea-growing area beyond.

Trellised seating area in French-style Fuxing Park, Shanghai

Two Days in Hong Kong

Hong Kong is a city of contrasts, with crowded, bustling streets and quiet, traditional fishing villages.

- **Arriving** Chek Lap Kok is Hong Kong's main airport, located 22 miles (35 km) from Central. The Airport Express train runs frequently between the airport and Central, 6am–1am daily.

Day 1

Morning Beat the crowds and take the Peak Tram up to the **Peak** *(pp318–19)* early in the day, walking around the flat Peak Circuit for breathtaking views of Victoria Harbour and beyond. Take the tram back to its lower terminus, and walk through the **Zoological and Botanical Gardens** *(p317)* to **Central** *(p316)*, the financial heart of Hong Kong, for a *dim sum* lunch in one of the area's numerous restaurants.

Afternoon Walk through **Sheung Wan's Markets** *(p321)* and along **Hollywood Road** *(p320)* to the incense-filled **Man Mo Temple** *(p320)*, before taking the tram back to Central and catching the iconic **Star Ferry** *(p321)* to **Tsim Sha Tsui** *(p322)* to watch the sunset from the waterfront. In the evening, head to **Temple Street Market** *(p323)* to haggle over souvenirs.

Day 2

Morning Take the ferry to Macau, and explore the center of this former Portuguese colony, starting from the **Largo do Senado** *(p333)*. Wander through the cobbled streets to the **Ruinas de São Paulo** *(p332)*, a ruined cathedral originally built by Jesuits. Then, climb up to the **Macau Museum** *(p332)* and the battlements of the **Fortaleza do Monte** *(p332)*, refueling with delicious Portuguese egg tarts and coffee as you go.

Afternoon Explore the **Barra** *(p334)* to see evidence of Macau's colonial past, before heading south to the Cotai Strip to visit **The Venetian** *(p333)*, one of Macau's most extravagant casino complexes, complete with artificial canals and Macanese gondoliers. Stay around for the evening to sample the local cuisine and watch a show, explore the casinos, or visit Asia's only greyhound racing venue, the **Canidrome** *(p338)*.

Spectators at a show Macau's ever-popular hotel-casino The Venetian

To extend your trip...
If you need a change of pace, head to one of Hong Kong's outlying islands. See **Lantau's Big Buddha** *(pp330–31)*, dine on seafood in laidback **Lamma** *(p330)*, or wander **Cheung Chau**'s atmospheric lanes *(p330)*.

Tourists on Sky Terrace 428 at The Peak, the highest viewing platform in Hong Kong

A Week in Guangxi & Yunnan

- **Airports** Arrive at Guilin Liangjiang airport, and depart from Lijiang Sanyi.
- **Transportion** Take a ferry from Guilin to Yangshuo, and a bus to return to Guilin airport to catch a flight to Kunming. Once in Yunnan, it is possible to travel to Dali and Lijiang by train or bus, hiring a car and driver for local excursions. Alternatively, for greater flexibility, you can hire a car from Kunming.
- **Booking ahead** Guilin: Li River cruise.

This itinerary focuses on two provinces in China's exotic southwest and combines the region's most beautiful scenery with opportunities to see fascinating ethnic minority cultures en route.

Day 1: Guilin

Renowned for its limestone karst peaks, the landscape around **Guilin** *(pp420–21)* has inspired poets since the 6th century AD. While the best scenery is south of the city, Guilin itself is a pleasant place to explore. Stroll along tree-lined Binjiang Lu, and see the remains of the city's Ming-era moats at **Rong Hu** and **Shan Hu** *(p420)*.

Day 2: Li River and Yangshuo

The **Li River Cruise** *(pp422–3)* is one of the highlights of a trip to China – and for good reason. Spend the day meandering down the river through scenery that seems lifted straight out of a Chinese scroll painting, with sheer-sided limestone cliffs emerging from the lush, rural countryside. Finish the day in the small but bustling town of **Yangshuo** *(pp424–5)*.

To extend your trip...
Drive to **Longsheng** *(p426)*, 56 miles (90 km) north of Guilin, and stay overnight at **Ping'an** village, nestled among terraced rice paddies.

View over the unusual landscape of the Stone Forest in Yunnan province

Day 3: Kunming

Fly to **Kunming** *(pp380–83)*, one of China's most relaxed provincial capitals. Historically, the city centered on **Cuihu Gongyuan** *(p380)*, and today many of the old buildings around the lake have been converted to quaint teahouses and restaurants, making this a great place to relax and sample one of Yunnan's most famous products, *pu'er* tea.

Day 4: Stone Forest

The bizarre limestone pillars of the **Stone Forest** *(pp384–5)* are the remains of a prehistoric seabed that was eroded by the wind and rain into the peculiar shapes visible today. A visit to the Stone Forest can be undertaken as a day trip from Kunming, but it is also possible to stay overnight at the site.

Maoniuping (Yak Meadow) cable car at Yulong Xue Shan mountain, Lijiang

Day 5: Dali

Once the capital of an ancient independent kingdom, today **Dali** *(pp392–3)* is a picturesque small town with cobbled lanes and stone houses. Wander the streets, take a boat trip on **Erhai** *(p394)*, or visit the **San Ta** pagodas *(p392)* just outside Dali – the oldest tower dates to around AD 800, when Dali was still an independent kingdom.

Day 6: Lijiang

Set against a stunning mountain backdrop, the labyrinthine **Lijiang Old Town** *(pp396–7)* is one of the most charming historic towns in China. Climb to the highest point in Lijiang, **Wan Gu Lou** *(p398)*, for superb views across the roofs of the old town. Lijiang is home to the Naxi minority, and you will see plenty of evidence of their unique culture around the town.

Day 7: Around Lijiang

Explore the beautiful valley around Lijiang. Drive out to the village of **Baisha** *(p398)* and on to **Yulong Xue Shan** *(p398)*, the snow-capped peak that dominates the valley. From here, it is possible to take a cable car to a glacier near the summit.

To extend your trip...
Continue north from Lijiang, hiking through the dramatic **Tiger Leaping Gorge** *(pp400–1)* and visiting the ethnically Tibetan hill town of **Shangri-La** *(p401)*.

For practical information on traveling around China, see pp614–19

A Week in Sichuan and Chongqing

- **Airports** Arrive at Chengdu Shuangliu airport, and depart from Yichang Sanxia.
- **Transportion** The first part of this tour is most easily done by car, though there are bus services along the same route. The stretch from Chongqing to Yichang is covered by boat.
- **Booking ahead** Chongqing: Three Gorges Cruise.

This week-long itinerary covers an area that is home to giant pandas, dense bamboo forests, and mouth-numbingly spicy food, as well as many important historic sights.

Day 1: Chengdu

Sichuan's provincial capital, **Chengdu** *(pp364–5)* is large but pleasant, with an abundance of excellent, if spicy, food. Work up an appetite with a visit to the **Panda Breeding Center** *(p366)* in the city's northeast, which breeds both red and giant pandas. Next, take a trip to the **Sanxingdui Museum** *(p366)*, full of exquisite archaeological finds unearthed nearby.

To extend your trip...
Take a short flight north to see the stunning scenery of **Huanglong** *(p375)* and UNESCO World Heritage Site **Jiuzhaigou** *(p376)*.

Red panda relaxing at the Panda Breeding Center just outside of Chengdu

Day 2: Huanglongxi and Leshan

The tiny historic village of **Huanglongxi** *(p374)* is a popular film location and an interesting place to break the journey from Chengdu to Leshan. Carved in the 8th century, the 230-ft (71-m) high **Leshan Buddha** *(pp370–71)* watches serenely over the treacherous confluence of three rivers. Descend from his ears to his toes on a steep staircase, or take a boat ride along the river to view the statue from the water.

To extend your trip...
Travel to the holy mountain of **Emei Shan** *(pp368–9)*, and spend two days hiking through the forests on the mountain's flanks, staying in monasteries en route.

Day 3: Zigong and Dazu

Drive through verdant Sichuanese farmland – this region is known as "China's rice bowl" due to the four rice crops each year – to **Zigong** *(p361)*, a longtime salt-mining town dotted with Qing-dynasty guildhalls and temples. Continue on to **Dazu** *(pp362–3)* and the Baoding Shan grottoes, which house a collection of lively, realistic carvings dating from the Tang dynasty.

Day 4: Chongqing

Return to city life in **Chongqing** *(pp356–7)*, a rapidly expanding port on the banks of the Yangzi. Explore the historic sights in the center, then try one of Chongqing's most famous dishes, hotpot. Head to the **Chaotian Men** docks *(p356)* to board the Three Gorges cruise.

Days 5–7: Three Gorges Cruise

During the three-day cruise from Chongqing through the **Three Gorges** *(pp358–60)* to **Yichang** *(p274)*, you can take in beautiful scenery and see the **Three Gorges Dam** *(pp274–5)*. Stops depend on the type of cruise, but a visit to the **Mini Three Gorges** *(p359)* or **Shennong Xi** *(p360)* is highly recommended.

Tourist boats navigating the Mini Three Gorges along the Yangzi River

Two Weeks on the Silk Road

- **Airports** Arrive at Xi'an's Xianyang airport, and depart from Kashgar airport.
- **Transportion** The distances covered are huge, so train travel in a sleeper berth is the most interesting and comfortable option – the scenery is wonderful. There are domestic airports in every overnight stop on this route. Local excursions are best made by hired car and driver, or by bus.
- **Booking ahead** Book all train tickets in advance, since services throughout the northwest get booked up well ahead of time.

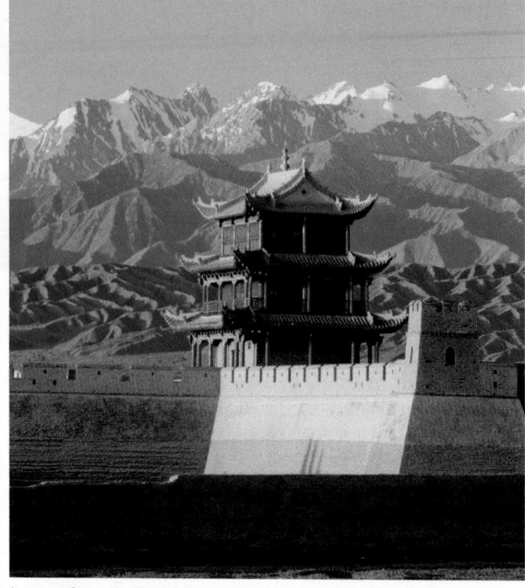
Jiayuguan fort on the Great Wall – once the last outpost of the Chinese Empire

This trip will take you along the Chinese section of the Silk Road, from the ancient imperial capital of Xi'an to the remote desert city of Kashgar.

Days 1 and 2: Xi'an

China's capital for 11 dynasties, **Xi'an** *(pp168–76)* has a wealth of important historical sights. Start at the wonderful **Shaanxi History Museum** *(pp172–3)* for an overview of the region's history, before moving on to see the world-famous **Terracotta Army** *(pp174–5)*, where hundreds of life-size terracotta figures still stand to attention more than two millennia after their burial in the tomb of China's first emperor. Take the time to explore Xi'an's religious sights, from the **Great Goose Pagoda** *(p170)*, originally built to house Buddhist scriptures, to the **Great Mosque** *(p169)* and the fascinating Muslim Quarter.

Day 3: Maiji Shan

Spectacular **Maiji Shan** *(pp484–5)* is home to one of China's most important collections of Buddhist sculptures and paintings. Precipitous stairways and balconies link the caves that honeycomb the sandstone cliff face, with the largest sculptures visible from afar.

Day 4: Lanzhou

Gansu's industrial provincial capital, **Lanzhou** *(pp488–9)* is a key transport link between the Chinese heartlands and the arid northwest. The city was an important stop on the Silk Road. Now home to the excellent **Gansu Provincial Museum** *(p489)*, it's worth taking time to stroll along the banks of the silt-laden Yellow River, which flows through the city.

To extend your trip...
Head south to the Tibetan town of **Xiahe** *(p486)* and watch Gelugpa monks praying at the beautiful **Labrang Monastery** *(p487)*.

Days 5 and 6: Jiayuguan

At the western end of the Great Wall, **Jiayuguan** *(p494)* was historically the last outpost of the Chinese Empire. Climb the ramparts of **Jiayuguan Fort** *(pp496–7)*, which dominates the narrow plain between two mountain ranges. Built in 1372, the fort controlled the only viable route between China and the oases of Central Asia and was of vital strategic importance. In the desert around Jiayuguan are a number of interesting Great Wall-related sites, including the **Great Wall Museum** and **Xuanbi Changcheng** *(p494)*.

The Terracotta Army standing to attention in Xi'an

For practical information on traveling around China, see pp614–19

Silk fabrics on sale at the Sunday market in Kashgar, Xinjiang province

Days 7 and 8: Dunhuang
A small oasis town, **Dunhuang** *(p498)* has two major draws for visitors. Most famously, the town is close to the **Mogao Caves** *(p501)*, a fabulous collection of centuries-old cave paintings and statues that have survived thanks to Dunhuang's arid climate. Less well known is the stunning desert scenery just south of the town, at **Mingsha Shan** *(p498)*, where sand dunes several hundred feet high loom over the edge of the oasis.

Days 9 and 10: Turpan
While modern-day **Turpan** *(pp508–9)* is a sleepy agricultural town that produces the sweetest grapes in China, echoes of a more vibrant past can be found in the nearby ruins of **Jiaohe** *(p508)* and **Gaochang** *(p509)*, both of which were abandoned to the desert sands over 500 years ago. Turpan is the hottest place in China, so if you visit during the summer, you may want to do nothing more than sip cooling drinks beneath the grape vines.

Day 11: Ürümqi
Capital of Xinjiang, **Ürümqi** *(p510)* is an interesting modern city, where Han, Uighur, and other ethnic minority cultures mingle; **Xinjiang Provincial Museum** *(p510)* has an excellent exhibit on the region's minorities, as well as a collection of preserved corpses found in Xinjiang's desert sands. The city is low on tourist attractions, but the parks, streets, and bazaars still provide plenty of interest.

To extend your trip...
Surrounded by forested mountains, **Tian Chi** *(p510)* offers a respite from north-west China's arid landscape.

Day 12: Kuqa
Until the 8th century, **Kuqa** *(p513)* was a thriving center of Buddhist scholarship. The town today is small and busy, and the strongly Uighur western end of town is a fascinating place to wander. It's also worth making the effort to visit the ruins of **Subashi** or the **Thousand Buddha Caves** *(both p513)*, both located outside the city.

Days 13 and 14: Kashgar
At the foot of the Pamirs, **Kashgar** *(pp514–15)* only became part of the Chinese Empire in the 18th century, and the different influences are very clear. Try to arrive in time for the Sunday market, when everything from camels to Iranian saffron is on sale and as many as 20,000 people descend on the city. While Kashgar Old Town has been redeveloped, it still retains plenty of charm, with the call to prayer booming out from the **Id Kah Mosque** *(p514)* and the scent of roasting lamb filling the air. Of the nearby sights, the **Aba Khoja Mausoleum** *(pp516–17)* is the most interesting and a beautiful example of Islamic architecture on the edge of China.

Beautiful wall paintings in the Mogao Caves near the small town of Dunhuang

Putting China on the Map

Stretching over 30 degrees of latitude and covering 3.7 million sq miles (9.6 million sq km) of land, the People's Republic of China is one of the largest countries in the world with almost 20 per cent of the planet's population. It is bordered by 14 countries and has a 12,400-mile (20,000-km) long Pacific coastline. The two largest cities – Beijing and Shanghai – have over 40 million inhabitants between them.

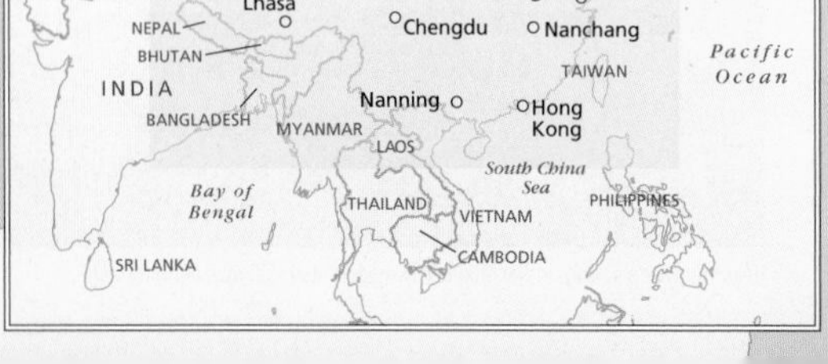

Central and Eastern Asia

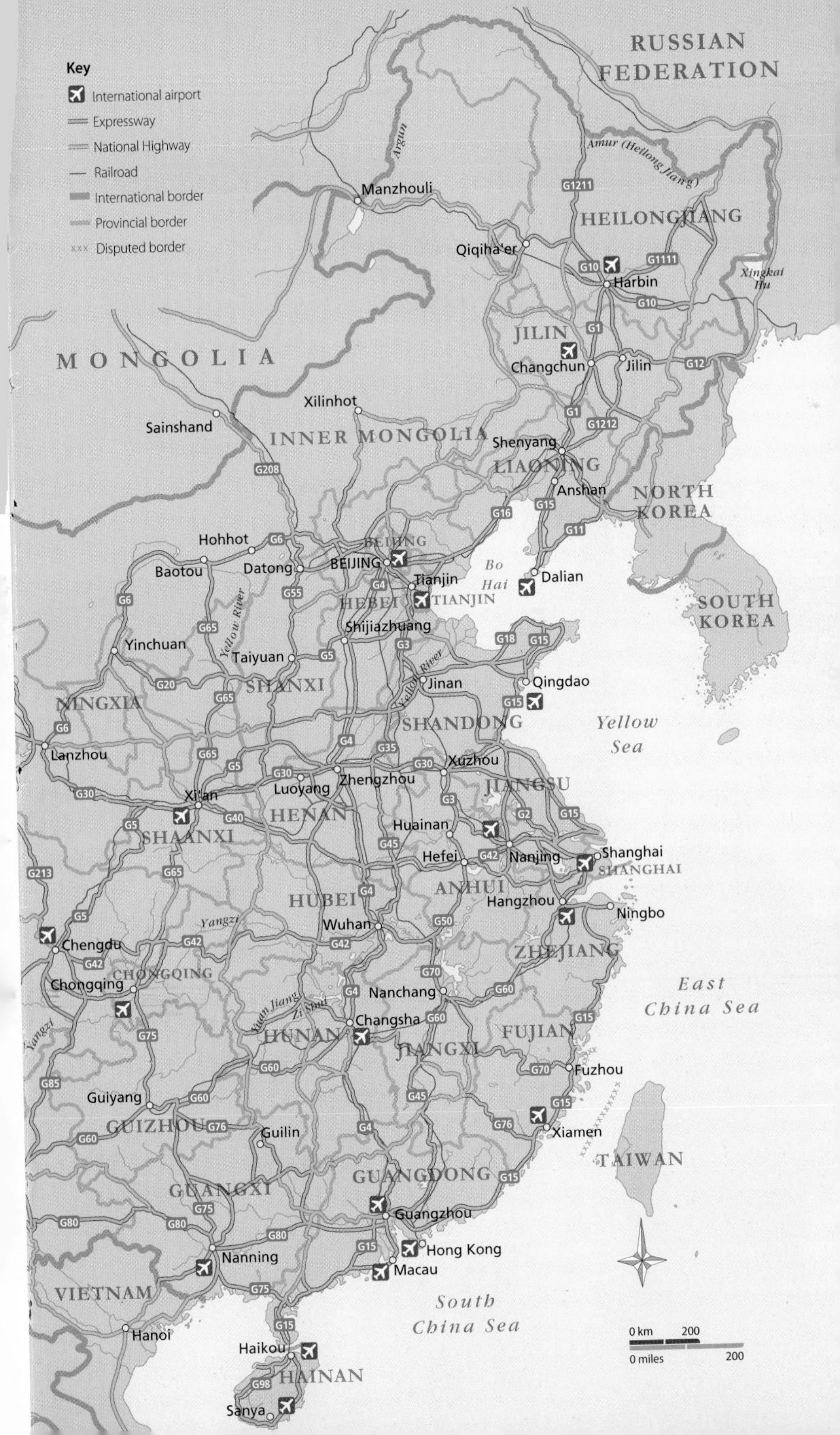

Key
International airport
Expressway
National Highway
Railroad
International border
Provincial border
xxx Disputed border

RUSSIAN FEDERATION
Argun
Amur (Heilong Jiang)
Manzhouli
G1211
HEILONGJIANG
Qiqiha'er
G10
G1111
Harbin
Xingkai Hu
G10
G1
JILIN
Changchun
Jilin
G12
MONGOLIA
Xilinhot
Sainshand
INNER MONGOLIA
G1
G1212
Shenyang
LIAONING
G208
Anshan
NORTH KOREA
G15
G16
G11
Hohhot
G6
BEIJING
Baotou
Datong
BEIJING
Bo Hai
Dalian
G4
Tianjin
G6
G55
HEBEI
TIANJIN
SOUTH KOREA
Yellow River
G65
Shijiazhuang
Yinchuan
G3
G18
G15
Taiyuan
G5
Yellow River
G20
SHANXI
Jinan
Qingdao
NINGXIA
G65
G15
SHANDONG
Yellow Sea
G6
G4
G35
Lanzhou
G65
G5
G30
G30
Xuzhou
Luoyang
Zhengzhou
G30
Xi'an
JIANGSU
G3
G40
HENAN
G2
G15
G5
Huainan
SHAANXI
G45
Nanjing
Shanghai
Hefei
G42
SHANGHAI
G213
G65
ANHUI
G4
HUBEI
Hangzhou
Ningbo
G5
Yangzi
Wuhan
G50
Chengdu
G42
G42
ZHEJIANG
G42
CHONGQING
G70
Chongqing
G4
Nanchang
G60
East China Sea
Yuan Jiang
Zi Shui
Yangzi
Changsha
G60
G15
G75
HUNAN
FUJIAN
JIANGXI
G60
G70
Fuzhou
G85
G45
Guiyang
G60
G15
G76
G76
Xiamen
GUIZHOU
G4
G60
Guilin
TAIWAN
GUANGDONG
G15
GUANGXI
G75
Guangzhou
G80
G80
G80
Nanning
G15
Hong Kong
Macau
VIETNAM
G75
South China Sea
Hanoi
G15
Haikou
0 km 200
0 miles 200
G98
HAINAN
Sanya

A PORTRAIT OF CHINA

Some 40 years after the late Deng Xiaoping's "reform and opening" policy allowed foreign travelers back into China, the country remains largely as mysterious to outsiders as it was in the 19th century, when gunboat diplomacy by foreign superpowers forced the last tottering dynasty to open up the country to foreign trade and exploration.

Drawn by this air of mystery, the number of visitors to China has been rising rapidly. Not one visitor will fail to be impressed by the splendor of China's greatest sights.

The Great Wall has been completely rebuilt in parts in modern times, but its dizzying loops across the horizon still leave most visitors lost for words. The Forbidden City, at the heart of Beijing, draws crowds that make its original majesty hard to imagine, but the labyrinth of side passages still leaves the more inquisitive visitor spellbound. Although images of Xi'an's Terracotta Warriors are familiar, nothing prepares visitors for coming face to face with an army of thousands. While China's incredible economic growth is clearly visible in the urban areas, rural life continues almost unchanged in whole swathes of the country beyond. Not far from the excitement and wealth of the shiny, high-rise cities, water buffalo pull the plow, and donkey carts are still a common form of transportation.

The success of the 2008 Beijing Olympics was a defining moment for China in terms of presenting the results of its economic development to the world and proving its ability to host a huge global event. The legacy of the Games was given added poignancy by the global economy crashing just weeks after. In the years since, China has emerged as a bona fide commercial pillar, not just for Asia but for the world, and a geo-strategic player that is on the brink of superpower status.

The high-rise skyline of Pudong, Shanghai – a symbol of China's booming prosperity

◀ Princess Iron Fan, a popular character in Chinese opera

The dizzying, hill-hugging loops of the Great Wall of China

Modern China

China's vast population, despite famines and civil wars, has grown from 400 million to approximately 1.39 billion in less than a century. This increase has driven a boom in consumerism, most evident in the cities where advertising hoardings for luxury brands and the latest fashions line streets of shops selling fast food, smartphones, and face-lifts.

Shanghai is said to represent the new entrepreneurial China, and visitors will immediately notice the billboards, the office towers, and the scores of glossy shopping malls found across the city. Urban Shanghai received a massive facelift in preparation for the 2010 World Expo, and new office blocks, roads, and metro lines were built. Shanghai's boom has spread well beyond the city limits, with manufacturing hubs and international trade zones sprawling out into the surrounding countryside.

There has been obvious, rapid economic development – luxury hotels, convenient public transportation, and excellent restaurants. However, these welcome refinements have been tempered by the destruction of traditional housing for the construction of highways that are choked with traffic. And yet for some people this commercialism has provided the disposable income to fund a return to traditional hobbies and pastimes.

Today, former occupants of crumbling courtyard houses may find themselves exiled to unfinished apartments in the suburbs, but in the spaces between the blocks, they've revived the tradition of walking their snuffling Pekinese. Songbirds flutter and call from delicate bamboo cages while their owners sit and chat. On bridges over ring roads, old men gather to fly colorful kites – now made from supermarket shopping bags.

Traditional courtyard housing in Lijiang, southwest China

Growing Too Fast?

International architecture on the Bund, Shanghai

As incomes and living standards have risen, so too have China's energy requirements. Almost 80 per cent of China's electricity generation is from coal-fired stations, and this – along with a boom in car ownership – has led to serious air pollution in many of the country's major cities.

With few opportunities for work in the countryside, tens of millions are moving to the cities in search of a better life. Living in poor conditions and often left unpaid by unscrupulous employers, they send whatever they can to families back home. Others staff the restaurants and run a million small businesses from shoe-shining to knife-sharpening. If your taxi driver doesn't know where he's going, it's often because he hasn't been in town long.

More established city-dwellers often blame the migrants for the rise in urban crime (although most countries would envy China's low crime figures), but complain when the services they provide vanish at Chinese New Year due to the workers returning home for the holiday.

Politics

The end of the 20th century saw communist regimes toppled across Europe, but the present government has made it clear that there will be no such change in China in the near future, though a thorough anti-corruption drive is under way. Politics, while almost invisible to visitors, still enters every aspect of life, including the training of tour guides to provide cultural and historical information that supports the view of China the Party wishes to promote.

The Hong Kong rush hour – much the same as in any international metropolis

Vehicles at a busy intersection in Shanghai

Despite the country's undemocratic rule, many Chinese people follow politics avidly. Dissatisfaction is widespread, particularly with regards to corruption, pollution, environmental degradation, and the expensive, rising cost of living. The global recession has hit certain sectors, such as manufacturing, very hard and unemployment is rising.

Family Life

Although freedom of marriage has been enshrined in Chinese law since 1950, it was only in 2003 that the formal requirement to obtain approval from the work unit was abolished. Today, as in the West, urban young people live together outside marriage (which is no longer illegal), and may try a few partners before settling down.

Divorce, unusual before the late 20th century, is now more common, and is attributed to an increase in work demands and extra-marital affairs. Attitudes to children, too, are changing. Long breached by anyone with connections or ready cash, the one-child policy is now being phased out. And there are signs that many members of the urban middle class, a small but growing percentage of the total population, wish to enjoy the treats they can now afford rather than have children. While in the 1970s it was considered fortunate to own a bicycle, now aspiring young urbanites can work towards owning a car and an apartment.

Minority mother and child

Unified by Language

The whole nation may have felt proud when Yang Liwei became the country's first astronaut in 2003, heralding China's entry to the exclusive club of space nations. The government likes to use such occasions to promote Han unity – "Han" is the name the Chinese majority use for themselves, as opposed to the 50 or so officially recognized minorities within China's borders *(see pp30–31)*. There's been a tendency to treat these minorities as unpredictable pets, and their mostly colorful costumes and traditional festivals have been put at the forefront of tourism promotion in recent years. It may not be ideal but it is a great improvement on the forced assimilation of past times.

Popstars performing an outdoor concert in Beijing

Almost everyone is educated in Mandarin *(Putonghua)*, the official language of China, but there are five completely different regional versions of Chinese, and a strong sense of local culture and tradition goes with them.

The Chinese people's common love of food also helps differentiate them, with preferences for spicy, vinegary, sweet, and other flavors being distributed geographically. Visitors to Sichuan and Guizhou will find the locals rightly proud of their uniquely fiery cuisine, while those visiting Guangdong and Guangxi will be astonished at the subtlety and delicacy of Cantonese food.

A space nation – China's first astronaut Yang Liwei

Culture and Religion

While traditional opera is now largely confined to shows for foreign tourists, modern art, films, and popular music have all flourished. Quality varies, but art galleries feature on tourist itineraries, resident students crowd bars to hear Chinese punk bands, and millions around the world flock to see big-budget martial arts epics.

Religion and traditional beliefs are making a small comeback which the government regards warily – it fears organizations of any kind not directly under its control. Many people are still struggling to cope with the end of government-organized everything, and for some the structure of organized religion provides a substitute. There may be many more opportunities to start businesses and make money, and all kinds of employment that simply didn't exist before Deng Xiaoping's reform policy kick-started the economy, but jobs no longer come with housing, healthcare, or any guarantees they'll last.

But the Chinese are used to turbulence, and are incredibly stoic about it. Their attitude to visitors varies from the studied indifference of the smart metropolitans, to the close interest in foreign wallets of the tourist touts, via frank curiosity, and the casual warmth and generosity of everyday folk.

China's modern consumer society – a smart shopping mall in Xi Dan, Beijing

Landscape & Wildlife – West

The west of China is made up of a high, arid mountain plateau and, further north, a harsh, dry desert. These areas are not suited to agriculture and therefore sparsely populated by humans – only animals that have adapted to the conditions survive here. At the eastern edge of the Tibetan plateau lie the mountains and wooded hills of central and west China, home to pockets of bamboo forest – the habitat of one of China's most famous and unique animals, the giant panda. Watered by rivers of melted snow from Tibet, the forests are also home to a great number of other animals, trees, and especially beautiful flowers *(see pp350–51)*.

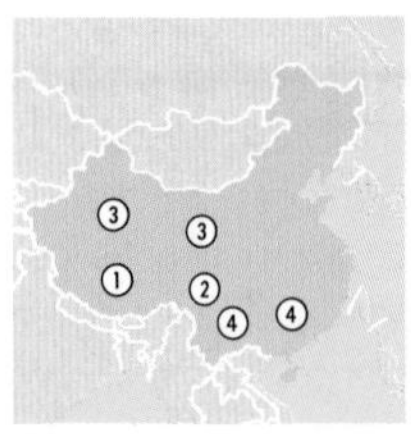

Key

① Tibetan High Plateau
② Mountains of Central & West
③ Deserts of North & Northwest
④ Bamboo Forest

Tibetan High Plateau

The vast, rocky Qinghai-Tibet Plateau lies between the Kunlun Mountains in the north, the Karakoram in the west and the Himalayas to the south. The altitude averages 15,994 ft (4,875 m), making it the world's highest plateau.

The blue poppy is one of the most famous Himalayan flowers. About 15 species of this genus *(Meconopsis)* grow in Yunnan and Tibet, and are used in traditional medicine.

The Himalayan blue sheep *(Pseudois nayaur)* is well adapted to the high crags of western China, where it is found mainly in Tibet, Sichuan, and Yunnan.

Snow leopards *(Panthera (Uncia) uncia)* have thick fur to protect them. Though protected, they are still poached for their valuable pelts.

Mountains of Central & West China

The central ranges have large areas of natural forest habitats, and are major wildlife refuges. Covering over 20,000 sq miles (52,000 sq km), they are home to many species, including the endangered golden monkey *(Rhinopithecus)*.

Rhesus macaques *(Macaca mulatta)* are common in Chinese forests. Though able to fend for themselves, they are used to people, and can be a nuisance begging for food.

Chinese fir *(Cunninghamia lanceolata)* is a common conifer, found typically in mixed needle-leaved-broadleaved forests in high sub-tropical sites.

The silver pheasant *(Lophura nycthemera)* is one of China's most beautiful birds. It is common in evergreen forests and bamboo thickets in southern and eastern areas.

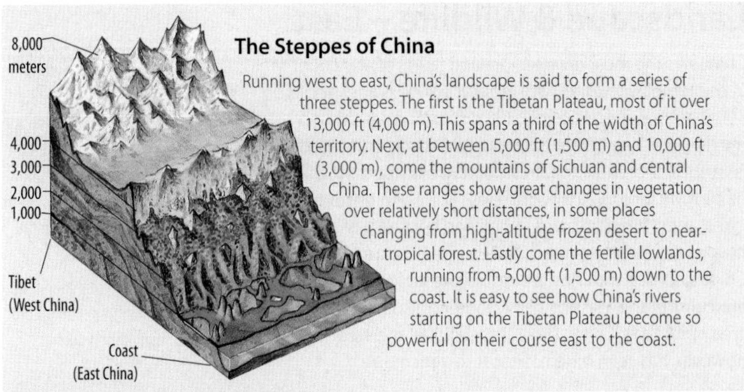

The Steppes of China

Running west to east, China's landscape is said to form a series of three steppes. The first is the Tibetan Plateau, most of it over 13,000 ft (4,000 m). This spans a third of the width of China's territory. Next, at between 5,000 ft (1,500 m) and 10,000 ft (3,000 m), come the mountains of Sichuan and central China. These ranges show great changes in vegetation over relatively short distances, in some places changing from high-altitude frozen desert to near-tropical forest. Lastly come the fertile lowlands, running from 5,000 ft (1,500 m) down to the coast. It is easy to see how China's rivers starting on the Tibetan Plateau become so powerful on their course east to the coast.

Deserts of North & Northwest

Deserts cover about 20 percent of China – mainly in the northwest. This is a challenging environment and few plants and animals are adapted to the deserts: reptiles and small rodents such as jerboas predominate.

Only about 600 of the two-humped Bactrian camel *(Camelus bactrianus)* survive in the deserts of China.

Wormwoods *(Artemisia spp.)* are typical low shrubs of dry steppe communities and can tolerate periodic droughts and even salty soils.

The deserts of northern China, close to Mongolia, are the habitat of the rare goitered gazelle *(Gazella subgutturosa)*; despite its rarity it is still targeted by trophy hunters.

Bamboo Forest

China has some 500 species of bamboo covering about 3 percent of the total forest area. They are found in 18 provinces and are a vital habitat for wildlife. Their almost indestructible culms (stems) are also a valuable resource.

Tall forests of muso bamboo *(Phyllostachys pubescens)* are managed to provide a sustainable crop of culms, which local people use in many ways *(see p417)*.

Golden pheasants *(Chrysolophus pictus)* are native to scrubby hillsides and forests in central southern China, from 2,625–8,200 ft (800–2,500 m).

The giant panda *(Ailuropoda melanoleuca)*, symbol of conservation, is slowly increasing in forest reserves in central and western China.

Landscape & Wildlife – East

China has the most diverse flora and fauna of any country in the temperate zone, with around 30,000 plant species, 500 mammal species, and 1,200 bird species. Although much of lowland China has been intensively cultivated for centuries, there still remain vast areas of important wild habitat, including 29 million acres (12 million hectares) of lakes, and 31 million acres (13 million hectares) of marsh, bog, and coastal salt marsh. The rugged nature of northeast China's borderlands has prevented the loss of its forest to agriculture, and, despite heavy logging, it is the largest area of forest in China. The accessibility of the steppe, however, has seen much of it lost to agriculture.

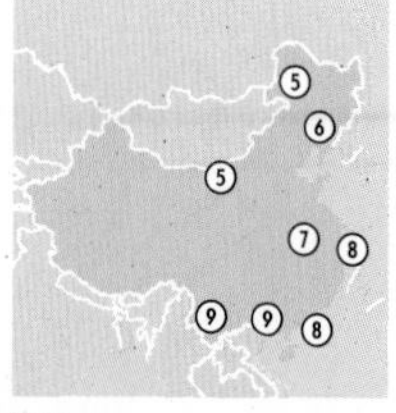

Key

⑤ Steppe Grasslands
⑥ Forests of Northeast China
⑦ Fertile Lowlands
⑧ Wetlands and Coasts
⑨ Jungle

Steppe Grasslands

The specialized grasses and drought-resistant herbs of the steppe are an important source of food for the nomadic herders. In addition, their roots hold together the topsoil, helping prevent erosion and desertification. Heavy cultivation in recent years has led to sandstorms in Beijing.

The steppe cat *(Felis libyca)* is common in the shrubby steppe habitats of the Heavenly Mountains (Tian Shan) of the northwest. It feeds on small mammals, birds, and reptiles.

The great bustard *(Otis tarda)* is, at up to 33 lb (15 kg), the heaviest flying bird. It nests in the open, on hummocks of dry grass.

The saiga antelope *(Saiga tatarica)* is one of the strangest steppe creatures. Its large nose filters dust and heats the air it breathes.

Forests of Northeast China

Forests here consist mainly of coniferous trees. Along with the evergreen fir, spruce, and pine, the deciduous larch is also common. To the south of these forest regions are mixed temperate broadleaf forests, with oaks and birch prominent.

Asiatic black bears *(Ursus thibetanus)* are found in many regions – once even as far south as Hainan. In colder areas they hibernate in winter.

The false acacia *(Robinia pseudoacacia)*, though native to eastern North America, has been extensively planted in China.

The beautiful azurewinged magpie *(Cyanopica cyana)* is a sociable species, moving in noisy flocks through the trees of forests and parks.

Under Threat

Pollution of the air, soil, and waterways is threatening many of China's delicate environments, special animals, and plants, especially when faced with large building projects like the Three Gorges Dam. In addition, the use of rare animals in medicinal "remedies" means that many species face extinction from poaching. However, the Chinese government is now paying some attention to conservation and reports that the giant panda, great crested ibis, and Chinese alligator are all increasing in numbers thanks to the protection of their habitat and improved ecosystems. Nevertheless there is still a long way to go.

Jungle

Tropical forests occur in the deep south of China – mainly on the island of Hainan, and also the basins of southern Yunnan. Many forests are secondary, or have been replaced through felling and grazing by a kind of savanna or by plantations, especially of rubber.

Fertile Lowlands

Intensively cultivated and denuded of natural vegetation, the huge lowland floodplains of major rivers, notably the Yellow and Yangzi, are a seemingly endless patchwork of fields. Grain crops, dominated by rice, are broken up by ponds with fish, ducks, and frogs.

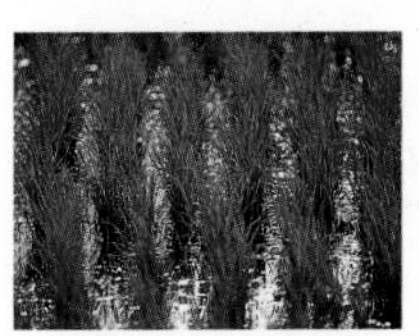

Rice fields or paddies occupy much of the fertile lowlands and hillsides in central and southern China.

The long-tailed shrike *(Lanius schach)*, often seen watching from a roadside wire or pole, is common in eastern and southern China.

Water buffalo *(Bubalus arnee)* are beasts of burden and used for plowing. They are at home in the muddy wet paddy fields of the south.

Wetlands & Coasts

Wetlands are some of the country's most diverse ecosystems, being prime habitats for rare or endemic plants and animals. The lakes and flooded river valleys are also vital staging posts for migrating birds, such as waterfowl and species of endangered crane.

The water arum *(Calla palustris)* grows around marshes and bogs in the northeast at altitudes of up to 3,600 ft (1,100m).

The mandarin duck *(Aix galericulata)* looks exotic and is a tree-hole nester, found mainly along wooded streams in the northeast.

Hawksbill turtles *(Eretmochelys imbricata)* still breed on a few beaches along the southern tropical coast, but are at risk from humans.

China's Peoples

There are about 55 different ethnic minorities in China, each with their own distinctive customs, costumes and, in many cases, languages. Though rich in culture, and varied, together they make up only about eight percent of the population, with the main group, known as Han Chinese, accounting for the rest. Modernization of society and intermarriage are inevitably leading to a dilution of these differences, but many groups remain proud of their heritage and retain their traditional beliefs and customs. Many have beautiful styles of dress (especially the women), and these costumes and cultures have become a major attraction to visitors, who bring trade to communities.

Almost 1.5 million Kazakh Muslims live in the north of Xinjiang province. Renowned for their horsemanship, the Kazakhs center their lives around their precious horses and farming.

There are around 10 million Uighur, a Muslim people with a language close to Turkish. They inhabit Xinjiang province in China's far northwest.

Northwest

A variety of mostly Islamic people inhabit this area dominated by desert, semi-desert, and mountains. The Uighur are the dominant minority and have their own Autonomous Region. Other groups include the Hui, Kazakhs, Kyrgyz, Uzbeks, Tajiks, and Tatars.

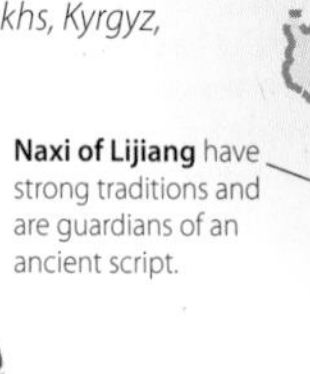

Naxi of Lijiang have strong traditions and are guardians of an ancient script.

Bai people live mainly in Sichuan, Yunnan, Guizhou, and Hunan, and number some 1.9 million. Their capital is Dali (Yunnan). Although traditionally farmers and fishermen, their colorful costumes attract a lot of tourism.

Southwest

The Tibetan plateau is home to more than 6.3 million Tibetans. With around 20 different minorities, the southwest of China has the most ethnic diversity. The Yi, the largest group in this region (8.7 million), live in Sichuan, Yunnan, and Guizhou.

The Dai and Hani of Xishuangbanna in southern Yunnan, in the tropical south, are mainly Buddhist farmers, and have a deep respect for the natural world.

Northeast

As well as the Mongolians, there are a few small groups of minorities in the northeast. These include about 130,000 Daur as well as the Oroqen, Hezhen, and Ewenki. There are also around 2 million Koreans (Chaoxian), while the largest group are the Manchu, with about with about 9.8 million.

The Oroqen are one of China's smallest minorities, with a population of about 8,500. They live mainly in Inner Mongolia and in Heilongjiang province. They live in conical houses with birch bark or skin roofs, supported by poles *(see p461)*.

The Muslim Hui have their own so-called Autonomous Region of Ningxia but have established communities in cities across China.

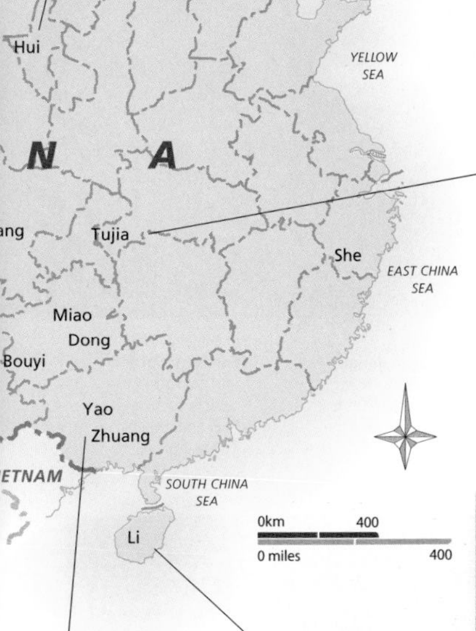

Central & East

The 700,000 She live mainly in Fujian and Zhejiang provinces. They are farmers, with a strong artistic tradition using bamboo. The Gaoshan, numbering about 4,000, are descendants of Taiwanese ethnic groups who settled on the mainland, notably in Fujian province.

The Tujia of Hunan, Hubei and Sichuan have a history stretching back over 2,000 years. There are about 8.4 million Tujia.

South

The largest minority in China is the Zhuang (16.9 million), who live mainly in their Autonomous Region of Guangxi, famous for the dramatic dragon-back rice terraces of Longsheng. They have linguistic and cultural links with the Dai who are ethnically related to Thai peoples. Renowned for their crafts and colorful festivals (see pp412–15), *the Miao (9.4 million) inhabit many areas in the southern provinces.*

There are 2.8 million Yao people.

The 1.5 million Li who inhabit the tropical island of Hainan are best known for their traditional weaving skills, producing colorful woven articles.

Language & Script

The Chinese script can be traced back to the oracle bones of the Shang dynasty (16th–11th centuries BC) that were inscribed with symbols representing words and used for divination. Despite changes brought about by different writing materials, Chinese characters have remained remarkably consistent. It is said that to read a newspaper takes knowledge of at least 3,000 characters but an educated person would be expected to know over 5,000. Since 1913 the official spoken language has been *Putonghua* (Mandarin) but there are many regional dialects. Although people from different parts of China may not be able to understand each other, they can use a shared written script.

Cang Jie, minister of the legendary Yellow Emperor, was supposedly inspired to invent the Chinese script one morning after seeing bird and animal tracks in the snow.

A Beautiful Script

Writing was elevated to an art form considered on a par with painting as a visual aesthetic *(see pp44–5)*. As the process changed from inscribing bone, brass, or stone to using a brush on silk and paper, a more fluid writing style became possible.

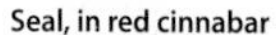

Seal, in red cinnabar – this may be a name seal, or inscribed with other characters.

Oracle bones display China's first examples of seal script. Questions were inscribed on the bones which were then burnt – the way cracks divided the inscriptions was deemed significant.

Writing materials were silk, stone, or paper, which was first invented around the 2nd century BC.

Cursive script *(cao shu)* has strokes that run into each other. Fluid and dynamic, it allows for great expressiveness.

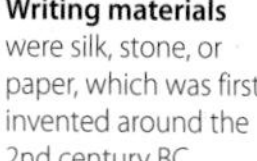

Bamboo slats were used from around the 5th century BC. These were tied together to make the earliest type of books. Used for administrative and philosophical texts, the script runs from top to bottom.

***The Diamond Sutra* (AD 868)** is the world's first block-printed book to bear a date. Printing was probably invented about a century earlier. Movable block printing was developed in the 11th century but had less social impact than in Europe because of the thousands of symbols required.

Chinese Characters

May be composed of pictographic, ideographic, and phonetic elements. The radical (or root), an element that appears on the left or at the top of a character, usually gives a clue as to sense. Here, in the character for "good," pronounced *"hao,"* the radical combines with another meaning element "child." The concept, therefore, is that "woman" plus "child" equals "good."

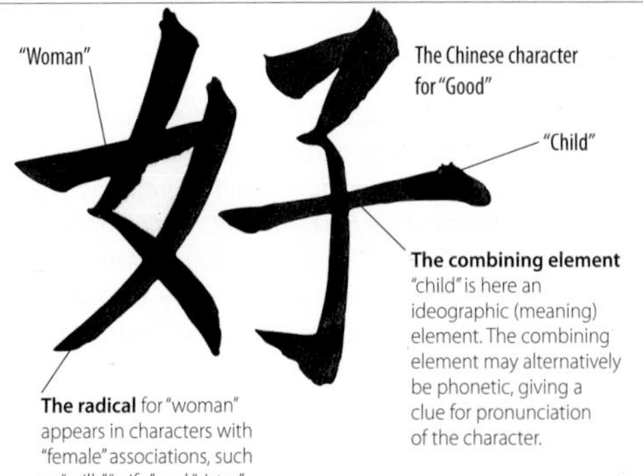
"Woman"
The Chinese character for "Good"
"Child"
The combining element "child" is here an ideographic (meaning) element. The combining element may alternatively be phonetic, giving a clue for pronunciation of the character.
The radical for "woman" appears in characters with "female" associations, such as "milk," "wife," and "sister."

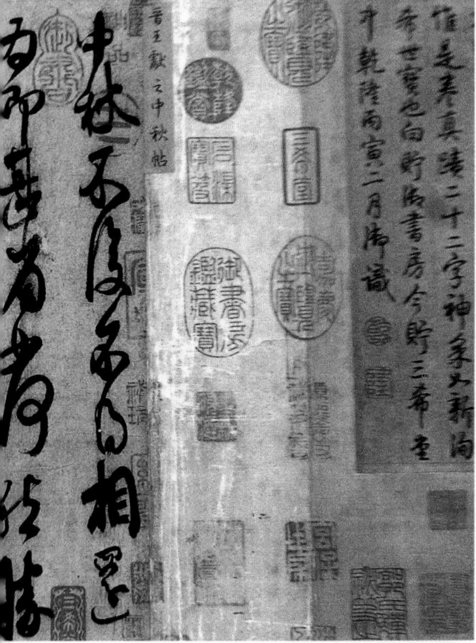

Pinyin is a Romanization system that was introduced in 1956. While Pinyin will never replace the character forms, it is an easier method for children to start learning the language and useful for input to computers.

Styles of Calligraphy

Zhuanshu, or seal script, was developed during the Zhou era and used for engraved inscriptions.

Lishu, or clerical script, probably evolved during the Han era and was used for stone inscriptions.

Kaishu, or regular script, developed from Lishu after the Han era, is the basis of modern type.

Cao shu, or cursive script, (literally grass script) has strokes that are reduced to abstract curves or dots.

Xingshu, or running script, has strokes that run together, and is a semicursive script.

Simplified script was introduced in 1956 to make it easier to learn to read.

Chinese typewriters were very difficult to use. The typist had to find each character in a tray of thousands. Computers have made typing Simplified script much easier – the user types in the Pinyin and gets a sub-menu of several possible characters.

Chinese Literature

Dating back to the 10th century BC, the earliest surviving Chinese texts include poetry and court records. Philosophical works, such as the Confucian *Analects* and Daoist *Daodejing* (or *Laozi*), appeared around the 6th century BC. During the Western Han dynasty (206 BC–AD 9), Sima Qian's *Shiji*, or *Historical Records*, established the genre of literary history; thereafter each dynasty wrote a history of the preceding one. Fully fledged novels began to appear early in the Ming period (1368–1644), and developed during the Qing dynasty. Although the arts were suppressed under Mao, since the 1980s Chinese authors have been allowed greater freedom of expression. In 2012 novelist Mo Yan was awarded the Nobel Prize for Literature.

Confucius, author of the *Analects*, and his disciples

Classics

Post-Qin dynasty, once Confucianism had become the state orthodoxy, five early works were canonized as the Five Classics: the *Book of Changes*, *Book of Documents*, *Book of Songs*, *Spring and Autumn Annals*, and *Book of Ritual*. These books were established as the basis for Chinese education.

The scholar class or literati achieved the status of government official through success in the civil service examinations, based on detailed knowledge of the Classics and accomplishment in writing.

Jia Baoyu prefers to flirt with the women rather than obey his father and study hard to advance his career.

Tang Poets

With early beginnings in the *Book of Songs* and *Elegies of Chu*, Chinese poetry reached its height more than 1,200 years later in the Tang period (618–907). The two greatest Tang poets are considered to be Du Fu and Li Bai. Others include the Buddhist Wang Wei, also 8th-century, and slightly later Bai Juyi (772–846).

Du Fu (c. 712–770) wrote of suffering in war, as well as of family life. His keynote is compassion, considered a Confucian virtue. His poems display enormous erudition.

Li Bai (c. 701–761) was a more ebullient figure. A prolific poet, his favorite subjects were moon-gazing and carousing. The theme of freedom from constraint is a Daoist one.

Epic Novels

In the Ming era, the novel developed from folk tales and myths into classics such as *Journey to the West, Romance of the Three Kingdoms* and *The Water Margin* – a tale of the heroic fight against corruption. Later, the Qing novels used a more elevated language and subtle characterization, culminating in the romantic novel *Dream of the Red Chamber*. These novels contain many characters that recur in other cultural contexts, from Beijing Opera to popular television serials and films.

Guandi, God of War, derives from Guan Yu, a general of the state of Shu, portrayed in *Romance of the Three Kingdoms*. This novel was based on historical figures from the Three Kingdoms Era (AD 220–80). A symbol for justice, honesty, and integrity, his image is found in temples throughout China.

Journey to the West is a comic fantasy based on the pilgrimage to India of the Buddhist monk Xuanzang. The late Ming novel centers on Monkey, one of the monk's companions, who represents carefree genius, bravery, and loyalty.

Dream of the Red Chamber

Perhaps the greatest Chinese novel, this portrays the decline of an aristocratic Qing household. Infused with a Daoist sense of transcendence, it focuses on the life and loves of the idle Jia Baoyu and 12 perceptively drawn female characters.

20th Century

In the early 20th century, fiction-writers and playwrights addressed social issues in a new realist style. However Communism demanded revolutionary themes. After the persecution of writers during the Cultural Revolution *(see pp70–71)*, experimental forms and styles gradually emerged. However, the books of Chinese authors may still be banned if they are openly critical of the government or are "spiritual pollutants;" though pirated versions are often widely available.

Mo Yan is a post-Cultural Revolution fiction-writer and recent Nobel laureate. Best known for his novel *Red Sorghum* (1986), made into a film, he writes in a rich style, often graphic, fantastic, and violent.

Lu Xun, early 20th-century writer of short stories and novellas, is known as the father of modern Chinese literature. His realist, satirical style is indebted to such writers as Dickens. He is renowned for his humorous depiction of Ah Q, an illiterate but enthusiastic peasant, done down by the forces of convention.

Religion & Philosophy

Traditionally, the three strands in Chinese religion and philosophy are Confucianism, Daoism, and Buddhism. An eclectic approach to religion allows the three to coexist, often within a single temple. Confucianism, the first to gain real influence, can be seen as a manifestation of the public, socially responsible self. Daoism represents a personal and wilder side; its emphasis on the relativity of things contrasts with Confucian concern for approved roles. Buddhism, a foreign import, is spiritual and otherworldly, offering an alternative to Chinese pragmatism. During the Cultural Revolution, religion was outlawed as contrary to Communist ideas. Today, people are largely able to express their beliefs.

Laozi, Buddha, and Confucius

Confucianism

Originated by Confucius (551–479 BC) and developed by later thinkers, Confucianism advocates a structured society in which people are bound to each other by the moral ties of the five principal relationships: parent-child, ruler-subject, brother-brother, husband-wife, and friend-friend. In Imperial China, Confucianism was the philosophy of the elite scholar-gentleman class. For much of the Communist era, it was reviled as a reactionary philosophy linked to the former ruling aristocracy.

Filial piety, or *xiao*, another Confucian precept, consists of obedience to and reverence for one's parents, and by extension respect for other family members and one's ruler.

Confucius was a thinker and teacher whose philosophy of family obligations and good government is based on the principles of *ren* (benevolence) and *yi* (righteousness). He died unknown, his disciples spreading his teachings.

The paying of respects to one's ancestors is based on filial piety and runs throughout Chinese culture. During the Qing Ming festival in April, Chinese traditionally clean and maintain their ancestors' tombs.

The birth of Confucius is celebrated in the philosopher's home town of Qufu *(see pp148–9)* in late September. Many thousands of his descendants, all surnamed Kong, still live in the city.

Scholars collated the Confucian Classics, including the *Lunyu (Analects)*, a series of Confucius's sayings, well after his death. The Classics were the basis of education until 1912.

Daoism

Strongly linked with early folk beliefs, Daoism incorporates the traditional concepts of an ordered universe, *yin* and *yang*, and directed energy, *qi (see pp38–9)*. Over time, Daoism developed into a complex religion with an extensive pantheon. Daoist philosophy encourages following one's intuition and following the grain of the universe by living in accordance with the Dao.

Laozi, the founder of Daoism, is a shadowy figure, who may have lived in the 6th century BC. The *Daode Jing*, which introduces the idea of Dao, or the Way that permeates reality, is attributed to him.

Han Xiangzi, one of the Eight Immortals, a popular group of Daoist adepts, is believed to have fallen from a sacred peach tree, which bestowed eternal life to him. He is usually shown playing a flute.

Daoist alchemists aimed to find an elixir for eternal life, winning influence with emperors. Daoism influenced scientific development, and contributed to the discovery of gunpowder in the 9th century.

In "Peach Blossom Spring" by Daoist poet Tao Qian, a fisherman chances upon a lost idyllic world and encounters Immortals. Daoist reverence for nature led to the creation of numerous paradises.

Buddhism

In China, the Mahayana school of Buddhism, which promises salvation to anyone who seeks it, is followed. Enlightened ones, *bodhisattvas*, remain in this world to help enlighten others. Through deeds and devotion believers gain merit and maintain their connections with the *bodhisattvas*, bringing them closer to nirvana.

The Guardian King of the South (left) is coiled by a snake; the King of the North holds a parasol. Kings of the four directions guard the entrance to many temples, protecting the main deity from evil influences.

The Laughing Buddha, or Milefo, is an adaptation of the Maitreya, the Future Buddha. His large belly and laughing face are signs of abundance and he is worshiped in the hope of a happy, affluent life.

Luohan or *arhats* are the Buddha's disciples and often appear in temples in groups of 18. Their holiness is thought to enable them to achieve extinction (nirvana) on death.

A Buddhist supplicant burns sticks of incense in aid of prayer. Buddhist temples throb with spiritual energy, as worshipers pray and make offerings to gain merit.

The Power of Qi

The Chinese philosophical notion of a cosmic *qi*, or breath that permeates the universe, dates from the Shang and Zhou periods. *Qi* is regarded as having created the cosmos and the Earth, and given rise to the complementary opposing negative and positive forces of *yin* and *yang*. Every physical change that occurs in the world is seen as a product of the working of *qi*. In the Daoist *Daode Jing*, *qi* is synonymous with Dao ("the Way"). The *qi* character *(right)* represents a bowl of rice with steam, where the rice's power or *qi* is manifested, rising above. The concept of *qi* runs through all areas of Chinese thought: it is a guiding principle in both traditional science and the arts.

Chinese character for *qi*, resembling a steaming bowl of rice

Harnessing Qi

Qi informs multiple practical and applied fields. When Chinese medicine became formalized during the 2nd century BC, for example, *qi* was established as its central concept. It was seen as the vital substance of living things, circulating in the body through a network of channels or meridians *(see p238)*.

Acupressure and acupuncture rely on the idea of *qi* circulating in the body. A person may suffer from inadequate or excessive *qi*, and the aim is to release or dampen the *qi* as appropriate.

The *cun* trigram is very *yin*. Its attributes are devotion and reception and it is connected to the element of earth.

***Qigong*, a practice** entailing deep-breathing exercises, is based on the concept of *qi*. Daoists traditionally associated lengthening the breath with lengthening life. Today, *qigong* is used to enhance wellbeing.

Martial arts emphasize the cultivation of *qi*. Through concentration, practitioners, such as monks of the Shaolin Monastery, perform extraordinary feats of fitness and endurance.

A ***feng shui*** practitioner sets up a *bagua* chart and other instruments to trace the flow of *qi* within an office building. *Feng shui* is popular in Hong Kong, where it is less frowned on as a superstitious practice.

Feng Shui

Chinese geomancy, or feng shui *("wind and water"), is based on ideas of* qi. Feng shui *posits that the appropriate layout of a building or room, for example the position of doorways, affects the flow of* qi *and hence the inhabitants' general wellbeing.*

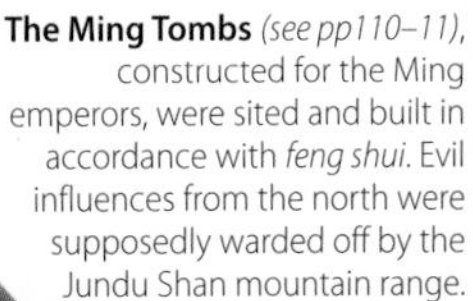

The Ming Tombs *(see pp110–11)*, constructed for the Ming emperors, were sited and built in accordance with *feng shui*. Evil influences from the north were supposedly warded off by the Jundu Shan mountain range.

The HSBC building on Hong Kong's Statue Square *(see p316)* is thought to enjoy outstanding *feng shui*, with harbor views and a large atrium allowing the free flow of *qi*.

Yijing

The Chinese classic, the Yijing (I Ching), *or* Book of Changes, *has been consulted as a divination guide book for thousands of years. In it, the* bagua *are combined into 64 hexagrams of six* yin *or* yang *lines each. The hexagrams represent even more complex states of* qi *than the* bagua.

The qian trigram, the trigram in which *yang qi* is strongest, consists of three unbroken lines.

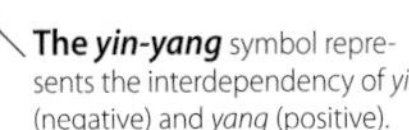

The *yin-yang* symbol represents the interdependency of *yin* (negative) and *yang* (positive).

Bagua Chart

Eight bagua, *or trigrams, ranged around a* yin-yang *symbol make up the basic* bagua *chart, an attempt to codify the working of* qi. *Each trigram consists of three lines –* yin *(broken) or* yang *(unbroken). Together they make up all possible permutations of such sets of lines and describe potential movement between different* qi *states.*

Confucius, in his later years, became very interested in the *Yijing*, and wrote numerous annotations to the text. Here he randomly divides yarrow sticks to create hexagrams and consults the *Yijing* to determine their meaning.

Divination sticks are often consulted nowadays to divine the future. Outside temples in Hong Kong, worshipers can be seen scattering the sticks on the ground. A practiced diviner reads the pattern by picking out *bagua* shapes.

Architecture

For over 2,000 years, the Chinese have used the same architectural model for both imperial and religious buildings. This has three elements: a platform, post-and-beam timber frames, and non-loadbearing walls. Standard features of building complexes include a front gate, four-sided enclosures or courtyards, and a series of halls in a linear formation running north. Most Chinese buildings were built of wood, but because wooden buildings tend to catch fire, only a few structures remain; the earliest date from the Tang period (AD 618–907).

Aerial view of the Forbidden City, showing the traditional linear layout

Hall

In every context, the Chinese hall, or *tang*, follows the same pattern: a platform of rammed earth or stone, and timber columns arranged in a grid. The front of the hall always has an odd number of bays. Between the columns and beams are brackets *(dougong)*, cantilevers that support the structure, allowing the eaves to overhang. The timber is brightly painted, the roof aesthetically curved, and tiled or thatched.

Gate of Heavenly Purity *(see p94)*
An archetypal Chinese hall, the central doorway and uneven number of bays emphasize the processional element.

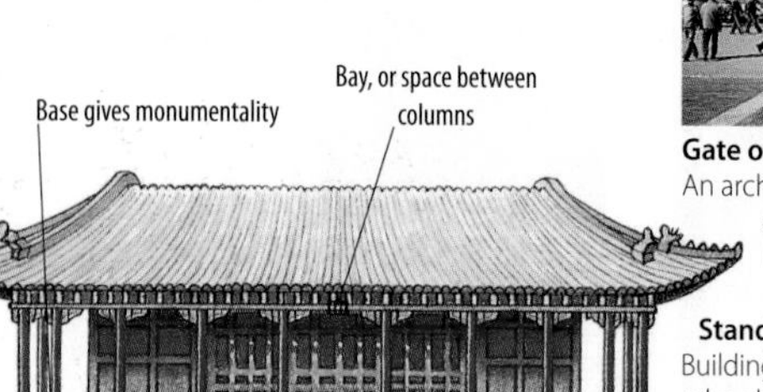

Standard Hall
Buildings in China conformed to a set of rules about proportions. This uniform architecture created a sense of identity – useful in a large and disparate country.

Storied Building (Lou) and Storied Pavilion (Ge)

Multi-story buildings in China predate pagodas and varied from two-storied private homes to huge seven- or more storied towers built to enjoy the scenery. Storied pavilions were used for storage and had doors and windows only at the front. Both types of building kept the standard elements of base, columns, and hanging walls.

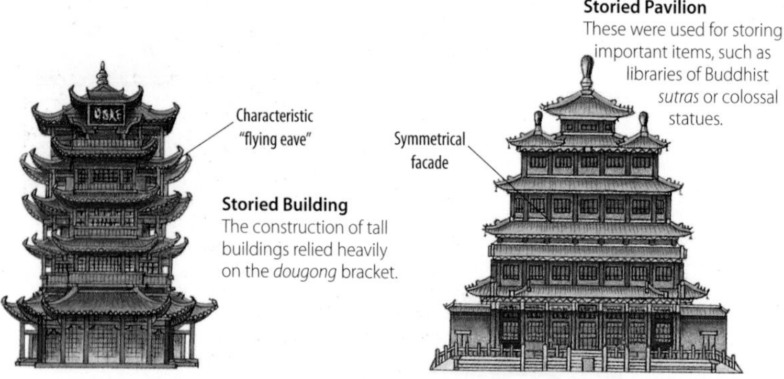

Storied Building
The construction of tall buildings relied heavily on the *dougong* bracket.

Storied Pavilion
These were used for storing important items, such as libraries of Buddhist *sutras* or colossal statues.

Pagoda

Based on the Indian stupa, the Chinese pagoda, or *ta*, was developed in the first century AD along with the arrival of Buddhism. Multi-storied pagodas appeared in Buddhist temple complexes (although later they often stood on their own) and were often intended to house a religious statue. They were built of brick, stone, or wood *(see p171)*.

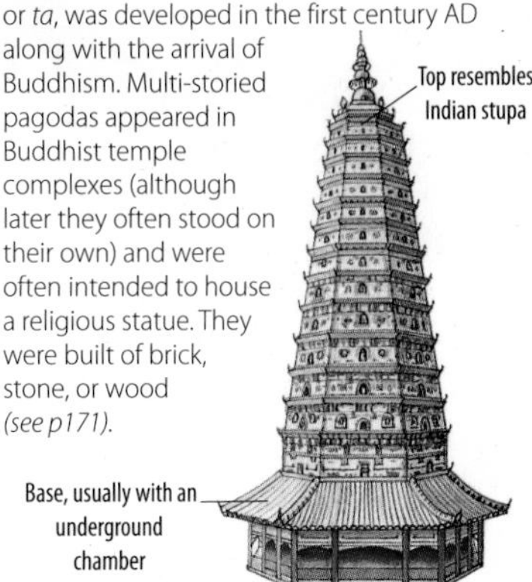

Ornamental Archway

The *pailou*, or *paifang*, is a memorial or decorative archway. Made of wood, brick, or stone, and sometimes with glazed tiles, it often bears an edifying inscription. *Pailou* were erected at crossroads, temples, bridges, government offices, parks, and tombs.

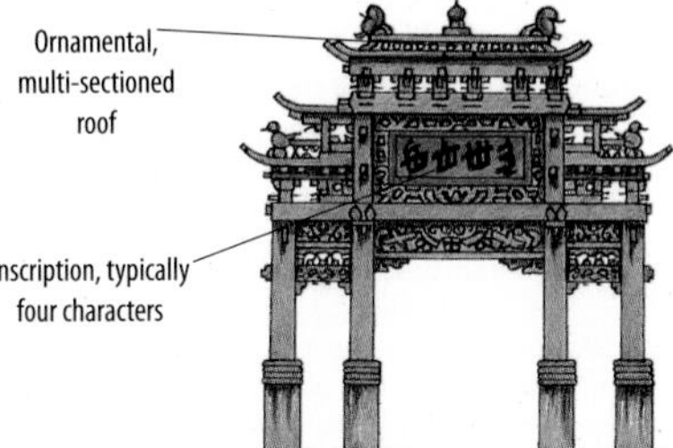

City Walls

Early defensive walls, like other early architectural forms, were made of earth – either pounded hard by pestles or moistened to make a clay and pressed around reed frames. Later walls were often built using brick. City walls were traditionally square, with the main gate to the south. The Chinese for "city" *(cheng)* also means "wall."

City Wall and Gate
The towers on top of walls can vary from small buildings to palatial multi-story structures.

Pingyao City Walls
Made of rammed earth and brick, rising 33 ft (10 m) high, the ramparts and watchtowers were an effective defense. The current structure *(see p144)*, collapsed in parts, is from the Ming dynasty.

Architectural Details

It is interesting to interpret the architectural detail on Chinese buildings. The use of yellow tiles, for example, was reserved for the emperor. The Nine-Dragon Screen, which occurs in the Forbidden City and elsewhere, is also imperial since the dragon symbolizes the *yang*, or male principle, and by extension the emperor.

Chiwen
Able to douse flames with water, the Chiwen often appears at the end of a roof ridge *(see p93)* as a protection against fire.

Dougong
A bracket *(dougong)* transmits the load from roof to column. It's a traditionally complex, nail-free, and ornamental construction method.

Chinese Inventions

Printed books, porcelain, silk, umbrellas, and kites are just a few of the everyday objects that originated in China and are used today throughout the world. Remarkably, the Chinese developed the technology to produce fine porcelain over 1,000 years before Europe. Philosophy played a part in two of the most famous Chinese discoveries. Seeking the elixir of life, Daoist alchemists stumbled upon gunpowder, while the magnetic compass was developed from an instrument used for geomancy and *feng shui*.

Wheelbarrow: used in agriculture, industry, and by the military. Like the plow, it vastly increased the efficiency of manual workers.

Cast iron: made by lowering the ore's melting point with phosphorus before heating it in very hot blast furnaces that had been developed over hundreds of years of firing pottery.

The decimal system developed alongside the writing system and led to mathematical advances.

The first paper was made from mulberry bark, bamboo, hemp, linen, and silk.

The crossbow had better range, penetration, and accuracy than the standard bow.

2000 BC	1800	1600	1400	1200	1000	800	600	400	200 BC
2000	1800	1600	1400	1200	1000	800	600	400	200

High-fired stoneware: first produced in the Shang dynasty, at the same time as the early glazes that added strength, color, and waterproofing.

***Kuan* or moldboard plow:** increased the efficiency of farmers. A cast-iron blade could cut through and plow previously unplowable land.

Great Leaps Forward

Early advances in technology spawned an agricultural revolution in China. Iron-bladed plows increased the amount of land that could be farmed and multiplied its productivity, enabling a larger population to be sustained. Paper, paper money, and printing were key to the efficient administration of a vast, populous, centrally controlled state. Increased manpower, organization, and technology advanced industrial production in mining and porcelain factories, for example, as well as boosting China's military might.

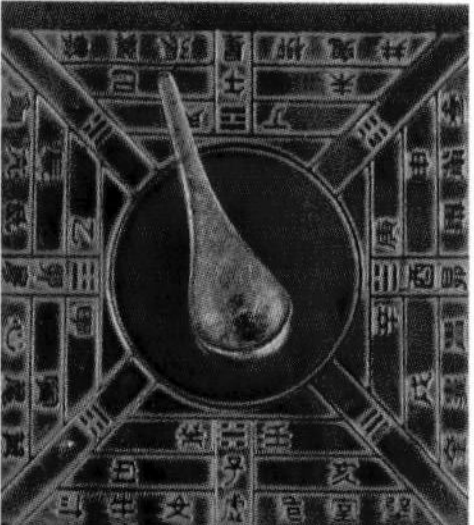

Magnetic compass: used for geomancy, the first compasses consisted of a loadstone spoon and bronze plate. Later examples would help Chinese sailors make huge voyages on trading trips.

Porcelain: ceramic technology reached a new peak in the 6th century with the discovery of "true" porcelain; hard, white, and translucent, it rings to the touch. Production methods would stay a closely guarded secret, keeping its value for export *(see p260)*.

Printing: woodblock printing was used to spread Buddhist teachings, and was well-developed by the time of the Diamond Sutra *(see p32)*. In 1041–8, Bi Sheng carved individual characters on pieces of clay, inventing movable block type.

Stirrup: this increased the efficiency of horses as tools for communication, transportation, and warfare.

Printing

The discovery of movable type did not really have any impact upon Chinese society, and most printers continued to carve the individual characters into a block. In Europe 400 years later, however, the discovery of movable type revolutionized society. This is because it is much easier to handle the 26 or so different blocks in a Roman alphabet than it is to handle the approximately 3,000 or more characters that are needed for a Chinese newspaper – without even allowing for duplicates. Woodblock carving, therefore, required far fewer resources.

AD 200 | 400 | 600 | 800 | 1000 | 1200 | 1400 | 1600 | 1800 | 2000 AD

Paper money: developed by merchants as certificates of exchange. Lighter than coins, bills were soon adopted by the government.

Gunpowder: first discovered by necromancers. It was originally used for fireworks and mining and not used for warfare until the 8th century.

Seismometer: invented by Chang Heng. It identified the direction of an earthquake when a ball fell from one of the dragons into a frog's mouth.

Cargo ship: designed with compartments, and equipped with fore-and-aft lugsails and stern-post rudders, these multi-masted ships were larger and technically superior to their European counterparts.

The abacus: invented during the Yuan dynasty. Because it is able to perform complex calculations, it is often referred to as the first computer and is still used in China today.

Traditional Arts

The earliest Chinese artifacts were found in royal tombs. These include bronzes, ceramics, and jades from the Shang and Zhou period, as well as terracotta warriors from the Qin period. Of the many rich art forms that subsequently developed in China, painting and pottery are perhaps the most important, and have reached the highest aesthetic level. Other significant art forms include sculpture, notably the Buddhist sculpture of western China. There are also many distinctive and popular forms of Chinese decorative art.

Buddhist sculpture in the Gandharan style

Ritual bronze tripod from an early royal tomb, decorated with a mythical animal design known as a *taotie*.

Wet and dry ink used to give the detail of the trees.

Textured strokes give the rocks depth.

Pottery

After inventing porcelain, China developed a huge range of potting, decorating, and glazing techniques that were imitated from Europe to Japan. Chinese ceramics led the world in aesthetic taste and technique up until the demise of the Qing dynasty.

Tang earthenware tomb figure representing a fierce warrior, with typical rough *sancai* (three-color) drip glaze. This was a lead-based glaze, fired at a low temperature.

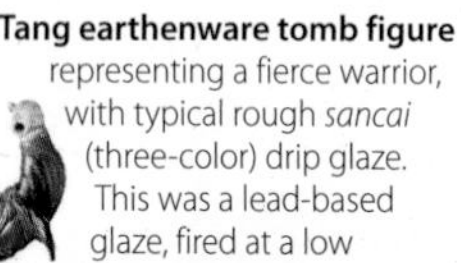

Song celadon bowl, with incised floral design. Celadon was the European name given to the refined gray-green glaze of this type of stoneware and porcelain.

Ming vase in the blue-and-white style known and imitated internationally. The technique involves underglaze painting in cobalt blue before the pot is fired.

Qing famille-rose vase, a delicate porcelain in a distinctive palette. The name comes from the use of bright pink enamel.

Bird-and-flower painting (including the depiction of fruit and insects) reveals the Chinese Daoist interest in observing the natural world. Despite the lightness of subject, the paintings have an intense, quasi-scientific depth.

Chinese Painting

Considered the highest traditional art form, Chinese painting is executed on silk or paper using a brush and inks or watercolors.

Landscape painting, associated with the scholar class, reached a highpoint in the Northern Song and Yuan periods. Huang Gongwang *(see below)*, a master of the Yuan, was admired for his simple calligraphic style.

Religious painting first appeared along the Silk Road with the arrival of Buddhism from India. The Chinese soon developed an individual style.

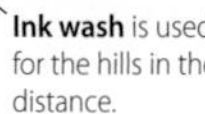

Ink wash is used for the hills in the distance.

Bamboo painting was a genre of the scholar class. Bamboo symbolized the scholar-gentleman who would bend but not break in the face of adversity.

Traditional Crafts

As well as the traditional high art forms of painting and pottery, China has a wealth of beautiful decorative arts. Delicate carvings in lacquer, ivory, and jade are popular, as are colorful cloisonné items, decorated inksticks (or cakes), snuff bottles, and fans.

Snuff bottles were produced in large numbers during the Qing period. Made of glass, jade, mother-of-pearl, or semiprecious stones, they were delicately carved or painted on the inside in exquisite detail.

Lacquer carving is distinctive for its deep red color and floral designs, and is often used on boxes.

Cloisonné is a style of enameling. Individual metal cloisons, usually made of copper, are soldered together and inlaid with different colored enamels. The object is then fired and polished.

Modern Arts

The birth of modern art in China at the start of the 20th century coincided with greater contact with the West. Experiments with new materials and styles in the visual arts, Western-style music, "spoken drama" *(huaju)*, cinema, and modern literary forms such as free verse all took root at this time. However, after 1949, this creativity was stifled by Soviet-influenced Socialist Realism. During the Cultural Revolution many artists were even persecuted on the grounds that their works were "reactionary." Since the 1980s and 1990s, however, there has been some liberalization in the arts and new, exciting forms have developed.

The Canton TV Tower in Guangzhou (inaugurated in 2010) exemplifies the evolution of high-rise Chinese architecture since the late 1990s.

This example of performance art is by Cang Xin, a Beijing-based conceptual artist, active since the mid-1990s. The title of this piece, *Unification of Heaven and Man*, alludes to classical Chinese philosophical concepts.

Shaven-headed man

Modern Art

This painting, *Series 2 No. 2*, is by Fang Lijun, leader of the Cynical Realism school, which came about as a reaction to the demise of the pro-democracy movement in 1989. Rejecting idealism, these artists comment on problems in China.

Sculpture entitled *Torso*, by Zhan Wang, a Shanghai-based conceptual artist. Zhan uses reflective steel sheets to give the illusion of solidity.

Orchestral and chamber music has been popular in China since the early 20th century. Today, there are many schools specializing in Western-style music, and several high-quality ensembles and artists on the world scene.

Chinese Cinema

From early classics such as *Street Angel* (1937), made in the (then) foreign enclave of Shanghai, Chinese cinema has scaled new heights of international success, with the work of such acclaimed directors as Zhang Yimou.

***Farewell My Concubine* (1993)**, directed by Chen Kaige, a post-Cultural Revolution filmmaker, who gave expression to new moral uncertainties, is set in the world of traditional Chinese Opera.

The Hong Kong film industry followed its own path and became primarily famous for its action movies. Renowned martial arts star Jackie Chan, seen above in an early acting and directorial debut, *Fearless Hyena*, made many films and successfully crossed over from Hong Kong to Hollywood.

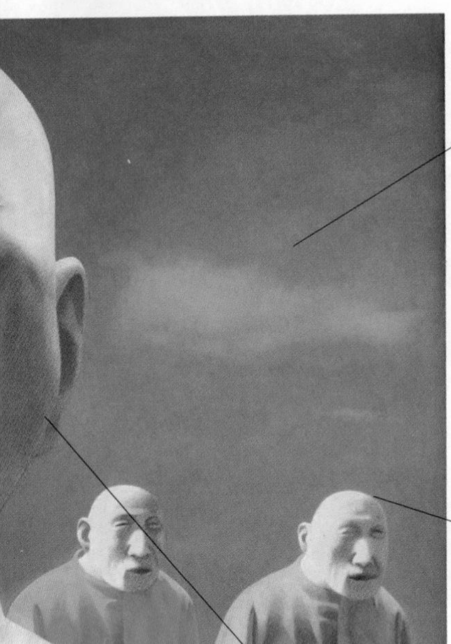

Background is a hazy blue, making it appear dream-like

Anonymous figures seem threatening

Main figure is yelling or yawning – is he angry or just bored?

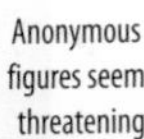

Li Yuchun is one of the best-selling singers in China today. Rock music only took off in the 1980s, with the likes of Cui Jian, the "grandad" of Chinese rock. The industry is closely following that of the West, with many stars emerging from TV talent shows.

Ballet in contemporary China mixes traditional Chinese and Western influences. Here, the ballet version of Zhang Yimou's film *Raise the Red Lantern* is performed by members of the National Ballet.

Modern theater provides an expression of Chinese life in the 21st century. Here, a scene from *Toilet*, a black comedy, is performed by the National Theater company in Beijing. The play broke taboos with its frank portrayal of urban life and treatment of homosexuality.

Festivals

An important part of Chinese culture and tradition, festivals are generally happy and colorful affairs that reaffirm ancient beliefs and customs. The biggest and most important festival is Spring Festival, or Chinese New Year. This brings families together for several days: the home is cleaned and everyone dresses up in new clothes; decorations are put up and gifts exchanged; and finally there is always time for a lively and noisy carnival climaxing in a brilliant display of pyrotechnics. Nearly all the festival elements and rituals are geared towards bringing good luck and prosperity. In business, all debts should be settled by Chinese New Year. Overall, the festivities last about 15 days but the whole country closes down for only three.

Hongbao
These decorative red envelopes symbolize luck and wealth and bring about both, as they contain money – they are typically given to children on New Year's Eve.

Lion Dance
Performed at New Year and other festivals. Usually two people are required to play the lion. The dance demands more martial arts skills than the Dragon Dance, also performed on these occasions.

Fireworks exploding over Hong Kong's Victoria Harbour

Firecrackers
Strings of firecrackers are set off at New Year, making the streets noisy and, potentially, dangerous places. Beijing tried to ban these in the center of the city supposedly driving people out to the suburbs for noisy fun.

Drummers
At the Spring Festival, processions of dancers and drummers march over the New Year period up until the Lantern Festival. Like the firecrackers, the noise of the drumming is supposed to keep the evil spirits away.

Festival Food

Each festival has its special food: *jiaozi* (boiled dumplings) are usually eaten for New Year, especially in the north of China; *yuanxiao* (glutinous rice balls) feature during the Lantern Festival and can be made with a sweet or savory filling; and *zongzi* (sticky rice pyramids wrapped in bamboo leaves) are served at the Dragon Boat Festival. The Mid-Autumn Festival, which falls on a full moon, brings mooncakes. Made to a thousand recipes with savory or sweet fillings, the cake symbolizes the moon.

A type of mooncake

Rice pyramids or *zongzi*

Traditional papercut of an astrological chart

Chinese Astrology

Each year is associated with one of 12 animal signs, which repeat in a cycle. At New Year people talk of welcoming, for example, the "Year of the Dog." In Chinese astrology, people born under a specific animal sign are supposed to have some of the characteristics attributed to the animal.

Dog 2018 – considered lucky in Chinese mythology.

Pig 2019 – associated with fertility and virility.

Rat 2020 – welcomed as a clever protector and bringer of wealth.

Ox 2021 – Laozi, the Daoist philosopher, is often shown sitting on an ox.

Tiger 2022 – in China he is deemed the king of the animals.

Rabbit 2023 – associated with longevity and believed to live in the moon.

Dragon 2024 – symbol of China, the emperor, and the positive *yang* element (*see pp38–9*).

Snake 2025 – an ancient ancestor, Fuxi, was thought to be half-human and half-snake.

Horse 2026 – symbol of freedom.

Sheep 2027 – signifying peace and creativity.

Monkey 2028 – associated with fun and genius, as in the story of the Monkey King.

Rooster 2029 – has five virtues: refinement, courage, assertiveness, benevolence, and reliability.

Spectacular Fireworks

New Year would not be complete without fireworks. Some major cities put on impressive all-night displays. Fireworks were originally intended to ward off evil spirits, or perhaps wake up the dragon who would create rain in the coming year and guarantee a good harvest.

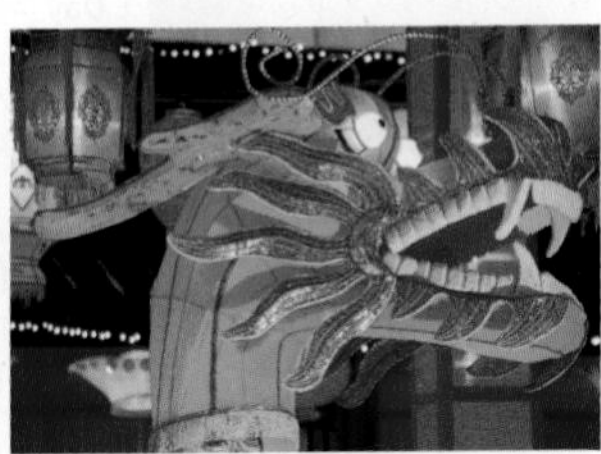

Colorful lanterns
Coinciding with the full moon, the Lantern Festival marks the end of the two-week New Year period. Lanterns may bear auspicious characters or be in animal shapes.

Tangerines
A New Year symbol of luck, tangerines are put on display at home – along with fresh flowers. The word for "tangerine" sounds like "luck" in Chinese while flowers signify a new beginning.

Duilian
These red scrolls at either side of the doorway bear Spring Couplets in classical Chinese expressing good wishes for the family in the coming year.

CHINA THROUGH THE YEAR

The traditional Chinese festivals are tied to the lunar calendar, which has 29.5 days a month, and this means the solar dates change every year. Festivals associated with Communism – National Day and Labor Day, for example – are usually fixed to the Western calendar. Religious festivals, kept alive in Hong Kong, Tibet, and other areas of the Chinese-speaking world, are gradually making a comeback in the People's Republic of China (PRC), and outlying areas such as Inner Mongolia have their own distinctive festivals. Some celebrations of foreign origin, such as Christmas, are also observed. Before the important New Year Festival, there are weeks of preparation. Most offices and many shops are closed for three days, but some tend to take a week-long break at this time. As most Chinese return to their family homes, travel is very difficult.

Colorful parade celebrating Chinese New Year

Spring (Feb–Apr)

This is the time of year when Chinese people try to settle old debts and make time to meet with friends and family members. The arrival of peach blossom is a signal of rejuvenation and the Spring Festival celebrates the start of the ancient cycle of plowing and sowing.

1st Lunar Month

Spring Festival (Chun Jie) The main festival – Chinese New Year *(see pp48–9)*. Gifts and red envelopes filled with money are exchanged and new shoes and clothes worn.

Lantern Festival *(Feb–Mar)* Coinciding with a full moon, this festival marks the end of the 15-day New Year period. A great many lanterns bearing auspicious characters or in animal shapes can be seen. *Yuanxiao* (sticky rice balls) are eaten.

2nd Lunar Month

Tibetan New Year The Tibetan New Year is marked by the eating of "barley crumb" food and an exchange of Tashi Delek blessings. It is followed by Monlam, the great prayer festival later in the month, and the Butter Lamp Festival, also known as the Lantern Festival.

A highly elaborate Tibetan butter sculpture

Hong Kong Arts Festival *(Feb–Mar)* A major international arts festival as well as the premier arts event in Hong Kong. A mix of overseas and local artists provide music, theater, dance, popular entertainment, film, and exhibition programs over three or four weeks.

International Women's Day *(Mar 8)* Women have a half or even a whole day's holiday, while men continue to work.

3rd Lunar Month

Tree-Planting Day *(Apr 1)* Promoted since the late 1970s by the reformist government, but not an official holiday, this is part of a greening campaign.

Qing Ming Festival *(Apr)* Festival for sweeping the graves and honoring the dead. Food is left on the grave and families often take a picnic with them.

Weifang International Kite Festival *(mid-Apr)* Flying kites is part of Qing Ming celebrations. Over 1,000 contestants compete at this festival in Shandong.

Water Sprinkling Festival *(mid-Apr)* Exclusive to the Dai people (Xishuangbanna, Yunnan, *see p389*). Marks the Dai lunar New Year, and involves blessing others by sprinkling or splashing them with water, which represents the quelling of the flames of a mythical tyrant demon.

Hainan Coconut Festival *(Apr)* Set up in 1992, and a showcase for the local coconut harvest.

Qing Ming Festival, sweeping or tending the ancestors' graves

Third Moon Fair *(Apr)* Dali area. This festival is exclusive to the Buddhist Bai minority in Yunnan. Events include fairs, horse-racing, singing, and dancing.
Tin Hau Festival *(Apr–May)* Celebrated in Hong Kong and coastal areas such as Fujian, the birthday of the Heavenly Queen or Mazu *(see p155)*, who looks after those at sea, is important for fishermen and sailors.

Summer (May–Jul)

Once the summer arrives, bringing warmer weather, festivals are often held outdoors. May sees the start of the traveling season, as many people go on trips around the country to see family and friends.

4th Lunar Month
International Labor Day *(May 1)* A week-long holiday around May Day during which travel can be difficult.
Youth Day *(May 4)* Commemorates the student movements of 1919, which sparked the evolution of modern China.
Buddha's Birthday *(May)* An important religious festival in Tibet but not officially observed in the PRC, though Buddhists may now do so privately. The festival has a higher profile in Hong Kong, where it is also known as the Festival of the Ten Thousand Buddhas. Buddhists pray for the washing away of sin and the attainment of wisdom and peace.
"Meet in Beijing" Festival *(May)* Music and arts festival, including opera, dance, instrumental and vocal concerts.

5th Lunar Month
Children's Day *(Jun 1)* Cinemas and other places of entertainment are free to children, who are also showered with presents.
Dragon Boat Festival (or Fifth Moon Festival) *(Jun)* commemorates the patriotic poet Qu Yuan who drowned himself. Originally religious but now just fun. Teams of rowers compete in long, decorated boats. Rice cakes *(zongzi)* are eaten. Hong Kong has several very colorful events, one with international teams.
Shanghai International Film Festival *(Jun)* First held in October 1993, this is the only accredited international film festival in mainland China, and it shows a range of new films from around the world. The main film prize is the Golden Goblet, and a prize is also awarded for young Asian movie talent.

Dragon Boat Festival – colorful, lively, and exciting to watch

Nadaam Fair, Mongolian sports festival and fair

6th Lunar Month
Founding of Chinese Communist Party *(Jul 1)* A day to mark the event that took place in 1921 in Shanghai.
Nadaam Fair *(late Jul)* Held in Hohhot, Bayanbulak, and elsewhere, in Inner Mongolia, and featuring horse-racing, wrestling, and archery. Women wear their traditional dress. It's also a trading fair.

Fall (Aug–Oct)

The weather may still be warm in the subtropical south, but in the high uplands and central areas it is cooling down. As the leaves turn golden, this is a popular time of the year to travel to festivals.

7th Lunar Month
Army Day *(Aug 1)* Marks the first Communist uprising against the Nationalists in 1927. The theme is unity between the army and the people.
Lovers' Festival *(Aug)* A romantic day, this celebrates the story of the earthly cowherd and celestial weaving girl who were separated by the gods but who are annually reunited in the heavens by a bridge of magpies on the seventh day of the seventh moon. It is also known as Seven Sisters Festival.
Shoton (Yogurt Festival) *(Aug–Sep)* Tibetan festival of opera. It takes its name from the yogurt served by pilgrims to the monks.
Nagqu Horse Race Festival *(Aug)* The most important folk festival in Tibet. This takes place in Nagqu. Over a thousand herdsmen compete in the traditional Tibetan sports of archery, horse-racing, and general horsemanship.
Zhongyuan (Hungry Ghost Festival) (Jul or Aug) Similar to Halloween, a traditional festival combining elements of ancestor worship and Buddhism, suppressed under Communism. Considered an inauspicious time to move house or marry.

Mid-Fall festival dragon

Qingdao International Beer Festival *(Aug)* Held in the eastern port city of Qingdao, Shandong, home of Tsingtao beer, brewed from the spring waters of nearby Lao Shan *(see p152)*.

8th Lunar Month
Teachers' Day *(Sep 1)* Not an established holiday, but it began in the 1980s in response to the anti-intellectualism of the Cultural Revolution.
Mid-Fall Festival or Zhong Qiu *(Sep)* Harvest or moon festival when moon cakes are eaten throughout the country and family reunions take place *(see p49)*.
Shaolin International Martial Arts Festival *(Sep)* Annual event since 1991 in the city of Zhengzhou.
Confucius's Birthday *(Sep 28)* Gradually regaining popularity in the PRC, after vilification of the sage (born in 551 BC) under the Communist regime. The day is celebrated at the Confucian temples in Qufu, Beijing, and elsewhere.
International Fashion Festival *(mid-Sep)* Dalian. The festival features two weeks of fashion shows by Asian designers, with a spectacular opening parade.

Qingdao International Beer Festival dancers

National day, well-drilled troops on the march

Corban Festival *(Sep)* Celebrated in Xinjiang, Ningxia, and among Hui people across China, this is a Muslim festival remembering Abraham's last-minute reprieve to sacrifice a goat instead of his son. Animals are slaughtered for a feast, accompanied with singing and dancing.

9th Lunar Month

National Day *(Oct 1)* A great rush of holiday-making takes place during this week-long break – one of China's two so-called Golden Week holidays, along with Chinese New Year. Parades – including a high-profile military show of strength in Tian'an Men Square – celebrate the founding of the PRC by Mao Zedong in 1949.

Double-Ninth (Chongyang) Festival *(Oct)* Double nine signifies double *yang* (in the *yin-yang* duality), connected with male assertiveness and strength. Traditionally, people do symbolic things like climb to high places, carry a sprig of dogwood, and drink chrysanthemum wine to ward off evil spirits at this festival, but it's not observed everywhere.

Hairy Crab Season *(Oct–early Dec)* Not strictly a festival, this is a two-month celebration of China's favorite winter delicacy, served in packed restaurants across the country but especially popular in Shanghai and eastern China.

Winter (Nov–Jan)

This season brings a drop in temperatures and relief from the humidity in the south, while central and northern regions usually experience bitter winters. The main traveling season is over but everyone enjoys the lengthy preparations for the Chinese New Year at home.

10th Lunar Month

Zhuang Song Festival *(Nov)* The Zhuang minority in Guangxi have their own folk-song and dance tradition. An International Folk Song and Arts Festival is held in Nanning.

11th Lunar Month

Winter Solstice *(Dec 22)* Chinese astronomers identified this day as early as the Han period. Historically, it has been an important festival, though less so now. In the north, people often eat dumpling soup or dumplings on this day to keep them warm. In the south, people may eat red-bean and sticky rice to drive away evil spirits.

Christmas Day *(Dec 25)* Although only a tiny number of the population is Christian, the commercial side of this celebration has taken off with Christmas trees and Shengdan Laoren, a Chinese version of Father Christmas, seen as a popular image. It's a public holiday in Hong Kong.

12th Lunar Month

New Year's Day *(Jan 1)* Overshadowed by the massive Chinese New Year celebrations that take place later in January or February, but still a recognized public holiday.

Public Holidays

New Year's Day (Jan 1)

Chinese New Year or Spring Festival (Jan–Feb)

Qing Ming Festival (Apr)

International Labor Day (May 1–3)

Dragon Boat Festival (May)

National Day (Oct 1)

Weekend Shifting

The weekends before and after the Spring Festival and October holidays are often shifted from year to year *toward* the three-day block to allow for a continuous run of seven days' holiday. To add to the confusion, the exact days of the holiday are usually not finalized until shortly beforehand. You may wish to avoid traveling during this period because many facilities are closed. Try to confirm the exact dates with a travel agent prior to making any plans.

The Climate of China

With many different climate zones across its vast landmass, China experiences all extremes of weather ranging from the hot, wet summers and warm winters of the subtropical southwestern coast and high temperatures of the Turpan Depression to the cool summers and long, dry winters of its mountainous regions. Rainfall is sparse in the arid northern uplands and the near-Siberian northeast but plentiful in the humid south and east.

The top of Hua Shan, Shaanxi

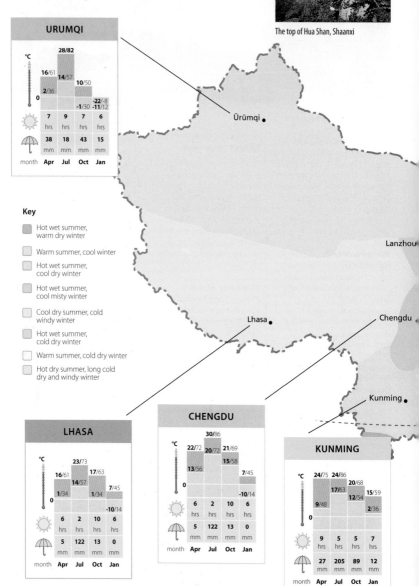

URUMQI

	Apr	Jul	Oct	Jan
°C	**16**/61	**28/82**	**10**/50	**-22**/-8
	2/36	**14**/57	**-1**/30	**-11**/12
hrs	7	9	7	6
mm	38	18	43	15

Ürümqi

Lanzhou

Lhasa

Chengdu

Kunming

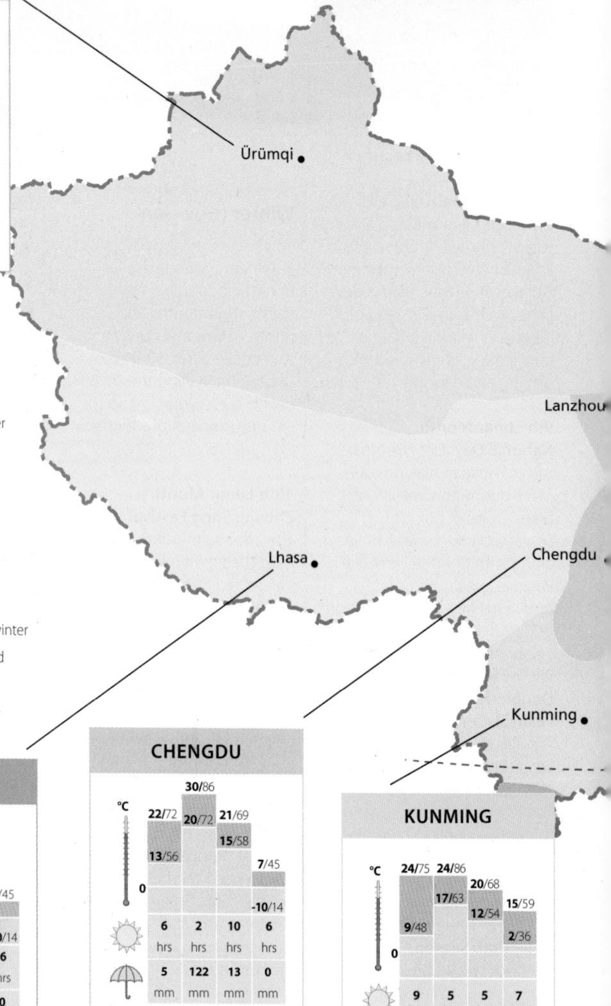

Key

- Hot wet summer, warm dry winter
- Warm summer, cool winter
- Hot wet summer, cool dry winter
- Hot wet summer, cool misty winter
- Cool dry summer, cold windy winter
- Hot wet summer, cold dry winter
- Warm summer, cold dry winter
- Hot dry summer, long cold dry and windy winter

LHASA

	Apr	Jul	Oct	Jan
°C	**16**/61	**23**/73	**17**/63	**7**/45
	1/34	**14**/57	**1**/34	**-10**/14
hrs	6	2	10	6
mm	5	122	13	0

CHENGDU

	Apr	Jul	Oct	Jan
°C	**22**/72	**30**/86	**21**/69	**7**/45
	13/56	**20**/72	**15**/58	**-10**/14
hrs	6	2	10	6
mm	5	122	13	0

KUNMING

	Apr	Jul	Oct	Jan
°C	**24**/75	**24**/86	**20**/68	**15**/59
	9/48	**17**/63	**12**/54	**2**/36
hrs	9	5	5	7
mm	27	205	89	12

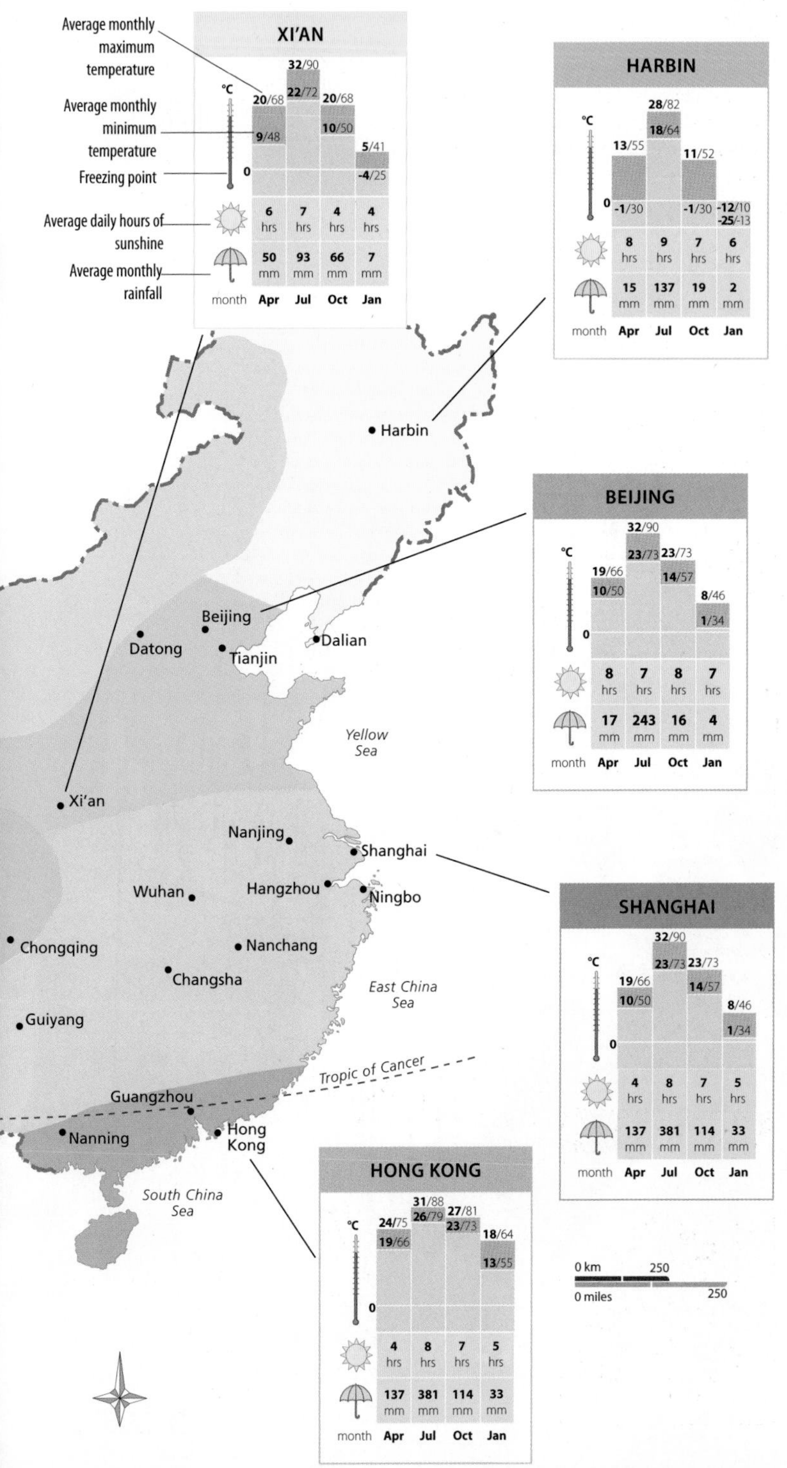
XI'AN
Average monthly maximum temperature
Average monthly minimum temperature
Freezing point
Average daily hours of sunshine
Average monthly rainfall
°C
20/68
9/48
32/90
22/72
20/68
10/50
5/41
-4/25
0
6 hrs
7 hrs
4 hrs
4 hrs
50 mm
93 mm
66 mm
7 mm
month
Apr
Jul
Oct
Jan
HARBIN
°C
13/55
-1/30
28/82
18/64
11/52
-1/30
-12/10
-25/-13
0
8 hrs
9 hrs
7 hrs
6 hrs
15 mm
137 mm
19 mm
2 mm
month
Apr
Jul
Oct
Jan
BEIJING
°C
19/66
10/50
32/90
23/73
23/73
14/57
8/46
1/34
0
8 hrs
7 hrs
8 hrs
7 hrs
17 mm
243 mm
16 mm
4 mm
month
Apr
Jul
Oct
Jan
SHANGHAI
°C
19/66
10/50
32/90
23/73
23/73
14/57
8/46
1/34
0
4 hrs
8 hrs
7 hrs
5 hrs
137 mm
381 mm
114 mm
33 mm
month
Apr
Jul
Oct
Jan
HONG KONG
°C
24/75
19/66
31/88
26/79
27/81
23/73
18/64
13/55
0
4 hrs
8 hrs
7 hrs
5 hrs
137 mm
381 mm
114 mm
33 mm
month
Apr
Jul
Oct
Jan
Harbin
Beijing
Datong
Tianjin
Dalian
Yellow Sea
Xi'an
Nanjing
Shanghai
Wuhan
Hangzhou
Ningbo
Chongqing
Nanchang
Changsha
East China Sea
Guiyang
Tropic of Cancer
Guangzhou
Nanning
Hong Kong
South China Sea
0 km 250
0 miles 250

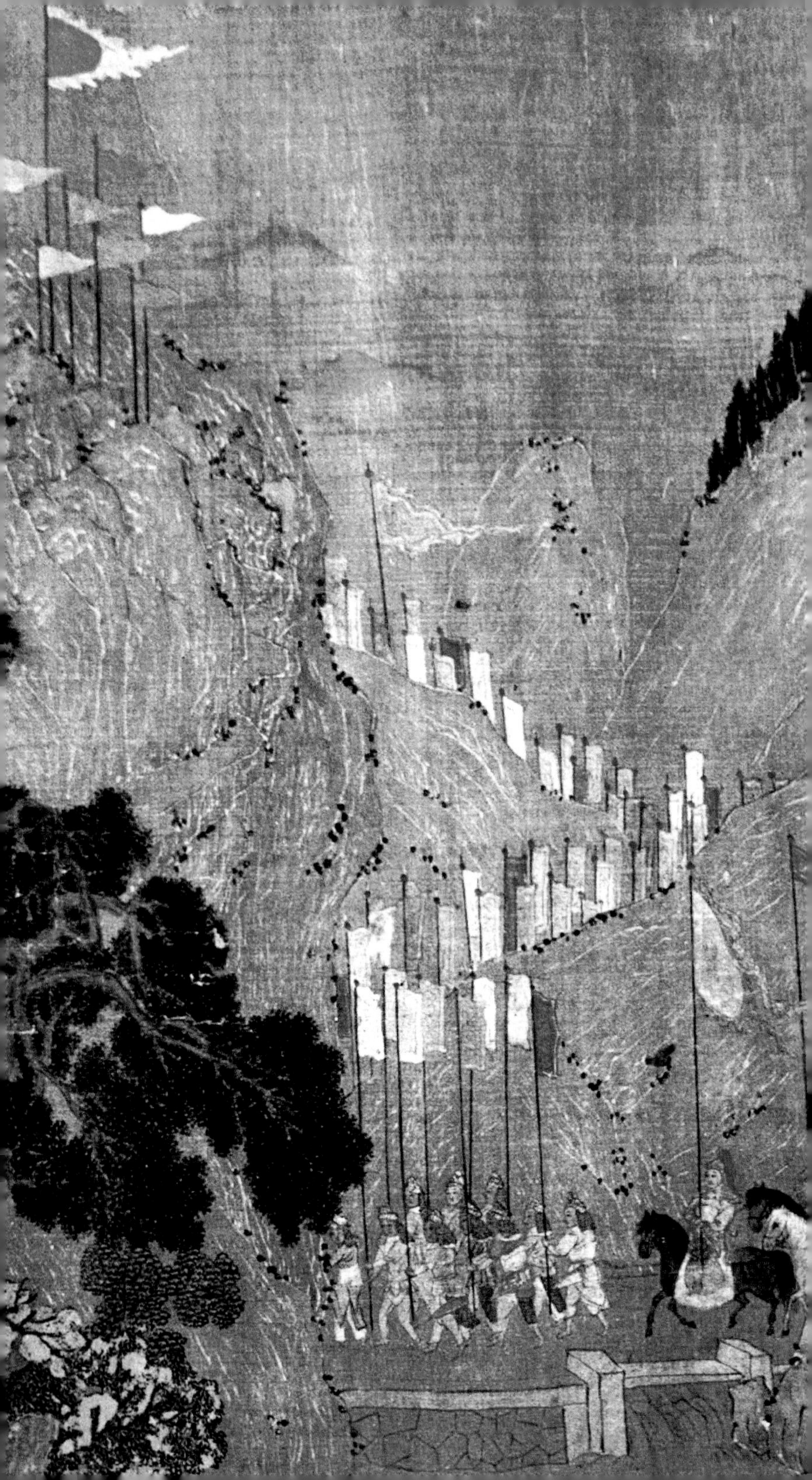

THE HISTORY OF CHINA

China boasts one of the longest single unified civilizations in the world. Its history is characterized by dramatic shifts in power between rival factions, periods of peace and prosperity when foreign ideas were assimilated and absorbed, the disintegration of empire through corruption and political subterfuge, and the cyclical rise of ambitious leaders to found each new empire.

First Settlers

From around 8000 BC, settlements of populations based on a primitive agricultural economy began to emerge in the eastern coastal regions and along the rich river deltas of the Huang He (Yellow River), the Yangzi, and the Wei. These civilizations focused on hunting, gathering, and fishing, and the cultivation of millet in the north and rice in the south. Each civilization is notable for its own distinct style of pottery, such as the bold earthenware of the Yangshao (5000–3000 BC) and the black ceramics of the Longshan (3000–1700 BC).

Bronze Age China & the First Kingdoms

The first dynasty in China was founded by the Shang around 1600 BC. The Shang lived in large, complex societies and were the first to mass-produce cast bronze. Power centered on the ruling elite who acted as shamans of a sort, communicating with their ancestors and gods through diviners. Elaborate bronze food and wine vessels were used both for banqueting and for making ancestral offerings. Inscriptions on oracle bones provide the first evidence of writing, dating from around 1300 BC.

In 1066 BC, the Zhou seized power, establishing their western capital at present-day Xi'an. The Western Zhou initially sustained many of the traditions of the Shang, but later reorganized the political system, and replaced the use of oracle bones with inscriptions on bronze and, later, writing on silk and strips of bamboo.

The Eastern Zhou period (770–221 BC) is divided into the Spring and Autumn period (named for the annals written by Confucius, 770–475 BC) and the Warring States period (475–221 BC). The Eastern Zhou period saw the capital moved to Luoyi (now Luoyang, Henan province) and was dominated by political conflict and social unrest as rival factions jockeyed for power. Some 25 emperors reigned during its duration. It also saw economic expansion and development as the use of iron revolutionized agriculture. It was in this climate of unrest that the philosophical ideologies of Confucianism, Daoism, and Legalism *(see p60)* emerged.

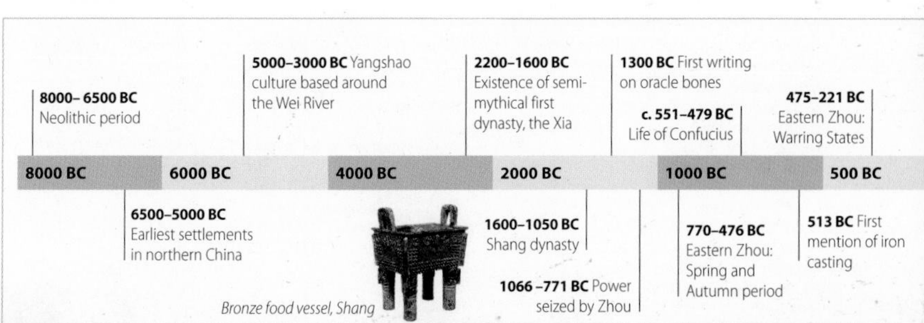
8000–6500 BC Neolithic period
5000–3000 BC Yangshao culture based around the Wei River
2200–1600 BC Existence of semi-mythical first dynasty, the Xia
1300 BC First writing on oracle bones
c. 551–479 BC Life of Confucius
475–221 BC Eastern Zhou: Warring States
8000 BC
6000 BC
4000 BC
2000 BC
1000 BC
500 BC
6500–5000 BC Earliest settlements in northern China
1600–1050 BC Shang dynasty
1066–771 BC Power seized by Zhou
770–476 BC Eastern Zhou: Spring and Autumn period
513 BC First mention of iron casting
Bronze food vessel, Shang

◀ Detail from *The First Emperor of the Han Dynasty Entering Kuan Tung* by Song painter Chao Po Chu

Dynasty Timeline

China was ruled by a succession of dynasties, broken by periods of fragmentation and civil war. The emperor's authority was divinely granted through a mandate of heaven and was thus unlimited. Leaders of succeeding dynasties claimed that the previous leadership had displeased the gods and had therefore had its heavenly mandate withdrawn.

Shang Dynasty

1600–1050 BC

The Shang dynasty marked the emergence of Bronze Age China and palace culture. A semi-divine king acted as a shaman and communicated with the gods.

Bronze tripod food vessel, Shang

Western Han

206 BC–AD 9

Gaozu	206–195 BC
Huidi	195–188 BC
Shaodi	188–180 BC
Wendi	180–157 BC
Jingdi	157–141 BC
Wudi	141–87 BC
Zhaodi	87–74 BC
Xuandi	74–49 BC
Yuandi	49–33 BC
Chengdi	33–7 BC
Aidi	7–1 BC
Pingdi	1 BC–AD 6
Ruzi	AD 7–9

Broken terracotta heads found at Jingdi's tomb

Eastern Han

AD 25–220

Guang Wudi	25–57	Shundi	125–144
Mingdi	57–75	Chongdi	144–145
Zhangdi	75–88	Zhidi	145–146
Hedi	88–105	Huandi	146–168
Shangdi	106	Lingdi	168–189
Andi	106–125	Xiandi	189–220

Tang

618–907

Gaozu	618–626	Wenzong	827–840
Taizong	626–649	Wuzong	840–846
Gaozong	649–683	Xuanzong	846–859
Zhongzong	684 & 705–710	Yizong	859–873
Ruizong	684–690 & 710–712	Xizong	873–888
Wu Zetian	690–705	Zhaozong	888–904
Xuanzong	712–756	Aidi	904–907
Suzong	756–762		
Daizong	762–779		
Dezong	779–805		
Shunzong	805		
Xianzong	805–820		
Muzong	820–824		
Jingzong	824–827		

Sancai-*glazed dancing tomb figures*

Five Dynasties and Ten Kingdoms

907–960

Based north of the Yangzi, five successive dynasties swiftly usurped one another, with no dynasty lasting for more than three reigns. The Ten Kingdoms to the south went through a similarly turbulent period.

Throughout this period and most of the Song dynasty, the northern frontiers were dominated by the semi-nomadic Liao dynasty (907–1125) in the east, and by the Western Xia (990–1227) in the west. In 1115, the Liao were overthrown by the Jin (1115–1234), who forced the Song southwards in 1127.

Yuan

1279–1368

Genghis Khan (1162–1227) united numerous Mongol-speaking tribes and captured Beijing in 1215. His grandson, Kublai, completed the conquest of China by finally defeating the Southern Song in 1279.

Kublai Khan	1279–1294
Temur Oljeitu	1294–1307
Khaishan	1308–1311
Ayurbarwada	1311–1320
Shidebala	1321–1323
Yesun Temur	1323–1328
Tugh Temur	1328–1329, 1329–1333
Khoshila	1329
Toghon Temur	1333–1368

Ming

1368–1644

Hongwu	1368–1398	Zhengde	1506–1521
Jianwen	1399–1402	Jiajing	1522–1567
Yongle	1403–1424	Longqing	1567–1572
Hongxi	1425	Wanli	1573–1620
Xuande	1426–1435	Taichang	1620
Zhengtong	1436–1449	Tianqi	1621–1627
Jingtai	1450–1457	Chongzhen	1628–1644
Tianshun (Zhengtong restored)	1457–1464		
Chenghua	1465–1487		
Hongzhi	1488–1505		

Western Zhou Dynasty

1066–771 BC

The Zhou founded their capital at Chang'an (Xi'an). They continued some Shang traditions, but reorganized the political system, dividing the nobility into grades. The feudal system of the Western Zhou broke down after the capital was sacked and the king slain.

Eastern Zhou Dynasty

770–221 BC

Spring and Autumn 770–475 BC

Warring States 475–221 BC

The Zhou dynasty ruled at its eastern capital of Luoyang alongside numerous rival states. This long period of almost constant warfare was brought to an end when the Qin emerged victorious.

Qin Dynasty

221–206 BC

Qin Shi Huang	221–210 BC
Er Shi	210–207 BC

Statue of attendant from the tomb of Qin Shi Huangdi

Period of Disunity

220–589

China was divided into the warring Wei, Wu, and Shu kingdoms. The Wei briefly re-united China under the Western Jin (280–316), the first of the six Southern Dynasties (280–589), with their capital at Jiankang (Nanjing).

The north was ruled by a succession of ruling houses – the 16 Kingdoms (304–439). The nomadic Toba Wei set up the Northern Wei dynasty, the first of five Northern Dynasties (386–581) with a capital first at Datong, then at Luoyang.

Sui

581–618

China was once more united by the short and decisive rule of the Sui.

Wendi	581–604
Yangdi	604–617
Gongdi	617–618

Emperor Wendi's flotilla on the Grand Canal

Northern Song

960–1126

Taizu	960–976
Taizong	976–997
Zhenzong	998–1022
Renzong	1022–1063
Yingzong	1064–1067
Shenzong	1068–1085
Zhezong	1086–1101
Huizong	1101–1125
Qinzong	1126–1127

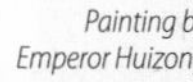

Painting by Emperor Huizong

Southern Song

1127–1279

Gaozong	1127–1162
Xiaozong	1163–1190
Guangzong	1190–1194
Ningzong	1195–1224
Lizong	1225–1264
Duzong	1265–1274
Gongdi	1275
Duanzong	1276–1278
Di Bing	1279

Emperor Zhengde's love of leisure led to a relaxation of imperial control

Qing

1644–1911

Shunzhi	1644–1661
Kangxi	1661–1722
Yongzheng	1723–1735
Qianlong	1736–1795
Jiaqing	1796–1820
Daoguang	1821–1850
Xianfeng	1851–1861
Tongzhi	1862–1874
Guangxu	1875–1908
Xuantong (Pu Yi)	1909–1912

Imperial dragon detail on the back of a eunuch's official court robe

Foundation of Imperial China

The Warring States period finally ended in 221 BC, when King Zheng of the state of Qin conquered the last of his rivals. Declaring himself the first emperor of China, or Qin Shihuang, he ruled over a short yet decisive period of history. The Qin state was based on the political theories of Legalism, which established the role of the ruler as paramount and espoused a system of collective responsibility. Following unification, Qin Shihuang conscripted thousands of workers to join together the defensive walls to the north, creating the Great Wall. He standardized the system of money, and weights and measures, and laid the foundations for a legal system. A ruthless ruler, Qin Shihuang died in the belief that his famous terracotta army would protect him in the afterlife from his many enemies.

Archer from Qin terracotta army

The founding of the Han dynasty (206 BC–AD 220) heralded a "golden age" in Chinese history. Emperor Gaodi (r. 206–195 BC) made Chang'an (Xi'an) the capital of the Western Han (206 BC–AD 9), and retained much of the centralized administration established by the Qin. Han society was founded on the principles propounded by Confucius, and the Confucian classics formed the basis of the civil service examination developed by subsequent emperors to select able men for state office. Daoism and *yin-yang* theory coexisted with ancestor worship and would form the basis of indigenous Chinese belief *(see pp36–9)*.

The Han empire expanded with regions of Central Asia, Vietnam, and Korea being brought under Chinese control. In 138 BC, General Zhang Qian was sent to establish diplomatic links with Central Asia and returned with tales of rich pastures and "heavenly horses." The fine thoroughbreds of Ferghana (in modern Uzbekistan) were traded in exchange for Chinese silk, starting the flow of goods along the fabled Silk Road *(see pp470–71)*.

Han rule was briefly interrupted as Wang Mang seized power in AD 9, only to be restored by Guang Wudi (r. AD 25–57), who established the Eastern Han capital in Luoyang. Once more, the Han expanded Chinese territory. Paper was by now in use for much official documentation and the first Chinese dictionary was produced. Buddhism began its spread to China with the first Buddhist communities being established in Jiangsu province.

Chariot and footmen, impressed into a tomb's brick, Han

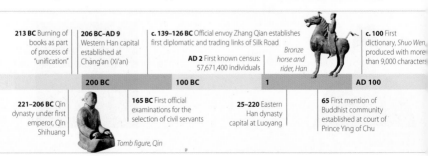

213 BC Burning of books as part of process of "unification"

206 BC–AD 9 Western Han capital established at Chang'an (Xi'an)

c. 139–126 BC Official envoy Zhang Qian establishes first diplomatic and trading links of Silk Road

AD 2 First known census: 57,671,400 individuals

Bronze horse and rider, Han

c. 100 First dictionary, *Shuo Wen,* produced with more than 9,000 characters

200 BC | 100 BC | 1 | AD 100

221–206 BC Qin dynasty under first emperor, Qin Shihuang

Tomb figure, Qin

165 BC First official examinations for the selection of civil servants

25–220 Eastern Han dynasty capital at Luoyang

65 First mention of Buddhist community established at court of Prince Ying of Chu

Sui emperors Yangdi and Wendi in a detail from *Portraits of the 13 Emperors* by Tang painter Yen Li Pen

Period of Division

From the rule of Hedi (r. AD 88–105), the Eastern Han declined. Civil war finally split the country in 220. The next 350 years were characterized by almost constant warfare as China was ruled by over 14 short-lived dynasties and 16 "kingdoms."

China was divided into the Northern and Southern dynasties (265–581), each region taking on its own distinct character. Foreign peoples took control of the north, such as the Toba branch of the Xianbei, who founded the Northern Wei in 386. These rulers were receptive to foreign ideas and religions, creating some of the finest Buddhist cave complexes first at Yungang, near their capital in Datong, and from 494, at Longmen, when they moved their capital to Luoyang.

Apsara from Buddhist cave, Northern Wei

As foreign invaders took control of the north, the Han Chinese retreated south to establish their new capital at Jiankang (Nanjing). In a climate of relative stability, the south became the economic and cultural center as the population shifted to the Yangzi delta. Philosophy and the arts flourished alongside a renewed interest in Daoism and a growing interest in Buddhism.

Unification & Stability

Following military successes against the Liang and the Chen, the Northern Zhou general Yang Jian (541–604) pronounced himself emperor, taking the name Wendi, and founded the Sui dynasty in 581. This brief but significant dynastic rule established political and social stability. Yang Jian undertook an extensive program of works including extending the Great Wall and the beginnings of the Grand Canal. The second emperor, Yangdi (569–617), restored diplomatic relations with Japan and Taiwan and extended trade to Central Asia.

190 Communications with Central Asia are cut

220 Civil war breaks out between the kingdoms of Wei, Shu, and Wu

late 3rd c. Renewed interest in Daoism

265–581 China divided into Northern and Southern dynasties

310 Massive exodus of Chinese upper classes to south

386–535 Northern Wei first of the ruling houses to adopt Buddhism

Colossal Buddha at Yungang Caves, Northern Wei

c. 6th C First true porcelain produced

581–618 Sui dynasty, initiated by Wendi's reunification of China

c. 7th C Woodblock printing first used in China

200 | 300 | 400 | 500 | 600

Tang Dynasty (618–907)

The Tang dynasty is widely regarded as one of China's golden ages, characterized by economic prosperity, territorial expansion, and political stability. During this period China reached its largest size to date: from Korea to Vietnam and across Central Asia to southern Siberia. Trade flourished by land and sea, stimulating the flow of luxury goods between East and West. Foreign religions were tolerated and Buddhism gained popular and imperial patronage. The arts and literature of the Tang are still considered to be among China's finest, notably the famous poets Li Bai and Du Fu.

Locator Map

Tang rule AD 750

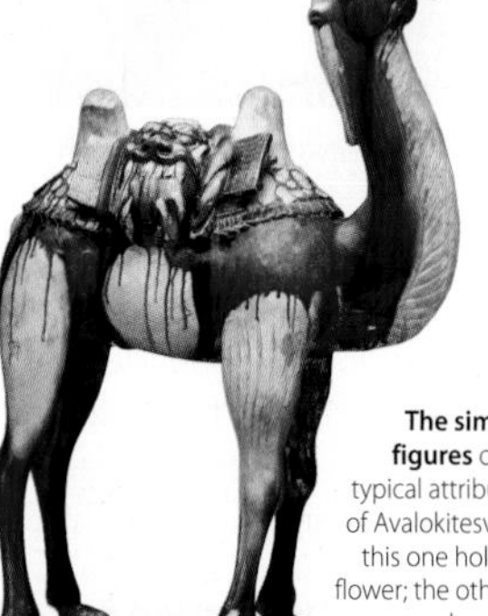

This pottery figure, decorated in three-color or *sancai* glaze, depicts life along the Silk Road. Merchants and pilgrims traveled the legendary route bringing with them objects crafted in gold and silver, textiles, exotic foods, and fine horses.

The similar figures carry typical attributes of Avalokitesvara: this one holds a flower; the other a vase and a sprig of willow.

Ample draped robes, typical of Tang style

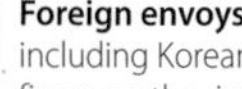

Foreign envoys, including Koreans (the figure on the right) and Westerners (standing next to the Korean), traveled to the Tang court for delegations and giving tribute, as seen in this tomb mural.

This silver cup, part of a hoard of buried treasure dug up in 1970, shows distinct Western influence, although the relief decoration is lavishly Tang.

Chang'an's (Xi'an's) elaborate city walls enclosed a population of one million by the 7th century, making Chang'an the largest city in the world. The cosmopolitan capital was populated by Sogdians, Turks, Uighur, Arabs, and Persians.

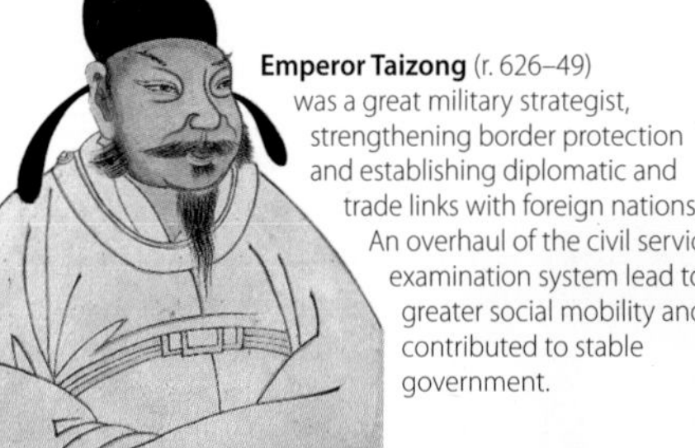

Emperor Taizong (r. 626–49) was a great military strategist, strengthening border protection and establishing diplomatic and trade links with foreign nations. An overhaul of the civil service examination system lead to greater social mobility and contributed to stable government.

Wu Zetian (r. 690–705), the only empress in Chinese history, manipulated her weak husband, Emperor Gaozong, and ruthlessly eradicated her opposition. Despite her scandalous nature, she became a strong ruler and brought peace and prosperity.

Inscriptions were written for wealthy donors who commissioned paintings on behalf of themselves or loved ones in order to accrue religious merit.

Avalokitesvara, one of the most popular *bodhisattvas*, is identified by the Amitabha Buddha in his crown.

Emperor Xuanzong (r. 712–56) or Minghuang, the Brilliant Emperor, ruled over a glorious period. A great scholar and patron of the arts, he poured his wealth into temple construction and founded the Academy of Letters (Hanlinyuan) in 754.

Dunhuang Silks

During the Tang dynasty, Buddhism gained popular and imperial support, particularly under the rule of the devout Wu Zetian. Buddhist communities became important centers for the translation of sutras *and the production of Buddhist arts, such as the fine silk paintings of Dunhuang.*

An Emperor's Love and Demise

In his later years, the Xuanzong emperor increasingly neglected his official duties as he became infatuated with his concubine, Yang Guifei. Intrigue and factions at court bred instability and in 750, General An Lushan, half-Sogdian half-Turkish by descent, seized control of the northeastern frontier. In 755, An Lushan stormed the capital forcing the court to flee for Sichuan. As they reached Mawai, Xuanzong's troops mutinied and demanded the emperor hand over Yang Guifei. She was strangled before his eyes, and the tragic story of their love affair has been immortalized by poets. Although An Lushan was eventually defeated, the Tang dynasty fell into decline.

Yang Guifei's plump figure became a classic *sancai* form

Glory of the Tang

The Tang dynasty (AD 618–907) marks a high point in Chinese history *(see pp62–3)*. During this golden age, China enjoyed an extended period of peace and prosperity. The arts flourished and were enriched by foreign styles, motifs, and techniques such as silverworking. Foreign religions, such as Nestorian Christianity, were tolerated and coexisted alongside native Daoism and Confucianism. Woodblock printing was invented by the Chinese some time during the 7th century and hastened the spread of Buddhism.

Sancai glazed horse, Tang

Following the An Lushan rebellion of 755, the Tang became increasingly inward-looking. The great Buddhist persecution of 841–6 was symptomatic of a dynasty in decline, it finally fell in 907.

The Liao Dynasty (907–1125)

The Liao dynasty, which at its largest covered much of Mongolia, Manchuria, and northern China, was ruled by semi-nomadic and pastoral people, the Qidan. The Liao maintained a dual administration, Qidan and Chinese, and even a prime-ministership, to ensure the survival of their own customs and traditions whilst utilizing the efficiency of Tang structures of government. In 1115, the Qidan were overthrown by another semi-nomadic people, the Ruzhen (Jurchen). With the support of the Northern Song, the Ruzhen took control of the north and founded the Jin dynasty. The Liao were forced westwards to the region of the Tian mountain range in present-day Xinjiang, where they established the Western Liao (1125–1211). The rest of northwest China was dominated by the Western Xia, a Tibetan-related people who recognized the Liao as their overlords.

Five Dynasties & Ten Kingdoms (907–60)

While the north of China was dominated by the insurgence of semi-nomadic peoples from the steppe regions, the south was ruled by a series of short military dictatorships. The Song dynasty was founded in 960 by Zhao Kuangyin, a military commander of the later Zhou (951–960), whose imperial name became Shizong. In the Yangzi delta and regions to the south, the Ten Kingdoms existed in relative peace and stability and were reunited by the Song in 979.

Painting of an official celebrating, Five Dynasties (923–38)

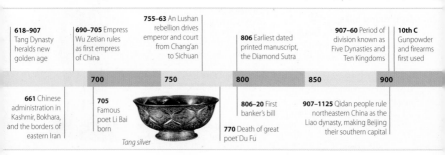

618–907 Tang Dynasty heralds new golden age

690–705 Empress Wu Zetian rules as first empress of China

755–63 An Lushan rebellion drives emperor and court from Chang'an to Sichuan

806 Earliest dated printed manuscript, the Diamond Sutra

907–60 Period of division known as Five Dynasties and Ten Kingdoms

10th C Gunpowder and firearms first used

700 | 750 | 800 | 850 | 900

661 Chinese administration in Kashmir, Bokhara, and the borders of eastern Iran

705 Famous poet Li Bai born

Tang silver

770 Death of great poet Du Fu

806–20 First banker's bill

907–1125 Qidan people rule northeastern China as the Liao dynasty, making Beijing their southern capital

The Song Dynasty (960–1279)

The Song presided over a period of cultural brilliance and unprecedented growth in urban life, during which the social makeup of China fundamentally changed. Less territorially ambitious than the Tang, the Song stimulated economic development through improved communications and transportation. New industries based on mass production began to emerge, notably the porcelain industry based in Jiangxi province. During the Southern Song, China underwent an industrial revolution producing raw materials such as salt and iron on a scale that would not be seen in Europe until the 18th century.

In this buoyant economic climate a new middle class emerged, stimulating demand for the new range of consumer goods. Power shifted from the aristocratic elite to government bureaucrats, who spent their spare time practicing poetry, calligraphy, and painting. Collecting and connoisseurship led to an artistic renaissance and the founding of the first imperial collections. Emperor Huizong was a great patron of the arts who used ancient precedents and values to buttress his own position. Neo-Confucianism and a renewed interest in Daoism marked a return to indigenous beliefs and traditional structures of power.

Early movable type, Song

The Northern Song repeatedly came under attack from the Western Xia in the northwest and the Jin in the northeast. Only 12 years after joining forces with the Song against the Liao, the Jin invaded the Northern Song capital at Bianliang (Kaifeng), capturing Emperor Qinzong and forcing the court to flee southwards. The capital of the Southern Song (1127–1279) was established at Lin'an (Hangzhou), south of the Yangzi.

Illustration of Song Emperor Huizong, r. 1101–25

Jin Dynasty (1115–1234)

The Jin were a semi-nomadic Tungusic people originating from Manchuria. War with the Song and persistent attacks from the Mongols resulted in a weakening of the Jin state, which by the early 13th century formed a buffer state between the Song in the south and the Mongols in the north. In 1227, Mongol and Chinese allied forces defeated the Jin and in 1234 the Jin emperor committed suicide. The Jin state was integrated into the rapidly expanding Mongol Empire.

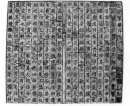

960–1126 Northern Song reunites China and bases capital at Bianliang (Kaifeng)
Detail of painting by Emperor Huizong
1127–1279 Southern Song dynasty with capital at Hangzhou, after being forced south by the Jin
1154 First issue of paper money (Jin)
1206–08 Song and Jin at war
950
1000
1050
1100
1150
1200
990–1227 Western Xia people establish kingdom dominating northwest China
1041–8 First attempts at printing with movable type
1090 First attested use of compass on Chinese ships
1115–1234 Jin dynasty founded in northeast China forcing Liao westwards
1214 Jin move capital from Beijing to Kaifeng in Henan province

Mongol Rule (1279–1368)

The Mongol leader Genghis Khan *(see p477)* united the various Mongol-speaking tribes of the steppes and in 1215 conquered northern China. He divided his empire into four kingdoms, each ruled by one of his sons. His grandson Kublai Khan (r. 1260–94), ruler of the eastern Great Khanate, finally defeated the Southern Song in 1279 and proclaimed himself emperor of the Yuan dynasty. China now became part of a vast empire which stretched from the East China Sea across Asia as far as Poland, Hungary, and Bohemia. Two capitals were maintained at Dadu or Khanbalik (present-day Beijing) and Yuanshangdu (Xanadu). The Silk Road opened once more, connecting China to the Middle East and Medieval Europe. Direct contact was now made for the first time between the Mongol court and European diplomats, Franciscan missionaries, and merchants. According to the writings of Marco Polo, the Italian merchant spent 21 years in the service of Kublai and his court.

Buddhist deity, Yuan

The Mongols ruled through a form of military government, in contrast to the bureaucratic civil service established by the Chinese. Although Chinese and Mongol languages were both used for official business, the Chinese were not encouraged to take up official posts. Muslims from Central and Western Asia took their place, and the Chinese increasingly retreated from official life.

As there were no clear rules for succession, civil war broke out in 1328 between Mongol nobles. The secret societies of the Red Turbans and the White Lotus led peasant rebellions and in 1368 General Zhu Yuanzhang forced the Mongols out of China, becoming the first emperor of the Ming dynasty.

Genghis Khan (c.1162–1227), Persian miniature

Ming Dynasty (1368–1644)

The Ming (literally "brilliant") dynasty was one of the longest and most stable periods in China's history. The founder of the Ming, Zhu Yuanzhang, rose from humble beginnings to become a general, ruling as the Hongwu emperor ("Vast Military Accomplishment"). During his reign, Hongwu introduced radical changes to both central and local government, which he made binding on his successors. The emperor's role became more autocratic as Hongwu dispensed with the position of prime minister, taking direct responsibility for overseeing all six ministries himself.

Hongwu appointed his grandson to be his successor. Upon his death his son, the Prince

1215 Mongols capture Beijing

1227 Genghis Khan dies, having united various Mongol-speaking tribes of the steppe

1234 Jin emperor commits suicide and Jin integrated into Mongol empire

Mongol on horseback

1250

1279–1368 Kublai Khan defeats Southern Song and rules China as emperor of the Yuan dynasty

1300

1328 Civil war breaks out between Mongol nobles

1350

1368–1644 Ming dynasty, founded by rebel leader General Zhu Yuanzhang

1400

1403 Construction of Great Walls in North China

Jade elephant, Ming

The existing battlements of the Great Wall, reinforced and joined together during the Ming dynasty

of Yan, who controlled the region around Beijing, led an army against his nephew, taking Nanjing and proclaiming himself Emperor Yongle ("Eternal Joy"). Yongle (r. 1403–24) moved the capital to his power base in Beijing, where he created a new city based on traditional principles of Chinese city planning. At its core lay the Forbidden City *(see pp92–5)*, the imperial palace and offices of government, surrounded by a grid system of streets, with four imperial altars at the cardinal points. The entire city was walled to provide both protection and enclosure. In 1421, Beijing became the official capital and would remain so until the present day. The Great Wall was reinforced, extended and faced with brick during the Ming dynasty.

By the 15th century, China had become a significant maritime power, its ships dwarfing those of contemporary Europe. Blue and white porcelain, silk, and other luxury items were in high demand in the foreign markets of Japan, Southeast Asia, and the Middle East. Yongle sent six maritime expeditions under the Muslim eunuch admiral Zheng He, which reached as far as the east coast of Africa. In 1514 Portuguese traders first landed in China, purchasing tea, which then became a fashionable drink in European society. Porcelain provided ballast for the ships, and other luxury items were brought back along with the cargo. Trade was dominated by the Dutch in the 17th century, only to be surpassed by the British a hundred years later. Jesuit missionaries, who arrived in the 16th century, claimed few converts but gained access to the emperor and the inner court.

Wedding jewelry, Ming

The arts thrived under the Xuande emperor (r. 1425–35), an artist and poet, who patronized the arts, notably the porcelain industry at Jingdezhen. In literature, the late Ming is noted for its great dramas and classical novels, such as *Journey to the West (see p35)*. Philosophy of the time reinforced the Neo-Confucianism of the Song.

The late Ming was dominated by peasant uprisings, incursions by Japanese pirates and Mongolian tribes, and excessive eunuch power. Rebellions within China eventually joined with external forces to end Ming rule.

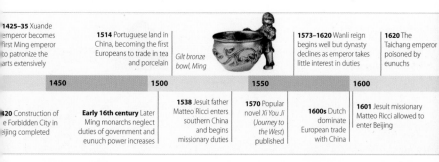

1425–35 Xuande emperor becomes first Ming emperor to patronize the arts extensively

1514 Portuguese land in China, becoming the first Europeans to trade in tea and porcelain

Gilt bronze bowl, Ming

1573–1620 Wanli reign begins well but dynasty declines as emperor takes little interest in duties

1620 The Taichang emperor poisoned by eunuchs

1450 | 1500 | 1550 | 1600

420 Construction of e Forbidden City in eijing completed

Early 16th century Later Ming monarchs neglect duties of government and eunuch power increases

1538 Jesuit father Matteo Ricci enters southern China and begins missionary duties

1570 Popular novel *Xi You Ji (Journey to the West)* published

1600s Dutch dominate European trade with China

1601 Jesuit missionary Matteo Ricci allowed to enter Beijing

Qing Rule (1644–1911)

The Manchu leader Nurhachi established the Later Jin in 1616, organizing the scattered tribes of the north into eight banner units *(see pp438–9)*. In 1636, the Manchu ruler Abahai changed the name to Qing, literally "pure," and prepared the way for the capture of Beijing in 1644. Under Manchu control, China was once more ruled by a foreign people. The Manchus were keen to adopt the Chinese method of rule, encouraging Chinese scholars into the service of the new empire. Dual administration at national and provincial levels meant Manchu and Chinese bureaucrats worked side by side using first Manchu and later Chinese as the official languages of government. However, despite the close interaction of Manchu and Chinese, the ruling Manchus were careful to maintain a distinct separation in order to protect their own privileges and cultural traditions.

Emperor Kangxi, r. 1661–1722

The first emperors of the Qing were enlightened rulers who presided over one of the largest and most populous countries in the world. The territorial aspirations of the Kangxi emperor brought the regions of Central Asia and southern Siberia once more under Chinese control. Kangxi *(see p128)* was succeeded by the Yongzheng emperor. It was his fourth son, the Qianlong emperor, "Lasting Eminence," (r. 1735–96) who heralded another golden age. An ambitious ruler, Qianlong was determined to extend China's borders beyond those of the Tang, personally leading campaigns to Burma, Vietnam, and Central Asia.

During the 18th century, contact with the West increased through Jesuit missionaries and trade. By the mid-18th century, the Chinese sought to control trade by refusing all official contact with Westerners and opening only Canton to foreign merchants. Pressure from European embassies increased as the British sent Lord Macartney in 1792–4 to establish diplomatic relations and open China to trade. China refused to grant a single concession to the British.

The Decline of the Empire

The 19th century is one of the most turbulent periods of Chinese history, as internal uprisings, natural disasters, and the relentless encroachment of the West culminated in the end of the empire. A succession of weak rulers were manipulated and controlled by the

Lord Macartney's massive entourage arriving at Qianlong's tent

1644–1911 Manchus establish Qing dynasty

1644–1800 Military expansion into Central Asia and Siberia; colonization of new territories Yunnan and Xinjiang

1650 First Catholic church in Beijing

1661–1722 Rule of Kangxi emperor. Appoints Jesuits to run Board of Astronomy

1723–35 Kangxi's son Yin Zhen seizes power, ruling under name of Emperor Yongzheng

1735–96 Qianlong, a great patron of the arts, rules over another golden age

The Shunzhi emperor, r. 1644–61

1747 Qianlong builds Yuanming Yuan *(see p109)* in Western style

1757 Chinese restrict all foreign trade to Canton

1650 1675 1700 1725 1750

A merchant testing tea quality in a Cantonese warehouse

Dowager Empress Cixi, who ruled for much of the late Qing from "behind the curtain." The Taiping Rebellion of 1850–64 devastated south and central China *(see p428)*.

Western powers, frustrated by the reluctance of the Chinese to open to foreign trade, brought the Chinese under increasing pressure. Keen to protect the trade of opium from their colonies in India, the British engaged in the First Opium War (1840–42), which culminated in the Treaty of Nanjing, resulting in the opening of four new ports to trade (known as "Treaty Ports"), the payment of huge indemnities, and the ceding of Hong Kong to Britain. Following the Arrow War (Second Opium War) with Britain and France (1856), the European forces divided China into "spheres of influence" – the British strongest along the Yangzi and in Shanghai, the Germans controlling Shandong province, and the French controlling the borders with Vietnam. In 1900 the Boxers allied with imperial troops and attacked the foreign legations in Beijing *(see p439)*. An eight-nation army defeated the onslaught, and Cixi fled to Xi'an, blaming everything on the emperor. The Chinese government paid once more for the loss of life and Cixi returned to Beijing until her death in 1908. The child emperor Pu Yi lived in the Forbidden City as the last emperor until his abdication. On 1 January 1912 the Republican leader Sun Yat-sen inaugurated the Chinese Republic.

From Empire to Republic

In the final years of the empire, many Chinese intellectuals recognized the need to modernize. Supporters of the Reform Movement of 1898 propounded the adoption of Western technology and education, and, following the Boxer Rebellion, a number of reforms were adopted. Elected regional assemblies were set up, further undermining the power of the Qing. In 1911 the empire collapsed completely. Sun Yat-sen *(see p303)* was elected provisional President of China, but was soon forced to resign in favor of General Yuan Shikai, who sought to become emperor. Yuan was forced to back down when governors revolted and he died soon after in 1916. China then came under the control of a series of regional warlords until it was united once more with the founding of the People's Republic of China in 1949.

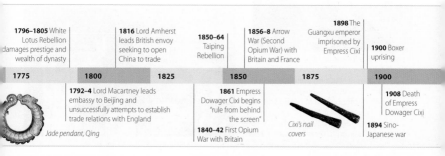

Sun Yat-sen, 1866–1925

1796–1805 White Lotus Rebellion damages prestige and wealth of dynasty

1816 Lord Amherst leads British envoy seeking to open China to trade

1850–64 Taiping Rebellion

1856–8 Arrow War (Second Opium War) with Britain and France

1898 The Guangxu emperor imprisoned by Empress Cixi

1900 Boxer uprising

1775 | 1800 | 1825 | 1850 | 1875 | 1900

1792–4 Lord Macartney leads embassy to Beijing and unsuccessfully attempts to establish trade relations with England

Jade pendant, Qing

1861 Empress Dowager Cixi begins "rule from behind the screen"

1840–42 First Opium War with Britain

Cixi's nail covers

1908 Death of Empress Dowager Cixi

1894 Sino-Japanese war

The Cultural Revolution

In 1966, Mao Zedong set in motion a chain of events that were to unleash the turmoil now known as the Cultural Revolution. Having socialized industry and agriculture, Mao called on the masses to transform society itself – all distinctions between manual and intellectual work were to be abolished and class distinction disappear. The revolution reached its violent peak in 1967, with the Red Guard spreading social unrest. The People's Liberation Army (PLA) finally restored order, but the subsequent years were characterized by fear, violence, and mistrust.

Children were encouraged to take part in the revolution. Their enthusiasm led to the destruction of family photographs and possessions. In some cases, children denounced their own parents.

The Red Guard

Mao appealed to students to form the Red Guard, in whom he entrusted the fate of the revolution. The movement rapidly gathered momentum and the Red Guard, who raised Mao to godly status, traveled China spreading Mao Zedong "Thoughts," smashing remnants of the past, vandalizing temples, and wreaking havoc.

Mass public meetings were held as part of the Socialist Education Movement, a precursor of the Cultural Revolution intended to reverse "capitalist" and "revisionist" tendencies perceived in social and economic life. Everyone was required to attend.

The *Little Red Book* was essential to the Red Guard and issued to every soldier under Lin Biao's command.

An injured cadre is carried away after being denounced. Shamings became the bench mark of public meetings. Many politicians and teachers were paraded and accused, leading to job loss and, in some cases, suicide.

Demonstrating their opposition to Soviet-style communism and their support for Maoism, Red Guards change a Beijing street sign in front of the Soviet Embassy from East Yangwei to Fanxiu Lu (Anti-Revisionism Road).

Lin Biao spread the study of the "Thoughts of Mao" and compiled the *Little Red Book*, which became obligatory reading for his army recruits. As head of the PLA, Lin Biao provided essential military backing and was Mao's named successor. He died in a plane crash over Siberia in 1971 amid rumors of an imminent usurpation.

Model operas were the pet project of Mao's third wife, Jiang Qing. She set about creating a politically correct revolutionary culture. Many artists and intellectuals were sent to the countryside for re-education.

May 7 Cadre Schools were set up by the central government in 1968. As many as 100,000 officials plus 30,000 family members were sent to perform manual labor and undergo ideological re-education. An unknown number of lower-ranking cadres were sent to thousands of other cadre schools.

Liu Shaoqi *(right)*, president from 1959–66, was one of a number of high officials to be denounced, imprisoned, and paraded in "struggle rallies." He died from his experiences.

Gang of Four

The Gang of Four, as they became known, orchestrated attacks on intellectuals and writers, high officials, the party, and the state and were responsible for some of the worst excesses of the Cultural Revolution. Zhang Chunqiao, critic and propagandist; Yao Wenyuan, editor-in-chief of *Shanghai Liberation Army Daily;* Wang Hongwen, a young worker; and Mao's third wife Jiang Qing, an ex-film star, dominated the political center unchallenged until Mao's death in 1976. Millions of Chinese citizens watched their televized trial in 1980–81. Jiang Qing, who was singled out by propagandists and became one of the most hated figures in China, was defiant until the end, railing against her prosecutors throughout the trial. She took her own life in 1991, while serving her life sentence.

Lynched effigies of members of the Gang of Four hanging from a tree

Chiang Kai-shek (1887–1975), leader of the KMT

Communists & Nationalists

After the fall of the empire, the political landscape changed dramatically and became dominated by two forces, the Nationalist Party or Kuomintang (KMT) and the Communist Party, founded in 1921. The Nationalists were led first by Sun Yat-sen from his power base in Guangzhou, then by General Chiang Kai-shek who seized power in 1926. In 1923 the two Parties formed a "united front" against the warlords, but in 1926 the Communists were expelled from the KMT. Chiang Kai-shek led his army to Nanjing where he tried to establish a Nationalist capital, and betrayed the Communist-led workers of Shanghai who were massacred by underworld gangsters. The Communists were driven underground and Mao Zedong retreated to the countryside.

High in the mountains of Jiangxi province, Mao and Zhu De founded the Jiangxi Soviet in 1930. From this inaccessible base, the Communists began to redistribute land to the peasants and institute new marriage laws. In 1934, Chiang Kai-shek drove the Communists from the area, forcing Mao to embark on the legendary Long March *(see pp262–3)*. Yan'an, where the march ended, became the new Communist Party headquarters and would remain so until 1945.

Japanese Attack

Domestic turmoil laid China open to attack, and in 1931 the Japanese occupied Manchuria, founding the puppet state of Manchukuo and placing the last Qing emperor, Pu Yi, at its head *(see p452)*. By 1937 the Japanese had occupied much of northern China, Shanghai, and the Yangzi valley, ruthlessly taking cities, wreaking death and devastation. The Japanese were finally driven from Chinese soil in 1945, and China was plunged into civil war.

The East Is Red

By 1947, the Communist policy of land reform was reaping rewards and gaining the support of people in the countryside. In 1948–9, the Communists gained decisive victories over the KMT. On 1 October 1949 Chairman Mao pronounced the founding of the People's Republic of China in Beijing. Chiang Kai-shek fled to Taiwan, establishing a Nationalist government and taking with him many imperial treasures.

Communist poster depicting Mao surrounded by the masses

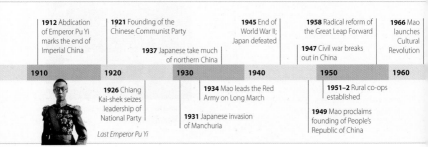

1910 | 1920 | 1930 | 1940 | 1950 | 1960

1912 Abdication of Emperor Pu Yi marks the end of Imperial China

1921 Founding of the Chinese Communist Party

1926 Chiang Kai-shek seizes leadership of National Party

Last Emperor Pu Yi

1931 Japanese invasion of Manchuria

1934 Mao leads the Red Army on Long March

1937 Japanese take much of northern China

1945 End of World War II; Japan defeated

1947 Civil war breaks out in China

1949 Mao proclaims founding of People's Republic of China

1951–2 Rural co-ops established

1958 Radical reform of the Great Leap Forward

1966 Mao launches Cultural Revolution

Zhou Enlai with President Nixon

In the early years of the People's Republic, the Chinese worked hard to rebuild a country devastated by years of turmoil. New laws sought to redress past inequities, redistributing land and outlawing arranged marriages. In 1957 the Party launched the Hundred Flowers movement, which encouraged freedom of expression. Unprepared for the resulting criticism, the Party branded intellectuals as "rightists" and sent them to the countryside for re-education. Frustrated with the slow rate of change, Mao launched the Great Leap Forward in 1958. Large communes providing food and childcare replaced the family, supposedly improving productivity. But unrealistic targets and falsified statistics concealed the disastrous effects. Agricultural failure coupled with natural disasters resulted in the starvation of millions.

His prestige dented, Mao sought to reassert his authority and launched the Cultural Revolution in 1966 *(see pp70–71)*. The greatest excesses were over by 1971, but real change did not come until Mao's death in 1976. Deng Xiaoping emerged as leader, implementing economic reforms that returned land to the peasants and allowed greater economic freedom. He introduced the one-child policy to rein in China's population growth.

The economic liberalization of the 1980s stimulated the economy but was unmatched by political freedom. On June 4, 1989, a democracy movement calling for political reform was brutally suppressed in Beijing's Tian'an Men Square and in other large cities. Many students and intellectuals fled abroad, but others remained incarcerated in China's jails until recently. Pressing on with economic reform, the 1990s saw the opening of Special Economic Zones, and stock exchanges in Shenzhen and Shanghai. By 1992, China's economy had become one of the largest in the world. The unprecedented rate of growth in the 1990s was reflected in the landscape as traditional buildings made way for modern highrises. The colonies of Hong Kong and Macau were returned to China and foreign investment flooded in, with entrepreneurs prospering.

The financial crisis of 2008 had a major effect on Chinese exports. Although it is still increasing steadily, China is no longer the world's fastest-growing major economy. In 2016, worries about the aging population led the government to change to a two-child policy. How the earth's most populous nation resolves its many issues is of great interest to the rest of a world on whose future China is going to have a massive impact.

Chinese traders on the Stock Exchange

Little Red Book
1976 Mao dies
1978 Deng Xiaoping emerges as leader
1993 Jiang Zemin becomes president; construction of Three Gorges Dam begins
2003 Chinese launch first manned spacecraft; Hu Jintao becomes president
2008 Beijing hosts the Olympics
1970
1980
1990
2000
2010
2020
1972 President Nixon is first American president to visit China
1989 Democracy movement suppressed in Tian'an Men Square
1997 Hong Kong handed back to China; Macau, two years later
2001 China admitted as member of World Trade Organization
2010 Shanghai hosts the 2010 World Expo. Guangzhou also hosts the Asian Games.
2013 Xi Jinping takes over as president

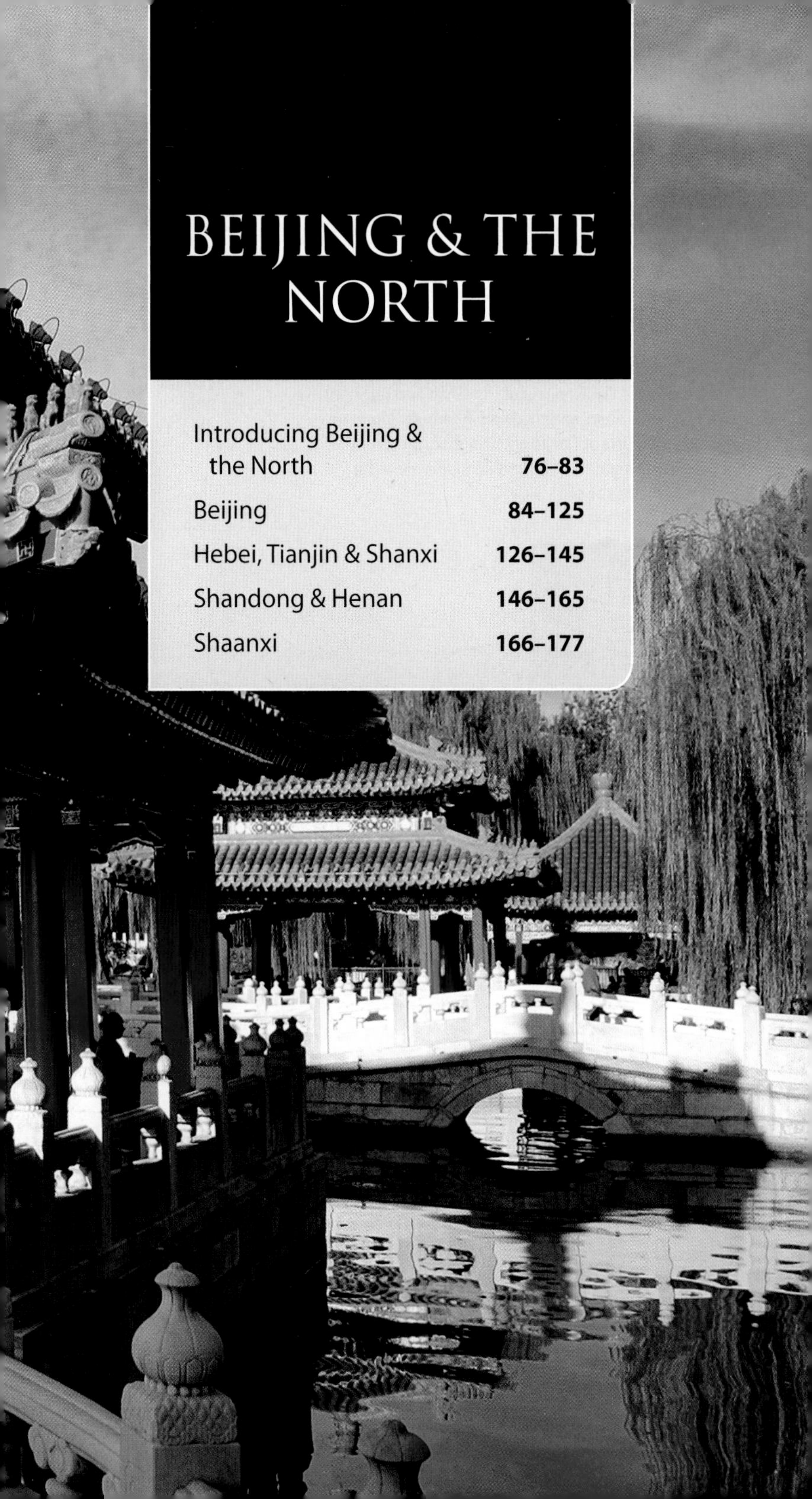

BEIJING & THE NORTH

Beijing & the North at a Glance

Threaded by the Yellow River and the Great Wall, China's north encompasses the six provinces of Hebei, Tianjin, Shanxi, Shandong, Henan, and Shaanxi, as well as Beijing, the nation's capital. From this vast domain, six ancient capitals governed China, leaving behind a wealth of dynastic sites, such as Beijing's magnificent Forbidden City, the Terracotta Army near Xi'an, and the Buddhist carvings at Longmen and Yungang. The region's religious sites include the Daoist peaks of Hua Shan and Tai Shan, the Buddhist Wutai Shan, and the Shaolin Temple. Along the coast are the ports of Tianjin and Qingdao, preserves of European architecture, and Shanhaiguan, where the Great Wall meets the sea.

Practicing *tai ji quan*, Temple of Heaven, Beijing

Vividly painted cave interior at the Yungang Grottoes, Datong, Shanxi

Key

Expressway

Main road

Minor road

Main railroad

Other railroad

Provincial border

Summit

Getting Around

Beijing has good air, rail, and bus links to the surrounding region. There are daily flights to Shanghai, Xi'an, Chengdu, Chongqing, Shenzhen, Guangzhou, Qingdao, Hangzhou, and Hong Kong. Express trains link Beijing directly with all the region's large cities, while many smaller towns are served by slower trains. Tianjin is a major north–south rail junction. There is also a comprehensive long-distance bus service, while faster private buses ply the popular tourist routes.

◀ Colorful pavilions in Bei Hai Park, Beijing

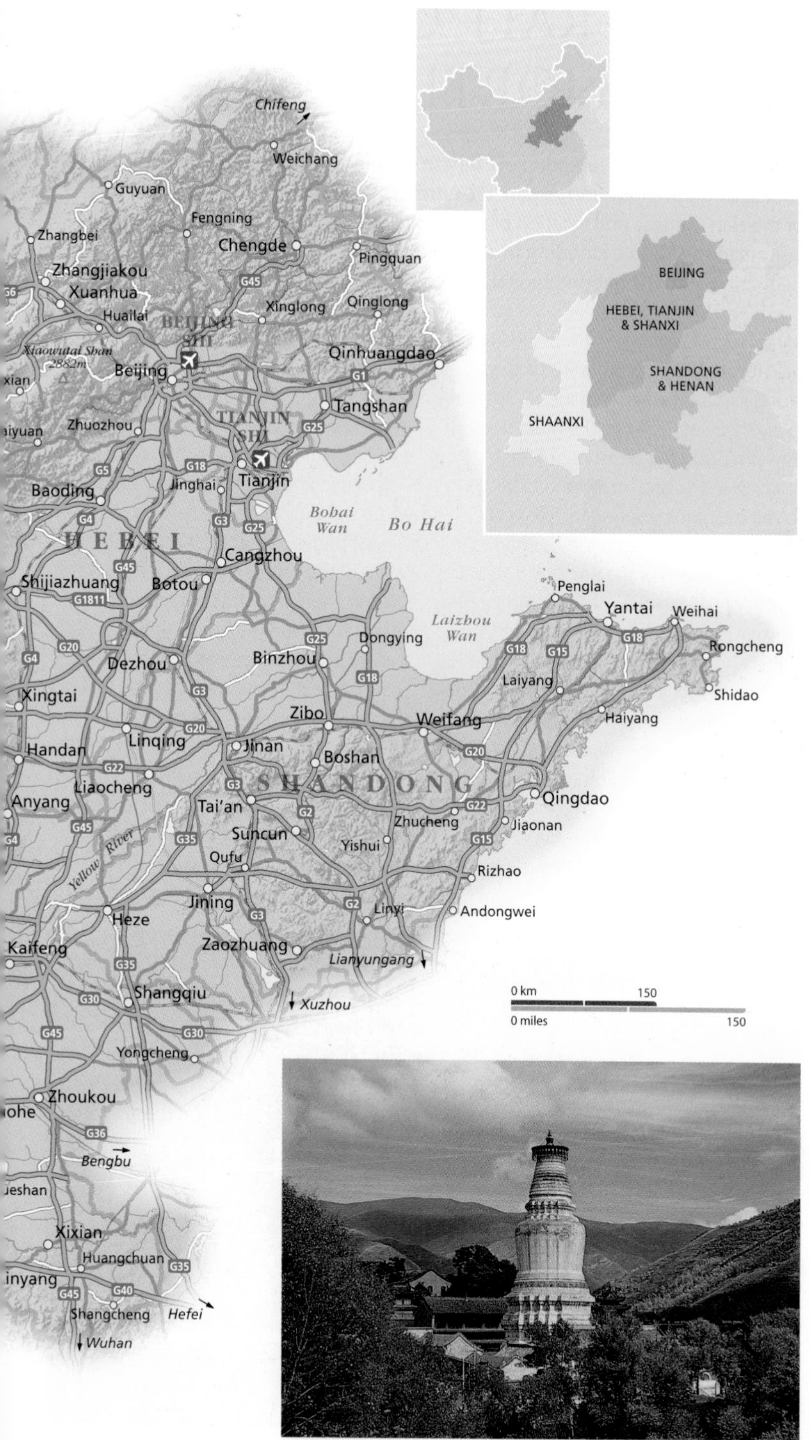

The imposing Great White Dagoba at Tayuan Si, Wutai Shan, Shanxi

For additional map symbols *see back flap*

A PORTRAIT OF BEIJING & THE NORTH

The Yellow River, the wellspring of Chinese culture and civilization, carves a course through the country's parched northern terrain, the historic homeland of the Han Chinese and location of the most significant monuments. Thus most visitors to the Middle Kingdom usually concentrate on these historic sites, beginning with the nation's capital, Beijing.

For millennia, the Yellow River (Huang He) has nurtured the communities strung along its banks while sporadically washing away their settlements. The great river flows through the provinces of Shaanxi, Shanxi, Henan, and Shandong, often forming a natural boundary between provinces. It also features in the names of Henan (South of the River) and Hebei (North of the River). In its long and looping journey it traverses a land rich in historic sights and cities, before spilling into Bo Hai (Bo Sea), north of the sacred mountain, Tai Shan. Occasionally, it comes across the vestiges of that other barrier, the Great Wall. Now a largely disintegrating bastion, the wall crawls across the face of north China, a reminder of the region's vulnerable position so close to the border with Inner Mongolia and erstwhile Manchuria. Although the Great Wall was built as a defensive fortification, it could not prevent the hordes of nomadic tribes, the so-called "barbarians," from entering China.

Neolithic finds and archeological sites wrote the province of Henan into the earliest pages of Chinese history. Here, South of the Yellow River, Luoyang and Kaifeng are two of the country's most important dynastic capitals; another ancient city, Anyang, was capital of the Shang dynasty. However, it is Xi'an in Shaanxi province that is more eclipsed by its past than any other ancient capital. Xi'an's most magnificent treasure is the Terracotta Army *(see pp174–5)*, created to guard the tomb of Qin Shi Huangdi, the Qin emperor who unified China. However Xi'an reached its zenith during the Tang

The Tower of the Fragrance of the Buddha overlooking Kunming Lake at the Summer Palace, Beijing

The modern skyline of Qingdao, Shandong province on China's east coast

dynasty *(see pp62–3)*, prospering because of its position at the eastern end of the Silk Road. The Grand Mosque and sizable Muslim population testify to Xi'an's cosmopolitan grandeur during that time.

Toward the end of the 13th century, the Mongol Kublai Khan established Beijing as his capital. But it was only in 1407, when the Ming Emperor Yongle moved his seat of power here, that Beijing achieved imperial status. Still organized along its grand Ming and Qing dynasty lines, it is a city of straight, wide boulevards and narrow, winding alleys around an ancient palatial core, the Forbidden City. The temples and palaces are today complemented by slick shopping streets and the commercial buzz of a people coming into their own in the 21st century.

Lighting incense sticks at Beijing's Lama Temple

The two adjoining provinces of Hebei and Shanxi are griddles in summer and iceboxes in winter, although Hebei's eastern seaboard towns benefit from cooling sea breezes. Shanxi, on the other hand, is sometimes affected by seasonal sand storms blowing in from the Gobi Desert. Hebei's fertile soil and productive agrarian economy contrast with landlocked Shanxi's mineral-rich terrain. Both provinces are heavily industrialized but there are still many sights that demand attention, such as the Buddhist monastery of Chongshan Si *(see p143)*, the holy mountain Tai Shan, and the port of Tianjin, Hebei's former capital. Despite modernization, Tianjin has preserved its European architecture, a legacy of its past as a foreign trading post. The Buddhist sculptures at the UNESCO World Heritage Site of the Longmen Caves in Luoyang *(see pp160–61)* are remarkable, while Shandong is best known for Qufu, the birthplace of Confucius *(see p149)*, the eminent philosopher-sage, whose teachings – which greatly influenced Chinese culture – are acceptable once more.

The kind of scenery that has inspired Chinese poets and artists for thousands of years, Hua Shan, Shaanxi

Beijing Opera

One among many hundreds of local operas across China, Beijing Opera began in the Qing dynasty. It is said that Emperor Qianlong (r. 1736–96), on a tour of the south, was rather taken by the operas of Anhui and Hebei and brought these troupes back to Beijing, where a new form of opera was established. The Guangxu emperor and Dowager Empress Cixi were also keen devotees and helped develop the art form. Beijing Opera has proved remarkably resilient, surviving the persecution of actors and the banning of most of the plays during the Cultural Revolution.

Emperor Qianlong, credited with starting Beijing Opera

Beijing Opera

Visually stunning and with a distinct musical style, the plays are based on Chinese history and literature. Beijing Opera is a form of "total theater" with singing, speech, mime, acrobatics, and symbolic visual effects.

Monkey is one of the favorite characters – clever, resourceful, and brave. He appears in Chinese classic literature *(see p35)*.

The colors of the painted faces symbolize the individual character's qualities. Red, for example, represents loyalty and courage; purple, solemnity and a sense of justice; green, bravery and irascibility.

The acrobatics of Beijing Opera combine graceful gymnastics and movements from the martial arts. Training is notoriously hard. The costumes are designed to make the jumps seem more spectacular by billowing out as they spin.

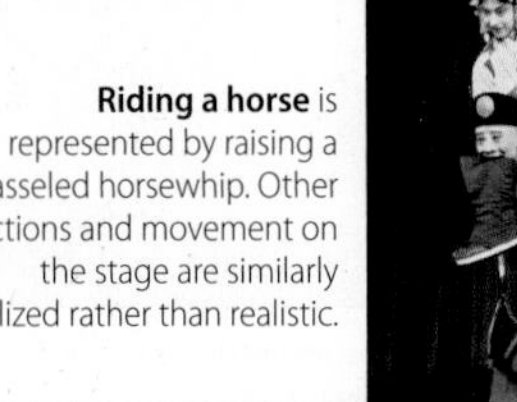

Riding a horse is represented by raising a tasseled horsewhip. Other actions and movement on the stage are similarly stylized rather than realistic.

Musical Instruments

Despite the dramatic visual elements of Beijing Opera, the Chinese say that they go to "listen" to opera, not to see it. The importance of the musical elements should not therefore be underestimated. Typically six or seven instrumentalists accompany the opera. The stringed instruments usually include the *erhu* or Chinese two-stringed violin, *sanxian* or three-stringed lute, and moon guitar, or possibly *pipa* (traditional lute). The main function of the instruments is to accompany the singing. Percussion instruments include clappers, gongs, and drums. These are used largely to punctuate the action; movement and sound are intimately linked. Wind instruments also sometimes feature, such as the Chinese horn, flute, and *suona*.

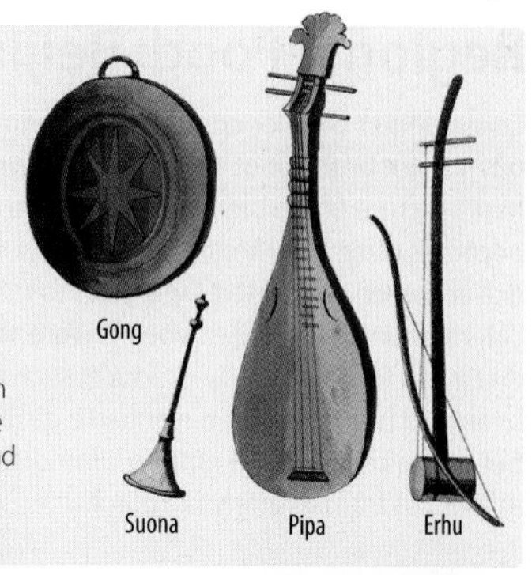

Mei Lanfang was the foremost interpreter of the female role type or *dan* during the opera's heyday in the 1920s and 1930s. Traditionally all female roles were played by male actors, although that has now changed.

The Four Main Roles

There are four main role types in Beijing Opera: the *sheng* (male) and *dan* (female) roles have naturalistic make-up. The *jing* or "painted faces," in contrast, have stylized patterned, colored faces, while the *chou* are comic characters.

Sheng: these may be young or old, with beard or without.

Dan: there are six parts within this role, from virtuous girl to old woman.

Chou: with a white patch on his face, the *chou* is usually dim but amusing.

Jing: the most striking looking, they also have the most forceful personality.

Regional Food: Beijing & the North

Communities developed beside the Yellow River before 6000 BC, but it is not until about 1500 BC, when written records started, that a picture of the dietary habits of the ancient Chinese becomes clear. They kept pigs and grew millet, wheat, barley, and rice and even fermented their grain to make alcoholic beverages. Later (around 1100 BC), soybeans were added to the Chinese diet, soon followed by by-products such as soy sauce and beancurd (tofu). Beijing never had a distinctive cuisine of its own, but as the center of the empire it imported elements and influences from a variety of sources.

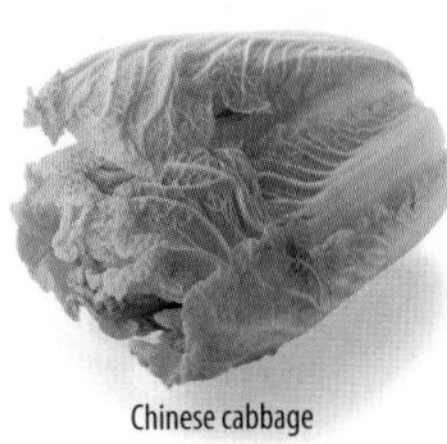
Chinese cabbage

Candied apples on the street, a feature of northern cuisine

The Palace Kitchen

Kublai Khan made Beijing the capital in 1271 and brought simple Mongolian influences to the northern Chinese cuisine – lamb, roasting, and the hot pot. Prior to that, the national capitals had been centered around the Yellow River valley in Xi'an, Luoyang, or Kaifeng. Elaborate preparation and expensive ingredients – shark's fin, bird's nest soup, and abalone, all imported from the south – feature, as well as artistic presentation and poetic names. Imperial cuisine can be summed up as the distillation of the creations of generations of Imperial Palace chefs over almost a millennium.

Shandong

As the birthplace and home of Confucius, the cuisine of Shandong is generally regarded as the oldest and best in China. Shandong has produced the largest number of famous master chefs, and it is even said

A whole Peking duck with traditional accompaniments

Regional Dishes & Specialties

Mu Shu Pork: stir-fried tiger lily buds, scrambled egg, black fungus, and shredded pork – eaten with pancakes.

Duck pears – like a duck's head

Peking duck – an imperial meal – must be the best known dish in north Chinese cuisine. The duck, a local Beijing variety, is carefully dried, and then brushed with a sweet marinade before being roasted over fragrant woodchips. Finally it is carved by the chef and eaten wrapped in pancakes with a special duck sauce, slivered scallions, and cucumbers. To accompany the duck, diners might also be served duck-liver pâté, and duck soup to finish. Another specialty of the region is Mongolian Hotpot; a simple one-pot dish which suited the nomadic way of life. Other regional specialties are made with local resources – carp from the Yellow River, king prawns and yellow croakers from the coast of Shandong, and not forgetting the aromatics – garlic, leeks, and scallions.

that the iron wok originated here as well. Shandong cuisine is popular in Beijing. As one of the most important agricultural areas of China, Shandong supplies Beijing with most of its food; its main crops are wheat, barley, sorghum, millet, and corn as well as soybeans and peanuts. Additionally, fisheries are widely developed along the Yellow River and the north China coast, particularly around the rocky Shandong peninsula where the specialties are fish, prawns, shellfish, abalones, sea slugs, and sea urchins. Fruits are also a Shandong specialty, and wines and beers – especially the famous Tsingtao beer *(see p152)* – are exported worldwide.

The art of pouring tea, shown in a Beijing restaurant

Tianjin

One of the largest cities in China, Tianjin occupies a rather unique position in Chinese cuisine. As a treaty port, Tianjin has acquired a cosmopolitan nature in many aspects of its daily life, particularly showing Russian and Japanese influences. Hence you will find a large number of beef and lamb dishes here, and the city is famous for its dumplings.

Some of the wide variety of foods on display at a night food market

Mongolian & Muslim Cuisine

The Chinese Muslim school of cooking derives mainly from the Hui, the Uighur, and the Mongolian minorities. The Hui are distributed throughout China, but their traditional area of settlement is in the north. The Uighur are mainly in the northwest, while the Mongols are traditionally nomadic and spread throughout the north. As Muslims they do not eat pork, so beef, lamb, and mutton cooked on skewers are important foods in their daily diet. Handmade noodles and flatbreads also feature.

On the Menu

Drunken Empress Chicken Supposedly named after Yang Guifei, an imperial concubine overly fond of her alcohol.

Stir-Fried Kidney-Flowers These are actually pork kidneys criss-cross cut into "flowers" and stir-fried with bamboo shoots, water chestnuts, and black fungus.

Fish Slices with Wine Sauce Deep-fried fish fillet braised in a wine sauce.

Phoenix-Tail Prawns King prawn tails coated in batter and bread crumbs, then deep-fried.

Lamb in Sweet Bean Sauce Tender fillet of lamb sliced and cooked in sweet bean paste with vinegar to give it that classic sweet and sour taste.

Hot Candied Apples A popular Chinese dessert.

Lamb and Scallions: sliced lamb rapidly stir-fried with garlic, leeks or scallions, and sweet bean paste.

Mongolian Hotpot: thinly sliced lamb, vegetables, and noodles dipped in boiling water and an array of sauces.

Sweet and Sour Carp: the quintessential Shandong dish traditionally made with Yellow River carp.

BEIJING

The capital of the People's Republic of China is one of the world's largest cities, with a population of around 20 million. Beijing first became an imperial capital during the Mongol Yuan dynasty (1279–1368), and both the Ming and Qing emperors ruled from the Forbidden City at its heart. Today, an all-pervading spirit of change has added an exciting new dimension to the city.

Expanding in concentric rings from the Forbidden City at its core, the grid-like layout of modern-day Beijing still echoes its Ming dynasty blueprint. Old Beijing survives in its temples, palaces, and old alleyways *(hutong)* that crisscross the city outside the second ring road, which itself charts the loop of the demolished City Wall. Within this ancient outline are huge avenues, vaulting flyovers, towering modern skyscrapers, shopping malls, and the vast expanse of Tian'an Men Square. The city that the 13th-century Mongol warlord Genghis Khan once put to the torch has undergone a dramatic face lift, as a result of the culmination of a quarter-century of reform, the pressures of a growing population, and the 2008 Olympics. Beijing is a microcosm of modern China and all its contradictions, a bustling mix of affluent shoppers, trendy youths, beggars, and plain-clothes police. Shopping is a popular pastime for middle-class Beijingers, and the capital offers some of the glitziest malls and most fashionable brand stores in Asia. Bars and cafés proliferate, and entertainment options range from traditional Beijing Opera and spectacular acrobatics to modern jazz and even raucous punk clubs. In the capital's many restaurants, China's diverse cuisine can be sampled across its range – from the fierce spices of Sichuan to the dainty morsels of Cantonese *dim sum*.

On the roads, the city's army of bicycles is under pressure from the huge influx of new cars and, indeed, are banned on the main roads, but for the time being pedal power is still one of the best ways to get around – if you can put up with the terrible pollution.

Pleasure cruise on Kunming Lake, Summer Palace

◀ The Long Corridor, in Beijing's Beihai Park

Exploring Beijing

Beijing's most significant sights and districts are marked on this map. At the core is the Forbidden City, with Tian'an Men Square and Qian Men to the south, and the sprawling shopping district of Wangfujing to its east. North of the Forbidden City stand the Drum and Bell Towers and farther northeast is the Buddhist Lama Temple. North of Beihai Park, Prince Kung's Mansion stands in a historic *hutong* quarter, the old alleyways that riddle the city. To the south, Tian Tan, known as the Temple of Heaven, is a majestic example of Ming dynasty architectural design. Beijing's environs are also dotted with impressive sites including the magnificent Great Wall and the scenic Ming Tombs.

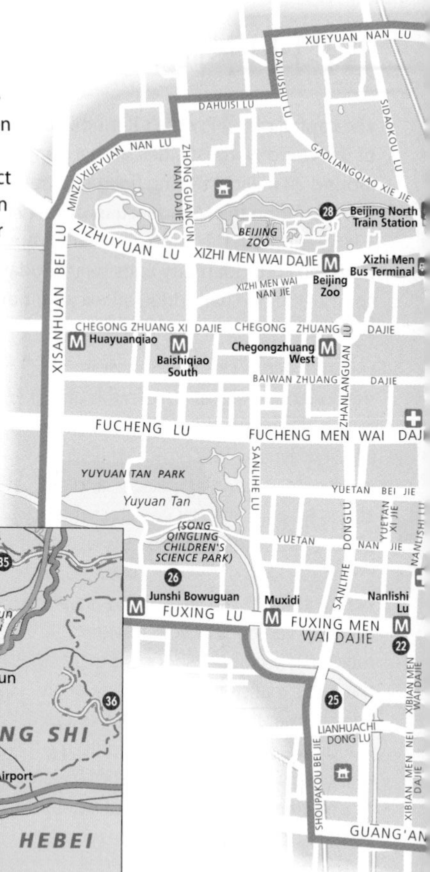

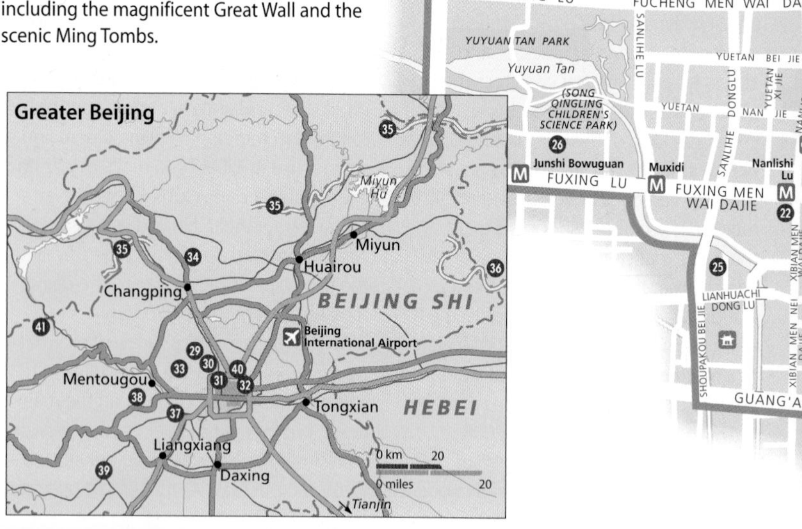

Sights at a Glance

Historic Buildings, Sites & Neighborhoods

1 *Tian'an Men Square pp88–9*
3 Qian Men
5 Dazhalan and Liulichang
7 *Forbidden City pp92–5*
10 Prince Gong's Mansion
11 Drum and Bell Towers
18 Ancient Observatory
29 *Summer Palace pp106–8*
30 Yuanming Yuan
34 *Ming Tombs pp110–11*
35 *Great Wall of China pp112–15*
36 Eastern Qing Tombs
37 Marco Polo Bridge
39 Peking Man Site
40 National Olympic Stadium
41 Chuandixia

Museums & Galleries

2 National Museum of China
4 Beijing Planning Exhibition Hall
16 National Art Museum of China
19 Southeast Corner Watchtower
20 Beijing Natural History Museum
22 Capital Museum
26 Military Museum of the Chinese People's Revolution

Temples, Churches & Mosques

6 South Cathedral
12 Lama Temple
13 Confucius Temple
15 Dong Yue Miao
21 *Temple of Heaven pp102–3*
23 Cow Street Mosque
24 Fayuan Temple
25 White Clouds Temple
27 White Tower Temple
31 Great Bell Temple
38 Tanzhe Temple

Shops & Markets

17 Wangfujing Street
32 798 Art Zone

Parks & Zoos

8 Jing Shan Park
9 Bei Hai Park
14 Di Tan Park
28 Beijing Aquarium
33 Xiang Shan Park

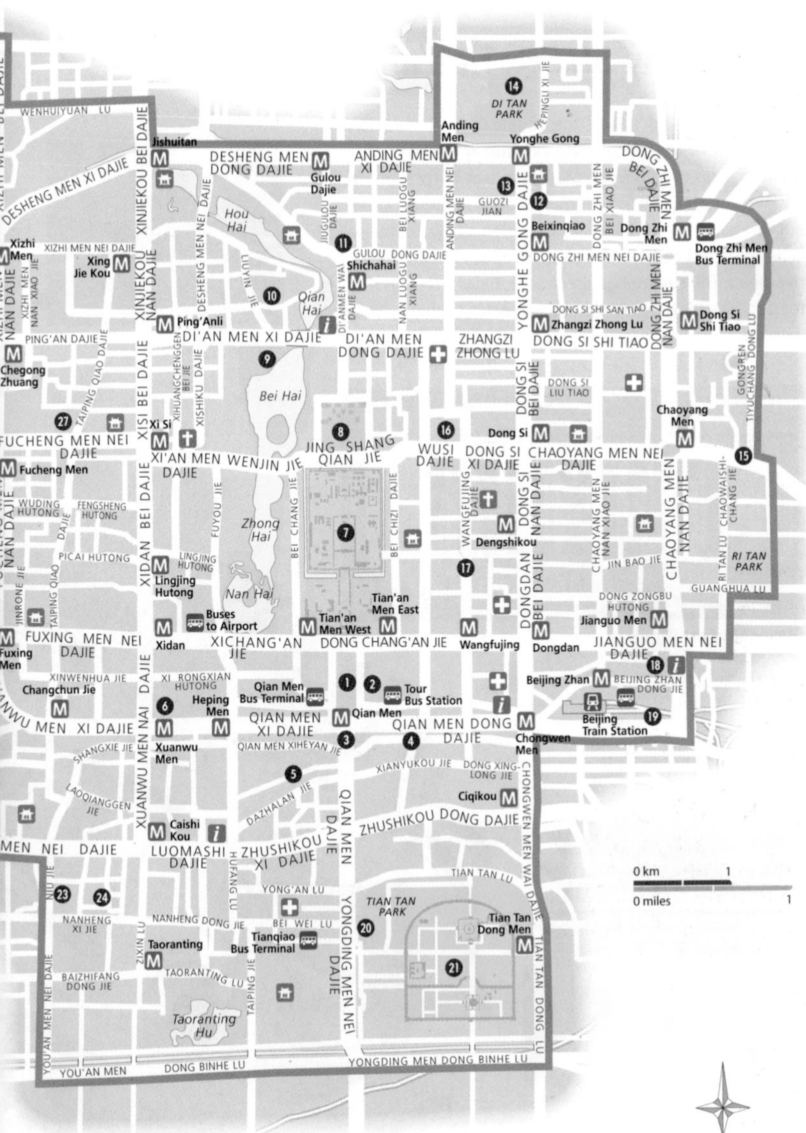

Key

National expressway

Main road

Provincial border

Great Wall of China

Getting Around

A system of ring roads encircles the city center, and the best way to explore this area is by taxi, by subway, or by bicycle *(see pp620–21)*. The bus service, though extensive, is generally slow and overcrowded. Organized tours are another option for a quick overview of the sights. Most hotels and agencies operate tour buses for visiting sights outside Beijing, although hiring a taxi for the day allows for greater flexibility.

For additional map symbols *see back flap*

❶ Street-by-Street: Tian'an Men Square

天安门广场

Tian'an Men Guangchang – the Square of the Gate of Heavenly Peace – is a vast open concrete expanse at the heart of modern Beijing. With Mao's Mausoleum at its focal point, and bordered by 1950s Communist-style buildings and ancient gates from Beijing's now leveled city walls, the square is usually filled with visitors strolling about as kites flit overhead. The square has also traditionally served as a stage for popular demonstrations and is most indelibly associated with the student protests of 1989 and their gory climax.

Modern buildings on Chang'an Jie

Great Hall of the People
Seat of the Chinese legislature, the vast auditorium and banqueting halls are open for part of the day, except when the National People's Congress is in session.

★ Zhengyang Men
Along with the Arrow Tower this tower formed a double gate known as the Qian Men. It now houses a museum on the history of Beijing.

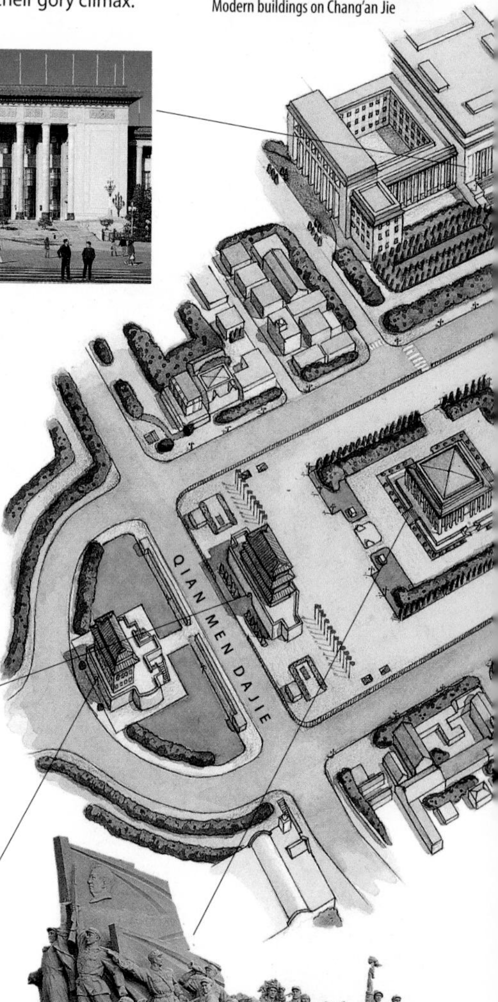

The Arrow Tower or Jian Lou, like Zhengyang Men, was first built in the Ming dynasty.

★ Mao's Mausoleum
Flanked by revolutionary statues, the building contains the embalmed body of Chairman Mao. His casket, raised from its refrigerated chamber, is on view mornings and afternoons..

For hotels and restaurants in this area see p558 and pp572–3

★ Tian'an Men
Mao proclaimed the founding of the People's Republic of China on October 1, 1949 from this Ming dynasty gate, where his huge portrait still remains.

BEIJING
Tian'an Men Square

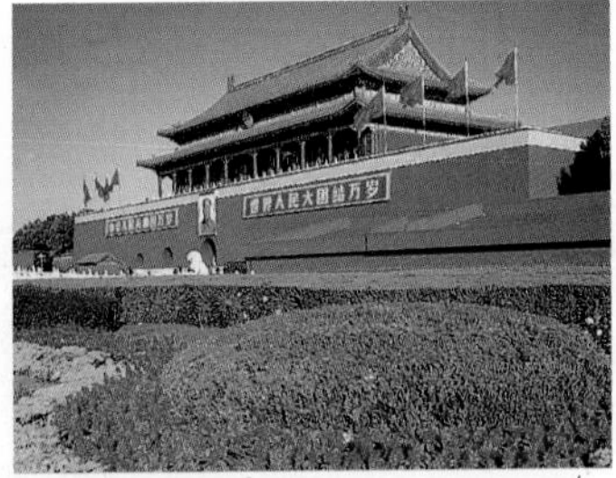

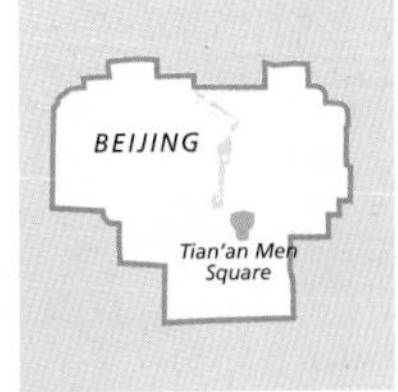

Locator Map
See Beijing Street Finder Map 3

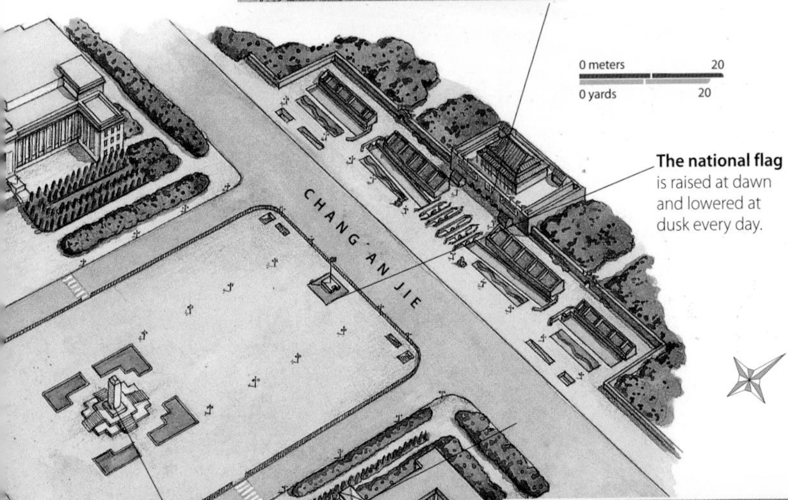

0 meters 20
0 yards 20
CHANG'AN JIE

The national flag is raised at dawn and lowered at dusk every day.

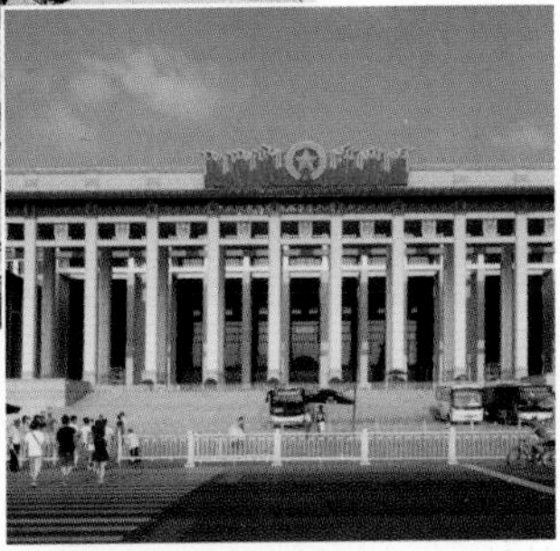

China National Museum
Built in 1959, this building was originally home to the Museum of Chinese History and the Museum of the Revolution, now merged. It reopened to great fanfare in 2011 after three years of renovation. The halls also host exhibitions from other world-class museums.

Bags, coats, and cameras must be left here before visiting Mao's Mausoleum.

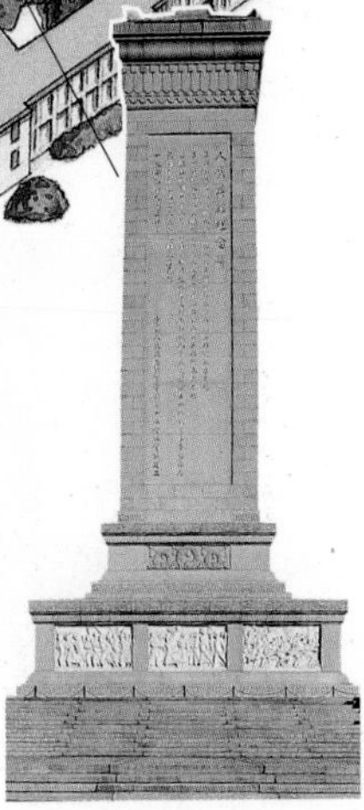

Monument to the People's Heroes
Erected in 1958, the granite monument is decorated with bas-reliefs of episodes from China's revolutionary history and calligraphy by Communist veterans Mao Zedong and Zhou Enlai.

Zhengyang Men, Qian Men – part of Beijing's central fortifications

❷ National Museum of China
中国国家博物馆

Tian'an Men Square. **Map** 4 D. Ⓜ Tian'an Men East. **Tel** (010) 6511 6440. **Open** 9am–5pm Tue–Sun. **W** **chnmuseum.cn**

Standing at more than 2 million sq ft (191,900 sq m), the National Museum of China is said to be the largest museum in the world. Its 49 rooms hold over a million cultural relics, including the cowboy hat worn by Deng Xiaoping on a trip to the United States and other noteworthy artifacts. Two permanent exhibitions cover China's ancient history and from 1840 to the present day, although the chaos of the Cultural Revolution is glossed over with just a single photograph.

❸ Qian Men
前门

Qian Men Dajie. **Map** 3 C2. Ⓜ Qian Men. **Open** 8:30am–3:30pm daily.

Qian Men, or the Front Gate, consists of two towers, the **Zhengyang Men**, on the southern edge of Tian'an Men Square, and the **Jiao Lou** (Arrow Tower) just to the south. Zhengyang Men (Facing the Sun Gate) was the most imposing of the nine gates of the inner city wall that divided Beijing's imperial quarters in the Forbidden City from the "Chinese City," where, during the Manchu Qing dynasty, the Chinese inhabitants lived.

Rising 131 ft (40 m), the gate stands on the north–south axis that runs through Tian'an Men Square and the Forbidden City. Its museum has dioramas of the old city walls, and photographs of Beijing's old streets.

Zhengyang Men
Tel (010) 6522 9386. **Open** daily.

❹ Beijing Planning Exhibition Hall
展览馆

20 Qian Men Dong Dajie. **Map** 3 C2. Ⓜ Qian Men. **Tel** (010) 6701 7074. **Open** 9am–5pm Tue–Sun, last entry 4pm. **W** **bjghzl.com.cn**

This impressive government museum, just east of the historic Qian Men area, offers a glimpse into what Beijing's future has in store. The highlight is a huge scale model of what the city should look like by 2020, complete with a regular

Beijing's City Walls

The earliest defensive walls around Beijing (then called Yanjing, later Zhongdu) were erected in the Jin dynasty (1115–1234) and modeled on the wall around Kaifeng *(see p156)*. The Mongol Kublai Khan rebuilt Zhongdu, naming it Dadu, and encompassed it with a 19-mile (30-km) wall. It was only during the Ming era (1368–1644) that the walls took on their final shape of an outer wall with seven gates, and an inner wall with nine gates. The magnificent inner wall was 38 ft (11.5 m) high and 64 ft (19.5 m) wide. The walls and most of their gates were unfortunately demolished in the 1950s and 60s to make way for roads. Of the inner wall, only Qian Men and Desheng Men survive, while the outer wall retains only Dongbianmen *(see p101)*. The old gates live on as place names on the second ring road, and as the names of stations on the Beijing Underground Loop line.

Arrow Tower of Qian Men

Shop selling Communist memorabilia, Dazhalan Jie

sound and light show. In contrast, the museum also has models and historical photographs of old Beijing, including a bronze model of the city as it looked in 1949.

❺ Dazhalan and Liulichang

大栅栏和琉璃厂

Map 3 C2. Ⓜ Qian Men.

South of Qian Men are the narrow and lively *hutong* *(see p97)* of the old Chinese quarter. The inner city wall and its gates separated the "Inner City" containing the imperial quarters of the Manchu emperors from the "Chinese City," where the Chinese lived apart from their Qing overlords. The district has been renovated to create a Qing dynasty appearance, complete with a tourist tram. Running west off the northern end of Qian Men Dajie is Dazhalan Jie, whose name "Big Barrier Street" refers to the now-demolished gates that were closed every night to fence off the residents from Qian Men and the Inner City. There are pricey *hutong* tours by rickshaw – drivers just wait in the street in Dazhalan.

Cyclists on restored Liulichang Jie

The area is a great place for browsing, and has several quaint Qing-era specialty shops. Located down the first alley on the left from Dazhalan Jie is the century-old pickle shop **Liubiju**, while **Ruifuxiang**, on the right-hand side of Dazhalan, is renowned for its silks and traditional Chinese garments. On the south side of Dazhalan Jie is the Chinese medicine shop **Tongrentang Pharmacy**, which has been in business since 1669 and enjoyed imperial patronage. On the same side of the road, the **Zhangyiyuan Chazhuang**, or Zhangyiyuan Teashop, has been supplying fine teas since the early 20th century. West of Dazhalan Jie is Liulichang Jie, a fascinating place to wander – it has everything from ceramics to antique Chinese books. Beware of so-called "antiques," which should be judiciously examined before buying.

❻ South Cathedral

南堂

141 Qian Men Xi Dajie. **Map** 3 A2. Ⓜ Xuanwu Men. **Open** 6am–9pm daily.

The first Catholic church to be built in Beijing, South Cathedral (Nan Tang) stands close to the Xuanwu Men underground station, on the site of Jesuit Matteo Ricci's former residence. Ricci was the first Jesuit missionary to reach Beijing. Arriving in 1601, he sent gifts of European curiosities such as clocks, mathematical instruments, and a world map to the Wanli emperor, thus gaining his goodwill, and was eventually given permission to establish a church.

Like many of China's churches, this restored building has suffered much devastation. Construction first began in 1605, and it subsequently burned down in 1775. It was rebuilt a century later, only to be destroyed once again during the Boxer Rebellion of 1900. The cathedral was rebuilt in 1904. Also known as St. Mary's Church, it is the city's largest functioning Catholic cathedral, and has regular services in a variety of languages including English, French, Italian, and Latin. Service timings are posted on the noticeboard. A small gift shop is located near the south gate.

Stained glass at the South Cathedral (Nan Tang)

❼ Forbidden City

故宫

Forming the very heart of Beijing, the Forbidden City, officially known as the Palace Museum (Gugong), is China's most magnificent architectural complex. Completed in 1420, the huge palace is a lasting monument of dynastic China from which 24 emperors ruled for nearly 500 years. The symbolic center of the Chinese universe, the palace was the exclusive domain of the imperial court and dignitaries until the abdication in 1912. It was opened to the public in 1949. The complex has a one-way south–north entry system and is now entered only via the Meridian Gate and exited via the Gate of Divine Prowess.

Chinese Lions

Pairs of lions guard the entrances of halls. The male is portrayed with a ball under his paw, while the female has a lion cub.

★ Golden Water

Five marble bridges, symbolizing the five cardinal virtues of Confucianism, cross the Golden Water, which flows from west to east in a course designed to resemble the jade belt worn by officials.

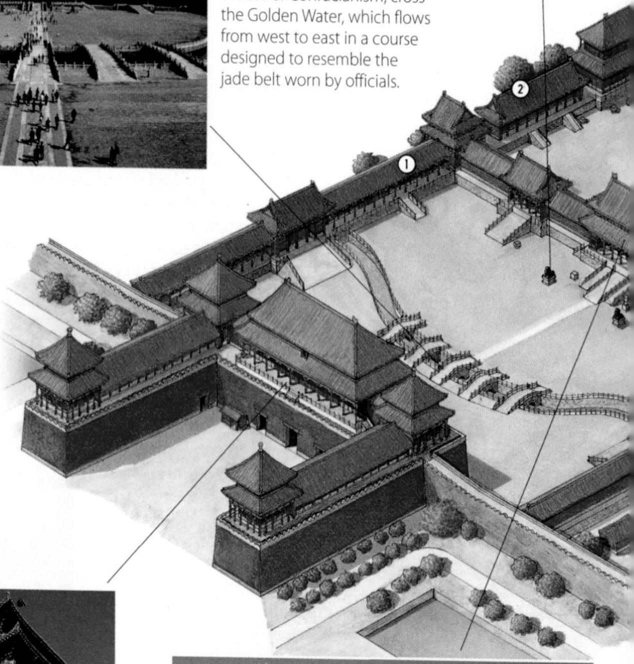

Outer Court

At the center of the Forbidden City, the Outer Court is easily its most impressive part. Most of the other buildings in the complex were there to service this city within a city.

Meridian Gate (Wu Men)

From the balcony the emperor would review his armies and perform ceremonies marking the start of a new calendar.

Gate of Supreme Harmony

Originally used for receiving visitors, the 78-ft (24-m) high, double-eaved hall was later used for banquets during the Qing dynasty (1644–1912).

For hotels and restaurants in this area see p558 and pp572–3

★ Marble Carriageway
The central ramp carved with dragons chasing pearls among clouds was reserved for the emperor.

VISITORS' CHECKLIST

Practical Information
N of Tian'an Men Square. **Map** 1 C5. **Tel** (010) 8500 7421. **Open** Apr–Oct: 8:30am–5pm daily; Nov–Mar: 8:30am–4:30pm daily. **en.dpm.org.cn**

Transportation
M Tian'an Men East.

Roof Guardians
An odd number of these figures, all associated with water, are supposed to protect the building from fire.

★ Hall of Supreme Harmony
The largest hall in the palace, this was used for major occasions such as the enthronement of an emperor. Inside the hall, the ornate throne sits beneath a fabulously colored ceiling.

KEY

① **Offices of the imperial secretariat**

② **Storehouses**

③ **Imperial sundial**

④ **The Hall of Middle Harmony** received the emperor before official ceremonies.

⑤ **Bronze cauldrons** were filled with water in case of fire.

⑥ **Hall of Preserving Harmony**

⑦ **Gate of Heavenly Purity**

Design by Numbers

The harmonious principle of *yin* and *yang* is the key to Chinese design. As odd numbers represent *yang* (the preferred masculine element associated with the emperor), the numbers three, five, seven, and the ultimate odd number – nine – recur in architectural details. It is said that the Forbidden City has 9,999 rooms and, as nine times nine is especially fortunate, the doors for imperial use usually contain 81 brass studs.

Palace door with a lucky number of studs

Exploring the Forbidden City

A short distance north through the Gate of Heavenly Purity lies the Inner Court with three impressive inner palaces. Further on through the Imperial Flower Garden stands the Shenwu Gate, the north gate of the Forbidden City, an exit from the palace that leads to a walk across to Jing Shan Park *(see p96)*. On the western and eastern flanks of the Inner Court, it is also possible to explore numerous halls, some of which house museum collections (entry fee payable).

The Pavilion of a Thousand Autumns in the Imperial Gardens

The Inner Court

Beyond the Hall of Preserving Harmony (Outer Court) lies a large but narrow courtyard with gates leading to the open areas east and west of the Outer Court and a main gate, the **Gate of Heavenly Purity**, leading to the Inner Court. Here lie three splendid palaces, mirroring those of the Outer Court but on a smaller scale. The double-eaved **Palace of Heavenly Purity** was used as the imperial sleeping quarters and for the reception of officials. It was here that the last Ming emperor, Chongzhen, wrote his final missive in red ink, before getting drunk, killing his 15-year-old daughter and his concubines, and then hanging himself on Jing Shan *(see p96)*, just north of the palace, as peasant rebels swarmed through the capital. Beyond lie the **Hall of Union**, used as a throne room by the empress, and the **Palace of Earthly Tranquillity**, the living quarters of the Ming empresses. During the Qing dynasty, the hall was used for Manchurian shaman rites, including animal sacrifice.

The Imperial Gardens

The **Imperial Flower Garden**, north of the three inner palaces and the Gate of Earthly Tranquillity, dates from the reign of the Ming Yongle emperor. It is symmetrically laid out with pavilions, temples, and halls as well as a rock garden and ancient trees. On the west and east sides of the garden are the charming Thousand Autumns Pavilion and Ten Thousand Springs Pavilion, each topped with a circular roof. Positioned centrally in the north of the garden, the **Hall of Imperial Peace** formerly served as a temple, and, on top of the lofty rockery in the northeast of the garden, the Imperial View Pavilion rises with long views over the gardens and beyond. During the Qing dynasty, sacrifices were performed in the gardens on the seventh day of the seventh lunar month (China's equivalent of Valentine's Day) by the emperor, empress, and imperial concubines to a pair of stars that represent lovers.

Eastern Palaces

On the east side of the Inner Court lies a much closer-knit series of smaller palaces and courtyards formerly used as the residences of imperial concubines. Nowadays, some of these areas serve as museums of jade, paintings, enamels, and antique collectibles, including the impressive Clock Exhibition Hall (housed in the **Palace of Eternal Harmony**) with its

Imperial five-clawed dragons on a glazed Nine Dragon Screen

Chinese Dragons

The Chinese dragon is a curious hybrid of sometimes many animal parts – snake's body, deer horns, bull's ears, hawk's claws, and fish scales. Endowed with magical characteristics, it can fly, swim, change into other animals, bring rainfall, and ward off evil spirits. The five-clawed dragon represented the power of the emperor, and therefore could only adorn his imperial buildings. The Chinese dragon is a beneficent beast offering protection and good luck, hence its depiction on screens and marble carriageways, and its significance, even today, in festivals such as Chinese New Year.

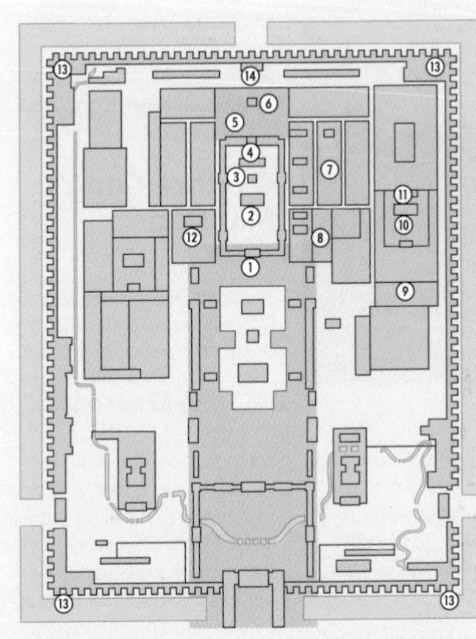

The Forbidden City

① Gate of Heavenly Purity
② Palace of Heavenly Purity
③ Hall of Union
④ Palace of Earthly Tranquillity
⑤ Imperial Flower Garden
⑥ Hall of Imperial Peace
⑦ Palace of Eternal Harmony
⑧ Palace of Abstinence
⑨ Nine Dragon Screen
⑩ Imperial Zenith Hall
⑪ Palace of Peaceful Longevity
⑫ Hall of Mental Cultivation
⑬ Arrow Tower
⑭ Gate of Divine Prowess

0 meters 300
0 yards 300

Key

Imperial buildings

Area illustrated *(see pp92–3)*

sizeable and fascinating display. Note that these are occasionally moved to other halls and at some an entry fee is payable. Among the collection are elaborate Chinese, British, and French timepieces, donated or collected by Qing emperors. In the southeast of the inner court is the **Palace of Abstinence**, where the emperor fasted before sacrificial ceremonies. Farther southeast stands a beautiful **Nine Dragon Screen**, a 100-ft (31-m) long spirit wall made from richly glazed tiles and similar to the screen in Beihai Park *(see p96)*. Screens were used to shield areas from sight and allow visitors to make themselves presentable. The screen leads on to the jewelry displays housed in a series of halls in the northeast of the complex, including the **Imperial Zenith Hall** and the **Palace of Peaceful Longevity**. These halls contain an array of decorative objects and tools used by the emperor. Northwest of the Palace of Peaceful Longevity is its flower garden, a tranquil strip of rockeries and pavilions.

Western Palaces

Much of the western flank of the Forbidden City is closed to visitors, but the halls west of the three inner palaces are accessible. **The Hall of Mental Cultivation** was used by Yongzheng *(see p115)* for his residence, rather than the Hall of Heavenly Purity where his father, Kangxi, had lived for 60 years. The East Warm Chamber of the Hall of Mental Cultivation was the site of the formal abdication by Pu Yi, the last emperor, on February 12, 1912 *(see p452)*.

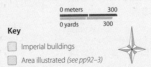

Tile relief by the Hall of Mental Cultivation

The Palace Walls

The wall around the Forbidden City is marked at each corner by an elaborate **Arrow Tower**, notable for their many eaves. The northern gate of the palace is called the **Gate of Divine Prowess** or Shenwu Men, and served as a combined bell and drum tower. The palace wall was enclosed within a moat and another wall ran around the grounds of the Imperial City. Beyond this lay the inner and outer city walls of Beijing. Damaged in the 1950s and 1960s, only a few parts of the Imperial City wall survive, while the city walls have all but vanished. However, the wall of the Forbidden City and its four gates have survived intact and can still be admired.

One of four arrow towers at each corner of the palace wall

Bei Hai with Jing Shan's summit in the background

❽ Jing Shan Park
景山公园

44 Jingshan Xi Jie, Xicheng. **Map** 1 C4. M Dong Si. **Tel** (010) 6404 4071. **Open** 6:30am–8:30pm daily.

Situated on Beijing's north–south axis, Jing Shan Park has its origins in the Yuan dynasty (1279–1368). Its hill was created from earth that was excavated while building the palace moat during the reign of the Ming Yongle emperor. In the early years of the Ming dynasty it was known as Wansui Shan (Long Life Hill), but was renamed Jing Shan (View or Prospect Hill) in the Qing era. Foreign residents also referred to it as Coal Hill (Mei Shan), supposedly because coal was stored at the foot of the hill, although other theories exist.

Until the fall of the Qing, Jing Shan was linked to the Forbidden City and was restricted to imperial use. The hill's purpose was to protect the imperial palaces within the Forbidden City from malign northern influences, which brought death and destruction according to classical *feng shui*. However, it failed to save the last Ming emperor Chongzhen, who hanged himself from a locust tree *(huaishu)* in the park in 1644 when rebel troops forced their way into Beijing. Another tree, planted after the original tree was cut down, marks the spot in the park's southeast. The park is dotted with several pavilions and halls, but the highlight of any visit is the superb view of the Forbidden City from the hill's Wanchun Ting (Wanchun Pavilion).

❾ Bei Hai Park
北海公园

1 Wenjin Jie, Xicheng. **Map** 1 C4. M Xisi. **Tel** (010) 6403 1102. **Open** 6:30am–9pm daily.

White Dagoba, Bei Hai Park

An imperial garden for more than 1,000 years, Bei Hai Park was opened to the public in 1925. Filled with artificial hills, pavilions, and temples, it is associated with Kublai Khan, who redesigned it during the Mongol Yuan dynasty. The Tuancheng (Round City), near the south entrance, has a huge, decorated jade urn belonging to him. The park is named after its extensive lake, **Bei Hai**, whose southern end is bordered by the inaccessible Zhong Nan Hai, the Communist Party Headquarters. In the middle of Bei Hai, Jade Island was supposedly made from the earth excavated while creating the lake. It is topped by the 118-ft (36-m) high **White Dagoba**, a Tibetan-style stupa built to honor the visit of the fifth Dalai Lama in 1651. Beneath the huge dagoba, **Yongan Si** comprises a series of ascending halls. The lake's northern shore has several sights, including the massive **Nine Dragon Screen**, an 89-ft (27-m) long spirit wall made of colorful glazed tiles. Depicting nine intertwining dragons, it was designed to obstruct evil spirits. The Xiaoxitian Temple lies to the west.

❿ Prince Gong's Mansion
恭王府

17 Qianhai Xi Jie, Xicheng. **Map** 1 B3. M Behai North. **Tel** (010) 8328 8149. **Open** mid-Mar–Oct: 8am–6:30pm daily; Nov–mid-Mar: 9am–6:30pm Tue–Sun. **W** **pgm.org.cn**

Beijing's most complete example of a historic mansion is situated in a charming *hutong* district west of Qian Hai. It was supposedly the inspiration behind the residence portrayed by Cao Xueqin in his classic 18th-century novel *Dream of the Red Chamber (see pp34–5)*. Built during the reign of the Qianlong emperor, the house is extensive and its charming garden is a pattern of open corridors and pavilions, dotted with pools and gateways. Originally built for Heshun, a Manchu official and the emperor's favorite, the residence was appropriated by the imperial household after he was found guilty of using regal motifs in his mansion design. It was later bequeathed to Prince Gong in the Xianfeng emperor's reign (r. 1851–61). The house is popular with tour groups, so early morning is the best time to visit and afterwards, the local *hutong* can be explored. Little is labeled in English, so a guided tour is recommended.

Elaborate arched gateway, Prince Gong's Mansion

For hotels and restaurants in this area see pp558-63 and pp572–3

Beijing's Courtyard Houses

At first glance, Beijing seems a thoroughly modern city, but a stroll through the its alleyways *(hutong)* reveals the charm of old Beijing. These *hutong* – weaving across much of central Beijing – are where many Beijing residents *(Beijingren)* still live. Typically running east to west, *hutong* are created by the walls of courtyard houses *(siheyuan)*. Formerly the homes of officials and the well-to-do, many were taken over by the state but they are now increasingly privately owned. The *hutong* are very easy to find: try the alleyways between the main streets south of Qian Men, or around Hou Hai and Qian Hai. The modernization of Beijing has destroyed many traditional *siheyuan*, but a few have been converted into hotels, allowing the visitor a closer look at this disappearing world.

Crowded courtyards As space became an issue in Beijing, additional buildings filled in the large courtyards. Several families may be living together in one *siheyuan*.

The main hall was the most northerly and usually reserved for the eldest of the family, such as the grandparents.

Wall adds privacy and keeps out spirits as they are unable to turn corners.

The open courtyard lets in both the sunlight and the wind and cold.

The number of halls and courtyards determines the grandeur of the residence.

Entrance is at the southeastern corner as prescribed by *feng shui*.

Walls were important to the Chinese psyche – even in the secure capital, they felt the need to retreat behind them.

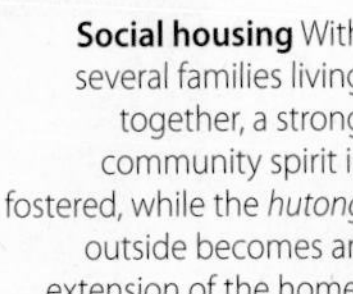

Social housing With several families living together, a strong community spirit is fostered, while the *hutong* outside becomes an extension of the home.

Typical Beijing *hutong*
You can take organized rickshaw tours of the *hutong*, sometimes with a visit to Prince Gong's Mansion *(see p96)*, but it can be more fun to explore them by yourself.

The Bell Tower as seen from Beijing's Drum Tower

⓫ Drum and Bell Towers

鼓楼

Northern end of Di'an Men Wai Dajie, Dongcheng. **Map** 1 C2. Ⓜ Gulou. **Tel** (010) 8402 7869. **Open** 9am–5pm daily.

Located on the north–south meridian that bisects the Forbidden City and Tian'an Men Square, the Drum Tower (Gu Lou) rises up from a historic Beijing *hutong* district *(see p97)*. The squat structure seen today was originally built in 1420 during the reign of the Ming Yongle emperor. Visitors can climb the steep stairs to look out over the city and inspect the 25 drums there. The one large and 24 smaller drums were beaten to mark the hours of the day. According to the official Chinese accounts, the original drums were destroyed by the foreign soldiers of the international army that relieved Beijing during the Boxer Rebellion *(see p439)*.

A short walk north of the Drum Tower, the Bell Tower (Zhong Lou) is an edifice from 1745, which replaced an earlier tower that had burnt down. Suspended within the tower is a 15-ft (4.5-m) high and 42-ton (42,674-kg) bell, that was cast in 1420. Visitors can pay to ring the bell for good luck.

⓬ Lama Temple

雍和宫

12 Yonghe Gong Dajie, Dongcheng. **Map** 2 E2. Ⓜ Yonghe Gong. **Tel** (010) 6404 4499. **Open** 9am–4pm daily.

Beijing's most spectacular temple complex, the Lama Temple (Yonghegong) was constructed during the 17th century and converted into a Tibetan lamasery in 1744. Its five main halls are a stylistic blend of Han, Mongol, and Tibetan motifs. The first hall has a traditional display – the plump laughing Buddha, Milefo, is back-to-back with Wei Tuo, the Protector of Buddhist Doctrine, and flanked by the Four Heavenly Kings. **Yonghe Hall** beyond has three manifestations of Buddha, flanked by 18 *luohan* – those freed from the cycle of rebirth. Even farther back, the Tibetan-styled **Falun Hall**, or Hall of the Wheel of Law, has a statue of Tsongkhapa, the founder of the Yellow Hat sect of Tibetan Buddhism *(see pp526–7)*.

The highlight, however, is encapsulated within the towering **Wanfu Pavilion** (Wanfu Ge) – a vast 55-ft (17-m) high statue of Maitreya (the Future Buddha), carved from a single block of sandalwood.

The striking main gateway of the colorful Lama Temple

Statue of Confucius at the main entrance, Confucius Temple

The splendid exhibition of Tibetan Buddhist objects at the temple's rear includes statues of the deities Padmasambhava (Guru Rinpoche), and the Tibetan equivalent of Guanyin, Chenresig, alongside ritual objects such as the scepter-like *dorje* (thunderbolt) and *dril bu* (bell), symbols of the male and female energies. Few captions are in English.

⓭ Confucius Temple
孔庙

13 Guozijian Jie, Dongcheng. **Map** 2 E2. Ⓜ Yonghe Gong. **Tel** (010) 6405 7214. **Open** 9am–5pm daily.

Adjacent to the Lama Temple, the Confucius Temple is the largest in China outside Qufu, the philosopher's birthplace in Shandong province *(see p148)*. The alley leading to the temple has a fine *pailou* (decorative archway), few of which survive in Beijing. First built in 1302 during the Mongol Yuan dynasty, the temple was expanded in 1906 in the reign of Emperor Guangxu. It is a tranquil place that offers respite from the city's bustle. Around 200 ancient stelae stand in the silent courtyard in front of the main hall (Dacheng Dian), inscribed with the names of those who successfully passed the imperial civil service exams. Additional stelae are propped up on the backs of *bixi* (mythical cross between a tortoise and a dragon), within pavilions surrounded by cypress trees. On a marble terrace in the main hall are statues of Confucius and some of his disciples.

⓮ Di Tan Park
地坛公园

N of the Lama Temple, Dongcheng. **Map** 2 E1. Ⓜ Yonghe Gong. **Tel** (010) 6421 4657. **Open** 6am–9pm daily.

An ideal place to stroll amid trees, Di Tan Park was named after the Temple of Earth (Di Tan), which was the venue for imperial sacrifices. The park's altar (Fangze Tan) dates to the Ming dynasty and its square shape represents the earth. Under the Ming, five main altars were established at the city's cardinal points – Tian Tan (Temple of Heaven) in the south *(see pp102–3)*, Di Tan in the north, Ri Tan (Temple of the Sun) in the east, Yue Tan (Temple of the Moon) in the west, and Sheji Tan (Temple of Land and Grain) in the center. Mirroring ancient ceremonies, a lively temple fair *(miaohui)* is held during the Chinese New Year *(see pp48–9)*, to welcome the spring planting season and appease the gods.

Guardian at entrance, Dong Yue Miao

⓯ Dong Yue Miao
东岳庙

141 Chaoyang Men Wai Dajie, Chaoyang. **Map** 2 F4. Ⓜ Chaoyang Men. **Tel** (010) 6551 3883. **Open** 8am–5pm daily.

On Beijing's eastern side near Chaoyang's Workers' Stadium, the mesmerizing Dong Yue Miao takes its name from the Daoist Eastern Peak, Dong Yue, also known as Tai Shan *(see pp150–51)*. It is fronted by a fabulous glazed Ming dynasty *paifang* inscribed with the characters "Zhisi Daizong," meaning "offer sacrifices to Mount Tai (Tai Shan) in good order."

This colorful and active temple, dating to the early 14th century, was restored at considerable cost in 1999, and is tended by Daoist monks. The main courtyard leads into the Hall of Tai Shan, where there are statues of the God of Tai Shan and his attendants. The greatest attractions here are over 70 "Departments," filled with vivid Daoist gods and demons, whose functions are explained in English captions. In Daoist lore, the spirits of the dead go to Tai Shan, and many Departments dwell on the afterlife. The Department for Increasing Wealth and Longevity, for example, offers cheerful advice.

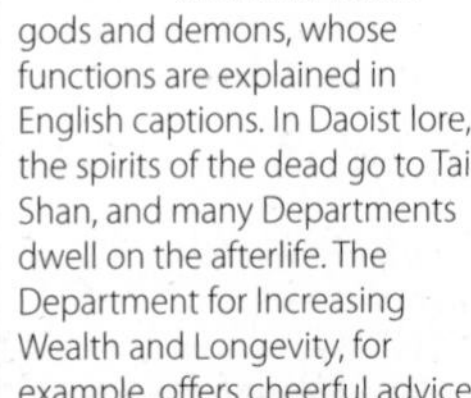

Corn laid out to form Chinese characters, temple festival, Di Tan Park

⓰ National Art Museum of China
中国美术馆

1 Wusi Dajie, Dongcheng. **Map** 2 D4. Ⓜ Dong Si. **Tel** (010) 6401 1816. **Open** 9am–5pm daily, last entry 4pm. **namoc.org**

Hosting exhibitions of Chinese and international art, as well as occasional photographic displays, the National Art Museum of China (Zhongguo Meishuguan) has 14 halls over three levels. This quite ordinary building holds an exciting range of Chinese modern art, which suffers less censorship than other media, such as film or literature. Magazines such as *Time Out Beijing* and *The Beijinger* carry details of current and forthcoming exhibitions, or check the website.

⓱ Wangfujing Street
王府井

Map 4 D1. Ⓜ Wangfujing. Foreign Language Bookstore: 235 Wangfujing Dajie. **Tel** (010) 6512 6903. **Open** 9:30am–9:30pm daily. Night Market: **Open** 5:30pm–10pm daily. St. Joseph's Cathedral: 74 Wangfujing Dajie. **Tel** (010) 6524 0634. **Open** early morning during services (in Mandarin only).

Bustling Wangfujing Street (Wangfujing Dajie), Beijing's original shopping street, is filled with department stores and giant malls such as the Sun Dong'an Plaza. Everything from curios, *objets d'art*, antiques, clothes, and books are available here. The huge **Foreign Language Bookstore** is a good place to buy a more detailed map of Beijing. The street has a lively mixture of pharmacies, laundry and dyeing shops, and stores selling silk, tea, and shoes.

The imposing facade of St. Joseph's Cathedral, Wangfujing Street

However, the street's highlight is the **Night Market**, with its endless variety of traditional Chinese snacks, including skewers of beef, and more exotic morsels such as scorpions. Other offerings include pancakes, fruit, shrimps, squid, flat bread, and more. The Wangfujing Snack Street, south of the Night Market, also has a range of colorful restaurants serving tasty dishes.

The impressive triple-domed **St. Joseph's Cathedral**, known as the East Cathedral, is at 74 Wangfujing Dajie. One of the city's most important churches, it has been restored at a cost of US$2 million. It was built on the site of the former residence of Jesuit Adam Schall von Bell (1591–1669) in 1655, and has been rebuilt a number of times after being successively destroyed by earthquake, fire, and then during the Boxer Rebellion *(see p439)*. It is fronted by an open courtyard and an arched gateway.

Delicious street food at the Night Market, just off Wangfujing Street

⓲ Ancient Observatory
古观象台

2 Dongbiaobei Hutong. **Map** 4 F1. Ⓜ Jianguo Men. **Tel** (010) 6524 2202. **Open** 9am–4pm daily.

Beijing's ancient observatory (Gu Guanxiangtai) stands on a platform alongside a flyover off Jianguo Men Nei Dajie. Dating to 1442, it is one of the oldest in the world. A Yuan dynasty (1279–1368) observatory was also located here, but the structure that survives today was built after the Ming emperors relocated their capital from Nanjing to Beijing. In the early 17th century, the Jesuits, led by Matteo Ricci (1552–1610) and followed by Adam Schall von Bell, impressed the emperor and the imperial astronomers with their scientific knowledge, particularly the accuracy of their predictions of eclipses.

Ecliptic armillary sphere, Ancient Observatory

The Belgian Jesuit Father Verbiest (1623–88) was appointed to the Imperial Astronomical Bureau, where he designed a set of astronomical instruments in 1674. Several of these were appropriated by German soldiers during the Boxer Rebellion of 1900, and were only returned after World War I. A collection of reproduction astronomical

The atmospheric Red Gate Gallery, Southeast Corner Watchtower

devices lies in the courtyard on the ground floor, some decorated with fantastic Chinese designs including dragons. Steps lead to the roof, where there are impressive bronze instruments, including an azimuth theodolite, used to measure the altitude of celestial bodies, and an armillary sphere, for measuring the coordinates of planets and stars.

Southeast Corner Watchtower (Dongbianmen Jiao Lou)

⓳ Southeast Corner Watchtower
东边门箭楼

Off Jianguo Men Nan Dajie, Chongwen. **Map** 4 F2. Beijing Railway Station. Red Gate Gallery: **Tel** (010) 6525 1005. **Open** 9am–5pm daily. For exhibition details visit **redgategallery.com**

About 2 km (1 mile) south of the Ancient Observatory, an imposing chunk of the Beijing City Walls *(see p90)* survives in the form of the 15th-century Southeast Corner Watchtower (Dongbianmen Jiao Lou). After climbing onto the Ming dynasty battlements, visitors can walk along the short but impressive stretch of attached wall to admire the towering bastion, pitted with archers' windows, and look down on the city below. The walls of the tower are engraved with graffiti left by soldiers of the international army that marched into the city to liberate the Foreign Legations during the Boxer Rebellion in 1900.

Within its splendid, cavernous interior, accessed from the battlements, the rooms reveal enormous red wooden columns and pillars, crossed with beams. The **Red Gate Gallery**, one of Beijing's most appealing art galleries, is situated within this superb setting. Originally founded in 1991 by Brian Wallace, an Australian who came to Beijing to learn Chinese, the gallery exhibits works in a wide variety of media by up-and-coming contemporary Chinese and foreign artists. Forthcoming exhibitions are listed on the gallery's website.

⓴ Beijing Natural History Museum
自然历史博物馆

126 Tianqiao Nan Dajie, Chongwen. **Map** 3 C3. Qian Men, then taxi. 2, 120. **Tel** (010) 6702 7702. **Open** 8:30am–5pm Tue–Sat. 1st floor. **bmnh.org.cn**

This museum is the largest of its type in China, with about 5,000 specimens arranged into three collections. The Paleontology Hall displays a selection of the prehistoric animals that populated China millions of years ago. The zoology section explains and illustrates the course of evolution, and a basement houses a macabre display of human cadavers, pickled corpses, limbs, and organs. The botany collection is less impressive.

㉑ Temple of Heaven

See pp102–3.

㉒ Capital Museum
北京首都博物馆

16 Fuxingmenwai Dajie. Muxidi. **Tel** (010) 6337 0491. **Open** 9am–5pm Tue–Sun. **en.capitalmuseum.org.cn**

This museum has an astounding collection of some 200,000 pieces of the best Chinese art and antiquities. An interesting film telling the story of Beijing is screened every 30 minutes. English captions on the exhibits are limited, so it is worth hiring an audio guide.

Dinosaur skeletons in the Paleontology Hall, Natural History Museum

㉑ Temple of Heaven

天坛

Completed in 1420, during the Ming dynasty, the Temple of Heaven, more correctly known as Tian Tan, is one of the largest temple complexes in China and a paradigm of Chinese architectural balance and symbolism. Now a UNESCO World Heritage Site, it was here that the emperor would make sacrifices and pray to heaven and his ancestors at the winter solstice. As the Son of Heaven, the emperor could intercede with the gods, represented by their spirit tablets, on behalf of his people and pray for a good harvest. Off-limits to the common people during the Ming and Qing dynasties, the Temple of Heaven is situated in a large and pleasant park that now attracts early morning practitioners of *tai ji quan (see p279)*.

Qinian Dian, where the emperor prayed for a good harvest

The Tian Tan Complex

The main parts of the temple complex are all connected on the favored north–south axis by the Red Step Bridge (an elevated pathway) to form the focal point of the park. The Round Altar is made up of concentric rings of stone slabs in multiples of nine, the most auspicious number. The circular Echo Wall is famed for its supposed ability to carry a whisper from one side of the wall to the other.

① Hall of Prayer for Good Harvests
② Red Step Bridge
③ Echo Wall
④ Imperial Vault of Heaven
⑤ Round Altar

Triple gates for emperor (east), officials (west) and gods (center)

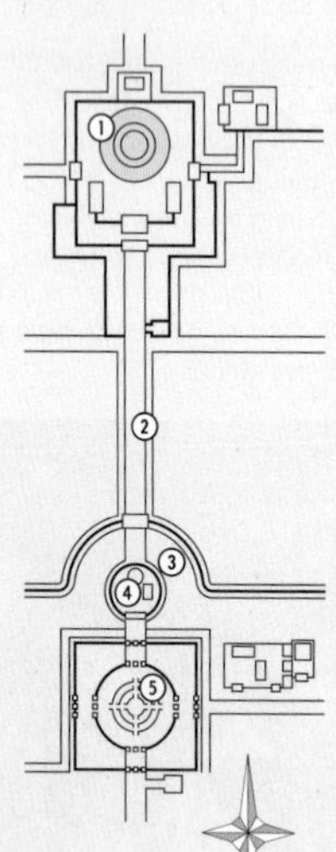

Key

Area illustrated

Imperial Vault of Heaven, store for the spirit tablets of the gods

The Round Altar, site of the emperor's sacrifice

Qinian Dian

Originally built in 1420, the Qinian Dian, or Hall of Prayer for Good Harvests, is often incorrectly called the Temple of Heaven. There is in fact no single temple building as such at Tian Tan, a more literal translation of which is Altar of Heaven – referring to the whole complex.

For hotels and restaurants in this area see p558 and pp572–3

VISITORS' CHECKLIST

Practical Information
Tian Tan Dong Lu (East Gate), Chongwen. **Map** 4 E4. **Tel** (010) 6702 5289. Temple Buildings: **Open** 8am–5:30pm daily (Jul–Oct: 6pm; Nov–Feb: 5pm). **en.tiantanpark.com**

Transportation
Tian Tan Dong Men. 6, 34, 35.

★ Caisson Ceiling
The splendid circular caisson ceiling has a gilded dragon and phoenix at its center. The hall is built entirely of wood without using a single nail.

★ Dragon Well Pillars
The roofs of the hall are supported on 28 richly decorated pillars. At the center, the four huge columns known as Dragon Well pillars represent the seasons, while the other 24 smaller pillars symbolize the months in a year plus the 2-hour time periods in a day.

KEY

① **Dragon and phoenix motifs** inside and out represent the emperor and empress.

② **Red** is an imperial color.

③ **Circular roof symbolizing the sky**

④ **Name plaques** are often written in the calligraphy of an emperor.

⑤ **The golden finial** is 125 ft (38 m) high and prone to lightning strikes.

⑥ **Blue** represents the color of heaven.

⑦ **Tablets** in memory of his ancestors were worshipped by the emperor.

⑧ **Symbolic offerings**

Marble Platform
Three tiers of marble form a circle 300 ft (90 m) in diameter and 20 ft (6 m) high. The balusters on the upper tier are decorated with dragon carvings to signify the imperial nature of the structure.

㉓ Cow Street Mosque
牛街清真寺

18 Niu Jie, Xuanwu. **Map** 3 A3. Ⓜ Caishikou, then taxi. **Tel** (010) 6353 2564. **Open** dawn–dusk daily. Avoid Fri (holy day).

Beijing's oldest and largest mosque dates back to the 10th century. It is located in the city's Hui district, near numerous Muslim restaurants and shops. The Hui, a Chinese Muslim minority group mainly from Ningxia province, are now scattered throughout China and number around 200,000 in Beijing. The men are easily identified by their beards and characteristic white hats.

The Cow Street Mosque is an attractive edifice, with Islamic motifs and Arabic verses decorating its halls and stelae. Its most prized possession is a 300-year-old, handwritten copy of the Koran *(Gulanjing)*.

Astronomical observations and lunar calculations were made from the tower-like **Wangyue Lou**. The graves of two Yuan dynasty Arab missionaries engraved with Arabic inscriptions can be seen here. The courtyard is lush with greenery, making it an idyllic escape from Beijing's busy streets. Visitors are advised to dress conservatively (covering arms, legs, and head). Non-Muslims are not allowed to enter the prayer hall.

Buddhist statuary in the main hall, Fayuan Temple

㉔ Fayuan Temple
法源寺

7 Fayuan Si Qian Jie, Xuanwu. **Map** 3 A3. Ⓜ Caishikou. **Tel** (010) 6353 4171. **Open** 8am–3pm daily.

A short walk east from Cow Street Mosque, the Fayuan Temple dates to AD 696 and is probably the oldest temple in Beijing. It was consecrated by the Tang Taizong emperor (r.626–49), to commemorate the soldiers who perished in an expedition against the northern tribes. The original Tang-era buildings were destroyed by a succession of natural disasters, and the current structures date from the Qing era.

The temple's layout is typical of Buddhist temples. Near the gate, the incense burner *(lu)* is flanked by the Drum and Bell Towers to the east and west. Beyond, the Hall of the Heavenly Kings (Tianwang Dian) is guarded by a pair of bronze lions, and has statues of Milefo (the Laughing Buddha) and his attendant Heavenly Kings. Ancient stelae stand in front of the main hall, where a gilded statue of Sakyamuni (the Historical Buddha) is flanked by *bodhisattvas* and *luohan* – those freed from the cycle of rebirth.

At the temple's rear, the Scripture Hall stores *sutras*, while another hall contains a 16-ft (5-m) Buddha statue. The grounds are busy with monks who attend the temple's Buddhist College.

Resplendent interior of the Cow Street Mosque

㉕ White Clouds Temple
白云寺

9 Baiyuanguan Jie, Xuanwu. Ⓜ Changchujie, then taxi or bus 9. **Tel** (010) 6344 3666. **Open** 8:30am–4pm daily.

Home to the China Daoist Association, the White Clouds Temple (Baiyun Guan) was founded in AD 739 and is Beijing's largest Daoist shrine. Known as the Temple of Heavenly Eternity, it was one of the three ancestral halls of the Quanzhen School of Daoism, which focused on right action and the benefits of good karma. Built largely of wood, the temple burned to the ground in 1166, and since then has been repeatedly destroyed and rebuilt. The structures that survive date largely from the Ming and Qing dynasties. A triple-gated Ming *pailou* (decorative archway) stands at the entrance. It is

For hotels and restaurants in this area see p588 and pp572–73

believed that rubbing the carved monkey on the main gate brings good luck. The major halls are arranged along the central axis, with more halls on either side. The Hall of the Tutelary God has images of four marshals who act as temple guardians, while the Hall of Ancient Disciplines is dedicated to the Seven Perfect Ones, disciples of Wang Chongyang, the founder of the Quanzhen School. The Hall of Wealth is popular with pilgrims who seek blessings from the three spirits of wealth, while the infirm patronize the Hall of the King of Medicine.

The temple grounds are full of Daoist monks with their distinctive topknots. It is most lively during the Chinese New Year *(see pp48–9)*, when a temple fair *(miaohui)* is held.

Buddhist monks, White Tower Temple

㉖ Military Museum of the Chinese People's Revolution

军事博物馆

9 Fuxing Lu, Haidian. M Military Museum. **Tel** (010) 6686 6244. **Open** 8:30am–5pm Tue–Sun. W **eng.jb.mil.cn**

Topped by a gilded emblem of the People's Liberation Army, the Military Museum of the Chinese People's Revolution is devoted to weaponry and revolutionary heroism. It is close to Muxidi, where the People's Liberation Army killed scores of civilians in 1989. Visitors are greeted by paintings of Mao, Marx, Lenin, and Stalin. The ground floor exhibits defunct F-5 and F-7 jet fighter planes, tanks, and surface-to-air missiles. The top gallery chronicles with pride many of China's military campaigns.

F-5 fighter planes, Military Museum of the Chinese People's Revolution

㉗ White Tower Temple

妙应寺

Fucheng Men Nei Dajie, Xicheng. **Map** 1 A4. M Fucheng Men. **Tel** (010) 6616 0211. **Open** 9am–4:30pm daily.

Celebrated for its distinctive Tibetan-styled, 167-ft (51-m) white *dagoba* (stupa or funerary mound) designed by a Nepalese architect, the White Tower Temple (Bai Ta Si) dates to 1271, when Beijing was under Mongol rule. In addition to its conventional Drum and Bell Towers, Hall of Heavenly Kings, and Main Halls, this Buddhist temple has a remarkable collection of small Tibetan Buddhist statues in one of its halls. Another hall has a collection of 18 bronze *luohan* (disciples).

㉘ Beijing Aquarium

北京水族馆

137 Xizhi Men Wai Dajie, Haidian. M Xizhi Men, then taxi. **Tel** (010) 6217 6655. **Open** 7:30am–4:30pm (to 5:30pm spring & summer). W **bj-sea.com**

Although situated within Beijing Zoo, which has some outdated conditions for keeping animals, the aquarium is a good way to spend a few hours (especially if traveling with children). The largest aquarium in China, it features a range of marine and freshwater tanks housing a large variety of creatures including sharks and stingrays, as well as whales and dolphins. There are also re-created habitats like coral reefs and an Amazon rainforest.

29 Summer Palace

颐和园

The sprawling grounds of the Summer Palace (Yihe Yuan) served the Qing dynasty as an imperial retreat from the stifling summer confines of the Forbidden City. Despite existing as an imperial park in earlier dynasties, it was not until the time of Emperor Qianlong, who reigned from 1736 to 1795, that the Summer Palace assumed its current layout. The palace is most associated, however, with Cixi, who had it rebuilt twice: once following its destruction by French and English troops in 1860, and again in 1902 after it was plundered during the Boxer Rebellion.

★ Longevity Hill
The Tower of the Fragrance of the Buddha dominates this slope covered with impressive religious buildings.

Marble Boat
Cixi paid for this extravagant folly with funds meant for the modernization of the Imperial Navy. The superstructure of the boat is made of wood painted white to look like marble.

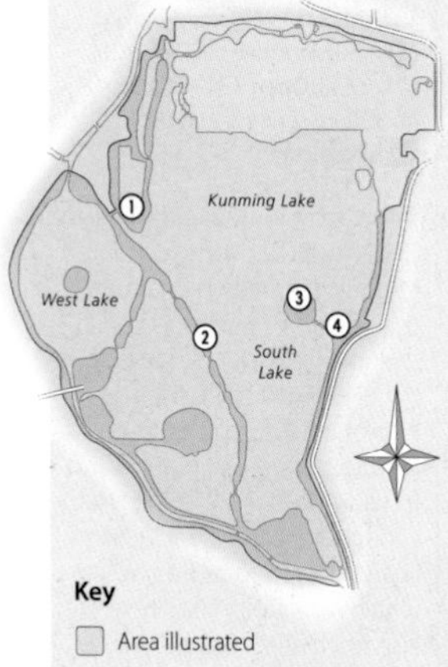

Plan of Grounds

The grounds of the Summer Palace cover 716 acres (290 hectares), with Kunming Lake lying to the south of Longevity Hill. South Lake Island is just off the east shore and a stroll around the entire shoreline takes about 2 hours.

① Jade Belt Bridge
② West Causeway
③ South Lake Island
④ Bronze Ox

0 meters 800
0 yards 800

KEY

① **The Bronze Pavilion**, weighing 207 tons (188 tonnes), is a detailed replica of a timber-framed building.

② **Boat pier**

③ **Temple of the Sea of Wisdom**

④ **Suzhou Street**

⑤ **Back Lake**

⑥ **The Garden of Harmonious Pleasures** was Cixi's favorite fishing spot.

⑦ **Hall of Jade Ripples**

⑧ **Hall of Happiness and Longevity**

For hotels and restaurants in this area see p558 and pp572–3

Empress Cixi, 1835–1908

Empress Dowager Cixi

Together with Tang-dynasty Empress Wu Zetian *(see p63)*, Cixi is remembered as one of China's most powerful women. Having borne the Xianfeng emperor's son as an imperial concubine, Cixi later seized power as regent to both the Tongzhi and Guangxu emperors (her son and nephew respectively). Cixi prevented Guangxu from implementing state reforms and, in her alliance with the Boxer Rebellion, paved the way for the fall of the Qing Dynasty in 1911.

VISITORS' CHECKLIST

Practical Information
6 miles (10 km) NW of Beijing. **Tel** (010) 6288 1144. **Open** 6:30am–8pm (Nov–Mar: 7am–7pm). Park sites close 2 hrs earlier.
summerpalace-china.com

Transportation
Beigongmen. from Yuyuan Tan Park, and Exhibition Center near zoo (not in winter or bad weather).

★ Garden of Virtue and Harmony
This three-story building served as a theater, where the court's 348-member opera troupe entertained Cixi, who watched from the surrounding gallery.

5

6

8

7

East Palace Gate (main entrance)

★ Long Corridor
The beams along the length of this 2,388-ft (728-m) walkway are decorated with over 14,000 scenic paintings.

Hall of Benevolence and Longevity
The principal ceremonial hall, this single-eaved building houses the throne upon which Cixi sat.

Exploring the Summer Palace

Like the imperial resort at Chengde *(see pp128–31)*, the palace grounds are arranged as a microcosm of nature, its hills *(shan)* and water *(shui)* creating a natural composition further complemented by bridges, temples, walkways, and ceremonial halls. Even after repeated restoration, the Summer Palace tastefully harmonizes the functional and fanciful, with administrative and residential quarters leading to the pastoral vistas of the grounds, as well as numerous peaceful temples and shrines.

Seventeen-Arch Bridge linking South Lake Island to the mainland

The grounds of the Summer Palace are extensive, but the main buildings can all be visited by those with a bit of energy and time. The main entrance at the **East Palace Gate** (Gong Dong Men) leads to the official and residential halls of the palace complex. Just inside the main gate stands the **Hall of Benevolence and Longevity** (Renshou Dian). Note the bronze statues in front of this ceremonial hall, including the symbol of Confucian virtue, the mythical *qilin,* a hybrid, cloven-hoofed animal with horns and scales. You will see signs here for **Suzhou Water Village**, which houses overpriced snack and souvenir stalls, and is not worth the extra entry fee.

By the lakeside to the west, the **Hall of Jade Ripples** (Yulan Tang) is where Cixi incarcerated the Guangxu emperor after the abortive 1898 Reform Movement. Cixi's residence, the **Hall of Happiness and Longevity** (Leshou Tang) is to the west of the **Garden of Virtue and Harmony** (Dehe Yuan) and north of the jetty from where Cixi would set sail across the lake. From here, the **Long Corridor** (Chang Lang) follows the lakeside, interrupted along its length by four pavilions. At the corridor's halfway point, a series of religious buildings ascends the slopes of **Longevity Hill** (Wanshou Shan), a sequence marked at the lakeside by a fabulous decorative gate *(pailou),* beyond which stands **Cloud Dispelling Gate,** with two bronze lions sitting alongside it. The first main hall, the **Cloud Dispelling Hall** (Paiyun Dian) is a double-eaved structure, above which rises the prominent, octagonal **Tower of the Fragrance of the Buddha** (Foxiang Ge). Behind the tower sits the rectangular brick and tile 18th-century **Temple of the Sea of Wisdom** (Huihai Si), its exterior decorated with green and yellow tiles and glazed Buddhist effigies, many of which have been vandalized. From here you can look down to the **Back Lake** (Hou Hu). West of the Tower of the Fragrance of the Buddha is the **Precious Clouds Pavilion** (Baoyun Ge), also called the **Bronze Pavilion**. Dating from the 18th century, the building is one of a handful that survived the destruction wrought by foreign troops.

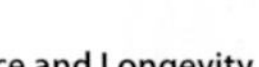

Bronze ox, believed to pacify the waters and prevent floods

The buildings at the north end of the lake are more than enough to fill a single day; however the southern end of the grounds can be blissfully free of crowds. Boat trips to **South Lake Island** depart from the jetty near the Marble Boat (north of which are the imperial boathouses). Alternatively, if time will allow, hire a boat for a leisurely row around Kunming Lake. **Dragon King Temple** (Longwang Miao) on South Lake Island is dedicated to the god of rivers, seas, and rain. The island is connected to the eastern shore by the elegant **Seventeen-Arch Bridge** (Shiqi Kong Qiao). A marble lion crowns each of the 544 balusters along the bridge's length, and a large bronze ox, dating back to 1755, reposes on the eastern shore. On the opposite shore, steep-sloped **Jade Belt Bridge** links the mainland to the West Causeway which slices through the lake to its southern point.

The unusual Bronze Pavilion, fashioned entirely from metal

Remnants of the Yuanming Yuan, once said to resemble Versailles

30 Yuanming Yuan
圆明园

28 Qinghua Xi Lu, Haidian. Ⓜ Yuanmingyuan Park. **Tel** (010) 6255 1488. **Open** 7am–7pm daily.

The Yuanming Yuan (Garden of Perfect Brightness, sometimes called the Old Summer Palace), now sits isolated from the main Summer Palace, but was a collection of princely gardens fused into the main mass by the Qing Qianlong emperor in the mid-18th century. He commissioned Jesuits at his court to design and construct a set of European-style buildings in one corner, which they likened to Versailles. Unfortunately, all the traditional Chinese halls were burned down by British and French troops during the Second Opium War in 1860. Later the European-style buildings were pulled down, and much of the remains carted away by the locals for building purposes. Chinese narrations of the devastation criticize both the marauding European troops and the ineffectual Qing rulers.

Today, Yuanming Yuan is a jumble of sad, yet graceful fragments of stone and marble strewn in the **Eternal Spring Garden** in the park's northeastern corner. A small museum displays images and models of the palace, depicting its scale and magnificence. The **Palace Maze** has been recreated in concrete to the west of the ruins. The rest of the park is a pleasant expanse of lakes, pavilions, gardens, and walks.

31 Great Bell Temple
大钟寺

31a Beisanhuan Xi Lu, Haidian. Ⓜ Dazhong Si. 300, 367. **Tel** (010) 8213 2630. **Open** 9am–4:30pm daily.

Home to a fascinating collection of bells, the 18th-century Dazhong Si follows a typical Buddhist plan, with the Heavenly Kings Hall, Main Hall, and the Guanyin Bodhisattva Hall. Its highlight is the 46.5 ton (47, 246 kg) bell – one of the world's largest – that is housed in the rear tower. The bell was cast between 1403 and 1424, and brought here from Wanshou Temple in the reign of the Qianlong emperor. Buddhist *sutras* in Chinese and Sanskrit embellish its surface. During the Ming and Qing dynasties, the bell was struck 108 times to bring in the New Year, and could be heard for 25 miles (40 km). The gallery above has a display on bell casting, and visitors can toss a coin into the bell for luck.

The Great Bell Temple or Dazhong Si

32 798 Art Zone
798艺术区

4 Jiuxianqiao Road, Chaoyang district. Ⓜ Wangjing South. **Tel** (010) 5978 9798. Ⓦ **798district.com**

A hip development in a renovated industrial area, the 798 Art Zone features many galleries, design studios, cafés, restaurants, and shops, all showcasing Beijing's thriving contemporary culture and art scene. It buzzes on weekends with a young, arty crowd.

33 Xiang Shan Park
香山公园

Wofosi Lu, Xiang Shan, Haidian district. Ⓜ Bagoumen, then taxi. 331 from Summer Palace, 360 from Zoo. **Tel** (010) 6259 9886. **Open** 6am–6:30pm daily. Botanical Gardens: **Open** 9am–4pm daily.

This wooded area, also known as Fragrant Hills Park, is at its scenic best in the fall, when the maples turn red. Its main draws are the fine views from **Incense Burner Peak**, accessible by a chairlift, and **Biyun Temple**, or Azure Cloud Temple, near the main gate. The temple is guarded by the menacing deities Heng and Ha in the Mountain Gate Hall. A series of halls leads to the Sun Yat-sen Memorial Hall, where his coffin was temporarily stored in 1925. At the temple's rear is the distinctive Diamond Throne Pagoda. About a mile (2 km) east of Xiang Shan Park, the **Beijing Botanical Gardens** contain some 3,000 plant species. China's last emperor, Pu Yi *(see p452)*, ended his days here as a gardener.

34 Ming Tombs: Chang Ling

明十三陵

The resting place for 13 of the 16 Ming emperors, the Ming Tombs (Shisan Ling) are China's finest example of imperial tomb architecture. The site was originally selected because of its auspicious *feng shui* alignment; a ridge of mountains to the north cradles the tombs on three sides, opening to the south and protecting the dead from the evil spirits carried on the north wind. The resting place of the Yongle emperor (1360–1424), the Chang Ling is the most impressive tomb and the first to be built. It has been beautifully restored, although the burial chamber, where Yongle, his wife, and 16 concubines are thought to be buried, has never been excavated.

★ Sacred Way
Part of the 4-mile (7-km) approach to the tombs, the Sacred Way is lined with 36 stone statues of officials, soldiers, animals, and mythical beasts.

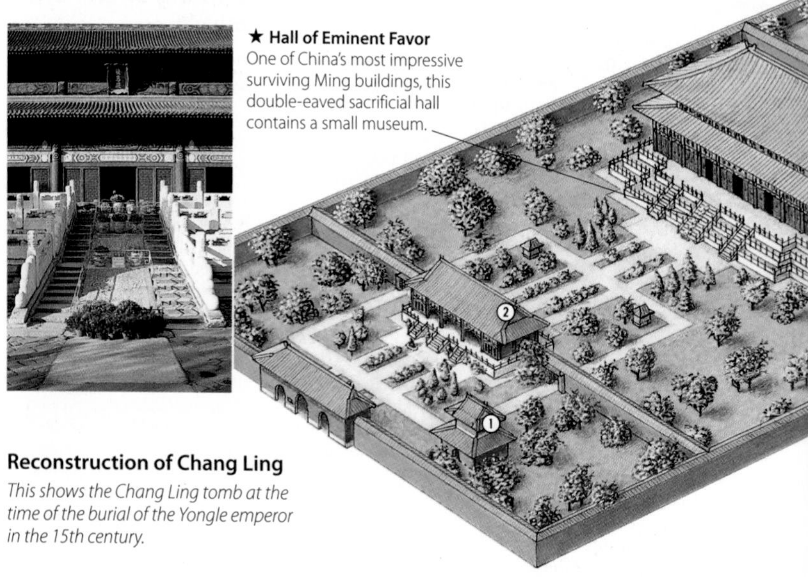

★ Hall of Eminent Favor
One of China's most impressive surviving Ming buildings, this double-eaved sacrificial hall contains a small museum.

Reconstruction of Chang Ling

This shows the Chang Ling tomb at the time of the burial of the Yongle emperor in the 15th century.

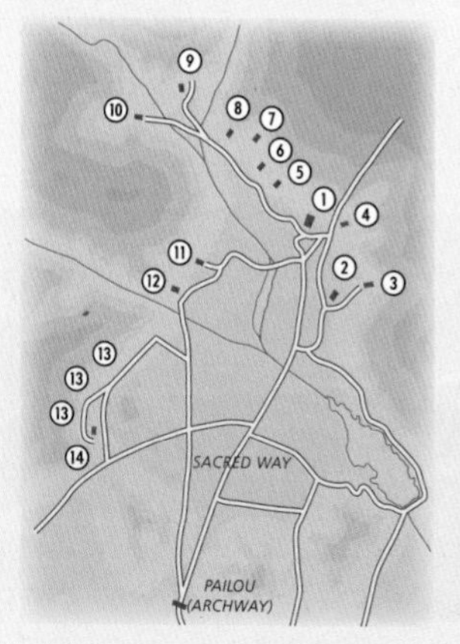

The Ming Tombs

The 13 tombs are spread over 15 square miles (40 sq km), so are best visited by taxi. Chang Ling, Ding Ling, and Zhao Ling have been restored and are very busy. Unrestored, the rest are peaceful places to visit but cannot at present be entered.

① Chang Ling (1424)
② Yong Ling (1566)
③ De Ling (1627)
④ Jing Ling (1435)
⑤ Xian Ling (1425)
⑥ Qing Ling (1620)
⑦ Yu Ling (1449)
⑧ Mao Ling (1487)
⑨ Tai Ling (1505)
⑩ Kang Ling (1521)
⑪ Ding Ling (1620)
⑫ Zhao Ling (1572)
⑬ Concubine cemeteries
⑭ Si Ling (1644)

0 kilometers 4
0 miles 4

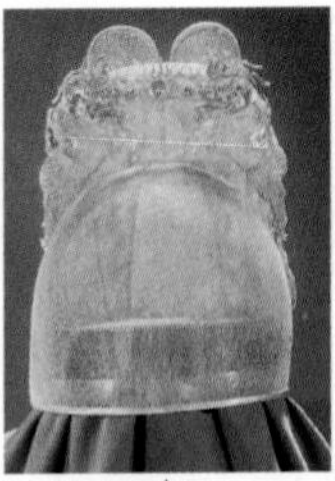

★ Ding Ling Treasures
Artifacts from the Wanli emperor's tomb, such as this threaded-gold crown decorated with two dragons, are on display in the main hall at Chang Ling.

VISITORS' CHECKLIST

Practical Information
32 miles (50 km) NW of Beijing. **Tel** (010) 6076 1148. **Open** Apr–Oct: 8am–5.30pm, Nov–Mar: 8:30am–5pm. interiors.
mingtombs.com

Transportation
Tourist bus 872 from Desheng Gate. Many tours to the Great Wall *(see pp112–14)* stop here.

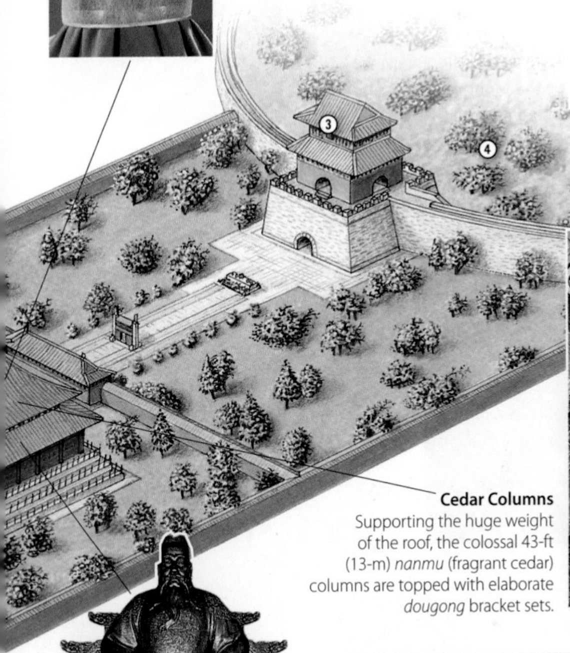

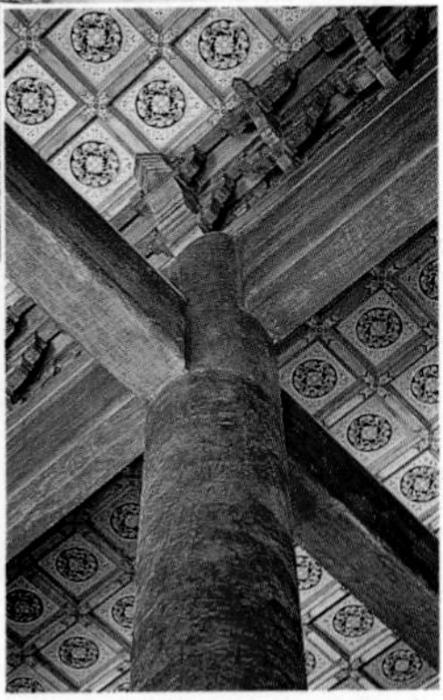

Cedar Columns
Supporting the huge weight of the roof, the colossal 43-ft (13-m) *nanmu* (fragrant cedar) columns are topped with elaborate *dougong* bracket sets.

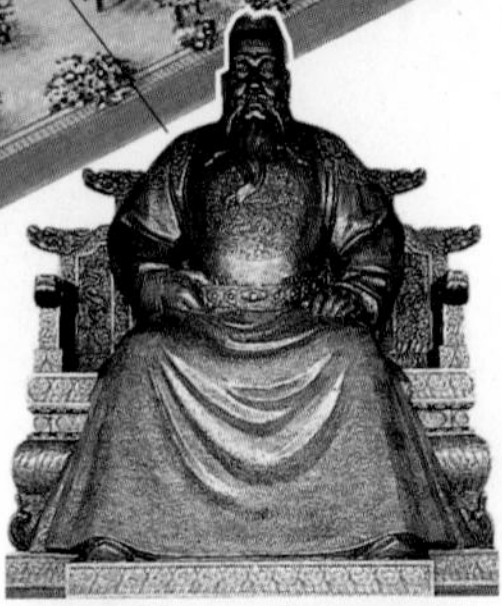

Statue of the Yongle Emperor
Yongle, the third Ming emperor, moved the capital from Nanjing to Beijing, where he then oversaw the construction of the Forbidden City.

Ding Ling Burial Chamber

Ding Ling, the tomb of the longest-reigning Ming emperor, Wanli (r. 1573–1620), is the only burial chamber of the 16 tombs to have been excavated and opened to the public. During the 1950s, archeologists were stunned to find the inner doors of the chamber still intact. Inside they found the treasures of an emperor whose profligate rule began the downfall of the Ming dynasty.

Side chambers were intended for others of Wanli's court, but were never used.

The central chamber contains three marble thrones, one for each of the dead.

The coffin chamber held the red lacquer coffins of Wanli and his two wives.

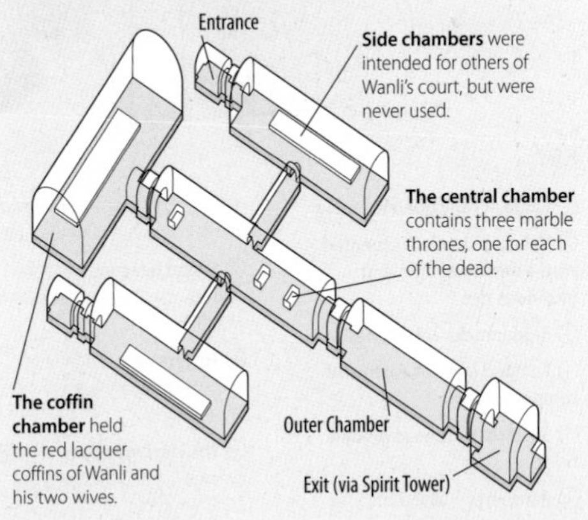

KEY

① **The Stele Pavilion** bears inscriptions dating from the Qing dynasty which revered the Ming emperors.

② **Gate of Eminent Favor**

③ **The Spirit Tower** marks the entrance to the burial chamber.

④ **An earthen mound**, surrounded by a circular rampart, covers the stone burial chamber.

㉟ Great Wall of China

长城

A symbol of China's historic detachment and sense of vulnerability, the Great Wall snakes over deserts, hills, and plains for several thousand miles. Originally a series of disparate earthen ramparts built by individual states, the Great Wall was created only after the unification of China under Qin Shi Huangdi (221–210 BC). Despite impressive battlements, the wall ultimately proved ineffective; it was breached in the 13th century by the Mongols and then, in the 17th century, by the Manchu. Today a UNESCO World Heritage Site, only select sections of its crumbling remains have been fully restored.

Crumbling Ruin
Most of the wall is still unrestored and has crumbled away leaving only the core remaining.

★ Panoramic Views
Because the wall took advantage of the natural terrain for defensive purposes, following the highest points and clinging to ridges, it now offers superb panoramic views.

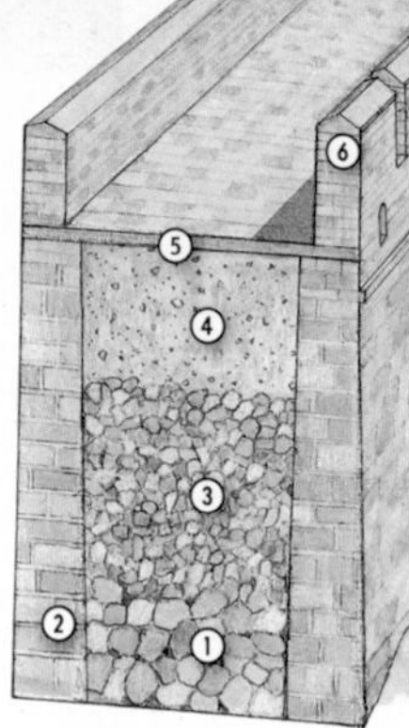

Reconstruction of the Great Wall

This shows a section of the wall as built by the most prolific wall builders, the Ming dynasty (1368–1644). The section at Badaling, built around 1505, is similar to this and was restored in the 1950s and 1980s.

★ Watchtowers
A Ming addition, these served as signal towers, forts, living quarters, and storerooms for provisions.

KEY

① **Large, locally quarried rocks**

② **Kiln-fired bricks, cemented with a mortar of lime and glutinous rice**

③ **Bigger rocks and stones**

④ **Tamped layer of earth and rubble**

⑤ **Surface of stone slabs and bricks**

⑥ **Ramparts** enabled the defending soldiers to fire down on their attackers with impunity.

⑦ **Signal beacons** were used to warn of attack by burning dried wolf dung.

⑧ **Towers** were spaced two arrow shots apart to leave no part unprotected.

⑨ **The carriageway** is on average (26 ft) 8 m high and (21ft) 7m wide.

For hotels and restaurants in this area see pp558–63 and pp572–85

Cannons
Another Ming addition, cannons were used to defend the wall and summon help.

TIPS FOR VISITORS

- The wall is exposed to the elements so be prepared for all outcomes: wear layers of clothing and a waterproof top, but also bring some sunscreen.
- Bring plenty of water.
- The wall can be very steep in places, so make sure you have strong footwear with a good grip such as hiking boots or tough waterproof running shoes.

Multi-Function Wall
The wall enabled speedy communications via smoke, flares, drums, and bells, as well as allowing for the rapid transportation of troops across the country.

The Great Wall of China (Ming Dynasty)

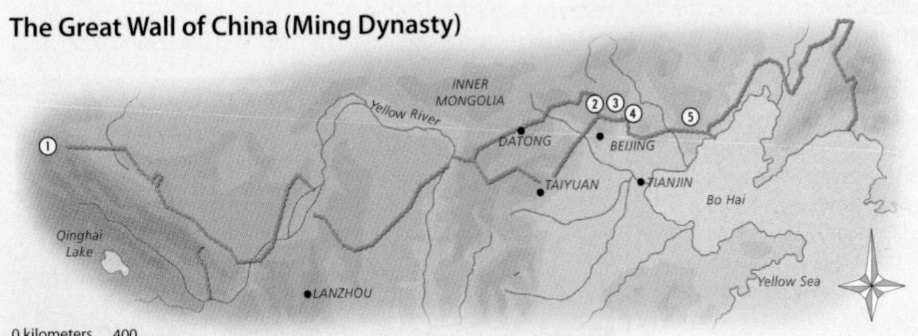

Most visitors travel to the wall from Beijing *(see p114)*, but it is worth seeing the wall anywhere along its length. Also impressive are the restored forts at Juyong Guan, Jiayuguan, and Shanhaiguan.

Places to visit
① Jiayu Guan *(see p494)*
② Badaling & Juyong Guan
③ Mutianyu & Huanghua Chen
④ Simatai
⑤ Shanhaiguan *(see p134)*

Exploring the Great Wall of China

A trip to the wall is a must for any visitor to Beijing. Most hotels will be able to organize this for you, usually combined with a visit to the Ming Tombs *(see pp110–11)*. However, be sure to find out whether there are any unwanted diversions planned to cloisonné workshops, jade factories, or Chinese medicine clinics. Small groups can have a more personalized visit, and see the more remote parts of the wall, by hiring a taxi for the day from Beijing and sharing the cost.

Ruins at Huanghua Cheng clinging to the steep hillside

Stall selling tourist paraphernalia at the Great Wall, Badaling

Badaling

44 miles (70 km) NW of Beijing. **Tel** (010) 6912 1737. 877 from Deshengmen (Beijing). from Beijing North. **Open** 7am–6pm daily.

Equipped with guardrails, cable car, pristine watchtowers, and tourist facilities, the restored Ming fortification at Badaling is the most popular section of the Great Wall. To fully appreciate the breathtaking view of the wall winding its way over the hills, get away from the crowds by walking as far as you can along the wall either east or west of the entrance. The ticket includes admission to the Great Wall Museum. The pass at **Juyong Guan** is on the way to Badaling and although restored, it is often quieter than Badaling. With unscalable mountains on either side it is easy to see why this spot was chosen for defense. There are also some authentic Buddhist carvings on a stone platform, or "cloud terrace," in the middle of the pass that date back to the Yuan dynasty (1279–1368).

Mutianyu

56 miles (90 km) North of Beijing, Mutianyu town, Huairou county. 6 from Xuanwu Men; 916 from Dongzhimen then taxi or minibus. **Open** 7am–6pm daily. plus chair lifts and slideway.

The appeal of Mutianyu lies in its dramatic hilly setting and slightly less intrusive tourist industry. With a series of watch-towers along its restored length, the wall you can see here dates from 1368 and was built upon the foundations of the wall built during the Northern Qi dynasty (AD 550–77).

Huanghua Cheng

37 miles (60 km) N of Beijing, Huairou county. 916 from Dongzhimen then taxi or minibus. **Open** 8am–4:30pm daily.

On the same stretch of wall as Mutianyu, Huanghua is an exhilarating section of Ming wall that is far less developed than other parts of the wall. The great barrier is split into two here by a large reservoir; most travelers take the right-hand route on the other side of the reservoir, as the left-hand section is more difficult to reach.

Devoid of guardrails, the crumbling masonry at Huanghua Cheng can be uneven and fairly treacherous in parts, so be careful. This is the best option for accommodation if you want to stay near the Great Wall.

Simatai

68 miles (110 km) NE of Beijing, Miyun county. 980 from Beijing to Miyun Gulou, then 51 to Simatai/Wtown. **Tel** (010) 8100 9999. **Open** 8am–5:30pm daily. (closed if windy). **wtown.com**

The wall at Simatai has been renovated, offering a more genuine impression of the original wall, though only the ten towers to the east of the town are currently open to the public and only with prior reservation via the website unless visitors buy a combination ticket for the town as well. The town has also been redeveloped as Beijing Wtown with historical exhibitions, hotels, shops, and restaurants in its restored streets and courtyards.

The restored section of the wall at Badaling, northwest of Beijing

36 Eastern Qing Tombs

清东陵

77 miles (125 km) E of Beijing, Zunhua county, Hebei province. M Sihui. from Sihui coach station to Zunhua, then taxi. **Tel** (0315) 694 5475. **Open** 8am–5pm daily. **qingdongling.com/idx**

The remoteness of the Eastern Qing Tombs east of Beijing and over the border in Hebei province makes them far less popular than the Ming ones *(see pp110–11)*, despite the fact that the setting is even more splendid. In fact, the Eastern Qing tombs make up the largest and most complete imperial cemetery in China, built on as grand a scale as the Forbidden City itself *(see pp92–5)*. Of the many tombs scattered throughout the area, only five are the burial places of Qing emperors: the tombs of the Shunzhi emperor (r. 1644–61), Kangxi (r. 1661–1722), Qianlong (r. 1736–95), and Xianfeng (r. 1851–61) are open, while that of the Tongzhi emperor (r.1862–74), at a distance from the main tomb grouping, is not. A 3-mile (5-km) Spirit Way, an approach lined with guardian figures, leads to Shunzhi's tomb, Xiao Ling, at the heart of the main tomb cluster, while several of the other tombs have their own smaller Spirit Ways. Southwest of here lies Yuling, Qianlong's tomb, with its incredible chamber adorned with Buddhist carvings and Tibetan and Sanskrit scriptures (rare features at imperial and principally Confucian tombs). The devious Empress Cixi *(see p107)* is buried at Ding Dong Ling to the west, in the right-hand tomb of a complex of twin tombs, the other being the resting place of Ci'an, eldest wife of the Xianfeng emperor. Although both tombs were built in 1879, Cixi had her magnificent tomb lavishly restored in 1895. The marble carriageway up to the Hall of Eminent Favor notably locates the carving of the phoenix *(feng)*, symbol of the empress, above the carving of the dragon *(long)*, symbol of the emperor. West of Ding Dong Ling, Ding Ling is partially open and approached via a set of stone animal statues. Look for the smaller tombs of imperial concubines, their roofs tiled in green (not the yellow of emperors and empresses).

Incense burners in front of a spirit tower at the Eastern Qing Tombs

Spirit Way to Emperor Shunzhi's tomb at the Eastern Qing Tombs

Emperor Yongzheng

The son of the Kangxi emperor and a maidservant, Yongzheng (r. 1723–35) chose not to be buried at the Eastern Qing Tombs, but perversely started a necropolis as far away as possible in the Western Qing Tombs (Yixian county, Hebei province). Perhaps, racked with guilt, he could not face burial alongside his father, whose will he had thwarted. For after Kangxi's death, Yongzheng seized the throne from his brother (his father's chosen successor), and declared himself the legitimate heir, ruthlessly eliminating any other brothers and uncles who may have been a threat to his rule. Despite this shaky start, Yongzheng was an able ruler and a devout Buddhist, punishing dishonesty among his officials and seeking to improve the morals and education of his people. Another possible reason for the switch was that he just wasn't satisfied with the Eastern Tombs and chose an area with a better natural setting. Whatever the reason, those keen on Chinese tomb architecture will enjoy the peace of the Western Qing Tombs. Nearby, moved in 1995 to a commercial cemetery, are the remains of Pu Yi, the last emperor of China.

Yongzheng in robes embroidered with symbols of his power

Brick stupas at Talin Si or Stupa Forest Temple

37 Marco Polo Bridge

芦沟桥

Wanping town, Fengtai district. 10 miles (16 km) SW of city center. M Wukesong, then bus 624. 339 from Beijing's Lianhuachi bus station. **Tel** (010) 8389 6510. **Open** 7:30am–6pm daily.

Straddling the Yongding River in Wanping town, the 876-ft (267-m) long marble bridge was first built during the Jin dynasty in 1189 but destroyed by a flood. The current structure dates to 1698. Known as Lugou Qiao in Chinese, the bridge acquired its English name after Marco Polo described it in his famous treatise *The Travels (see p249)*. At the bridge's eastern and western ends are stelae inscribed by the Qing emperors Kangxi and Qianlong. The poetic observation by Qianlong on a stele at the eastern end reads "*lugou xiaoyue*," meaning "Moon at daybreak at Lugou." The balustrades along the length of the bridge are decorated with more than 400 carved stone lions, each one slightly different in appearance. Local legend has it that these fierce-looking statues come alive during the night. Despite the widening and extensive restoration work done over the centuries, a surprising amount of the bridge is original.

Stone lion, Marco Polo Bridge

In addition to its antiquity, it is significant as the site of the disastrous Marco Polo Bridge Incident. This is where, on July 7, 1937, the Japanese Imperial Army and Nationalist Chinese soldiers exchanged fire – an event that led to the Japanese occupation of Beijing and a full-scale war. For those with a keen interest in this period of history, the incident is marked by some rather gruesome displays in Wanping's **Memorial Hall**.

38 Tanzhe Temple

潭柘寺

Mentougou district. 28 miles (45 km) W of Beijing. M to Pingguo Yuan (1 hr), then bus 931, or taxi. **Tel** (010) 6086 1699. **Open** 8am–4:30pm daily.

This enormous temple dates back to the 3rd century AD, when it was known as Jiafu Si. It was later renamed Tanzhe Temple, after the adjacent mountain Tanzhe Shan, which in turn got its name from the nearby Dragon Pool (Long Tan) and the surrounding cudrania (*zhe*) trees. It has a splendid mountainside setting, its halls rising up the steep incline. The temple is especially famous for its ancient trees, among which is a huge ginkgo known as the Emperor's Tree. A slightly smaller tree close by is called the Emperor's Wife.

The most fascinating sight, however, is the **Stupa Forest Temple** (Talin Si) near the parking lot, with its marvellous collection of brick stupas hidden among the foliage. Each stupa was constructed in memory of a renowned monk. The towering edifices were built in a variety of designs, including the graceful *miyan ta* or dense-eave stupa, characterized by ascending layers of eaves. The earliest among them dates from the Jin dynasty (1115–1234).

The Marco Polo Bridge, known locally as Lugou Qiao

39 Peking Man Site
周口店北京猿人遗址

Zhoukoudian village. 30 miles (48 km) SW of Beijing. 917 from Beijing's Tianqiao bus station to Fangshan, then bus 38 or taxi. **Tel** (010) 6930 1272. **Open** Apr–Oct: 9am–4pm daily; Nov–Mar: 8:30am–4:30pm daily.

Unearthed from a cave at Zhoukoudian in the 1920s, the 40-odd fossilized human bones and primitive implements were identified as the prehistoric remains of Peking Man *(Homo erectus Pekinensis)*, who lived here over 500,000 years ago. It was thought that this exciting discovery provided the much sought-after missing link between Neanderthals and modern humans. Designated a UNESCO World Heritage Site, the area is geared toward specialists, although the small museum has an interesting display of tools, ornaments, and bone fragments. Sadly, Peking Man himself is not actually here and the site has suffered neglect.

The prehistoric Peking Man Site at Zhoukoudian

40 National Olympic Stadium
奥林匹克体育中心

Olympic Green. Olympic Green. **Tel** (010) 8437 5700. **Open** 9am–10pm daily.

Beijing's National Olympic Stadium was designed to be the stunning centerpiece of China's massive building program for the 2008 Olympics. It is part of the city's "Olympic Green" development, which includes a large landscaped park, an Olympic Village, and many other stadia including the National Indoor Stadium and Swimming Center.

Swiss architects Herzog and de Meuron won the competition for the stadium with a bird's nest-like structure of apparently random, intertwined ribbons of steel and concrete that simultaneously form both facade and structure. The gaps in the concrete lattice of the roof are filled with translucent inflated bags, making the building waterproof while allowing light to filter down to the spectators.

The National Stadium is one of the most striking buildings to be found anywhere in the world, and visitors are able to take tours around it. During the winter it is turned into a ski center. Plans to turn the area around the stadium into a shopping and entertainment complex are ongoing and include the Xin'ao Plaza mall next to the subway station.

The futuristic structure of the National Olympic Stadium

41 Chuandixia
川底下

Near Zhaitang town. 56 miles (90 km) NW of Beijing. M to Pingguo Yuan (1 hr), then bus 929 to Zhaitang (2 hrs) or taxi. **Tel** (010) 6981 8988. **Open** daily. W **cuandixia.com**

Despite the rather laborious expedition required to get here, a trip to the tiny village of Chuandixia (Under the River) is well worth the effort as the crumbling hamlet survives as a living museum of Ming and Qing dynasty village architecture. Situated on a steep mountainside, it is a picturesque outpost of courtyard houses *(siheyuan)* and rural Chinese buildings. Because of the close-knit nature of the original village all the courtyards were inter-connected by small lanes. The entry ticket allows access to the entire village, all of which can be explored in a few hours. Look out for the Maoist graffiti and slogans that survive on the boundary walls; similar graffiti from the Cultural Revolution has been white-washed in most other towns.

Chuandixia's population consists of about 70 people spread over a handful of families. Accommodations can be arranged for those wanting to explore the surrounding hills or simply experience the rural hospitality. Alive to the opportunities brought by tourism, quite a few of the old homesteads provide basic facilities at a reasonable price.

Traditional Ming and Qing dynasty houses, Chuandixia village

Shopping and Entertainment in Beijing

Beijing's shopping scene has undergone a dramatic change and slick department stores coexist with older retail outlets. Its vast array of retail options range from shopping malls and department stores to specialist stores, boutiques, antique and silk markets, and street vendors. The main shopping street Wangfujing Dajie *(see p100)* is very popular with Beijingers and visitors from out of town, but a raft of malls offer up stiff competiton. Regrettably, many of the traditional shops no longer exist with the exception of those on Dazhalan Jie *(see p91)*. Beijing also has a lively entertainment scene, with a growing number of pubs, bars, and clubs, and numerous venues for traditional Beijing Opera, theater, and music.

Shopping

Visitors can buy anything from traditional handicrafts, collectibles, carpets, and silks to electronic goods, furniture, antiques, and designer clothing in Beijing. Many stores listed here arrange packaging and shipping as part of their service.

Antiques, Crafts & Curios

Genuine antiques *(gudong)* are hard to find. Objects dating between 1795 and 1939 cannot officially be taken out of the country without a certificate; anything older may not be exported at all *(see p587)*. The best market for antiques and curios is **Panjiayuan Market** in the southeast of town. Open all week, for the best deals, visitors should get there at sunrise during weekends to rummage through the Bodhisattva statues, ceramics, screens, calligraphy, and variety of ornaments. The **Beijing Curio City**, just to the south, also has a vast collection of ceramics, furniture, jewelry, and Tibetan art on several floors. The large **Hong Qiao Market** near the Temple of Heaven *(see pp102–3)* is good for collectibles, souvenirs, and pearls, especially the third and fourth floors. Be aware, however, that many of the goods on sale here are not original items. Visitors could spend a few hours browsing through **Liulichang** *(see p91)* for its lacquerware, ceramics, paintings, and crafts. Nearby **Liulichang Antiques Market** is the largest in the city, though beware that some goods here may be fake.

Books

It is advisable to take your own reading material when traveling to China, as the choice of imported and English-language fiction in Beijing is quite limited. But a fine selection of photographic, cultural, and travel books on China can be found. **Page One**, which has four separate mall locations, has an excellent selection of international and Chinese books across many of the most popular subjects. It also hosts regular literature, culture, and art events, as well as author talks and book-signings.

The Bookworm should be your first choice for books; it has a great selection to either buy or borrow.

Department Stores & Shopping Malls

Since China's economic rise, there has been an explosion of opportunities for the newly monied to spend their cash. As well as the department stores along Xidan Dajie, hundreds of shopping malls have sprung up in the capital to sate the locals' desire for foreign designer labels and luxury goods. For the visitor, these malls provide an escape from the hustle-and-bustle of the streets of Beijing, and they are also the best places to find larger clothing sizes. The outdoor **Taikoo Li** in Sanlitun is especially good for this, while **Parkview Green** remains the city's best overall shopping mall.

Carpets & Textiles

Beijing's markets sell a variety of carpets *(ditan)* from Tibet, Gansu, and Xinjiang, but visitors should bargain hard on all purchases. The **Qian Men Carpet Company** on Xingfu Dajie has fine handmade carpets from Xinjiang, Mongolia, and Tibet. Other shops worth visiting are the carpet stores on **Liulichang**, the **Liangma Antique Market**, and the stalls at **Panjiayuan Market**.

The cramped Silk Street Alley Market has been transformed into the multi-story New Silk Street Alley Market; experienced shoppers say it lacks the character of the old place and visitors should haggle for good prices. The **Yuanlong Silk Corporation** sells silk fabric and a large selection of ready-made silk garments, and the long-established **Beijing Silk Store** south of Qian Men has good-value silk and tailors onsite who can make outfits. For upscale, made-to-measure clothes, try the Na-Li Mall in Sanlitun, a small strip of boutiques just north of Bar Street where it is still fine to haggle.

Entertainment

The arts scene in Beijing received a huge boost with the opening in 2007 of the futuristic **National Center for the Performing Arts**, known colloquially as The Giant Egg, which stages operas, concerts, and plays. English-language theater is increasingly popular, as are art exhibitions and music concerts. The rock, punk, and jazz live music scene is rapidly expanding.

Only a limited number of foreign films are admitted to be screened in cinemas each year. Many embassies and bars show movies (either in English or with subtitles). There is a good cinema at Taikoo Li in Sanlitun. All European and Hollywood films are pirated on release, and appear in the markets as DVDs and VCDs of variable quality. Check out the listings in the English-language entertainment magazines found in the expat pubs on Sanlitun Lu, as well as in hotels. *The Beijinger* has good listings.

Beijing Opera

Traditional performances of Beijing Opera *(jingju)* are staged in the splendid **Zheng Yici Theatre**, the sole surviving wooden theater in China which was formerly a temple, where shows begin on most nights at 7:30pm. The **Huguang Guildhall** has a similarly distinguished setting, with daily performances at 6:30pm, while shows at the modern **Mei Langfang Theatre** start at 7:30pm. Another major venue is the **Liyuan Theatre**, where shows are tailored to tourists, and have subtitles in English. The **National Center for Performing Arts** also stages traditional Chinese operas.

Traditional Theater

The city's numerous teahouses are excellent venues for the enjoyment of a variety of performances such as traditional Chinese music, storytelling, Chinese opera, acrobatics, and martial arts.

The extraordinary body-bending feats of Chinese acrobats *(zaji)* can be seen at several places in the capital. Popular performances are held nightly at the **Chaoyang Theatre** at 4, 5:30, and 7pm, and the China Acrobatics Troupe stages performances at the **Tianqiao Acrobatic Theater** every afternoon at 5:30pm. More expensive shows featuring opera and acrobatics take place at the **Laoshe Teahouse** throughout the afternoon and evenings. For something more exciting, the **Red Theatre** holds a Vegas-style Kung Fu show at 7:30pm.

Pubs, Bars & Clubs

The capital's bar scene is lively and varied, with a strong focus on the Nali Patio area of Taikoo Li (North Sanlitun Lu), where microbrewery-pub pioneers **Great Leap Brewery #12** has its central location; and South Sanlitun Lu, which sits on the opposite side of Gongti Bei Lu to Nali Patio, where uber-chic modern speakeasy **Janes and Hooch** serves cool cocktails with jazzy lounge music. For mainstream clubs, such as **Modo**, the Gongti (Workers' Stadium) area is the place to be, though there's also a thriving alternative scene; check online for the current favorites.

DIRECTORY

Antiques, Crafts & Curios

Beijing Curio City
21 Dongsanhuan Nan Lu, W of Huawei Bridge, Chaoyang district.
Open 9:30am–6:30pm daily.

Hong Qiao Market
9 Tiantan Jie, Hong Qiao Lu, Chaoyang District.
Map 4 E3.
Open 9:30am–7pm daily.

Liulichang Antiques Market
Liulichang Xijie.
Map 3 B2.

Panjiayuan Market
Panjiayuan Lu, Chaoyang district. **Open** 8:30am–5:30pm Mon–Fri, 4:30am–5:30pm Sat & Sun.

Books

The Bookworm
Building 4, Nan Sanlitun Lu.
W beijingbookworm.com

Page One
Taikoo Li Sanlitun, Chaoyang district.
W pageonegroup.com

Department Stores & Shopping Malls

Parkview Green
9 Dongdaqiao Rd, Chaoyang district.
W parkviewgreen.com

Taikoo Li
19 Sanlitun Lu, at jnct with Gongti Bei Lu.
W taikoolisanlitun.com

Carpets & Textiles

Beijing Silk Store
50 Dashilan'r Xijie. **Map** 3 C2.
Open 8:30am–8:30pm daily.

Liangma Antique Market
27 Liangmaqiao Lu, Chaoyang district.

Qian Men Carpet Company
F1, Building 3, 59 Xingfu Dajie. **Map** 4 F3. **Open** 9:30am–5:30pm daily.

Yuanlong Silk Corporation
55 Tiantan. **Map** 4 D4.
Tel (010) 6702 2288.

Beijing Opera

Huguang Guildhall
10 Dongzhimen Nan Jie.
Map 3 B3.
Tel 186 1235 9093.
W huguangguildhallopera.com

Liyuan Theatre
175 Yongan Lu, Xicheng.
Map 3 C3.
W www.liyuantheatreopera.com

Mei Langfang Theatre
32 Ping'an Lixi.
W www.bjmlfdjy.cn

National Center for the Performing Arts
Xi Chang'an Jie.
Tel (010) 6655 0000.
W chncpa.org

Zheng Yici Theatre
220 Qian Men Xiheyan Dajie.
Map 3 C2.
Tel (010) 8315 1650.

Traditional Theater

Chaoyang Theatre
36 Dongsanhuan Bei Lu.
Tel 135 5252 7373.
W chaoyangtheatre.com

Laoshe Teahouse
3 Qian Men Xi Dajie, Xuanwu. **Map** 3 C2.
Tel (010) 16303 6830.
Open 10am–midnight daily (performances: 7:50–9:20pm)
W laosheteahouse.com

Red Theatre
44 Xingfu Dajie, Dongcheng. **Map** 4 F3.
Tel 135 5252 7373.
W redtheatrekungfu.com

Tianqiao Acrobatic Theater
1 Beiwei Donglu, Nan Dajie.
Map 3 C4.
Tel (010) 6303 7449.

Pubs, Bars & Clubs

Great Leap Brewery #12
12 Xinzhong Jie.
Tel (010) 5208 6138.

Janes and Hooch
Courtyard 4, Gongti Bei Lu.
Tel (010) 6503 2757.

Modo
4/F, U-Town Shopping Mall, Chaowai Jie.
Tel 132 6401 2084.

BEIJING STREET FINDER

The map references given for all sights, hotels, restaurants, shopping, and entertainment venues described in this chapter refer to the following two maps. The page grid superimposed on the schematic map below shows which parts of Beijing's city center are covered in this *Street Finder*. An index of the street names marked on the maps follows on the opposite page. The key, set out below, indicates the scales of the maps and shows what other features are marked on them, including subway, train, and bus terminals, hospitals, and tourist information centers. Beijing has extended a long way beyond the main city center and the Greater Beijing map on page 86 gives an idea of the areas to the north, west, and south of central Beijing. Getting used to the directional system of road naming *(see opposite)* is vital to getting around easily in cities.

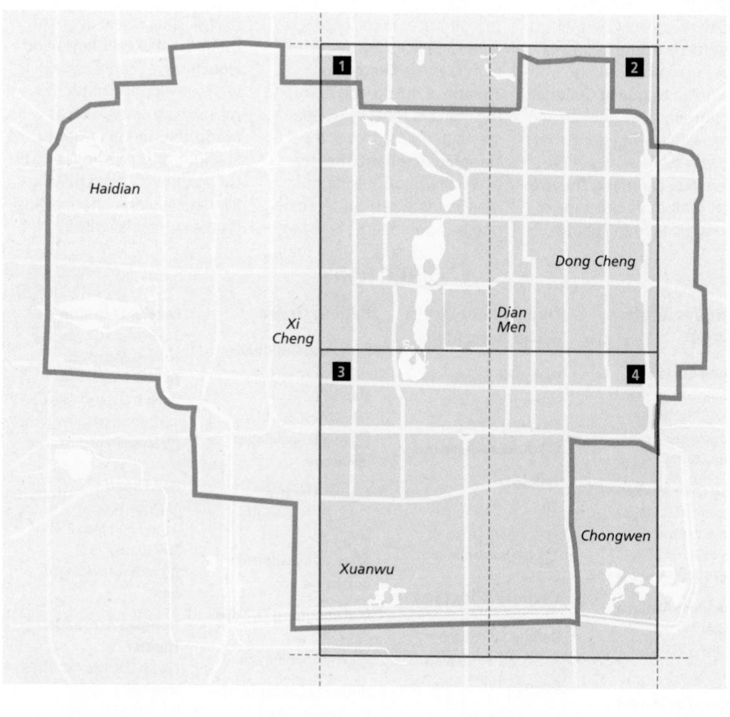

Key to Street Finder

- Major sight
- Place of interest
- Other important building
- Train station
- Bus station
- Subway station
- Tourist information
- Hospital
- Temple
- Church
- Mosque

Scale of Map Above

0 kilometers 2

0 miles 2

Scale of Maps 1–4

0 meters 500

0 yards 500

Street Finder Index

In street names, the suffix "jie" meaning street, or "lu" meaning road are often interchangeable. Therefore, when asking for directions or an address, note that Tian Tan Jie may also be known as Tian Tan Lu. Many streets are also called "dajie" or avenue. Directionals such as "zhong" (middle), and the four cardinal points – "dong" (east), "xi" (west), "bei" (north), and "nan" (south) – are often added to street names. The other key word mentioned here is "hutong" (alleyway).

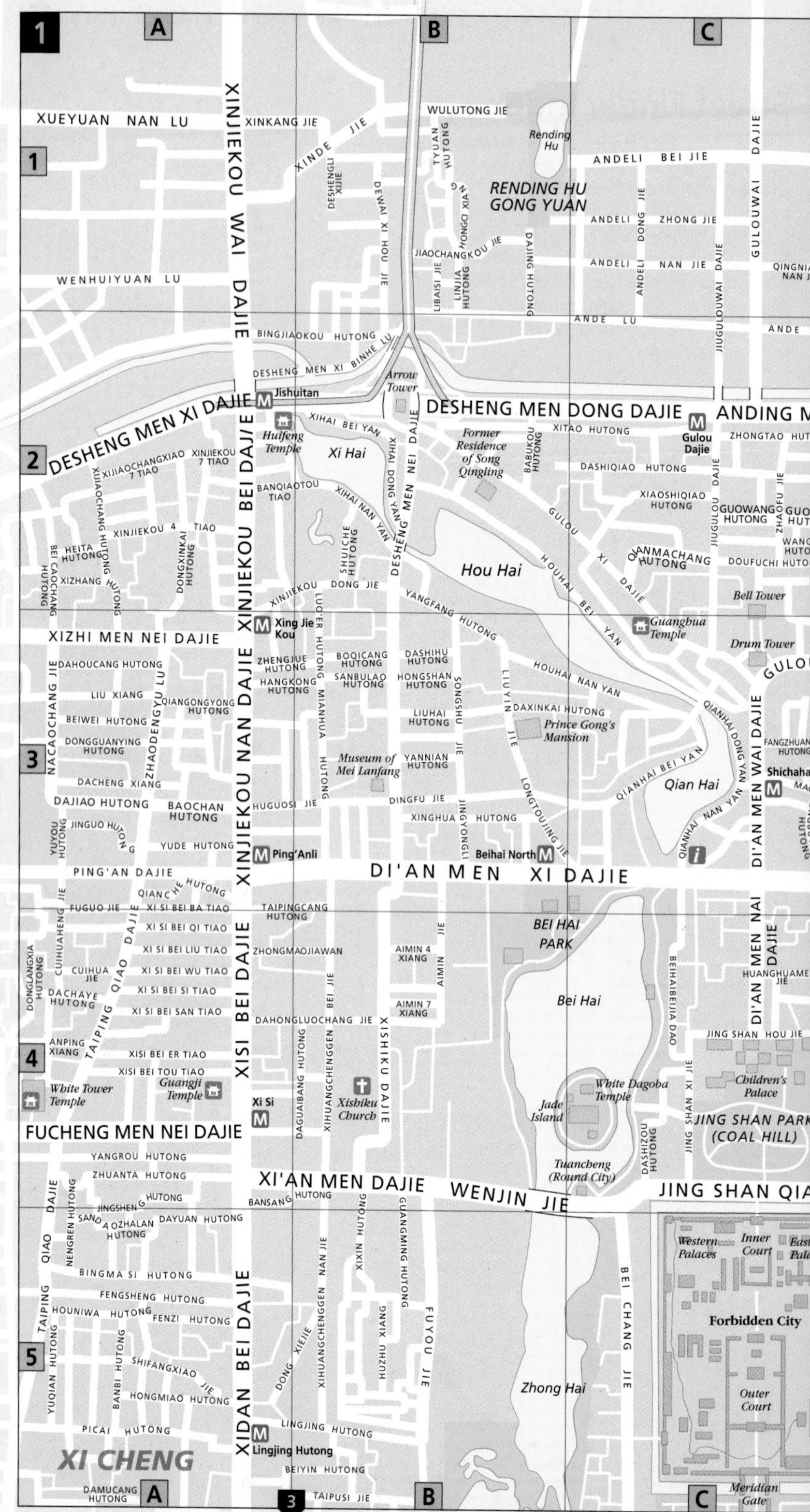

1
A
B
C
1
2
3
4
5
XUEYUAN NAN LU
XINKANG JIE
XINDE JIE
WULUTONG JIE
TYUAN HUTONG
Rending Hu
RENDING HU GONG YUAN
ANDELI BEI JIE
ANDELI ZHONG JIE
ANDELI NAN JIE
ANDELI DONG JIE
GULOUWAI DAJIE
QINGNIAN NAN JIE
DESHENGLI XIJIE
DEWAI XI HOU JIE
HONGCI XIANG
JIAOCHANGKOU JIE
DAJING HUTONG
LIBAISI JIE
LINJIA HUTONG
WENHUIYUAN LU
XINJIEKOU WAI DAJIE
BINGJIAOKOU HUTONG
ANDE LU
JIUGULOUWAI DAJIE
DESHENG MEN XI BINHE LU
Arrow Tower
Jishuitan
DESHENG MEN XI DAJIE
DESHENG MEN DONG DAJIE
ANDING MEN
XIHAI BEI YAN
Huifeng Temple
Xi Hai
XIHAI DONG YAN
DESHENG MEN NEI DAJIE
Former Residence of Song Qingling
BABUKOU HUTONG
XITAO HUTONG
Gulou Dajie
ZHONGTAO HUTONG
DASHIQIAO HUTONG
XIAOSHIQIAO HUTONG
JIUGULOU DAJIE
GUOWANG HUTONG
ZHAOFU JIE
WANG HUTONG
XIJIAOCHANGXIAO 7 TIAO
XINJIEKOU 7 TIAO
XIJIAOCHANG HUTONG
BANQIAOTOU TIAO
XIHAI NAN YAN
GULOU XI DAJIE
HOUHAI BEI YAN
QIANMACHANG HUTONG
DOUFUCHI HUTONG
XINJIEKOU 4 TIAO
DONGXINKAI HUTONG
SHUICHE HUTONG
Hou Hai
HEITA HUTONG
BEI CAOCHANG HUTONG
XIZHANG HUTONG
XINJIEKOU DONG JIE
XINJIEKOU BEI DAJIE
YANGFANG HUTONG
Bell Tower
Guanghua Temple
Drum Tower
XIZHI MEN NEI DAJIE
Xing Jie Kou
DAHOUCHANG HUTONG
ZHENGJUE HUTONG
BAOCHAN HUTONG
DASHIHU HUTONG
HANGKONG HUTONG
SANBULAO HUTONG
HONGSHAN HUTONG
LUOYER HUTONG
MIANHUA HUTONG
SONGSHU JIE
HOUHAI NAN YAN
GULOU
LIU XIANG
QIANGONGYONG HUTONG
ZHAODENGYU LU
BEIWEI HUTONG
LIUHAI HUTONG
LIUYIN JIE
DAXINKAI HUTONG
Prince Gong's Mansion
QIANHAI DONG YAN
DI'AN MEN WAI DAJIE
DONGGUANYING HUTONG
FANGZHUANG HUTONG
NACAOCHANG JIE
Museum of Mei Lanfang
YANNIAN HUTONG
QIANHAI BEI YAN
Qian Hai
Shichahai
DACHENG XIANG
LONGTOUJING JIE
DAJIAO HUTONG
XINJIEKOU NAN DAJIE
HUGUOSI JIE
DINGFU JIE
XINGHUA HUTONG
JINGYONGLI
QIANHAI NAN YAN
JINGUO HUTONG
YUYOU HUTONG
YUDE HUTONG
Ping'Anli
Beihai North
PING'AN DAJIE
DI'AN MEN XI DAJIE
QIANCHE HUTONG
FUGUO JIE
XI SI BEI BA TIAO
TAIPINGCANG HUTONG
XI SI BEI QI TIAO
BEI HAI PARK
CUIHUAHENG JIE
XI SI BEI LIU TIAO
ZHONGMAOJIAWAN
AIMIN 4 XIANG
AIMIN JIE
DI'AN MEN NEI DAJIE
DONGLANGXIA HUTONG
CUIHUA JIE
XI SI BEI WU TIAO
BEIHAIBEIJIA DAO
HUANGHUAMEN JIE
DACHAYE HUTONG
XI SI BEI SI TIAO
BEI JIE
Bei Hai
TAIPING QIAO DAJIE
XI SI BEI SAN TIAO
AIMIN 7 XIANG
DAHONGLUOCHANG JIE
XISHIKU DAJIE
JING SHAN HOU JIE
ANPING XIANG
XISI BEI ER TIAO
Children's Palace
XISI BEI TOU TIAO
XISI BEI DAJIE
DAGUAIBANG HUTONG
XIHUANGCHENGGEN BEI JIE
White Tower Temple
Guangji Temple
Xishiku Church
White Dagoba Temple
JING SHAN XI JIE
Xi Si
Jade Island
FUCHENG MEN NEI DAJIE
JING SHAN PARK (COAL HILL)
DASHIZUO HUTONG
YANGROU HUTONG
Tuancheng (Round City)
ZHUANTA HUTONG
XI'AN MEN DAJIE
WENJIN JIE
JING SHAN QIAN
HUTONG
BANSANG HUTONG
JINGSHENG HUTONG
SANDAOZHALAN HUTONG
DAYUAN HUTONG
NENGREN HUTONG
XIXIN HUTONG
GUANGMING HUTONG
XIHUANG CHENGGEN NAN JIE
Western Palaces
Inner Court
Eastern Palaces
BINGMA SI HUTONG
BEI CHANG JIE
FENGSHENG HUTONG
FUYOU JIE
Forbidden City
HOUNIWA HUTONG
FENZI HUTONG
HUZHU XIANG
BANBI HUTONG
SHIFANGXIAO JIE
DONG XIEJIE
XIDAN BEI DAJIE
YUQIAN HUTONG
HONGMIAO HUTONG
Zhong Hai
Outer Court
PICAI HUTONG
Lingjing Hutong
LINGJING HUTONG
XI CHENG
BEIYIN HUTONG
DAMUCANG HUTONG
TAIPUSI JIE
Meridian Gate
3

2
LIUYIN GONG YUAN
QINGNIAN HU GONG YUAN
Qingnian Hu
DI TAN PARK
Temple of Earth
Hepinglibeijie
Lama Temple
Confucius Temple
ANDING MEN WAI DAJIE
ANDING MEN NEI DAJIE
XI DAJIE
ANDING MEN
DONG DAJIE
DONG ZHI MEN BEI DAJIE
Anding Men
Yonghe Gong
Andingmenxibin
Beijing Capital International Airport Train Station
Dong Zhi Men
Dong Zhi Men Bus Terminal
NANGUAN GONG YUAN
JIAODAOKOU DONG DAJIE
DONG ZHI MEN NEI DAJIE
Beixinqiao
JIAODAOKOU NAN DAJIE
YONGHE GONG DAJIE
DONG ZHI MEN NAN DAJIE
Dong Si Shi Tiao
South Luogu Alley
Zhangzi Zhong Lu
ZHANGZI ZHONG LU
DONG SI SHI TIAO
DONG CHENG
MEISHUGUAN HOUJIE
DONG SI BEI DAJIE
CHAOYANG MEN BEI DAJIE
National Art Museum of China
Fuwangfu Temple
Dong Si
Chaoyang Men
WUSI DAJIE
DONG SI XI DAJIE
CHAOYANG MEN NEI DAJIE
Dang Yue Miao
Capital Theater
St. Joseph's Church
Dengshikou
WANGFUJING DAJIE
DONG SI NAN DAJIE
CHAOYANG MEN NAN DAJIE
Zhihua Temple
Sun Dong'an Plaza
Mahakala Temple
JIN BAO JIE
4

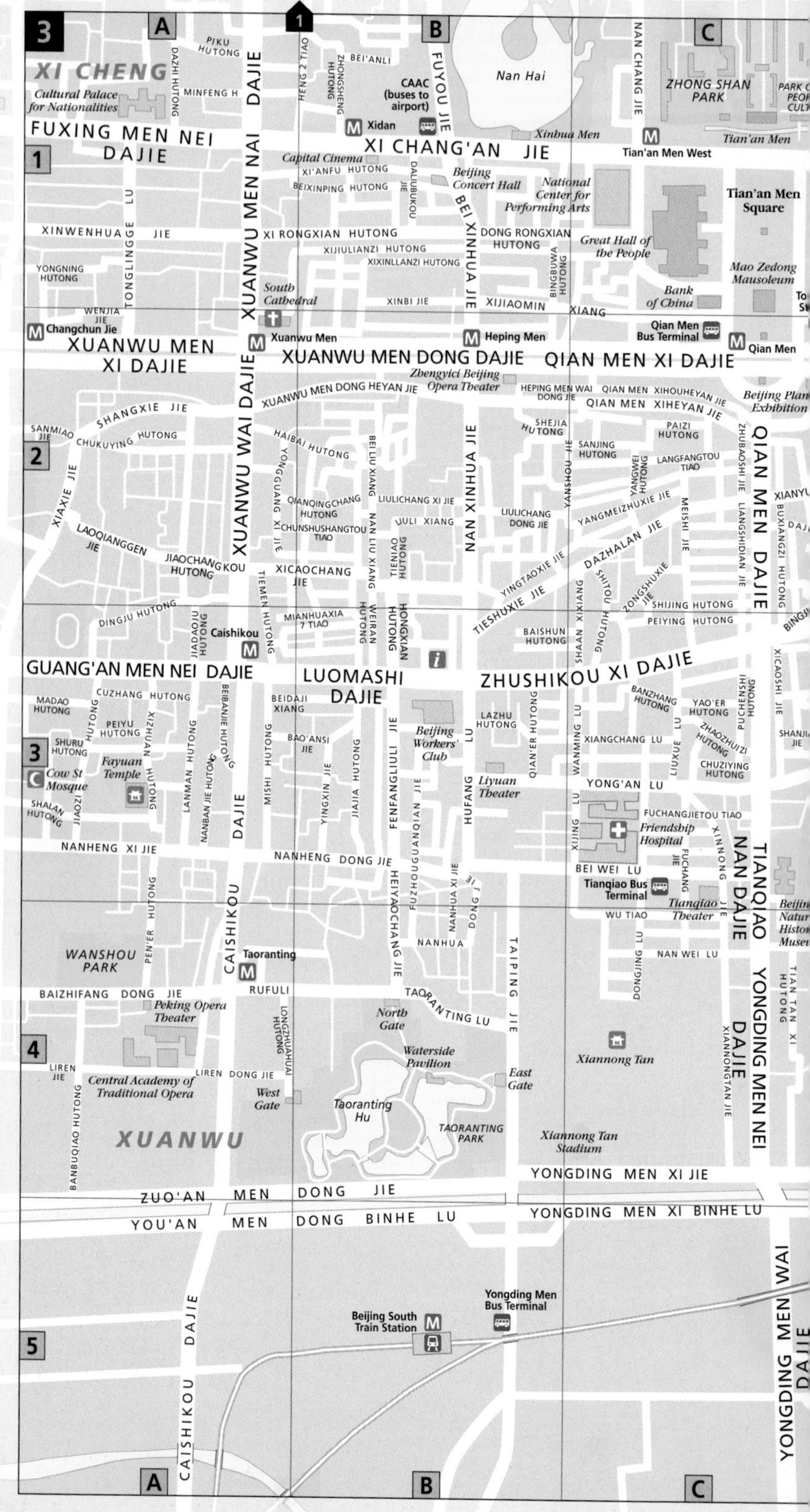
3
A
1
B
C
XI CHENG
Cultural Palace for Nationalities
PIKU HUTONG
DAZHI HUTONG
MINFENG H
FUXING MEN NEI DAJIE
XUANWU MEN NAI DAJIE
HENG 2 TIAO
ZHONGSHENG HUTONG
BEI'ANLI
CAAC (buses to airport)
Xidan
FUYOU JIE
Nan Hai
Xinhua Men
NAN CHANG JIE
ZHONG SHAN PARK
Tian'an Men
XI CHANG'AN JIE
Tian'an Men West
Capital Cinema
XI'ANFU HUTONG
BEIXINPING HUTONG
DALIUBUKOU JIE
Beijing Concert Hall
National Center for Performing Arts
Tian'an Men Square
TONGLINGGE LU
XINWENHUA JIE
XI RONGXIAN HUTONG
XIJIULIANZI HUTONG
XIXINLLANZI HUTONG
BEI XINHUA JIE
DONG RONGXIAN HUTONG
Great Hall of the People
Mao Zedong Mausoleum
YONGNING HUTONG
BINGBUWA HUTONG
South Cathedral
XINBI JIE
XIJIAOMIN XIANG
Bank of China
WENJIA JIE
Changchun Jie
Xuanwu Men
Heping Men
Qian Men Bus Terminal
Qian Men
XUANWU MEN XI DAJIE
XUANWU MEN DONG DAJIE
QIAN MEN XI DAJIE
Zhengyici Beijing Opera Theater
XUANWU MEN DONG HEYAN JIE
HEPING MEN WAI DONG JIE
QIAN MEN XIHOUHEYAN JIE
QIAN MEN XIHEYAN JIE
Beijing Planning Exhibition
SHANGXIE JIE
SANMIAO JIE
CHUKUYING HUTONG
HAIBAI HUTONG
SHEJIA HUTONG
PAIZI HUTONG
2
XIAXIE JIE
YONGGUANG XI JIE
BEI LIU XIANG
NAN XINHUA JIE
YANSHOU JIE
SANJING HUTONG
YANGWEI HUTONG
LANGFANGTOU TIAO
ZHUBAOSHI JIE
QIAN MEN DAJIE
QIANQINGCHANG HUTONG
LIULICHANG XI JIE
CHUNSHUSHANGTOU TIAO
LIULI XIANG
LIULICHANG DONG JIE
YANGMEIZHUXIE JIE
MEISHI JIE
LIANGSHIDIAN JIE
BUXIANGZI HUTONG
LAOQIANGGEN JIE
JIAOCHANGKOU HUTONG
NAN LIU XIANG
TIEMEN HUTONG
TIENIAO HUTONG
XICAOCHANG JIE
YINGTAOXIE JIE
DAZHALAN JIE
SHITOU HUTONG
ZONGSHUXIE JIE
DINGJU HUTONG
JIADAOJU HUTONG
Caishikou
MIANHUAXIA 7 TIAO
WEIRAN HUTONG
HONGXIAN HUTONG
TIESHUXIE JIE
SHAAN XIXIANG
SHIJING HUTONG
PEIYING HUTONG
BAISHUN HUTONG
GUANG'AN MEN NEI DAJIE
LUOMASHI DAJIE
ZHUSHIKOU XI DAJIE
XICAOSHI JIE
MADAO HUTONG
CUZHANG HUTONG
BEIBANJIE HUTONG
BEIDAJI XIANG
Beijing Workers' Club
LAZHU HUTONG
QIAN'ER HUTONG
BANZHANG HUTONG
YAO'ER HUTONG
PEIYU HUTONG
XIZHUAN HUTONG
BAO'ANSI JIE
XIANGCHANG LU
ZHAOZHUZI HUTONG
SHANJIA JIE
3
SHURU HUTONG
Fayuan Temple
LANMAN HUTONG
NANBAN JIE HUTONG
MISHI HUTONG
YINGXIN JIE
JIAJIA HUTONG
FENFANGLIULI JIE
HUFANG LU
WANMING LU
CHUZIYING HUTONG
Cow St Mosque
Liyuan Theater
YONG'AN LU
SHALAN HUTONG
JIAOZI
FUZHOUGUANQIAN JIE
XIJING LU
FUCHANGJIETOU TIAO
Friendship Hospital
NANHENG XI JIE
NANHENG DONG JIE
NANHUA XI JIE
DONG JIE
HEIYAOCHANG JIE
BEI WEI LU
Tianqiao Bus Terminal
FUCHANG JIE
XINONG JIE
TIANQIAO NAN DAJIE
WU TIAO
Tianqiao Theater
Beijing Natural History Museum
WANSHOU PARK
PEN'ER HUTONG
CAISHIKOU
Taoranting
NANHUA
TAIPING JIE
DONGJING LU
NAN WEI LU
YONGDING MEN NEI DAJIE
TIAN TAN XI HUTONG
BAIZHIFANG DONG JIE
RUFULI
TAORANTING LU
Peking Opera Theater
North Gate
4
LONGZHUAHUAI HUTONG
Waterside Pavilion
Xiannong Tan
XIANNONGTAN JIE
LIREN JIE
LIREN DONG JIE
East Gate
Central Academy of Traditional Opera
West Gate
Taoranting Hu
TAORANTING PARK
XUANWU
BANBUQIAO HUTONG
Xiannong Tan Stadium
YONGDING MEN XI JIE
ZUO'AN MEN DONG JIE
YONGDING MEN XI BINHE LU
YOU'AN MEN DONG BINHE LU
YONGDING MEN WAI DAJIE
Yongding Men Bus Terminal
Beijing South Train Station
5
CAISHIKOU DAJIE
A
B
C

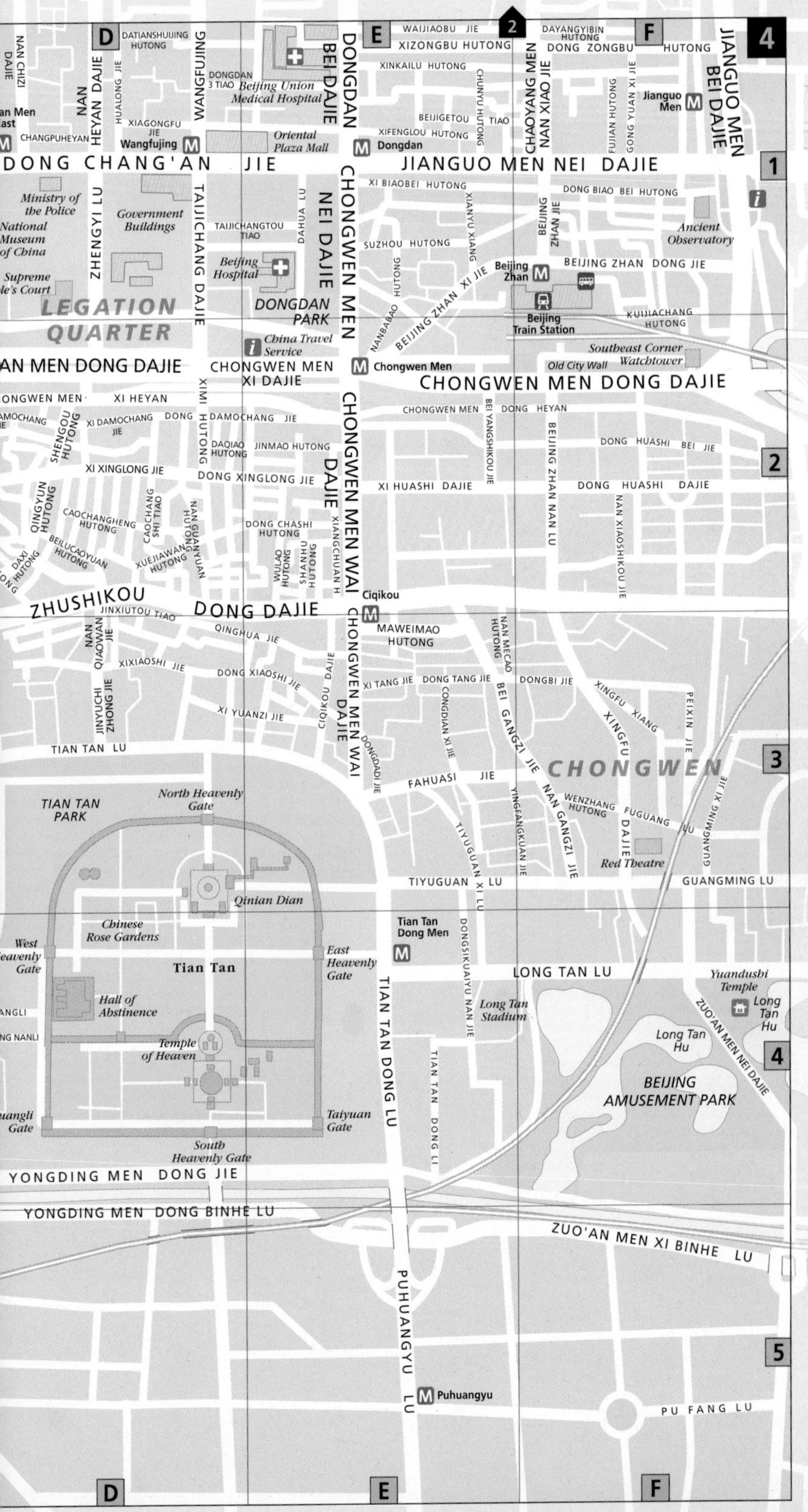

4
D
E
F
1
2
3
4
5
DONG CHANG'AN JIE
JIANGUO MEN NEI DAJIE
DONGDAN BEI DAJIE
WANGFUJING
Beijing Union Medical Hospital
Oriental Plaza Mall
Dongdan
Wangfujing
Jianguo Men
JIANGUO MEN BEI DAJIE
CHAOYANG MEN NAN XIAO JIE
DONG ZONGBU HUTONG
XIZONGBU HUTONG
WAIJIAOBU JIE
DAYANGYIBIN HUTONG
XINKAILU HUTONG
BEIJIGETOU TIAO
XIFENGLOU HUTONG
CHANGPUHEYAN
NAN HEYAN DAJIE
HUALONG JIE
XIAGONGFU JIE
DATIANSHUIJING HUTONG
DONGDAN 3 TIAO
NAN CHIZI DAJIE
Ministry of the Police
Government Buildings
National Museum of China
Supreme People's Court
ZHENGYI LU
TAIJICHANG DAJIE
TAIJICHANGTOU TIAO
Beijing Hospital
DONGDAN PARK
LEGATION QUARTER
CHONGWEN MEN NEI DAJIE
XI BIAOBEI HUTONG
SUZHOU HUTONG
DONG BIAO BEI HUTONG
Ancient Observatory
BEIJING ZHAN DONG JIE
Beijing Zhan
Beijing Train Station
BEIJING ZHAN XI JIE
NANBABAO
KUIJIACHANG HUTONG
Southeast Corner Watchtower
Old City Wall
China Travel Service
CHONGWEN MEN XI DAJIE
Chongwen Men
CHONGWEN MEN DONG DAJIE
XI HEYAN
CHONGWEN MEN DONG HEYAN
XI DAMOCHANG JIE
DONG DAMOCHANG JIE
XIMI HUTONG
DAQIAO HUTONG
JINMAO HUTONG
SHENGOU HUTONG
XI XINGLONG JIE
DONG XINGLONG JIE
XI HUASHI DAJIE
DONG HUASHI DAJIE
DONG HUASHI BEI JIE
BEIJING ZHAN NAN LU
NAN XIAOSHIKOU JIE
CHONGWEN MEN WAI DAJIE
QINGYUN HUTONG
CAOCHANGHENG HUTONG
CAOCHANG SHI TIAO
NAN GUANYUAN HUTONG
XUEJIAWAN HUTONG
BEILUCAOYUAN HUTONG
DONG CHASHI HUTONG
WULAO HUTONG
SHANHU HUTONG
XIANGCHUAN H
Ciqikou
ZHUSHIKOU DONG DAJIE
JINXIUTOU TIAO
QINGHUA JIE
NAN QIAOWAN JIE
XIXIAOSHI JIE
DONG XIAOSHI JIE
XI YUANZI JIE
JINYUCHI ZHONG JIE
CIQIKOU DAJIE
MAWEIMAO HUTONG
NAN MECAO HUTONG
XI TANG JIE
DONG TANG JIE
DONGBI JIE
XINGFU XIANG
XINGFU DAJIE
PEIXIN JIE
CONGDIAN XI JIE
BEI GANGZI JIE
NAN GANGZI JIE
CHONGWEN
DONGDADI JIE
FAHUASI JIE
TIAN TAN LU
WENZHANG HUTONG
FUGUANG LU
GUANGMING XI JIE
Red Theatre
YINGFANGKUAN JIE
TIYUGUAN XI LU
TIYUGUAN LU
GUANGMING LU
TIAN TAN PARK
North Heavenly Gate
Qinian Dian
Chinese Rose Gardens
West Heavenly Gate
East Heavenly Gate
Tian Tan
Hall of Abstinence
Temple of Heaven
Guangli Gate
Taiyuan Gate
South Heavenly Gate
Tian Tan Dong Men
DONGSIKUAIYU NAN JIE
LONG TAN LU
Long Tan Stadium
Yuandushi Temple
Long Tan Hu
ZUO'AN MEN NEI DAJIE
BEIJING AMUSEMENT PARK
TIAN TAN DONG LU
TIAN TAN DONG LI
YONGDING MEN DONG JIE
YONGDING MEN DONG BINHE LU
ZUO'AN MEN XI BINHE LU
PUHUANGYU LU
Puhuangyu
PU FANG LU

HEBEI, TIANJIN & SHANXI

With its northern borders adjoining Inner Mongolia and the western tip of erstwhile Manchuria, Hebei divides into a long southern plateau and a mountainous north, dotted with fragments of the Great Wall. Despite these barriers, the Manchu army flowed through the Shanhaiguan Pass in 1644 to impose 250 years of foreign rule on the Chinese. Hebei borders Shanxi to the west and envelops the wealthy conurbations of Beijing and Tianjin – Hebei's former capital and a repository of foreign concession-era architecture.

Shanxi (West of the Mountains), its northern edge protected by the Great Wall, was once a buffer zone against the hostile Mongol and Turkic tribes. It is largely a mountainous plateau, heavily industrialized, with the Yellow River (Huang He) flowing the length of its western border. Leaving Beijing, most visitors first explore Chengde, with its imperial park and temple architecture, or the celebrated Buddhist carvings at Yungang, outside Datong. Other key sights include the magnificent Hanging Temple clinging to a cliff face, the peaceful hills around Wutai Shan, one of China's four sacred Buddhist mountains, and the charming Ming and Qing architecture in the ancient walled town of Pingyao.

Sights at a Glance

Towns & Cities

- 2 Beidaihe
- 3 Shanhaiguan
- 4 Tianjin
- 5 Shijiazhuang
- 6 Datong
- 10 Taiyuan
- 11 *Pingyao pp144–5*

Temples & Monasteries

- 1 *Chengde pp128–31*
- 8 Hanging Temple
- 9 *Wutai Shan pp140–42*
- 12 Shuanglin Si

Historic Sites

- 7 *Yungang Grottoes pp138–9*
- 13 Qiao Jia Dayuan

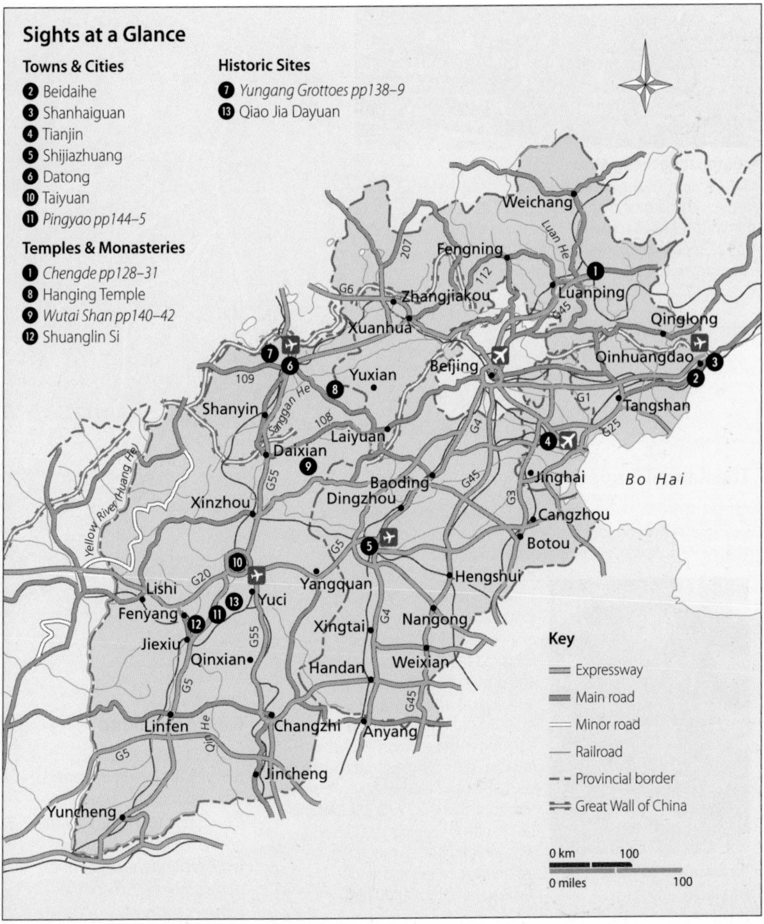

Key

- Expressway
- Main road
- Minor road
- Railroad
- Provincial border
- Great Wall of China

0 km 100
0 miles 100

◀ A traditional Chinese building illuminated at night

For map symbols *see back flap*

❶ Chengde

承德

The mountain resort at Chengde (Bishu Shanzhuang) was chosen by the Kangxi emperor in 1703 as a means of eluding the hot summers in the Forbidden City. Set in a river valley surrounded by mountains, the park was strategically secure and allowed the hardy Manchu to engage in hunting and martial sports. The rural setting beyond the Great Wall reminded the Manchu rulers of their homelands to the northeast. The eclectic temple design of the surrounding Eight Outer Temples put visiting Mongol and tribal chieftains at ease, so the emperor could exploit their allegiances.

Tibetan Buddhist designs to make the Mongol allies feel at home

Shuxiang Si

Putuozong

Northwest Gate

BISHU SHANZHUANG

West Gate

CHENGDE CITY

★ Putuozongcheng Miao
Built to resemble the Potala Palace in Lhasa, the temple is the largest of the Eight Outer Temples and has displays of *thangkas* (Tibetan religious scrolls), Tibetan religious ornaments, and two scaled-down sandalwood pagodas.

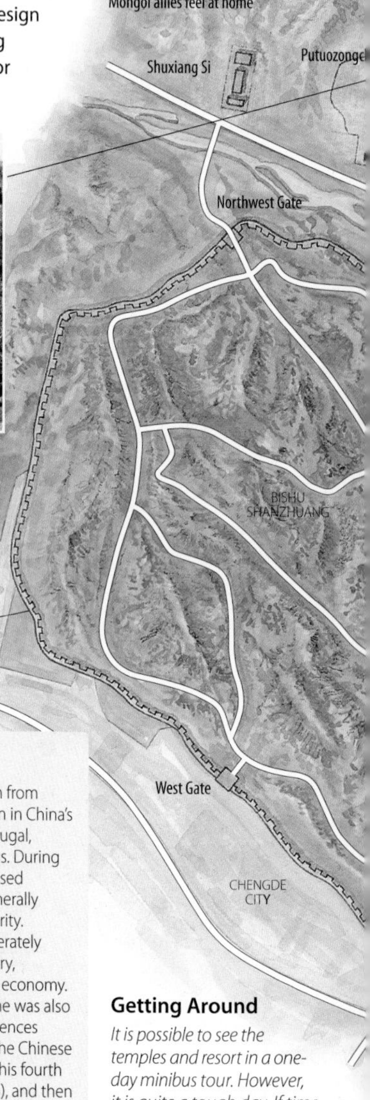

The wall is over 6 miles (10 km) long.

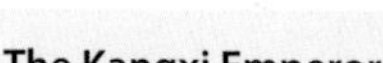

The Kangxi Emperor

Kangxi (1654–1722) was the second Qing emperor to reign from Beijing, and held on to power for 61 years, the longest reign in China's history. His rule was, in comparison with other emperors, frugal, practical, and conscientious. During his reign the empire increased in size and wealth, and generally enjoyed peace and prosperity. He taxed the farmers moderately and protected the peasantry, building up a healthy rural economy. An outstanding militarist, he was also a patron of the arts and sciences inviting Jesuit scholars to the Chinese court. He was followed by his fourth son, Yongzheng (r.1723–35), and then his grandson Qianlong (r.1736–95), who idolized him so much that he resigned as emperor after 60 years so as not to outdo him.

The Kangxi emperor pictured in his library

Getting Around

It is possible to see the temples and resort in a one-day minibus tour. However, it is quite a tough day. If time allows, try a more leisurely walk around the resort one day and hire a taxi for the temples the next.

For hotels and restaurants in this region see pp558–9 and pp573–4

Xumifushou Zhi Miao
This temple was built to impress the visiting Panchen Lama who came to Chengde on the occasion of the Qianlong emperor's birthday in 1780.

VISITORS' CHECKLIST

Practical Information
Chengde. 150 miles (250 km) NE of Beijing. **Tel** (0314) 216 1132. Bishu Shanzhuang: **Open** 8am–5:30pm daily. Outer Temples: **Open** daily (not all open at the same time).

Transportation
1, 5, 15, 30 from Chengde station.

Puning Si
PUYOU SI
Xumiufshou Zhi Miao
East Gate
Anyuan Miao
Yongyousi Pagoda
Pule Si
Puren Si
0 meters 800
0 yards 800
Imperial Palaces
ain Gate

★ Puning Si
This temple combines Han Chinese designs at the front with typical Tibetan structures at the back. The highlight is the majestic wooden statue of Guanyin in the main hall *(see pp130–31)*.

Pule Si
The most impressive hall in Pule Si, the Temple of Universal Joy, is the yellow-tiled twin conical-roofed hall which has strong echoes of the Temple of Heaven in Beijing.

★ Bishu Shanzhuang
The southern section of the resort contains an array of simple but elegant palaces, cool shaded lakes, and waterside pavilions, best viewed from a rowing boat.

Key
Town area
Road

Puning Si, Chengde

普宁寺

One of the most impressive outer temples at the Imperial Summer Retreat at Chengde, Puning Si (Puning Temple) was built in 1755 by the Qianlong emperor to commemorate the defeat of Mongol rebels. The whole temple complex is a harmonious synthesis of Chinese and Tibetan styles of architecture. As part of a series of halls ascending the slope of a mountain, the temple's pinnacle is the Mahayana Hall, in which towers one of the world's largest wooden statues, a vast 72-ft (22-m) high representation of the Buddhist goddess of compassion, Guanyin.

Buddhist Symbols

Guanyin's hands hold an array of Buddhist symbolic instruments – the pure sound of the bell is said to drive away evil spirits.

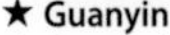

★ Guanyin

The huge effigy of Guanyin, also known to Buddhists as Avalokitesvara, is fashioned from five different types of wood. Viewing galleries can be climbed for views above ground level.

KEY

① **Diyu** houses a macabre display of Buddhist punishments.

② **The terrace buildings** form a three-dimensional mandala *(see p540)*, a physical representation of Buddhist cosmology.

③ **One of two attendant statues**

④ **Viewing gallery**

⑤ **Amitabha Buddha**, Guanyin's teacher, is shown perched on the top of her head.

⑥ **Tibetan elements** of the buildings are the bricks, the red-and-white coloring, and the shape of the windows.

⑦ **Miaoyan Shi** was where the emperor rested when visiting.

⑧ **Defensive wall**

⑨ **Gatehouse**

Prayer Wheels
In Tibetan Buddhism, sacred mantras and prayers are inserted into the decorated cylinders and activated by spinning the wheel clockwise.

VISITORS' CHECKLIST

Practical Information
5 miles (8 km) NE of Chengde, Hebei province. **Open** 8am–5:30pm daily. Chengde Intl. Travel Service, (0314) 205 8209.

Transportation
6 from Lizhengmen Dajie in Chengde.

★ Mayahana Hall
Called Dacheng Ge in Chinese, the 122-ft (37-m) high hall symbolizes the palace of Buddha on Mount Sumeru, the center of the Buddhist world.

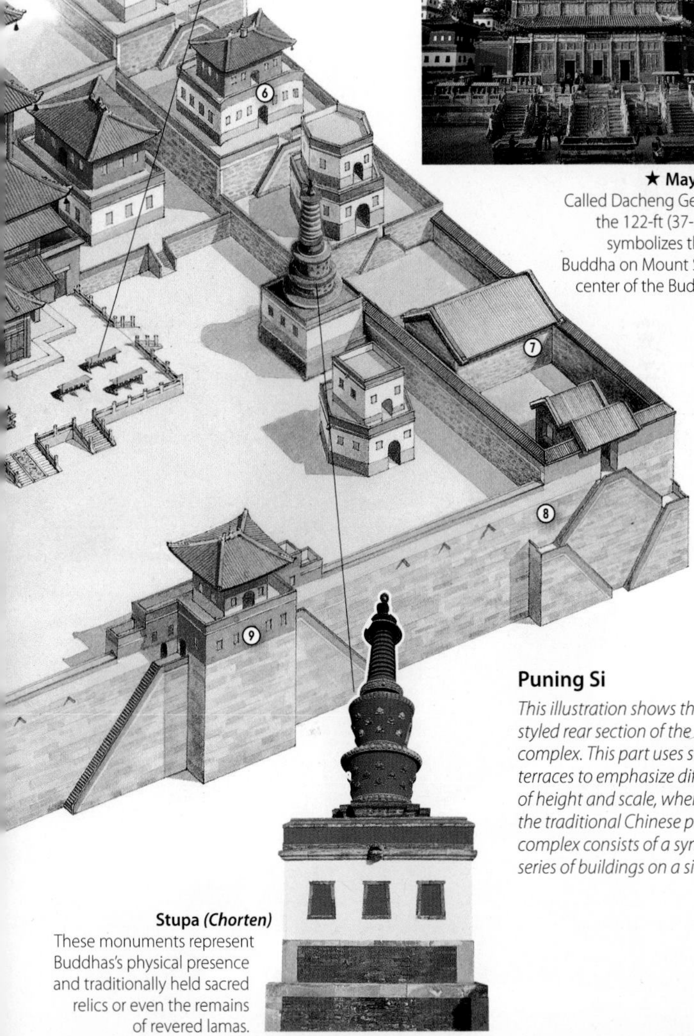

6

7

8

9

Puning Si

This illustration shows the Tibetan-styled rear section of the temple complex. This part uses several terraces to emphasize differences of height and scale, whereas the traditional Chinese part of the complex consists of a symmetrical series of buildings on a single axis.

Stupa *(Chorten)*
These monuments represent Buddhas's physical presence and traditionally held sacred relics or even the remains of revered lamas.

Beidaihe, one of northern China's premier resorts

❷ Beidaihe
北戴河

186 miles (300 km) E of Beijing. ✈ to Qinhuangdao, 9 miles (15 km) NE of Beidaihe, then express bus.

Despite its immense coastline, China has very few good-quality beaches, except perhaps in Hainan Island in the south. Nevertheless, the coastal town of Beidaihe, north China's breezy seaside retreat, is a pleasant enough escape from Beijing's intolerable summer heat. Discovered in the 19th century by British railway engineers, it soon became popular with foreign nationals from Tianjin, and villas, summer holiday homes, and golf courses soon sprang up. These were later taken over by Chinese Communist Party cadres, and party leaders still gather in Beidaihe for their annual conference in August.

Sadly, many of the elegant European-style villas are now obscured by garish modern seafront properties. During summer (April–October), Beidaihe's beaches are packed with hawkers and domestic holidaymakers. The best way to spend one's time is to sample the array of seafood, or hire a bike or tandem from one of the outlets on Zhonghaitan Lu for panoramic rides along the coast. The hilly **Lianfengshan Park** in the west of town is covered in cypresses and pines, and its hilltop Sea-Viewing Pavilion provides a good vantage point for views of the coast. The restored **Guanyin Temple**, dedicated to the Goddess of Compassion, is also located here. Beidaihe's three beaches are dotted with statues of revolutionary workers. **Middle Beach** is the most popular, while West Beach is quieter. Nearby, **Tiger Rocks** is a popular spot to watch the sunrise. **East Beach**, 4 miles (6 km) northeast of Beidaihe, gets covered in seaweed and shells at low tide.

Lianfengshan Park
Open 8am–6pm daily. 5, 21.

❸ Shanhaiguan
山海关

218 miles (350 km) E of Beijing.
W shgjq.com

A short hop up along the coast from Beidaihe, Shanhaiguan (The Pass Between the Mountain and the Sea) is where the Great Wall meets the sea. The town is steeped in history and is fortified by a Ming-era wall. The charming area within the walls is segmented by *hutong* (historic alleys), and serviced by a few hotels.

Shanhaiguan promotes its Great Wall links. **The First Pass Under Heaven** in the east of town is a formidable section of wall attached to a huge gatehouse. The Manchus overcame half-hearted resistance here and headed for Beijing to establish the Qing dynasty. Visitors can climb up on the ramparts, or access its tower, which displays Qing weapons and costumes. To the south is the **Great Wall Museum**, worth visiting for its photographs and models of the wall. Also on display are tools that were used to build it, as well as the various weapons that were used in its defense. There are some English captions, and the exhibits are well displayed.

A more stirring section of the wall lies 2 miles (3 km) north of town at **Jiao Shan** (open Apr–Oct), where bracing climbs can be made up its steep incline – or take a cable car. **Lao Long Tou** (Old Dragon Head) marks the end of the Great Wall at the sea, 3 miles (4 km) south of town. This part of the wall has been completely reconstructed and, despite the tour buses, is worth visiting. Visitors can head west along the beach to explore Haishen Miao (Temple of the Sea God).

Great Wall Museum
Tel (0335) 505 1313. **Open** 8am–5pm daily. **W scb-museum.com/english**

The aptly named Lao Long Tou, where the Great Wall reaches the sea

◀ Xumifushou Zhi Miao, a UNESCO World Heritage Site in Chengde

❹ Tianjin
天津

50 miles (80 km) SE of Beijing. 10,000,000. Main train station (central), Tianjin south station (30-min drive from center). High speed train from Beijing's south station takes 30 mins. West bus station, Northeast bus station, bus station No. 1, CAAC (buses to airport), South bus station. Tanggu Harbor. **en.tjtour.cn**

Hebei's former capital, the municipality of Tianjin is China's fourth largest city and a major seaport. The city's appeal lies in its Western concession architecture, a legacy of its past as a foreign trading post since 1858. The former powers, led by Britain and France, and followed by Japan, Germany, Austro-Hungary, Italy, and Russia, built schools, banks, and churches.

In the north of town, the **Ancient Culture Street** is a re-creation of an ancient Chinese street. The **Tianhou Temple**, dedicated to the Goddess of the Sea, is on the street's west side. To the southwest, close to the Old Chinese Town, the **Confucius Temple** was damaged during the Cultural Revolution, and restored in 1993. About a mile (1.6 km) northeast across the Hai River is the gaunt **Wang Hai Lou Cathedral** (Wang Hail Lou Jiao Tang). Outside, a plaque in Chinese relates the church's turbulent history. It was destroyed by a mob in 1870, and again during the 1900 Boxer Rebellion. The 1976 Tang Shan earthquake damaged it for the third time, and it was repaired in 1983. North of the cathedral, the Qing-era **Dabei Monastery** is reached via a colorful market selling incense sticks and Buddhist talismans. People pay their respects to Milefo (the Laughing Buddha) at the entrance and to Guanyin in her own hall. A popular attraction is the **Tianjin Eye**, one of the tallest Ferris wheels in the world, standing at 394 ft (120 m). On **Jiefang Bei Lu** are many of Tianjin's colonial buildings, including the Astor Hotel, whose guests included China's last emperor, Pu Yi. The highly original and hugely popular **China House Museum** is a beautiful old French house that has been redecorated by Zhang Lianzhi, a collector of Chinese porcelain. To the south, at the end of Binjiang Dao, Tianjin's biggest thoroughfare and shopping area, are the three green domes of the French-built **Xi Kai Cathedral** (Xi Kai Jiao Tang), open on Sundays (8am–6pm).

Deity, street market

Beautiful tiled wall at the Tianhou Temple, Tianjin

Dabei Monastery
40 Tianwei Lu. **Tel** (022) 2626 1769.
Open 9am–4pm.

China House Museum
72 Chifeng Dao. **Tel** (022) 2712 3366.
Open 9am–6:30pm.

Tianjin City Center

1. Ancient Culture Street
2. Tianhou Temple
3. Confucius Temple
4. Wang Hai Lou Cathedral
5. Dabei Monastery
6. Jiefang Bei Lu
7. China House Museum
8. Xi Kai Cathedral

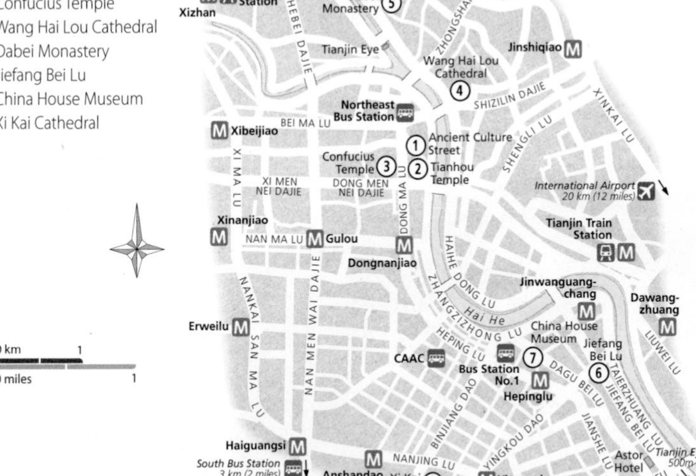

❺ Shijiazhuang
石家庄

155 miles (250 km) SW of Beijing. 9,300,000. 26 Donggang Lu, (0311) 8588 5777.

The capital of Hebei often suffers from unfair comparisons to both Beijing and the former provincial capital, Tianjin. An industrial town dating from the modern railway age, Shijiazhuang has just a few sights, including the **Hebei Provincial Museum** in the east of town, which displays ancient musical instruments, historical relics such as a jade burial suit, and a miniature terracotta army. To the west along Zhongshan Lu is the **Martyrs' Memorial**, a park which honors two doctors as Heroes of the Revolution. Both men, a Canadian named Norman Bethune and an Indian named Dwarkanath Kotnis, served the Communist Party in the early 20th century.

Hebei Provincial Museum
Tel (0311) 8604 5642.
Open 9am–5pm Tue–Sun.

Environs: Most of the area's main sights lie outside Shijiazhuang, and are easily accessed by train, bus, or minibus. Lying a short train or bus journey 9 miles (15 km) north of town, the ancient walled town of **Zhengding** is known for its temples and pagodas. The most renowned is **Dafo Si** (Great Buddha Temple), also known as Longxing Si. Its highlight is the gargantuan 69-ft (21-m) high bronze statue of Guanyin (the Goddess of Compassion) that stands in the Dabei Ge (Pavilion of Great Mercy). Fashioned over 1,000 years ago during the Song dynasty, the multi-armed statue is a riveting sight. Visitors can climb the gallery surrounding the statue for a closer look.

West of Dafo Si, the 135 ft (41 m) **Lingxiao Ta** (Lingxing Pagoda) in Tianning Si is a restored Tang-dynasty structure built from wood and brick, while **Kaiyuan Si's** Tang-dynasty pagoda rises up just off Yanzhao Dajie, Zhengding's main street. Also here is China's sole surviving Tang-dynasty Bell Tower (Zhong Lou). Dotted around Zhengding are several temples and pagodas, including the Confucian Temple, Chengling Ta (Chengling Pagoda) at Linji Si, and the Hua Ta (Hua Pagoda) at Guanghui Si, with its many intriguing motifs that represent the Buddhas, elephants, and whales.

Kaiyuan Si's Tang pagoda, Zhengding

About 25 miles (40 km) southeast of Shijiazhuang, near Zhaoxian town, the 1,400-year-old **Zhaozhou Bridge** (Zhaozhou Qiao) is a graceful feat of engineering. Built over ten years by the mason Li Chun and completed in AD 605, the 167-ft (51-m) long bridge satisfied several requirements.

Qiao Lou at Cangyan Shan Si (Hanging Palace), Cangyang Shan

The gentle bow had to be level enough to convey imperial soldiers, yet high enough to evade flood waters, while relying on the soft riverbanks for support. The main arch (forming an arc rather than a semicircle) is an effortless span of 28 stone blocks. Supported on each end of the arch are two smaller ones that are designed to lighten the structure of the bridge and allow the passage of flood waters.

About 50 miles (80 km) southwest of Shijiazhuang is a group of monasteries and pagodas tucked away among the cypresses and sheer drops of **Cangyan Shan** (Cangyan Mountains). The Cangyan Shan Si also known as the Hanging Palace, situated hundreds of steps up the mountainside, dates from the Sui dynasty. One hall, the Qiao Lou, is spectacularly slung between two cliffs, suspended on a bridge over the void. In the valleys and on the slopes beyond, the trail continues to explore the dramatic landscape, passing several shrines.

Dafo Si
Tel (0311) 8878 9987.
Open 8am–5pm daily.

Lingxiao Ta
Tel as above. **Open** as above.

Zhaozhou Bridge
Tel (0311) 8729 1010.
Open 9am–6pm daily.

Cangyan Shan
from Shijiazhuang. **Tel** (0311) 8202 2613. **Open** 9am–4pm daily.

The graceful stone Zhaozhou Bridge (Zhaozhou Qiao)

For hotels and restaurants in this region see pp558–9 and pp573–4

6 Datong
大同

165 miles (265 km) SW of Beijing. 3,000,000. CITS Datong, (0352) 510 1326.

Situated near the southern flank of Inner Mongolia, Datong has some splendid sights that are worth exploring despite the abundance of coal mines and power stations that blight the surrounding landscape.

The city was twice a dynastic capital, under the Northern Wei (AD 386–534), and the Liao (AD 907–1125), both non-Chinese. The Northern Wei were fervent Buddhists who carved and decorated the **Yungang Caves** nearby, while a significant relic of the Liao era survives in the **Huayan Si** (Huayan Temple), located in an alley off Da Xi Jie, west of the crossroads in the old town. Completed by the Jin, the temple was much restored by later dynasties. Raised up on a 13-ft (4-m) terrace, Huayan Si's Great Treasure Hall (Daxiong Bao Dian) is one of China's largest Buddhist halls. Within the hall sit five gilded and enthroned Ming-era statues with attendants. The ceiling panels are decorated with Sanskrit letters, flowers, and dragons. A short walk east of the crossroads on Da Dong Jie is **Jiulong Bi** (Nine Dragon Screen), a 148-ft (45-m) tiled spirit wall built to front the palace of the 13th son of Hongwu, the first Ming emperor. Less than a mile south of the crossroads on Da Nan Jie is the **Shanhua Si**. Erected during the Tang era, it was subsequently destroyed by fire and rebuilt in the 12th century. The main hall has five Buddhist statues, flanked by 24 divine generals.

Gilded Buddhist statuary, Mahavira Hall, Huayan Si, Datong

Huayan Si
Open 9am–6pm daily.

Shanhua Si
27. **Tel** (0352) 205 2898.
Open 9am–6pm daily.

7 Yungang Grottoes

See pp138–9.

8 Hanging Temple
悬空寺

40 miles (65 km) SE of Datong. from Datong to Hunyuan, then taxi. **Tel** (0352) 832 2142. **Open** 8am–6pm daily.

One of China's five sacred Daoist mountains, Heng Shan is also known as Beiyue (Northern Peak). The mountain range is a huge draw, its highest peak daring climbers to scale its 6,600 ft (2,000 m) slopes – a tradition started by the first emperor, Qin Shi Huangdi, and kept alive by later rulers. Its main attraction, however, is the spectacular Xuankong Si. Supported by slender wooden pillars, the temple seemingly clings precariously to the canyon's walls. The Northern Wei were the first to build here, but flood waters from the Heng River below regularly washed the buildings away. The current edifice dates from the Qing dynasty. The temple's 40-odd halls are hewn from natural caves and hollows in the rock, and are covered with wooden facades. They are connected by walkways and bridges, and contain statues of Confucian, Buddhist, and Daoist gods in stone, iron, and bronze. The Sanjiao Dian (Three Religions Hall) has statues of Confucius, Buddha, and Laozi all seated together.

The spectacular Hanging Temple (Xuankong Si), Heng Shan

❼ Yungang Grottoes

云岗石窟

Carved into sandstone cliffs, the caves at Yungang are one of China's most celebrated accomplishments of Buddhist art. The assembly of over 51,000 statues was started by the Northern Wei dynasty in AD 453 to atone for their persecution of Buddhism. Hellenistic, Persian, Central Asian, and Indian influences are evident in the carvings, testifying to the many influences entering China via the Silk Road. When the capital moved from Datong to Luoyang, in 494, work at Yungang all but stopped. The statues are accompanied by English explanations. Note that individual caves are occasionally closed for routine maintenance or renovation.

★ Exterior of Cave 6
The wooden temple facade has protected the beautifully carved 50-ft (16-m) stone pagoda and the rest of the sculptures within.

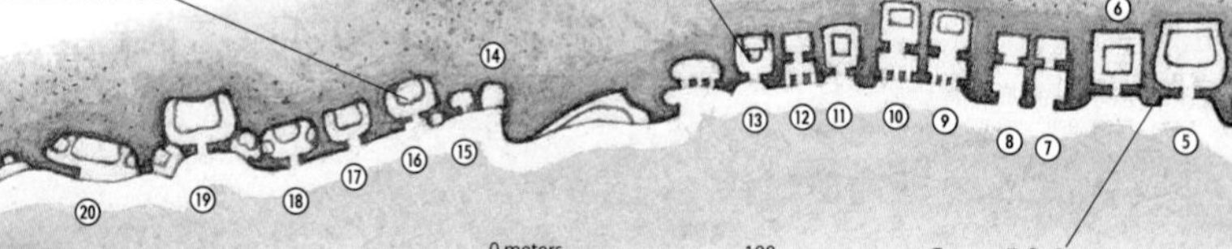

Cave 16 Has finely featured carving especially Buddha's head.

Cave 13 Look for the small figure supporting the Buddha's arm.

Caves 5 & 6
Protected by wooden frontage.

Caves 16–20 These are the oldest caves, built between 453 and 462 by the monk Tan Hao.

Detail of Cave 10
Built as a pair along with Cave 9, this cave is also divided into two chambers. The interior is densely decorated with colorful bas-reliefs and statues in niches.

★ Main Buddha, Cave 20
The simplicity and balance of the tableau shows great artistic merit. This cave would have been shielded by a wooden screen.

★ Seated Buddha, Cave 5
Marking a move from the more stylized earlier Buddhas, this one has a more corpulent and naturalistic air. Protected by the wooden facade, the cave is in good condition.

Musicians, Cave 12
This cave is decorated with devotees of music and dance. The colorful walls provide excellent evidence for the development and use of musical instruments in China at the time.

View of the central section of the Yungang Caves, Datong

VISITORS' CHECKLIST

Practical Information
10 miles (16 km) W of Datong.
Tel (0352) 320 6818. **Open** 8:30am–6pm daily. **tour.yungang.org**

Transportation
28 from Datong bus station, 26 from the long-distance bus station, 4 from train station.

Interior, Cave 3
The Buddhas here have rounded fleshy faces and full lips, indicating that they are later creations, perhaps Sui dynasty (581–618).

Pagoda in Cave 2
Nearly square in construction, this cave has a carved square pagoda linking ceiling and floor. The statues in the cave have suffered a little due to exposure to the weather.

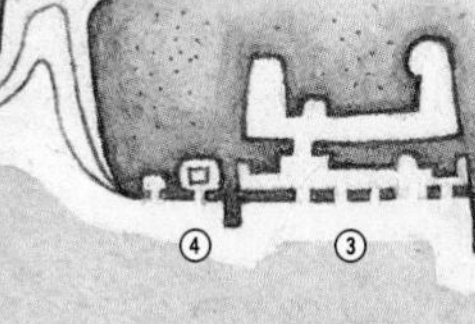
④
③

Artistic Influences, Cave 18

The colossal Buddha recalls the style of Gandhara (see p471). *This Buddhist stronghold and meeting point for many of the Silk Roads sought to recreate the solemnity, dignity, and aweinspiring nature of Buddha. A more realistic style can be seen in the five smaller* arhats *on each side and the crown worn by the* bodhisattva.

The bared shoulder was replaced by the more Chinese robe and girdle *(see Cave 5).*
The realistic faces of these *arhats* show the personal input by the artists.
Statue has webbed fingers, one of the marks of Buddha.

Exterior of Cave 18 showing the colossal Buddha

9 Wutai Shan

五台山

The monastic village of Taihuai, nestling in the valley ringed by Wutai Shan's five mountain peaks (or terraces), has the largest concentration of temples, as well as most of Wutai Shan's hotels and restaurants. Wutai Shan was the site of over 300 temples during the Qing dynasty, but many were destroyed. Tsongkhapa, the founder of the Buddhist Yellow Hat Sect (which has the Dalai Lama as its head), lived here and the mountains and its shrines are revered by Lamaist Buddhists. In winter, the roads are often closed due to snow. Late spring and summer is the best time to visit, but also the most crowded.

Luohou Si
Inside this temple is a wooden lotus flower decorated with eight wooden petals that, when rotated, open to reveal carved Buddhist figures.

★ Tayuan Si
This temple is dominated by its distinctive Ming dynasty and Tibetan-styled Great White Dagoba (Da Bai Ta), which rises to a height of 164 ft (50 m). The dagoba is topped with a bronze cap with bells.

KEY

① **Ming Qing Jie**

② **Pu Hua Si**

③ **Shu Xiang Si**

④ **Wan Fo Dong**

⑤ **San Ta Si**

⑥ **Shou Ning Si** is a little bit off the beaten track in the hills.

⑦ **Guang Hua Si**

⑧ **Jin Jie Si**

⑨ **Shang Cai Dong** sits at the foot of the hills in view of the cable car to the north.

Taihuai
West of the Qingshui River, the village is thronged by pilgrims, monks, and lamas. Visitors come for its Buddhist temples and to shop for religious talismans.

★ Xian Tong Si
The highlight of this, the largest temple on Wutai Shan, is the Bronze Hall. Made entirely from metal, it is decorated with thousands of small Buddhist figures.

VISITORS' CHECKLIST

Practical Information
149 miles (240 km) N of Taiyuan. CITS 400 600 888. **Open** daily. by minibuses, taxis, or through tourist office.

Transportation
to Taiyuan, then bus to Taihuai. from Datong or Taihuai. from Beijing to Shahe, then bus.

6

5

★ Pusa Ding
To reach Pusa Ding (Bodhisattva Summit), a temple complex dating from the Ming and Qing dynasties, there is a climb of 108 steps. A significant number – it is the number of beads on a Buddhist rosary.

7

Qi Fo Si
This temple is not visited as much as the other more famous temples and as such will be a quieter spot to take in the scenery. It also has a white stone pagoda.

8

9

0 meters 100
0 yards 100

Key
Built-up area
Road

The Cult of Manjusri

Known as Wenshu in China, Manjusri is the Buddhist *bodhisattva* of Wisdom and the patron deity of Wutai Shan. A disciple of Sakyamuni (Buddha), Manjusri is often portrayed riding a lion or holding a sword – for cleaving both ignorance and suffering. Many of Wutai Shan's temples and halls are dedicated to Wenshu and the deity's association with the mountain dates as far back as the 1st century AD, when a visiting Indian monk had a vision of the *bodhisattva*. Many more sightings have been recorded since.

Manjusri or Wenshu, patron deity of Wutai Shan

Exploring Wutai Shan

Wutai Shan was originally worshiped by followers of the Dao (Daoists) pursuing the secrets of immortality, before attracting devotees of Buddha who built many temples in his name. If visitors explore around Taihuai they will find many temples scattered among the peaks and in more distant parts of the region. Most can be reached without much difficulty, with a chairlift to some parts, and the effort rewards the adventurous with the chance to admire some of China's oldest buildings.

The thickly wooded slopes of Wutai Shan

Wutai Shan's Temples

The first temples appeared on Wutai Shan during the Eastern Han dynasty. The five peaks of Wutai Shan are each topped with a temple, but they are hard to reach and tend to attract only devout pilgrims. Several temples can be visited either by hiking, by bus, or by minibus tour from Taihuai (including those through CITS), although other trips, such as to Nanchan Si, involve longer expeditions.

With lovely views over the valley, **Nanshan Si** (South Mountain Temple), around 2 miles (3 km) south of Taihuai, is one of the largest temples on Wutai Shan, most notable for its 18 superbly crafted *arhat* effigies. Three miles (5 km) southwest of Taihuai, immediately above Nanshan Si and part of the same temple complex, is **Youguo Si**. **Longquan Si** (Dragon Spring Temple), at the top of 108 steps through a marvelous marble archway, features the Hall of Heavenly Kings (with an effigy of Milefo – the future Buddha, also known in this chubby incarnation as the Laughing Buddha), the attractively decorated and designed Puji Pagoda, and the Guanyin Hall, among other structures.

Two more temples within easy reach of Taihuai include the Ming dynasty **Bishan Si**, which contains some intriguing Buddhist sculptures, and **Zhenhai Si**.

Considerably farther away is the remote **Nanchan Si**, about 44 miles (70 km) south of Taihuai on the road to Taiyuan, which contains one of China's oldest surviving wooden halls (AD 782). The main hall has somehow avoided destruction – a miracle considering the many anti-Buddhist purges during China's history. Despite much restoration work, the hall's original Tang-dynasty design, a rarity in Chinese temple hall architecture, is preserved. **Foguang Si** (Buddha's Light Temple), about 25 miles (40 km) south of Taihuai, also features a Tang dynasty hall dating to the 9th century. The hall is especially notable for its fine *dougong* *(see p41)* bracket-work, Tang and Song dynasty wall paintings, and collection of Ming dynasty *arhats*.

The elaborately carved archway at Longquan Si

Wutai Shan Temples

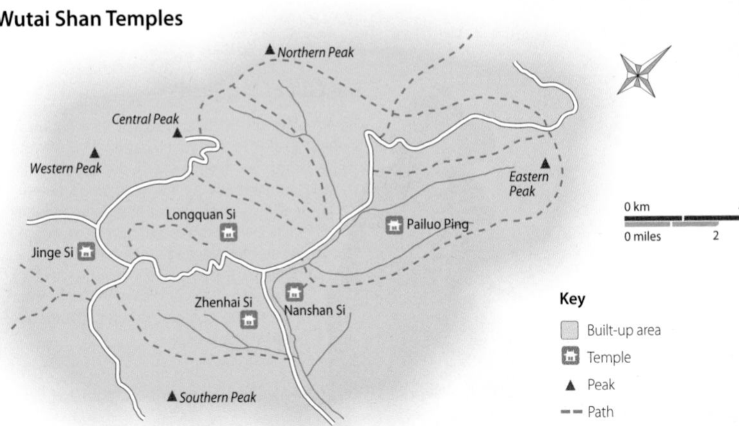

The Buddhist Chongshan Si, Taiyuan

⑩ Taiyuan
太原

254 miles (408 km) SW of Beijing. 2,600,000. CITS 38 Pingyang Lu, (0351) 821 1111.

A heavily industrialized city, Taiyuan lies on the banks of the Fen River at the heart of Shanxi and makes a convenient base for trips to Pingyao *(see p144)* and Wutai Shan *(see pp140–42)*. Between the years 471–221 BC Taiyuan was the capital of the Zhao Kingdom, and became a flourishing center of Buddhism by the 6th century AD. Because of its strategic position, bordering the hostile nomadic tribes to the north, the city underwent heavy fortification during the Tang dynasty. However, fearing its ambitions, the Song ruler had it torched to the ground. The city was rebuilt a few years later.

The Buddhist monastery **Chongshan Si** is hidden down an alleyway northeast of Wuyi (May 1) Square. A temple has existed here since the 7th century, although the current building dates from the 14th century. A fire reduced much of the temple to ashes in 1864, but considerable rebuilding has taken place. The Hall of Great Compassion (Dabei Dian) houses the striking Qianshou Guanyin (Thousand-Armed Goddess of Compassion), the central figure in the trinity of statues. The multi-armed and multi-eyed goddess stands over 26 ft (8 m), her arms fanned out behind her. Also displayed in the temple are *sutras* (Buddhist scriptures) and scrolls from the Song, Yuan, and Ming eras. In the east of town, the **Twin Pagoda Temple** (Shuangta Si) was built on imperial instruction during the late Ming era. Also known as Yongzuo Temple, its 13-story, 164-ft (50-m) high pagodas have come to symbolize Taiyuan. Formerly housed in Chunyang Temple, the **Shanxi Provincial Museum** is now located in a modern, purpose-built facility on the banks of the Fen River. Its collections are arranged over four floors and are beautifully presented, although there are few explanations of the items in English. Displays include relics, bronzes, Chinese currency, statuary, and a collection of Buddhist *sutras*.

Guardian deity, Jinci Temple

Chongshan Si
Open 8am–4:30pm daily.

Shanxi Provincial Museum
13 Bin He Xilu. **Tel** (0351) 878 9015.
Open 9am–5pm Tue–Sun.
old.shanximuseum.com

Environs: The bustling **Jinci Si**, 15 miles (25 km) southwest of town at the base of Xuanwang Shan (Xuanwang Mountain), dates to the Northern Wei, although much of its architecture is from the Song period. The main entrance leads straight to the Ming-era Mirror Terrace, originally used as a theatrical stage. To the west, a canal runs through the temple complex, crossed by a bridge that leads to a terrace supporting four iron statues. Lying beyond is the carved Hall of the Sacred Mother (Shengmu Dian), one of China's oldest surviving wooden buildings. Inside the hall, a group of ceramic Song-era figures waits on a central figure of the Sacred Mother.

About 25 miles (40 km) south-west of Taiyuan, the **Tianlong Shan Grottoes** in the Tianlong Mountains constitute a small, but significant, collection of Buddhist cave art. A total of 21 caves dot the eastern and western sides of the mountain, with worn and damaged statues dating from the Eastern Wei to the Tang dynasties. The best-preserved specimen to behold is the large seated Buddha in Cave No. 9.

Jinci Si
Tel (0351) 602 0038. **Open** 8am–5pm daily (Apr–Sep: to 6pm).

Tianlong Shan Grottoes
Tel (0351) 634 9668.
Open 8:30am–5pm daily.

The temple spring at Jinci Si, Taiyuan

⑪ Pingyao
平遥

Surrounded by one of China's few intact Ming city walls, Pingyao's streets are lined with a wealth of traditional Chinese buildings, including courtyard houses, temples, and more than 3,000 historic shops. Pingyao's treasure trove of Ming and Qing architecture is a legacy of the town's affluent days as a banking center, which ceased when the Qing dynasty defaulted on loans and abdicated, leaving the banks empty. The transferral of the country's finances to Shanghai and Hong Kong turned the city into a backwater, saving it from development and, ultimately, preserving its character.

★ Rishenchang
This extensive museum of early banking is the site of China's first draft bank, founded in 1824.

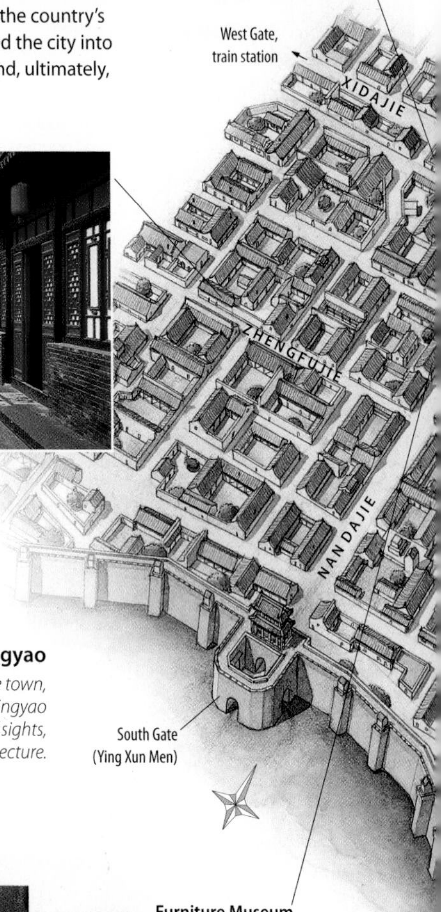

West Gate, train station

XIDAJIE

ZHENGFUJIE

NAN DAJIE

County Magistrate's Residence
Pingyao's justice department during the Ming and Qing dynasties, these offices represented the secular world while the Daoist temples, mirroring the County Yamen on the other side of Nan Dajie, represented the spiritual realm.

Southeast Pingyao

The most notable part of the car-free town, the southeast corner and center of Pingyao has the largest concentration of sights, museums, and heritage architecture.

South Gate (Ying Xun Men)

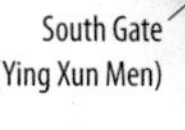

★ City Walls
The 39-ft (12-m) high, crenellated enclosure dating from 1370 is said to resemble the outline of a tortoise. Its head lies at the South Gate, its four feet at the East and West Gates, and its tail at the North Gate.

Furniture Museum
As well as this rickshaw, there are rooms in this typical Qing dynasty compound that are furnished as bedrooms, kitchens, and opium dens.

0 meters 30
0 yards 30

For hotels and restaurants in this region see pp558–9 and pp573–4

VISITORS' CHECKLIST

Practical Information
62 miles (100 km) S of Taiyuan. 40,000. Zhao Pi Nan Jie 58. **Open** daily. (joint ticket for all sights).

Transportation
West, South & North gates.

★ Bell Tower
Rising above Nan Dajie, the Bell Tower is a charming structure decorated with ornamented eaves.

North Gate (Gonji Men)

The Tianjixiang Museum has a small collection of local artifacts.

These three adjoining Daoist temples were last rebuilt in 1859, after burning down during a temple fair.

DONG DAJIE

NGHUANGMIAOJIE

Upper East Gate

Watchtowers punctuate the length of the wall every 164 ft (50 m).

Kuixing Tower
This extravagant and unusually designed eight-sided pavilion rises above the battlements. It is named after a star in the 28 constellations of the Chinese zodiac.

⓬ Shuanglin Si
双林寺

4 miles (6 km) SW of Pingyao. **Open** 8:30am–6:30pm daily (to 5pm in winter).

This temple has a long history, dating back 1,500 years to the Northern Wei, which had its capital at Datong *(see p137)*. The current temple was built during the Ming and Qing dynasties and contains over 2,000 Buddhist statues, some from the Song dynasty. The effigies are arranged in ten halls around three courtyards. The expertly fashioned figures' expressions vary from the sublime through the comic to the sinister. The lifelike *luohans* in the second hall each reveal an individual persona and the *bodhisattvas* in the third hall are well worth seeking out.

Classic courtyard at the extensive Qiao Jia Dayuan

⓭ Qiao Jia Dayuan
乔家大院

12 miles (20 km) N of Pingyao. between Taiyuan and Pingyao can drop you off. **Tel** (0354) 532 1045. **Open** 8am–6pm daily. **qjdywhyq.com**

This magnificent courtyard house was the setting for director Zhang Yimou's classic 1991 film *Raise the Red Lantern*, starring Gong Li. Dating from the 18th century, the vast complex, comprising 313 rooms, is an exquisite exercise in architectural balance, its linked courtyards pervaded by a sense of equilibrium. Enclosed by a 33-ft (10-m) high fortified wall, the house was built by Qiao Guifa, a merchant who made his fortune in tofu and tea.

SHANDONG & HENAN

The swathe of territory comprising Shandong and Henan, irrigated by the final sweep of the Yellow River (Huang He), sustained some of China's earliest settled societies. The Shandong Chinese are proud of their many treasures, which include sages Confucius and Mencius, as well as the Yellow River, and Tai Shan, China's holiest Daoist peak, and the former German colony of Qingdao, with its Bavarian cobbled streets and Teutonic architecture. (Qingdao may be testament to humiliating 19th-century foreign ambitions, but it was German expertise that helped brew China's famous Tsingtao beer.) The Yellow River enters Shandong (East of the Mountains) from the west, after slicing Henan (South of the River) into two uneven chunks. Henan's historic sights cluster around the river in the province's north, in an area that was the cradle of Chinese civilization as early as 6000 BC. The ancient capitals of Anyang, Kaifeng, and Luoyang are located here. The impressive Longmen Caves, with their Buddhist carvings, lie outside Luoyang. Other sights include the sacred Daoist mountain of Song Shan, home to the Shaolin Temple and its band of warrior monks, and the Northern Song capital of Kaifeng, with its fine Buddhist architecture and historic Judaic links.

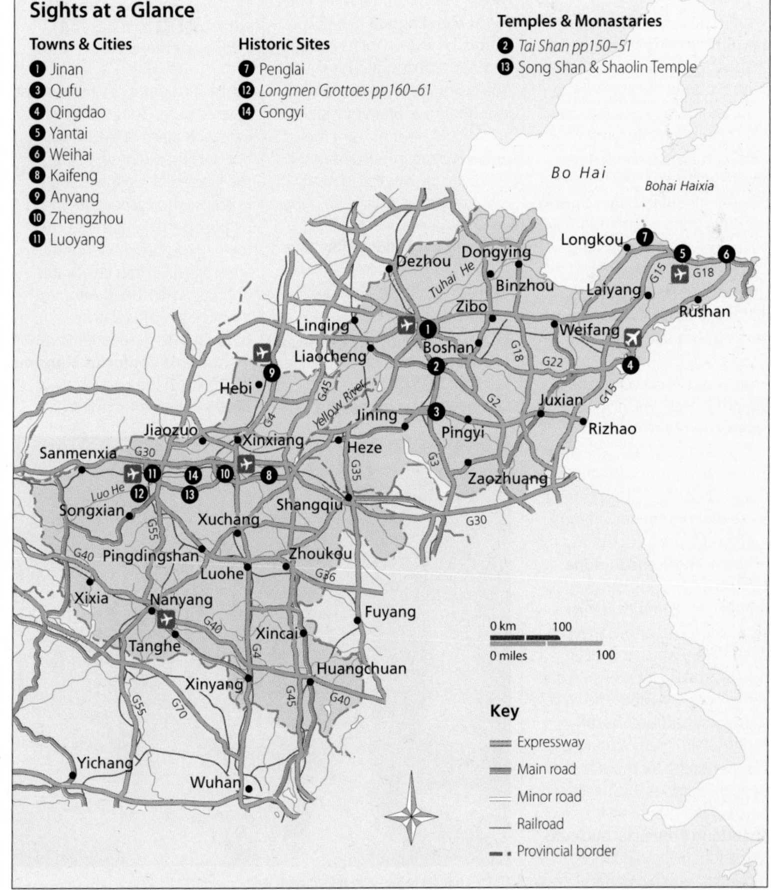

◀ Longmen Caves – an important and busy tourist attraction

For additional map symbols *see back flap*

A view of the skyline of Jinan, the capital of Shandong from across Daming Lake

❶ Jinan
济南

216 miles (350 km) S of Beijing.
5,900,000.
17386 Jingshi Lu, (0531) 8267 6232.
travelshandong.com/cities/jinan

South of the Yellow River as it makes its final thrust for the sea, Shandong's capital is visited primarily by travelers en route to Tai Shan, Qingdao, and Qufu. It was known for its natural springs, many of which have now dried up. The most famous of these, the **Black Tiger Spring**, still flows somewhat erratically out of tiger-headed spouts.

In the north of town, the park surrounding **Daming Hu** (Big Brilliant Lake) is filled with ponds, gardens, and temples, and is a good place for a stroll. To the southwest is the **Li Qingzhao Memorial Hall** which commemorates one of China's most famous female poets who lived in the 12th century. There is a statue of her as well as portraits and extracts from her writings.

In the southeast of the city, the slopes of **Thousand Buddha Mountain** (Qianfo Shan) are dotted with Buddhist statues. Several temples are situated on the summit, which is over an hour's climb up the steps. A cable car service is available. The earliest statuary dates from the 6th century, with many additions compensating for those broken by Red Guards. A short walk north of the mountain is the **Shandong Provincial Museum**. Its exhibits include Buddhist carvings, Neolithic pottery fragments (some from Long Shan nearby), and dinosaur fossils. It is also the home of China's oldest existing book, though only a reproduction is on display.

Environs: Near Liubu village, 21 miles (33 km) southeast of Jinan, the **Si Men Pagoda** (Four Gate Pagoda) is known for its antiquity and unusual design. This squat, one-story stone structure with four doors is topped by a steeple, and would have housed the remains of an important monk. The pagoda, erected in AD 611, is the oldest of its kind in China.

Thousand Buddha Mountain
18 Jing Shiyi Lu, off Qianfoshan Lu. **Open** 6:30am–6:30pm daily. K51, K54.

Shandong Provincial Museum
14 Jingshiyi Lu. **Open** 9am–5pm Tue–Sun.
sdmuseum.com/english

❷ Tai Shan

See pp150–51.

❸ Qufu
曲阜

112 miles (180 km) S of Jinan. 160,000. from Jinan. CITS 1 Donguamendajie, (0537) 449 1491.

As the birthplace of China's most revered sage, Qufu occupies a hallowed place in the minds of not only the Chinese, but also the legions of Japanese and Koreans who come here on pilgrimage. In September the town comes alive during the annual festival that celebrates Confucius's birthday. Although the sage lived in relative obscurity, his descendents dwelt in the grand **Confucius Mansion** (Kong Fu) in the heart of town. Wielding immense political

Covered corridor to the Confucius Temple at Qufu

authority and wealth, the Kong family – referred to by the Chinese as the First Family Under Heaven – built a palatial mansion occupying over 40 acres (16 ha). Arranged on a traditional north–south axis, the mansion is divided into residential and administrative quarters, with a temple in the east and a garden at the rear. Most of the halls date from the Ming era. The Gate of Double Glory in the north was used for the emperor's visits, while to the east stands the Tower of Refuge, where the family assembled in times of strife.

Next to the mansion, the **Confucius Temple** (Kong Miao) is a lengthy complex of memorial gateways, courtyards, halls, stele pavilions, auxiliary temples, gnarled cypresses, and ancestral shrines. Originally a simple shrine in 478 BC, the year after Confucius's death, the temple grew gradually over the centuries before suddenly expanding during the Ming and Qing eras. Beyond the entrance stand 198 stone stelae, listing the names of as many as 50,000 successful candidates in the imperial examinations, during the Yuan, Ming, and Qing dynasties. Some are supported on the backs of mighty *bixi*, primitive, turtle-like dragons. A long succession of gateways leads to the 11th-century Kuiwen Pavilion, a triple-roofed building. Confucius instructed his disciples from the Apricot Pavilion, accessed through the Great Achievements Gate. On top of a marble terrace with columns that are elaborately carved with dragons, the Great Achievements Hall (Dacheng Dian) forms the temple's splendid nucleus. Beyond, the Hall of the Sage's Relics houses carved stone plates with scenes from the sage's life. The Lu Wall in the eastern section is where one of his descendents hid his books to save them from Emperor Qin Shi (259–210 BC), who wished to burn them. The books were rediscovered during the Han era.

Carved column, Confucius Temple

Mencius Temple at Zoucheng, south of Qufu

In the north of town, the walled **Confucius Forest** (Kong Lin) contains the grave of Confucius and other members of the Kong clan. The forest is mostly pines and cypresses interspersed with shrines and tombstones.

Not far south of Qufu, **Zoucheng** (now a city), is the home town of Mencius (372–289 BC), the Confucian philosopher, second in importance only to Confucius himself. The tranquil Mencius Temple consists of 64 halls set around five large courtyards. As in Qufu, the philosopher has both a Mansion and Graveyard.

Confucius Mansion
Open 7:30am–4:30pm daily. 5, K01.

Confucius Temple
Open 7:30am–4:30pm daily. 5, K01.

Confucius

The teachings of Confucius (551–479 BC), China's most renowned philosopher, profoundly influenced the culture of China as well as other nations, including Japan, Korea, and Vietnam. Born in the state of Lu during an age of uninterrupted war, Confucius (whose name was derived from his Chinese name, Kong Fuzi or Master Kong) was prompted by the suffering around him to develop a practical philosophy built upon the principle of virtue *(ren)*, in the hope that rulers would govern in a just manner. Finding no audience among his native rulers, he communicated his beliefs to a body of disciples and embarked on a journey in search of a ruler who would apply his rules of governance. He died unrecognized and never recorded his philosophy in writing, but his thoughts were compiled by his followers into a volume called the *Analects (Lunyu)*, and promulgated. Championed by successive thinkers including Mencius, Confucius's philosophy later achieved predominance and formed the basis for the civil service examination system, a major hurdle to a career in officialdom right until the 20th century.

The philosopher-sage, Confucius

❷ Tai Shan

泰山

Having played a part in China's earliest creation myths, Tai Shan (Peaceful Mountain) has held sway over the Chinese imagination for millennia. It is ascended year-round by legions of pilgrims and travelers, making it China's most sacred and most climbed mountain. Despite the crowds, a supernatural presence permeates Tai Shan, best experienced via a slow ascent with plenty of pit stops at wayside shrines and monuments. Many tourists stay overnight at hotels on the mountain and watch the sunrise from the cloud-wreathed peak, which is where Tai Shan's most significant temples can be found, attracting droves of devout worshipers.

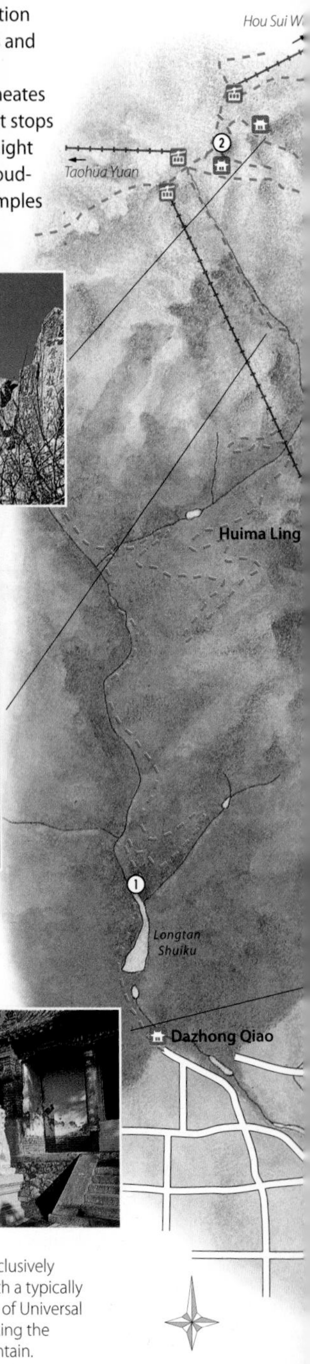

Taohua Yuan

Huima Ling

Longtan Shuiku

Dazhong Qiao

★ Yuhuang Miao
Dedicated to the supreme deity of Daoism, the Jade Emperor Temple marks the conclusion of the ascent at 5,070 ft (1,545 m) and houses a statue of the Jade Emperor and wall paintings.

★ Shiba Pan
The last and most punishing part of the climb, the steep Path of Eighteen Bends is visible from Zhong Tian Men (the halfway point), and brings weary travelers to Nan Tian Men, the last gate on Tai Shan, but not the summit.

Puzhao Si
Tai Shan's shrines are not exclusively Daoist and this temple – with a typically Buddhist name (the Temple of Universal Light) – is easily visited if taking the Western Route up the mountain.

KEY

① **Heilong Tan (Black Dragon Pool)**

② **Bixia Ci**, dedicated to the Princess of the Azure Clouds, attracts would-be mothers to the summit.

③ **Yi Tian Men (First Gate under Heaven)**

Mountain of Emperors

The most exalted of China's five Daoist mountains, Tai Shan has been an essential imperial climb since the time of Qin Shi Huangdi. Emperors ascended Tai Shan to gain assurance that their heavenly mandate would be maintained; an abortive ascent could signal Heaven's favor was in question. Several sights have imperial associations: Huima Ling (Horse Turns Back Ridge) marks the spot where Emperor Zhenzong's horse refused to go any farther and the ruler had to continue by sedan chair. Tai Shan's importance is further evinced by two other notables who clambered up its slopes: Confucius and Mao Zedong.

Qin Shi Huangdi, first emperor of China

VISITORS' CHECKLIST

Practical Information
Tai'an, 45 miles (70 km) S of Jinan. near train station, (0538) 806 6077. Tai Shan Race (Sep).
Open daily; cable car: 6:30am–5:30pm.

Transportation
at Jinan. 3 from Jinan.

Key

- Minor road
- Path
- Built-up area

Climbing Tai Shan

Two routes lead to the summit. The Central Route is more popular, following the traditional imperial way and taking travelers past the most notable monuments. Despite having fewer historical sights and not being particularly wellmarked, the Western Route boasts lovely natural scenery, including Heilong Tan. Many travelers ascend by the Central Route and descend by the Western Route.

Stone Sutra Valley
North of Doumu Gong is a further Buddhist contribution to this Daoist peak, a large flat rock carved with the text of the Diamond Sutra, the first block-printed book to bear a date.

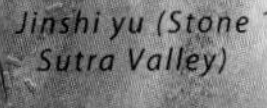

Hong Men Gong
This Ming dynasty temple, Red Gate Palace, is the first of numerous shrines dedicated to the Princess of the Azure Clouds (Bixia).

★ Dai Miao
This temple is the town's main attraction and a natural departure point for climbing the mountain. The main building, the Tiankuang Dian, is an immense yellow-eaved hall that contains a massive dimly lit Song dynasty fresco depicting the Zhenzong emperor as the God of Tai Shan.

For additional map symbols *see back flap*

❹ Qingdao

青岛

A world away from China's drab industrial towns, the breezy seaside city of Qingdao is a colorful port on the Shandong Peninsula. Known to foreign nationals as Tsingtao, where its namesake beer is brewed, pretty Qingdao's charms derive from its German textures, namely cobbled streets, red roof tiles, distinctive stonework, and tree-lined avenues. The city came under German jurisdiction in 1897, it was returned to China in 1922. Modern-day Qingdao is an entrepreneurial, forward-thinking city, with high ambitions, as shown by the world's largest 26-mile long- (42-km)-long Haiwan Bridge to Huangdao. The city holds the Qingdao International Sailing Week in August, attracting many visitors.

The former Governor's Residence

Exploring Qingdao

In 1897, Kaiser Wilhelm took over Qingdao after two German missionaries were killed by the Boxers *(see p439)*. The Qing court was forced to cede the city to Germany for 99 years, but it was returned to China in 1922, after eight years under Japanese occupation. The Japanese took over the port again between 1938 and 1945.

Wandering about at leisure is the best way to see Qingdao's main sights, most of which lie in the **German Concession** in the southwest of town that roughly stretches between Tai'an Lu and Xiaoyu Shan Park. The Germans built the imposing train station, equipped with a belfry, to mark the end of the line they laid to the provincial capital of Ji'nan. Reproduced on the label of Tsingtao beer, the octagonal Huilai Pavilion, which hosts craft exhibitions, lies at the tip of **Zhanqiao Pier**. The 1,444 ft (440 m) pier juts into Qingdao Bay off the frenetic No. 6 beach.

The busy Zhongshan Lu running north is Qingdao's premier shopping street. To the east is **St. Michael's Church**, whose twin spires preside over an atmospheric part of town filled with steep cobbled streets and iron balconies. Southeast of the Catholic church is the charming **Lutheran Church**, with its distinctive clock tower and white clock face. Built in 1910, its exterior has sandy yellow walls and red clay tiles, while the frugal interior is open to visitors. The 128-ft (39-m) clock tower is also open, and visitors can climb up its steep stairway to enjoy the view of the coast. Farther east in Xinhao Shan Park is the former **Governor's Residence**. This grand mansion once played host to Yuan Shikai and Mao Zedong. A short walk to the south, the **Qingdao Museum** is worth exploring for its collection of relics, including calligraphy and paintings from the Yuan and

Qingdao City Center

① Zhanqiao Pier
② St. Michael's Church
③ Governor's Residence
④ Lutheran Church
⑤ Qingdao Museum
⑥ Huashi Lou
⑦ Badaguan

Key to Symbols *see back flap*

Chinese Beer

Tsingtao beer can

Tsingtao, which swears by its magic ingredient of mineral water from Lao Shan, is China's most famous beer *(pijiu)*. Built by homesick Germans in 1903, the Tsingtao brewery is China's largest, with exports to over 40 countries. Once the best (and most expensive) in China, Tsingtao faces stiff local competition as international breweries invest heavily in joint ventures in what is the fastest growing beer market in the world. Vast amounts of beer are drunk during the town's Beer Festival in the last two weeks of August. You can visit the brewery (which also has a museum and bar) and receive free samples.

For hotels and restaurants in this region see p559 and pp574–5

An expanse of sand on one of Qingdao's many beaches

Ming eras. Visitors can stroll down Qingdao's waterfront past its many beaches. No. 1 beach is the longest and busiest, while farther east, No. 2 beach is more attractive. Its clean stretch of sand leads to **Huashi Lou**, a stone mansion with a turret that was once the residence of a Russian aristocrat. The genteel **Badaguan** area to the north is known for its villas and sanatoriums set amid tree-lined streets.

St. Michael's Church
15 Zhejiang Lu. **Tel** (0532) 8286 5960. **Open** 8am–5pm Mon–Fri (from noon Sun) 7am, 6pm Sun.

Lutheran Church
15 Jiangsu Lu. **Tel** (0532) 8286 5970. **Open** 8:30am–5pm daily Sun.

Qingdao Museum
51 Meiling Lu. **Tel** (0532) 8889 6286. **Open** 9am–5pm (Nov–Apr: to 4:30pm) Tue–Sun.
qingdaomuseum.com/en

VISITORS' CHECKLIST

Practical Information
236 miles (380 km) E of Jinan. 8,170,000. 33 Donghai Lu, (0532) 587 3081. Beer Festival (Aug). **qdta.cn**

Transportation
Qingdao North railway station. Long distance bus station, CAAC (buses to airport). Passenger ferry terminal, local ferry terminal.

Environs: A 25-mile (40-km) bus ride from Qingdao, the vast mountainous region of **Lao Shan** is a famous retreat with temples, waterfalls, and hiking trails. The area is steeped in Daoist lore and throughout the ages envoys were dispatched here in search of the elixir of life. The Song-era **Great Purity Palace** is located a third of the way up Mount Lao Shan. The palace was built by the first Song emperor as a place to perform Daoist rituals for the dead. From the palace, paths lead to the summit. Visitors can climb the stairs located half-way up, or take the cable car for dramatic views. The area was once dotted with Daoist temples, but only a few survive today. The most famous is the Song-dynasty **Taiqing Temple** near the coast, not far from where the Shandong writer Pu Songling (1640–1715) lived. Many more temples survive on Lao Shan's slopes along with caves, the highest and deepest of which is the Mingxia cave in front of Xuanwu Peak. Lao Shan is also known for its mineral water, a vital ingredient of Tsingtao beer.

Qingdao's skyline, similar to the modern architecture of Pudong, Shanghai

Gateway to the Yantai Museum, housed in a fine Qing-era guildhall

❺ Yantai
烟台

149 miles (240 km) NE of Qingdao. 6,500,000. from Shanghai, Dalian and Tianjin. 180 Jiefang Lu, (0535) 623 4144.

Formerly known as Chefoo and overshadowed by the dynamic port of Qingdao to the south, Yantai is a deepwater harbor town situated on the north coast of the Shandong peninsula, famous for its clocks, fruit, and locally produced wine. The name Yantai, meaning "Smoke Terrace," refers to the wolf-dung-burning beacons erected along the coast in the Ming dynasty to warn of sudden raids by pirates or the Japanese. In 1863, the city became a British treaty port and a substantial number of foreign merchants moved here, although its rise was eclipsed by the development of Qingdao at the end of the 1900s. The British were followed by the Germans, the Americans, and finally the Japanese. Despite its history as a treaty port, very little foreign architecture survives here, as the town never had a foreign concession.

Most travelers pass through en route to Penglai to the west, but the **Yantai Museum** is definitely worth a visit. Housed in a splendid Qing dynasty guildhall built for sailors and merchants, the museum's exhibits pale by comparison to the building's elaborate architectural detail and wood and stone carvings.

The impressive main hall, known as the Palace of the Empress of Heaven, was dedicated to Tianhou, the Empress of Heaven and Protector of Seafarers, by sailors from Fujian, who had taken shelter in Yantai during a fierce storm. All the component parts of the hall were designed by craftsmen from the southern provinces of Fujian and Guangdong, and shipped to Yantai where it was assembled in 1864. It is a fine example of the southern style, with a double roof decorated in mythical ceramic, stone, and wood figures. The entrance hall to the guildhall is elaborately carved with parables and episodes from Chinese literature and mythology, including the Eight Immortals who Crossed the Sea, battle scenes, figures, fabulous creatures, and several scenes from the *Romance of the Three Kingdoms (see p35)*. Arab figures playing musical instruments lie beneath the eaves, while the beams take the shape of a woman with her infant child. The temple has a garden and is equipped with a stage, employed for performances and events celebrating the Goddess Tianhou.

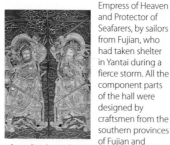

Ornate Qing dynasty doors, Yantai Museum

Yantai also has several parks, including the small and central **Yuhuangding Park**, and **Yantai Shan Park**, a hillside haven above the sea. East of here are Yantai's two rather forlorn beaches. Both are a bit of a disappointment, and are surrounded by buildings and construction. The town's waterfront, however, is a pleasant place for a leisurely stroll. Toward the eastern headland, fishermen can be seen repairing their nets or simply relaxing.

Yantai Museum
257 Nan Dajie. **Tel** (0535) 623 2976. **Open** 9am–4pm Tue–Sun.

❻ Weihai
威海

37 miles (60 km) E of Yantai. 2,500,000. from Yantai, Qingdao, Beijing & Shanghai. daily from Dalian, every afternoon to Inch'on (South Korea). CITS 602 Beiyang Dasha, (0631) 581 8616.

The port city of Weihai was the site of the mauling of China's European-built North Sea (Beiyang) Fleet by a Japanese flotilla during the 1894–5 Sino-Japanese War. Afterwards,

Museum of the 1895 Sino-Japanese War, Weihai

The Penglai pavilion, mythical abode of the Eight Immortals

between 1898 and 1930, the city was a rather unproductive British Concession and was known as Port Edward, but little remains of the town's British heritage. Today, Weihai's chief diversion is **Liugong Island** (Liugong Dao), 3 miles (5 km) off the coast, reached by ferry. Providing shelter for Weihai harbor, the island forms a natural stronghold and served as the base for the doomed Chinese North Sea Fleet.

The island's main sight is the **Museum of the 1895 Sino-Japanese War** (or Jiawu War Museum). The conflict between the two nations resulted in the ceding of Taiwan and the Liaodong Peninsula (including Dalian) to Japan. Not far from the jetty, the museum functions for the "patriotic education" of Chinese visitors, with displays of photographs and artifacts salvaged from ships, as well as reminders of the island's days as a station for the British Royal Navy.

The rest of the island is a pleasant place to explore, with several hiking trails heading off into the forested hills. Its International Beach is popular for its long stretches of sand and calm waters. Ferries connect Weihai with Dalian and Incheon in South Korea. Accommodation is not available on the island.

Museum of the 1895 Sino-Japanese War
Liugong Island. from Weihai (20 minutes). Ferry back to Weihai: summer 7am–6pm; winter 8:30am–4:30pm, every 30 mins. **Open** 7:30am–5pm daily.

7 Penglai
蓬莱

43 miles (70 km) NW of Yantai.
from Yantai every hour.

Associated with the Eight Immortals of Daoism, who drank wine here before making their mythical crossing of the sea without the aid of boats, the castle-like pavilion complex of **Penglai Ge** affords dramatic views out to sea from its breezy clifftop perch. Accessible by bus, the pavilion dates back to 1061, though Penglai entered folklore when China's first emperor, Qin Shi Huangdi, foraged in the area for herbs that bestow immortality.

The imposing complex has a large network of buildings, pavilions, halls, temples, gardens, and crenellated walls. Many of the buildings are thickly covered in ivy and vines. Among its six main halls, which have been extensively renovated, the Tianhou Palace is dedicated to Tianhou, the Empress of Heaven, and enshrines a golden statue of the goddess. The statue is backed by a fine mural of dragons frolicking in the sea and amongst the clouds. The castle is at its liveliest on the occasion of the goddess's birthday, on the 23rd day of the third month of the Chinese lunar calendar *(see p51)*, when a lively temple fair is held. The goddess is invoked with incense sticks and prayer. The complex now has a cable car and a theater.

Penglai Ge is also known for the mirage that is supposed to occur here every few decades. Witnesses have described seeing an island, complete with buildings, inhabitants, and trees arising from the mist. Visitors can watch a video recording of the mirage in the Tianhou Palace for a small fee. Penglai is usually busy on weekends when large tour groups visit the pavilion. It is quieter on weekdays, and can be easily visited as a daytrip from Yantai.

Penglai Ge
from Penglai. **Tel** (0631) 564 8106. **Open** 8:30am–5pm daily.

The Empress of Heaven

The Empress of Heaven, Tianhou, is also known by the Chinese as Mazu, Niangniang, and Tianshang Shengmu. She is the Daoist equivalent of Guanyin, the Buddhist Goddess of Compassion. In the coastal provinces of Guangdong and Fujian, she is worshiped as the Goddess of the Sea, and is the guardian deity of seafarers. She was supposedly originally a woman named Lin Mo, born in AD 960 on Meizhou Island in Fujian *(see p297)*. From a tender age, Lin Mo was famous for helping sailors in distress, and after her death at age 27, her red-clothed apparition was seen by fishermen and sailors in danger. Confusingly, in Cantonese, her name is pronounced as Tinhau, and she is also known as A-Ma in Macau.

Goddess Tianhou depicted on a Chinese pirate flag

❽ Kaifeng

开封

South of the Yellow River as it snakes into Shandong Province is the ancient walled city of Kaifeng, the capital of seven dynasties, which reached its zenith as the capital of the Northern Song (960–1126). Its glory days as a burgeoning Song city are pictorially recorded in the 16-ft (5-m) long scroll "Going Upriver During the Qingming Festival," now kept in Beijing's Forbidden City. However, its prosperity could not prevent the Yellow River from repeatedly flooding the city, with a heavy loss of life. Significant buildings were also washed away, including the synagogue. Today, Kaifeng is an attractive city with fine examples of temple and pagoda architecture and some lively markets.

The ornately decorated Shanshaan Gan Guildhall

Exploring Kaifeng

Much of modern Kaifeng lies within the old city walls. In the west of the city is the large and peaceful Baogong Hu (Baogong Lake). Within walking distance to the south of the lake, the Kaifeng Museum on Yingbin Lu houses three stelae that originally stood outside the old Jewish synagogue. They record the history of the city's Jewish community. The No. 4 People's Hospital on Beitu Jie sits on the remains of the synagogue in the Jewish quarter. All that can be seen today is the iron cover over an old well. Nearby is the Kaifeng Jewish History Memorial Center. Outside the city walls, 6 miles (10 km) to the north, is the Yellow River Viewing Point. From the pavilion, there are expansive views across the vast silt plain of the winding river. Adjacent to the pavilion stands an iron statue of an ox, that was originally a charm to protect the city from floods.

Shanshan Gan Guildhall

Xufu Jie, off Shudian Jie. **Tel** (0378) 595 7411. **Open** 8am–6:30pm daily.

The exuberant Qing-dynasty hall was built by merchants of Gansu, Shanxi, and Shaanxi provinces as housing. It sports a drum and bell tower, as well as a spirit wall. The building's eaves have vivid scenes from merchant life, while the eaves in the main hall are carved with animals, birds, and gold bats (symbols of luck).

Da Xiangguo Si

36 Ziyou Lu. 5, 9. **Tel** (0378) 595 0090. **Open** 8:30am–10pm daily.
Yanqing Guan: Baogong Hu Dongbei Shengli Jie. **Open** daily.

Kaifeng's most celebrated temple is Da Xiangguo Si (Prime Minister's Temple). Originally built in 555, it was China's principal temple during the Song era, when it accommodated 64 halls and a huge legion of monks. Swept away by flood waters in 1642 at the end of the Ming dynasty, it was rebuilt around 1766. The octagonal pavilion at the back of the temple houses a statue of Guanyin, known as Qianshou Guanyin or the Thousand-Armed Goddess of Compassion. Carved from a single tree and covered in gold leaf, it is the temple's finest statue, and its four-sided arrangement is a rare feature. The main hall has a frieze of *luohan* *(see p37)*. A sprawling open-air market lies near the temple.

To the west is the **Yanqing Guan** (Yanqing Temple), a small Daoist shrine known for the unusual design of its Pavilion of the Jade Emperor. This ornate, octagonal building, covered in turquoise tiles and carved brickwork, has a bronze image of the Jade Emperor inside.

Iron Pagoda

Iron Pagoda Park, Beimen Dajie. **Tel** (0378) 286 2279. **Open** 7am–7pm daily.

The 13-story Iron Pagoda (Tie Ta) rises up just within the Song dynasty ramparts in the northeast of the city. This brick pagoda was built in 1049 and is covered with brown glazed tiles, which give the tower its metallic luster as well as its name. Visitors can no longer climb the pagoda, although you can still explore the beautiful grounds. The pagoda is Kaifeng's best-known landmark.

The magnificent Qianshou Guanyin, Da Xiangguo Si

Prayer flags in front of Da Xiangguo Si

lie to its northwest and south respectively. The park is marked by several amusement rides for children, as well as the Qing-dynasty Dragon Pavilion, and is an excellent place to watch the locals relaxing in their leisure time.

VISITORS' CHECKLIST

Practical Information
44 miles (70 km) E of Zhengzhou.
4,800,000.
kaifeng.gov.cn

Transportation
Zhengzhou.
Southern bus station, West bus station.

Longting Park

N of Zhongshan Lu. **Tel** (0371) 2566 0808. **Open** daily. Millennium City: **Open** 8am–7pm daily.

Songdu Yu Jie, built on the Imperial Way – Kaifeng's main thoroughfare during the Song dynasty – leads north up to Longting Park. It features reproduction Song-dynasty restaurants and shops selling antiques, calligraphy, and knick-knacks. The street gets more touristy as it heads northward to Yangjia Hu (Yangjia Lake), originally part of the imperial park, and now surrounded by tourist attractions and amusement parks such as the popular **Millennium City**. Longting Park itself stands on the site of the Song-dynasty Imperial Palace and its surrounding park. The Xibei Hu and Yangjia Hu lakes

Fan Pagoda

1 mile (1.5 km) SE of Kaifeng. 8. **Open** 8am–5:30pm daily. joint entrance fee for pagoda & parks.

Hidden away (albeit reachable by bus) south of the city walls and just west of the Yuwangtai Park (Yuwangtai Gongyuan), the Northern Song-dynasty Fan Pagoda (Po Ta) is Kaifeng's oldest Buddhist structure, built in 997. Known for its carved brickwork, the three-story pagoda once stood nine stories and 263 ft (80 m) high. Visitors can climb right to the top for views of the surrounding factories and houses.

China's Jews

It is not known when Jews *(youtairen)* first came to Kaifeng, but evidence suggests that Jewish merchants arrived in China in the 8th century, along the Silk Roads. Chinese Jews were given seven surnames (Ai, Jin, Lao, Li, Shi, Zhang, and Zhao) by imperial decree in the Ming era. According to one story, in 1605 Jesuit Matteo Ricci traveled to Kaifeng because he was told there was a community here who believed in one god. Expecting to meet Catholics he was surprised to find they were in fact Jewish. The community struggled in isolation over the years, and all but disappeared after the synagogue, damaged by flooding, was torn down in 1845. There are still a few Jewish families here but they are not recognized by the Chinese government, nor rabbis as they trace their origin through their paternal lineage.

Kaifeng City Center

① Shanshan Gan Guildhall
② Da Xiangguo Si
③ Iron Pagoda
④ Longting Park
⑤ Fan Pagoda

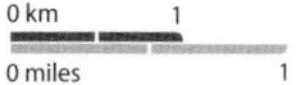

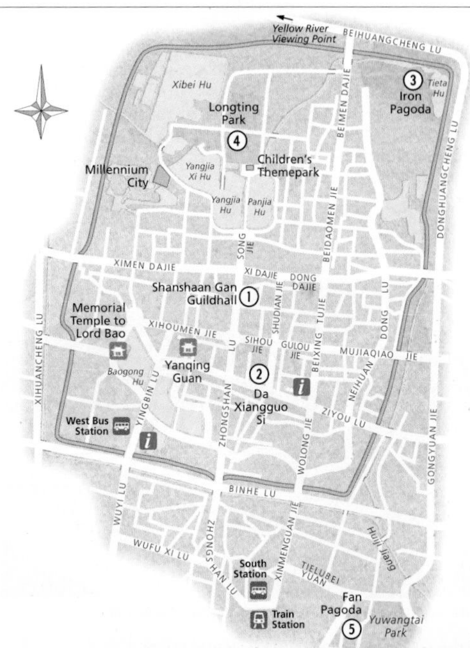

Key to Symbols *see back flap*

❾ Anyang
安阳

124 miles (200 km) N of Zhengzhou. 5,250,000. CITS, 37 Wenfen Dadao, (0372) 591 0100.

Archeological excavations have identified Anyang, in northern Henan, as the site of Yin, the capital of the Shang dynasty. In the late 19th century, peasants unearthed bones etched with ancient Chinese symbols, identified as "oracle bones" or bones used for divination *(see p32)*. Further discoveries of bronzes, jade, and royal tombs, helped form a picture of the long forgotten city of Yin. The **Museum of Yin Ruins** (Yinxu Bowuguan), in the north of town, exhibits fragments of oracle bones, pottery, and bronze vessels, as well as six chariots, drawn by skeletal horses. To the east is the ostentatious **Tomb of Yuan Shikai**, a general who helped force the Qing abdication in return for the presidency, but later tried to have himself enthroned as emperor. The bustling **Old City**, centered around the Bell Tower south of Jiefang Lu, is also worth exploring. To the southwest, stands the octagonal **Wenfeng Pagoda**, originally built in the 10th century and restored during the Ming era.

Wenfeng Pagoda, Anyang

Museum of Yin Ruins
18. **Open** 8:30am–5pm daily.

Tomb of Yuan Shikai
8, 23 or 35 to Yuan Lin. **Open** 8:30am–5pm daily.

Traditional three door gateway, Baima Si (White Horse Temple), Luoyang

❿ Zhengzhou
郑州

440 miles (700 km) SW of Beijing. 8,600,000. Nongye Lu (Crn Huayuan Lu), (0371) 6585 2309.

Henan's capital is a fast-developing megacity that is often used as a stopover en route to Kaifeng, Luoyang, and the Shaolin Temple. The **Shang City Walls** to the east of town are all that remain of the city that existed here 3,000 years ago. To the west is **Chenghuang Miao** (Temple of the City God), with its roof sculptures of dragons and phoenixes. The **Henan Provincial Museum**, in the north of town, has a superb collection of relics with English captions, while the fourth floor houses porcelain and pottery. For fine views of the Yellow River, visit the **Yellow River Scenic Area**, 17 miles (28 km) northwest of town.

Henan Provincial Museum
8 Nongye Lu. **Tel** (0371) 351 1062. **Open** 9am–5pm Tue–Sun.

⓫ Luoyang
洛阳

75 miles (121 km) W of Zhengzhou. 6,400,000. (Longmen Station for high-speed trains). Jiudu Xi Lu, (0379) 633 0500.

Luoyang's industrial face conveys little of its impressive history. The city was the site of the ancient Zhao court, where the sage Laozi was keeper of the archives. It was also the site of China's first university in 29 BC, and was capital to 13 dynasties from Neolithic times till AD 937.

East of Wangcheng Park is the **Luoyang City Museum**, which exhibits Shang bronzes, jade carvings, and Tang era *sancai* (three-color) porcelain. Visitors flock here each spring to attend the Peony Festival, when hundreds of peonies – brought here on the orders of the Tang Empress Wu Zetian – bloom in Wangcheng Park.

Most of Luoyang's sights lie outside the city. **Guanlin**, 4 miles (7 km) south, is dedicated to Guan Yu *(see p35)*, a heroic general of the Three Kingdoms period. Stone lionesses line the path to the main hall housing an impressive statue of Guan Yu. About 8 miles (12 km) east of town is **Baima Si** (White Horse Temple). Claiming to be China's oldest Buddhist monastery (AD 68), Baima Si remains active, with a constant stream of worshipers. The monks' tombs lie in the first courtyard, while the main hall has a statue of the Buddha.

Luoyang City Museum
Tel (0379) 6990 1002. **Open** 8:30am–5pm daily.

Guanlin Si
81. **Open** 8am–6pm daily. 

A Shang-era war chariot and charioteer from an imperial tomb, Anyang

The Yellow River

China's second-longest river, at 3,400 miles (5,464 km), the Huang He or Yellow River gets its name from its vast silt load, picked up as it carves its way through the soft clay of the Loess plateau. As the river slows, it deposits much of this silt, elevating the river bed above the surrounding plains – outside Kaifeng it is up to 35 ft (10 m) higher than the city – making flooding likely. It has also changed its path completely many times, sometimes running south of the Shandong peninsula, each time with widespread devastation. In 1642 an estimated 300,000 people died when the river broke through the dykes and took the southern route. These disasters have earned the river the nickname "China's Sorrow." Rapid economic growth has led to vastly increased water usage in north China and the Yellow River now regularly runs dry in its lower reaches.

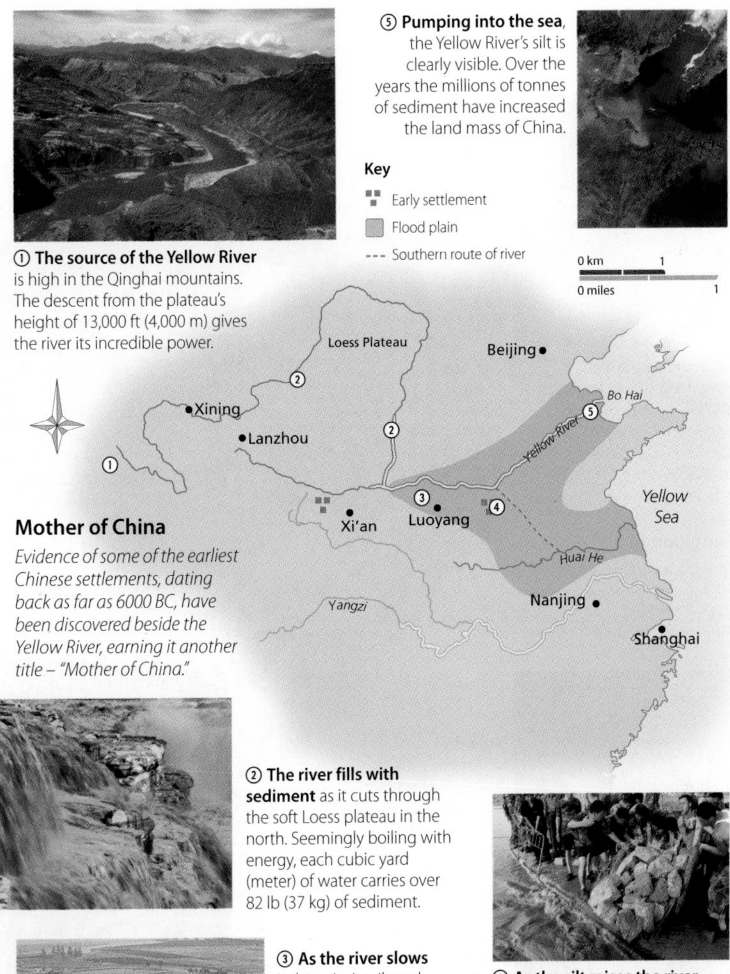

⑤ **Pumping into the sea**, the Yellow River's silt is clearly visible. Over the years the millions of tonnes of sediment have increased the land mass of China.

① **The source of the Yellow River** is high in the Qinghai mountains. The descent from the plateau's height of 13,000 ft (4,000 m) gives the river its incredible power.

Mother of China

Evidence of some of the earliest Chinese settlements, dating back as far as 6000 BC, have been discovered beside the Yellow River, earning it another title – "Mother of China."

② **The river fills with sediment** as it cuts through the soft Loess plateau in the north. Seemingly boiling with energy, each cubic yard (meter) of water carries over 82 lb (37 kg) of sediment.

③ **As the river slows** it deposits its silt and enriches the soil, making the local farmland one of the most productive areas of China.

④ **As the silt raises the river bed** those living close to the river have to work together to rebuild the dykes and keep the river banks in good condition.

⓬ Longmen Grottoes

龙门石窟

This outstanding collection of Buddhist statuary was started by the Northern Wei rulers (AD 386–534) – creators of the Yungang Grottoes *(see pp138–9)* – after they moved their capital from Datong to Luoyang. The Sui and Tang dynasties further added to the grottoes, especially during the rule of Tang dynasty Empress Wu Zetian, before anti-Buddhist purges halted its development. The number of headless statues as a result of vandalism and theft creates a solemn mood, although today the caves are well cared for. The caves are best visited in the afternoon, when they are mostly in the shade.

View across the Yi River looking onto Fengxian Si and the west bank caves

★ Vairocana Buddha

Over 56 ft (17 m) tall, this colossal statue's face was reputedly modeled after Empress Wu Zetian. The statue's enigmatic smile has earned it the nickname the "Eastern Mona Lisa."

Fengxian Si ①

This grotto, on the west bank, is largest of all the caves and dates back to AD 675.

Ananda

This statue is of Ananda, a disciple of Sakyamuni, the founder of Buddhism. A master of memory, he compiled the Buddhist *sutras.*

Smashed Ananda

Some statues were damaged in the late-Tang dynasty, as Buddhism fell out of favor. Other figures were stolen by souvenir-hunters or attacked by Red Guards during the Cultural Revolution.

★ **Heavenly King**
Holding a votive pagoda in one hand and crushing a demon under his feet, this sculpture of a Heavenly King is remarkable for its sense of movement and realistic posture.

Exploring the Longmen Grottoes

There are around 1,400 caves or niches and over 100,000 statues (with English captions) in total clustered inside a few caves, largely within a half-mile (1-km) section on the west bank of the Yi River.

The well-preserved Lotus Flower Grotto ② was built c. 527 as a complete entity, and not added to over the years. It derives its name from the large lotus flower in the center of its domed roof, surrounded by musical water spirits – *apsaras*. The Ten Thousand Buddha Grotto ③ is a typical Tang dynasty cave built in 680. The many figures of Buddha create an overwhelming sense of the presence of the great teacher. The Prescription Grotto ④ has 140 inscriptions recording many treatments for a wide variety of diseases and conditions carved on the walls on either side of the entrance. The list has been added to over a period of 150 years and so provides a unique record of typological changes over time. The three Binyang San Dong Grottoes ⑤ took 24 years to build and were completed in 523. On the main wall there are five very large Buddhist images: the central one, of Sakyamuni, is flanked by four bodhisattvas all in the ascetic and rather formal Northern Wei style. Together with the statues on the side walls, the three groups of figures symbolize the Buddhas of the past, present, and future. There were two large reliefs of the emperor and empress worshiping Buddha that were stolen in the 1930s and they now reside in museums in the USA. The southern Binyang Grotto has some beautiful sculptures that were completed in 641. These figures have serene features and can clearly be seen as a transition between the artistic styles of the solemn, austere Northern Wei and the lively naturalism of the Tang artists as displayed at Fengxian Si.

Seated Buddha, Sakyamuni, in the Binyang San Dong Grottoes

VISITORS' CHECKLIST

Practical Information
4 miles (6 km) S of Luoyang. **Tel** (0379) 598 1342. **Open** Mar–Oct: 7:30am–6:30pm daily; Nov–Feb: 7:30am–5pm daily. **W lmsk.cn/en**

Transportation
53, 81 from the Luoyang train station or taxi.

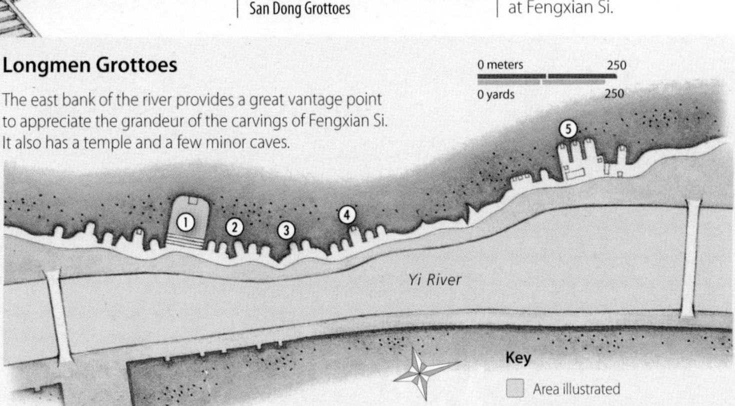

Longmen Grottoes
The east bank of the river provides a great vantage point to appreciate the grandeur of the carvings of Fengxian Si. It also has a temple and a few minor caves.

The monumental Forest of Stupas, Shaolin Temple

⑬ Song Shan & Shaolin Temple

嵩山和少林寺

50 miles (80 km) W of Zhengzhou. 1 from Dengfeng East Long Distance Bus Station to Shaolin Temple. Dengfeng: 146 Zhongyue Jie, (0371) 6287 1139.

The Central Peak of China's five sacred Daoist peaks, Song Shan soars 4,895 ft (1,492 m) high. Its sights can be best explored by staying at **Dengfeng**, at the foot of Taishi Shan, where numerous trails lead past temples and pagodas, and offer splendid views. Just 3 miles (5 km) east is the vast **Zhongyue Miao** (Central Peak Temple). Possibly China's oldest Daoist shrine, it was consecrated more than 2,200 years ago, although what exists today is more recent.

About 2 miles (3 km) north of Dengfeng is the **Songyang Academy**. A Confucian college that was one of China's four great centers of learning, its courtyard has two tall cypresses, said to have been planted 2,000 years ago by the Han Emperor Wudi. Farther uphill, the 12-sided **Songyue Si Pagoda**, dating from the 6th century AD, is China's oldest brick pagoda. Just 6 miles (10 km) southeast of Dengfeng, the Gaocheng Observatory dates from the Yuan era. Its pyramidal tower is China's oldest intact observatory. Shaolin, literally "Young Forest," is the name of the fighting order of monks who reside in the Buddhist **Shaolin Temple**, 8 miles (13 km) northwest of Dengfeng. Founded in the 5th century AD, it acquired its martial spirit under Bodhidarma, an Indian monk who arrived here in 527. He devised a system of exercises that evolved into *shaolin quan*, or Shaolin Boxing, the origin of all the great Chinese martial arts. The temple has burned down repeatedly and today its mystique has been dulled by commercialization. It remains a place of pilgrimage for martial arts devotees, who flock here to develop *gong fu* (skill), popularly known as kung fu, although many schools have moved to Dengfeng. The large temple has several halls. Toward the back, the Standing in the Snow Pavilion marks the spot where the monk Huihe chopped off his arm to commune more closely with Zen Buddhism. Behind, the Pilu Pavilion's floor is marked with pits where monks practiced their footwork. Within the Chuipu Hall, terracotta figures depict various styles of Shaolin Boxing.

Bodhidarma statue, Shaolin Temple

The Forest of Stupas, a short walk from the temple, is a large assembly of brick pagodas commemorating renowned Shaolin monks. Each September, the famous *wushu* (martial arts) festival is held here. The cave where Bodhidarma reputedly sat in meditation for nine years is up the mountainside.

Zhongyue Miao
Tel (0371) 6290 5589.
Open 8am–5pm daily.

Shaolin Temple
Open 8:10am–5:30pm daily.
shaolin.org.cn/en

⑭ Gongyi

工艺

50 miles (80 km) W of Zhengzhou. from Luoyang or Zhengzhou.

Just outside the sleepy town of Gongyi, a historic collection of Song-era imperial tombs and a group of Buddhist grotto art can be found. The seven surviving tombs of Song emperors are marked by burial mounds and statuary. Scattered over a vast area southeast of town, the tombs can be seen from buses shuttling between Luoyang and Zhengzhou. About 5 miles (8 km) north of Gongyi, the **Buddhist Grottoes** *(shiku)* have carvings from the Northern Wei period.

Buddhist Grottoes
Tel (0371) 6415 7150.
Open 8am–6pm daily.

Buddhist carvings in the grottoes outside Gongyi

◀ Striking Buddhist sculptures at the Longmen Grottoes

Kung Fu

Chinese martial arts are loosely referred to as *gong fu* or kung fu in the West. *Gong fu* means "skill" and can describe the accomplishments of a calligrapher or pianist, as much as a martial artist. No one is certain when the fighting arts came to the country, but it is clear that China has the largest number and most colorful of fighting styles, including Drunken Boxing and Praying Mantis Fist. Although there is considerable blurring between them, kung fu divides into internal *(neijia)* and external *(waijia)* schools. The internal schools tend to stress internal power or *qi* *(see pp38–9)*, using evasion and softness to lead an attacker off balance, while *waijia* forms seek to overwhelm an opponent with physical strength and power. Kung fu employs many weapons, including the spear, broadsword, pole, and whip and even encompasses training in the use of everyday objects, such as the fan, umbrella, or stool, as weapons.

Bodhidarma, the founder of Chan (Zen) Buddhism, was an Indian monk who visited the Shaolin Temple. He invented a system of exercises for the monks who were often seated in meditation. It was from these exercises that Shaolin Boxing developed.

Shaolin monks endure a rigorous training regimen. Here, they perform an acrobatic version of the horse stance *(mabu)*, a painful exercise that is essential for developing a powerful stance and a deep "root" for stability while fighting.

Xingyi Quan (Shape Mind Fist) is, of the *neijia* practices, probably the closest to a hard school. Although its strikes and blocks are linear and powerful, relaxation is paramount. The basics of this explosive fighting style are simple to learn, but tricky to master.

Bagua Zhang (Eight Trigram Palm), an internal art, incorporates circular movements into all footwork and strikes. Bagua practitioners were traditionally seen by other stylists as unpredictable, elusive, and ferocious adversaries.

Bruce Lee *(right)* in *The Chinese Connection*

Kung Fu Film Industry

The Chinese and Hong Kong film industry entertains its audience with stylized versions of kung fu in movie plots that typically hinge on themes of vengeance and retribution. Famous actors have included Bruce Lee, Jackie Chan, and Jet Li and a host of lesser known B-movie actors and actresses. Hallmark films include *Drunken Master 2* (Jackie Chan), *Enter the Dragon* (Bruce Lee), *Crouching Tiger, Hidden Dragon* (Zhang Ziyi and Yun-Fat Chow), and the *Once Upon a Time in China* series (Jet Li). The martial arts employed in cinema are very different from the real thing. Movements are choreographed and stunts are practiced repeatedly to give the impression of a real fight, without the dangers inherent in real combat.

SHAANXI

At the heart of China, bordered by the Yellow River to the east, the dusty province of Shaanxi has had its lion's share of splendor. In 1066 BC, the Western Zhou dynasty established its capital at Hao, near modern-day Xi'an *(see pp168–73)*. It was from here, about 850 years later, that China was unified by its first emperor, Qin Shi Huangdi *(see p60)*. This set the stage for Xi'an to serve as the seat of political power to successive dynasties including the Western Han, the Sui, and the Tang, for over a millennium. By the 9th century, Xi'an, known then as Chang'an, was the largest and wealthiest city in the world, immersed in the riches that spilled along the Silk Road. At the peak of the Tang era, Xi'an's population of over a million people worshiped at as many as 1,000 temples within the confines of a vast city wall.

The city's treasures are abundant, from the silent army of Terracotta Warriors just northeast of Xi'an, fashioned to guard the tomb of China's first emperor, to the impressive Shaanxi History Museum, with thousands of exhibits ranging from Shang and Zhou bronze vessels to Tang-era ornaments and funerary items.

Xi'an's other key sights include the extensive Eight Immortals Temple associated with Daoist legends, and the two Goose Pagodas with their strong connections to Tang-era Buddhism. Many visitors also make a trip to the holy mountain of Hua Shan, to the east of Xi'an, for its stimulating combination of energetic hiking opportunities and quiet sanctity.

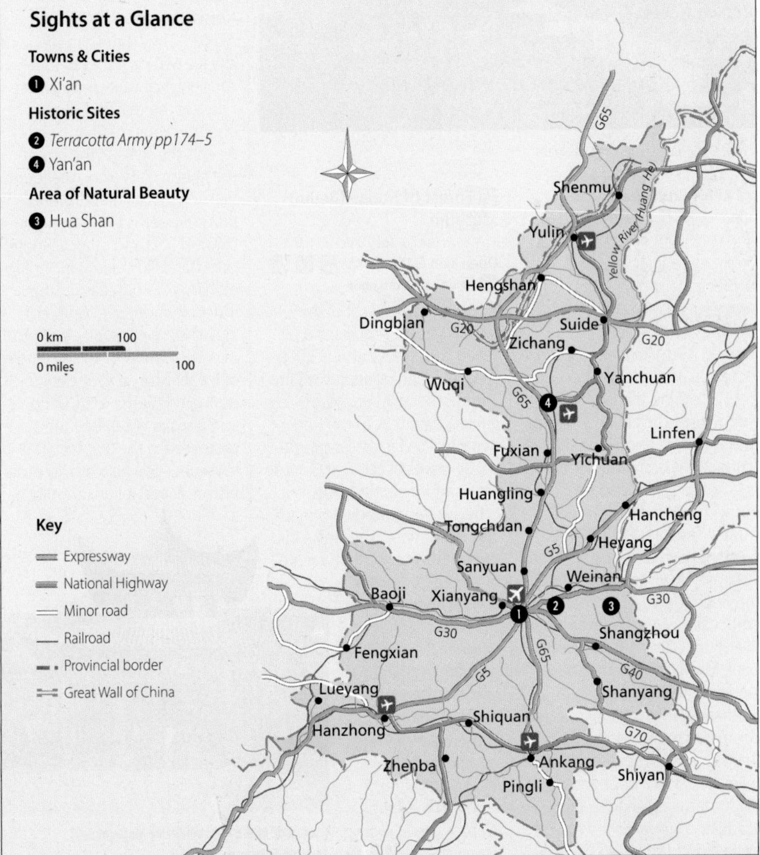

◀ The granite-peaked Hua Shan, with prayer flags adorning the route

For additional map symbols *see back flap*

❶ Xi'an

西安

Capital of modern Shaanxi, Xi'an has served as capital to 11 dynasties over a period of 4,000 years, including the Western Zhou, Western Han, Qin, Western Wei, Northern Zhou, Sui, and Tang. The Chinese trace its lineage back even further to the mythical Yellow Emperor, who made Xianyang his capital (2200–1700 BC). Xi'an peaked during the Tang dynasty, when its position at the eastern end of the Silk Road *(see pp470–71)* transformed it into a bustling metropolis, luring foreign merchants and faiths, including Nestorian Christians, Muslims, Zoroastrians, Manicheans, and Buddhists. The city declined later but has some splendid sights and a thriving tourist economy.

A view of the South Gate, Xi'an City Walls

Xi'an City Walls

Open South Gate: 8am–10pm daily, other gates: 8am–6pm daily.

Unlike many city walls in China, including Beijing's mighty ramparts – now mostly flattened – Xi'an's walls are still intact, forming a 9-mile (14-km) long rectangle around the city center. In 1370, during the reign of Hongwu, the first Ming emperor, these walls were built on the foundations of the Tang imperial palace, using rammed earth, quicklime, and glutinous rice extract. The 39-ft (12-m) high bastions have bases up to 59 ft (18 m) thick. Visitors can climb the walls at several locations, particularly at the steps east of the South Gate or at the West Gate, for walks along the busy ramparts. Though striking in themselves, the walls are modest compared to the mighty bastion that once encompassed 30 sq miles (78 sq km) of Chang'an, Xi'an's name during the Tang era. Bikes can be rented to cycle around the walls.

Forest of Stelae (Beilin) Museum

18 Wenyi Bei Lu. **Tel** (029) 721 0764.
Open 8am–6:15pm daily.
W beilin-museum.com

A short distance east of the South Gate, this museum's seven halls house about 3,000 stelae – stone pillars carved for commemorative purposes – the earliest dating from the Han dynasty. The tablets bearing dense reams of classical Chinese may only interest scholars, but others are engraved with maps and illustrations. The stelae in the first hall comprise a record of the 12 Confucian classics, including the *Book of Songs (Shijing)*, the *Book of Changes (Yijing or I Ching)*, and the *Analects (Lunyu)*. These were carved on 114 stone tablets in 837, upon the orders of the Tang Wenzong emperor, as the standard texts

Detail from the Nestorian tablet at the Forest of Stelae Museum

to eliminate copyist's errors, and were kept at the Imperial Academy in Xi'an. The Daqin Nestorian Tablet in the second hall is topped with a cross and was carved in 781 to commemorate the arrival of Nestorian Christianity in Xi'an. The characters at the top of the stele refer to Rome (or Daqin), and Nestorian Christianity, the "Revered Religion." Branded heretical for believing in the separation of Christ's human and divine attributes, the first Nestorians arrived in Xi'an in AD 635. They thrived in the city for two centuries before suddenly vanishing altogether.

Inside the third hall, an engraved map of Chang'an reveals the scale of the city at the height of its glory. The fourth hall houses calligraphic renditions of poems by Su Dongpo (1037–1101) and other Chinese poets, and illustrations including etchings of Bodhidarma, the Indian founder of Chan (Zen) Buddhism *(see pp164–5)*. Useful reference material for the study of local history and society during the Song, Yuan, Ming, and Qing eras can be found preserved in the fifth hall. The museum's side halls display more historical and religious artifacts.

The facade of the Forest of Stelae Museum, once the Temple of Confucius

Drum and Bell Towers

Open 8:30am–6pm daily.

The enormous Bell Tower, with its distinctive green three-tiered roof, is situated on a busy roundabout in the center of Xi'an, where the city's four main streets converge. Standing on a brick platform, this wooden structure was first built in 1384, two blocks west of here, before being relocated to its current site in 1582. It was later restored in 1739. The tower, which formerly housed a large bronze bell that was struck each morning, now stores a collection of bells, chimes, and musical instruments. A balcony running all along the outside offers splendid views of the town's main roads and heavy traffic. The Drum Tower, built in 1380, is situated to the west of the Bell Tower on the edge of the old Muslim Quarter, for centuries the home of Xi'an's Hui minority, which currently numbers around 30,000. Within its restored interior drumming performances take place daily.

Iron bell in the Bell Tower

The Great Mosque

Open 8am–6:30pm daily.

First built during the Tang dynasty, and located in the heart of the Muslim Quarter west of the Bell Tower, Xi'an's Chinese-styled Great Mosque (Da Qingzhen Si) is one of the largest in China. Constructed in 742, when Islam was still a young religion, the mosque's surviving buildings date to the Qing dynasty and have been restored. A serene oasis of tranquillity, the mosque has four courtyards, the first of which contains a 30-ft (9-m) high decorated wooden arch, built in the 17th century, while the third houses the Introspection Minaret, an octagonal pagoda with a triple-eaved roof. Housed within the hall to the south of the minaret is a Ming-dynasty handwritten copy of the holy Koran. Located beyond two fountains is the main prayer hall, capped in turquoise tiles, its ceiling carved with inscriptions from the Koran. The prayer hall is usually closed to non-Muslims. Avoid visiting the mosque on Fridays, the Muslim holy day.

Also worth exploring is the Muslim Quarter, with its winding streets, low houses, excellent ethnic cuisine, and resident Hui community.

Arabic script on a stone arch in the Great Mosque's courtyard

VISITORS' CHECKLIST

Practical Information

744 miles (1,200 km) SW of Beijing. 8,000,000. 159 Beiyuanmen, (029) 8763 0166. **en1.xian-tourism.com:81**

Transportation

Xi'an Xianyang International Airport, 25 miles (40 km). Xi'an train station. Shaanxi province long-distance bus station, CAAC (buses to airport), to Xi'an train station and 5 more routes.

Xi'an City Center

1. Xi'an City Walls
2. Forest of Stelae (Beilin) Museum
3. Drum and Bell Towers
4. The Great Mosque
5. Eight Immortals Temple
6. Small Wild Goose Pagoda
7. Shaanxi History Museum
8. Great Wild Goose Pagoda

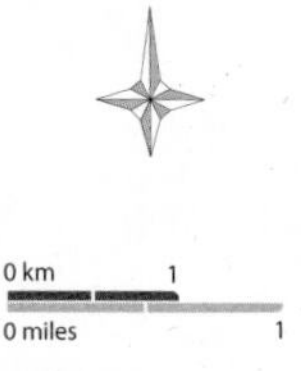

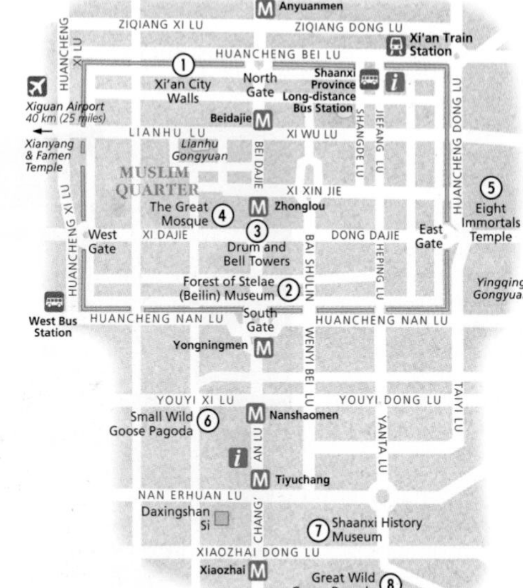

Key to Symbols *see back flap*

Eight Immortals Temple

Open 8am–6pm daily.

East of Xi'an's walls, this is its largest Daoist shrine, built on the site of a temple originally consecrated to the Thunder God, whose presence had been indicated by subterranean rumblings. It was later named Baxian Gong, after the Eight Immortals of Daoist mythology, who were glimpsed here during the Song dynasty. The halls and courtyards of this active temple teem with monks and nuns. Of particular interest are a series of slabs attached to the wall in the main courtyard, inscribed with Daoist literature and illustrations, including extracts from the *Neijing*, the bible of Daoist yogis and alchemists. Other plaques are etched with curious Daoist designs, including a tablet illustrated with the five mystic symbols denoting the five Daoist sacred mountains. On the left and right of the **Lingguan Hall** are statues of the guardian beings, the White Tiger and Green Dragon, and an effigy of Wang Lingguan, the protector of Daoism. Statues of the Eight Immortals line either side of their hall.

Stele Pavilion Eight Immortals Temple

At the rear of the complex, the **Doumu Hall** is dedicated to the important Daoist Goddess Doumu, also called Doulao, the Queen of the Big Dipper. Also at the rear is the Hall of Master Qiu, where the Dowager Empress Cixi and the Guangxu emperor sought refuge when they fled Beijing's Forbidden City at the end of the Boxer Rebellion in 1900 *(see p439)*. Above the door of the hall is a tablet inscribed with the characters *yuqing zhidao*, meaning the Dao of Jade Purity, Cixi's dedication to the abbot. The temple hosts a popular religious festival on the first and fifteenth day of every lunar month. An excellent street market of curios, fakes, and memorabilia is held on Wednesdays and Sundays in the road outside the temple.

The Small Wild Goose Pagoda, originally 15 stories high

Small Wild Goose Pagoda

72 Youyi Xi Lu. 7, 8. **Tel** (029) 8780 3591. **Open** 9am–6pm daily. Xi'an Museum: **W xabwy.com**

Southwest of the South Gate, the 43-m (141-ft) high Small Wild Goose Pagoda, Xiaoyan Ta, is attached to the remains of a temple, Jianfu Si. One of the city's Tang relics, it was built to store *sutras* (scriptures) brought back from India. Its brick tower, completed in AD 709, was meant to protect the *sutras* from fire, which often destroyed wooden temples. At the back of the complex is the **Xi'an Museum**, storing 130,000 cultural relics.

Shaanxi History Museum

See pp172–3.

Great Wild Goose Pagoda

Yanta Lu. 41, 610 from train station. **Open** 8am–5pm daily. (separate fee to climb the pagoda).

This Tang-dynasty pagoda, built in AD 652, is attached to the extant Ci'en Si (Ci'en Temple). Known as Dayan Ta, the pagoda was built in memory of the Gaozong emperor's mother, Empress Wende. The monk Xuanzang, who traveled to India via Central Asia and returned with bundles of *sutras (see p491)*, officiated at the temple, translating the hundreds of scriptures from Sanskrit into Chinese. The 210-ft- (64-m-) high pagoda, built on his orders for their storage, is a square, sturdy structure with a brick exterior and wood interior. At the height of the Tang dynasty, Xi'an's extent was almost seven times larger than it is today, enclosing within its walls both the temple and pagoda.

The Dayan Ta can be climbed, and visitors pay to ring the bell here for good luck. The large temple complex, smaller now than during its Tang heyday, can also be explored. Its main hall contains three statues of the Buddha flanked by 18 *luohan* or *arhats (see p37)*.

At the back of the pagoda is a huge relief depicting scenes from Xi'an's history. North of the pagoda is a giant fountain which has nightly shows timed to music.

A visitor lighting a candle in the courtyard, Great Wild Goose Pagoda

History of the Pagoda

Considered an archetypal element of Chinese architecture, the pagoda originates from India in concept and form as a development from the Buddhist stupa. However, Chinese architectural forms and styles were soon used in the design of pagodas, as can be seen by the pillar pagodas in the Yungang caves that clearly show multi-storied buildings. Over 1,500 years pagodas developed a variety of forms from pillars to squat tombs to soaring multi-story towers. Made of stone, brick, or wood, they could also be square or multi-sided. As they became uniquely Chinese they were also used slightly differently. Originally the focal point of the temple, they were superseded in this by the more functional hall. *Feng shui* led to pagodas being built without a temple on hills outside towns or overlooking rivers, to bring good luck or prevent floods.

The Indian stupa was a symbolic tomb and receptacle for Buddhist relics that inspired the pagoda. However the stupa form was largely dropped until the 13th century when the Yuan imported Tibetan Buddhist stupas (also known as dagobas), popularizing the form for later dynasties.

This Dali pagoda is a beatiful example of a stone close-eaved pagoda. From a square base it is 260-ft (69-m) high, tapering to a lotus bud spike that recalls the Indian stupas.

Octagonal pagodas may have come about as a result of Tantric Buddhism, which used a cosmology with eight cardinal points.

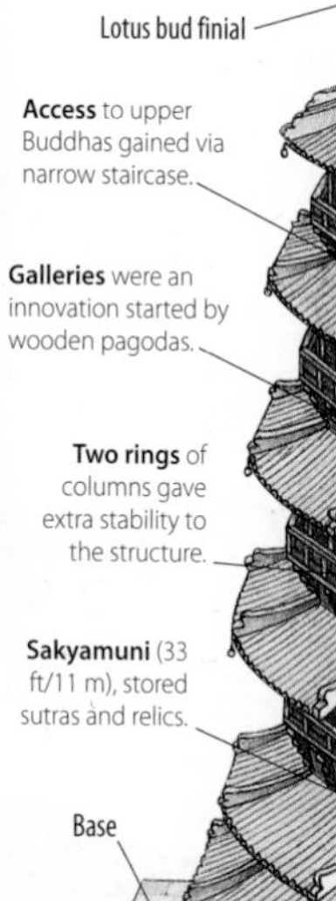
Lotus bud finial
Access to upper Buddhas gained via narrow staircase.
Galleries were an innovation started by wooden pagodas.
Two rings of columns gave extra stability to the structure.
Sakyamuni (33 ft/11 m), stored sutras and relics.
Base

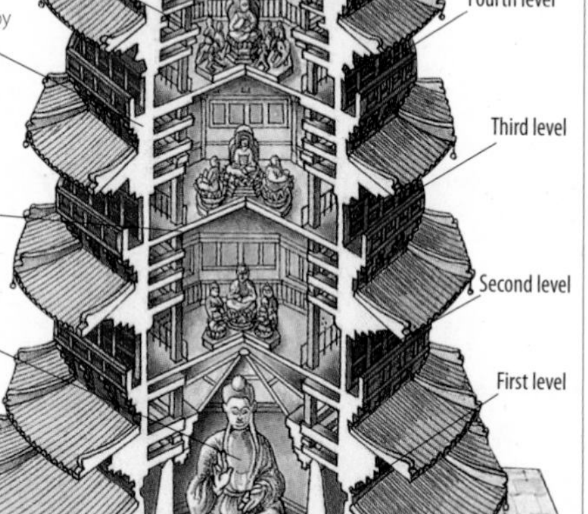
Fifth level
Fourth level
Third level
Second level
First level

Yingxian Pagoda

The wooden pagoda at the Fogong Si, Yingxian, is one of the finest surviving pagodas. Built in 1056, the octagonal building is called the Sakyamuni Pagoda.

Shaanxi History Museum

陕西历史博物馆

One of Xi'an's premier attractions, this roomy, modern museum contains over 370,000 relics chronicling Shaanxi civilization and culture from as far back as prehistoric times. The collection is strong in ceramics, bronzes, jade pieces, gold and silver items, ancient coins, and calligraphy mainly from the pre-Ming periods, reflecting Xi'an's later decline. Look out also for some interesting Tang-dynasty frescoes and the chance to examine some of the renowned terracotta soldiers *(see pp174–5)* up close. Exhibits are well displayed and accompanied by both Chinese and English captions.

Tang-dynasty style architecture of the modern Shaanxi History Museum

★ Shang Cooking Pot

The ogre-mask motif of this vessel is indicative of the Shang society's absorption in the world of nature spirits and supernatural beings. The bronzes of the Shang era are regarded as the dynasty's most significant creative achievement.

Zhou Wine Decanter

Capped with a lid in the shape of a tiger and incorporating a tail-shaped handle, this ox-shaped *zun* (a type of wine vessel) was excavated in 1967. The elaborate surface pattern is typical of Zhou-dynasty animistic design.

Entrance

Key to Floorplan

- Pre-history
- Shang and Zhou dynasties
- Qin dynasty
- Han dynasty
- Northern and Southern dynasties
- Tang dynasty
- Song to Qing dynasties
- Special exhibitions
- Non-exhibition space

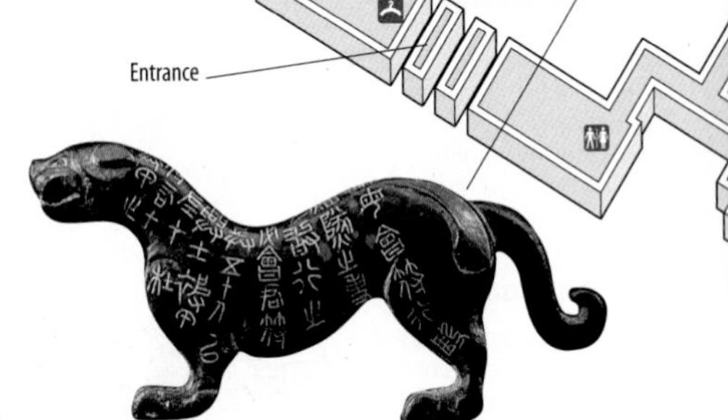

Tiger-Shaped Tally

Inscribed with the archaic script used for Qin official texts, this remarkable bronze artifact was issued to generals to authorize the mobilization of troops.

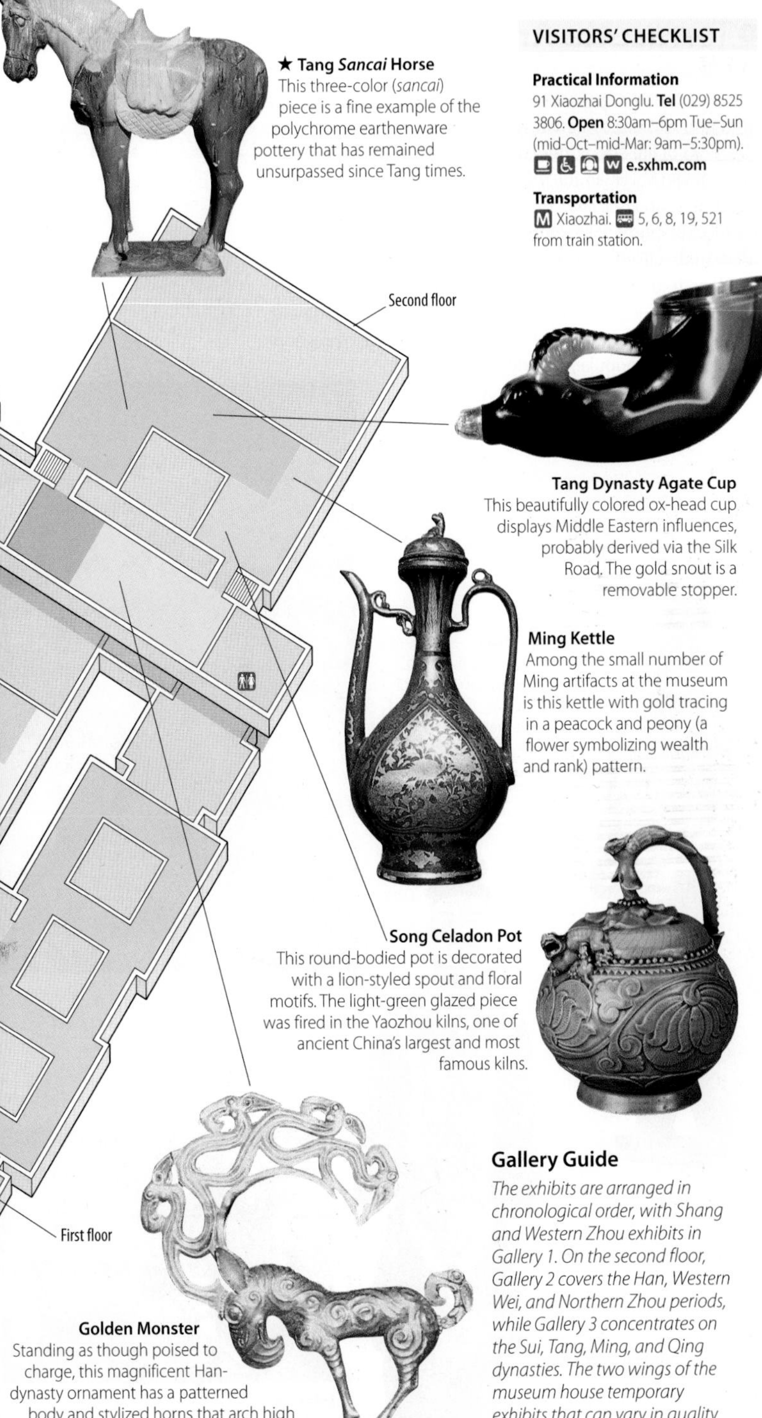

★ Tang *Sancai* Horse
This three-color (*sancai*) piece is a fine example of the polychrome earthenware pottery that has remained unsurpassed since Tang times.

VISITORS' CHECKLIST

Practical Information
91 Xiaozhai Donglu. **Tel** (029) 8525 3806. **Open** 8:30am–6pm Tue–Sun (mid-Oct–mid-Mar: 9am–5:30pm). **e.sxhm.com**

Transportation
Xiaozhai. 5, 6, 8, 19, 521 from train station.

Tang Dynasty Agate Cup
This beautifully colored ox-head cup displays Middle Eastern influences, probably derived via the Silk Road. The gold snout is a removable stopper.

Ming Kettle
Among the small number of Ming artifacts at the museum is this kettle with gold tracing in a peacock and peony (a flower symbolizing wealth and rank) pattern.

Song Celadon Pot
This round-bodied pot is decorated with a lion-styled spout and floral motifs. The light-green glazed piece was fired in the Yaozhou kilns, one of ancient China's largest and most famous kilns.

Golden Monster
Standing as though poised to charge, this magnificent Han-dynasty ornament has a patterned body and stylized horns that arch high over the beast's back and end in a face.

Gallery Guide

The exhibits are arranged in chronological order, with Shang and Western Zhou exhibits in Gallery 1. On the second floor, Gallery 2 covers the Han, Western Wei, and Northern Zhou periods, while Gallery 3 concentrates on the Sui, Tang, Ming, and Qing dynasties. The two wings of the museum house temporary exhibits that can vary in quality and explanation.

❷ Terracotta Army
兵马俑

The Terracotta Army (Emperor Qinshihuang's Mausoleum Site Museum) was discovered in 1974 by peasants digging a well. The ranks of life-size pottery figures were made to guard the tomb of Qin Shi Huangdi, the ruler who unified China over 2,200 years ago *(see p60)*. Excavations yielded three pits and over 7,000 figures. Pit 1 contains the infantry; Pit 2 (still being excavated) is filled with cavalry and soldiers; and Pit 3 (partially unexcavated) seems to be the command center, with 70 high-ranking officers. Each warrior, originally colored with pigment and holding a weapon, has an individually crafted expression. The site is very popular, so arrive before 10am. A guide is recommended to appreciate it fully.

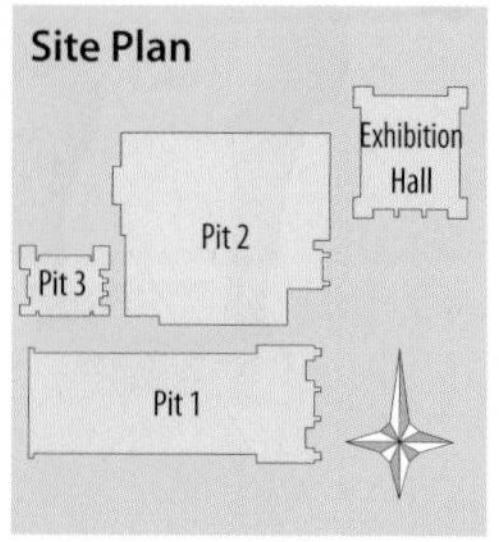

★ Army in Pit 1
The most impressive pit contains over 6,000 warriors, arrayed in battle formation. The rear of the vault is strewn with smashed heads and fragments yet to be assembled.

The pottery horses have been assembled from broken fragments, like the warriors around them.

High-Ranking Officer
Dressed commandingly in a long, two-layered knee-length tunic, this imposing figure is distinguished both by his regalia and by being taller than the pottery infantry figures he appears to oversee.

Original Decoration
All of the figures were originally painted in vivid colors similar to this replica. Some retain traces of paint, but most of them faded after exposure to air.

Infantry
The pottery warriors were originally equipped with weapons, including swords, spears, and bows and arrows, many of which have rotted.

★ Kneeling Archer
Cloaked in upper-body armor and kneeling in a state of preparation, this archer is alert although his wooden bow has disintegrated. His square-toed shoes are studded for extra grip.

VISITORS' CHECKLIST

Practical Information
19 miles (30 km) E of Xi'an. **Tel** (029) 8139 9047. **Open** 8:30am–6pm daily (winter: 5:30pm). **bmy.com.cn**

Transportation
306, 914, 915 from Xi'an train station.

The earth-walled corridors that house the warriors were originally roofed with wooden rafters.

Individual Details
The intricacy is astonishing, especially in the careful execution of individual hairstyles on the hand-sculpted heads. Further artistry is evident in the detailed belts, clothing, and footwear.

Restoring the Army
The work to excavate and restore the terracotta figures continues to this day. Each warrior is unique and must be painstakingly reassembled by a team.

Qin Shi Huangdi's Tomb

The Terracotta Army is just one part, the defending army, of a complex necropolis. A mile west of the pits, a large hill, yet to be fully excavated, is believed to be the burial mound of Emperor Qin Shi, a tyrant preoccupied with death and the legacy he would leave behind. He spared no expense, enlisting 700,000 people over 36 years in the tomb's construction. Historical sources portray a miniature plan of his empire: a floor cut by rivers of mercury beneath a ceiling studded with pearls to represent the night sky. The complex is also said to contain 48 tombs for concubines who were buried alive with the emperor, a fate also reserved for workers, to prevent the location and design of the tomb from becoming known. Two marvelous bronze chariots, originally housed in wooden coffins, were unearthed near the burial mound, and laboriously reassembled. Half actual size, one is made up of over 3,600 metal pieces.

One of the bronze chariots, on display in the Exhibition Hall

Colorful fresco in the tomb of Yi De, Qian Ling

Xi'an: Farther Afield

The sights around Xi'an are best visited by the Western Tour buses that depart from Xi'an train station in the morning. Located 15 miles (25 km) northeast, the modern city of Xianyang, China's first dynastic capital, is mainly visited for its museum and the surrounding imperial tombs. Housed in a former Confucian Temple, the tranquil **Xianyang City Museum** displays relics from Qin and Han times, and its highlight is an army of 3,000 miniature terracotta soldiers excavated from a nearby tomb. **Mao Ling** (Mao Tomb), 25 miles (40 km) west of Xi'an, is the tomb of the Han emperor Wudi (141–87 BC). The largest of the Han tombs in the surrounding region, it has a museum that houses stone sculptures and further relics from the tomb complex. The impressive **Qian Ling** (Qian Tomb), 50 miles (80 km) northwest of Xi'an, is the burial site of the Tang Gaozong emperor and his wife, the indomitable Wu Zetian *(see p63)*. The Imperial Way is lined with stone figures, while the southeast section of the area contains 17 lesser tombs, including the vividly frescoed tombs of Prince Zhang Huai, the emperor's second son, and crown prince Yi De, the emperor's grandson. The mountainside mausoleum of the Tang Taizong emperor lies at **Zhao Ling** (Zhao Tomb), 43 miles (70 km) northwest of Xi'an.

Stele in Yi De's Tomb, Qian Ling

Situated 74 miles (120 km) northwest of Xi'an, the remote **Famen Temple** is well worth the long journey. This shrine is one of China's first Buddhist temples, and a venerated place for Buddhist pilgrims the world over. It was built in the 2nd century AD to house a finger bone of Sakyamuni (the Historical Buddha) donated by the Indian king Ashoka, who was dispensing Buddhist relics *(sarira)* among Buddhist lands. The sacred bone enjoyed extensive veneration, and was periodically removed from the temple crypt and paraded through the streets of Xi'an during the height of the Tang era. After the dynasty's fall, the crypt was lost in obscurity, possibly as a result of anti-Buddhist purges. It is surprising that the crypt remained hidden for so long, as pagodas often have vaults for storing relics and Buddhist ornaments. In the 1980s, an exploration following a partial collapse of the pagoda exposed the crypt, along with its relics and Tang-dynasty riches. Today, the finger bone is once again preserved in a crypt, while the temple museum displays many Tang-era artifacts. The sacred bone is occasionally taken abroad, as it was in 2003, when it went to Taipei in Taiwan.

Xianyang City Museum
53 Zhongshan Jie. 59 or K630 from Xi'an to Xianyang, then bus 7, 19, or 24. **Tel** (029) 3323 1998. **Open** 9am–5:30pm Tue–Sun.

Mao, Qian & Zhao Ling
59 or K630 from Xi'an to Xianyang, then taxi. **Open** 8am–6pm daily (Dec & Jan: 8:30am–5:30pm).

Famen Temple
Tel (0917) 525 4002. from Xi'an station, bus 2. **Open** 8am–5:30pm daily (winter: 8:30am–5pm).
fmscf.org

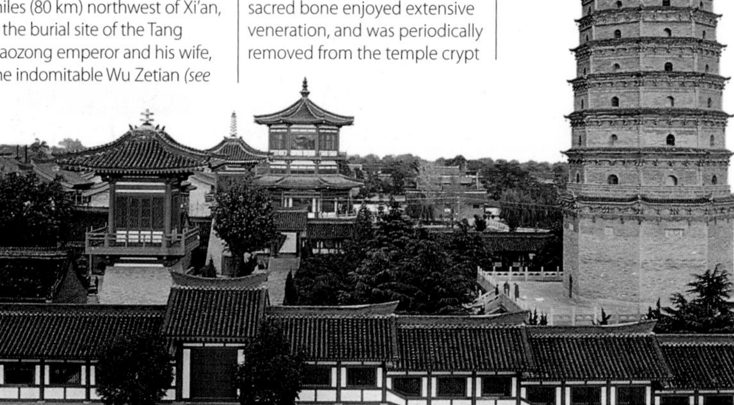

The 12-storied pagoda at the Famen Temple, now restored to its former glory

For hotels and restaurants in this region see p559 and p575

Pilgrims and hikers winding their way up North Peak, Hua Shan

❸ Hua Shan
华山

75 miles (120 km) E of Xi'an. from X'ian to Menyuan, then bus. bus 1 (suspended Jan–Mar) at 8am, from X'ian train station to Huayin, then shuttle to entrance. **Tel** 400 0913 777. **Open** 7am–7pm daily (Dec–Feb: 9am–5pm daily). Cable car available.

The westernmost and loftiest of China's five Daoist peaks, the 8,563-ft (2,610-m) high Hua Shan is characterized by steep ascents, precipitous gullies, and peerless views. Crowned by five peaks (North, South, East, West, and Central), and towering southwest of the Yellow River as it loops east along the Henan–Shanxi border, Hua Shan (Flower Mountain) was traditionally likened to a lotus bloom. Also known by its other name, Xiyue (Western Peak), the mountain is believed to be presided over by the Daoist God of Hua Shan. For centuries, it was a magnet for hermits and ascetics in pursuit of immortality, and its crags and crannies still teem with Daoist myths. Its numerous temples have dwindled over the years, although several survive perched on the mountain.

Hikers can either drift to North Peak by cable car from the station at the eastern base, or make the strenuous 3-5-hour trek along with hordes of pilgrims from Huayin. From North Peak, you can either descend or follow the trail along the ridge to the other four peaks lying to the south. Spring and autumn are the best seasons to climb Hua Shan, since summers and winters are extreme. Night-time ascents can also be made. It is best to carry food with you, though refreshments are available from vendors and at hotels along the trail. Wear shoes or boots with a rugged grip as certain sections are treacherous. Near the summits, bunches of padlocks hang on chains. According to the custom, couples have their names engraved on them and then lock them here forever. Accommodation is available in Huayin and on the mountain itself for overnight stays and watching the sunrise from East Peak.

Padlocks engraved with couples' names, Hua Shan

❹ Yan'an
延安

155 miles (250 km) N of Xi'an. 200,000. from Xi'an and Beijing. CITS (0911) 238 9063.

Quiet Yan'an, within the Loess hills of northern Shaanxi, is best explored by train from Xi'an. The town was the Communist Party's headquarters for a decade after the culmination of the Long March *(see p262)* in October 1935. In the north of town, the **Yan'an Revolution Memorial Hall** houses a display of Communist relics, including Mao's stuffed horse, weapons, photographs, and uniforms (few captions are in English). Nearby, the **Wangjiaping Revolution Headquarters Site** is where Mao and other front-rank party leaders worked and lived. The **Fenghuang Shan Lu Revolution Headquarters Site**, the early residence of the Communists, houses memorabilia of prominent officers. Perched on a hill southeast of town, and with impressive views, is the Ming-dynasty **Yan'an Bao Pagoda**, which sometimes features on Communist memorabilia.

Yan'an Revolution Memorial Hall
Baota Qu. 6. **Tel** (0911) 821 3666. **Open** 8:30am–4:30pm daily.
yagmjng.com

Wangjiaping Revolution Headquarters Site
Wangjiaping. 1, 8. **Tel** (0911) 233 5979. **Open** 7am–6pm Tue–Sun.

CENTRAL CHINA

Central China at a Glance

Dominated by the mighty Yangzi River, China's central region encompasses the east coast port city of Shanghai and the six provinces of Jiangsu, Anhui, Zhejiang, Jiangxi, Hunan, and Hubei, that fan out from it to the north, south, and west. The region is rich in historic sights as well as natural beauty, including the attractive city of Nanjing, with its largely intact city wall, and the splendid scenery around Zhejiang's West Lake and Anhui's Huang Shan mountain. The cultured cities of Hangzhou and Suzhou lie on the banks of the Grand Canal, one of the greatest engineering feats in China's early history. A more up-to-date colossal feat of construction, the Three Gorges Dam, on the Yangzi River in Hubei, is the world's largest.

View from Jiuhuashan, a sacred Buddhist mountain.

Tranquil scene in Shizi Lin (Lion Grove Garden), Suzhou

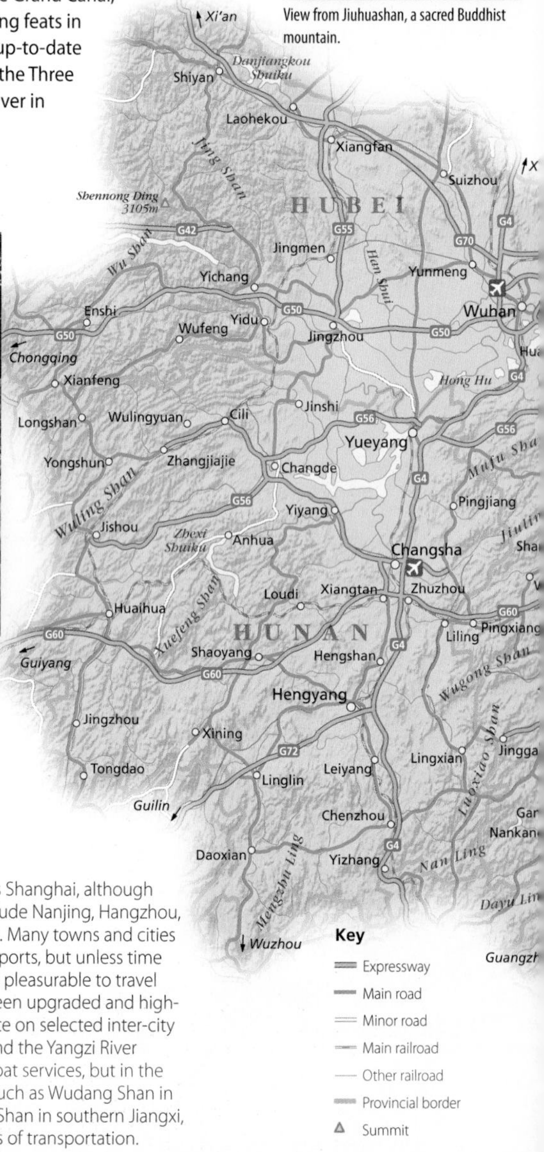

Key

Expressway

Main road

Minor road

Main railroad

Other railroad

Provincial border

Summit

Getting Around

The region's main airport hub is Shanghai, although other international airports include Nanjing, Hangzhou, Wuhan, Ningbo, and Changsha. Many towns and cities in the region have domestic airports, but unless time is really an issue, it can be more pleasurable to travel by train. The rail network has been upgraded and high-speed CRH "bullet" trains operate on selected inter-city routes. Both the Grand Canal and the Yangzi River operate tourist ferry or canal-boat services, but in the remote mountainous regions such as Wudang Shan in northern Hubei, and Jinggang Shan in southern Jiangxi, bus travel is the quickest means of transportation.

◀ The Shanghai skyline by night

Temple buildings on the island of Putuo Shan, off the east coast of Zhejiang

A PORTRAIT OF CENTRAL CHINA

From the modern city of Shanghai to the historic and picturesque canal towns, central China encapsulates the essence of the country and its culture. The region can also be considered the crucible of modern China, as many of the stirring historical events that shaped the nation took place here in the early 20th century.

The Yangzi (Chang Jiang), which flows into the East China Sea just below Shanghai, is the thread that binds all of central China together. The combination of water and silt has fertilized vast areas, especially around Wuhan, referred to as "China's Grain Basket," or the "Land of Fish and Rice." Despite its tendency to flood, the river has for centuries been a vital conduit for China's trade, crowded with sampans and junks, as observed by Marco Polo in the 13th century, as well as tea clippers in the 19th century and ferries and cruise ships today. The river has also accelerated the country's development: without the Yangzi there would have been no Grand Canal and no Shanghai. Now, with the controversial construction of the Three Gorges Dam, the river has been used again to supply the requirements of China's vast, sprawling population.

Shanghai, which actually sits on the Huangpu River, a small tributary of the Yangzi, is something of an upstart, despite its reputation. A small provincial town until the mid-19th century, it evolved to become China's greatest city. Even after the Cultural Revolution it remained the country's fashion and shopping capital as well as a great industrial powerhouse. It is, today, one of the most visible symbols of "new" China's vitality and dynamism. Shanghai has experienced massive urban renewal after hosting many international events, and the city has positioned itself as a world financial center.

Politically too, Shanghai's impact has been enormous; it was the site of the first meeting of the Chinese Communist Party and the spawning ground for the Cultural Revolution and the Gang of Four, all of whom had strong connections with the city.

The Yangzi Bridge in Wuhan city, opened in 1957, spans the Yangzi River from Hanyang (north bank) to Wuchang (south bank)

Tour boats on one of Tongli's many canals

In fact, nearly all of the major political events of 20th-century China took place in its central provinces. Nanjing, the first Ming capital, was also Chiang Kai-shek's Republican center. Chairman Mao was born and educated, and began his revolutionary activities in Hunan. In Jiangxi, the 1927 Nanchang Uprising was the rallying point for the creation of the Red Army, while the same province was the starting point of the Long March. That revolution should ignite so easily was not surprising, since Anhui, Hunan, and Jiangxi, large parts of which are mountainous and remote from the Yangzi and seats of power, have always been associated with appalling poverty.

Detail from the Ming Palace Ruins, Nanjing

However, long before the fall of the last emperor, this was where many of the greatest features of pre-Revolutionary Chinese culture flowered during the brilliance of the Song and Ming dynasties. Before establishing their capital in Beijing, the Ming left their mark on Nanjing, as evidenced by the huge Ming tomb and formidable city wall, while Hangzhou, a former Song capital, is the location of the West Lake, one of China's most scenic places. Just as remarkable are the region's gardens and workshops producing silk embroidery and porcelain. Suzhou, in Jiangsu, has to some extent retained some of its ancient charm and is renowned for its private gardens, which have survived the upheavals of recent history largely intact. Porcelain production continues alongside the historic imperial kilns of Jingdezhen, while silk, produced throughout parts of the region, is still a major export, as it was a thousand years ago.

Considering that central China is a heavily populated region largely shaped by man's manipulation of nature, it is surprising that there are still large areas of wilderness to enjoy. This is best illustrated in the legend of the Wild Man, China's equivalent of the Yeti, who is said to haunt Shennongjia in Hubei. For those wishing to escape urban or pastoral China, there are many opportunities, from the scenic beauty around Taihu Lake in Jiangsu to the mountain vistas at Hunan's Wulingyuan and Zhejiang's Yandang Shan.

Suspension bridge at the Divine Cliffs, Yandang Shan

Traditional Chinese Gardens

The Chinese garden developed as a synthesis of two concepts linked in Daoist philosophy *(see p37)* – scenery and serenity: the contemplation of nature in isolated meditation led to enlightenment. Therefore, the educated and wealthy built natural-looking retreats for themselves within an urban environment. The garden creates poetic and painterly concepts, and aims to improve on nature by creating a picture that looks natural but is in fact entirely artificial. For this the Chinese garden designer used four main elements: rocks, water, plants, and architecture.

Classical Chinese garden design was considered a type of three-dimensional landscape painting or solid poetry.

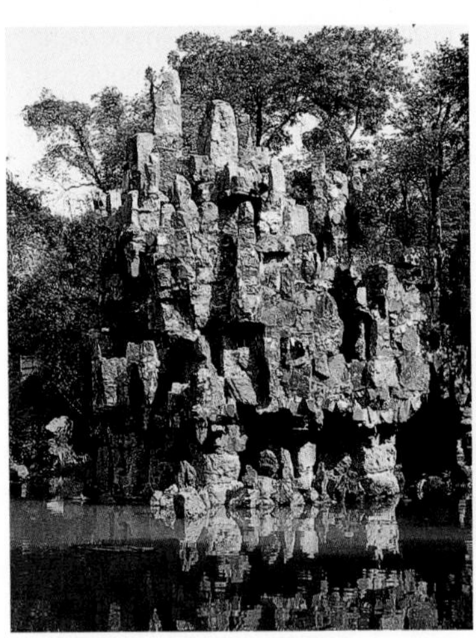

Rocks: There were two main kinds of rock – the eroded limestones from lakes, often used as sculptures, or the yellow rock piled up to recall mountains and caves to the mind of the viewer. The beauty and realism of the rockery usually determined the success or failure of the garden.

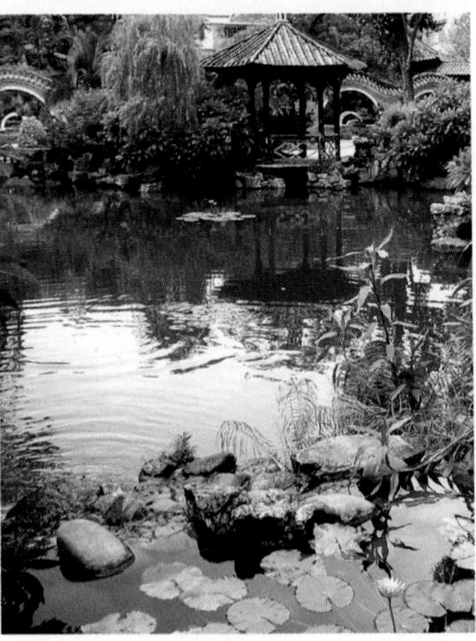

Water: An essential element of life, water could be used in the garden as a mirror and so appear to increase the size of the garden. Water also serves as a contrasting partner and therefore a balance to the hard stone. Finally it is a home for goldfish, symbols of good fortune.

Corridors, paths, and bridges link the different areas and give the artist control over how the views are presented to the visitor.

Interiors of pavilions were important as the venues for creativity. A lot of care was taken to select an appropriate and poetic name for each building.

Patterns and mosaics brighten up the garden and are also symbolic. Cranes represent longevity, while the *yin* and *yang* symbol often appears where a path forks in two.

Garden Views

Using these four elements the garden is like a series of tableaux painted onto a roll of silk. One by one they come before your eyes just as the artist intended them to. As you follow the paths, you see just what he wanted you to see. These may be borrowed views, where the scenery from somewhere else is made to look part of the picture; hidden views, where you round a corner to come upon an unexpected scene; or contrasting views where leafy bamboo softens the view of rock, or opposite views as the *yin* element water balances the *yang* element rock.

A moon gate is a round door that neatly frames a view as though it were a picture. Gates can be square-, jar-, or even book-shaped.

Patterned screens allow in a certain amount of light and may be used to cast patterned shadows on white walls. They are also sometimes used to give tempting partial views through to other areas of the garden.

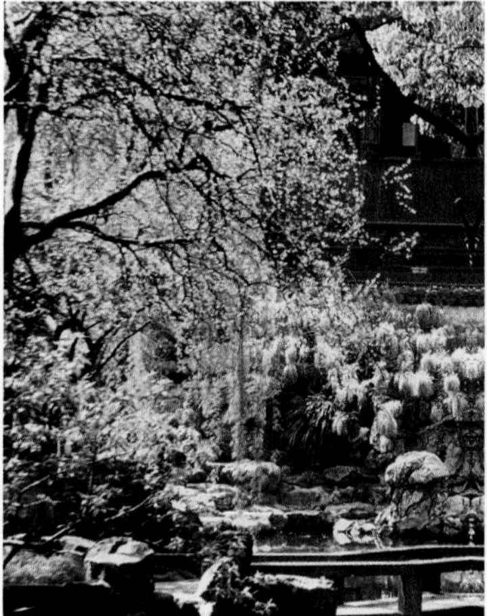

Plants: Plants were used sparingly and usually for their symbolic qualities. Thus the lotus is purity, as it flowers from the mud; bamboo is resolve, it is difficult to break; plum is vigor, as it blooms in winter; the pine is longevity, for it is an evergreen; the imperial peony is wealth.

Buildings: An intrinsic part of the garden, these pavilions and waterside halls provide a place for contemplation and, more importantly, a specific viewpoint, as well as shelter from the sun and rain. They could range from open kiosks to multi-story halls and meeting rooms.

Penjing

Dating as far back as the Tang dynasty (618–907), *penjing* is the art of creating a miniature landscape in a container. Not limited to small trees, the artist may use rocks and specially cultivated plants to portray a scene of natural beauty, as though it were a landscape painting. As well as being beautiful, the harmony in these creations is seen as the spiritual expression of man's relationship with nature, the meeting of the temporal with the omnipresent. Often part of a Chinese garden will be devoted to the display or cultivation of this delicate art.

The Chinese art of *penjing*, the forerunner to Japanese bonsai

Regional Food: Central China

Traditionally referred to as the "Lands of Fish and Rice," central China is one of the country's leading agricultural regions along with with some of the most fertile land. Both wheat and rice are grown here as well as barley, corn, sweet potatoes, peanuts, and soybeans. Freshwater fisheries abound in the network of lakes and rivers, while deep-sea fishing has long been established in the coastal provinces. In the holy mountains of Huang Shan and Jiuhua Shan, Buddhist vegetarianism has also influenced the region's cuisine. Hunan's cuisine is like Sichuanese food but even spicier *(see pp352–3)*.

Garlic chives and bok choi

Market stall displaying the wide variety of dried goods available

Shanghai

The characteristics of Shanghai cuisine are summarized as "exquisite in appearance, rich in flavor, and sweet in taste." A favorite winter delicacy is the hairy crab from the Yangzi estuary (although overfishing means they tend to come from elsewhere). A relatively new city, Shanghai has not really developed its own cuisine, although it has its own famous filled dumplings called *xiao long bao*. Instead the city's main influences are older schools of cuisine – Huaiyang and Suzhe. Another culinary influence is the Buddhist school of cuisine. Strangely, the best Buddhist vegetarian restaurants are to be found in Shanghai – a city with a racy reputation. Maybe the sinners want to redeem themselves by abstaining from meat occasionally. Dishes tend to have have similar names to meat dishes and, thanks to the skillful use of soy sauce, tofu, gluten, and agar, they can look and even taste like meat.

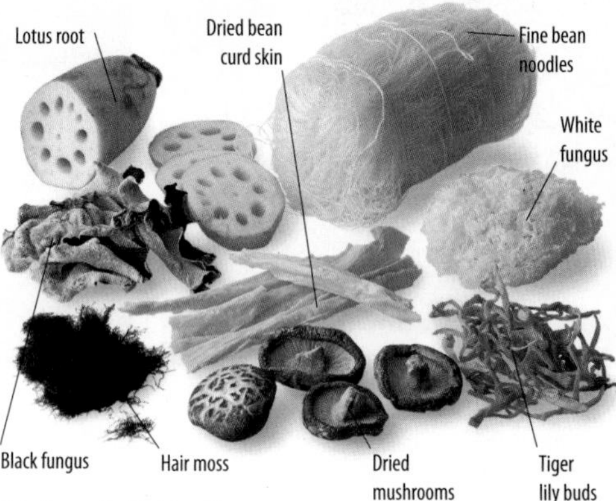

Eight-Treasure Buddha's Special

Regional Dishes & Specialties

Fermented bean curd

Two of the area's great cities, Nanjing and Hangzhou, were at different times capitals in central China. Whenever there was a change of capital, the vast imperial kitchens changed location, bringing the staff with them, which resulted in a cross-fertilization of recipes and methods from one region to another. One favorite imperial dish despite its lowly name is Beggar's Chicken – a whole chicken is stuffed with vegetables and herbs, wrapped in lotus leaves, and encased in clay before being baked. The clay container is then broken at the table releasing the beautiful aromas. A central China specialty (but actually enjoyed all over) is red fermented bean curd. This has a pungent, cheese-like flavor that is also very savory and appears in vegetarian and meat dishes alike. Freshwater crabs are best during October and November, simply steamed with spring onions, ginger, soy, sugar, and vinegar.

Lions' Heads: pork meatballs braised with Chinese leaf – meant to look like lions' heads and manes.

Huaiyang & Suzhe

Based specifically around the deltas of the Huai and Yangzi Rivers, Huaiyang cuisine is most famous for its excellent fish and shellfish – the freshwater crabs from Tai Hu are superb. Suzhe cuisine, however, covers a wider area – the provinces of Jiangsu and Zhejiang – and includes culinary centers such as Nanjing and Hangzhou that both served as capital cities. Along with stews flavored with a light stock, the region is famous for its "red cooking" – food braised in soy sauce, sugar, ginger, and rice wine. "Chinkiang Vinegar" is black rice vinegar from Zhenjiang, Jiangsu, and is acknowledged to be the best rice vinegar in China.

Eels, a popular ingredient from the rivers of central China

The province of Zhejiang produces China's best rice wines from Shaoxing and top-quality hams from Jinhua. It is also worth trying the Long Jing (Dragon Well) green tea grown around West Lake in Hangzhou.

Park cafés – popular places to snack on some filled dumplings

Anhui

Further inland is the little-known Anhui cuisine, which has a long history, but is often overlooked by visitors. Despite being landlocked, Anhui still enjoys a lot of fish thanks to its network of lakes and rivers. The province is also one of the leading agricultural regions in China, producing a great number and variety of crops and vegetables. One of Anhui's famed ingredients are its tender white bamboo shoots. These crisp shoots feature prominently in the vegetarian cuisine prepared in the lofty Buddhist mountain retreats and are often combined with a variety of exotic woodland mushrooms. Finally the world-famous Keemun red tea – it is actually black – comes from the humid hills of Qimen in south Anhui.

ON THE MENU

Beggar's Chicken A whole chicken stuffed with flavorings and cooked in a clay pot.

Fried Prawns in Shells Prawns still in their shells are rapidly fried and then braised in a soy and tomato sauce.

Three-Layer Shreds Steamed shredded ham, chicken, and pork with bamboo shoots and black mushroom – should be called five-layer shreds.

Freshwater Crabs Simply steamed with scallions, ginger, soy, sugar, and vinegar.

Steamed Belly Pork with Ground Rice Also known as double-braised pork, this long-cooked dish melts in your mouth.

Eight-Treasure Buddha's Special A generic name for a delicious vegetarian dish which can actually contain any number of different ingredients.

Tofu Casserole: tofu with sea cucumbers, ham, prawns, mushrooms, bamboo shoots, and bok choi in a stew pot.

Squirrel Fish: a bream is filleted, coated with batter, deep-fried, and served with a sweet-and-sour sauce.

Sweet and Sour Spare Ribs: deep-fried bite-size pork spare ribs braised in soy, sugar, and vinegar.

SHANGHAI

Straddling both banks of the Huangpu River, close to the mouth of the mighty Yangzi on China's eastern seaboard, Shanghai is the nation's largest and most dynamic city, with a population of more than 24 million people. It is an autonomous municipality, and an explosion of economic and industrial development has made it one of the fastest growing cities in the world.

By Chinese standards, the development of Shanghai, which means "above the sea," is a recent phenomenon. In the 13th century it became a minor county seat and so it remained until the mid-19th century when British commercial ambitions led to war with China. The ensuing Treaty of Nanking allowed the British to trade freely from certain ports, including Shanghai. The city soon became an outpost of glamor, high living, and ultimately decadence. It was divided into "concessions," where foreign nationals lived in miniature versions of first Britain, then France, the US, and Japan. The Bund, or quay along the Huangpu, is still lined with concession-era buildings, evidence of a time when Shanghai was the third largest financial center in the world. In 1949, the Communists took over and the city was stripped of its grandeur. However, in 1990, the Pudong area across the river from the Bund was declared a Special Economic Zone, and a revival started. Investments poured in; flyovers, malls, and hotels sprang up, and shining metal and glass skyscrapers towered above the Huangpu. This infrastructure boom skyrocketed into the new millennium. Both airports are state-of-the-art, with Pudong serviced by a 268-mph (431-km/h) maglev train, and the city is a hub of China's impressive high-speed network. Today, from the Shanghai Tower, China's tallest building, to the latest street fashions, Shanghai is the best place in the country to get a feel for the China of the future.

Exterior of the renowned Shanghai Museum

◀ Oriental Pearl Tower – a prime example of modern architecture in China

Exploring Shanghai

Of Shanghai's three main areas, the Old City to the south is typically Chinese, with alleys, markets, and temples. It is also the site of the Yu Gardens (Yu Yuan), Shanghai's finest traditional garden. The former concession areas comprise the French Concession to the Old City's west and the British and American Concessions – collectively known as the International Settlement – to its north. Here are the Bund – the riverside promenade lined with grand colonial buildings, including the Fairmont Peace Hotel and the Waldorf Astoria Hotel – and the city's two main shopping streets, Nanjing Road and Huaihai Road. Pudong, Shanghai's newest district, on the Huangpu's east bank, has some of the world's highest commercial buildings.

Sights at a Glance

Historic Buildings, Sites & Neighborhoods

1 *The Bund pp192–3*
5 Pudong
7 Site of the First National Congress of the Chinese Communist Party
9 French Concession
10 Shanghai Exhibition Center
15 Soong Qingling Memorial Residence
17 Longhua Cemetery of Martyrs

Temples & Churches

11 Jing'an Temple
12 Jade Buddha Temple
16 Xujiahui Catholic Cathedral

Parks & Gardens

3 People's Park and Square
6 *Yu Gardens and Bazaar pp198–9*
8 Fuxing Park
14 Lu Xun Park

Museums

4 *Shanghai Museum pp196–7*
13 Jewish Refugee Museum

Town

19 Song Jiang

Shops & Markets

2 Nanjing Road

Area of Natural Beauty

18 She Shan

Getting Around

The city metro is the best way of getting around Shanghai. Its network is rapidly expanding, with many new lines completed before the 2010 World Expo, and several more under construction *(see p620)*. Taxis are convenient, cheap, and plentiful. There are plenty of buses, but these tend to be crowded and slow due to the traffic congestion, especially during the morning and evening rush hours. Each bus has its own schedule, which can be complicated to follow.

For additional map symbols *see back flap*

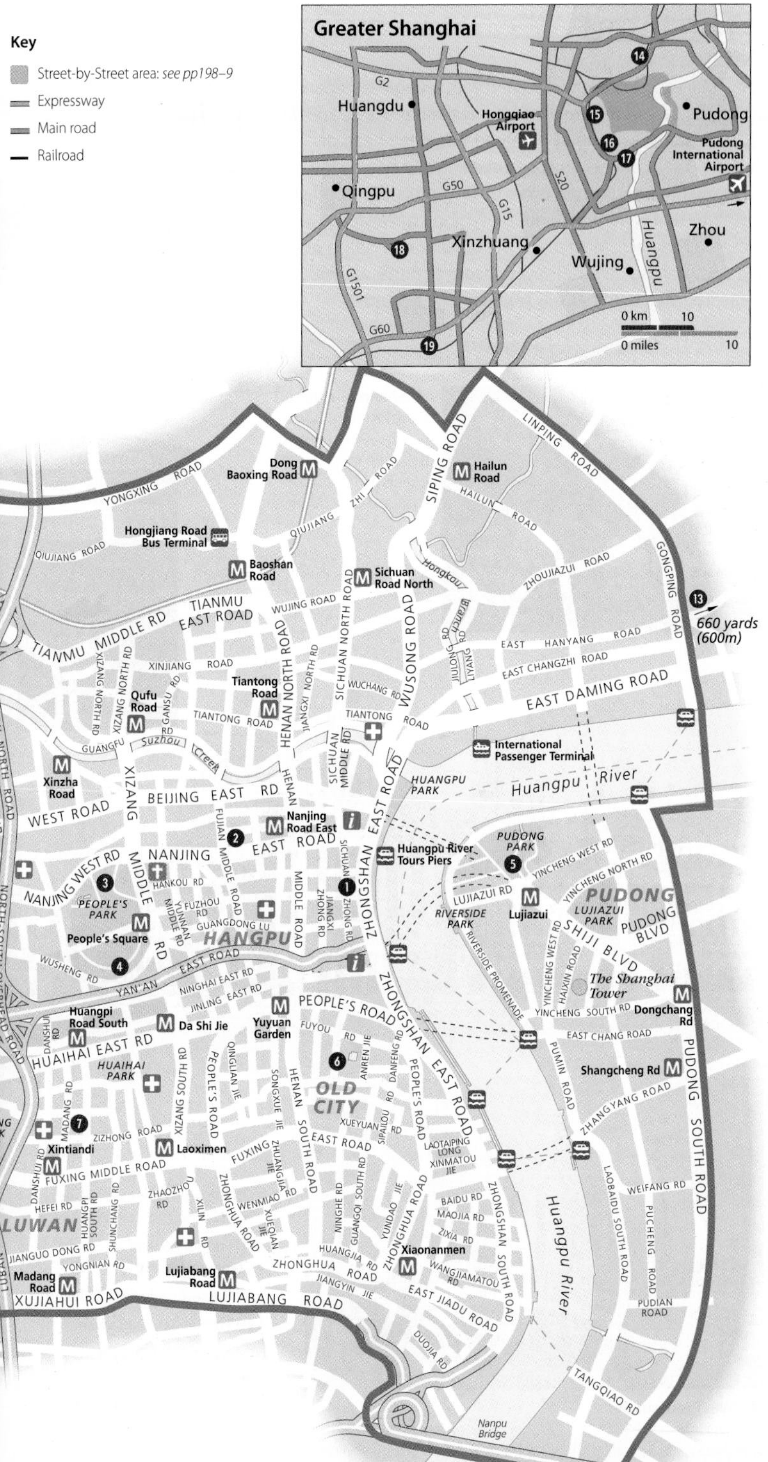

Key
Street-by-Street area: see pp198–9
Expressway
Main road
Railroad
Greater Shanghai
Huangdu
Hongqiao Airport
Pudong
Pudong International Airport
Qingpu
G2
G50
G15
S20
G1501
G60
Xinzhuang
Wujing
Zhou
Huangpu
0 km 10
0 miles 10
Dong Baoxing Road
Hailun Road
Hongjiang Road Bus Terminal
Baoshan Road
Sichuan Road North
660 yards (600m)
Tiantong Road
Qufu Road
Xinzha Road
International Passenger Terminal
Huangpu River
HUANGPU PARK
Nanjing Road East
Huangpu River Tours Piers
PUDONG PARK
PEOPLE'S PARK
People's Square
Lujiazui
PUDONG
LUJIAZUI PARK
RIVERSIDE PARK
HANGPU
The Shanghai Tower
Dongchang Rd
Huangpi Road South
Da Shi Jie
Yuyuan Garden
HUAIHAI PARK
Shangcheng Rd
OLD CITY
Xintiandi
Laoximen
LUWAN
Xiaonanmen
Madang Road
Lujiabang Road
Huangpu River
Nanpu Bridge
YONGXING ROAD
QIUJIANG ROAD
TIANMU MIDDLE RD
TIANMU EAST ROAD
WUJING ROAD
SIPING ROAD
LINPING ROAD
HAILUN ROAD
ZHOUJIAZUI ROAD
GONGPING ROAD
EAST HANYANG ROAD
EAST CHANGZHI ROAD
EAST DAMING ROAD
XINJIANG ROAD
TIANTONG ROAD
HENAN NORTH ROAD
SICHUAN NORTH ROAD
WUSONG ROAD
BEIJING EAST RD
NANJING EAST ROAD
NANJING WEST RD
XIZANG MIDDLE RD
ZHONGSHAN EAST ROAD
YINCHENG WEST RD
YINCHENG NORTH RD
LUJIAZUI RD
SHIJI BLVD
PUDONG BLVD
RIVERSIDE PROMENADE
YAN'AN EAST ROAD
PEOPLE'S ROAD
HUAIHAI EAST RD
EAST CHANG ROAD
PUDONG SOUTH ROAD
ZHANGYANG ROAD
FUXING MIDDLE ROAD
FUXING EAST ROAD
HENAN SOUTH ROAD
ZHONGHUA ROAD
EAST JIADU ROAD
ZHONGSHAN SOUTH ROAD
XUJIAHUI ROAD
LUJIABANG ROAD
WEIFANG RD
LAOBAIDU SOUTH ROAD
PUDIAN ROAD
TANGQIAO RD
NORTH-SOUTH OVERHEAD ROAD

❶ The Bund

外滩

Some places are forever associated with a single landmark, and in the case of Shanghai it is surely the Bund. Also known as Zhongshan East 1 Road, the Bund was at the heart of the post-1842 concession era, flanked on one side by the Huangpu River and on the other by the hotels, banks, offices, and clubs that were the grandiose symbols of Western commercial power. Most of the old buildings are still in place and a walk along here can easily absorb a couple of pleasant hours. The area is immensely popular on weekends.

The Bund, at its peak the third biggest financial center in the world

★ Shanghai Pudong Development Bank
Built in 1921, this was said to be the most beautiful building in Asia. Inside there are delightful murals.

★ Customs House
The entrance hall is decorated with some handsome marine mosaics.

★ River Promenade
The riverside of the Bund is a wonderful place for taking a stroll, watching the river traffic, and viewing the varied Pudong skyline.

KEY

① **The bronze lions'** paws and head are rubbed for good luck.

② **Former Bank of Communications**

③ **Russo-Asiatic Bank Building**

④ **Former Bank of Taiwan**

⑤ **North China Daily News Building**

⑥ **Chartered Bank Building** of India, Australia, and China.

★ Views of Pudong
In the evening the Bund throngs with people enjoying the river breeze and the spectacular lights of Pudong's modern skyline (*see p195*).

Bank of China
Blending 1920s American and traditional Chinese styles, this impressive block was built by a rival of Sassoon, H. H. Kung.

Former Palace Hotel
The Palace Hotel was built in 1906 and was one of the best hotels in Shanghai. It is now called the Swatch Art Peace Hotel.

Fairmont Peace Hotel
The most distinctive building on the Bund was built in 1930 by the millionaire Sir Victor Sassoon. Famous visitors include actor Charlie Chaplin and playwright Noel Coward.

Chen Yi's statue
The bronze statue looking down the Bund is not Chairman Mao but Chen Yi, revolutionary commander and first mayor of Shanghai after 1949.

❷ Nanjing Road
南京路

Ⓜ Nanjing Road East, Nanjing Road West.

Running west from the Bund, Nanjing Road has historically been considered Shanghai's foremost shopping street, despite competition from areas such as chic Huaihai Road. The street is divided in two – Nanjing Road East runs from the Bund to People's Square, after which it becomes Nanjing Road West, a total length of 6 miles (10 km). The traditional "shopper's paradise" is along pedestrianized Nanjing Road East, which is filled with upscale brand malls, stores, and boutiques. Theaters, cinemas, restaurants, and beauty salons complete the picture. Before 1949, all the major stores were located here. One of them, the Sun Department Store, is now the **Shanghai No.1 Department Store**, which attracts 100,000 customers every day with its exotic window displays. The pedestrianized section of Nanjing Road East between People's Park and the Bund, with its numerous 1930s European-style buildings, is perpetually busy. The road culminates on People's Square in front of the **Pacific Hotel**, with its impressive exterior and fine plasterwork interior, and the dark and brooding **Park Hotel**, once one of the city's most fashionable hotels, as well as China's tallest building when it was built in 1934. Farther west, the area between Nanjing Road West and Jing'An Temple metro station was formerly known as Bubbling Well Road after the well near Jing'an Temple. It is more upscale and less crowded, with exclusive shopping and residential developments such as Plaza 66, Westgate Mall, and the **Shanghai Center** *(see p206)*. There is a clutch of designer shops, restaurants, and apartments around the Portman Ritz-Carlton Hotel, opposite the Shanghai Exhibition Center.

The Park Hotel, formerly one of the most fashionable addresses in town

The impressive Shanghai Grand Theater

❸ People's Park and Square
人民广场

Nanjing Road West. Ⓜ People's Square. **Open** 6am–6pm daily.

Opposite The Park Hotel is the oval-shaped former Racecourse, now occupied by People's Square and incorporating the pleasantly landscaped People's Park (Renmin Gong Yuan), the Shanghai Museum and Shanghai Grand Theater. Most people visit the park to walk, gossip, exercise, or simply watch the world go by. The park is ringed by gleaming glass-and-metal skyscrapers. Facing it on its eastern side is **Mu'en Tang**, the Merciful Baptism Church that was built in 1929 as the American Baptist Church. An inter-denominational survivor of China's many revolutions, it is open to all and foreign nationals are welcome, but the services are only in Chinese.

Within the park itself is the elegant glass box of **MOCA Shanghai**, the Museum of Contemporary Art. Its two floors house regularly changing exhibitions of cutting-edge art and design. At the northwest corner of the park is the old racecourse clubhouse *(see p203)*.

Opposite the Shanghai Museum is the **Shanghai Urban Planning Exhibition Hall**, which traces the huge urban development projects that have taken place in recent years. The highlight is a whole floor dedicated to a scale model of Shanghai, showing all existing and approved buildings.

At the northwest corner of People's Square is the **Shanghai Grand Theatre** *(see p206)*, made almost entirely of glass and topped by a spectacular convex roof. It is worth a visit for a meal with a view in one of its restaurants or just to look around, and tours are also available.

✝ Mu'en Tang
316 Xizang Middle Rd. **Tel** (021) 6322 5069. **Open** 7am–8pm daily. ✝ 7:30 & 10am, 2 & 7pm Sun.

MOCA Shanghai
Tel (021) 6327 9900. **Open** 10am–6pm daily. **mocashanghai.org**

Shanghai Urban Planning Exhibition Hall
100 Renmin Ave. **Tel** (021) 6318 4477. **Open** 9am–5pm Tue–Sun.

Shanghai Grand Theatre
Tel (021) 6386 8686. **Open** 9am–5pm daily. **shgtheatre.com**

❹ Shanghai Museum

See pp196–7.

❺ Pudong

浦东

East bank of Huangpu. M from People's Square to Lujiazui. People's Square. Cross-River ferry terminal.

In the mid-20th century, Pudong, facing the Bund on the other side of Huangpu, was a squalid huddle of slums and brothels and the home of the notorious gangster Du Yuesheng, or Big-Eared Du. In 1990, it acquired the status of Special Economic Zone, and became one of the largest building sites in the world. The transformation has been remarkable – a forest of skyscrapers grew as investment poured in. The 1,500-ft (457-m) **Oriental Pearl TV Tower** offers views across the city from halfway up, and houses some of the collections of the **Shanghai History Museum**. The 1,379-ft (421-m) **Jinmao Tower**'s 88th-floor observation deck has views down on the Pearl. Both are surpassed by the **Shanghai Tower Pudong**, the world's second-tallest building after Dubai's Burj Khalifa, with the world's highest observation deck on its 118th floor.

Also in Pudong is the **China Art Museum**, which has a large collection of Chinese modern art.

Oriental Pearl TV Tower
1 Century Blvd.
Tel (021) 5879 1888.
Open 8am–9:30pm daily.

Shanghai History Museum
Tel (021) 6372 3500.
Open 8am–9:30pm.

Shanghai Tower Pudong
Huayuan Shiqiao Lu and Yincheng Zhong Lu.
Open 9am–9pm daily.

China Art Museum
205 Shangnan Rd. **Tel** 400 921 9021.
Open 10am–5pm Tue–Sun.
sh-artmuseum.org.cn

The Old Racecourse

The Old Racecourse was the center of Shanghai's social life in the early 20th century, and its Race Club was one of the most profitable corporations in China. It also had a swimming pool and a cricket pitch. After the Communists came to power in 1949, it became a symbol of Western decadence, and was turned into a park and a square that was used for political rallies and was finally landscaped to accommodate the Shanghai Museum. All that remains is its old grandstand clock tower and clubhouse on the park's west side.

A view of Shanghai's Old Racecourse before 1949

The modern skyline of Pudong, with a bridge over the Wusong River

❹ Shanghai Museum

上海博物馆

With a collection of over 140,000 pieces, the Shanghai Museum displays some of the best cultural relics from China's Neolithic period to the Qing dynasty, a span of over 5,000 years. While the highlights are the bronze ware, ceramics, calligraphy, and painting, it also has excellent displays of jade, furniture, coins, and Chinese seals or "chops." The museum was established in 1952, and the current building opened in 1995 with a design that recalls some of the exhibits and symbolizes "a round heaven and a square earth."

Shanghai Museum, reminiscent of a Shang-dynasty bronze *ding* pot

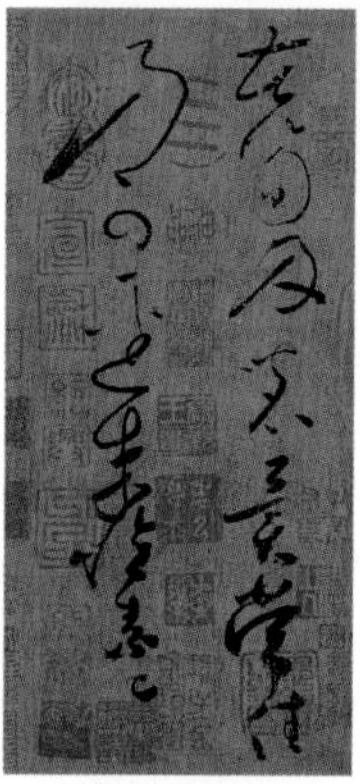

Calligraphy
To the Chinese, calligraphy is more than mere communication, it is one of the highest art forms. This cursive script *(see p33)* was painted by Huai Su (AD 737) in typically wild movements that combine delicate and forceful strokes.

Third floor

★ Sancai Pottery Figures
The major technical advance of the Tang dynasty (618–907) in ceramics was the development of *sancai* (three-color) pottery. This grave figure is a superb piece of polychrome pottery.

Celadon Ware
Celadon's simple beauty and strength made it highly desirable. This example of Longquan ware from the Southern Song dynasty (1127–1279) elegantly captures the movement of the coiled dragon.

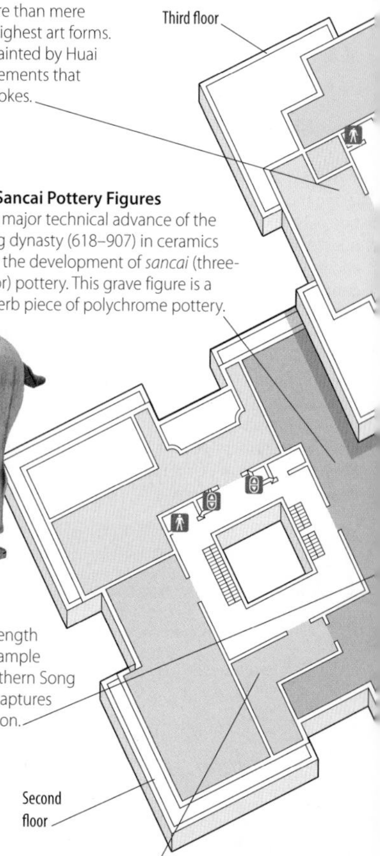

Second floor

Key to Floorplan

- Bronzes
- Sculpture
- Ceramics
- Zande Lou ceramics
- Paintings
- Calligraphy
- Seals
- Jade
- Furniture
- Coins
- Ethnic minorities gallery
- Temporary exhibitions
- Non-exhibition space

Zande Lou Ceramics is a privately donated collection of 130 pieces and includes some outstanding Qing imperial items.

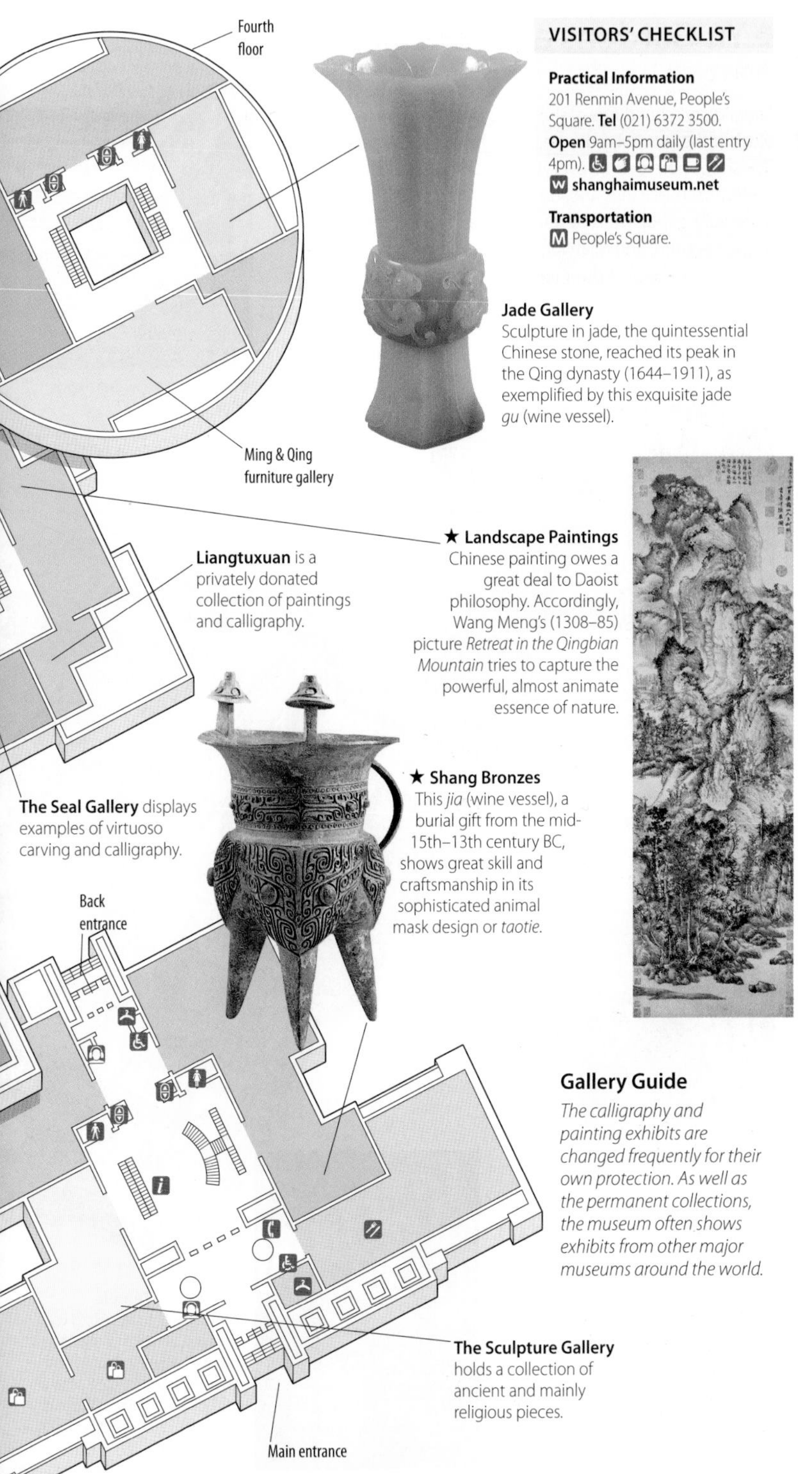

Jade Gallery
Sculpture in jade, the quintessential Chinese stone, reached its peak in the Qing dynasty (1644–1911), as exemplified by this exquisite jade *gu* (wine vessel).

★ Landscape Paintings
Chinese painting owes a great deal to Daoist philosophy. Accordingly, Wang Meng's (1308–85) picture *Retreat in the Qingbian Mountain* tries to capture the powerful, almost animate essence of nature.

Liangtuxuan is a privately donated collection of paintings and calligraphy.

The Seal Gallery displays examples of virtuoso carving and calligraphy.

★ Shang Bronzes
This *jia* (wine vessel), a burial gift from the mid-15th–13th century BC, shows great skill and craftsmanship in its sophisticated animal mask design or *taotie*.

The Sculpture Gallery holds a collection of ancient and mainly religious pieces.

VISITORS' CHECKLIST

Practical Information
201 Renmin Avenue, People's Square. **Tel** (021) 6372 3500.
Open 9am–5pm daily (last entry 4pm).
W shanghaimuseum.net

Transportation
M People's Square.

Gallery Guide

The calligraphy and painting exhibits are changed frequently for their own protection. As well as the permanent collections, the museum often shows exhibits from other major museums around the world.

❻ Yu Gardens and Bazaar

豫园

The old-style buildings of the Yu Gardens Bazaar are not really old, but the fanciful roofs are nevertheless very appealing. The shops here peddle everything from tourist souvenirs to traditional medicines and, despite inflated prices, the area is incredibly popular. It is best to arrive early and go straight to the beautiful and relatively peaceful Ming-dynasty Yu Gardens (Yu Yuan). A dumpling lunch, before the restaurants get too busy, will set you up for a hectic afternoon of shopping and haggling, followed by a cup of tea in the quaint Huxinting teahouse.

Yu Gardens Bazaar – modern shops in old-fashioned buildings

Yu Gardens Bazaar
Despite being a bit of a tourist trap, there is plenty of fun to be had wandering among the stalls and haggling over prices.

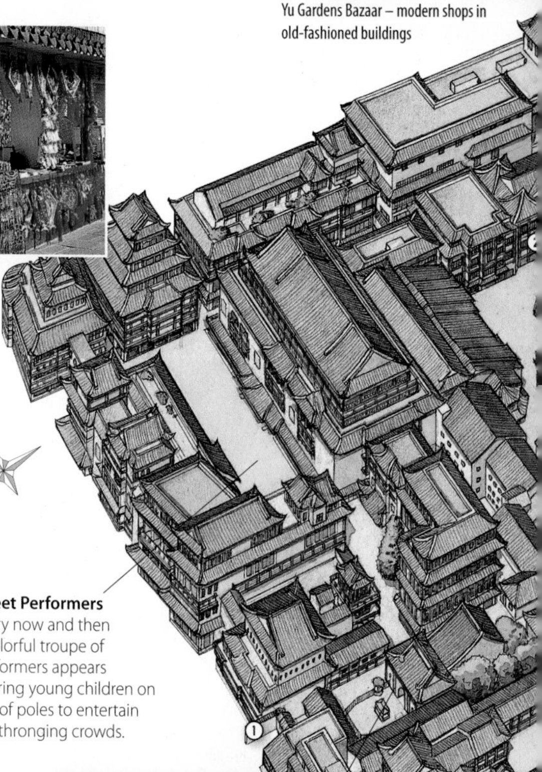

Street Performers
Every now and then a colorful troupe of performers appears bearing young children on top of poles to entertain the thronging crowds.

①

KEY

① **Shanghai Old Street** (Fangbang Road) and an entrance to the Bazaar.

② **Restaurants** surround the lake – you can see the dumplings being made in the morning.

★ City God Temple
Dating back to the Ming era, the temple once housed the patron god of Shanghai and encompassed an area as large as the bazaar. Now this small restored temple is very popular with tourists.

VISITORS' CHECKLIST

Practical Information
269 Fangbang Middle Road (Shanghai Old St), Old City. **Tel** (021) 6326 0830. City God Temple: **Open** 8:30am–4pm daily. Yu Gardens: **Open** 9am–5pm daily. Huxinting Teahouse: **Open** 9:30am–9pm daily.

Transportation
M Yuyuan Garden. 11, 26 and 64.

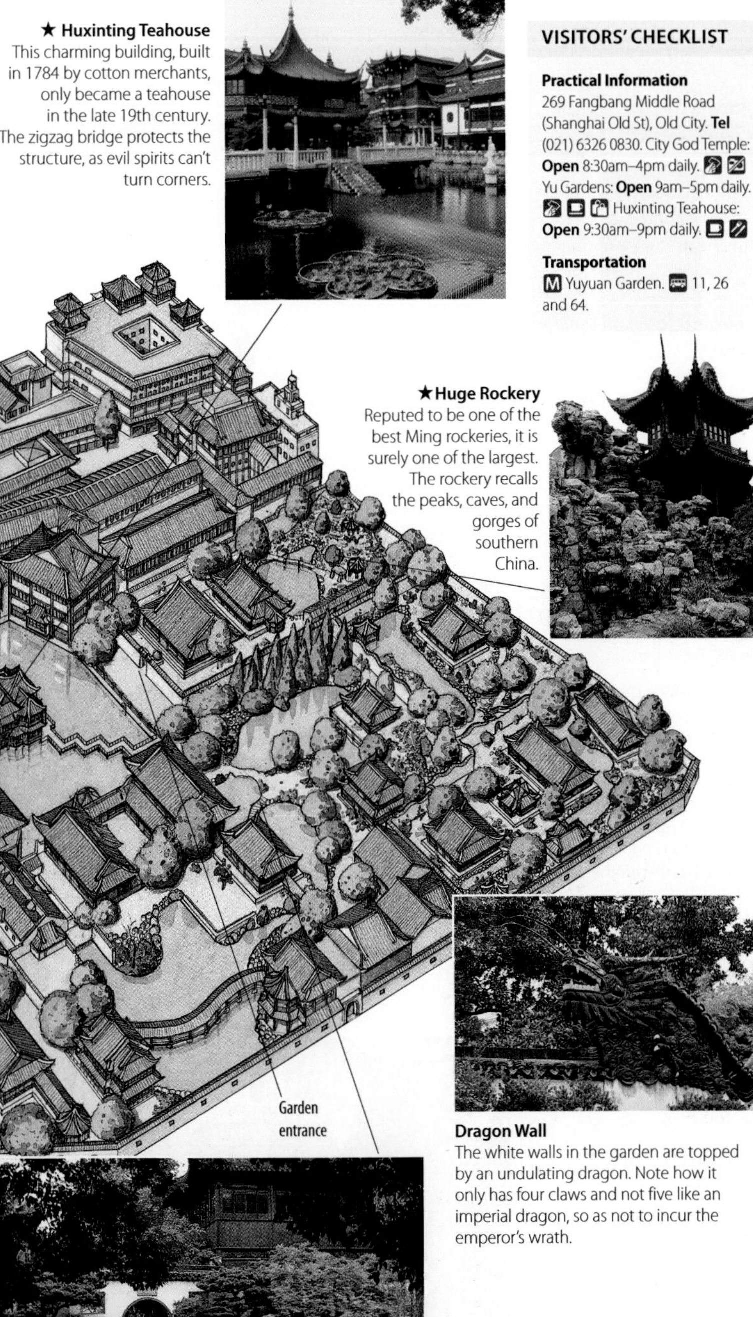

★ Huxinting Teahouse
This charming building, built in 1784 by cotton merchants, only became a teahouse in the late 19th century. The zigzag bridge protects the structure, as evil spirits can't turn corners.

★ Huge Rockery
Reputed to be one of the best Ming rockeries, it is surely one of the largest. The rockery recalls the peaks, caves, and gorges of southern China.

Dragon Wall
The white walls in the garden are topped by an undulating dragon. Note how it only has four claws and not five like an imperial dragon, so as not to incur the emperor's wrath.

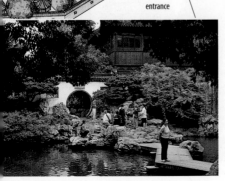

Yu Gardens Scenic Areas
The walls divide the garden into six scenic areas, which makes it feel like a maze and seem larger than it really is. The garden gets very busy in the afternoon and on weekends so try to come early if possible.

Entrance, First National Congress of the Chinese Community Party

❼ Site of the First National Congress of the Chinese Communist Party
中共一大会址纪念馆

374 Huangpi Road South. Ⓜ Huangpi Road South. **Tel** (021) 5383 2171. **Open** 9am–4pm Tue–Sun.

This house in the French Concession was the venue for a historic meeting, where representatives of China's communist cells met to form a national party on July 23, 1921. Officially, there were 12 participants including Mao Zedong, but it is believed that many others also attended. The police discovered the meeting and the delegates were forced to escape to a boat on Nan Lake, in Zhejiang. The house has a reconstruction of the meeting, with the original chairs and teacups used by the delegates. The exhibition hall tells the history of the Chinese Communist Party.

❽ Fuxing Park
复兴公园

Fuxing Middle Road. Ⓜ Huangpi Road South. Sun Yat-sen Memorial Residence: 7 Xingshan Rd. **Tel** (021) 5306 3361. **Open** 9am–5pm daily. Zhou Enlai's Former Residence: 73 Sinan Rd. **Tel** (021) 6473 0420. **Open** 9am–5pm daily.

The French bought this private garden, located in the French Concession, in 1908. It was known then as the "French Park," and has elements of a formal Parisian *jardin,* with meandering paths flanked by cherry trees. It was renamed Fuxing, meaning "revival," in 1949, and houses a large statue of Marx and Engels.

Close by on Xiangshan Road is the **Sun Yat-sen Memorial Residence**, a typical Shanghai villa where the leader and his wife, Soong Qingling, lived between 1918 and 1924. The interior is just as it was in Sun's time, with many of his personal items such as his gramophone and books. South of the park, 73 Rue Massenet (now Sinan Road) was the **Former Residence of Zhou Enlai**, who lived here when he was head of the city's Communist Party in the 1940s. It is furnished in a spartan style and is another excellent example of a European-style Shanghai villa.

Statue of Sun Yat-sen, Sun Yat-sen Memorial Residence

❾ French Concession
法国花园

Ⓜ Shaanxi Road South.

The former French Concession, stretching from the western edge of the Old City to Avenue Haig (Huashan Road), comprises European-style villas and tree-lined boulevards, shops, and cafés. It's residents were mainly White Russians and Chinese and it had its own electrical system, judiciary, and police force, whose highest ranking officer, "Pockmarked Huang," was the leader of the infamous Green Gang that controlled the opium trade.

Today, the Concession is centered around **Huaihai Road** and Yan'an Road – vibrant streets lined with megamalls, boutiques, restaurants, and bars – and the area around the stylish Art Deco facades of the **Jinjiang Hotel** complex. The hotel's compound includes the Grosvenor Residence, pre-War Shanghai's most exclusive property. The VIP Club, in the hotel's old wing, retains its 1920s architecture. The surrounding streets come alive at night with lively bars and clubs *(see p207)*. Another interesting building is the Tudor-style manor, **Ruijin Guesthouse**, at the corner of Fuxing Middle Road and Shaanxi South Road, which serves as a hotel. **The Children's Palace** at the western end of Yan'an Road was part of a 1920s estate, and is now a children's arts center, with performances and exhibitions.

The European-style villa that was Zhou Enlai's former residence

The Huangpu River

The Huangpu River is a mere 68 miles (110 km) in length from its source, Dianshan Lake, to its junction with the Yangzi River, 17 miles (28 km) downstream from Shanghai. As a spectacle, however, it is fascinating and there is much for the eye to take in, from the redeveloped waterfront at the Bund, and burgeoning modern metropolis of Pudong, to the bustling docks that line the Huangpu all the way to the wide, windblown mouth of the Yangzi. The boat departs from the wharves on the Bund south of Yan'an Road *(see pp190–91)*. The one-hour trip takes visitors as far as the Yangpu Bridge, but there is also the longer 3 ½ -hour trip, all the way to the Yangzi River.

④ Shanghai Docks
The Shanghainese proudly claim that nearly a third of all China's international trade enters via the perennially busy Huangpu River.

⑦ The Yangzi River
The color of the water changes markedly here, as the oily Huangpu meets the muddy and turbulent Yangzi. A lighthouse marks the confluence of the two.

⑥ Wusong Fort
The site of a decisive battle against the British in 1842, it consisted of a crescent-shaped fort with ten imported cannons.

③ Yangpu Bridge
Built in 1993, this is one of the world's longest cable-stay bridges – cables are anchored to each tower.

② Huangpu Park
At the northern tip of the Bund, this park is the home of the Monument to the People's Heroes.

⑤ Gongqing Forest Park
This large and pleasantly landscaped park was reclaimed from marshland and is popular with the Shanghainese on weekends.

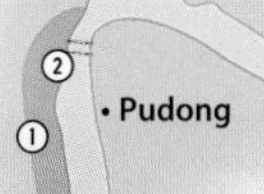

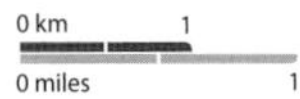

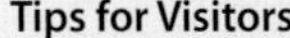

① The Bund
The central road area of the Bund was redeveloped for the 2010 World Expo. Most traffic was diverted underground and the roads turned into parks and walkways.

Tips for Visitors

Length: 37 miles (60 km). One-hour trip: 10 miles (16 km).
Boat trips: The boats vary in size and facilities,.so make sure you know what you are getting. The more expensive ones do provide food and sometimes entertainment.
Times: Boats leave from Zhongshan Lu on the Bund (where you can buy tickets), to the Huangpu Bridge and back.

Facade of the Soviet-style Shanghai Exhibition Center

⑩ Shanghai Exhibition Center
上海展览中心

1000 Yan'an Middle Rd. Ⓜ Jing'an Temple. **Tel** (021) 6279 0279. **Open** 9am–4pm daily.

The enormous Shanghai Exhibition Center is one of the few reminders of the influence the Soviet Union once had in Shanghai. Built in 1954, it was known as the Palace of Sino-Soviet Friendship, and was designed as a place for exhibiting China's technological and agricultural advances following the founding of the People's Republic in 1949. Ironically, the building stands on the site of the estate of millionaire Silas Hardoon – Shanghai's biggest capitalist in the 1920s. The Center is worth seeing for its grimly florid Soviet-style architecture. It has an impressively ornate entrance, with columns decorated with red stars, and a gilded spire. Today, it is an exhibition and convention center.

Nearby on Xinle Road, in the former French Concession, is the old **Russian Orthodox Church** with its distinctive onion-shaped domes. It served thousands of refugees from the Russian Revolution in 1917. The area around Julu Road and Changle Road, nearby, has a number of interesting Art Deco and early 20th-century villas and mansions constructed by Shanghai's wealthy residents.

⑪ Jing'an Temple
静安寺

1686 Nanjing West Rd (near Huashan Rd). Ⓜ Jing'an Temple. **Tel** (021) 6256 6366. **Open** 7:30am–3:45pm daily.

Located opposite the attractive Jing'an Park, which contains the old Bubbling Well Cemetery, Jing'an Temple (Temple of Tranquillity) is one of the city's most revered places for ancestor worship. Founded in the Three Kingdoms Period (AD 220-80), it reopened in 2006 after being completely rebuilt. In the 1930s, it was Shanghai's wealthiest Buddhist temple, headed by the influencial abbot Khi Vehdu, who was also a gangster with a harem of concubines and White Russian bodyguards.
It is said his body-guards went with him everywhere, carrying bulletproof briefcases as shields in the event of an attack. The temple was closed during the Cultural Revolution, but has reopened to become one of the best examples of an active Buddhist shrine in the city. It is a popular place to offer coins and pray for financial success.

⑫ Jade Buddha Temple
玉佛寺

170 Anyuan Rd. Ⓜ Changshou Road then taxi. **Tel** (021) 6266 3668. **Open** 8am–4:30pm daily.

The most famous of Shanghai's temples, Yufo Si lies in the northwest part of the city. It was built in 1882 to enshrine two beautiful jade Buddha statues that were brought from Burma by the abbot Wei Ken. The temple was originally located elsewhere, but shifted here in 1918, after a fire damaged the earlier structure. After being closed for almost 30 years, it reopened in 1980, and today has some 100 monks. Built in the Southern Song-dynasty style, it has sharply curved eaves and figurines on the roof. Its three main halls are connected by two courts. The first hall is the **Heavenly King Hall**, where the four Heavenly Kings line the walls. The **Grand Hall of Magnificence** houses three incarnations of the Buddha, while the **Jade Buddha Chamber** contains the first jade statue – that of a large reclining Buddha. The finer of the two statues, however, lies upstairs. Carved from a single piece of jade, this jewel-encrusted seated Buddha is exquisite. Visitors should note that photography is forbidden here.

Wall detail, Jade Buddha Temple

Golden Buddhas in the Jade Buddha Temple

For hotels and restaurants in this area see pp559-60 and pp575–7

Old Shanghai

Until 1842, Shanghai was a minor Chinese river port, worthy of a protective rampart but otherwise undistinguished. In that year the Chinese government capitulated to Western demands for trade concessions, resulting in a number of ports along China's eastern seaboard, including Shanghai, becoming essentially European outposts. Their key feature was that of extra-territoriality – foreign residents were answerable only to the laws of their own country. Thus the Americans, British, and French had their own "concessions" – exclusive areas within the city with their own police forces and judiciary – a situation that attracted not only entrepreneurs, but refugees, criminals, and revolutionaries. This mix was a potent one and Shanghai's reputation for glamor and excess derives from the politically combustible period between the two world wars. It all came to an end in the 1940s with the Japanese invasion and wartime occupation of Shanghai.

The Bund, also known as Zhongshan East No. 1 Road or, more colloquially, "Waitan," was the wide thoroughfare running along the Huangpu River. This was where all the major financial players in Shanghai commerce built their offices and created the distinctively grandiose skyline.

The Great World was a quintessential Shanghai creation, a mixture of freakishness, fashion, sex, and theater under one roof, owned by the gangster Pockmarked Huang.

The Racecourse, located in the area of today's People's Square, was a part of expatriate life, where, just as in the numerous clubs and institutions for non-Chinese, wealthy expats could socialize as if they were home.

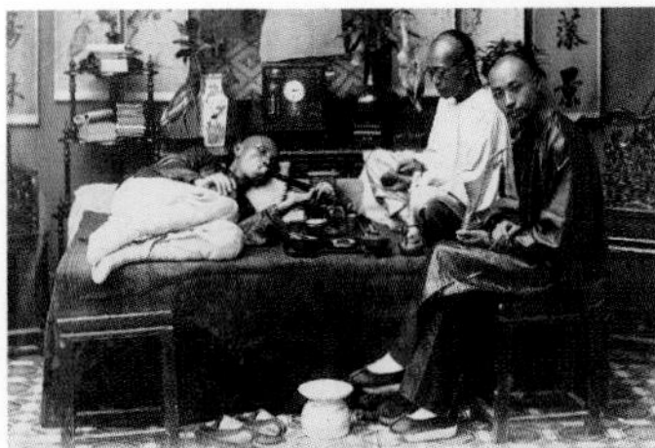

Opium, trafficked commercially with claims for free-trade by British companies like Jardine Matheson, was the foundation of Shanghai's prosperity and dens dotted the city. When the mercantile veneer was jettisoned, opium became the currency of Shanghai's gangster underworld.

Nanking Road was, and still is, Shanghai's retail hub. Divided in two parts (the western end is Bubbling Well Road), it was home to China's first department stores, where Chinese and expatriates mixed on an equal footing.

Brightly colored boats alongside the lake pier at Hongkou Park (Lu Xun Park)

⓭ Jewish Refugee Museum
犹太难民纪念馆

62 Changyang Rd. Ⓜ Dalian Road. **Tel** (021) 6512 6669. **Open** 9am–4:30pm daily.

From 1933 to 1941, Shanghai absorbed more than 20,000 Jewish refugees fleeing persecution in Europe. This museum is housed in a former synagogue. The focus is on photographs and refugees' stories.

⓮ Lu Xun Park
鲁迅公园

2288 Sichuan Bei Rd. Ⓜ Hongkou. **Tel** (021) 6540 0009. **Open** 6am–6pm. The Memorial Hall closes at 4pm.

To the north of Suzhou Creek and Waibaidu Bridge lies the Japanese section of the former International Settlement, which once had a Zen temple, a Japanese school, and specialist Japanese shops. The area's most interesting spot is Lu Xun Park – a pleasant place to watch the Chinese taking boat rides, playing chess, practicing *tai ji quan*, or simply relaxing. Originally known as Hongkou Park, it now has a name that reflects its strong associations with the great Chinese novelist Lu Xun (1881–1936), who lived nearby. His most famous work is *The True Story of Ah Q*, which lampooned the Chinese national character. Lu Xun was also an early proponent of the *baihua* or plain speech movement, which championed the simplification of the Chinese script and the use of spoken Chinese in literature. **Lu Xun's Tomb**, where his ashes are interred, is also in the park. To the right of the main park entrance is a **Memorial Hall** dedicated to the novelist, where visitors can view early editions of his work and his correspondence with intellectuals such as George Bernard Shaw. To the south is **Lu Xun's Former Residence** on Shanyin Road, where he spent the final three years of his life.

Statue, Lu Xun's Tomb

Lu Xun's Former Residence
9 Dalu Xincun, Shanyin Rd. **Tel** (021) 56 66 9711. **Open** 9am–4pm Tue–Sun.

⓯ Soong Qingling Memorial Residence
宋庆龄故居

1843 Huaihai Middle Rd. Ⓜ Hengshan Rd. **Tel** (021) 6474 7183. **Open** 9am–4:30pm daily.

At the southwestern edge of the city is the fine villa that was the residence of Soong Qingling, wife of the revolutionary leader Dr. Sun Yat-sen. All the Soong siblings – three sisters and a brother – came to wield a lot of influence in China. Of the three sisters, Soong Meiling married Chiang Kai-shek, the head of the Nationalist Republic of China from 1928 to 1949; Ailing married H. H. Kung, the director of the Bank of China and Soong Qingling married Sun Yat-sen. Her brother, known as T. V. Soong, became Chiang Kaishek's finance minister. Soong Qingling stayed in China once the Communists took over and became an honorary Communist heroine. She lived in Shanghai after her husband's death, initially in the house they had shared in the former French Concession *(see p200)*, before moving to this villa. She died in Beijing in 1981.

The house is a charming example of a mid-20th-century Shanghai villa. It has some wonderful wood paneling and lacquerwork. Her limousines are still parked in the garage, and some of her personal items are also displayed.

Soong Qingling Memorial Residence – a charming early 20th-century villa

⓰ Xujiahui Catholic Cathedral
徐家汇堂

158 Puxi Rd. M Xujiahui. **Tel** (021) 6438 2595. **Open** 9–11am daily.

The red-brick Gothic Cathedral of St. Ignatius that stands at a southwestern corner of Shanghai has long been associated with foreign nationals. The land originally belonged to a member of the Xu clan, Xu Guangqi (1562–1633), who was converted to Catholicism by Matteo Ricci. Upon his death, Xu left land to the Jesuits for the building of a church, seminary, and observatory. The cathedral, with its 164-ft (50-m) twin towers, was built in 1906. It was partly destroyed during the Cultural Revolution, but was rebuilt, and now holds Sunday services attended by over 2,000 worshipers. The interior is a mix of traditional Catholic decoration and Chinese embellishment. Xu Guangqi is buried nearby in Nandan Park.

⓱ Longhua Cemetery of Martyrs

龙华烈士陵园

180 Longhua West Rd. M Longhua Road. No. 41. **Tel** (021) 6468 5995. **Open** 9am–3:30pm Tue–Sun. Longhua Si: 2853 Longhua West Rd. **Tel** (021) 6456 6085. **Open** 7am–4:30pm daily.

This site honors those who died for the communist cause before the People's Republic was established in 1949. At the center is a Memorial Hall, while many commemorative sculptures dot the park. The cemetery is situated on the site of the Nationalist Party's execution ground, where many Communists were put to death in 1927 by gangs working for Chiang Kai-shek.

Nearby is **Longhua Temple** and an octagonal pagoda. A temple has existed on this site since AD 687, and a pagoda since AD 238–251. The foundations of the current pagoda, with its upturned eaves, date to 977, while the temple buildings were built during the late Qing era. The temple is very active, and the monks can be heard chanting at around 3:30pm. The surrounding area is pretty in the spring.

Commemorative statue at the Longhua Cemetery of Martyrs

⓲ She Shan
佘山

22 miles (35 km) SW of Shanghai. M Sheshan. from Wenhua Guangchang bus stop or Xi Qu bus station in Shanghai. Cathedral: **Tel** (021) 5765 1521. **Open** 8am–4:30pm daily.

She Hill or She Shan is a mere 328-ft (100-m) high, and is surmounted by the red-brick Catholic She Shan Cathedral. In the 1850s, European missionaries built a small chapel here. Later, a bishop took refuge in the area and vowed to build a church. The basilica, dating from 1925 to 1935, is the biggest in Southeast Asia. Services, often in Latin, take place on Christian holidays and particularly in May, when pilgrims stream here. The route to the top of the hill represents the Via Dolorosa (the Way of Suffering), the road that Christ took to his crucifixion. It is a pleasant walk past bamboo groves, and the views from the summit are terrific. An ancient observatory on the hill houses an ingenious earthquake-monitoring device: a jar with dragon heads around the outside and a pendulum inside. Each dragon has a steel ball in its mouth. When an earthquake occurred, the pendulum would swing and knock a dragon, causing its mouth to open and a ball to drop out, thereby pointing out the direction of the earthquake.

Exterior of the grand She Shan church, Our Lady of China

⓳ Song Jiang
松江

25 miles (40 km) SW of Shanghai. M Song Jiang Xincheng. from Xi Qu bus station in Shanghai, then No. 14 to town. Sonjiang Mosque: 21 Gangbeng Alley. **Tel** (021) 5782 3684.

On the Shanghai–Hangzhou railway line, Song Jiang is a small county town. Its sights include a Song-dynasty square pagoda in Fangta Park and close by, a 13-ft (4-m) high Ming screen wall, decorated with carvings of legendary beasts. West of Song Jiang is Sonjiang Mosque, part of which dates to the Yuan dynasty and is said to be one of the oldest Islamic buildings in China. It is still a place of worship.

Shopping & Entertainment in Shanghai

Shanghai has always been China's premier shopping destination. Before World War II, the city's glamorous foreign community demanded the finest goods, and Shanghai's reputation for novelty and quality continues today, with stores that cater to all tastes and budgets. This is also a culturally vibrant city, with regular performances of opera, theater, acrobatics, Western classical music, and jazz. The city's nightlife is buzzing with plenty of fashionable bars and restaurants, as well as cinemas and nightclubs.

Shops & Markets

Shanghai's best-known shopping street is Nanjing Road, which is lined with stores *(see p194)*. **Plaza 353**, in the historic Dong Hai Plaza, is a hip mall with stores and dining options. The most interesting local market is just off Nanjing Road, on Jiangyin Road. Huaihai Road in the former French Concession is also well known, and packed with upscale fashion boutiques and stores.

Clothes & Textiles

All the major brand names from around the world are represented here, along with some Hong Kong chain stores, though the latter often don't have sizes that fit foreign visitors. The main streets are Nanjing Road, Shaanxi South Road, Huaihai Road, and Maoming Road, as well as the malls of Pudong. For silk, try the **No. 1 Department Store** *(see p194)*, but the best quality is sold at stores such as **Isetan**. For fashion boutiques, there are a number of independent stores clustered at Taikang Road and at Xinle Road for youth fashion. The city has also revived its tradition of fine tailoring, and **W. W. Chan & Sons Tailor Ltd** provides quality at good prices.

Antiques

Although Shanghai offers a range of antiques, there are two potential hazards in buying them. First, the market is flooded with fakes that visitors might mistake for the real thing, and second, it is illegal to export antiques that do not bear a government-approved seal. Bargains are hard to come by and the best-quality items are not likely to be much cheaper than at home. The main markets are near the Old City on **Dongtai Road** and **Fangbang Middle Road** *(see p198)*, where the Treasure Tower is one of the largest indoor antiques markets in China. Hongkou district's **Duolun Road** has a row of restored shops selling antiques, books, and art.

Arts & Crafts

All traditional Chinese arts and crafts are widely available across Shanghai. The **Yu Yuan Old Street** is great for items such as tea, teapots, teaware, and other souvenirs, but remember to always bargain hard. For porcelain, the best buys are the fine reproductions of classical porcelain, available at the **Shanghai Museum**, which although expensive, are far better than anything else in the market. Handicrafts made by China's ethnic minorities such as Tibetans, as well as by people of neighboring countries such as Nepal, are available at specialist shops on Nanjing Road such as **Duo Yun Xuan Art House** and **Room with a View**. Jewelry shops abound all over the city, but jade, although available, is difficult to classify. Cultured pearls are a safer bet for buyers, and are available in stores such as **Shanghai Pearl City**. For Chinese art, there are galleries around Moganshan Road near Suzhou Creek.

Entertainment Guides & Tickets

There are a number of English-language publications, such as the bi-weekly *City Weekend* and monthly *that's Shanghai* and *Time Out Shanghai*, which carry details of current events, as well as restaurant reviews. Mainstream events are listed in local Chinese newspapers. A useful website is Culture.sh.cn, the city's primary ticket agency for theater, concerts, and sports events. Tickets can also be arranged through the tourist office, directly at the venue, or even through your hotel.

Performing Arts & Music

Shanghai is home to several international-standard venues – such as the **Shanghai Grand Theatre** *(see p194)* and the **Shanghai Oriental Art Center** – that stage national and international opera performances, music, dance, and theater. Another very popular cultural venue is the **Shanghai Centre** *(see p194)*, which also puts on Chinese acrobatic shows, jazz, and western classical concerts and opera. Era, a lavishly staged acrobatics show, is performed nightly at **Shanghai Circus World**. A hot venue is the **Mercedes-Benz Arena**, which was built for the World Expo and now hosts international concerts, theater, music and dance shows, and sports events. Traditional Beijing Opera can be seen at the **Yifu Theater** and occasionally at the old **Lyceum Theater** (Lan Xin). The Art Deco **Majestic Theater** also has a program of ballet and local opera, while modern Chinese and international theater is performed at the **Shanghai Dramatic Arts Center**. There are also concerts (mostly at the weekend) at the **Shanghai Music Conservatory Auditorium**. Jazz music is most famously available at the **House of Blues & Jazz** and at the **JZ Club** on Fuxing Road.

Cinemas

Apart from Chinese and Hong Kong films, films from Europe and the US are also screened in cinemas and bars. Halls such as **UME International Cineplex (Baoshan)**, **Shanghai Film Art Center**, and **Studio City** show foreign films (often censored), either in their original language with Chinese subtitles or dubbed into Chinese with English subtitles.

Bars & Nightclubs

Shanghai's nightlife is China's most brash, diverse, and pulsing. Bars come and go, and what's "in" one month may close down the next. Bars tend toward the avant-garde, and are heavily influenced by what is fashionable in Tokyo, New York, and London. Prices for drinks can be high, and many bars have dancing, live music, film nights, and comedy spots. The best areas are the Bund, Xintiandi, Fuxing West Road, Yongfu Road, and Sinan Road. **Boxing Cat Brewery** on Fuxing Road is popular for happy hour beers and Southern US bar food. **Big Bamboo**, a Canadian sports bar, is one of the city's most popular late-night hangouts. Popular cocktail lounges include **Constellation**, located at the trendy Sinan Mansions (a redevelopment of a clutch of heritage villas), and **Hollywood**, a hip club and lounge with DJs and dancing. Current reviews, including details of which clubs have DJs from London and New York, are to be found in *that's Shanghai* and *Time Out Shanghai*, as well as online at www. smartshanghai.com.

Amusement Parks

Shanghai has two huge amusement parks in the shape of a **Disneyland** in Pudong, and **Shanghai Happy Valley**, about 35 miles (40 km) west of downtown Song Jiang. Both have excellent rides, although you can expect to wait 1–2 hours for your turn.

DIRECTORY

Shops & Markets

Plaza 353
Nanjing East Rd.
Tel (021) 6353 5353.

Clothes & Textiles

Isetan
1038 Nanjing West Rd.
Tel (021) 6272 1111.

No. 1 Department Store
830 Nanjing Rd. Pedestrian St.
Tel (021) 6322 3344.

W. W. Chan & Sons Tailor Ltd.
165D Maoming South Rd.
Tel (021) 5404 1469.

Arts & Crafts

Duo Yun Xuan Art House
422 Nanjing East Rd.
Tel (021) 3313 4800.

Room With a View
479 Nanjing East Rd.
Tel (021) 6352 0256.

Shanghai Museum
201 Renmin Avenue.
Tel (021) 6372 3500.

Shanghai Pearl City
558 Nanjing East Rd.
Tel (021) 6322 3911.

Yu Yuan Old Street
269 Fangbang Middle Rd. (Shanghai Old Street).
Tel (021) 6655 9999.

Performing Arts & Music

House of Blues & Jazz
60 Fuzhou Rd.
Tel (021) 6323 2779.
W bluesandjazz shanghai.com

JZ Club
158 Julu Rd.
Tel (021) 5309 8221.
W jzclub.cn/en

Lyceum Theater
57 Maoming South Rd.
Tel (021) 6256 2926.

Majestic Theater
66 Jiangning Rd.
Tel (021) 6217 4409.

Mercedes-Benz Arena
1200 Expo Avenue.
Tel 400 181 6688.
W mercedes-benz arena.com/en

Shanghai Centre
1376 Nanjing West Rd.
Tel (021) 6279 8663.
W shanghaicentre. com/theatre

Shanghai Circus World
2266 Gonghe New Rd.
Tel (021) 6652 2395.
W era-shanghai.com/ era/en

Shanghai Dramatic Arts Center
288 Anfu Rd.
Tel (021) 6473 4567.
W china-drama.com

Shanghai Grand Theatre
300 Renimin Avenue.
Tel (021) 6386 8686.
W shgtheatre.com

Shanghai Music Conservatory Auditorium
20 Fenyang Rd.
Tel (021) 6431 3701.
W shcnmw.com

Shanghai Oriental Art Center
425 Dingxiang Rd, Pudong.
Tel (021) 6854 1234.
W en.shoac.com.cn

Yifu Theater
701 Fuzhou Rd.
Tel (021) 6322 5294.

Cinemas

Shanghai Film Art Center
160 Xinhua Rd.
Tel (021) 6280 6088.

Studio City
10/F, Westgate Mall, 1038 Nanjing West Rd.
Tel (021) 8537 9075.

UME International Cineplex (Baoshan)
Nuoya Xintiandi Square, 318 Mudanjiang Rd.
Tel (021) 6218 7109.
W ume.com.cn

Bars & Nightclubs

Big Bamboo
132 Nanyang Rd.
Tel (021) 6256 2265.

Boxing Cat Brewery
82 & 519 Fuxing Rd.
Tel (021) 6431 2091.

Constellation
86 Xinle Rd.
Tel (021) 5404 0970.

Hollywood
Building 4, 570 Yongjia Rd.
Tel 137 6407 9136.

Amusement Parks

Disneyland Shanghai
Chuansha New Town, Pudong New Area.
Tel (021) 3158 0000.
W shanghaidisney resort.com

Shanghai Happy Valley
888 Linhu Rd.
Tel (021) 5779 9922.
W sh.happyvalley.cn

JIANGSU & ANHUI

The provinces of Jiangsu and Anhui lie to the north and west of Shanghai respectively. Jiangsu, one of China's most fertile and populated areas, is largely rural. Its southern region is dominated by the Yangzi River, along which lie the major cities, including Nanjing, the provincial capital, with a profusion of historic sights, and the cities of Suzhou and Yangzhou, known for their gardens, canals, and silk production. The province is developing at a fast rate but still retains its charm, especially in the small towns where traditional architecture can be seen. Anhui's main sights lie in the south, where vast spreads of paddy fields are watered by the Huai River. The area south of the Yangzi River is dominated by mountain ranges offering spectacular scenery. Huang Shan, the Yellow Mountain, is Anhui's most popular scenic area, while the Buddhist mountain, Jiuhua Shan, is more serene. The towns of Shexian and Yixian in the southeast are renowned for their traditional old houses with fine wooden carvings.

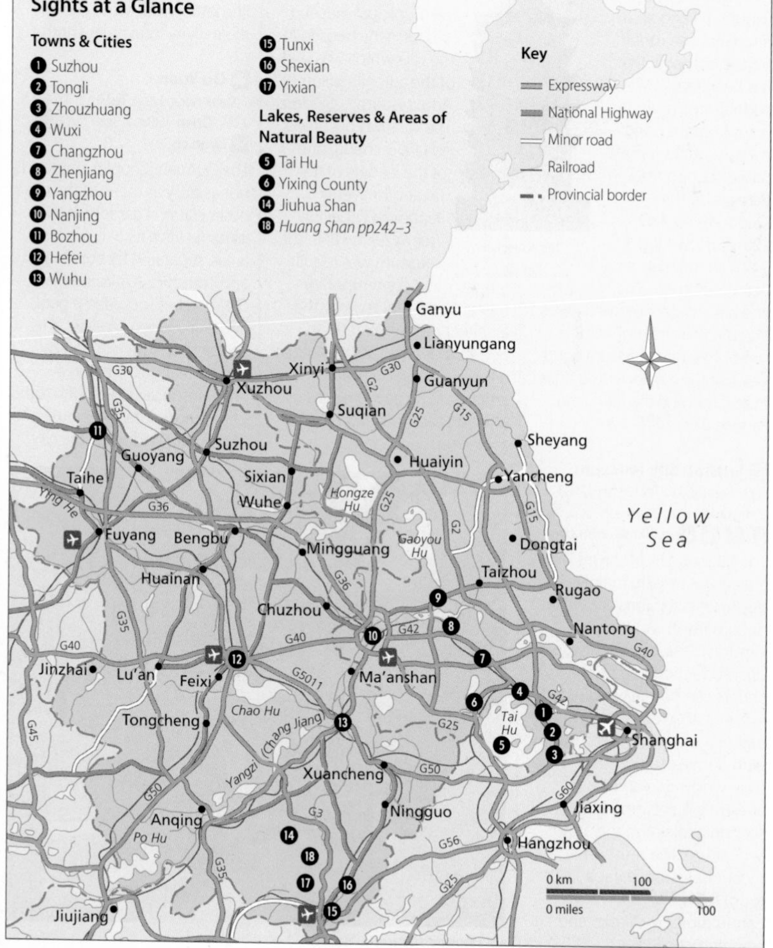

Walkway along a rock face in Anhui province

For additional map symbols *see back flap*

❶ Suzhou
苏州

A network of canals, bridges, and canalside housing characterizes the city of Suzhou. Its history dates back to the 6th century BC, when the first canals were built to control the area's low water table. The construction of the Grand Canal *(see p223)* 1,000 years later brought prosperity as silk, the city's prized commodity, could be exported northwards. During the Ming dynasty, Suzhou flourished as a place of refinement, drawing an influx of scholars and merchants, who built themselves numerous elegant gardens. The city has plenty of sights, and is dissected by broad, busy roads laid out in a grid.

Beisi Ta

1918 Renmin Lu. **Tel** (0512) 6753 1197. **Open** 8am–6pm daily.

The northern end of Renmin Rd is dominated by the Beisi Ta (Northern Pagoda), a remnant of an earlier temple complex, that has been rebuilt. The pagoda's main structure dates from the Song dynasty, but its foundations supposedly date to the Three Kingdoms era (AD 220–65). Towering 249 ft (76 m) high, it is octagonal in shape, and has sharply upturned eaves. Visitors can climb right to the top, from where there are good views of the city, including Xuanmiao Guan and the Ruiguang Pagoda *(see pp218–19)*.

The octagonal Beisi Ta

Suzhou Silk Museum

2001 Renmin Lu. **Tel** (0512) 6753 5943. **Open** 9am–5pm Tue–Sun.
szsilkmuseum.com

The Suzhou Silk Museum is a pleasure to visit, mainly because its exhibits are well-documented with English captions. It traces the history of silk production *(see pp214–15)* and its use from its beginnings in about 4000 BC to the present day. Exhibits include old looms with demonstrations of their workings, samples of ancient silk patterns, and a section explaining the art of sericulture. The museum's most interesting exhibit is its room full of live silk worms, eating mulberry leaves and spinning cocoons.

Suzhou Museum

204 Dongbei Jie. **Tel** (0512) 6757 5666. **Open** 9am–5pm Tue–Sun.
szmuseum.com

The municipal museum was formerly housed in the villa which was part of the adjoining Humble Administrator's Garden. The villa was occupied by Li Xiu-cheng, one of the leaders of the Taiping Heavenly Kingdom Rebellion *(see p428)* in 1860. The museum was rebuilt in a contemporary-meets-traditional style by the architect I. M. Pei in 2006. It houses more than 30,000 cultural relics, including excavated artifacts, Ming and Qing dynasty paintings and calligraphy, and ancient arts and crafts.

The charming garden of Ou Yuan

Humble Administrator's Garden

See pp212–13.

Shizi Lin

23 Yuanlin Lu. **Tel** (0512) 6777 3263. **Open** 7:30am–5pm daily.
szszl.com

The Shizi Lin (Lion Forest Garden) is considered by many the finest in Suzhou. Visitors unfamiliar with Chinese garden design may find it rather bleak, though, as rocks are its main feature. Ornamental rocks were a crucial element of classical gardens, and symbolized either the earth or China's sacred mountains. Dating to 1342, the garden was originally built as part of a temple. The large pool is spanned by a zigzag bridge and buildings with unusually fine latticework, while part of the rockery forms a labyrinth.

Ou Yuan

7 Xiaoxinqiao Lane. **Tel** (0512) 6727 2717. **Open** 7:30am–5pm daily.
oygd.cn

The Ou Yuan (Couple's Garden) is not as busy as many of the city's other classical gardens. It takes its name from its two garden areas, separated by buildings and corridors. A relaxing place, Ou Yuan has rockeries, a pool, and a fine, open pavilion at its center that is surrounded by several teahouses. It is in a charming locality filled with some of the most attractive houses, canals, and bridges in the city.

Mural in the Hall of Literary Gods, Xuanmiao Guan

VISITORS' CHECKLIST

Practical Information
32 miles (50 km) NW of Shanghai. 6,000,000. 345 Shiquan Jie, (0512) 6530 5887.
envisitsz.com

Transportation
Suzhou train station; Suzhou North for high-speed trains. North station, Nanmen, Wu Xian. tours of Grand Canal.

Museum of Opera and Theater

14 Zhongzhangjia Xiang. **Tel** (0512) 6727 3334. **Open** 8:30am–4:30pm daily. **kunopera.com.cn**

Housed in a beautiful Ming dynasty theater of latticed wood, the Museum of Opera and Theater (Kunqu Bowuguan) is a fascinating and highly visual museum. Its display halls are filled with examples of old musical instruments, delicate hand-copied books of scores and lyrics, masks, and costumes. Other exhibits include a life-size orchestra and vivid photographs of dramatists and actors. Traditional Suzhou Opera, known as *kun qu* or *kun ju*, is renowned as the oldest form of Chinese opera, with a history of about 5,000 years.

The museum is the venue for occasional performances, while the adjacent teahouse stages daily shows of *kun*-style opera and music.

Xuanmiao Guan

94 Guanqian Jie. **Tel** (0512) 6727 6616. **Open** 7:30am–5pm daily.

The Daoist Temple of Mystery was founded during the Jin dynasty but, like many Chinese temples, has been rebuilt many times. The Hall of the Three Pure Worshipers dates to the Song dynasty, and is the largest ancient Daoist hall in China. The intricate structure of the roof in particular is worth scrutiny. Located in Suzhou's commercial center, the temple was associated with popular street entertainment, and although the musicians and jugglers have gone, it retains a casual atmosphere.

Suzhou City Center

1. Beisi Ta
2. Suzhou Silk Museum
3. Suzhou Museum
4. Humble Administrator's Garden
5. Shizi Lin
6. Ou Yuan
7. Museum of Opera and Theater
8. Xuanmiao Guan
9. Shuang Ta
10. Yi Yuan
11. Silk Embroidery Research Institute
12. Wangshi Yuan
13. Canglang Ting
14. Pan Men Scenic Area
15. Confucian Temple

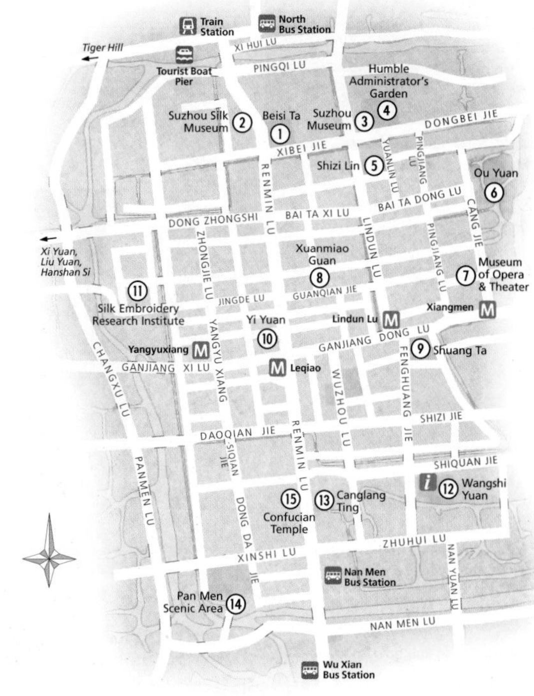

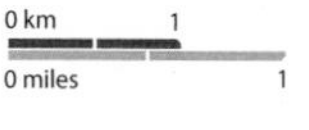

Key to Symbols *see back flap*

Humble Administrator's Garden

拙政园

Suzhou's largest garden, Zhuozheng Yuan, the Humble Administrator's Garden is also considered the city's finest. It was established in the 16th century by a retired magistrate, Wang Xianchen, and developed over the years as subsequent owners made changes according to the fashion of the day. A 16th-century painting shows that originally the garden was less decorative than it is now. The garden is separated into three principal parts, east, central, and west. The eastern section has colorful flowers but is of less interest than the other two. There is also a museum that explains the history and philosophy of Chinese gardens.

Covered walkway – a way to enjoy the garden even in the hot sun

★ Mandarin Duck Hall

Split into two equal rooms, this arrangement allowed visitors to enjoy the cooler north-facing chamber in summer, and the warmer south-facing one in winter.

KEY

① **The Wavy Corridor** rises up and down over the water as if going over waves.

② **Western section of the garden**

③ **The central part** of the garden imitates the scenery of China south of the lower Yangzi.

④ **Little Flying Rainbow Bridge**

★ Fragrant Isle

This pavilion and terrace is supposed to resemble the deck and cabin of a boat. As it projects out over the water, it gives excellent views of the garden from all sides.

The Humble Administrator's Garden

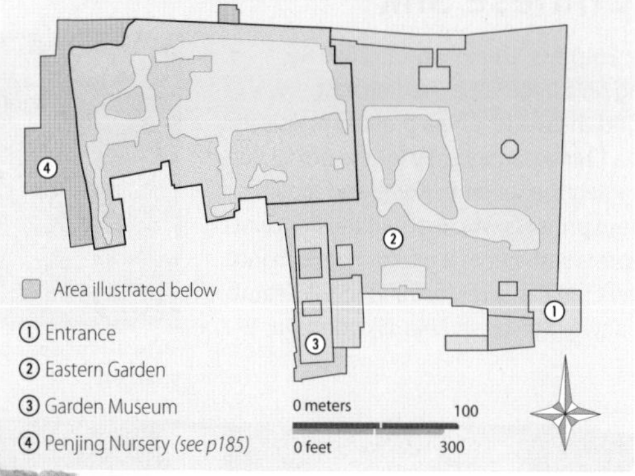

Area illustrated below

① Entrance

② Eastern Garden

③ Garden Museum

④ Penjing Nursery *(see p185)*

0 meters 100

0 feet 300

VISITORS' CHECKLIST

Practical Information
178 Dongbei Jie, Suzhou. **Tel** (0512) 6751 0286. **Open** 7:30am–5:30pm daily (mid-Nov–Feb: to 5pm). includes the Garden Museum. **en.szzzy.cn**

Orange Pavilion
Artificial mountains were an important element in Chinese gardens and were ideal for contemplation.

Entrance to the central section

Secluded Pavilion of Firmiana Simplex and Bamboo
The most famous view of the garden, the "borrowed view" *(see p185)* of Beisi Ta, the Northern Pagoda reflected in the water, is visible from here.

★ Hall of Distant Fragrance
The main hall of the garden, is named after the perfume of the large lotus pond nearby that delicately wafts in.

The History of Chinese Silk

According to legend it was the Empress Xi Ling who, in 2640 BC, encouraged silkworm breeding on a large scale. Trading vast quantities of the material around the world, China profited massively from the industry. It remained a Chinese monopoly for the next 3,000 years or so until refugees smuggled the secret to Korea and Japan. Another story tells that a Chinese princess who married the Prince of Khotan secretly brought silkworms with her as a gift for her husband. The Western world, which knew China as Seres, or Land of Silk, learnt the secret of silk production via two monks who hid silkworms in their bamboo staffs.

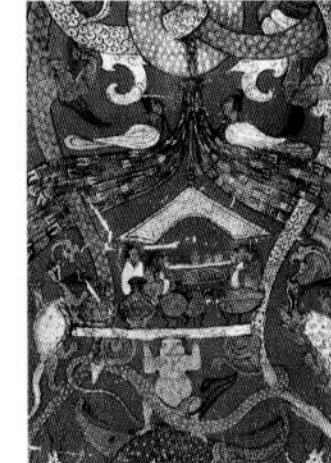

Silk burial offering dating from c.200 BC

Imperial Gift

Silk was originally reserved for use by the imperial household, an example of which is this gorgeous robe embroidered with the imperial symbol of the five-clawed dragon. The imperial yellow symbolizes the earth.

Silk was traded extensively *(see pp470–71)* as an important source of income and indeed was often used as a form of payment of taxes or for payment of salaries.

This traditional pattern suggests waves and mountains and therefore the boundless nature of the Chinese Empire.

Justinian was the Byzantine emperor who stole the secret of silk in AD 600. Silk had for long been fashionable in the Roman Empire but they had no idea how it was made, even thinking that it grew on trees.

Women produced silk in their own home – and it took up a large part of the day for six months of the year. The state also had many workshops producing and weaving silk. By the Tang dynasty, all classes of society in China were allowed to wear silk.

Silk embroidery became an important art and the women of distinguished families could make a considerable fortune by skillful embroidery.

Meaning of Symbols

Ax is one of the 12 symbols of sovereignty that were reserved for the emperor. The ax stands for the power to punish.

Goblets are a symbol of imperial loyalty. These sacrificial goblets are also symbolic of ancestor worship.

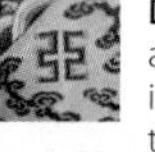

Double qi is another of the 12 imperial symbols that represents the emperor's power to judge his subjects.

The Production of Silk

Thousands of years of intensive breeding have rendered the silk moth, *Bombyx mori*, a blind, flightless, egg-laying machine whose larvae hold the secret of silk. The genius of the Chinese lay in the discovery of the potential of its ancestor, a wild, mulberry-eating moth unique to China.

Farming silkworms: the eggs are first kept at 65° F (18° C) rising to 77° F (25° C), at which point they hatch. The silkworms (actually caterpillars) are now kept at a constant temperature and fed mulberry leaves at 30-minute intervals day and night until fattened, they are ready to enter the cocoon stage.

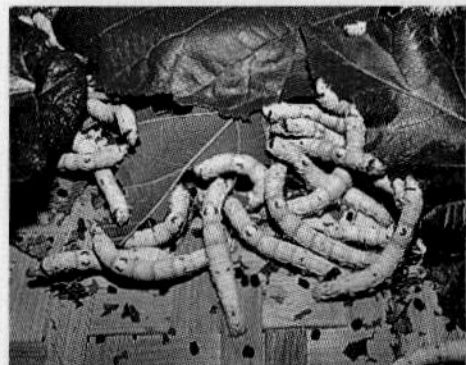

Silken saliva: the silkworms' saliva glands secrete a clear liquid, that solidifies into silk threads as it dries, and a gum that sticks these together.

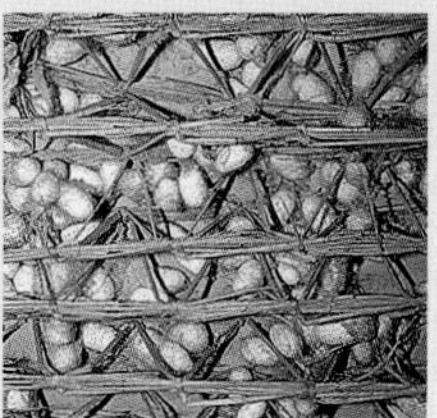

Cocoons: when they are ready to pupate, with a figure-of-eight motion, they spin their sticky secretion into cocoons.

Making silk: the cocoons are steamed to kill the pupae and soaked to soften the sticky gum and allow the silk strands to be separated. Several strands are woven to make one silk thread.

Chinoiserie was popular in Europe and America at various times from the 17th century onwards. Chinese factories created a range of Chinese-style designs solely for export.

Silk has special qualities in that it retains warmth and yet is lightweight and cool and can therefore be worn in comfort both in winter and summer.

China's silk industry is still strong today although a lot of the "silk" that is on display in cheap markets is actually rayon.

The octagonal Song dynasty twin pagodas, Shuang Ta

Shuang Ta

22 Dinghui Si Xiang. **Open** 8am–5:30pm daily.

Once part of a temple, these 98-ft (30-m) high twin pagodas date to the early Song era. According to an inscription, they were first built in AD 982 by the students Wang Wenhan and his brother in honor of their teacher, who helped them pass the imperial civil service exams. Twin pagodas are commonly found in India but are a rarer feature of Chinese temples, where pagodas were largely built as single edifices.

Yi Yuan

1265 Renmin Lu. **Tel** (0512) 6524 9317. **Open** 7:30am–4:30pm daily.

The Garden of Happiness is one of Suzhou's newer gardens, dating from the late Qing dynasty. It was built by a government official who utilized rocks and landscape designs from other abandoned gardens. The garden appears to have originally covered a larger area; today its central feature is a pool encircled by rockeries and spanned by a zigzag bridge. The best viewpoint is from the Fragrant Lotus Pavilion, while another pavilion that juts into the pool is known for catching cooling breezes. Look out for the calligraphy by famous scholars and poets.

Silk Embroidery Research Institute

272 Jinde Lu. **Tel** (0512) 5887 1762. **Open** daily.

Housed in the Huan Xiu (Surrounded by Beauty) Mountain Villa, this institute creates exquisitely fine silk embroidery, work that is mainly done by women. In order to produce the painting-like effect of their designs, the women sometimes work with silk strands that are so fine, they are almost invisible. They specialize in double-sided embroidery – for example, a cat with green eyes on one side and blue on the other.

Wangshi Yuan

11 Kuojia Tou Xiang. **Tel** (0512) 6529 3190. **Open** 7:30am–5:30pm daily.

It is said that the Master of the Nets Garden was named after one of its owners – a retired official who wished to become an accomplished fisherman. Dating to 1140, it was completely remodeled in 1770 and for many people, is the finest of all Suzhou's gardens. Although small, it succeeds, with great subtlety, in introducing every element considered crucial to the classical garden *(see pp184–5)*. It includes a central lake, discreet connecting corridors, pavilions with miniature courtyards, screens, delicate latticework, and above all, points which "frame a view," as if looking at a perfectly balanced photograph. The best-known building is the Pavilion for Watching the Moon, from where the moon can be viewed in a mirror, in the water, and in the sky. Regular performances of Chinese opera, including local *kun ju*, take place here.

Canglang Ting

3 Canglang Ting Jie, Renmin Lu. **Tel** (0512) 6519 4375. **Open** 7:30am–5pm daily (mid-Apr–Oct: to 5:30pm). **W** szclp.com

The Canglang Ting (Dark Blue Wave Pavilion Garden) – whose name is suggestive of a relaxed and pragmatic approach to life – is perhaps Suzhou's oldest garden, first laid out in 1044 by a scholar, Su Zimei, on the site of an earlier villa. His successor, a general in the imperial army, enlarged it in the 12th century, and it was rebuilt in the 17th century. It is known for its technique of "borrowing a view," allowing the scenery beyond the garden's confines to play a role in its design. Here, it is achieved by lowering walls on the north side of some of the pavilions, allowing

The Pavilion for Watching the Moon, Wangshi Yuan

For hotels and restaurants in this region see p560 and p577

Gateway to the Confucian Temple

views across water; elsewhere the southwest hills can be seen. The central feature is a mound that is meant to resemble a wooded hill. Gardens were ideal places for contemplation and writing poetry, clearly visible in the engravings of verses and poems dotting Canglang Ting.

Liu Yuan and Xi Yuan

Liu Yuan: 338 Liuyuan Lu. **Tel** (0512) 6533 7903. **Open** Apr–Oct: 7:30am–5:30pm; Nov–Mar: 1:30–4:30pm.
Xi Yuan: 18 Xiyuan Lu. **Tel** (0512) 6534 9545. **Open** 7:30am–5:30pm daily.

Originally a pair, these two gardens lie near each other to the west of the old moated area. The Liu Yuan (Garden for Lingering in), was restored in 1953, and its four scenic areas are connected by a long corridor. The Xi Yuan (West Garden) once belonged to a devout Buddhist, and is more temple than garden. The Jiechuang Temple, with its tiled roof and red beams, is a fine example of southern-style architecture. Adjoining it is the Hall of Five Hundred Luohan.

Pan Men Scenic Area

See pp218–19.

Confucian Temple

613 Renmin Lu. **Tel** (0512) 6519 4343. **Open** 9am–4:30pm daily.

The original Song dynasty temple was rebuilt in 1864 after it was destroyed in the Taiping Rebellion *(see p428)*. Its main hall, dating from the Ming dynasty, has several stone carvings including China's oldest surviving city map, depicting Suzhou, or Pingjiang as it was known in 1229. A star chart dating from 1247 maps the positions of stars and celestial bodies in the heavens. It is one of the earliest surviving maps of its kind.

Tiger Hill

8 Sanmen Nei Lu. **Tel** (0512) 6532 3488. **Open** 7:30am–6:30pm daily.

In the city's northwest is the popular Tiger Hill (Huqiu Shan), the burial place of He Lu, the King of Wu and founder of Suzhou. His spirit is said to be guarded by a white tiger who appeared three days after his death and refused to leave.

Ceremonial urn, Tiger Hill

The main attraction is the Song-dynasty leaning pagoda (Yunyan Ta or Cloud Rock Pagoda), built in brick, which leans more than 7 ft (2 m) from the perpendicular at its highest point. Some 10th-century Buddhist *sutras* and a record of the year that it was constructed (959–61) were discovered during one of the attempts to prevent it from falling. The park is quite large, with pools and flowerbeds filled with blooms in spring and early summer. One of the many boulders is split in two, allegedly the result of He Lu's swordsmanship. He is supposedly buried nearby along with 3,000 swords.

Hanshan Si

24 Hanshansi Long. **Tel** (0512) 6723 6213. **Open** 7am–5:30pm daily.

First constructed in the Liang dynasty, the Cold Mountain Temple was named after a Tang-dynasty poet-monk. A stone rendition of him and his fellow monk, Shi De, is to be seen here. The temple was rebuilt in the 19th century, after it was destroyed during the Taiping Rebellion. Located close to the Grand Canal, it was immortalized by the Tang-dynasty poet Zhang Ji, who arrived here by boat and anchored nearby. His poem "Anchored at Night by the Maple Bridge" is inscribed on a stone stele, and contains the lines that made Hanshan Si famous: "Beyond Suzhou lies Hanshan Temple; at midnight the clang of the bell reaches the traveler's boat." The bell alluded to here was subsequently lost, and the temple's current bell, which you can ring for luck, was presented by Japan in 1905. Nearby, a beautiful arched bridge offers views along the Grand Canal.

Incense burners in the grounds of Hanshan Si

Pan Men Scenic Area

盘门

Set in the southwest corner of the old city of Suzhou, this once-overlooked area has been extensively restored – gone are the pretty canalside shacks – but it still contains some of the city's most interesting historical sights. Pan Men is a unique fortified gate that once controlled access to the city by both land and water. It is said to date back to 1351, although most of the present construction is more recent. Other highlights include the charming Wu Men Bridge and the views of the city and canals from the Ruiguang Pagoda.

Hall of Attractive Scenery
This three-story pavilion houses a tranquil tea room with views to the platform of the Western Stage in front.

★ Pan Men
This gate and attached section of wall (dating back to 1351) are all that remains of the city's ancient fortifications. It is the only land and water gate in China.

KEY

① **Double-doored water gate**

② **Wu Zixu's Memorial Temple**

③ **Entrance Gate** This is the main entrance to the park. Pay here for access to the park and also a separate fee to climb the pagoda.

④ **Ornamental *pailou* or gate**

⑤ **300-ft (90-m) section of city wall**

★ Wu Men Bridge
This graceful bridge spanning the Grand Canal is the tallest in Suzhou and its design dates back to the Song dynasty, although it has since been rebuilt a few times. It has steps built into it and a lovely view from the top.

VISITORS' CHECKLIST

Practical Information
1 Dong Da Lu, SW corner of the city. **Tel** (0512) 6526 0004. **Open** 8am–5pm daily. for scenic area (including Pan Men and Wu Men Bridge), separate fee for Ruiguang Pagoda.

Transportation
from the train station, tourist bus 2 and 5.

View from Ruiguang Pagoda
After a climb up narrow stairs, looking down into the heart of Suzhou itself reveals a city dotted with large pockets of green – the beautiful gardens that have made the city so famous.

★ Ruiguang Pagoda
This seven-story, 140-ft (43-m) high pagoda dates back to the Song dynasty. It is constructed of brick with wooden platforms, and has simple Buddhist carvings at its base.

Hall of Four Auspicious Merits
The name of this hall is inspired by Buddhist teachings. At each side of the hall at the end of covered walkways are smaller pavilions, one containing a drum and the other a bell.

Houses fronting a canal in Zhouzhuang's Old Town

❷ Tongli
同里

16 miles (25 km) SE of Suzhou. 55,000. Suzhou train station. **Tel** 400 698 2990. **tongli.net**

A pretty little water town typical of the region, sometimes called "Venice of the East," Tongli gives visitors a good idea of what Suzhou must have been like in its heyday. All its houses open out on to a network of canals that are spanned by dozens of stone bridges and are busy with transportation and trading boats. Some of its buildings are open to the public, such as **Jiayin Hall**, the former home of Liu Yazi, an early 20th-century actor renowned for his rather bizarre collection of gauze caps. The other interesting sight is **Tuisi Yuan**, a classical garden dating from the late Qing period.

Tuisi Yuan
Open 7:30am–5:30pm daily.

One of Tongli's numerous tree-lined canals, spanned by a stone bridge

❸ Zhouzhuang
周庄

50 miles (80 km) W of Shanghai. 32,000. from Shanghai, Suzhou. to Tongli. Old Town: tickets from Quangong Lu. **Tel** 400 8282 900. **zhouzhuang.chinadaily.com.cn**

A small town on the Grand Canal, which links Suzhou and Hangzhou, Zhouzhuang was once a flourishing port, specializing in silk, pottery, and grain. It attracted scholars and officials who built fine bridges and houses between the Yuan and Qing eras. The charming **Old Town** can be explored on foot or via a boat tour on the canals. Among the sights are the Ming-era Hall of Zhang Residence with 70 rooms, and the Hall of Shen's Residence, with 100 rooms connected to the main hall. The Chengxu Temple, located near the museum, is a Song-dynasty Daoist shrine.

❹ Wuxi
无锡

25 miles (40 km) NW of Suzhou. 6,400,000. services from Hangzhou & Suzhou. **Tel** (0510) 12301. **en.wuxi.gov.cn**

The highlights of a trip to Wuxi are the scenic Tai Hu (Lake Tai), the Grand Canal, and the lakeside cherry blossoms in spring. According to legend, the town was established 3,500 years ago as the capital of the Wu Kingdom and was a center for the production of tin. When the mines ran dry (Wuxi means "without tin"), the capital moved west, but Wuxi remained significant due to its location on the Grand Canal. **Xihui Park** was established in 1958, and houses the Jichang Yuan garden. At the park's entrance, a path leads to the Dragon Light Pagoda on top of Xi Shan. A cable car connects Xi Shan to nearby Hui Shan. The **Wuxi Museum** has exhibits dating back 6,000 years.

Xihui Park
2 Huihe Lu. **Open** 5:30am–10pm daily.

Wuxi Museum
71 Huihe Lu. **Tel** (0510) 8572 7500. **Open** 9am–5pm daily. **wxmuseum.com**

The scenic cable car ride, Xihui Park, Wuxi

❺ Tai Hu
太湖

3 miles (5 km) SW of Wuxi. Meiyuan Kaiyuan Temple. 1, 68, 157.

One of China's largest lakes, Tai Hu is famous for its rocks, an indispensable feature of a traditional garden *(see pp184–5)*. The lake's northern shores are fringed with scenic spots, including **Mei Yuan** (Plum Garden), spectacular in spring when its 4,000 fruit trees blossom. **Yuantou Zhu** (Turtle Head Promontory) is a favorite with the Chinese, with teahouses and pretty lake views. Nearby, **Sanshan Island** is a former bandit's haunt with temples and tall Buddha statues. However, none is as tall as the 289-ft (88-m) Lingshan Buddha on Ma Shan peninsula, a short bus ride from the other sights. The area also has a handful of lakeside theme parks.

Mei Yuan and Yuantou Zhu
Open 8am–4:30pm daily.

◀ Tourists exploring Zhouzhuang by boat on the historic Grand Canal

The Grand Canal

The Grand Canal (or Jinghang Canal), started in 486 BC, was built in sections over the next 1,000 years, with the aim of linking the Yangzi with the Yellow River, and one capital with another. It remains the world's largest man-made waterway. The earliest northern section was built for military reasons but large-scale construction began in the 7th century AD under the Sui Wen Di emperor, involving over 5 million conscripted males aged between 15 and 55, supervised by a vast and brutal police force. Linking the comparatively populous north with the southern rice-producing region, it reached Beijing only in the 13th century. In the early 20th century, a combination of the altered course of the fickle Yellow River and the rise of the railways saw its gradual demise.

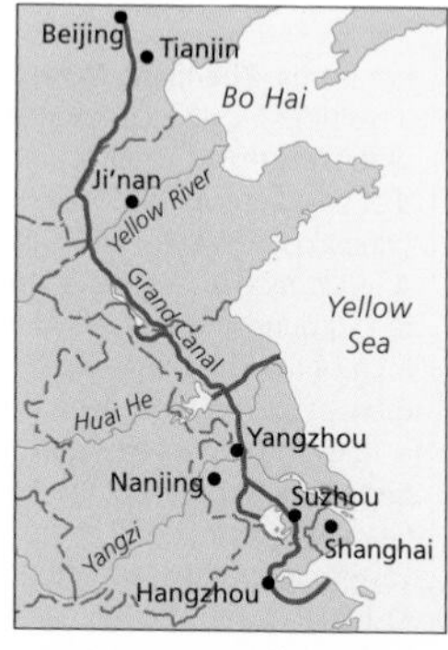

This map shows the route of the 1,112-mile (1,900-km) canal from Beijing to Hangzhou. Crossing the traditional battlefields between north and south, the canal supplied food throughout the empire. The hilly terrain led to the first recorded use of double locks in AD 984.

Key

The Sui Yang Di emperor is said to have celebrated the completion of his work by touring the canal with a flotilla of dragon boats hauled by the empire's most beautiful women.

Tourist boats are now the only way to enjoy a journey on the canal as road and rail transportation is favored by the locals. Regular overnight tourist boats services run between Hangzhou and Suzhou or Wuxi, whilst boats can also be chartered for daytrips between the major tourist stops.

Barges splutter their way along the canal laden with agricultural produce and factory supplies. The busiest sections are in the south, and north of the Yangzi to the border with Shandong.

The canal banks are lively with people performing domestic tasks. Families, even if they have houses, may live on board the boats when they are working.

Pottery shop selling typical ceramic items, Ding Shan

6 Yixing County

宜兴

70 miles (118 km) W of Suzhou. bus service between Wuxi and Yixing. **yixing.gov.cn**

The county's main town, Yixing, is a busy transportation hub that provides connections to the entire region. This fertile area of canals and farmland is known for its pottery, produced at **Ding Shan** for 3,000 years. Its name *yixing* or "purple sand" is derived from its distinctive deep maroon color. The town's streets are lined with factories and pottery shops, the latter full of items such as traditional little pots in all shapes and sizes. Ding Shan's tourist office also organizes factory visits.

A short journey from town, the **Pottery Exhibition Hall** displays a range of objects, from fine, early Yixing-ware to the prized miniature teapots. Nearby are the **Karst Caves**, comprising three groups – Zhanggong, Linggu, and Shanjuan. The highlight of Zhanggong's 72 caves is the Hall of the Sea Dragon King, which can hold several thousand people, while Linggu has an underground waterfall.

Pottery Exhibition Hall
150 Ding Shan Beilu. **Open** 7:30am–4:30pm daily.

Karst Caves
Open daily.

7 Changzhou

常州

25 miles (40 km) NW of Wuxi. 4,600,000. (0519) 8199 7800.

Often overlooked, this city on the Grand Canal is worth visiting for its old center, crisscrossed by streets of traditional houses and canals. The two main streets, Bei and Nan Dajie, are lined with shops selling silks and the locally made painted combs. The 7th-century **Tianning Si** has 83 Buddha statues decorating its roof, while the Song-era **Yizhou Pavilion** is associated with the poet Su Dongpo, who stayed here when he visited the city.

8 Zhenjiang

镇江

90 miles (150 km) NW of Suzhou. 3,100,000. 92 Zhongshan Xi Lu, (0511) 8521 7773. **zhenjiang.jiangsu.net**

Set on the banks of the Yangzi River, Zhenjiang's prosperity was linked to the construction of the Grand Canal *(see p223)*. In the 19th century, the city was ceded to foreign powers. The former **Royal Hotel** is a fine example of European pastiche, while the old British Consulate now houses the **Zhenjiang Museum**. Its exhibits include a photograph of the *Amethyst*, the British ship that sailed upriver in 1949 to bring aid to the British in Nanjing. After coming under heavy fire, it ran aground and was stranded for months. The ship finally managed to rejoin its fleet.

To the museum's west, **Jin Shan Park** is the site of the Jin Shan Temple, founded in the Eastern Jin dynasty, and the Cishou Pagoda, one of a pair built in the Tang era. The climb to the top reveals splendid views of the Yangzi. To the city's northeast lies **Beigu Shan** hill with its beautiful **Lingyun Ting** pagoda. Farther east is **Jiao Shan**, an island famed for its scenery, accessible by cable car or boat. Above the island's fortifications, Xijiang Lou tower offers fine views of the river.

Zhenjiang Museum
85 Boxian Lu. **Tel** (0511) 8528 5032. **Open** 9am–5pm Tue–Sun.

Jin Shan Park
62 Jinshan Xilu. 2, 104. **Tel** (0511) 8551 2992. **Open** 6am–6pm daily.

The southern-style Tianning Si (Temple of Heavenly Peace), Changzhou

Calligraphy

Calligraphy raises ordinary Chinese script into a high art form and is traditionally regarded as highly as painting or poetry as a method of self-expression. The beauty of calligraphy may seem hard to appreciate for most visitors who do not read Chinese. Freestyle calligraphy, however, which transforms ordinary characters almost into figurative and abstract paintings, can easily be appreciated for its artistry. The Chinese viewer, taught from a young age the basic sequence of strokes, can mentally trace the characters as they were created by the artists and so experience their spiritual world. As they are limited to the same eight strokes, the artists' individual styles – the variations in stroke weight, angle, and vigor – are easily appreciated. Experts consider the balance and proportional weight of the strokes, the structure of the character, and its unity and harmony.

The Four Treasures

The main tools of the calligrapher are known as "The Four Treasures of the Study" – ink sticks, ink stone, brushes, and paper. Anhui is especially famed for the quality of its ink and brushes.

Ink sticks are made from soot – pine wood or tung oil – mixed with glue and even spices. Inks are usually black although colors are available.

Each character is made up of eight types of stroke performed in a set order.

Thicker dashes look less crowded

The seal is carefully positioned on the page. The cinnabar ink stamp may be the name of the artist or some poetry.

The ink stone is used to grind the ink stick with the right amount of water. A thick ink is glossy and strong, while thin ink can be lively or subtle.

Graceful downstroke to the left

Finely tapered hook stroke

Paper, invented around AD 100, was made from mulberry or bamboo fibers. Much cheaper than the silk it replaced, paper is classed by its weight, as this affects how fast it absorbs the ink.

Brush rests were used to hold other brushes or so the artist could put down his brush and contemplate.

Brushes permitted greater freedom for expression than engraving bone or stone and led to more fluid scripts. Supposedly made from many varieties of fur, the tip should be round yet pointed, even and strong.

Practice is crucial. The hand must always know what it is about to do; there is no room for indecision. There are three levels of practice – tracing, copying, and working from memory. Each step up allows the artist to add more individuality.

❾ Yangzhou

扬州

One of the Yangzi River delta's great cities, Yangzhou has always been known for its prosperity, culture, and cuisine. Its location on the Grand Canal dictated the rise and fall of its fortunes. The city declined with the fall of the Song dynasty and the diminished use of the canal, but revived again in the Ming era, when the canal was restored and used to transport silk, rice, and salt. The salt merchants in particular built elegant villas and gardens, especially in the 18th century when Yangzhou was part of the imperial inspection tours. Despite development, the city has much to offer, including its several gardens.

Villas and barges on the Yechunyuan Canal in Yangzhou

Daming Si

8 Pingshan Tang Lu. **Tel** (0514) 8733 1089. **Open** 8am–5:30pm daily.
W damingsi.com

Sitting atop a hill, the Temple of Abundant Light dates to the 5th century AD, but was rebuilt after being destroyed in the Taiping Rebellion *(see p428)*. The central **Jian Zhen Hall** was erected in 1973 in honor of the monk Jian Zhen, who traveled to Japan in 753. Credited with introducing many aspects of Chinese culture to Japan, he is revered by the Japanese, who funded the main hall's construction and modeled it on the Tosho-dai Temple in Nara, Japan. Nearby is a natural spring with a teahouse.

Hanlingyuan Museum

98 Pingshantang Dong Lu. **Tel** (0514) 8762 5587. **Open** 8am–5pm.

The magnificent Western Han tomb of Liu Xu, ruler of the Guangling Kingdom, is five levels deep. Its second air-tight layer comprises 840 *nanmu* (cedar) bricks joined by hooks. The third level housed the warehouse, the fourth level the king's living quarters, and the fifth level, a coffin on wheels. The tomb was equipped with every imaginable luxury, including a bathroom.

Shou Xi Hu

28 Da Hongqiao Lu. **Tel** (0514) 8735 7803. **Open** 7:30am–6pm daily.
W shouxihu.com

Yangzhou's most popular sight, the Thin West Lake is a slim version of Hangzhou's famous West Lake *(see pp248–9)*. It winds through a park filled with willow trees, pavilions, and bridges. The handsome **Wuting Qiao** (Five Pavilion Bridge) is its most famous structure, built by a salt merchant in 1757 to honor the Qianlong emperor's visit to Yangzhou. To the west is Ershisi Qiao (Twenty-Four Bridge), so called because it has 24 steps and 24 posts and is 24 m (78 ft) long. **Bai Ta** (White Dagoba) is a Tibetan-style stupa, modeled on the one in Beijing's Bei Hai Park *(see p96)*. In the Xu Garden, the **Listening to Orioles Pavilion** has fine woodwork, while the **Pinyuan Lou** offers views that supposedly demonstrate the rules of perspective as compiled by the Song artist Guo Xi. East of the lake, the Imperial Jetty is where Qianlong's barge was moored.

Yangzhou Museum

Wenchang Xi Lu. **Tel** (0514) 8522 8028. **Open** 9am–4pm Tue–Sun.
W yzmuseum.com

Housed in a complex on the western side of Mingyue Lake, Yangzhou Museum contains some splendid items, including an ancient boat salvaged from the Grand Canal, and a collection of unusual woodblock prints.

Ge Yuan

10 Yanfu Dong Lu. **Tel** (0514) 8736 1638. **Open** 7:15am–5:45pm daily.
W ge-garden.net

Yangzhou's most famous garden, Ge Yuan was once owned by the painter Shi Tao, and later by a salt merchant. Its name derives from the leaves of its bamboo plants, that resemble the character *"ge"* meaning "self." Its central feature is its rockeries, but it also has some fine pavilions.

Wuting Qiao (Five Pavilion Bridge), Shou Xi Hu

Wang Shi Xiao Yuan

18 Dongquan Men Lishi Jiequ.
Tel (0514) 8732 8869.
Open 8am–5pm daily.

Located on a street of historic homes including that of former president Jiang Zemin, the grand Wang Shi Xiao Yuan was the residence of a wealthy salt merchant. Dating to the Qing era, it has nearly 100 rooms. The interior is lavishly furnished, and its main Spring Hall contains a German chandelier and marble wall panels.

Garden Tomb of Puhaddin

17 Jiefang Nan Lu. **Open** 8am–6pm daily. **Closed** (tomb only): Sat.

Said to be the 16th descendant of the Prophet Mohammed, Puhaddin was a teacher who lived in Yangzhou until his death in 1275. His grave is enclosed in a building filled with inscriptions from the holy Koran. Other noted Muslim figures from the Song and Ming eras are buried nearby. Puhaddin also built the tiny **Xianhe Mosque**, located southwest on Ganquan Road. Its wall is covered in arabesques, a legacy of the Persian traders who once frequented the city.

The Tang-dynasty Shi Ta or Stone Pagoda

He Yuan

66 Xuning Men Jie. **Tel** (0514) 8723 9626. **Open** 7:30am–5pm daily.

This small garden creates an illusion of space and depth by the clever arrangement of its features, including shrubs, trees, and a walkway. Named after one of its 19th-century owners, it is divided in two, with some pavilions decorated in southern-style latticework, although northern influences prevail in its overall layout and style. A few teahouses also dot the garden.

VISITORS' CHECKLIST

Practical Information

37 miles (60 km) NE of Nanjing.
4,500,000. 8 Fengle Shang Jie, 400 710 0400.

Transportation

Yangzhou Taizhou.
East and West bus stations.

Wenchang Ge

The round Wenchang Ge (Promoting Literature Pavilion) is all that remains of the old Confucian Academy. Founded by the first Ming emperor, Hongwu, who believed in education for all, the academy originally had two pavilions. To the north, the **Si Wang Ting** (Pavilion of the Four Views) was a part of the Ming-era Provincial College, and was used as an observatory. Lying west of Wenchang Ge, the Tang-dynasty **Shi Ta** (Stone Pagoda) was once part of a temple located outside the city walls. It was moved here in the Song era.

Yangzhou City Center

1. Daming Si
2. Hanlingyuan Museum
3. Shou Xi Hu
4. Yangzhou Museum
5. Ge Yuan
6. Wang Shi Xiao Yuan
7. Garden Tomb of Puhaddin
8. Xianhe Mosque
9. He Yuan
10. Wenchang Ge
11. Si Wang Ting
12. Shi Ta

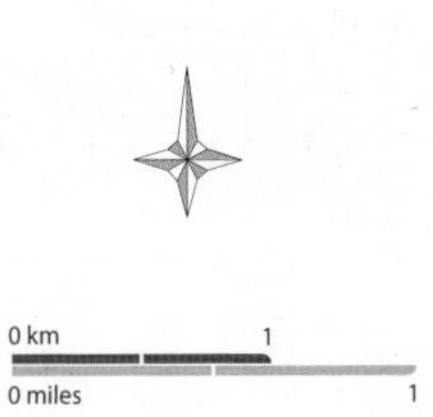

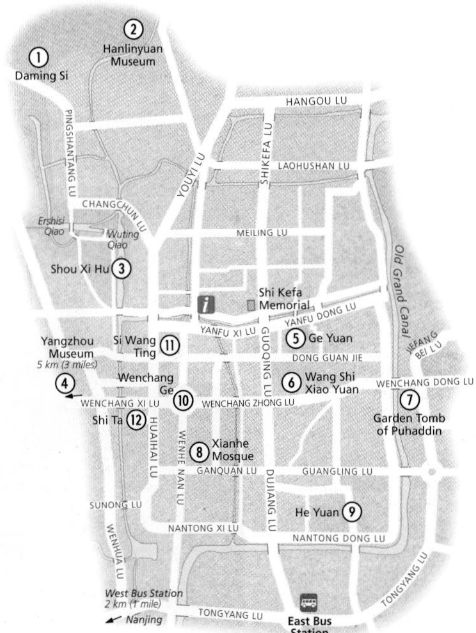

Key to Symbols see back flap

⑩ Nanjing

南京

Of all China's great cities, Nanjing, or Nanking as it was once known, is the most attractive. The capital of Jiangsu province, it is picturesquely set on the banks of the Yangzi, close to the magnificent Purple Mountain. This city of lakes is still enclosed within its grand city wall, and its streets are shaded by plane trees. Meaning "southern capital," it was the capital of several regional kingdoms up to AD 220. Later, it was China's capital under the early Ming. It was also the capital of the 19th-century Taiping Heavenly Kingdom and the first Chinese Republic under Dr. Sun Yat-sen. Today, Nanjing is a fast-developing city, with good restaurants and a lively nightlife.

Garden and pavilions at the Taiping Heavenly Kingdom History Museum

Exploring Nanjing

Although the medieval city walls give the impression that Nanjing is a small city, it is in fact fairly spread out. A lot of ground can be covered on foot, but visitors will also need to use the city's local transportation, either the metro system, the comprehensive bus service, or one of the reasonably priced taxis.

Zhonghua Gate

See pp230–31.

Taiping Heavenly Kingdom History Museum

128 Zhanyuan Lu. **Tel** (025) 5220 1849. **Open** 8:30am–5:30pm daily.

This museum commemorates the anti-dynastic Taiping Heavenly Kingdom Rebellion of 1851–64 *(see p428)*. The building was used by one of the rebellion's leaders, or Heavenly Princes, while one section – the Zhan Yuan or Viewing Garden – originally belonged to the first Ming emperor, Hongwu. Today, the renovated halls are filled with memorabilia and photographs relating to the rebellion, which overran large parts of China. After the rebels claimed Nanjing as their base, they came very close to toppling the Qing dynasty in Beijing, but were eventually defeated by the Qing army under Western leadership in 1864. On display are weapons and uniforms, samples of Taiping currency, and documents explaining the Heavenly ideology, which aimed to change China's feudalistic society into one based on equality. Their aims included the modernization of the education system which was still based on Confucian classics, the redistribution of land, and equality of the sexes.

Bailuzhou Park

Tel (025) 8662 7126. **Open** 6am–10pm daily. 14, 23, 43, 87, 88, 301.

The White Egret Park was once the property of the Ming General Xu Da, and later became the Chinese quarter during the centuries of Manchu rule. The pavilions were all destroyed during the Taiping Rebellion, but the park was restored in 1951, and the area still abounds in traditional houses.

Fuzi Miao

Gongyuan Lu. **Tel** (025) 5265 1345. **Open** 9am–10pm daily. **njfzm.net**

The origins of Fuzi Miao (Temple of Confucius) go back to 1034, but the current buildings date to the late 19th century, with later additions. The temple was the seat of Confucian study for over 1,500 years. Its halls feature a small exhibition of folk arts. The surrounding streets are flanked by houses with upturned eaves and whitewashed walls – many of which are being restored in typical southern style. Nearby, the attractive canal bank has plenty of boats that ply the short distance to Zhonghua Gate.

The distinctive double-eaved main hall of the Fuzi Miao

Chaotian Gong

Mochou Lu. **Tel** (025) 8446 6460. **Open** 8am–5pm daily.

The substantial Chaotian Gong (Heaven-Facing Palace) was once a place of ancestor worship, a seat of learning, and a Confucian temple. Its mid-19th-century buildings such as halls, towers, and walkways, stand on an ancient temple site dating to AD 390. It now houses the Municipal Museum, displaying Shang bronzes and fragments of the legendary porcelain pagoda destroyed in the Taiping Rebellion. The pagoda was built in the 15th century by the Ming Yongle emperor to honor his mother, and was covered in glazed white bricks. The attractive museum is a quiet place to learn more about Nanjing's fascinating history.

Nearby along Tangzi Jie, house No. 74 has colorful paintings dating to the Taiping occupation that were discovered in 1952. The house was occupied by a follower of the Taiping Eastern Prince, Yang Xiuqing. The paintings – of animals and birds – are more interesting for their historical associations than for their deft execution.

Detail from the Sun Yat-sen Hall, Tianchao Gong

Tianchao Gong & Xu Yuan

292 Changjiang Donh Lu. **Tel** (025) 8457 8700. **Open** 8:30am–6pm daily (Nov–Mar: to 5pm). **njztf.cn/en**

The Tianchao Gong (Presidential Palace), together with the surrounding classical Xu Yuan Garden (Balmy Garden), were originally built by a Ming prince. Under the Qing dynasty, it became the seat of provincial government until 1853, when it was seized by the leader of the Taiping Rebellion, Hong Xiuquan, as his headquarters. Finally, after the overthrow of the Qing empire, the palace housed the Republican Government, from where both Dr. Sun Yat-sen and Chiang Kai-shek ruled China. Inside, there is an exhibition devoted to the Taiping Rebellion and to Dr. Sun Yat-sen. The surrounding Xu Yuan Garden is a popular weekend spot with the locals.

VISITORS' CHECKLIST

Practical Information

125 miles (200 km) NW of Shanghai. 8,100,000. 202/1 Zhongshan Bei Rd, (025) 8342 8999. **cityofnanjing.com**

Transportation

Nanjing (North and South train stations), Zhonguamen. Zhongyang Men station, Hanfu Jie station, CAAC (buses to airport), Nanjing (South). to Shanghai, Wuhan & Chongqing.

Nanjing City Center

1. Zhonghua Gate
2. Taiping Heavenly Kingdom History Museum
3. Bailuzhou Park
4. Fuzi Miao
5. Chaotian Gong
6. Tianchao Gong & Xu Yuan
7. Meiyuan Xincun
8. Ming Palace Ruins
9. Nanjing Museum
10. Xuanwu Lake
11. Drum and Bell Towers
12. Nanjing Yangzi River Bridge
13. Mochou Lake
14. Memorial Hall of the Victims in Nanjing Massacre by Japanese Invaders *(p237)*

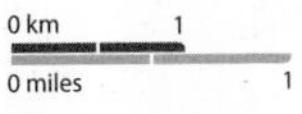

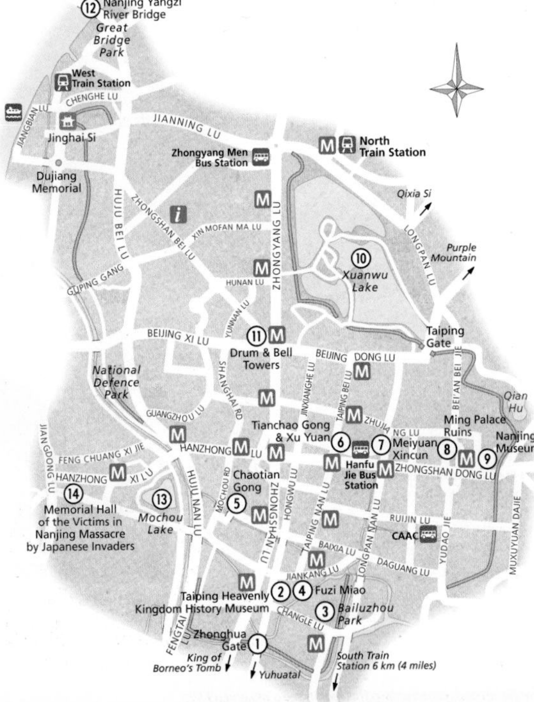

Key to Symbols *see back flap*

Zhonghua Gate

中华门

Built under the orders of the first Ming emperor, Hongwu, from 1368 to 1386, the walls surrounding the capital were the most extensive in the world at the time. The 40-ft (12-m) high walls snaked 20 miles (33 km) around the city's natural contours. Given that the city was elsewhere protected by river and mountain, Zhonghua Gate was a key element in Nanjing's southern defences. Its walls were cemented by a super-strong mortar made with glutinous rice. Certainly the emperor's show of defense was effective – no enemy attempted to breach the walls via Zhonghua Gate. Today the gate's impressive remains are open to visitors and an interesting museum has been built into the battlements.

The city wall adjacent to Zhonghua Gate, Nanjing

★ Inner Citadels

Behind the main gate are three courtyards or citadels. During an attack, enemy forces that breached the main gate could be trapped in these courtyards. The cavities in the walls concealed soldiers waiting in ambush.

Reconstruction of Zhonghua Gate

The main gate tower sat adjacent to the top of the wall, with the citadels protruding into the city. Today, only the brick walls remain – none of the gatehouses has survived.

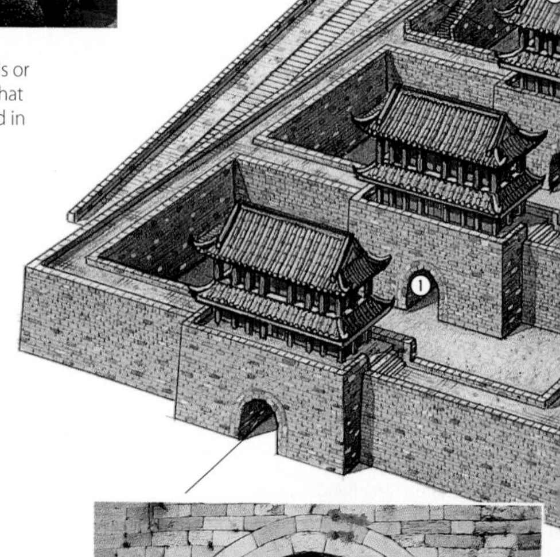

KEY

① **Portcullises** blocked passage through the gateways. The grooves are still visible.

② **Four gatehouses**, sitting above each arched gateway, contained armaments and supplies.

③ **Decorative** ***wen***

④ **The main gate tower** acted as the first line of defense, providing protection from enemy fire and a lookout point.

★ Arched Gateways

Four arched tunnels, each as long as 174 ft (53 m), run through the battlements. Each gate had massive double doors and a portcullis.

★ Signed Bricks
Numerous bricks are stamped with the name of the kiln where they were fired and even the name of the brick-maker himself, together with the date of manufacture.

VISITORS' CHECKLIST

Practical Information
Zhonghua Lu. **Tel** (025) 8662 5752.
Open 8:30am–8pm daily.

Transportation
16 from city center.

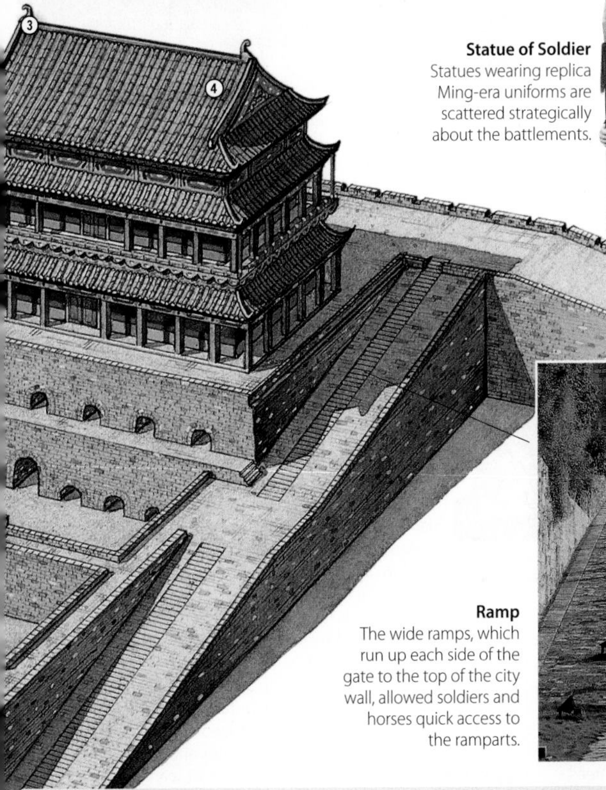

Statue of Soldier
Statues wearing replica Ming-era uniforms are scattered strategically about the battlements.

Ramp
The wide ramps, which run up each side of the gate to the top of the city wall, allowed soldiers and horses quick access to the ramparts.

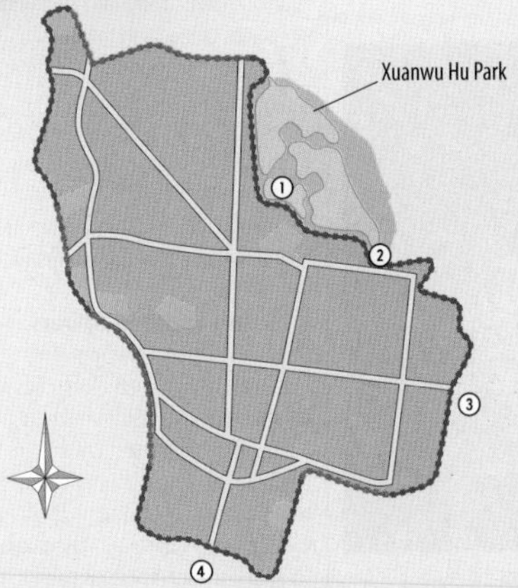

Nanjing's City Walls

Originally 20 miles (33 km) long, much of the wall, about 75 per cent, remains. The most impressive sections are near the refurbished Xuanwu Gate in the north and the long strip in the east. Parts, but not all, of the existing wall can be walked along.

1. Xuanwu Gate
2. Taiping Gate
3. Zhongshan Gate
4. Zhonghua Gate

Xuanwu Hu Park

0 km 1
0 miles 1

Key

Existing wall
Path of destroyed wall

Meiyuan Xincun

18–1 Hanfu Lu. **Tel** (025) 8454 2362. **Open** 7:30am–8:30pm daily.

The former Chinese Communist Party office was headed in 1946–7 by Zhou Enlai *(see p256)*, who lived here during negotiations with the Kuomintang after the Japanese surrender. The restored building houses a museum commemorating these events.

Ming Palace Ruins

311 Zhongshan Donglu. Mingugong. **Tel** (025) 8480 3110. **Open** 8am–6pm daily.

The old Ming Palace (Ming Gugong) was built in the 14th century for the first Ming emperor, Hongwu, who made Nanjing his capital. Within a century of its construction, this splendid palace was severely damaged by two fires. Later, the Manchus and then the Taiping soldiers completed its destruction. All that remains are ten marble bridges, the old Wu Men or Meridian Gate, and a large number of pillar bases with finely sculpted details. The pillars also give an idea of the layout of the palace buildings. Along its main axis, the palace would have had three major courtyards enclosed by enormous halls raised on platforms. These were flanked on either side by altars and temples. Beijing's Forbidden City *(see pp92–5)* is a larger version of this palace complex. The grounds have plenty of trees, which offer shade in summer.

Sculptural detail, Ming Palace Ruins

Xuanwu Lake, with the city's skyscrapers in the background

Nanjing Museum

321 Zhongshan Donglu. **Tel** (025) 8480 7923. **Open** 8am–4:30pm daily. **njmuseum.com/en**

Nanjing Museum, founded in 1933, is one of China's better museums and worth a visit. Its highlights include wonderful ornate sedan chairs, bronzes from the Zhou dynasty, and model trading ships. The collection of jade and lacquerware includes a jade burial suit consisting of rectangles of jade sewn together with silver thread, dating from the Eastern Han dynasty. Also on display are bricks from the city wall, pictures of the old city, and relics from the Taiping Heavenly Kingdom Rebellion. Many of the exhibits are captioned in English, which makes the museum even more interesting.

Purple Mountain

See pp234–5.

Xuanwu Lake

Xuanwu Park. **Tel** (025) 8361 4286. **Open** 7am–9pm daily. **xuanwuhu.net**

In the northeast corner of the city an especially fine stretch of the Ming city walls skirts the western shore of the enormous Xuanwu Lake, situated in Xuanwu Park. At well over 1 mile (1.6 km) long, the lake was an important water source for the city, as well as a popular imperial resort for many centuries. During the Song dynasty, it was also used for naval exercises. The park was opened to the public after the fall of the Qing dynasty in 1911.

Xuanwu Lake has five small islands named after the five continents, which are linked by bridges and causeways. They offer a variety of entertainment options with teahouses, restaurants, pavilions, boats of various types, an open-air theater, and even a small zoo. The most scenic is Yingzhou Island, delightfully laid out with lily pads, trees, and flowers. Although the park can get crowded, especially on weekends, it is a charming place to relax. The most convenient entrance is through the triple-arched Xuanwu Gate in the old city wall on Zhongyang Road.

Drum and Bell Towers

Gulou. **Open** 8am–5pm daily.

The much-restored Drum Tower dates back over 600 years to 1382, and is fronted by a traditional gateway. It was built to house several drums that were beaten through the night to mark the change of the

Marble pillar bases marking the layout of the palace, Ming Palace Ruins

watch, and occasionally to sound alarms. Today, only one large drum remains. The tower also houses a collection of amateur paintings, and a part of it has been converted into a teahouse. A short distance to the northeast is the Bell Tower (Dazhong Ting), constructed during the Ming dynasty and rebuilt in 1889. The huge bronze bell, cast in 1388, is one of the largest in China.

The area surrounding the towers was the administrative center of the old city. It is now a busy place, full of offices and heavy traffic.

Nanjing Massacre

Monument to the Nanjing Massacre

The Nanjing Massacre, or the Rape of Nanking as it is also known, is still an object of friction between the Chinese and the Japanese. In 1937, when the invading Japanese army succeeded in capturing Nanjing, a large number of civilians stayed behind instead of fleeing, following an appeal made by the Chinese government. While the government fled, the occupying army proceeded to carry out a brutal campaign of murder, pillage, and rape on the civilian population. It is thought that up to 400,000 people were killed in the incident. After Japan's surrender in 1945, the government returned to Nanjing and the city regained its status as the capital of China until the Communists shifted the capital back to Beijing in 1949.

Daqiao Gongyuan (Bridge Park) with Nanjing Yangzi River Bridge behind

Nanjing Yangzi River Bridge

Daqiao Nanlu. **Tel** (025) 5878 5703. Elevator: **Open** 8am–5pm daily.

This piece of engineering, completed in 1968, is one of the great achievements of the Chinese Communists, who took over the project after the Russians marched out in 1960. According to the official Chinese version, the bridge was built from scratch, as the Russians took the original plans with them when they left. The double-decker bridge, designed for road traffic as well as trains, is almost a mile (1.5 km) long, and is one of the longest in China. Before it was built, ferries used to carry entire trains across the river, one carriage at a time. An elevator takes visitors to the top of one of the towers, from where there are excellent views across the river. Also worth noting are the Soviet-style sculptures that decorate the bridge. The best approach to the bridge is through the Daqiao Gongyuan (Bridge Park).

Mochou Lake

Tel (025) 8665 1047. **Open** 5:30am–9:30pm daily.

Just outside the city wall in western Nanjing, Mochou Lake (Mochou Hu) is named after the legendary heroine Mochou. Her name, meaning "Without Sorrow," was bestowed because her singing was so sweet that it banished all sorrow. Surrounding the lake, Mochou Lake Park is especially pretty when the lotus flowers on the water are in full bloom. An open-air stage and a teahouse lie along the water's edge. The **Square Pavilion** contains a statue of Mochou in a pond, while the **Winning Chess Pavilion** next door was where the first Ming emperor, Hongwu, played chess with his general.

Square Pavilion with a statue of the legendary maiden Mochou, Mochou Lake Park

Purple Mountain

紫金山

Overlooking the city, Zijin Shan, or the Purple Mountain, is said to take its name from the color of the rocks. It is a picturesque area of gentle hills shaded by woodland and bamboo groves, dotted with villas. It also contains several of the most important points of interest in Nanjing, such as the Mausoleum of Dr. Sun Yat-sen, Ming Xiao Ling, and the Linggu Temple complex. Seeing everything will take a whole day and, although there are food stalls around, visitors are advised to take along a picnic. The energetic can make the long climb to the summit for splendid views over the city; alternatively you can take a cable car from outside the eastern wall.

Statue of Sun Yat-sen, "Father of Modern China," in his mausoleum

Purple Mountain Observatory
Alongside more modern equipment, the observatory houses a display of bronze instruments that date back to the 15th century. However, similar pieces were used by the Chinese as long as 3,000 years ago.

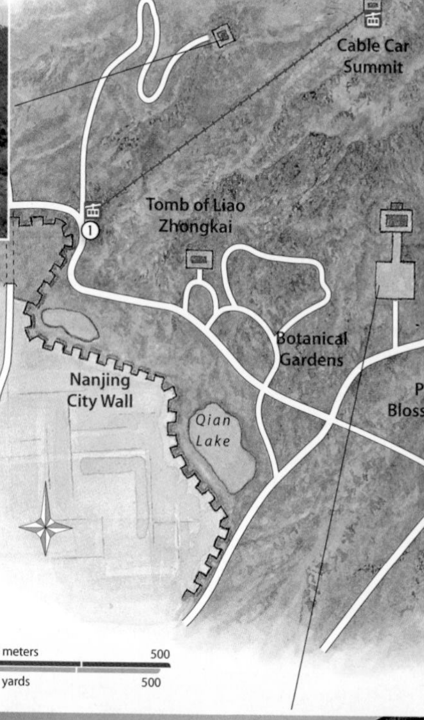

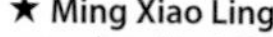

KEY

① **The cable car** goes to the summit in two stages and is recommended for the views.

② **The Music Stage** was built in 1933 as part of Sun Yat-sen's mausoleum.

★ Ming Xiao Ling
This tomb was completed in 1405 for the first Ming emperor, Hongwu, and his wife. Although much of it was destroyed in the Taiping Rebellion *(see p428)*, enough remains to give a sense of the grandeur of the original.

Museum of Dr. Sun Yat-sen
Set in a pretty building, this museum is often overlooked by visitors. Four floors of exhibits chronicle Sun Yat-sen's life with paintings, photographs, and personal effects.

VISITORS' CHECKLIST

Practical Information
Jiangsu province, 2 miles (3 km) E of Nanjing. Purple Mountain: **Tel** (025) 8444 6111. **Open** 24 hours daily. Ming Xiao Ling: **Open** 7:30am–6pm daily. Museum of Dr. Sun Yat-sen: **Open** 8:30am–5pm daily.

Transportation
M Muxuyuan. from the train station. There is a shuttle service in the park.

Linggu Pagoda
Built in 1929, this 199-ft (61-m) high pagoda was designed by Henry Murphy, at the behest of Chiang Kai-shek, in memory of the soldiers killed in the 1911 revolution *(see pp68–9)*.

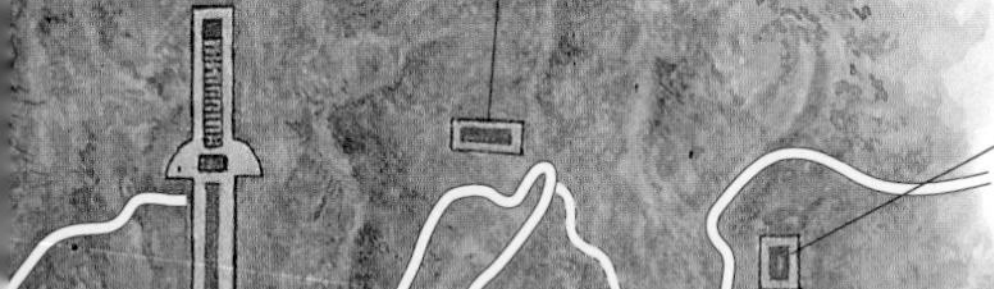

Guanghua Pavilion

★ Linggu Temple and Beamless Hall
Originally founded in AD 514, the temple was moved here by Ming Emperor Hongwu to make room for his tomb. It is most notable for the beamless hall, built in 1381 without using any wood in the construction.

★ Mausoleum of Dr. Sun Yat-sen
Despite the use of blue tiles, instead of the emperor's yellow ones, this grand mausoleum has imperial resonances. Completed in 1929, the blue and white colors represent the Nationalist Party.

For additional map symbols *see back flap*

Exploring the Purple Mountain

Also known as Zhongshan Mountain, after Sun Yat-sen's Mandarin name, the Purple Mountain (Zijin Shan) is best explored by starting from the easternmost site at the Linggu Temple and slowly working your way west back to the city. To fully explore the area requires a long day, but if time is scarce, half a day will do for visiting Sun Yat-sen's Mausoleum, the most popular site on the mountain, and one other. However, it is also pleasant just to get away from everybody else and wander the network of shady woodland paths that crisscross the hillside, and to visit the many smaller visitor attractions.

Lake beside the Linggu Temple at the foot of the Purple Mountain

Linggu Temple, Beamless Hall, and Pagoda

The Linggu Temple was originally sited where the Ming Emperor Hongwu wanted to build his tomb (Ming Xiao Ling), and so he had it moved to this site. The only original building that remains is the Beamless Hall. Built in 1381, it is a brick vaulted edifice constructed without any wooden beams. This was supposed to be the solution to a timber shortage, but, with few exceptions, it failed to be adopted. The nearby Linggu Pagoda was erected in memory of those soldiers who lost their lives in the 1911 revolution. It is inscribed in the handwriting of Chiang Kai-shek saying "repaying the country with extreme loyalty." The building is meant to combine the future and the past in that it is an old style of building – a pagoda – but constructed using modern materials: reinforced concrete. From the top, there is a great view of the thick green leafy carpet that cloaks the mountain.

Stone sculpture from the Xiao Ling sacred way

Museum of Dr. Sun Yat-sen

Slightly off the tourist trail, this museum is inside a beautiful building that once held a Buddhist library. The collection of paintings, black-and-white photos, and artifacts chronicles in detail the life of the "father of the people." The top two floors have captions in English. The Buddhist library of *sutras* is now housed in a separate building out the back.

Sun Yat-sen's Mausoleum (Zhongshan Ling)

The revolutionary leader died in 1925 and a competition was held to design his tomb. The winner was Y. C. Lu, a graduate of Cornell University School of Architecture. The tomb is approached up a typically long marble stairway of 392 steps and comprises a square hall with a life-size marble statue of the man leading to a round, domed building that contains his sarcophagus inset in the floor. There are other memorials in the area such as the **Music Stage**, an auditorium popular with picnicking visitors and the Guanghua Pavilion.

Xiao Ling Tomb

Although much of it is derelict, the site is mainly of interest as the first of the Ming tombs. The sacred way, an avenue of stone statues of pairs of animals and officials, some sitting, some standing on duty, is also impressive. Unusually it does not run south to north but winds its way up the hillside. South of the tomb lies the scenic area of **Plum Blossom Hill**, especially pretty in spring when the trees bloom pink. To the west lie the **Botanical Gardens**, a huge area with colourful planting, lawns, hills, and lakes. Nearby lies the **Tomb of Liao Zhongkai** (assassinated in Guangzhou in 1925) and his wife He Xiangning, prominent Nationalists who followed Sun Yat-sen.

Observatory

Built in the 1930s, the observatory is slightly run down these days. The main point of interest for the casual visitor is the small collection of copies of bronze Ming and Qing astronomical instruments.

Approach to the tomb of the first Ming emperor, Hongwu

Memorial to the 300,000 victims of the Nanjing Massacre

Memorial Hall of the Victims in Nanjing Massacre by Japanese Invaders

418 Shuiximen Lu. M Yun Jin Lu. **Tel** (025) 8661 2230. **Open** 8:30am–4:30pm Tue–Sun. W **nj1937.org**

Just west of Mochou Park, this site recalls the Japanese atrocities, known as the Nanjing Massacre *(see p233)*, that took place during the city's occupation in World War II. In the garden, shards of bone and piles of skulls are grim mementoes. Amid a photographic chronicle of the events, one room focuses on the post-War reconciliation between the two nations.

Martyrs' Memorial, Yuhuatai

Around Nanjing

There are plenty of interesting sites around Nanjing that are worth seeing along with the Purple Mountain. All can easily be reached by taxi, or in the case of Qixia Si, by bus.

Yuhuatai

215 Yuhua Lu. M Zhonghuamen. **Tel** (025) 5241 1523. **Open** 8am–5pm daily.

According to legend, Yuhuatai, south of Zhonghua Gate, is where a 5th-century monk gave a sermon that was so moving that flowers rained down from the sky. Chinese visitors still collect the colored pebbles that are found here. Sadly, the park became an execution ground during the Chinese Revolution (1927–49), and thousands lost their lives here. The **Martyrs' Memorial** consists of nine gigantic, 98-ft (30-m) high figures in typical Soviet realist style. Behind it is a pagoda, from where there are good views across the city.

Tomb of the King of Boni

9 Weijiu Lu. Over 1 mile (2 km) NW of Yuhuatai. M Tianlong Temple. **Tel** (025) 5235 5833. **Open** 8:30am–5pm daily.

Situated close to Yuhuatai, the Tomb of the King of Boni was discovered in 1958. The rulers of Boni (a medieval state on the island of Borneo) had been sending tribute to China since AD 977. In the mid-14th century, the first Ming emperor, Hongwu, greatly expanded the existing tribute system, whereby foreign nations paid "tribute" to China in the form of gifts and precious goods. He sent envoys to all of China's tributary states including Boni, to ensure that this economic exchange continued. The King of Boni arrived in Nanjing in 1408, but died during his stay. His tomb is marked with a tortoise stele and a sacred pathway with statues on either side. As the site is not clearly signposted it is advisable to have the tomb's name written in Chinese in order to ask for directions.

Qixia Si and Thousand Buddha Cliffs

Qixia Shan. 9 miles (15 km) NE of Nanjing. M Maqun, then bus 138. **Tel** (025) 8576 1831. **Open** 7am–5pm daily. W **en.njqixiashan.com**

One of the largest Buddhist seminaries in the country, Qixia Si was originally founded in AD 483, but the current building dates from 1908, at the end of the Qing dynasty. It consists of two principal temple halls; one has walls that are extensively covered with flying *apsaras* (celestial maidens), while the other houses a statue of an upright Vairocana Buddha, known as the Cosmic Buddha who is the embodiment of Truth and Knowledge. To the east stands an octagonal stone pagoda built in AD 601, which bears carvings of scenes from the life of the Buddha.

Behind the halls are the **Thousand Buddha Cliffs**. These are in fact just over 500 Buddha statues carved into the cliff face, but "thousand" is often used in China to denote "many." The earliest statues date to the 5th century Qi dynasty, while most were carved during the Song and Tang dynasties. Some statues were badly defaced during the bloody Taiping Rebellion *(see p428)* and again during the Cultural Revolution *(see pp70–71)*, but enough remain to make the visit worthwhile. Visitors can spend a few enjoyable hours walking in the woods behind the cliffs.

Octagonal stone pagoda with carvings of the Buddha's life, Qixia Si

Traditional Medicine

Medicine in China dates back some 4,000 years and evolved as a result of the search for the elixir of life, research in which many emperors took a keen interest. Over the centuries an approach was adopted that would today be called holistic – the importance of diet, emotional health, and environment was emphasized. Today, treatment is still founded on the use of herbs, diet, and acupuncture. Daoist philosophy is an integral ingredient, the most notable aspect being *qi* *(see pp38–9)*, the vital force of living things. *Qi* gives rise to the opposite and interdependent forces of *yin* and *yang*, signified in the universe and body by wet and dry, cold and heat, etc. Unlike Western medicine, where an outside force, such as bacteria or a virus, is assumed to cause disease, in Chinese medicine a medical problem is caused by a *yin-yang* imbalance within the patient. When *yin* and *yang* are out of balance, the flow of *qi* has been depleted or blocked; Chinese medical practitioners seek to return the balance.

10th-Century Channel Chart

Qi flows through channels that radiate throughout the body from the vital organs to the extremitites. This chart clearly illustrates a channel that runs from the intestines through the arm to the finger tips. Applying pressure to the specified points will moderate the flow of *qi*.

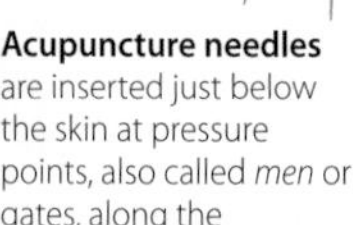

Acupuncture needles are inserted just below the skin at pressure points, also called *men* or gates, along the channels. Acupuncture has even proved an effective anesthetic.

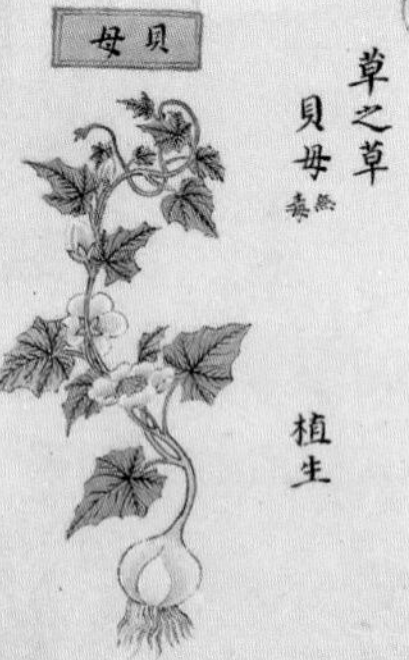

The *Bencao Gangmu*, a pharmacopeia of medicine listing all known diseases and their treatments, was compiled by the naturalist Li Shizhen during the 12th century.

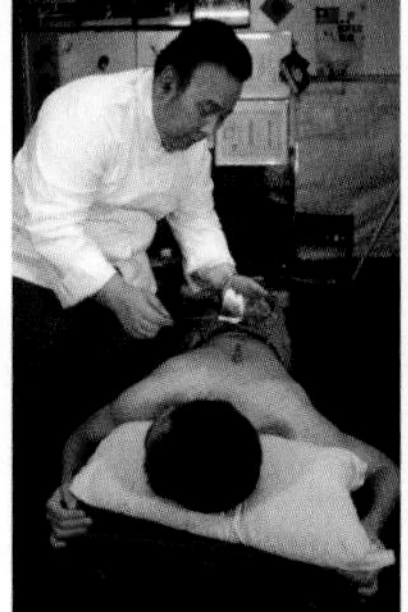

Moxibustion, used in chronic cases, involves burning artemisia leaves to heat up the pressure points. The heat is conveyed by needles, but the moxa is sometimes held so close to the skin that it singes.

A mixture of herbs, fungus, roots, bark, and sometimes dried animal products, such as ground antler, are carefully combined and dispensed to the patient, who boils the ingredients to make a powerful decoction.

Plaque over the beautifully decorated entrance to the Guangji Si, Wuhu

11 Bozhou
亳州

155 miles (250 km) NW of Hefei. 5,350,000.

Bozhou's **Medicinal Market** – the largest of its kind in the world – attracts over 6,000 traders from China and Southeast Asia. Every conceivable plant, insect, and animal limb, in whole and powdered form, can be found in its halls. Most business takes place in the morning.

The 17th-century **Flower Theater** has wood and brick carvings and painted friezes around the stage. The town's museum exhibits a Han-dynasty jade burial suit of the father of Cao Cao, the Three Kingdoms warlord, who built the **Underground Tunnel** to conceal the army, if attacked.

Medicinal Market
Zhongyao Shiyang. **Open** Mon–Fri.

Underground Tunnel
49 Renmin Zhong Lu.
Open 8am–6pm daily.

12 Hefei
合肥

93 miles (150 km) W of Nanjing. 7,600,000. 100 Dongliu Lu. **Tel** (0551) 353 7378.

Anhui's provincial capital grew into a flourishing industrial center after 1949, when the new Communist government supported the growth of industry in areas that had been previously impoverished. Visitors are likely to pass through Hefei while exploring the province.

The **Provincial Museum** has some interesting exhibits including bricks from Han-dynasty tombs, a cranium belonging to *Homo erectus* discovered in Anhui, and an exhibition on the "Four Treasures of the Study" *(see p225)*, mainly ink sticks, ink stones, brushes, and paper, for which the province is known. Baohe Park, set around a pretty tree flanked by a lake, has a **Memorial Hall** devoted to the great Song dynasty administrator, Lord Bao. The 16th-century **Mingjiao Si** temple stands 16 ft (5 m) above the ground, while nearby **Xiaoyaojin Park** has a 3rd-century well and is good for walks.

Li Bai's Tomb, Caishiji

Provincial Museum
268 Huaining Lu. **Tel** (0551) 373 6655.
Open 9am–5pm Tue–Sun. **ahm.cn**

Lord Bao Memorial Hall
72 Anhui Wuhu. **Tel** (0551) 6288 5950.
Open 9am–5pm (6pm in summer).

Mingjiao Si
44 Huaihe Lu. **Tel** (0551) 265 6284.
Open 6:30am–6pm daily.

13 Wuhu
芜湖

78 miles (125 km) SE of Hefei. CITS, Beijing Xi Lu. **Tel** (0553) 388 3881.

The province's main ferry port has little to offer. Its few sights include the **Guangji Si** on Zhe Shan, founded in AD 894, and the nearby **Zhe Ta** (Ocher Pagoda), from where there are views over the town. Some streets in the town's center are lined with old houses with thatched roofs and mud walls, and make for a nice stroll. Wuhu is a good base for visiting **Li Bai's Tomb** at Caishiji, 4 miles (7 km) from Ma'an Shan, the first stop south of Wuhu on the railway line. Li Bai (AD 701–62), a Tang-dynasty poet, was a famous drunk and is said to have died drowning in the moon's reflection. His tomb stands at the top of a long series of steps behind a Qing-dynasty temple, and overlooks the Yangzi. It may only contain Li Bai's clothes, as his final resting place is still the subject of debate.

Li Bai's Tomb
Caishiji. 12.
Tel (0555) 668 3504.
Open 8am–5:30pm daily.

Environs: Some 37 miles (60 km) southeast of Wuhu, **Xuancheng** is the site of the Alligator Breeding Center, which has increased the population of this endangered species. Found only in Anhui, the wild population remains small, but the captive population now runs into thousands, and it may soon be possible to reintroduce these reptiles back into the wild.

Alligators sunning themselves in Xuancheng's breeding center

⓮ Jiuhua Shan
九华山

100 miles (160 km) SE of Hefei. Chizhou Jiuhuashan. from Nanjing, Hefei, Tongling, or Chizhou. (0566) 283 3798. **jiuhuashan.gov.cn**

One of the four mountains holy to Chinese Buddhists, Jiuhua Shan has been sacred since the Korean monk Jin Qiaojue – thought to be a reincarnation of Bodhisattva Ksitigarbha – died here in AD 794. It is also an important place of pilgrimage for the recently bereaved, who come to hold services for those who have passed on.

Over 60 temples, linked by paths from Jiuhua village, dot the mountain. The first is the Qing-dynasty **Zhiyuan Si**, with a honeycomb of halls. Farther up is the oldest temple, **Huacheng Si**, a part of which possibly dates to the Tang era. Beyond, an ornamental gate marks the path up the mountain. From here, one option is an hour-long walk that passes Yingke Song (Welcoming Pine), and bears left past a series of temples until **Baisui Gong**, where the preserved body of the priest Wu Xia sits at prayer. Visitors can either walk back or take the funicular railway. The other option is the path going to the right at Yingke Song and leads to **Feng Huang Song** (Phoenix Pine) to the summit at **Tiantai Zhengding** (Heavenly Terrace), where a huge Buddha statue is due to be built. The four-hour walk to the summit can be shortened by taking the cable car from Feng Huang Song, and returning by taxi.

A restored Ming-dynasty shop, Lao Jie (Old Street), Tunxi

⓯ Tunxi
屯溪

44 miles (70 km) SE of Huang Shan. 28 Binjiang Xi Lu, (0559) 251 2449. **hsta.gov.cn**

An important transportation hub for visiting the popular Huang Shan *(see pp242–3)*, the town of Tunxi has numerous fine examples of traditional classical architecture. In certain areas, such as along **Lao Jie** (Old Street), restored houses dating to the Ming dynasty have been converted into shops selling souvenirs and antiques, while others serve as tourist restaurants. The high standard of restoration gives visitors a clear picture of a typical Ming-era town. Many of the houses bear the decorative "horsehead gables" *(see opposite)*, which originally had a practical use as fire baffles.

The serene Jiuhua Shan or Nine Glorious Mountains

⓰ Shexian
歙县

16 miles (25 km) NE of Tunxi. minibus from Tunxi.

Formerly known as Huizhou, Shexian is renowned for its wealth of well-preserved Ming-dynasty houses, once owned by wealthy salt merchants. Many of these houses lie along the lanes off Jiefang Jie and along Doushan Jie, still occupied exactly as they were as far back as the 14th century.

The wealthy Huizhou tradesmen also erected many memorial archways *(paifang)* in Shexian county, but the most famous is the complex of seven Ming and Qing arches at **Tangyue,** a village about 4 miles (7 km) west of Shexian. The arches acknowledge the political career, filial piety, chastity, and charity of a successful local family.

⓱ Yixian
黟县

22 miles (35 km) NW of Tunxi. minibus from Tunxi, Hongcun and Xidi **Open** daily. **Tel** (0559) 555 3333.

The UNESCO World Heritage Sites of **Hongcun** and **Xidi**, known for their Ming and Qing houses, lie in the vicinity of Yixian. About 7 miles (11 km) to the northeast, Hongcun dates to 1131. Ringed by mountains, it is known as "a village in a Chinese painting." The village is laid out in the shape of a water buffalo and is watered by a network of canals that feed the Moon Pond and South Lake, representing the buffalo's stomach, while the canals represent its intestines.

Xidi, 5 miles (8 km) north of Yixian, has a maze of lanes flanked by over 100 houses, dating mainly from the late Ming and early Qing eras. Some have charming courtyards, while their interiors are often decorated with carved wooden screens and panels. Some houses feature performances of local arts. **Nanping**, 3 miles (5 km) west of Yixian, also has fine examples of classical architecture.

For hotels and restaurants in this region see p560 and p577

Huizhou Architecture

Shexian county is home to the descendants of a group of people who played a key role in the Chinese economy 400 years ago. Today, the people of southern Anhui province are mostly farmers, but from the 14th to 17th centuries, their forefathers were the wealthy merchants of Huizhou, famous the length and breadth of China for their commercial acumen and integrity. They used their money to build large family houses, with whitewashed exteriors and beautiful wood interiors. The distinctive features of these houses are a result of social and environmental factors, and are attempts to deal with the weather, earthquakes and the risk of attack by bandits. Many of these houses still remain, sometimes a little run down, but still a testament to the enterprise of the Huizhou traders.

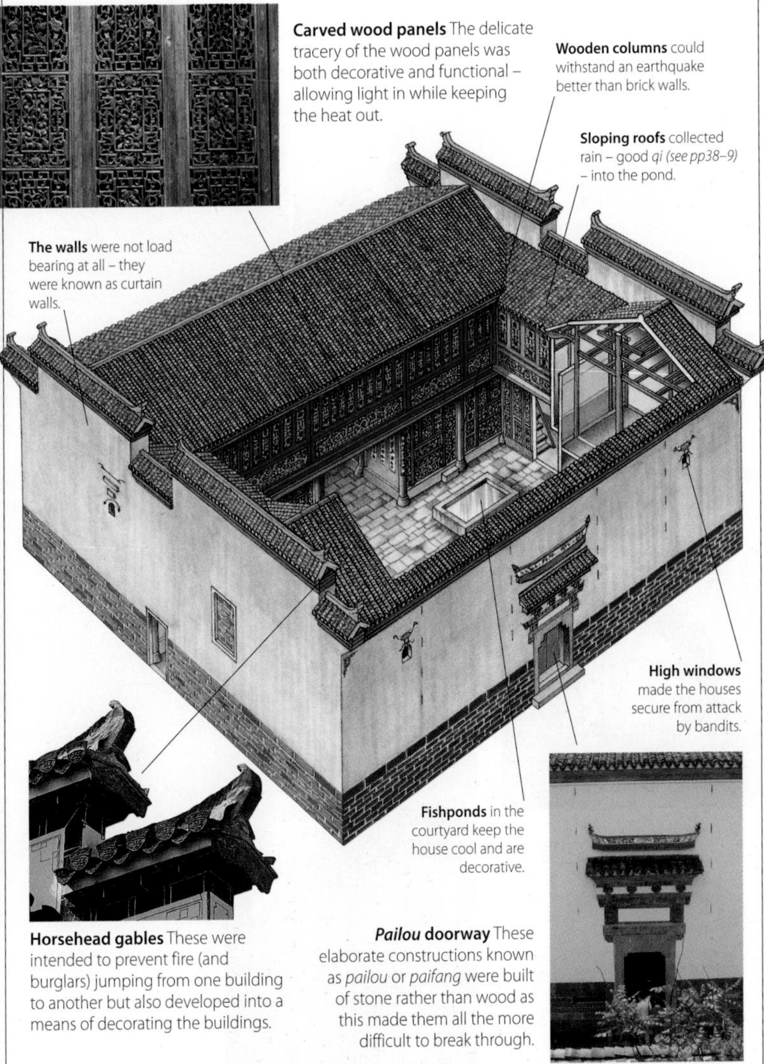

Carved wood panels The delicate tracery of the wood panels was both decorative and functional – allowing light in while keeping the heat out.

Wooden columns could withstand an earthquake better than brick walls.

Sloping roofs collected rain – good *qi* *(see pp38–9)* – into the pond.

The walls were not load bearing at all – they were known as curtain walls.

High windows made the houses secure from attack by bandits.

Fishponds in the courtyard keep the house cool and are decorative.

Horsehead gables These were intended to prevent fire (and burglars) jumping from one building to another but also developed into a means of decorating the buildings.

***Pailou* doorway** These elaborate constructions known as *pailou* or *paifang* were built of stone rather than wood as this made them all the more difficult to break through.

⓲ Huangshan

黄山

Reputed to be the most beautiful mountain range in the country, the startling, cloud-cloaked peaks of Huangshan (Yellow Mountain) have for centuries been celebrated by poets and painters. Although the main peak is under 6,200 ft (1,900 m), the 70 sheer rock cliffs are spectacular to hike, and the winding concrete steps are usually very crowded. Even when shrouded in mist as is the norm, the scenery of precipitous peaks, bamboo groves, and ancient, twisted pines is unusually beautiful. Accommodation is available in pretty Wenquan or nearby Tangkou. Consider spending a night at the top for spectacular, but not solitary, sunsets and sunrises.

Taiping

①

Guangming Ding (Bright Summit Peak) 6035 ft

Lianhua Feng (Lotus Flower Peak) 6145 ft

Shen Quan Feng 5340 ft

Banshan

Wen

★ Feilai Shi

The "Rock Flown From Afar," a massive, rectangular boulder poised at an unlikely angle, overlooks the "Western Sea," an endless vista of mountain peaks and cascading clouds.

Western Trail

This path, more physically demanding than the eastern route, cuts through splendid rock formations, along narrow, and very steep, flights of steps.

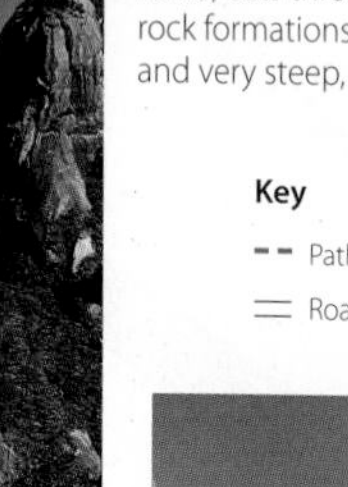

Key

-- Path

═ Road

KEY

 **Qingliang Tai** (Refreshing Terrace) is a popular spot for watching the sunrise.

Welcoming Guest Pine

Ying Ke Song, featured on endl postage stamps, appears to be the visitor up the mountain an said to be over a thousand yea

View from the Top
The summit with its stunning views takes about 3 hours to explore. Head to Paiyun Ting, "Cloud Dispelling Pavilion," at the top of the Taiping cable car, for the best views of the sunset.

VISITORS' CHECKLIST

Practical Information
125 miles (200 km) S of Hefei. **Tel** (0559) 566 1111. **Open** daily. Cable car: 8:40am–4pm daily.
huangshanguide.com

Transportation
Tunxi. Tunxi. from Huangshan city; from Nanjing or Hefei to Tangkou (5 hr); from Tunxi to Tangkou (1.5 hr).

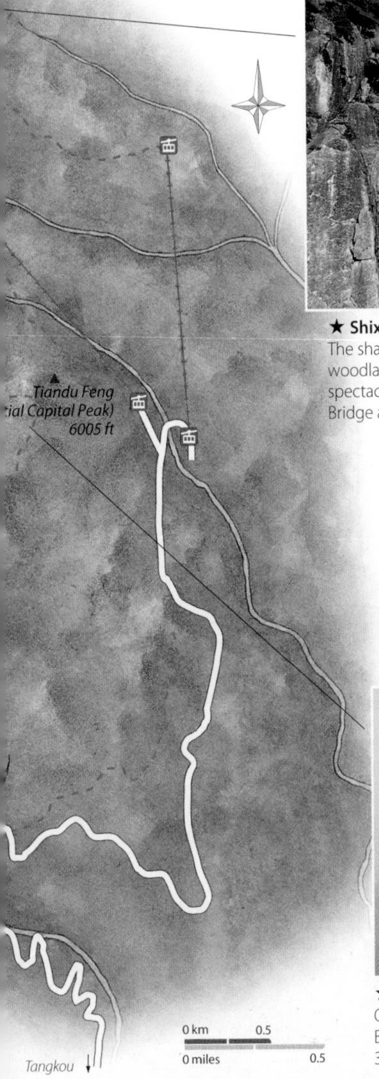

★ Shixin Feng
The shard-like "Beginning to Believe" peaks, rising above woodland and glistening streams, offer one of the most spectacular views at Huangshan. Access is via the Immortals' Bridge at the eastern end of the summit.

Tiandu Feng
ial Capital Peak)
6005 ft

Exploring Huangshan

The eastern route (5 miles/8 km) takes about 3 hours; the western route (9 miles/15 km) up to twice that. Some hikers choose to take the eastern route up and the western route down. Three cable cars allow you to bypass much of the walking, but the line-ups are usually very long, especially on weekends, when you may have to wait for up to 2 hours.

★ Aoyu Bei
On the approach to Tiandu Feng, Aoyu Bei (the Carp's Backbone), is a disconcertingly exposed and narrow 30-ft (9-m) arch with sheer drops down both sides.

0 km 0.5
0 miles 0.5
Tangkou

For additional map symbols *see back flap*

ZHEJIANG & JIANGXI

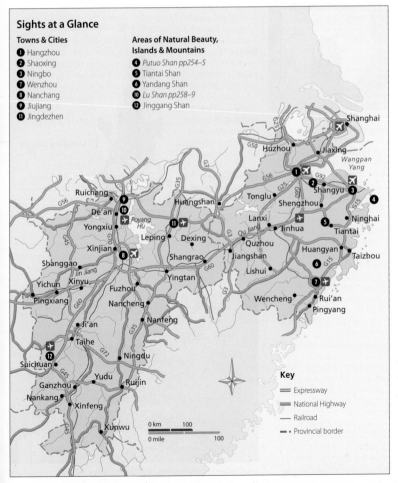

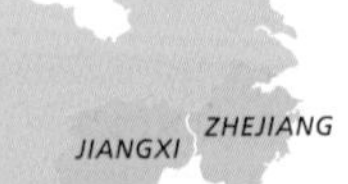

Lying immediately to the south of Shanghai, Zhejiang is bordered by Jiangxi to its southwest. Northern Zhejiang is a vast region of fertile farmland, with canal towns such as the provincial capital of Hangzhou, and lovely Shaoxing. Hangzhou and the great port of Ningbo are the region's chief industrial and commercial centers. Just off Zhejiang's coastline are some 18,000 islands, among them the holy shrine of Putuo Shan. The south of the province is rugged and mountainous, with superb scenery at Yandang Shan.

Landlocked Jiangxi is sparsely populated compared to the rest of central China. Its northern reaches are a fertile plain watered by Poyang Hu, the largest freshwater lake in China, and the rivers that feed it. Nanchang, the provincial capital, prospered in the 7th century, following the construction of the Grand Canal. With the growth of coastal treaty ports in the mid-19th century, Jiangxi's economy declined. Later, in the early 20th century, civil strife forced millions into exile. The rugged Jinggang Shan mountains in southern Jiangxi, where most of the fighting took place, are rich in revolutionary associations. In the province's northeast lie the porcelain town of Jingdezhen and the charming mountain resort of Lu Shan.

Sights at a Glance

Towns & Cities

1 Hangzhou
2 Shaoxing
3 Ningbo
7 Wenzhou
8 Nanchang
9 Jiujiang
11 Jingdezhen

Areas of Natural Beauty, Islands & Mountains

4 *Putuo Shan pp254–5*
5 Tiantai Shan
6 Yandang Shan
10 *Lu Shan pp258–9*
12 Jinggang Shan

Key

Expressway
National Highway
Railroad
Provincial border

0 km 100
0 mile 100

◀ Boats on West Lake, Hangzhou, with Leifeng Pagoda in the background

For additional map symbols *see back flap*

❶ Hangzhou

杭州

Renowned in medieval China as an earthly paradise, Hangzhou became the splendid capital of the Southern Song dynasty between 1138 and 1279. Later, when the conquering Mongols chose what is now Beijing as their new capital, Hangzhou continued to be a thriving commercial city. Its glories were extolled by Marco Polo, who allegedly visited Hangzhou at the height of its prosperity and described it as "the City of Heaven, the most magnificent in all the world." Although most of the old buildings were destroyed in the Taiping Rebellion, the attractive West Lake and its surrounding area have been extensively restored and are well worth visiting.

Entrance archway to Yue Fei Mu (Tomb of Yue Fei)

Yue Fei Mu

80 Bei Shan Rd. **Tel** (0571) 8798 6653. **Open** 7:30am–5:30pm daily.

Just north of the West Lake lies the tomb of the Song General Yue Fei, a Chinese hero revered for his patriotism. His campaigns against the invading Jin were so successful that his overlords began to worry that he might turn against them. He was falsely charged with sedition and executed, only to become a martyr.

The Yue Fei Temple is a late 19th-century construction, and the tomb lies beside it. The central tumulus belongs to Yue Fei, while the smaller one is his son's, who was also executed. The kneeling figures in iron represent his tormentors – the prime minister, his wife, a jealous general, and the prison governor. It was customary to spit on them, but this is no longer encouraged.

Huanglong Dong Park & Qixia Shan

North of West Lake (Xi Hu).

Huanglong Dong Park, nestling in the hills, is very attractive with its teahouses, ponds, and flowers, and a pavilion where musicians perform traditional music in summer. To the east is **Baoshu Ta**, a 20th-century rebuild of a Song-era pagoda. Looming close by is Qixia Shan (Lingering Clouds Mountain), with the **Baopu Daoist Compound** located halfway up its slopes. This active temple has services on most days.

Wood panel carving at Baopu Daoist Temple

Hu Qingyu Tang Museum of Chinese Medicine

95 Dajing Xiang. **Tel** (0571) 8781 5209. **Open** 8:30am–5pm daily.

This interesting museum is housed in a beautiful old apothecary's shop. It was established by the merchant Hu Xueyan during the Qing dynasty and traces the history of traditional Chinese medicine, which goes back thousands of years. It is still an active dispensary and pharmacy.

West Lake

See pp248–9.

Former Residence of Hu Xueyan

18 Yuanbao Jie. **Tel** (0571) 8606 4752. **Open** 8am–5:30pm daily.

Hu Xueyan's small but perfectly formed mansion is a great place both to learn about this former merchant's rags-to-riches-to-rags story and to appreciate a sublime example of Qing architecture.

China National Tea Museum

88 Longjing Rd. **Tel** (0571) 8796 4221. **Open** 8:30am–4:30pm Tue–Sun. **www.teamuseum.cn**

Tracing the history of tea production *(see p299)*, this museum explores the different varieties of tea, its cultivation, and the development of tea-making and tea-drinking vessels.

Longjing Village

SW of Tea Museum.

The village of Longjing (Dragon Well) produces one of China's most famous varieties of green tea. Visitors can wander around the tea terraces, catching glimpses of the different stages of production – cutting, sorting, and drying – and also buy the tea.

Inside the main hall of the Hu Qingyu Tang Museum of Chinese Medicine

Lingyin Si

1 Fayun Nong, Lingyin Rd. **Tel** (0571) 8796 8665. **Open** 7am–6pm daily.
en.lingyinsi.org

The hill area known as Feilai Feng (The Peak that Flew Here) is home to some of the city's main sights, including Lingyin Si. Founded in AD 326, this temple once housed 3,000 monks who worshiped in more than 70 halls. Though now much reduced in size, it is still one of China's largest temples. It was damaged in the 19th century Taiping Rebellion, and then again by fire in the 20th century. It is said to owe its survival to Zhou Enlai *(see p256)*, who prevented its destruction during the Cultural Revolution. Still, some parts of the temple are ancient, such as the stone pagodas on either side of the entrance hall that date from AD 969. Behind this hall is the **Great Buddha Hall**, with an impressive 66-ft (20-m) statue of the Buddha carved in 1956 from camphor wood.

The **Ligong Pagoda** at the entrance was built in honor of the Indian monk Hui Li, who gave the mountain its eccentric name. Hui Li thought it was the spitting image of a hill in India and asked whether it had flown here. Feilai Feng is known for the dozens of Buddhist sculptures carved into the rock, many dating from the 10th century.

VISITORS' CHECKLIST

Practical Information

108 miles (180 km) SW of Shanghai. 8,700,000. 228 Yan'an Lu, (0571) 5719 6123.
en.gotohz.com

Transportation

Train station, East & South train stations. East, North & West bus stations, CAAC (to airport).

Buddha sculptures at Feilai Feng

Six Harmonies Pagoda

84 Zhijiang Lu. **Tel** (0571) 8659 1401. **Open** 6:30am–5:30pm daily.

Standing beside the railway bridge on the northern shore of the Qiantang River, Liuhe Ta is all that is left of an octagonal temple first built in AD 970 to placate the tidal bore, a massive wall of water that rushes upstream during high tide. Over 197-ft (60-m) high, it served as a lighthouse up until the Ming dynasty.

Hangzhou City Center

① Yue Fei Mu
② Huanglong Dong Park & Qixia Shan
③ Hu Qingyu Tang Museum of Chinese Medicine
④ West Lake
⑤ Former Residence of Hu Xueyan
⑥ China National Tea Museum
⑦ Longjing Village
⑧ Lingyin Si
⑨ Six Harmonies Pagoda

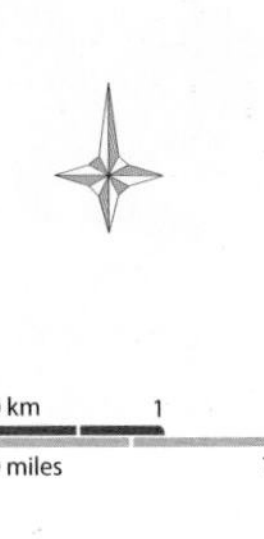

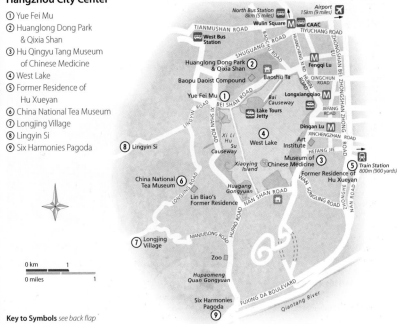

Key to Symbols *see back flap*

West Lake

西湖

Long considered one of the scenic wonders of China, covering over 3 square miles (8 sq km), West Lake (Xi Hu) is situated at the heart of Hangzhou. Surrounded by gentle green hills, the lake's willow-shaded causeways and fragrant cover of lotus blossoms have long been an inspiration for artists. Originally the lake was an inlet off the estuary of the Qiantang River, becoming a lake when the river began to silt up in the 4th century. The lake had a tendency to flood, so several dykes were built, including the Bai and Su Causeways. Hiring a private boat from the eastern shore for an afternoon on the water is highly recommended, as is a leisurely stroll along the shady causeways.

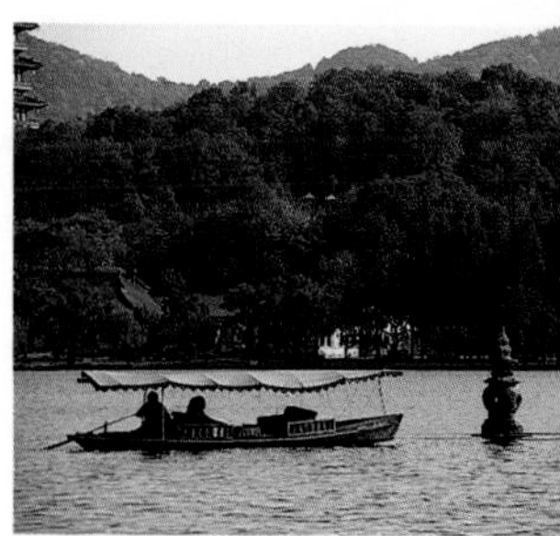

★ Three Pools Reflecting the Moon
Three small stone pagodas rise from the waters near Xiaoying Island. At full moon candles are placed within and their opening are covered in paper to create reflections resembling the moon.

XI LI HU

Huagang Garden
This garden is intended as a place for viewing fish. Designed by a Song-dynasty eunuch, its pools are filled with shimmering goldfish in a restful setting of grasses and trees.

★ Xiaoying Island
Often called San Tan Yin Yue Island, referring to the three moon-reflecting pagodas off its shores, Xiaoying Island consists of four enclosed pools fringed by pavilions first built in 1611. The zig-zagging Nine Bend Bridge was built in 1727.

KEY

① **The Seal Engravers Society** is open in the summer months.

② **Zhejiang Provincial Museum**

For hotels and restaurants in this region see p560 and p578

★ Su Causeway

The longer of the two causeways takes its name from the Song-dynasty poet Su Dongpo, who also served as governor. Linked by six stone bridges, the causeway is a peaceful thoroughfare running along the lake's western edge.

VISITORS' CHECKLIST

Practical Information

Hangzhou.
Zhejiang Provincial Museum: 25 Gushan Rd. **Tel** (0571) 8797 1177. **Open** 9am–5pm Tue–Sun.
W zhejiangmuseum.com

Transportation

regularly from eastern shore near Hubin Rd. Boats for hire on Gu Shan Island.

Bridge to Quyuan Garden

This bridge leads to a stunning garden surrounded by lotus flowers. It is considered one of the ten prospects from where the lake can be seen to best advantage.

GU SHAN

XI HU

BEI LI HU

Marco Polo

Whether Marco Polo ever visited China is much disputed. However, according to the book he dictated to a ghostwriter who embroidered it substantially, Polo became governor of nearby Yangzhou for three years during the Yuan dynasty. He describes Hangzhou as paradise and the finest city in the world, with fascinating markets, pleasure boats, and prostitutes. Hangzhou was indeed a cosmopolitan city, ever since the Southern Song dynasty made it their capital. *The Travels of Marco Polo*, however, may be based on earlier journeys by his father and uncle, and stories from other merchants.

Engraving of Marco Polo, 1254–1324

Bai Causeway

Named after the 9th-century poet-governor Bai Juyi, this dyke leads to Gu Shan, an island first landscaped during the Tang dynasty, and now containing a teahouse and the provincial museum.

Lu Xun's Former Residence, Shaoxing

❷ Shaoxing
绍兴

47 miles (67 km) SE of Hangzhou. 4,900,000. 288 Zhongxing Zhong Rd, (0575) 8520 0067. **en.sx.gov.cn**

Despite the proliferation of new buildings, this canal town has retained its charm, with its narrow streets, arched bridges, and whitewashed houses. Ancient Shaoxing was the capital of the Yue kingdom during 770–221 BC. It remained important over the years, even when Hangzhou became the Song capital. Today, it is a scenic place to explore for its waterways.

The **Qing Teng Shu Wu** (Green Vine Study), former home of the 16th-century writer and artist Xu Wei, lies off Dacheng Long, an alley not far from Jiefang Nan Road. Regarded as the best example of traditional domestic architecture in China, the house has a simple ornamental garden, while one of its rooms displays Xu's expressive art.

There are also several houses associated with Lu Xun, perhaps the best-known modern Chinese writer, born here in 1881. Most of them are clustered together on Lu Xun Road. **Lu Xun's Former Residence** is a fine example of domestic architecture, though it is a bit empty now that most of his personal items have been moved to the nearby Luxun Memorial Hall. Opposite is Sanwei Shuwu, the school where he studied.

Shaoxing's most famous bridge, the 13th-century **Bazi Qiao**, resembles the Chinese character for number 8, and lies in an area of old streets off Baziqiao Zhi Jie, north of Lu Xun Lu.

The town makes a good base for several excursions. The scenic **Dong Hu** (East Lake) is nearby. Visitors can also take a boat to **Yu Ling**, allegedly the tomb of Yu the Great, founder of the Xia kingdom (2200 BC). Farther out is **Lan Ting** (Orchid Pavilion), where China's greatest calligrapher, Wang Xizhi (AD 321–79), threw a party where, so one story goes, guests had to drink cups of wine as they floated past and compose a poem, recorded by the host.

Stone lion, Tianye Ge

Qing Teng Shu Wu
10 Qian Guan Xiang.
Open 8:30am–5pm daily.

Lu Xun's Former Residence
235 Lu Xun Zhong Rd. **Tel** (0575) 8513 2080. **Open** 8:30am–5pm daily.

❸ Ningbo
宁波

90 miles (145 km) SE of Hangzhou. 3,500,000. 510 Heqing Bei Lu, (0574) 8911 5389. **english.ningbo.gov.cn**

China's greatest port between the Song and Ming eras, Ningbo is located upstream from the coast on the Yong River. It was later eclipsed by Shanghai, but has regained some importance due to its deep natural harbor. The town has had a long association with commerce. When Shanghai and Guangzhou prospered in the 19th and early 20th centuries, Ningbo's residents were employed as "compradors," agents or mediators by the foreign companies.

Ningbo's main sight is the **Tianye Ge**, a 16th-century private library, the oldest in China. It resembles a traditional garden with bamboo groves, rockeries, and pavilions, one of which exhibits ancient books and scrolls. To the southeast off Kaiming Jie, is the 14th-century Tianfeng Pagoda. The former foreign concession lies at the northern end of Xinjiang Bridge, with a 17th-century Portuguese church and a riverside Bund. Outside the city, **Baoguo Si** temple's Mahavira Hall is the oldest surviving wooden building in the Yangzi delta region.

Tianyi Ge
5 Tianyi Jie. **Tel** (0574) 8729 3856. **Open** 8am–5:30pm daily (to 5pm in winter). **tianyige.com.cn/en**

Charming narrow streets around Tianye Ge, Ningbo

◀ Pavilion on bridge over West Lake, Hangzhou

❹ Putuo Shan

See pp254–5.

The Guoqing Si monastery, at the foot of Tiantai Shan

❺ Tiantai Shan
天台山

118 miles (190 km) SE of Hangzhou. **Tel** (0576) 8388 1002. **Open** 7am–9pm daily.

The Heavenly Terrace Mountain – Tiantai Shan – is the seat of the Tiantai Buddhist sect, which also has strong links with Daoism *(see pp36–7)*. A pilgrimage site since the Eastern Jin, today it is especially popular with Japanese Buddhists, who regard China as the Buddhist motherland. The sect's founder, the monk Zhiyi, spent most of his life on the mountain, where the imperial court helped him to construct a temple. This wonderfully scenic spot, with its paths, streams, and woodlands, is ideal for walking. Several famous plants such as Hua Ding cloud and mist tea, and the Tiantai mandarin orange, as well as a variety of medicinal plants, were discovered here.

The first of Tiantai Shan's monasteries, **Guoqing Si**, lies at its foot, 2 miles (3 km) from Tiantai village. From here, a road leads to the 3,609 ft (1,100 m) **Huading Peak**. Visitors can then walk to Baijingtai Si (Prayer Terrace Temple) on the summit or to Shiliang (Stone Beam) Waterfall, near the Upper Fangguang Monastery, where there are a number of inscriptions, including one by the famous Song artist, Mi Fu.

The **Zhenjue Si** (Monastery of True Enlightenment) houses Zhiyi's mummified body in a pagoda in its main hall.

Huading Peak Temples
Open 6am–5pm daily.

❻ Yandang Shan
雁荡山

50 miles (80 km) NE of Wenzhou. from Wenzhou to terminus at Yandang Zhen or Ningbo. **Tel** (0577) 6224 3338. **yds-en.com**

This is a beautiful area of sheer hills, luxuriant slopes, and monasteries. Its highest peak, Baigang Shan, reaches 3,773 ft (1,150 m). The **Big Dragon Pool Falls** (Dalongqiu Pubu) cascade 623 ft (190 m), making them one of China's highest. The path leading to them weaves among towering columns of rock, where, on the hour, a cyclist performs a high-wire act. The largest area is **Divine Peaks** (Ling Feng), excellent for hiking among caves and strangely shaped peaks. The **Divine Cliffs** area (Ling Yan), reached by cable car, has walkways and a suspension bridge. From the bus terminus at Yandang Zhen, there are several walking trails.

Big Dragon Pool Falls
Open daily.

Divine Peaks
Open daily.

❼ Wenzhou
温州

160 miles (257 km) S of Ningbo. 9,100,000. Area 1, Wenzhou Sports Center, (0577) 8815 7168.

Located on the southeast coast of Zhejiang province, Wenzhou has always been a seafaring city. It is still a busy port and its booming economy is mainly due to heavy investment in manufacturing and textiles by overseas Chinese. A good base for visiting nearby Yandang Shan, the city also offers a few sights of its own. The most popular, **Jiangxin Park**, is on an island in the Ou River, easily be reached by the regular ferry service from Wangjiang Dong Road. Completely devoid of traffic, the park's pretty gardens, pavilions, pagodas, and footbridges make it a pleasant place to spend a few hours. It also has a working lighthouse. Stretching between Jiefang Road and Xinhe Road to the south of the Ou River is what is left of the old town. Here and there are a few particular buildings of interest such as the 18th-century British-built Protestant church, the 19th-century Catholic church, and the Miaoguo Temple, whose origins are Tang-dynasty.

Jiangxin Park
Jiangxin Dao. from Jiangxin Matou, Wenzhou. **Open** 7am–9pm daily.

Walkway with panoramic views, Yandang Shan

❹ Putuo Shan

普陀山

Nestled among numerous islands in the Zhou Shan archipelago, Putuo Shan is one of the four sacred Buddhist mountains, having strong associations with the goddess of compassion and mercy, Guanyin. It has been considered holy since the 10th century, and although the temples suffered greatly at the hands of the Red Guards during the Cultural Revolution, they are still impressive and full of fascination. A small, attractive island, fringed with bright blue waters and sandy beaches, Putuo Shan has become a very popular place of pilgrimage. Minibuses ply the roads between the major temples and sights, but the island's hills, caves, and beaches are best explored on foot.

To the summit
A cable car links a minibus stop with the summit of Foding Shan from where there are wonderful views across the island and out to sea.

★ Puji Si
Surrounded by beautiful camphor trees, this extensive temple is located at the island's tourist center. The first temple was built here in the 11th century, although the current temple is far newer.

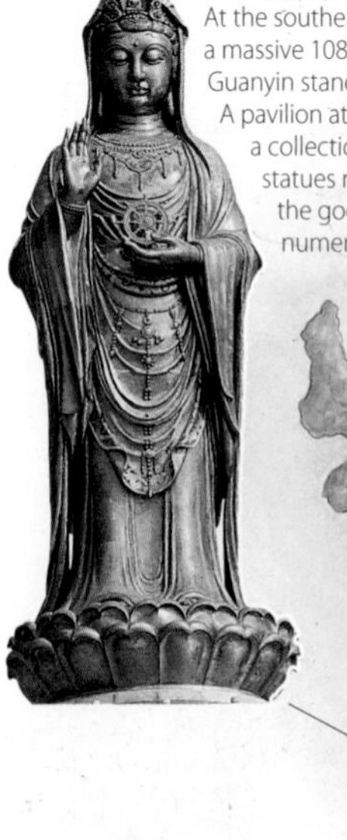

★ Guanyin Colossus
At the southern tip of the island a massive 108-ft (33-m) statue of Guanyin stands near the shore. A pavilion at its base exhibits a collection of some 400 statues representing the goddess in her numerous incarnations.

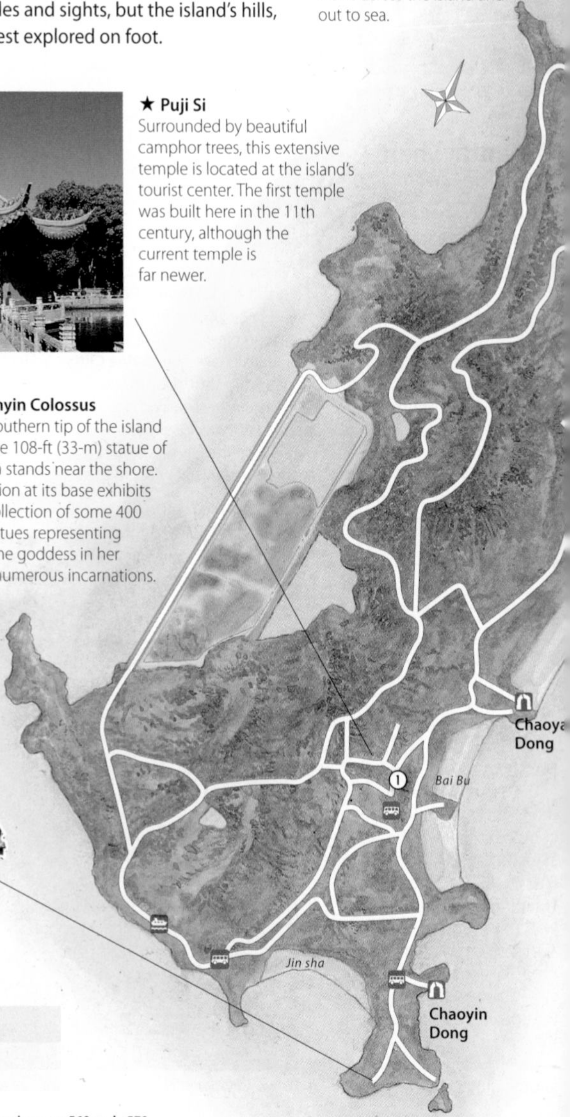

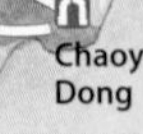

Bai Bu

Jin sha

Chaoyin Dong

KEY

① Duobao Pagoda

For hotels and restaurants in this region see p560 and p578

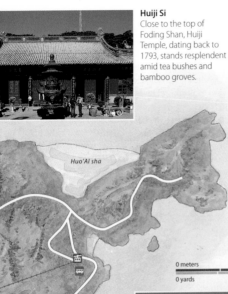

Huiji Si
Close to the top of Foding Shan, Huiji Temple, dating back to 1793, stands resplendent amid tea bushes and bamboo groves.

VISITORS' CHECKLIST

Practical Information
50 miles (80 km) E of Ningbo, off coast of Zhejiang. (0580) 319 1919. for island access, plus minimal fees for separate sights. Guanyin Festival (early Apr, mid-Aug & early Nov).

Transportation
Zhou Shan. Shanghai to Shenjiamen, then ferry. from Shanghai (fast ferry: 4 hrs; slow ferry: 13 hrs), Ningbo (fast ferry: 2 ½ hrs; slow ferry: 5 hrs), and Zhou Shan (30 mins).

Huo'Al sha

Key
- - Path
Road

0 meters 500
0 yards 500

Gufo Dong

Shancai Dong

Fanyin Dong

Qian Bu Sha
The loveliest of Putuo Shan's beaches, Qian Bu Sha (Thousand Step Beach) stretches along the eastern coast and is separated from Bai Bu Sha (Hundred Step Beach) by a headland and cave, Chaoyang Dong, concealing a teahouse.

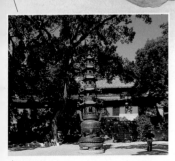

★ Fayu Si
The 200 halls of this charming temple pile up against the flank of a hill overlooking the sea. The Dayuan Hall, unusual for its domed roof and beamless arched ceiling, was brought here from Nanjing in the late 17th century.

The Legend of Hui'e

Hui'e, a Japanese monk who had purloined a Guanyin figure from the holy Buddhist mountain Wutai Shan, was sailing home when his ship was caught in a violent storm. Fearing for his life, he vowed to build a temple to Guanyin if he were saved. The seas suddenly calmed, and the ship floated gently towards the nearby shores of Putuo Shan. Believing that Guanyin was choosing the island, Hui'e built the promised temple and became a devoted hermit, spending the rest of his life on Putuo Shan.

Frieze of Hui'e sailing near Putuo Shan

For additional map symbols *see back flap*

8 Nanchang

南昌

Founded during the Han era, this provincial capital flourished under the Ming dynasty as a center of trade. However, it is best remembered as the scene of a significant uprising led by the Communist leader Zhou Enlai, who took control of the city for a few days in 1927. Although Nanchang was soon recaptured by the Nationalists, the incident started a chain of events that ultimately led to the formation of the People's Republic of China. Despite being largely an industrial city, Nanchang has numerous sights, including a good museum and several sites with revolutionary associations.

Offering incense sticks in front of the Youmin Si

Bayi Square

Memorial Hall to the Martyrs of the Revolution: 399 Bayi Dadao. **Tel** (0791) 8626 2566. **Open** 9am–4pm Tue–Sun.

The huge, open space of Bayi (August 1) Square is surrounded by some impressive, if slightly chilling, examples of Soviet-inspired revolutionary architecture. At the southern end is the **Monument to the Martyrs**, a theatrical sculpture of revolutionary fervor topped by a rifle, while the vast **Exhibition Hall** is decorated with a glittering red star. Just north of the square is the **Memorial Hall to the Martyrs of the Revolution**, which exhibits archival photographs of events in China between the 1920s and 1940s.

Zhu De's Former Residence

2 Dong Ming De Lu. **Open** 8am–5:30pm daily.

This attractive wooden house dates from 1927, when it housed the fledgling revolutionaries, Zhu De and Zhou Enlai, who led the uprising that briefly captured the city on August 1 of that year. Their army, consisting of about 30,000 rebels, held the city until the Kuomintang forces drove them out. Although the operation was a failure, it is considered a defining moment in 20th-century Chinese history, and celebrated as the day of the birth of the Red Army.

Youmin Si

181 Ming De Lu. **Tel** (0791) 8622 2301. **Open** 8am–6pm daily. Bayi Park: **Open** 8am–6pm daily.

This Buddhist temple, founded in the Liang era in the 6th century, is one of Jiangxi's principal shrines. It was damaged during the Cultural Revolution, and has now been restored. One of its three halls has a 33-ft (10-m) high Buddha standing on a lotus. The temple also houses a Ming-dynasty bronze bell and a cast during the Tang era in AD 967.

Just south of the temple is **Bayi Park** (August 1st Park), formerly the site of the imperial examination halls. It is a pleasant expanse of water and greenery, with an enclosed garden known as Old Man Su's Vegetable Plot, after its Song-dynasty owner.

August 1st Nanchang Uprising Memorial Museum

380 Zhongshan Lu. **Tel** (0791) 8661 3806. **Open** 8am–5pm daily.

The striking building housing this museum was the headquarters of the Communist forces led by Zhou Enlai, which captured the city in 1927. Its three floors are filled with period furniture and weaponry.

Teng Wang Pavilion

7 Yanjiang Lu. **Tel** (0791) 8670 2036. **Open** 7:30am–6pm daily (winter: 8am–5:30pm). **W cntwg.com**

This impressive pavilion was first built in 653, during the early Tang era and immortalized by the poet Tang Bo. There have been about 26 versions of the pavilion since then – the latest was erected in 1989 to replace

Zhou Enlai (1898–1976)

Premier Zhou Enlai in 1973

Zhou Enlai, one of the early members of the Chinese Communist Party, became the nation's prime minister in 1949. His pragmatism and diplomacy helped him survive the constant upheavals of Mao Zedong's chairmanship. To the West, he represented the reasonable and affable side of the Chinese people, while to his countrymen, he was the only member of the government to understand their problems. He is credited with curbing some of the excesses of the Cultural Revolution. When he died, the outpouring of grief in China was spontaneous and heartfelt.

The stately Teng Wang Pavilion, on the banks of the Gan Jiang

VISITORS' CHECKLIST

Practical Information
312 miles (500 km) SW of Hangzhou. 5,100,000. 8 Hongcheng Lu, (0791) 8620 0289.

Transport
Nanchang Changbei. Nanchang West (high-speed). Long Distance Bus Station, CAAC (buses to airport).

the one destroyed by fire in 1926. The 197-ft (60-m) high structure is in the Southern Song style. Visitors can take a lift to the top for views of the city. Occasional evening performances of dance and music or local opera are also held in the tiny theater.

Provincial Museum

2 Xinzhou Jiangxi Lu. **Tel** (0791) 8659 2509. **Open** 9am–5pm Tue–Sun.
jxmuseum.cn

By the river, in the west of the city, this museum's building outshines its collection. However, the exhibits are interesting, and include fossils found in Jiangxi, and a range of porcelain from the kilns at Jingdezhen, dating from the 4th century to the Qing era. There are also funeral items from the Spring & Autumn period and the Ming era, such as statuary, jade belts, and jewelry. Some were discovered in the tomb of the son of Hongwu, founder of the Ming dynasty.

Shengjin Ta

Zhishi Jie. 5. **Open** 7am–6pm daily.

Formerly part of a temple, this 194-ft (59-m) high brick pagoda was first built in the late Tang dynasty, but was entirely rebuilt in the 18th century. Like many pagodas, its construction was said to avert disaster, while its destruction heralded the fall of the city. The pagoda is located in a pedestrianized neighborhood with a handful of teahouses, barber shops, and grocery stores.

Eight Hermits Hall

259 Qingyunpu Lu. **Tel** (0791) 8527 3565. 20. **Open** 8am–6pm daily.

The Eight Hermits (Ba Da Shanren) Memorial Hall was the retreat of China's great painter Zhu Da, who flourished at the end of the Ming era and the early Qing dynasty. He was a descendant of the Ming imperial family who went into hiding here after their fall, in what was originally designed as a Taoist retreat. His paintings, strikingly spare and direct, are reproduced here.

Nanchang City Center

① Bayi Square
② Zhu De's Former Residence
③ Youmin Si
④ August 1st Nanchang Uprising Memorial Museum
⑤ Teng Wang Pavilion
⑥ Provincial Museum
⑦ Shengjin Ta

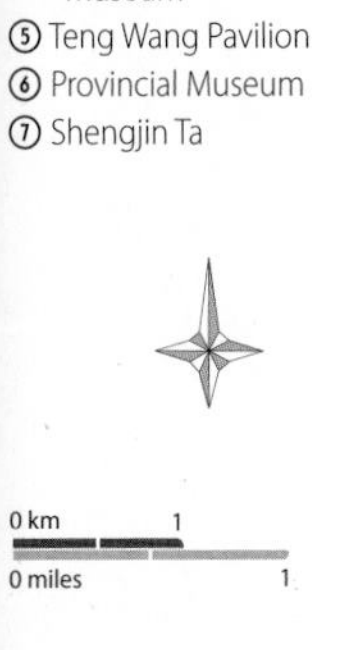

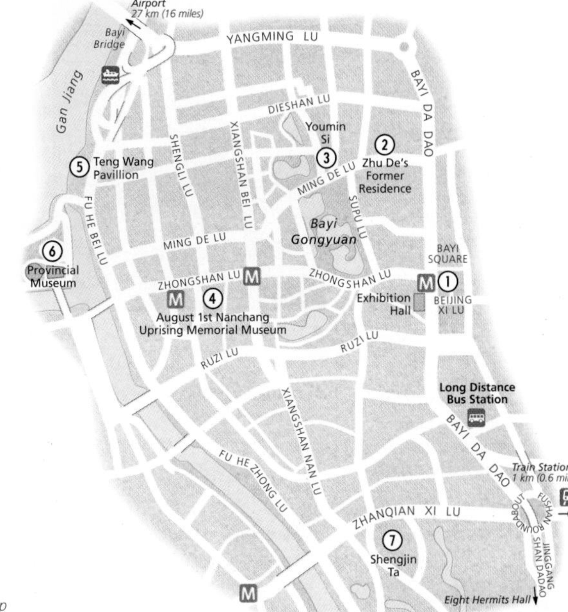

Key to Symbols *see back flap*

Xunyang Lou, an impressive re-creation of a Tang-era tavern

❾ Jiujiang

九江

80 miles (130 km) N of Nanchang. 4,700,000. Jiujiang Airport, 25 miles (40 km) S of Jiujiang. 6 Lufeng Lu, (0792) 898 2268. **jjwqb.gov.cn/English**

The gateway to Lu Shan, the ancient port of Jiujiang, was used for shipping rice and tea and, during the Ming dynasty, porcelain from Jingdezhen. Badly damaged during the Taiping insurrection, it was later opened to foreign trade in 1861 and became noted for its tea bricks.

The older and livelier part of town lies close to the river, separated from the industrial section by two lakes. Yanshui Ting, the Misty Water Pavilion, is located on a small island on Gantang Hu. It was most recently rebuilt in the Qing dynasty and contains a museum showing old photos of Jiujiang. **Nengren Si** was founded in AD 502. Closed during the Cultural Revolution, it now houses a flourishing community of monks.

The **Xunyang Lou** is a modern reincarnation of a Tang-dynasty wooden tavern that was the setting for a raucous scene in the Chinese classic *The Water Margin* *(see pp34–5)*.

Nengren Si
168 Yuliang Nan Lu. **Open** daily.

Xunyang Lou
908 Binjiang Lu. **Open** 7am–6pm daily.

❿ Lu Shan

庐山

During the 19th century, this beautiful area of highland scenery was developed by Edward Little, a Methodist minister and property speculator, as a resort area for Europeans. Later it became a favorite retreat among Chinese politicians; Chiang Kai-shek had a summer residence here and from 1949 Lu Shan was popular with Mao and his ministers. Today, despite the summer crowds, Lu Shan remains a refreshing place for walks among lakes, hills, and waterfalls.

★ Floral Path
This walk skirts the edge of the western cliffs, giving marvelous views over the Jinxiu Valley. The path leads to the Immortal's Cave, once inhabited by a Daoist monk.

★ Dragon's Head Cliff
Magnificent views combine with the sound of the wind in the pine forest and the roaring of waterfalls in the Stone Gate Ravine.

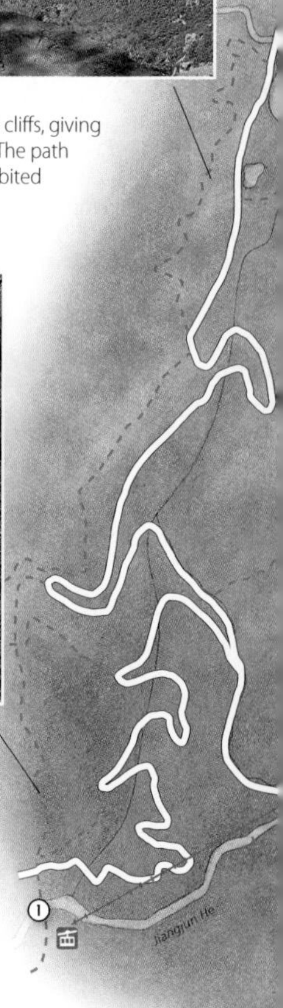

Jiangjun He

KEY

① **Suspension Bridge**

② **Lu Shan Museum**, housed in Mao's former villa.

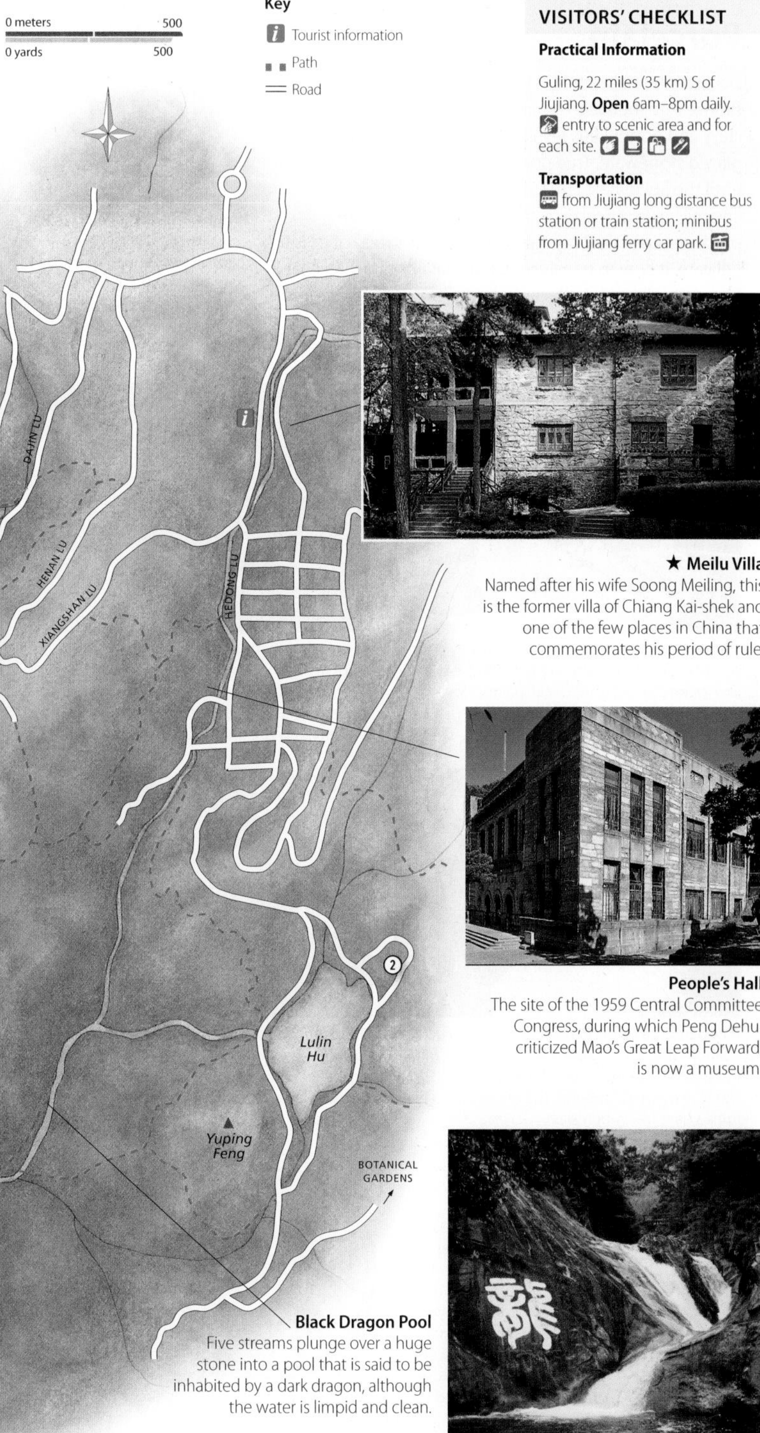

★ Meilu Villa
Named after his wife Soong Meiling, this is the former villa of Chiang Kai-shek and one of the few places in China that commemorates his period of rule.

People's Hall
The site of the 1959 Central Committee Congress, during which Peng Dehui criticized Mao's Great Leap Forward, is now a museum.

Black Dragon Pool
Five streams plunge over a huge stone into a pool that is said to be inhabited by a dark dragon, although the water is limpid and clean.

VISITORS' CHECKLIST

Practical Information

Guling, 22 miles (35 km) S of Jiujiang. **Open** 6am–8pm daily. entry to scenic area and for each site.

Transportation

from Jiujiang long distance bus station or train station; minibus from Jiujiang ferry car park.

For additional map symbols *see back flap*

Porcelain

Despite Chinese pottery's long history, it was not until the Bronze Age (between about 1500 and 400 BC) that special clays and hotter kilns resulted in a harder, sometimes glazed stoneware. True porcelain, however, did not appear until the Sui dynasty (AD 581–618). A far finer type of ceramic, true porcelain is smooth and polished, and produces an almost crystalline ring when struck; at its most delicate, it is even translucent. Porcelain became popular in Europe during the 16th century, and the Portuguese, and later the Dutch and English, set up a lucrative trade between China and the rest of the world.

Blue and White Ming porcelain is seen by some as the epitome of Chinese style. The elegance of the designs and the depth of color are astounding.

Jingdezhen clay is the key to the quality of the porcelain and is a mixture of fine white kaolin and "petuntse" (a crushed feldspar rock). The resulting fine powder is washed, strained through silk, and dried.

As on a production line, each artisan performs a single task in the porcelain-making process. The clay is centered on a wheel and thrown into a rough shape, sculpted into a finer piece with scrapers, and brushed with water to create a smooth surface.

A cobalt blue underglaze may be added before coating with a clear glaze of limestone ash, the finest petuntse, and water. The glaze absorbs the blue dye and fuses into the original clay to form a hard glassy porcelain.

Firing is a crucial stage in making porcelain – fluctuations in temperature can ruin thousands of pieces in one go. The best porcelain is fired inside clay "saggars" – cases that protect them from dust and sudden variations in heat.

Rose medallion porcelain was made specially for export. Often these pieces were made to Western designs in terms of shape and decoration. Sometimes dinner sets displaying a family or even a royal crest were produced, and designs were sent from Europe to be reproduced by the Chinese.

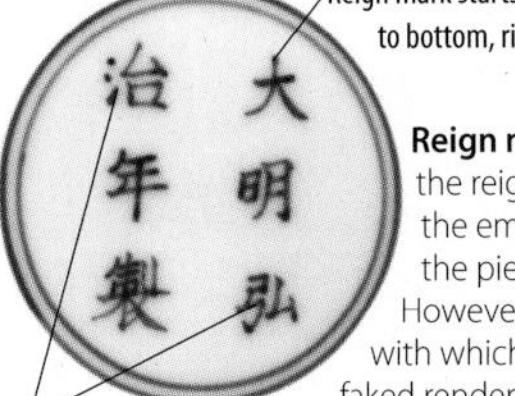
大明弘
治年製
Reign mark starts here and reads top to bottom, right to left
Characters for Emperor Hongzhi

Reign marks show the reign name of the emperor when the piece was made. However, the ease with which they can be faked renders accurate dating the task of experts.

Porcelain Timeline

Han

A key development during this period was the art of glazing. Simple pots began changing from everyday items to works of art.

Tang

Technical advances during the Tang dynasty saw the production of new types of porcelain, most famously the *sancai* (tri-colored) pieces illustrating figures from the Silk Road.

Song

Beautiful Song porcelain is characterized by simple shapes glazed in a single, rich color. New shapes were developed, as well as the cracked glazing technique.

Yuan

Porcelain from the Mongol dynasty absorbed foreign influences. Cobalt blue underglaze was introduced, and later perfected during the Ming period.

Ming

The Ming dynasty was the era of imperial patronage of Jingdezhen and large-scale exportation to the West. The kilns flourished and the artisans returned to a richer palette of colors and pictorial design.

Qing

The latter part of this dynasty was often characterized by overly elaborate design and poor quality, but the early part of the Qing saw the production of delicate *famille rose* porcelain.

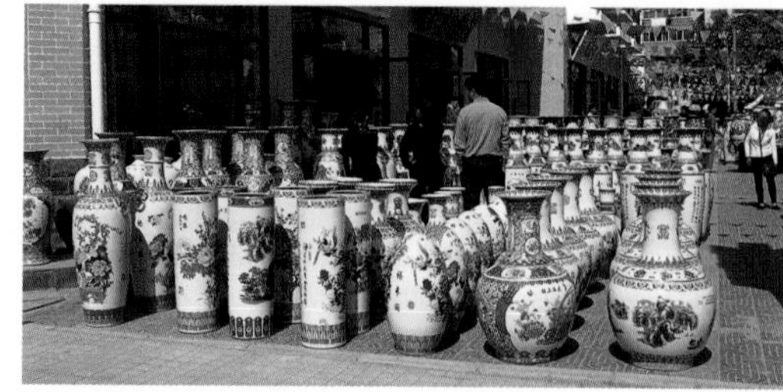

One of Jingdezhen's many pottery shops

⓫ Jingdezhen
景德镇

108 miles (174 km) NE of Nanchang. 1,550,000. Lianhuatang Lu, (0798) 822 2903.

For centuries the ceramic capital of China, Jingdezhen is still one of the country's major porcelain producers. Although pottery kilns were operating here as far back as the Han dynasty, it was the discovery of real porcelain, during the Five Dynasties era (907–79), which depended on locally found clay rich in feldspar, that brought Jingdezhen its pre-eminence. During the Ming dynasty, its location near the imperial capital of Nanjing increased its importance and it became famous for fine porcelain with a blue underglaze. Although the quality of the porcelain is lower than in the past, the main reason for visiting Jingdezhen is still ceramic production. Visiting a factory or one of the ancient kiln sites will need to be arranged though CITS but there are also several places of interest that can be visited independently.

Detail from museum entrance

The **Ceramic History Exposition** (Taoci Lishi Bolanqu) is located in a rural setting on the western edge of town. Displays of items taken from ancient kiln sites around Jingdezhen and of potters at work effectively make this museum interactive. It is housed in an elegant Ming house, a rare survivor among the many that would once have graced the town. The adjacent **Ancient Pottery Factory** (Guyao Cichang) gives demonstrations of the ancient techniques used in the making of porcelain.

The **Porcelain Museum** (Taoci Guan) houses a collection of beautiful porcelain from the Song, Ming, and Qing dynasties, as well as some of the finer creations produced since the establishment of the PRC in 1949. The main porcelain market is on Jiefang Road. Porcelain in all shapes and sizes is sold here, from classical-period reproductions to garden ornaments and sentimental reproductions of dogs and cats. For a view across the roofs of town, visitors can climb the wooden four-story **Longzhu Ge** (Dragon Pearl Pavilion).

Ceramic History Exposition
Zhonghua Bei Lu. **Tel** 400 118 1728. **Open** 2–5:30pm daily.
chinaguyao.com

Porcelain Museum
21 Lianshe Beilu. **Tel** (0798) 822 8005. **Open** 7:30am–4:30pm daily.

The wooden Longzhu Ge, with views across Jingdezhen

The Long March

During the 1920s the outlawed Communist leaders sought refuge from the Kuomintang (KMT) at remote rural bases, or "soviets," in Sichuan, Hunan, and in Jiangxi province, at Jinggang Shan, the headquarters run by Mao Zedong and Zhu De. In October 1934, with the KMT closing in, the Jiangxi Soviet was forced to break out and join thousands of revolutionaries on a tactical retreat. Covering, largely at night, an average of 20 miles (32 km) a day, the Communists marched 5,900 miles (9,500 km) in a year. The march, however, was not a strategic success and many did not survive it.

The Red Army – outlawed, harried and hungry – had to fight battles, outwit their better-equipped enemy, and cross inhospitable terrain in all seasons.

⑧ **Yan'an** was the end point of the march on October 19, 1935. Mao arrived with 5000 marchers and established the Yan'an Soviet as an independent communist state.

⑦ **Crossing the** remote, boggy and freezing Aba Grasslands brought enormous losses. A subsequent meeting with rival Zhang Guotao firmly established Mao's primacy.

⑥ **Daxue Shan**, the Great Snowy Mountains, are some of the highest in the country. Crossing the passes was the most challenging episode of the Long March, and led to the death, through altitude sickness, exhaustion, and exposure, of many Red Army soldiers.

④ **At Lu Shan Pass**, the Red Army reached the pass just ahead of the KMT, deceived their pursuers, and gained an unexpected victory.

⑤ **The Luding Chain Bridge** *(see p377)* was the only means of crossing the Dadu River. Blocked by KMT troops who had removed most of the bridge's planks, 22 Red Army soldiers took the bridge by crawling along the remaining chains, with the loss of seven men.

③ **Zunyi** was taken despite heavy losses in January 1935. Mao emerged from the ensuing conference as leader of the Communist Party and commander of the Red Army; the Soviet-supported general was expelled.

Many prominent Long Marchers became China's future leaders, including (from left) Bo Gu (Communist leader until 1935), Zhou Enlai, Zhu De, and Mao Zedong.

① **Jinggang Shan** was the base of the Jiangxi Soviet whose position was steadily being eroded by advancing KMT troops. Led by Mao Zedong, the Long March started from here on October 16 ,1934.

② **The crossing of** the Xiang River was the marchers' first major battle. Accounted a disaster, huge amounts of equipment were lost in the waters.

The thickly wooded slopes of Jinggang Shan

⓬ Jinggang Shan
井冈山

Ciping, 220 miles (350 km) SW of Nanchang. 🚌 ℹ 2 Tianjie Lu, (0796) 655 0550. 🎫 for most revolutionary and scenic sights.

There are two reasons for visiting Jinggang Shan: its scenery, which has been featured on Chinese banknotes, and its revolutionary associations. The mountain range, of which the main peak is Jinggang Shan, sometimes known as Wuzhi Feng (Five Fingers Peak), reaches to 5,200 ft (1,586 m). There are magnificent views, especially at sunrise, as well as a great variety of plants, birds, butterflies, and other insects.

The village of **Ciping** was destroyed during the civil war of the 1930s but was rebuilt after 1949 as a sort of shrine to the Communist struggle and to the Long March in particular. There are a number of buildings commemorating the way of life of the early revolutionaries, forced here in the late 1920s by Chiang Kai-shek's persecution, which culminated in a massacre of striking workers in Shanghai in 1927. It is possible here to gain some idea of what life was like for the revolutionaries, as they developed their strategy before the epic walk to Shaanxi. A short distance away is the watching post at **Huangyang Jie**, where the Red Army repulsed Kuomintang troops in 1928. Located at about 3,300 ft (1,000 m), Ciping was the center of the Jinggang Shan revolutionary base during the 1920s and 1930s and is now the site of local government. Its location at the center of the mountain range and growing collection of hotels make it a good base for exploring the area. The beauty of the area is a startling contrast with its image as a gritty, revolutionary stronghold. There are the 33-ft (100-m) **Shuikou waterfalls**, located in a luxuriant valley surrounded by rocks amid bamboo, azaleas, and pine forest. **Wulong Tan**, a few miles north of Ciping, is composed of several limpid pools into which stream a number of rapids and waterfalls. A cable car can take you to the top and give you magnificent views over the whole area, whilst for those with enough energy, much of the area can be enjoyed on foot.

Monument outside Wulong Tan

Pearl Pool, one of the five waterfalls at Wulong Tan

HUNAN & HUBEI

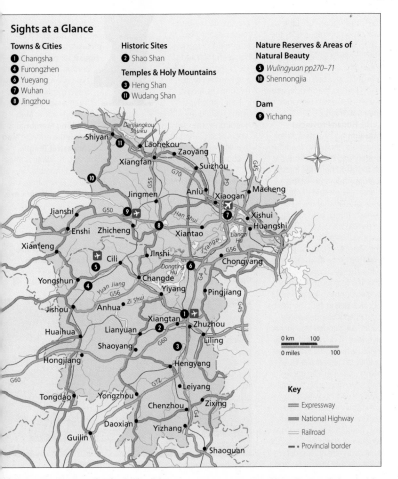

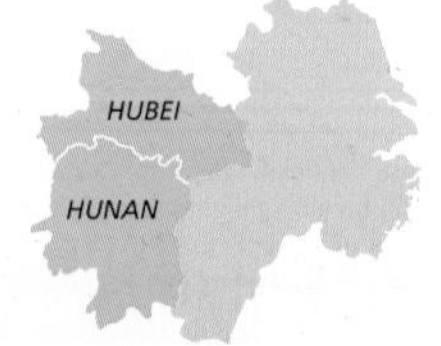

Hunan and Hubei are central China's westernmost provinces. Hubei is dominated by the mighty Yangzi River, and its capital Wuhan is a great industrial city on the river. The mountainous Three Gorges in western Hubei near Yichang is the site of the world's largest dam, completed in 2007. The scenic Shennongjia Forest Reserve, home of the legendary Wild Man, and Wudang Shan, known for its martial arts school, are spectacular sights worth visiting, although remote and difficult to access.

Hunan's fertile farmlands lured millions of migrants during the political upheavals in north China between the 8th and 11th centuries. An important grain producer during the Ming and Qing dynasties, by the 19th century the population had outgrown the land, and the ensuing unrest was exploited by the Taiping Heavenly Kingdom Rebellion *(see p428)*. The region's poverty also had a great impact on China's history in the 20th century. As the birthplace of Mao Zedong, Hunan's revolutionary credentials are still one of its principal attractions, both in Changsha, the capital, and in Mao's birthplace at Shao Shan. Other popular sights include Dongting Hu, China's second-largest lake, in the northeast, the temples at scenic Heng Shan in the south, and the wonderful mountain scenery of Wulingyuan in the northwest.

Sights at a Glance

Towns & Cities

1. Changsha
4. Furongzhen
6. Yueyang
7. Wuhan
8. Jingzhou

Historic Sites

2. Shao Shan

Temples & Holy Mountains

3. Heng Shan
11. Wudang Shan

Nature Reserves & Areas of Natural Beauty

5. *Wulingyuan pp270–71*
10. Shennongjia

Dam

9. Yichang

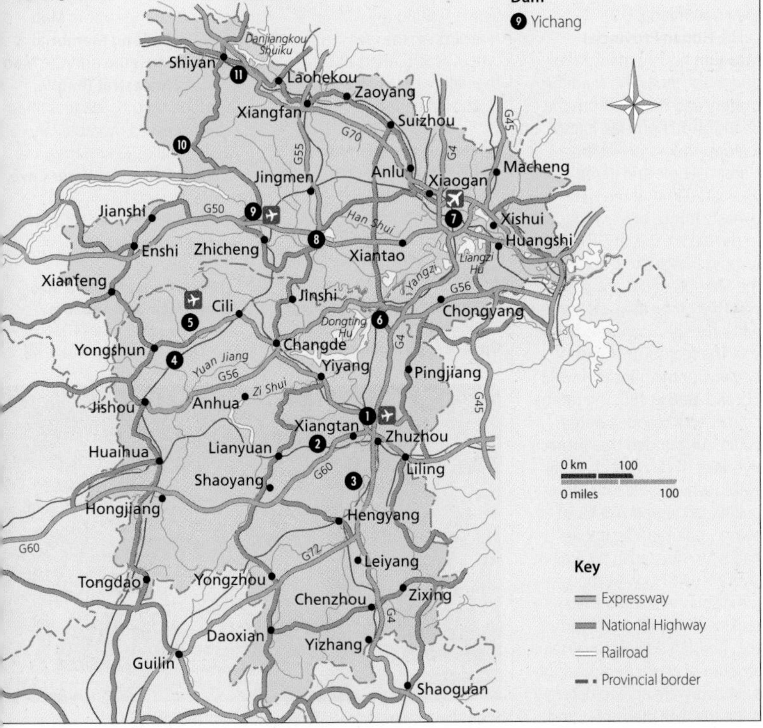

0 km 100
0 miles 100

Key

- Expressway
- National Highway
- Railroad
- Provincial border

◀ The hanging restaurant near Three Travelers' Cave, Yichang

For additional map symbols *see back flap*

No. 1 Teachers' Training College, Changsha

❶ Changsha
长沙

207 miles (333 km) S of Wuhan. 7,500,000. 88, 1 Duan, Furong Zhong Rd. **Tel** (0731) 8228 5589.

An important ancient city, Changsha was the capital of the Chu kingdom until the unification of China under the Qin in 280 BC. Much later, the city's profile was raised once more when in 1903 it became a treaty port, open to foreign trade. During the Sino-Japanese war in 1938 it was damaged by the Kuomintang.

The **Hunan Provincial Museum** houses many items of interest, including Neolithic pottery and bronzes from the Shang and Zhou eras. It also features the history of the Hunan people and items excavated from three Han-dynasty tombs at Mawangdui, to the east of the city. The first tomb belonged to the wife of the Marquis of Dai, the second was that of the Marquis himself, while the third contained their son. The Marquis, Li Cang, became prime minister in 193 BC, and died in 186. The tombs contained a wooden outer coffin, surrounded by a protective layer of clay and charcoal, within which were four other coffins, lacquered and handsomely painted. The bodies had been dressed in several layers of silk. His wife's body (on display in a liquid-filled tank) was so well preserved that her skin retained a certain amount of elasticity. Amazingly scientists were able to determine that she died at 50, and was suffering from tuberculosis and arthritis. According to the customs at the time, the tombs were filled with foods and furnishings to comfort that part of the soul that remains on earth, and a silk banner that mapped the Han belief system. Close by is the pleasantly landscaped **Martyrs' Park**.

Among the numerous sites related to Mao Zedong, the most interesting is the **No. 1 Teacher's Training College**, where he studied from 1913 until 1918. Although he famously failed his art exam, by drawing a circle and calling it an egg, he was declared student of the year in 1917. At college, he devoted much of his time to organizing student societies, a useful practice for his future role as leader. Mao returned as a teacher between 1920 and 1922. Visitors can follow a self-guided route through the rebuilt college, which is still active, visiting the dormitories, the well where Mao bathed, and the halls where he held political meetings.

Mao statue, No. 1 Teachers' Training College

Hunan Provincial Museum and Martyrs' Park
50 Dongfeng Rd. **Tel** (0731) 8451 4630. **Open** 9am–5pm Tue–Sun (but call ahead of your visit for the latest information).
hnmuseum.com

Hunan First Normal College
356 Shuyuan Rd. **Tel** (0731) 515 0619. **Open** daily. **hnfnu.edu.cn**

❷ Shao Shan
韶山

48 miles (80 km) SW of Changsha. daily from Changsha.

The birthplace of Mao Zedong, China's leader from 1949 until his death in 1976, Shao Shan is really two towns. The newer one is near the train station, while the village of Shao Shan Dong, where the "Great Helmsman" spent his early years, is 4 miles (6 km) away. At the height of the Mao phenomenon during the Cultural Revolution, special pilgrimage trains, crowded with Red Guards, brought almost 8,000 worshipers a day – which is a lot fewer than visit these days. The buildings connected with Mao are now preserved as museums. **Mao's Family House**, where he was born in 1893, is typically rural, except for its displays of memorabilia. Nearby lie the sizable **Mao Zedong Memorial Museum** and the **Mao Ancestral Temple**. Overlooking the village is Shao Peak, accessed by cable car. About 2 miles (3 km) from the village is **Dripping Water Cave**, where, legend has it, Mao pondered over the Cultural Revolution in 1966.

Mao's Family House & Mao Zedong Memorial Museum
Shao Shan Chong. **Tel** (0731) 5568 5157. **Open** 8:30am–4pm daily.

Stone tablets engraved with Mao's poems, Shao Peak, Shao Shan

For hotels and restaurants in this region see pp560–61 and pp578–9

Grand gateway of the Zhusheng Si Monastery, Nanyue

3 Heng Shan
衡山

85 miles (135 km) S of Changsha. **Tel** (0734) 567 3377. from Changsha to Nanyue. **Open** daily.

One of the five holy Daoist mountains, Heng Shan, at 4,232 ft (1,290 m), is a cluster of wooded peaks, dotted with temples dating back some 1,300 years ago. The gateway to Heng Shan is **Nanyue**, a 2-hour bus journey from Changsha. It is a pleasant little town with two main streets, and a couple of significant temples. **Nanyue Damiao** has been a place of worship for both Buddhist and Daoists since the early 8th century AD, although the current buildings, modeled on Beijing's Forbidden City, date from the 19th century. The other, **Zhusheng Si**, is an 8th-century Buddhist monastery, rebuilt in the 18th century.

The mountain can be explored on foot or by minibus, but it is a 9-mile (15-km) walk to the top. There is a cable car to the summit from about halfway. A number of monasteries and temples lie along the path that meanders through lush countryside before reaching the **Martyrs' Memorial Hall**, honoring those who died in the 1911 revolution. Next is the 7th-century **Xuandu Si**, Hunan's main Daoist temple. The route finally leads to **Shangfeng Si**, also the minibus terminus. Just beyond is the summit marked by **Zhurong Gong**, a tiny stone temple. Visitors can stay at a hotel near the top for views from the **Terrace for Watching the Sunrise**.

4 Furongzhen
芙蓉镇

249 miles (400 km) NW of Changsha. to Mengdonghe, then bus or boat. from Mengdonghe.

Mengdonghe is the jumping-off point to Furongzhen (Wang Cun), the location of the 1986 film *A Small Town Called Hibiscus*. Furongzhen means Hibiscus Town and the film was an adaptation of the novel *A Town Called Hibiscus* by Gu Hua. It was one of the first books to show how the political upheavals of the 1950s and 1960s affected people in rural China. Furongzhen is an attractive town with stone streets and old wooden buildings. Its **Tujia Museum** on Hepan Jie is devoted to the culture of the indigenous Tujia people *(see p31)*. Visitors can also go rafting near Furongzhen, on the Yuan Jiang River.

5 Wulingyuan

See pp270–71.

6 Yueyang
岳阳

90 miles (145 km) N of Changsha. 5,400,000. at Chenglingji. 121 Yunmeng Lu, (0730) 828 2222.

Situated on the banks of the Yangzi and the shores of Dongting Hu, China's second largest freshwater lake, Yueyang is an important stopping point for river ferries and trains on the Beijing to Guangzhou line. Its main sight, **Yueyang Tower**, was once part of a Tang-era temple. The current structure, dating from the Qing era, is an impressive sight, with its glazed yellow-tiled roofs overlooking the lake. Nearby are two pavilions, Xianmei Ting and Sanzui Ting; the latter was where Lu Dongbin, one of the Taoist Eight Immortals *(see pp36–7)*, came to drink wine. To the south is **Cishi Ta**, a pagoda built in 1242 to propitiate flood-causing demons.

A 30-minute boat ride from Yueyang is the small island of **Junshan Dao**, a former Daoist retreat that is now famous for its silver needle tea.

Yueyang Tower
Dongting Beilu. 12 or 15. **Tel** (0730) 831 5588. **Open** 7am–6:30pm daily.

A river boat at the scenic Junshan Dao (Junshan Island)

Cult of Mao

When he became Chairman in 1949, Mao Zedong was already a figure of almost mystical stature, having led the Red Army since 1934. He was an ideologue and whilst his impatience at the pace of reform led to decisions that often brought disaster, skillful maneuvering by the party meant that he remained a heroic figurehead. The Cultural Revolution *(see pp70–71)* of 1966–76, was, at the expense of millions of lives, a calculated attempt to make Mao a deity. The years after his death saw a diminution of his status, but since the 1990s his popularity has revived. Once again Mao is considered by millions to be *weida* – Great – though more as a liberator than a leader.

Mao's portrayal, not only as a deity but as a man of the people, was part of the ambiguity of the cult. Nonetheless, Mao remains at the center of the image surrounded by adoring women.

Poster Art

In the 1960s the Chinese propaganda machine turned out posters featuring Mao by the million. He was often portrayed as a benevolent avatar, a god come among the people to transform their lives.

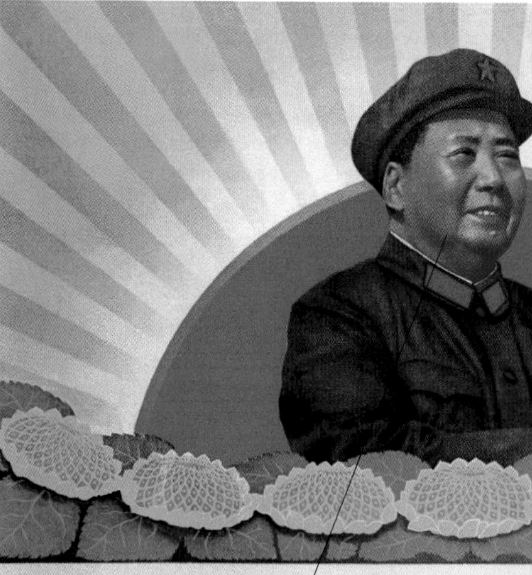

"Celebrate the birth and life of Chairman Mao for 10,000 years."

Mao's face was always a ruddy red, as artists were told to avoid grey and to imbue him with cherub-like youth.

A Mao study group discusses Mao's philosophy in the late 1960s. His thought briefly became a modern substitute for the Confucian philosophy that had dominated Chinese intellectual life for millennia.

The thoughts of Chairman Mao were collected in 1961 in a volume, known as the *Little Red Book*, which was distributed to all Red Guards.

Pilgrims at Shao Shan, Mao's birthplace *(see p266)*, pay their respects. At the height of the Cultural Revolution, several trains a day pulled into Shao Shan to disgorge thousands of fervent pilgrims. In the 1980s this traffic all but ceased but was revived again in the 1990s.

"Chairman Mao is the red sun in our hearts," this poster asserts. The uppermost characters say "the East is Red," the name of a piece of music that became an anthem of the Cultural Revolution.

Early poster art was slightly different in character from later propaganda. Although this poster asks people to march forward under the banner of Mao Zedong, revolutionary Soviet-endorsed communism, rather than Maoism, is celebrated on the flags.

Light always radiates from behind Mao, just as a halo might appear behind a god in a temple.

Mao memorabilia is widely available in China, although many of the pieces on sale at markets today have been produced specifically for the tourist market.

Since Mao's death the Party has had to tread a delicate line between condemnation of his excesses and praise for his achievements. His portrait still hangs at the north end of Tian'an Men Square and his image is on all Chinese banknotes; perhaps his posthumous function is as a symbol of a united China.

Domestic shrines with a figure of Mao to whom family members would address their revolutionary prayers started replacing Daoist and Buddhist shrines during the 1960s. Mao shrines are still seen, although the Party disapproves.

Mao Attacked

In 1994 Mao's private physician, Li Zhisui, wrote *The Private Life of Chairman Mao*, in which Mao is portrayed as vain, cold, and contemptuous of his colleagues and of the suffering of the Chinese people. The book was instantly banned by the Chinese government. At the time of publication, Li was living in the United States and so escaped persecution. The book provides some surprising insights into Mao's habits and opinions. However, many critics, even those unsympathetic to Mao's politics, claim that the book is simply opportunistic.

The jacket of Li's biography

❺ Wulingyuan

武陵源

Often called Zhangjiajie, this 243-square-mile (391-sq-km) scenic preserve is a karst landscape *(see pp418–19)* of enormous beauty, with rocky pinnacles rising from a coverlet of dense subtropical vegetation. Wulingyuan covers three natural reserves – Zhangjiajie, Tianzi Shan, and Suoxi Yu – and contains well over 500 species of tree, including the dawn redwood, which was believed to be extinct until it was re-identified in 1948. It is also a haven for fauna, including giant salamanders, rhesus monkeys, and a wide variety of birds. The park is often cloaked in fog, adding atmosphere but obscuring most views. Summers are excessively humid.

★ Xianren Qiao
The Bridge of the Immortals is a spectacular, narrow, and unfenced of rock over a deep chasm.

★ Huang Shi Zhai
At 3,450 ft (1,050 m), Huang Shi Zhai is the highest area in Wulingyuan. The climb up the 3,878 steps requires a good 2 hours; there is also a cable car if the stairway sounds too daunting.

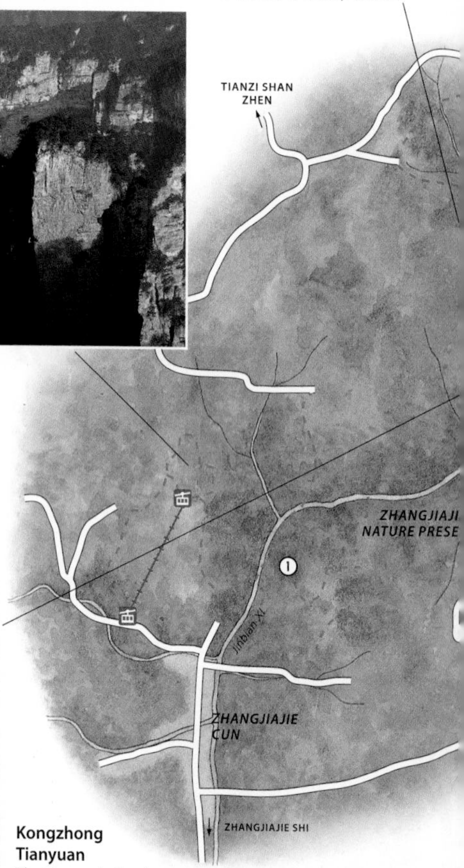

TIANZI SHAN ZHEN

ZHANGJIAJI NATURE PRESE

Jinbian Xi

ZHANGJIAJIE CUN

ZHANGJIAJIE SHI

Kongzhong Tianyuan
The Heavenly Garden is an isolated outcrop covered in a mantle of green and surrounded by clusters of slender pinnacles and towering peaks.

KEY

① **Jin Bian Yan**, a sandstone pea which stands at 1,312 ft (400 m).

② **Boat trips** on Baofeng Hu's pristine waters are included in the price of admission.

Tianzi Ge
In the northern part of the preserve, the pinnacle of this hill allows views of a valley forested with dozens of fine, splinter-like tors. Numerous underground caverns are found throughout the surrounding area.

VISITORS' CHECKLIST

Practical Information
190 miles (305 km) NW of Changsha. **Open** daily. 89 Ziwu Zhong Rd, Zhangjiajie Shi, (0744) 829 8777. valid for 3 days.
zhangjiajietourism.us

Transportation
at Zhangjiajie Shi (Zhangjiajie City). to Zhangjiajie Shi. to Zhangjiajie Shi; a tourist bus runs direct from the long-distance bus station.

Key

Cable car

Path

Road

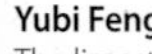

Yubi Feng
The limestone columns of the Emperor's Brushes are featured on Chinese stamps and resemble traditional Chinese calligraphy brushes.

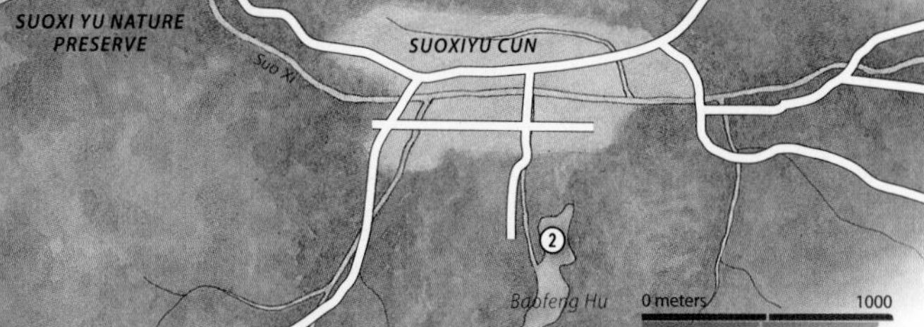

★ Huanglong Dong
Although garishly illuminated, 7-mile (11-km) Yellow Dragon Cave loses none of its impact. Boat tours drift down its subterranean river.

loring Wulingyuan
nain entrance is just past Zhangjiajie Cun. w the left path for a 4-hour walk that includes ng Shi Zhai. The right path presents several ns, taking you, eventually, away from the ds. Accommodations are available in gjiajie Cun, as well as Suoxiyu Cun, which ood base for exploring the east and north e park. Simple inns are scattered throughout eserve.

❼ Wuhan

武汉

An important port on the Yangzi, Hubei's capital is an amalgamation of three older cities. Wuchang, capital of the State of Wu (770–221 BC), and Hanyang, founded in the Sui era (AD 581–618), are ancient settlements, while Hankou was founded in 1861 when it became a treaty port for foreign trade. As a result, the city was a center for early Chinese industrialization, when iron and steel works were built here in the 19th century. It was also the site of the first uprising of the 1911 Revolution that led to the fall of the Qing dynasty and the formation of Republican China.

Ancestral musical instruments at the Hubei Provincial Museum

Hubei Provincial Museum

160 Donghu Rd. **Tel** (027) 8679 4127.
Open 9am–5pm Tue–Sun.
hbww.org

Among the highlights of this excellent museum on the shore of Dong Hu are items excavated from the tomb of the Marquis of Yi, an eminent figure from the Warring States period. He died in 433 BC and was buried in a lacquered coffin, accompanied by his concubines, his dog, and thousands of bronze, stone, and wooden items. Many of these are on display, but the most impressive is the panoply of bronze bells, which produce two notes each when struck.

Ferry rides are available to explore the scenic area around Dong Hu, with its many pavilions and gardens.

Mao's Villa

142 Donghu Rd. **Tel** (027) 6888 1888.
Open 9–11am & 2:30–5:30pm daily.

This pleasant villa (Mao Zedong Bieshu) was Mao's hideaway from 1960 to 1974, where he stayed for long periods during the first years of the Cultural Revolution. It is set in the grounds of the Donghu Hotel, and visitors can see his living quarters, conference room, bomb shelter, and swimming pool.

Yellow Crane Tower

Wuluo Rd. **Tel** (027) 8887 1394.
Open 8am–6pm daily.
cnhhl.com/en

The Yellow Crane Tower on She Shan, south of the Yangzi in Wuchang district, is a reconstruction of a 3rd-century edifice that burned down in 1884. According to legend, it was built to honor one of the Daoist Eight Immortals, who paid his tavern bills by drawing cranes on the walls. The 164-ft (50-m) high pavilion is a handsome Qing-style building. It can be climbed for fine views across the city. On the eastern part of the hill is **Changchun Guan**, a Daoist temple with a pharmacy, where a doctor dispenses locally collected herbs. To the south is Hong Ge, a red-brick building that housed the **Former Headquarters of the Hubei Military Government** (Hong Lou) during the 1911 uprising provoked by Sun Yat-sen *(see p303)*. Sun Yat-sen's statue stands in front of the building. Behind the pavilion itself is an enormous bronze temple bell which, for a small fee, visitors may strike.

Enormous bronze bell behind the Yellow Crane Tower

Yangzi Bridge

This impressive 361-ft (110-m) long bridge was built in 1957 by the Communists. Before its construction, all road and rail traffic crossed the river by ferry. A second bridge was built a short way downriver in 1995.

Key to Symbols *see back flap*

Wuhan City Center

① Hubei Provincial Museum
② Mao's Villa
③ Yellow Crane Tower
④ Yangzi Bridge
⑤ Gui Shan
⑥ Guiyuan Si
⑦ Hankou

Daoist priests depicted in a wall painting at Changchun Guan

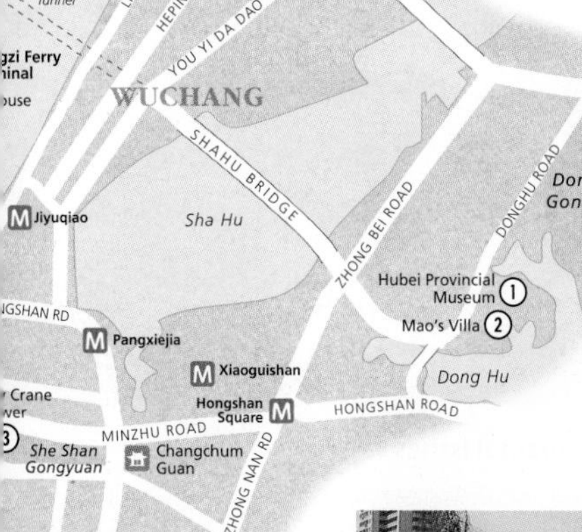

Gui Shan

Wuhan's industrial quarter of Hanyang has a few sights of interest, most of which lie on or around Gui Shan, or Turtle Hill. This was named after a magic turtle that defeated a water demon and prevented the Han and Yangzi rivers from flooding. The **Guqin Tai** (Lute Terrace), famous for its massive TV tower, was where the legendary musician Bo Ya would come to play his lute. After the death of his friend, the woodcutter who could understand his music, Bo Ya destroyed his lute and vowed never to play again. A couple of tombs survive on the eastern part of the mountain. Near the tomb of **Xiang Jing Yu** (1895–1928), one of the first women leaders in Communist China, lies that of a semi-mythical hero from a much earlier era – **Lu Su**, a Wu general from the Three Kingdoms period.

VISITORS' CHECKLIST

Practical Information
500 miles (800 km) W of Shanghai. 10,100,000. 6 Baofeng Rd, (027) 8366 9955.

Transportation
Hankou train station, Wuchang; Wuhan for high-speed trains. CAAC (buses to airport), Hankou bus station, Hanyang, Wuchang. Yangzi ferry terminal.

Guiyuan Si

20 Cuiwei Lu. **Tel** (027) 8462 0877. **Open** 7:30am–6pm daily.

Buddha statue, Guiyuan Si

This Buddhist temple in western Hanyang was founded in the early Qing era (1644–62), although the current buildings are late Qing and early Republican. It has a few ancient relics including a Northern Wei Buddha statue, but is most famous for its hall of 500 *arhat* statues sculpted in the 1820s, including a statue of Buddha carved from a single piece of jade.

Hankou

From 1861, the district of Hankou was the site of the former foreign concession. This area has several fine examples of European-style colonial architecture. The best are located between the river and Zhongshan Dadao, particularly along Yanjiang Dadao and Jianghan Road. The old **Customs House** looking over the river is a vast Renaissance-style building with a striking gray-stone portico and Corinthian capitals.

Colorful kites on sale on the Yangzi riverfront

Jingzhou Museum, part of the Taoist Kaiyuan Temple

8 Jingzhou
荆州

Jingzhou municipality. 130 miles (210 km) W of Wuhan. 6,600,000. 52 Jingdong Lu, (0716) 846 6429.

A worthwhile stop if cruising the river, the ancient town of Jingzhou is about 5 miles (8 km) to the west of its modern counterpart Shashi. The old town is ringed by walls 22 ft (7 m) in height, which were constructed by General Guan Yu of the State of Shu (AD 221–63). Within the walls stands the **Jingzhou Museum**. This has a large collection of ancient silk and fabrics and finds from a Western Han tomb of a court official called Sui, including his gory but well-preserved corpse, with organs.

Jingzhou Museum
134 Jingzhong Lu. **Tel** (0716) 849 4808. **Open** 9:30am–4:30pm Tue–Sun. **jzmsm.org**

9 Yichang
宜昌

Yichang District. 190 miles (305 km) W of Wuhan. 52 Jiefang Lu, (0717) 676 0392.

Yichang, which was once a treaty port for foreign traders, is now associated with the Gezhou Dam, completed in 1986 and the controversial Three Gorges Dam, completed in 2008. You can visit the site of the Three Gorges Dam at Sandouping, which lies 24 miles (38 km) upstream. The town is also a starting point for a visit to scenic Shennongjia *(see p278)*.

The Three Gorges Dam
乔家大院

The construction of the Three Gorges Dam, at over 600 ft (180 m) high and more than a mile (2 km) across, was intended to provide a significant amount of China's energy, curb the Yangzi's tendency to flood, and channel some of the country's wealth, for long concentrated along the coastal regions, into China's heartland. However, creating a 400-mile (645-km) long reservoir has also meant the relocation of many thousands of people, the obliteration of important cultural sites, and long-term environmental damage.

Three Gorges Dam seen from the low-water side

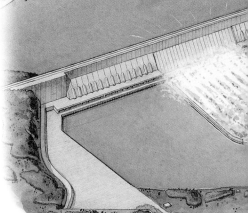

Environmental Issues

Hundreds of miles downstream, the rapidly growing municipality of Chongqing has been pumping untreated waste and chemicals into the Yangzi. With the river no longer able to flush this away, the fear is that it could all collect in a 400-mile (645-km) long cesspool. Additionally, the reduced flow of the water could substantially increase the silting up of subsidiary waterways, further harming the fragile ecosystem and closing the migration routes of many fish species and rare freshwater dolphins.

Part of the Three Gorges before the water levels rose 575 ft (175 m)

For hotels and restaurants in this region see pp560–61 and pp578–9

★ Jar Hill Observation Platform
This high point provides an excellent bird's-eye view of the dam as well as a museum showing the history of the construction.

VISITORS' CHECKLIST

Practical Information
Sandouping, 32 miles (51 km) W of Yichang. (0717) 676 3498.
sxdaba.com

Transportation
4 from Yichang train station to Yemingzhu, then bus 8 to Liuzhashou reception center, or hire a minibus or taxi.

KEY

① **The Ship Lifting Tower** is simply a large and very powerful elevator for ships less than 80-ft (25-m) long – faster than using the 5-level lock.

② **The Yangzi Sculpture** is a large lump of eroded rock that is said to be from the Yangzi River.

★ 5-Level Double Ship Lock
At over a mile long (1,600 m) this lock can raise or lower ships a total vertical distance of 370 ft (113 m) and is, not surprisingly, the largest lock system in the world. It takes nearly 3 hours to pass through the lock gates.

Dense virgin forests lining a gorge at Shennongjia

⑩ Shennongjia
神农架

144 miles (230 km) NW of Yichang. ✈ at Hongping, 25 miles (40 km) from Songbai. 🚌 from Yichang to entrance at Muyu, then hire a car. ℹ 100 Yiling Da Dao, (0717) 690 8026. from Yichang tourist office & Forestry Office Travel Service, Muyu.

This remote and little-visited forest reserve has some remarkable scenery. It is covered with rare trees and several hundred species of plants used in traditional medicine, samples of which were introduced to the West by the botanist Ernest Wilson in the early 20th century. It is also home to many of China's rarest animals, including the splendid golden monkey.

Inside the reserve, at **Xiaolong Tan**, is a museum dedicated to the legendary Chinese Wild Man *(ye ren)*, who is like the Himalayan Yeti and just as hard to find. The first reported sighting was in 1924. Walking trails around Xiaolong Tan lead into the heart of the reserve, providing an excellent opportunity to see the rare golden monkeys, giant salamanders, and golden pheasants. Some trails follow forest roads, others meander gently across meadows, while the crudest lead to mountain tops. Foreign visitors can explore the Muyu area, where peaks reach 10,187 ft (3,105 m). It may be possible to visit the main town of Songbai, but only if accompanied by a tour guide.

⑪ Wudang Shan
武当山

250 miles (400 km) NW of Wuhan. ✈ Shiyan Wudangshan Airport, 12 miles (19 km) from Wudang Shan. Bus 2 runs to the mountain. 🚆 from Wuhan or Xiangfan to Wudang Shan town. 🚌 from Shiyan, Xiangfan or Liuliping train stations to Wudang Shan town, or direct from Wuhan or Xi'an.

The many peaks of Wudang Shan – the highest reaching 5,289 ft (1,612 m) at **Tianzhu** (Heavenly Pillar) **Peak** – have been associated with Daoism since the Tang era. Wudang Shan has also been known for its martial arts since the Song-dynasty monk Zhang Sanfeng created a style called Wudang boxing, from which *tai ji quan* later developed. The entry point is the town of Wudang Shan, which many Chinese tourists now visit for the temple museum of **Tai Shan Miao** and the ruins of Yuxu Gong temple. Wudang Shan lies to the south of town, and there are several ways of reaching it. A path near the railway station takes eight hours to reach the summit at Tianzhu Peak. Blue tourist buses and minibuses go about three-quarters of the way up, from where it is another 2 hours on foot to the top. Other options are sedan chairs and a cable car that runs between a point called Qiongtai and the summit. Going up by bus, visitors first pass the **Martial Arts School** and then the **Zixiao Gong** (Purple Cloud Palace), an impressive Ming temple. Inside the main hall is a beautiful spiral cupola. From the minibus terminus, a short diversion leads to the **Nanyan Gong** temple at the very edge of the cliff. Nearby is **Dragon Head Rock**, which projects horizontally from the edge and is covered in sculpted designs. The main path goes past **Lang Mei Xian Ci**, a shrine dedicated to the monk Zhang Sanfeng. The path eventually divides into two at Huanglong Dong. Of the two paths, it is easier to take the one leading straight on to the group of temples at Tianzhu Peak. At the summit, the peak is surmounted by **Jindian Gong** (Golden Hall), built of gilded copper and bronze in 1416. It has a statue of the Ming emperor Zhen Wu, who retreated to Wudang Shan in the 15th century. The views from Tianzhu, of razor-edge cliffs covered in mist, are magnificent.

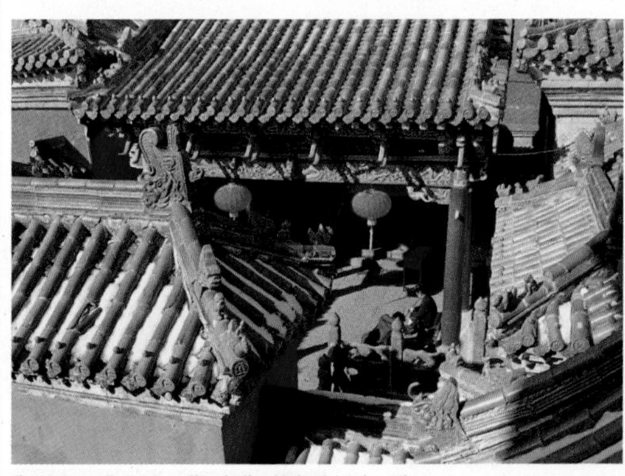
The Ming-era Zixiao Gong (Purple Cloud Palace), Wudang Shan

◀ The Yangzi River, winding its way through the Three Gorges

Tai Ji Quan (Tai Chi)

Practiced daily by millions of Chinese, *tai ji quan*, or "Supreme Ultimate Fist," is a slow-moving, graceful form of kung fu *(see p165)*. Developed over a thousand years ago by Daoist recluses and monks, *tai ji quan* is based on the movements of birds and animals and the Daoist concept of *yin* and *yang*, or equal opposites. All of the movements, each with their own names and prescribed patterns, have elements of *yin* and *yang*; movements contract and expand, sink and rise, move inwards and outwards. The movements follow one another fluidly and sets can involve anywhere from 12 to 108 moves, and take up to an hour to complete. *Tai ji quan* does have martial aspects, but is utilized chiefly to improve the flow of *qi (see pp38–9)*, or vital energy, through the body. The exercises leave the practitioner feeling revitalized and relaxed.

Zhang Sanfeng, an official, retired from the court in disgust to Wudang Shan. Inspired by a battle between a crane and a snake, he came up with the basis for *tai ji quan,* combining kung fu and Daoist health principles.

The Sword set involves the use of a weapon to aid balance and concentration. The simple sword form, with some 50 movements, is related to the water element, whilst the sabre is related to fire.

Movements of the Tai Ji Quan Set

Tai ji quan's *numerous schools have different sets and movements. "Whip to one side" is a common move often repeated in a set.*

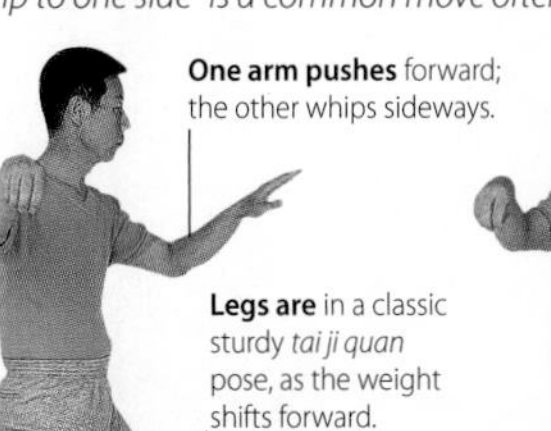

One arm pushes forward; the other whips sideways.

Legs are in a classic sturdy *tai ji quan* pose, as the weight shifts forward.

As the body turns to a 45 degree angle, the feet turn and the weight shifts to the back leg.

The trunk sinks, while the back remains upright. Arms are poised as if to ward off attack.

The front leg slides forward, the body sinking *(yin)* close to the ground in a powerful position ready to sweep upward *(yang).*

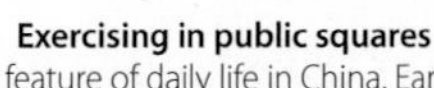

Exercising in public squares is a feature of daily life in China. Early in the morning, crowds of mostly elderly people perform *tai ji quan* in large groups, executing the movements in graceful unison.

THE SOUTH

The South at a Glance

Encompassing the provinces of Fujian, Guangdong, and Hainan, as well as Macau and Hong Kong, the south is China's most familiar region, mainly because millions of immigrants from the area have moved overseas, taking their cooking and traditions with them. Yet, with the exception of Hong Kong and Guangzhou, the area rarely features on travelers' itineraries. There is much to enjoy here from the ancient Ming city of Chaozhou and Wuyi Shan's superb scenery, to the historic ports of Quanzhou, Xiamen, and Shantou along the coasts of Guangdong and Fujian, and the tropical beaches of Hainan.

Fishermen laboring on the beach at Meizhou Island

The active Buddhist temple Nan Putuo Si, Xiamen

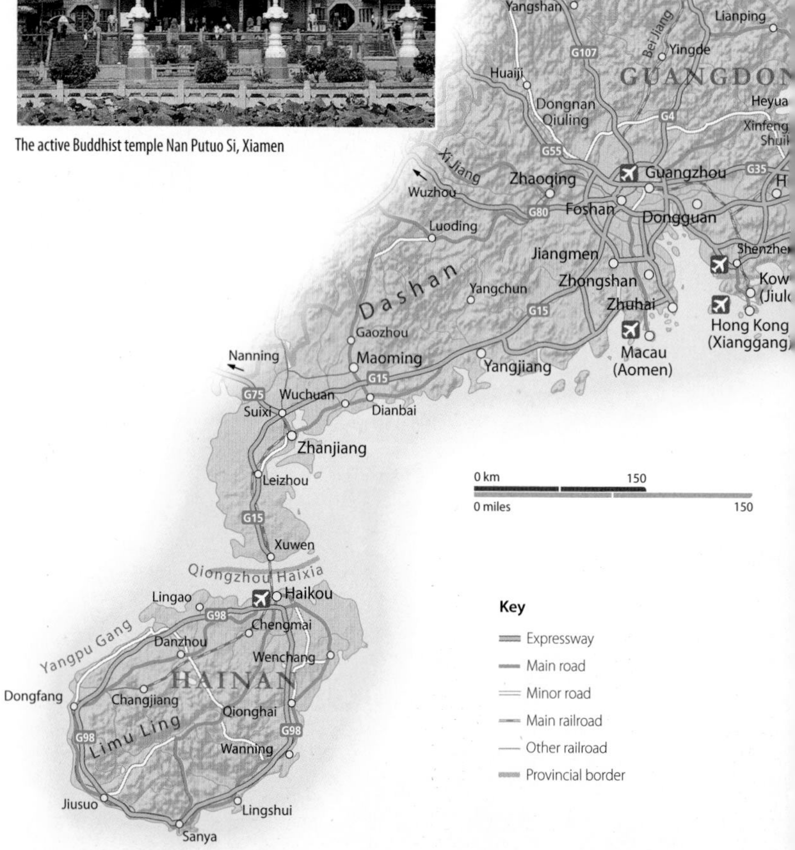

Changsha
Lianzhou
Shaoguan
Qujiang
Yangshan
Lianping
Bei Jiang
Yingde
G107
Huaiji
GUANGDON
Heyua
Dongnan Qiuling
G4
Xinfeng
Shui
G55
Xi Jiang
Zhaoqing
Guangzhou
G35
Wuzhou
G80
Foshan
Dongguan
Luoding
Jiangmen
Shenzhe
Zhongshan
Kow (Jiul
Yangchun
Dashan
Zhuhai
G15
Hong Kong (Xianggang)
Gaozhou
Macau (Aomen)
Nanning
Maoming
Yangjiang
G15
G75
Wuchuan
Suixi
Dianbai
Zhanjiang
Leizhou
G15
Xuwen
Qiongzhou Haixia
Lingao
Haikou
G98
Chengmai
Yangpu Gang
Danzhou
Wenchang
HAINAN
Dongfang
Changjiang
Qionghai
Limu Ling
G98
G98
Wanning
Jiusuo
Lingshui
Sanya

0 km 150
0 miles 150

Key

Expressway
Main road
Minor road
Main railroad
Other railroad
Provincial border

◀ Night-time view of the Hong Kong skyline

Pucheng
Wuyishan
Wenzhou
Songxi
Nanchang
Jianyang
Zherong
Shaowu
G15
Futun Xi
G3
Jian 'ou
Fu'an
Jiufeng Shan
Taining
Ningde
Nanping
Jiangle
G70
Min Jiang
Luoyuan
FUJIAN
Lianjiang
Sanming
G72
G3
Fuzhou
Yong 'an
Liancheng
Fuqing
G25
G72
Daiyun Shan
Putian
G15
Daimao Shan
Zhangping
Wuyi Shan
Hui'an
Longyan
G25
Nan 'an
Quanzhou
Shanghang
G76
Tong 'an
Jinjiang
Zhangzhou
Xiamen
Dabu
Xingning
Zhangpu
G15
G78
Yunxiao
Fengshun
Chaozhou
Jieyang
Chenghai
Shantou
Puning
Chaoyang
G15
Lufeng

Women of the Hui'an minority, Chongwu

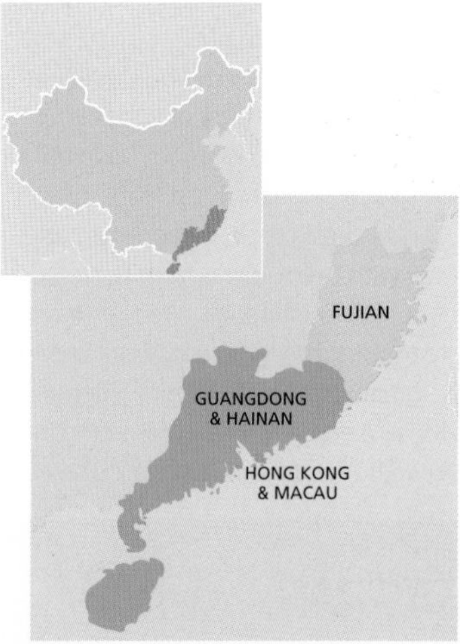

FUJIAN
GUANGDONG & HAINAN
HONG KONG & MACAU

Traffic moving slowly along the bustling Gloucester Road in Wan Chai, Hong Kong

Getting Around

The main airport hubs are at Hong Kong and Guangzhou. Hong Kong offers connections to destinations all over the world, while Guangzhou has direct flights to cities throughout China and Asia. Xiamen, Fuzhou, Sanya, and Haikou also have airports with several domestic flights. Trains, some air-conditioned, link much of the region although routes can be circuitous. The extensive bus network offers varying degrees of comfort depending on the destination. There are frequent ferry services, particularly between Hong Kong, Macau, and various mainland ports.

For additional map symbols *see back flap*

A PORTRAIT OF THE SOUTH

An enduring maritime tradition has influenced life and culture in the south. The long coastline along the South China Sea gave the ports of Fujian and Guangdong easy access to trade routes leading East and West. Trade also brought the British and Portuguese to the south, ultimately leading to the colonization of Hong Kong and Macau. Only Hainan Island remained isolated from the developments that took place across the sea on mainland China.

Guangdong and Fujian are particularly mountainous, and although the mountains are not especially high, they have isolated the provinces from the political mainstream of the center and north of the country. Consequently, the south has tended to look outwards, across the sea, and over the centuries has been far more inclined than much of China to deal with foreigners – either by design or default.

From the 7th century onwards, Arab traders introduced Islam to China through ports such as Guangzhou (Canton) and Quanzhou, and took silk, porcelain, and tea away with them. It was from these ports that China launched its overseas naval expeditons. The Ming emperors sponsored the great voyages of Admiral Zheng He, a Muslim eunuch, who crossed the Indian Ocean from Fuzhou to Africa in the early 1400s. Almost a century later, Portuguese vessels ventured up the Pearl River to Guangzhou, an expedition that eventually led to the colonization of Macau in 1557. The British soon followed, but their nefarious policy of flooding the Chinese market with opium led to the two Opium Wars (1839–42 and 1856–60), after which China ceded Hong Kong and the tip of the Kowloon Peninsula to Britain.

Over the centuries, waves of southern Chinese migrated overseas, first to Southeast Asia, and later westward as far as North America, as indentured labor. Their global presence is one of the reasons why visitors consider this the most familiar region in China.

The Cantonese culinary tradition is distinct and known the world over. The local cuisine, however, may encompass

Hong Kong Island's glittering skyline, seen from Kowloon across Victoria Harbour

Tiled roofs above the harbor at Meizhou Island

outlandish ingredients not used in overseas restaurants; it is said, with some justification, that the Cantonese will eat anything.

Teas from the south are exported throughout the world and Fujian produces some of China's finest, including oolong. The area has cultivated the arts of tea-brewing and -tasting, and so-called "tea art halls," where resident brew-masters demonstrate techniques associated with particular varieties of tea, are still found in Fuzhou, the province's capital.

A traditional Hakka dwelling

The south's largely subtropical climate has encouraged a gregarious lifestyle, which tends to manifest itself in an active, open-air streetlife. The local language of Cantonese is quite different from Mandarin, the national language. The sound is distinctive, even to the untrained ear. The region's other major dialect is Fujianese *(Minnan hua)*.

The south is home to several ethnic communities, including the Hakka and the Li. The Hakka migrated to south and central China from the north. The impressive round mansions of the Fujianese Hakka are a highlight of a trip to the interior. The Li are Hainan's original people, who settled here almost 2,000 years ago and lived a primeval existence until the 1930s. The Central Highlands around Tongshi offer glimpses into their unique culture.

Strong overseas connections have meant that in the last 30 years, money has poured back into the south. China's more flexible modern economy, as well as large investments from Hong Kong, have also enhanced the region's affluence. Development has been rapid, propelling the growth of new cities, such as Shenzhen, helped by their status as Special Economic Zones. Inspired by Hong Kong's sleek, contemporary architecture, construction has been frantic and the proliferation of high-rise buildings has transformed the skyline of historic cities.

There are still many hidden gems to explore among the region's skyscrapers and new developments. Chief among these are Guangzhou's Nan Yue Tomb, the rarely visited Chaozhou with its still-intact Ming city wall, and one of China's oldest mosques in Quanzhou. Some of the finest examples of colonial architecture can be seen in Macau and on the islet of Gulang Yu in Xiamen. Tropical Hainan's main appeal lies in its beaches, but the mountainous center is worth exploring as well. Finally, there is Hong Kong, a frenetic, cosmopolitan city that vibrates day and night with an energy that is in keeping with its status as a global financial center.

Women of the Hui'an minority, Chongwu

Rice

Rice has long been vital to the Chinese as both a food staple and a cash crop. So intrinsic to life is the grain that *"Chi fan le ma?"* (Have you eaten rice today?) is one of the most common greetings in China. Rice-growing is thought to have its origins in southern China around 10,000 BC, although the flooded-field method that allowed larger yields and required massive irrigation projects was not perfected until thousands of years later. Today, rice is grown throughout much of China and accounts for 30 percent of the world's total.

Rice plants, like most other cereals, produce dense flower-heads, with the grains tightly packed inside protective husks.

An endless chain of wooden pallets pulls water from a lower source to the fields by the pedaling power of laborers. Although much irrigation is now mechanized, numerous ingenious devices, many of them ancient technology once fashioned from bamboo, are still used to water the fields.

Japonica rice

Glutinous rice

Japonica, a sub-species of *Oryza sativa*, is the most common rice in China, and is generally short grained and slightly sticky. Glutinous rice, grown in the south-east, becomes a sticky mass when cooked. It is often served wrapped in bamboo leaves.

Rice Products

The Chinese have found many uses for their pervasive staple. During the Ming dynasty, builders used water in which glutinous rice had been cooked as mortar mix to strengthen defensive walls. Rice straw, the leaves of the plant left after harvest, is pulped to produce a fine white paper, perfect for paintings and kites. Husks are used as fertilizer, packing material, or simply fed to animals. Rice is ground to produce rice flour that can be rolled and pulled to create a huge range of noodles. Numerous rice wines are sold in China, some of them quite palatable, including sweet Shaoxing, made from glutinous rice.

Extracting juice from rice to ferment and make into *jiu* (wine or spirits)

Water buffalo pull plows, harrows, and other agricultural implements. These sturdy animals thrive in the waterlogged conditions, produce valuable manure, and require less maintenance than tractors.

Terraced Hillsides

Vast areas of China are dominated by rice cultivation, and paddy fields have transformed the landscape, especially in the subtropical regions of the south, where cascades of terraces clothe many hillsides. Low mud banks trap the water as it trickles down the slopes, creating an attractive sequence of narrow, contour-hugging fields which are worked mainly by hand. Farmers are not completely reliant on rainfall because the water flow is carefully controlled, as is the depth, which is typically 6 in (15 cm). Ever resourceful, some farmers raise edible fish such as grass carp in the paddy waters.

Cultivating Rice

In much of rural China, rice-growing is very much a hands-on activity, and traditional methods are still used, especially in hilly country. The work is labor-intensive, but the two or three harvests a year that are possible in the south make the efforts worthwhile.

Rice seedlings are grown in special protected beds. After about 40 days they are transplanted by hand to the paddies.

Planting is tiring, back-breaking work, and in some areas is now mechanized. Teams of workers wade through the paddy fields planting the seedlings one by one.

At harvest time, the fields are drained before the rice plants are cut either by hand-held sickle or by machine.

To dry the rice, mounds of freshly harvested grain are raked out in a thin layer and left to warm in the sun.

Winnowing, tossing or pouring the rice from a basket, separates the dried rice grains from their husks – the wind carries away the chaff.

Regional Food: the South

The southern school of Chinese cooking, called by the generic name Cantonese, is centered around Guangzhou, where the Pearl River delta runs into the South China Sea. Situated at the mouth of this estuary lies Hong Kong, another culinary center of China. Fish, of course, plays a major role in this coastal economy and rice is the dominant food grain. Other food crops include tea, peanuts, sugar cane, and subtropical fruits such as bananas, pineapples, oranges, and lychees. Large-scale emigration from the south has meant that Chinese food served outside China is likely to be southern Chinese cooking.

Bitter melon and water spinach

Lush and colorful vegetables on display in the market

Guangzhou (Canton)

The epicenter of Chinese cuisine, Guangzhou owes its culinary primacy to its geography. As a port it had a well-off, cosmopolitan merchant class who could afford expensive foods. It also has a subtropical climate and a summer that lasts for almost six months, with the rest of the year divided into autumn and spring: there is no winter. As a result, crops grow luxuriantly all year round and supplement the abundance of fish. Despite this fecundity, the size of the population the land has to support means that it has always struggled to provide enough food. Therefore the Cantonese also eat less-expensive "delicacies" not popular in other provinces such as frog's legs, turtles, dogs, snakes, and nearly every kind of animal there is. Food is almost a religion to the Cantonese and the locals claim that in Guangzhou "there is a restaurant every five steps."

A selection of *dim sum* dishes

Regional Dishes & Specialties

Soy-cured bacon and sausages

Most people probably associate Cantonese cuisine with *dim sum* (meaning "dot on the heart" or "snack"), delectable, dainty bites of steamed or fried food: dumplings with prawn or pork fillings, miniature spareribs, deep-fried spring rolls, paper-wrapped prawns, chicken feet, or glossy custard-filled tarts. These snacks are to be eaten during the day for breakfast or lunch with pots of tea, never as dinner. Other famous specialties are the fish and shellfish dishes, and roast meats – duck, *cha siu* (roast pork), and suckling pig. Key to the southern school of cuisine are its various sauces. Although such fresh food is often quickly steamed with a few simple aromatics, sauces such as oyster, hoi sin (sweet soy bean and garlic), mushroom, lemon, black bean and *chu hou* (soy bean, garlic, and ginger) are also used to add flavor.

Steamed Seabass: steamed with scallions and ginger, and seasoned with light soy sauce, rice wine, and sesame oil.

Chaozhou & Dongjiang

Chaozhou (also known as Teochew) is a richer cuisine than Cantonese. This cuisine specializes in fresh shellfish and seafood, so the emphasis is on buying live animals or fish, be it at a market or restaurant. Stocks are flavoured with fish sauce, hot sauce, or red rice vinegar. Dongjiang is a more rustic and salty cooking – soy-cured bacon and air-dried sausages are a specialty – and it also uses more poultry. This cooking is also sometimes known as Hakka, meaning "guest people," which refers to the immigrants from northern China who settled in the south some time after the invasion by Mongols in the 13th century. Later there were other large-scale migrations overseas, one of the reasons why most Chinese restaurants in the West serve only southern Chinese (Cantonese) food.

Dried vegetable and spices stall

Fish drying in a shop in Hong Kong

Hong Kong

Although mainly Chinese, Hong Kong is a unique city in China: as an international port, it has been open to outside influences. So, while most of the restaurants are Cantonese, you will also find all the regional Chinese cuisines here alongside those from other Asian countries and Europe. A gastromomic supermarket, Hong Kong doesn't really have a specialty dish although some claim that "smelly beancurd" (a pungent type of fermented tofu) fulfils that role. Hong Kong is a 24-hour city and, all day every day, all the food places, from the humble street stands to the luxury banqueting halls, are filled with people eating. The story goes that you could visit a different restaurant each day for a year and never eat the same dish twice.

On the Menu

Seafood with Vegetables A popular dish of prawns, squid, and scallops stir-fried with whatever vegetables are available and noodles.

"White-Cut" Chicken A whole chicken blanched in boiling water or stock, then left to cool in the liquid under cover for 6–8 hours. Tender and moist.

Stir-Fried Squid with Black Bean Sauce In fact any seafood such as crab, lobster, or prawns may be substituted for the squid. This can also be made with chilies for a more spicy alternative.

Eight-Treasure Stuffed Beancurd The stuffing is pork and prawn – vegetarians should stick with the Eight-Treasure Buddha's Special *(see p186–7)*.

Steamed Chicken with Dried Mushrooms Chicken pieces steamed with Chinese mushrooms – simple but great.

Lobster with Ginger and Scallions: lobster braised with aromatics and served on a bed of soft noodles.

Oyster Sauce Beef: stir-fried beef with mushrooms and vegetables, all cut to the same size, in oyster sauce.

Roast Meats: choice cuts of suckling pig, duck, pork, and chicken served cold with tasty dipping sauces.

FUJIAN

The sea and mountains form the essential features of the province of Fujian. Its major cities thrive as coastal ports, while inland there is the spectacular, rugged beauty of Wuyi Shan.

Fujian's historical importance dates back almost as far as the Warring States period (475–221 BC), when the Yue people, defeated by the State of Chu (today's Hubei and Hunan), migrated southwards to settle in this part of China and Vietnam. Those who came to what is now Fujian were called Min Yue, later known as the Min people. Even today the Fujianese are sometimes referred to as Min and the southern Fujian language as Minnan Hua. The native people who preceded them are thus called the Ancient Min. Very little survives from this period, apart from the mysterious 3,000-year-old boat-shaped coffins found lodged high above the river in the Wuyi Mountains. The main attractions are strung along the busy coastline and include the historic ports of Xiamen and Quanzhou, as well as Fuzhou, the capital of Fujian, which was a major maritime center for more than 1,000 years. Other attractions are the historic stone town of Chongwu and the small island of Meizhou, birthplace of the important Goddess of the Sea. Inland, Fujian's hinterland was until recently, wild and unspoiled enough to protect the last South China tigers, now thought to be extinct. It is also the home of the Hakka people, whose traditional dwellings can be seen at the rural settlements around Yongding *(see p296)*.

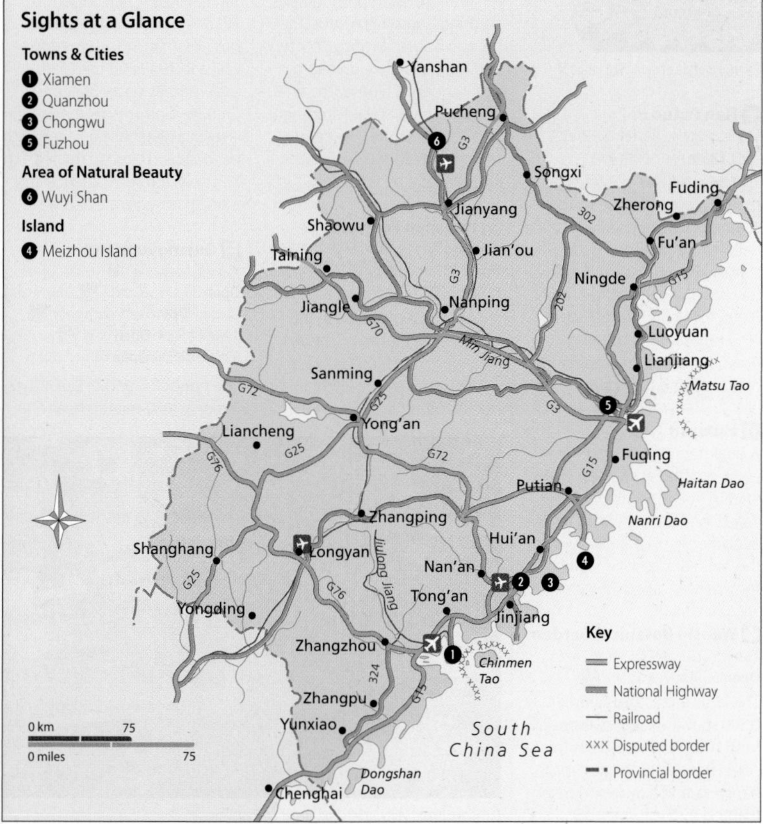

Traditional Fujian *tulou* (earthen dwellings) in a Hakka village

For additional map symbols *see back flap*

❶ Xiamen

厦门

An attractive city with a bustling nautical atmosphere, Xiamen was known as Amoy in the 19th century. It was first settled in the Song dynasty (AD 960–1279) but did not become a significant port until the Ming dynasty. It also served as an important stronghold against the Manchus when they invaded in the 17th century. The resistance was led by the legendary pirate and Ming loyalist Zheng Chenggong, also known as Koxinga, who is commemorated in the city. Xiamen became an early treaty port in the 19th century, when the foreign community established itself on Gulangyu Island. The city was also declared one of China's first Special Economic Zones in the 1980s.

Colorful rooftop dragon, Nan Putuo Si

Nan Putuo Si

515 Siming Nan Lu. **Tel** (0592) 208 7282. **Open** 4am–6pm daily.

This busy temple was founded in the Tang era in the extravagant southern style *(see p306)*. Its three halls hold a wealth of Buddhist statuary. The Heavenly King Hall has an image of Wei Tuo, Protector of Buddhist Doctrine, who holds a stick pointing down to signify that the temple offers lodging to pilgrims.

Huxiyan

A quaint temple lies high on a rocky outcrop at Huxiyan (Tiger Stream Rock). Another temple, Bailu Dong (White Deer Cave), is even higher up the hill. Built in the Ming era, its main draw is the fine view across the city.

Wanshi Botanical Garden

25 Huyuan Lu. **Tel** (0592) 202 4785. **Open** 6:30am–6pm daily.

This large scenic area houses over 6,300 species of plants, especially from south China and Southeast Asia. These include eucalyptus, bamboo, and a redwood tree planted by the former US President Richard Nixon. A bullet-scarred rock marks the spot where Koxinga killed his cousin.

Overseas Chinese Museum

493 Siming Nan Lu. **Tel** (0592) 208 5345. **Open** call for details.

In this museum, the first section focuses on the story of Fujianese emigration, using photographs, paintings, and mementos. The second houses bronzes, pottery, and artworks once owned by non-resident Chinese. The final section covers the environment and natural world. The centerpiece is the 50-ft (15-m) long skeleton of a sei whale.

Hulishan Fortress

Huandao Nan Lu. **Tel** (0592) 209 9603. **Open** 7:30am–5:30pm daily (summer: to 6pm).

Situated along the coast, this 19th-century fortress features a cannon made for the Qing government by the German manufacturer Krupp in 1891.

Cannons guarding the ramparts at Hulishan Fortress

Almost 46-ft (14-m) long and weighing 49 tons (50,000 kg), it had a firing range of 6 miles (10 km). Taiwan's islands are visible from the ramparts – a fascination for locals, who were forbidden entry to the site until 1984.

Jimei School Village

Open 9am–4:30pm Tue–Sun.

Located 9 miles (15 km) north of the city, Jimei School Village was founded by the philanthropist Tan Kah Kee (Chen Jiageng) in 1913. A successful Singapore businessman, he returned to China in 1950 and held various government posts. Built in Chinese-Gothic style, the college is set in a beautiful park filled with pagodas and close to the sea. Tan Kah Kee's former residence and a small museum are also here.

Gulangyu Island

Xiamen Seaworld: **Tel** (0592) 206 9350. **Open** 8am–9pm daily. Shuzhuang Garden: **Open** 8am–6pm daily. Sunlight Rock: **Open** daily. Koxinga Memorial Hall: **Open** 8am–5:30pm.

The tranquil island of Gulangyu lies only a 10-minute boat ride

Gulangyu Island's tiny streets and elegant colonial houses

For hotels and restaurants in this region see p561 and p579

from Xiamen, with attractive buildings and no traffic apart from battery-powered buggies. The island first became important in 1842 after the signing of the Treaty of Nanking, when the resident representatives of the foreign powers established themselves here. It soon grew into a European-style town with churches, consulates, and spacious villas. In 1903, it was designated an International Settlement for Europeans and Japanese, complete with a municipal council and Sikh police force, and it retained this status until the end of World War II. The island still retains an atmosphere reminiscent of southern Europe.

Spread over nearly 1 square mile (2.5 sq km), Gulangyu Island is very pleasant to explore on foot, with its tiny streets and elegant houses fronted by pretty flower gardens. Between the two ferry terminals is **Xiamen Seaworld**, which houses an interesting collection of sharks, seals, dolphins, penguins, and tropical fish. To the southeast is the **Statue of Koxinga**, which commemorates

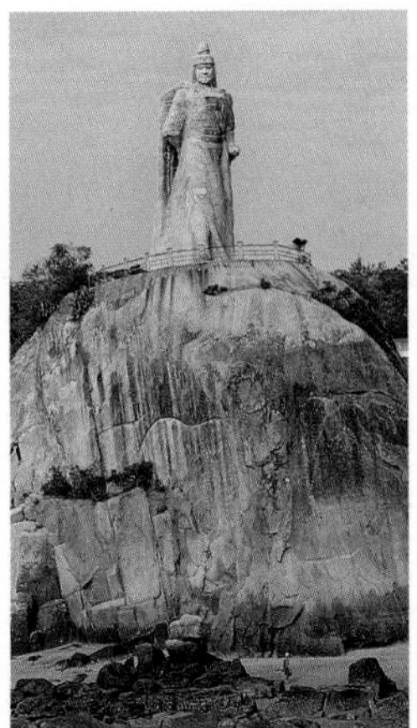

Statue of the legendary rebel commander Koxinga, Gulangyu

Xiamen's famous rebel. Koxinga and his fleet held out against the encroaching Manchus for years. He is also credited with ousting the Dutch from Taiwan. Farther south along the coast is **Shuzhuang Garden**. Built in 1931 as a private villa, the garden opened to the public in 1955. Today visitors are enticed by its numerous tropical plants and flowers, as well as its complex of traditional Chinese gardens.

VISITORS' CHECKLIST

Practical Information
155 miles (250 km) SW of Fuzhou. 3,500,000. 2/F Huajian Building, 78 Xinhua Lu, (0592) 204 6847. **english.visitxm.com**

Transportation
Hubin Nan Lu bus station, Xiahe Lu bus station, Songbo bus station. to Gulangyu Island from Dongdu International Cruise Terminal.

Adjacent to the gardens is the attractive, but usually crowded **Gangzaihou Beach**. Close by to its north is **Sunlight Rock**, the island's highest point which can easily be reached by cable car. At the foot of the rock is the **Koxinga Memorial Hall**, which houses a handful of Koxinga's personal possessions, such as his jade belt and parts of his robe, as well as other historical items.

Farther toward the southwestern coast is **Yingxiong Shan**, with an unusual open-air aviary at the top of the building. It is filled with colorful parrots, egrets, and tropical pigeons.

Xiamen City Center & Gulangyu Island

① Nan Putuo Si
② Huxiyan
③ Wanshi Botanical Garden
④ Overseas Chinese Museum
⑤ Xiamen Seaworld
⑥ Statue of Koxinga
⑦ Shuzhuang Garden
⑧ Gangzaihou Beach
⑨ Sunlight Rock
⑩ Koxinga Memorial Hall
⑪ Yingxiong Shan

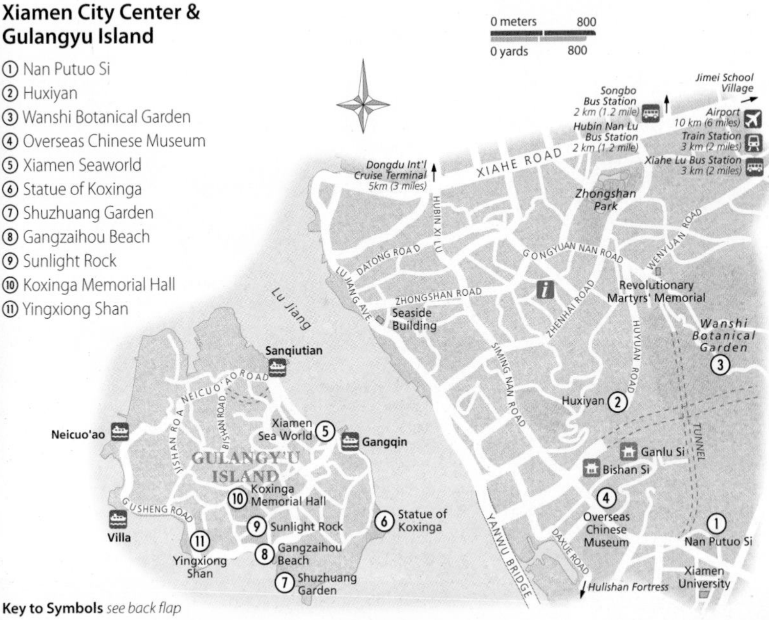

0 meters 800
0 yards 800
Songbo Bus Station 2 km (1.2 mile)
Jimei School Village
Airport 10 km (6 miles)
Hubin Nan Lu Bus Station 2 km (1.2 mile)
Train Station 3 km (2 miles)
Xiahe Lu Bus Station 3 km (2 miles)
Dongdu Int'l Cruise Terminal 5km (3 miles)
XIAHE ROAD
Zhongshan Park
HUBIN XI LU
DATONG ROAD
GONGYUAN NAN ROAD
WENYUAN ROAD
LU JIANG AVE.
ZHONGSHAN ROAD
Seaside Building
ZHENHAI ROAD
Revolutionary Martyrs' Memorial
Lu Jiang
Wanshi Botanical Garden
HUYUAN ROAD
SIMING NAN ROAD
Sanqiutian
NEICUO'AO ROAD
Huxiyan
TUNNEL
Neicuo'ao
Xiamen Sea World
Gangqin
GULANGYU ISLAND
JISHAN ROAD
BISHAN ROAD
Ganlu Si
Bishan Si
Koxinga Memorial Hall
GUSHENG ROAD
Statue of Koxinga
Overseas Chinese Museum
Sunlight Rock
Villa
Nan Putuo Si
Yingxiong Shan
Gangzaihou Beach
YANWU BRIDGE
DAXUE ROAD
Shuzhuang Garden
Hulishan Fortress
Xiamen University

Key to Symbols *see back flap*

Earthen Dwellings of Yongding

The Hakka people were driven south from the Yellow River plains by war in the late Tang and early Song dynasties. It is perhaps due to their past experiences of persecution, and to their presence in a new land (their official minority name is Kejia, which means "guest people"), that they adopted a fortress-like style of rammed-earth buildings called *tulou*. Capable of housing several hundred people, these round or square buildings are constructed around a courtyard containing a maze of storage sheds and public meeting rooms. Hukeng is one of the more accessible towns in the Yongding area with several Hakka dwellings. The train from Xiamen to Longyan takes 75 minutes (the bus takes 4 hours) after which it is a 2-hour bus ride to Hukeng.

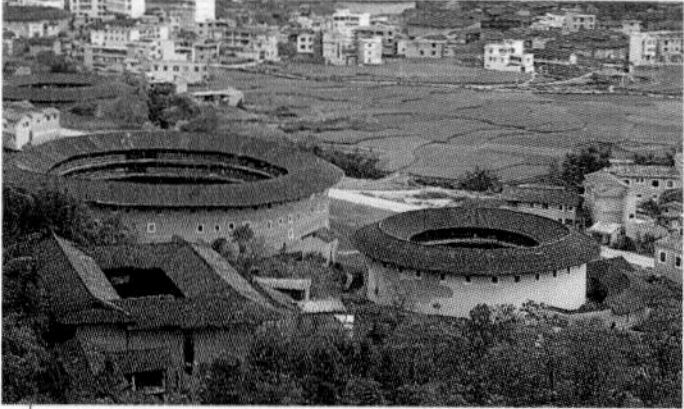

Numerous *tulou* are located in the countryside surrounding Yongding. Although the round houses are the most celebrated, other styles are found in the vicinity: massive square dwellings similar in scale to the round houses and smaller rammed-earth residences facing onto a central courtyard.

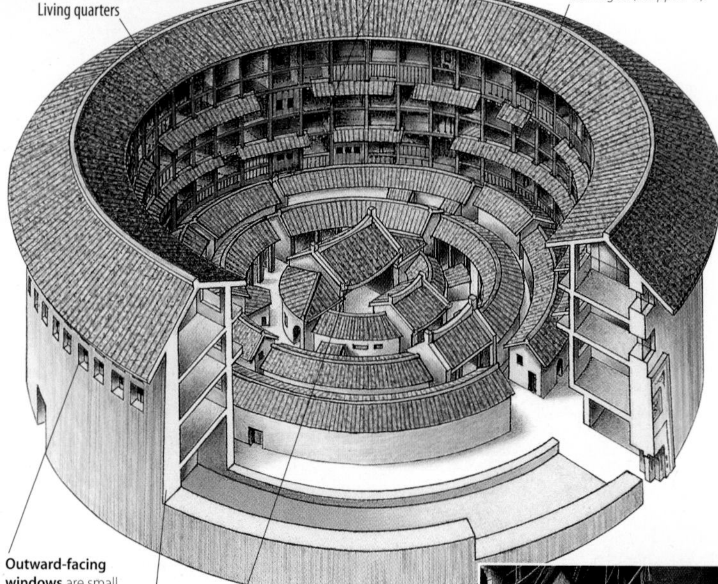

Grain storage

Thick fire walls divide the building into eight segments, echoing the Daoist octagonal symbol, the *bagua* (see pp38–9).

Living quarters

Outward-facing windows are small and trapezoidal and only located in the upper stories for security.

An ancestral hall at the center of the inner buildings may be used for ceremonies such as weddings.

Outer walls are thick for defense, often as wide as 5 ft (1.5 m) at the base, tapering towards the top.

The lower level is dedicated to communal Hakka life. Outdoor sculleries for washing and food preparation are located in front of the kitchens and dining rooms.

◀ An enchanting view of Nine Bend Creek, with Wuyi Shan in the background

Entrance to Qingjing Mosque, one of China's oldest extant mosques

❷ Quanzhou
泉州

62 miles (100 km) N of Xiamen. 1,400,000. 401 Fengze Jie, (0595) 2217 7719.

Located on the Jin River, Quanzhou was China's principal port during the Song and Yuan dynasties. The city's trade with India and elsewhere resulted in a permanent community of foreign residents. It was known to Arab geographers as Zaitun, from which the word "satin" is derived. Although Quanzhou's importance declined during the Ming dynasty, the town still offers insights into its maritime past.

Left partially roofless by a 17th-century earthquake, the **Qingjing Mosque** was first built in 1009, with extensive repairs in 1309, 1350, and 1609. Unlike other mosques in southern China that follow the traditional Chinese architectural style, this one is an elegant stone structure with an obvious Arabian influence. The surviving gate is supposedly modeled on a mosque in medieval Damascus. Its museum details the port's significance as a trade center.

In the north, the **Kaiyuan Si** was built in AD 686 and called Lianhua Si (Lotus Temple), after a lotus miraculously grew on a mulberry bush that still exists to the west of the Great Hall. In the Song period, 1,000 monks worshiped here. Among the temple's three halls, the Sweet Dew Vinaya Hall has a splendid ceiling and a throne on which sits Bodhisattva Ksitigarbha, Guardian of the Domain of Death. On each side of the halls are two ancient pagodas with carvings.

North of Kaiyuan Si is the **Qingyuan Shan** scenic area with the enormous **Laojun Yan**, a Song-dynasty sculpture of the Daoist Laozi *(see p37)*.

Northeast of the city center lies the **Quanzhou Maritime Museum**. One of its highlights is a Song trading vessel dating to 1274. Found in 1973, it was made of cedar wood and would have had sails of bamboo and hemp. At that time, such ships traveled to Arabia, Africa, and Asia, exporting porcelain and silks and importing spices, ivory, and glass. The museum also has stone carvings relating to Nestorian Christianity and to the Arab presence in the city.

Qingjing Mosque
108–112 Tumen Jie. **Tel** (0595) 2219 3553. **Open** 8am–5:30pm daily.

Kaiyuan Si
176 Xi Jie. **Tel** (0595) 2238 3285. **Open** 8am–6pm daily.

Maritime Museum
425 Donghu Jie. **Tel** (0595) 2210 0561. **Open** 8:30am–5:30pm daily.

❸ Chongwu
崇武

20 miles (32 km) E of Quanzhou. from Quanzhou to Hui'an, then minibus to Chongwu.

The Chongwu Peninsula's importance as a defensive stronghold was bolstered by the construction of the stone town of Chongwu in 1387, as a bastion against pirates. As part of its defense, the granite houses had flat roofs, making them almost invisible from beyond the forbidding 22-ft (6½-m) high boundary wall. The main inhabitants are the Hui'an people, whose women wear distinctive cropped blue tops and wide black trousers. Fishing and stone-carving are the main industries today, but the walls and old streets of Chongwu's fortress days still make a striking impression.

❹ Meizhou Island
梅州岛

35 miles (56 km) NE of Quanzhou. from Putian to Wenjia, then ferry. **Open** 7am-7pm daily

For the Fujianese, this island near Putian is associated with Mazu, Goddess of the Sea and Protector of Sailors *(see p155)*. Mazu is the deification of a 10th-century girl, whose powers enabled her to make maritime predictions, and her birthday is the island's main festival, celebrated on the 23rd day of the third lunar month. Numerous temples to the goddess dot the island, all the way up the hillside where her statue proudly stands on the summit. The main temple, **Mazu Miao**, is a short walk uphill from the pier. Rebuilt many times, it now resembles Beijing's Forbidden City. Due to the effort involved in getting here, it may be worthwhile staying overnight in one of the island's numerous hotels.

Statue of Mazu, Meizhou Island

Flat-roofed houses below the level of the wall, Chongwu

European-style architecture on Zhongzhou Island, Fuzhou

5 Fuzhou
福州

155 miles (250 km) N of Xiamen. 7,200,000. 121 Dong Jie, (0591) 8711 9928.

With its scenic location on the Min River, Fujian's capital was a major maritime port for over 1,000 years. It was the center of a lucrative trade, first in tea and sugar and later in cotton, lacquer, and ceramics. When the explorer Marco Polo visited Fuzhou in the 13th century, he recorded that the city was garrisoned by imperial troops. The city still has large numbers of troops due to its proximity to Taiwan.

Wuyi Square, with its statue of Mao Zedong, marks the city center. Just north is the 10th-century **Bai Ta** (White Pagoda), while to the west is **Wu Ta**, a black granite pagoda from the same era. Northwest of Wu Ta, the **Lin Zexu Memorial Hall** commemorates Lin Zexu, a Qing-dynasty official who destroyed an opium shipment in protest at the British trade, an act that led to the First Opium War *(see p69)*. Farther north is the **Three Lanes and Seven Alleys** area of well-preserved traditional buildings. To its northwest lies Xi Hu Gongyuan (West Lake Park), where the **Fujian Museum** contains a 3,500-year-old boat coffin.

Cang Shan, south of the river, was once the site of the foreign concession area. **Zhongzhou Island** (in the middle of the river) is a development with foreign restaurants. About 6 miles (10 km) east of the city is **Gu Shan**, with wooded walks and the restored **Yongquan Si**, built in AD 908.

Lin Zexu Memorial Hall
16 Aomen Lu. **Tel** (0591) 8762 2782.
Open 9am–5pm daily (summer: to 5:30pm).

Fujian Museum
96 Hutou Jie. **Tel** (0591) 8375 7627.
Open 9am–5pm Tue–Sun.
fjbwy.com

6 Wuyi Shan
武夷山

218 miles (350 km) NW of Fuzhou. to Wuyi Shan city (Wuyi Shan Shi), then bus 6 to park. China Travel Building, San Gu Jie, (0599) 511 9966.

Magical Wuyi Shan, a hilly area renowned for its oolong tea, offers some of the most stunning scenery in southern China. Its sheer, mist-shrouded sandstone mountains, known as the Thirty-Six Peaks, are threaded by the Jiuqu River and covered in lush vegetation. First visited by the Han Emperor Wudi (r. 141–87 BC), Wuyi Shan came to be regarded as a sacred place by subsequent emperors.

The best way to enjoy the landscape is to take a raft along the river as it meanders through gorges known collectively as **Jiu Qu Xi** (Nine Bend Creek). Above the fourth bend, mysterious 3,000-year-old coffins are lodged high in the cliffs. Made of *nanmu* (cedar), they are about 16 ft (5 m) long; each contains a single individual wrapped in silk and hemp. How they got here, however, remains a mystery.

Several trails lead to the summits. The table-top shaped **Da Wang Feng** is the most difficult, while an easier climb is **Tianyou Shan**, the traditional spot from where to watch the sunrise. The highest peak is **Sanyang Feng** at 2,356 ft (718 m). A path also leads to the **Shuilian Dong**, with a teahouse next to a waterfall.

Lacquerware – a Chinese Craft

Made from the sap of the "lac" tree *(Rhus verniciflua)*, lacquer was used long before the Han dynasty as a timber preservative – it hardens easily, even in damp conditions. It was later used in making plates and cups by applying layers of sap on wood or cloth, and painting the final layer. The modern craft, which appeared in the Yuan dynasty, uses the same basic method of applying layers on a wooden base, but before the lacquer completely hardens, it is deeply and intricately carved. The surface is then inlaid with gold, silver, or tortoiseshell, and usually painted red.

A lacquered screen

For hotels and restaurants in this region see p561 and p579

The Story of Tea

Tea *(cha)* has long been an integral part of Chinese traditional culture. Its legendary origins in China date back over 5,000 years, although some believe that it was introduced from India about 1,800 years ago. At first it was drunk as a tonic; now it is simply an indispensable part of daily life for almost all Chinese. It is widely grown throughout the warmer and wetter southern areas of China, particularly in Fujian, Yunnan, and Zhejiang. Although tea comes in many forms, all tea comes from the same species, *Camellia sinensis*. The most common Chinese teas – green, black, and oolong – have differing appearance and taste due to the process of fermentation, although the flavor of the tea does vary depending on where it is grown, and whether other ingredients have been added such as chrysanthemums in *huacha*. Tea is always drunk clear, never with milk or lemon. Sugar is added only in the northwestern Muslim areas, while the Tibetans drink theirs with butter.

Shen Nong was the mythological emperor who discovered tea, according to Chinese lore. A wise ruler, he pronounced that all drinking water should be boiled. One day, tea leaves fell from a tree into a pot of boiling water and the resulting brew delighted him.

By the Tang dynasty, tea was drunk throughout the empire. Before the 8th century, tea merchants commissioned Lu Yu to explain the advantages of the drink. He produced the *Cha Jing*, a compendium of tea, which systemized its production and traditions.

The tea trade was a key element in Britain's interest in China. The Portuguese were the first Europeans to enjoy tea, and the Dutch the first Europeans to deal in tea commercially, but it was the British who became the greatest tea traders as the fashion for tea spread from Holland to England in the late 17th century.

Upscale tea shops abound in the larger city centers. Highly prized specialty teas, such as the Fujianese oolong *tie guanyin*, can be purchased and sometimes sampled.

Tea plantations, many of them terraced, cover the hillsides of the southern interior. Up to five harvests can take place in a year. Picking is still done mostly by hand – an experienced picker can harvest 70 lb (32 kg) in a day – but mechanical methods are becoming common.

GUANGDONG & HAINAN

Located at the southernmost tip of continental China are the province of Guangdong and the island of Hainan, just off its coast in the South China Sea. Guangdong's capital, the great city and port of Guangzhou (Canton), stands on one of China's longest rivers, the Pearl (Zhu Jiang), while Haikou, the capital of Hainan, is located on the island's north coast, about 30 miles (50 km) to the south of the mainland.

Guangdong is perhaps the most familiar part of China, since a large proportion of the Chinese diaspora is of Cantonese origin. The province also lies very close to Hong Kong, whose inhabitants are mostly Cantonese. Given its long-standing contacts with the outside world, it is not surprising that Guangdong was only fully integrated into China in the 12th century, when large numbers of Han settlers migrated here from the north. Today, it is a key area of China's economic development, most evident in cities such as Guangzhou and Shenzhen. Despite the recent development, there are several places of historical interest, as well as some beautiful areas of natural beauty, which are well worth visiting.

Formerly administered as part of Guangdong, the tropical island of Hainan is now a separate province. A place of exile for centuries, its superb beaches on the southern coast have been developed as thriving tourist resorts. There are still vestiges of the indigenous Li culture to seek out, and some wild mountains to explore at the island's center.

GUANGDONG

HAINAN

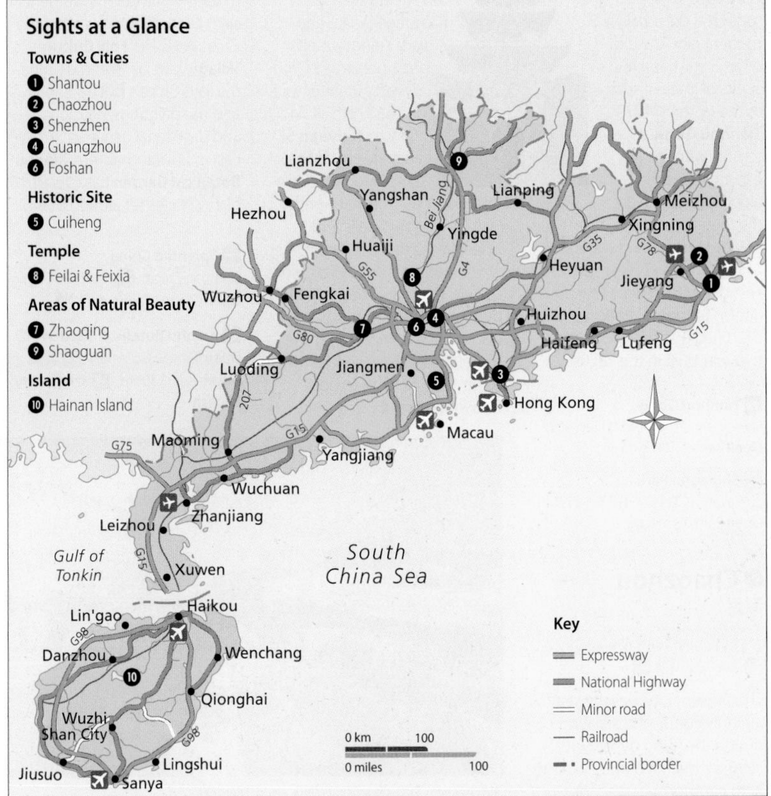

◀ Night view of Guangzhou, dominated by the Guangzhou Tower

For additional map symbols *see back flap*

The dramatic Shipaotai fortress and moat, Shantou

❶ Shantou
汕头

260 miles (420 km) E of Guangzhou. 5,300,000. 7 Changping Lu, (0754) 8861 0689.

This city was originally a fishing village, whose strategic location on the Han Jiang estuary was exploited by foreign traders from 1858. Known then as Swatow, it soon became a major center for trade. In 1980, it was declared a Special Economic Zone and today it is essentially a modern city. The old quarter still has a few sights of interest such as the restored 1879 **Tianhou Gong**, a temple with vibrant carvings. Nearby along **Anping Lu** are the remains of old colonial houses and warehouses. About 2 miles (3.2 km) to the east of Anping Lu at the waterfront is **Shipaotai Park**, home to a fortified gun emplacement that was built in the 1870s.

Tianhou Gong
Shengping Lu. **Tel** (0754) 8845 4097.
Open 7am–5:30pm daily.

Shipaotai Park
20 Haibin Lu. **Tel** (0754) 8854 3120.
Open 8am–6pm daily.

❷ Chaozhou
潮州

275 miles (440 km) E of Guangzhou. 2,600,000.

This ancient city was the seat of a highly cultured civilization during the Ming dynasty. Its fortunes declined rapidly in the 17th century, when almost 100,000 people were massacred for opposing the Manchu regime. Later, during the 19th century, terrible famines and poverty led to mass emigration.

Today, the remains of the 23-ft (7-m) high **Ming City Walls** run along the banks of the Han River, defining the eastern boundary of the old city center. Extending up to Huancheng Lu in the west, the old city is Chaozhou's most fascinating quarter, where its historic past is visible on streets such as Zhongshan Lu and Jiadi Xiang, with its well-preserved Qing-dynasty architecture. To the north of Jiadi Xiang is **Kaiyuan Si**, an active Buddhist temple founded in AD 738, with pretty courtyards and several colorful halls, one of which has a gorgeous vaulted ceiling. The grand **Guangji Men,** overlooking the Han, has steps leading up to a trail along the top of the wall. Across the river is the 10th-century temple **Hanwen Gong Ci**, and downstream is the renovated Ming-dynasty pagoda **Fenghuang Tai.**

Guangji Men, Chaozhou

Kaiyuan Si
32 Kaiyuan Lu. **Tel** (0768) 222 5571.
Open 6am–5pm daily.

❸ Shenzhen
深圳

85 miles (135 km) SE of Guangzhou. 10,500,000. from Hong Kong and Macau. Chuanbu Lu, Luohu, (0755) 8247 7051.

Shenzhen was the first town to become a Special Economic Zone as part of Deng Xiaoping's economic reforms. SEZ status transformed this tiny village near Hong Kong into a booming metropolis in a few years. Today, it is an important business center and transportation hub. On its western outskirts are a host of theme parks. **Splendid China** and **Window on the World** have scale models of famous monuments such as the Eiffel Tower and the Great Wall,. The **Folk Culture Village**, part of Splendid China, displays China's folk traditions, and has paintings, pavilions, and traditional dance shows. East in Liantang district, **Xianhu Botanical Garden** has over 9,000 plant species set around a lake.

Splendid China
Shennan Dadao. Hua Qiao Cheng.
Open 10am–9:30pm daily.

Xianhu Botanical Garden
Open 4am–9:30pm daily. (free 4–8am & 6–9:30pm). **szbg.ac.cn/english**

Aircraft on the Russian carrier at Minsk World, Shenzhen

Sun Yat-sen

For many, Sun Yat-sen, who planned the overthrow of the last Chinese dynasty and the establishment of a republic, is the father of modern China. Born in Guangdong in 1866, he studied medicine and was greatly influenced by the leader of the Taiping Rebellion, and fellow Cantonese, Hong Xiuquan *(see p428)*. A failed uprising in Canton (Guangzhan) in 1895 forced him abroad, where he spent 15 years raising money in support of his cause (in London he was abducted and held in the Chinese legation). Abroad when the Qing dynasty fell in 1911, he was made president of the new republic in 1912. Power struggles soon forced him from office. He died in 1925 before he was able to establish an independent government, with the aim of uniting the country.

"The World Belongs to All" is a slogan reflecting Sun's democratic notions: the right to vote, the right to recall, and the powers of legislation and amendment.

Sun Yat-sen working in the office of his Guangzhou headquarters, from where he strove to create the circumstances that would lead to a democratic and united China.

Chiang Kai-shek (standing), who, like Sun, married a Soong sister *(see p204)*, used Sun's theories of political tutelage to justify military dictatorship.

Discussing the organization of a new government in 1911, before Sun Yat-sen (second from left) became president. He resigned when general Yuan Shikai sought to become emperor in 1913, plunging China back into civil war.

Seen here as Generalissimo in 1922, Sun Yat-sen established a military government in Guangzhou, the base of the Nationalist Revolution.

On National Day portraits of Sun Yat-sen are brandished together with those of Marx and Engels in Tian'an Men Square. Sun Yat-sen, despite his Kuomintang connections and his antipathy to class war, is seen as a revolutionary who paved the way for communism.

❹ Guangzhou

广州

Guangdong's capital, known as Canton to its 19th-century foreign residents, is an ancient and significant port. During the Tang dynasty, the city's trade links across Asia gave it a sizable Muslim community. Later, Western merchants made their first contact with China through this port. Today, Guangzhou is an affluent, bustling city, with a handful of interesting sights, including the 2,000-year-old tomb and excavated palace gardens of the Nan Yue kings. While the city's modern infrastructure is comprehensive, Guangzhou's architectural heritage has also been carefully preserved in places. South of the city, Shamian Island was the site of the foreign concession and is filled with charming colonial-style buildings.

A variety of foodstuffs, grains, and spices on sale, Qingping Market

Qingping Market

Qingping Lu. Ⓜ Huangsha. **Open** daily.

Just across the road from Shamian Island *(see pp306–7)* is one of China's largest and most famous markets, devoted to all types of produce. On sale are medicines, spices, vegetables, dried seafood, grains, fish, meat, and live animals, including cats, dogs, and endangered species. Fortunately, the numbers of endangered animals on sale have drastically reduced in recent years. For some visitors, the atmosphere is too gory, while for others it is exhilaratingly Chinese.

Hualin Si

31 Hualin Si Qian Jie. Ⓜ Changshou Lu. **Tel** (020) 8139 6228. **Open** 8am–5pm daily.

The city's liveliest Buddhist temple, founded in 526, was one of the shrines visited by Bodhidarma, the founder of Chan Buddhism *(see p165)*. Hualin Si has a main hall with 500 images of *luohan* or *arhats* (those freed from the cycle of rebirth); one of them, sporting a broad-brimmed hat, is thought to be the merchant Marco Polo.

Devotees lighting incense sticks, Hualin Si

Sacred Heart Church

56 Yide Lu. Ⓜ Haizhu Square. **Tel** (020) 8333 6761. **Open** 8.30–11:30am, 2:30–5pm (weekdays); 8am–5pm (weekends). ✝ 3:30pm Sun (English).

A Gothic-style Roman Catholic church, the Sacred Heart Church (Shi Shi Jiaotang) was built by the French between 1863 and 1888. The land was granted to France as compensation for its losses during the Second Opium War. The church's twin spires rise to a height of 190 ft (58 m), and its bell tower contains four bronze bells cast in France.

Peasant Movement Institute

42 Zhongshan Si Lu. Ⓜ Peasant Movement Institute. **Tel** (020) 8333 3936. **Open** 9am–5:30pm Tue–Sun.

The city's revolutionary past is on display in this former Ming Confucian temple. In 1924, the building became a training school for peasant revolutionaries, who were taught by leaders such as Mao Zedong and Zhou Enlai *(see p256)*. The school closed in 1926 as the relationship between the Communists and the KMT soured *(see p72)*.

Nan Yue Palace Gardens

Zhongshan Lu. Ⓜ Gongyuanqian. **Open** 11am–2:30pm & 5–10pm daily.

This extraordinary site contains the excavated gardens that surrounded the palace of Zhao Tuo, the founder of the ancient Nan Yue kingdom *(see p306)*. A Qin general from Hebei province, he founded an independent kingdom after the fall of the Qin dynasty. The site is covered by a corrugated roof, and a raised pathway leads past the main sights. To the northeast, a paved lake and an ornamental stream are clearly visible, while in the southwestern corner are the remains of an even older Qin dynasty shipyard. The site's small museum exhibits stone slabs, pillars, and rooftiles, many of which bear the inscription "Panyu," which is Guangzhou's original name.

Huaisheng Mosque

56 Guangta Lu. Ximenkou.
Open to Muslims only.

Founded during the Tang dynasty by Abu Waqas *(see p307)*, this is one of China's oldest mosques. Much of the mosque has been reconstructed, though it contains an unusual minaret, thought to have been used as a beacon for boats, and numerous stone stelae.

Guangxiao Si

109 Guangxiao Lu.
Ximenkou. **Tel** (020) 8108 8867. **Open** 6:30am–5pm daily.

Supposedly founded during the Western Han dynasty, the Guangxiao Si (Temple of Glorious Filial Piety) is one of the city's most attractive sights. Built over the palace of the last Nan Yue king, it became a temple in the 5th century and was later visited by Bodhidarma, the founder of Chan Buddhism. None of the original buildings survive, and most of the current halls date to the 19th century. The pillared main hall has several Buddha images, while the three pagodas behind it are of great antiquity. Of these, one was built over a hair of Hui Neng, the Sixth Chan Buddist Patriarch (AD 638–713) who came from Guangzhou, while the other two are 10th-century structures.

Ancient pagoda, Guangxiao Si

Liu Rong Si

87 Liurong Lu.
Gongyuanqian.
Tel (020) 8339 2843.
Open 8am–5pm daily.

Liu Rong Si, the Six Banyan Temple, was established in AD 537 to house a portion of the Buddha's ashes, which were brought from India and enshrined in the Flower Pagoda (Hua Ta). Rebuilt in 1097, the 187-ft (57-m) octagonal pagoda appears to have nine stories from the outside, but in fact has a total of 17. The pagoda's wooden eaves are covered in intricate carvings of birds, insects, and lions. At the top is an enormous bronze pillar with reliefs of meditating figures.

Little remains of the original temple, which was associated with Hui Neng. The Hall of the Sixth Patriarch contains a bronze figure of him, cast in AD 989. The temple was named by the exiled Song dynasty poet Su Dongpo *(see p310)* in appreciation of the trees in the temple. His calligraphic characters that read "Liu Rong" are engraved into stone over the gateway.

VISITORS' CHECKLIST

Practical Information
94 miles (150 km) NW of Hong Kong. 12,900,000. Huaxia Hotel, 2 Qiaoguang Lu, (020) 2201 3396.

Transportation
Baiyun airport. Guangzhou station and East train station. Provincial bus station, Liuhua and Tianhe bus station. to Hong Kong from Lianhuashan Port.

Guangzhou City Center

1. Qingping Market
2. Hualin Si
3. Sacred Heart Church
4. Peasant Movement Institute
5. Nan Yue Palace Gardens
6. Huaisheng Mosque
7. Guangxiao Si
8. Liu Rong Si
9. Chen Jia Ci
10. Nan Yue Tomb
11. Orchid Garden and Islamic Cemetery
12. Yuexi Gongyuan
13. Shamian Island

Key to Symbols *see back flap*

Chen Jia Ci

34 Enlong Li, Zhongshan Qi Lu. Ⓜ Chen Clan Academy. **Tel** (020) 8181 4371. **Open** 8:30am–5:30pm daily.

This temple, in the gloriously colorful southern style, was built in 1890 with funds donated by members of the Chen clan. It was to act as a temple of ancestor worship and as a school. Though obviously Chinese, these southern temples are quite different from their northern counterparts. Less severely classical, their halls are generally lower and broader. Roofs and, as in the case of the first hall here, facades, are often smothered in fantastic designs and sculpted figures from operas.

Brick relief of a traditional opera on the facade of Chen Jia Ci

Nan Yue Tomb

867 Jiefang Bei Lu. Ⓜ Yuexiu Park. **Tel** (020) 3618 2920. **Open** 9am–5:30pm, last entry 4:45pm daily.

This is the site of the 2,000-year-old tomb of Zhao Mo, grandson of Zhao Tuo. Zhao Tuo, a Qin general from Hebei province, was sent here in 214 BC to control southern China. After the fall of the Qin, Zhao Tuo established the Nan Yue kingdom. Shortly after his grandson's death, the kingdom was reclaimed by the Han kings.

The tomb contains magnificent burial items made of gold and precious stones, including a jade burial suit. Many of the captions are in English, and a video recounts the story of the excavation that took place in 1983.

Orchid Garden and Islamic Cemetery

901 Jiefang Bei Lu. Ⓜ Yuexiu Park. **Open** 6am–9pm daily.

This charming garden has bamboo groves and ponds overhung with palms. The orchids are in greenhouses, and the best time to see them is late winter to early spring. Along the garden's western edge, the cemetery contains

Shamian Island

沙面岛

Leased to the French and British after the Chinese were defeated during the Second Opium War (1856–60), this island is really little more than a sandbank about half a mile (800 m) long. Before being allowed to settle on Shamian Island, foreigners had previously been compelled to remain in their warehouses on the mainland. Soon after the French settled at the east end and the British at the west, the streets filled with European-style villas, banks, and churches. Chinese people were long forbidden to enter the island, so an exclusively European way of life prevailed on this strange outpost.

Christ Church served the Protestants among the British community at the west end of the island.

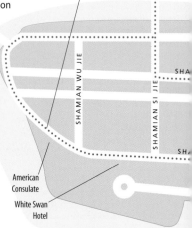

SHAMIAN WU JIE

SHAMIAN SI JIE

American Consulate

White Swan Hotel

Cannon in Shamian Gongyuan

The two cannons in Shamian Gomgyuan were manufactured in the neighboring city of Foshan for use during the mid-19th century Opium Wars.

For hotels and restaurants in this region see p561 and pp579–80

what is said to be the tomb of Abu Waqas, the uncle of the Prophet, credited with bringing Islam to China. Though closed to non-Muslims, it can be viewed through a screen.

Yuexiu Gongyuan

988 Jiefang Bei Lu. Ⓜ Yuexiu Park. **Tel** (020) 8666 1950. **Open** 6am–9pm daily.

Spread over 222 acres (90 ha), Yuexiu Park is one of the largest municipal parks in China. It is split into several parts by Huanshi Zhong Lu and Yingyuan Lu. The most striking building, the **Sun Yat-sen Memorial Hall**, is in the southernmost section off Dongfeng Zhong Lu. Built in 1931 in traditional style with a blue tiled roof, it marks the spot where Dr. Sun Yat-sen *(see p303)* was proclaimed head of the Nationalist government in 1923.

Most of the other sights lie in the middle of the park, including the **Five Rams Statue** – the city symbol that commemorates the myth that Guangzhou was founded by Five Immortals riding five rams, who planted sheaves of corn to ensure that famine would never strike.

Nearby, the **Municipal Museum** is housed in the Zhenhai Lou, a Ming watch-tower. It has 1,200 exhibits dating from 4000 BC to the present, and includes a Christian tract that inspired the Taiping Rebellion *(see p428)*.

Sun Yat-sen Memorial Hall, Yuexiu Gongyuan

Art Museum

13 Luhu Lu. **Tel** (020) 8365 9337. **Open** 9am–5:30pm Tue–Sun; last entry 5pm. **W gzam.com.cn**

This contemporary museum exhibits shows by major Chinese artists. On permanent display is an exhibition of the works of political cartoonist Liao Bingxiong, who was criticized in 1958 for his Rightist leanings. No flip-flops allowed.

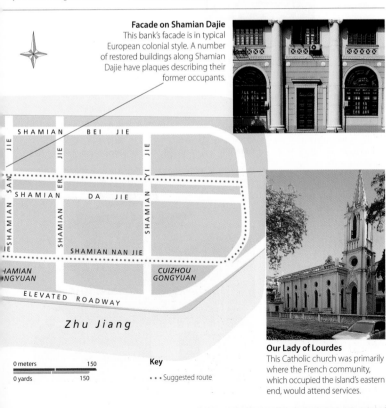

Facade on Shamian Dajie
This bank's facade is in typical European colonial style. A number of restored buildings along Shamian Dajie have plaques describing their former occupants.

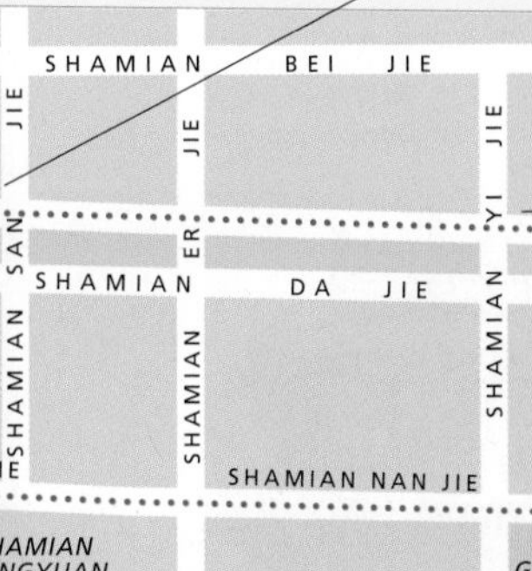

Our Lady of Lourdes
This Catholic church was primarily where the French community, which occupied the island's eastern end, would attend services.

The bedroom at Sun Yat-sen's residence, Cuiheng

❺ Cuiheng
翠亨

15 miles (25 km) E of Zhongshan town. bus 12 from Zhongshan East bus station.

Zhongshan county, located 56 miles (90 km) south of Guangzhou, is the birthplace of Sun Yat-sen *(see p303)*, whose name is Sun Zhongshan in Mandarin. This revolutionary leader was born in Cuiheng village on the outskirts of Zhongshan town in 1866. The Portuguese-style house in which he lived with his parents between 1892 and 1895 is now part of a memorial garden devoted to his life. Nearby, other houses belonging to the same period have been restored and are also open to the public.

Sun Yat-sen's Residence
Cuiheng Dadao. **Tel** (0760) 8550 1691.
Open 9am–5pm daily.

❻ Foshan
佛山

21 miles (35 km) SW of Guangzhou. 7,200,000. minibuses from Guangzhou. Crowne Plaza, 118 Fenjiang Zhong Lu, (0757) 8380 8888.

Foshan has been known since the Song dynasty for its fine ceramics, particularly figurines with a pale blue glaze. Visits to factories can be arranged through the tourist office. Nearby, the **Zu Miao** was founded in AD 1080 as a metallurgists' guild temple. It is lavishly decorated with ceramic figures, made in nearby Shiwan, representing scenes from traditional opera and folk stories. At the rear of the complex is a museum dedicated to local kung fu master and Bruce Lee's instructor, Yip Man, and Wong Feihung, whose exploits have inspired countless martial arts movies. Free martial arts shows are held twice daily. Near the entrance is a garden displaying cannons that were used against the British in the 19th century Opium Wars.

Elaborate stone roof of Zu Miao, Foshan

Zu Miao
21 Zumiao Lu. Zumiao.
Open 8:30am–6pm daily.

❼ Zhaoqing
肇庆

60 miles (95 km) W of Guangzhou. 3,900,000. from Guangzhou and Foshan. to Hong Kong. Xinghu Plaza, 10 Duanzhou Lu, (0758) 222 9908.

This attractive city was the home of the Italian Jesuit priest Matteo Ricci in the late 16th century, until he was expelled by a local official in 1589. Today, it is famous for the limestone scenery at **Qixing Yan** (Seven Star Crag), 1 mile (1.5 km) north of the Xi River. Located beside a lake, the mist-covered peaks lie in the shape of the Big Bear constellation, and some believe them to be fallen stars. They can be explored via a network of bridges and causeways.

The city's sights include the **Chongxi Ta**, a pagoda overlooking the Xi River. Built in the Ming period, it is the tallest pagoda in Guangdong. The old **City Walls** still stand on Jianshe Lu, while in the western suburbs, the **Plum Monastery** is associated with Hui Neng, the Sixth Chan Buddhist Patriarch.

A short bus ride northeast of the city is the forested reserve of **Dinghu Shan**, which offers numerous scenic walking trails.

Qixing Yan
Tel (0758) 223 4728.
Open 7:30am–6pm daily.

The Piyun Tower perched atop Zhaoqing's ancient city walls

The grand gateway of Feilai Gusi along the banks of the Bei River

❽ Feilai & Feixia
飞来 和 飞霞

52 miles (85 km) NW of Guangzhou. to Qingyuan. Feilai and Feixia Temples: depart daily from Qingyuan's Wuyi Dock. **Open** 8am–5:30pm daily.

The busy industrial town of Qingyuan is the access point for two picturesque temples located at **Feilai** and **Feixia** on the Bei River, that can only be reached by boat. The boats, which depart early in the morning and return in the afternoon (it's best to charter them with a group), pass fishermen whose cormorants – trained to fish for them – sit patiently on the prows of sampans. The first temple, **Feilai Gusi**, was founded about 1,400 years ago and is situated on the steep riverbank of a gorge. Steps lead up from the river to its ornate gateway. Its current buildings are mainly from the Ming dynasty. A short walk through the various buildings leads to a modern pavilion, from where there are superb views along the river.

Located a short distance farther along the gorge is Feixia Gusi comprising two late 19th-century Daoist temples, Feixia and Cangxia. Feixia is much larger than Feilai, and its stone halls and temples are surrounded by a fine set of walls. Cangxia, located up the hillside, is often being refurbished as a result of regular flooding. There are, however, some impressive frescoes and hiking paths.

❾ Shaoguan
韶关

144 miles (230 km) N of Guangzhou.

Shaoguan town has only a handful of sights, such as the Fengcai Lou, a reconstruction of an ancient city gate, and the Dajian Chan Monastery founded in AD 660, but there are three worthwhile places of interest in the vicinity. The **Nanhua Si** (Southern China Temple), 16 miles (25 km) to the southeast, was founded in AD 502 and became renowned for its connection with Bodhidarma, the founder of Chan (Zen) Buddhism who meditated here for 36 years. One of the halls contains a statue of him, said to have been cast from his corpse; another has a statue of a monk walking on stilts. The bell tower has a large, 700-year-old bronze bell cast in the Song dynasty.

Statue of a monk walking on "improbable stilts," Nanhua Si

About 31 miles (50 km) northeast of town, **Danxia Shan** is a 112-sq-mile (290 sq-km) park on the banks of the Jin. It has rocky outcrops in fascinating shapes, with trails leading to their summits. A boat or bus takes visitors farther along the river to Danxia Shan itself. Meaning "Cinnabar Cloud," it has red sandstone cliffs, with paths leading past hillside monasteries.

About 11 miles (18 km) south of Shaoguan is **Shizi Yan**, a cave where the prehistoric remains of *Homo erectus* were found. The museum displays arrowheads, pottery, and artifacts from local prehistoric sites.

Nanhua Si
Tel (0751) 650 1223.
Open 8am–5pm daily.

Danxia Shan
Open daily.

Shizi Yan
Open daily.

⑩ Hainan Island

海南

Although China's largest island became a part of the Chinese empire during the Han dynasty, it remained a backwater and place of exile until the mid-20th century. It was so remote that its ethnic Li people still lived a primitive hunter-gatherer existence until as late as the 1930s. In 1988, the island became a Special Economic Zone, but the local economy only took off when tour operators realised the potential of the south coast beaches. Hainan is today an independent province with much to offer. Beyond the tropical beaches around the southern city of Sanya, attractions include impressive mountain scenery in the southwest, and coffee plantations on its east coast.

Fish being laid out to dry in Xincun on the east coast

Haikou

175 miles (285 km) N of Sanya. 2,100,000. mainland ferries from Xingang pier.

The island's capital is a busy port and transportation hub, with the ambience of a tropical Asian city. To its southeast, **Wugong Ci** (Five Officials Memorial Temple) was built in 1889 to honor a group of scholars who were banished here during the Tang and Song dynasties for criticizing their government. One of its halls commemorates the Song-era poet Su Dongpo, who was also exiled here between 1097 and 1100.

To the west of the city center is a massive fortification at **Xiuying**, constructed by the Chinese in the 19th century to resist the French. Thick stone walls conceal six large cannons, that are connected by subterranean passages. Farther southwest is the tomb of **Hai Rui**, an upright Ming dynasty official who was exiled to Hainan for criticism.

Wuzhi Shan City & the Central Highlands

Wuzhi Shan City: 130 miles (220 km) SW of Haikou. from Sanya and Haikou. Nationality Museum: **Open** 9am–5:30pm daily.

The central mountainous region is worth a visit for its spectacular landscape and to explore the island's ethnic culture. The main town is the pleasant **Wuzhi Shan City** (also known as Tongshi), the capital of the autonomous Li and Miao governments. The **Nationality Museum** offers an excellent insight into all aspects of Hainan's history and culture. The city's surrounding countryside has remnants of traditional Li houses and barns. About 31 miles (50 km) northeast of town is the 6,125-ft (1,867-m) high **Wuzhi Shan**, which is sacred to the Li people. It is a pleasant hike to the mountain's summit. Also northeast of Wuzhi Shan City, the town of **Qiongzhong** is surrounded by some beautiful scenery, including the 984-ft (300-m) high waterfall at Baihua Shan.

The East Coast

Wenchang: 60 miles (100 km) SE of Haikou. Xinglong Tropical Botanical Garden: **Tel** (0898) 6255 4410. **Open** 7:30am–5:30pm daily.

The town of **Wenchang** is the ancestral home of the Soong sisters *(see p204)*, two of whom, Qingling and Meiling, married the revolutionary leaders Sun Yat-sen and Chiang Kai-shek. Its main attractions are the beaches and coconut groves at Dongjiao Yelin and Gusong, a fishing village 25 miles (40 km) east of Wenchang. A further 36 miles (60 km) south of Bo'ao, on the outskirts of Wanning town, **Dongshan Ling** has curiously shaped natural rock formations. Farther south, Xinglong is known throughout China for its coffee, and the **Xinglong Tropical Botanical Gardens**, 2 miles (3 km) south of town offer coffee and tea tastings. South of Xinglong is **Lingshui**, the principal town of the Lingshui Li Autonomous County, that is home to a large number of Li people who have lived on Hainan since 200 BC. The Communist Museum commemorates China's first Communist government which that was formed in Hainan in 1928. Many of Lingshui's narrow streets remain unchanged since the early 1900s and are lined with quaint shops and houses. Just 6 miles (10 km) south of Lingshui is **Xincun** and with a large Hakka

Calligraphy at Dongshan Ling ridge

The pristine, palm-fringed beach at Yalong Bay

VISITORS' CHECKLIST

Practical Information
15 miles (25 km) S of Guangdong. 8,450,000. Datong Lu, (0898) 6675 4379. Li People San Yue San Festival (the 3rd day of the 3rd lunar month).

Transportation
train–ferry shuttle from mainland destinations. from Beihai, Guangzhou and Hai'an.

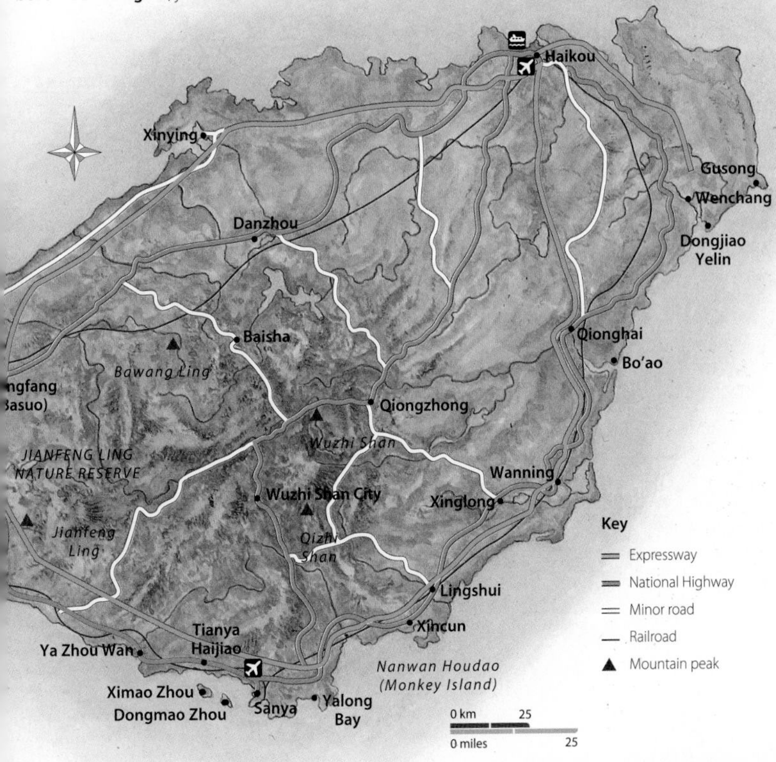

population *(see p296)*. Close by and accessible only by boat, **Monkey Island** has a sizable colony of Guangxi macaques and is a popular day trip from Xincun.

Sanya & the South Coast

175 miles (285 km) S of Haikou. 680,000.

Hainan's main attractions are the tropical beaches near the town of Sanya. The busiest beach is **Dadonghai**, just south of town, with hotels, restaurants, and shops. The area's best beach is to the east of town at **Yalong Bay**, with a 4-mile (7-km) stretch of pristine sand lined with upmarket hotels. The beach at **Tianya Haijiao**, 16 miles (25 km) northwest, is known for its famous rock that appears on the old 2-yuan note. The other attraction is **Ximao Zhou Island**, a 2-hour boat ride off the coast. It is popular for snorkeling and hiking.

Jianfeng Ling Nature Reserve

65 miles (115 km) NW of Sanya. to Dongfang (Basuo) from Sanya, then local bus and auto-rickshaw. **Open** 8:30am–6:30pm daily.

Pleasantly situated in the mountains, this highland rain forest, with its huge trees, ferns, and vines as well as species of birds and butterflies, offers great walks and hikes.

Key
Expressway
National Highway
Minor road
Railroad
Mountain peak

0 km 25
0 miles 25

For additional map symbols *see back flap*

HONG KONG & MACAU

Although tiny and relatively recently developed, Hong Kong and Macau are rich and fascinating oddities. They owe their unique identities as administrative regions separate from China to the trade that flourished between East and West from the 16th century onwards, and to the British and Portuguese powers that annexed and held them until 1997 and 1999 respectively.

The Portuguese were the first Europeans to settle at "A-Ma Gau" or the Bay of A-Ma – the region's patron goddess – in 1557. Today, Macau, as it came to be known, is a charming haven of pastel-colored colonial mansions and glitzy casinos, the proceeds of which, along with tourism, keep this tiny region financially afloat.

In the 1800s, China's attempt to destroy Britain's lucrative opium trade drove the British to blockade Chinese ports and eventually secure Hong Kong as their own trading enclave in 1841. The area, hitherto inhabited by farmers and fisherfolk, quickly flourished. After World War II and the four-year Japanese occupation, trade resumed and Hong Kong's manufacturing industry boomed. It soon grew into a densely packed, high-rise city built by ambitious colonial administrators and millions of Chinese migrants escaping the turmoil convulsing their Communist homeland. In its final years as a British territory, Hong Kong's status as a major financial center was established. Despite the 1997 Asian financial crisis, it retains its sleek international gloss, its enterprise, and its breathtaking visual impact. Standing in Kowloon and gazing at the skyscrapers scaling Hong Kong Island's hills, writer Pico Iyer's description sums it up succinctly: "a dream of Manhattan, arising from the South China Sea."

Spirals of fragrant incense hanging in Daoist Man Mo Temple, Hong Kong

◀ Night-time view of Central's modern skyscrapers, Hong Kong

Exploring Hong Kong & Macau

The bustling heart of Hong Kong is broken in two and divided by Victoria Harbour. Its key sights, cultural attractions, shopping, and eating spots are found along the northern shore of Hong Kong Island, and at, or close to, Kowloon's southern tip. Between Kowloon and the border with the rest of China lie the New Territories, with their rugged mountains and most of Hong Kong's modern, high-rise dormitory towns. The other major islands – Lamma, Cheung Chau, and Lantau – are west of Hong Kong Island, and beyond these is Macau. A passport is necessary to leave or arrive in both Macau and Hong Kong, as they are still administered as autonomous regions of China.

Locator Map
See also Map pp282–3

Sights at a Glance

Historic Sites, Neighborhoods & Towns

1 Central
2 Wan Chai
3 Causeway Bay
7 Lan Kwai Fong
8 The Central-Mid-levels Escalator
9 Hollywood Road
13 Tsim Sha Tsui Waterfront
15 Nathan Road
24 Lung Yeuk Tau Heritage Trail
28 Aberdeen
32 Stanley
36 *Macau pp332–5*

Museums

14 Hong Kong Museum of Art
16 Hong Kong Science Museum
17 Hong Kong Museum of History
21 Heritage Museum

Parks, Gardens & Areas of Natural Beauty

5 Hong Kong Zoological & Botanical Gardens
6 *The Peak pp318–19*
23 Sai Kung Town & Peninsula Beaches
25 Kadoorie Farm & Botanic Garden
26 Mai Po Marshes
27 Maclehose Trail
30 Deep Water & Repulse Bays

Temples & Monasteries

10 Man Mo Temple
20 Wong Tai Sin Temple
22 10,000 Buddhas Monastery
31 Hong Kong Life Saving Society

Other Attractions

4 Happy Valley Racecourse
12 Star Ferry
29 Ocean Park

Shops & Markets

11 Sheung Wan's Markets
18 Temple Street & Jade Markets
19 Flower Market

Islands

33 Lamma Island
34 Cheung Chau Island
35 Lantau Island

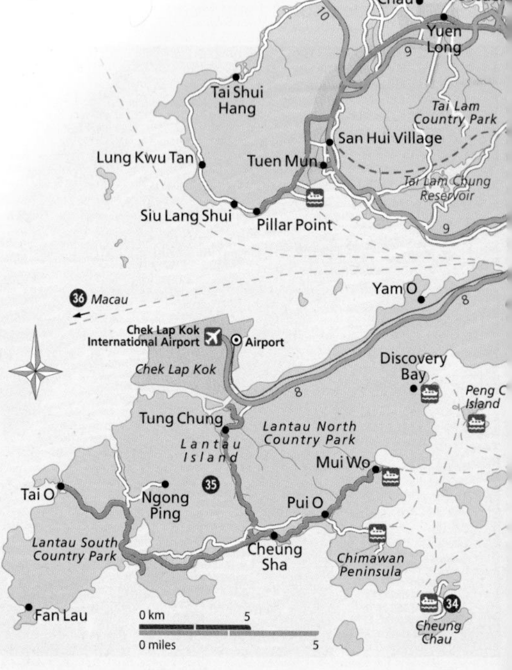

Hong Kong Island & Kowloon

For Street Finder Maps see pp340–43

Getting Around

The best way to get around Hong Kong's central areas is on foot. The efficient MTR (Mass Transit Railway), which is the city's subway system, serves the central districts, has a fast airport line, and links the center with the New Territories and China *(see p620)*. Buses, trams, and taxis operate from all major nodes and are cheap by international standards. The Star Ferry *(see p321)*, shuttles between Hong Kong Island and Kowloon, while regular inter-island ferries link Hong Kong with the main islands. The fast, sleek Macau-bound ferries leave from their own terminal just west of the inter-island ferry terminal.

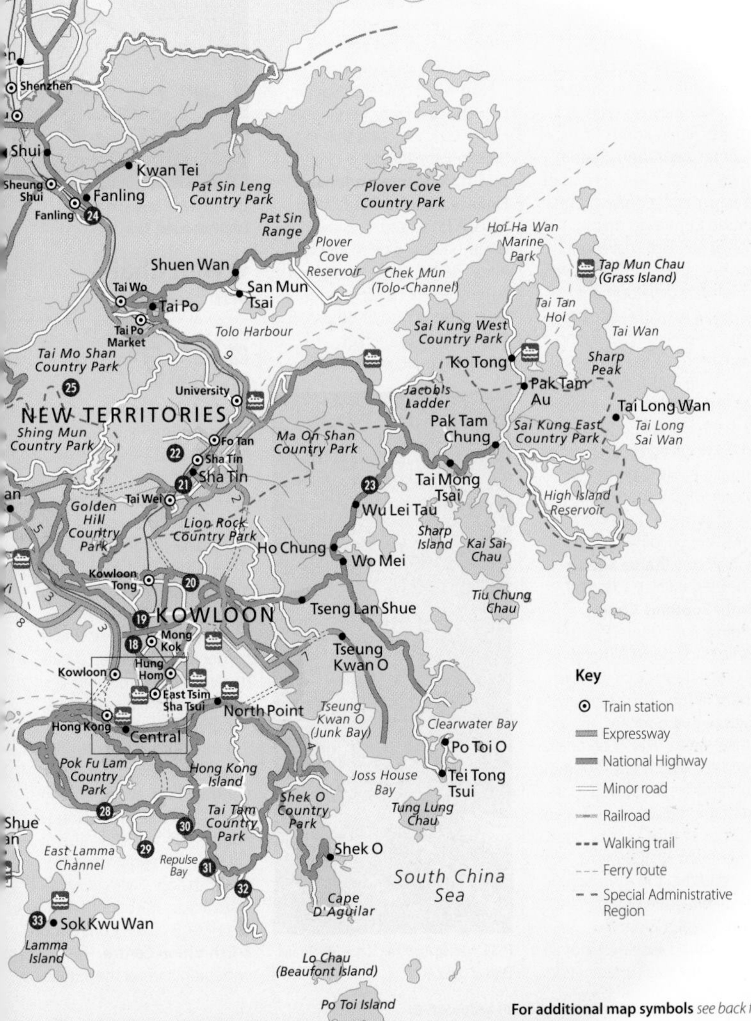

For additional map symbols *see back flap*

The Two IFC Tower near the Star Ferry Terminal

❶ Central
中環

Hong Kong Island. **Map** 2 C3. Ⓜ Central. Star Ferry from Kowloon.

The sleek, corporate cathedrals of local banks and businesses tower over the ever-teeming streets of Hong Kong's financial epicenter. Apart from Statue Square, which is at the heart of the area, there are few cultural sights in Central, as many colonial buildings have long since disappeared, making way for high-rise development. The desire for real estate has always been strong, and land reclamation started almost as soon as the British took over in 1841. This continous reclamation has made Hong Kong Island and Kowloon creep even closer. Central is easily explored on foot, allowing visitors a close view of some of the most interesting buildings, especially those around **Statue Square**.

The elegant Neo-Classical **Former Supreme Court Building**, surmounted by the blindfolded figure of Themis, the Greek goddess of justice, is the sole surviving colonial structure in the square. Completed in 1911, it originally served as Hong Kong's Supreme Court and latterly served as the seat of the region's government. It will house the Court of Final Appeal from 2016 onwards.

Beyond this, the municipal-style architecture of the square's center is rather disappointing. However, not all the structures lack imagination. The modernistic, but *feng shui*-friendly girders of the **HSBC (Hong Kong & Shanghai Banking Corporation) Headquarters** loom over the square. Designed by British architect Sir Norman Foster and completed in 1985, it was at that time one of the most expensive buildings, costing more than HK$5 billion. Be sure to rub the paws of the regal-looking lions outside for luck. The stark spike of the **Bank of China** headquarters rises behind the HSBC building. Designed by the renowned Chinese-born architect I. M. Pei, its harsh, angular lines go against all *feng shui* guidelines, and it is seen as an aggressive statement that offsets the benign energies of the HSBC Headquarters.

Northwest of Statue Square, near the Star Ferry Terminal, is Hong Kong's second-tallest building, the 88-story, 1,362-ft (415-m) **Two International Finance Centre (IFC)**, built in 2003. A hotel and a residential tower have also been erected here. The IFC Mall at the tower's base is one of Hong Kong's largest, adding to Central's collection of upmarket shopping malls, such as **The Landmark**. The International Commerce Centre across the water in Kowloon is even taller than the IFC, at 1,587 ft (484 m), and marks a shift away from Hong Kong Island's north shore for competitive hi-tech architecture.

HSBC building *(right)* on Statue Square and Bank of China *(left)*

Hong Kong's dramatic skyline is showcased in a nightly sound and light show – crowds gather on the Tsimshatsui waterfront to see the city at its best.

The roof of the Convention & Exhibition Centre, Wan Chai

❷ Wan Chai
灣仔

Hong Kong Island. **Map** 3 F3. Ⓜ Wan Chai. Star Ferry from Kowloon.

Made famous in Richard Mason's 1957 novel *The World of Suzy Wong*, Wan Chai's colorful red light district has now largely given way to new development, fancy bars, restaurants, and hotels. The Wan Chai MTR is a good starting point for a walking tour. A trip down Lockhart Road, just around the corner from the MTR, reveals the area's few remaining ties with its past in the form of a handful of go-go bars.

A 5-minute walk north of the MTR across Gloucester Road is **Central Plaza**, at one time the tallest, and still one of Hong Kong's grandest skyscrapers. There are splendid views from the 46th floor. Facing Central Plaza across Harbour Road is the HK$4.8 billion **Convention & Exhibition Centre**. The sweeping lines of the extension

For hotels and restaurants in this area see p561 and pp580–81

at its northern end are intended to create the impression of a bird taking flight. This was the venue for the 1997 ceremony during which Britain handed Hong Kong back to China. The glass walls offer fine harbor views, and outside are a large promenade and a pleasant sitting area.

The historic Noonday Gun, fired daily at noon, Causeway Bay

❸ Causeway Bay
銅鑼灣

Hong Kong Island. Ⓜ Causeway Bay. Eastbound (to Shau Kei Wan) trams.

A neon-lit crush of giant department stores, such as Sogo, and malls like Hysan Place and Times Square, and the ever-present crowds of shoppers is the first view of Causeway Bay when emerging from the MTR. East of the MTR sprawls **Victoria Park**, Hong Kong's largest public park and a serene place to swim, play tennis, or practice *tai ji quan*. Close to the harbor, also known as the typhoon shelter, is the **Noonday Gun**, which has been fired daily since the 1840s and retained as a charity fundraising event. The enclosure housing the gun opens for half an hour after noon, where a small plaque explains the origins of the tradition, celebrated in Noel Coward's song "Mad Dogs and Englishmen."

Most of the land that Causeway Bay stands on is reclaimed, and the reclamation work continues today along the harborside between Central and Causeway Bay.

❹ Happy Valley Racecourse
香港賽馬會

Hong Kong Island. Happy Valley. For race night details, call (0852) 1817. **W hkjc.com/english**

The racecourse at Happy Valley crackles with nervous energy during the Wednesday race nights, as tens of thousands of eager gamblers shout their way through the evening. Horse-racing is a passion in Hong Kong; it's the only legal gambling opportunity available to local people. The industry is carefully controlled, with only the Hong Kong Jockey Club allowed to run the betting.

Formerly a malaria-ridden marsh, Happy Valley was used for the racecourse as it was the widest stretch of flat land on Hong Kong Island. The first race was held here in 1845. Today, the huge stand holds up to 54,000 spectators. Racing is open all year except between July and September. Happy Valley's small Racing Museum details Hong Kong's racing history.

Happy Valley Races

Hong Kong's punters are crazy about horse-racing. A single race at Happy Valley or at Sha Tin in the New Territories, often attracts more bets than an entire week of racing in Britain, and in 2016, the turnover reached a record HK$107 billion. The government collects significant tax revenues from the races, and although revenue has always been lost to illegal betting syndicates, the Hong Kong government still took HK$21 billion in gambling tax revenue in 2016.

A thrilling finish at Happy Valley Racecourse

❺ Hong Kong Zoological & Botanical Gardens
香港動植物公園

Albany Road. **Map** 2 B4. Ⓜ Central or Admiralty. 12, 12A, 12M, 23, 23B, 103. **Tel** (0852) 2530 0154. **Open** 6am–7pm daily. **W lcsd.gov.hk**

Opposite Hong Kong Park, just across Cotton Tree Drive, lie the Zoological and Botanical Gardens, established in 1864. The gardens house dozens of exotic animals such as lemurs, orang-utans, and the world's largest collection of buff-cheeked gibbons, while its aviaries have a colorful collection of birds. Hundreds of plants, including some ancient trees, provide welcome shade in this oasis of quiet. There is also a playground, some sculptures and fountains.

❻ The Peak

山頂

Cooling sea breezes, shaded woodland walks and spectacular views of the city, harbor, and outlying islands make the Peak an unmissable Hong Kong experience. Ever since colonial days, the Peak has been the place to live in the city. Governors and rich merchants built houses here in the mid-1800s to escape the worst of the summer heat and humidity. The Peak's inhabitants were hauled up the sheer slopes in sedan chairs and coolies were employed to carry supplies to the hilltop mansions. When the Peak Tram (actually a funicular railway) was built in 1888, the trip was slashed from an hour's slog to a pleasant, if alarmingly steep, 10-minute ride. Despite the new accessibility, Chinese were excluded from buying real estate on the Peak well into modern times. Today, anyone with the means can acquire these properties – among the world's most expensive.

★ Peak Circuit
This flat 2½-mile (4-km) circuit offers breathtaking views over Victoria Harbour to the north, and Aberdeen and Lamma Island to the south.

Victoria Peak Garden
A steep trudge towards the summit leads to these well-manicured gardens, which were once part of the Governor's Lodge (destroyed after World War II). Sadly, the summit is fenced off and houses telephone masts.

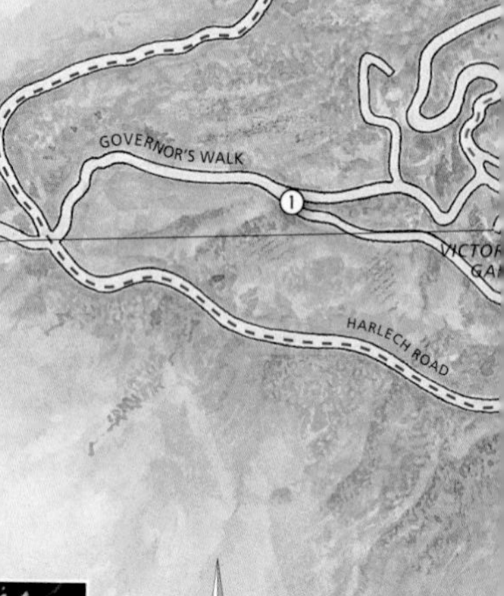

Pok Fu Lam Reservoir
A 3-mile (5-km) path descends through the peaceful woods of the Country Park and past the reservoir. It emerges on Pok Fu Lam Road, where frequent buses head back to the city center.

KEY

① **Governor's Walk** winds from the garden to Harlech Road. It tends to be overgrown and slippery.

② **This old route** to Central is pleasantly shaded but unrelentingly steep. To avoid the busy traffic near the bottom, detour onto Tregunter Path.

③ **Peak Galleria** houses pleasant shops and cafés.

For hotels and restaurants in this area see p561 and pp580–81

★ The View
Equally stunning by day or night, the panorama of harbor activity and highrises is endlessly fascinating. Clouds and smoggy haze, however, often obscure the views; early mornings tend to be clearer.

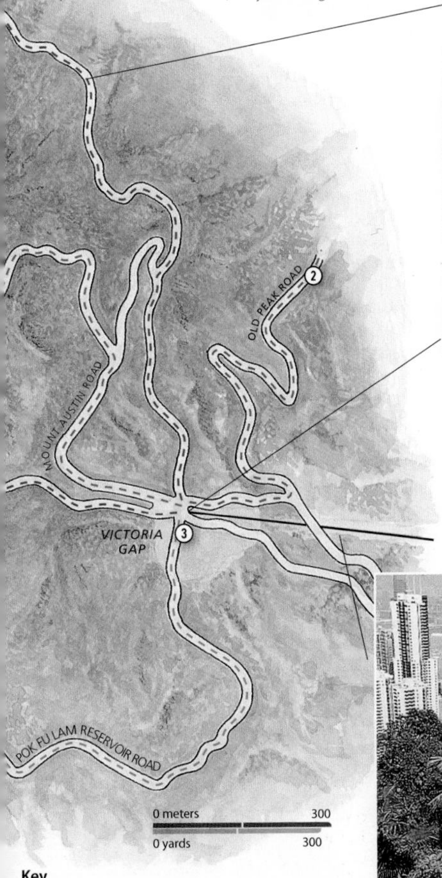

VISITORS' CHECKLIST

Practical Information
The Peak Tower, 128 Peak Road.
Map 2 A5. **Tel** (0852) 2849 0668.
thepeak.com.hk

Transportation
Lower Peak tram terminal, Garden Road. 15c at Central bus terminal (Pier 7); minibus 1 at Central (Two IFC).

OLD PEAK ROAD
MOUNT AUSTIN ROAD
VICTORIA GAP
POK FU LAM RESERVOIR ROAD
0 meters 300
0 yards 300

Key
- To Victoria Peak Garden
- Peak Circuit
- To Pok Fu Lam Resevoir
- Old Peak Road to Central
- Peak Tram

Peak Tower
This imposing mall at the tram terminus contains over 30 shops, Madame Tussauds, many cafés offering good views, and a 360° viewing terrace.

★ Peak Tram
With one of the best safety records in the world, the Peak Tram has been trundling up the hair-raisingly steep 27° incline between St. John's Cathedral and Victoria Gap for over a century.

For additional map symbols *see back flap*

❼ Lan Kwai Fong
蘭桂坊

Central. **Map** 2 B3. Ⓜ Central.

It is only at night that Lan Kwai Fong ("Orchid Square") really starts to buzz, attracting office workers, including plenty of city suits, to its many bars, clubs, and restaurants. It houses some of the trendiest pubs and entertainment hangouts in Hong Kong, and the street is especially packed with revelers on Fridays and Saturdays, although most places remain open until late throughout the week. The partying spills across D'Aguilar Street to tiny Wing Wah Lane's bars and good-value Thai, Malay, and Indian restaurants, most of which have outdoor dining spaces.

The bustling Lan Kwai Fong, dotted with trendy bars and restaurants

❽ The Central–Mid-Levels Escalator
中環半山自動扶手電梯

Central. **Map** 2 B3. Ⓜ Central.
Open Downhill 6am–10pm; uphill 10am–midnight.

All the roads between Queen's Road Central and Conduit Road are linked by a 2,598-ft (792-m) long string of escalators. This is the longest covered outdoor escalator system in the world, and took two-and-a-half years and more than HK$205 million to build. On a hot day, it is the best way to get between Central, the Mid-Levels, and SoHo (South of Hollywood Road). Many bars,

Entrance to the Central–Mid-Levels Escalator

cafés, restaurants, and market stalls cluster round the Escalator. Good Spring Company, on Cochrane Street, sells bitter health tonics from a brass urn. Inside, its herbalist consultants, some of whom speak English, can tailor-make a brew for those who are curious.

Partly as a result of the completion of the Central–Mid-levels Escalator, SoHo has been transformed from a sleepy district into a thriving entertainment area. Elgin, Shelley, and Staunton Streets are excellent places to find food and drink. A plaque on Staunton Street marks the site of the house in which Dr. Sun Yat-sen *(see p303)*, seen by many as China's revolutionary forefather, met with fellow members of his society in the late 1890s. It also marks a historical trail of 13 sites connected with him.

❾ Hollywood Road
荷李活道

Central. **Map** 2 B3. Ⓜ Central, then Escalator.

The many antique shops here no longer offer the bargains they once did, but Hollywood Road still has shops selling ancient ceramics, mammoth ivory carvings, and delicate snuff bottles. The stalls on Upper Lascar Row are a good hunting ground for antiques, old coins, and kitsch. Haggling is acceptable here. Some home furnishings shops, located at the eastern end, sell traditional items such as teardrop-shaped silk lampshades.

❿ Man Mo Temple
文武廟

124–126 Hollywood Rd. **Map** 2 A3. Ⓜ Central, then Escalator. **Tel** (0852) 2540 0350. **Open** 8am–6pm daily.

Atmospheric Man Mo Temple stands at the corner of Ladder Street. Inside its red and gold interior, smoke curls from giant incense spirals hanging from the ceiling, and flames in large brass urns devour paper offerings to the dead, such as the ubiquitous Hell bank-notes. Built in 1847, the temple was dedicated to two deities, Man and Mo (the Gods of Literature and War), believed to be real men – the 3rd-century administrator Cheung Ah Tse and the

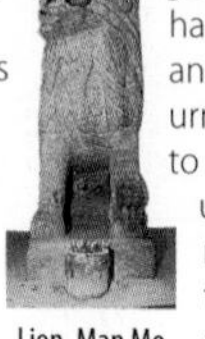

Lion, Man Mo Temple

Lighting a joss stick at Man Mo Temple

The city's Star Ferry service – an unmistakable sight in Hong Kong

3rd-century soldier Kwan Yu – who were deified by the emperors. Their statues can be seen at the back of the main chamber. The temple served as a courthouse and community center for the Chinese in the 19th century, as it sits in the historic heart of the Chinese city.

⓫ Sheung Wan's Markets
上環街市

Hong Kong Island. **Map** 2 A2. Ⓜ Sheung Wan.

The short stroll from Central's slick modernity into the western district of Sheung Wan feels like entering a different city. Beneath the scruffy 1950s tenement blocks, the area between Queen's Road West and Wing Lok Street teems with Chinese medicine and dried seafood wholesalers. This is the world's largest center for the shark's fin trade, an exorbitantly priced delicacy, usually used in soups. The piles of fins on view explain why the world shark population is fast declining.

Apart from dried goods, fresh produce is available in the many fruit, vegetable, and "wet" markets clustered around Gage Street. Live produce, of the feathered, finned or webbed kind, is usually sold in the wet markets, while the fruit and vegetable markets sell a wonderful selection of fruit and typical Chinese fare, including fresh, still-steaming beancurd and rubbery "1,000 year eggs," which are not, in fact, that old, but given an aged look by the mineral earth they are stored in. These places are not to be missed, although the squeamish may want to avoid the meat and fish sections.

Fresh fruit piled high at a market in Sheung Wan

⓬ Star Ferry
天星小輪

Star Ferry Terminals: Central, Wan Chai and Kowloon. **Map** 3 D2, 3 F3, 3 E1. **Tel** (0852) 2367 7065. **W** **starferry.com.hk**

Few activities in Hong Kong can compete with the sheer excitement and romance of jumping on these old 1960s ferries that chug ponderously between Kowloon and Hong Kong Island. They are by far the best and cheapest way to view the city skyline by day or night. The main route links the Kowloon peninsula (just near the Clock Tower) with the Star Ferry Terminal at Central, but it is also possible to reach the Convention Centre and Wan Chai from Kowloon aboard these jolly green boats. Touted as Hong Kong Island's most dependable sight, the Star Ferry service was started by Mr. Dorabjee Nowrojee, a Parsi gentleman, way back in 1898. At that time, the only people allowed on first-class decks were Europeans, and a collar and tie were obligatory.

Forecourt of the Hong Kong Cultural Centre

⓭ Tsim Sha Tsui Waterfront
尖沙咀沿岸

Kowloon. **Map** 1 B5. Ⓜ Tsim Sha Tsui. Star Ferry. Star Ferry Concourse. Hong Kong Space Museum: 10 Salisbury Rd. **Tel** (0852) 2721 0226. **Open** 1–9pm Mon & Wed–Fri, 10am–9pm Sat, Sun and public hols.

The Tsim Sha Tsui waterfront is a popular tourist destination with some of the ritziest arcades, museums, and hotels in the city. The Star Ferry *(see p321)* pier is also located here. East of the pier is the **Hong Kong Cultural Centre**, which houses a concert hall and theater. Adjacent to the Centre is the Space Museum, ideal for children with its interactive exhibits and space theater. Other attractions include the Avenue of Stars honoring the city's film greats and an elevated walkway for views of the city skyline.

⓮ Hong Kong Museum of Art
香港藝術館

10 Salisbury Road, Tsim Sha Tsui. **Map** 1 B5. Ⓜ Tsim Sha Tsui. Star Ferry. **Tel** (0852) 2721 0116. **Closed** for renovation until 2019; call for details. free Wed. **W hk.art.museum**

The Museum of Art is renowned for its exhibitions of traditional Chinese watercolors, calligraphy, and exquisite craftware from Southern China and Asia. Also on display are more than 3,000 objects in ceramics, jade, bronze, lacquer, enamel, glass, and ivory, as well as furniture and fine porcelain.

⓯ Nathan Road
彌敦道

Kowloon. **Map** 1 B4. Ⓜ Tsim Sha Tsui.

Also known as the Golden Mile on its lower reaches, Nathan Road is Kowloon's main transportation artery. Running north through the center of the peninsula, it is bright, busy, and packed with hotels and shops. The term Golden Mile, however, flatters the area – far more glitzier enclaves can be found in Central. Nonetheless a stroll along Nathan Road is definitely an essential Hong Kong experience. You'll find crowds of shoppers and workers, tangled neon signage, bustling tailoring shops, and the stark contrast between smart hotels, Cantonese canteens, and grim tenement blocks, such as the once-notorious Chungking Mansions, making for a chaotic and insightful journey. The road's far northern end offers glimpses of the past. Here, the ramrod-straight Boundary Street still marks the line of the 1860 border, the year Britain forced China to cede Kowloon to expand the burgeoning island colony.

Neon sign, Nathan Road

⓰ Hong Kong Science Museum
科學館

2 Science Museum Rd, Tsim Sha Tsui East. **Map** 1 C3. **Tel** (0852) 2732 3232. Ⓜ Tsim Sha Tsui. **Open** 10am–7pm Mon–Wed & Fri, 10am–9pm Sat, Sun & public hols. free Wed. **W hk.science.museum**

A great destination for children, the Science Museum is packed with fun interactive displays on its four floors that detail basic scientific principles, including electricity and gravity, and a fun "World of Mirrors" on the ground floor. There are also good displays on technology, which demonstrate the workings of various types of machinery ranging from the combustion engine to computer chips, as well as robotics and virtual reality.

Model of a DNA molecule at the Hong Kong Science Museum

⓱ Hong Kong Museum of History
香港歷史博物館

100 Chatham Road South, Tsim Sha Tsui East. Ⓜ Tsim Sha Tsui. **Map** 1 C3. **Tel** (0852) 2724 9042. **Open** 10am–6pm Mon, Wed–Fri, 10am–7pm Sat, Sun & public hols. **W hk.history.museum**

The pursuit of profit and the resulting change of pace in much of Hong Kong has eroded most of its historical and cultural heritage. The excellent Museum of History shows what the region looked like before the skyscrapers arrived. Walk around replicas of traditional villages, street blocks, and shops, or linger over fascinating displays of old photographs. There is also a display of Bronze Age daggers, pottery, and arrowheads found on Lamma and Lantau Islands *(see pp330–31)*.

⓲ Temple Street and Jade Markets
廟街及玉石市場

Yau Ma Tei. **Map** 1 B2. Ⓜ Jordan or Yau Ma Tei.

Haggling is an essential skill at the Temple Street night market, which only livens up after 8pm. Although cheaper bargains are available elsewhere, the atmosphere and range of items, including fake designer labels, shoes, Mao memorabilia, and pirated DVDs, are unbeatable. Adding to the experience are fortune tellers, street performers, and food vendors. The market snakes north from Ning Po Street to Man Ming Lane. The daytime Jade Market is a good place to pick up inexpensive trinkets, although cheaper jade can be found in Guangzhou *(see pp304–5)*, and elsewhere in China.

Colorful selection of blooms on sale at the Flower Market in Mong Kok

⓳ Flower Market
花市

Flower Market Road, Mong Kok, Kowloon. Ⓜ Prince Edward.

The Flower Market is less frenetic and more convenient than Temple Street, and is well worth a visit. Colorful blooms and clever bamboo creations line Flower Market Road, just north of Prince Edward Road West. A huge array of cut flowers, potted plants, seeds, and bulbs are sold throughout the year. The market is especially busy in the days leading up to Chinese New Year. At the end of Flower Market Road is the small Bird Market, with a few stalls selling elegant bamboo cages.

⓴ Wong Tai Sin Temple
黃大仙祠

Wong Tai Sin, Kowloon. Ⓜ Wong Tai Sin. **Tel** (0852) 2327 8141. **Open** 7am–5pm daily.

The temple at Wong Tai Sin is one of Hong Kong's largest, busiest, and most interesting places of worship. The complex contains altars and shrines to Buddhist, Confucian, and Daoist deities. It is primarily dedicated to the god Wong Tai Sin, a shepherd reputed to have performed healing miracles. Beside the main temple are fortune-tellers, some of whom can reveal your fortune in English for a hefty fee, mostly through palm and face reading.

Some worshipers try to divine what lies in store for them by shaking small canisters of bamboo sticks until one emerges from the stack. Each is marked with a numeral and a corresponding meaning. Also used are *bui*, or "Buddha's lips," two pieces of wood shaped like orange-segments. A question is asked, the *bui* are thrown, and the "lips" answer yes or no, depending on which way they land.

Wong Tai Sin Temple, one of Hong Kong's busiest places of worship

Life-size *arhats* line the path up to 10,000 Buddhas Monastery

㉑ Heritage Museum 香港文化博物館

1 Man Lam Rd, Sha Tin, New Territories. **M** Che Kung MTR. **Tel** (0852) 2180 8188. **Open** 10am–6pm Mon, Wed–Fri (10am–7pm Sat, Sun & public hols). **W** **heritagemuseum.gov.hk**

This excellent modern museum tells the story of Hong Kong's 6,000-year-old human history. The largest of the city's museums, it has five permanent exhibitions and plenty of space for temporary shows. The New Territories Heritage Hall illustrates prehistoric human life, the rise of village society, colonial rule, and the large-scale development of the New Territories towns. There is also a display on Cantonese opera, which explains the elaborate ritual and color symbolism involved and contains exquisitely crafted costumes. Beautiful calligraphy scrolls hang from the second floor. The Children's Discovery Gallery on the ground floor is a fun look at Hong Kong's natural habitat.

㉒ 10,000 Buddhas Monastery 萬佛寺

221 Pai Tau Village, Sha Tin, New Territories. **M** Sha Tin MTR. **Tel** (0852) 2691 1067. **Open** 9am–5pm daily.

Ruby-lipped, life-size golden *arhats* line the steep path up to the 10,000 Buddhas Monastery, a 15-minute walk from the northern exit of the Sha Tin MTR station. Cross the road and follow the clear signposts to the temple, which is at the top of the wooded hill. The main temple houses hundreds of tiny golden Buddhas that line shelves reaching up to the ceiling. There are more images outside, including two statues depicting languid *boddhisattvas* astride different animals. Still more statues peep from the monastery's bright-red, nine-story pagoda. The small annex above the main temple contains the embalmed body of the temple's founding monk, covered in gold leaf and placed in a glass case.

Pagoda, 10,000 Buddhas Monastery

㉓ Sai Kung Town & Peninsula Beaches 西貢海灘

New Territories. **M** Choi Hung MTR then taxi or minibus 1A or 1S to Sai Kung Town.

It may seem incredible, but just a few miles from Kowloon's bustling streets, it is possible to find empty beaches, clear surf, and seclusion on the shores of the rugged Sai Kung Peninsula.

The area is best accessed via Sai Kung Town, a pleasant place to wander among the stalls selling fish near the sea-front, and to eat at the profusion of seafood restaurants.

Some of the most pristine beaches on the peninsula can be found at **Tai Long Wan**, where there is a small village with a couple of basic cafés and shops. The best way to reach this spot is to take bus 94 from Sai Kung Town to Pak Tam Au, on the MacLehose Trail *(see p327)*, and then hike to Tai Long Wan. A reasonable level of fitness is required for the 4-mile (6-km) hike and remember to bring with you a good map and plenty of fluids for the journey.

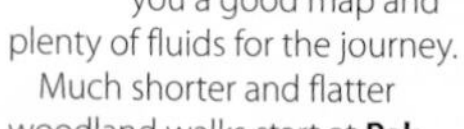

Much shorter and flatter woodland walks start at **Pak**

The beaches and emerald waters of the Sai Kung Peninsula

◀ Hong Kong Harbor at dusk

Tam Chung Visitor Centre. Maps are available here for numerous walks, including a worthwhile nature trail. Take a taxi or bus 94.

Alternatively, hire a *kaido*, a small ferry, from Sai Kung Town for a tour of the many small islands off the peninsula. It is easy to find eager operators near the jetty, although without speaking Cantonese, travelers will need a map to point out where they would like to go, as most of the operators don't speak English.

One of the buildings along the Lung Yeuk Tau Heritage Trail

㉔ Lung Yeuk Tau Heritage Trail

龍躍頭文物徑；

Fanling, New Territories. M Fanling MTR, then 54K minibus.

For a glimpse of pre-colonial times in rural Hong Kong, spend a couple of hours exploring the mile-long **Lung Yeuk Tau Heritage Trail** near Fanling. This passes five *wais* (walled villages) and six *tsuens* (villages), mostly built by the Tangs, one of the five great New Territory clans. The buildings are in various states of repair, from dilapidated ruins to pristine walled compounds and some modern houses. Most of these are still lived in. Among the best-preserved buildings is the large **Tang Chung Ling Ancestral Hall**, founded in 1525 and still used today by the Tangs to pay respects to their ancestors and to hold celebrations. **Tong Kok**, a *wai*, also has dozens of old houses.

㉕ Kadoorie Farm & Botanic Garden

嘉道理農場暨植物園

Lam Kam Rd, New Territories. Tai Po Market MTR then 64K bus. **Tel** (0852) 2483 7200. **Open** 9:30am–5pm daily, but check in advance for irregular closed days. W **kfbg.org.hk**

This working organic farm and wildlife refuge is nestled in the wooded foothills of Hong Kong's tallest mountain, 3,140-ft- (957-m-) high **Tai Mo Shan**. It is a great place to escape the crowds and modernity of downtown, with an easy hike to the top. There are terraced vegetable plots and groves of fruit trees, a small enclosure of orphaned animals, including wildcats, deer, and birds of prey, and a walking trail. You will need a good half-day to see everything the farm has to offer.

㉖ Mai Po Marshes

米埔自然保護區

New Territories. M Sheung Shui MTR then 76K bus or taxi. **Tel** (0852) 2526 1011. on weekends. Permits: deposit and advanced booking required. W **wwf.org.hk**; W **wetlandpark.com**

Wedged between Hong Kong and the urban sprawl of Shenzhen, this globally important wetland is home to a range of wildife species. Pollution has taken its toll elsewhere along the Pearl River delta, making this 940-acre (380-ha) park the last refuge for many species. Apart from herons and egrets, otters and the very rare black-faced spoon-bill can be seen. There are numerous bird hides for keen bird-watchers. Contact HKTB *(see p339)* for details of guided weekend tours. Nearby, the government-run **Hong Kong Wetland Park** explores the area's diverse ecosystems and occupies a 150-acre (61-ha) area.

㉗ MacLehose Trail

麥理浩徑

New Territories. Tai Mo Shan: taxi from Tsuen Wan MTR. W **hiking.gov.hk**

Strung east–west across the middle of the New Territories, this 62-mile (100-km) route takes in huge, wild, and high areas from Tuen Mun in the west to the lovely Sai Kung Peninsula in the east. The trail is divided into 10 manageable stages, and it is possible to walk for long stretches without seeing a soul. One of the most scenic sections takes in **Tai Mo Shan**, Hong Kong's highest peak with views, on a clear day, down to the distant city. The far eastern stage is also very beautiful, concluding at Tai Long Wan's lovely beaches *(see p326)*. Sturdy shoes, fluids, and maps (from the Government Publications Centre) are essential. The record for completing the entire trail is just under 11 hours as part of the annual Oxfam Trailwalker race.

A scenic waterway in Mai Po Marshes

A traditional fishing sampan moored in Aberdeen's bustling harbor

㉘ Aberdeen
香港仔

Hong Kong Island. 🚌 70 from Central's Exchange Square bus station.

Once a quiet fishing village, Aberdeen is today the largest separate town on Hong Kong Island, with a population of more than 60,000. Named in 1845 after the British Colonial Secretary, the Earl of Aberdeen, the harbor housed Hong Kong's first dockyard, which was built in the 1860s.

A short bus ride from Central *(see p316)*, the Aberdeen district has a rather unattractive town center, edged by massive high-rise apartment blocks, commercial towers, and factories. What it lacks in aesthetic appeal, however, it makes up for in bustle and atmosphere. The boat-filled harbor is the big attraction in Aberdeen as it is the center of all activity. Many of the boats found here are actually part-time residences for Hong Kong's fishermen and their families; so much so that the district still has the characteristics of a traditional fishing village. Tiny sampans dodge among the wooden fishing fleet and the large, palatial floating restaurants. Pushy operators on the waterfront offer tours by sampan that take visitors past the fishing boats, the houseboats, and small harbor-side shipyards.

Alternatively, for a quicker (and free) tour, jump aboard the shuttles to the floating restaurants moored here, such as the **Jumbo Floating Restaurant**. The first and most famous of the floating restaurants, it is a massive, palatial hulk that is part Las Vegas-style casino and part Chinese temple, with the kitchen producing upmarket Cantonese classics.

The garish Jumbo Floating Restaurant lights up Aberdeen Harbour

㉙ Ocean Park
海洋公園

180 Wong Chuk Hang Road, Aberdeen. 🚌 Ocean Park City Bus 629 from Central Star Ferry and Admiralty MTR. **Tel** (0852) 3923 2323. **Open** 10am–6pm daily (to 7:30pm Sat, Sun & pub hols). **W** **oceanpark.com.hk**

With the arrival of a mega-competitor in the shape of Lantau Island's Disneyland *(see p331)*, Ocean Park, Hong Kong's first amusement park, has fought back with several new attractions. It is much better than it ever was, gives Disney a run for its money, and attracts great crowds of people every day. There is plenty to do for adults and children alike, and it's easy to spend a day exploring the eight themed areas of this pleasant complex. The Waterfront area is one of the most enjoyable sections, with a collection of Asian animals, including the theme park's pride, four giant pandas. A scenic cable car skirts the edge of Deep Water Bay, dropping passengers in Marine World. Here, a large and impressive aquarium captivates visitors with close-up views of schools of fish and an under-water tunnel through a tank of sharks. Numerous thrilling rides are found throughout the grounds, including the Hair Raiser, a roller coaster that juts out over the sea, the dizzying Mine Train, and The Rapids, which guarantees a good soaking.

30 Deep Water and Repulse Bays
深水灣及淺水灣

Hong Kong Island. 6 and 260 from Central's Exchange Square bus station.

Several good beaches line these two scenic bays located along the road from Aberdeen to Stanley. Deep Water Bay is a pretty spot favored by the wealthy, with many luxurious houses. The long stretch of beach lined by cypress-like trees is reminiscent of the French Riviera. Upmarket apartment blocks, inhabited by Hong Kong's business elite, surround the long, well-tended beach at Repulse Bay. The beach is a popular summer destination and gets very crowded in high season and on weekends. The pricey Verandah Restaurant – the only surviving section of the stately Repulse Bay Hotel, which was torn down in the 1980s – is a good stopping point for a drink or to indulge in afternoon tea. Just behind the Verandah there is a supermarket for picnic supplies and a few cafés.

The popular beach at the seaside town of Stanley

Statue of *Bodhisattva* of Mercy Guanyin, Hong Kong Life Saving Society

31 Hong Kong Life Saving Society
香港拯溺協會

Repulse Bay, Hong Kong Island. **Open** 7am–7pm daily.

At the far southern end of Repulse Bay is the Hong Kong Life Saving Society. The building also serves as a temple, and is a great place for children to explore. Garish statues – a menagerie of gods, animals, and mythical beasts – are scattered across the grounds in amongst the life-saving equipment. Among the gods is a large statue of Guanyin, the *bodhisattva* of Mercy, to whom the temple is dedicated. Several other gods are represented, including a number of smiling bronze Buddhas. Rubbing their bald heads is said to bring good luck. Some believe that crossing the Bridge of Longevity also adds three days to a person's life.

32 Stanley
赤柱

Hong Kong Island. 6, 6X, 260 from Central's Exchange Square bus station. 9am–6pm daily.

This pre-colonial fishing village today resembles a British seaside town, complete with English-style pubs. The extensive sprawl of market stalls selling clothes, beachwear, silk, jade, trinkets, and furniture draws weekend crowds. The area also has a good selection of Thai, Italian, Spanish, Vietnamese, and Chinese restaurants.

Beside the square is **Murray House**, a large Neo-Classical building housing some fine restaurants with bay views. Dismantled and rebuilt here in 1998, it originally stood on the site now occupied by the Bank of China tower in Central. Next to it **Tin Hau Temple**, built in 1767, is one of the island's oldest and most evocative shrines. The festival of Tin Hau *(see p51)* is celebrated in late April or early May with dances and boat races.

On the other side of town is the beautifully kept **Stanley Cemetery**, dating to the earliest colonial days. It contains the gravestones of early residents and soldiers killed in World Wars I and II, including those who died in the Japanese internment camp built nearby. Stanley Beach, on the other side of the peninsula, is a long stretch of sand and the venue for the local dragon boat races, held each year in June.

Lamma Island, with hilltop views of the sea and Hong Kong Island

㉝ Lamma Island
南丫島

from Central (pier 4) and from Aberdeen (via Mo Tat).

Good seafood restaurants and pubs, a relaxed atmosphere, pleasant hilltop walks, and the absence of cars make leafy, low-key Lamma the perfect escape from the city bustle. Its two main villages, **Yung Shue Wan** on the west coast and restaurant-packed **Sok Kwu Wan** on the east coast, are a half-hour ferry ride from Central. Yung Shue Wan is an expat stronghold with two or three English-style pubs and some good restaurants. A steep climb leads to the hills above Yung Shue Wan, where there are fine views of the sea and Hong Kong Island. Visitors can hike between the two villages, but should plan their walk around the infrequent return ferry from Sok Kwu Wan. The harbor at Sok Kwu Wan is home to the **Lamma Fisherfolk's Village**, a fascinating floating exhibition that looks at the life of a fisherman and the skills and traditional techniques of the trade.

㉞ Cheung Chau Island
長洲

from Central (pier 5). Bun Festival (May).

This charming island, just 45 minutes by ferry from Hong Kong Island, has plenty to offer, from lounging on its beaches to exploring the traditional shops and shrines along its narrow lanes and eating at the many seafood places at the harbor's edge on Pak She Praya Road. The squid with shrimp paste is a local speciality. The southern coast offers the best walks, with sea views and wood-land pathways threading past striking rock formations.

The island's earliest settlers arrived here some 2,500 years ago; their only surviving relics are the geometric etchings on a rock below Warwick Hotel. In the 19th century, the island was a haven for pirates, and the notorious Cheung Po-Tsai supposedly hid plunder here. The fishing community is now depleted due to excessive fishing over the past 50 years.

Close to the harbor, the 1783 **Pak Tai Temple** is dedicated to the island's patron deity, who is credited with saving islanders from the plague in 1777. The annual Bun Festival *(see p339)* is celebrated here in May, when young men scale 40-ft (12-m) high bamboo towers covered in buns.

Colorful sampans and fishing boats in Cheung Chau harbor

㉟ Lantau Island
大嶼山

from Central (pier 6) to Mui Wo (Silvermine Bay).

Twice the size of Hong Kong Island, Lantau was ceded to the British in 1898 along with the other islands and the New Territories. Despite the addition of a bridge and the huge airport at Chek Lap Kok, large tracts of the island still remain virtually uninhabited, including two country parks in which are the peaks that form the island's backbone and numerous hiking trails.

Lantau's seclusion has made it a popular place for religious retreats. The most striking of these is **Po Lin Monastery**, located on a hilltop on the Ngong Ping plateau. The mon-astery grounds are grand and colorful, and the over-the-top,

Tai O Fishing Village
Traditional stilt houses cluster on the muddy banks of the small estuary at this rural fishing settlement.

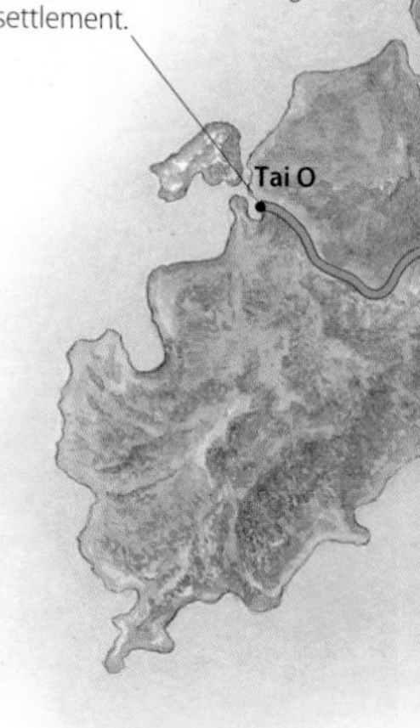

For hotels and restaurants in this area see p561 and pp580–81

gaudy main temple is well worth a visit. The **Big Buddha**, an 85-ft (26-m) statue perched at the top of a 268-step flight of stairs, is the monastery's biggest draw. Since the Buddha's consecration in 1993, the monastery has been overrun with tourists. There are also bauhinia and orchid gardens and basic vegetarian food is served in the monastery canteen.

The area around Ngong Ping is also a great place for walks and picnics. Keen hikers stay at the SG Davis Youth Hostel before making a pre-dawn hike up **Lantau Peak** to watch the spectacular sunrise.

At the island's western end, the sleepy fishing village of **Tai O** has narrow streets and tiny residences reminiscent of rural China. Once a major salt trading center, today the old saltpans are being used as fish-breeding ponds. Tai O has a few temples and many shops selling live seafood and dried fish, the local speciality.

The Big Buddha at Po Lin Monastery

In the east of the island, **Discovery Bay** is the starting point for a gentle walk to a Trappist Monastery. Its chapel is open to visitors willing to observe the vow of silence taken by the monks.

Lantau's popular attraction, the multi-billion dollar **Hong Kong Disneyland**, is modeled after the original Disneyland in California, and the 311-acre (126-ha) area includes a park featuring Mickey Mouse and his friends, as well as original attractions designed especially for Hong Kong, themed hotels, an arboretum, and a retail and dining center.

Ngong Ping & the Big Buddha
Bus 2 from Mui Wo. Also taxi or cable car from Tung Chung MTR.

Disneyland
MTR to Disneyland Resort via Sunny Bay station.

Tung Chung is connected to Po Lin Monastery by a 4-mile (6-km) cable car.

Hong Kong Disneyland is built on reclaimed land, which was once Penny's Bay.

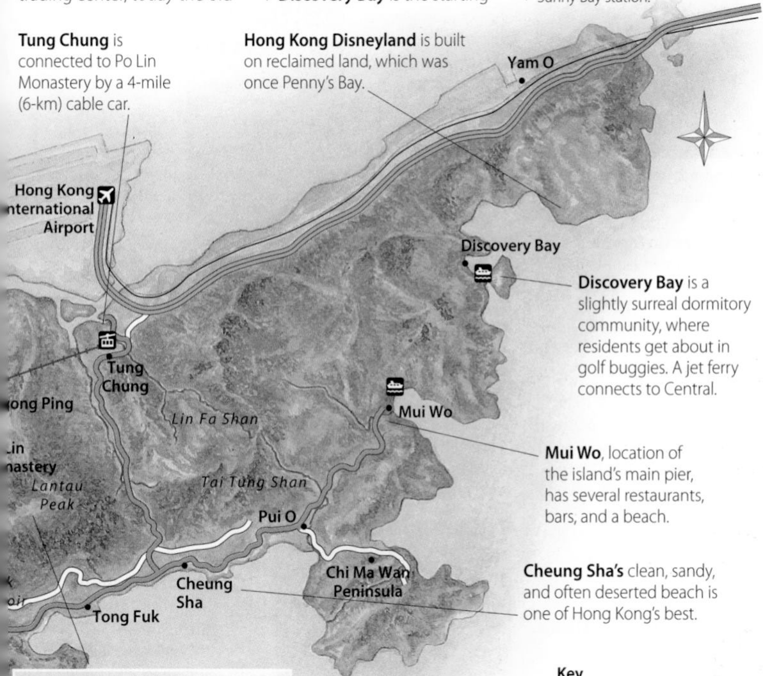

Discovery Bay is a slightly surreal dormitory community, where residents get about in golf buggies. A jet ferry connects to Central.

Mui Wo, location of the island's main pier, has several restaurants, bars, and a beach.

Cheung Sha's clean, sandy, and often deserted beach is one of Hong Kong's best.

Key

- National Highway
- Major road
- Minor road
- Railroad

Lantau Peak
The only way up this 3,065-ft (934-m) high peak is via a steep path through tea gardens. It is an ideal spot for watching the sunrise.

For additional map symbols *see back flap*

36 Macau

澳門

An hour by ferry from Hong Kong, Macau was once seen as principally a sleepy side-trip offering a break from the buzz and bustle of the British enclave. Economically backward, it traded on the preservation of colonial-era buildings and as a gambling weekend resort. But even before the Portuguese colony's return to China in 1999, two years after Hong Kong, a complete restructuring of the tiny territory was underway, with vast public works projects including harbor reclamation, an airport, new bridges, and the fusing of the islands Taipa and Coloane into one. The connecting land, known as the Cotai Strip, is filling up with luxurious hotel-casinos, anchored by a copy of Las Vegas's The Venetian, with sampans floating amongst the gondolas. In some aspects, Macau now out-glitzes neighboring Hong Kong.

Historic cannon on the ramparts of Fortaleza do Monte

Fortaleza do Monte

Rua de Monte. **Open** 7am–7pm daily. Macau Museum: Praceta do Museu de Macao, No. 112. **Tel** (0853) 2835 7911. **Open** 10am–6pm Tue–Sun. (free on 15th of each month).

W macaumuseum.gov.mo

Built between 1617 and 1626, this fortress housed the original Portuguese settlement at Macau. Its thick ramparts, surmounted by ancient cannons, still occupy a commanding position and appear as invincible as they did in 1622, when the invading Dutch forces were defeated.

Dug into the hill beneath the fort is the informative **Macau Museum**. Its escalators and stairs are an air-conditioned route to the hilltop fortress, passing through re-creations of Portuguese and Chinese life. Beginning with the arrival of Portuguese traders and Jesuit missionaries, the exhibitions compare the two cultures at the time of contact and cover the development of Macau and its unique traditions.

Ruinas de São Paulo

Rua de São Paulo.
Open daily.

All that is left of this once grand cathedral, built by the Jesuits and perched precariously atop a steep flight of steps, is its magnificent, crumbling facade. Its most outstanding features are the ornate figures on the facade, comprising a "sermon in stone" that records some of the main events from the Christian scriptures.

The cathedral was built by Japanese Christian converts who fled to Macau in the 16th century following religious repression. In the 18th century, Macau also expelled the Jesuits and the building was converted into barracks until it was destroyed by a fire in 1835. Only extensive structural work in the 1990s stopped the facade from crumbling. The attached museum houses paintings, sculptures, and relics from Macau's churches.

The magnificent façade of the Ruinas de São Paulo

Old Protestant Cemetery

Praca Luis de Camões.
Open 8:30am–5:30pm daily.

The gravestones at this cemetery at the corner of the Camões Gardens are crammed with fascinating historical details that give some wonderful insights into the lives led by early colonists. Many of them were Britons, who traded, married, or fought in and around Macau before Hong Kong was established as a British territory.

Gravestone, Old Protestant Cemetery

Among the notable people buried here are Robert Morrison, the first Protestant missionary to venture to China, and the artist George Chinnery. The gravestones speak of short but heroic lives, such as that of the brave Lieutenant Fitzgerald killed after "gallantly storming" a gun battery at Canton (now Guangzhou). The inscription on Robert Morrison's tomb states that he produced the first Chinese version of the Old and New Testaments. The adjoining Camões Gardens are named after the renowned Portuguese poet Luis Vaz de Camões, the author of the 16th-century epic *The Lusiads*.

Guia Fort & Lighthouse

Estrada de Cacilhas. **Tel** (0853) 2859 5481. **Open** 9am–6pm daily.

The Guia Fort was built between 1622 and 1638, and offers great views over the town. Initially it served as a fort to defend the border with China, but in 1865 a lighthouse was added. A pleasant way to get here is to take the cable car to the hilltop. A small chapel stands next door and there are several gentle walking trails around the hill.

Colonial facade on Largo do Senado

The Venetian

Cotai Strip. **Tel** (0853) 2882 8888. **venetianmacao.com**

Inspired by The Venetian in Las Vegas, Macau's most spectacular hotel-casino recreates a miniature Venice, complete with campanile, Rialto Bridge, and gondolas with singing gondoliers. The mega-resort is suites-only and offers themed shopping as well as a theater seating up to 1,800 people. There is the usual array of slot machines, blackjack, baccarat, roulette, and *keno* (bingo), as well as some Chinese games, including the dice game *dai sui* and the *mahjong*-style *pai kao.* Gambling is Macau's lifeblood, contributing more than half the government's revenue. Macau also hosts horse-racing, held twice a week, and greyhound-racing, four times a week *(see p338)*.

Largo do Senado

The symbolic heart of Macau, the Largo do Senado or Senate Square has numerous stately colonial buildings set around it, including the Leal Senado, or Loyal Senate, which now houses the municipal government, the General Post Office, and the Santa Casa de Misericordia, an old refuge for orphans and prostitutes. There are also numerous restaurants and the tourist office. The striking, wavy black and white tile patterns snaking across the square make it a great place to take photographs by day or floodlit by night.

VISITORS' CHECKLIST

Practical Information

560,000. 9 Largo de Senado, (0853) 2833 3000. Macau Arts Festival (May). **macautourism.gov.mo**

Transportation

Taipa Island. From terminal on Avenida Amizade and Cotal Strip to Hong Kong, Hong Kong Airport, and Shenzhen Airport.

Praia Grande

Perhaps the best way to get a flavor of Macau's colonial architecture is to take a stroll on the Avenida de Praia Grande. Although land reclamation has encroached on the waterfront and robbed the Praia Grande of some of its elegance, it is still a charming place with many grand houses in excellent condition. The monument to Jorge Alvares, the first Portuguese explorer to reach China, stands near the corner of Avenida do Dr. Mario Soares. One of the most handsome buildings is the old Governor's Residence. Although it is not open to the public as it is a private residence, a good view can be had from the road.

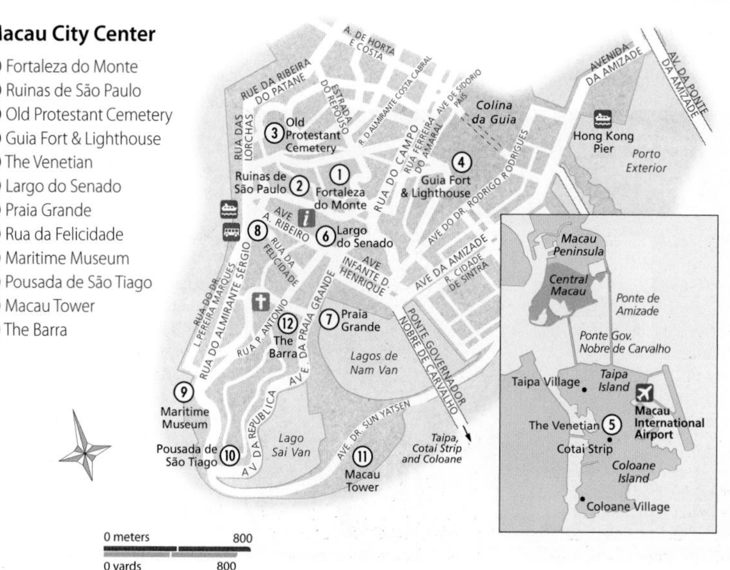

Rua da Felicidade

A variety of sweet scents waft from the Rua da Felicidade, or "Street of Happiness," where tasty and colorful Macanese biscuits and cakes are baked and sold. The area once teemed with brothels, hence its somewhat ironically bestowed name. Today, it is a charming, cobbled street lined with small eateries, which makes it a good place for a quick lunch stop.

A scale model of a Chinese junk, Maritime Museum

Maritime Museum

Largo do Pagode da Barra 1.
Tel (0853) 2859 5481.
Open 10am–6pm Wed–Mon.
museumaritimo.gov.mo

Small-scale but interesting exhibits make this museum worth a visit for insights into the maritime past upon which Macau's wealth was built. Displays include models of Chinese junks, Portuguese ships and fishing boats, a mock Hakka village *(see p296)*, a dragon boat, and a small aquarium. There is also a nice bar on the esplanade outside, open during museum hours.

Pousada de São Tiago

Avenida da Republica, Fortaleza de São Tiago da Barra. **Tel** (0853) 2837 8111. **Closed** at the time of publication. Call for up-to-date information.

Well worth a visit for a drink on the terrace, a night's stay, or a meal at its restaurant, this tiny but enchanting hotel was once a fortress hewn from the rock on which it stood in the 17th century. The chapel to São Tiago, Portugal's patron saint of soldiers, remains to this day. The structure is more a rocky grotto than a smart hotel, which only adds to its charm. A natural spring runs through the lobby and the corridors are paved with flagstones. Its rooms are traditionally decorated in Portuguese style. The hotel also runs a good restaurant, La Paloma.

Macau Tower

Largo da Torre de Macau.
Tel (0853) 2893 3339.
Open 10am–9pm Mon–Fri, 9am–9pm Sat & Sun.
macautower.com.mo

The Macau Tower, the peninsula's most visible attraction, is 1,107 ft (338 m) high. The tower provides a great view; in fact, visitors can see Hong Kong's surrounding islands on a clear day. However, it is not the ideal place for those who don't like heights. Glass-sided elevators rocket visitors skywards, and the restaurants and viewing galleries at the top are also partially glass-bottomed. For the truly adventurous, it is possible to don overalls and a harness, and explore parts of the tower's exterior with the adventure sports company A. J. Hackett, which runs a number of activities, including bungy trampolining and a dizzying skywalk around the tower's outer rim at a height of over 764 ft (233 m).

The modern Macau Tower

The Barra

Located south of Largo de Senado, Rua Central and Rua P. Antonio cut through the Barra district, where Macau's first European residents settled. A 40-minute walk through narrow streets sided with old colonial buildings will bring you to the Neo-Classical olive green front of **Teatro Dom Pedro V** dating back to 1873. Farther down, **São Lourenço** is a plain but beautifully proportioned church set high off the street. Eventually you reach tiny **Largo do Lilau**, a pretty cobbled square with a fountain and the restored **Mandarin's House** dating from 1881. Another 545 yds (500 m) along, the finely collonaded **Quartel dos Mouros**, once a Muslim barracks, is now a post office. Beyond lies the **A-Ma Temple**, Macau's oldest.

Avenida da Republica, near the Pousada de São Tiago

Regional Food: Macau

When the Portuguese arrived in Macau 450 years ago, the peninsula was virtually uninhabited. The settlers cooked using Portuguese methods, but with local Chinese ingredients and Southeast Asian herbs and spices picked up from their other outposts in Africa, Goa, Malacca, Indonesia, and Japan. As the years went by, and links home were established, some of the grander families continued using Portuguese recipes made with the traditionally correct ingredients, while the less well-off incorporated more Cantonese-style dishes and ingredients, and over time the two cuisines fused together to form a separate Macanese cuisine.

A selection of Cantonese sweetmeats in a Macau shop

Portuguese

Bacalhau is the most famous Portuguese ingredient. This dried and salted cod is integral to Iberian cookery and in Macau is cooked in every way possible. Distinguishing other Portuguese influences is difficult but good signs include the liberal use of olive oil, almonds, *chorizo* (paprika sausage), rabbit, and saffron. Other non-Chinese foods that are available are bread, cakes, cheese, olives, and coffee. Macau is also home to a well-developed wine culture, and naturally almost all the wines on offer are Portuguese. These are generally better quality than on the mainland and even better value.

Other Influences

The other obvious change to Cantonese cuisine is the more generous use of herbs and spices: coriander and chilies in peri-peri dishes from Africa; fish sauce from Southeast Asia; hot and spicy curries from Goa; *feijoada* and sweet potatoes from Brazil; tamarind from Malacca.

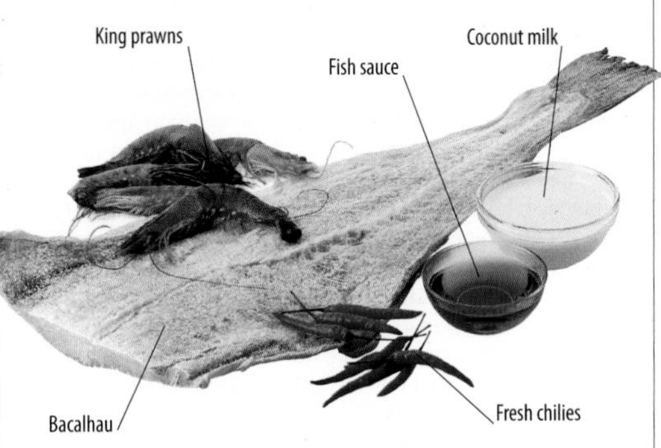

A selection of typical Macanese ingredients

Regional Dishes & Specialties

Saffron strands

There are very few totally Cantonese-inspired dishes in the Macanese cuisine. Tacho – a winter casserole of beef, pork, chicken, and Chinese sausage is perhaps the most Cantonese of all Macanese dishes. As expected, *bacalhau* dishes feature prominently. There are *Bacalhau Guisado* (salted cod stew), *Bacalhau a Gomes de Sa* (salted cod in Gomes de Sa Style), and *Pasteis de Bacalhau* (salted cod cake) to name just a few. Other popular dishes include *Caril de Camarao* (shrimp curry). There are traditional Portuguese dishes like *Caldo Verde* (cabbage and potato stew) and *Carne de Porco a Algarvia* (braised pork with clams). At first sight, *Pasteis de Nata* (egg tartlets) look similar to the Cantonese ones in Hong Kong, but they taste quite different and have a flakier pastry shell.

Galinha Africana (African chicken) *derives from a West African recipe in which char-grilled chicken is coated in a spicy peanut and coconut sauce, then roasted.*

Shopping in Hong Kong and Macau

Label-mad Hong Kong is a paradise for shoppers, and is jammed with opportunities to buy, from swanky designer boutiques in modern shopping malls to inexpensive street markets. It is a competitive destination for some electronic and computing items as well as good-quality, custom-made suits, shirts, and *cheongsams* – the tight-fitting, traditional Chinese silk dresses. Visitors are unlikely to find good bargains, however, especially if comparing prices with those in China. Hong Kong's main advantage is the sheer, unrivaled profusion of items on sale. Don't be afraid to haggle in markets and smaller stores, though prices are usually fixed in smarter shops and department stores.

Markets

Street markets are one of the best bargain-hunting grounds in Hong Kong, as long as you're prepared to sift through the ever-present fake designer goods. The **Temple Street Night Market** *(see p323)* in Yau Ma Tei is perhaps the most celebrated for its atmosphere, its prices, and the range of accessories, clothes, trinkets, and other memorabilia. The **Jade Market**, just south of the night market, sells exactly what it advertises. A visit to the market at **Stanley** *(see p329)*, on Hong Kong Island's southern coast, is as much fun for the trip out on the dramatic winding roads across the island as it is for the shopping. It is a good place to shop for touristy arts, crafts, clothes, and accessories.

Western Market is a more sedate place, located in the western district of Sheung Wan. The handsome colonial-era building outshines the nondescript restaurants on the ground floor, while the middle floor spills over with a huge variety of Chinese silks and brocades.

Shopping Centers, Malls & Department Stores

Even seasoned department-store junkies can overdose on the huge variety available in Hong Kong's sprawling shopping malls. **Harbour City**, with its massive extended malls containing hundreds of individual shops, even dwarfs the big liners that dock near the mall in Kowloon's Tsim Sha Tsui district. Across Victoria Harbour on Hong Kong Island, **The Landmark** in Central and **Pacific Place** in Admiralty are the places to head to for designer clothing labels such as Chanel, Prada, and Versace, and super-chic consumables from Louis Vuitton, Bulgari, and Tiffany. **Sogo** in Causeway Bay *(see p317)* is another mammoth department store, while **Island Beverley**, nearby, crams hundreds of small outlets into its dozen or so floors, and sells modish street fashion at affordable prices.

Antiques & Jewelry

Hollywood Road *(see p320)* in Central is best for antiques, and is full of emporia selling everything from huge terra-cotta tomb guards to delicate little snuff bottles. Established names include **Honeychurch Antiques**, specializing in antique Asian porcelain and paintings, **Gorgeous Arts & Crafts**, which stocks, among other things, antique hats and hairpins, and **Dragon Culture**, offering a good selection of pottery, bamboo carvings, and snuff bottles. **Gallery EXIT** is a good place to find works by new Asian artists. There are also some good antique shops in Macau *(see pp332–5)*, immediately to the south of the Ruinas de São Paulo.

Electronics, Cameras & Computers

Tsim Sha Tsui and the rest of Kowloon are generally the places to head to for electronics and gadgetry. Once the bargain basement of international electronics retail, **Nathan Road** *(see p322)* is still packed with camera and electronics outlets, but prices aren't as competitive as they once were. Be wary, as there are numerous tales of less-than-honest vendors. If you plan to shop here anyway, do your homework, make sure you compare like for like, ask questions (ensuring that your purchase is compatible with your home country's voltage), and you may find a bargain.

Star House, opposite the bus terminal and the Star Ferry at Tsim Sha Tsui, is convenient and contains a number of computer boutiques on its second floor. Farther north, the **Mongkok Computer Centre** houses more retailers. Its prices are generally lower than elsewhere, and visitors can try bargaining. However, if you would like to keep your shopping more straightforward, the **Fortress** chain stores are reasonably priced and a safe bet for cameras and handhelds. They will provide warranties and guidance on foreign voltages.

Chinese Arts & Crafts

While it may be possible to find the wares on offer in **Yue Hwa** at cheaper prices over the border, it is a convenient place to go to when buying last-minute presents. The store in Jordan is packed with silk goods, carvings, ceramics, jade, and teapots. The **Lock Cha Tea House**, inside Hong Kong Park, in Admiralty, is a cosy, friendly place, where visitors can sample delicate green and jasmine teas and buy some exquisite traditional teapots. Souvenirs designed by local artists can be found at **Macau Creations**. For a modern take on Chinese style, the upmarket **G.O.D.** (Goods of Desire) chain offers smart interior goods at reasonable prices.

Clothes

Needless to say, the malls and department stores are the best places for clothes. However, **Joyce** is also a good destination for shoppers seeking a large range of smart labels under one roof. Great value Gap-style clothing can be found at one of the many **Giordano** stores in town. **Shanghai Tang** in Central offers traditional Chinese clothes and home decor with a luxurious, contemporary twist. For Europeans who despair of finding essentials in their size, there is always the well-known British **Marks & Spencer** chain of stores.

Party-goers may want to sift through the stylish, modern and retro street fashion offerings at the independent boutiques around Granville Road and Kimberley Street in Kowloon. Legendary for its tailors and shirt-makers, Hong Kong is still the place to come. Take a chance with the stores in Tsim Sha Tsui or go for established names such as **David's Shirts** or the renowned **Sam's Tailor**, who has made elegant outfits for an illustrious clientele. For end-of-line designer bargains, it's best to head to the **Citygate Outlets** mall in Tung Chung, home to a collection of brand-name outlets.

Hong Kong's markets are awash with fake designer wear, whose quality and cut are often far inferior to the real thing. If looking for authentic labels, it is best to avoid the street markets altogether, and shop only at the larger department stores and boutiques.

DIRECTORY

Markets

Jade Market
Kansu and Battery Sts, Yau Ma Tei.
Map 1 B1.
Open 10am–3:30pm daily.

Stanley Market
Stanley, Hong Kong Island.
Open 9am–6pm daily.

Temple Street Night Market
Temple St, Yau Ma Tei.
Map 1 B2.
Open 6pm–midnight daily.

Western Market
Des Voeux Rd Central, Sheung Wan. **Map** 2 A2.
Open 10am–7pm daily.

Shopping Centers, Malls & Department Stores

Harbour City
3 Canton Rd, Tsim Sha Tsui. **Map** 1 A4.
Tel (0852) 2118 8666.

Island Beverley
1 Great George St, Causeway Bay.
M Causeway Bay.

The Landmark
15 Queen's Rd Central.
Map 2 C3.
Tel (0852) 2500 0555.

Pacific Place
88 Queensway. **Map** 3 D4.
Tel (0852) 2844 8988.

Sogo
555 Hennessy Rd, Causeway Bay.
Tel (0852) 2833 8338.
M Causeway Bay.

Antiques & Jewelry

Dragon Culture
231 Hollywood Rd, Central.
Map 2 A2.
Tel (0852) 2545 8098.

Gallery EXIT
3/F, 25 Hing Wo St, Tin Wan, Aberdeen.
Tel (0852) 2541 1299.

Gorgeous Arts & Crafts
Shop J, Goodview Court, 49–59 Square St, Sheung Wan. **Map** 2 A3.
Tel (0852) 2973 0034.

Honeychurch Antiques
29 Hollywood Rd, Central.
Map 2 B3.
Tel (0852) 2543 2433.

Electronics, Cameras & Computers

Fortress
Shop 335–337, Level 3, Harbour City, Canton Rd, Tsim Sha Tsui.
Map 1 A4.
Tel (0852) 3101 1413.

Mongkok Computer Centre
8a Nelson St, Mongkok.
M Mongkok.
Tel (0852) 2384 6823.

Star House
3 Salisbury Rd. **Map** 1 A5.

Chinese Arts & Crafts

G.O.D.
48 Hollywood Rd, Central.
Map 2 B3.
Tel (0852) 2805 1876.
Shop 105, Stanley Plaza, Stanley.
Tel (0852) 2673 0071.

Lock Cha Tea House
G/F, The K.S. Lo Gallery, Hong Kong Park, Admiralty.
Map 2 D4.
Tel (0852) 2801 7177.

Macau Creations
T1, Macau Tower Entertainment Centre, Largo da Torre de Macau.
Tel (0853) 2833 3311.

Yue Hwa
301–309 Nathan Rd, Jordan.
Map 1 B2.
Tel (0852) 3511 2222.

Clothes

Citygate Outlets
20 Tat Tung Rd, Tung Chung. M Tung Chung.
Tel (0852) 2109 2933.

David's Shirts
Shop 108B, The Galleria, 9 Queen's Rd Central.
Map 2 C3.
Tel (0852) 2524 2979.

Giordano
27 Des Voeux Rd, Central.
Map 2 C3.
Tel (0852) 2921 2028.

Joyce
232 Pacific Pl, Admiralty.
Map 3 D4.
Tel (0852) 2523 5944.

Marks & Spencer
Times Square, 1 Matheson St.
Map 1 A4.
M Causeway Bay.
Tel (0852) 2923 7972.
Central Tower, 28 Queen's Rd Central.
Map 2 B3.
Tel (0852) 2921 8323.

Sam's Tailor
Shops K & L, Burlington Arcade, 94 Nathan Rd, Tsim Sha Tsui.
Map 1 B4.
Tel (0852) 2367 9423.

Shanghai Tang
Shanghai Tang Mansion, 1 Duddell St, Central.
Map 2 C3.
Tel (0852) 2525 7333.

Entertainment in Hong Kong & Macau

Hong Kong's entertainment options are incredible. There are several good venues attracting local and international musicians, Chinese opera groups, and theater and comedy shows, particularly during the arts festival in February and March. The city's nightlife is booming, and bars, dance venues, pubs, and music clubs are plentiful. The younger crowd have discovered an appetite for house and techno music, although they retain their liking for Cantopop, the homegrown pop genre. Karaoke bars are also a favorite with locals.

Macau also has its fair share of diversions, from vast casino gaming floors and glittering shows to excellent restaurants.

Entertainment Guides

Visitors will be spoilt for choice in terms of good listings in Hong Kong. Perhaps the best is the free, weekly *HK Magazine*, available in cafés and bars across the city, which offers a thorough guide to eating, drinking, shopping, and entertainment. The Friday edition of the *South China Morning Post* is useful as it contains a guide to weekend events. The Hong Kong edition of *Time Out* is another great source of local information.

Bars & Pubs

Hong Kong's best clubs, bars, and pubs cluster around Lan Kwai Fong *(see p320)* in Central, along Wyndham Street, and SoHo. For delicious cocktails in a sumptuous setting, head to subterranean bar **Le Boudoir**, located on Wyndham Street.

If you want to drink with the jet-set, there are a number of super-smart bars including **Felix** above the Peninsula Hotel, with sensational harbor views. Alternatively, try **SEVVA** on the roof of Central's Prince's Building, or the fashionable **Drop** in SoHo, which turns into a lively club later on into the evening.

If you are in the mood for a more laid-back drink in a British-style pub atmosphere, you'll find it at **The Globe** in SoHo.

Nightclubs

Nightclubs vary hugely from down-at-heel, free-to-enter clubs with occasional live music to slick, cutting-edge venues for the rich and famous. Cover prices vary but a typical mid-range fee would be around HK$100. Looking out over Wyndham Street, **Dragon-i** is a smart club with an exclusive reputation, playing dance music and often hosting international disc jockeys. **Volar** in D'Aguilar Street is great for house music. **Drop** *(see Bars and Pubs left)* and **Magnum Club** are also popular clubs near Lan Kwai Fong.

Music & Arts Venues

There's no shortage of venues for large musical, operatic, and dramatic productions. These include the **Hong Kong Cultural Centre**, which sometimes offers free concerts, the **Hong Kong Convention & Exhibition Centre** in Wan Chai, and the **Hong Kong Coliseum** in Hung Hom. Close to the Coliseum, the **Ko Shan Theatre** is the place to go for Chinese opera and orchestral music performances. The **Hong Kong Arts Centre, The Fringe Club**, and **The Hong Kong Academy of the Performing Arts** all offer more intimate venues for an excellent and diverse range of arts from dance to stand-up comedy. **The Wanch** is a tiny place that hosts local folk and indie acts.

The **Macau Cultural Centre** is also worth a visit. It hosts art, history, and architecture exhibitions and runs a busy calendar of music, theater, opera, and dance, particularly in May during Macau's arts festival.

Sports

Spring heralds the start of the dragon-boating season; check with the HKTB for race details. The Rugby Sevens tournament in March is a huge, boisterous event for Hong Kong's expats, many of whom see its main purpose as an opportunity to drink large quantities of beer. For those interested in the actual game, 50 matches are played by the assembled internationals in 72 hours. Hong Kong is also host to a number of professional tennis tournaments from October to December.

Gambling

Horse-racing at the tracks in **Sha Tin** and **Happy Valley** *(see p317)* is the only spectator sport where you can gamble legally in Hong Kong. It is the biggest such spectator event in the region and race days or nights are well worth attending for the atmosphere alone. Macau also has its own, less fevered horse-racing nights as well as an excellent greyhound-racing track, the rather grandly titled **Canidrome**. Macau, of course, is best known for its glitzy casinos, running all day and night. The most spectacular of them is **The Venetian**, complete with miniature campanile, Rialto Bridge, gondolas, and themed shopping.

Children's Entertainment

Hong Kong's favorite attractions are two state-of-the-art amusement parks: **Ocean Park** *(see p328)*, the region's oldest amusement park, and **Disneyland** *(see p331)*, offering a massive range of rides, attractions, and entertainment. Up in the New Territories, **Kadoorie Farm & Botanic Garden** *(see p327)* has a small zoo of orphaned native animals, including muntjac deer and wild cats. In a similar vein, but much more central is the enchanting **Edward Youde Aviary** in Hong Kong Park, which is built to resemble a tropical rain forest and has elevated walkways.

Traditional Festivals

One of Hong Kong's grandest annual celebrations is the **Chinese New Year** *(see pp48–9)*. Victoria Park becomes a huge open-air market and there are spectacular harbor fireworks that rival any display in the world. The **Birthday of Tin Hau**, the Goddess of the Sea, is more low key. Parades and lion dances take place at the larger temples, including the one at Joss House Bay in the New Territories, and temples and fishing boats are decorated all over Hong Kong. The **Cheung Chau Bun Festival** in May is a fun week-long celebration on Cheung Chau Island *(see p330)*. It culminates in the eating of huge piles of buns offered, some say, to the unhappy spirits of victims of the island's pirate past, and a procession of "floating" children, carried aloft on themed floats. The **Dragon Boat Festival** in June is marked with a great flourish, making it one of the region's most exciting events. Other traditional festivals celebrated in Hong Kong include the **Hungry Ghost Festival** in mid/late August and the **Mid-Autumn Festival** in late September/early October.

DIRECTORY

Hong Kong Tourism Board (HKTB)

Hong Kong International Airport Arrivals Hall. Kowloon: Star Ferry Concourse. **Map** 1 A5. **Tel** (0852) 2508 1234. **W discoverhongkong.com**

Bars & Pubs

Le Boudoir
Basement, 65 Wyndham St, Central. **Tel** (0852) 2530 3870. **W french-creations.com/boudoir**

Drop
Basement, On Lok Mansion, 39–43 Hollywood Rd, Central (entrance on Cochrane St). **Map** 3 B3. **Tel** (0852) 2543 8856. **W drop.com.hk**

Felix
Peninsula Hotel, Salisbury Rd, Kowloon. **Map** 1 B4. **Tel** (0852) 2696 6778.

The Globe
Garley Building, 45-53 Graham Street, Central. **Map** B3. **Tel** (0852) 2543 1941. **W theglobe.com.hk**

SEVVA
25/F, Prince's Building, Chater St, Central. **Map** 2 C3. **Tel** (0852) 2537 1388. **W sevva.hk**

Nightclubs

Dragon-i
The Centrium, 60 Wyndham St. **Map** 2 B3. **Tel** (0852) 3110 1222. **W dragon-i.com.hk**

Magnum Club
3–4/F, 1 Wellington St, Central. **Map** 2 B3. **Tel** (0852) 2116 1602. **W magnumclub.com.hk**

Volar
B/F 44 D'Aguilar St, Central. **Map** 2 B3. **Tel** (0852) 2810 1510. **W volar.com.hk**

Music & Arts Venues

The Fringe Club
2 Lower Albert Rd, Central. **Map** 2 C3. **Tel** (0852) 2521 7251. **W hkfringeclub.com**

Hong Kong Academy of the Performing Arts
1 Gloucester Rd, Wan Chai. **Map** 3 E3. **Tel** (0852) 2584 8500. **W hkapa.edu**

Hong Kong Arts Centre
2 Harbour Rd, Wan Chai. **Map** 3 E3.**Tel** (0852) 2582 0200. **W hkac.org.hk**

Hong Kong Coliseum
9 Cheong Wan Rd, Hung Hom, Kowloon. Hung Hom MTR. **Tel** (0852) 2355 7234. **W lcsd.gov.hk/hkc**

Hong Kong Convention & Exhibition Centre
1 Expo Drive, Wan Chai. **Map** 3 F3. **Tel** (0852) 2582 8888. **W hkcec.com**

Hong Kong Cultural Centre
10 Salisbury Rd, Tsim Sha Tsui. **Map** 1 B5. **Tel** (0852) 2734 2009. **W lcsd.gov.hk/hkcc**

Ko Shan Theatre
77 Ko Shan Road, Hung Hom. **Tel** (0852) 2740 9222. **W lcsd.gov.hk/kst**

Macau Cultural Centre
Av. Xian Xing Hai S/N Nape, Macau. **Tel** (0853) 2870 0699. **W ccm.gov.mo**

The Wanch
54 Jaffe Road, Wan Chai. **Map** 3 F4. **Tel** (0852) 2861 1621. **W thewanch.hk**

Gambling

Canidrome
Avenida General Castelo Branco, Macau. **Tel** (0853) 2833 3399.

Happy Valley Racecourse
Happy Valley, Hong Kong Island. **Tel** (0852) 1817. **W hkjc.com**

Sha Tin Racecourse
Tel (0852) 1817. **W hkjc.com**

The Venetian
Estrada de Baia de N. Senhora de Esperanca, S/N. Taipa, Macau. **Tel** (0853) 2882 8877. **W venetianmacao.com**

Children's Entertainment

Disneyland
Penny's Bay, Lantau Island. M Disneyland Resort. **Tel** (0852) 2203 2000. **W hongkongdisneyland.com**

Edward Youde Aviary
Hong Kong Park, Cotton Tree Drive, Central. **Map** 2 C4. **Tel** (0852) 2521 5041. **W lcsd.gov.hk/parks**

Kadoorie Farm & Botanic Garden
Lam Kam Rd, New Territories. **Tel** (0852) 2483 7200. **W kfbg.org.hk**

Ocean Park
180 Wong Chuk Hang Rd, Aberdeen. **Tel** (0852) 3923 2323. **W oceanpark.com.hk**

HONG KONG STREET FINDER

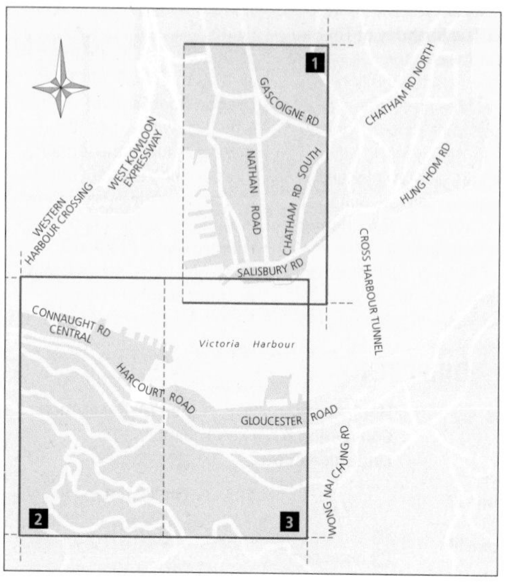

Key to Street Finder

- Place of interest
- Other important building
- Train station
- MTR station
- Bus station
- Ferry terminal
- Tram station
- Tourist information
- Police station
- Hospital
- Temple
- Railroad
- Tramline

Scale of Maps 1–3

0 meters 250

0 yards 250

Street Finder Index

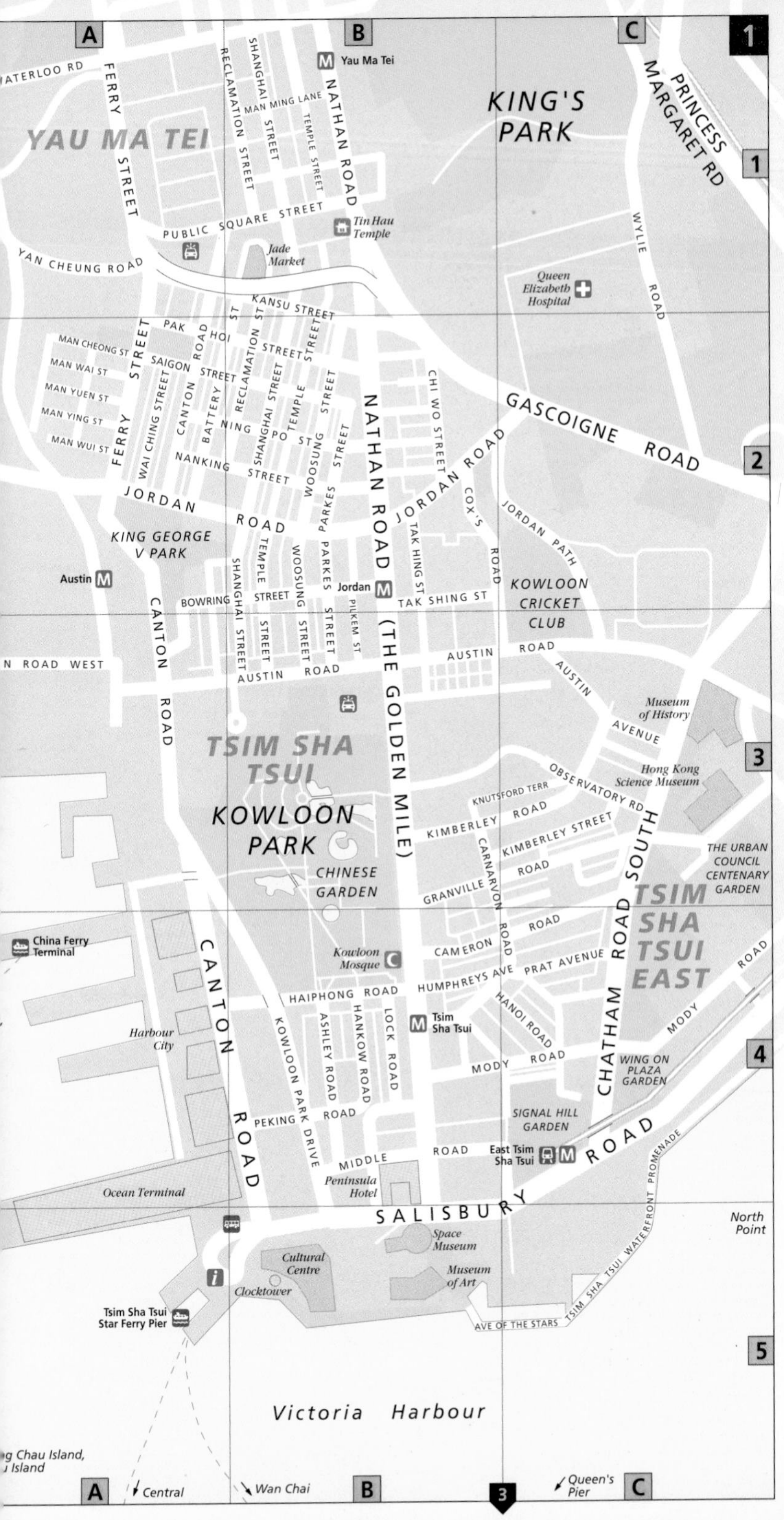

A
B
C
1
Yau Ma Tei
KING'S PARK
YAU MA TEI
WATERLOO RD
FERRY STREET
RECLAMATION STREET
SHANGHAI STREET
MAN MING LANE
TEMPLE STREET
NATHAN ROAD
PRINCESS MARGARET RD
PUBLIC SQUARE STREET
Tin Hau Temple
Jade Market
YAN CHEUNG ROAD
WYLIE ROAD
Queen Elizabeth Hospital
KANSU STREET
PAK HOI STREET
MAN CHEONG ST
MAN WAI ST
MAN YUEN ST
MAN YING ST
MAN WUI ST
SAIGON STREET
WAI CHING STREET
CANTON ROAD
BATTERY STREET
NING PO ST
TEMPLE STREET
CHI WO STREET
GASCOIGNE ROAD
2
NANKING STREET
WOOSUNG STREET
PARKES STREET
JORDAN ROAD
COX'S ROAD
JORDAN PATH
TAK HING ST
KING GEORGE V PARK
Austin
Jordan
KOWLOON CRICKET CLUB
TAK SHING ST
BOWRING STREET
PILKEM ST
NATHAN ROAD (THE GOLDEN MILE)
AUSTIN ROAD WEST
AUSTIN ROAD
AUSTIN AVENUE
Museum of History
TSIM SHA TSUI
3
Hong Kong Science Museum
OBSERVATORY RD
KNUTSFORD TERR
KOWLOON PARK
KIMBERLEY ROAD
KIMBERLEY STREET
CARNARVON ROAD
THE URBAN COUNCIL CENTENARY GARDEN
CHINESE GARDEN
GRANVILLE ROAD
CHATHAM ROAD SOUTH
TSIM SHA TSUI EAST
China Ferry Terminal
Kowloon Mosque
CAMERON ROAD
PRAT AVENUE
HUMPHREYS AVE
HAIPHONG ROAD
HANOI ROAD
MODY ROAD
Harbour City
KOWLOON PARK DRIVE
ASHLEY ROAD
HANKOW ROAD
LOCK ROAD
Tsim Sha Tsui
4
WING ON PLAZA GARDEN
SIGNAL HILL GARDEN
PEKING ROAD
MIDDLE ROAD
East Tsim Sha Tsui
Peninsula Hotel
Ocean Terminal
SALISBURY ROAD
TSIM SHA TSUI WATERFRONT PROMENADE
North Point
Space Museum
Cultural Centre
Museum of Art
Clocktower
Tsim Sha Tsui Star Ferry Pier
AVE OF THE STARS
5
Victoria Harbour
Central
Wan Chai
Queen's Pier

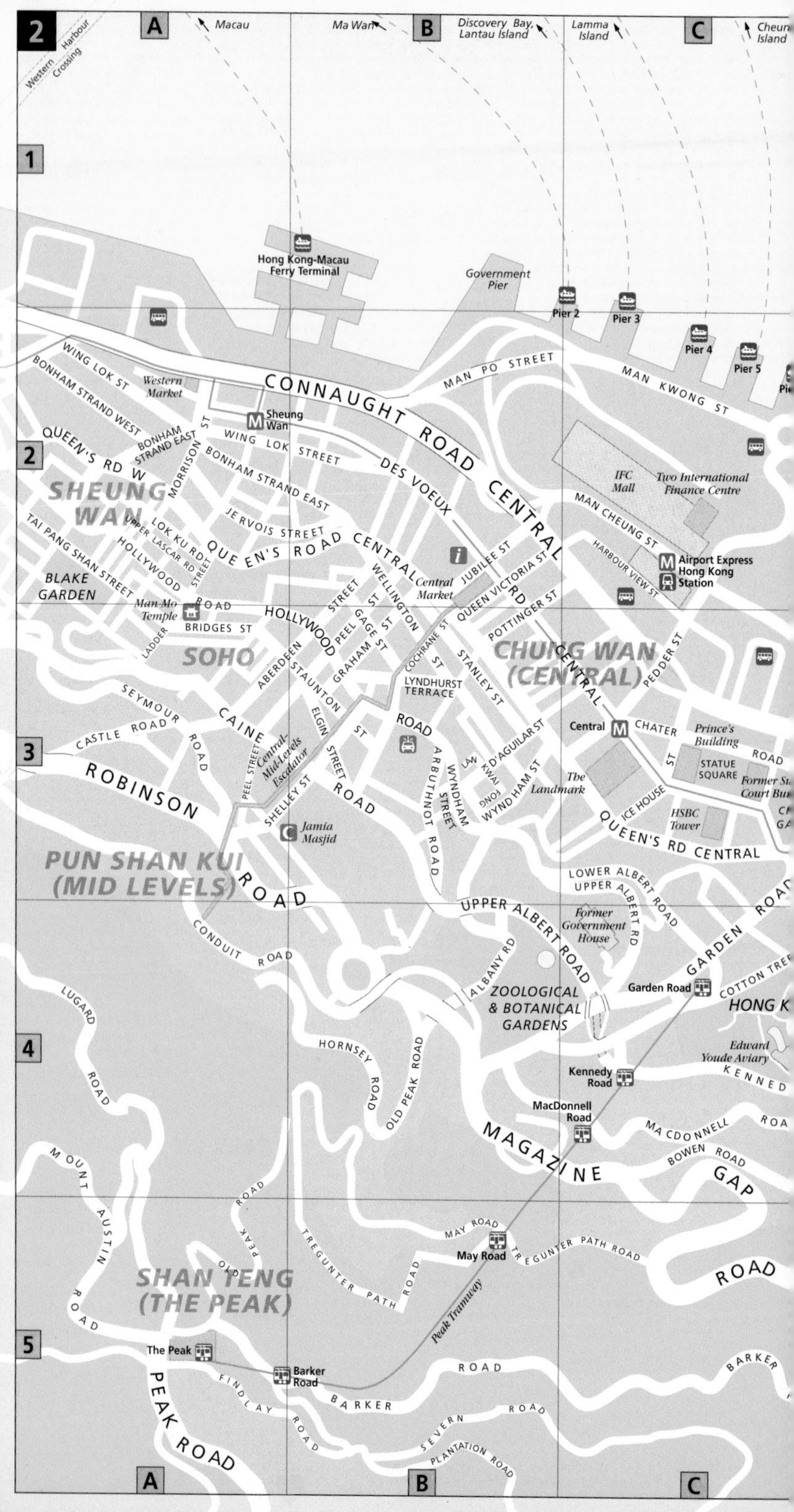
A
B
C
1
2
3
4
5
Macau
Ma Wan
Discovery Bay, Lantau Island
Lamma Island
Western Harbour Crossing
Hong Kong-Macau Ferry Terminal
Government Pier
Pier 2
Pier 3
Pier 4
Pier 5
CONNAUGHT ROAD CENTRAL
MAN PO STREET
MAN KWONG ST
WING LOK ST
BONHAM STRAND WEST
Western Market
Sheung Wan
WING LOK STREET
BONHAM STRAND EAST
QUEEN'S RD W
MORRISON ST
DES VOEUX RD CENTRAL
IFC Mall
Two International Finance Centre
MAN CHEUNG ST
HARBOUR VIEW ST
Airport Express Hong Kong Station
SHEUNG WAN
JERVOIS STREET
LOK KU RD
UPPER LASCAR RD
TAI PANG SHAN STREET
HOLLYWOOD
QUEEN'S ROAD CENTRAL
WELLINGTON
JUBILEE ST
QUEEN VICTORIA ST
Central Market
BLAKE GARDEN
Man Mo Temple
HOLLYWOOD ROAD
BRIDGES ST
LADDER
PEEL ST
GAGE ST
COCHRANE ST
POTTINGER ST
SOHO
ABERDEEN
STAUNTON
GRAHAM ST
STANLEY ST
CHUNG WAN (CENTRAL)
PEDDER ST
LYNDHURST TERRACE
SEYMOUR
CAINE ROAD
ELGIN ST
Central
CHATER ROAD
Prince's Building
CASTLE ROAD
Central-Mid-Levels Escalator
D'AGUILAR ST
STATUE SQUARE
Former Supreme Court Building
ROBINSON ROAD
PEEL STREET
SHELLEY ST
ARBUTHNOT ROAD
LAN KWAI FONG
WYNDHAM STREET
WYNDHAM ST
The Landmark
ICE HOUSE
HSBC Tower
Jamia Masjid
QUEEN'S RD CENTRAL
PUN SHAN KUI (MID LEVELS)
LOWER ALBERT ROAD
UPPER ALBERT RD
UPPER ALBERT ROAD
CONDUIT ROAD
Former Government House
GARDEN ROAD
ALBANY RD
ZOOLOGICAL & BOTANICAL GARDENS
Garden Road
COTTON TREE
HONG K
LUGARD ROAD
HORNSEY ROAD
OLD PEAK ROAD
Edward Youde Aviary
KENNEDY
Kennedy Road
MacDonnell Road
MAGAZINE GAP ROAD
MACDONNELL ROAD
BOWEN ROAD
MOUNT AUSTIN ROAD
OLD PEAK ROAD
TREGUNTER PATH ROAD
MAY ROAD
May Road
TREGUNTER PATH ROAD
SHAN TENG (THE PEAK)
Peak Tramway
The Peak
Barker Road
BARKER ROAD
FINDLAY ROAD
SEVERN ROAD
PLANTATION ROAD
PEAK ROAD

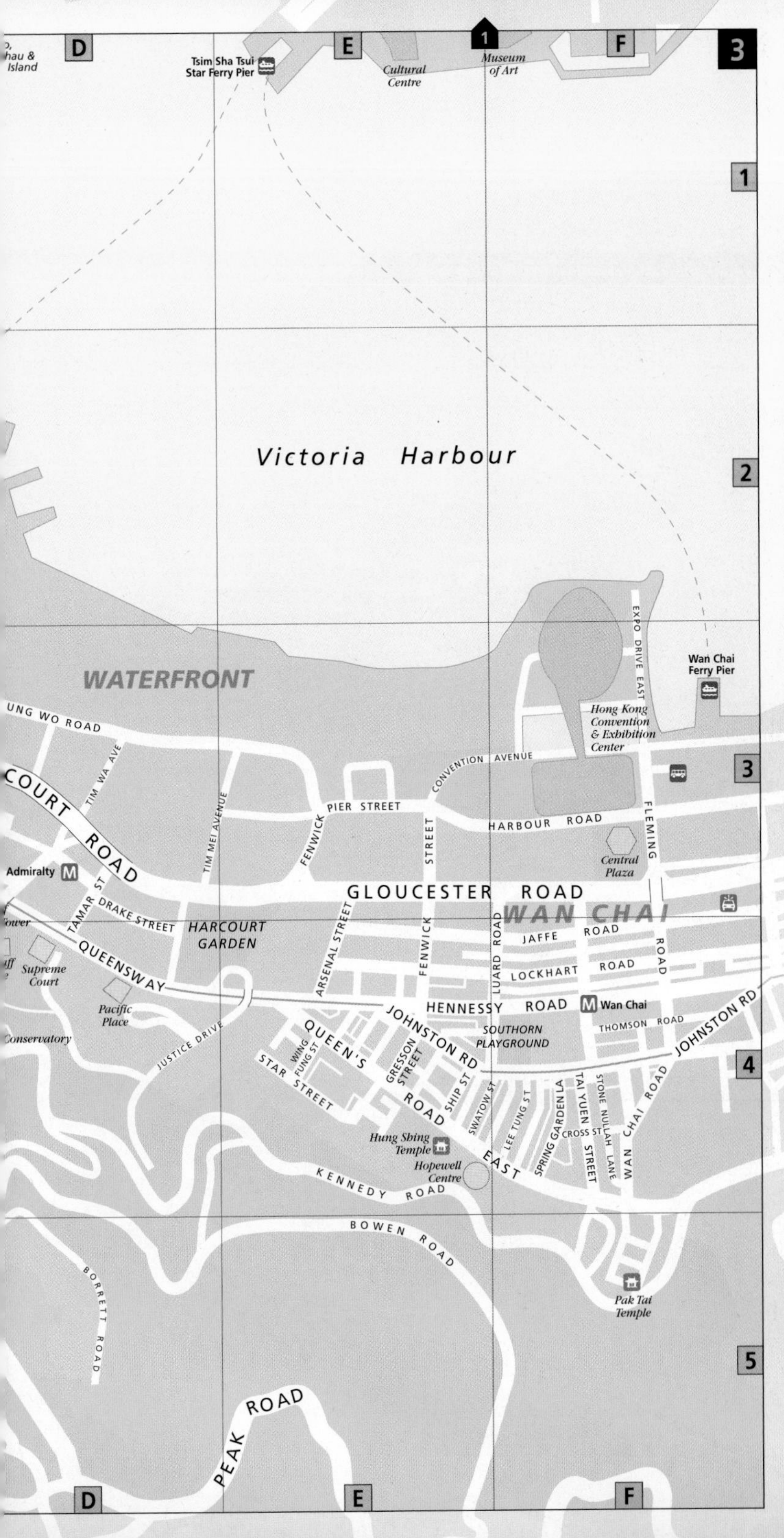

D
E
1
F
3
Tsim Sha Tsui Star Ferry Pier
Cultural Centre
Museum of Art
1
Victoria Harbour
2
WATERFRONT
Wan Chai Ferry Pier
EXPO DRIVE EAST
Hong Kong Convention & Exhibition Center
3
CONVENTION AVENUE
HARBOUR ROAD
FLEMING ROAD
Central Plaza
PIER STREET
FENWICK STREET
TIM MEI AVENUE
TIM WA AVE
COURT ROAD
Admiralty
GLOUCESTER ROAD
WAN CHAI
TAMAR ST
DRAKE STREET
HARCOURT GARDEN
ARSENAL STREET
LUARD ROAD
JAFFE ROAD
LOCKHART ROAD
QUEENSWAY
Supreme Court
Pacific Place
HENNESSY ROAD
Wan Chai
JOHNSTON RD
THOMSON ROAD
SOUTHERN PLAYGROUND
Conservatory
JUSTICE DRIVE
QUEEN'S ROAD EAST
WING FUNG ST
STAR STREET
GRESSON STREET
SHIP ST
SWATOW ST
LEE TUNG ST
SPRING GARDEN LA
TAI YUEN STREET
CROSS ST
STONE NULLAH LANE
WAN CHAI ROAD
4
Hung Shing Temple
Hopewell Centre
KENNEDY ROAD
BOWEN ROAD
BORRETT ROAD
Pak Tai Temple
5
PEAK ROAD
D
E
F

THE SOUTHWEST

The Southwest at a Glance

Some of China's most evocative landscapes are found in the southwest: the fertile Red Basin of eastern Sichuan, deep gorges along the Yangzi River, the mountainous fringes of the Tibetan Plateau, Xishuangbanna's tropical forests, and the karst hills of Guizhou and Guangxi. Cultural highlights include the sites of Buddhist art at Le Shan and Dazu, and the remains of Ming city walls at Dali and Songpan. Ethnic minority communities include Tibetans in the west, Miao and Dong in Guizhou and Guangxi, Dali's Bai, Lijiang's Naxi, and the Dai of Xishuangbanna. There are wildlife preserves for giant pandas in Sichuan, waterfowl at Cao Hai, and elephants in Xishuangbanna; and trekking opportunities at Tiger Leaping Gorge, Emei Shan, and along the Lao border in southern Yunnan.

The stepped and calcified Mirror Pools in Huanglong, Sichuan

The Miao village of Xijiang nestled into a terraced valley near Kaili, Guizhou

Getting Around

The major cities and destinations, such as Chengdu, Chongqing, Kunming, Guiyang, Guilin, Lijiang, and Jinghong, are all served by air. Train lines, though more restricted, offer fairly direct services connecting the provincial capitals with most of the larger cities. A comprehensive network of buses covers much of the region, with comfortable express coaches and surfaced roads linking key sites, though travel through remoter areas on local buses can be rough and slow-going, particularly in Guizhou and Guangxi. It is also possible to spend a few days taking a ferry down the Yangzi from Chongqing, or to take a scenic day trip along the Li River between Guilin and Yangshuo in Guangxi province.

◀ The ancient Miao village of Xijiang in Guizhou

Key

Expressway
Main road
Minor road
Main railroad
Other railroad
International border
Provincial border
 Summit

Dai women selling their produce at a market in Jinghong, Xishuangbanna

Songpan
Pingwu
Guangyuan
Xi'an
Wanyuan
Bazhong
Jiangyou
Mianyang
Nanbu
Dazhou
Fengjie
Deyang
Nanchong
Wanzhou
Yangzi
Chengdu
Liangping
Suining
Hechuan
Wuhan
CHONGQING SHI
Leshan
Neijiang
Chongqing
Qianjiang
Zigong
Luzhou
Qijiang
Youyang
Yibin
Xiushan
Chishui
Dalou Shan
Xuyong
Junlian
Fenggang
Tongren
Daguan
Zunyi
Gaoyuan
Zhaotong
Bijie
Changsha
Zhenyuan
Jinping
Weining
Yungui
GUIZHOU
Guiyang
Kaili
Liping
Duyun
Anshun
Sanjiang
Longsheng
Quanzhou
Qinglong
Dushan
Jinwan Dashan
Luodian
Guilin
Zhenfeng
Xingyi
Nandan
Rongshui
Anlong
Hechi
Lipu
Hezhou
Tuoniang Jiang
Buliu He
Hongshui He
Tianlin
Liuzhou
Huangyao
Guangnan
GUANGXI
Bose
Wuxuan
Guangzhou
Tiandong
Mashan
Wuzhou
Yanshan
Funing
Guiping
Litang
Pingguo
Cenxi
Jingxi
Nanning
Yulin
Hekou
Chongzuo
Bobai
Pingxiang
Qinzhou
Hanoi
Hepu
Beihai
G5
G93
G42
G65
G75
G50
G76
G85
G60
G72
G80
G7211

SICHUAN & CHONGQING
GUIZHOU & GUANGXI
YUNNAN

0 km 150
0 miles 150

For additional map symbols *see back flap*

A PORTRAIT OF THE SOUTHWEST

The southwest's stunning landscapes, from the impossibly steep limestone hillocks along the Li River, to the deep gorges cut by the upper reaches of the Yangzi, make it one of China's most picturesque regions. The area's ethnic diversity, evident in the traditional culture and lifestyles of its numerous minority communities, also adds to its attraction as an exotic tourist destination.

The southwest's isolation has meant that for much of its past it has forged its own path. The area roughly covered by today's Yunnan has always had closer ties with its neighbors to the south and west than with China's traditional dynastic centers. During the period of the Warring States (475–221 BC), Zhuang Qiao, a Chu general, was sent here to subdue the tribes, but after a long campaign he was impelled to stay, establishing the Kingdom of Dian at what is now Kunming in around 300 BC. For the next 500 years, the kingdom existed as a loose conglomerate of tribute-paying tribal chiefs.

In the 8th century, the Kingdom of Nanzhao emerged in Dali, extending its territory into Vietnam and Myanmar. The dynasty grew wealthy on trade along the southern Silk Route, until it was conquered by the Yuan Emperor Kublai Khan in the 13th century. Through much of the Ming and Qing eras, the area that is now Yunnan, Guizhou, and Guangxi was ruled as a colonized outpost, dominated by tribal chieftains.

During the 1800s, the dispossessed, ground down by merciless warlords and extra imperial taxes, revolted in two major uprisings: the Muslim Uprising of 1856 (also known as the Du Wenxiu Rebellion), which lasted until 1873 and centered on Kunming, and the Taiping Rebellion (which lasted from 1850–64), begun in Guangxi *(see p428)*. Both uprisings were brutally suppressed by the Qing and colonizing forces, sending the region into a downward spiral of provincial obscurity and abject poverty. The Miao minority revolted again in 1870. When the Communists marched through during the Long March in 1934, they encountered a population ready for revolution and took on many recruits.

Fishing boats on the banks of peaceful Er Hai (Ear Lake) near Dali

Worshipers wreathed in incense smoke at Chengdu's main Daoist temple, Qingyang Gong

Sichuan, the region's largest province, has long been a part of China – an enigmatic bronze-working culture flourished here around 1000 BC, with its capital at Sanxingdui, north of modern Chengdu. After the fall of the Han dynasty in AD 220, the province's fertile eastern part became the agriculturally self-sufficient Kingdom of Shu during the Three Kingdoms period (AD 221–63), whose wealth sponsored great religious works under the Tang and Song dynasties such as the huge Buddha at Leshan. Sichuan remained a crucial outpost during the ensuing eras. Chongqing, its major city, was targeted for heavy industry under the Communists and is today the world's largest municipality, after separating from Sichuan in 1997. It's from Chongqing that the Three Gorges Cruise down the Yangzi begins *(see pp358–60)*, still the main reason to visit the city.

Bai women in traditional dress, Shaping

Sichuan's heavily populated eastern plains give way to sparsely populated foothills and the Aba grasslands plateau, inhabited mainly by ethnic Tibetans. On the fringes of this frontier, the last few remaining pandas live in what is left of Sichuan's bamboo groves. For a fashionable metropolis, the capital Chengdu is surprisingly laid-back, a characteristic that is best seen in the many teahouses found in parks, temples, and old courtyards.

Yunnan stretches from the Tibetan foothills in the north, where the head-waters of the Yangzi gather strength, to Xishuangbanna and the Laotian border in the south, through which the Mekong flows. Today, Yunnan is quickly becoming one of the country's foremost tourist destinations. Northwest of Kunming lie the pretty towns of Dali and Lijiang, surrounded by villages inhabited by the indigenous Bai and Naxi peoples. Xishuangbanna's landscape and culture, on the other hand, are reminiscent of Vietnam, Laos, and Myanmar. The regular markets, where minority people gather, are very colorful.

Most tourists head to Guangxi for the stunning karst landscapes surrounding Guilin and Yangshuo. The charms of Guizhou and Guangxi lie, however, in the less-visited areas of hilly rural landscape, peppered with wooden villages and inhabited by minority peoples – the Miao in particular are renowned for their ultra-sociable festivals. The region's poverty, due to its poor farmland, has allowed natural sights such as the magnificent Detian Falls, and the lush Maling Canyon to remain relatively untouched.

Limestone peaks coated in vegetation, Li River area

The Flora of Southwest China

Southwest China has the greatest variety of flora in the whole country, and Yunnan province in particular can claim the diversity prize, having some 15,000 species of plant, or about half the country's total. Many garden plants originate from this part of China, including the ubiquitous rhododendron and magnolia. The reason for this richness lies in its unique geography: in a very short distance the environment changes from high altitude mountain plateau to moist subtropical jungle on the Tropic of Cancer in the south, with isolated valleys that restrict access and cross-pollination in between.

A major tourist site, the Tropical Botanical Gardens at Xishuangbanna are also where research into tropical forest ecosystems takes place.

Mountains & Valleys

The landscapes of this region are dominated by seemingly endless vistas of mountain ranges and deep valleys. In northern Yunnan, western Sichuan, and southwest Tibet lie the headwaters of three of the world's great rivers: from west to east, the Nu Jiang (Salween), the Lancang Jiang (Mekong), and the Jiansha Jiang (Yangzi). All originate high in the mountains of Tibet and Qinghai.

Magnolia *(Magnolia campbellii)*, with its showy pink flowers, is native to the Himalayas and China. It was discovered by George Forrest, a Scottish plant hunter, in 1904 but was not brought into cultivation until 1924.

Mountain slopes, lush with beautiful plants such as rhododendrons and magnolias.

Wild rhododendrons grow in this region, a center of diversity for many plants. Most of the modern hybrid garden forms originate from wild species introduced from southwest China.

Poppy *(Meconopsis integrifolia)* grows high in the mountains of southwest China at 8,850–16,7306 ft (2,700–5,100 m), its foliage protected by soft silky hairs. First collected by renowned botanist E. H. Wilson, the poppy is used in traditional medicine.

Many slipper orchid species thrive in the alpine meadows of the Sichuan mountains above 7,800 ft (2,400 m) and *Cypripedium tibeticum* is one of the most attractive.

Camellias, of which there are many beautiful garden species, are grown mainly for their lovely flowers. Also, more than 200 kinds of tea in China are based on *Camellia sinensis*.

Tropical Forest or Jungle

A rare habitat in China, jungle covers only about 0.5 per-cent of the country, but it contains 25 percent of China's species. One of the largest remaining areas lies in the southwest, in Xishuangbanna prefecture, Yunnan province. Here, the rainy season is between April and October, the annual rainfall is about 60 in (1,500 mm), and humidity and temperatures are high. Jungle is also found on Hainan Island, and in southern Guangxi Province.

Typically dense patch of natural tropical forest in Xishuangbanna, southern Yunnan

Pomelo or Chinese grapefruit *(Citrus maxima)* has been cultivated in southern China for thousands of years. The flowers are followed by very large fruits with green rind and sweet, juicy flesh.

Dragon's blood *(Dracaena cochinchinensis)* plays an important role in traditional Chinese medicine. Its red, blood-like sap is collected and used in a variety of preparations to improve the circulation of the blood. Endangered in the wild, it is now being planted to ensure supplies continue.

Musella *(Musella lasiocarpa)*, closely related to the banana, is a beautiful but rare plant in Yunnan and Guizhou provinces. It is low-growing and has a dense yellow flowerhead, reminiscent of a globe artichoke.

The jungle floor is carpeted with ferns and shrubs while above, lianas and figs drape and strangle tree branches. Mists and monsoon rains constantly dampen the air, so epiphytes (plants growing on trees) flourish.

The red dwarf banana *(Musa coccinea)* is one of the prettiest banana plants and is popular in gardens. About 6½ ft (2m) tall, it has bright red flowers that last up to two months. It is now scarce because of over-collection and habitat destruction.

Famous Plant-Hunters

The beginning of the 20th century saw a number of intrepid botanists and explorers set out to discover and bring back new and exotic plants from around the world. Among the most famous were George Forrest (1873–1932), E. H. Wilson (1876–1930), Joseph Rock (1884–1962), and Frank Kingdon Ward (1885–1958). Although only one of the early pioneers, Kingdon Ward achieved renown exploring and collecting botanical specimens in Yunnan province just before and after World War I, and also later in Tibet. Among his most celebrated discoveries are several rhododendron species. In the 1920s he brought back seeds of the beautiful blue poppy *Meconopsis betonicifolia*, which inspired the title of the most famous of his many books: *The Land of the Blue Poppy*.

Frank Kingdon Ward, explorer and collector

Regional Food: the Southwest

Subject to hot summers and mild winters with plenty of rain, the southwest enjoys year-round crop growth, making it one of China's "rice bowls." The Sichuan basin also yields a wealth of subtropical products such as fruits, tea, and herbal medicines and its spicy cooking has become the region's dominant cuisine. By contrast, the cooking of Yunnan is underrated despite some wonderful produce; while the cuisines of Guizhou and Guangxi lie somewhere between Sichuanese spiciness and the subtle, delicate flavors of the Cantonese kitchen.

Eggplants and yard-long beans

Fruits and deep-fried snacks on sticks, typical of the southwest

Sichuan

The cuisine of Sichuan has the reputation of being richly flavored and peppery hot but, in fact, a lot of Sichuanese dishes are not hot at all. After all, the chili is a relatively recent import from the Americas that was not widely cultivated here until the 19th century. According to Sichuanese chefs, chilies do not paralyze the tastebuds, but stimulate the palate. Each dish should be a balance of flavors such as sweet, sour, bitter, hot, salty, aromatic, and fragrant. When the palate is stimulated by the heat of the chili, it becomes sensitized and can appreciate even more flavors at the same time. The most famous regional spice is the Sichuan peppercorn *(hua jiao)*. This dried berry has an aromatic, lemony heat that makes the mouth tingle, even numbing it against the chilies' heat. The final secret of Sichuan food is the purity of the salt collected from the wells of Zigong *(see p361)*.

A selection of Sichuan spices

Regional Dishes & Specialties

Fresh water chestnuts

Most visitors to China will at some time come across versions of Gongbao Chicken and Ma Po Doufu. However, outside Sichuan these dishes are likely to lack the depth of flavors and balance of textures of the original. Each region of China has its own "preserved vegetables" but Sichuan's pickles are among the best – mustard root pickled in a spicy sauce. Yunnan's "Crossing the Bridge Noodles" is said to have been created by the wife of a Qing-dynasty scholar to prevent the noodles cooling on the way to her husband studying in an island pavilion. The dish consists of a chicken broth with a hot, insulating layer of oil on top served with noodles, slices of ham, vegetables, and egg to be added to it at the table. Another specialty is Steam Pot Chicken cooked with vegetables and often medicinal herbs; as it steams, a flavorful broth is created in the pot.

Gongbao Chicken: the best-known Sichuan dish is named for an official from Guizhou who rose to be governor of Sichuan.

Yunnan

Yunnan's tropical climate means the province is a haven for vegetable-lovers, with an excellent variety of fresh produce on offer. Several products distinguish Yunnan on the map of gastronomy – firstly the highly prized *pu'er* tea. Dried into bricks, this is strong and black and often taken as a medicine. Just as famous is Yunnan ham, which rivals the ham from Jinhua in Zhejiang. Unusually for China, Yunnan is also known for its milk products, with cheese eaten in the area around Dali.

When the long rainy season ends, a profusion of mushrooms fills the hills and forests of the region, sending the locals out to collect these delicacies. Finally, the tropical climate means that all sorts of exotic fruits grow here and many turn up in the area's dishes.

Vegetables on sale in a street market in Guizhou

Stall selling *zongzi*, parcels of sticky rice wrapped in bamboo leaves

Guizhou & Guangxi

Relatively poor provinces, Guizhou and Guangxi are known for their famine cuisine especially among the minorities, but despite the stories the average visitor will be hard pressed to find bee grub stir-fries and the like.

Fiery hotpots are a specialty of Guizhou, including those made with dog, but these can easily be avoided *(see p405)*. The predominant flavors are spicy and sour. The province's most distinguished product is Maotai. A strong spirit distilled from sorghum and other grains, it is drunk at formal occasions.

Guangxi cuisine includes Cantonese-style sweet and sour dishes along with more rustic Zhuang minority food. *Zongzi* are also a favorite and the pyramids of sticky rice can be savory or sweet.

On the Menu

Aromatic and Crispy Duck Quite different to Peking Duck, this is marinated, steamed, and then deep-fried. A special version – Tea Smoked Duck – is smoked using tea, cypress, and camphor wood chips.

Twice-Cooked Pork Another traditional Sichuan dish that is extremely popular. The secret is that the pork is first boiled, then stir-fried till tender.

Steamed Beef in a Basket Spicy beef coated with ground rice and steamed – served in the bamboo steamer basket.

Toban Fish A whole fish deep-fried then braised with chili, garlic, ginger, scallions, soy, sugar, wine, chili bean paste *(toban jiang)*, and vinegar.

Ants Climbing Trees Minced pork with rice vermicelli – the minced pork forms the "ants" and the vermicelli the "trees".

Ma Po Doufu: "pockmarked" tofu – a classic dish that combines ground meat, tofu, and chilies in a spicy gravy.

Hot and Sour Soup: this dish, when made properly, derives its pungency solely from the use of ground white pepper.

Fish-Fragrant Aubergine: "fish-fragrant" sauces use the same seasonings as traditional fish cookery.

SICHUAN & CHONGQING

SICHUAN
CHONGQING

The province of Sichuan and the neighboring municipality of Chongqing cover 220,078 sq miles (570,000 sq km) and are home to almost 120 million people. This vast region can be divided into three distinct geographical zones. In the east is Chongqing, a municipality based around the heavily industrialized Chongqing city, with a rural strip running east along the Yangzi River and its famous Three Gorges *(see pp358–60)*. In the center lies the hugely fertile Red Basin, whose laid-back capital Chengdu sits surrounded by chequerboard fields and well-irrigated plains. The wealth generated by this fertile land helped sponsor the temples on Emei Shan's forested slopes and the startling Buddhist sculptures at Dazu and Leshan. In contrast, northern and western Sichuan are covered by the snow-capped foothills of the Himalayan range, with peaks rising to well over 16,400 ft (5,000 m), a thinly settled region whose culture is predominantly Tibetan. Northwest of Chengdu is the Wanglang Nature Reserve, home to the critically endangered giant panda, while to the far north is the beautiful alpine scenery around Songpan and Jiuzhaigou.

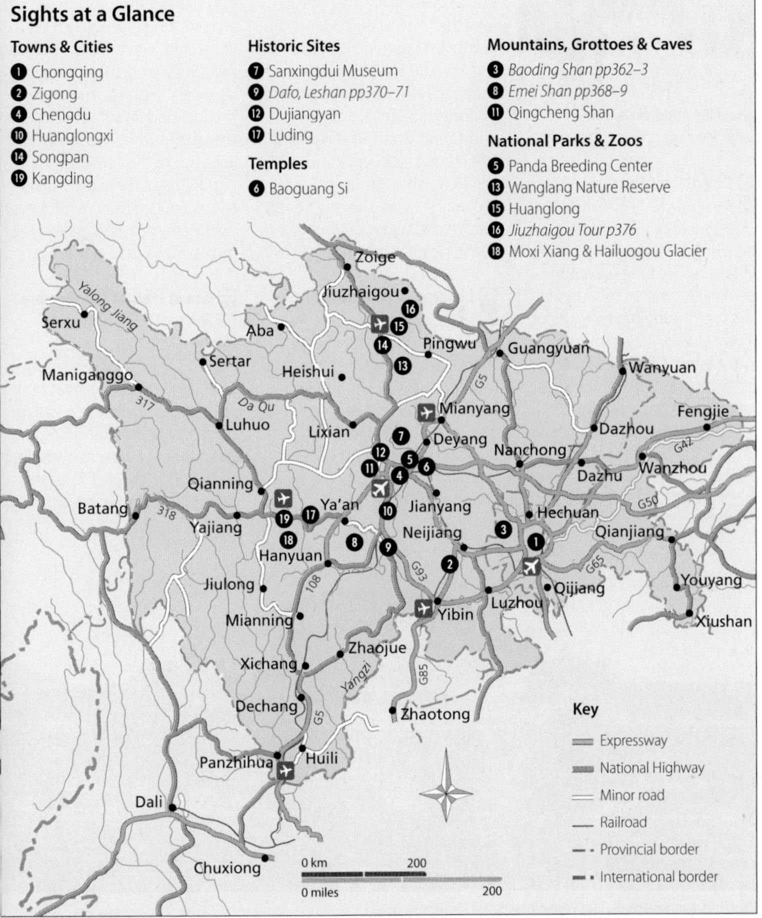

The colorful mineral pools of Huanglong, Sichuan

For additional map symbols *see back flap*

❶ Chongqing

重庆

Believed to have been founded as the capital of the shadowy State of Ba in 1000 BC, this port is situated on a peninsula at the junction of the Yangzi and Jialing Rivers. Also known as Shan Cheng (Mountain City), due to the hills covering the peninsula, it is one of the Yangzi valley's "three furnaces" owing to its stifling summer humidity, made even worse by pollution. The main reason to visit Chongqing, a lively, rapidly modernizing city with few historic sights, is to catch a Yangzi ferry downstream through the Three Gorges *(see pp358–60)*. In 1997, Chongqing became the administrative center of the new city-province of Chongqing Shi, which stretches 311 miles (500 km) east to Hubei.

View of the interior of the Three Gorges Museum

Chaotian Men

Ⓜ Xiaoshenzi and a 10-min walk.

Chaotian Men (Gate Facing Heaven) is Chongqing's wharf district right at the tip of the peninsula, where cruise boats line the muddy banks, readying themselves for their journey into eastern China. A viewing platform overlooking the river junction was constructed in 2000, and offers splendid views on a windy day, though often visibility is impaired by the heavy fogs caused by intense pollution.

Luohan Si

7 Luohansi Jie. Ⓜ Xiaoshenzi

Open 8am–6pm daily.

This Qing-style temple is famed for its hall crowded with *luohan* (those freed from the cycle of rebirth). The Indian Buddhist pantheon has just 18 *luohan*, but the Chinese have added hundreds of their own, including Buddhist figures, folk heroes, and even Daoists. The hall has 524 life-size statues; some sit serenely, while others have grotesque faces. The most easily identifiable figure is Ji Gong, a comic peasant hero near the exit.

Liberation Monument

Ⓜ Linjiangmen.

Situated in the heart of downtown Chongqing, the Liberation Monument is a plain-looking clock tower commemorating the Communists' defeat of Kuomintang forces in 1949. It is surrounded by a busy shopping district.

The Liberation Monument (Jiefangbei) in downtown Chongqing

Three Gorges Museum

236 Renmin Lu. Ⓜ Zengjiayan.

Open 9am–5pm daily.

This museum, also known as Chongqing Museum, houses a superb collection of Eastern Han tomb relics (AD 25–220) from sites around Sichuan. Peculiar to the region are 20-in (50-cm) long mausoleum bricks, illustrated with figures depicting religious and secular themes. A recurrent image is that of the dragon-bodied sun god, Rishen, associated with Fuxi, legendary ancestor of the Chinese. The highlight is a frieze of soldiers and chariots passing a nobleman being entertained. Upstairs is a display of Ba-era boat coffins.

Great Hall of the People

173 Renmin Lu. Ⓜ Zengjiayan.

Open 8:30am–5pm daily.

This 213-ft (65-m) high rotunda, seating 4,200 people, was built in 1954 as a conference hall to commemorate Chongqing's important war-time role. Inspired by Beijing's Temple of Heaven *(see pp102–3)*, it is now a part of

The extravagant Great Hall of the People, now part of the Renmin Hotel

For hotels and restaurants in this region see p562 and pp581–82

the Renmin Hotel and is used for concerts. Its striking exterior, with three tiers of red-pillared eaves beneath a blue canopied roof, stands out from the modern highrises that are encircling it.

Stilwell Museum

63 Jialing Xin Lu, Liziba. Fotugyan.
Open 9am–5pm daily.

This is the former home of General Stilwell (1883–1946), who was based here between 1942 and 1944 as Commander of the US forces and Chiang Kai-shek's Chief of Staff. The 1930s building has period furnishings, with informative displays on "Vinegar Joe's" (the General's nickname) career. Opposite this museum is the small Flying Tigers museum, with maps and photographs of the Tomahawk fighter planes of the American volunteer pilots.

Hongyan Cun

52 Hongyan Cun. 6 miles (10 km) W of Chongqing. Xietaizi.
Open 8:30am–5pm daily.

This group of whitewashed buildings was the base of the Nationalist-Communist "United Front" government during World War II. Among the prominent people based here were the Communist leader Zhou Enlai and his wife, Deng Yingchao. Chairman Mao briefly visited Hongyan Cun (Red Crag Village) after Japan surrendered in 1945, to attend the US-sponsored talks with the Kuomintang forces led by Chiang Kai-shek. The buildings now house a collection of sparsely captioned wartime photographs. More appealing is the hilly parkland surrounding the site.

Ciqi Kou

9 miles (14 km) W of Chongqing.
Ciqikou

Founded 1,700 years ago on the banks of Jialing Jiang, Ciqi Kou (Porcelain Port) was a famous porcelain production center during the Ming era, and is something of a museum piece. Its riverfront lanes, preserved in their original flagstoned state, are flanked by old timber, adobe, and split-stone buildings with carved stonework, latticed windows, and gray-tiled roofs. Teahouses are everywhere, and there are about 100 to choose from. A couple of traditional ones overlook the river and occasionally host opera shows. Busy markets sell food and local arts and crafts. Porcelain is no longer made here, but Ciqi Kou is now popular with modern and traditional painters.

VISITORS' CHECKLIST

Practical Information
200 miles (330 km) SE of Chengdu. 9,700,000.
10/F, 177 Bayi Lu, near Liberation Monument, (023) 6382 1162.

Transportation
Jiangbei airport.
Caiyuanba bus station, CAAC (to airport). Chaotian Men docks.

Visitors at a colorful and bustling market in Ciqi Kou

Chongqing City Center

1. Chaotian Men
2. Luohan Si
3. Liberation Monument
4. Three Gorges Museum
5. Great Hall of the People
6. Stilwell Museum

0 meters 800
0 yards 800

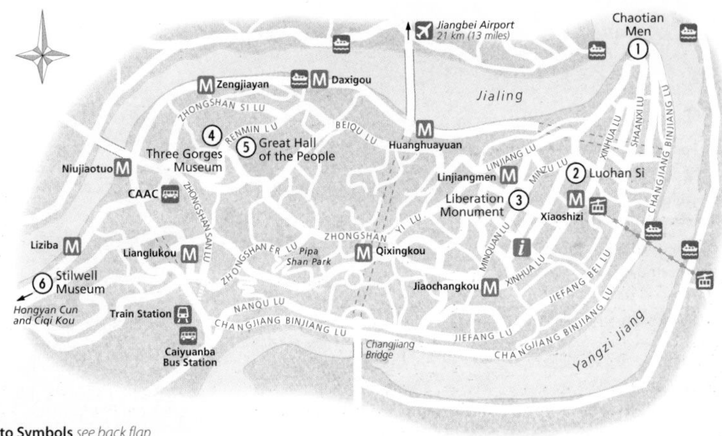

Key to Symbols *see back flap*

The Yangzi and Three Gorges
长江三峡

Before the 20th century, rugged mountains would have virtually isolated Sichuan from eastern China if it hadn't been for the 400-mile (650-km) stretch of the Yangzi linking Chongqing with Yichang in Hubei province. The journey was a perilous one, the river tearing through the sheer-sided Three Gorges. Today, with the shoals cleared, the journey makes a popular cruise through spectacular scenery, with regular stops at famous sights. The landscape has been irrevocably changed by the Three Gorges Dam, which filled to its maximum capacity in 2009, making the cruise even more leisurely and extending the cruising season.

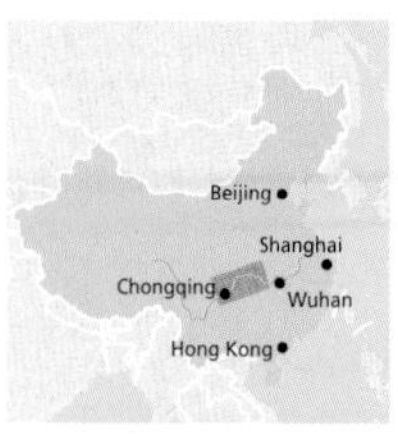

Area illustrated below

★ Shibao Zhai
This outstanding monastery *(see p360)* sits on an island, with Lanruo Dian (Orchid Palace) built into the cliff above.

Landscape near Chongqing
The gentle farmland around Chongqing, fascinating for its depiction of day-to-day life, does little to prepare you for the wild, spectacular gorge scenery downstream.

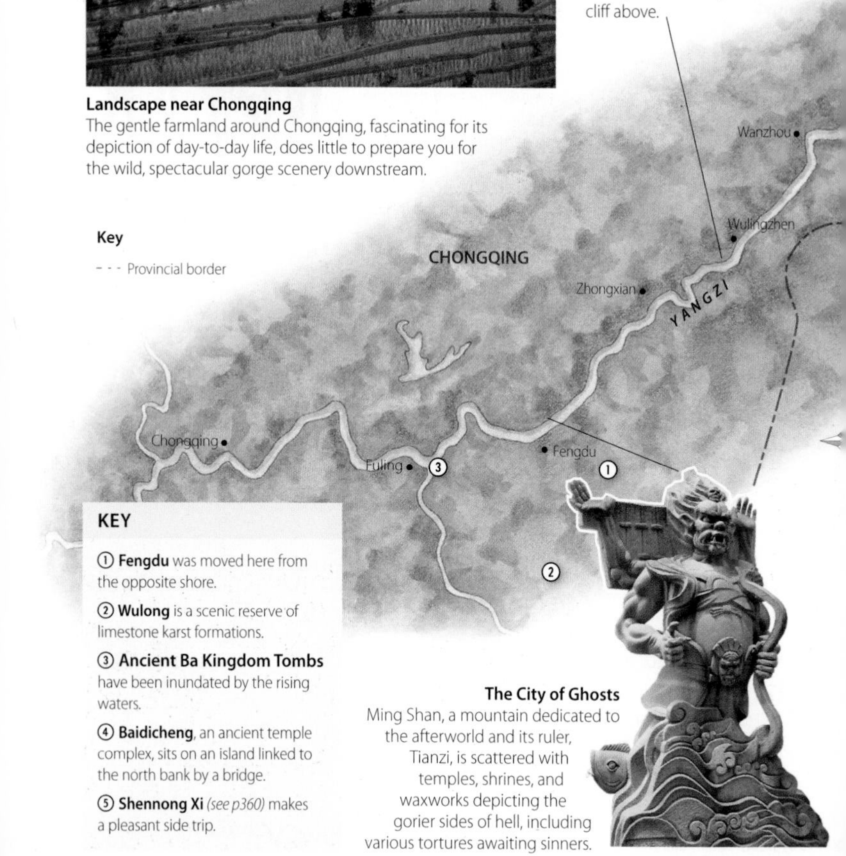

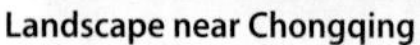

Key

- - - Provincial border

CHONGQING

Wanzhou
Wulingzhen
Zhongxian
YANGZI
Chongqing
Fuling ③
Fengdu ①
②

KEY

① **Fengdu** was moved here from the opposite shore.

② **Wulong** is a scenic reserve of limestone karst formations.

③ **Ancient Ba Kingdom Tombs** have been inundated by the rising waters.

④ **Baidicheng**, an ancient temple complex, sits on an island linked to the north bank by a bridge.

⑤ **Shennong Xi** *(see p360)* makes a pleasant side trip.

The City of Ghosts
Ming Shan, a mountain dedicated to the afterworld and its ruler, Tianzi, is scattered with temples, shrines, and waxworks depicting the gorier sides of hell, including various tortures awaiting sinners.

For hotels and restaurants in this region see p562 and pp581–82

The Three Gorges
Though the river is no longer the vicious torrent described by earlier travelers, the steep walls and tight channels of Qutang Xia, Wu Xia, and Xiling Xia still present an awesome spectacle.

VISITORS' CHECKLIST

Practical Information
Chongqing to Yichang or Wuhan. 10/F, 177 Bayi Lu, Chongqing, (023) 6382 1162 (Chongqing CITS). excursions extra. **yzcruises.com**

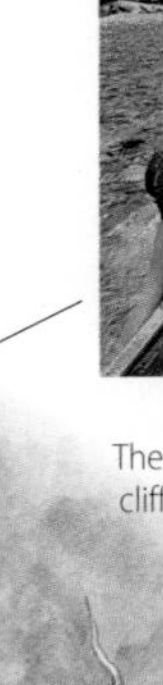

★ Mini Three Gorges
The Mini Three Gorges feature the cliffs of Longmen Xia and troupes of wild monkeys.

★ Qutang Xia
The first and shortest of the stunning Three Gorges, the once violent waters of Qutang Gorge were described by the Tang poet Li Bai as "a thousand seas poured into a single cup."

Three Gorges Dam
Before reaching Yichang, there's a chance to see the world's largest hydroelectric project in operation *(see pp274–5)*. Most cruises now end above the dam.

Cruising the Yangzi

Planned for more than a century, the Three Gorges Dam was completed in 2009. Its 32 hydroelectric generators produce around 2 percent of China's total power requirements. Construction required the relocation of millions of people, the rebuilding of several towns above the new waterline, and the loss of some priceless archeological sites. A few key historic buildings were relocated; where this was not possible, protective dikes were built instead. The drama of the landscape has undoubtedly diminished, but the reservoir is so long that the impression of being a river remains.

Tour sailing up the narrows of Shennong Xi in a sampan

Shennong Xi

One of the highlights of the whole Yangzi cruise is detouring up the ever-narrowing waters of Shennong Stream. The cliffs are pocked with post-holes marking the route of a Han-dynasty plank road, built for military access. Farther upstream in Baidi Cheng, Shennong Xi's hanging coffins have been carved into the gorge's walls by the long-vanished Bai people. Burial goods and cliffside paintings link the Bai with both Sichuan's earliest-known civilization, the Ba, and also the local Tujia ethnic group *(see pp30–31)*.

If the waters are too low to navigate this stream, most cruises include a trip up the Mini Three Gorges instead *(see p359)*.

Wulong

from Wulong town. **Open** 9am–6:30pm daily (last ticket sold 4pm).

About 62 miles (100 km) south of the Yangzi port of Fengdu, Wulong is a scenic reserve of limestone karst formations *(see pp418–19)* scattered in the countryside around Wulong town. The key area is **Tiansheng Sanqiao**, the "Natural Three Bridges," where a former underground river system has collapsed, leaving a complex of vast sinkholes and soaring stone archways, all overgrown with luxuriant vegetation. **Tianlong Tiankeng**, the largest sinkhole, is 1,804 ft (550 m) wide and 890 ft (270 m) deep. Around 2 miles (3 km) of well-formed paths and an outdoor elevator provide access for visitors to navigate around the site.

Shibao Zhai

The most striking aspect of Shibao Zhai (meaning Precious Stone Fortress) is the beautiful 12-story Lanruo Dian, whose curly eaves are said to resemble an orchid, built in 1750 and rising 184 ft (56 m) up the rock wall above the small temple. The "Precious Stone" of the name relates to a legend about a rock in the monastery with a hole, through which every day trickled just enough rice to feed all the monks. But when one of them greedily enlarged the hole, hoping to sell the surplus, the rice stopped flowing. Shibao Zhai has been protected from rising waters by a large dike, but sadly, the medieval village at its base has been drowned.

Choosing a Cruise

Which itinerary: Some cruises sail to Shanghai, but the scenery is bleak east of Wuhan. Book Chongqing to Yichang or Wuhan (extra day). Cruises upstream (west) are cheaper, but may sail through the night.
Cruises: Some English spoken, accommodation varies (dorm to 4-star), check excursions on itinerary, book privately (cheaper than CITS).
Public ferries: No English, very basic conditions, food is bad (bring some), no excursions, tickets from Chaotian Men Dock, Chongqing.
When: Sep and Oct are best; May and Nov riskier; rainy season in summer.

Trackers

Before the rapids were cleared in the 1950s, boats could only make it upstream with the help of trackers, teams of barely paid men who were harnessed together to literally pull the boat, inch by inch, through the Three Gorges' torrents. Paths cut into the bank to make their work easier and slightly less hazardous – or copies of them above the new maximum waterline – can be seen in several places through the gorges.

Towing a barge on Shennong Xi, a tributary of the Yangzi River

Gateway to the Wangye Miao teahouse

❷ Zigong
自贡

135 miles (215 km) W of Chongqing. 3,200,000. 3 Binjiang Lu, (0813) 230 3175.

Salt has been mined in Sichuan for at least 2,500 years, and for much of that time Zigong has been at the center of its production, luring traders from all over China. Brine is drawn from artesian wells beneath the city, along with natural gas used to fuel the evaporation process. Chinese well-drilling techniques, mainly the use of bamboo cables and heavy iron drill-bits, were borrowed by the West during the 1850s, and later adapted for mining oil reserves. Until the 1960s, Zigong was full of bamboo pipelines and 328-ft (100-m) high wooden derricks. Even today one can visit some of these older mines and vintage architecture built to display the salt-merchants' wealth.

The **Zigong Salt Museum** was built in 1736 as the Xiqin Guildhall, a meeting place for salt merchants from Shaanxi province. This lavish building features elaborate flying eaves, and a gilded, wood-carved interior based around a large galleried atrium, where plays were once performed. Exhibits cover the entire history of salt mining, from Han dynasty illustrations, to huge metal drill-bits and cutaways showing the drilling process. Other contemporary buildings of interest are two teahouses with charming antique interiors, where locals sit and chat. The most attractive of these is the 19th-century Wangye Miao, a smaller version of the Xiqin Guildhall, which perches castle-like on a rocky outcrop overlooking the Fuxi Jiang on Binjiang Lu. The other, Huanhou Gong, is a former butchers' guildhall on Zhonghua Road, whose carved entrance-way opens into a sloping courtyard surrounded by private wood-paneled booths.

The **Shenhai Well**, just north-east of the center, was easily the deepest in the world when drilling reached a depth of 3,285 ft (1,001 m) in 1835, producing a daily output of 494 cubic ft (14 cubic m) of brine and 300,175 cubic ft (8,500 cubic m) of natural gas. The 59-ft (18-m) high timber derrick, bamboo pipes, cables, and buffalo-powered winches used in the drilling and retrieving processes are on show, along with gas-powered evaporation pans used to refine salt, which is still produced and packed on site. Zigong's other form of subterranean wealth is its fossils, found at a major Jurassic site in the northeastern suburb of Dashanpu that has now been roofed over as a **Dinosaur Museum**. In 1985, extensive excavations were carried out with British assistance, unearthing hundreds of skeletons, including the stegosaur-like *Gigantspinosaurus sichuanensis*, and the 30-ft (9-m) long, carnivorous *Yangchuanosaurus hepingensis*. Assembled skeletons are displayed in the main hall, along with partially excavated remains in the original diggings.

Zigong Salt Museum
107 Jiefang Lu. **Tel** (0813) 220 5577. **Open** 9am–5:30pm daily. **zgshm.cn**

Shenhai Well
262 Da'an Jie. **Tel** (0813) 510 6214. **Open** 8:30am–5:30pm daily.

Dinosaur Museum
Shenhai Jing Lu, Dashanpu. **Tel** (0813) 580 1234. **Open** 8:30am–5:30pm daily. Last entry 5pm. **zdm.cn**

The main entrance of the Zigong Salt Museum

Mining Salt in Sichuan

An essential part of imperial tax since the Western Han era, salt was extracted from saltwater pools on the coasts. In Sichuan, however, mining from briny grounds was cheaper than importing heavily taxed salt from the coast. With deep drilling and the installation of bamboo pipes in the 11th century, salt production in Sichuan relied on ingenious artesian wells for centuries before European technology was able to catch up. During this time entrepreneurs opened up mines and workers flocked to the area, leading a bureaucracy alarmed at the tax losses to ban deep drilling – although the mines were soon opened again. By the 17th century, the Sichuanese had devised a method of capturing the natural gas that escapes from briny deposits to fuel their evaporating stoves.

Salt mine model, Xiqin Guildhall

Carvings of Dazu

Combining elements from Confucianism, Daoism, and Indian Tantric Buddhism, the carvings at Baoding Shan, Dazu are a unique example of the harmonious synthesis of these philosophies and religions. Though most are religious in theme, the carvings vary greatly in style. A few are naturalistic depictions of daily life, but most of them are monumental and even surreal, with fanged guardian gods and serene Buddhas at the point of enlightenment surrounded by cartoon-like details of Buddhist parables. The main colors used are reds, blues, and greens.

③ **Wheel of Transmigration** A giant, toothy demon holds a segmented disc depicting the possible states of reincarnation, from Buddha-hood down to animals and ghosts.

⑧ **1,000-armed Guanyin** In fact it has 1,007 gilded arms that seem to flicker like flames from the central figure of Guanyin, each palm holding a different symbol of the *bodhisattva*.

⑪ **Reclining Buddha** This 50-ft (15-m) long Buddha lies on his side, his stylized face making the lifelike busts of officials and donors arranged in front appear even more striking. The adjacent Nine-Dragon Spring refers to the legend of Buddha being washed at birth by dragons.

⑰ **Filial Duty** A Confucian theme of honoring parents for the sacrifices they make for their children illustrates the flexible nature of Chinese belief at this predominantly Buddhist site.

⑳ **Buddhist Hell** Buddha and *bodhisattvas* gaze down at drunken sinners, while animal-headed demons mutilate others on Knife Mountain and in Knee-Chopping Hall.

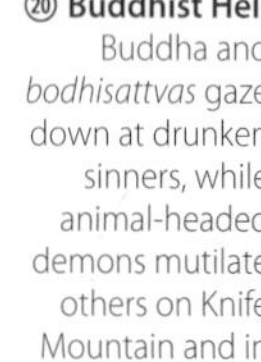

㉔ **Dao Sages** These ancient figures of wise old men appear to be representatives of Daoist philosophy.

㉘ **Stone Lion** The lion is assigned to Wenshu, the incarnation of Wisdom in Buddhist teaching. Here, this twice life-size statue guards the entrance to the Cave of Full Enlightenment.

④ **The Three Sages** Three serene figures sit in eternal contemplation of life, the infinite, and everything. The Chinese characters declare the site as Baoding Shan.

⑮ **Parental Care** This expression of the Confucian theme of the duty of parental love at a Buddhist site is an illustration of how religious philosophies could co-exist during the Tang dynasty.

㉙ **Enlightenment Buddha** The centerpiece of Baoding Shan's only true cave, this represents the reward of perfecting the self through cycles of reincarnation.

Baoding Shan

There are 31 caves in total so be sure to allow enough time to explore the site fully.

0 meters 30
0 yards 30

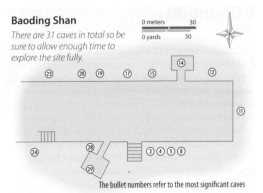

⑭ ㉓ ⑳ ⑲ ⑰ ⑮ ⑫ ⑪ ㉔ ㉘ ③④⑤⑧ ㉙

The bullet numbers refer to the most significant caves

❸ Baoding Shan, Dazu
宝顶山

9 miles (15 km) NE of Dazu. from Caiyuanba station, Chongqing (2hrs) to Dazu; minibus to caves (30 mins). **Open** 8:30am–5pm. includes Bei Shan. Fee required for video.

The hills around Dazu are riddled with caves and grottoes decorated with more than 50,000 carvings dating as far back as the Tang dynasty in the 7th century. The best collection of statuary with the finest craftsmanship and richest content can be found at Baoding Shan; the monk Zhao Zhifeng oversaw the work between 1179 and 1245. The bulk of these carvings decorate over thirty separate niches carved into the soft limestone walls of a 28-ft (8-m) high, horseshoe-shaped gully known as Dafo Wan (Big Buddha Bend) after the large sculpture of the reclining Sakyamuni Buddha.

Other carvings worth noting at Baoding Shan are the pastoral scenes of buffalo-herding in Cave 5, a whole tableau of activity that stands as a beautiful allegory of the search for enlightenment. The Cat and Mouse between Caves 3 and 4 is a light-hearted carving with a wonderfully naturalistic cat looking up at a mouse climbing a bamboo stalk. The Dazu grottoes are more secular and real to life than other grottoes – that is to say, they relate the abstract Buddhist doctrines through the lives of ordinary people. The realistic carvings include not only the statues of Buddha and *bodhisattvas*, but also monarchs, ministers, military officers, officials, monks, the rich, and even the poor.

The site has been listed as a World Cultural Heritage Site by UNESCO since 1999.

Environs: Bei Shan, just over a mile (2 km) north of Dazu, was originally a military camp whose carvings were commissioned by the general Wei Junjing in 892. The caves are somewhat dark and few sculptures stand out. The most outstanding sculpture is in Cave 136, which houses a Wheel of Life carving, Puxian the patron saint of Emei Shan *(see pp368-9)*, and the androgynous Sun and Moon Guanyin.

One of the sculptures in the Bei Shan grottoes, Dazu

❹ Chengdu
成都

The capital of Sichuan, Chengdu is a modern city with a relaxed culture, typified by its pleasant gardens and teahouses. A distinct part of city life, teahouses are found in parks and other spaces, and are often no more than a collection of rickety chairs and tables. The city's roots go as far back as the enigmatic Ba-Shu era *(see p366)*, though it first became a capital during the Three Kingdoms (AD 221), later gaining a reputation for its silk brocade and for being the first place in the world to print paper money. While Chengdu sprawls for miles, most sights are concentrated around the city centre, with one or two notable exceptions.

Business as usual at the bustling teahouse in Wenshu Yuan

Wenshu Yuan
66 Wenshu Yuan Jie. Ⓜ Wenshu Monastery. **Open** 8am–4:30pm daily.

This busy Chan Buddhist temple is dedicated to Wenshu, the incarnation of Wisdom, whose lion is depicted in sculptures and paintings in the monastery's elegantly austere halls. The small gilded pagoda to one side is said to contain the skull of Xuanzang, a famous Tang dynasty pilgrim and hero of *Journey to the West (see p35)*. After a visit, relax at the teahouse or restaurant.

Adjacent to the temple, **Wenshu Fang** is an area of antique alleys and restored period buildings, thick with snack stalls and shops.

Incense for sale at Wenshu Yuan

Yong Ling Museum
10 Yongling Lu. 48 from Xinanmen. **Open** 8:30am–5:30pm daily.

A large mound in the northwest of town was excavated in 1942 to uncover Yong Ling, the Tomb of Wang Jian, self-appointed Emperor of Sichuan, who fought his way to power in AD 907 and died in 918. The relics include a 20-ft (6-m) long stone platform that formed the base for a multi-layered wooden sarcophagus, carved with a 22-figure female orchestra. Life-size busts of warriors, sunk up to their waists in the floor, support the platform. The statue of Wang Jian enforces the impression of a modest man, though his self-indulgent son lost the empire to the Late Tang in AD 925.

Du Fu's Thatched Cottage
28 Caotang Lu. **Open** 8am–6pm daily.

The Tang dynasty's most celebrated poet, Du Fu, arrived in Chengdu during a nationwide uprising in AD 759. He spent the next four years living in poverty in a tumbledown thatched cottage on the outskirts of the city, where he wrote around 240 soulful poems contrasting the forces of nature with the turmoil of contemporary life. Admirers first founded gardens here in the 10th century, although the traditional arrangement of pools, bridges, trees, and pavilions dates from 1811. Simple whitewashed halls display antique collections of Du Fu's poems, and a museum gives an outline of his life in models and paintings.

Qingyang Gong
9 Xi Er Duan. 58 from Renmin Pk. **Open** 8am–5pm daily.

The name of this sprawling Daoist temple, meaning Green Goat Palace, refers to the obscure final words of Daoism's mythical founder, Laozi, that those who understood his teachings could find him at the green goat market. The story is commemorated at the Bagua Pavilion, where a life-sized statue of Laozi riding his buffalo is surrounded by coiled dragons and also at the Three Purities Hall, where there are two bronze statues of what are supposedly goats, although the right-hand animal has tiger paws, a unicorn's horn, a snake's tail, and other attributes of animals in the Chinese zodiac.

Renmin Park
9 Citang Jie. **Open** 6:30am–10pm daily. Ⓜ People's Park.

This is the best of Chengdu's parks, with year-round floral displays, ponds, terraces draped in wisteria, and a hall hosting weekend shows of shadow-puppetry. The Martyrs' Monument, commemorates the 1911 rail dispute that mobilized opposition to the Qing and eventually led to their demise.

Worshipers outside the Daoist Qingyang Gong

Wuhou Ci

231 Wuhou Ci Dajie. 58 from Renmin Pk. **Open** Jul–Oct: 8am–9:30pm (Nov–Jun: till 6:30pm) daily. **wuhouci.net.cn**

Meaning "Shrine to the Minister of War," Wuhou Ci commemorates Zhuge Liang (AD 181–234), a brilliant military strategist from the Three Kingdoms period. In 1672, the complex was expanded to include temple-like halls, filled with statuary of Three Kingdoms' characters, guarding **Liu Bei's Tomb**. The Three Kingdoms Hall has statues of Liu Bei, robed in gold along with his grandson, while another room has statues of Zhuge Liang. The last hall is used for Sichuan theater.

East of Wuhou Ci, **Jin Li** alley has colorful Song-style houses, shops and stalls, and is a good place to sample Chengdu's famous street food.

Sichuan Museum

251 Hanhua Nan Lu. 58 from Renmin Pk. **Tel** (028) 6552 1555. **Open** 9am–5pm Tue–Sun. **scmuseum.cn**

A trove of ethnographic and cultural artifacts on three levels, this museum's lower floor is full of animated Han dynasty pottery models of musicians, court figures, acrobats, and warriors; while the upper two stories focus on bronze sculptures and Tibetan Buddhist artifacts. A wing at the rear features silk brocade.

Across the road, **Songxian Qiao Curio Market** is a wonderful place to browse among porcelain, wooden screens, and Cultural Revolution momentos.

Jinsha Museum

227 Qingyang Dadao. 901 tourist bus. **Open** daily. **jinshasitemuseum.com**

This museum occupies the site of a previously undocumented Shang dynasty settlement, which was discovered during building work in 2000. Thousands of artifacts, animal bones, graves, and house foundations indicate that Jinsha was a major center for the later Ba-Shu culture. The glass-sided **Exhibit Hall** is built over the excavations, exposing sacrificial pits where valuables were ceremonially buried.

VISITORS' CHECKLIST

Practical Information

200 miles (330 km) NW of Chongqing. 7,400,000. Renmin Nan Lu 4 Duan.

Transport

Shuangliu Airport. North Train Station, South train station. Chandianzi bus station, CAAC (buses to airport), Xinnanmen Bus Station, Zhaojuesi bus station.

A striking moon gate at Wuhou Ci

Chengdu City Center

① Wenshu Yuan
② Yong Ling Museum
③ Du Fu's Thatched Cottage
④ Qingyang Gong
⑤ Renmin Park
⑥ Wuhou Ci
⑦ Sichuan Museum

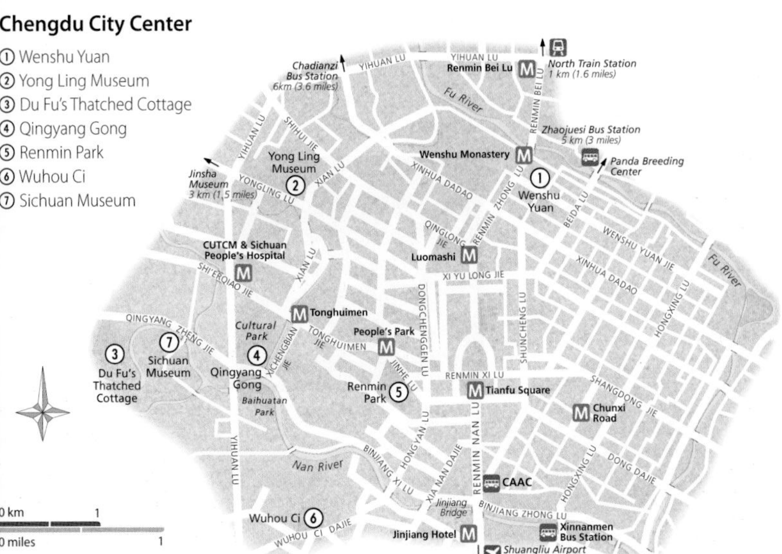

Key to Symbols *see back flap*

A bizarre yet exquisitely crafted Sanxingdui mask

❺ Panda Breeding Center
大熊猫繁殖基地

9 miles (15 km) NE of Chengdu. 87, 198, or Tourist Bus 902. **Open** 7:30am–6pm daily. **W** **panda.org.cn**

This research base set up in 1987 has bred and raised over 100 giant panda cubs, with well over the usual captive survival rate. While so far this has been for the benefit of zoos, the center's main aim is to start returning pandas to the wild. One of the best places to see pandas in China, it houses around 30 red and over 50 giant pandas. Mostly inactive, they can be seen chewing piles of arrow bamboo or sleeping.

❻ Baoguang Si
宝光寺

14 miles (24 km) NE of Chengdu. or taxi. **Open** 8am–5pm daily.

A place of worship since the Han dynasty, Baoguang Si owes its current name and reputation to the Tang Emperor Xizong, who took refuge here in AD 881 during a rebellion. He called the temple Baoguang, or Shining Treasure, after he saw a light underneath a wooden pagoda in the temple, which was supposedly emanating from buried holy relics. The pagoda, which he ordered to be rebuilt in stone, still stands as the 13-story, 98-ft (30-m) high **Sheli Ta**, just inside the entrance. Its top, however, broke off during an earthquake.

The temple has well-tended gardens planted with ginkgos, besides a dozen or more halls filled with holy relics, including a room dedicated to the Gelugpa sect of Tibetan lamaism, and a stone stele carved with Buddha images from AD 540. Baoguang Si's biggest draw is its Qing-era **Luohan Hall**, where 518 brightly painted, life-size sculptures of Buddhist saints are joined by 59 Buddhas and Bodhidarma – the Indian founder of Zen Buddhism – along with a huge phoenix statue. Among the statues are the Emperors Kangxi and Qianlong, with their distinctive beards, boots, and capes. Also within the compound is a little vegetarian restaurant.

❼ Sanxingdui Museum
三星堆博物馆

30 miles (50 km) N of Chengdu in Guanghan. 6 from Guanghan. **Tel** (0838) 565 1526. **Open** 8:30am–6pm daily (last adm 5pm). **W** **sxd.cn**

In the 1980s, archeologists began excavating at Sanxingdui, where farmers had been finding ancient pieces since 1929. They unexpectedly uncovered traces of an ancient city, over 3,000 years old, tentatively believed to have been the capital of the Ba-Shu culture. Numerous sacrificial pits were found containing an extraordinary trove of bronze, gold, and jade artifacts. Key pieces in the museum include a 7-ft (2-m) high bronze figure with huge, coiled hands, a giant "spirit tree" hung with mystical animals, and several leering, 3-ft (1-m) wide masks whose eyes protrude on stalks. Also on display are smaller, finely detailed pieces, along with accounts of the excavations. Highly individual in style, though evoking the contemporary Shang bronzes of eastern China, the Sanxingdui artifacts reveal a very high degree of craftsmanship. The finds perhaps challenge the popular theory that China evolved from a single culture living by the Yellow River.

Sichuan Opera

Elaborately costumed actors at an opera performance

Sung in the Sichuanese dialect, this 300-year-old tradition lacks the formality of Beijing Opera, but instead is filled with wit and dynamism, its high-pitched singing accompanied by percussion and wind instruments. Acrobatics are a major part of the performance. *Bianlian*, the Sichuanese trick of face-changing, allows each actor to portray many characters; with a swift move of the hand, makeup is added, or a layer of mask removed. Once widely performed in small, casual theaters and teahouses, Sichuan Opera is sadly in decline as a form of popular entertainment. In Chengdu, it is still possible to enjoy tourist-oriented shows. Tickets are available at Jinjiang Theater on Huaxing Zheng Jie and Jin Li, near Wuhou Ci. Many tour operators run excursions to theaters, giving an explanation of the plot and a fascinating glimpse backstage.

For hotels and restaurants in this region see p562 and pp581–2

Giant Pandas

The famously rare giant panda occurs only in China, and, due to its lack of close genetic relatives, is considered a "living fossil." The wild panda population of around 1,600 is increasing, though with perhaps only another 340 in zoos worldwide, they remain seriously endangered. There is added concern following the 2008 Sichuan earthquake, which seriously affected the panda population and habitat. Pandas feed primarily on bamboo. They have developed large molars for grinding up the stalks, but are not well adapted to digesting them and so spend almost all their waking hours eating. Bamboo flowers and dies off simultaneously over huge areas, periodically depriving giant pandas of their food source. In the past, they could travel to other regions to find more bamboo to eat, but now their habitat has been carved up by development. Some 49 reserves are dedicated to panda preservation in China, including the Wanglang reserve in north Sichuan *(see p375)*.

Pandas eat between 35 and 65 lbs (15 and 30 kg) of bamboo a day, despite having a carnivore's digestive tract. They only digest 20 percent of the nutrients, so spend the rest of the day asleep, conserving energy.

The panda's paw is adapted to its special diet. The wrist is modified into a sort of opposable "thumb" that helps it to grasp delicate bamboo stems.

Pandas are not prolific breeders, even in the best-equipped zoos, as they only have a brief breeding window (for only a few days in spring) and they are extremely choosy about whom they mate with.

Pandas in the wild are occasionally seen in family groups, but mostly they live a solitary existence for much of their 25 years in a clearly defined territory marked out by scent. One theory for their striking coloration is that it helps them recognize each other in the forests.

Breeding programs in Sichuan saw 9 births in 2014, with a 100 percent survival rate. Artificial insemination is usually used. Incubators reduce the high infant mortality found in the wild.

A panda baby weighs just 3½ oz (100 g) at birth – compared to the adult's 440 lb (200 kg). The cub is carried by the mother for 90 days and stays on with her for up to three years.

❽ Emei Shan

峨眉山

Rising to 10,167 ft (3,099 m), Emei Shan has been considered holy by both Daoists and Buddhists since the Eastern Han dynasty. Many of the temples nestled on the mountain's lush slopes are dedicated to the Bodhisattva of Universal Benevolence, Puxian, who is said to have ascended the mountain during the 6th century atop a six-tusked elephant. Emei Shan is also a storehouse of botanic diversity, with over 3,200 plant species found on the mountain – 10 percent of China's total. Many can be seen in monastery gardens, including the white-petaled handkerchief tree; the ginkgo, long thought to be extinct in the wild; and the straight-trunked *nanmu*, a favored wood for temple pillars. The most visible of Emei's animals are the aggressive monkeys, who pester hikers for handouts – keep food packed away.

★ The Summit
Emei's three main peaks are the crests of an undulating ridge, with a sheer drop of over 3,000 ft (1,000 m) on the front face.

Hikers
Hawkers hoist sedan chairs for those who have had enough of walking. To cut down some of the trekking, take a bus from Baoguo to the cable car leading to Wannian Si, or, easiest of all, to the cable car going all the way to the summit at Jieyin Dian.

Baoguo Si
One of the most important temples on Emei, Baoguo Si contains a massive bronze bell. Cast during the Ming dynasty, it is rung with a large swinging tree trunk and is said to be audible for 10 miles (16 km).

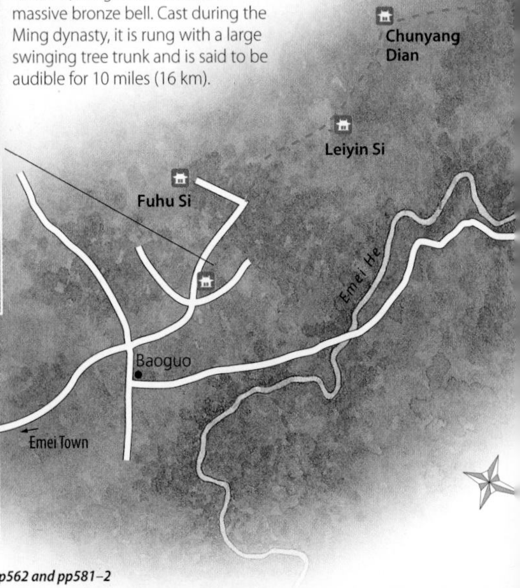

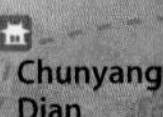

Fuhu Si

Emei He

Baoguo

Emei Town

KEY

① **Xixiang Chi** (Elephant Bathing Pool) is at the spot where Puxian is said to have stopped to wash his elephant.

For hotels and restaurants in this region see p562 and pp581–2

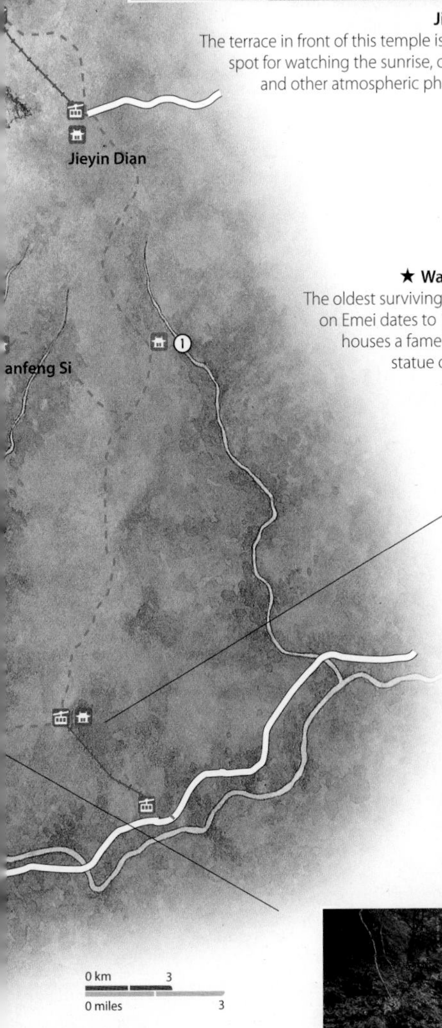

ing

fo Ding
) ft

Jin Ding
10,095 ft

Jin Ding Si
The terrace in front of this temple is a favorite spot for watching the sunrise, cloud seas, and other atmospheric phenomena.

Jieyin Dian

anfeng Si

VISITORS' CHECKLIST

Practical Information
96 miles (160 km) SW of Chengdu. near Baoguo Si, (0833) 552 0444. **Open** daily.

Transportation
to Emei town. from Chengdu Xin Nan Men bus station or Le Shan to Emei town or Baoguo; Emei town to Baoguo (20 min).

Key

- Path
- Road

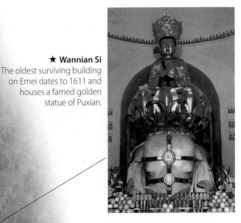

★ Wannian Si
The oldest surviving building on Emei dates to 1611 and houses a famed golden statue of Puxian.

Exploring Emei Shan

It takes about three days to climb and descend Emei Shan; basic accommodations and food are available at numerous temples. Pack rain gear and wear stout footwear as the flagstone paths can be slippery, particularly from October to April when hawkers sell straw soles and metal crampons to attach to boots. Warm clothing is essential at the summit year round.

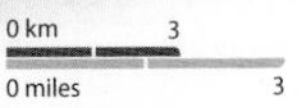

★ Qingyin Ge
Reached over a pair of arched bridges, the Pure Music Pavilion is set in lowland forest at the junction of two streams. The nearby temple is the most romantic place to spend a night on Emei Shan.

For additional map symbols *see back flap*

⑨ Dafo, Leshan
乐山大佛

The enormous 230-ft (71-m) high Dafo (Great Buddha) is carved into the red sandstone face of Lingyun Hill overlooking the treacherous confluence of the Min, Dadu, and Qingyi Rivers below. In AD 713 a monk, Haitong, decided to safeguard passing boats by creating a protective icon in the cliffs – though he was also practical enough to realize that the resultant rubble would fill in the shoals. By the time Dafo was completed, other temples had been built around it and on the adjacent Wuyou Hill. In 1996 the Buddha was included by UNESCO on the list of World Heritage Sites.

Jiazhou Huayuan
This museum, located in a pretty temple, gives a full account of Dafo's history and construction, with interesting models.

★ Dafo (Great Buddha)
Up close, the remains of a drainage system can be seen. The statue must be restored every decade to survive plant invasion and pollution.

KEY

① **Nine Turns Staircase** is a steep, narrow set of steps down to the toes.

② **Ancient shrines and temples close by**

③ **Wuyou Hill** was cut off from Lingyun Hill around 250 BC to reduce the river's currents. Wuyou's Buddhist temple was founded in AD 742.

④ **Guardian figures flank the Buddha**

★ Buddha's Feet
At his huge 26-ft (8-m) feet you can really appreciate one of the world's biggest Buddhas. His other statistics are equally impressive: each ear droops 23 ft (7 m), his shoulders span 92 ft (28 m), while his nose measures 18 ft (5.6m).

Haitong, Sculptor and Monk

When Haitong's idea was accepted, funds were raised by public subscription and regional government contributions from the salt revenue (*see p361*). The monk lived in a cave behind Dafo's head and when a local official threatened to blind Haitong unless he could take a cut of the funds, the monk gouged his own eyes out to prove his sincerity. However, the project was only completed in AD 803 after his death, and after Wei Gao, the regional governor, donated his own salary to finish off the legs and feet.

Haitong, a pious monk devoted to his project

VISITORS' CHECKLIST

Practical Information
Leshan, 96 miles (154 km) SW of Chengdu. **Tel** (0833) 230 2296.
Open May–Sep: 7:30am–7:30pm; Oct–Apr: 8am–6pm.

Transportation
from Chengdu Xinnanmen bus station to Leshan, then bus 3 to Dafo. from Leshan to Wuyou Si, then walk to Dafo.

Mahao Cave Tombs
Dating from the Eastern Han dynasty (AD 25–220), these grottoes were built to house the remains of local nobles, with carved scenes of cavalry and some early Buddha figures.

★ Haoshang Bridge
This elegant, part-covered structure is built in an "antique" style and links the Great Buddha with outlying temples on the adjacent hills.

Dafo or Great Buddha, best seen from a river boat, hired from Leshan

Qingcheng Shan's ornate front gateway, with sharply upturned eaves

⑩ Huanglongxi
黄龙溪

31 miles (50 km) SW of Chengdu. from Chengdu Xinnanmen bus station.

Consisting of just seven narrow lanes on a quiet riverbank surrounded by fields, the delightfully dated village of Huanglongxi served as one of the sets in the martial-arts romance *Crouching Tiger, Hidden Dragon*. Most of its timber-framed, stone buildings date from the Qing dynasty. Of its three temples, **Gulong Si** is the largest, with a few slightly shabby halls and a low entrance guarded by two stone lions, above which is a theater stage used during temple fairs. At the other end of the village, **Nanwu Chaoxi Si** is a tiny nunnery with a painted stone carving of the dragon spirit Nanwu in human form, with red hair and a mustache. **Zhenjiang Si** is mostly closed to the public, but does have a pleasant, relaxed riverfront teahouse.

⑪ Qingcheng Shan
青城山

43 miles (70 km) NW of Chengdu. from Chengdu. to Dujiangyan then taxi. **Tel** (028) 8728 8159. **Open** 8am–6pm daily.

As its name "Green Wall Mountain" suggests, this renowned Daoist retreat is beautifully forested. Its two separate sections are dotted with Daoist temples linked by stone paths, ideal for rambling. The front face is reached from the main entrance in town, while the wilder rear face, with steeper gradients and narrower paths, lies 9 miles (15 km) farther west. **Jianfu Gong**, outside the entrance, is the best-preserved shrine. The main temple on the mountain's front face lies halfway up at **Tianshi Dong**. Ming-dynasty panels decorate its main hall, the complex surrounding a cave where the Han dynasty Daoist master Zhang Ling once taught. Situated on the 4,134-ft (1,260-m) summit, 2 hours on foot and accessible by cable car, **Shangqing Gong** was first built in the 4th century AD and houses a tearoom. From here, it is a short climb to the **Laojun Ge**. On the lower slopes of the peak's rear face is the huge **Tai'an Temple**.

⑫ Dujiangyan
都江堰

37 miles (60 km) NW of Chengdu. from Chengdu. from Chadianzi bus station, Chengdu. **Tel** (028) 8728 3890. **Open** 8am–6pm daily. for Irrigation Scheme Area.

The sprawling town of Dujiangyan is primarily known for the Dujiangyan Irrigation Scheme, built in 256 BC by the Sichuanese governor Li Bing. He organized the building of an artificial island to tame and divide the flood-prone Min Jiang into two channels that could be regulated and tapped to provide a steady flow for crop irrigation. Li Bing's project is still fully functional and was made a UNESCO World Heritage Site in 2000, but it was affected by the construction of Zipingpu Dam, 5 miles (9 km) north. During the 2008 Sichuan earthquake, the dam cracked causing extensive damage to the town. Some

A ferry on the scenic Yuecheng Hu (Moon Wall Lake) at Qingcheng Shan

◀ Crowds viewing Leshan's Dafo (Great Buddha) from various vantage points

Songpan's east gate and impressive stone wall

scientists have suggested that building work at the dam may have triggered the earthquake. After collapsing, **Erwang Miao** (Two Kings Temple) was rebuilt according to the original plans.

⓭ Wanglang Nature Reserve
王朗自然保护区

210 miles (350 km) N of Chengdu. Access via hired minibus from Pingwu. **Tel** (0816) 882 5312. **Open** daily. **slack.net/~rd/wanglang/home.htm**

In the heart of the Min Shan Mountains, this high-altitude nature reserve is remote and difficult to access, but there is a good chance of seeing rare animals, including takin, musk deer, and serow, along with abundant birdlife. A few **pandas** inhabit the reserve, but you are highly unlikely to encounter these elusive animals since they generally stay hidden deep inside Wanglang's impenetrable bamboo thickets.

From the research base and accommodation center (where rooms must be booked in advance), the 7-mile (12-km) long **Baisha Gou** road passes through old-growth pine forest and boggy moorlands to a scree-strewn alpine gully dotted with rhododendron thickets and splashes of hardy flowers. Alternatively, **Baixiong Gou** is 6 miles (9 km) from camp via high ridges where goat-like serow and takin are sometimes seen. At the end of the road, there are boardwalks through dense stands of bamboo and juniper.

⓮ Songpan
松潘

190 miles (305 km) N of Chengdu. from Chadianzi bus station, Chengdu.

Founded as a Ming-dynasty garrison post to guard a 8,200-ft (2,500-m) mountain pass, Songpan is an administrative center and busy marketplace for nearby Tibetan, Qiang, and Hui communities. It derives its ancient character from the surviving original cross-shaped street plan with high stone walls and its north, south, and east gates. Walled-in courtyards in front of the south gate were once the "customs area" for searching caravans coming into town. The Min Jiang, bisecting Songpan's center, is crossed by the covered **Gusong Qiao**, the Ancient Pine Bridge whose two-tiered roof is decorated with carved animals. Songpan's two large mosques, one in the center of town and the other along the river outside the north gate, resemble standard Chinese temples except in their use of green and yellow paint and the Arabic script over their doors. Shops sell beaten copper pots, turquoise jewelry, sheepskin coats, yak butter, and wind-dried yak meat. Just outside the north gate, two tour companies organize overnight guided horse treks to nearby villages. Sleeping arrangements are out in the open air or in tents and food is basic. Trekkers should have the itinerary and fees agreed, in writing, before setting off to avoid argument.

Lantern at the east gate, Songpan

⓯ Huanglong
黄龙

40 miles (65 km) NE of Songpan. from Chengdu or Songpan. Huanglong Temple Fair (Jul/Aug).

Huanglong is a 2½-mile (4-km) long valley, 9,845 ft (3,000 m) above sea level in the foothills of the snow-capped Min Shan range. Deposited minerals from the river descending the valley have created 12 terraced pools and calcified cascades, whose yellow rocks give Huanglong (Yellow Dragon) its name. Of the four nearly ruined temples, the **Huanglong Temple**, at the valley's upper end, has a statue of Huanglong's patron saint, and hosts an annual temple fair featuring a horse race.

Calcified terraces in Huanglong

⓰ Jiuzhaigou Tour

九寨沟

One of China's most scenic reserves and a UNESCO World Heritage Site, Jiuzhaigou (Nine Stockades Gully) covers 280 sq miles (720 sq km) of mountain valleys dotted with Tibetan villages. Beneath the snow-capped mountains, the valley floors are strung with extraordinarily blue lakes, said to be the broken slivers of the Tibetan goddess Semo's mirror. Broad waterfalls, heavily encrusted with lime deposits, connect many of the lakes. Aside from herds of yaks, birds are the most evident wildlife, including rare mandarin ducks. A panda sighting is unlikely.

Tips for Walkers

Getting around: Buses are included in admission. Hiking follows roads and boardwalks. Nuorilang is a convenient base.
When to go: Avoid summer weekends. Sep–Oct has fall colors and fewer crowds. Winters are well below freezing with deep snow.

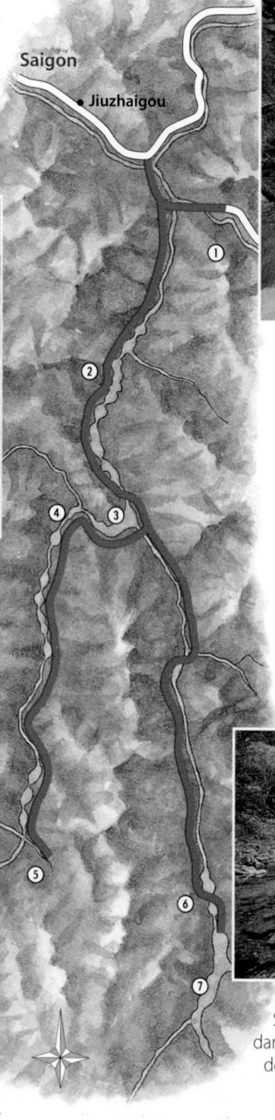

① Zharu Temple
This small temple, its interior adorned with bright murals, is home to a growing population of Tibetan lamas.

Saigon

Jiuzhaigou

③ Nuorilang Falls
Jiuzhaigou's most renowned cataract is best seen in full flood in late spring, when the water foams wildly in multiple ribbons over its stony outcrops.

② Shuzheng Zhai
A Tibetan stockaded village, replete with Buddhist shrines and water-powered mills, sits halfway along a string of deep blue pools and reed beds.

④ Pearl-Beach Falls
Water tumbles down a calcified slope, spraying pearl-like drops on its rocky ridges.

⑤ Primeval Forest
An atmospheric coniferous forest at the far end of the reserve is far from crowds.

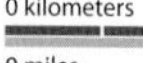

0 kilometers 4

0 miles 4

Key

Tour route

Other road

⑥ Five-Colored Pool
Surrounded by a fringe of ferns and dark woods, this pool's kingfisher-blue depths are enhanced by green algae in the shallows, and milky-white swirls that seep in after rain.

⑦ Long Lake
This pool is not only the largest, but also the highest in the park, sitting at 10,170 ft (3,100 m).

The debris-laden Hailuogou Glacier descending the southeastern slopes of Gongga Shan

17 Luding
泸定

168 miles (270 km) W of Chengdu. from Chandianzi bus station, Chengdu

The small market town of Luding is surrounded by mountains above the banks of Dadu Jiang. The 328-ft (100-m) **Luding Chain Bridge** over the Dadu, comprising 13 iron chains spanned by wooden planks, was built in 1705 to improve transportation across the region. The Luding Chain Bridge became a national icon in May 1935 due to an incident during the Long March *(see p262)*. The Nationalist forces had removed the bridge's planks to trap the Red Army on the south side of the river, but "22 Heroes" clambered along the chains and managed to capture a Nationalist camp on the opposite side. The bridge is flanked on either side by gateways, while a museum on the river's far side exhibits contemporary photos.

The historic 18th-century Luding Chain Bridge

18 Moxi Xiang & Hailuogou Glacier
磨西和海螺沟

33 miles (53 km) S of Luding. from Chandianzi bus station, Chengdu. Treks organized by hotels.

The tiny village of **Moxi Xiang**, with its large Qiang population, is a staging post for trips up the adjacent Hailuogou (Conch Valley) to the **Hailuogou Glacier**, whose tongue, at 12,205 ft (3,720 m), makes it the lowest and most accessible glacier in Asia. Moxi's wooden church sheltered the Red Army in 1935, before they attempted crossing the passes over Daxue Shan – Great Snow Mountain *(see p262)*. The glacier descends the southeastern side of Sichuan's highest peak, the 24,790-ft (7,556-m) Gongga Shan. A road runs through the pine forests from Moxi to the trailhead, from where it is a 2-mile (3½-km) walk or a cable car ride. Look beyond its debris-blackened snout to the crevassed slopes above, to catch a glimpse of Gongga Shan beyond.

Moxi's early 20th-century church

19 Kangding
康定

31 miles (50 km) W of Luding. from Chandianzi bus station, Chengdu.

Lying between China and Tibet, Kangding is a bustling trading depot situated in a valley on the Zheduo River. During the Qing era, the town developed on the tea trade between Tibet and China and was the place where porters would exchange bricks of tea for Tibetan goods such as wool and copperware. Ethnically, the region is inhabited largely by the Khampa, a Tibetan people whose heavy turquoise jewelry, forward manners, and habit of carrying knives match their reputation for toughness. The central **Anjue Lamasery** is a focus for the Khampa community. The town is also home to Qiang, Hui, and Han Chinese people. To the southeast, Paoma Shan (Horse Race Mountain) is the venue for the annual horse-racing, which takes place in the 4th month of the Chinese lunar calendar, and is where the Khampa demonstrate their equestrian skills. Heading west from Kangding, it is 311 miles (500 km) to the fringes of Tibet, with a long but worthwhile detour taking in Dege and its Scripture Printing Lamasery.

YUNNAN

Located along China's southwest frontier, Yunnan offers an unmatched diversity of landscapes, climate, and people. The Tibetan highland frames its northwestern fringes; tropical rainforests and volcanic plains lie to its south. In the center are plains and hills, crisscrossed by some of Asia's great rivers – the Yangzi, Salween, and Mekong.

The seat of the pastoral Dian Kingdom founded in the 3rd century BC, Yunnan was for centuries an isolated frontier region that resisted Han influences and upheld local identities. Even today, the province is home to a third of China's ethnic minorities and has much in common with neighboring Myanmar, Laos, and Vietnam. The province's capital, Kunming, is one of the more relaxed cities in China; nearby are the astonishing rock formations of the Stone Forest (Shi Lin). Several minority villages dot the tropical forests of Xishuangbanna, while in the north, Dali is home to the indigenous Bai people. Farther north is the UNESCO World Heritage Site of Lijiang, capital of the Naxi Kingdom, with cobbled streets and distinctive architecture. Tiger Leaping Gorge, an impressive, steep-sided ravine, offers superb, accessible two-day hikes.

Kunming is well connected to the rest of China, but the bulk of the province has only limited train services. Bus travel is necessary to access most of Yunnan.

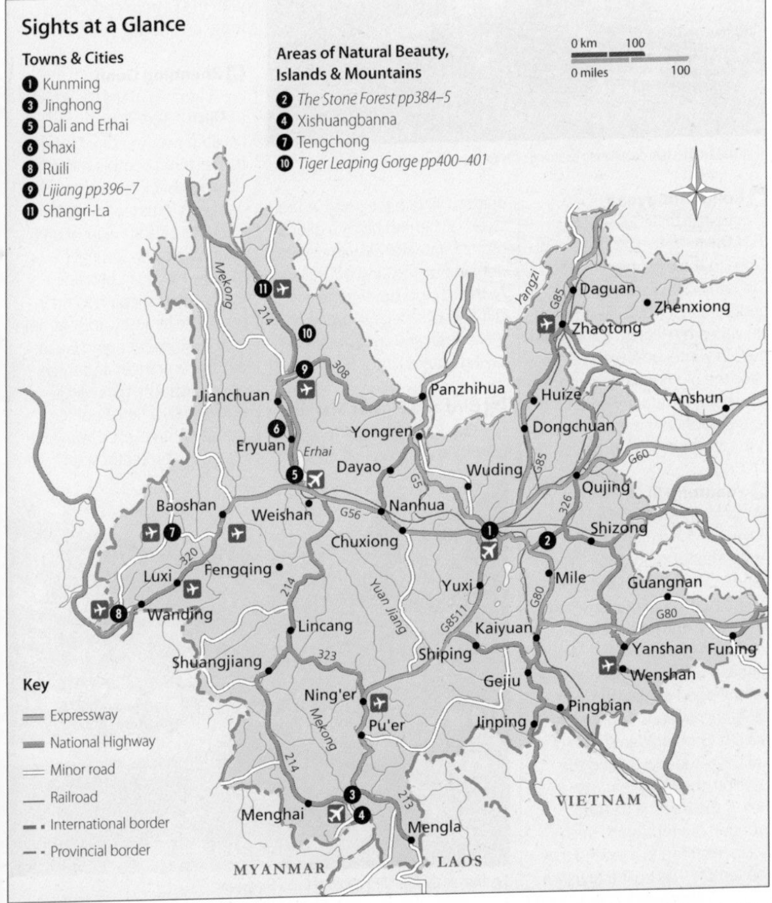

The striking limestone pillars of the Stone Forest

For additional map symbols *see back flap*

❶ Kunming

昆明

The capital of Yunnan province, Kunming rests at 6,500 ft (2,000 m) above sea level. Its clement weather and floral wealth have earned it the nickname "City of Eternal Spring." An ancient city that first came to prominence as part of the Nanzhao Kingdom *(see p394)*, Kunming had grown into a thriving city with a cosmopolitan character by the 13th century. Kunming is fast becoming indistinguishable from the redeveloped metropolises found throughout the country, but it is still considered one of China's more laid-back cities, with lakeside vistas just to the south.

High-rise architecture dominating Kunming's city center

Cuihu Gongyuan

67 Cuihu Nan Lu. **Tel** (0871) 6531 8808. **Open** dawn–10pm daily.

Close to the city's historic heart, this park has pavilions and bridges, and its lotus-filled ponds are visited by migrant red-beaked gulls in winter. Just west of the park, the old **French Legation** now holds temporary exhibitions. To the northwest is the university district, with its student cafés.

Yuantong Si

30 Yuantong Jie. **Tel** (0871) 6519 3762. **Open** 9am–5:30pm daily.

At the foot of Yuantong Hill lies Yunnan's largest Buddhist complex, a popular pilgrimage spot. Renovated and rebuilt many times, it has an imposing Ming gateway, while a bridge over the central pond crosses through a Qing-era pavilion. Enshrined here is a 6-ft (3-m) golden statue of Maitreya Buddha. Behind the pavilion, the Ming-dynasty Great Hall of the Buddha has two wooden dragons on its main pillars, referring to a legend that the temple was built to pacify a dragon living in the pond. A Thai-style hall behind holds a gilded bronze statue of Sakyamuni, donated by the King of Thailand. At the back of the temple is a cliff cut with steps allowing a view of religious poems and sayings carved into the rock.

Bird and Flower Market

The many stalls lining the crammed alleyways off Jingxing Jie sell an eclectic variety of goods. In both covered and outdoor sections of the market exotic houseplants and colorful songbirds are on sale alongside *tai ji quan* swords, jewelry, old coins, bamboo pipes, and Cultural Revolution mementos.

Xi Si Ta

Dong Si Jie. **Open** 7am–8pm.

The 13-storied Tang-era Xi Si Ta (Western Pagoda) has statues in the niches of each story. Close by, Dong Si Ta (Eastern Pagoda) is a more attractive replica standing in a garden. Although visitors cannot enter the temples associated with both pagodas, a small fee permits entry into Xi Si Ta's courtyard, where people come to relax on sunny afternoons. Both pagodas are surrounded by small parks, with the Eastern park offering more greenery.

Zhenqing Guan

Cnr of Tuodong Lu and Chuncheng Lu. **Open** 8:30am–5pm.

Located near the City Museum, this restored complex of stone courtyards and smartly painted halls was founded in 1419 to honor the Daoist warrior deity Zhen Wu. Today it is full of friendly monks in brocade robes, their hair pinned up in buns. The largest Daoist temple in Kunming, Zhenqing Guan has five entrances and three courtyards. The gateway is guarded by a fierce golden statue of three-eyed Wan Ling Guan, the protector spirit,

Pavilions on the fish-filled waters of Cuihu Gongyuan

wearing a severed demon's head as a belt buckle and brandishing an iron pagoda to scare off evil. Inside, the main hall features an intricately bracketed domed ceiling and murals of the Taoist pantheon, while the adjacent Dulei mansion is dominated by a statue of the Thunder God and a model of the globe wrapped in animals of the zodiac. The complex sometimes hosts musicians, including a full traditional Chinese orchestra.

City Museum

93 Tuodong Lu. **Tel** (0871) 6315 3256. **Open** 9:30am–4:30pm daily.

Though less interesting than the Provincial Museum, this museum houses a few relevant artifacts. The most striking is the Song-dynasty **Dali Sutra Pillar**, a 20-ft (7-m) sculpture in pink sandstone, commissioned by the Dali King Yuan Douguang in honor of General Gao Ming. Seven tiers swarm with lively images of guardian gods and captive demons, and at the top is a ring of Buddhas holding up the universe. On the upper floors are fascinating displays on the "Flying Tigers" – a group of American volunteers who flew for the Chinese Air Force during World War II – and the Tea Horse Road, a trade route that for centuries transported fragrant Yunnanese tea from the subtropics to Tibet.

Provincial Museum

6393 Guangfu Lu. **Tel** (0871) 6728 6223. **Open** 9am–5pm Tue–Sun. **ynmuseum.org**

This museum is housed in a purpose-built five-story building south of the center. On the first floor are splendid bronze drums *(see p429)* excavated from tombs on the shore of Lake Dian and dating back more than 2,000 years to the Warring States and Western Han periods. The drums are embellished with relief dioramas, largely showing typical scenes of rural life, although there are also wrestling scenes, a dramatic image of an ox battling a tiger, and a strange picture of a bamboo house transformed into a coffin. The most ornate of the drums were used to store cowry shells, then a form of currency. The others served as musical instruments or elements in sacrificial rites. Even today, bronze drums play an important role at weddings, festivals, and funerals for some of Yunnan's minority groups. Other halls are arranged chronologically, starting with dinosaur skeletons. The ground floor holds temporary exhibitions.

The pink sandstone Dali Sutra Pillar

VISITORS' CHECKLIST

Practical Information

208 miles (335 km) SE of Dali. 6,500,000. 1118 Huancheng Nan Lu, (0871) 6356 6701. **chinakunming.travel**

Transportation

Kunming Changshui airport. Kunming train station, North train station. Western, South, and East bus stations.

Kunming City Center

① Cuihu Gongyuan
② Yuantong Si
③ Bird and Flower Market
④ Xi Si Ta
⑤ Zhenqing Guan
⑥ City Museum

Key to Symbols *see back flap*

The double-eaved Jin Dian, made entirely of bronze

Jin Dian

7 miles (12 km) NE of Kunming. 71 from Kunming's North train station. **Open** 7:30am–6pm daily.

Well-kept flower gardens and leafy pine woods are reason enough to visit this secluded spot in the city's northeastern suburbs. However, the park's ostensible focus is the Jin Dian (Golden Temple) located on top of its central hill. Originally built in 1602 during the Ming dynasty, and rebuilt in 1671 as the summer residence of the Ming rebel general Wu Sangui, this unusual two-tiered shrine is made entirely of bronze. Its overall construction imitates the more conventional wooden temples, with screens, columns, and flying eaves. Just over 20-ft (6-m) high and weighing nearly 300 tons (272,155 kg), the temple sits atop a base of Dali marble and is almost completely black with the patina of age. In the courtyard stand ancient camellia trees, one of which is 600 years old. The main hall, with bronze lattices, beams, and statues, houses two magical swords used by Daoist warriors. Fragrant with camellias, the gardens here serve as popular picnic spots. Visitors can either take a bus or hire a bike to reach the base of the hill, from where it's an easy hike up to the temple.

Situated on the hill behind Jin Dian is another Daoist shrine with a tower that houses a 14-ton (12,700-kg) bronze bell. Dating to 1423, it was retrieved from Kunming's demolished southern gates.

Qiongzhu Si

7 miles (12 km) NW of Kunming. C61 from Kunming's Western bus station. **Open** 8:30am–6pm daily.

With its origins in the Tang-era, Qiongzhu Si (Bamboo Temple) has burned down and been rebuilt several times. Today, this elegant Buddhist structure, with fine black-and-red woodwork, stands on Yuan-dynasty foundations. Besides housing three impressive Buddha statues, the temple is famous for its dazzling array of life-size clay sculptures, created over ten years toward the end of the 19th century by a supremely talented Sichuan sculptor, Li Guangxiu. The sculptor and his five assistants were commissioned to produce clay figures of the 500 *arhat* or *luo- han* (those freed from the cycle of birth and death) for the main building. Today, these sculptures are the highlight of the temple, though at that time they were regarded as so distressing and absurd that Li Guangxiu never worked again. Along one wall a set of snarling, outlandish figures – one with arms longer than his body, another with eyebrows to his knees – ride foaming waves swarming with sea creatures. Elsewhere, three shelves of figures depict Buddhist virtues and faults. Many aspects of human life and folly are portrayed in these beautiful characters: reaching for the moon; playing with a pet monster; yawning, debating, and eating a peach. While Li Guangxiu's skill at rendering facial expressions and gestures makes these figures unique, many are thought to be caricatures of his contemporaries, probably the reason they were so disliked at the time.

Also worth a glance is a 14th-century stone tablet, housed in the main hall. It records imperial China's dealings with Yunnan in Chinese and Mongolian scripts. A pleasant teahouse lies within the temple grounds.

An aerial view of the extensive Qiongzhu Si (Bamboo Temple)

Haigeng Park viewed against the expanse of Lake Dian

Lake Dian & the Western Hills

from Kunming. **Tel** (0871) 6842 7475. **Open** 8:30am–5pm daily. Haigeng Park:

The 25-mile (40-km) long Lake Dian (Dian Chi), just south of Kunming, is surrounded by fertile farmland. Plying the waters of the elongated lake are *fanchuan*, traditional junks with bamboo masts and square canvas sails, once used for fishing. **Daguan Pavilion** on the north shore makes a pleasant spot for a stroll, while a few miles south is **Haigeng Park**, with green willows and eucalyptuses, offering good views of the lake.

The most rewarding way to see the lake is from the Western Hills (Xi Shan), about 10 miles (16 km) southwest of Kunming. The undulating contours of the "Sleeping Beauty Hills" are said to resemble a reclining woman with tresses flowing into the lake. The path leading to the summit holds a treasury of temples. Visitors can either climb up or take a minibus. The first temple, a mile (2 km) from the entrance, is **Huating Si**. Designed originally as a country retreat for Gao Zhishen, who ruled Kunming in the 11th century, it has been rebuilt several times. The attractive gardens, dotted with stupas and ponds, contain interesting figures, including the four fierce-looking Guardians of the Directions, the gilded, blue-haired Buddhas, and a set of 500 *arhat*.

From Huating Si, a steep, winding road leads deep into the forest for 1 mile (2 km) to **Taihua Si**, established by Xuan Jian, a wandering Chan (Zen) Buddhist monk in 1306, and dedicated to Guanyin, the Goddess of Compassion. It is well known for its garden of camellias and magnolias, and excellent views. A cable car runs directly from here to the Dragon Gate ticket office, but it is also possible to walk up. The path leads past **Sanqing Si**, a complex of temples, halls, and pavilions, which formerly served as a summer palace for a 14th-century Mongolian prince.

A picturesque pavilion with a pond and garden, Taihua Si

Just half a mile away is the **Dragon Gate Grotto**, a set of chambers, steps, and tunnels excavated from the mountain. The mammoth construction task, which involved swinging from ropes and hacking at the rock with chisels, was begun by the late 18th-century monk Wu Laiqing, and took 70 years to complete. Worth exploring along the way are niches with several fantastic statues, including those of Guanyin and the Gods of Study and Virtue. A cable car runs from near Sanqing Si to the summit at **Grand Dragon Gate**, a balcony perched at 8,200 ft (2,500 m), from where there are fine views over Lake Dian.

The Burma Road

For 1,500 years, the southern Silk Route ran through Yunnan, across Burma, and into India, traversing thick jungle and bandit-ridden mountains. In the 1930s, the Chinese government, driven west by the invading Japanese, reopened the route to use as a supply line into China from Burma. The 684-mile (1,100-km) road was built by 300,000 laborers, with primitive tools, and connected Kunming with the railhead at Lashio in British Burma. After the beginning of World War II, it became a strategic lifeline for the Allied troops, bringing in food, arms, and medical supplies. Provisions arrived by rail from Rangoon, and were then trucked to China on this route. After the Japanese occupied Lashio in 1942, another road, built under the command of US General Stilwell *(see p357)*, linked Ledo in India to the Burma Road at Bhamo.

The Burma Road in the 1930s, snaking through the hills

❷ The Stone Forest
石林

Celebrated as a natural wonder, the limestone pillars of the Stone Forest (Shi Lin) are Yunnan's most visited sight. The bizarre, tightly packed formations, some as tall as 100 ft (30 m), have been given imaginative names such as "Rhinoceros Gazing at the Moon" and "Everlasting Fungus." Resembling a petrified forest, the area is shot through with winding pathways, ponds, and look-out points. So popular is this place that the central paths can get clogged with tour groups. Head to the edges of the forest to find a quiet corner, but keep in mind that it is easy to get lost in this otherworldly landscape. Alternatively, spend the night nearby and explore first thing in the morning.

③ ★ Wangfeng Ting
Many of the paths lead to the central Peak Viewing Pavilion, a good meeting point, with views over the forest to help you gain your bearings.

① Xiao Shi Lin
The Minor Stone Forest, a smaller rock cluster to the north of the main forest, is a little quieter. Each evening, Sani minority dances are performed at an amphitheater here.

Fluted shape created by retreating water

Shi Lin's Formation

Fossils found in the area reveal that Shi Lin was underwater during the Permian period, 270 million years ago. The retreating sea left a limestone seabed that has been eroded since by wind and rain into today's weird, twisted shapes.

② Ode to Plum Blossom
Many of the rocks are cut with calligraphy, including one of Mao Zedong's most loved poems, executed in his elegant flowing script.

The Sani

The area around Shi Lin is home to the Sani, one of the many subgroups of the Yi minority. Spread throughout the southwest, the Yi have their own written language, with six dialects, and numerous tracts on medicine, history, and the genealogy of ruling families. Much of Yi society was feudal well into the 20th century, and some groups still practice shamanism. The Sani are known for their embroidery, widely available at Shi Lin, and many local Sani work at the forest as tour guides and dancers.

A Sani tour guide, posing at Shi Lin

④ ★ **Jianfeng Chi**
This ornamental pool is ringed by jagged ridges. A narrow walkway runs from here across the top of the forest.

VISITORS' CHECKLIST

Practical Information
60 miles (100 km) E of Kunming.
Tel (0871) 771 9006.
Open 8am–6pm daily. Torch Festival (end of the 6th lunar month).

Transportation
from Kunming. from Kunming's East bus station.

Sharp edge or *karren*

⑤ **Wife Waiting for Husband**
This formation, reminiscent of a woman waiting patiently, sits in the quiet area right at the back of the forest, on the route of the overhead walkway.

The wavy shapes and thin edges were created by chemicals in standing water dissolving the limestone.

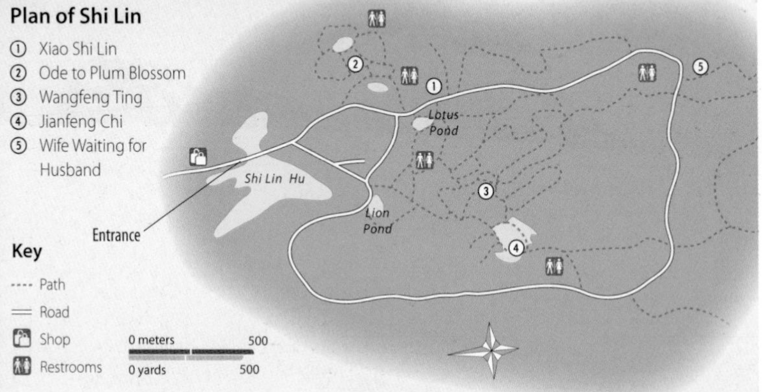

Pagoda at Manting Park

❸ Jinghong
景洪

323 miles (520 km) SW of Kunming. 371,000. 233 Manting Lu, (0691) 222 8222.

The tropical region of Xishuangbanna, in the far south of Yunnan, resembles its neighbors, Myanmar and Laos, more than dynamic modern China. Jinghong, its fast-growing capital, was founded in the 12th century by the Dai warlord Bazhen. It is today an incongruous mix of concrete architecture and palm-lined streets. With an attractively torpid pace of life, it is an ideal introduction to the region and its indigenous Dai culture *(see opposite)*.

Wat Manting, situated southeast of the city center, is Xishuangbanna's largest Buddhist temple. Built entirely of wood and raised off the ground on stilts, it has a simple interior, with vivid frescoes illustrating Buddhist themes. Next door is a school where Dai boys learn Buddhist lore. Behind the temple, **Manting Park**, once the quarters for royal slaves, is a lush place with numerous resident peacocks. There are several paths leading across the tiny river to replicas of temples and pagodas. There are nightly enactments of the Dai Water Splashing Festival *(see p389)*. Located in the west of town is the lovely **Tropical Flower & Plant Garden**, a must-see for those interested in the incredibly diverse flora of the region. It is bursting with tropical plants – over 1,000 species – quite a few with labels in English. In the early afternoon, tour groups are entertained by displays of traditional Dai dancing. A prominent monument commemorates a summit Zhou Enlai *(see p256)* held here with the Burmese leader U Nu in 1961 to defuse border tensions.

Budding plant, Tropical Flower & Plant Garden

Wat Manting
Manting Lu. **Open** 7:30am–5:30pm and 7:40–9:40pm daily.

Tropical Flower & Plant Garden
Xuanwei Dadao. **Open** 7:30am–6:30pm daily.

Environs: Located 20 miles (30 km) southeast of Jinghong, **Ganlanba** makes a good base for exploring the surrounding area. To the southeast of the small town, the **Dai Minority Park** is a collection of refurbished Dai villages, with traditional bamboo and wood houses raised on stilts. Near the park's center stands the 700-year-old, gilded **Wat Ben Pagoda**. The town's main attraction, however, is its picturesque setting in lush jungle beside the Mekong River. Several cafés here offer advice on daywalks and bike rental.

Popular with domestic visitors, the **Wild Elephant Valley**, 30 miles (50 km) north of Jinghong, is home to a herd of wild elephants. Visitors are not allowed to wander off the paths without a guide. Raised treetop walkways allow for observing the wild elephants, while a chairlift provides a bird's-eye view. Near the southern entrance is a bird and butterfly zoo. The reserve's frequent elephant displays are best avoided, since the animals are coaxed into performing with spears.

A visit to **Banla Village**, 24 miles (38 km) west of Jinghong, is the most accessible way to experience Aini culture (a subgroup of the officially recognized Hani minority). The village is attractive, with stilted houses overlooking rice terraces and tea plantations. Besides dance recitals held at the village hall, visitors can also see the distinct Aini dress, with embroidered tunics, silver breastplates, and ornate headdresses.

The lush Tropical Flower and Plant Garden, Jinghong

◀ The stunning beauty of Jade Dragon Snow Mountain

The Dai

In China, the Dai people live in the lush lands of Xishuangbanna. Once spread as far north as the Yangzi Valley, the Dai were driven south during the 13th century by Mongol expansion, and are now found throughout Thailand, Laos, Myanmar, and Vietnam. The Dai in all of these countries share a similar culture, following Theravada Buddhism rather than Mahayana, the Buddhist school practiced in much of the rest of China, and speaking their own language with its own script. Known as skillful farmers, the Dai have always flourished in fertile river basins, growing rice, sugar cane, rubber trees, and bananas. Dai cuisine is well worth trying, with sweet flavors and unusual ingredients not found elsewhere in China. Rice is steamed inside bamboo or pineapple, and exotic specialties include ant eggs and fried moss.

Traditional Dai homes are made of bamboo and raised on stilts, with the livestock penned underneath and generations of the same family living above. The well outside will likely have a shrine over it, water being sacred to Dai culture.

Dai women traditionally wear a sarong or long skirt, a bodice, and a jacket. Hair is tied up, fixed with a comb, and often ornamented with flowers. Gold-capped teeth are considered attractive and married women wear silver bands on their wrists.

Many Dai men have impressive tattoos of animals, flowers, geometric patterns, or Dai script. Traditionally, when a boy reaches 12 years, he has his torso and limbs decorated. This rite of passage has largely died out in mainstream Dai culture, but it is still undertaken in some very rural areas.

Markets in rural Dai homelands offer the only opportunity for some to buy products they can not produce themselves. Huge social occasions usually held on a Monday, they attract villagers for miles around. A lot of hard bargaining – as well as gossip and flirting – goes on.

Water Splashing Festival

Originally a solemn Buddhist rite celebrating the defeat of a demon, Poshui Jie, the Water Splashing Festival is today a joyous and hedonistic carnival. Water is liberally hurled at friend and stranger alike, and becoming thoroughly drenched is seen as fortuitous. The festival also features a massive market on the first day; dragon-boat racing, fireworks, and elephant and peacock displays on the second; and the biggest drenching of all, along with much singing and dancing on the third.

Yunnan's Water Splashing Festival a celebration in mid-April, usually the 13th to the 16th

4 Xishuangbanna

西双版纳

In climate and culture, the subtropical far south of Yunnan, Xishuangbanna, feels a part of Southeast Asia. The region is home to China's last snippets of primeval rain forest, as well as a huge diversity of flora and fauna, including a third of China's bird species. A third of the population is Dai *(see p389)*; another third is made up of the numerous other minorities. Most of the population lives in small villages and the area's appeal lies in the opportunity to hop between towns, explore the countryside by bike, and trek through the jungle.

Pillar-like palm trees at Menglun's Botanic Gardens

East to Laos

This route travels through cultivated flat lands and highland forest to the Laotian border, which you can cross, provided you have the required visa.

The small settlement of **Manting**, a few miles east of Ganlanba *(see p388)* is full of traditional wooden Dai houses. The town's **Fo Si** and **Dadu Ta** are excellent reconstructions of 12th-century temples destroyed in the Cultural Revolution.

About 25 miles (40 km) to the east lies **Menglun**, a dusty couple of streets beside the Luosuo Jiang. The superb **Botanic Gardens**, across a suspension bridge on the opposite bank, were set up to research medicinal uses of local plants. With over 3,000 different species, there's plenty to see, even for the not-so-botanically minded, including the celebrated Dragons' Blood Trees whose sap is used to heal wounds, as well as bamboo and ancient cycad groves. If stopping over, there is an excellent resort nearby.

Leaving the gardens behind, the road to **Mengla** travels through a tract of thick tropical jungle, the largest of Xishuangbanna's five wildlife reserves, which gives way to rubber plantations. Mengla itself is a rather drab and unattractive town.

A short taxi ride north of Mengla, the **Wangtianshu Aerial Walkway**, a chain of slender bridges 130 feet (40 m) up in the tree canopy, allows for unrivaled views of the jungle below. It's another 9 miles (15 km) to the Yao minority village of **Yaoqu**. There's a hostel, and from here it is possible to trek into remote regions – you are advised to hire a guide.

Shangyong is the last village before the Laos border crossing at Mohan and though not really worthy of a trip in itself, it's interesting as a center for Xishuangbanna's Miao population *(see pp412–13)*.

Botanic Gardens
Menglun. **Tel** (0691) 871 5406.
Open 7:30am–6:30pm daily.
W english.xtbg.cas.cn

Wangtianshu Aerial Walkway
19 miles (30 km) N of Mengla. **Tel** (0691) 817 5911. **Open** 8:30am–6pm daily.
W ynskytree.com

West to Myanmar

Western Xishuangbanna is less developed than the east, with rougher roads and sketchier transportation. The many fascinating villages inhabited entirely by minorities, however, make the rigors of travel worthwhile.

Sprawling **Menghai** is unremarkable, but useful as a base for exploring villages and the countryside by bike. It's renowned for its *pu'er* tea and hosts a lively daily market.

The monastery at **Jingzhen** is known for its *busu*, an octagonal pavilion for delivering sermons. The main temple has beautiful decorative wall paintings. A bit farther on at **Mengzhe**, the hilltop **Manlei Si** is a bizarre-looking, frilly octagon built in the 18th century, which holds an important collection of *sutras* written on palm fiber. **Xiding**, an attractive Aini village, holds a large Thursday market.

Gelanghe is dominated by the Aini, whose women wear elaborate silver headdresses. A sub-group, the Ake, who wear their long hair in braids, live in a settlement just north of town on the way to the lake.

Heading south towards the

Life of the Buddha wall paintings, Jingzhen monastic complex

Manfeilong Ta, supposed to resemble emerging bamboo shoots

border, **Menghun** is a sleepy town with a huge, bustling Sunday market, beginning at dawn and finished by noon. Most participants are Dai, but you will also see Aini and Bulang. There's also a rather run-down 19th-century monastery in town.

The border town of **Daluo** is the end of the line for westerners who are not allowed to travel to Myanmar unless being met at the border as part of an official tour. The cross-border market, which attracts hill tribes and Burmese traders, makes the trip to this outpost worth it.

Damenglong to Bulang Shan

Damenglong, 44 miles (70 km) south of Jinghong, comes alive on market days and is a popular spot for trekking and temple-hopping. On the way, it's worth stopping at **Gasa** to explore **Manguanglong Si**, a monastery with a lovely dragon-shaped stairway.

Manfeilong Ta is a half-hour walk north of Damenglong and its nine graceful spires make it the most impressive of the local temples. Built in 1204 to enshrine what is purported to be Buddha's footprint, it is popular with Buddhist pilgrims and is the center of festivities during the Tan Ta Festival in late October or early November. Another Buddhist monument, **Hei Ta**, is rather rundown, but set in a very pleasant location.

The **walk to Bulang Shan** is a simple, well-established three-day walk along the Nana Jiang and its tributaries, passing through dense jungle and villages of the Dai, Aini, Bulang, and Lahu minorities. Hire a guide and be careful not to stray off the path into Myanmar. From Damenglong it's 6 miles (10 km) to the Dai village of **Manguanghan**, then a further 8 miles (13 km) to the Bulang village of **Manpo**, which makes a good place to spend the night. The next day is a 14-mile (22-km) tramp through heavy jungle on winding paths to **Weidong**, and the following day is an easy hike of 6 miles (10 km) along the road to Bulang Shan, which offers rudimentary accommodations and a daily bus to Menghai.

Tips for Explorers

Getting around: Cars with drivers are available in Jinghong. Local buses are frequent along main roads. Bikes can be hired from cafés in the tourist areas.
Trekking: Numerous trekking organizations are based in Jinghong. A guide is recommended for jungle treks. This is a sensitive border region – do not walk unguided near the Myanmar border. Take plenty of food and water, sunscreen, a raincoat, a hat, and a first aid kit.
Accommodation: Basic accommodation is available in most villages, sometimes in locals' homes.

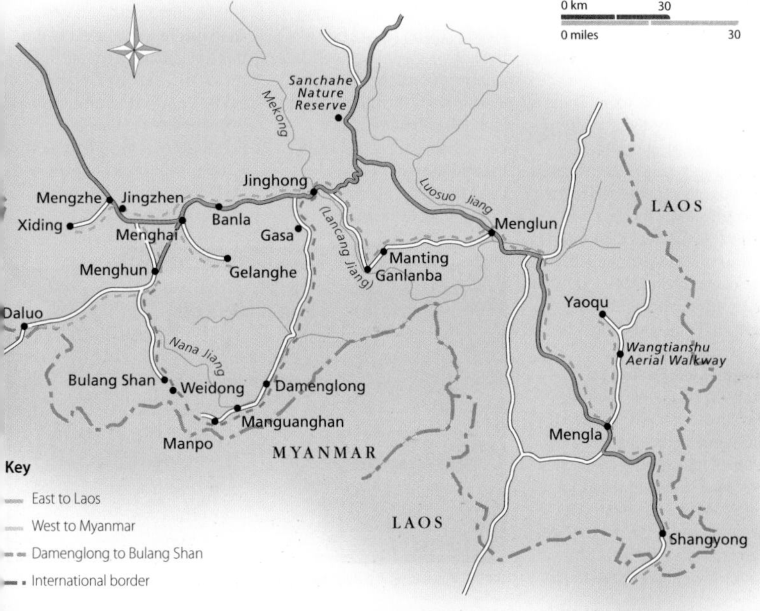

5 Dali and Erhai

大理 与 洱海

Sandwiched between Erhai to the east and the Cang Shan range to the west, the picturesque little town of Dali draws innumerable visitors. The old town, surrounded by the remains of the Ming city walls, is characterized by cobbled lanes and stone houses. In the nearby countryside, numerous Bai villages offer a glimpse into traditional culture, and are particularly interesting on market days. Other activities include hiking in the mountains and watching traditional cormorant fishing on Erhai. The best time to visit is during the Spring Fair, when hundreds of Bai come for five days of bareback horse-racing, wrestling, dancing, and singing.

Looking north over the city's rooftops from Nancheng Men

Exploring Dali

Dali's old town center, just 1½ miles (4 km) across, can be explored in a single morning. It takes about half an hour to walk from the South Gate to the North Gate across town. There is plenty to interest visitors, from small souvenir shops to tea-houses and traditional masseurs. Crowds of shoppers and farmers also arrive here for the daily vegetable market on Renmin Lu. The best vantage point is at the top of Nancheng Men (South Gate), from where there are views to Erhai and Cang Shan.

Huguo Lu & Fuxing Lu

Running east–west through the center of town, Huguo Lu, nicknamed Foreigners' Street, is full of guesthouses and cafés that serve pizzas and cappuccinos. Most of the old town's sights lie along the main north–south artery, Fuxing Lu. The Drum Tower, lying close to the Dali Museum, once signaled the close of the city gates each evening. Farther north along Fuxing Lu, the square outside the library is a popular venue for a game of cards or dominoes. Still farther is the quiet Yu'er Park, full of fruit trees and ponds, while tucked away in the streets to its north is Dali's Catholic church, with extravagant flying eaves.

The Dali Museum, set in picturesque grounds

Dali Museum

111 Fuxing Lu. **Tel** (0872) 267 0196. **Open** 9am–5pm Tue–Sun.

Just inside Nancheng Men, the Dali Museum was originally the mansion of the Qing governor, and later served as the headquarters of Du Wen Xiu, leader of the 1856–73 Muslim Uprising. It is worth visiting for its tranquil courtyards, filled with bougainvillea and lantana. The huge bronze bell hanging outside in a pavilion came from the old Bell Tower. Inside, the most interesting relics are a collection of Buddhist figurines from the Nanzhao Kingdom *(see p394)*, and statues of serving girls and an orchestra excavated from a Ming-dynasty tomb. A hall at the back houses copies of scroll paintings, including one depicting the founding of the Nanzhao Kingdom.

San Ta

1 mile (2 km) NW of Dali. **Tel** (0872) 266 6346. **Open** 7am–6:30pm daily.

The distinctive San Ta (Three Pagodas) that symbolize Dali stand within the monastery of Chongwen Si, which was destroyed during the Qing dynasty and rebuilt in 2005. A 20-minute walk or short bus ride north of town, the pagodas are best visited early. The 16-tiered, square-based **Qianxun Ta** is the tallest of the three at 230 ft (70 m), and is also the oldest, dating to around AD 800. Each tier is embellished with fine marble figures. Buddhist relics including *sutras* (scriptures), copper mirrors, and gold ornaments were found during a renovation in 1979,

For hotels and restaurants in this region see p562 and pp582–3

The splendid San Ta just north of town

and are displayed in a museum behind the pagodas. The two smaller octagonal pagodas were built in the 11th century, and are 138 ft (42 m) high. As well as serving as reliquaries, they were built to appease the gods and thus gain protection against natural disasters. The characters inscribed in front of the Qianxun Ta read "subdue forever mountains and rivers."

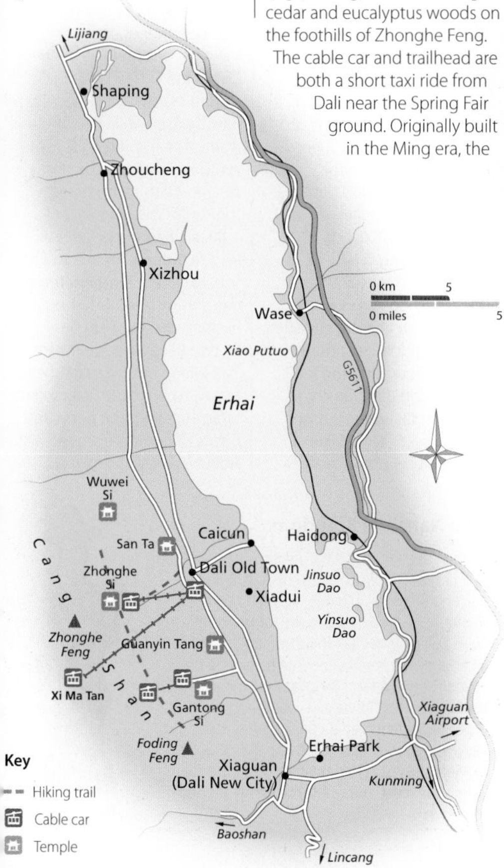

Zhonghe Si

W of Dali.

A steep walk or a short cable-car ride from Dali's western edge, Zhonghe Si sits among cedar and eucalyptus woods on the foothills of Zhonghe Feng. The cable car and trailhead are both a short taxi ride from Dali near the Spring Fair ground. Originally built in the Ming era, the temple has been reconstructed and serves both Daoists and Buddhists. The views from here over the lake and town are superb. From here you can hike the spectacular 7-mile (11-km) Jade Belt trail to Gantong Si, or the 6-mile (9-km) hike along a stone path to **Wuwei Si**, where monks study *tai ji quan*. Visitors can stay the night at a small hostel near Zhonghe Si.

VISITORS' CHECKLIST

Practical Information

210 miles (350 km) W of Kunming. 500,000. 39 Yita Lu, (0872) 251 3033. Spring Fair (15th day of the 3rd lunar month – April or May).

Transportation

Xiaguan airport, 18 miles (30 km) from Dali. to Xiaguan, then 30 mins by bus to Dali.

Guanyin Tang & Gantong Si

Approx 3 miles (5 km) S of Dali.

Dedicated to the Buddhist Goddess of Compassion, Guanyin Tang sits at the foot of Foding Shan. From the back of the temple, a 20-minute cable-car journey or a 2-hour hike will take you to Gantong Si, once the largest shrine in the area. Despite only two partially restored halls surviving, the temple remains impressive. Between Gantong Si and Zhonghe Si is the midway station for the Xi Ma Tan cable car, which runs from Dali Old Town to Xi Ma Tan (Horse-Washing Pool), high up in the Cang Shan.

A bustling market at one of the many towns around Dali

A fisherman and his cormorants on Erhai's jade waters, Dali

Erhai

Open 8.30am-6pm daily.

Located 2 miles (3 km) east of Dali, Erhai is a symbol of natural fecundity to the Bai. The 25-mile (40-km) long lake has numerous ferry services and is home to 50-odd species of fish. Any café in Dali can arrange a tour on the lake; most trips usually involve visits to small temples, or excursions to scenic spots on the eastern shore. Visitors can also accompany a cormorant fisherman *(see p424)* and watch the trained birds catch fish. A variety of tour boats, from big, virtual floating pagodas for large groups to smaller craft, leave from Caicun on Erhai's western shore.

Tours usually take in **Jinsuo Dao**, across the lake near its eastern shore. Once a summer retreat for Nanzhao royalty, it is now home to a fishing village. Farther north lies **Xiao Putuo**, a tiny rocky crag topped with a Buddhist temple.

At the southern tip of the lake, **Erhai Park** was once a royal deer ranch during the Nanzhao Kingdom. A lush path leads up to a peak that offers splendid views.

Surrounding Villages

Dotting the shores of Erhai are several villages worth exploring, especially on market days. One of the numerous minibuses, that congregate just outside Dali's North Gate can easily be flagged down as they hop from village to village. Lying 12 miles (20 km) north of Dali, **Xizhou** was an important military outpost during the Nanzhao period. Today, it has about 90 significant Bai mansions, their rooms arranged around a courtyard. Most lie northwest of the central square, and one of them has been converted into the pleasant Linden Centre hotel. A few miles northeast of Xizhou is **Zhoucheng**, a larger Bai village that is home to workshops producing the area's distinctive tie-dye cloth. Just north of here, **Shaping** is a sleepy village that transforms every Monday, when it hosts a huge market. On sale are a variety of local produce and livestock, as well as delicious wild honey, condiments, and traditional Bai clothing. The scale, bustle, and color make this one of the great highlights of the area.

A Bai woman from Shaping

On the eastern side of the lake, **Wase** village is a maze of narrow back lanes. It has a simple government guesthouse and its own Monday market, which is less touristy than the one at Shaping. Boats return to Dali from **Haidong**, 6 miles (10 km) south of Shaping.

6 Shaxi
沙溪

60 miles (100 km) N of Dali. from Dali or Lijiang via Jianchuan.

Tiny mud-brick Shaxi, a traditional Bai village set in the bowl of a river valley, is a relic of Yunan's **old tea-horse road**. This is the trade route along which tea and other goods such as salt were once ferried between China and Tibet. The Chinese sought sturdy Tibetan ponies for military uses while the Tibetans wanted coarse *pu'er* tea from southern Yunnan, which was steamed into compressed "bricks" for the journey.

Shaxi's handful of lanes all lead to **Sideng**, the old town square, where **Xingjiao Temple** dates from 1451. Its famous Buddhist frescoes are protected by two fierce gate guardians. The village hosts a market each Friday, when the usually sedate village fills with the noise and bustle of farmers from the hills. About 9 miles (15 km) from

The Nanzhao Kingdom

In the 8th century, the Bai unified under a ruthless prince, Pileguo, who vanquished his rivals by inviting them to a banquet and setting fire to the tent. He then founded the Nanzhao Kingdom, with Dali as its capital. The city's strategic location, in a valley shielded by mountains, helped protect it against two attacks by invading Tang armies, and established its control over the southern Silk Road trade. At its zenith, the kingdom stretched across southwest China and into Burma and parts of Vietnam. It survived until the 13th century, when the great Mongol Kublai Khan founded the Yuan dynasty.

Nanzhao figurine

A historic bridge in the Shaxi Valley

Shaxi, **Shibao Shan** is a wooded hillside that offers pleasant walks. Tucked among the pine trees is a series of caves with carvings dating from the Nanzhao Kingdom *(see opposite)*.

❼ Tengchong
腾冲

150 miles (250 km) W of Dali.

A thriving settlement during the Han era, Tengchong prospered from the southern Silk Road trade. Today a remote backwater, it has preserved more of its traditional wooden architecture than nearby Baoshan. Set amid jungle, volcanoes, and hot springs, Tengchong is also a major seismic zone, and has experienced 70 earthquakes since records began in the 16th century.

Tengchong's destructive earthquakes have left the town bereft of historic buildings, although a lone gate tower survives at the eastern end of Fengshan Lu. Along western Guanghua Lu is the main market, held every morning. Tengchong's most renowned product – Burmese jade – is traded in a large market at the northern edge of town. Burmese traders, distinctive in their sarongs and sandals, can be seen around town. Be cautious of their goods unless you are an expert. Just west of town, **Laifeng Shan Park** is a pine forest criss-crossed with paths. Near the top of the hill, **Laifeng Monastery** is now a museum and holds exhibits on local history.

Laifeng Shan Park
Open 8am–7pm daily.

Environs: The sights out of town are best visited on a tour, which can be arranged by any large hotel in Tengchong. **Heshun**, 2 miles (4 km) west of town, was founded in the Ming dynasty and is still as pretty as a postcard despite its growing popularity with visitors. Funds from thousands of former residents now living abroad have kept the traditional courtyard houses, ornate pavilions, and gardens in an excellent state of repair. One of the finest buildings is the wooden library, which was built in 1928.

As a result of its fragile fault-lines, the entire region is dotted with volcanoes, dry lava beds, geysers, and hot springs. The most impressive of the 100-odd small volcanoes lie 12 miles (20 km) north of town. **Dakong Shan** is 820-ft (250-m) high, and beside it is the smaller **Heikong Shan**, only 262 ft (80 m) high, but over 328 ft (100 m) deep. Just 7 miles (12 km) southwest of Tengchong, **Rehai** or "Hot Sea" is an area of geo-thermal springs, popular among the Chinese who throng here for a bath in the mineral-rich water.

Heshun
Tel (0875) 515 8998. **Open** 7:30am–8pm daily.

Dakong and Heikong Shan
Open daily.

Rehai
Tel (0875) 586 8899. **Open** 8:30am–6:30pm daily.

❽ Ruili
瑞丽

115 miles (185 km) SW of Tengchong.
from Kunming.

Ruili, on the Myanmar border, is in every way a frontier town – slightly exotic, with a touch of the illicit. Although much Burmese heroin passes through here, and gambling and prostitution are rife, the town should not necessarily be avoided as the presence of Burmese traders and Dai and Jingpo minorities makes it one of the most intriguing places in southwest China. An interesting jade and gem market lies in the north of town, parallel to **Nanmao Jie**. The town really comes to life at night, when gambling and food stalls are set up in the back streets. Numerous hotels advertise tours into Myanmar, often to watch transvestite shows, but the frontier is closed to all foreign visitors except those being met by Burmese officials for a pre-arranged tour.

Lush Tengchong countryside, with hills in the background

❾ Street-by-Street: Lijiang

丽江

Set in a picturesque valley with a stunning mountain backdrop, Lijiang's Old Town, Dayan, is a labyrinth of cobbled alleys lined with wooden houses, cafés, and the workshops of traditional craftsmen. Home to the Naxi people, Dayan is one of the most pleasant urban scenes in China. Lijiang came to international attention in 1996 when an earthquake killed over 300 people and devastated the city. Money poured into Dayan's relatively sensitive reconstruction, and numerous hotels as well as an airport were built. Lijiang has been a UNESCO World Heritage Site since 1999.

A typical narrow street in the center of the Old Town

Heilong Tan Gongyuan

DONG DAJIE

YU HE

XINHUA JIE

Water Wheels
Heralding the entrance to the Old Town, these water wheels are ornamental. Lijiang once had numerous mills.

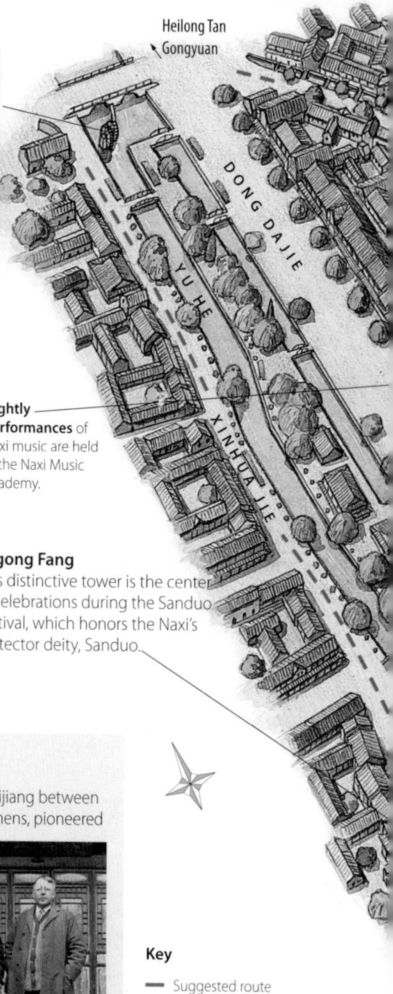

Nightly performances of Naxi music are held at the Naxi Music Academy.

Kegong Fang
This distinctive tower is the center of celebrations during the Sanduo Festival, which honors the Naxi's protector deity, Sanduo.

Joseph Rock

An eccentric Austrian botanist, Joseph Rock lived in Lijiang between 1922 and 1949. He gathered over 80,000 plant specimens, pioneered the use of photography in the field, and wrote reports for *National Geographic*. He was a defender of Naxi culture and compiled the first dictionary of the language. His expedition entourage was huge, and included cooks, hundreds of mercenaries, and servants to carry such dubious necessities as his gramophone, gold dinner service, and collapsible bathtub.

Joseph Rock (right) with the Prince of Choni, 1925

Key

— Suggested route

0 meters 100

0 yards 100

View of the rooftops of Dayan from Wangu Lou

VISITORS' CHECKLIST

Practical Information
315 miles (525 km) NW of Kunming. 1,210,000. Tourism Development Building, Xueshan Lu, (0888) 511 1169. Bangbang Festival (15th day of 1st lunar month); Sanduo Festival (8th day of 2nd lunar month). to Dayan. **ljta.gov.cn**

Transportation
Lijiang Sanyi airport. 

The canals are helpful if you get lost. Walk against the current to head towards the water wheels.

XINYI JIE

★ Mishi Xiang
With a canal bubbling beside it, this is one of Dayan's most charming streets. Locals stop for a drink from the well here, outside the Blue Page Vegetarian restaurant.

Old Town Center

The old town is a cobweb of narrow cobbled alleyways, criss-crossed with canals and free of traffic. It's extremely pretty and very popular. If you want to escape the crowds head off into the alleys away from the major tourist routes, where local people still live, or visit early in the morning.

WUYI JIE

GUANGYI JIE

★ Sifang Jie
Market Square is the heart of Lijiang. Naxi gather here to play cards and chat. Local men who enjoy falconry often display their hawks. There are dancing performances daily at 11am, 2:10pm, and 4:10pm.

Yu He runs south from Heilong Tan (Black Dragon Pool), north of Dayan.

Lou

Exploring Lijiang & Beyond

Shizi Shan (Lion Hill) divides the Old Town (Dayan) from the New Town, where most hotels and other amenities can be found. There are a few sights just south of Dayan, on Shizi Shan, and clustered around Heilong Tan (Black Dragon Pool), north of Dayan. The countryside surrounding Lijiang is dotted with Naxi hamlets, many of which have interesting temples. Some of these can be reached by bicycle; otherwise by a short bus trip.

Wan Gu Lou, a perfect vantage point for viewing Dayan

Wan Gu Lou

Shizi Shan. **Tel** (0888) 517 5060.
Open 7am–8pm daily.

Standing at the highest point in Lijiang, this 108-ft (33-m) pavilion is accessible from either the Old Town or from Minzhu Lu on the west side of the hill. A four-story edifice with huge wooden pillars, it offers superb views overlooking the Old Town.

Mu Fu

49 Guanyuang Xiang, SW of the Old Town. **Tel** (0888) 512 2572.
Open 9am–5:30pm daily.

The Mu were Lijiang's ruling family up to 1723 and the mansion they built for themselves at the south end of the Old Town contained over 100 buildings. What was left of the mansion was destroyed in the 1996 earthquake, after which it was rebuilt in Han, Naxi, Bai, and Tibetan architectural styles.

Heilong Tan Gongyuan

1 Minzhu Lu. **Tel** (0888) 518 8041.
Open 7am–8pm daily. included in adm to Lijiang Old Town.

On the northern edge of town, Black Dragon Pool Park is stunningly picturesque, with the elegant Deyue Lou placed at the center of a carp-filled pool, and backdropped by the peak of Yulong Xue Shan (Jade Dragon Snow Mountain). The **Dongba Cultural Research Institute**, in the southwest corner of the park, is an academic institution for the preservation of Naxi culture – there are about 30 dongba shamans here, studying and translating Naxi religious texts. In the north of the park stands a set of halls transported during the 1970s from what was once Lijiang's biggest monastery, **Fuguo Si**. The grandest is the 66-ft (20-m), triple-roofed Wufeng Lou (Five Phoenix Hall), built in 1601. The **Museum of Naxi Culture**, by the park's north gate, holds exhibitions on Naxi dress and customs.

Environs: Baisha, a sleepy village 6 miles (10 km) north of Lijiang, was, until Kublai Khan's invasion, the capital of the Naxi Kingdom. Today there's little evidence of its past importance, with most visitors drawn by the 15th-century temple murals at Dabaoji Gong, or by the chance to consult Dr. Ho, a traditional Chinese physician. Made famous by travel writer Bruce Chatwin, the elderly doctor speaks good English and will doubtlessly track you down and offer his tonic herb tea in exchange for a small donation.

Beiyue Si in the village of Yulong, a couple of miles north of Baisha, is dedicated to the protector deity Sanduo, depicted with a white hat and spear. The temple has been managed by the same family for almost 1,000 years.

Built in 1756, the small lamasery **Yufeng Si** is just outside Yulong at the foot of the mountain. A huge ancient camellia tree produces thousands of flowers each spring and is cared for with impressive dedication by the monks. A Naxi orchestra often practices here in the afternoon.

Red chilies drying

The magnificent **Yulong Xue Shan** mountain dominates the countryside surrounding Lijiang. To access this mountain that was first scaled in the 1960s, you'll need to either join an organized tour or hire a taxi. Once inside the mountain park you'll find a plethora of scenic spots and activities to do. Ride Asia's highest chairlift up to the snowline at 14,780ft (4,506m) or watch the spectacular "Impressions Lijiang," a show staged daily in an outdoor amphitheater at the foot of the mountain. Be prepared for changeable conditions and take care in the thinner air.

The jagged peaks of Yulong Xue Shan (Jade Dragon Snow Mountain)

For hotels and restaurants in this region see p562 and p583

The Naxi

The Naxi minority, numbering about 326,000, live in Sichuan and Yunnan, with Lijiang as their spiritual capital. Descended from Tibetan nomads, the Naxi society is matrilineal, though local rulers were always male. There are strong matriarchal influences throughout Naxi society and in particular in the Naxi language. For example, nouns become superlative when the word "female" is added and diminutive with the addition of "male." A "female stone," therefore, is a boulder; a "male stone" a pebble. The script, called Dongba, consists of about 1,400 pictograms and is the only hieroglyphic writing system still in use. The Naxi religion, also called Dongba, is polytheistic and mixes elements of Daoism and Tibetan Lamaism with older animist beliefs. The main Naxi deity is Sanduo, a protector war god depicted in white, carrying a white spear and riding a white horse. He is celebrated each year with the sacrifice of a goat and, of course, much singing and dancing.

Naxi society's matriarchal nature results in the women controlling businesses, but also doing most of the work. Inheritance passes through the female line to the eldest daughter. Naxi men are expected to while away their time as gardeners or musicians.

Traditional shawls have an upper blue segment which represents night, a lower sheepskin band to represent daylight, and small circles recalling the stars. Two circles on the shoulder areas depict the eyes of a frog, an ancient Naxi deity.

Dongba shaman are invited to chant scriptures at weddings, funerals, on New Year's Day, and at festivals. A few of these shaman survived the purges of the Cultural Revolution and are training a new generation in ancient Naxi ritual.

Naxi music is unique – a combination of Daoist rite, Confucian ceremony, and literary lyrics, played on venerable instruments such as the flute, reed pipes, lute, and zither.

This page of pictographic Dongba script is from the Naxi manuscript "Sacrifices to the High Deity." It is one of numerous Dongba documents translated by Joseph Rock *(see p396)*.

⑩ Tiger Leaping Gorge

虎跳峡

This popular trek follows the roaring Yangzi River (also known as Jinsha Jiang) through one of China's deepest gorges, supposedly named after a tiger escaped hunters by leaping across its narrowest point. With peaks on either side soaring to over 16,400 ft (5,000 m), the gorge makes for a thrilling trek. The 18-mile (30-km) trail along the ridge is well marked, though at times arduous, and passes through rustic hamlets that allow visitors to rest up amid beautiful countryside. The walk can easily be completed in two days, but many hikers decide to stay an extra night. If time is tight, day-long bus tours from Lijiang head into the gorge along the lower road, which runs the length of the gorge.

Bendiwan
A tiny village with superb views, Bendiwan has numerous guesthouses and is a convenient place to overnight 10 miles (16 km) from Qiaotou.

★ Views of the Gorge
Starting at the Qiaotou end of the gorge provides magnificent views right from the start. The peaks of Jade Dragon Snow Mountain rise far above the river.

The 24 Bends
When coming from Qiaotou, the 24 Bends are the toughest part of the trail and consist of rather more than 24 grueling switchbacks. Some hire horses at Nuoyu for this part of the trip.

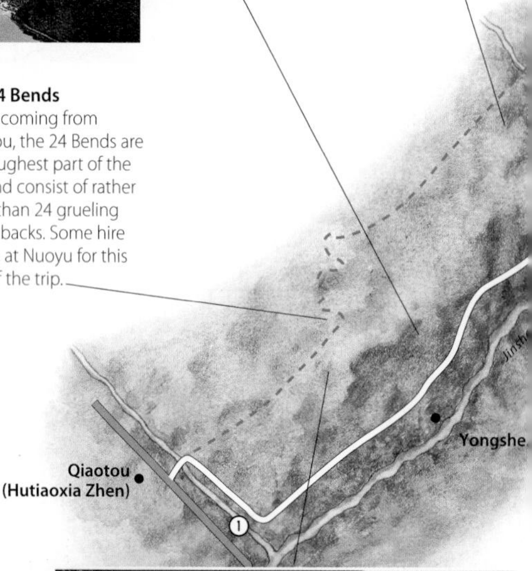

Qiaotou (Hutiaoxia Zhen)

Yongshe

①

KEY

① **Relatively new lower road**

② **A short diversion** down a steep, winding trail leads to Longdong Waterfall.

③ **Original ferry crossing**

④ **The "new" ferry** crossing is sometimes closed. Check at Walnut Grove or Daju before departing.

⑤ **Follow the path** down to the river to judge for yourself whether any animal could have made this jump.

Farms at Nuoyu
The lovely village of Nuoyu is just 2 hours from Qiaotou. A few guesthouses here offer dorm beds and meals, as well as horses.

For hotels and restaurants in this region see p562 and pp582–3

VISITORS' CHECKLIST

Practical Information
50 miles (80 km) NW of Lijiang. for access to the gorge, and ferry crossing.

Transportation
from Lijiang to either Daju or Qiaotou; last bus from Daju to Lijiang at 1:30pm.

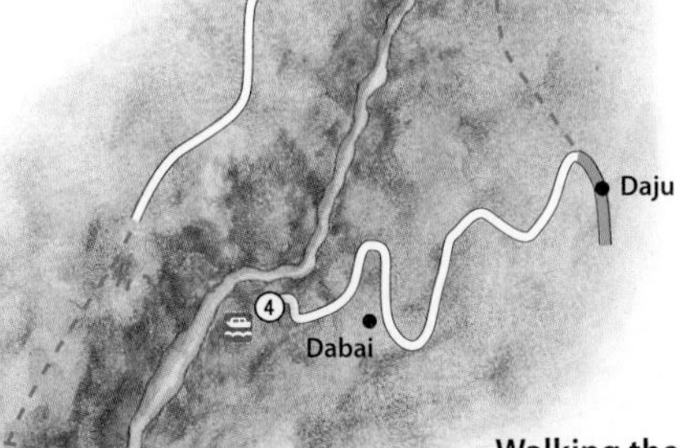

Walking the Gorge

The upper trail follows the peaks between Qiaotou and Daju, either of which can be used as a starting point. Both Bendiwan and Walnut Grove are about a day's walk from either end, so make good spots to overnight. Don't attempt the trek on your own, or in heavy rain or thick mist. Landslides do occur in the area so be wary, especially after the rains in July and August.

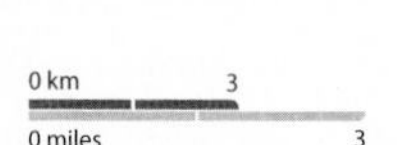

Key

- Major road
- Minor road
- Path

★ **Walnut Grove**
This quiet village of terraced fields, walnut trees, and stone-and-timber houses is 14 miles (23 km) from Qiaotou and a great place to rest up. The views of the gorge's narrowest section are not to be missed.

Traditional Tibetan buildings at Ganden Sumtseling Gompa

⓫ Shangri-La
香格里拉

105 miles (175 km) NW of Lijiang. 3 hrs from Lijiang. 105 Kangzhu Dadao, (0887) 822 6951.

After officially changing its name from Zhongdian in 2002, Shangri-La is named for the fictional land in the 1933 novel by James Hilton. The city is the capital of Diqing Tibetan Autonomous Region and worth visiting if you're not able to visit Tibet. The ramshackle town filled with blocky architecture does not quite live up to the paradise billing, especially after the old Tibetan town burned down in a catastrophic fire in 2014. Just north is the largest Tibetan monastery in the southwest, Ganden Sumtseling Gompa (Songzanlin Si), home to over 600 monks. It was built by the fifth Dalai Lama almost 400 years ago, destroyed during the Cultural Revolution, and re-opened in 1981. There are several Tibetan villages and two hotels in the monastery complex.

Environs: There is a good choice of trips out into the countryside – geographically, part of the Tibetan plateau – to **Baishui Tai**, for example, a set of limestone terraces, or to **Bita Hai**, an emerald lake and home to many endangered species. These trips are best arranged with local agencies, who can also organize overland journeys through the beautiful and remote countryside between here and Sichuan.

GUIZHOU & GUANGXI

Guizhou and Guangxi share a dramatic mountainous landscape of weathered limestone (karst) pinnacles, which hide some of China's largest cave systems. Despite the abundant rainfall, the region possesses poor soil, which discouraged Han settlement until the late Ming period. As a result, the area saw little development, and many indigenous groups, especially the Miao and Dong, have retained their traditional customs, including several well-known festivals. Guangxi is also home to the Zhuang, China's largest ethnic minority, and officially became the Guangxi Zhuang Autonomous Region in 1958.

Still among China's least-developed regions, Guizhou and Guangxi do have a few sights that are well-visited by tourists and easily accessible. The city of Guilin in eastern Guangxi is famous for the Li River cruise, which passes through an astonishing karst landscape and ends at the small town of Yangshuo. Kaili, a convenient base for exploring Miao villages, is becoming more accessible and popular with tourists. For determined travelers with time on their hands, long bus journeys are rewarded with the beautiful Detian Falls surrounded by karst hills, stunning scenery near the Vietnamese border, the wooden Dong villages around Zhaoxing, and the calm waters of bird sanctuary Cao Hai.

Sights at a Glance

Villages, Towns & Cities

1. Guiyang
2. Anshun
8. Miao Villages
9. Zunyi
11. Guilin
13. Longsheng
14. Sanjiang
15. Zhaoxing
16. Huangyao
17. Guiping
18. Nanning
20. Pingxiang
22. Beihai

Waterfalls, Caves & Areas of Natural Beauty

3. Longgong Dong
4. Huangguoshu Falls
5. Zhijin Dong
6. Weining & Cao Hai
7. Xingyi & Maling Canyon
10. Chishui
12. Yangshuo
19. Zuo Jiang
21. Detian Falls

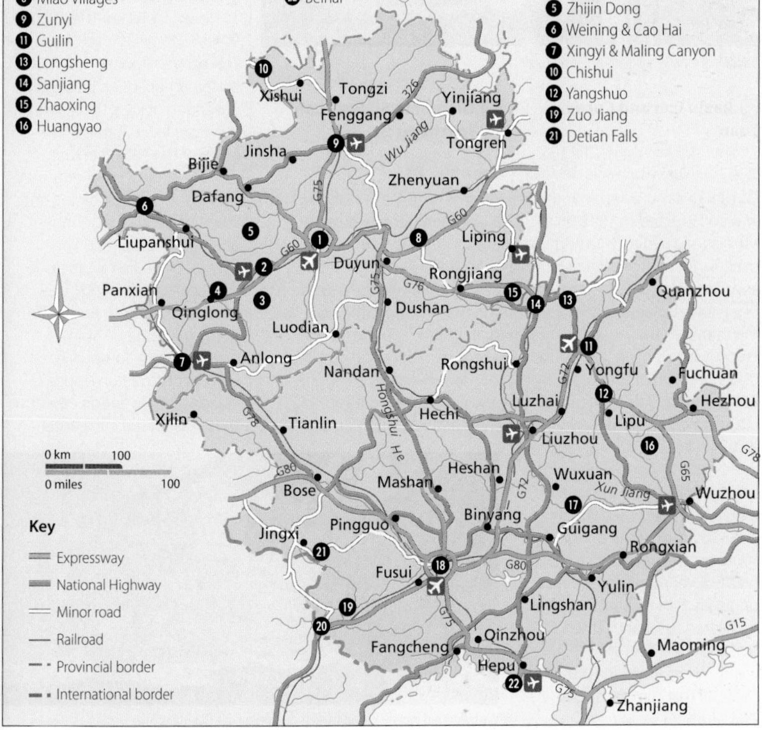

0 km 100
0 miles 100

Key

- Expressway
- National Highway
- Minor road
- Railroad
- Provincial border
- International border

◀ Zhuang girl walking through rice fields

For additional map symbols *see back flap*

❶ Guiyang

贵阳

Founded during the Han dynasty, Guiyang remained a minor provincial center until it became the capital of Guizhou in the early 20th century. The city is situated in a valley along the little Nanming River, protected from the unlucky northern direction by high hills. Guiyang means "Precious Sun," which reflects the general Chinese opinion of the province's damp climate. An easy-going place, Guiyang is a steadily modernizing city surrounded by parklands, with a couple of historic relics dotted among its tower blocks. The Huaxi District to its south includes rural parks, a few villages inhabited by the Bouyei minority *(see p406)*, and a well-preserved Ming-era town.

Jiaxiu Lou and the arched Fuyu Qiao over Nanming River

Traditional temple buildings in Cuiwei Yuan

Jiaxiu Lou and Cuiwei Yuan

2 Cuiwei Xian Nanming Lu. **Tel** (0851) 8550 3811. **Open** 8am–8pm daily.

The small Jiaxiu Lou pavilion was constructed in 1598 on a tortoise-shaped rock jutting out over Nanming River. It was built as an inspirational meeting place for scholars studying for the imperial civil service exams. The pavilion is now a teahouse decorated with antique poetry scrolls. Its upper floor offers views of Guiyang's modern downtown district. The 95-ft (29-m) high, three-storied wooden tower is connected to the riverbank by the arched Fuyu Qiao (Floating Jade Bridge). On the bridge's southern side, adjacent to Jiaxiu Lou, Cuiwei Yuan garden was originally part of a temple dedicated to Guanyin,the Buddhist Goddess of Compassion. Founded around 1500, all that remains today are late Qing-era buildings.

Qianming Si, Jue Yuan & Wenchang Ge

City center, N of the river.
Open daily.

A few examples of Guiyang's classic architecture survive around the city center. The most interesting is Qianming Si, located on Yangming Lu on the north bank of the river. Its main point of interest is the street market outside, selling bonsai trees, pets, fishing gear, and Cultural Revolution memorabilia. Jue Yuan on Fushui Nan Lu is another temple, whose main attraction is the excellent vegetarian restaurant out front, which uses generous quantities of chilies to spice up the tofu, vegetable, and gluten dishes. Just off Wenchang Bei Lu, Wenchang Ge features an elegant three-story tower with flared and pointed eaves built between 1609 and 1669. It was originally part of the east city wall.

Provincial Museum

168 Beijing Lu. **Tel** (0851) 8682 2762.
Open 9am–5pm Tue–Sun.

The second floor of this dusty building houses an interesting collection of local finds, though there are few captions. The pride of the collection are a 3-ft (1-m) high Han-era bronze horse and chariot, and some glazed clay figurines from a Ming tomb near Zunyi. Ethnological displays include silverware, batiks, and embroideries from Guizhou's many minorities. A shiny new museum complex is under construction opposite Guiyang's convention center, northeast of the city center.

Vermilion-red joss sticks and trinkets on sale outside Qianming Si

For hotels and restaurants in this region see p562 and p583

Stone steps leading up a thickly forested hill, Qianling Shan Park

Qianling Shan Park

187 Zaoshan Lu. **Open** 6:30am–10pm daily. 1 or 2 northbound.

This scenic park comprises an unexpected patch of forested hills to the north of the city. A flagstoned path leads uphill past several shrines, trees hung with red ribbons, and groups of monkeys to **Hongfu Si**, the main attraction. Entry to the temple is past a 33-ft (10-m) marble stupa and a tiled screen depicting the infant Buddha being washed by nine colorful dragons. The temple was originally founded in 1672, although its present buildings were constructed later, including a Luohan Hall with several hundred painted statues of Buddhist saints. On the hilltop above, Kanzhu Pavilion offers fine views of the city.

Huaxi District

11 miles (17 km) S of Guiyang. 210.

The small town of Huaxi is the location of Guizhou University and the attractive Huaxi Park, a 2-sq-mile (5-sq-km) stretch of woodland, river, and ornamental gardens. A handful of Bouyei villages lie close by, including **Zhenshan**, built entirely in stone. The village is known for its Ground Opera, derived from local animistic rituals, where dancers wear stylized wooden masks.

Just 8 miles (12 km) to the south of Huaxi is **Qingyan**, a garrison outpost founded in 1373. Its 33-ft (10-m) high city walls, dating to the 18th century, are still intact, along with watchtowers, stone gateways, and 17 temples.

VISITORS' CHECKLIST

Practical information

660 miles (1,100 km) NW of Guangzhou. 3,050,000.
Floor 7, Longquan Building, 1 Hequan Lu, (0851) 8690 1575.

Transportation

Longdong Bao Airport.
CAAC (buses to airport), East bus station, Jinyang bus station.

Dog Meat

Characters for "dog meat" on a restaurant sign

One thing to look out for in Guizhou is the locals' fondness for eating dog meat, a habit shared by people in parts of Guangxi and other Southeast Asian countries. Rather like chilies, dog meat is considered "warming" in Chinese medicine, and also a remedy for male impotence. The meat is often served as a hot pot. However, visitors shouldn't worry about being served dog meat by accident, since it is an expensive luxury, generally served only in specialist restaurants. If you're concerned, look for the characters shown above, pronounced "gou rou."

Guiyang City Center

1. Jiaxiu Lou
2. Cuiwei Yuan
3. Qianming Si
4. Jue Yuan
5. Wenchang Ge
6. Provincial Museum
7. Qianling Shan Park

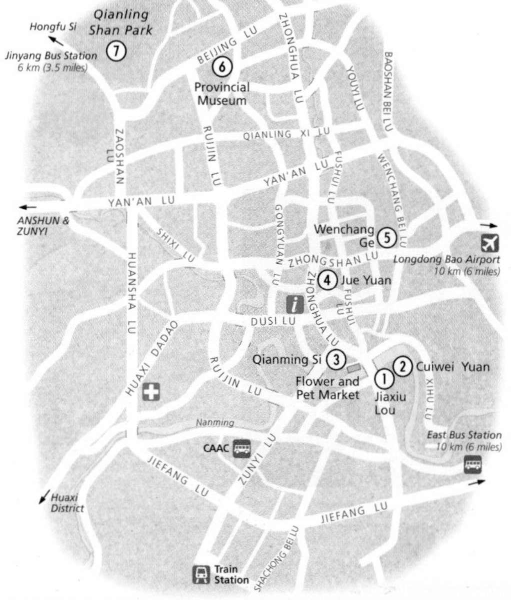

Key to Symbols *see back flap*

Traditional houses of the Bouyei community near Anshun

❷ Anshun
安顺

62 miles (100 km) SW of Guiyang.

Founded as a garrison town in the 13th century, Anshun grew into a prosperous trading post, mainly because of its strategic position along the overland trade routes between central and southwestern China. Today's city survives on tourism, subsistence farming, and its traditional batik industry, which capitalizes on the highly developed textile skills of the local Bouyei minority. The Bouyei number around 3 million and live throughout western Guizhou and nothern Vietnam. A writing system for the Bouyei language was devised in the 1950s and has been used to record their rich folk literature.

Surrounded by karst hills, Anshun has one of Guizhou's most scenic landscapes, despite the frequent gusts of coal dust from nearby mines. It also has numerous street markets, and offers easy access to several of the surrounding traditional villages. The busy town center lies at the intersection of Zhonghua Nan Lu and Tashan Lu. The **Bai Ta** (White Pagoda), one of Anshun's two surviving Ming structures, overlooks the center from Xixiu Hill. The other, **Wen Miao**, is a Confucian temple and lies in the town's northeastern back streets. The 600-year-old temple was once embellished with superb stone carvings. Today, what survives are its front pillars, covered in beautiful spiraling dragons and considered to be the finest in the country.

The area around the city center bustles with rural commerce. Rows and rows of shops selling beautiful batik products, including wall hangings and colorful banners, are situated outside the **Batik Factory** on Zhonghua Nan Lu.

Environs: Lying about 9 miles (15 km) east of Anshun are eight fortified villages, locally known as **Yunfeng Ba Zhai**. Founded by Ming-dynasty troops, each village contains a scattering of old structures. **Tiantai Shan**, 24 miles (40 km) northeast of town, is a 1,300-ft (400-m) hill with a cluster of thickly forested crags, whose summit is crowned by a Buddhist temple dating from 1616. Another 18 miles (30 km) southwest of Anshun, **Zhenning County** has a concentration of traditional Bouyei villages. The houses are built of skillfully laid drystone walls, with roofs tiled in hand-cut slates, overlapping like fish scales. The village of **Shitou Zhai**, built almost entirely in stone, is known for its traditional batik.

Fruit sellers at the Sunday market, Anshun

❸ Longgong Dong
龙宫洞

17 miles (27 km) SW of Anshun. from Anshun's East bus station. **Tel** 400 966 1984. **Open** 8am–6pm daily. **china-longgong.com**

Longgong Dong (Dragon Palace Caves) comprise a 9-mile (15-km) long complex of 90 or

A strikingly designed, contemporary batik, filled out in red and orange

Anshun Batik

Several ethnic groups across southwestern China have been traditionally involved in creating batik. For almost 1,000 years, the Bouyei around Anshun have been using batik as a background to embroidery on clothing, and since the establishment of a factory in Anshun in the 1950s, have come to monopolize the indigenous textile market. The designs, which were originally of abstract plants and animals, are drawn with wax on cloth. The cloth is then dyed in indigo before being boiled to remove all traces of the wax, leaving the pattern in white on a blue background. The earlier monochromatic batiks have now given way to multi-colored, mass-produced designs, which include stylized representations of zodiac animals, scenes from Bouyei legends, and mythical creatures. Today, Anshun's batik is in great demand across China.

For hotels and restaurants in this region see p562 and p583

Tour boats used to explore the watery Longgong Dong

more caves, connected by an underground river. Only six caves, covering 2,800 ft (855 m), are open to exploration, accessed by boat through the flooded eastern entrance, Tian Chi (Heaven's Pool), which is partially concealed by a 130-ft (40-m) high waterfall. Inside, the largest cavern is about 260-ft (80-m) high. The caves can be explored both by boat and on foot. Yulong Dong and Long Gong are the most spectacular caverns here, with colorfully lit stalactites and stalagmites, and scores of oddly shaped rock formations.

❹ Huangguoshu Falls
黄果树瀑布

40 miles (65 km) SW of Anshun. from Anshun and Guiyang. **Tel** (0851) 3359 2136. **Open** 7am–6pm daily. Last entry 5pm. **hgscn.com/en**

Immensely popular in China, the Huangguoshu Da Pubu (Yellow Fruit Tree Falls) on the Sanche River rise to a height of 250 ft (77 m). During the summer rains in June and July the river becomes a torrent, and the 266-ft (81-m) wide curtain of water creates an awesome spectacle as it hits the Rhinoceros Pool below. It does not, however, rank as China's largest cataract; in fact, during drier months, its flow shrinks to a pretty network of streams pouring over the rock face. Low water levels during this time of the year make it possible to wade across the streams.

Staircases and bridges connect viewing areas opposite the falls. **Shuilian Dong**, a 440-ft (134-m) long tunnel, runs behind the falls, where natural "windows" look out through the curtain of water. Visitors should be prepared to get wet.

Of the remaining dozen or so water features along the Sanche, the pick of the crop lies upstream at **Doupotang Falls**, which though only a quarter of the height of Huangguoshu, are a staggering 340-ft (105-m) wide. About 3 miles (5 km) downstream at **Tianxing** are a series of small caves, some karst spires rising 66 ft (20 m), and the Yinlianzhuitan (Silver Chain Cascades), where water tumbles into a network of streams between rocky islets.

❺ Zhijin Dong
织金洞

60 miles (100 km) N of Anshun. from Anshun and Guiyang to Zhijin town. Taxis and minibuses available to the caves. **Tel** (0857) 781 2015. **Open** 9am–5pm daily. compulsory. **gzzjd.com**

Extending for over 7 miles (12 km) into limestone hills, these caves are ranked as the largest in China, and are also among the biggest in the world. One of the largest caverns stands at a height of 200 ft (60 m), and is almost 800ft (250 m) long. Paths and stairways link the caves between fossilized waterfalls and elephantine stalactites and stalagmites. The imposing rock formations have each been given descriptive names, such as "Puxian Riding the Elephant," "Goddess and Snake," and the aptly named and impressive "Old Woman and Daughter-in-Law."

The largest cavern, **Guanghan Dong**, contains the immensely elegant, 56-ft (17-m) stalagmite known as the "Silver Rain Tree." The obligatory guided tour, which lasts for more than 2 hours, requires a minimum of ten people, so smaller groups may have to wait for more sightseers to arrive before they can explore the area.

The Huangguoshu Falls, spectacular even during drier periods

Punting on Cao Hai, with the Yunnanese border on the horizon

6 Weining & Cao Hai
威宁 / 草海

200 miles (320 km) W of Guiyang. to Weining, or to Liupanshui, then bus. Yi Torch Festival (Jun/Jul).

The rugged hills of northwest Guizhou contain a large number of coal veins, and as a result the region's settlements are largely industrial mining towns. On the border with Yunnan is the 7,200-ft (2,195-m) high Weining Plateau, whose main town is the small, chaotic, and ugly Weining, inhabited by Hui, Yi, and Da Hua Miao. The Muslim Hui, scattered throughout China, are descendants of Arab and Persian traders who came to China along the Silk Road during the Tang and Yuan dynasties. The Yi community number around 8.7 million and are spread through southwestern China. Their torch festival is a major annual event featuring archery contests, bonfires, and wrestling. The Da Hua Miao *(see p412)* differ from the Miao near Kaili in both language and embroidery patterns, which feature the stylized flower motif inspired by their name Da Hua, meaning "Big Flower."

Immediately southwest of Weining is Cao Hai, known throughout China prominent spots for bird-watching. The 17-sq mile (45-sq km) nature reserve was set up in 1992. The shallow, blue, oval-shaped lake is ringed with low hills and fringed with reed beds that attract tens of thousands of wintering birds between November and March. Its most important annual visitors include a large flock of 400 endangered black-necked cranes, along with Eurasian cranes, barheaded geese, and several duck species.

It is possible to observe the abundant birdlife by either walking around the shore where the cranes congregate, or hiring a punt to approach flocks of wild fowl out on the lake. Boats can also be rented for a tour of the lake.

7 Xingyi & Maling Canyon
兴义 和 马岭河峡谷

190 miles (305 km) SW of Guiyang. to Xingyi. Maling Canyon: White-water rafting arranged by hotels. **Open** 8am–6pm daily.

In the far southwestern corner of Guizhou, the small and remote market town of Xingyi is surrounded by low, rounded limestone hills and flat paddy fields. Northeast of Xingyi, just outside the suburbs, lies the 9-mile (15-km) long slash of Maling Canyon. About 330-ft (100-m) deep in places, the canyon has been carved by a fast-flowing river. Ground-level springs gush down mossy cliffs in miniature waterfalls. The river's currents and cataracts make for exciting white-water rafting trips from Maling's upper section, 16 miles (25 km) northeast of town. The canyon's lower section features several walking tracks and bridges which zigzag down to the water level and then follow the river, sometimes through natural tunnels, for some distance upstream.

River running through the lower section of Maling Canyon

Chinese Cranes

The lakes and marshes of China are vital to the survival of eight of the world's 15 species of crane, many of which are highly endangered. Most breed in northern China, in particular at Zhalong Nature Reserve in Heilongjiang province. All are migratory, but several species – including the tropical sarus and China's sole endemic variety, the black-necked crane – occur only in the central and southwestern parts of the country. Aside from being naturally elegant birds, cranes have spectacular mating "dances," where they energetically leap and flap around to attract their lifelong partners. As a result of this display, the crane is a Chinese symbol of fidelity and longevity. The Daoist God of Longevity, Shou Lao, is often depicted riding a crane.

Courting cranes pair for life. They cement the bond with elaborate courtship displays, during which the couple loop necks, toss their heads back, throw around twigs and pebbles, and leap high into the air, parachuting down with wings spread.

The crane is a symbol of good fortune, wisdom, and the quest for spiritual improvement, as well as fidelity – so it is often seen on official and imperial clothing.

Trailing legs

Cranes migrate great distances, with some species covering up to 2,500 miles (4,000 km) between their summer breeding grounds and winter quarters. The younger birds learn the routes in a V-formation behind their elders.

Cruising speed of up to 44 miles per hour (70 km/h)

Demoiselle cranes are gregarious and have been recorded in flocks several thousand strong. Their diet is mostly frogs, fish, and insects, though they can also eat grain and carrion.

Common cranes are a very vocal species, and their deep booms, loud honks, and raucous croaks are produced by a specially adapted windpipe or trachea.

Miao Festivals & Crafts

The Miao people, or Hmong as they call themselves, believe they originated on the Himalayan plateau, migrating over the last few thousand years to their current homelands in southwestern China, Laos, Cambodia, Vietnam, and Myanmar. As Miao communities tend to exist in remote mountainous areas, each village has developed its own customs, and can be identified by their distinct ornamentation, such as the fine silverwork and embroidery once made and worn by unmarried girls. These are displayed at the many Miao social festivals, where mass dancing is featured.

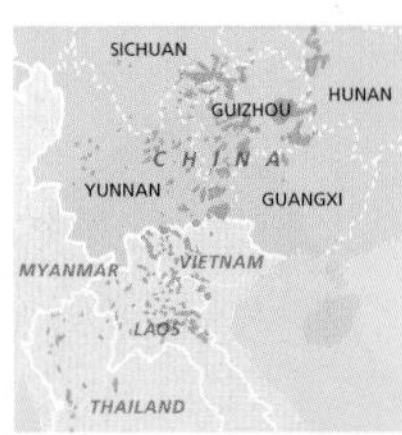

Miao Communities of Asia

Miao population

Huge horns adorn these fabulous headdresses.

Miao People in the Kaili area call themselves Hei Miao, or Black Hmong, irrespective of their colorful clothing, which identifies the wearer's village or region. This woman is from the Leigong Shan area.

Da Hua Miao, or Big Flower Miao, from western Guizhou, wear wax-resist (batik) dyed skirts, and for festivals, bright red headgear.

Sisters' Meal Festival

Amid three days of drinking and dancing at this important festival, teenage girls choose their husbands. The man offers a packet of sticky rice; she returns it with two chopsticks buried inside if she agrees, or chilies if she refuses.

This Gejia headpiece with orange tassels shows that this Gejia girl is unmarried. The designs are unusual in that they embellish their batik work with embroidery.

The Changjiao, or Long-horned, Miao of western Guizhou bundle several pounds of their own and ancestors' hair around horn-like headpieces for festivals.

◀ The beauty of Yangshuo Karst, Yangshuo

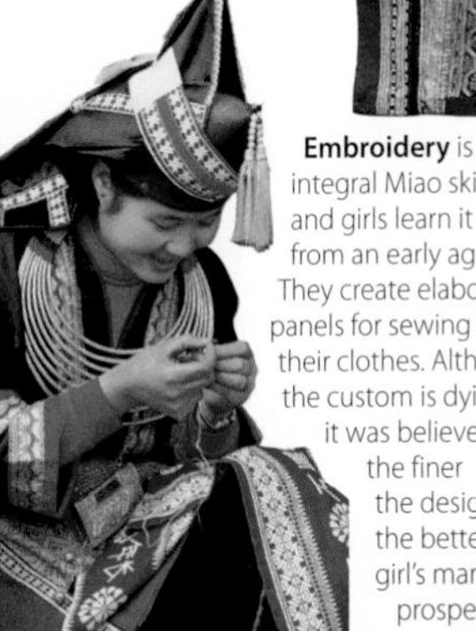

Embroidery is an integral Miao skill, and girls learn it from an early age. They create elaborate panels for sewing on to their clothes. Although the custom is dying, it was believed, the finer the design, the better a girl's marriage prospects.

This jacket is typical of dark geometric Gejia pieces. It is heavily embroidered and incorporates batik work of abstract buffalo and plant motifs.

Miao silverwork ranges from simple earrings to twisted, weighty necklace chains and fantastic headpieces with bells, horns, and animal figurines.

Elaborate silverwork, including headpieces, breast-plates, and necklaces, are collected by families of Hei Miao girls from the time they are born.

Traditional long pleated skirt

Dragon-boat races are held in the Kaili region at least twice a year, celebrating a local victory over invading Chinese armies. Villages send a team of rowers and a long, narrow boat with carved wooden dragon-head prows.

Two buffalo going head-to-head is a feature of Miao festivals, but buffalo are cherished creatures and there is usually no bloodshed.

Only men play the *lusheng*, usually at festivals. This instrument is made from a gourd with a mouthpiece and a dozen or so bamboo pipes. It produces a nasal humming sound.

8 Miao Villages
凯里苗寨

China's Miao *(see pp412–13)* consider the area around Kaili and the ancient town of Zhenyuan their homeland. In between, the terrain rises to rough hills, planted with pine trees and split by river valleys. A few villages maintain traditional wooden houses and cobbled streets; others are not so pretty, but host large festivals. Markets come close to a festival atmosphere and operate on a five-day cycle. Numerous buses run from Kaili, but to reach remoter places, hiring a taxi – or hiking – is necessary.

The traditional village of Langde, tucked into a steep valley

Kaili

105 miles (170 km) E of Guiyang. Yingpanpo Hotel, 53 Yingpan Dong Lu, (0855) 822 2506.

Kaili is a large town of busy streets and unremarkable architecture. Backstreet markets add a bit of color, and there's also a dusty **Minorities Museum**, displaying local silver and embroidery. Hilltop Dage Park is crowned by a wooden pagoda, unusual in its Daoist iconography and statues ritualistically smeared with bloody chicken feathers.

Minorities Museum

5 Guangchang Lu. **Open** 9am–5pm Tue–Sun.

Langde & Xijiang

This route includes the most accessible traditional villages served by buses from Kaili. Possible as a daytrip if you hire a taxi, otherwise, plan to overnight at Xijiang.

Langde is an easy 20-minute walk from the main road. It is entirely traditional, with 50 wooden houses knotted into a fold in the hillside. At Langde's center is a pond and a dancing ground cobbled in concentric rings around a wooden pole adorned with buffalo horns and painted dragons.

Lei Shan is a down-at-heel collection of concrete buildings at the foot of **Leigong Shan** (7,150 ft/2,178 m). Some of the region's remotest villages are found on the mountain and it's possible to organize hiking trips between them. From Lei Shan, it's another 18 miles (30 km) on a good road to **Xijiang**, the area's largest Miao village at around 1,200 wooden homes. The best times to visit are during the fall New Rice Tasting Festival, or Miao New Year's celebrations.

Eastern Route

There are several buses daily from Kaili via Taijiang and Shidong through to Zhenyuan. Both towns host major festivals, with extra transportation during events. Each can be done as a daytrip, but Taijiang does have several hotels, and there are a few basic guesthouses in Shidong.

Taijiang is an untidy market town 34 miles (55 km) from Kaili. It transforms during the Sisters' Meal Festival, when thousands of villagers descend to watch Miao girls choose their husbands. At other times, the old village of **Fanpai** is a more photogenic place to spend a day.

Shidong is a partially wooden riverside village of half-a-dozen lanes. You can shop for beautifully designed silverwork and embroideries on market days, or see them worn during dragon-boat races, held at least twice a year. Afternoon races are accompanied by furious drumming, and the day winds down with a dance in which everyone present – sometimes 10,000 people – joins in.

The terraced slopes of Leigong Shan

Western Route

Frequent buses ply the route from Kaili to Shibing; change here for connections to Zhenyuan. There are some basic accommodations in Chong'an and hotels in Shibing.

Pleasantly rural **Matang** is home to the majority of Gejia, a Miao sub-group. The road passes close by, but you'll need to hire a taxi from Kaili if you don't want to walk the last 2 miles (3 km). About 6 miles (10 km) west of Matang, **Xianglu Shan** (4,265 feet/1,300 m) is where Zhang Xiumei, one of the leaders of the Miao Rebellion, was defeated by government troops in 1872. An annual Hill-Climbing Festival is held here in his honor.

The riverside town of **Chong'an** uses its old core of wooden shops for a lively market, somewhere to experience crowds bargaining for everything from ducklings to home-made spirits. Right on the roadside, **Feiyun Dong** is a curious Daoist shrine founded in 1443, whose few moss-covered halls (one contains a museum of Miao artifacts) are built right into a natural arrangement of grottoes and vegetation. From **Shibing**, a modern place on the south bank of Wuyang He, it is possible to hike up Yuntai Shan, which features the ruins of a Ming-dynasty temple and a handful of paved hiking trails.

A battery of old stone water-powered mills, Chong'an

Miao woman with baby

Zhenyuan

75 miles (125 km) NE of Kaili.
93 Xinglong Jie, (0855) 572 5366..

An old garrison town, Zhenyuan is squeezed by flanking cliffs into two long streets either side of Wuyang He. In the old town on the north bank, Qing-dynasty buildings with wavy eaves and ornate stonework have been restored. East of the old town, a stone Ming-dynasty bridge leads to Qinglong Dong. The temple complex is built into the over-hanging cliffs, where water seeps onto shrines dedicated to Buddhist, Daoist, and Confucian deities. It's also possible to cruise a stretch of the Wuyang He west of Zhenyuan, through a series of limestone gorges.

Festivals

Jan Drum Festival, Gaowu, near Taijiang

Feb/Mar Lusheng Festivals across region

Apr/May Sisters' Meal, Taijiang & Shidong

Jun/Jul Dragon-boat Races at many riverside villages and towns

Jul/Aug Hill-Climbing Festival at Xianglu Shan

Aug/Sep New Rice Tasting Festival in villages around Kaili and Lei Shan; Lusheng Festival, Chong'an

Oct/Nov Lusheng Festival and horse races, Yongxi, near Zhenyuan

Dec Miao New Year, Xijiang and villages around Kaili

Steps leading up to the Monument to the Red Army Martyrs, Zunyi

❾ Zunyi
遵义

150 km N of Guiyang.

The largest city in northern Guizhou, Zunyi is encircled by a gray mass of cement factories and bustling transportation terminals that conceal a quiet and clean older quarter, southwest of Fenghuang Shan. The city holds a special place in the history of the Chinese Communist Party (CCP). In January 1935, Zunyi was invaded by the Red Army during the Long March *(see p262)*. Having suffered major defeats at the hands of the Nationalists, Communist leaders including Mao, Zhou Enlai, and Otto Braun, the Soviet advisor, convened the Zunyi Conference. During the three-day meeting, Mao emerged as the party leader and severed ties with the Russians, a vital step that helped the CCP defeat the Nationalists and eventually emerge as China's ruling party. **Zunyi Conference Museum**, contains the original gray brick conference hall (now closed to the public) and a collection of old photographs. Further on, revolutionary sites line the streets behind the museum, including the former **Red Army Political Department** – housed in a French Catholic church – on Yangliu Jie, and the **Zunyi Folklore Museum** on Hongjun Jie. Across the river, in Fenghuang Shan Park, the **Monument to the Red Army Martyrs** commemorates the heroes of the Long March.

Carved detail, Monument to the Red Army Martyrs

Conference Museum
80 Ziyin Lu. **Open** 9am–5pm daily.

Environs: About 6 miles (10 km) south of Zunyi, **Yang Can Mu** is the final resting place of a local military official, Yang Can, who died around 1250. The stone reliefs of this well-preserved Song-era mausoleum are beautiful, depicting plants, guardian figures, and dragons curling around an ornamental gateway. There is also a portrait of Yang Can in court robes.

❿ Chishui
赤水

150 miles (250 km) NW of Zunyi.

On the banks of Chishui He in northwestern Guizhou on the Sichuan border, Chishui is encircled by sandstone hills. The subtropical forests covering these hills are divided into nature reserves, reached by minibus from town. The finest is **Shizhang Dong**, 23 miles (37 km) south of town, with a 236-ft (72-m) waterfall. Some 10 miles (16 km) southwest, **Sidong Gou** is a valley whose red-silted river gives Chishui its name, "Red Water." It runs over four waterfalls and through a forest thick with bamboo. Locals harvest the edible bamboo shoots, and the mature stems are split and woven into matting. The region is also famous for its *baijiu*, an alcoholic drink produced in **Maotai**, 50 miles (80 km) southeast in Xishui county *(see p571)*.

Nature Reserves
minibus from Chishui.
Open 8am–5pm daily.

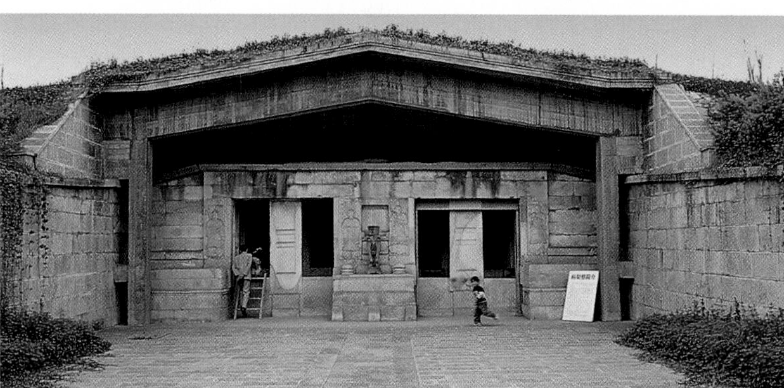

Façade of the elegant Song-dynasty mausoleum, Yang Can Mu

For hotels and restaurants in this region see p562 and p583

Bamboo

A fast-growing, long-lived type of grass found throughout central and southern China, bamboo is put to a huge array of uses. The culms (stems) are turned into pipes, hats, furniture, mats, and cooking utensils, while the shoots of certain varieties are cooked and eaten. The body of the plant is a rhizome (a horizontal, underground stem) that, according to type, clumps or runs, putting out regularly spaced shoots that can grow up to 2 ft (60 cm) per day until they reach full height. Plants might flower only every few decades, or even just once per century, after which they die back. Bamboo has become part of the religion, philosophy, and culture of the Chinese: it represents Confucian values of devotion and righteousness; the segments on its straight stem symbolize the steps along the straight path to enlightenment; and its strength, grace, and longevity have made it the subject of a great many poems and paintings.

In the wild, bamboo covers the hillsides in tall, dense, waving green forests, a sight often called a "bamboo sea." In gardens, smaller plants are often used as symbolic elements *(see p185)*.

Bamboo painting – or *mozhu* – is an esteemed art considered to be on a par with calligraphy *(see p225)*. Using a monochrome ink the painter attempts to convey the bamboo's spirit rather than its exact form in just a few fluid and almost abstract brush strokes.

Split bamboo can be woven into many useful objects, such as lattice screens and blinds for use around the home as well as baskets such as these, used for carrying chickens to market.

Whole bamboo stems are versatile enough to be sawn, drilled, bent, or spliced, while keeping their strength. Items of furniture like these teahouse chairs can be made by a skilled craftsman in a matter of minutes.

The strength of bamboo is such that, in the south of the country where it is easily available, bamboo is preferred over steel poles as scaffolding, even for high-rises. China's urban boom is being built on the back of this giant grass.

Karst

Huge areas of China's southwest comprise visually spectacular landscapes featuring karst – weathered limestone formations. In China, limestone has been created from fossilized prehistoric sea-floor sediments, brought to the surface by geological upheavals. The exposed alkaline limestone is then eroded by the natural acidity of rainwater. Above ground, this creates anything from closely packed "stone forests," poking a few meters skyward, to the huge conical hills covering half of Guizhou, and the tall, elegant pinnacles around Guilin. Underground, percolating water and subterranean rivers carve out long, interlinked caverns, hung with oddly shaped rock formations.

Stone forests, such as Shi Lin outside Kunming *(see pp384–5)*, are karst formations created by the retreating waters of ancient seas, and wind and rain erosion.

Karst Formation

Southwest China's thick and fractured pure limestone has led to a dramatically eroded landscape. The warm, wet climate speeds up the weathering of limestone by acid rainwater and chemicals in rotting plants.

1 Surface streams lose water to cave systems developing in the limestone. Surface drainage is diverted down sink holes to below the water table.

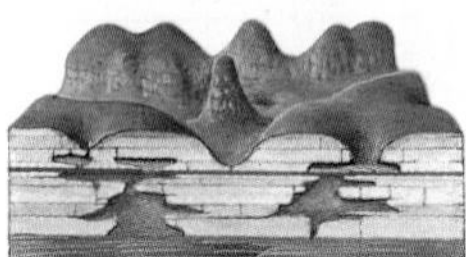

2 Peaks develop from the land left after erosion by the streams. The cave system gets larger as fast-moving subsurface streams bore through the limestone, and the water table drops.

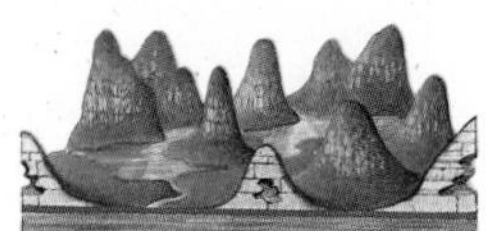

3 Much of the limestone has eroded past the caves down to a layer of shale. Limestone peaks remain, many fractured with small, waterless caves.

Sinkholes, or *tiankeng* (heavenly pits), are formed by repeated cave-ins of thinning layers of limestone. The holes can be disturbingly massive. This one at Xiaozhai, Chongqing, is almost as wide as it is deep –2,200 ft (666 m).

The limestone of southern China's crust is exceptionally thick and extensive, enabling the creation of spectacular karst.

Karst Landscape

This cut-away artwork shows an idealized karst landscape, with all the features shown together. Karst topographies usually have a thick layer of cave-riddled limestone, and then, depending on the area's geology and the age of the formation, a few of the features shown here.

The Li River *(see pp422–3)* cuts through an impressive variety of karst hills. Cruises start in Guilin with *fenglin*, which gradually give way to dense *fengcong*.

***Fenglin* karst**, which translates as peak-forest karst, is characterized by peaks that rise near vertically, like trees, 100 to 250 ft (30 to 80 m) above the surrounding flat floodplains. These dramatic tower-like karsts are found in and around the city of Guilin *(see pp420–21)*.

A losing stream runs along the surface and then disappears underground, joining the subterranean drainage system.

Caves that open out into large halls filled with stunning limestone formations are found throughout karst areas. Minerals deposited by losing streams and water drainage create the strange shapes.

***Fengcong* karst**, or peak-cluster karst, differ from the straight-sided *fenglin*. Their peaks are more cone-shaped and one hill meets the next across a depression or doline. Superb *fengcong* landscape can be seen near the small town of Xingping *(see p423)*.

⓫ Guilin

桂林

Guilin is renowned for its karst peaks, most under 650 ft (198 m) high. Dotted throughout the city, they are particularly concentrated along the Li River *(see pp422–3)* to the south of town. Guilin dates back to the Qin era, and by the 6th century AD, its hills were already inspiring poets. Under the Ming, it emerged as a provincial capital, a position it lost in 1914 to Nanning. Guilin today is a tidy tourist city, with about ten parks enclosing some fine peaks and limestone caves. Guilin means "Osmanthus Forest," and has an avenue of these sweet-scented trees along the riverside Binjiang Lu.

Elephant Trunk Hill, which resembles an elephant drinking water from the Li River

Rong Hu & Shan Hu

Rong Hu Bei Lu & Shan Hu Bei Lu. Pagodas: **Open** 8am–9pm daily.

The conjoined Rong and Shan Lakes lie on either side of Zhongshan Lu, which runs through the heart of town. Originally a part of the Ming city's moats, the lakeshores have been paved and pleasantly planted with shady banyan and willow trees. On the shore of the westerly Rong Hu stands an 800-year-old banyan tree, that gives the lake its name. On the lake's northern shore lies **Gu Nan Men**, Guilin's old South Gate, the only remnant of the Ming city walls. Several classical-style arched bridges join the two banks. Shan Hu, on the eastern side of Zhongshan Lu, is overlooked by the twin 130-ft (40-m) pagodas, **Riyue Shuang Ta,** built in an antique style.

One of the two Riyue Shuang Ta

Xiangbi Shan

Off Minzhu Lu. 2, 58. **Tel** (0773) 223 5151. **Open** 6:30am–6:30pm daily.

The most famous of the city's rock formations, the 328-ft (100-m) high Xiangbi Shan (Elephant Trunk Hill), with a hole through one end, resembles the stylized form of an elephant taking a drink from the adjacent Li River. According to legend, a baggage elephant in an imperial convoy was abandoned by the riverside by an uncaring emperor after it became sick. Nursed back to health by an elderly couple, the elephant refused to rejoin the returning convoy and was killed by the emperor and turned into a hill, the one that stands here to this day. The small stupa at the summit is said to be the hilt of the emperor's sword sticking out of the elephant's back. Along the path to the summit stands an old, crumbling pagoda.

Qixing Gongyuan

Qixing Lu. 58. **Open** 7am–8pm daily.

The pleasant Qixing Gongyuan (Seven Stars Park) covers an area of 1 sq mile (2 sq km) along the eastern shore of the Li River. It is named after the four peaks on Putuo Hill, and three on Crescent Hill. Seen together, the peaks form the shape of the Great Bear or Big Dipper constellation, which governs fate in Chinese mythology. Covered in thick scrub, they provide shelter to about 100 half-wild monkeys. There are several trails and pathways ascending to viewing pavilions.

Guilin's crags are renowned for their carvings and caves. Crescent Hill is known for the 200-odd poems and commentaries carved into its overhangs, some of which are believed to date back to the Tang dynasty. Putuo Hill, which houses the 22-story high Putuo Si, is hollowed out by Qixing Yan (Seven Stars Cave), a broad cavern with a small subterranean waterfall and surprisingly few rock formations. The 246-ft (75-m) Luotuo Shan (Camel Hill), standing on its own to the north of the park, resembles a seated single-humped camel. From its summit, there are views away to the south of Chuan Shan and Ta Shan (Pagoda Hill), topped with a Ming-dynasty pagoda.

The pleasant Qixing Gongyuan (Seven Stars Park)

For hotels and restaurants in this region see p562 and p583

Colorfully illuminated formations inside Ludi Yan (Reed Flute Cave)

Jingjiang Prince's Palace & Duxiu Feng

1 Wangcheng Lu, off Xihua Li.
Tel (0773) 280 3149. **Open** 7:30am–6:30pm daily.

Complete with its own encircling wall and four gates, this palace resembles a miniature Forbidden City. It was originally built for the Ming prince Zhu Shouqian in 1372, pre-dating Beijing's palace by 34 years. Having housed 14 successive Ming princes, it later served as Sun Yat-sen's headquarters in the 1920s. Today, it houses the Guangxi Teacher Training College. A sloping marble slab, carved with clouds at the entrance, indicates an imperial residence, while the absence of the usual dragons indicates that the palace was for a prince, not an emperor.

Within the palace grounds lies **Duxiu Feng** (Solitary Beauty Peak), whose 707-ft (216-m) spike protects the palace from the unlucky northern direction. At its foot is a tag carved by the Song-dynasty governor Wang Zhenggong, extolling Guilin's charms. Steps lead to the summit, offering splendid views.

Fubo Shan

Binjiang Lu. **Open** 7am–7pm daily.

A tall, yellow-gray rock rising from the river, Fubo Shan is believed to calm the rough waters below, hence its name, "Wave-Subduing Hill." Grottoes around the peak are filled with Song-dynasty carvings and at the foot of the hill, a dramatic stalactite named the "Sword-Testing Stone" hangs inches above the floor.

Ludi Yan

3 miles (5 km) NW of city center.
3, 58. **Open** 8am–5:30pm daily.

Used as a hideout by Guilin's residents during the Japanese invasion in the 1940s, Ludi Yan (Reed Flute Cave) contains 33-ft- (10-m-) high tunnels winding for 546 yards (500 m) through Guangming Hill. Inside, its numerous rock formations are illuminated with neon lights.

VISITORS' CHECKLIST

Practical Information
235 miles (378 km) NE of Nanning. 800,000. 11 Binjiang Lu, (0773) 225 9922.

Transportation
Liangjiang International Airport. Guilin Train Station. Guilin bus station, CAAC (buses to airport), Minibus station (to Yangshuo).

Guilin City Center

1. Rong Hu
2. Shan Hu
3. Xiangbi Shan
4. Qixing Gongyuan
5. Jingjiang Prince's Palace & Duxiu Feng
6. Fubo Shan

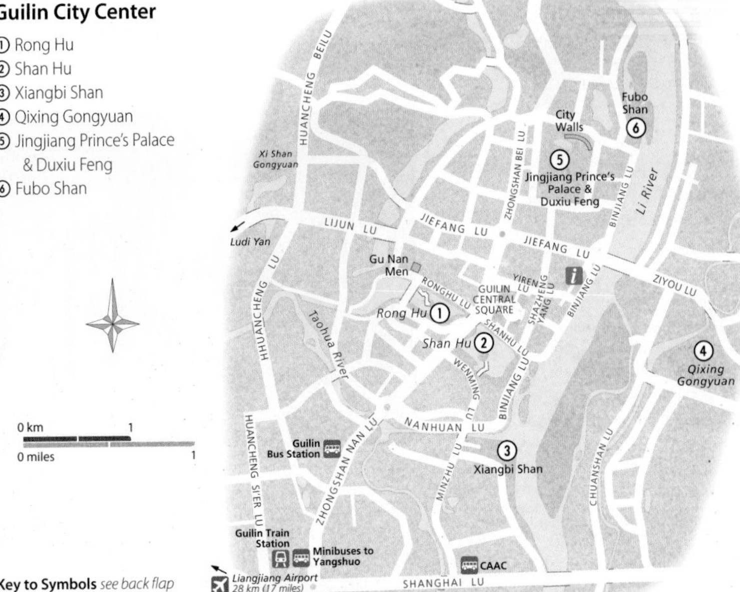

Key to Symbols *see back flap*

Li River Cruise

漓江

The cruise along the Li River (Li Jiang) from Guilin south to Yangshuo passes through landscape that seems lifted straight out of a Chinese scroll painting. The shallow river weaves between sheer-sided, 980-ft (300-m) karst peaks, all weathered into intriguing shapes and interspersed with the villages and bamboo groves so typical of southern China's rural areas. People here still travel the river on low bamboo rafts, often using trained cormorants to catch fish *(see p424)*. Cruises take about 6 hours and usually include a buffet lunch. Foreign visitors sail in boats with English-speaking guides, although this costs more.

Bamboo rafts, for navigating the river during winter's low waters

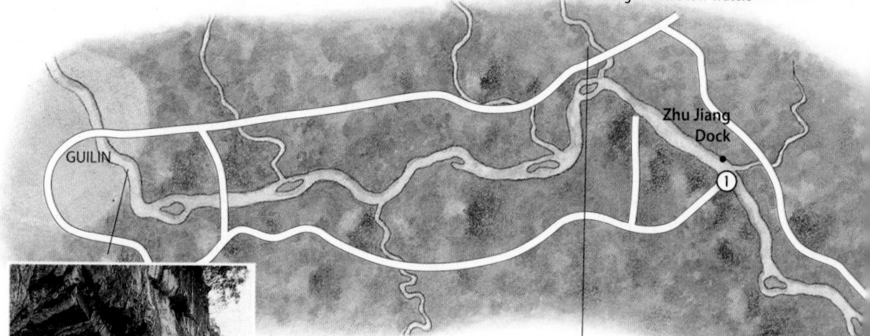

GUILIN

Zhu Jiang Dock

①

★ Elephant Trunk Hill

Located on the riverside in downtown Guilin, Elephant Trunk Hill (Xiangbi Shan) is an endearing symbol of the city *(see p420)*. It resembles an elephant who has placed its trunk in the Li River waters for a drink.

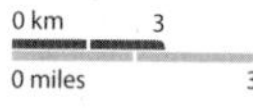

KEY

① **The pier at** Zhu Jiang is where many tours begin.

② **In winter**, tours may start at Yangdi, if water levels are too low upstream.

③ **Fish Tail Peak**

④ **Nine Horse Fresco Hill** is a cliff face stained brown by minerals, creating a mural resembling galloping horses.

⑤ **Yellow Cloth Shoal**, a shallow patch of yellow river stones, is easily seen even during high water.

⑥ **Snail Hill**

⑦ **Five Fingers Hill**

Daxu

Downstream from Guilin, Daxu is a Song-era market town, whose cobbled main street still retains many timber-and stone-houses over a century old, as well as an attractive Qing bridge just outside town.

Pointed *fengcong* karst formations near Yangdi

VISITORS' CHECKLIST

Practical Information
Guilin to Yangshuo 52 miles (85 km), 6 hrs. 11 Binjiang Lu, Guilin, (0773) 225 9922 (CITS for booking).

Transportation
to starting point and from Yangshuo provided.

★ Penholder Peak
Just past Yangdi and facing Writing-Brush Mountain, this sharp, vertical outcrop does indeed resemble a traditional Chinese penholder. This section of hills is the beginning of the most spectacular mountain ranges.

★ Scenery at Xingping
Xingping, an old, wooden town and ferry port, marks the start of a spectacular 12-mile (20-km) stretch of scenery. Pick of the peaks are Five Fingers Hill and swirly patterned Snail Hill.

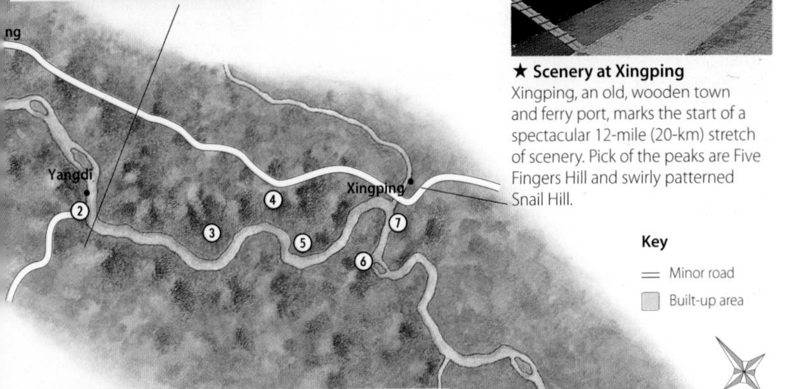

Dragon Head Hill
Visitors to Yangshuo are greeted by this imposing peak, said to resemble the head of a dragon with its gaping jaws wide open.

⓬ Yangshuo

阳朔

A small town at the end of the Li River Cruise *(see pp422–3)*, Yangshuo is surrounded by some spectacular karst hills interspersed with green paddy fields. It was nothing more than a rural marketplace until the late 1980s, when it became popular with visitors taking the cruise from Guilin. Though not as tranquil as it used to be, Yangshuo remains a good base to explore the surrounding peaks and river, as well as a few caves and outlying villages. Hiring a bicycle is one of the easiest ways to explore the area. Local specialties include grapefruit-like pomelos and "beer fish" – served at most restaurants in town. Yangshuo has become one of Asia's favorite rock-climbing centers, with more than 200 short routes mapped out.

Ferries moored along the Li River, with karst hills rising in the distance

Xi Jie

A 275-yd (250-m) long cobbled street running between the highway and the Li River, Xi Jie (West Street) is lined with restored rural architecture dating from the Qing dynasty. Today, it is lined with restaurants, cafés, guesthouses, and souvenir shops that attract crowds of visitors. Restaurants serve Western cuisine such as wood-fired pizzas and steak, as well as local specialties including a variety of fresh fish dishes. Shops sell a range of inexpensive Chinese souvenirs, from Mao memorabilia and wooden theater masks to antique wooden panels, batiks, silk T-shirts, scroll paintings, and modern and traditional clothes. A few shops also sell factory-reject designer wear at bargain prices. The C.Source Residence, a hotel located about halfway down the street, was built in the 19th century as an inn for merchants from Jiangxi. The docks area at the river end, where ferries pull in from Guilin, is covered in ornamental paving and offers good views of the angular peaks upstream. In the area north of the highway are some lovely back alleys, and a lively produce market where locals shop.

The forested Bilian Feng (Green Lotus Peak), overlooking the river

Bilian Feng & Yangshuo Gongyuan

Open daily.

Situated close to the center of town are two 328-ft (100-m) high peaks which can be climbed. To the southeast of town, overlooking the river, is the towering Bilian Feng (Green Lotus Peak), with a steep track to the summit. The second peak, Xilang Shan, is situated in Yangshuo Gongyuan to the west of town. It has an easier set of steps that lead to a viewing pavilion. The park is also a pleasant place to stroll and watch sessions of early-morning *tai ji quan*.

Jianshan Si & Underground Caves

3 miles (5 km) S of Yangshuo. or cycle. **Open** 8:30am–5pm daily.

The only temple in the area around Yangshuo, Jianshan Si is

Cormorant Fishing

The Chinese have used tame cormorants to fish for thousands of years, and this unusual technique is still practiced in southern areas. Fishermen set off on bamboo rafts after dark, with cormorants wearing collars to prevent them from swallowing their catches. The birds swim just below the surface alongside the raft towards a light hanging from the bow. When a bird has made a catch, the fisherman pulls it from the water and retrieves the fish from the bird's beak. Hour-long viewing trips can be organized during the summer months through most hotels.

Cormorant fishing at night using lanterns

built in a simple, late Qing-dynasty style, with wing-like horsehead gables protecting its doorway. Located nearby, the Black Buddha, Assembled Dragons, and New Water Caves are a series of underground caverns discovered in the 1990s. Lit up with colored lights, these cool, damp caves are far smaller than the other well-known caves in the region, and the temple and caves are becoming popular with tourists.

Pomelos on sale at a market

Yueliang Shan

4 miles (7 km) S of Yangshuo. or cycle. **Open** 7am–6:30pm daily.

The distinctive crescent-shaped arch that pierces Yueliang Shan (Moon Hill) has made it the most famous of Yangshuo's peaks. Stone steps, steep in places, lead to the base of the arch, a half-hour climb through bamboo thickets and bushes. The view of the Li River valley from the far side of the arch is magnificent, with fields laid out below, encircling the jagged karst pinnacles. The best time to visit is during the summer rains, when the fields are bright green. If traveling by bicycle, visitors should take the main road south of town. Close by, **Longtan Village** has several unrestored old buildings, with white-washed brick walls, wooden doors, and tiled roofs supporting intricate "flying eaves" drawn out into points.

Fuli Village

5 miles (8 km) E of Yangshuo. or cycle.

The pretty village of Fuli is a quiet rural center except when it hosts a busy produce market on dates ending in 1, 4, or 7. One of the best in the region, it is visited by throngs of villagers who bargain for livestock, seasonal fruit, plastic buckets, wooden pipes, all kinds of vegetables, and bamboo fans – a famous local product. To the north is Donglang Shan, a narrow hill often paired with Yangshuo's Xilang Shan in local legends.

VISITORS' CHECKLIST

Practical Information

44 miles (70 km) S of Guilin. 60,000. 8th Fl, 362 Zhongshan Zhong Lu, Da Shijie. For rock climbing: visit Insight Adventures, 53 Xianqian Jie, (0773) 881 1033.

Transportation

from Guilin. tours and boat trips available.

The pretty countryside surrounding Assembled Dragons Cave, Yangshuo

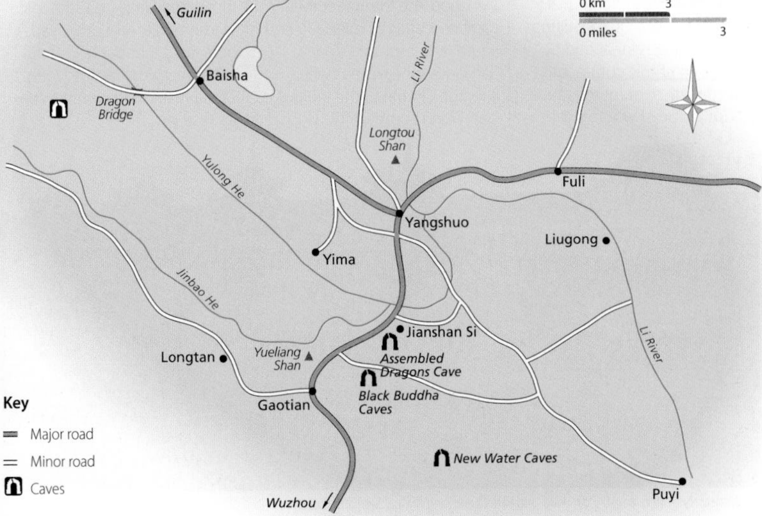

A view of the complex terracing on Longji Titian, Longsheng

⓭ Longsheng
龙胜

56 miles (90 km) NW of Guilin. 170,000. minibuses from Longsheng to Ping'an.

The high ridges of the Rongshui River valley surround the township of Longsheng, which serves as a good base for exploring the adjoining countryside dotted with Zhuang and Yao villages. To the southwest is a steep range of 3,280-ft (1,000-m) high hills, known as **Longji Titian** (Dragon Backbone Terraces), whose lower and middle reaches have been covered in rice terracing by the Zhuang people *(see p430)*. The Zhuang, who form the majority of Longsheng's population, live in traditional wooden houses. On the hilltops lie a few villages inhabited by the Yao, an ethnic community that consists of numerous sub-groups, some of whom still depend on hunting rather than farming. They are also especially skilled in embroidery, weaving, and dyeing. The Zhuang village of **Ping'an** sits near the top of a ridge in the heart of Longji Titian. It offers basic accommodations in traditional wooden buildings, as well as walking trails leading to other settlements in the area.

⓮ Sanjiang
三江

90 miles (145 km) NW of Guilin. 360,000.

Situated on the Rongshui River, Sanjiang was the base of resistance against the Japanese during World War II, when Danzhou, the former regional capital located 22 miles (35 km) south, was captured. Today, Sanjiang is the main town of a region central to the indigo-clad Dong community, which has a population of around 2.8 million. Typical Dong architecture, consisting of wooden houses, towers, and bridges, can be found in several villages up in the hills to the north. The hospitable Dong usually offer visitors their favorite *you cha* or oil tea, a bitter soup made with rice and fried tea leaves.

On the south bank of the river is an 11-story **Drum Tower**, the largest in the region. It was built in 2003, using entirely traditional techniques. The structure is supported by four 154-ft (47-m) pillars, each carved from separate tree trunks. The third story of the tower houses a large drum.

The small **Fulu Buddhist Nunnery**, situated on the hill behind, is a little unusual, since the Dong community is mainly animist. The nunnery's three halls contain a mix of statuary representing both religions.

Bamboo shoots for sale, Sanjiang

Situated to the north of the river, the County Museum stands next to the Government Guesthouse. The museum exhibits several scale models of traditional Dong architecture, photographs, and maps displaying Sanjiang's strategic wartime role. Also displayed here are a number of colorful costumes worn by the Dong, Zhuang, and Yao communities for festivals.

The intricately crafted *fengyu qiao*, wind-and-rain Chengyang Bridge, Sanjiang County

Dong Architecture

The Dong, who dwell in forested hill country where stone is of poor quality, make efficient use of timber. Nails are avoided, and even the largest structures are skillfully pegged together. As incomes rise in the region, there's been a resurgence of traditional building with villages competing with one another to sponsor the construction of bridges and towers. Drum towers are usually square-based, with multiple octagonal eaves. Originally they served as watchtowers and rallying places for the village, many with adjoining theater stages for use during festivals. Elaborate, covered wind-and-rain bridges are also places for villagers to meet, and are believed to ward off inauspicious energy.

Traditional drum tower in one of Chengyang's pretty rural hamlets

Environs: The most accessible Dong villages lie 11 miles (18 km) north of Sanjiang at **Chengyang**, a group of hamlets on the far side of the Linxi He, accessible by bus or taxi from Sanjiang. Connecting Chengyang to the main road are over 100 bridges. One of the most exquisite is a *fengyu qiao*, a wind-and-rain bridge, dating from 1916, for which an entrance ticket is required. The 256-ft- (78-m-) long bridge, built from pegged cedar – no nails are said to have been used – took 12 years to complete. The roof is especially elaborate, with five raised pavilions, each built in a different regional style. These beautifully built bridges not only served a practical function, but acted as shrines to river spirits as well. Most of the altars have now been moved to the riverbank, as the incense is considered a fire hazard.

Basic accommodations are available for visitors interested in exploring the ethnic villages and surrounding countryside. Each hamlet in Chengyang houses a small drum tower, while the surrounding fields are irrigated by bamboo pipes fed by huge, spindly waterwheels, also made from plaited bamboo.

The highland market town of **Dudong** lies 2 hours by bus north of Sanjiang, on a separate road past numerous Dong villages. Situated near the Hunanese border, it provides basic accommodations for visitors. A cobbled walking track leads uphill to **Gaoding**, a cluster of six drum towers and 100-or-so dark-roofed wooden houses.

⑮ Zhaoxing
肇兴

75 miles (120 km) NW of Sanjiang. from Sanjiang.

One of the most attractive Dong villages, sprinkled with fish ponds and bisected by a stream, Zhaoxing sits in a wide, flat valley and is famed throughout China for its impressive collection of traditional architecture (although there are a few modern buildings found on its outskirts). The town is divided into five sections, each inhabited by a different clan, and each possessing its own drum tower, theater, and wind-and-rain bridge. The original structures were destroyed during the Cultural Revolution, and although they have been rebuilt since, they are charmingly well-worn and impressively intricate. The bridges and theaters are embellished with mirror fragments and detailed moldings.

The Dong community here still makes and wears traditional dark-blue clothing, which is hand-beaten with wooden mallets until soft, and then varnished with egg white to ward off mosquitoes.

Numerous muddy tracks lead through the surrounding rice terraces. One trail leads 4 miles (7 km) uphill to the small village of **Tang'an**, packed with wooden buildings. **Jitang**, 2 miles (3 km) southwest of Zhaoxing, is also worth the steep climb. It has some old drum towers that survived the vandalism of the early 1970s.

A cluster of Dong wooden houses, Zhaoxing

⓰ Huangyao
黄姚

68 miles (110 km) SE of Yangshuo. 3,000. from Yangshuo or Guilin.

This sizeable rural village survives almost completely intact from Qing times. Its atmospheric cobbled streets, stone bridges, and old houses are laid out along a small river beneath a ring of limestone peaks. Many houses have heavy wooden doors and elaborate "fire-baffle" end walls – to direct heat and flames in a certain direction – drawn up into a decorative oval shape, while the village gates are guarded by short brick watchtowers with gun slits at the front, left over from days of banditry. The most impressive building is an **ancestral hall** built in the southern Chinese style, with atriums separated by carved wooden screens.

Huangyao's rural Chinese setting and beautiful scenery draws artists and photographers, and has been used as a location in such films as *The Painted Veil* (2006). Huangyao is neither as developed for tourism as many other old villages in China, nor does it attract the same volume of tourists. By late afternoon, the streets are generally empty except for a few chickens and dogs. At night the back lanes are hung with attractive red lanterns.

Xi Shan's tea plantation surrounded by mist-covered forest, Guiping

⓱ Guiping
桂平

205 miles (330 km) S of Guilin.

Located at the confluence of the Yu and Xi Rivers, Guiping is an unremarkable modern city surrounded by lush mountain scenery. Its importance as a regional center has declined, due to the cessation of river traffic during the 1990s. Its main industry is now sugar cane.

Guiping is renowned for its high-quality green tea, *Xishan cha,* which grows on **Xi Shan** (West Mountain), on the outskirts of town. The long leaves of tea are processed and rolled into what look like miniature black cheroots. They are steeped one at a time to produce a faintly bitter, yet refreshing brew.

Lion statute from Longhua Si, Guiping

Xi Shan itself can be easily ascended from town. The 2-hour hike, past tea plantations and through bamboo groves, passes a number of Tang-era Buddhist temples. **Longhua Si**, deep in the forest on the upper slopes of the mountain, was built during the Song dynasty and heavily renovated during the 1980s. It contains numerous Buddhist statues. The temples sell tea, which is said to be superior to

A depiction of imperial forces recapturing Nanjing from the Taiping rebels in 1864

The Taiping Rebellion

After being defeated in the 1840–42 Opium Wars, China was forced to pay a huge indemnity to Britain. Taxation was increased, causing great hardship in poor rural areas such as southern Guangxi. People's discontent with the weak Qing rule was fueled by Hong Xiuquan, who formed a 10,000-strong militia, known as the Taiping Tianguo (Kingdom of Heavenly Peace), at Jintian village in January 1851. Marching north, the Taiping captured Nanjing, making it their capital in March 1853. Influenced by Hong's personal interpretation of Christianity, the Taiping initially planned the overthrow of the Qing dynasty along with traditional religions, aiming to establish an egalitarian society. However, poor military planning and Hong's paranoia saw the movement falter. In July 1864, imperial forces wrested back Nanjing after a siege in which Hong died. It is thought that 20 million people were killed during the 13-year-long Taiping Uprising, one of the world's bloodiest civil conflicts.

that sold in Guiping shops. The summit offers splendid views of the river plains.

Environs: A 40-minute journey by bus from Guiping, the hamlet of **Jintian** lies 16 miles (25 km) north of town. From the bus stop, it's a 3-mile (5-km) walk across rural fields to the location of the first head-quarters of Hong Xiuquan's Taiping Army. A low-key museum houses weapons, paintings, and maps recording the main events of the Taiping Uprising.

Waterfall pouring down a Xi Shan rock face, Guiping

⓲ Nanning
南宁

235 miles (380 km) SE of Guilin. 2,480,000. 5/F Block A, 26 Jinhu Lu, (0771) 262 6228.

Nestled in the southern half of the province, only 120 miles (200 km) from the Vietnamese border, the Guangxi capital of Nanning is somewhat removed from the rest of the province. Founded in the Song dynasty, Nanning became the provincial capital in 1914, until it was occupied by the Japanese forces during World War II. Reinstated as the capital in 1949, Nanning later served as an important center for supplies going to North Vietnam during the Vietnam War in the 1960s. In 1979, relations with Vietnam soured, and China went to war with its southern neighbor; Nanning once more became a military stronghold. Today, the city is expanding rapidly, partly as a consequence of cross-border traffic, which resumed in the 1990s.

Nanning makes a useful transit point for those heading to Vietnam or towards sights located in the southwestern corner of the province, such as the Detian Falls and the Zuo Jiang *(see pp430–31)*. Nanning itself has only a handful of monuments and sights, but is a nice enough place with a laid-back atmosphere and many bustling markets. It is also the main city of the Zhuang minority *(see p430)*, who make up over 60 percent of the population.

The busy shopping district of **Xingning Lu**, with its well-restored European-style buildings, is a reminder that Nanning was opened to foreign trade in 1907. The **Provincial Museum** on Minzu Dadao has a display of over 50 antique bronze "Dongson" drums in many different styles, some of which are about 2,000 years old.

On Renmin Dong Lu, **Renmin Park** is planted with a variety of tropical plants such as giant taro, heliconias, bird-nest ferns, and philodendrons. To the east of the city on Chahua Yuan Lu, **Jinhua Cha Gardens** exhibits the rare Golden Camellia, only found in the mountains of Guangxi and quite possibly now extinct in the wild. Unusual for a camellia, its petals are large and rather tough.

Provincial Museum
34 Minzu Dadao. **Tel** (0771) 270 7025. **Open** 9am–5pm Tue–Sun.

Renmin Park
1 Renmin Dong Lu. **Open** 6am–7pm daily.

Dongson Drum

Named for an archeological site in Vietnam, the oldest Dongson drums are over 2,200 years old. They appear to have originated in Thailand or Vietnam, from where their use spread across Southeast Asia. The typically narrow-waisted drums are made from bronze and reach up to 3 ft (1 m) in height, in styles that vary greatly from region to region. In Guangxi, timpani are marked with a 12-pointed star and are often decorated with frog figurines, while their middles are finely chased in stylized designs of warriors in boats wearing feathered headdresses. Originally used as storage vessels, later, as Ming historians observed, they came to symbolize chiefly authority amongst the Zhuang. They were played during agricultural ceremonies, and still feature as percussion instruments in some festivals amongst Guizhou's Miao community.

Bronze drum from Nanning

Vegetable vendors with their baskets at an outdoor market, Nanning

Ancient rock art on the cliff of Hua Shan along the Zuo Jiang

⑲ Zuo Jiang
左江

110 miles (180 km) SW of Nanning. to Ningming. to Ningming. sampan to Hua Shan from Ningming. Hua Shan and Longrui Nature Reserve:

A river tour up the peaceful Zuo Jiang in a sampan hired from Ningming, a small settlement on the railroad between Nanning and Pingxiang, takes visitors past prehistoric rock art and towering karst scenery. Produced almost 2,000 years ago between the Warring States and the late Han periods, the paintings of over 2,600 human figures are scattered across 70 locations along the river. Painted in red-brown ochre, they mainly depict mass shamanistic ceremonies. The designs show marked similarities to those on bronze Dongson drums *(see p429)* that have been found in Vietnam and southern China. It is believed that the artists were the Luo Yue, ancestors of the indigenous Zhuang.

The first paintings are about 12 miles (20 km) upstream from Ningming, but the largest concentration is situated at **Hua Shan** (Flower Mountain), about 2 hours along the river. A steep cliff rising 33 ft (10 m) above the water is covered in as many as 1,200 stick figures, mostly male, engaged in what appears to be a ritual dance. A frequently recurring symbol is a small circle, thought to represent a bronze drum, around which several figures seem to dance with their arms raised as if to invoke the gods. A few carry swords or ride on the back of beasts. Only two of them are clearly women, depicted with long, flowing hair. Other figures include dogs, a horse, farmers, and rowers in a dragon-boat race. A shaman, identifiable by his elaborate headdress, appears at the center of all this activity.

Panlong, a tiny hamlet on the river between Ningming and Hua Shan, has gorgeous views of the rural peaked landscape. Lodging is available here in a handful of pretty wooden buildings. Paths lead from Panlong through the **Longrui Nature Preserve**, meant to protect the very rare white-headed leaf monkey. A sighting of these black-and-white primates amongst the dense forest and undergrowth is unlikely, but its rugged paths are well worth exploring.

Gateway on the Vietnamese border, Pingxiang

⑳ Pingxiang
凭祥

120 miles (195 km) SW of Nanning.

Surrounded by vast fields of sugar cane and the jagged hills so typical of this region, Pingxiang is a busy market town

A group of Zhuang women in traditional clothes

The Zhuang Community

With a population of around 17 million, the Zhuang form China's largest ethnic minority. Most live in the Guangxi Zhuang Autonomous Region, although there are also communities in adjoining provinces and Vietnam. They speak their own language, which uses the Roman alphabet instead of Chinese characters. Visitors will see bilingual road signs all across the region, particularly in Guilin and Nanning. Apart from their language, it is hard to distinguish urban Zhuang from the Han Chinese, although in the country the men often dress in turbans and black pyjamas, while the women wear blue embroidered jackets. The Zhuang are mainly animistic, which explains the lack of Buddhist and Daoist temples in Guangxi. One of their most famous festivals is Buffalo Soul Day, held in honor of the Buffalo King's birthday on the eighth day of the fourth lunar month (Apr/May). On this day, all buffalos are washed and groomed, fed a special rice dish, and given the day off work.

The magnificent Detian Falls surrounded by spectacular karst hills

and the railhead for the crossing into Vietnam. Visitors require a valid visa to enter Vietnam at the border crossing, **Youyi Guan** (Friendship Pass), another 9 miles (15 km) away. The current border was demarcated as early as the Ming era, and a good stretch of the original 33-ft (10-m) stone wall still stands, along with a restored watch-tower and gateway under which visitors pass. The tower's second floor houses a diorama of the area and offers views into Vietnam. An early 20th-century European-style building on the Chinese side was built by the French when they controlled this region, known then as Indo-China. For those crossing into Vietnam, the rail line for Hanoi resumes 3 miles (5 km) away on the far side at Dong Dang.

㉑ Detian Falls
德天瀑布

125 miles (200 km) W of Nanning. via Daxin to Shuolong, then minibus from Shuolong to falls, 10 miles (16 km).

A spectacular set of broad cataracts dividing China from Vietnam, Detian is the second largest transnational waterfall in the world, after Niagara Falls on the US-Canada border. The two attractions, however, have little else in common. Detian does not possess the sheer force of Niagara, but is more gently beautiful, falling in stages, and surrounded by an emerald karst landscape of jagged hills and plowed fields. It is possible to swim in the broad pool beneath the falls, and to take a bamboo raft into the spray near its base. Remember that a border runs through the center of the river – do not stray too far across. A road running along the top of the falls leads to a stone tablet from the 1950s that marks out the border.

㉒ Beihai
北海

135 miles (215 km) S of Nanning. to Hainan Island.

A tropical port city of about 400,000 people, Beihai is one of the departure points for ferries to Hainan Island *(see pp310–11)*. Many of the city's residents are ethnic Chinese from Vietnam, whose expulsion from that country in the late 1970s sparked a brief attempt by China to invade its neighbor.

Established over 2,000 years ago, the city prospered during the Han era, when it was a busy port. The old Colonial Quarter, on the northern seafront along Zhuhai Lu, is a mile-long (1½-km)stretch of narrow lanes and disintegrating 1920s plasterwork, at least one former church, and several colonnaded shopfronts.

About 3 miles (5 km) south of the center along Sichuan Lu is the Beihai International Passenger Port, which also serves as a working fishing port.

Beihai's other attraction, **Yin Tan** (Silver Beach), lies 6 miles (10 km) south of town, but it does not compare with the lovely beaches of Hainan.

Located about 20 miles (32 km) offshore from Beihai, volcanic **Weizhou Island** offers attractive beaches amid groves of banana trees. It also has a Gothic church built by French churchmen in 1882.

Facade of an old colonial church on Weizhou Island

THE NORTHEAST

The Northeast at a Glance

Lying in the peripheral corner of China, the northeast (Dongbei) abounds in raw beauty and mineral wealth, and was inhabited for centuries by indomitable tribes including the Khitan, Mongols, and Jurchen (Manchu), the latter ruling China for over 250 years. Today, the region's three provinces of Liaoning, Jilin, and Heilongjiang form China's industrial heartland, although the many lakes, mountains, and rugged borderlands offer scenic getaways. In Liaoning, Shenyang's palaces are testament to its great Manchu past, while Dalian is a fast-moving city with architectural marvels. The city of Jilin, once the capital of Manchukuo (1933–45), the puppet state installed by the Japanese, has stunning winter landscapes. Changchun, the capital of Jilin province, has a thriving automobile industry, while Heilongjiang is famed for its Harbin Ice Festival.

The ornate *paifang* or gateway to the rugged scenery of Bingyu Valley (Bingyu Gou), Liaoning

Sights at a Glance

1. Shenyang
2. Jinzhou
3. Dandong
4. Bingyu Valley
5. Dalian
6. Changchun
7. Jilin
8. *Changbai Shan pp454–5*
9. Harbin
10. Mudanjiang Jingpo Hu
11. Zhalong Nature Reserve
12. Wudalianchi & the River Border

◀ Cattle being led through the snow, northeast China

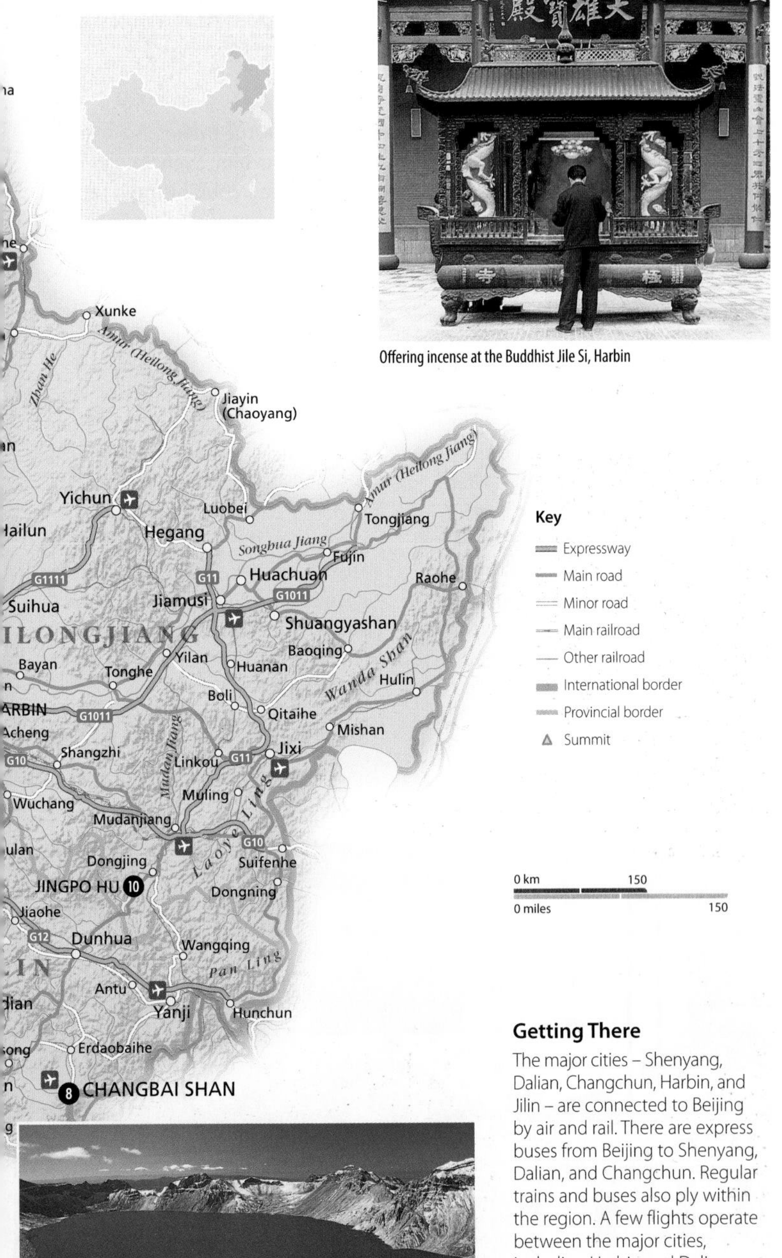

Offering incense at the Buddhist Jile Si, Harbin

The icy blue waters of the volcanic Tian Chi – Heaven's Lake – in Changbai Shan

Getting There

The major cities – Shenyang, Dalian, Changchun, Harbin, and Jilin – are connected to Beijing by air and rail. There are express buses from Beijing to Shenyang, Dalian, and Changchun. Regular trains and buses also ply within the region. A few flights operate between the major cities, including Harbin and Dalian. In winter, popular destinations such as Jilin and Harbin are relatively easy to reach, while remoter areas such as Jingpo Hu and Changbai Shan are more difficult to access. Within cities, taxis are the best option.

A PORTRAIT OF THE NORTHEAST

Sandwiched between Russia, Korea, and Inner Mongolia, the three northeastern provinces constitute China's easternmost extent. Even though the prevalent culture is Han Chinese, the northeast's geography, history, and extended external boundaries have shaped a distinct regional identity. The region's attractions range from the bustling sprawl of its big cities to the rugged and sublime terrain beyond, and the cultural mix of its border towns.

It is hard to categorize the northeast (Dongbei) – it enjoys hot summers but glacial winters, and although heavy industry and socialist planning blight some cityscapes, others sport elegant pockets of colonial architecture. While parts of the region have been reveling in China's economic boom, others have suffered from chronic unemployment.

Encompassing the three provinces of Liaoning, Jilin, and Heilongjiang, the northeast was a latecomer to the Chinese empire and is sometimes considered as little more than an appendix to the rest of the country. As part of former Manchuria, however, it was the cradle of the magnificent civilization that ruled China from 1644 until 1912. Shenyang, Liaoning's present capital, became the Manchu capital in 1625, and the site of the Imperial Palace. Here they perfected their Eight Banner system of color-coded hereditary social and administrative divisions *(see pp438–9)*. Taking advantage of the overthrow of the Ming dynasty in 1644, they moved their capital to the Forbidden City in Beijing. Even today, the region's Manchu population take great pride in their heritage and still adhere to the Eight Banners.

In more recent times, the northeast attracted the attentions of Russia and Japan, both of which have helped shape the region's destiny. At the end of the

Stately Russian architecture in Daliqu district, Harbin

Facade of the Puppet Emperor's Palace, Changchun

19th century the Russians, interested in the ice-free port of Lushun (Dalian), tried to annex parts of Manchuria and built part of the Trans-Siberian Railway line, before being humiliated by Japan. The area suffered again during the Japanese occupation of the 1930s and 40s, when it was renamed Manchukuo and Pu Yi was installed as Puppet Emperor. The brutal occupation left deep scars on the region's psyche along with some pitiful sights, such as the Unit 731 Museum near Harbin.

Door handle, Confucius Temple

Japanese occupation came to an end after World War II, ushering in a period of industrialization under Chairman Mao. His camaraderie with Russia in the 1950s resulted in the installation of a Stalinist state-sector economy. The peaceful relationship was shortlived and conflicts soon flared along the border.

The northeast's rich mineral wealth has made it China's industrial heartland. However, under-investment and ruthless downsizing with huge state-sector layoffs have resulted in high unemployment.

Centuries of hardship have molded the character of the *Dongbeiren* (north-easterners). Resolute, unaffected, forthright, and hospitable, they are looked upon by their compatriots as a hardy, stalwart people, prone to hard drinking. Taller and stockier than their southern cousins, they speak Mandarin with a coarse, albeit intelligible accent.

Unlike the sophisticated cuisine of Hong Kong and Shanghai, the local food – including *jiaozi* (dumplings), *dun* (stews), and *tudou* (potatoes) – is hearty and filling. The temperament of the people matches the vigorous landscapes that range from dense forest to volcanic regions and the tough terrain along the Russian and North Korean borders. These areas offer plenty of outdoor options including trekking and bird-watching, particularly in Zhalong Nature Reserve. The border town of Dandong has a thriving tourist industry, catering mainly to North Korean visitors.

Despite the unfortunate effects of industrialization, there is much worth seeing. The onion domes and Byzantine ornamentation visible in Harbin's buildings are distinctly Russian, a legacy of the city's cross-cultural links. Dalian, on the Yellow Sea, is a dynamic and progressive city that has enjoyed the same economic success as Shanghai. Known as the "Hong Kong of the North," it adds an affluent touch to the northeastern rustbelt.

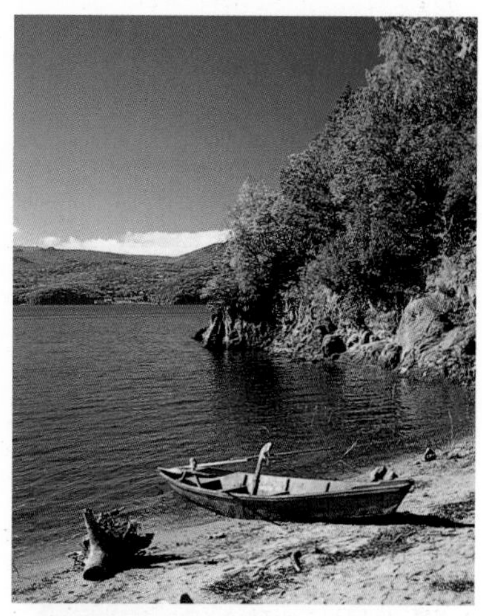
A secluded bay by the blue waters of the volcanic Jingpo Hu, Heilongjiang

The Manchu Dynasty

The final overlords of the Middle Kingdom, the Manchus from the northeast took advantage of a China weakened by peasant rebellion to invade and establish the Qing or "pure" dynasty in 1644. This foreign Manchu court preserved much of China's governing apparatus and over time absorbed local ways. Despite providing some of China's most illustrious emperors, including Kangxi *(see p128)* and Qianlong, the Qing declined into an ineffectual torpor. Coupled with the seizure of territories by foreign powers, the Qing failure to modernize led to the collapse of Manchu legitimacy and the final downfall of the dynasty.

The queue, a long plaited hairstyle that has come to symbolize Chinese tradition was a Manchu import imposed on Han Chinese men.

The Court at the Forbidden City

Like the Ming before them, the Manchu Qing established their court in Beijing. The Manchus were the last dynastic occupants of the Forbidden City. Served by as many as 3,000 eunuchs, they were immersed in a court life of arcane ceremony and ritual until the dynasty was unseated by the founding of the Republic of China in 1912.

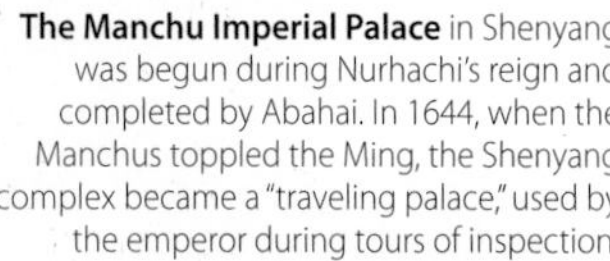

Nurhachi (1559–1626), the first Manchu emperor, organized the scattered tribes of the northeast into eight banner units in the early 17th century. He moved his capital to Shenyang, but did not live to see the subjugation of China. After his death, his son Abahai established the Qing dynasty in 1636 and proceeded to invade China.

The Manchu Imperial Palace in Shenyang was begun during Nurhachi's reign and completed by Abahai. In 1644, when the Manchus toppled the Ming, the Shenyang complex became a "traveling palace," used by the emperor during tours of inspection.

Elaborate summer camping trips in Inner Mongolia were undertaken by the early Qing rulers, as a break from Confucian court life. They hunted, practiced archery, and slept in yurts, in order to preserve their Manchu vigor.

Qianlong (r. 1735–96), the fourth Qing emperor, was a generous patron of the arts. His lengthy reign was also marked by territorial expansion, including the absorption of Xinjiang, and was largely a period of Chinese prosperity.

Yuanming Yuan, the Garden of Perfect Brightness *(see p109)*, was designed by Jesuits for the Qianlong emperor. Much of its grandiose architecture was destroyed by French and English troops in 1860.

Jesuit missionary Adam Schall von Bell (1591–1666) impressed the Manchu court with his knowledge of astronomy. The Jesuits realized that having influence in China required mastering the Confucian Classics and Mandarin.

In 1793, Lord Macartney arrived with elaborate gifts from King George III, seeking to establish trade between Britain and China. Macartney was rebuffed by the Qianlong emperor, who refused Britain a single concession.

The Boxer Rebellion

The Boxers, a band of xenophobic rebels from north China who rose up to rid China of the "foreign devils," drew from superstitious rituals that they believed made them invulnerable. Cixi, seeking an opportunity to strike back at the foreign powers, allied herself to their cause. The rebels laid waste to Beijing's Legation Quarter in 1900, while besieging the district's foreign population. The siege was finally lifted by an eight-power allied force. The Qing government was forced to sign the Boxer Protocol which, among other conditions, allowed the stationing of foreign troops in Beijing.

Boxer massacre of Chinese Christians

The Empress Dowager Cixi *(see p107)* was deeply conservative and a shrewd manipulator. Dismissive of foreign powers, she appointed pro-Boxer Prince Duan as Minister of Foreign Affairs.

Trans-Siberian Railway

The term Trans-Siberian Railway refers to three services: the Trans-Siberian, the Trans-Mongolian, and the Trans-Manchurian. In 1891 Russia decided to join the extremities of its empire by rail. A short cut through Manchuria was negotiated with China and the line was completed in 1903. War with Japan forced the Russians to cede the railroad to them in 1905 and build a new line skirting Manchuria – the Trans-Siberian route was finished in 1916. The Trans-Mongolian route was added in the 1940s and 50s. In an era of jet travel, this epic week-long journey is an experience not to be missed.

Conductor and train on the Trans-Siberian Railway

Orthodox priest running a mobile religious service in Manchuria at the turn of the 20th century. Today the historic Russian presence in the northeast can still be seen in Harbin, Lushun, and border towns like Manzhouli.

Steam trains were finally replaced in 2002, although electrification began in 1939. Because of differences in the track widths of the Chinese and Russian lines, huge cranes lift the carriages up onto the correct width "bogeys" when crossing the border.

The train carves its way through the grasslands of the north Manchurian plain.

This 1907 poster advertises the romance of a winter trip on the Trans-Siberian Railway. The poster's distinct Japanese feel derives from Japan's occupation of Manchuria and Korea at the time.

The standard of luxury is reasonable. (The Chinese deluxe carriage has showers.) If the dining car doesn't appeal, at each stop there's a throng of vendors on the platforms selling goods.

The longest railway service in the world at nearly 6,000 miles (9,500 km), it takes up to 7 days to cover the journey.

Key

- Trans-Siberian
- Trans-Mongolian
- Trans-Manchurian

RUSSIAN FEDERATION
Yekaterinburg
Moscow
Omsk
Lake Baykal
Irkutsk
Ulan-Ude
KAZAKHSTAN
MONGOLIA
Harbin
Vladivostok
CHINA
Beijing

Trans-Manchurian Railway

The Vostok *makes the 6-day trip once a week from Beijing through Shanhaiguan and Harbin, before heading through the spectacular Manchurian plain, the huge expanse of Russia, and back.*

The Trans-Mongolian is probably the most interesting route of the three: it goes through China – past the Great Wall and Datong, site of the Yungang Caves; via Mongolia and its grasslands; and finally through the expanse of Russia. However, it also requires three visas.

Lake Baykal's cliffs proved problematic for the builders. They had to chisel miles of tunnels out of solid rock and construct many bridges. It was worth it in the end because the southern end of the lake provides all three lines with some of the most picturesque scenery of the trip.

Looking out the window occupies most of your time on the trip – when not meeting other travelers.

Travelers' Tips

- You can book tickets through Seat 61 W **seat61.com**
- Summer is the peak season; fall is quieter; the train is heated, but winter can be very cold outside.
- Bring dried noodle snacks, hot chocolate, a bowl, and cutlery as there is boiling water on tap.
- Arrange for at least one or two stops on the way – separate ticket required for each stop.
- Be prepared to drink vodka.

Moscow is the end (or indeed start) for the three Trans-Siberian Railway services. It is possible to go on to St. Petersburg and the Baltic Sea. However, Moscow has plenty of museums, churches, and grand architecture to see, and deserves a few days of exploration.

LIAONING, JILIN & HEILONGJIANG

HEILONGJIANG
JILIN
LIAONING

Stretching from Shanhaiguan – the Great Wall's terminus at the Yellow Sea – to the Siberian borders in the north, the provinces of Liaoning, Jilin, and Heilongjiang cover 309,000 sq miles (800,000 sq km), an area larger than Spain and Portugal. With a population of over 100 million, they offer a variety of landscapes, from seaside ports to expanses of uninhabited forests and mountains.

The region was once part of erstwhile Manchuria, and the lavish palace of the Manchu kings at Shenyang in the heart of Liaoning stands testament to their might. On Liaoning's balmier southern coast, Dalian features scenic coastal drives and fine, sandy beaches. With the only ice-free port in the area, it was coveted by both Japan and Russia, and occupied continuously by one or the other between 1895 and 1955.

Japan's imperialist stamp also survives in Jilin's capital, Changchun, from where China's last emperor, Pu Yi, ruled the Japanese state of Manchukuo as a mere puppet. In Heilongjiang, the city of Harbin has heavy Russian overtones, clearly evident in its buildings and restaurants, while strong Korean influences color Dandong town, situated along the North Korean border. Also straddling the border is the rugged, spectacular Changbai Shan Reserve, which abounds in lush, jagged peaks and hiking opportunities. Its volcanic lake, Tian Chi, is China's deepest, rumored to be home to a mysterious aquatic beast.

Other natural attractions include Liaoning's Bingyu Valley with its towering rock formations, Heilongjiang's volcanic lakes – Wu Da Lian Chi and Jingpo Hu – and the huge bird sanctuary at Zhalong Nature Reserve, whose marshy expanse supports hundreds of species of birds during the summer breeding season.

A secluded sandy cove in the Bangchuidao Scenic Area, Dalian

◀ Interior of St. Sofia Church in Harbin

❶ Shenyang
沈阳

Capital of Liaoning province and the largest city in the northeast, Shenyang may lack the panache of Dalian, but it serves as an important transportation and industrial hub at the heart of the province. Of strategic importance in the state of Yan during the Warring States period (475–221 BC), the town was first called Shenyang during the Mongol Yuan dynasty, before rising to prominence as the first Manchu capital in 1625, when it was known as Mukden and was chosen as the setting for the Imperial Palace, a splendid rival to Beijing's Forbidden City.

A throng of visitors outside the Dazheng Hall, Imperial Palace

Imperial Palace

171 Shenyang Lu. **Tel** (024) 2484 3001. **Open** summer: 8:30am–5:30pm, winter: 9:30am–4:30pm. **Closed** Mon am. interiors. **W** **en.sypm.org.cn**

Second only in scale to the Forbidden City in Beijing, the Imperial Palace, also called Shenyang Gugong, is Shenyang's premier historical sight, situated in what was the center of the old city. Its construction began in 1625, during the reign of Nurhachi (1559–1626), leader of the Manchus. In 1644, Manchu troops breached the Great Wall at Shanhaiguan *(see p134)* and swarmed into China to establish the Qing dynasty. Serving as the imperial residence of both Nurhachi and his son and heir Abahai, the palace is composed of 300 rooms. While its features reflect a pronounced Manchu and Mongol influence, the palace was obviously an attempt to emulate its Ming counterpart, the Forbidden City, Beijing.

The palace is divided into three sections. The dominating feature of the central section is the **Chongzheng Hall**, from where Abahai oversaw political affairs and received envoys from vassal lands and border territories. In the courtyard behind the hall, the **Qingning Palace** is where the emperor and his concubines resided. The Phoenix Tower, the tallest structure in the imperial grounds can be found here too.

In the western section, the **Wensu Pavilion** formerly housed one of seven copies of the 36,078-volume *Siku Quanshu* (Complete Library of the Four Treasures), an encyclopedic collection of Chinese literature compiled in the Qing era, of which only four sets survive. The **Dazheng Hall** is the central feature of the eastern section, fronted by pillars emblazoned with sinuous dragons. It was here that Shunzhi (Aisin Gioro Fulin) was crowned as the first Qing emperor, before he conquered China in 1644. In front of the hall stand the Ten King Pavilions, once used as offices by the chieftains of the "Eight Banners" – the Manchu system of land and hereditary divisions. The palace has undergone extensive restoration, and the halls are all open to visitors. It achieved UNESCO World Heritage Site status in 2004.

Mao Statue

Zhongshan Square.

The statue of Mao Zedong situated in Zhongshan Square in downtown Shenyang stands as a reminder of a vanished era. Mao statues tower over public squares across China, including such far-flung outposts as Lijiang *(see pp396–8)* in Yunnan and Kashgar *(see pp514–15)* in Xinjiang, but this example is perhaps the most histrionic, depicting Mao's giant monolithic figure as a superman in an overcoat.

North Pagoda

27 Beita Jie. **Tel** (024) 8662 5665. **Open** 9–11:30am, 2–4:30pm.

Built between 1643 and 1645, Bei Ta is the only one of four temples and pagodas situated on the city boundaries in an excellent state of repair. The surviving features of the original pagoda are the Great Hall and Falun Temple.

Wei Tuo Buddha, North Pagoda

18 September Museum

46 Wanghua Nanjie. **Tel** (024) 8832 0918. **Open** 9am–4pm Tue–Sun. **W** **918museum.org.cn**

The Jiuyiba Lishi Bowuguan commemorates the occupation of Shenyang on September 18, 1931 by Japanese troops. Its exhibits make up the most comprehensive chronicle of the Japanese aggression in Manchuria. Some of the displays can be rather gruesome.

Zhaoling Mausoleum's ornate west wall and gateway

VISITORS' CHECKLIST

Practical Information

440 miles (700 km) NE of Beijing. 5,000,000. Bldg A, 290 Shigu Dalu, (024) 2295 8888.

Transportation

Shenyang Airport. South or North train stations. South bus station (provincial trains), Express bus station (national trains), CAAC (buses to airport).

Zhaoling Mausoleum

12 Taishan Lu, Beiling Gongyuan, North Shenyang. **Tel** (024) 8691 0461. **Open** summer: 7am–5pm; winter: 8am–4pm. interiors.

The huge Beiling Park houses the tomb of Abahai (1592–1643), the son of Nurhachi, and his wife, Empress Borjijit. One of the best-preserved of China's imperial tombs, the Zhaoling Mausoleum was built between 1643 and 1651. Its layout is typical of imperial Chinese tombs *(see pp110–11)*, and is accessed through Zhenghong Gate to the south. The pavilion furthest east of the gate was used as a dressing room for visiting emperors, while the westernmost pavilion was the site for sacrificing animals. A spirit way *(shendao)*, lined with animal statues, leads to the Hall of Eminent Favor (Ling'en Dian). Behind the hall lie the tree-covered imperial burial mounds, formally called Zhao Ling (the Luminous Tomb), and a lovely dragon screen.

Mythical animal, Zhaoling Mausoleum

East Tomb

3 miles (5 km) E of Shenyang. 210 Dong Ling Lu. **Open** summer: 7:30am–5:30pm; winter: 8am–4:30pm.

Completed in 1651, the impressive East Tomb (Dong Ling), or Fuling Tomb, is the final resting place of Nurhachi (1559–1626) and his wife Yehenala. Arranged attractively on the slopes of Mount Tianzhu near the Hun River, the three-storied tomb has a flight of 108 steps leading to its main gate. The number 108 is sacred to the Chinese; in the Daoist celestial order, 108 represents the 36 stars of heaven and the 72 stars of hell. The number is sacred to Buddhists, too, reflected in the 108 beads on Buddhist rosaries and the number of *luohan* (disciples) in some Buddhist sects. Photography is not allowed inside.

Shenyang City Center

① Imperial Palace
② Mao Statue
③ North Pagoda
④ 18 September Museum
⑤ Zhaoling Mausoleum

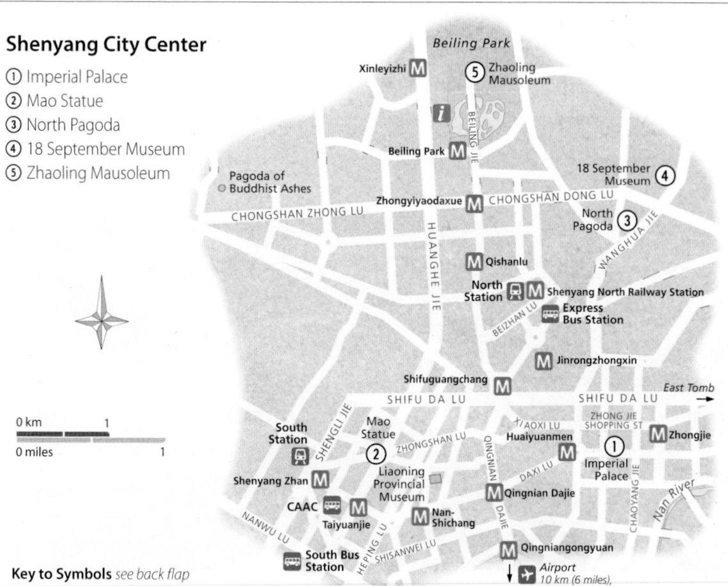

Key to Symbols *see back flap*

The impressive Bijia Shan, connected to the mainland by an isthmus at low tide

❷ Jinzhou
锦州

125 miles (200 km) SW of Shenyang. 3,000,000. 797 Sidalin Lu, Jinzhou Qu, Dalian Shi, Liaoning Sheng, (0411) 8483 2601.

An industrial city on the eastern shores of the Liaoning Gulf, Jinzhou is visited mainly for its storehouse of Jurassic period fossils, of which more than 300 are housed in the private **Wenya Museum** (Bowuguan). Set up by the amateur collector Du Wenya, this collection is in the process of changing location, so call to check the latest details before visiting. The star attraction is a specimen of *dushi kongzi niao (Confuciusornis dui hou)*, a winged, avian dinosaur with feathered features that was unearthed in 1998 in western Liaoning, a region rich in dinosaur remains.

Jutting out of Jinzhou Bay, 21 miles (34 km) south of town, is **Bijia Shan** (Penholder Mount). It is connected to the mainland by an isthmus that emerges from the sea at low tide. The island's peaks – which resemble a Chinese pen rest – support several Buddhist temples and offer magnificent views over the bay. Visitors who wish to walk to Bijia Shan along the isthmus should check the timings of low-tide before planning a trip. An alternative way of reaching the island is by taking a fishing boat.

Wenya Museum
10, 125. **Tel** (0416) 332 1222. **Closed** for relocation; call for up-to-date information.

Bijia Shan
110 yards (100 meters) west of train station. **Tel** (0416) 358 2477. **Open** 8am–5pm daily.

❸ Dandong
丹东

172 miles (277 km) SE of Shenyang. 7,500,000. 31 Weidu 6 Lu, (0415) 221 1050.

Presided over by a statue of Mao Zedong in the heart of town, Dandong is located along the Yalu Jiang (Yalu River) in the eastern part of Liaoning province. It would have been little more than an obscure outpost, ignored by travelers, if it were not for its proximity to North Korea. Today the largest border town in China, Dandong has an unmistakable Korean stamp, from the *shaokao* (barbecue) dishes, to the signs in *hangul* (the Korean script), and the Korean shops and souvenirs.

Within reach of Dandong are several other interesting sights, and the town acts as a useful launch pad to Changbai Shan *(see pp454–5)* and the stunning mountain lake of Tian Chi. Dandong's trademark sight, the **Yalu Jiang Duan Qiao** (Yalu River Bridge), is near the high-speed train station, and reaches out into the river alongside the bridge connecting China with North Korea – this railroad line runs all the way from Beijing to Pyongyang. The steel bridge ends halfway along its full span, the remainder having been dismantled by the Koreans. The surviving half in Chinese

The Yalu Jiang Duan Qiao, that once connected China with North Korea

Dramatic karst hills rising up from the river, Bingyu Valley

territory bears the scars of combat, having been strafed in 1950 by US fighter planes during the Korean War. The ruin serves as a monument to the **Kang Mei Yuan Chao Zhanzheng** (War to Resist US Aggression and Aid Korea), as the Chinese refer to their part in the conflict. Boats and speedboats offer cruises along the Yalu River for visitors who want to get within 2 or 3 ft of the hermit kingdom. It is permitted to take photographs of North Korea, though there are few photogenic features – just factories, civilians, and Stalinist housing. Those who wish to learn more about China's contribution to the Korean War can visit the **Museum to Commemorate Aiding Korea and Resisting America**, with a plethora of exhibits on the war. Even though the captions are almost exclusively in Chinese, the nationalistic refrain is evident.

Located 31 miles (50 km) northwest of town, the 2,760-ft (840-m) **Fenghuang Shan** (Phoenix Emperor Mountain) is associated with Daoist mythology. It supports a crop of temples and caves, besides offering some excellent hiking trails. A good time to visit is during the temple fair *(miao-hui)*, held every April. The **Hushan Great Wall**, a little-visited and restored stretch of the Great Wall, is located 20 km (12 miles) northeast of Dandong, near Jiuliancheng town, over-looking the Yalu River and the North Korean border. This section of the wall, dating from the reign of the Ming Wanli emperor, is its easternmost point. The **Great Wall Museum** displays relics associated with the defensive barrier. The North Korean border is not always clearly marked, so hiking around this area is not advised, in case visitors inadvertently cross over into North Korea.

A traffic policewoman on duty

Yalu Jiang
Duan Qiao 15. **Tel** (0415) 212 2145. **Open** 7am–6:30pm daily.

Fenghuang Shan
Fengchen City. **Open** 6am–7pm daily.

4 Bingyu Valley
冰峪沟

149 miles (240 km) NE of Dalian. from Dalian to Zhuanghe, then bus. from Dalian to Zhuanghe, then bus to Bingyu Fengjingqu. **Tel** (0411) 8864 4189.

A picturesque river valley, sprawling Bingyu Gou offers long riverside walks and hikes in fabulous trekking terrain overlooked by jagged peaks, karst rock formations, temples, and cliffs hollowed out by numerous caves. Opportunities for climbing, fishing, and rafting are also available. The valley can be reached via the town of Zhuanghe, northeast of Dalian. Accommodations are available for those who wish to stay overnight. It is best to avoid the holiday periods as well as weekends during summer, when the valley receives crowds of visitors.

Steps leading to a Daoist temple on Fenghuang Shan

❺ Dalian

大连

Sparkling with self-assurance and confidence, Dalian is northeast China's most dynamic and attractive city. It is famed throughout China for its top-notch hotels, progressive economy, modern and European-style architecture, football team, and cleanliness. The city resembles Shanghai in its port setting, cosmopolitanism, Special Economic Zone status, and history of foreign control, but has the added attraction of a coastline dotted with scenic beaches and lawns. Located at the southernmost point of northeast China near the tip of the Liaodong peninsula, Dalian enjoys sea breezes and a warmer winter than other parts of the region.

Bangchuidao Scenic Area, with the finest beaches on China's east coast

Exploring Dalian

The city of Dalian has few temples or monuments of note, but most visitors come for its beaches, seafood, shopping, and striking modernity. Serving as a dazzling hub from which major streets radiate, **Zhongshan Square** (Zhongshan Guangchang) is laid out with lawns and encircled by a ring of colonial buildings dating from the Russian and Japanese eras. At night, locals gather here to dance and listen to music, and to watch the occasional cultural performances that are held. The most interesting buildings along the square's periphery are the Dalian Hotel (Dalian Binguan) at No. 4 to the south, and the Bank of China (Zhongguo Yinhang) on the northern rim at No. 9.

Dalian's main shopping area is **Tianjin Jie**, a pedestrianized stretch of shops northwest of Zhongshan Square. Beneath Shengli Square to the west is a huge underground shopping center, while the Friendship Store lies farther east on Renmin Lu.

Dotting Dalian are several tree-lined streets and spacious parks. Southwest of Zhongshan Square is **Labor Park** (Laodong Gongyuan), with its hallmark giant football at the center. It is known for hosting the Locust Flower Festival each spring. Farther southwest is Dalian's other main square, **Renmin Square**. Formerly known as Stalin Square, it was originally overlooked by a large statue of a Russian soldier, that now stands in nearby Lushun. The square is pleasantly laid out with grass and is lit at night.

Dalian is famous for its beaches and these can easily be reached by bus or taxi. In the northeast of the Dalian peninsula, just off Binhai Lu near the Eighteen Bends, is the scenic **Donghai Park**. Covering 1,112 acres (450 ha), this seaside park has a 3,937-ft (1,200-m) long coastline. It was founded to celebrate Dalian's centennial anniversary, and has striking statues of oversized seacreatures, including a giant octopus and a shark. There are fine sea views, and the water is clean though rather cold until mid-July for swimming. The pebble beach is popular with visitors, who often bring tents and beach towels and spend the day here.

Farther south along the coastal Binhai Lu, the **Bangchuidao Scenic Area** (Bangchuidao Jingqu) has the best beaches on China's east coast, once reserved for party officials and now open to all. Binhai Lu makes for a marvelous walk with fantastic views over the cliffs across the Yellow Sea. The next stop is the more touristy **Tiger Beach Scenic Area** (Laohutan Jingqu), which sports an amusement park and an aquarium. Several miles west, the **Fujiazhuang Scenic Area** (Fujiazhuang Jingqu) is also rather boisterous and crowded, and farther still is the Xinghai Beach Scenic Area, housing the huge and immensely popular **Sun Asia Ocean World**. This aquarium has a 381-ft (116-m) long under-water tunnel and several tanks filled with sealife that attract children in droves.

Statue of a rowing team in midstroke, Xinghai Square

◀ Ice sculptures at Harbin Ice and Snow Festival, Heilongjiang province

Just off the coast, Xinghai Square was built to commemorate the return of Hong Kong to China in 1997.

Donghai Park
Binhai Bei Lu. **Tel** (0411) 8273 1569. **Open** 6am–9pm daily.

Bangchuidao Scenic Area
Tel (0411) 8289 3888. 404, 703. **Open** 8am–7pm daily.

Sun Asia Ocean World
Tel (0411) 8458 1113. Convention and Exhibition Center. **Open** hours vary. **sunasia.com**

Environs: Lying 22 miles (35 km) southwest of Dalian, **Lushun** enjoys an excellent strategic position, its harbor benefiting from the perennial ice-free waters. Known as Port Arthur, it was the chief naval base for the Chinese Beiyang fleet from the mid-19th century, and was seized by the Japanese during the Sino-Japanese War (1894–5). Returned to China soon after, the port fell to the Russians in 1897, who developed the base for their Pacific fleet, but Japan wrested Lushun back in 1905, forfeiting it only at the end of World War II. Among the surviving Russian architecture is the **Railway Station**, built in 1898 as the South Manchuria Railway terminus *(see pp440–41)*. The **Japanese-Russian Prison**, which incarcerated Russian, Japanese, and Chinese prisoners, also has a gory torture room and gallows. These can be seen on a guided tour that takes in the compound and the collection of interesting photographs on display. All photography is prohibited here. North of the bay and near the station, **Baiyu Hill** is topped with rows of cannons and a tower, plus great views.

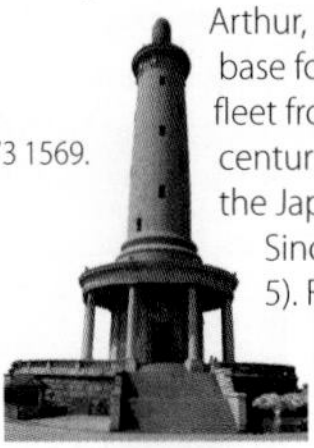

Tower at the top of Baiyu Hill in Lushun

A cruise liner docked near Xinghai Square

VISITORS' CHECKLIST

Practical Information
180 miles (300 km) S of Shenyang. 3,400,000. Locust Flower Festival (Spring). 4/F Wanda Guangchan, (0411) 836 91165.

Transportation
Dalian Airport. Dalian Station, Dalian North (high-speed trains). Dalian bus station, CAAC (to airport), Heishijiao bus station. from Yantai and Weihai.

Japanese-Russian Prison
139 Xiangyong Jie. 2, 3, 5.
Tel (0411) 8661 0675/6. **Open** 9am–3:30pm daily (winter: to 3pm).

Dalian City Center

1. Zhongshan Square
2. Tianjin Jie
3. Labor Park
4. Renmin Square
5. Donghai Park
6. Bangchuidao Scenic Area
7. Tiger Beach Scenic Area
8. Fujiazhuang Scenic Area
9. Sun Asia Ocean World

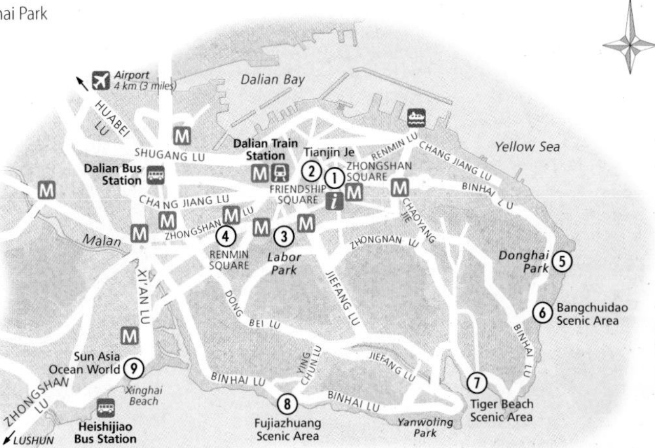

Key to Symbols *see back flap*

Living quarters at the Puppet Emperor's Palace, Changchun

6 Changchun
长春

185 miles (300 km) NE of Shenyang. 2,200,000. Xiangtan airport. to Dalian, Shanghai and Tianjin. 2055 Xi'an Da Lu, (0431) 8896 5966.

The sprawling modern capital of Jilin province is cheerfully known as "Eternal Spring" despite its brutal winter. The city was badly damaged at the end of World War II, which ended its ignominious phase as the capital of the Japanese-controlled state of Manchukuo, when it was known as Hsin-Ching. Industrialized after the war, Changchun today has emerged as an attractive, green city in China's northeastern "rust belt," famed for its car production.

Changchun's only major sight of interest is the **Puppet Emperor's Palace**, the residence of the "Last Emperor," Pu Yi, whom the Japanese installed as the Emperor of Manchukuo. Located in the city's northeast, the palace, with its period furnishings and old photographs, serves as an apt epitaph to the tragic folly of Pu Yi's life. The palace lacks the majesty of the Forbidden City, and instead is suggestive of the sanctuary of an exiled monarch. Renovations have, however, restored much of its former grandeur. It is now a fascinating museum of artifacts relating to the 13 powerless years that Pu Yi spent here. Scenes from Bertolucci's 1987 epic film *The Last Emperor* were filmed here. Other period buildings include the **Manchukuo State Council Building** on Xinmin Dajie in the southeast of town, a further relic of the Japanese occupation. Open to the public, the building is a government structure that features a brass Otis elevator that once ferried Pu Yi aloft.

In the northeast corner of People's Square on the main street of Renmin Dajie stands **Banruo Temple**, an active Buddhist temple dating to 1921. Inside the main hall is a statue of Sakyamuni with attendant *arhats* *(see pp36–7)*. Changchun is also famous for its cinematic output and the city's film studio can be visited, although it is only really of interest to specialist film buffs.

Official buildings at the Puppet Emperor's Palace, Changchun

Puppet Emperor's Palace
5 Guangfu Lu. 264. **Tel** (0431) 8286 6611. **Open** 8:30am–5:20pm. **W** wmhg.com.cn

The Last Emperor

Aisin Gioro or Pu Yi ascended the Qing throne at the age of three in 1908 after the death of his uncle, the Guangxu emperor. His brief reign as the Xuantong emperor was brought to an end on February 12, 1912, when he abdicated the throne in the Forbidden City to make way for the new Republican government. The powerless Pu Yi continued to live in the palace until 1924, before furtively escaping to live in the Japanese concession in Tianjin. He was later installed as the Japanese puppet emperor of Manchukuo, residing in his palace in Changchun. At the end of World War II, he was arrested and handed over to the Chinese Communists, who imprisoned him in 1950. In 1959, Mao granted him amnesty. Pu Yi never returned to the Forbidden City, and he died of cancer, childless and anonymous, in 1967, after working for seven years as a gardener at the Beijing Botanical Gardens.

Pu Yi (1905–67), China's "Last Emperor"

7 Jilin
吉林

60 miles (100 km) E of Changchun. 2,000,000. to Shanghai Dalian, Tianjin. Room 502, Caoyang Sijicheng, Song Jiang Dong Rd, 138 4461 3826.

Known as Kirin during the Japanese occupation between 1931 and 1945, the city of Jilin is a little-visited industrial settlement on either side of the Songhua or Sungari River. Like many other cities in the northeast, Jilin has a short history and was a small village until the 17th century, when it was fortified. It was heavily industrialized during the Japanese occupation, when the huge hydro-electric power station at Fengman on the Songhua River was constructed. The station generates one of Jilin's major winter attractions – *shugua* or needle-like white frost that covers the branches of the riverside pine and willow trees. As warm water from the power station flows into the Songhua, its temperature rises and it remains unfrozen. Evaporating water droplets from the river condense along the branches of trees and freeze, producing a sparkling display of ice-rimmed branches, resembling pieces of coral. As with Harbin, winter is the main tourist season, and Jilin also stages an ice festival, which includes sporting events and photography contests, from January to the end of February.

Pleasant walks along paths, and past shrines and pavilions are possible in hilly **Beishan Park** in the west of town. The park has an array of Daoist and Buddhist temples that are worth investigating, including the Guandi Temple (Guandi Miao), the Three King Temple (Sanwang Miao), and the Jade Emperor's Temple (Yuhuang Ge), with a gaggle of fortune-tellers in front.

Locals are proud of the city's attractive **Catholic Church**, built by the French in the early 19th century. It rises up west of Jilin's main bridge on Songjiang Lu, the road along the north bank of the river. Vandalized during the Cultural Revolution, the church became the city's emblem after it reopened in 1980. East of the church is the **Confucius Temple** (Wen Miao), dedicated to the great sage. Candidates of the imperial civil service examinations came here to pray for his help and blessings. The sedate temple provides an escape from Jilin's modern face.

Catholic Church, Jilin

In the south of the city, the **Meteorite Shower Museum** houses a scattering of rock fragments that rained down around Jilin in 1976, including a vast specimen weighing nearly 2 tons (1,770 kg).

The delicate frost that covers Jilin's trees each year

Statues at the scholars' altar, Confucius Temple, Jilin

Beishan Park
Open daily.

Catholic Church
3 Songjiang Lu. **Open** for services.

Confucius Temple
2 Nanchang Lu. **Open** 8:30am–9pm daily.

Environs: Formerly known for its temples and hiking opportunities, **Zhuque Shan** (Rosefinch Mountain) has earned a reputation for its ski slopes. Its restaurant, which stands on a heated platform, provides panoramic views over the hills.

About 15 miles (24 km) southeast of Jilin is the picturesque **Songhua Lake** (Songhua Hu), covering a vast and panoramic area surrounded by peaks. It provides an excellent getaway from town, offering hiking and boating in a huge forested park setting. Every winter, a state-of-the-art ski resort operates on the slopes around the lake, attracting cross-country fans. At the lake's southern end is the Fengman Dam, the site of the city's hydro-electric power station. Due to the river's annual flooding, four sluice gates are opened to keep Jilin from being submerged.

Zhuque Shan
Taxi from Jilin train station. **Open** 8:30am–4:30pm daily. Ski gear available.

Songhua Lake
from train station to lake, then taxi to ski resorts. Resort: **Tel** 400 688 0999.
lakesonghua.com

8 Changbai Shan

长白山

Listed as a UNESCO Biosphere Reserve, Changbai Shan (Ever-White Mountains) is the largest of China's nature reserves at 760 sq miles (1,965 sq km), with a rich abundance of fauna and flora. Thick belts of deciduous and coniferous forest harbor important medicinal plants like ginseng, and endangered animals like the Siberian (or Manchurian) Tiger, while above the tree line lies the only alpine tundra in East Asia. The real highlight is Tian Chi (Heaven's Lake), a glittering volcanic crater that straddles the mountainous border with North Korea. This is China at its wildest and most spectacular, with opportunities for hiking amid dramatic scenery, although the area is only open to exploration during summer and early fall.

White birch
Despite heavy deforestation, there are still healthy numbers of over 80 species of trees such as these white birch.

★ Changbai Waterfall
Tian Chi releases huge quantities of water (the mountains are capped with snow between October and June) creating this dramatic 225-ft (68-m) high waterfall near the volcanic crater.

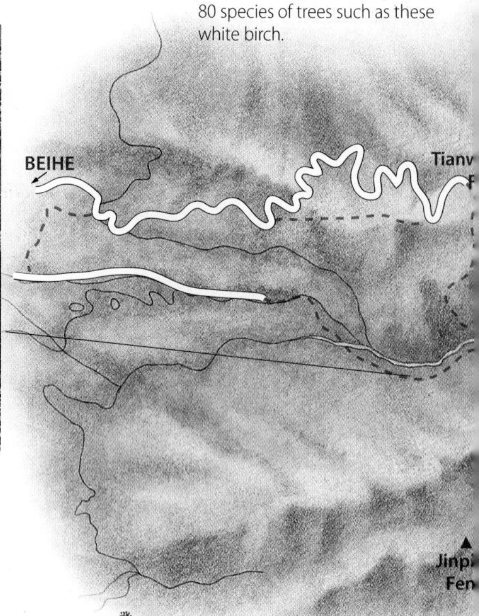

BEIHE

0 kilometers 1

0 miles 1

Key

International border

Path

Ginseng

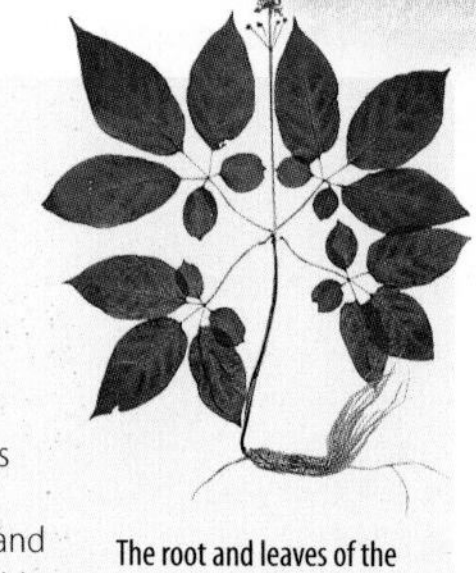

The root of the ginseng *(Panax ginseng)* plant has been valued in China for thousands of years for its healing and rejuvenating properties. Native to Korea and northeast China, ginseng is a slow-growing herbaceous perennial that is widely farmed (although wild specimens are most highly prized). Ginseng from northeast China is especially esteemed and was once protected under imperial edict to prevent overharvesting. Its efficacy does not develop until the plant is around six years of age. Premium-quality wild ginseng is very expensive costing US$150–450 per gram. However, buyer beware; the market is awash with fake produce.

The root and leaves of the ginseng plant

For hotels and restaurants in this region see pp562–3 and pp583–4

VISITORS' CHECKLIST

Practical Information
16 miles (25 km) S of Baihe; 350 miles (560 km) E of Jilin. CITS, (0432) 6245 3416.
Open 8:30am–4pm daily. Last bus back to Baihe 4pm. from Jilin (CITS).

Transportation
or to Baihe, then bus or taxi.

★ Tian Chi – Heaven's Lake
The volcano last erupted in 1702, wiping out most of the surrounding forest. The deep waters of Tian Chi (China's deepest lake) are said to harbor an aquatic beast similar to the Loch Ness Monster.

NORTH KOREA

Hot Springs Near Tian Chi
Many springs reach temperatures of over 176° F (80° C) – hot enough for local hawkers to boil eggs and for visitors to take therapeutic dips in steamy pools.

Bai Yun Feng

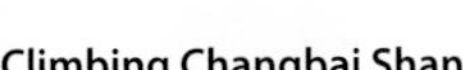

Climbing Changbai Shan

Due to heavy snowfall, Changbai Shan is only open to trekking from June to October. Although a tempting 8 miles (13 km) in circumference, Tian Chi cannot be circumnavigated as it overlaps with North Korea. Prepare for unpredictable weather conditions as it can get very cold (and carry plenty of food and water). The more sedentary (and winter visitors) can hire a 4-wheel-drive taxi all the way to the main peak. Visitors can overnight in one of the hotels on Changbai Shan or in Baihe. Tours are easy to find and usually include two nights in a hotel.

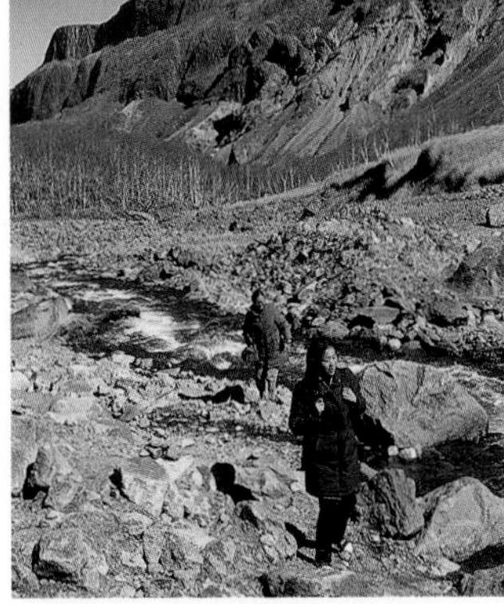

Trekking opportunities
Even at peak periods, it is easy to enjoy and explore the wilderness and beauty of Changbai Shan at leisure – however, be very careful not to stray into North Korea.

9 Harbin

哈尔滨

Situated in the far north of China close to the vast sub-Siberian plains, Harbin is the pleasant capital of Heilongjiang province. It was a simple fishing hamlet on the Songhua River until the Russians linked it to both Vladivostok and Dalian *(see pp450–51)* by rail at the close of the 19th century. The railroad and the Bolshevik Revolution brought large numbers of Russians to the city, prompting a change in Harbin's fortunes. Once called "Little Moscow" for its charming pockets of Russian architecture, Harbin still vaguely resembles an outpost of Imperial Russia. While the city's summer is quite pleasant, its winter temperatures dip below -22°F (-30°C), perfect weather for its spectacular Ice Festival.

People walking and relaxing along Harbin's riverbank

Exploring Harbin

Harbin's most interesting sites lie within the Daoli district (Daoli Qu), which stretches from the main train station to the Songhua River. The district's downtown area is lined with upmarket boutiques, fur shops, and department stores. Visitors can walk north along the pedestrianized shopping street of **Zhongyang Dajie** to explore the picturesque cobbled alleys and architectural legacies of the grand Russian era. Numerous shops and buildings on Zhongyang Dajie have been restored, and their histories recorded in English on exterior plaques. The lanes leading off Zhongyang Dajie are ideal for a stroll, while along its length are several good bars and restaurants. Lined with ice sculptures in winter, the streets here are alive with the bustle of pavement cafés during summer.

A motorcycle taxi in Harbin

East of Zhongyang Dajie is the **St. Sofia Cathedral**, the city's most spectacular Russian edifice. Dating from 1907, it is also the largest Russian Orthodox church in the Far East. This Byzantine-style red-brick cathedral is topped with a green, onion-shaped dome. It houses the Architecture and Arts Centre, a rewarding photographic exhibit of the Russian influence on Harbin.

To the north, **Zhaolin Park** is the setting for some of the smaller ice sculptures of the annual Ice Festival (Bingdeng Jie), officially held every year from January 5 to February 25. In winter, the park is transformed into a glistening wonderland of brightly lit ice sculptures, ranging from simple statues to buildings, monuments, and temples.

Close by, Harbin's riverfront is dotted with interesting sights. The **Flood Control Monument** at the northern end of Zhongyang Dajie was erected in 1958 to commemorate the river's flood-prone history. Stretching along the riverbank is **Stalin Park**, China's last public memorial to Joseph Stalin. In summer, boat trips can be taken along the river and across to **Sun Island Park** (Tai Yang Dao) on the northern bank. The park has a variety of recreational attractions and can also be reached by cable car. In winter, the river freezes over completely, and visitors can hire go-carts or simply walk across. An annual ice sculpture exhibition is held at Harbin Ice and Snow World, in the northern part of Sun Island. Another part of the island is home to the Siberian Tiger Park, where the endangered Manchurian tiger is being bred. Visitors may want to give this rather dismal place a miss, as the fenced-off area seems much too small for the big cats, who are constantly being teased with live chickens by noisy busloads of tourists.

South of the main railway station, the **Provincial Museum** has a rather uninspiring collection of exhibits with no English captions. Farther east along Dong Dazhi Jie are some of Harbin's Buddhist temples, all of which were damaged during the Cultural Revolution. The quiet **Jile Si** is home to an active

The splendid Byzantine-style Church of St. Sofia

For hotels and restaurants in this region see pp562–3 and pp583–4

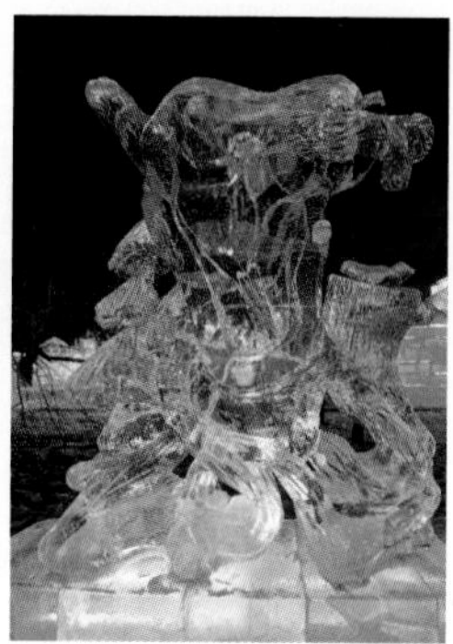
An intricate ice sculpture at Harbin's Ice Festival in Zhaolin Park

Buddhist community. The complex follows a typical Buddhist temple layout with Drum and Bell Towers, a Hall of Heavenly Kings, and a main hall, adorned with statues of Sakyamuni (the Historical Buddha) and various *bodhisattvas*. Adjacent is the seven-tiered **Qiji Futu Pagoda**, standing within the largest temple complex in the province. Nearby on Wenmiao Jie, the Confucian Temple is a sizeable shrine also worth visiting.

St. Sofia Cathedral
Diduan Jie. **Tel** (0451) 8467 9456. **Open** 8:30am–5pm daily.

Sun Island Park
3 Jingbei Lu. **Tel** (0451) 8819 2966. **Open** 8am–5pm daily.

Jile Si
9 Dong Dazhi Jie. **Open** 8am–5pm daily.

Environs: Twelve miles (20 km) southwest of Harbin in the small village of Pingfang, the **Unit 731 Museum** is the city's most notorious sight. Formerly operated by the Japanese army's 731 Division, the gruesome remains of the experimental base are now open to the public. It housed a top-secret research unit that subjected over 30,000 Chinese, Korean, British, Mongolian, and Russian prisoners to some truly horrendous experiments. The Japanese destroyed the base at the end of World War II, and it was only after the dogged efforts of a Japanese journalist in the 1980s that the existence of the base was exposed. Nobody was ever prosecuted due to an immunity deal given by the USA in return for the results of their experiments. The museum is largely limited to photographs and all captions are in Chinese, but the site survives as a somber monument to the atrocities of World War II.

The elegant, seven-tiered Qiji Futu Pagoda in the northeast of town

Unit 731 Museum
47 Xinjiang Dajie. **Tel** (0451) 8710 8731. **Open** 9–11am & 1–4pm Tue–Sun. 338, 343.

VISITORS' CHECKLIST

Practical information
340 miles (550 km) N of Shenyang. 4,750,000. 48 Daoliqu Shisidaojie, (0451) 8765 6661. Ice Festival (Jan/Feb), Harbin Festival (Jul). **harbin.gov.cn**

Transportation
Harbin bus station, CAAC (buses to airport).

Harbin City Center

① Zhongyang Dajie
② St. Sofia Cathedral
③ Zhaolin Park
④ Flood Control Monument
⑤ Stalin Park
⑥ Sun Island Park
⑦ Provincial Museum
⑧ Jile Si
⑨ Qiji Futu Pagoda

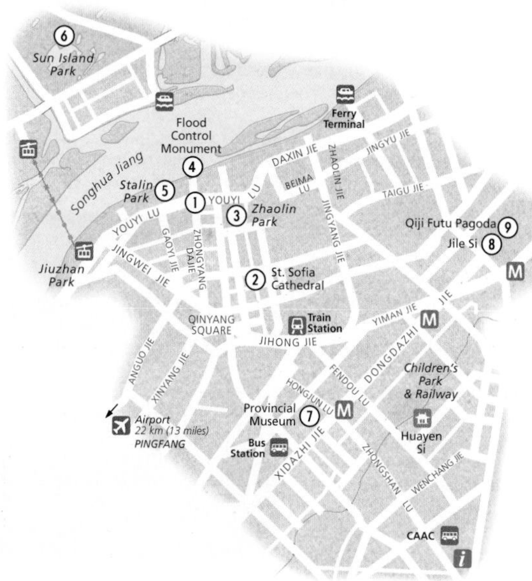

0 km 1
0 miles 1

Key to Symbols *see back flap*

Diving off the edge of Diaoshuilou Pubu (Diaoshuilou Waterfall), Jingpo Hu

⑩ Jingpo Hu
镜泊湖

62 miles (100 km) SW of Mudanjiang. **Tel** (0453) 627 0180. to Mudanjiang or Dongjing, then bus or taxi to Jingpo Hu (2 hours). 158 Jingfu Jie, Mudanjiang, (0453) 6911 186. **Open** daily.

An attractive, 31-mile (50-km) long winding strip of water, Jingpo Hu was carved from the Mudan River by volcanic eruptions 50,000 years ago. The surrounding forested slopes are clearly reflected in the lake's waters, hence its name, "Mirror Lake." In summer, bus-loads of visitors – largely Chinese and Russian – gather at Jingpo Shanzhuang, a village on the northern shore equipped with abundant resort facilities. Tourism has spoiled some of the lake's natural beauty, but much of its huge body of water and the luxuriant wooded hills are still tranquil and worth exploring. The 131-ft (40-m) wide waterfall **Diaoshuilou Pubu** lies at the northern end of the lake. Its cascade is most impressive in the wetter summer months, while in winter, it freezes into a spectacular curtain of ice.

Visiting the lake is possible in winter, although temperatures can also dip well below freezing point through to April, with fewer transportation and accommodations options. July and August are the wettest and busiest months, and booking ahead at lake-side hotels is recommended. An alternative is to stay in Mudanjiang city to the north, from where buses depart for Jingpo Hu. Activities include boating, fishing, and hiking and boat tours around the lake can also be arranged. Not far from the waterfall is a Korean minority village.

Several volcanic features dot the surrounding area, including lava caves and the **Dixia Senlin** (Underground Forest), 31 miles (50 km) northwest of Jingpo Hu. Not actually subterranean, the forest has grown spectacularly in the fertile soil of ten dormant volcanic craters. The delicate ecosystem here supports a varied animal and plant population including black bears, leopards, purple pines, firs, and dragon spruces. Taxis and buses leave regularly from Jingpo Hu's main gate to Mudanjiang and Dixia Senlin. It is also worth looking out for tour buses to the lake that include trips to Dixia Senlin.

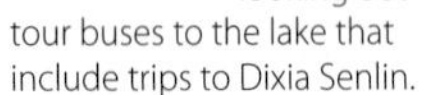

A visitor enjoying a ride on a jet ski at Jingpo Hu

Dixia Senlin
50 km NW of Jingpo Hu. **Tel** (0453) 627 0180. **Open** 7am–4:30pm daily.

⑪ Zhalong Nature Reserve
扎龙自然保护区

17 miles (27 km) SE of Qiqiha'er. to Qiqiha'er, then bus 306. **Tel** (0452) 244 2155. **Open** 7am–6pm daily.

China's largest wetland reserve, the 518,700-acre (210,000-ha) Zhalong Nature Reserve lies in the Songhua-Nen River plain, along a major bird migratory route from the Arctic to Southeast Asia. Zhalong's reed beds, ponds, and marshland provide an ideal home to almost 300 species of birds, including swans, storks, ducks, geese, egret, white ibis, and other waterfowl. Established in 1979, the reserve is one of the few breeding grounds in the Far East for the marsh grassbird *(Megalurus pryeri)*. Six of the world's 15 varieties of crane are also found here. The most famous are the endangered red-crowned crane *(Grus japonensis)*, a tall bird with black-and-white plumage and a red crest that is the symbol of longevity in China, and the white-naped crane *(Grus vipio)*, both of which are bred at a research center here. Other rare bird species that visit Zhalong include the swan goose *(Anser cygnoides)* and the Siberian crane *(Grus leucogeranus)*. Birds arrive in spring, and begin breeding in summer. The best time to visit the reserve is from April to June. It is advisable to take binoculars, as Zhalong's population of waterfowl can be elusive.

The marshlands at Zhalong Nature Reserve, important to migrating birds

For hotels and restaurants in this region see pp562–3 and pp583–4

Fossils of Northeast China

China has long been an excellent hunting ground for fossil collectors. Over 130 million years ago much of northern China was volcanic, richly forested, and teeming with life. As the volcanoes erupted they covered the land with dust, hot ash, and mud, and for many years fossils of all kinds have been uncovered, from simple, shellfish-like ammonites through to complete skeletons of large dinosaurs. More recently, the area of northeast China has captured the imagination because of the discovery of at least five feathered species of dinosaurs. The feathers were not only used for flight, but also for insulation and perhaps decoration. Such has been the excitement – and indeed money – generated by these discoveries that fossils have become big business in the area. Locals are discovering and illegally selling what they find, and even going so far as to create fake fossils that have fooled the scientists.

Dragonfly fossils like this reveal even the delicate tracery of the insect's wings. This amazing detail was retained thanks to a thin dusting of fine volcanic ash that was followed by a thick layer of mud, preventing oxidation and rapid decay.

Paleontology has become a booming business in China and placed the country at the heart of important debates about evolution. Therefore the government has been keen to sponsor further research and museums.

This *Dicynodont* was a plant-eating reptile the size of a pig, with two large front teeth – its name means "two dog teeth." One of the most common dinosaur fossils, it has been found all over the world.

Dinosaur eggs are classified by size and shell type because it is difficult to tell what species they were laid by. Some are very similar to birds' eggs, further strengthening the theory that birds descended from a specific group of dinosaurs.

Microraptor gui was a four-winged creature – its legs were feathered too – that glided from tree to tree. The outline of the feathers can clearly be seen, and some think that it might represent an intermediate stage between dinosaurs and birds.

One of the five volcanic lakes at Wudalianchi

⓬ Wudalianchi & the River Border
五大连池

Heilongjiang Sheng, Heihe Shi, 232 miles (375 km) N of Harbin. from Harbin or Qiqiha'er to Beian, then bus. from Harbin. **Tel** (0456) 729 6999. **Open** 8:30am–6pm daily.

A large and popular nature reserve situated in a volcanic field, Wudalianchi lies in a region in western Heilongjiang inhabited by the ancient Daur minority. Its name, meaning "Five Big Connected Lakes," is derived from the five bodies of water created by a succession of volcanic eruptions, the most recent occurring in the 18th century. The resulting lava, which blocked the Bei River and created the lakes, has turned Wudalianchi into a volcanic spa, with geothermal springs and sulphurous waters that have a reputation throughout China for their curative powers.

The 14 volcanoes of the Wudalianchi Geopark add a measure of drama and character to the region's flat terrain. To the west of Number 3 Lake are the two principal volcanic vents, **Lao Hei Shan** (Old Black Hill) and **Huoshao Shan** (Fire Burn Hill). The sites of the most recent eruptions, which took place in 1719–21, both volcanoes are popular with visitors and can be climbed for panoramic views of the area. Surrounded by fields of lava, Lao Hei Shan generated most of the magma that spilled out into the surrounding area. However, like all the volcanoes at Wudalianchi, it is now dormant. Visitors can also bathe in the area's pungent hot-water springs and taste the local mineral water. Apparently bursting with dissolved minerals and curative powers, the waters are sought by a devoted band of the ill and infirm, as well as elderly Chinese, who flock to Wudalianchi to avail of treatment in the numerous sanatoriums that have opened here. The waters are also the star attraction of the annual Water Drinking Festival of the local Daur people, held every May.

Underground caverns dot the area, including the freezing **Crystal Palace** and **Bai Long Dong** (White Dragon Cave), subterranean ice caves decorated with ice sculptures and crowded with visitors in summer. The nearest settlement is the village of Wudalianchi, which has several hotels. Since the guided tours available often make costly and needless diversions, visitors may find it more efficient to travel independently by regular taxi or tuk-tuk.

Bai Long Dong
Near Shenyu Guangchang.
Tel (0456) 729 6999. **Open** 8am–5:30pm daily.

Environs: The **Heilong Jiang** (Black Dragon River, known as the Amur in Russia), that lends its name to this province, demarcates a long section of the border between China and Siberia. Several of northeast China's ethnic tribes traditionally settled in this region, making their living from the river, although many have now been assimilated into the larger Han Chinese population. It is possible to see Siberian forests and small settlements along the border. Since most parts of this region require a permit, it is advisable to check with Harbin's Public Security Bureau.

Connected to Harbin by train, the large border town of **Heihe** sees a healthy cross-border trade with the Russian port town of Blagoveshchensk, which can be visited with a tourist visa for Russia, arranged in Beijing. Hour-long cruises along the Heilong Jiang are also available. At the northern tip of Heilongjiang is **Mohe**, whose main attraction is the spectacular aurora borealis (northern lights) in winter. The town records almost 22 hours of daylight in June.

The frozen Heilong Jiang, used for traveling through the heavily forested terrain

River Border Minorities

Although the majority of the population in Heilongjiang is Han Chinese, the River Border is home to several minorities, including the Oroqen, Hezhen, and Ewenki. Traditionally these nomadic peoples eke out a living in this inhospitable environment. They rely on animal furs for clothes and local plants for medicines, and, when on the move, even construct tents out of birch bark. The Oroqen are hunters, descended from Khitan nomads. They speak an Altaic language and are noted for their shaman and animistic customs and rituals. Numbering a few thousand, the Hezhen are one of China's least populous tribes but their skill at fishing is legendary. The Ewenki supplement their fishing and hunting mainly through breeding reindeer. For all these peoples, however, this way of life is slowly dying out: hunting has been banned in some of the mountain reserves, forcing the nomads to settle down as farmers, while others have left for the cities in search of an easier life.

The Ewenki are dependent on reindeer, which are well adapted to survive in the cold climate. However this nomadic and traditional way of life is rapidly disappearing.

Ewenki tents traditionally have a frame made out of birch poles that are covered with birch bark in summer and with animal skins in winter. Practical *feng shui* means that the entrance is usually south-facing to avoid the wind from the north.

The Oroqen are expert hunters who even make clothes from the animals that they kill for food. Subsidies are now enticing some of them to settle down as farmers.

The Hezhen are legendary for their fish-skin shirts, trousers, and even shoes. The dried skins of carp, pike, and salmon are stitched together to make waterproof items that are highly prized.

The Oroqen's traditional hunting grounds have suffered from encroachment by industry as well as general deforestation and finally by China's newfound enthusiasm for wildlife reserves that have closed off large areas of the wilderness from hunting.

INNER MONGOLIA & THE SILK ROADS

Inner Mongolia & the Silk Road

This massive region, forming a giant northwesterly arc linking Siberia with Central Asia, takes up a third of China's landmass. Geographically it ranges from forest to sandy desert to grassland, while ethnically these lands are home to several Chinese minorities, notably Mongolians, Uighur, and Hui, as well as, among others, Russians, Kazakhs, and Kyrgyz. Three provinces – Inner Mongolia, Ningxia, and Xinjiang – are officially designated autonomous regions. The main attractions in Xinjiang and Gansu are the dusty oasis towns of the Silk Road, replete with Buddhist cave paintings, evocative ruins, and chaotic markets, while elsewhere the appeal is the beauty of China's last great wildernesses.

A monk prays at the Gao Miao, Zhongwei

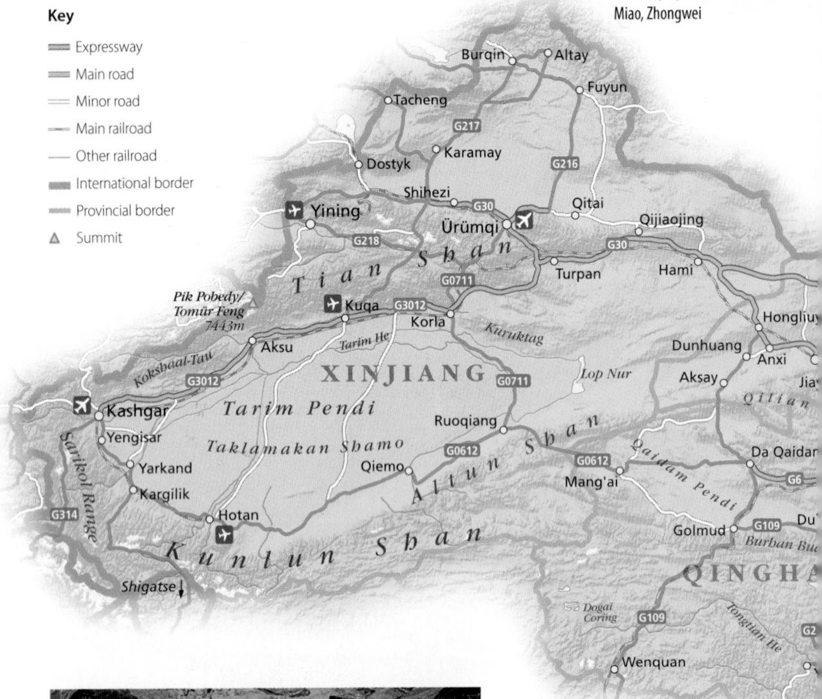

Key

- Expressway
- Main road
- Minor road
- Main railroad
- Other railroad
- International border
- Provincial border
- Summit

Burqin
Altay
Fuyun
Tacheng
G217
Karamay
Dostyk
G216
Shihezi
G30
Yining
Ürümqi
Qitai
Qijiaojing
G218
Tian Shan
G30
Turpan
Hami
G0711
Pik Pobedy/ Tomür Feng 7443m
Kuqa
G3012
Korla
Hongliu
Kuruktag
Aksu
Tarim He
Dunhuang
Anxi
Kokshaal-Tau
G3012
XINJIANG
G0711
Lop Nur
Aksay
Kashgar
Tarim Pendi
Ruoqiang
Qilian
Yengisar
Taklamakan Shamo
Altun Shan
Da Qaidam
Yarkand
G0612
Qiemo
G0612
Qaidam Pendi
Sarikol Range
Kargilik
Mang'ai
G6
G314
Hotan
Golmud
G109
Burhan Bu
Kunlun Shan
QINGHA
Shigatse
Dogai Coring
G109
Tongtian He
Wenquan

Buddha sculpture at Bingling Si, Gansu, still retaining some of its original color

Getting Around

There are airports in the major towns and cities, while the rail network is confined to trunk routes linking major centers. Independent travelers will need to use local bus services, which are comprehensive but crowded and uncomfortable. Because of the distances involved, visitors are likely to focus on one area at a time – the Silk Road or the Mongolian grasslands, for example.

◀ Jiayuguan Fort, the farthest outpost safeguarding the civilized world of the Ming dynasty

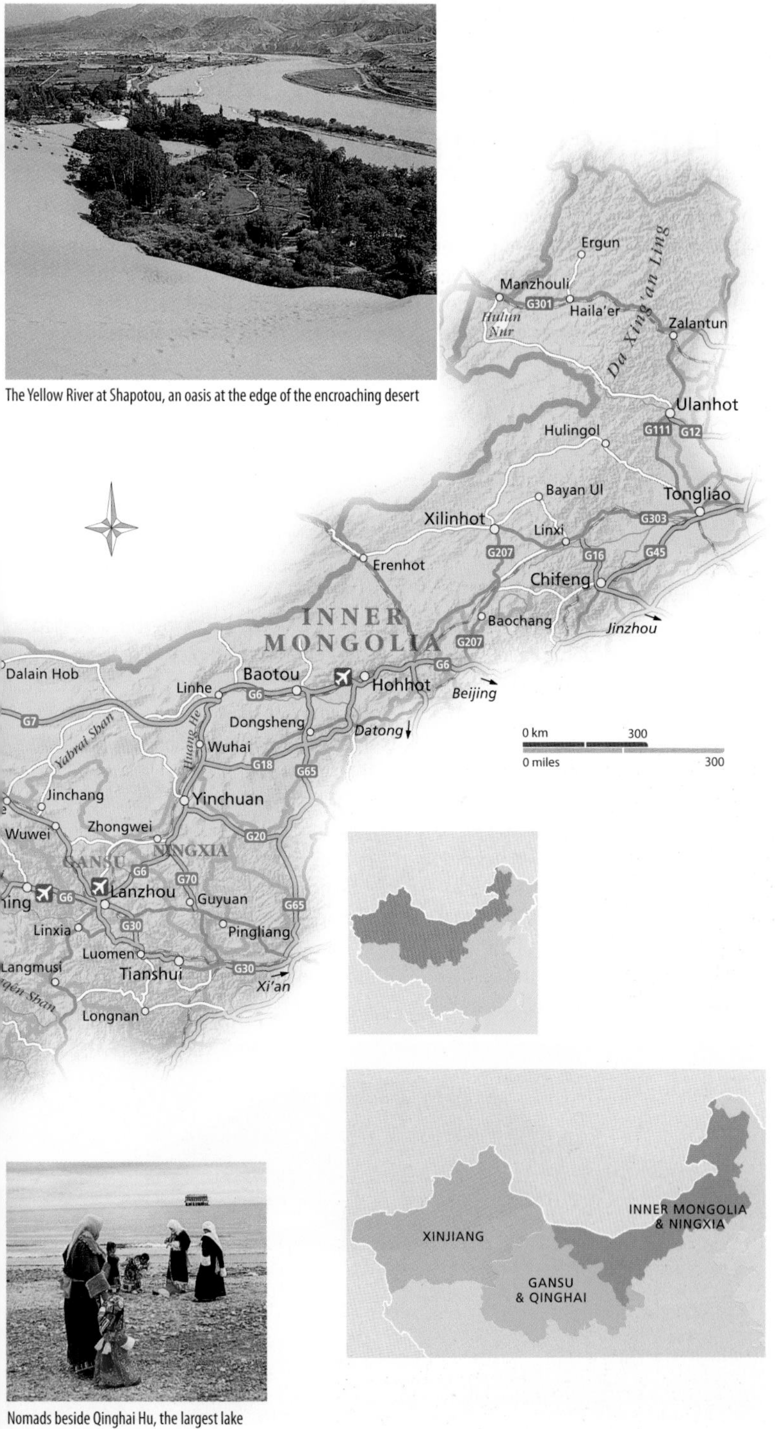

The Yellow River at Shapotou, an oasis at the edge of the encroaching desert

Nomads beside Qinghai Hu, the largest lake in China

For additional map symbols *see back flap*

A PORTRAIT OF INNER MONGOLIA & THE SILK ROAD

This vast region, comprising Inner Mongolia, Ningxia, Gansu, Qinghai, and Xinjiang, covers a significant proportion of the total area of China. Although sparsely populated, the area's appeal lies in its magnificent landscape, the distinctive lifestyles of its indigenous peoples, and its Silk Road past. This fabled trade route's legacies are visible everywhere, from historic sights to religious traditions.

Bordering the Mongolian Republic and Russia to the north, the Central Asian states to the west, and the Indian subcontinent to the south, this region is now indissolubly attached to China as a result of vigorously pursued Chinese hegemony. Today, although the local population is largely Han, they have little in common with the area's indigenous peoples. Only the eastern portion of Gansu seems naturally to form part of China proper. Gansu to the west of Lanzhou and the other provinces are at best indifferent to, and at worst in uneasy thrall to the government in Beijing, which has often ruled with callous disregard for local sentiments. For the Chinese, there still lingers a historic suspicion of the "barbarians" living beyond the frontier marked by the course of the Great Wall. However, historic cultural identities have been retained, and this, together with the region's distinctive geography, means that Inner Mongolia and the northwest have a different character to most of China. Because of this, these three areas – Ningxia, Xinjiang, and Inner Mongolia – are not officially provinces but so-called Autonomous Regions, where the Hui, Uighur, and Mongolian peoples theoretically have a measure of self-government. In practice, any autonomy is superficial, though local languages are spoken and religions practiced reasonably freely.

Although the communities are united by their ethnic minority status, the region is by no means a cohesive entity. For example, the Mongolians and Uighur are only connected by the fact of their inclusion within the political borders of China. Mongolia's grasslands are inhabited

Dramatic sand dunes near Crescent Moon Lake, Dunhuang

Incense burner in the inner courtyard of the Gao Miao, a multi-denominational temple in Zhongwei

by a traditionally nomadic people who maintain their livelihoods through the grazing of sheep and horses. Xinjiang, the homeland of the Turkic-speaking Uighur, on the other hand, is a stony desert relieved by oases dependent upon an ancient but sophisticated system of underground irrigation channels. The one feature that links the region is the extreme nature of its climate and terrain. While much of Xinjiang is flat and featureless, it is fringed by some of the world's highest mountains, including the Pamirs to the southwest and Tian Shan to the northwest.

At its center sits the immense Taklamakan Desert, the world's second-largest shifting sand desert. Only the Sahara is bigger. Summers here are unbearably hot, and its winters are dry and very cold. Qinghai is a mountain plateau, while arid Ningxia and Gansu are rendered habitable only by the presence of the Yellow River. Inner Mongolia, composed of grassland, steppe, desert, and mountain, has short, pleasant summers but dramatically cold, wind-swept winters.

Historically, this area's most significant period was during the great days of the Silk Road, when caravans carrying silk, spices, and tea crossed the inhospitable terrain, stopping at oasis towns along the way. Centuries later, this region became the domain of Genghis Khan, the Mongol warlord *(see p477)*. These desert gardens are still markets where local products, from raisins to saddles and daggers, are traded just as they have been for centuries.

The most significant Silk Road monuments are the Mogao Caves in Dunhuang, perhaps the greatest repository of Buddhist murals, sculpture, and manuscripts. Other Buddhist sites such as the Labrang monastery in Gansu and Ta'er Si in Qinghai owe their origins to the influence of Tibetan Buddhism. Besides visiting caravanserais, grottoes, and monasteries, it is worth exploring the grasslands, mountains, and lakes such as Qinghai Hu, as some of China's last great wilderness areas can be seen here. In recent decades, efforts to bind these western regions into the national mainstream have turned the larger cities into prosperous metropolises. However, in rural areas and smaller towns, a distinctive frontier atmosphere and a powerful sense of history endure.

Statue inside the Fuxi Miao, Tianshui

Tibetan nuns gathering outside their nunnery in Xiahe, Qinghai

Mongols of the Steppe

In the 13th century Genghis Khan *(see p477)* united the steppe-land tribes into a confederation that briefly ruled much of the Eurasian continent. Today, the Mongolian nation is divided into two parts: the Mongolian Republic to the north, and the Inner Mongolia Autonomous Region in China. Traditionally, Mongols are nomadic herders who travel and work on horseback, mostly on the vast, grass-rich steppe. Their diet consists largely of meat and dairy products, including fermented mare's milk, the intoxicating *airaq*. In Inner Mongolia, most of the Mongolian minority now lead a sedentary life of farming. They are striving, however, to keep their traditions alive, by staging the annual Nadaam Festival, for example.

Motorbike travel has replaced the horse for many families and it is not unusual to see an entire family astride a bike, which is just as likely to be seen parked outside a *ger* as a horse.

Equestrian Skill

The key to the Yuan Empire's success was the Mongolians' horse-riding prowess. Horsemanship is still valued, and many learn to ride before they can walk. The sturdy Mongolian pony remains an integral feature of life in the countryside for nomadic herders.

The name Mongol, first used during the Tang dynasty, referred to several tribes. This illumination from 1350 shows that the essential lifestyle of Mongolians changed little up to the 20th century.

***Gers* (yurts)** are the traditional felt homes of the nomads. They are found in the rural grasslands. Permanent encampments of *gers* are found closer to Hohhot.

The frame comes apart for easy transportation. The wooden poles (orange like the sun) are called *uni;* between ten and fifteen of them support each of the *khanas*, or sections of wall.

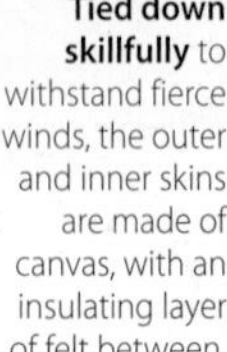

Tied down skillfully to withstand fierce winds, the outer and inner skins are made of canvas, with an insulating layer of felt between.

The principal traditional garment, the *deel*, is a long gown tied with a brilliant sash at the waist. It is worn by both women and men and comes in different weights – lined with sheepskin for winter, quilted for spring, and made of light cloth for summer.

Mongolian wrestling, a favorite event at the Nadaam Festival along with equestrianism and archery, has no weight classes and no time limits. The winner is the one who throws or trips his opponent in such a way that some part of his body touches the ground.

Colorful banners are carried by riders at the competitive Nadaam Festival.

Leather saddles have replaced the less comfortable traditional wooden version.

Hardy Mongolian pony

Buddhism is the main religion among Mongols. Tibetan influence became very strong at the Mongolian court of Kublai Khan and by the 16th century Lamaist Buddhist images had found a place in every *ger*.

Inside is warm and comfortable. A stove sits in the center of the *ger*, while the back is reserved for the family altar and is the place for elders and honored guests.

Desertification

The incursion of dry soil into fertile lands, desertification is caused by overworking the soil and inappropriate irrigation, a major problem in China. In Inner Mongolia, it is severely affecting the traditional way of life, as it destroys grazing pastures. Poor farmers swarm to the area to harvest *facai* or "get rich" grasses, removing the topsoil's anchoring root-structure. Mongols have been encouraged to abandon the pastoral life and settle as farmers and so increase the pressures on the land.

Once-rich grassland reduced to infertile sand

The Silk Road

In reality several ancient trading routes between China and Europe, the Silk Road – the term was coined in the 19th century by Baron von Richthofen – first became busy in the Han dynasty, exposing the Chinese capital Chang'an (Xi'an), and ultimately all of China, to the influences and styles of an alien world. Technologically advanced, with a large workforce and a monopoly on some highly valued products, China was well placed to benefit from a massive expansion in trade.

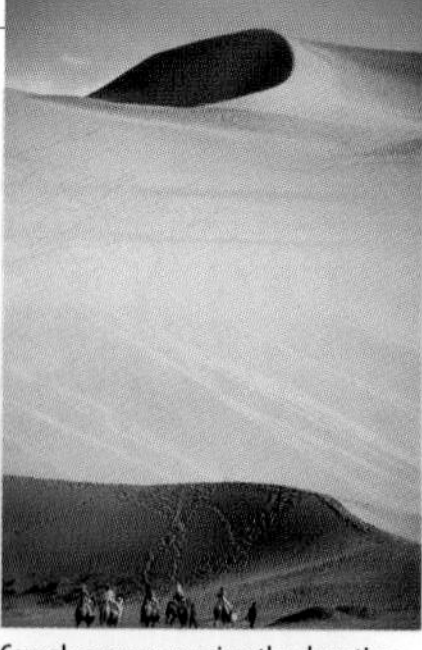

Camel caravan crossing the daunting Silk Road dunes

Silk Road Commerce

The merchants who used the Silk Road dealt not only in spices, silk, porcelain, and jade but also in gold and silver, wool, Arab horses, and many other commodities. However, it was silk (see pp214–15)*, a mysterious Chinese invention, that particularly captivated the West.*

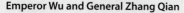

This piece of silk dating from 1500 BC was discovered in what was Bactria, today's Afghanistan, indicating that a network of trading routes had been established long before the heyday of the Silk Road under the Tang.

***Rome** was a major importer of silk and knew China as "Seres" – the land of silk. This gold Roman coin was found along the Silk Road in Xinjiang.*

Emperor Wu and General Zhang Qian

In the 2nd century BC the Han Emperor Wudi saw that his cavalry's horses – better suited to pulling carts – were struggling against the fast horses of his enemy, the Xiongnu. He subsequently sent Zhang Qian, his general, to Sogdiana and Ferghana to obtain some of their legendary horses. Although the mission failed, the information Zhang Qian brought back about the riches he saw led to the development of trade along the Silk Road, and the Ferghana horses did eventually make it to China.

Statue of one of Ferghana's "heavenly horses"

Gold and silver were not highly prized in China until after contact with the West. These precious metals became fashionable in the Tang dynasty, as shown by this gold teacup with Middle Eastern styling.

This Chinese incense burner shows that silverworking techniques must have made it to China along with the vogue for precious metals.

The Silk Road was a series of routes linking China in the east with the Roman Empire to the west. The principal routes looped south and north of the Taklamakan Desert, to join with other branches from Siberia and India as they headed through Central Asia and Persia as far as the Mediterranean. The route flourished in periods of calm and declined in times of war.

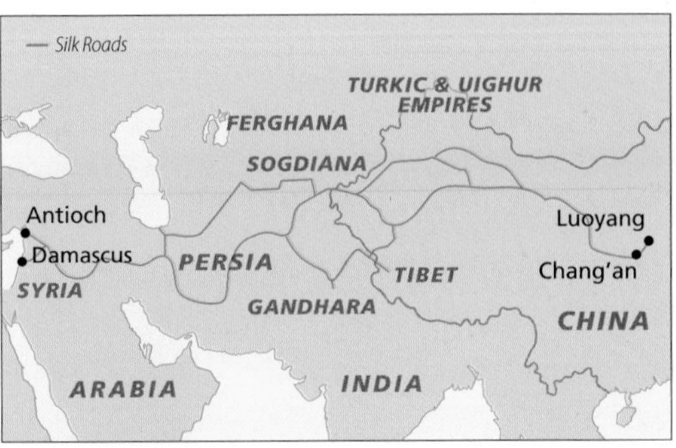

Foreign Ideas and Religions

Contact with foreigners meant traders brought back religions such as Buddhism, which eventually became the national religion, as well as philosophies and artistic styles.

Most artistic influences came from Gandhara, a center of Buddhism. The area's unique artistic styles developed after its conquest by Alexander the Great in the 4th century BC. This Gandharan-inspired Chinese bust recalls the graceful sculptures of Classical Greece.

Detail from the Catalan Map

Made in the 14th century for Charles V of France, this map gives an indication of the extent of geographical knowledge as it stood during the later Middle Ages. The inclusion of China was helped by Marco Polo's account.

This cross is evidence of Nestorianism in China around the 8th century AD. Other religions to make it to China include Islam, Judaism, and Manicheanism, a Babylonian religion based on the opposing principles of Light and Darkness.

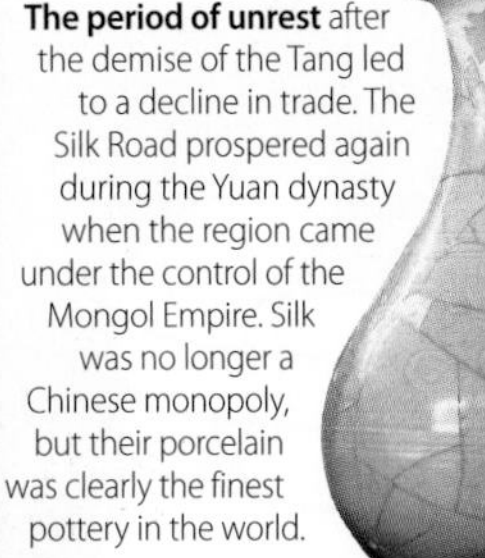

The period of unrest after the demise of the Tang led to a decline in trade. The Silk Road prospered again during the Yuan dynasty when the region came under the control of the Mongol Empire. Silk was no longer a Chinese monopoly, but their porcelain was clearly the finest pottery in the world.

The final decline came with the large ships of the 15th century that could travel with less cost, harassment, and danger. Dwindling use saw the gradual abandonment of the caravanserais that had been the merchants' refuges.

INNER MONGOLIA & NINGXIA

This area comprises two autonomous regions, Inner Mongolia, stretching across northern China in an enormous arc, and Ningxia, China's smallest province after the island of Hainan. The region's main attractions are its great landscapes and the unique cultures of its minority people.

Much of Inner Mongolia consists of rolling grasslands dotted with the traditional tents (*gers* or yurts) of the nomadic Mongols. The capital, Hohhot, is the most convenient place to join a tour and experience their traditional way of life, while the more adventurous can head north to the towns of Xilinhot and Haila'er, where vast tracts of untouched wilderness lie waiting to be explored. The historic Mongolian homeland was made up of the independent Republic of Mongolia, Inner Mongolia (now in China), and parts of Siberia. Bordering Inner Mongolia to the south, Ningxia was first established in 1928. In the 1950s, it became part of Gansu, and in 1958 was designated an autonomous region for the indigenous Hui Muslims *(see p479)*. Living in pockets throughout China, the Hui are the descendants of Muslim Silk Road traders, but they are now largely assimilated with the Han culture. Despite some industrialization, Ningxia is a largely undeveloped region with a smattering of interesting sights. At the foot of the scenic Helan mountains near the capital, Yinchuan, stand the crumbling tombs of the Western Xia dynasty. The Xumi Shan Caves near Guyuan are another key sight, with a wealth of Buddhist carvings.

Sights at a Glance

Towns & Cities

1. Hohhot
2. Baotou
3. Dongsheng
5. Haila'er
6. Manzhouli
8. Yinchuan
11. Zhongwei

Mountains, Grottoes & Caves

9. Helan Shan
12. Guyuan

Monasteries & Stupas

10. *108 Dagobas p481*

Historic Site

7. Xanadu

Area of Natural Beauty

4. Xilinhot

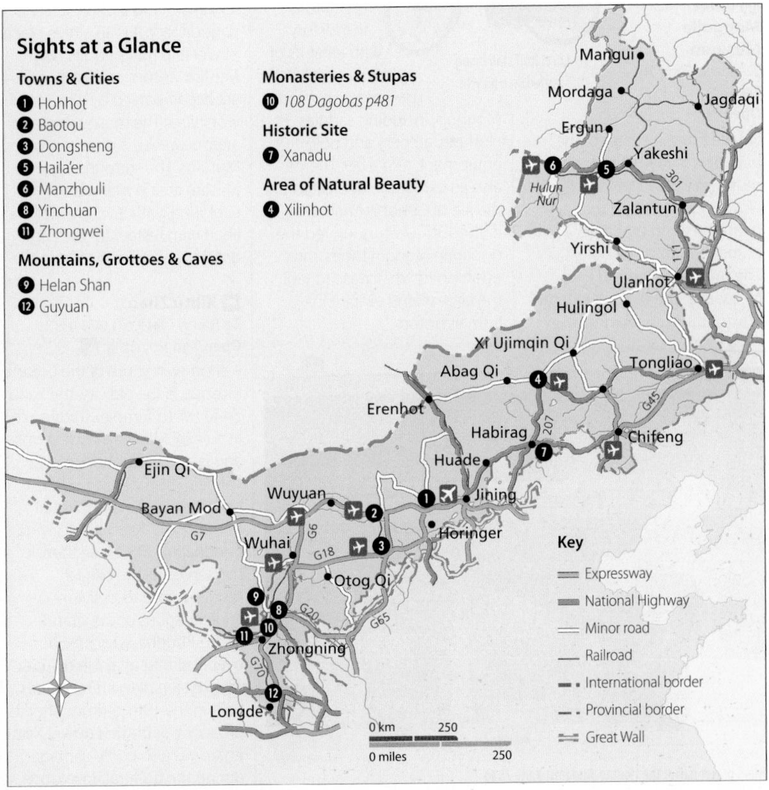

Key

Expressway
National Highway
Minor road
Railroad
International border
Provincial border
Great Wall

0 km 250
0 miles 250

Yurts in the Xilamuren grassland, Inner Mongolia

For additional map symbols *see back flap*

❶ Hohhot

呼和浩特

290 miles (480 km) W of Beijing. 1,980,000. 10 miles (16 km) E of town. Hohhot CITS, (0471) 691 8568.

Dinosaur skeletons on display at the Inner Mongolia Museum

A small Buddhist settlement since the Ming era, Hohhot became the capital of Inner Mongolia in 1952. Although it has expanded considerably, the city has kept some of its charm, visible in traditional mud-brick houses in the south, as well as a few temples and an excellent museum. However, the surrounding grasslands and the traditional way of life they support are the main interest. The greenery in summer makes it the best time to visit the city. Hohhot is largely inhabited by Han Chinese, with a small Mongol and Hui population.

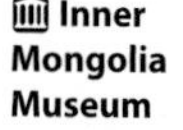

Inner Mongolia Museum

27 Xinhua Dong Jie. **Tel** (0471) 461 4000. **Open** 9am–5pm Tue–Sun.

Situated in the center of the new part of town, this modern museum is definitely worth visiting for an insight into the history and traditions of the Mongolian people. The museum's ground floor focuses on the region's natural environment, displaying an excellent collection of fossils discovered in Inner and Outer Mongolia. This includes the skeleton of a woolly rhinoceros unearthed from a coal mine in Manzhouli *(see p478)*, and several other impressive dinosaur skeletons. On the museum's upper floors, the focus is on culture and history, with exhibits of the paraphernalia used by the nomadic Mongols, including saddles, clothing, archery and polo equipment, and a *ger*. There's also an exhibition dedicated to the life of Genghis Khan, who, in the 13th century, united the disparate Mongol tribes and established what was arguably the largest land empire in human history.

Local fruit stall being carried on a bicycle

Great Mosque

28 Tongdao Nan Jie. **Tel** (0471) 639 1363. **Open** daily.

In the old southwestern part of the city, the attractive Great Mosque (Qingzhen Da Si) is best known for its fusion of both Chinese and Arab architectural influences. The main building, dating from the Qing dynasty, is constructed in black brick, while its minaret has a Chinese-style pagoda roof. It is an active place of worship that permits non-Muslim visitors, especially if they are accompanied by a local Hui worshiper. The mosque's prayer area, however, is reserved for Muslims. The surrounding Muslim area is well worth exploring, with its narrow alleys lined with restaurants selling delicious noodles and kabobs.

Xilitu Zhao

Da Nan Jie. **Tel** (0471) 631 0332. **Open** 8am–6pm daily.

A short walk south of the Great Mosque in the old city, the Xilitu Zhao (Xilitu Temple) started off as a small Ming-dynasty temple and is one of Hohhot's oldest shrines. This Tibetan-Buddhist temple became the spiritual home of the 11th Grand Living Buddha in 1735. Since then, it has served as the official residence of successive reincarnations of the Grand Living Buddha, who presides over Buddhist affairs in the city. This version of the temple was built in the 19th century, after its predecessor burned down. Xilitu Zhao was also badly damaged during the Cultural Revolution,

Main prayer hall at the Tibetan-Buddhist Xilitu Zhao

but has since been heavily restored. It is essentially Chinese in style, with a few Tibetan elements. Its *dagoba* (Tibetan-style stupa), for example, features Sanskrit writing, Chinese dragons, and Tantric Tibetan murals that vividly depict the horrors of hell in gory detail. The temple is still active and the monks here are friendly and some speak English. They are usually happy to show visitors around.

Da Zhao

Da Nan Jie. **Tel** (0471) 630 3154. **Open** 8:30am–6:30pm daily.

The largest Buddhist temple in the city, the Da Zhao is located in a narrow alley just west of Da Nan Jie. Similar in style and layout to the Xilitu Zhao, it was originally built in 1579, and renovated during the 1990s. The shrine was dedicated to the Qing Emperor Kangxi in the late 17th century, and murals in the main hall commemorate his visit. An astounding 10-ft (3-m) silver Sakyamuni Buddha is among the temple's many treasures.

Da Zhao also boasts an extensive collection of musical instruments and dragon sculptures, and is the venue for Buddhist festivals held through the year.

Wusutu Zhao, Hohhot's Mongolian-style temple

Wu Ta Si

48 Wutasi Qian Jie. **Tel** (0471) 597 2640. **Open** 8:30am–5:30pm daily (until 5pm in winter).

Just south of Qingcheng Park, amid the remains of the old city, the Indian-style Wu Ta Si (Five Pagodas Temple) is one of Hohhot's most attractive buildings. It was constructed in 1727 as part of another temple that has now disappeared. The distinctive five pagodas surmount a solid-looking base that contains a smallish temple with 1,563 images of the Buddha carved into its walls, each differing slightly from the others. Inside is a rare Mongolian cosmological map carved onto a large stone that illustrates a zodiac and the positions of numerous stars.

Guardian, Wusutu Zhao

Wusutu Zhao

7 miles (12 km) NW of Hohhot. **Open** 8am–6pm daily.

Founded in 1606, the predominantly Mongolian-style Wusutu Zhao includes some Chinese and Tibetan features. Inside the monastery there are Ming-dynasty murals on display as well as some intricate woodcarvings with imperial dragon motifs. The name "wusutu" means "near to water" in Mongolian. The nearby grasslands and Daqing mountains make pleasant day-trips from town.

Bai Ta

9 miles (15km) east of Hohhot **Open** dawn–dusk daily.

Bai Ta (White Pagoda) is a seven-storied, octagonal structure. It was first built in the 10th century to house Buddhist scriptures dating from the Liao dynasty *(see p64)*. Over 180ft (55m) high, and made of wood and brick, it has some striking carvings inspired by Chinese mythology and nature, including coiled dragons, flowers, and birds. A winding staircase leads to the top, from where there are panoramic views. Bai Ta is best reached by taking a taxi from town.

The open grasslands, traditional home to nomadic Mongols

The Grasslands

Mongolia's history is linked to its grasslands, and for many people, the classic image of the Mongolian landscape is unbroken grassy steppe spreading to the horizon. The steppe provides fodder for the horses and sheep that support the Mongolians' nomadic lifestyle. The three grassland areas accessible from Hohhot are Xilamuren, 50 miles (80 km) north; Huitengxile, 75 miles (120 km) northeast; and Gegentela, 93 miles (150 km) north. The easiest way to explore them is by taking a tour that includes a stay in a village of traditional tents *(gers)*, where visitors attend a banquet and watch Mongolian sports. Though obviously stage-managed, they do show something of Mongolian culture. One can also travel independently by hiring a horse, or negotiating an overnight stay in a *ger* belonging to a local.

Buddhist mural outside a hall at Wudang Zhao monastery, Baotou

❷ Baotou
包头

105 miles (170 km) W of Hohhot. 2,070,000. from Beijing. Baotou CITS, Wulan Dao, (0472) 211 8966.

The largest city in Inner Mongolia, Baotou was once an arid and undeveloped region, inhabited by Mongolian herders of sheep and horses. Today, it is an industrial community made up largely of Han Chinese, with a visible Mongol presence. The town is divided into three principal areas – **Donghe**, the oldest part, lies to the east, while the western area consists of **Qingshan**, the main shopping district, and **Kundulun**, the industrial hub. While Qingshan resembles any modern Chinese town, with its tower blocks and array of shops, Kundulun is a depressing leftover from the Communist era, with large, bleak squares, and no sign of greenery. Donghe has undergone dramatic urban regeneration in the 21st century, but a few traditional mudbrick houses remain.

Environs: The region's best-preserved Lamaist monastery, **Wudang Zhao** lies 43 miles (70 km) northeast of Baotou in a tranquil valley. Built in 1749 in the Tibetan flat-roofed style, it quickly became an important place of pilgrimage, and was home to several hundred monks belonging to the Yellow Hat Sect. It houses a collection of Buddhist murals from the Qing era. Just 6 miles (10 km) south of Baotou lies a section of the **Yellow River** that inscribes a huge northerly loop, enclosing an area called the Ordos that was not conquered by the Chinese until the Qing era. The irrigation projects made possible by the Yellow River have made this area a fertile oasis. There is little to see besides the river, but its sluggish progress through the flat landscape is impressive.

South of Baotou is the great Gobi, a desert that stretches across the northern reaches of Inner Mongolia and the Republic of Mongolia. The **Resonant Sand Gorge,** 37 miles (60 km) south of Baotou, is filled with sand dunes, some of which soar 295 ft (90 m) high. Visitors slip and slide on the dunes, and its name refers to the sound made by the falling sand. Paragliding and camel rides are also available, and a chairlift shuttles visitors from the main road.

Plaque in four scripts, Wudang Zhao

Wudang Zhao
Tel (0472) 535 0546.
Open 8:30am–5pm daily.

Resonant Sand Gorge (Xiangsha Wan)
Tel (0477) 396 3366. **Open** usually 8am–7pm daily.

❸ Dongsheng
东胜

62 miles (100 km) S of Baotou. 160,000.

Reasonably attractive, the small town of Dongsheng serves mainly as a base for visiting **Genghis Khan's Mausoleum** (Ejin Horo Qi), a rather uncomfortable bus trip 30 miles (50 km) to the south. It is almost certain that Genghis Khan is not buried here, as his real tomb is thought to lie in the Hentei Mountains near Ulan Batur in the Republic of Mongolia. However, scholars believe that this site contains a few relics of the Great Khan, and it has grown into a place of pilgrimage for many Mongolians. The mausoleum consists of three conjoined halls, each echoing the shape of a *ger* (Mongolian tent) decorated with murals. The middle hall has a large statue of Genghis with a map of his empire. Some of the halls are bedecked with hangings, and contain *gers*, altars, and other religious paraphernalia. Special ceremonies are held here four times a year to honor Genghis Khan, attracting pilgrims from all over Mongolia.

Genghis Khan's Mausoleum
Tel (0477) 396 5179. **Open** 7:30am–6:30pm daily (winter: 8am–5:30pm).

Sacrificing Aobao near Genghis Khan's Mausoleum, a place of pilgrimage for Mongolians

For hotels and restaurants in this region see p563 and p584

Genghis Khan

Born in 1162 to the head of the Kiyat-Borjigen tribe, Genghis Khan (or Chinggis Khan) was given the name Temujin. A born fighter, as a teenager he killed his half-brother and in 1206 he was proclaimed Genghis Khan (meaning universal king). He unified Mongolia's warring fiefdoms into a huge army of up to 200,000 warriors that invaded China and much of Asia, and eventually created one of the greatest land empires in history. The secret of his success was the skilful use of cavalry and the toughness of the Mongolians, who could survive on very little. Their dietary needs were met either from their horses or from the countryside. Genghis died in 1227, before the capture of Peking, after falling from his horse. In fact it was after his death that the Mongol armies made most of their conquests, but it was thanks to his organization and determination in the first place.

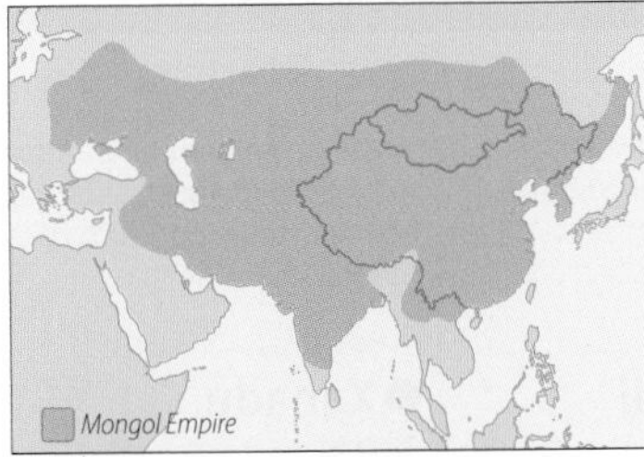

The empire of Genghis Khan's successors at its greatest extent shown on a modern map

Genghis Khan was a supreme organizer and tactician. He also created the first Mongolian code of law, the "Yasak," and promoted the growth of trade between China and Europe.

The Mongolian bow's unique shape gave it a better range than standard bows.

Lance for close-quarters fighting

Mongolian horses were small but sturdy

The cavalry were supreme horsemen and able to fight on the move.

The Mongolian Warrior

This Persian picture, painted 100 years after Genghis Khan's death, shows him fighting the Tatars. The key to Mongolian success was their horsemen. They were disciplined, mobile, and heavily armed, and their ferocity and skill were unmatched at the time.

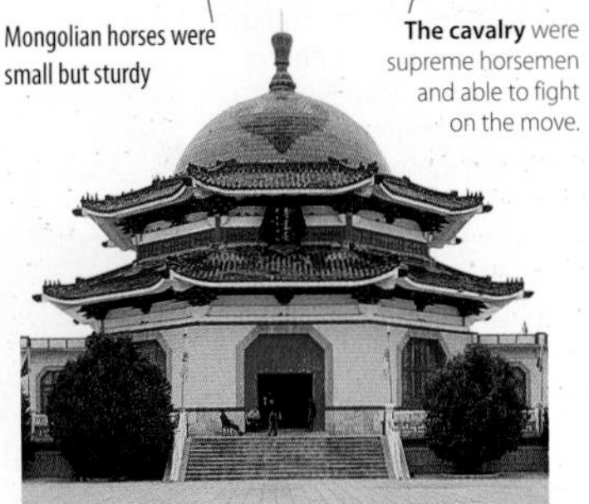

Genghis Khan's Mausoleum is perhaps reminiscent of a Mongolian *ger* or tent. After his death his body was carried by thousands of his followers and taken back to Mongolia. The actual site of his burial is unknown.

The vast expanse of the Hulunbuir grasslands around Haila'er

❹ Xilinhot
锡林浩特

420 miles (700 km) NE of Hohhot. ✈ W of Xilinhot. 🚆 to Erlianhot, then bus. 🚌 from Hohhot, check with PSB if a permit is required. ℹ Xilinhot Travel Agency, (0479) 824 9165.

Situated right in the heart of the province's grasslands, Xilinhot's main draw is a visit to the Mongolian wilderness, inhabited by nomadic sheep- herders in their *muchang jia* (pastureland homes). The tours available here are quieter and cheaper than the ones around Hohhot. Independent trips can also be organized through private tour agents.

❺ Haila'er
海拉尔

570 miles (950 km) NE of Xilinhot. ✈ Haila'er Dongshan, E of Xilianhot. 🚆 🚌 ℹ CTS Haila'er, 20 Ali He Lu, (0470) 822 4017.

Near the Russian border, Haila'er is Inner Mongolia's northernmost town. This small settlement on the banks of the Amur River is a good base for visiting the grasslands in summer. The town's main sight is the network of tunnels used by the Japanese army during World War II. Built by Chinese prisoners, they were used as defensive bunkers along Haila'er's northwestern ridge, which marked the western boundary of Japan's advance into China. Beyond Haila'er lie the **Hulunbuir grasslands**, an expanse of rolling plains threaded by rivers and inhabited by herds of sheep and horses, best accessed on a grassland court.

❻ Manzhouli
满洲里

130 miles (215 km) W of Haila'er. 🚆 from Haila'er & Harbin. 🚌 from Haila'er. ℹ Lantian Travel, (0470) 622 3003.

For long inhabited only by nomads, the border town of Manzhouli became a permanent settlement in 1901, as a stop on the Trans-Manchurian and Trans-Siberian railways. Steam locomotives can still be seen in the shunting yards at Zalainuo'er. Russian influences are apparent in the architecture, mainly the wooden cottages with painted shutters and stucco buildings in pre-Revolutionary style. The main attraction, however, is **Dalai Hu** or Hulun Nur to the south. Surrounded by marshy grasslands, it is one of China's largest lakes, where migratory swans, geese, and cranes come to nest. The tourist office arranges grassland tours, on which visitors can stay in *gers* (tents).

❼ Xanadu
夏那都

280 miles (450 km) NE of Hohhot. 🚌 to Duolun, then taxi. arranged by agencies in Xilinhot.

Close to Inner Mongolia's border near Duolun lie the remains of Yuanshangdu or Xanadu, the site of the legendary palace of Kublai Khan, grandson of Genghis Khan *(see p477)*. One of China's greatest emperors, Kublai Khan and his magnificent summer palace were exalted in Samuel Taylor Coleridge's poem, which begins with the lines "In Xanadu did Kubla Khan a stately pleasure-dome decree." The palace was abandoned by the Khan during his lifetime, and later crumbled. Only a few weathered walls and embankments remain, but the grasslands setting is beautiful.

Manzhouli, the last stop in China on the Trans-Manchurian railway line

For hotels and restaurants in this region see p563 and p584

8 Yinchuan
银川

450 miles (750 km) SW of Hohhot. 1,290,000. 15 miles (25 km) SE of Yinchuan. Ningxia CITS, 375 Beijing Dong Lu, (0951) 673 2858.

The stately Gulou (Drum Tower) in Yinchuan's old town

Situated in the north of Ningxia, in the lee of the Helan mountains, Yinchuan is well protected from the harsh desert climate, and makes a good base from which to explore the surrounding sights. Watered by the Yellow River, this lush and leafy city was the capital of the little-known Western Xia Kingdom from around the 11th century onward. The Kingdom has left few traces of its short existence except for a set of dagobas, and a handful of imperial tombs located 12 miles (20 km) west of the city *(see p480)*. This mysterious dynasty materialized in the 1030s, in the area north of Han China. Following a period of expansion in the late 11th century, the Western Xia empire included all of modern-day Ningxia, as well as parts of Shaanxi, Gansu, Qinghai, and Inner Mongolia. Although the Chinese considered them barbarians, they achieved a considerable level of sophistication, partly through the assimilation of Tang culture, until their kingdom was sacked by the invading Mongols in 1227.

Sign advertising a fortune teller outside Haibao Ta

Today, Yinchuan is a pleasant and lively city, with a handful of interesting things to see. It consists of two parts, the new town (Xin Cheng) to the west near the railway station, and the old town (Lao Cheng or Xingqing), 4 miles (7 km) east, where most of the sights are located.

Jiefang Jie, the old town's main thoroughfare, has two well-restored traditional Chinese towers. One is the large **Gulou** (Drum Tower), while farther east lies the **Yuhuang Ge** (Yuhuang Pavilion), which dates back to the Ming dynasty. Just south of the Drum Tower, Gulou Jie is the heart of the city's busy shopping district and is lined with department stores.

West of Gulou Jie stands the 13-story, octagonal **Xi Ta** (West Pagoda), built within the grounds of the Chetian Temple, originally built in the 11th century.

Southeast of Gulou, is the **South Gate** (Nan Men) which resembles a miniature version of Beijing's Tian'an Men. A short walk southwest of Nan Men, **Nanguan Mosque** is a modern building constructed in 1981 to replace the original 1915 shrine. It is an active place of worship that caters to Yinchuan's Hui population. Unlike most mosques in China, it has hardly any Chinese features and is built in a distinct Middle-Eastern style. In the northern reaches of the old town, the ancient **Haibao Ta** stands in the grounds of an active monastery. According to records, the 177-ft (54-m) tower, also known as the Northern Pagoda (Bei Ta), was first built in the 5th century AD. It was rebuilt in the 18th century in the original style, after an earthquake destroyed it in 1739. It is an unusually angular structure, with ledges and niches at every level. It is worth making the climb to the top of its nine stories, as there are terrific views across the city to the Yellow River and Helan mountains. The only sight in the west of Yinchuan is the **Ningxia Provincial Museum**, worth visiting for its large collection of Western Xia artifacts. The museum also has informative exhibits on the Silk Road and Hui culture. Followers of Islam, the Hui descended from Arab and Persian traders who came to China during the Tang and Yuan dynasties.

Gulou and Yuhuang Ge
Jiefang Jie. **Open** 8:30am–5pm daily.

Nanguan Mosque
Yuhuangge Nan Jie. **Tel** (0951) 410 6714. **Open** 8am–5pm daily.

Ningxia Provincial Museum
E side of Renmin Guangchang. **Tel** (0951) 508 5062. **Open** 9am–4:30pm Tue–Sun. **nxbwg.com**

The 1,500-year-old Haibao Ta in northern Yinchuan

The striking Xi Xia Wang Ling (Western Xia Tombs) in Helan Shan

9 Helan Shan
贺兰山

12 miles (20 km) W of Yinchuan. from Xinyue Sq or taxi. Ningxia CITS, 375 Beijing Dong Lu, (0951) 673 2858.

Looming over Yinchuan, about 12 miles (20 km) to the west, the 11,667-ft (3,556-m) high mountain range of Helan Shan has some interesting historical places to visit. At the foot of its eastern slopes lie the **Xi Xia Wang Ling**, the royal tombs of the Western Xia dynasty (1038–1227). Spread over a large area, these crumbling but still impressive mounds commemorate nine Xia kings. The **Gunzhong Pass**, farther north, makes for pleasant hikes in the surrounding hills if the weather is fine. Located 5 miles (8 km) north of the pass are the 39-ft (12-m) twin pagodas, **Baisikou Shuang Ta**, decorated with Buddha statues. Nearby, at **Suyu Kou**, are hundreds of rock paintings of uncertain age depicting animals and human figures. These sights can all be visited in a day by hiring a minibus or car from Yinchuan.

Xi Xia Wang Ling
22 miles (35 km) W of Yinchuan.
Open 8am–6:30pm daily.

10 108 Dagobas

See p481.

11 Zhongwei
中卫

106 miles (170 km) SW of Yinchuan. Zhongwei Travel Service, 33 Gu Lou Xi Jie, (0995) 701 4880.

The pleasant town of Zhongwei lies between the Tengger Desert to the north and the Yellow River to the south. This small settlement can easily be explored on foot or by cycle-rickshaw. At its center lies a traditional **Drum Tower** (Gulou) dating to the Ming era. Zhongwei's main sight is the 15th-century **Gao Miao**, a rather bizarre temple which serves Buddhists, Daoists, and Confucians alike. It was originally built for Buddhists, but somehow developed ecumenically, which is reflected in the welter of well over 200 chapels and rooms. Rebuilt several times, the temple, in its present form, is an interesting amalgamation of architectural styles.

Painting on upper pavilion, Gao Miao

Carved entrance of the multi-denominational Gao Miao, Zhongwei

Environs: About 9 miles (15 km) west of Zhongwei, the spectacular resort of **Shapotou** lies on the banks of the Yellow River, between riverbank vegetation on one side and the striking sand dunes of the desert on the other. Accessed by minibus from Zhongwei, the Shapotou Desert Research Center was founded in 1956 to reclaim fertile land from the desert. It has met with some success, as seen in the groves of trees and surrounding cultivation. It is now a resort, offering camel rides and trips downriver on traditional rafts that are kept afloat with inflated sheep skins. Sand sleds are available to rent for those who wish to speed down the sand dune slopes.

Gao Miao
Gulou Bei Jie. **Open** 7:30am–6pm daily (8am–5:30pm in winter).

Shapotou
Tel (0955) 398 8699. **Open** 8:30am–5pm daily. **spttour.com**

12 Guyuan
固原

200 miles (330 km) S of Yinchuan. Xumi Shan Caves: from Guyuan to Sanying, then taxi.

In the southern part of Ningxia, Guyuan serves as a base for visiting the **Xumi Shan** (Treasure Mountain) **Caves**, 31 miles (50 km) to the north-west. Set in dramatic sandstone hills, these Buddhist grottoes – numbering well over a hundred – are relics from the greatest era of the Silk Road, mostly the period covering the Northern Wei, Sui, and Tang dynasties. They contain more than 300 well-preserved Buddhist statues, the most famous being a colossal Maitreya (Future) Buddha, which stands 62 ft (19 m) high in Cave 5.

⑩ 108 Dagobas

108塔

Set in the desert near the town of Qingtongxia Zhen, the 108 Dagobas stand in 12 gleaming rows, spread out in a perfect triangular formation overlooking the Yellow River. A Buddhist monument, it is not clear exactly what their purpose is. Traditionally it has been thought that they were placed here during the Yuan Dynasty (1279–1368) but there may be some link to the Western Xia Empire. The number 108 is significant in Chinese numerology: there are 108 prayer beads in a Buddhist rosary – and the same number of possible sins or worries.

VISITORS' CHECKLIST

Practical Information
50 miles (85 km) S of Yinchuan.
Tel (0953) 301 2868.
Open 8am–6:30pm daily.

Transportation
or from Yinchuan to Qingtongxia Zhen, minibus or taxi.

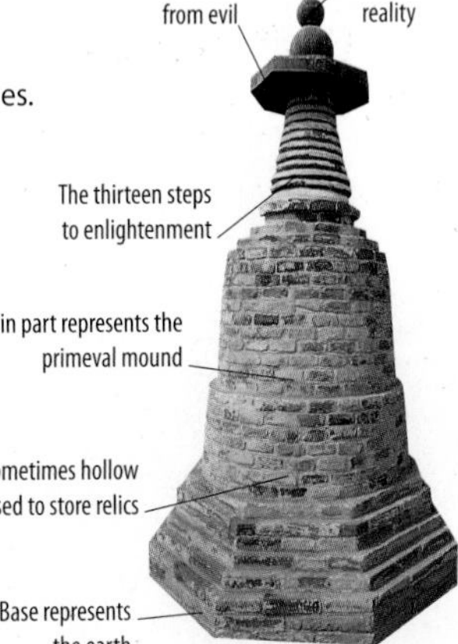

★ Hillside Location
Impressive as the dagobas are, a good reason for visiting them is to get out in the peaceful surrounding hills and do a bit of walking. Here you can find quiet temples at the top of some testing steps as well as flowing calligraphy carved into the rockfaces.

★ The Dagobas
Like the Indian stupa, the dagoba is a deeply symbolic icon. In early Buddhist art, Buddha was never shown in human form, instead a stupa became his symbol.

Viewing the Dagobas
The best view is from a boat on the river – if the water level is high enough. The site is in excellent condition as a result of an overzealous restoration.

Western Xia Empire

Western Xia coin

This mysterious dynasty materialized in the early 11th century when they established the Great Xia Empire in the area north of what was Han China. Known as Tanguts – and probably from Tibet – they were briefly strong enough to build up a small empire and force tribute from the Song rulers in China. However, they were so thoroughly defeated by the Mongols in 1227 that little evidence of their existence remains except for some coins, books, and a famous stele covered in their feathery script (now in Xi'an).

GANSU & QINGHAI

For centuries, Gansu and Qinghai were regarded as frontier provinces that marked the outer limits of ancient China. A harsh and rugged region, Gansu connects the Chinese heartland with the vast desert regions to the northwest. The Hexi Corridor, running 750 miles (1,200 km) between two mountain ranges and dotted with oases, formed a link between China and the West. The Silk Road passed through here, as did the Great Wall, and later, the region's only railroad line. The Yellow River flows through Lanzhou, for centuries a major stop along the Silk Road. To the southwest lies the Tibetan town of Xiahe and its splendid Labrang Monastery. In the desert landscape northwest of Lanzhou are two great historical relics – the mighty Ming fortress of Jiayuguan and the cave art at Dunhuang.

Lying between Gansu and Tibet, Qinghai is a vast mountain plateau inhabited by a mere 5.5 million people. In every respect – culturally, historically, and geographically – it is part of the Tibetan Plateau, and was once the Tibetan province of Amdo, becoming a province of China only in 1928. Due to its remoteness, it has been used as the site for several prison camps for political dissidents. The province, however, abounds in natural beauty, with lush valleys around the capital of Xining, and miles of unspoilt wilderness around Qinghai Hu, China's largest lake. It also houses one of the country's greatest Tibetan lamaseries, Ta'er Si, and provides access into Tibet from Golmud and Xining across some of the highest mountains in the world.

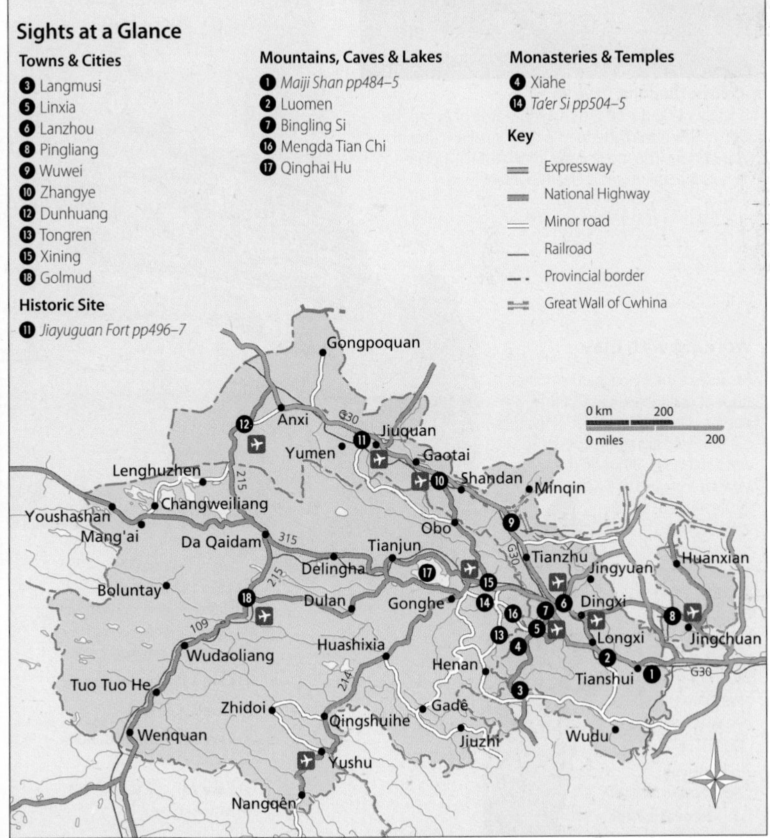

◀ The steep stairway up the side of Maiji Shan, Gansu

For additional map symbols *see back flap*

❶ Maiji Shan

麦积山

The site of one of China's most important groups of Buddhist carvings, 465-ft (142-m) high Maiji Shan (Corn Rick Mountain) was designated a UNESCO World Heritage Site in 2014. It is likely that the first sculptures were made around the end of the 4th century AD, and work continued up to the Qing dynasty. It provides an invaluable insight into the development of Chinese Buddhist artistic style. Almost 200 caves survive and are reached by a series of precipitous stairways. However, many of the best caves are closed and the gloomy interiors have to be viewed through grilles, so bring a flashlight.

Maiji Shan, said to resemble a corn rick or haystack from afar

★ Colossal Buddha: Cave 98

This finely worked 53-ft (16-m) high statue of Amitabha Buddha is portrayed attended by two smaller statues of Avalokitesvara. The move away from classical Indian-style Buddha sculptures is clearly evident here.

Working with Clay

Because of the friable nature of the stone at Maiji Shan, many of the statues were not hewn out of the rock but modeled from clay stuck onto a wooden frame. Although they are not as well preserved as a result, they are more lively and with more detail than similar carvings in the Buddhist caves at, for example, Dunhuang. There are a few stone statues at Maiji Shan, but these have been carved from specially imported rock.

Statue showing details of dress and hairstyle

KEY

① **Cave 133** is actually a tomb and home to many sculptures and engravings. It is considered one of the most exquisite holy caves.

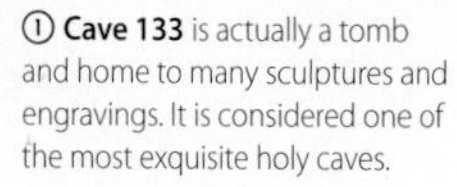

② **Cave 135, Cave of Heaven**

③ **Cave 5, Calf Hall**

④ **Cave 3, Thousand Buddha Corridor**

⑤ **Cave 43** is the tomb of a Wei-dynasty empress.

For hotels and restaurants in this region see p563 and p584

Upper Seven Buddhas: Cave 4
The upper gallery of Buddhas includes this magnificent Song-dynasty guardian. The cave complex itself is said to have been built by the local governor Li Yunxin, as early as the 6th century.

VISITORS' CHECKLIST

Practical Information
22 miles (35 km) SE of Tianshui.
Tel (0938) 273 1407. **Open** 8am–6pm. for an additional large fee, the closed caves may be opened. **517mjs.cn**

Transportation
from Beidao and Tianshui.

★ Colossal Buddhas: Cave 13
These huge statues originally date from the Sui dynasty and were then repaired during the Ming dynasty. The myriad holes around the statues were probably used to support a protective framework.

Middle Seven Buddhas: Cave 9
These figures show a transitional phase between Indian-influenced sculpture and later Song-era figures, with pure Chinese characteristics. The statues are well-proportioned and slim in stature, with realistic drapes to their clothes.

★ Gallery Views
There are excellent views across the countryside from the network of walkways on the cliff face of Maiji Shan. If time allows, a hike around the arboretum at the foot of the cliff is recommended.

Rock carvings and paintings at Lashao Si

❷ Luomen
洛门

155 miles (250 km) SE of Lanzhou. Water Curtain Thousand Buddha Caves: minibus from Luomen. **Open** 8am–6pm daily.

The small town of Luomen serves as a base for visiting the **Water Curtain Thousand Buddha Caves** (also known as Shuilian Dong), situated in a spectacular gorge in the nearby mountains. Remote and accessible only by a rough road, the caves cannot be reached in bad weather as the road becomes unusable. The main attractions are a 98-ft (30-m) Sakyamuni (the Historical Buddha), carved into a rock face, and Lashao Si, a temple built into a cave in the mountainside that has paintings and carvings dating from the Northern Wei dynasty (AD 386–534). Visitors can reach Luomen by bus or train from Tianshui, or from Lanzhou.

❸ Langmusi
郎木寺

236 miles (380 km) S of Lanzhou. from Lanzhou, Linxia, or Xiahe to Hezuo, then direct bus to Langmusi.

The remote mountain town of Langmusi is inhabited by a mix of Tibetan, Hui, and Han Chinese. While the hills offer miles of unspoilt country with trails for walking and riding, several active temples dot the town. Built in 1413, the **Dacang Langmu Gansu Gompa** (also known as Saichi Si) is the place of worship for several hundred monks, who study astrology and medicine as well as Tibetan Buddhist theology. Traditional sky-burials, where the dead are left for vultures, take place in the surrounding hills, though visitors are not usually permitted to watch.

Dacang Langmu Gansu Gompa
Open 8am–5pm daily.

❹ Xiahe
夏河

175 miles (280 km) SW of Lanzhou. Monlam (Great Prayer) Festival (Feb/Mar).

Perched at a height of 9,514 ft (2,900 m) in a mountain valley at the edge of the Tibetan plateau that is now a part of Gansu, Xiahe is a significant Tibetan monastery town that attracts many devout Buddhist pilgrims to its **Labrang Monastery** every year. As a result, the town's population is a mix of Hui, Tibetan, and Han Chinese.

Xiahe's location offers many opportunities to explore the surrounding grasslands on horseback, bicycle, or on foot. Guest houses and travel agencies in town can arrange excursions. The town itself comprises a single main street, running along the Daxia River. The commercial part is at the eastern end; the Labrang Monastery is in the center; while the Tibetan quarter is at the western end, offering glimpses of the Tibetan way of life. This town is worth a visit, especially for those not going to Tibet.

Environs: Lying near **Sangke** village, 6 miles (10km) southwest of Xiahe, is a lake surrounded by the Sangke grasslands, used by nomads for grazing their yaks. This huge area of grass and flowers can be accessed by road, although a fee is charged. 19 miles (30 km) north of Xiahe lie the even more vast and picturesque **Ganjia grasslands**.

Breathtaking scenery around Langmusi

For hotels and restaurants in this region see p583 and pp584–85

Labrang Monastery

拉卜楞寺

The most important center of the Yellow Hat Sect (Gelugpa) outside Tibet, the Labrang Monastery (Labuleng Si) attracts thousands of Tibetan pilgrims each year. As a result of the Cultural Revolution the monastery was closed until 1980 and the number of monks reduced from 4,000 to about 1,500. Set in an auspicious location with mountains to the north and the Daxia River to the south, the impressive monastery buildings are joined by a haphazard maze of alleyways that makes it a fascinating place to wander around.

Main prayer hall, Labrang Monastery

Exploring the Labrang Monastery

This monastery was founded in 1709 during the forty-eighth year of the reign of the Qing Kangxi emperor by a local monk, E'ang Zongzhe. He became the first generation Living Buddha, or Jiemuyang, who ranks third in the Tibetan hierarchy after the Dalai and Panchen Lamas. The monastery's buildings came through the Cultural Revolution relatively unscathed, but in 1985 a fire seriously damaged the Grand Sutra Hall, which has subsequently been fully restored. Today the sprawling monastery complex dominates the town. If it weren't for the ring of prayer wheels that encircle the monastery, it would be difficult to see where the town ends and the monastery starts.

The monastery is built in a typical Tibetan style and consists of six grand halls for the study of scriptures or *sutras*, 18 Buddha temples, offices for the Living Buddha, and many hundreds of residences for the monks. The monastery is also an academic institution and holds an assortment of around 60,000 *sutras* and specialized books. The large halls are colleges for the monks to study a variety of degrees such as mathematics, astronomy, medicine, and other more esoteric subjects.

The Grand Sutra Hall is the grandest of the buildings and can hold up to 4,000 monks. It is an impressive sight to see the monks chanting outside the hall each morning as they wait to go in and pray. Labrang has a multitude of prayer wheels set in a long line that encircles the monastery. Spinning these was, and still is, a way for the largely illiterate Tibetan people to pray.

Within the prayer wheels stands the **Gongtang Pagoda**, south of the main road. At nearly 100-ft (31-m) high it comprises five levels topped with a gold-colored stupa containing thousands of *sutras* and Buddha statues. You can climb up to the upper level and get an oustanding view over the monastery and town. Parts of Labrang can only be visited as a member of a tour group, although much of the monastery can be freely explored. There are a couple of tours in English each day. Visitors should be sensitive to the religious nature of the site.

Senior Yellow Hat monk

Xiahe is also famous for its Monlam festival. Seen by thousands who have come from all over the country, a huge *thangka* of Buddha is unfurled and sanctified on a screen to the south of the Daxia River. There follow several days of festivities, including processions, musical performances, and dances.

View over the monastery with the gleaming Gongtang Pagoda to the left

VISITORS' CHECKLIST

Practical Information

Xiahe, 175 miles (280 km) SW of Lanzhou. **Tel** (0941) 712 1095.
Open 8am–noon, 2–6pm daily.
required for main temple.
Monlam Festival *(see p50)*.

Transportation

Linxia, Lanzhou, Langmusi, or Tongren.

Bunches of noodles tied up and ready for sale, Linxia

❺ Linxia

临夏

62 miles (100 km) SW of Lanzhou. 250,000. from Lanzhou, Xining, and Xiahe.

A pleasant place for ambling leisurely through streets bustling with locals, the modern town of Linxia has a predominantly Muslim character. It was once a stopover for travelers passing between Lanzhou and the South Pass along the Silk Road. The town is still a good place to break the journey between Lanzhou and Xiahe. However, it offers very few attractions aside from its numerous mosques. The most prominent is the large and impressive **Nanguan Mosque**, just off the main square.

Linxia's appeal lies in its colorful markets and teahouses. The markets are lined with shops selling carved gourds, carpets, and saddlery. Most interesting are the distinctive local spectacles, made from ground crystal lenses, which many elderly men can be seen wearing. At the top end of Jiefang Nan Lu, in the south of town, is the great night market with numerous stalls stocked with aromatic curry-flavored breads *(bing)* and huge piles of noodles – fresh and dried.

The area around Linxia is home to the Dongxiang minority, who speak their own Altaic language and are supposedly descendants of Mongol troops garrisoned here in the 13th century.

❻ Lanzhou

兰州

A large industrial city and Gansu's capital, Lanzhou has for long been the key transport link between the Chinese heartlands and the northwest. Located at the eastern end of the Hexi Corridor, the town was a crucial stop on the Silk Road. The Yellow River flows through the center of the city, and for centuries Lanzhou was the principal point for crossing the river. In fact, until the 19th century, a bridge created by chaining together a flotilla of boats was used. The first iron bridge was built in 1907. Although most of the attractions lie well away from the center, Lanzhou offers good food, shopping, and an excellent museum.

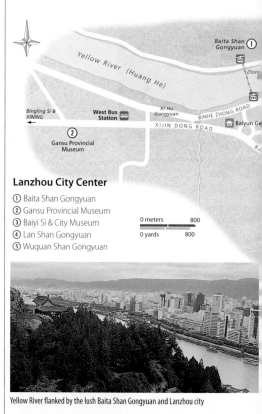

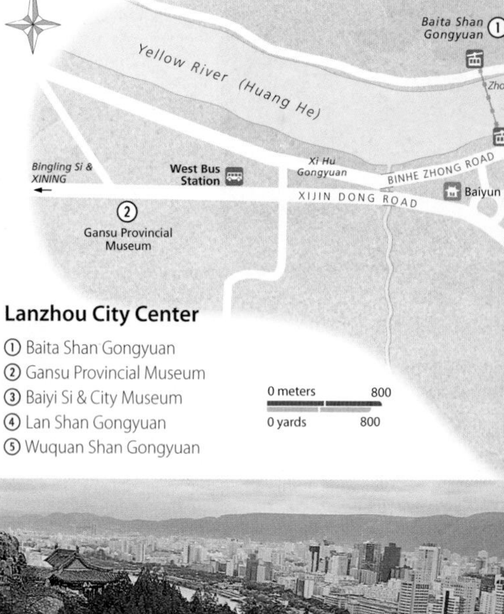

Yellow River flanked by the lush Baita Shan Gongyuan and Lanzhou city

Baita Shan Gongyuan

Open 6am–6pm daily.

To the north of the river, near Zhongshan Bridge, is Baita Shan Gongyuan (White Pagoda Hill Park). It takes its name from the 13th-century pagoda, Bai Ta, which was built as part of a temple at the hill's summit. Steps have been carved into the steep slopes, and the walkways are dotted with teahouses, mosques, a plant nursery, and assorted pavilions. Chairlifts take visitors to the top from a spot on the other side of the river.

Gansu Provincial Museum

3 Xijin Xi Lu. **Tel** (0931) 233 9133. **Open** 9am–5pm Tue–Sun.

This museum is set in an old Soviet-style building west of town. The ground floor has a natural history section with a mammoth skeleton found in the Yellow River in 1973. Captioned in English, the history section upstairs is best known for the striking 2,000-year-old bronze Flying Horse, with its hoof resting on the back of a swallow, that was discovered in an Eastern Han tomb in Wuwei. and worth a visit for this alone. Also worth seeing are the bronze chariots, with horses and attendants, from a tomb in the same area, as well as a fine collection of Yangshao pottery dating from the late Neolithic period. Other relics include Silk Road carvings, wooden spills, statuary, and writing tablets. In the garden, a mock tomb recreates burials in the Jiayuguan area in the late 3rd and early 4th centuries. A large exhibit commemorates the Long March.

Flying Horse statue at Lanzhou's train station

Key to Symbols *see back flap*

Baiyi Si and City Museum

110 Qingyang Dong Lu. **Open** 9am–5:30pm daily.

Baiyi Si, with its temple and accompanying stupa, was built during the Ming dynasty (1368–1644) and now houses Lanzhou's small City Museum Qingyang Lu. The small temple's unusual location, dwarfed by the department stores of Lanzhou's main shopping district, makes it appear strikingly out of place,

Ornamental door knob, Rui Yuan Si, Wuquan Shan

Lan Shan Gongyuan

Open 8:30am–5pm daily.

South of the city, Lan Shan Gongyuan (Lan Shan Park) can be reached by chairlift from Wuquan Shan Gongyuan. The 20-minute ride to the top is a pleasant way to escape the summer heat. It is a great spot to watch the sunsets and the city lights at night. There are an amusement park and several eateries. A trail leads to Wuquan Shan Gongyuan.

VISITORS' CHECKLIST

Practical Information

425 miles (680 km) W of Xi'an. 2,180,000. Lanzhou CITS, 10/F, Tourism Building, Nongmin Xiang, (0931) 883 5566.

Transportation

Lanzhou Zhongchuan airport, 42 miles (70 km) N of city. Lanzhou train station. CAAC (buses to airport), East bus station, Main bus station, West bus station.

Wuquan Shan Gongyuan

Tel (0931) 824 3247. **Open** 7am–8pm daily.

Also set in the south of town, Wuquan Shan Gongyuan (Five Springs Hill Park) resembles a traditional garden, with its weathered rocks, cascading streams, elaborate doorways, and myriad pavilions. The hill is said to be the place where the

Gateway designed as a quatrefoil moon in Wuquan Shan Gongyuan

Han General Huo Qubing quartered his cavalry as he mounted an expedition to the northwest. According to one legend, he cut at the rocks until the water he needed for his horses and men gushed forth. Of the several temples on the site, **Chongqing Si** dates back to 1372, and houses an iron bell cast in 1202. Despite its venerable origins, modern materials like concrete have been used several times in restoring the temple, and it is now an artistic blend of Soviet and traditional Chinese design. Another one of the oldest buildings in the park, the Ming-dynasty **Jingang Palace** houses an impressive 16-ft (5-m) bronze Buddha, reputedly cast in 1370.

The enormous seated Buddha carved into a cliff, Cave 172, Bingling Si

❼ Bingling Si
炳灵寺

56 miles (90 km) SW of Lanzhou. [bus] to Liujia Xia Reservoir, then boat to caves. **Tel** (0930) 887 9070. **Open** Apr–Oct, when the water level in reservoir is high. [tours] [boat] from Lanzhou.

The magnificent group of Buddhist caves at Bingling Si (Bright Spirit Temple) is one of the most intriguing sights in Gansu. Buddhism arrived in China along the Silk Road, and these caves are among the earliest significant Buddhist monuments in the country. Carved into sheer cliffs, the caves stretch for about a mile (1.6 km) along a 196-ft (60-m) high gorge. Isolated by the waters of the Liujiaxia Reservoir on the Yellow River, the splendid sculptures and paintings were saved from damage during the Cultural Revolution, and remain in surprisingly good condition. Known as the Thousand Buddha Caves, there are, in fact only 183 of them, of which 149 can be more appropriately described as niches.

The caves were created about 1,600 years ago during the Northern Wei and Western Jin dynasties. It is believed that the artists hung down the cliffs on ropes and chiseled out sculptures from the rock-face. The style of work is similar to the Buddhist caves at Datong and Luoyang. Most of the caves contain rock-cut statues, clay sculptures, and colorful frescoes. One of the earliest caves, No. 169, dates to AD 420 and contains a Buddha and two *bodhisattvas* that are among the oldest and best preserved in China, though an additional fee is required to access the cave. Most of the other caves were completed during the Tang era. The most impressive cave, No. 172, has an 89-ft (27-m) high seated statue of Maitreya (the Future Buddha).

Work on the sculptures continued long after the Silk Road had lost its importance, and there are examples of work from the Song, Ming, and Qing dynasties. The paintings reached their height during the Song and Ming dynasties, although there are some older and comparatively cruder paintings dating back to the Tang period.

Getting to the caves can be slightly uncertain, as access depends on the water level in the reservoir. Fall is usually the best time of year to visit Bingling Si. It is a two-hour bus journey from Lanzhou to the reservoir and dam, where a visitor center sells tickets and arranges transport by boat to the caves. The boat trip takes around an hour, passing through some beautiful countryside with fishermen busy at work, and wheat and rice being cultivated on the riverbanks.

❽ Pingliang
平凉

195 miles (325 km) E of Lanzhou. [bus]

Hidden in the hills in a mountainous region near the Gansu–Ningxia border is the sleepy town of Pingliang. Surrounded by beautiful peaks, some of which rise to heights of 6,890 ft (2,100 m), it remains one of the least-visited parts of the province and is mostly used as a convenient base for exploring **Kongtong Shan**, a Daoist monastery, 6 miles (10 km) west of town. Perched dramatically on a clifftop of the same name, the monastery sits above a glittering lake and a few other temples scattered across the landscape. The surrounding area is excellent for taking long walks across the lush green hills.

Carved stele, Kongtong Shan, Pingliang

Kongtong Shan's lush north peak, Pingliang

For hotels and restaurants in this region see p563 and pp584–5

The Spread of Buddhism

Buddhism's establishment in China was a long process and the date of its arrival is uncertain. The earliest sign of the religion in China is associated with the foundation of the White Horse Temple *(see p158)* during the Han dynasty near the imperial capital of Luoyang. Based on the teachings of Buddha, who lived in northern India during the 6th century BC, Buddhism was probably disseminated along the Silk Route by immigrants from Central Asia from the 1st century AD onwards. In China, Buddhism surged in popularity during periods of instability, when Confucianism's veneration for authority *(see p36)* did not sit well with the populace, and it was eventually adopted by China's rulers. The Mahayana school *(see p37)* took hold in China, breaking into different sects, such as the Chan sect, which gained a large following in Japan as Zen Buddhism.

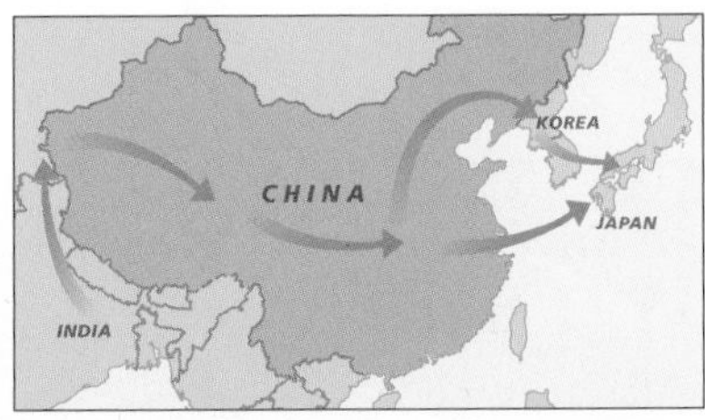

Mahayana Buddhism started in India in the 1st century AD, finally spreading to Japan, via China, around AD 600.

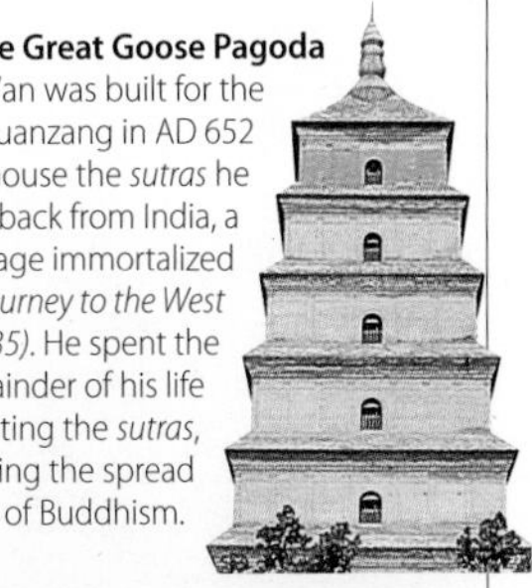

The Great Goose Pagoda in Xi'an was built for the monk Xuanzang in AD 652 to house the *sutras* he brought back from India, a pilgrimage immortalized in *Journey to the West (see p35)*. He spent the remainder of his life translating the *sutras*, aiding the spread of Buddhism.

The caves at Dunhuang *(see pp500–501)* were the last stop before the Silk Road crossed the perilous Taklamakan Desert. The frescoes and carvings, which were sponsored by traders hoping for a safe journey, are among the most important early Buddhist works in China.

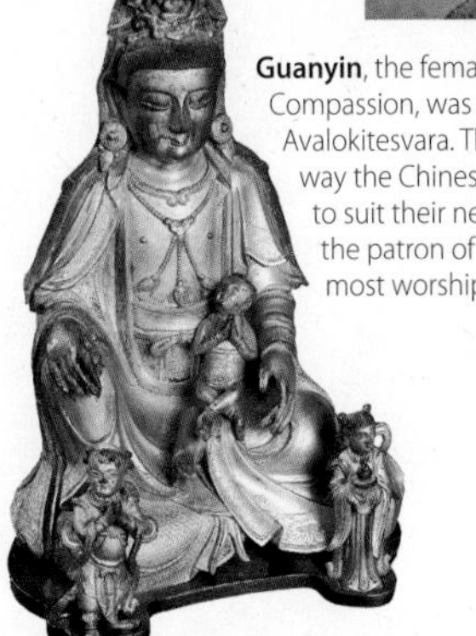

Guanyin, the female Goddess of Compassion, was originally the male deity Avalokitesvara. This sex change is one way the Chinese adapted Buddhism to suit their needs. Guanyin became the patron of motherhood and is the most worshiped figure in China.

The early Tang dynasty was a time of Buddhist renaissance, with the religion gaining imperial patronage. In the 9th century, however, rebellions provoked a period of Buddhist suppression.

❾ Wuwei
武威

160 miles (270 km) NW of Lanzhou.

Between Lanzhou and Zhangye, this town is where Gansu's most celebrated relic, the bronze Flying Horse, was discovered in 1969. Found in an Eastern Han tomb in the grounds of **Leitai Si**, a few miles north of town, the statue now sits in the Provincial Museum in Lanzhou *(see p489)*, and its symbol can be seen all over Wuwei. The tomb, a series of empty passageways, houses replicas of its original relics and is open to visitors.

Other sights are the brick **Luoshi Ta**, off Bei Dajie, and farther east, the old **Bell Tower** inside a lively temple. To the south is **Wen Miao**, a museum in the grounds of a temple. The South Gate (Nan Men) has been reconstructed and adds a little old-world grandeur to a rapidly changing town.

Leitai Si
Bei Dajie. **Tel** (0935) 221 5852.
Open 9am–5pm daily. 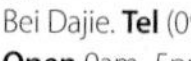 tomb.

❿ Zhangye
张掖

310 miles (515 km) NW of Lanzhou.

Once a stopover on the Silk Road, Zhangye has several sights of interest. At its center is a Ming-era **Gulou** (Drum Tower), with a large bell. To the east, **Daode Guan** is an active Daoist shrine also dating to the Ming era. South of the Gulou on Nan Dajie lies **Tu Ta**, a former Buddhist monastery featuring a large stupa. Also nearby is the **Dafo Si**, which houses the largest reclining Buddha in China in its hall. Lying 37 miles (60 km) south of Zhangye, in the Tibetan town of Mati, is **Mati Si**, a fascinating complex of Buddhist caves carved into a cliff.

A traditional incense burner in the grounds of Dafo Si, Zhangye

A view of the Tu Ta stupa, Zhangye

⓫ Jiayuguan
嘉峪关

450 miles (750 km) NW of Lanzhou.
from Dunhuang.

Traditionally regarded as China's final outpost, the last point of civilization before the desert, Jiayuguan is visited mainly for its Ming-era fort *(see pp496–7)*. The nearby **Great Wall Museum** documents the history of the wall from the Han to the Ming eras. Exhibits include photographs of remote sections of the wall as well as scale models.

Several other sights lie around Jiayuguan. About 6 miles (10 km) north of the fort is **Xuanbi Changcheng** (Overhanging Wall), a restored section of the wall dating to the 16th century, that once linked the fort to the Mazong Mountains. In the same area, the **Hei Shan** rock carvings depict scenes from daily life during the Warring States period. Situated 4 miles (6 km) southwest of town is the **First Beacon Tower**, a desolate outpost that marks the start (or end) of the western part of the Ming-dynasty Great Wall. About 12 miles (20 km) northeast of town are the **Wei-Jin Tombs** (AD 220–420), whose bricks are painted with complex scenes of everyday life. The **Qilian Shan** peaks, 75 miles (120 km) to the south, cradle the 14,110 ft (4,300 m) Qiyi Bingchuan (July 1st Glacier), best visited on a tour, or by train and taxi.

Great Wall Museum
Outside Jiayuguan Fort. **Tel** (0937) 639 6110. **Open** 9am–5pm daily.

The 16th-century ramparts of Xuanbi Changcheng, Jiayuguan

◄ Colorful rock formations at Zhangye Danxia Landform Geological Park, Gansu

The Great Game

The "Great Game" was the name, popularized by Rudyard Kipling in *Kim*, of the covert war fought by the Russian and British empires for influence in the deserts and mountains of Central Asia during the 19th century. Afghanistan was the first target for these two great empires and both sides vied for influence, with the British eventually succeeding in establishing a sympathetic regime in 1880. Meanwhile, in Xinjiang, Uighur Muslims broke free of China and set up the independent state of Eastern Turkestan in 1863 under Yakub Beg. The Russians invaded the Ili Valley and, when China took Xinjiang back in 1877, negotiated to establish consulates in the area. The British response was to set up a trade mission in Kashgar and take a more aggressive approach in Tibet. In 1907 the stand-off ended with the Anglo-Russian Convention, which clearly defined territorial limits.

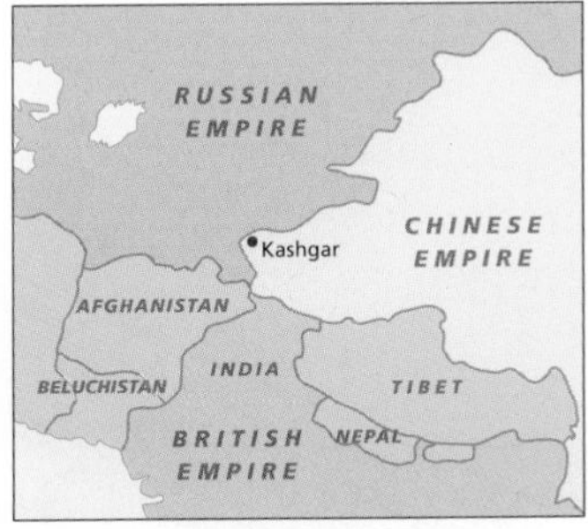

Central Asia was where the Russian, British, and Chinese empires touched. Fearful of the Russian threat to India, the British wanted to cultivate a buffer zone around its border, using Afghanistan, Eastern Turkestan, and Tibet.

Yakub Beg (1820–77) was the self-made king of Eastern Turkestan at the height of the Great Game. Originally from Uzbekistan, he arrived in Kashgar in 1865 and quickly established an independent state. He was often approached by British and Russian envoys seeking alliances, but China resumed control soon after his death.

The Pamir Mountains held the passes that Alexander the Great and Timur (Tamerlane) had used to invade India. Russian advances here in 1885 and 1896 led to the mobilization of British troops, but treaties establishing new frontiers prevented war both times.

The Open Mouth (1899), a *Punch* cartoon, shows the British Lion and Russian Bear trying to get their hands on a scared Chinaman. China, weakened by internal strife, was repeatedly forced to sign unfair treaties handing over land and allowing the superpowers to establish trade missions that were used to spy on the other side.

Tibet became involved when Britain placed it in China's sphere of influence. In response, Tibet refused to acknowledge British attempts to set up a trade mission, resulting in the attack on Gyantse in 1903 *(see p547)* by Younghusband.

⓫ Jiayuguan Fort

嘉峪关

At the western extremity of the Great Wall stands the Jiayuguan Fort, dominating the stony plain that separates two mountain ranges. Built of tamped earth in 1372, in the distinctive, embattled Ming-dynasty style, it was dubbed the "Impregnable Defile Under Heaven." It was of enormous strategic importance as it controlled the only military and trade link between China and the deserts of Central Asia. The frontier lay some way farther west, but for the Chinese Jiayuguan was the last outpost of civilization, beyond which lay barbarian country, a place of perdition, fit only for exiled officials and banished criminals.

Detail Inside Tower
As shown by these wooden doors, the interiors of the towers were beautifully painted in typical Ming style.

Trap Court
This was used to lure the enemy into a place from where they could be attacked from above. It also served as a holding bay for caravans.

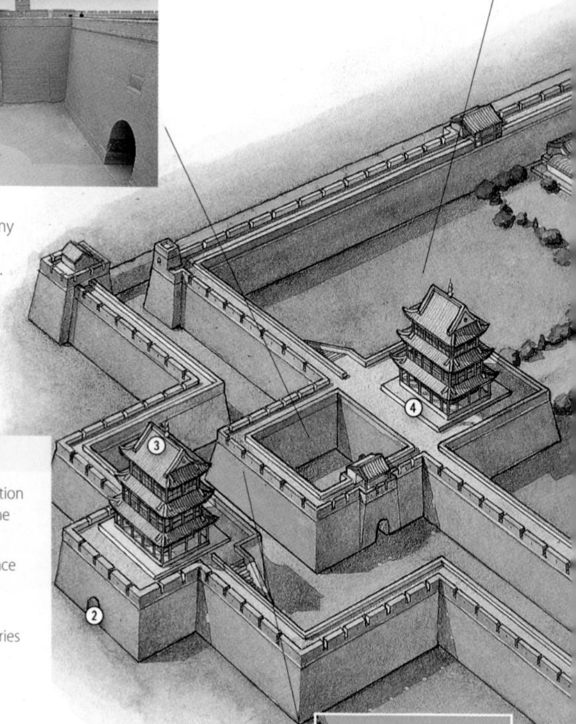

KEY

① **Corner Towers** gave protection to archers while they fired on the attacking troops.

② **The "Gate of Sighs"** was once inscribed with the sorrowful graffiti of those leaving China.

③ **Jiayuguan Men** is three stories high with typical Ming-style upturned eaves.

④ **Rou Yuan Men or Gate of Conciliation**

⑤ **Accommodations** for the generals and their families.

⑥ **Wenchang Hall** served as the official meeting point for visiting dignitaries coming from the interior of China.

⑦ **Outer wall of the fort**

⑧ **The inner wall** is fortified by a 6-ft (1.8-m) parapet and embrasured towers.

★ Fort Walls
Built of tamped earth and bricks, the mighty 35-ft (10-m) high walls were designed to be accessed by horses via ramps that lead from the gates to the battlements. The total length of the walls is about half a mile (750 m).

★ Guanghua Men
Rising 56 ft (17 m) above the fortress walls, the gate tower was originally completed in 1506, although like the others it has been extensively renovated.

VISITORS' CHECKLIST

Practical Information
3 miles (5 km) W of Jiayuguan. **Tel** (0937) 639 6058. **Open** 8:30am–8pm daily (Nov–Jun: to 6pm). includes Great Wall Museum and the Overhanging Great Wall.

Guandi Temple
This provided spiritual nourishment for the troops. The temple would have offered a mixture of Buddhist, Daoist, and Confucian ceremonies.

Old Theater
This was a later Qing-dynasty addition to the fort and was used for entertaining the troops stationed both at the fort and at garrisons along the Great Wall.

End of the Great Wall of China
The wall stretches out either side of the fort closing off the plain. The wall is made of tamped earth, a raw material in ready supply in the desert.

A camel ride across the dunes at Mingsha Shan, Dunhuang

⓬ Dunhuang
敦煌

225 miles (375 km) W of Jiayuguan. 8 miles (14 km) W of town. 6 miles (10 km) E of town. Duhuang CITS, Mingshan Lu, (0937) 882 2474.

The oasis town of Dunhuang once prospered as the last stop on the Silk Road before the Taklamakan Desert. Today it thrives instead on tourism and wind and solar energy projects in the surrounding wilderness. Despite its remote location, it is a tidy, modern place, and it caters well to the many foreign and domestic tourists who use it as a base for visiting the famous grottoes at Mogao *(see pp500–501)*. The items of interest at the **City Museum** (Shi Bowuguan) are a few Chinese and Tibetan manuscripts from Mogao's famous Cave 17, which escaped the looting of explorers and archeologists, and some models of Mogao's most famous caves. The museum also has silks and domestic items found near the beacon towers that were once part of China's outermost line of defense. There is a souvenir night market every summer evening along the town's main thoroughfare, Yangguan Zhong Lu. The range of items on sale includes leather shadow puppets, Chinese scroll paintings, jade items, coins, Tibetan horns, and Buddha statues. Just 3 miles (5 km) south of Dunhuang is **Yueya Quan** (Crescent Moon Lake), a small freshwater lake that has survived amid the surrounding sand dunes for thousands of years.

Printed textiles, Dunhuang market

The dunes are known as **Mingsha Shan** (Singing Sand Mountains) and tower several hundred feet high. The dunes were named after the sound of sand being crunched under foot. For some remarkable views, visitors can climb the dunes – preferably in the cool of the evening. There is also a range of activities, including paragliding, sand-tobogganing, and camel rides.

Situated in the middle of fields about 2 miles (4 km) west of Dunhuang is the nine-story **Baima Ta** (White Horse Pagoda). This Tibetan-style pagoda was built in memory of a horse belonging to the monk Kumarajiva, who came from the Silk Road kingdom of Kuqa *(see p513)*. The horse died here in AD 384.

City Museum
1390 Mingshan Lu.
Tel (0937) 881 8162.
Open 9am–6pm Tue–Sun.

Yueya Quan
Tel (0937) 888 3388.
Open 6am–9pm daily (closed in monsoon).

Environs: About 12 miles (20 km) southwest of Dunhuang lies **Dunhuang Gucheng** (Dunhuang Ancient City), a film set built in the 1990s that was never dismantled. Its location and panoramic views are impressive, but it is rather dog-eared on closer inspection. However, the set has become a regular tourist stop with souvenir stores and even accommodations in yurts.

Lying 50 miles (80 km) west of Dunhuang are two Han-dynasty gates, **Yu Men Guan** (Jade Gate Pass) and **Yang Guan** (South Pass). Separated by 3 miles (5 km) of desert, they were once linked by the Great Wall. Abandoned over 1,000 years ago and under constant attack by the desert, the two towers remain quite impressive, particularly Yu Men Guan, its 33-ft (10-m) walls still standing firm after centuries in this desolate spot.

Yueya Quan and Mingsha Shan dunes, Dunhuang

The Race for the Silk Road Oases

A scholarly reflection of the political rivalry between the great powers at the end of the 19th century was the race between a group of explorer-archeologists to locate (and plunder) the lost towns of the Silk Road. Between them, they succeeded in uncovering a huge number of long-forgotten, desert-scoured towns. These pioneers furthered the knowledge of life along the Silk Road and saved many items from further degradation. However, they also removed vast quantities of priceless works of art, to the eventual annoyance of the Chinese government. These are now scattered in museums around the globe. Initial interest in the region by the British was based on strategic considerations *(see p495)*; then, as stories of lost cities emerged, the interest of antiquarians around the world was aroused. Controversial though they were, their excavations captured the world's imagination.

Tales of buried cities being uncovered by sandstorms emerged at the end of the 19th century. The Gaochang Ruins, discovered by von Le Coq, were found to have been a major Buddhist and Nestorian center *(see p471)*.

Sven Hedin (1865–1952), from Sweden, was the first of many government-sponsored adventurers to explore these isolated regions. The others were Albert von Le Coq from Germany, Count Otani of Japan, Paul Pelliot of France, Sir Aurel Stein from Great Britain, and Langdon Warner from the USA.

This Buddha's head came from the Bezeklik Caves, discovered by von Le Coq in 1904. These caves held some beautiful murals protected over the years by the encroaching sand. Von Le Coq simply cut them from the walls and sent them home to Germany. Unfortunately, the murals were destroyed by bombing during World War II.

This silk painting is from the Mogao Caves, which were reached by Aurel Stein in 1907. He befriended the Abbot, Wang, and gained access to the newly discovered silks and manuscripts of Cave 17.

This fresco of a *bodhisattva* and other wall paintings at the Mogao Caves were considered sacred, so the collectors could not remove them *(see p500)*. But Stein and the others negotiated with Abbot Wang to carry off thousands of historic items.

The Cave Paintings of Dunhuang

Protected by their relative isolation, the cave paintings at Dunhuang form the most fascinating repository of Buddhist art in China. For over 700 years, between the 4th and 11th centuries AD, Buddhist monks excavated and painted these caves, until invasion and the encroachment of Islam brought work to a halt. The paintings were all but forgotten until 1907, when the explorer Sir Aurel Stein stumbled across the caves and the Daoist priest who guarded them, Wang Yuanlu. Among the many thousands of items uncovered by Stein is the *Diamond Sutra*, the world's earliest printed book (in scroll form), and many of the patterns used by the monks to reproduce elements of the paintings.

Cave 275: Sixteen Kingdoms 366–439
This early cave of the Northern Liang Period is dedicated to the Maitreya or Future Buddha, who is depicted in wall paintings and statues.

Cave 272: Sixteen Kingdoms 366–439
These *devas* (Buddhist angels) are in rapture as they listen to the Buddha's teaching.

Cave 254: Northern Wei 439–534
This cave shows stories of Buddha's early life, including the Sacrifice of the Prince. The murals are richer in content than in earlier caves and the artwork has become more accomplished.

Cave 249: Western Wei 535–56
On the north wall there is a wonderfully lively hunting scene showing the backward-shooting hunter – a feat only made possible with the invention of the stirrup.

Cave 428: Northern Zhou 557–80
Stories of the Good Prince, an earlier incarnation of Buddha, abound. Here he offers himself to a starving tigress so she may feed her cubs.

Cave 419: Sui 581–618
Under the short-lived Sui dynasty, China was reunified. Both the north and south adopted Buddhism as their religion. This harmony allowed the development of a more Chinese artistic style and was a highly fruitful time for Dunhuang. This cave portrays the Good Prince on a hunting trip with his brothers.

Cave 420: Sui 581–618
This fresco portrays a journey on the Silk Road, the route via which Buddhism came to China, as well as pictures of buildings in a style of which no real example survives.

Cave 220: Early Tang 618–704
Rich patrons would often feature in murals. This cave portrays ten generations of the wealthy Zhai family.

Cave 217: Early to High Tang 618–780 Detail of the Western Paradise of Amitabha Buddha
This cave contains some wonderful, unfinished paintings of *bodhisattvas.*

Cave 17: Late Tang 848–906
A detail from the famous cave where the massive library of *sutras* was first found by Abbot Wang.

ve 263: Western Xia 1036–26
der the Western Xia dynasty ɔt of older caves were simply ecorated. This was originally ave of Northern Wei origin.

The Dunhuang cliff face, home to 1,000 years of Buddhist history

Mogao Caves
莫高窟

Mogao, 15 miles (25 km) SE of Dunhuang. **Tel** (0937) 882 5000. **Open** Apr–Oct: 8:30am–6pm daily; Nov–Mar: 9:30am–5:30pm daily. **mgk.org.cn**

The caves at Mogao were dug into cliffs that rise out of an otherwise largely flat and featureless desert landscape. Getting there is relatively easy, if you are travelling independently, as Dunhuang is crawling with Mogao-bound minibuses. The drivers wait until every seat is taken before setting off, but the half-hour journey is cheap.

Of the 600 surviving caves, only about 20 are open to the public. The entrance fee includes a Chinese-speaking guide, although it is worthwhile, for an additional fee, engaging an English-speaking guide, since the tour party is likely to be smaller and the choice of caves less rigidly laid down. The caves that include portrayals of tantric sex can also sometimes be opened for a supplementary payment. The guides are generally fairly knowledgeable about the history of the caves and the paintings and sculptures within. You are, however, recommended to take your own flashlight and to remember that photography is not allowed in the caves (unless you have a very expensive permit), a rule that is rigorously enforced. The standard tour lasts half a day, and includes about 15 of the caves, as well as the museum, which exhibits some of the ancient manuscripts found here. In an effort to relieve pressure on the site, visitor numbers have been officially limited to 6,000 a day. In high season, it is advisable to book your ticket in advance from the ticket office in central Dunhuang (Welcome Garden District 15, Bldg 102); tickets are also available at the modern Mogao Digital Exhibition Center, which is the access point for the caves. The Center features state-of-the-art screens showing high-quality footage of the caves' interiors. Shuttle buses run from the Center to the caves.

Statue from pagoda at Mogao caves

Facade of Cave 96, covering a 100-ft (30-m) statue of Buddha

For hotels and restaurants in this region see p563 and p584

The beautifully decorated door of Longwu Si's prayer hall, Tongren

⓭ Tongren

同仁

75 miles (125 km) NW of Xiahe. from Xiahe or Xining. Lurol Festival (6th lunar month); Buddhist Festival (1st lunar month).

Known as Repkong in Tibetan, Tongren is a transit point between Xiahe and Xining. This small town offers fascinating insights into the life of the Tibetan people. On the outskirts of town lies the colorfully decorated lamasery, **Longwu Si**, containing fine relics in its many halls. Initially built in 1301 during the Yuan dynasty, today's modern reconstruction houses three colleges and an assortment of lamaseries belonging to the Yellow Hat sect – a branch of Tibetan Buddhism *(see pp526–7)*. At dusk, visitors can watch the resident monks debating, using elaborate formalized body language to make a point. Sometimes, if you're lucky, they can also be seen making sand mandalas. Beyond the monastery, the valley runs south to a series of quaint Tibetan villages set amongst terraced fields. Situated in another village, Wutun, 4 miles (7 km) north of the town center, the **Upper** and **Lower** monasteries are home to some of the best Tibetan artists in the world. Both monasteries are magnificently decorated, with every surface of their assembly halls carved and painted with traditional Repkong designs. The residents of this village speak a mixture of Tibetan, Mongolian, and other dialects.

⓮ Ta'er Si

See pp504–5.

⓯ Xining

西宁

144 miles (232 km) W of Lanzhou. 1,200,000. Xining CITS, 14/F, 49 Xiaguan Dajie, (0971) 613 3844.

Although blessed with very few sights, Qinghai's capital, Xining, is home to an intriguing mix of minorities, mostly Hui Muslims and Tibetans with a sprinkling of Kazakhs and Mongols. It is the starting point of the railroad to Lhasa; trains depart daily. From the 16th century, it served as a stopover on the Silk Road's lesser-used southern route, and is now a good base for exploring Qinghai. Xining lies in a remote valley, and, at 7,464 ft (2,275 m), experiences a cool summer and freezing winter.

A devotee in Xining's Great Mosque

The **Dongguan Great Mosque**, one of the largest and most impressive in northwest China, is situated on Dongguan Dajie, close to the city center. It was originally built in the 14th century, and combines elements of Arabic and Chinese design, with minarets and flying eaves. Enclosed within is a public square that fills with thousands of worshipers for Friday prayers.

One of Xining's more intriguing sights is **Ma Bufang's Former Residence** on Weimin Xiang, once the home of a local warlord. After decades, the buildings have been restored to their former glory, their rooms tiled with jade and filled with fancy imported goods.

Xining's ethnic mix is best appreciated at **Shuijing Xiang Market**, in the west of town off Xi Dajie, where over 3,000 stalls sell all manner of provisions and food, especially hot breads, mutton dishes, and kabobs. It is also a good place to stock up on snacks before heading off on a trip to Qinghai Hu, to the west of town.

The grand 14th-century Dongguan Great Mosque, Xining

Mengda Tian Chi nature reserve along the banks of the Yellow River

⑯ Mengda Tian Chi
孟达天池

124 miles (200 km) SE of Xining. [bus] to Guanting or Xunhua, then taxi. [icon]

The remarkably beautiful Tian Chi, or "Heavenly Lake," forms the core of the Mengda Nature Reserve, situated along the Yellow River. In contrast to most other parts of the province, the land here is fertile and abounds with vegetation. Most of the reserve is woodland, offering opportunities for scenic walks and bird-watching. Accommodations are available at the reserve, while trips can be arranged through tour operators in Xining. The trip to Mengda Tian Chi from Xunhua is spectacular, winding along a precipitous road that cuts into the cliffs along the Yellow River. Xunhua is home to the Turkic-speaking Salar people, who have been here for centuries but originate from modern-day Uzbekistan.

⑰ Qinghai Hu
青海湖

93 miles (150 km) W of Xining. Bird Island: **Closed** Nov–Feb. [icons]

The largest lake in China, Qinghai Hu covers a vast area of over 1,740 sq miles (4,500 sq km). Its location on the Tibetan plateau, at a height of 10,500 ft (3,200 m) above sea level, and its sheer size means that it is best visited on an organized tour. The lake is home to many Tibetan nomads, who graze their yaks and sheep near the lake, and in summer, numerous herds can be spotted grazing.

A medallion with Tibetan calligraphy

The lake's icy salt water is home to large quantities of fish, which feed a thriving bird population. Most trips to the lake center around a visit to **Bird Island**, a rocky outcrop on the western side where colonies of swans, cormorants, bar-headed geese, and rare black-necked cranes, among others, flourish during the Feb–Jun breeding season. On the southern shore, the Qinghai Lake Tourist Center offers opportunities for boating, fishing, horse-riding, and trekking. Basic accommodation is available in settlements around the lakeshore.

⑱ Golmud
格尔木

474 miles (762 km) W of Xining. [icons] Golmud CITS, 60 Bayi Zhong Lu, (0979) 849 6150.

In the far west of Qinghai, Golmud is perched at 9,186 ft (2,800 m) on the southern edge of the desolate Qaidam Basin. The only sizable town for several hundred miles, it is the second largest city in the province after Xining, with a largely Han Chinese population.

The town's bus service, which runs to Lhasa in Tibet, is not particularly cheap and very few people use it now that the 625-mile (1,000-km) railroad to Lhasa has been built. Trains run to Lhasa along this, the highest railroad in the world, from several starting points, including Beijing, Chengdu, and Golmud. The trains' carriages are pressurized, in order to make the journey – which crosses the 16,600 ft (5,100 m) Tanglha Pass – more comfortable.

From Golmud, it is possible to travel onwards by bus across the Qaidam Basin and into remote parts of Xinjiang.

Golmud itself is largely unappealing, although the surrounding lunar-looking landscape has a rugged charm best appreciated on the way out.

Colorful Tibetan prayer flags on the shore of Qinghai Hu

⓮ Ta'er Si

塔尔寺

Nestled into a hillside, this walled temple complex, also known as Kumbum Monastery, is one of the most important Tibetan Buddhist sites in China. Tsongkhapa, founder of the Gelugpa sect *(see p526)*, was born here in 1357, and the first temple was built in his honor in 1577. The monastery was closed for a period under Communist rule, although the buildings were afforded protection during the Cultural Revolution, and reopened in 1979. A major restoration project has been undertaken since an earthquake rocked the complex in 1990. Ta'er Si is easily accessible from Xining, and so is popular with both tourists and pilgrims.

★ Great Golden Roof Hall
This temple was built at the spot where Tsongkhapa was born and a tree is said to have grown with an image of the Buddha on each leaf. It contains a silver stupa holding his image.

Pilgrim
Turning a hand-held prayer wheel and fingering prayer beads, the devout walk clockwise around the perimeter of the complex.

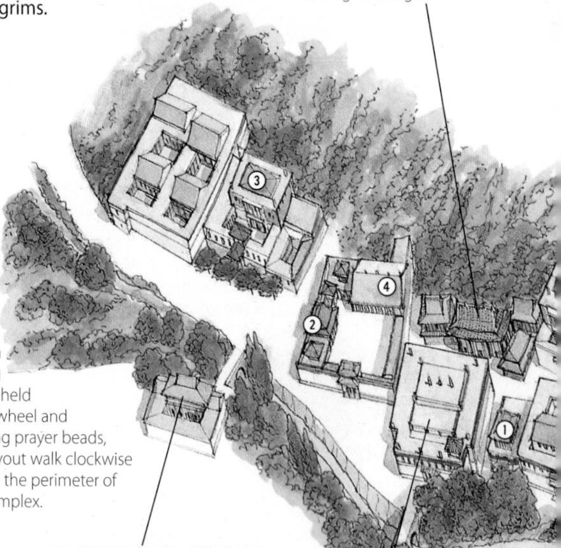

★ Hall of Butter Sculpture
This strongly fragrant exhibition is packed with intricately carved yak butter sculptures. The gaudily painted figures depict scenes from Buddhist lore.

★ Great Hall of Meditation
This evocative chamber, where up to 2,000 monks could gather to chant *sutras*, is hung with silken *thangkas*. The flat roof rests on grand pillars, each wrapped in an exquisite carpet.

KEY

① **Grand Kitchen**

② **Prayer Hall**

③ **Dinkejing Hall**

④ **Nine Room Hall**

⑤ **Visitors who climb** these steps are rewarded with views across the valley.

⑥ **Dafangzhang Hall**

Local monk
Ta'er Si is a working monastery and houses over 650 monks who spend their life studying Buddhist teachings. There were once as many as 3,500 resident monks.

VISITORS' CHECKLIST

Practical Information
Huangzhong. 17 miles (28 km) S of Xining. **Tel** (0971) 223 2357. **Open** 8:30am–5pm daily. Monlam: 8th–15th of 1st lunar month; Saga Dawa: 8th–15th of 4th month; Tsong-khapa: 20th–26th of 9th month.

Transportation
from the train station in Xining.

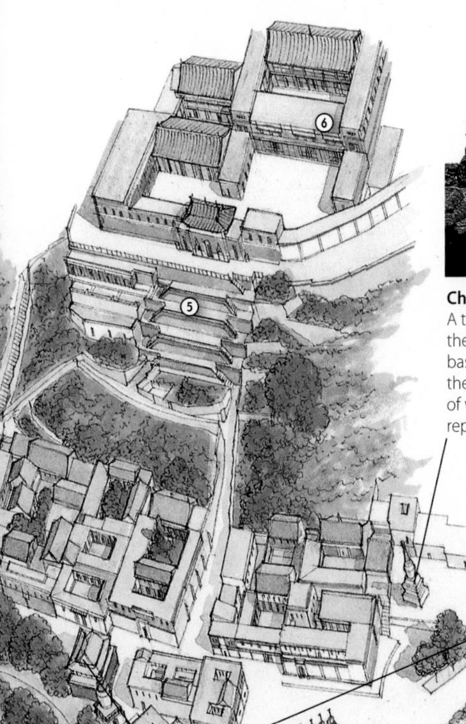

Chorten
A towering *chorten* of 46 ft (13 m) marks the monastery's entrance. The square base symbolizes earth, the dome water, the steps fire, and the parasol wind, all of which is topped by a crown representing the ethereal sphere.

Lesser Golden Roof Hall
A truly bizarre pavilion, this temple is dedicated to animals. Stuffed deer, sheep, and goats draped in ceremonial scarves peer down from the upper story.

Prayer Hall
This time-worn temple is still used for religious tutelage. The external murals are new, however, and show a mix of Chinese and Tibetan influences.

XINJIANG

A vast and isolated region made up of desert ringed by high mountain ranges, Xinjiang (meaning "new frontier") shares borders with eight countries. Almost 50 percent of the population is made up of ethnic minorities. Strings of oasis towns developed along the branches of the Silk Road flanking the northern and southern edges of the Taklamakan Desert over 2,000 years ago, and the region, which came under the influence of traders from the east and west, is home to both Christian churches and Buddhist temples. Turkic tribes settled here in the 6th century, later adopting Islam. Sporadic Chinese control was established over parts of Xinjiang from the time of the Han Dynasty onward, but there were frequent revolts and interludes of outright independence as late as the early 20th century before Chinese rule was finally secured in the 1950s. Although tensions remain, unlike in neighboring Tibet, the Chinese authorities generally avoid placing restrictions on foreign travelers in Xinjiang.

Highlights of a visit include the Tian Shan range and Tian Chi (Heaven Lake) outside the capital, Ürümqi, and atmospheric Silk Road towns such as Turpan and Kashgar, set against a backdrop of desert and mountain. It is also possible to travel along the spectacular Karakoram Highway toward Pakistan, or west into Kyrgyzstan and Kazakhstan over high mountain passes.

Sights at a Glance

Towns & Cities

1 Turpan
2 Ürümqi
5 Ghost City
8 Kuqa
9 Kashgar
11 Yengisar
12 Yarkand
13 Kargilik
14 Hotan

Lakes, Mountains & Areas of Natural Beauty

3 Tian Chi
4 Altay
6 Sayram Lake
7 Yining & Ili Valley
10 Karakoram Highway

Key

Expressway
National Highway
Minor road
Railroad
International border
Provincial border
xxx Disputed border

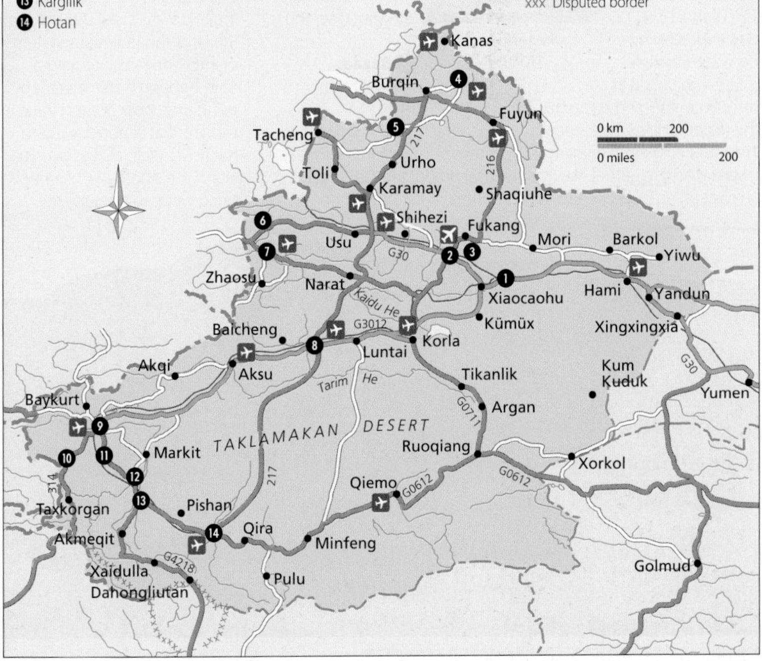

◀ The beautiful Tian Chi, surrounded by mountains

For additional map symbols *see back flap*

The graceful Emin Ta and Iranian-style mosque

❶ Turpan
吐鲁番

116 miles (187 km) SE of Ürümqi. 255,000. Daheyan, 33 miles (54 km) N of Turpan, then minibus. Turpan CITS, Jiaotong Hotel, (0995) 853 5809.

This oasis town on the northern Silk Road lies in the Turpan depression – one of the lowest areas on earth – and is largely an Uighur settlement. The Uighur descended from nomadic Siberian tribes who united in the 7th century and settled in the region in the 9th century. They later converted to Islam as it spread across Central Asia. It is an easy-going place, famous for its grapes, with mud-brick houses and dusty streets often covered with trellised vines. The original Silk Road settlements of Jiaohe and Gaochang lie outside town along with other sights. In summer, the heat is intense, and it is best to use donkey carts or taxis.

Dried fruit on sale, Turpan bazaar

Emin Ta
1½ miles (2.5 km) SE of town. **Open** 9am–8pm daily (mid-Oct–mid-Apr: 10am–6:30pm).

This is perhaps the most interesting of Turpan's numerous mosques because of its old minaret (Emin Ta), constructed in 1778, that rises like a stout but graceful chimney beside it. Built by Prince Suleiman in honor of his father, Prince Emin, the minaret is broad at the base and tapers toward the top. The neighboring Governor's Mansion is a reconstruction of an aristocratic Uighur dwelling.

Bazaar
Laocheng Xi Lu. **Open** daily.

The small Turpan market is an interesting place to browse for local products including a variety of medicinal potions, decorated knives, clothing, fabric, nuts, and fruit (especially raisins).

Turpan Museum
Gaochang Lu. **Open** 10am–7pm Tue–Sun.

This large, modern museum houses an impressive collection of artifacts, including ancient silks, which have been excavated from the Tang-dynasty Astana tombs outside Turpan. There are also dinosaur fossils from the Taklamakan Desert and well-preserved mummies.

Jiaohe Ruins
6 miles (10 km) W of Turpan. minibus or cycle. **Open** 9am–6pm daily.

Although less important and smaller than Gaochang, the ruins of Jiaohe are better defined. Jiaohe was founded as a garrison town but came under Uighur jurisdiction in the 6th century. It was finally abandoned during the Yuan era, perhaps due to failing water supplies. The ancient city occupies a position on a steep plateau, with its street plan clearly visible, and is well worth a visit.

Returning from Jiaohe, visitors can stop off to see the *karez* irrigation site. Used throughout Xinjiang, this ingenious system of irrigation taps into natural underground water sources by using a network of subterranean tunnels that channel water to the fields. Wells dug at intervals along the length of the tunnels bring water to the surface.

The ruined city of Jiaohe set against a backdrop of hills on a steep plateau

For hotels and restaurants in this region see p563 and p585

The dramatic Flaming Mountains near Turpan

Grape Valley

7 miles (8km) NE of Turpan. minibus from town. **Open** daily.

An attractive desert oasis to the north of Turpan, Grape Valley (Putao Gou) is best visited in the summer. With vines and trellises bulging with grapes, it is a pleasant place to stop for lunch, with plenty of grapes and raisins to eat (for a fee). There is a winery nearby, as well as brick silos for drying the grapes.

Flaming Mountains

Flaming Mountains Scenic Area: minibus from town. **Open** daily.

The road east to Bezeklik leads past these sandstone mountains, made famous in the novel *Journey to the West (see p35)*, a fictionalized account of the journey of the pilgrim monk Xuanzang to India. In the book, the mountains (Huoyan Shan) are described as being on fire, and at certain times of day, a combination of sun and shadows makes them seem to flicker as though glowing red-hot.

Bezeklik Caves

31 miles (50 km) E of town. minibus from town. **Tel** (0995) 868 9116. **Open** 8am–9pm daily (mid-Oct–mid-Apr: 10am–6:30pm).

Picturesquely situated in a desert gorge high above the Sengim River, the Bezeklik Caves once formed part of a Buddhist monastery between the 6th and 14th centuries. The caves originally stored a collection of Buddhist murals in the Indo-Iranian style, which showed unusually marked Western influences. Sadly, only fragments remain, as after centuries of neglect, they were all removed in the early 1900s by the German explorers von Le Coq *(see 499)* and Grunwedel, and placed in a Berlin museum, where they were later destroyed by Allied bombs during World War II.

Buddha mural in the Bezeklik Caves

Astana Graves

25 miles (40 km) SE of Turpan. minibus from town. **Open** 10:30am–6:30pm daily.

The cemetery of the ancient city of Gaochang is located at Astana, a few miles northwest of Gaochang. The tombs, dating from between the 3rd and 8th centuries AD, were systematically excavated from 1959 and revealed several corpses, mummified by the dry desert air. They had been wrapped in silks and buried with many everyday items, including pottery, wooden carvings, coins, and documents relating to military and domestic transactions such as land tenures. Most items are now on display at museums in Turpan and Ürümqi, but the three tombs that are open to visitors display Tang-era paintings and a few preserved corpses.

Gaochang Ruins

29 miles (46 km) SE of Turpan. **Tel** (0995) 869 3628. minibus from town. **Open** 8am–9pm daily (mid-Oct–mid-Apr: 10am–6:30pm).

Southeast of the Astana tombs lie the ruins of Gaochang city, surrounded by 33-ft (10-m) high walls. Founded as a garrison town in the 1st century AD, by the 4th century Gaochang had become a regional capital. A cosmopolitan city with traces of Nestorian Christianity and Manichaeism (a Persian dualistic religion), it was visited by the monk Xuanzang in AD 630, on his journey to India in search of Buddhist *sutras*. From the 9th to the 13th centuries, the city was the Uighur capital, but was abandoned during the early Ming era. The ruins are extensive, but little is recognizable, apart from a Buddhist temple outside the southwest walls.

The Bezeklik Caves situated in a spectacular river gorge

❷ Ürümqi
乌鲁木齐

911 miles (1470 km) NE of Kashgar. 3,115,000. Urumqi CITS, 16/F, 33 Renmin Lu, (0991) 282 1428.

Capital of Xinjiang since the 19th century, Ürümqi sits amid beautiful scenery, with the snow-laden Tian Shan to the east. It served as the base for a succession of warlords well into the 20th century, including the infamous Yang Zengxin who, in 1916, invited all his enemies to dinner and then beheaded them. Today a growing metropolis with a population of over 3 million, Ürümqi is a modern Chinese city, with designer stores and highrises. Many Han Chinese have settled here since 1949 and now make up the majority. Resident minorities include Uighur, Manchu, Kazakh, Mongolian, and Tajik.

Ürümqi is a major transport hub, with many connections to eastern China and the rest of Xinjiang, as well as a rail link to Kazakhstan. Most visitors come to see Tian Chi (Heaven Lake), but the city has other attractions such as its lively markets and the fascinating mix of ethnic peoples. The fine **Xinjiang Provincial Museum** devotes a section to archeological finds, especially from around Turpan, including some preserved corpses, silk paintings, and lovely brocades. A section dedicated to local peoples includes *gers*, jewelry, and traditional clothes. In the north of the city, the scenic **Hong Shan Park** has a small 18th-century pagoda, and offers wonderful views.

Pagoda in Hongshan Park, Ürümqi

Tian Shan peaks surrounding the deep-blue waters of Tian Chi

Xinjiang Provincial Museum
Xibei Lu. **Tel** (0991) 455 2826.
Open 10am–6pm Tue–Sun.

❸ Tian Chi
天池

62 miles (100 km) E of Ürümqi. **Tel** (0994) 835 8888. from Ürümqi. **Open** Apr–Oct: 8am–8pm daily; Nov–Mar: 10:30am–4pm Tue–Sun. Horses available for exploring lake area.

A refreshing break from the arid deserts of northwestern China, Tian Chi (Heaven Lake) is a beautiful stretch of water surrounded by luxuriant meadows and pine forests. It lies at an elevation of 6,500 ft (1,980 m), enclosed by snow-capped peaks including the majestic Bogda Feng, which reaches a height of almost 20,000 ft (6,000 m). A wonderful place for spending a day, Tian Chi offers many opportunities for leisurely walks and hikes in the lake area and through the neighboring countryside dotted with Kazakh *gers*.

The once-nomadic Kazakhs today make their living from tourism. Very friendly and hospitable, they can arrange guides and horse treks around the lake and into the hills.

Summer is the best time to visit Tian Chi, as access can be difficult during the winter snows. There are usually plenty of accommodations available in local Kazakh *gers* around the lake. Staying overnight can be far more fun and interesting than the daytours, which are sometimes a bit tacky.

Grapes and Wine

Nearly every household in the region is involved in grape production, either in cultivation, or in drying inside ventilated barns. In Xinjiang, the use of grapes for making wine was first recorded by a Chinese emissary in 138 BC, although grapes were possibly cultivated here as early as the Shang era. In fact, all wine-making in China was learned from the peoples of the western regions. By the Yuan era, wine production, based in Xinjiang, was substantial, and by the Ming period, varieties such as the crystal, the purple, and the seedless green rabbit-eye grape were grown. Today, wine production is thriving in China, and most of these varieties are still grown.

Fruit vendor weighing grapes at the marketplace in Ürümqi

For hotels and restaurants in this region see p563 and p585

Islam in China

Islam probably came to Xinjiang via the Silk Road in the 9th century, some 200 years after Arab sailors had landed in southern China. By the Ming dynasty, Muslims had flourished and become fully integrated into Han society without losing their dress and dietary customs. Despite hostile regimes and upheavals, there is now a significant Muslim population of over 20 million. These comprise the Xinjiang nationalities – Uighur, Kazakhs, Kyrgyz, Tajiks, Tatars, and Uzbeks of the northwest – and the large contingent of Chinese-speaking Hui, scattered around the country. It is generally accepted that all Muslims in China are Sunni of the Hanafi School, which is one of four schools of Islamic law. It is considered the oldest and most liberal school and is traditionally tolerant of differences within Muslim communities.

Mosques in China retain most traditional Islamic features, but the pagodas and upturned eaves are clear signs of Chinese architectural influences.

The muezzin, as in all Muslim communities, calls the faithful to prayer five times a day. Today, the call is usually recorded and broadcast by loudspeaker.

Inside the mosque the congregation members, usually men, prostrate themselves before the *mihrab*, a niche in the wall indicating the direction of Mecca. The main hall is reserved for Friday prayers.

Dongxiang Muslims hail from Gansu province and speak Mongolian. They have left pastoral herding in favor of a sedentary farming life.

The Hui are said to be the descendants of the Arab and Persian traders who arrived in the Tang dynasty and married into Chinese families. They are China's biggest Muslim minority.

The Koran was first translated into Chinese in 1927. Through interpretations of scholars, the Koran is a vital part of Islamic life.

The breathtaking alpine scenery of Kanas Lake Nature Reserve, Altay

❹ Altay
阿勒泰

404 miles (650 km) N of Ürümqi. ✈ Altay, then bus. 🚌 from Ürümqi to Burqin, then 93 miles (150 km) N via bus or car to reserve.

In contrast to the arid deserts of southern Xinjiang, the far north is covered in forests, lakes, and streams, overlooked by high mountains. The Altay region, bordering Mongolia, Russia, and Kazakhstan, is famous for its natural beauty, best seen in the **Kanas Lake Nature Reserve** (which can be visited from Burqin). Centered around an alpine lake set at 4,490 ft (1,370 m) in the glorious Altay mountains, the reserve supports a diversity of wildlife. The area is wonderful for walking, and boat trips are available on the lake. Tours from Ürümqi operate all year.

❺ Ghost City
魔鬼城

Near Urho, 62 miles (100 km) N of Karamay. 13,000. ✈ Karamay, then bus. 🚌 from Karamay. **Tel** (0990) 696 4700.

Rising above the ocean of oil rigs, along the Junggar Basin, is a collection of wind-shaped rock formations known as the Ghost City. Made famous by the movies filmed there, including *Crouching Tiger, Hidden Dragon*, it is now a popular destination. Camel rides, mountain bikes, and four-wheel vehicles can be hired.

❻ Sayram Lake
塞里木湖

75 miles (120 km) N of Yining. 🚌

The jewel-like Sayram Lake, or Sailimu Hu, is a vast stretch of water set amid magnificent mountain scenery and flowering meadows. Located at 6,560 ft (2,000 m), the lake area is chilly for most of the year, and only warm in summer when it is also covered in flowers. Reached by bus from Yining, it is a beautiful spot, despite the road to Urumqi running nearby, and it is possible to stay in simple lakeside guesthouses or *gers* (yurts).

❼ Yining
伊宁

420 miles (700 km) W of Ürümqi. 430,000. ✈ 🚌 from Ürümqi. Ili Valley: 🚌 from Yining.

Close to the border with Kazakhstan, Yining is the capital of the Ili Kazakh Autonomous Prefecture. In recent centuries,

Woman tending her sheep in a flower-covered meadow on the shores of Sayram Lake

For hotels and restaurants in this region see p563 and p585

A traditional shop in one of Yining's Uighur bazaars

Russia has noticeably influenced Yining as it was occupied by Russians in 1872, when Yakub Beg ruled the region (then known as Eastern Turkestan), and later, during the period of Sino-Soviet friendship in the 1950s, a number of Russians resided here. After relations between China and the USSR broke down in the early 1960s, there were violent border clashes along the Ili River. More recently, Yining has been the scene of several Uighur uprisings, which were quelled.

Small, but pleasant and friendly with tree-lined streets, Yining is known for its fruit, local honey beer, and hard cheese. The town has undergone a building boom that has changed the face of the old Uighur quarter south of Qingnian Park, though the areas bazaars still remain a lively attraction.

About 3 miles (5 km) south of town, the **Ili Valley** (Ili Gu) is a scenic farm area of fields and meadows home to the Xibo people, a tiny minority whose capital is at Chapucha'er. Related to the Manchu, the Xibo were sent here during the Qing era to maintain sovereignty in the region. They have kept themselves separate from the Han and other local communities, and retain their own language and script.

Grapes for sale on the street, Yining

8 Kuqa

库车

380 miles (630 km) SW of Ürümqi. 75,000. Yinyan Travel Service, (0997) 723 3228. Fri.

This small oasis town, essentially an Uighur settlement, has an interesting history. An independent state until the 8th century, when it fell under Chinese rule, the kingdom had strong links with India. Its significance as a Buddhist center dates back to the 4th century, when the Buddhist scholar Kumarajiva flourished. Born here, he went to school in Kashmir, northern India, and came back to China as a teacher and linguist, translating Sanskrit texts into Chinese. The town became a focal point from where Buddhism was disseminated throughout China. Several large monasteries were founded on the vast wealth generated by the Silk Road trade. In the 7th century, the monk Xuanzang passed through Kuqa and claimed to have defeated its ruler in a philosophical debate. With the arrival of Islam in the 9th century, however, most traces of its Buddhist past disappeared.

Mainly a stopover on the long journey to Kashgar, Kuqa is effectively two towns – New Kuqa and Old Kuqa. The old town has a bustling bazaar atmosphere, and a few dusty, narrow lanes lined with traditional mud houses. Built in 1923, the attractive green-tiled **Great Mosque** bears no traces of Chinese influence in its traditional arabesque design.

One of the main reasons to visit Kuqa is the **Thousand Buddha Caves** at Kizil, 43 miles (70 km) west of town. The caves date to AD 500–700 and the frescoes, in a mixture of Indo-Iranian and Greek styles, are fascinating for their total absence of Chinese influence. Unfortunately, the caves were looted at the beginning of the 20th century by archeological explorers. While most of the caves have been stripped of their frescoes, some of the cave decoration has survived, notably the musicians in Cave 38 and the domestic and agricultural scenes in Cave 175.

About 19 miles (30 km) north of Kuqa lie the ruins of the ancient city of **Subashi**.

Thousand Buddha Caves

Hired car or taxi. **Open** 10:30am–7pm daily. arranged by the Kuqa tourist office.

The Thousand Buddha Caves at Kizil, outside Kuqa

❾ Kashgar

喀什

In the far west of Xinjiang, the Silk Road town of Kashgar lies at the foot of the Pamir Mountains, with the Taklamakan Desert to the east. As the meeting point of the northern and southern Silk Roads and the gateway to the West, it was once a place of great significance. A Chinese garrison was established here in AD 78, but the area succumbed to the spread of Islam in the 9th century, and Kashgar did not become part of the Chinese Empire again until the 1700s. Later, a Central Asian warlord, Yakub Beg *(see p495)*, established a state centered on Kashgar and ruling most of modern Xinjiang, but he died in 1877 and China annexed the province. Today, Kashgar is a busy market town and transport hub, and despite rampant modernization retains much of its old charm.

Farmers waiting to trade livestock at market, Kashgar

Market

Near Ayziret Lu. **Open** daily. Livestock market: Pamir Dadao. **Open** Daily; best day is Sunday.

One of China's most famous markets lies in the northeast suburbs, just beyond the river. The market is no longer the wild spectacle of past decades, with much of the retail action now contained within a modern covered bazaar that operates all week. This is still one of the most colorful parts of the city to explore, however, with plenty of traditional crafts and unusual folk remedies on sale amid the modern hardware. On Sundays the market becomes much livelier, with dozens of temporary traders setting up shop around the peripheries. The photogenic Sunday livestock bazaar – originally part of the main market – now takes place on the far northwest outskirts, best reached by taxi.

Id Kah Mosque

Id Kah Square. **Tel** (0998) 282 3235. **Open** 9am–4pm Sat–Thu, 9am–1pm Fri (closed during services).

The largest mosque in Xinjiang, and one of the largest in China, Id Kah Mosque (Aitiga'er Qingzhen Si) was probably founded in 1738, although it possibly stands on the site of a smaller mosque from the 15th century. Built in the Central Asian style and altered over the centuries, the mosque's current structure dates back only as far as 1838, and was badly damaged during the Cultural Revolution *(see pp70–71)*. The main gate, flanked by a pair of small minarets, is a confection of marzipan-like yellow brick and tiling. Inside the gate is an octagonal pavilion and a pool, as well as a 100-columned space which can accommodate as many as 7,000 worshipers. Modestly dressed non-Muslims are allowed to enter outside of prayer times. Visitors should remove their shoes when entering carpeted areas.

Uighur Quarter & Preserved Old Town

Areas to E of Id Kah Mosque.

Kashgar's sprawling Uighur Quarter, which was originally ringed by fortified walls, has undergone government modernization programs in recent years. Many of the original mudbrick courtyard houses and labyrinthine alleys have been replaced with a somewhat more orderly cityscape, complete with modern sanitation. Little of the original old town survives, but lively commerce has resumed amid the new buildings and widened alleyways, with traditional goods and street food on offer. A pocket of the true old town has been preserved farther east, covering a low hilltop by the river. Here, old-style dwellings survive, many inhabited by traditional craftsmen who make a living selling their wares to curious tourists.

The Id Kah Mosque, with Kashgar city and the Pamirs on the horizon

Scenic view of the Preserved Old Town of Kashgar

Tomb of Yusuf Haji Hajup

Open 10am–6pm daily.

This favorite son of Kashgar was an 11th-century Uighur thinker and poet, renowned for his epic poem *The Knowledge of Happiness*. He was originally buried outside the city, but his tomb was relocated close to Kashgar's main square when threatened by a flooding river. Although it has a plain interior, the external structure is impressive. Topped with a blue dome and a cluster of minarets, the tomb is encased in blue-and-white tiles with Arabic motifs.

Apak Khoja Mausoleum

See pp516–17.

Shipton's Arch

25 miles (40 km) NW of Kashgar.

Situated in the mountains northwest of Kashgar is Shipton's Arch. At 1,500 ft (460 m), it is regarded as the world's tallest natural arch. Known to Uighurs as Toshuk Tagh, "the holed mountain," the arch was first recorded by English diplomat and mountaineer Eric Shipton in the 1940s. It has become an increasingly popular daytrip destination from Kashgar. There are concrete steps and a viewing platform for ease of access, but the journey still involves a lengthy off-road drive, so it is necessary to travel with an experienced guide.

VISITORS' CHECKLIST

Practical Information

920 miles (1,473 km) SW of Ürümqi. 507,000. Uighur Tours, 144 Seman Lu, (0998) 298 0770. Sun. **uighurtour.com**

Transportation

International bus station, Long-Distance bus station, CAAC (buses to airport).

Ruins of Ha Noi

22 miles (35 km) NE of Kashgar.

The remains of the Tang-era town of Ha Noi lie in a desert setting northeast of Kashgar. Abandoned in the 12th century, little survives today beyond the **Mor Pagoda**, a remnant of a large Buddhist temple.

Opal

18 miles (30 km) W of Kashgar.

Mon.

Opal, or Wupoer, has a weekly market that is far less sanitized than the one in Kashgar. Livestock is traded alongside household goods. The town is also home to the tomb of the 11th-century scholar Mohammed Kashgari, who compiled the first Turkic-Arabic dictionary.

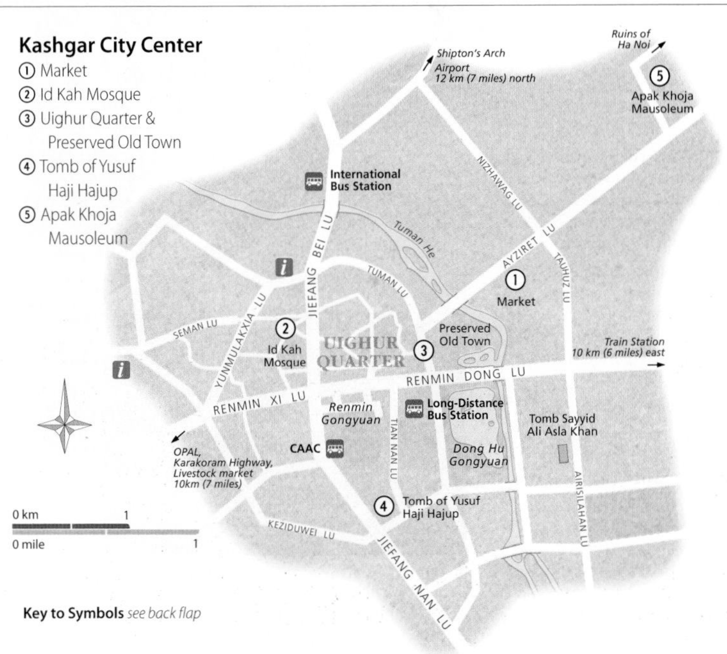

Key to Symbols *see back flap*

Apak Khoja Mausoleum
香妃墓

Built in the 17th century, the Apak Khoja Mausoleum and nearby buildings form one of the best examples of Islamic architecture in China. The mausoleum is the burial place of the family of Apak Khoja, a celebrated Islamic missionary. However, the monument is also known as Xiangfei's Tomb, as it may be the burial place of Apak Khoja's granddaughter, Ikparhan, said to be the legendary "fragrant concubine" Xiangfei. The wife of a defeated rebel leader, she was captured by the Qian-dynasty Emperor Qianlong and taken back to Beijing to be his imperial concubine. Refusing to submit to him she was, depending on which story you believe, either murdered or driven to suicide by the emperor's mother. Others claim she died of old age.

The entrance to the Apak Khoja complex lined with plane trees

★ Geometric Decorations
Floral and geometric patterns are common in Islamic art because creating images of animate objects was considered to be in God's realm (flowers were considered inanimate).

★ Tombs
Decorated with blue-glazed tiles, the tombs of the Apak Khoja family lie on a raised platform, draped in colorful silks.

KEY

① **The casket of Ikparhan** is labeled inside the tomb hall. The carriage which supposedly carried her body back from Beijing is also on display.

② **The four corner minarets** lack the slender grace of most other towers. Instead their charm derives from the colorful striping of the tiles and the exquisite detailing of Islamic motifs and patterns.

③ **The dome** is 56 ft (17 m) in diameter. After years of disrepair, the structure was retiled in recent years.

④ **Top corners of entrance mirror the surrounding minarets**

⑤ **Arabesques** are beautiful floral patterns where a main stem branches into a series of secondary stems that may either branch again or rejoin the main stem, and so on.

For hotels and restaurants in this region see p563 and p585

VISITORS' CHECKLIST

Practical Information
Just over 2 miles (4 km) NE of Old Town center. Mausoleum: **Open** 9:30am–8pm daily. Mosque: **Open** daily *(prayer day Fri).*

Transportation
from People's Square. Also possible to cycle or walk.

Apak Khoja Mausoleum
Considered the holiest Muslim site in Xinjiang, the mausoleum provides resting places for 72 members of the Afaqi family, enclosing the tombs of five generations.

Minaret decoration
Each of the windows is screened in a different geometric pattern. The surrounds are adorned with graceful arabesques while the turret is topped with an inverted lotus dome, scalloped edges, and finial.

Mausoleum Entrance
The impressive facade of the mausoleum has a tiled *iwan* niche-style entrance typical of mosques in Central Asia.

The Apak Khoja Complex

Although Islam came to Xinjiang via Arab and Persian traders on the Silk Road in the 9th and 10th centuries, it was not until the 15th century that it became the dominant religion of the area, and Kashgar became an important Islamic center. The Apak Khoja complex is a significant architectural ensemble comprising a mausoleum, four prayer halls, a lecture hall, and a cemetery. There is also a gateway covered in decorative, blue-glazed tiles and a pond in the courtyard for worshipers to cleanse themselves before entering the mosque. The halls are graced by exquisitely painted wooden beams supported by pillars with delightful *muqarnas* – an Islamic feature of projecting niches – on the capitals.

Arabic *muqarnas* on mosque pillar

Truck passing a checkpoint on the Karakoram Highway, with the Pamir Mountains in the background

⑩ Karakoram Highway
中巴友谊公路

SW from Kashgar into Pakistan.

Once a spur of the Silk Road, the Karakoram Highway (Zhongba Gonglu) was the only route over the Karakoram Mountains to and from India. During the 1970s and 1980s, a road was built across the mountains following the old caravan route, to link China and Pakistan. The 808-mile (1,300-km) route from Kashgar to Islamabad in Pakistan is one of awe-inspiring beauty. Camels and yaks, tended by Tajik herdsmen, graze in the highland pastures. A highlight of the first section of the route is the stunning **Lake Karakul**, beyond which rises mighty Muztagh Ata, one of the highest mountains in Xinjiang, at 24,636 ft (7,509 m).

The last town in China is **Tashkurgan**, a wildly remote outpost that has been earmarked for major investment by the government to encourage cross-border trade. An airport is under construction. Beyond it is the 15,750-ft- (4,800-m-) high **Khunjerab Pass**, the gateway to Pakistan. The Pakistan border post lies just beyond at Sost. The border is closed in winter, and visas are required in advance to cross into Pakistan. However, it is possible to travel along the highway from Kashgar as far as Tashkurgan without a permit, stopping over at Lake Karakul. This is one of the wildest and most dramatic parts of Xinjiang, home to the Tajik people.

⑪ Yengisar
英吉沙

37 miles (60 km) S of Kashgar.

The small, sleepy town of Yengisar, on the southern arm of the Silk Road, is renowned for its locally produced knives. For centuries, the town has been manufacturing hand-crafted knives for Uighur men, who carry them as traditional accoutrements. Knives of all shapes and sizes are sold in dozens of shops. While most of the knives produced are factory-made, traditional knife-making skills are still practiced by artisans in the center of town. Using basic tools, the workers at the **Yengisar Country Small Knife Factory** produce exquisite designs fashioned from fine woods, their handles inlaid with silver or horn. It is sometimes possible to visit the factory, even though a big board outside bears a "No Entrance" sign. The knives, which make attractive gifts, require special arrangements to be taken home.

Polished knives displayed at a stall in the Sunday Market, Yengisar

For hotels and restaurants in this region see p563 and p585

Jade

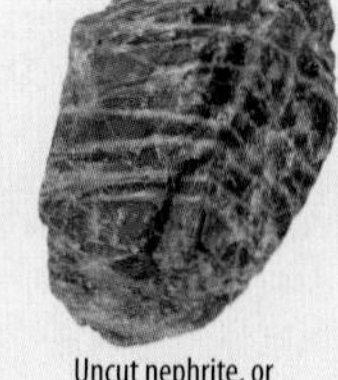

Uncut nephrite, or true jade

Jade, or nephrite, has been carved and polished by the Chinese for several thousand years, along with jadeite, soapstone, and chalcedony. While the latter are known as *yu*, nephrite is *zhen yu*, or true jade. Initially used as a tool, jade came to be widely used as jewelry during the Han era. By the Qing period, carvers were producing a variety of decorative pieces including intricate jade animals. Always thought of as being green, jade can in fact be brown, black, or the prized "mutton fat" jade – a cloudy white. To the Chinese, it symbolizes longevity and purity, and is worn as an amulet to ward off disease. The country's only source of nephrite is Xinjiang, particularly around Hotan, so a sophisticated supply system must have existed even in Neolithic times.

⓬ Yarkand

莎车

106 miles (170 km) SE of Kashgar.

For centuries an important commercial center on the southern arm of the Silk Road, Yarkand was, like Kashgar, prominent in the Great Game – the power struggle between China, Russia, and Britain *(see p495)*. The old town, with its adobe walls and narrow streets, has a few interesting sights. The **Altunluq Mosque** has beautifully painted ceilings, and in its courtyard is the **Tomb of Amannisahan** (1526–60) – the poet wife of one of the local Khans – built in 1992. Behind the mosque is a sprawling cemetery housing the tombs of the Khans of Yarkand. There is also a lively Sunday market.

A vendor pulls a cart of radishes, Yarkand

⓭ Kargilik

椰城

144 miles (230 km) SE of Kashgar.

This town was a convenient stop between Hotan and Kashgar on the southern arm of the Silk Road. The colorful old Uighur town is worth exploring, while the town's main attraction, the 15th-century **Jama Masjid**, sits within the arcaded bazaar.

⓮ Hotan

和田

249 miles (400 km) SE of Kashgar. 322,000. Hotan CITS, 49 Tunken Lu, (0903) 251 6090. Sun.

The oasis town of Hotan, or Hetian, was an early center for the spread of Buddhism before Islam arrived in the 9th century. Formerly the capital of the Yutian kingdom, it has been, like most Silk Road cities, periodically subsumed into the Chinese Empire. For centuries, the town's jade, carpets, and silk have been considered the finest in China, and are still produced in factories across town. According to legend, the secret of silk was first introduced to the region by a Chinese princess betrothed to a local prince, who smuggled silk moth eggs in her hair in AD 440. Craftsmen carve fine jade items at the Jade Factory on Tanai Lu, while the Carpet Factory across the river is a friendly place also worth a visit, especially for those wishing to buy a carpet, as they are available here at bargain prices. Visitors interested in silk production can head out to the village of Jiya, 7 miles (12 km) to the northeast of Hotan.

The chaotic local market takes place on Fridays and Sundays in the northeast of town in the area around the Jiamai Mosque. Though not as large as its famous counterpart in Kashgar, it is a colorful affair with livestock, fruit, silks, and carpets on sale.

At the end of the 19th century, the first rumors of the region's lost cities – which inspired several expeditions – emanated from here. A detailed map, indicating the location of the buried cities, lies in the small **Hetian Regional Museum**. Other items of interest include fragments of silk, wooden utensils, and jewelry excavated from nearby lost cities, as well as the mummified corpses of a 10-year-old girl and a 35-year-old man with Indo-European features, which are 1,500 years old. The ruined city of **Melikawat** lies over 18 miles (30 km) south of town. All that remains of this once significant Buddhist center are crumbling walls and shards of glass and pottery.

Hetian Regional Museum
342 Beijing Xi Lu. **Tel** (0903) 251 9286. **Open** 10am–1:30pm, 4–7:30pm Thu–Tue.

Craftsmen at the open-air market in Hotan

TIBET

Tibet at a Glance

Bordered on three sides by some of the world's highest mountain ranges – the Himalayas, the Karakoram, and the Kunlun – Tibet has remained in relative isolation. Sheltered first by its inaccessibility and then, in the age of air travel, by Chinese occupation, the "Roof of the World" is now open to foreign visitors. Its one major city, Lhasa, retains its spiritual core: the Jokhang; the venerable palace of the Dalai Lamas, the Potala; and great monasteries such as Drepung and Sera. Wherever you go, Tibet offers panoramic vistas of high-altitude desert fringed by peaks, but the turquoise depths of Lake Namtso and the sky-scraping peaks of Mount Everest are particularly worth visiting.

Thangka hanging on a door at the Jokhang Temple, Lhasa

Muztag Feng 6973m
Hoh Xil Sh
Gozha Co
Bairab Co
Kashgar
Orba Co
Lumajangdong Co
Dog Corin
Rutog
G219
Lugu
Gomo
Nganglong Kangri 6596m
XIZANG ZIZHI
(TIBET)
Gar
Gegyai
Qagcaka
S301
Oma
Gar Xincun
Sênggê Zangbo
Gar Zangbo
Gerze
Zhaxi Co
Langqên Zangbo
Gangdisê Shan
Ngangla Ringco
S301
Cozhe
Bogcang Zangbo
Nyima
G219
Lunggar
Coqen
Tangra Yumco
Gyaring
Barga
La'nga Co
Zhari Namco
Ngangze Co
Burang
Kangmar
Paryang
Himalayas
Lungsang
Zhongba
Dogxung Zangbo
SHIGA
Saga
G219
Ngamring
G318
Lhatse
7 SAKYA MONA
Tingri
Xixabangma Feng 8027m
Zhangmu
THE NEPAL BORDER 9
8 EVEREST BASE
Mt Everest 8848m
Yac

Sights at a Glance

Towns & Cities

1 Lhasa
5 Gyantse
9 The Nepal Border

Areas of Natural Beauty

4 Namtso Lake
8 Everest Base Camp

Temples & Monasteries

2 *Samye Monastery pp544–5*
3 Tsurphu Monastery
6 Shigatse & Tashilunpo
7 Sakya Monastery

Key

Main road
Minor road
Railroad
International border
Disputed border
Provincial border
Summit

◀ Yamdrok Lake, the largest lake in south Tibet, seen from the Kamba-la Pass

Potala Palace seen from the rooftop of the Jokhang, Lhasa's holiest temple

Getting There

Visitors mostly arrive mostly by air from Chengdu, the capital of Sichuan, or Kathmandu, Nepal. An overland route also connects Kathmandu and Lhasa, but while individual travelers can leave, only tour groups may enter this way. The bus route from Golmud in Qinghai has been superseded by a high-speed railway line, and most people take the train to Lhasa from Xining or Chengdu. No independent travel is allowed for foreigners in Tibet, and a permit is required ahead of travel by road, rail, or air in the region. The best option is to arrange a tour with an agency in Lhasa, that will also handle permits.

A PORTRAIT OF TIBET

Tibet's reputation as a land of exotic mystery is due to centuries of geographic isolation and a unique theocratic culture, based on Buddhism but influenced by an older shamanistic faith called Bon. In 1950, China marched into Tibet and annexed the country. Despite this upheaval, the traditional culture and values of the Tibetans remain strong and continue to lure and enchant visitors.

Since the introduction of Buddhism in the 7th century, the religion has permeated all aspects of Tibetan life, with monasteries acting as palaces, administrative centers, and schools. Ruled by priests, Tibet was feudal in outlook and resisted all modernization. The country thus entered the 20th century without an army, lay education, or roads, and with few technologies more sophisticated than the prayer wheel.

Buddhism was introduced in Tibet by Songsten Gampo (AD 608–50). A remarkable ruler who also unified the country, Songsten Gampo was converted to Buddhism by his Chinese and Nepalese wives. The next religious king, Trisong Detsen (742–803), consolidated the Buddhist faith, inviting the Indian teacher Padmasambhava (Guru Rinpoche) to Tibet and founding Samye Monastery. A revival of the native Bon religion in the 8th century led to Buddhist persecution, and though the religion re-emerged later, the kingdom disintegrated into several principalities.

In the 13th century, Tibet submitted to the Mongols, and in 1247 the Mongols appointed the head lama of Sakya Monastery as Tibet's ruler. Subsequently, Tsongkhapa (1357–1419) established the Gelugpa or Yellow Hat sect. His disciples became the Dalai Lamas, rulers of Tibet for 500 years. Each new Dalai Lama is seen as a reincarnation of the previous one. In 1950, the Chinese took advantage of a tenuous claim to the territory and invaded. In the uprising that followed in 1959, the 14th Dalai Lama (b. 1935) fled to India, where he still heads the Tibetan Government-in-Exile. By 1970, more than a million Tibetans had died either directly at the hands of the Chinese or through famine caused by incompetent agricultural policies. Tibet's cultural heritage was razed, and thousands of monasteries were destroyed.

Sprawling Ganden Monastery, built in the early 15th century

Buddha's all-seeing eyes on the Kumbum, Gyantse

Some monasteries that were ravaged during the Cultural Revolution have now been repaired and returned to their former roles, but creating or owning an image of the Dalai Lama is still illegal.

The ancient city of Lhasa is the heart of Tibet, though Han Chinese immigrants now outnumber ethnic Tibetans. A spectacular railroad linking Golmud in Qinghai to Lhasa means that immigrant numbers will continue to grow. However, the old quarter, home of the Potala Palace and the Jokhang Temple, illustrates the determination with which Tibetans have held onto their cultural traditions. A common sight here are the pious pilgrims, swinging prayer wheels and performing prostrations as they make *kora* – holy circuits – around the temple.

Most of Tibet is desert, and the average altitude is over 13,000 ft (4,000 m), with temperatures well below freezing in winter. Many customs arose as a response to life in this harsh environment. Sky burials, for example, in which the dead are left in the open for vultures, are practical in a land where firewood is scarce and the earth too hard to dig. Polyandry (the practice of having more than one husband at a time) and celibacy of the clergy were necessary forms of population control.

A Tibetan mandala, a ritual tantric diagram

Almost a quarter of Tibetans are nomads, keeping herds of *dzo* (a cross between a yak and a cow) and living in tents. Their livestock provide products vital for everyday Tibetan life – yak butter is used in the ubiquitous butter tea and burnt in smoky chapel lamps.

Tibet's roads are few, and journeys are always time-consuming. The busiest route is the Friendship Highway between Lhasa and the Nepalese border, which passes through Shigatse, Gyantse, and the dramatic Sakya Monastery. It is a long, bumpy, but rewarding diversion from here to the Everest base camp, which offers great views of the forbidding peak. Lhasa, too, can be a good base for exploring some of the other isolated destinations. The monasteries of Drepung, Sera, Ganden, and Tsurphu are easily accessible, while Samye and Lake Namtso are farther away. Note that you will need to outline every place you wish to visit to the tour operator who applies for your permit; if a place is not mentioned on your permit, you may not be allowed in.

Monks debating under a tree, a common sight at Sera Monastery, near Chasa

Tibetan Buddhism

The Mahayana school of Buddhism, which emphasizes compassion and self-sacrifice, came to Tibet from India in the 7th century. As it spread it took on many aspects of the native, shamanistic Bon religion, incorporating Bon rituals and deities. Like most Buddhists, Tibetans believe in reincarnation – consecutive lives that are better or worse depending on the karma, or merit, accrued in the previous life. For many Tibetans, Buddhism suffuses daily life so completely that the concept of a religion separate from day to day occurences is completely foreign – there is no word for religion in Tibetan.

Chortens hold the ashes of spiritual teachers. The square base symbolizes Earth; the pinnacle crown represents the ethereal sphere.

The Gelugpa or Yellow Hat sect was founded in the 1300s by the reformist Tsongkhapa. Dominant in Tibetan politics for centuries, the sect is led by the Dalai Lama and Panchen Lama *(see p524, p548)*.

Monks and Monasteries

At the height of monastic power there were some 6,000 monasteries in Tibet, and numerous Buddhist sects. Most families sent a son to become a monk and live a life of celibacy and meditation.

The Nyingma order is the oldest and most traditional of all the sects. It was founded during the 600s by Guru Rinpoche.

A soul can take one of two paths: the light path leads to auspicious rebirths until final liberation, the dark to poor rebirths and hell.

At the axle the three evils – a snake (anger), a pig (ignorance), and a cockerel (desire) – eternally chase each other's tails.

Wheel of Life

The continuous cycle of existence and rebirth is represented by the Wheel of Life, clutched in the jaws of the Lord of Death, Yama. Achieving enlightenment is the only way to transcend the incessant turning of the wheel.

Bon – Tibet's Pre-Buddhist Faith

Bon, an animistic faith with emphasis on magic and spirits and the taming of demons, was Tibet's native religious tradition before the arrival of Buddhism. Many Tibetan legends concern the taming of local gods and their conversion to the new faith. Much of today's Buddhist iconography, rituals, and symbols, including prayer flags and sky burials – where the deceased is chopped to pieces and left on a mountainside for vultures – are Bon in origin. The faith has been revived by a handful of Bon monasteries in Tibet.

A 19th-century bronze figure of a Bon deity

Spinning a prayer wheel clockwise sends a prayer written on coiled paper to heaven. The largest wheels contain thousands of prayers and are turned by crank or water power.

Prayer and Ritual

Worship in Tibet is replete with ritual objects and customs, many of which help with the accrual of merit. Koras, which are always followed clockwise, can be short circuits of holy sites or fully fledged pilgrimages. The most auspicious kora *is around Mount Kailash, considered the center of the universe; nirvana is guaranteed on the 108th circuit.*

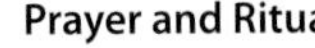

The outer ring illustrates the 12 factors that determine karma, including spiritual awareness (a blind man with a stick) and acts of volition (a potter molding pots).

The inner wheel depicts the six realms into which beings can be reborn – gods, demigods, humans, animals, ghosts, and demons.

This ritual drum, made from the upper part of two skulls, has extra potency as a tool of prayer because it is fashioned from human remains.

A worshiper spins a hand-held prayer wheel, rings a Tibetan bell called a *drilbu*, and holds offerings of banknotes, all in aid of prayer.

Mani stones are carved with the Sanskrit mantra *"om mani padme hum"* (hail to the jewel in the lotus), a powerful Buddhist chant.

The Tibetan Pantheon

An overwhelming plethora of deities, buddhas, and demons, many of them reincarnations or evil aspects of each other, make up the Tibetan pantheon. Buddhas, "awakened ones," have achieved enlightenment and reached nirvana. Bodhisattvas *have postponed the pursuit of nirvana to help others achieve enlightenment.*

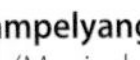
Jampelyang (Manjushri) represents knowledge and learning. He raises a sword of discriminating wisdom in his right hand.

Buddhist Deities

Jowo Sakyamuni: the historical Buddha
Jampa (the Maitreya): the future Buddha
Dipamkara (Marmedze): the past Buddha
Guru Rinpoche (Padmasambhava): earthly manifestation of Buddha who spread Buddhism throughout Tibet
Chenresig (Avalokitesvara): multi-armed *bodhisattva* of compassion
Drolma (Tara): female aspect of compassion

Dharmapalas, defenders of the law, fight against the enemies of Buddhism. Originally demons, they were tamed by Guru Rinpoche, who bound them to the faith. Mahakala, one of the most common *dharmapalas*, is a wrathful manifestation of Chenresig.

Nomadic Life

The Chang Tang, a high plateau covering almost 70 percent of Tibet, is home to about a quarter of Tibetans, many of whom are nomads (or *Drokpa)*, as the harsh, arid climate precludes farming. Their existence has barely been touched by modern life, and they still herd sheep, goats, and *dzo* (a cross between a yak and a domesticated cow), as they have for centuries. The animals are adapted to high altitude, having larger lungs and more hemoglobin than lowland animals. Despite being perfectly adapted to the climate, the nomads' way of life is under threat as the Chinese government pushes them to resettle in permanent camps.

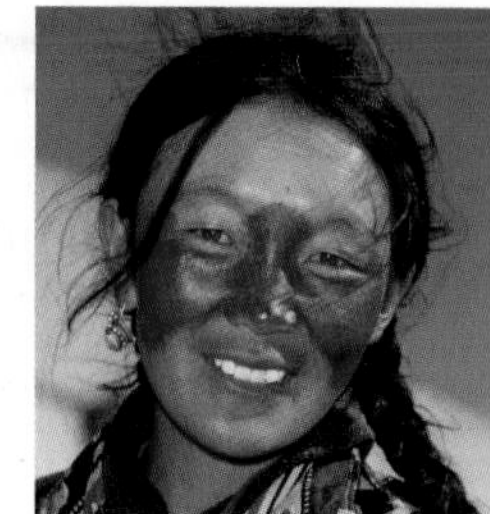

Dried yogurt is thought to protect the skin from the sun, but men don't use it at all; women smear it on with a tuft of wool as a cosmetic.

These men enjoy cups of salted tea made with yak butter, a popular drink throughout Tibet. The salt combats dehydration and the fat gives much-needed energy. They wear knee-length *lokbars*, with a black strip at the edge, the traditional dress for male nomads.

Traditionally, nomads wear belted robes made out of goatskin called *lokbars* that double as blankets at night. The fleece is worn on the inside, while the sturdy hide is exposed to wind and snow. The sleeves are extra long to keep hands warm. Women braid their hair and wear their wealth as jewelry. Coral, in particular, is highly valued.

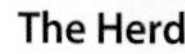

The Herd

Nomads rely totally on their herds for food, clothing, shelter, and sometimes income, so no part of any animal goes to waste. Goats, for example, provide milk for yogurt, skins for clothing, wool for trading, and dung for fuel.

Each household has a home tent, four-sided and made out of the coarse hairs found on a yak's belly. Often, the tent is pitched in a pit and surrounded by stone wind-breaks. Another cloth tent may be used for traveling.

A woman spreads yak dung over a windbreak wall. Once it has dried, she will scrape the dung off the wall and use it to fuel fires for cooking. Such tasks are strictly demarcated by gender; women do all the milking, churning, cooking, weaving, and fuel gathering, and so work harder than the men for most of the year.

A nomad pours yak butter from a churn for adding to strong, salty tea. The nomadic diet is basic; the staple is *tsampa*, roasted barley flour that, often eaten dry and on its own, provides about half of a nomad's calories. Goat's milk yogurt, radishes, and occasional meat stews supplement the diet.

The wool of the yaks, sheep, and goats in the nomad's herd is woven using a loom, creating robust textiles for tent walls, blankets, and clothing. The incomes of many nomads have been augmented by the popularity of cashmere wool, which is the soft down on a goat's underbelly.

Moving the Herds

Nomads on the Chang Tang do not move continuously, nor do they move far – only around 10 to 40 miles (15 to 65 km), as the growing season is the same all over the plateau. Indeed, they try to minimize travel, declaring that it weakens livestock. Some families even build a house at their main encampment. In the fall, after the herds have eaten most of the vegetation at the main encampment and the growing season has ended, the nomads move their livestock to a secondary plain for grazing. Here livestock must forage for eight to nine months on dead vegetation. Later the nomads may move some of their herds farther up the hills. They then return to their original encampment.

A herder driving his yaks over a snowy mountain pass

TIBET

The enormous Tibetan plateau stretches across an awesome 463,323 sq miles (1,200,000 sq km). Its northern expanse is the Chang Tang, a vast, uninhabited, high-altitude desert, dotted with enormous brackish lakes. Nearly all the main sights and cities, as well as half of Tibet's population of 2.8 million people, are concentrated in the less harsh southern region.

The fertile valley created by the Yarlung Tsangpo river is bordered by the Himalayas along Tibet's southern boundary. A mere 14 million years old, the Himalayas are the youngest mountains on earth, and also the highest, with over 70 peaks reaching elevations of 23,000 ft (7,000 m) or over, including Mount Everest, the world's highest at 29,029 ft (8,848 m). The spectacle of these snow-clad peaks is perhaps what led to Tibet being called the "Land of Snows." In reality, at an average altitude of over 13,000 ft (4,000 m), the thin air intensifies the sunshine making acclimatization and sunscreen essential.

Tibet's eastern reaches are riddled with gorges carved out by three of China's rivers – the mighty Yangzi, the Salween, and the Mekong. Eastern Tibet, also known as Chamdo, is one of the few regions of Tibet where it rains frequently – the mountains of the southeast are cloaked in mysterious, unexplored forests.

The wide, open spaces of northern and western Tibet are home to nomads who live a hardy pastoral existence. These wilderness areas are slowly shrinking as a result of the encroaching industrial world.

However, despite rapid development and seven decades of Chinese occupation, Tibet still clings strongly to its cultural heritage, most visible in the revitalized monasteries. Tourism, too, is a growing industry as more areas are opening up, allowing visitors tantalizing glimpses of a once-forbidden world.

Main prayer hall at Ganden Monastery, the first Gelugpa monastery in Tibet

◀ Namtso Lake, a popular tourist destination

❶ Lhasa

Tibet's capital since the 7th century, Lhasa is an intoxicating introduction to Tibet. The Dalai Lama's splendid but poignantly empty seat, the Potala Palace, dominates the city from its site on top of Marpo Ri. Today much of Lhasa is made up of modern Chinese boulevards. However, older traditions endure in the richly atmospheric Tibetan quarter, a short way east from the center. The revered Jokhang Temple is the hub of this area. Around it is the neighborhood known as the Barkhor, which retains much of its medieval character, with smoky temples and cobbled alleys.

Lhasa City Center

Key

Street-by-Street area: *see pp534–5*

0 meters 500
0 yards 500

Key to Symbols *see back flap*

Strikingly colored mural at the Lukhang Temple

Potala Palace

See pp538–9.

Lukhang

Ching Drol Chi Ling Park.

Picturesquely located on an island in the lake behind the Potala, and cloaked by willows in summer, this temple is dedicated to the king of the water spirits *(lu)*, who is depicted riding an elephant at the back of the main hall. The upper floors are decorated with striking 18th-century murals representing the Buddhist Path to Enlightenment. Their great attention to detail and vivid stories offered visual guidance to the Dalai Lamas *(see p524)*, who retired here for periods of spiritual retreat.

Buddhist myths dominate the walls on the second floor, while the top-floor murals depict the esoteric yogic practices of the Indian tantric masters. They also illustrate episodes in the life of Pema Lingpa, ancestor of the 6th Dalai Lama who is credited with the Lukhang's original design in the 17th century.

Ramoche

Xiao Zhao Si Lu.

Open 7:30am–8pm daily.

The three-story Ramoche, just north of the Barkhor area *(see pp534–5)*, is the sister temple to the Jokhang. It was built in the 7th century by Songtsen Gampo *(see p524)* to house the statue of Jowo Sakyamuni (Tibet's most venerated Buddha image) brought by his Chinese wife Wencheng. According to legend, the threat of Chinese invasion after the king's death compelled his family to hide the statue in a secret chamber inside the Jokhang. It was replaced by a bronze statue of an eight-year-old Sakyamuni *(see p527)*, part of the dowry of another of his wives, the Nepalese Princess Bhrikuti.

The temple features some huge prayer wheels, and is not as busy as the Jokhang. Next door is the **Tsepak Lhakhang**, a chapel with an image of Jampa, the Tibetan name for the Future Buddha *(see p527)*.

Prayer wheels at the Ramoche Temple

The New Summer Palace of the Dalai Lamas in the Norbulingka

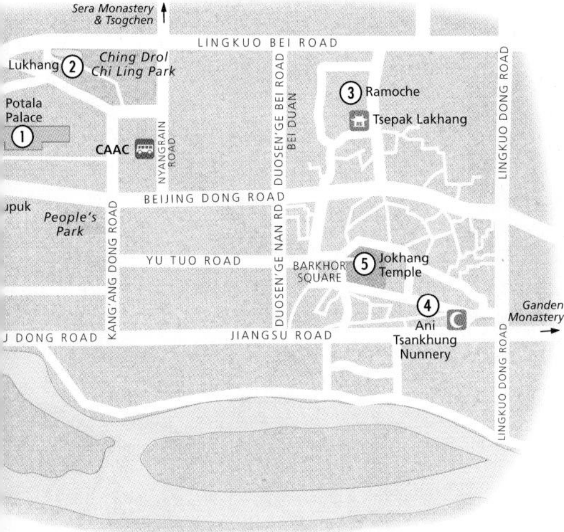

Ani Tsankhung Nunnery

29 Linkuo Nan Xiang. **Open** 8am–6pm daily.

Situated in the old Tibetan quarter, the Ani Tsankhung Nunnery is difficult to find. Wandering through the busy back alleys south of the Barkhor area in search of the place can be a wonderful experience. It is located in a yellow building on the street running parallel to and north of Jiangsu Lu. The nunnery's main hall contains a beautiful image of Chenresig, the multi-armed *bodhisattva* of compassion *(see p527)*, and behind it lies a meditation chamber used by Songtsen Gampo in the 7th century. An air of serenity pervades this quaint place, with its flower bushes and spotless compound. The nunnery's main attraction is the warm welcome the curious nuns give to the few visitors that come here.

Jokhang Temple

See pp536–7.

Tibet Museum

19 Norbulingka Road. **Tel** (0891) 683 5244. **Open** 9:30am–noon, 2:30–5:30pm Tue–Sun.

This building presents a rather one-sided version of Tibetan history. Ignoring the propaganda, the more than 30,000 relics are worth a visit. The most interesting displays are of rare Tibetan musical instruments and medical tools.

Norbulingka

21 Norbulingka Road. **Tel** (0891) 682 6274. **Open** 9:30am–6pm daily.

Today a pleasantly scrubby park, the Norbulingka (Jewel Park) was once the summer palace of the Dalai Lamas. Founded by the 7th Dalai Lama in 1755 and expanded by his successors, the park contains several palaces, chapels, and other buildings, and is a charming place for a leisurely afternoon. The path west from the entrance leads to the oldest palace, the **Kelsang Potrang**, used by the 8th to the 13th Dalai Lamas. Its main hall has a wealth of *thangkas (see p540)* and a throne. More diverting is the **Takten Migyur Podrang** (New Summer Palace), just north of here, which was built for the present Dalai Lama in 1954. Its audience chamber holds murals depicting events from Tibetan history, from the tilling of the first field to the building of the great monasteries, including the Norbulingka. Next to the chamber are the Dalai Lama's meditation room and bedroom, preserved exactly as he left them in 1959, when he escaped from this palace disguised as a Tibetan soldier and began his journey to India. The Assembly Hall where he held state has a golden throne and murals depicting scenes from the Dalai Lama's court, and episodes from the lives of Sakya Thukpa (Sakyamuni, the Historical Buddha) and Tsongkhapa, founder of the Gelugpa order of monks *(see p524)*.

VISITORS' CHECKLIST

Practical Information

560,000. Tibet Vista, Jia Cuo 3–070 Beijing Xi Lu, (0891) 681 7201. **tibettravel.org**

Transportation

Lhasa Gonggar Airport, 40 miles (65 km) from Lhasa. Lhasa Station. Main bus station, CAAC (buses to airport).

Brightly painted doorway, Norbulingka

Street-by-Street: The Barkhor

八廓街

Lhasa's liveliest neighborhood, the fascinating Barkhor bustles with pilgrims, locals, and tourists eager to visit the Jokhang Temple *(see pp536–7)* – by dusk the crowds are enormous. The pilgrimage circuit or *kora* that runs clockwise around the Jokhang is Tibet's holiest, and has been since the 7th century. Many of the buildings in the Barkhor are ancient, some dating back to the 8th century. Despite the efforts of conservationists, some important buildings have been demolished and replaced with less attractive traditional architecture; the market stalls that once did brisk business here have been removed. Still, the Barkhor's cobbled alleyways maintain a unique, archaic character.

Butter stall
A stall selling yak butter for burning candles. Candles, though, are not allowed inside Jokhang.

★ Jokhang Temple
The magnificent Jokhang, Tibet's most important religious structure, sits at the heart of the Barkhor, and is the structure around which the rest of Lhasa developed.

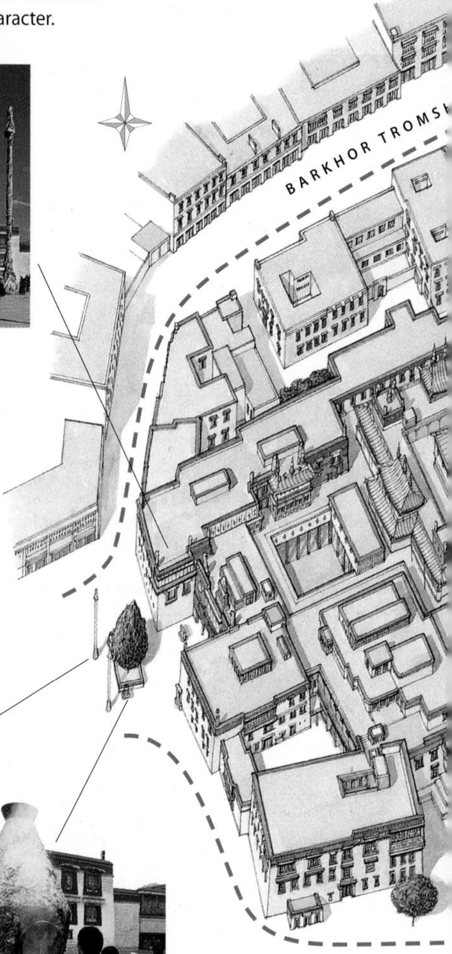

Key

— *Kora* (holy route)

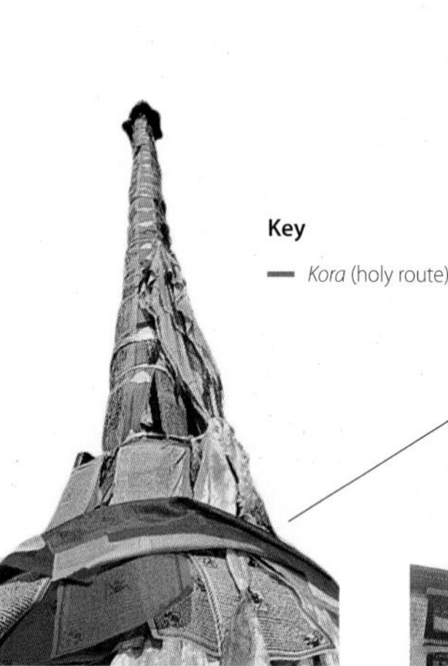

Prayer flags
Two poles laden with flags stand outside the Jokhang. Vertical flagpoles originated in the Amdo region *(see p483)*, and represent battle flags that have become signs of peace.

Incense burner
Juniper bushes are burnt in the four stone incense burners, or *sangkang*, which mark the route of the *kora*.

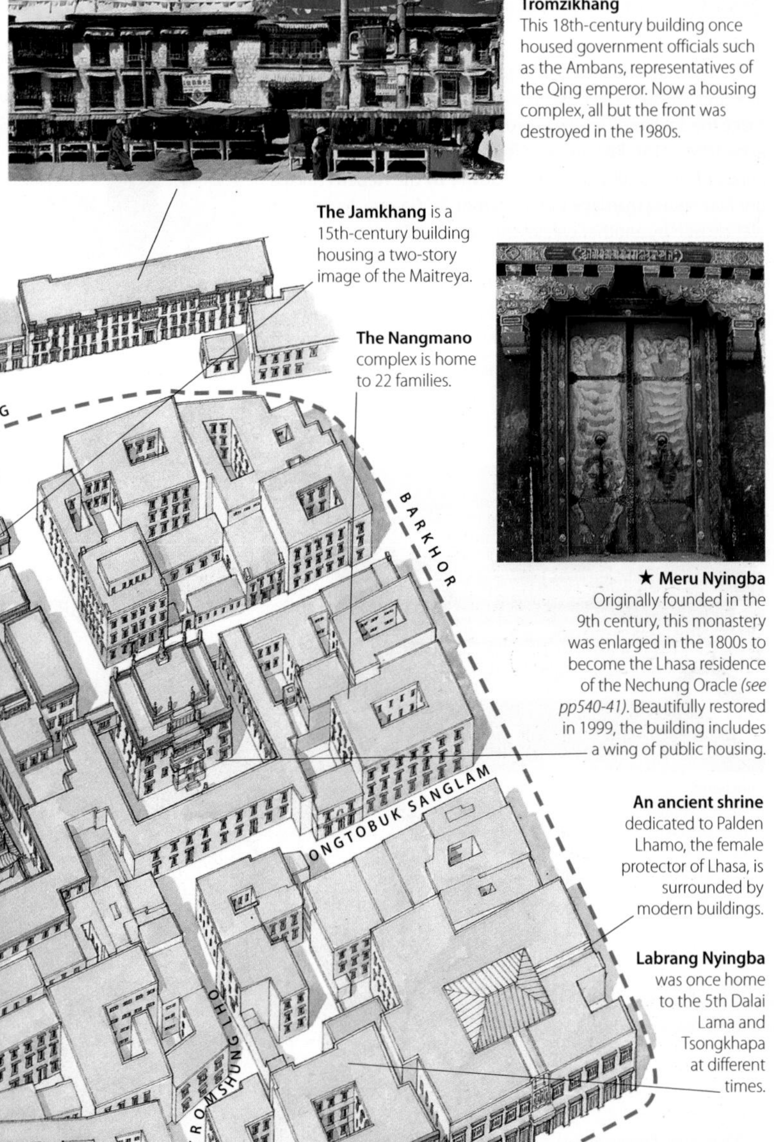

Tromzikhang
This 18th-century building once housed government officials such as the Ambans, representatives of the Qing emperor. Now a housing complex, all but the front was destroyed in the 1980s.

The Jamkhang is a 15th-century building housing a two-story image of the Maitreya.

The Nangmano complex is home to 22 families.

★ Meru Nyingba
Originally founded in the 9th century, this monastery was enlarged in the 1800s to become the Lhasa residence of the Nechung Oracle *(see pp540-41)*. Beautifully restored in 1999, the building includes a wing of public housing.

An ancient shrine dedicated to Palden Lhamo, the female protector of Lhasa, is surrounded by modern buildings.

Labrang Nyingba was once home to the 5th Dalai Lama and Tsongkhapa at different times.

Barkhor Street
This ancient street surrounds the Jokhang Temple and is popular with tourists and pilgrims, who can be seen spinning prayer wheels and chanting throughout the day.

Jokhang Temple

大昭寺

The constant bustle, gaudy paraphernalia of worship, flickering butter lamps, and wreaths of heady incense make the Jokhang Temple one of Tibet's most memorable experiences. The Jokhang was founded in AD 639 to house an image of the Buddha brought as dowry by the Nepali Princess Bhrikuti on her marriage to King Songtsen Gampo. Its location was chosen by another wife of the king, the Chinese consort Princess Wencheng. She declared that a giant female demon slumbered beneath the site and a temple must be built over her heart to subdue her. After the king's death, Wencheng's own dowry image of Jowo Sakyamuni was moved from the Ramoche *(see p532)* to the Jokhang, where it was thought to be safer from invading forces.

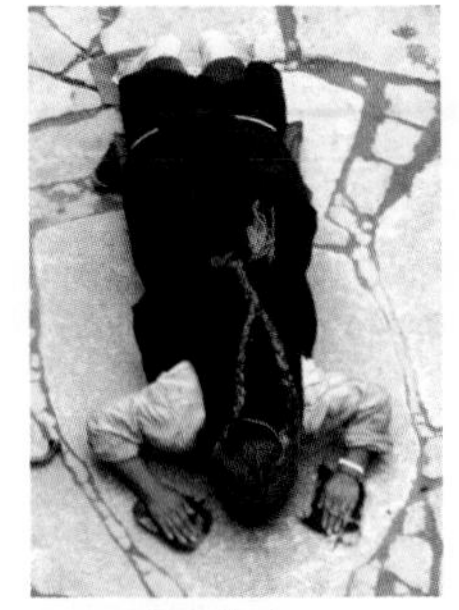

Prostrating pilgrim
The Jokhang is Tibet's most venerated site. Pilgrims bow and pray on the flagstones just outside the temple doors.

Courtyard
This open courtyard, or *dukhang*, is the focus for ceremonies during festivals. The long altar holding hundreds of butter lamps marks the entrance to the interior.

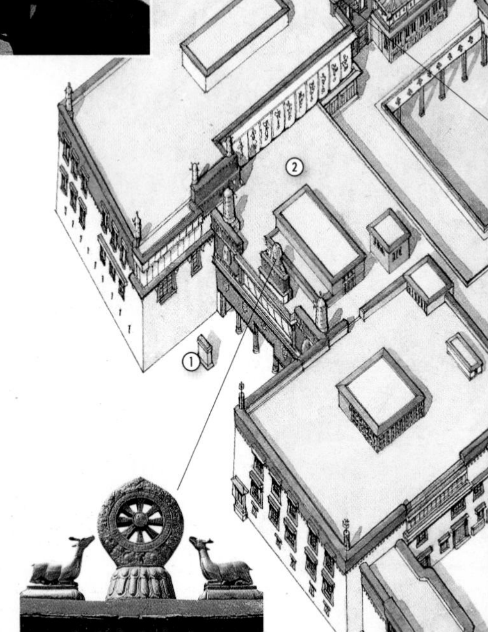

KEY

① **This stele** is inscribed with the terms of the Sino-Tibetan treaty of AD 822, guaranteeing mutual respect for the borders of the two nations.

② **Just inside the entrance** are the four Guardian Kings, the Chokyong, one for each cardinal direction.

③ **The Chapel of Songtsen Gampo**, where the king is flanked by Wencheng on the right and Bhrikuti on the left.

④ **The Chapel of Tsongkhapa** has an impressive and accurate image of the founder of the Gelugpa order.

⑤ **The Jampa** enshrined here is a copy of the one brought to Tibet by Princess Bhrikuti.

Roof ornament
Spokes of the Wheel of Law represent the eight paths to enlightenment.

VISITORS' CHECKLIST

Practical Information
The Barkhor, Lhasa. **Open** 8–11:30am (pilgrims, small groups and individual visitors), 11:30am–5:30pm (tourists) daily. Visit from left to right. Monlam, during the first lunar month.

★ Chapel of Chenresig
A large statue of Chenresig, the *bodhisattva* of compassion, dominates this room. The doors and frames, crafted by Nepalis in the 7th century, are among the few remains of the original temple.

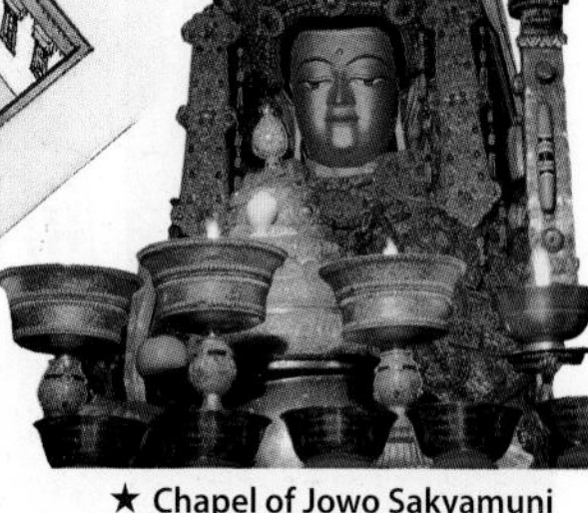

★ Chapel of Jowo Sakyamuni
Pilgrims crowd around this impassive statue of the 12-year-old Sakyamuni to make offerings and pray. Part of Princess Wencheng's dowry, it is the most revered image in Tibet.

★ Inner Sanctum
This houses some of the Jokhang's most important statues, including images of Guru Rinpoche, the Jampa, and a thousand-armed Chenresig. The chapels lining the walls are visited clockwise, and there's a line for the holiest, with monks at hand to enforce crowd discipline.

Prayer Wheels
Pilgrims spin the wheels on a route that surrounds the inner chapel called the Nangkor, one of the three sacred circuits of Lhasa.

Potala Palace

布达拉宫

Built on Lhasa's highest point, Marpo Ri, the Potala Palace is the greatest monumental structure in Tibet. Thirteen stories high, with over a thousand rooms, it was once the residence of Tibet's chief monk and leader, the Dalai Lama, and therefore the center for both spiritual and temporal power. These days, after the present Dalai Lama's escape to India in 1959, it is a vast museum, serving as a reminder of Tibet's rich and devoutly religious culture, although major political events and religious ceremonies are still held here. The first palace was built by Songtsen Gampo in 631, and this was merged into the larger building that stands today. There are two main sections – the White Palace, built in 1645 under orders from the 5th Dalai Lama, and the Red Palace, completed in 1693.

★ Golden Roofs
Seeming to float above the palace, the gilded roofs (actually copper) cover funerary chapels dedicated to previous Dalai Lamas.

★ Chapel of the 13th Dalai Lama
The bejeweled stupa of the 13th Dalai Lama, containing his mummified remains, is nearly 43 ft (13 m) high.

KEY

① **The base** is purely structural, holding the palaces onto the steep hill.

② **Red Palace Courtyard**

③ **The Chapel of the 5th Dalai Lama** contains a stupa gilded with around 6,600 lb (3,700 kg) of gold.

④ **Maitreya Chapel**

⑤ **East Sunshine Apartment**

⑥ **Eastern Courtyard**

⑦ **School of Religious Officials**

⑧ **Defensive Eastern Bastion**

⑨ **Thangka Storehouse**

★ 3D Mandala
This intricate mandala of a palace, covered in precious metals and jewels, embodies aspects of the path to enlightenment.

View from the Red Palace
On a clear day, the view over the valley and on to the mountains beyond is unequaled, although the newer parts of Lhasa are less impressive.

VISITORS' CHECKLIST

Practical Information
Beijing Zhong Road, Lhasa. **Tel** (0891) 633 9615. **Open** 9:30am–5pm daily. Best arranged via a travel agent. Tickets are timed. interior. Not suitable for those who find stairs a problem, best tackled once acclimatized to the altitude. **potalapalace.cn**

White Palace
The entrance to the main building has a triple stairway – the middle set of stairs is for the sole use of the Dalai Lama.

Heavenly King Murals
The East Entrance has sumptuous images of the Four Heavenly Kings, Buddhist guardian figures.

Western Hall
Located on the first floor of the Red Palace, the largest hall inside the Potala contains the holy throne of the 6th Dalai Lama.

Exploring Around Lhasa

Lhasa's environs are dotted with the major monasteries of Drepung, Nechung, Sera, and Ganden. Easily accessible from Lhasa by bus, minibus, or hired vehicle, these are ideal for day trips. Agencies in Lhasa hire out Land Cruisers along with a driver and guide. Vehicles can take up to five people – if looking to share the cost with others, check the bulletin boards in backpacker hotels. Make sure that any monasteries you plan to visit are listed on your travel permit.

A typically gory Tantric painting at Nechung Monastery

Drepung Monastery

5 miles (8 km) W of Lhasa.
Open 9am–4pm daily (chapels close noon–3pm).

Drepung, meaning "rice heap," was founded in 1416 by Jamyang Choje, a disciple of Tsongkhapa, the founder of the Gelugpa or Yellow Hat order of monks *(see p524)*. In its heyday in the 17th century, it was Tibet's richest monastery, with four colleges and 10,000 monks; today there are around 500 to 600.

The site is vast and the easiest way to get around is to follow the pilgrims, who circle the complex clockwise. From the entrance, turn left to the **Ganden Palace**, built in 1530 as a residence by the 2nd Dalai Lama. His rather plain apartments are upstairs on the seventh floor. The courtyard is usually busy with wood-carvers and block-printers creating prayer prints at great speed. Next is the **Tsogchen** or Main Assembly Hall, the most atmospheric building in the complex. About 180 pillars hold up the roof, and the room is draped with *thangkas* and hangings and decorated with suits of armor. There is plenty of statuary, with the finest images in the **Chapel of the Three Ages** at the back of the Main Assembly Hall.

At the hall's entrance, stairs lead to the upper floor from where it is possible to see the massive head and shoulders of the **Maitreya Buddha**, the Future Buddha or Jampa, rising up three stories. Pilgrims prostrate before it and drink from a holy conch shell. The **Tara Chapel** next door contains wooden racks of scriptures and a statue of Prajnaparamita, the Mother of Buddhas and an aspect of the goddess Tara; the amulet on her lap contains a tooth said to belong to Tsongkhapa. Behind the Tsogchen, the little **Manjusri Temple** has a relief image of the Bodhisattva of Wisdom, Jampelyang, chiseled out of rock. The circuit continues north to the Ngagpa College, then to various colleges toward the southeast.

Each building contains fine sculptures, though some might prefer to skip them and rest in the courtyard outside the Tsogchen. Those who are acclimatized can walk round the Drepung *kora* or pilgrim circuit, which passes rock paintings and the cave dwellings of nuns, and offers great views.

Nechung Monastery

4 miles (7 km) W of Lhasa.
Open 8am–4pm daily (chapels close noon–3pm).

A 15-minute walk southeast from Drepung, Nechung Monastery was the seat of the Tibetan Oracle. The Oracle not only predicted the future, but also protected the Buddha's teachings and his followers. During consultations with the Dalai Lama, the Oracle, dressed in an elaborate and weighty

Thangkas and Mandalas

Thangkas are religious paintings mounted on brocade that carry painted or embroidered images inside a colored border. Seen in temples, monasteries, and homes, they depict subjects as diverse as the lives of Buddhas, Tibetan theology and astrology, and mandalas or geometric representations of the cosmos. The Tashilunpo Monastery *(see p548)* displays gigantic *thangkas* during its festivals each year. Mandalas are often used as meditation aids by Buddhists and are based on a pattern of circles and squares around a central focal point. The Potala Palace in Lhasa *(see pp538–9)* has a splendid three-dimensional mandala made of precious metal. Monks spend days creating mandalas of colored sand that are swept away on completion to signify the transient nature of life.

Mandala symbolizing the universe

Monks engaged in group debates at Sera Monastery

costume, would go into a trance before making his pronouncements, concluding the session in a dead faint. Tibet's last Oracle fled to India in 1959, and now the monastery has only a few caretaker monks. Nechung's decor is startling as the courtyard outside is filled with gory paintings and demon torturers. Within the chapels, leering sculptures of skulls loom out of the gloom. The airy Audience Chamber on the second floor is a welcome respite. Here, the Dalai Lama used to consult the Oracle. The roof-level chapel is dedicated to Padmasambhava, the Tantric Buddha, also known as Guru Rinpoche.

Sera Monastery

2 miles (4 km) N of Lhasa.

Open 9am–5pm daily.

Founded in 1419 by disciples of the Gelugpa order, Sera Monastery was famous for its warrior monks, the Dob-dob. Once home to 5,000 monks, today there are less than one-tenth that number, although the energetic renovation suggests that this may improve.

Activity centers around its three colleges, visited in a clockwise circuit. Turn left from the main path to reach the first college, Sera Me, that was used for instruction in Buddhist basics. Sera Ngagpa, a little farther up the hill, was for Tantric studies, and Sera Je, next to it, was for teaching visiting monks. Each building has a dimly lit main hall and chapels toward the back that are full of sculptures. The largest and most striking building in the complex is the **Tsogchen** located farthest up the hill. It features wall-length *thangkas*, a throne that was used by the 13th Dalai Lama, and images of him and of Sakya Yeshe, the founder of Sera monastery. At the top of the path stands the open-air debating courtyard. The monks assemble here for debates and their ritualized gestures – clapping hands and stamping when a point is made – are fascinating to watch. The Sera *kora*, or pilgrim circuit that heads west from the main entrance, takes about an hour to complete and passes some beautiful rock reliefs.

Rock painting, Sera Monastery

Ganden Monastery

28 miles (45 km) E of Lhasa.

Open 9am–4pm daily.

The farthest-flung of Lhasa's monasteries, Ganden is probably the one most worth visiting, with its scenic setting high on the Gokpori Ridge. A guide and a driver are required, but if travel restrictions ease, traveling on a local minibus full of excited pilgrims is a more interesting option. Minibuses depart from the west side of the Barkhor. The monastery was founded in 1410 by Tsongkhapa, and its main building, the **Serdung Lhakhang**, has as its centerpiece a huge gold and silver *chorten* (stupa or funerary mound) with Tsongkhapa's remains. However, the buildings are not its main appeal. Its highlight is the *kora*, which takes an hour to walk. The circuit offers fine views of the landscape and a *chorten* or two that pilgrims (and visitors if they wish) must hop around on one leg.

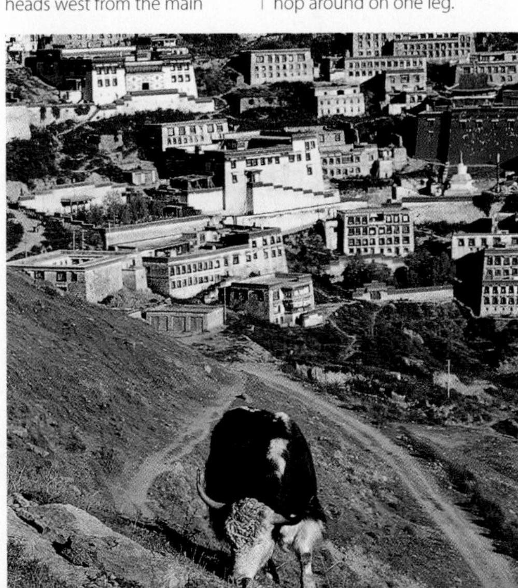

A domestic yak on the steep hills surrounding Ganden Monastery

❷ Samye Monastery
桑耶寺

With its ordered design, wealth of religious treasures, and stunning location, Samye makes a deep impression on visitors. Tibet's first monastery, Samye was founded in the 8th century during Trisong Detsen's reign, with the input of the great Buddhist teacher Guru Rinpoche. Indian and Chinese scholars, invited to Samye to translate Buddhist scriptures into Tibetan, argued over the interpretation of doctrine, and so Trisong Detsen held a public debate to decide which form of Buddhism should be followed in Tibet. The Indian school won out and Chinese religious influence gradually waned. Today the monastery has a well-worn and eclectic feel, having been influenced by numerous sects over the years.

★ Jowo Sakyamuni Chapel
Samye's most revered chapel centers on an image of Sakyamuni at age 38. He is flanked by two protector deities and ten *bodhisattvas*.

★ Chenresig Chapel
This chapel centers on a stunning statue of Chenresig, with an eye painstakingly painted on each of its thousand hands.

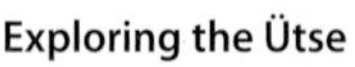

Exploring the Ütse

The Ütse is dimly lit, so take a flashlight to explore. The entrance leads directly into the Main Hall, with the Chenresig Chapel to the left and the Gongkhan Chapel to the right. The Jowo Sakyamuni Chapel is at the far end of the Main Hall. Numerous chapels and the Dalai Lama's quarters are located on the second story. The third story has an open gallery lined with impressive murals.

View of Samye Monastery
A superb view of the monastery can be had from the surrounding hills. From here it is easy to see that the monastery is laid out as a 3-D mandala *(see p540)*.

KEY

① **Monks** live in quarters on the upper level of the outer wall.

② **The outer wall** facing the Ütse is lined with prayer wheels and elaborate murals of Buddha.

③ **The mural** to the left of the entrance on the third story depicts the 5th Dalai Lama receiving the Mongol Khan Gushri and his retinue.

④ **Gongkhan Chapel** is packed with draped statues of fierce demons. A stuffed snake guards the exit.

⑤ **The inscription** on this stone stele (AD 779) declares that King Trisong Detsen has proclaimed Buddhism as the state religion.

⑥ **The Main Hall** houses images and statues of Guru Rinpoche and the Buddhist kings Trisong Detsen and Songtsen Gampo.

◄ A herder and his flock alongside the Yamdrok Yumtso, a sacred lake

Guru Rinpoche
An 8th-century monk-king from Swat in modern-day Pakistan, he is said to have subdued evil demons and established Buddhism in Tibet. Images of him carrying a thunderbolt are found throughout the complex.

VISITORS' CHECKLIST

Practical Information
93 miles (150 km) SE of Lhasa.
Open 9am–6pm daily. unless fee paid. Samye Festival, 15th day of 5th lunar month.

Transportation
Travel to Samye must be arranged by a travel agency.

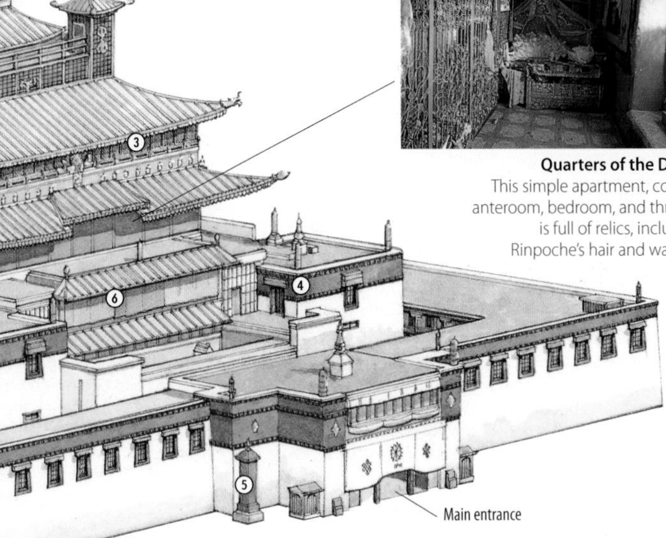

Quarters of the Dalai Lama
This simple apartment, consisting of anteroom, bedroom, and throne room, is full of relics, including Guru Rinpoche's hair and walking stick.

Plan of Samye Complex

Samye's design echoes Tibetan Buddhism's cosmology of the universe. Many of the 108 buildings have been destroyed, but the four *ling* chapels representing the island continents that surround Mount Sumeru (the Ütse) are still intact. Jampa Ling holds an impressive mural of the complex as it once was. The circular monastery wall is topped with 1,008 *chortens* that represent Chakravla, the ring of 1,008 mountains that surrounds the universe.

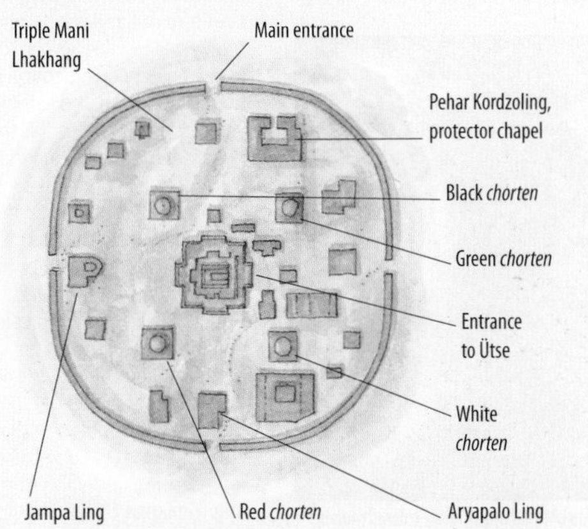

Nomad tents at the edge of the breathtaking Namtso Lake

❸ Tsurphu Monastery
楚布寺

Tolung Valley. 45 miles (70 km) W of Lhasa. must be organized by a travel agency. **Open** 9am–2pm daily.

At an altitude of 14,700 ft (4,480 m), this monastery was founded in the 12th century by the Karmapa or Black Hat order and is important as the traditional home of the Karmapa Lama, the third most important religious leader in Tibet after the Dalai and Panchen Lamas *(see pp524 and 548)*. The present incumbent, the 17th Karmapa, fled to India in 1999 at the age of 14. His departure was significant as he was the only senior Tibetan Buddhist official recognized by both the Chinese authorities and the Dalai Lama. The flood of daily pilgrims who came for blessings has now stopped and the monastery is rather quiet, though several hundred monks still reside here.

The Karmapa's throne, an object of great veneration, is in the audience chamber of the main hall. Here, a *chorten* (stupa or funerary mound) contains the relics of the 16th Karmapa, who died in Chicago in 1981. The *kora* from behind the monastery takes 3 hours, and provides magnificent views but beware – visitors must be acclimatized.

One of the many brightly colored murals at Tsurphu Monastery

❹ Namtso Lake
纳木错湖

125 miles (200 km) NW of Lhasa. Rent a 4WD from Lhasa; a day trip is possible, but staying overnight at the lake is preferable. **Open** daily.

With its classic Tibetan scenery of azure water beneath snow-capped peaks and grasslands dotted with herds of yaks, this lake is the most popular overnight jeep trip from Lhasa. About 45 miles (70 km) long and 19 miles (30 km) wide, it is the second largest saltwater lake in China after Qinghai Hu *(see p503)*.

The Eight Auspicious Symbols

The Eight Auspicious Symbols represent the offerings that were presented to Sakyamuni Buddha after he attained enlightenment. Born as Siddhartha Gautama, prince of the kingdom of Kapilavastu, he renounced his princely life at the age of 30 and went in search of answers to the meaning of human suffering and existence. After years of penance, Siddhartha attained enlightenment after meditating under a Bodhi tree in Bodh Gaya, India. Tibetans regard the symbols as protective motifs and use them to decorate flags and medallions as well as tiles in Buddhist temples, monasteries, and homes. The Conch Shell is blown to celebrate Sakyamuni's enlightenment; the Endless Knot represents harmony, and the never-ending passage of time; and the Wheel of Law symbolizes the Buddha's eightfold path to enlightenment. Other symbols include the Golden Fish, representing liberation from the Wheel of Life, and the Lotus Flower that represents purity.

Conch Shell

Endless Knot

Wheel of Law

The flat land around it offers good grazing and draws nomad encampments in summer. From November to May, the lake freezes over and the access road is often impassable. Basic accommodation is available at the Tashi Dor peninsula, on the lake's southeast shore. Bring a warm sleeping bag and a flashlight. The lake is at the incredible height of 15,500 ft (4,718 m), so visitors must be thoroughly acclimatized.

Highly decorated doorway to the main chapel, Kumbum, Gyantse

❺ Gyantse
江孜

158 miles (255 km) SW of Lhasa. must be organized by a travel agency.

Attractive, if dusty, Gyantse is the sixth largest town in Tibet, famous for its carpets and usually visited en route to Nepal *(see p551)*. Often called "Heroic City," it was originally capital of a 14th-century kingdom, and the remnants of its old **Dzong**, or fort, watch over the town. Heavily bombarded during the British invasion in 1904, when it was captured at great loss of life to the Tibetans, it is today a dramatic ruin with a small museum. Here, Chinese propaganda describes the "heroic battle fought to defend the Chinese motherland," although at that time China had no authority over Tibet. The Dzong offers good views from its roof. About 650 ft (200 m) northwest is a compound housing the **Kumbum** and **Pelkor Chode Monastery**.

The Kumbum, constructed around 1440, is a six-story and 115-ft (35-m) high *chorten*, honeycombed with chapels. It is built in an architectural style unique to Tibet and this is the finest extant example. A clock-wise route leads up past chapels full of statuary and decorated with 14th-century murals – *kumbum* means "a hundred thousand images." On the sixth floor, painted pairs of eyes, signifying the all-seeing eyes of Buddha, look out in each of the cardinal directions. The staircase in the eastern chapel leads into the *chorten's* dome with views from the top. Built 20 years after Kumbum, the Pelkor Chode Monastery was designed for all the local Buddhist sects to use; its Assembly Hall has two thrones, one for the Dalai Lama and one for the Sakya Lama *(see p550)*. The main chapel has a statue of Sakyamuni, the Historical Buddha, and some impressive wooden roof decorations. At the top, the Shalyekhang Chapel has some fine mandalas *(see p540)*.

On the way to Gyantse, it is worth taking a detour to see beautiful **Yamdrok Lake**, one of the four holy Tibetan lakes.

Dzong
Open 9:30am–6pm daily.

Kumbum and Pelkor Chode Monastery
Open 9am–7pm daily. (chapel is occasionally closed noon–3pm).

The British Invasion of Tibet

Alarmed by the growing influence of Tsarist Russia in the 19th century, Britain's viceroy in India sent a diplomatic mission to Tibet in an effort to build links and facilitate the free flow of trade. When the mission failed, an expeditionary force – part of the Great Game *(see p495)* – of 1,000 soldiers and 10,000 porters, led by the dashing 26-year-old Colonel Francis Younghusband, invaded Tibet in 1903. As the force traveled towards Lhasa, they killed almost 700 peasants, who were armed with little more than magic charms to ward off bullets. Then, in the world's highest battle, the British captured Gyantse Fort with only four casualties, while the Tibetans lost hundreds of men. The force proceeded to Lhasa, where an agreement allowed Britain to set up trade missions.

Francis Younghusband

Kumbum, Gyantse, a three-dimensional mandala

❻ Shigatse and Tashilunpo

日喀则

Capital of the Tsang region, Shigatse sits at an elevation of 12,800 ft (3,900 m). To its north, the Drolma Ridge rises steeply, with the ruins of the ancient Dzong, once home to the kings of Tsang, crowning its eastern end. Shigatse holds a powerful position in Tibet and was the capital for a spell during the early 17th century. After Lhasa regained its status, Shigatse continued to hold sway as the home of the Panchen Lama, Tibet's second most important religious ruler, whose seat is located at Tashilunpo Monastery, the town's grandest sight. Worth exploring for a day or two, Shigatse is the most comfortable place in Tibet after Lhasa, with decent food and accommodations on offer.

A group of carpet-weavers tying richly colored wool into intricate knots

Gang Gyen Carpet Factory

9 Zhu Feng Lu. **Tel** (0892) 882 6192.
Open 9am–1pm & 3–7pm Mon–Sat.
W tibetgang-gyencarpet.com

This factory, where local women produce beautiful carpets, first skeining the wool then weaving it, is the place to come if you are in the market for a Tibetan carpet. The process is sufficiently interesting to warrant a visit even if you have no intention of buying. A project initiated by the 10th Panchen Lama in 1987, the business is part-owned by the monastery. Shipping can be arranged on the premises.

Shigatse Dzong

The leaders of Tsang once ruled from the mighty fortress of **Shigatse Dzong**, in the north of town, built in the 14th century by Karma Phuntso Namgyel, a powerful Tsang king. It once resembled a small Potala, but was destroyed by the Chinese in 1959 during the Tibetan uprising and rebuilt on a smaller scale in 2007. You can walk around the Dzong but you can't enter it. A *kora* or holy route, marked by prayer flags and *mani* stones, leads here from the west side of Tashilunpo. Keep your distance from the packs of stray dogs.

Tibetan Market

At the Dzong's southern base on Tomzigang Lu stands a small Tibetan market selling souvenirs, such as prayer wheels and incense, and a few Tibetan necessities – medicine, legs of lamb, and large knives. Just to the west of the market is an old traditionally Tibetan neighborhood of narrow lanes and tall whitewashed walls.

Stall selling religious paraphernalia at the Tibetan Market

Tashilunpo Monastery

1 Jijilangka Lu. **Tel** (0892) 882 2114.
Open summer: 9am–12:30pm & 4–6pm Mon–Sat; winter: 10am–noon & 3–6pm Mon–Sat.

A huge monastic compound of golden-roofed venerable buildings and cobbled lanes, Tashilunpo would take several days to explore fully. It was founded in 1447 by Genden Drup, retrospectively titled the 1st Dalai Lama. It grew suddenly important in 1642, when the 5th Dalai Lama declared his teacher, the monastery's abbot, to be a reincarnation of the Amithaba Buddha and the fourth reincarnation of the Panchen Lama, or 'Great Teacher'. Ever since, it has been the seat of the Panchen Lamas, who are second in authority to the Dalai Lama.

The 11th Panchen Lama

The death of the 10th Panchen Lama in 1989 brought Tibet's leaders and the Chinese government into conflict over succession. Like the seat of the Dalai Lama, the Panchen Lama's position is passed on through reincarnation. Traditionally, upon the death of either of these leaders, top monks scour the land hoping to identify the new incarnate. In 1995, after an extensive search, the Dalai Lama named a six-year-old boy, Gedhun Choeki Nyima, as the 11th Panchen Lama. The chosen boy and his family soon disappeared and have not been seen since. Keen to hand pick the next Dalai Lama's teacher, the Chinese authorities sanctioned a clandestine ceremony thatordained Gyancain Norbu as the "official Panchen Lama" and immediately whisked him off to Beijing.

Gyancain Norbu, the China-sanctioned 11th Panchen Lama

Majestic Tashilunpo Monastery with Drolma Ridge rising behind

VISITORS' CHECKLIST

Practical Information
172 miles (278 km) W of Lhasa. 120,000. Arrange travel to Shigatse through a travel agency in Lhasa. Tashilunpo: 2nd week of 5th lunar month.

Head up the main path to the back of the compound for the most impressive sights. The gold and silver *chorten* straight ahead holds the remains of the 4th Panchen Lama. Built in 1662, it was the only funeral *chorten* in the monastery to escape destruction during the Cultural Revolution. The larger, jewel-studded *chorten* just to the west holds the remains of the 10th Panchen Lama, who died in 1989; it was constructed in 1994 at a cost of 8 million US dollars.

Continue west for the Jampa Chapel, which holds the monastery's most impressive artifact, an 85-ft (26-m) golden image of, the Future Buddha, made in 1914. It took almost a thousand artisans four years to complete using more than 600 lbs (275 kg) of gold.

The Wheel of Law, an auspicious symbol

The complex of buildings on the east side is the Kelsang. It centers around a courtyard where monks can be observed praying, debating, and relaxing. The 15th-century Assembly Hall on the west side holds the imposing throne of the Panchen Lamas.

Those with energy left can follow the monastery *kora*, which takes about an hour. It runs clockwise around the outside of the walls before heading up to the Dzong. You'll pass colorful rock reliefs, some of Guru Rinpoche, and the huge white wall where a *thangka* of Buddha is exposed to the sun during the three-day long Tashilunpo Festival.

Summer Palace of the Panchen Lamas

Zhade Dong Lu. **Open** 9:30am–noon & 4–6pm daily.

South of Tashilunpo Monastery is the Panchen Lamas' summer palace, constructed in 1954. There are some excellent wall paintings inside the complex, and the gardens are a pleasant place to stroll.

Shigatse City Center

1. Gang Gyen Carpet Factory
2. Dzong
3. Tibetan Market
4. Tashilunpo Monastery
5. Summer Palace of the Panchen Lamas

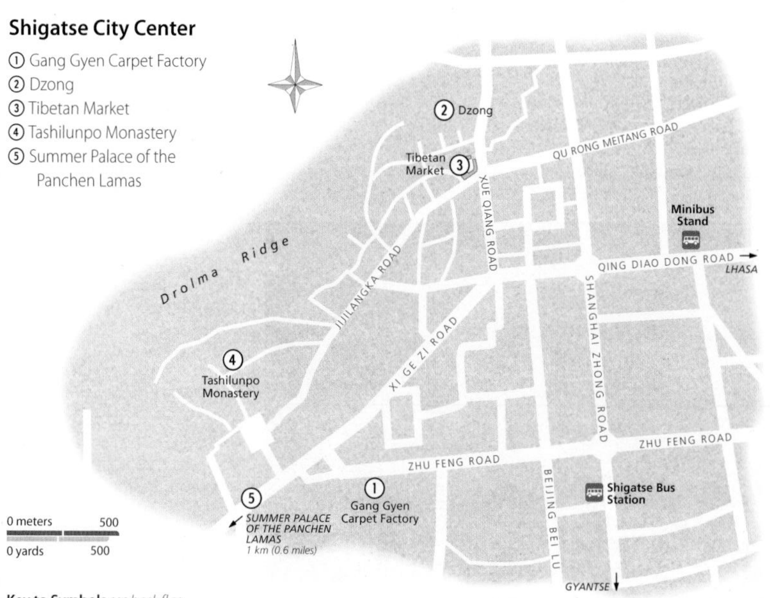

Key to Symbols *see back flap*

❼ Sakya Monastery
萨迦寺

250 miles (402 km) SW of Lhasa. Travel must be arranged by a travel agency in Lhasa. **Open** 9am–6pm Mon–Sat. travel permit required *(see p523)*.

The town of Sakya is dominated by the huge, fortress-like monastery that looms up from the gray plains. Sakya, or "Gray Soil" in Tibetan, was the capital of all Tibet in the 13th century, when monks of the Sakyapa order formed an extraordinary alliance with the Mongols. In 1247, the head of the Sakyapa order, Sakya Pandita, traveled to Mongolia and made a pact whereby the Mongols were the overlords while the Sakya monks ruled as their regents – the first time a lama was also head of state. His nephew, Phagpa, later became the spiritual guide to the conqueror of China, Kublai Khan. In 1354, Mongol power waned, and in-fighting among the religious sects led to a decline in Sakya's influence.

Originally, there were two monasteries on either side of the Trum River, but the northern one was destroyed during the Cultural Revolution *(see pp70–71)*. The mid-13th century **Southern Monastery**, built by Phagpa, is a typical Mongol structure, with thick walls and watchtowers. The entrance leads to a courtyard with an enormous prayer pole in the center. To the left is the **Puntsok Palace**, the traditional home of one of the two head lamas, who now lives overseas. Apart from the statue-filled chapel, its rooms are mainly empty. Moving clockwise, the next chapel, the **Purkhang**, holds images of Jowo Sakyamuni and Jampelyang among others, while wall murals depict Tantric deities. The **Main Assembly Hall** has 40 huge wooden pillars, one of which was said to have been gifted by Kublai Khan, while another is said to have come from India on the back of a tiger. The elaborately decorated hall has rich brocades, statues, and butter lamps and holds thousands of religious texts *(sutras)*. The fine central Buddha image enshrines the remains of Phagpa. The chapel to the north has 11 silver *chortens* containing the remains of previous Sakya lamas. Sakya houses are traditionally painted gray with red and white vertical stripes; the colors are supposed to symbolize the *bodhisattvas* Chana Dorje, Jampelyang, and Chenresig respectively.

Detail from wall painting at Sakya Monastery

Houses in Sakya town, painted gray with red and white stripes

❽ Everest Base Camp
珠峰大本营

Rongphu: 336 miles (610 km) SW of Lhasa. 4WD from Lhasa, 2 days; must be arranged through a travel agency in Lhasa. Travel permit required *(see p523)*.

Despite the spine-jarring, 4-hour trip off the Friendship Highway – which connects Lhasa to the Nepal border at Zhangmu – the craggy lunar landscape en route to Everest is enchanting. Rongphu is a good place for a stop and at 16,500 ft (4,980 m) is the highest monastery in the world. Although it has some good murals, the interior is not as riveting as its stunning location in front of Everest's forbidding north face in the Rongphu Valley. The monastery was founded in 1902 on a site that had been used by nuns as a meditation retreat for centuries, and is now home to some 30 monks.

Everest Base Camp lies 5 miles (8 km) to the south. The trip across the glacial plain takes about 15 minutes by vehicle or 2 hours on foot. Private vehicles must stop 2½ miles (4 km) from the base camp at a jumble of tents and makeshift teahouses, with visitors continuing on a bus or on foot. Whichever way, the views of Mount Everest, the world's highest mountain at a staggering 29,029 ft (8,848 m), are absolutely unforgettable.

The entire Rongphu and Everest area has been designated a nature reserve that covers 13,100 sq miles (34,000 sq km), and borders three national parks in Nepal. There is a spectacular viewpoint at the Pangla Pass, from which you can see Everest (known as Chomolungma in Tibetan), Cho Oyo, Lhotse, Makalu, and Gyachung. Most people try to arrive at this pass either to see the sun rise or set over the Himalayas.

For hotels and restaurants in this region see p563 and p585

Everest Base Camp, with magnificent views of the world's highest mountain

The rarefied air at this altitude (17,000 ft/5,150 m) makes any strenuous activity impossible, however, so unless visitors are properly acclimatized, it is best to go back to the Friendship Highway and carry on to the town of Shegar for the night.

9 The Nepal Border
尼泊尔边境

Zhangmu: 466 miles (750 km) SW of Lhasa; Gyirong: 510 miles (820 km) SW of Lhasa. Taxi or 4WD from Lhasa, 2 days (direct), or 5–6 days (via Gyantse, Shigatse and Everest Base Camp). All travel must be arranged through a travel agency in Lhasa. Travel permit for all places (between Shigatse and border) required *(see p523)*.

The Friendship Highway connecting Lhasa to the Nepal border has long been an important link for trade and tourism. However, a devastating earthquake in 2015 destroyed the border bridge and the facilities. It is expected to take many years before the crossing is fully functional again. In the interim, a second crossing at Gyirong, further west, has been upgraded, and opened to tourists. However, monsoon landslides have caused setbacks here, too, and the stuation remains uncertain. Be sure to contact a tour operator in Tibet well in advance of any overland journey, and be prepared to make alternative arrangements. There are regular flights between Lhasa and Kathmandu.

When the border is open, the route heads southwest from Shigatse to **Tingri**. This is a traditional Tibetan town with good views of the Cho Oyu. After climbing for 56 miles (90 km) the road begins a steep, winding descent through densely wooded mountains. At Xiamude, the road to the original crossing at Zhangmu heads south, while that to Gyirong continues west, skirting the vast **Paiku Lake** and passing the local administrative hub of Zongga before bearing south to the frontier. If the border is open, single-entry Nepal visas are usually available on arrival, with the fee payable in US dollars.

The Friendship Highway

The 466-mile (750-km) route between Lhasa and the Nepal border, known as the Friendship Highway, is probably the most popular journey for visitors to Tibet and includes some important sight-seeing detours along the way. When the border crossing is open, many agencies in Lhasa and in Kathmandu in Nepal can arrange the trip, sort out the necessary permits, and provide an appropriate four-wheel drive vehicle, a driver, and guide. Depending on the itinerary, which usually includes the towns of Shigatse and Gyantse, the trip can take up to a week. Visitors must ensure that the contract specifies exactly what they want and what they are paying for.

The Friendship Highway, winding across the plateau to Nepal

TRAVELERS' NEEDS

WHERE TO STAY

An abundance of accommodation options are available in China for most of the year. Four- and five-star hotels, increasingly run by either major international chains or expanding Chinese hotel companies, are plentiful in major cities and tourist destinations. In other cities and towns, there are many mid-range hotels and budget options to choose from. Ideally, rooms should be booked in advance, but if you have not done so, do not panic, unless you are traveling during one of the high seasons – the first week of May and October, and Chinese New Year (Spring Festival). Although you may want to book some of your stay (the first few nights, for example, to ease your arrival), it is perfectly feasible to turn up at your hotel of choice, bargain cheerfully, and book yourself a room at a sizable discount.

Hotel Chains

Visitors in search of international standards of comfort and service should stick either to five-star hotels managed by familiar Western chains or to the luxury Asian brands. **Starwood** hotels (such as Sheraton, W, and Westin) are well represented in China. Other international chains – such as **Accor**, **Hilton**, **Hyatt**, **Kempinski**, **Marriott, Ritz-Carlton**, and **Shangri-La** – all have hotels in the major cities; check their websites for details.

Chinese-run hotels do their best to emulate Western operations. The published rack rates of Chinese four- and five-star hotels are indeed comparable, but the level of service does not match their Western counterparts just yet. Standards are fast improving, however, and there is a willingness to please, especially away from the main tourist areas.

The Chinese star system of grading hotels is meaningless. Although authorities have devised a checklist of facilities that hotels must provide within each grade, there is no proper system of monitoring the standard of these services. Therefore, no matter how poorly these facilities may be maintained, no star is ever lost once it is given. Rather than be involved in this system, some international hotels choose to go starless. These establishments can be far superior to Chinese-run properties. As a general rule for Chinese-run hotels, the newer the hotel, the better the facilities.

Visit www.ctrip.com and www.elong.com to find the best deals, check out the location and prices of hotels, and make online bookings.

Budget Hotels & Other Types of Accommodations

Budget travelers will find a choice of inexpensive options all across the mainland and in Hong Kong. Away from the larger cities, dormitory beds for around ¥40 are easily available. Youth hostels with spotless facilities and beds costing about ¥50 are beginning to open up in some metropolises. Many universities will also rent out vacant rooms.

Palatial lobby of Shangri-La Hotel in Suzhou *(see p560)*

Spacious and comfortable suite at Amanfayun in Hangzhou *(see p560)*

At the upper end of the budget spectrum, the **Motel 168** and **Jinjiang Inn** chains offer excellent rooms with free Internet, private bathroom, and TV at affordable rates. **Home Inns** and **Green Tree Inns** are good budget brands with free Internet. Rooms at all these chains can be booked online.

Camping is not an option in China. Pitching a tent, except in the most far-flung places, is certain to attract attention, and you are likely to get a visit from the police. Staying in a *ger*, the round homes of the nomadic Mongols and Kazakhs, can be arranged in Inner Mongolia and Xinjiang. However, these overnight camps are targeted at tourists, so it may not be an authentic experience. Some monasteries and lamaseries have pilgrims' inns where you are welcome to stay for a minimal fee, but conditions can be very austere. On holy mountains, such as Emei Shan, you will find many temples that offer basic but atmospheric accommodations for travelers.

◀ A selection of ornate and colorful traditional prayer wheels

Harbor views from Upper House in Hong Kong *(see p561)*

Choosing a Hotel

The newest hotels are usually the best, as most owners seem to resist carrying out repairs unless they are absolutely necessary. New hotels are constantly springing up in various parts of the country in the hope of benefiting from the growth in domestic tourism. Some are one-off operations started by private businesses, but most belong to Chinese chains building pan-China hotel portfolios. Hotels run by the police, banks, tobacco companies, post offices, and other businesses are aspiring to compete with long-standing establishments run by local governments. Any hotel with a decent website or the word "business" in the title is likely to be relatively new and offer good services.

Booking a Hotel

In China, the real price of a hotel room is what the customer is willing to pay. Locals always ask for a discount, and you should too. The days of official surcharges for non-Chinese customers are long gone. Although many hotels still quote higher prices to foreign visitors, they are amenable to hard bargaining and will bring their rates down drastically, especially if the room in question would otherwise go empty. Discounts of 10 to 20 percent are standard, 30 to 40 percent very common, and 50 percent not unusual. Try for larger discounts, especially in locations with seasonal demand.

Booking online in advance via sites such as **ctrip.com**, **elong.com**, or **hostelworld.com** is another good way to obtain a bargain. This is also true of most foreign-run hotels.

The introduction of double beds of various sizes in Chinese-run hotels (rather than the standard twin single beds) has led to some confusion. Older hotels and a few newer ones do indeed have regular "single rooms," with a single bed in a relatively small space for a cheaper price. However, rooms described as "single" usually refer to those with a double bed, and can be occupied by two people, although they usually cost slightly less than twin-bed rooms of the same size.

The display of certain credit card symbols at hotels does not guarantee that the international versions of these cards will be accepted. It is therefore important to confirm that your card will be accepted before checking in. Most of the upper-tier hotels do take credit cards; in smaller establishments, be prepared to pay in *renminbi.*

Costs

The prices quoted by major international hotels do not include service charges or local bed taxes, although the latter are rarely levied. Many Chinese-run upper-end hotels have begun to levy service charges of between 5 and 15 percent. Foreign visitors should check their bills carefully before paying. Note that minibar contents are as overpriced in China as anywhere else. Costs for phone calls from even modest hotels are usually computer-monitored, and a service charge will be added on top of the actual cost of the call. Most Chinese-run and many foreign-owned hotels in China offer free Wi-Fi. Check before booking, and if the hotel you choose charges for Internet use, pick somewhere down the street that doesn't.

Traditionally designed courtyard at The Linden Centre in Dali *(see p562)*

Seasonal Demand

While rooms are readily available in China for most of the year, the busiest travel periods are during the week-long national holidays, principally around the Chinese New Year (January or February), May 1 (Labor Day), and October 1 (National Day). Unlike the West, very few people in China have discretionary holidays, so almost everyone in the country seems to be traveling at the same time. This is particularly true of the Chinese New Year (also known as the Spring Festival), when cheaper accommodation can be difficult to find. Transport costs also shoot up. Train tickets, which have fixed prices, sell rapidly when they go on sale 30 days in advance.

Spring and fall, with their milder temperatures and lower humidity, are more popular seasons for traveling than summer or winter, which are both extreme. In summer, some of the cooler destinations within reasonable reach of large cities – such as the island of Putuo Shan, served by short flights and ferries from Shanghai – can be very crowded and expensive during weekends, but very cheap during the week. Other events that affect transport costs and room availability are the festivals of ethnic minorities, particularly in the southwest, and trade events such as the biannual fair in Guangzhou.

Richly furnished lobby at the Cachet Boutique hotel in Shanghai *(see p559)*

General Observations & Precautions

Check-out time is usually noon, but visitors can pay half the nightly rate to keep the room until 6pm. A polite request may get you a free extension of an hour or two. Chinese regulations require all non-residents to be out of hotel rooms by 11pm, but this is widely ignored. Although foreign-exchange facilities are usually open seven days a week at most of the better hotels, these facilities can be used only by registered guests.

Many hotels, including some establishments with foreign management, advertise facilities such as nightclubs, hair and beauty salons, and karaoke bars, but these are often fronts for prostitution. Be wary of unexpected telephone calls to your room offering *anmo*, or massage. It is best to disconnect your phone if you wish to avoid being solicited.

Though it is simpler to arrange transport services through your hotel, be aware that this might cost more than it would if you found a taxi on your own. It can be better to simply walk onto the street and flag down a passing vehicle, though taxis hovering near the doors of hotels in popular tourist destinations should be approached with caution.

When surveying hotels, remember that the pictures you see on brochures and websites usually date to the time of opening, and are unlikely to represent the current condition of the rooms. In addition, do not be swayed by the promise of fitness centers, swimming pools, saunas, or Jacuzzis, especially in Chinese-run hotels in remote areas, as the presence of these in brochures does not indicate that they are still working or fit for use. Most importantly, the rates mentioned are not fixed.

The imposing facade of Shangri-La Hotel in Xian *(see p559)*

Facilities for Children & the Disabled

Children are welcome everywhere in China, although special facilities for them in hotels are rare. Most hotels allow children under 12 years to stay with their parents free of charge. Most hotels will also add an extra bed for an older child for a nominal (and usually negotiable) fee. Groups of four, including two children over 12, can sometimes share a room, though parents may be required to pay for two rooms. However, many older,

Chinese-run hotels have three- and four-bed rooms that are ideal for families.

In general, China is not an easy destination for the disabled. Only the newest and best international hotels make any serious effort to provide wheelchair access or fully adapted rooms. Most places have standard suites with inconveniently placed light switches, although some have wider bathroom doors to allow wheelchairs. However, most hotels have elevators, so booking a ground-floor room is not necessary.

Tipping

As tipping is not very common in China, hotel staff don't usually expect to be tipped. The international hotels will be charging you a 5 to 15 percent service charge on top of your bill in any case. Some Chinese hotels have started to add these charges as well.

Recommended Hotels

The hotels on pages 558–63 cover a huge variety of accommodation options from simple hostels and budget hotels to historic establishments and luxury retreats. They are listed by price within each area. Luxury hotels number among the most upscale options in town, with high standards of rooms and service par for the course.

China's boutique hotel industry is booming of late, and this category can include everything from slick and trendy operations in a city, to rural homestays with just a few rooms. There are many historic options for visitors to choose from, from Art Deco gems in Shanghai to one of China's first hotels to cater to foreigners in Harbin. Those who enjoy the flexibility of a self-catered stay should look for properties in the apartment category. China has many budget options where rooms are neat and clean and there are also numerous hostels where guests can stay in communal dormitories. Hotels that fall under the Business category feature amenities such as business centers and meeting rooms with audio and visual technology.

Finally, hotels featured as DK Choice are special establishments that are highly recommended for an exceptional quality, be it a great spa, beautifully designed rooms, or an ecologically sustainable outlook.

Classy interiors at the luxurious Waldorf Astoria Shanghai on the Bund hotel in Shanghai *(see p560)*

DIRECTORY

Hotel Chains

Accor
Tel 844 382 2267 (US).
Tel 0871 663 0624 (UK).
W accorhotels.com

Hilton
Tel 400 820 0500 (China).
Tel 1-800 445 8667 (US).
Tel 08705 909 090 (UK).
W hilton.com

Hyatt
Tel 1-800 233 1234 (US).
Tel 0845 888 1234 (UK).
W hyatt.com

Kempinski
Tel 400 120 9262 (China).
Tel 1-800 426 3135 (US).
Tel 00800 4263 1355 (UK).
W kempinski.com

Marriott
Tel 400 830 0251 (China).
Tel 800 962 509 (HK).
Tel 1-888 236 2427 (US).
Tel 00800 1927 1927 (UK).
W marriott.com

Ritz-Carlton
Tel 400 830 0253 (China).
Tel 1-800 542 8680 (US).
Tel 0800 234 000 (UK).
W ritzcarlton.com

Shangri-La
Tel 400 120 5900 (China).
Tel 1-866 565 5050 (US).
Tel 0800 028 3337 (UK).
W shangri-la.com

Starwood (Sheraton, W, Westin)
Tel 400 890 3588 (China).
Tel 3051 2777 (Hong Kong).
Tel 1-888 625 4988 (US).
Tel 020 3564 6335 (UK).
W starwood.com

Budget Hotels

Green Tree Inns
W 998.com

Home Inns and Motel 168
Tel 400 820 3333.
W homeinns.com

Jinjiang Inn
Tel 400 820 9999.
W jinjianginns.com

Booking a Hotel

Useful websites:
W ctrip.com
W elong.com
W hostelworld.com

Where to Stay

Beijing

Downtown Backpackers ¥
Hostel **Map** 2 D3
85 Nanluoguxiang, Dongcheng district
Tel *(010) 8400 2429*
W backpackingchina.com
Cheerful place close to the city's most funky *hutong* (alleyway). Great for visitors on a tight budget.

YoYo Hotel ¥
Budget
10F Middle Section of Sanlitun, Chaoyang district
Tel *(010) 6417 3388*
W yoyohotel.cn
Located in one of the city's popular nightspots, this boutique hotel offers stylish, good-value rooms.

Hotel de Cour SL ¥¥
Boutique **Map** 2 E5
70 Yanyue Hutong, Dongcheng district
Tel *(010) 6523 9598*
W hotelcotecourbj.com
Elegant rooms combine modern amenities with antique surrounds.

Red Wall Garden ¥¥
Boutique **Map** 2 E4
41 Shijia Hutong, Dongcheng district
Tel *(010) 5219 0221*
W redwallgardenhotel.com
This traditional hotel in a historic *hutong* area has modern facilities, great restaurants, and a tea room.

The Aman at the Summer Palace ¥¥¥
Luxury
1 Gongmenqian St, Summer Palace, Haidian district
Tel *(010) 5987 9999*
W amanresorts.com
Stay in century-old pavilions at this retreat next to the Summer Palace.

Brickyard Retreat ¥¥¥
Boutique
12 Mutianyu Village, Huairou district
Tel *(010) 6162 6506*
W theschoolhouseatmutianyu.com
Stay at the eco-resort or hire a well-appointed village home with amazing views of the Great Wall.

China World Summit Wing ¥¥¥
Luxury **Map** 4 F1
1 Jianguomenwai Ave, Chaoyang district
Tel *(010) 6505 2299*
W shangri-la.com
Up in the China World Trade Center, rooms at this hotel have luxurious interiors, great views, and a built-in air-filtration system.

DK Choice

Duge Courtyard Boutique Hotel ¥¥¥
Luxury **Map** 2 D3
26 Qianyuanensi Hutong, Nanluoguxiang, Dongcheng district
Tel *(010) 6445 7463*
W dugehotel.com
This hideaway was part-created by jeweler and interior designer Jehanne de Biolley. Each of the seven rooms is unique, and the burnished-gold Imperial Suite will make guests feel like royalty.

Hotel Eclat ¥¥¥
Luxury
9 Dongdaqiao Lu, Chaoyang district
Tel *(010) 8561 2888*
W eclathotels.com/beijing
This slightly offbeat luxury hotel boasts a superb art collection.

The Opposite House ¥¥¥
Boutique
1 Taikoo Li Sanlitun Bei Lu, Chaoyang district
Tel *(010) 6417 6688*
W theoppositehouse.com
Featuring an impressive green-glass exterior, this is an arty hotel, club, and restaurant.

Park Hyatt ¥¥¥
Luxury
2 Jianguomenwai St, Chaoyang district
Tel *(010) 8567 1234*
W beijing.park.hyatt.com
Rooms at this 63-story hotel boast marble baths and butler service.

The Peninsula Beijing ¥¥¥
Luxury **Map** 2 E5
8 Goldfish Lane, Wangfujing
Tel *(010) 8516 2888*
W beijing.peninsula.com
Beijing's grand dame of style and service houses a highly rated spa.

Price Guide
Prices are based on one night's stay in high season for a standard double room, inclusive of service charges and taxes.

¥	under ¥400
¥¥	¥400 to ¥1,000
¥¥¥	over ¥1,000

Hebei, Tianjin & Shanxi

BEIDAIHE: Beihuayuan Hotel ¥¥
Rooms with a view
316 Lianfeng Lu
Tel *(0335) 4680 555*
A large hotel with great ocean views. There are few English-speakers here, so be prepared to use a phrase book.

CHENGDE: Mountain Villa Hotel ¥¥
Budget
11 Lizhengmen
Tel *(0314) 209 5511*
Clean, basic rooms in a well-known hotel at a great location, opposite the main entrance to the Mountain Resort.

DATONG: Garden Hotel ¥
Business
59 Danan St
Tel *(0352) 5865 888*
W datonghotels.com
Well located and geared for foreigners, this hotel wins plaudits for service. It features a restaurant serving Brazilian as well as Chinese food.

TAIYUAN: Chateau Star River Taiyuan ¥¥
Luxury
2 Xinghe West Rd
Tel *(0351) 7698 866*
W chateaustarriver.com
Beautiful hotel with a pool. Non-Chinese speakers may struggle to make themselves understood.

Opulent suite at the China World Summit Wing in Beijing

TIANJIN: The Astor Hotel Tianjin ¥¥
Historic
33 Taier Zhuang Rd
Tel *(022) 5852 6888*
W starwoodhotels.com
This restored 1863 hotel evokes a bygone era. Ask for a room in the old wing for a taste of antiquity.

TIANJIN: St Regis Tianjin ¥¥
Luxury
158 Zhangzizhong Rd
Tel *(022) 5830 9999*
W starwoodhotels.com
Along the picturesque Hai River, this hotel offers flawless service.

TIANJIN: Tangla Hotel Tianjin ¥¥
Luxury
219 Nanjing Rd
Tel *(022) 2321 5888*
W tanglahotels.com
The spacious, well-furnished rooms at the Tangla come with spectacular city views.

Shandong & Henan

JI'NAN: Sofitel Silver Plaza ¥¥
Luxury
66 Luoyuan Dajie
Tel *(0531) 8606 8888*
W sofitel.com
This modern hotel incorporates European elements in its decor.

LUOYANG: Aviation Hotel ¥¥
Business
8 Tiyuchang Lu
Tel *(0379) 6338 9777*
Staid, reliable accommodation with English-speaking staff. Breakfast included.

QINGDAO: Huiquan Dynasty Hotel ¥¥
Rooms with a view
9 Nanhai Lu
Tel *(800) 860 0668*
W hqdynasty.com
Ask for a room with a sea view at this chic hotel opposite the beach.

QINGDAO: Shangri-La ¥¥
Luxury
9 Xiang Gang Zhong Lu
Tel *(0532) 8388 3838*
W shangri-la.com/qingdao/shangrila
Enjoy the full array of facilities at this deluxe hotel close to stores, restaurants, and the coast.

QINGDAO: Hyatt Regency ¥¥¥
Rooms with a view
88 Donghai East Lu
Tel *(0532) 8612 1234*
W qingdao.regency.hyatt.com
A smart hotel near Sho Lao Ren beach. Rooms on the upper floors have fine views.

Shaanxi

XI'AN: Xiangzimen International Youth Hostel ¥
Boutique
16 Xiangzimiao Jie
Tel *(029) 6286 7888*
W yhachina.com
Antique building with Chinese-style decor near the city wall's south gate and street food markets.

XI'AN: Citadines Central Xi'an ¥¥
Apartments
36 Zhubashi Lu
Tel *(029) 8576 1188*
W citadines.com
Spacious, clean apartments with kitchenettes and well-equipped rooms. Great location.

XI'AN: Shangri-La Hotel ¥¥
Luxury
38B Keji Lu
Tel *(029) 8875 8888*
W shangri-la.com/xian/shangrila
This beautiful hotel is within walking distance of the local attractions. Friendly staff, modern rooms, and a huge gym.

XI'AN: Sheraton Xi'an ¥¥
Business
262 Fenghao Dong Lu
Tel *(029) 8426 1888*
W sheratonhotels.com
Business-friendly hotel with large rooms featuring walk-in showers. Excellent breakfasts on offer.

XI'AN: Sofitel Xi'an on Renmin Square ¥¥
Luxury
319 Dong Xin St
Tel *(029) 8792 8888*
W sofitel.com/xian
Located within the city walls, this stylish property offers spotless rooms and excellent breakfasts.

Shanghai

Magnolia ¥¥
B&B
36 Yangqing Lu, Xuhui district
Tel *(138) 1794 0848*
W magnoliabnbshanghai.com
Five rooms spread over four floors in a house built in 1927, brimming with an authentic feel.

Cachet Boutique Shanghai ¥¥¥
Boutique
931 Nanjing Xi Lu, Jing'an district
Tel *(021) 6217 9000*
W cachethotels.com
The Philippe Starck-designed Cachet is in a vibrant location and has an in-house gallery showcasing contemporary Chinese art.

Designer rooms at Cachet Boutique Shanghai

Fairmont Peace Hotel ¥¥¥
Historic
20 Nanjing Dong Lu, Huangpu district
Tel *(021) 6318 6888*
W fairmont.com
Shanghai's most famous heritage hotel, this Art Deco gem is outstanding in terms of its decor and historical interest.

Hyatt on the Bund ¥¥¥
Luxury
199 Huangpu Lu, Hongkou district
Tel *(021) 6393 1234*
W shanghaithebund.hyatt.com
A modern hotel with all the latest amenities, a spa, and a restaurant.

DK Choice

Mansion Hotel ¥¥¥
Historic
82 Xinle Lu, Xuhui district
Tel *(021) 5403 9888*
W mansionhotelchina.com
Beautifully renovated 32-room hotel in the heart of the French Concession. Set in what was once an infamous gangster's home, the hotel is a special treat for those interested in Shanghai's racy history.

The Peninsula Hotel ¥¥¥
Luxury
32 Zhongshan Dong Yi Lu, near Beijing Dong Lu, Huangpu district
Tel *(021) 2327 2888*
W shanghai.peninsula.com
Experience superlative luxury at The Peninsula, from its elegant rooms to the open-air terrace.

The Puli Hotel and Spa ¥¥¥
Luxury
1 Changde Rd, Jing'an district
Tel *(021) 3203 9999*
W thepuli.com
A sleek, urban resort with spacious rooms, a knockout restaurant, and a fancy spa.

For more information on types of hotels *see p554*

Sophisticated interiors of the deluxe Amanfayun in Hangzhou

Les Suites Orient ¥¥¥
Boutique
1 Jinling Dong Jie
Tel *(021) 6320 0088*
W lessuitesorient.com
This smart hotel fuses Art Deco design with traditional Oriental style. Iconic views over the river.

Waldorf Astoria Shanghai on the Bund ¥¥¥
Luxury
2 Zhong Shan Dong Yi Lu
Tel *(021) 6322 9988*
W waldorfastoria3.hilton.com
With flawless service and vistas across the skyline, this is a multi-award-winning hotel.

Waterhouse at South Bund ¥¥¥
Historic
3 Maojiayuan Rd, Huangpu district
Tel *(021) 6080 2988*
W waterhouseshanghai.com
A 1930s warehouse with an original frontage houses a swanky boutique hotel with designer furniture.

The Westin Bund Center ¥¥¥
Luxury
88 Henan Zhong Lu, Huangpu district
Tel *(021) 6335 1888*
W westin.com/shanghai
Attractive hotel with a distinctive roof, Vegas-style light effects, and rooms with large windows – most with views.

Jiangsu & Anhui

NANJING: Orange Hotel ¥¥
Budget
224 Zhongyang Lu
Tel *400 819 0099*
W orangehotel.com.cn
Great-value accommodation in the city center, within walking distance of many attractions.

NANJING: InterContinental Nanjing ¥¥¥
Luxury
1 Zhongyang Lu
Tel *(025) 8353 8888*
W ihg.com
Towering over the city center, this hotel offers great views.

SUZHOU: Hotel Soul Suzhou ¥¥
Boutique
27–33 Qiaosikong Xiang
Tel *(0512) 6777 0777*
W hotelsoul.com.cn/en
Eye-catching trendy decor and a Suzhou-style rooftop garden.

DK Choice

SUZHOU: Scholars Boutique Hotel (Pingjiangfu) ¥¥
Boutique
60 Bai Ta Dong Lu
Tel *400 888 7388*
W pingjiangpalace.com
This charming retreat set in a traditional courtyard is surrounded by centuries-old Suzhou gardens. Rooms have smart, contemporary interiors.

SUZHOU: Shangri-La Hotel Suzhou ¥¥¥
Luxury
168 Tayuan Lu
Tel *(0512) 6808 0168*
W shangri-la.com/suzhou/shangrila
Impeccable service and huge, well-appointed rooms.

TUNXI: Huangshan Tunxi Lodge ¥¥
Boutique
15 & 17 Lao Jie
Tel *(0559) 258 0388*
W the-silk-road.com
Book online for lower rates at this hotel with traditional rooms.

Zhejiang & Jiangxi

HANGZHOU: West Lake Youth Hostel ¥
Hostel
62–3 Nan Shan Lu
Tel *(0571) 8702 7027*
W westlake-youth-hostel.hangzhouhotel.org
Bright and spacious dorms and rooms on the lake, near Leifeng Pagoda. Book well ahead.

HANGZHOU: Xihu State Guesthouse ¥¥
Boutique
18 Yang Gong Causeway
Tel *(0571) 8797 9889*
W xihustateguest.hotel.com.tw/eng
A guesthouse with efficient staff, stunning grounds, and lake views.

DK Choice

HANGZHOU: Amanfayun ¥¥¥
Luxury
22 Fayun Jie, Xi Hu Jie
Tel *(0571) 8732 9999*
W amanresorts.com
Amanfayun is a quiet, ultra-expensive resort for the rich and famous, hidden in a picturesque valley amid the verdant natural beauty of the tea gardens.

NANCHANG: Grand Skylight International Hotel Nanchang ¥¥
Business
1 Ganjiangbei Dajie
Tel *(0791) 8206 6666*
W grandskylight-intl.com
A quiet hotel with helpful staff, business facilities, and good food.

WENZHOU: Shangri-La Wenzhou ¥¥
Luxury
1 Xiangyuan Lu
Tel *(0577) 8998 8888*
W shangri-la.com/wenzhou/shangrila
The city's best hotel, situated in a skyscraper and renowned for its excellent service and river views.

Hunan & Hubei

CHANGSHA: Dolton Hotel ¥¥
Business
159 Shaoshan Bei Lu
Tel *(0731) 8416 8888*
W doltonhotel.com
This hotel features a business center, plus an on-site health club.

DK Choice

CHANGSHA: Wyndham Grand Plaza Royale Furongguo Changsha ¥¥¥
Luxury
106 Furong Zhong Lu
Tel *(0731) 8868 8888*
W wyndham.com
Though a little way out of town, this lavish hotel lives up to its five-star rating. The lobby is truly majestic and the rooms well appointed. Some guests say the breakfast buffet is the best in China.

WUHAN: Bingo International Youth Hostel ¥
Budget
1 Guishan Bei Lu
Tel *(027) 8477 0648*
W wuhanbingohostel.com
Hip hostel with clean, modern rooms and dorms, plus cats.

Key to Price Guide *see p558*

WUHAN: Jinjiang Inn Wuhan ¥
Budget
Jiangtan Pedestrian St, 2 Dongting Lu
Tel *(027) 8277 6600*
W jinjiang.com
Excellent-value hotel in a superb location. Helpful staff, too.

WUHAN: Marco Polo Hotel Wuhan ¥¥
Business
159 Yanjiang Dajie
Tel *(027) 8277 8888*
W marcopolohotels.com
This riverfront property with large, airy rooms is a good choice for corporate travelers.

Fujian

FUZHOU: Best Western Fuzhou Fortune Hotel ¥¥
Business
220 Hualin Lu
Tel *(0591) 8819 9999*
W bestwestern.com
A well-appointed hotel offering spacious rooms with free Wi-Fi. Complimentary breakfast.

FUZHOU: Howard Johnson Riverfront Plaza Fuzhou ¥¥
Business
6 Jiangbin Dong Dajie
Tel *(0591) 8862 9999*
W plazariverfrontfuzhou.hojochina.com
Business-oriented hotel with large, well-maintained rooms. Facilities include pool, spa, and gym.

FUZHOU: Shangri-La Hotel ¥¥
Luxury
9 Xinquan Nan Lu
Tel *(0591) 8798 8888*
W shangri-la.com/fuzhou/shangrila
A comfortable hotel with an old-fashioned feel and one of the best Korean restaurants in town.

XIAMEN: Remy's Garden Hotel ¥
Boutique
65 Kangtai Lu, Gulangyu Island
Tel *(0592) 219 6957*
Unusual, snug place offering one- and two-bedroom apartments, some with terraces, on Gulangyu Island. Book in advance.

XIAMEN: Xiamen International Youth Hostel ¥
Hostel
41 Nanhua Lu
Tel *(0592) 208 2345*
W yhachina.com
Friendly hostel with mixed dorms. Beds have curtains for privacy. Laundry and storage facilities.

DK Choice

XIAMEN: Seaview Resort ¥¥¥
Luxury
3999 Huandao Nan Lu
Tel *(0592) 502 3333*
W xmseaview.com
Top-class resort located just outside the city center. Rooms come with baths the size of hot tubs, and many have private pools or gardens. Dine at one of the lovely restaurants dotted around the stunning gardens. Attentive staff. Book ahead.

Guangdong & Hainan

GUANGZHOU: Journey House Youth Hostel ¥
Hostel
Apartment 3902, Lin He Community A5, 164 Linhe Zhong Lu
Tel *(020) 3880 4573*
Clean hostel with kitchen, air con, and Wi-Fi. Shared bathrooms.

GUANGZHOU: The Ritz-Carlton Guangzhou ¥¥¥
Luxury
3 Xing'an Lu, Pearl River New City
Tel *(020) 3813 6688*
W ritzcarlton.com
Plush opulence and impeccable service; home to one of the city's top restaurants, Lai Heen.

DK Choice

HAINAN: Banyan Tree Sanya ¥¥¥
Luxury
Luhuitou Bay, 6 Luling Lu
Tel *(0898) 8860 9988*
W banyantree.com
Forty-nine pool villas are scattered around a sculpted tropical lagoon on Hainan Island. The hotel offers very high standards of service.

SHENZHEN: Today's Hotel ¥
Budget
161 Dawei Cun, Dongchong
Tel *(0755) 8440 3000*
This hotel has spacious rooms with balconies and views and is just a short walk from the beach.

SHENZHEN: St Regis Shenzhen ¥¥¥
Luxury
5016 Shennan Dong Lu
Tel *(0755) 8308 8888*
W stregis.com
One of Shenzhen's tallest buildings. Rooms come with various extras, including a butler service.

Hong Kong & Macau

HONG KONG: Hullet House ¥¥¥
Historic **Map** 1 A3
2A Canton Rd, Tsim Sha Tsui, Kowloon
Tel *(0852) 3988 0000*
W hulletthouse.com
In a stunning colonial building, this hotel features suites with private balconies.

HONG KONG: J Plus Boutique Hotel ¥¥¥
Boutique
1–5 Irving St, Causeway Bay
Tel *(0852) 3196 9000*
W jplushongkong.com
Designed by Philippe Starck, with quirky rooms. Rates include breakfast and evening cocktails.

DK Choice

HONG KONG: Upper House ¥¥¥
Boutique **Map** 3 D4
Pacific Place, 88 Queensway
Tel *(0852) 2918 1838*
W upperhouse.com
A stylish haven from one of Asia's trendiest designers, Andre Fu. Enjoy fabulous city views from the luxurious apartment-like studios, which come with espresso machines and iPods.

HONG KONG: W Hong Kong ¥¥¥
Luxury **Map** 1 A3
1 Austin Rd West, Kowloon
Tel *(0852) 3717 2222*
W w-hongkong.com
The W boasts Hong Kong's highest rooftop pool. Stylish rooms with superb views.

MACAU: Pousada de Mong-Ha ¥¥
Boutique
Colina de Mong-Ha
Tel *(0853) 2851 5222*
W ift.edu.mo/pousada
Rooms are decorated in traditional Portuguese style at this quiet inn.

Fashionable studio at the Upper House in Hong Kong

For more information on types of hotels *see p554*

Sichuan & Chongqing

DK Choice

CHENGDU: The Loft Design Hostel ¥
Hostel
4 Xiaotong Alley, Zhongtongren Lu
Tel *(028) 8626 5770*
W dragontown.com.cn/loft
A stylish and quirky hostel in a converted factory, with both dorms and private rooms with en-suite bathrooms. The staff are helpful in assisting with travel arrangements and tours.

CHENGDU: BuddhaZen Hotel ¥¥
Boutique
B6–6, Wenshufang Jie
Tel *(028) 8692 9898*
W buddhazenhotel.com
Lovely hotel with well-appointed rooms. The in-house restaurant serves delicious local food.

CHONGQING: Beity Hot Spring Tourism Resort ¥¥
Luxury
Beidi Yiyuan, 288 Nongke Dadao
Tel *(023) 6571 8888*
W cqbeity.cn
Surrounded by mountains, villas at this popular resort are scattered around a lake. Rooms come with hot tubs and there also huge outdoor springs for guests to soak in.

CHONGQING: Somerset Jiefangbei Chongqing ¥¥
Apartments
Block B Hejing Building, 108 Minzu Lu
Tel *(023) 8677 6888*
W somerset.com
Serviced apartments with panoramic views of the city. There is a pool plus great facilities for kids.

Yunnan

DK Choice

DALI: The Linden Centre ¥¥
Boutique
5 Chengbei, Xizhou town
Tel *(0872) 245 2988*
W linden-centre.com
An eco-friendly hotel where guests can experience traditional village life in comfort. The 14 rooms are set around a scenic courtyard in a national heritage site. Rates include breakfast and local excursions.

KUNMING: Lost Garden Guest House ¥
Hostel
7 Yiqiutian, Huanggong Dong Jie, Cuihu Nan Lu
Tel *(0871) 6511 1127*
W lostgardenguesthouse.com
Spotless rooms and a small Western-style restaurant are to be found at this charming hostel.

KUNMING: Green Lake Hotel ¥¥
Luxury
6 Cuihu Nan Lu
Tel *(0871) 6515 8888*
W greenlakehotelkunming.com
Elegant public spaces and rooms beside Kunming's famous lake.

LIJIANG: No.188 Boutique Hotel ¥
Boutique
188 Bayi Lower Section, Qiyi Jie
Tel *(0888) 888 8177*
Pleasant rooms with traditional decor. Run by a friendly manager. Great location in the Old Town.

LIJIANG: Intercontinental Lijiang Ancient Town Resort ¥¥
Luxury
276 Xianghe Lu
Tel *(0888) 588 8888*
W ihg.com/intercontinental
Thoughtfully designed rooms with extras such as Wi-Fi and iPod docks. The lobby boasts stunning views of Jade Dragon Snow Mountain. Large breakfast buffet.

SHANGRI-LA: Banyan Tree Ringha ¥¥¥
Boutique
Hong Po Village, Jian Tang town, Shangrila county
Tel *(0887) 828 8822*
W banyantree.com
This peaceful rural retreat offers accommodations in luxuriously appointed Tibetan-style villas.

Guizhou & Guangxi

GUILIN: Lakeside Inn ¥
Guest House
1-1-2 Sha Lake Building, Shan Lake North Rd
Tel *(0773) 280 6806*
W guilin-hostel.com
Beautifully located by the lakeside, this tiny guesthouse offers excellent hospitality.

GUILIN: Aroma Tea House ¥¥
Guest House
9 Ronghu Nan Lu
Tel *(0773) 228 3265*
W aroma-tea-house.com
This friendly lakeside hotel offers a unique style of decor. It hosts an impressive collection of Chinese antiques and modern art.

GUILIN: Shangri-La Hotel Guilin ¥¥
Luxury
111 Huancheng Bei Er Lu
Tel *(0773) 269 8888*
W shangri-la.com/guilin/shangrila
The plushest hotel in Guilin offers a pool and rooms with river views. It operates tours, too.

NANNING: Nanning Marriott Hotel ¥¥
Luxury
131 Minzu Dadao
Tel *(0771) 536 6688*
W marriott.com
Guests enjoy comfortable rooms, professional service, and a spa.

YANGSHUO: Tea Cozy ¥¥
Boutique
212 Xiatang Village, Yulonghe Scenic Area
Tel *(0773) 881 6158*
W yangshuoteacozy.com
Traditional Chinese-style rooms with tastefully fitted wooden furnishings. Breathtaking views.

Liaoning, Jilin & Heilongjiang

DALIAN: Howard Johnson Parkland Hotel ¥¥¥
Business
95 Huizhan Lu
Tel *(0411) 8499 0000*
W hotelparklanddalian.hojochina.com
Rooms at this quiet hotel come with sea or mountain views.

HARBIN: Kazy International Hostel ¥
Hostel
27 Tongjiang Jie
Tel *(0451) 8765 4211*
W snowtour.cn
A popular hostel in a former church with both private rooms and dorms. Good central location.

Spacious room at The Linden Centre, in Dali, Yunnan

Key to Price Guide *see p558*

DK Choice

HARBIN: Modern Hotel ¥¥
Historic
89 Zhongyang Jie
Tel *(0451) 8488 4000*
W modern-hotel.hotelsharbin.com
Built in 1906 in the Old City, this is now a government-preserved historical site, but it is still possible to stay in the atmospheric old rooms.

SHENYANG: Shenyang Rich Gate Hotel ¥¥
Business
128 Harbin Lu
Tel *(024) 2259 8888*
W richgatehotel.com
Comfortable, well-maintained rooms, and gym facilities.

Inner Mongolia & Ningxia

HOHHOT: Anda Guesthouse ¥
Hostel
Qiaokao Xi Jie
Tel *(0471) 691 8039*
W andaguesthouse.com
This friendly, family-run hostel has dorms and doubles ranged around a small courtyard.

HOHHOT: Shangri-La Hotel Hohhot ¥¥¥
Luxury
5 Xilin Guole Nan Lu
Tel *(0471) 336 6888*
W shangri-la.com
Hohhot's first international deluxe hotel has a plethora of restaurants and leisure facilities.

XILINHOT: Yuanhe Jianguo Hotel ¥¥
Business
6 Nanjing Lu
Tel *(0479) 829 9299*
W yhjghotel.com
A high-end business hotel with comfortable, modern rooms and excellent buffet breakfasts.

YINCHUAN: Yuehai Hotel ¥¥
Luxury
1A Helanshan Lu
Tel *(0951) 569 6888*
Deluxe hotel with a gym, pool, and a garden with a pagoda.

YINCHUAN: Kempinski Hotel Yinchuan ¥¥¥
Luxury
160 Bei Jing Zhong Lu
Tel *(0951) 516 5888*
Yinchuan's most sophisticated accommodation, with an array of in-house restaurants.

Gansu & Qinghai

DUNHUANG: Dunhuang Hotel ¥
Budget
373 Mingshan Bei Lu
Tel *(0937) 885 2999*
Centrally located, this hotel has small but comfortable rooms and a good buffet breakfast.

DUNHUANG: Silk Road Dunhuang Hotel ¥¥
Luxury
Dunyuet Lu
Tel *(0937) 888 2088*
W the-silk-road.com
Offering views of the dunes, this resort has atmospheric rooms with traditional design touches.

LANZHOU: Legend Hotel ¥¥
Business
529 Tianshui Nan Lu
Tel *(0931) 853 2888*
W lanzhoulegendhotel.com
This high-rise hotel has English-speaking staff and comfy rooms.

XIAHE: Nirvana Hotel ¥
Guesthouse
247 Ya Ge Tang
Tel *(0941) 718 1702*
Dorms and doubles are offered in this welcoming guesthouse with authentic Tibetan decor.

Xinjiang

KASHGAR: Kashgar Old Town Youth Hostel ¥
Hostel
233 Wusitangboyi Lu
Tel *(0998) 282 3262*
W kashgaroldcity.hostel.com
In the old part of town, this basic but welcoming hostel has rooms set around a bright courtyard.

KASHGAR: Tianyuan International Hotel ¥
Business
8 Renmin Dong Lu
Tel *(0998) 280 1111*
A centrally located hotel with comfortable rooms. Free Wi-Fi.

DK Choice

TURPAN: Silk Road Lodges ¥¥
Boutique
Muna'er Lu, Muna'er village
Tel *(0995) 856 8333*
W silkroadlodges.com
Located in a traditional Uighur settlement, guests can experience local village life first hand while relaxing in comfortable surroundings. There are fine views overlooking the vineyards.

Restaurant at the Silk Road Dunhuang Hotel, Dunhuang

ÜRÜMQI: Jinjiang Inn ¥
Budget
93 Hongqi Lu
Tel *(0991) 281 5000*
In a central location, this excellent budget hotel has spotlessly clean rooms.

ÜRÜMQI: Bayinhe Hotel ¥¥
Boutique
71 Wenhua Lu
Tel *(0991) 221 9999*
This modern hotel has stylish rooms, some with city views.

Tibet

LHASA: Phuntsok Khasang International Youth Hostel ¥
Hostel
48 Duosenge Bei Lu
Tel *(0891) 692 7618*
W yhachina.com
This backpacker stalwart near the Potala Palace offers an array of dorms, singles, and doubles.

LHASA: Shambhala Palace ¥¥
Boutique
16 Taibeng Gang Wengdui Xingka Sangdong Yuan
Tel *(0891) 632 6695*
W shambhalaserai.com
Packed with Tibetan fabrics and handicrafts, this is an atmospheric guesthouse in the old town.

LHASA: St Regis Lhasa ¥¥
Luxury
22 Jiangsu Lu
Tel *(891) 680 8888*
W starwoodhotels.com
This hotel offers a blend of international luxury and Tibetan style.

SHIGATSE: Shigatse Hotel ¥¥
Business
12 Shanghai Zhong Lu
Tel *(0892) 880 0336*
A favorite with tour groups, this large hotel has clean rooms with touches of Tibetan decor.

For more information on types of hotels *see p554*

WHERE TO EAT & DRINK

Can any other nation rival China's obsession with food? Instead of "How are you?" Chinese people greet each other with *Ni chi fan le ma?* – "Have you eaten yet?" Once your travels begin, you may ask yourself a similar question – have you really eaten Chinese food before? For the Middle Kingdom serves up cuisine of such variety and delight that mealtimes there will soon dissolve the taste memories of the pale imitations of Chinese food from back home. As you travel around the country you will enjoy a culinary journey, too. From the wheat noodles, lamb kabobs, and Peking duck of the north, venture east to taste the braised crabs and abalone of Shanghai, west to try the fiery feasts of Sichuan, and south to "dot the heart" with a thousand different Cantonese *dim sum*.

The sleek elegance of Crystal Jade in Beijing *(see p572)*

A Divine Pleasure

"Food is a divine pleasure," runs a traditional saying. China's fascination with food stems from the ancient worship of gods and spirits, when emperors were carried to temples or sacred peaks to guarantee good harvests with sacrifices of meat and rice wine. Today, any event can prompt a feast where families bond, relationships grow, disputes are resolved, and business deals are concluded. For Chinese people, food is not just a social lubricant, but the cornerstone of their culture.

A Famine Cuisine

One of China's problems has been: how can such a large population (almost a fifth of the world's people) feed itself when less than 12 percent of its land is arable? The answer lies in centuries of innovation in the fields and in the kitchen. The Chinese have developed a "famine cuisine," cherishing wild plants like bamboo shoots, lotus roots, seaweed, fungi, and moss, and utilizing every part of domesticated or wild animals. Bustling markets, and even some mealtimes, are not for the squeamish, but the daring will learn how fish heads, pig's trotters, chicken intestine, duck webs, sea slugs, and bull's testicles can be prepared as delicacies. Imagine how many lives scorpions, fried and full of protein, could save in a famine?

The First Fast Food

Although boiling and steaming are popular, Chinese cuisine is best known for stir-frying. Meat and vegetables are cut into small pieces and fried briefly in hot oil, thus saving on fuel and equipment without sacrificing the taste. There is little saving in terms of work time, but labor is the one resource of which China has no shortage.

The Culinary Arts

According to records, China's earliest master of gastronomy, Yi Yin, cooked for the first Shang emperor way back in the 16th century BC. One cookbook from the 6th century AD still sets the standards for today's chefs: a recipe states that roasted suckling pig should "melt in the mouth like ice." Over the centuries, countless men of letters have sung the glories of food. Song-dynasty poet Su Dongpo penned a famous ode to pork, and even today Dongpo pork remains Hangzhou's most celebrated dish.

The ancient philosophy of *yin* and *yang* – the blending of contrasts and duality of nature – applies to culinary matters in China as much as to spiritual ones. Achieving the right harmony of *yin* (soft, cold, dark, and feminine) and *yang* (strong, hot, bright, and masculine) will ensure good health, not just a good meal. Cooling *yin* foods – for example, most vegetables, crab, tofu – must complement warming *yang* – meat, chilies. Hence, in menu planning, there should be meat dishes as well as vegetable, hot and cold, sweet and sour, plain and spicy. Even meat dishes rarely contain meat alone, while the basic ingredients of stir-frying –

Scorpion kebabs – cooking renders the sting ineffective

Steaming food on the street – simple, fast, and efficient

scallions and ginger – are *yin* and *yang*, as well. Additionally, a balanced diet should include appropriate proportions of both *fan* (grains) and *cai* (vegetables), and not too much meat.

You Are What You Eat

Nutritionists were attached to the Zhou court back in the 7th century BC, for the Chinese have long recognized the medicinal value of food. In the Chinese chef's repertoire there is a dish or an ingredient for every poorly organ or ailment. Some foods that are meant to boost your *qi*, such as ginseng and bird's nest soup, require a small leap of faith as to their efficacy; others, such as iron-rich duck blood, are more obvious. In some cases, as in other cultures, animal parts are believed to strengthen the human equivalent: try duck brain for increasing your intelligence, ox tongue for eloquence, and bull's testicles for greater sexual potency.

The Five Flavors

The Chinese are not really recipe-bound. Amid the drama of the flaming stir-fry, they seem to take a more flexible approach, finely judging the right quantity of each ingredient. Nevertheless, Chinese chefs are very particular about flavor, aroma, color, and texture. Each of these properties has been elevated to an art form with a special vocabulary and set of rules. If *xian* (an elusive, sweet but natural freshness) captures the soul of a food, *cui* (a crisp crunchiness like the skin of perfect Peking duck) is the goal of most Chinese cooking. Trained Chinese palates distinguish five different flavors – sweet, sour, bitter, pungent, salty – and only the right combinations work. Foods rich in flavor combine well with textured foods of little taste, such as sea cucumbers and shark's fin that absorb and heighten the foods cooked with them.

Rice and chopsticks

Symbolism in Food

In a culture obsessed with symbolism and eating, there are many foods that have earned special meaning and are consumed on certain occasions. Round mooncakes, dotted with moon-like duck-egg yolks, are a must for family reunions at the Mid-Autumn Festival. At the Spring Festival dinner, the whole family cooks *tangyuan*, round sweet dumplings made of glutinous rice flour, because *yuan* can also mean "reunion." Fish is particularly auspicious, because the character for fish (*yu*) sounds like the one for "abundance" and offers the hope of good fortune in the year ahead. *Jiaozi* (meat dumplings) are another New Year favorite, as their shape is said to resemble the symbol for prosperity. Birthdays are often celebrated with noodles, a symbol of longevity.

Recommended Restaurants

One thing guaranteed in China is that you will never go hungry, as even the smallest village will have at least a couple of basic restaurants, while major cities are overrun – in Shanghai, for example, there are more than 20,000 restaurants, from hole-in-the-wall noodle joints to some of the most cutting-edge and expensive establishments in the world. The listings on pages 572–85 feature as wide a selection of restaurants as possible, from inexpensive to upmarket. While focusing on Chinese cuisine such as traditional places serving noodles, hotpot, or stew, there is also a good choice of great cafés, pizza parlors, and restaurants serving international cuisine.

Establishments highlighted as DK Choice have been selected in recognition of a special feature – this could be exceptional cuisine, a fantastic atmosphere, excellent value, or a combination of these.

Cooking Chinese-style – balancing colors, tastes, and textures

Types of Restaurant

Whether you are looking to eat in the splendor of an imperial pavilion in Beijing, a chic Shanghai café, or a busy Sichuan teahouse, you will find a wide variety of restaurants in China. Freed from state control, entrepreneurs are constantly thinking up tempting new ways to indulge in the country's favorite pastime. You never have to walk far to find restaurants and when you do, do not let first appearances put you off – in contrast to the delicacy of the food, many gourmet restaurants boast simple decor and harsh lighting. Look instead for happy crowds of diners and a different concept of "atmosphere." In Chinese eyes, the more lively and noisy *(renao)* a restaurant is, the better.

Typical restaurant – busy and noisy with a utilitarian decor

Open All Hours

Early to bed, early to rise was the pattern of Chinese lives until the 1990s, leaving some foreign visitors caught out when planning mealtimes. While Chinese stomachs still demand food earlier than their Western counterparts, social and professional hours are diversifying. You can breakfast on the street by 6am, but many hotels will serve breakfast until 10am or later. Lunch is typically from 11:30am until 2:30pm, after which some restaurants shut until the evening shift starts around 5pm. In the evening, closing times can be very late, while some places never shut. Booking is rare except for the most popular and high-end establishments. Usually you can simply turn up; if the restaurant is full, you may have to wait until a table comes free or have a drink at the bar. Sometimes the owner will come to your rescue by setting up a makeshift table in the corner, or even out in the backyard.

Hotel Food

If you are tired and hungry, and staying at one of China's more expensive hotels, then room service can provide comfort with imitations of Western food. But try to make it downstairs, as most hotels offer a range of cuisines within the premises.

In the main cities, some of the best restaurants are located in hotels, and you can sample some excellent upscale Chinese cuisine. Contrary to opinion, hotel restaurants do not always serve overpriced, deliberately bland Chinese food to appease foreign palates. However, home to one of the world's top cuisines, China has a lot to offer. The more intrepid diner who makes a few forays outside the comfort of four-star hotel restaurants will be sure to reap handsome dividends.

Street Food

As China smartened up for the Beijing Olympics and the Shanghai Expo, street vendors were sometimes forced to play hide-and-seek with the authorities. Yet their portable stalls form a vital part of the everyday life of China, selling cheap and popular foods such as breakfasts of dough sticks *(youtiao)* and beancurd *(doujiang)*, or snacks like scallion pancakes *(jianbing)*, sweet potatoes *(fanshu)* roasted in old oil drums, deep-fried beancurd cubes *(zhadoufu)*, and local fruits.

A reliable way to locate delicious street food is to stroll through a night market *(yeshi)*, a culinary and visual feast where clouds of steam escape from bamboo steamers and the sky glows red from the flames of oil drum stoves. The sizzle of cooking and clamor of vendors shouting for business should stir your appetite, and if deep-fried scorpions or cicadas on skewers prove too exotic, be assured that plenty of other foods will take your fancy. If the food is hot and freshly cooked for you, hygiene problems are rare. The market off Wangfujing Dajie *(see p100)*, in Beijing, is the most famous, but track down night markets wherever you go, to enjoy the local delicacies and specialties.

Dunhuang night market – food stalls for shoppers buying spices, silks, and carpets

Stall-holder making some *xiaochi* or "little eats" in Dalian

Little Eats

Cheap and nourishing snacks such as those found at night markets are known collectively as *xiaochi*, or "little eats." Restaurants that specialize in them are called *xiaochidian*; they sell different types of noodles or dumplings, stuffed buns or pancakes. Open early for breakfast, they may serve simple stir-fried dishes too, and shut only when the last guest leaves. The setting is usually basic, but the food is hearty, tasty, and very reasonably priced. Every city has its own local varieties, but the ultimate "little eats" are the *dim sum* of Cantonese cooking *(see p288)*.

Fast Food

The popularity of fast food giants McDonald's, Pizza Hut, and KFC, now found in all cities, has spurred Chinese firms to compete. Yonghe King is an impressive Taiwanese chain serving up all-day breakfasts of soyabean milk, *congee* (a savory rice porridge), and spring onion pancakes, while 85°c is a rapidly expanding coffee, cake, and bread chain. If the street stalls are a little too basic, food courts in department stores or malls are worth exploring and are clean and usually air-conditioned.

Themed Restaurants

As urban tastes grow ever more sophisticated, restaurateurs race to catch up, opening restaurants with a special theme, cuisine, or setting, like a train carriage or mock prison. The character of these places is often nostalgic, such as the old Beijing style (Lao Beijing), where each guest is loudly greeted, and staff in pre-Revolution uniforms clatter the teacups in welcome on your table. The walls of Cultural Revolution restaurants are covered with bittersweet memorabilia of that era, while many Sichuan eateries have concentrated on rustic decor to increase the appeal.

The Other China

There is not only a wide spread of regional cuisines across Han China, but also a whole range of ethnic specialties offered by the many minority nationalities from the Korean border to the Tibetan plateau. The minorities' restaurants are an "exotic" attraction for Chinese as well as foreign tourists. In Dai restaurants, offering the Thai-like cuisine of southern Yunnan, guests are greeted with scented water, given a lucky charm, and later invited to join in the singing and dancing. In Uighur restaurants, serving food from the Muslim northwest, belly dancing is sometimes on show.

Pretty colored dumplings

Vegetarian Surprise

The Chinese understanding of a good life is inextricably associated with meat. They find it hard to understand why someone who could afford to eat meat would choose not to. Nevertheless, you will find a few vegetarian restaurants in big cities, often attached to Buddhist temples, serving excellent vegetarian dishes to worshipers and non-worshipers alike. Many of these have meaty names, and are made in exact imitation of their meat-filled namesakes. Ordinary restaurants can lay on good vegetarian meals too, as long as you can repeat: *"Wo chi su"* ("I eat vegetables") a few times and don't mind the odd bit of meat or chicken stock turning up in your bowl every now and then.

Foreign Food

Western restaurants, now found in all major cities, typically offer Indian, Thai, Italian, and French, or a fusion of international food. Some have justifiably earned wide acclaim, such as Maison Boulud in Beijing, and M on the Bund in Shanghai.

In smaller cities, Western restaurants are harder to find, although Italian cuisine is the most common – ravioli and spaghetti are easy concepts for the dumpling- and noodle-loving Chinese to appreciate. Other Asian cuisines – mainly Korean, Japanese, and Thai – are also well represented, and more readily accepted.

Uighur bread stall in the market at Linxia, Gansu

Food Customs and Etiquette

Confucius was renowned for his silence at meals. The good news, however, is that 2,500 years later, the Chinese are actually quite informal at mealtimes. In fact, a busy Chinese restaurant can be a deafening place as waiters crash plates about and diners shout orders at the waiters. It may seem daunting but just join in and expect praise for your chopstick skills – even if you struggle, your willingness to try will be appreciated.

Business dinner in a private room, still an enjoyable event

Earning Some Face

The Chinese do not expect visitors to be fully versed in proper banquet etiquette, but awareness of a few essentials can earn "face" both for yourself and your host, whatever the occasion. The other guests will appreciate that you have some respect for Chinese culture and traditions.

When attending, or hosting, a formal meal, note that the guest of honor is usually placed on the seat in the middle, facing the door. The host, traditionally positioned opposite the guest, now more often sits to his or her left.

If you come as a guest, be punctual and do not sit down until you are given your seat – seating arrangements can be very formal and based on rank.

Once seated, do not start on the food or drink before your host gives the signal. Some of the delicacies on offer may test your courage; be gracious and try everything – it is an insult if the food is untouched – but leave some food on the plates. Empty bowls imply that the host is too poor or mean to lay on a good spread.

The Art of Ordering

If you are someone's guest, you may be asked to order something, or state some sort of preference – if you do not do so, a ten-course banquet could soon appear. Feel free to name your favorite dish, or point at the object of your desire, often swimming in a fish tank at the entrance to the restaurant. Freshness is all important in Chinese cuisine.

English-language menus are becoming more common, and an increasing number of restaurants actively encourage visitors to get out of their chairs and choose ingredients from tanks, cages, and supermarket-type shelves. Your Chinese friends (and waiters and onlookers) will likely be delighted by any interest you show in the whole experience. In the end, when language or phrase book fail, point at whatever appeals on other tables, or even head into the kitchen to find what you need.

A meal might begin with cold starters such as pickled vegetables, ten-thousand-year old eggs, seasoned jellyfish, or cold roasted meats.

When selecting main courses, remember to aim for harmony and balance – an equilibrium of *yin* and *yang*. For example, with sweet and sour pork, you might order a spicy chicken dish. Different cooking methods are also important: a steamed fish or roast pork add variety to a series of stir-fried foods. You shouldn't need to ask for a side order of vegetables as they are usually part of the dishes – unless you want something specific.

The last dish is usually soup, or *tang*. Then comes *fan*, a grain staple such as rice, noodles, or bread *(mantou)*, without which a Chinese diner may feel they have not eaten. At informal meals you can have rice at the start of the meal, but not at a banquet, or your host will assume his dishes are inadequate.

Desserts are not a Chinese tradition, but fresh fruit is almost always served in Chinese restaurants, especially at banquets, and succulent fruit is available nationwide.

Filling up on rice at an informal meal in a market, Dali

Invited to Dinner

A formal meal often takes place in a private room and usually begins with a toast. The host serves his guest with the choicest morsels, and then everyone is permitted to help themselves. Serving chopsticks or spoons may be provided; if not, simply use your own pair.

Confucius said that it was uncivilized to have knives on the table, but if you are really struggling, most restaurants will readily provide you with knives and forks.

The host almost always orders more dishes than necessary. While it is polite to try everything, don't feel it is necessary to finish it all.

How to Hold Chopsticks

1) Place the first chopstick in the crook of your thumb and forefinger. Support it with the little and ring fingers, and keep it there with the base of the thumb.
2) Hold the second chopstick like a pencil, between middle and index fingers, anchored by the pad of your thumb.
3) When picking up food, keep the lower stick stationary and the tips even. As the index finger moves up and down, only the upper stick should move, using the thumb as an axis.

Third finger acting as a rest for the lower stick

Thumb and first finger controlling the top stick

Good Neighbors

It is courteous to keep your neighbors' tea cups filled. To thank an attentive neighbor, tap your first two fingers together on the table. This tradition dates back to the Qing Emperor Qianlong, who liked to tour the country in disguise. Once, at a teahouse, he took his turn to pour the tea. His companions, who should have been pressing their foreheads to the floor, maintained his disguise by tapping their fingers in a mini-kowtow. If you don't want your cup refilled, don't empty it.

Crabs – difficult to eat with chopsticks

Dos and Don'ts

The Chinese are fairly relaxed about table manners. Slurping shows appreciation, enables better appreciation of flavor, and sucks in air to prevent burning the mouth. Holding your bowl up to your mouth, to shovel rice in, is another practical solution. You may happily reach across your neighbors, but do not spear food with your chopsticks, and do not stand them upright in a bowl of rice either, as it looks like incense sticks offered to the dead. If you have finished with the chopsticks lay them flat on the table or on a rest. You shouldn't suck greasy fingers, or use them to pick bones out of your mouth – spit bones or shell onto the table, into the saucer that was under your bowl, or into a napkin. Toothpicks are ubiquitous, but do cover the action with your free hand. And don't be shy about shouting for attention. Eating alone is very strange to the Chinese way of thinking. Eating in a group – sharing the dishes and the experience – greatly increases the enjoyment.

The End of the Meal

A platter of fresh fruit and steaming hot towels signal the end of the meal. Just as you should await the start of a meal, do not stand up before your host, who will rise and indicate that the dinner has ended and ask if you've had enough. The answer is "yes," or *bao le*.

An old lady demonstrating the perfect noodle technique

The person who invited you usually shoulders the full weight of the bill, so accept graciously. Offering to pay is fine, even polite; insisting too hard suggests that you doubt the host's ability to pay.

The capitalist habit of tipping was wiped out after Mao's Communist Party took over. Politically acceptable today, it is still rare, as is "going Dutch."

Prices are fixed and written down in most restaurants, and on bills, although there is the occasional story of restaurants overcharging foreigners.

There is no service charge except in the more upmarket and expensive restaurants, which are also the only places likely to accept international credit cards.

The Business of Banquets

The business banquet is the apex of the Chinese dining experience, and almost all significant deals are clinched at the banquet table. In addition to the above, further rules apply: arrive 15 minutes early; if you are applauded as you come into the room, applaud back; reply to the welcome toast with your own short speech and toast; avoid sensitive subjects; show respect to your elders and superiors by ensuring that the rim of your glass is lower than theirs when clinking glasses, and drain your drink in one swift movement.

What to Drink

Tea, of course, is the most popular drink in China. There are countless arguments for drinking the infusion of the bush *Camellia sinensis*, and just as many legends about its origin *(see p299)*. While tea is the most popular drink, there is a wide range of others for the visitor. Beer is popular with meals but wine is also drunk in many upmarket restaurants. Chinese spirits can range from the extremely pleasant to the almost dangerous. Likewise, approach "health tonics" like snake wine with caution – as if the reptilian "sediment" in the bottle isn't enough, they can be fiercely alcoholic.

Tea plantation in the Fujian hills, south China

Types of Tea

Green is the most common, baked immediately after picking. Flower tea is a mixture of green tea with flower petals. Black tea colors during the fermentation process and the reddish brew that results explains its Chinese name – red tea. The most highly prized is oolong, a lightly fermented tea. Brick tea is black or green, pressed into blocks. Eight Treasure tea (babaocha) *has many ingredients including, dates, dried longan, and wolfberry, and Tibetans enjoy yak butter tea.*

Lid keeps leaves in the cup, not the mouth

Gaiwan or three-piece teacup

Saucer to prevent fingers burning

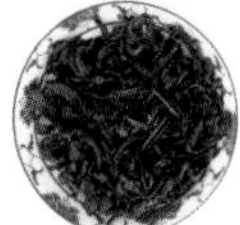
Black: *hongcha,* actually called "red tea" in Chinese.

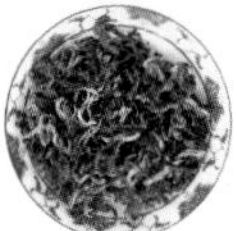
Green: *lucha,* uses leaves dried without fermentation.

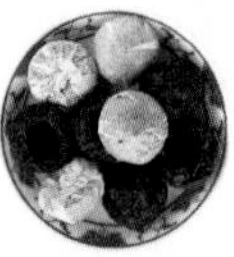
Pu'er: from Yunnan, is often compressed into "bricks."

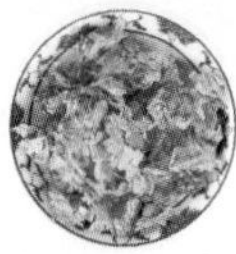
Flower: *huacha,* a mix of petals – jasmine, rose, and chrysanthemum.

The famous "Hairy Peak" green tea

Coffee

As café culture enters China, coffee drinking is becoming fashionable among the middle classes. A Starbucks can be found in practically every major city in China.

Tea and Coffee Drink

Those who want a fashionable coffee drink, but cannot do without their daily shot of tea, can try this blend of tea and coffee.

Soft Drinks

Even as a cold drink, tea is dominant; iced tea is very popular, especially with the young. Besides the usual array of fruit juices, there is pomegranate juice in Xinjiang, hawthorn juice in Beijing, and lychee and sugar cane juice down south. As well as the global drink brands, there are local challengers like Tianfu Cola, and the energy drink Jianlibao, made with honey. As China overcomes its dairy aversion, milk and yogurt drinks multiply, as well as soyabean *(doujiang)* and Hainan's famous coconut milk.

Sugar cane juice

Iced green tea

Coconut milk drink

Tsingtao beer

Yanjing beer

Beer

Alcoholic drinks have been brewed in China for over 10,000 years, but European-style beer was introduced only in the early 20th century. China is now the world's biggest brewer, so you are never far from a light lager, and even a darker brew. Each city usually has its own local brewery.

Wine

As a result of joint ventures with French and other winemakers, the quality of Chinese wine is rapidly improving. The Chinese consume almost exclusively red wine – it is considered good for the heart, and a lucky color too.

Great Wall

Dragon Seal

Spirits

For millennia the Chinese have been distilling grains into *baijiu* or "white spirits" ranging from strong to deadly. They are classified into three types: the *qingxiang*, or light bouquet, group includes Fenjiu from Shanxi; Guizhou's famous Maotai is a classic *jiangxiang*, soy bouquet; while *nongxiang*, strong bouquet, is championed by Sichuan giant Wuliangye.

Maotai – "eight times fermented and seven times distilled" – is favored for toasts at banquets. At the other end of the scale, *erguotou* is cheap and effective – the people's drink.

Maotai

Erguotou

Rice Wine

Despite being called "wine," some care is required as this can vary in strength from a mild 15–16% alcohol, to the double- or triple-fermented wines at up to 38% ABV. Good rice wine is best drunk warm and goes well with cold starters.

Shaoxing rice wine

Shaoxing: This is among the best of the *huangjiu* (yellow spirits), noted for its moderate alcohol content (about 16%) and mellow fragrance.

Strong rice wine

Drinking Culture

Teahouses are enjoying a bit of a revival in China, as appreciation of tea culture recovers after years of proletarian austerity. While *cha* (tea) stimulates quiet contemplation, *jiu* (alcohol) lubricates noisy celebrations. Despite reveling in the drunkenness of their poets such as Li Bai *(see p34)*, the Chinese have not been as badly affected by alcoholism as many other societies. Public drunkenness is frowned upon – except maybe in the ever more popular karaoke bars. Traditionally, only soup was drunk with meals, but this is changing, especially when eating with foreigners. "*Gan bei!*" or "dry the cup" is the clarion call to toasting bouts and drinking games. Beware the legendary capacity of the northeast Chinese, and don't drink alone or on an empty stomach.

Lan Kwai Fong, Hong Kong – home to the most popular bars and restaurants in the city

Where to Eat & Drink

Beijing

Biteapitta ¥
Middle Eastern
2/F Tongli Studio, 43 Sanlitun North, Sanlitun Houjie, Chaoyang
Tel *(010) 6417 6095*
Enjoy hummus, tasty pita sandwiches, and other Middle Eastern fare in this bright restaurant, a perfect pit stop before heading on to the bars.

Donghuamen Night Market ¥
Street Food **Map** 2 D5
Donghuamen Dajie
A fun market popular with tourists that sells snacks from all over China – from the ordinary (dumplings and chicken skewers) to the bizarre (bugs on a stick).

Huajia Yiyuan ¥
Regional **Map** 2 E3
235 Dongzhimen Nei Dajie
Tel *(010) 5128 3315*
This is a great destination for a fun *renao* (literally, "heat and noise") experience, as well as for the opportunity to sample the city's staple dishes. Peking duck is a good choice, as is the spicy crayfish. Live Chinese opera and magic shows are often performed.

Kejia Yuan ¥
Regional
2 Tuanjie Hu Beilu, Chaoyang
Tel *(010) 6582 5010*
A rustic and attractive venue that serves food from the Hakka ethnic minority. The tasty, hearty specialties, such as braised pork tofu, are authentic and popular.

Let's Burger ¥
American
B1/F, Sanlitun Village North, Sanlitun Lu, Chaoyang
Tel *(010) 6415 2772*
Enjoy fabulous, innovative burgers and milkshakes in a playful and stylish setting.

Warm lighting in the elegant dining area at Agua, in Beijing

There is an impressive array of delicious condiments, including blue-cheese sauce.

Saveurs de Corée ¥
Korean **Map** 2 D3
128–1 Xiang Er Hutong, Jiaodaokou
Tel *(010) 5741 5753*
Delicious MSG-free food in a charming setting. There is an à la carte list, as well as a range of set meals that are easy on the pocket.

A Thousand and One Nights ¥
Middle Eastern
3–4 Gongti Bei Lu and 6 Chaoyang Park Lu
Tel *(010) 6532 4050*
Authentic Arabian cuisine, along with hookahs, belly dancing, and other Middle Eastern-flavored entertainment. The kabobs and the hummus are delicious. Syrian-Lebanese fare is also available.

Casalingo ¥¥
Italian
18 Xuanwai Dajie
Tel *(010) 6391 6361*
Stylish and surprisingly affordable, this restaurant on the first floor of JW Marriott serves excellent pizzas. Great service, and the Italian chef is very gregarious.

Crescent Moon Muslim Restaurant ¥¥
Middle Eastern **Map** 2 E4
16 Dongsi Liutiao, 100 yards west of Chaonei Beixiaojie
Tel *(010) 6400 5281*
Popular, rough-and-ready Xinjiang joint, thanks to its chunky lamb kabobs and hearty chicken and potato stews, served with naan bread and home-made yogurt to cool down the heat.

Crystal Jade ¥¥
Regional
87 Jianguo Lu, Chaoyang
Tel *(010) 6533 1150*
Order fabulous *dim sum* at this famous Asian chain that also offers traditional dishes such as BBQ pork ribs. A value-for-money restaurant despite the regal decor and formal service.

Price Guide
Prices are the equivalent of a meal for two made up of a range of dishes, served with tea, and including service charges.

¥	under ¥200
¥¥	¥200 to ¥500
¥¥¥	over ¥500

Da Dong ¥¥
Regional **Map** 2 D5
301 Wangfujing Dajie
Tel *(010) 6528 8802*
Da Dong is rightly famous for its Peking roast duck, but all the dishes are innovative and worth a try. Excellent quality. Book ahead.

DK Choice

Dali Courtyard ¥¥
Regional **Map** 2 D3
67 Xiaojingchang Hutong, Gulou Dong Dajie
Tel *(010) 8404 1430*
Easily one of the most beautiful courtyard restaurants in Beijing, this lovely venue serves up unusual spicy dishes from the Yunnan province. The fixed-price seven-course menu does not offer much choice, but there is a separate vegetarian one. Don't miss the Yunnan goat's cheese and cured ham, if available.

Element Fresh ¥¥
International
8-3-3, Building 8, 19 Sanlitun Nan Lu, Chaoyang
Tel *(010) 6417 1318*
Fast service, great coffee, and inexpensive Western classics make this bright and sleek spot busy from breakfast time till the evening. The fresh and healthy salads are a must-order.

Hatsune ¥¥
Japanese
S8–30, 3/F, Taiko Li South, 19 Sanlitun Lu, Chaoyang
Tel *(010) 6415 3939*
A long-standing favorite for its unbeatable fresh sushi, this restaurant offers its own unusual take on classic dishes.

Karaiya Spice House ¥¥
Regional
3/F, S9-30, Taikoo Li South, 19 Sanlitun Lu, Chaoyang
Tel *(010) 6415 3535*
Come to Karaiya for fiery Hunan fare tempered to the Western

Minimalist decor at TRB Hutong, in Beijing

palate. Classic dishes include ribs covered with spicy peanuts, and steamed Mandarin fish.

Middle 8th ¥¥
Regional
S8–40, Bldg 8, Sanlitun Village South, Sanlitun Nan Lu, Chaoyang
Tel *(010) 6413 0629*
Enjoy fresh and spicy Yunnanese cuisine in a fun and lively setting. This restaurant is famous for its mushroom dishes; the mushrooms and ribs wrapped in leaves are a must-try.

The Veggie Table ¥¥
Vegetarian **Map** 2 D2
19 Wudaoying Hutong
Tel *(010) 6446 2073* **Closed** *Tue*
Vegan and organic food on a menu that spans the world – the Indian *dal* (lentil) dishes and Middle Eastern favorites such as hummus are big hits. Lively vibe.

Vineyard Café ¥¥
Café **Map** 2 D2
31 Wudaoying Hutong, off Yonghegong Dajie
Tel *(010) 6402 7961* **Closed** *Mon*
This converted courtyard spot is a great place to refuel on Western staples. The coffee is good, as are the popular brunches.

Agua ¥¥¥
Spanish
4/F, Nali Patio, 81 Sanlitun Beilu, Chaoyang
Tel *(010) 5208 6188*
The Spanish chef truly excels at this fine-dining establishment, a rooftop branch of the Hong Kong restaurant. The suckling pig is sublime, as is the seafood.

Capital M ¥¥¥
International **Map** 3 C2
3/F, 2 Qianmen Pedestrian St
Tel *(010) 6702 2727*
A wonderful place for a cocktail, a special dinner, or even Sunday brunch while soaking up the views of Tian'anmen Square. Among the most celebrated dishes are the slowly baked, salt-encased leg of lamb and the legendary pavlova.

Duck de Chine ¥¥¥
Regional
4 Gongti Bei Lu, Chaoyang
Tel *(010) 6501 8881*
Duck de Chine is a stylish venue attracting a young crowd. The classic duck dish, served with non-traditional sides with a French twist, is a specialty.

Huang Ting ¥¥¥
Regional **Map** 2 E5
B2 Peninsula Palace Hotel, 8 Jinyu Hutong
Tel *(010) 8516 2888, ext 6707*
Outstanding *dim sum* and classic regional dishes are served by two expert Hong Kong chefs at Huang Ting. The interior, with its aged pine floor, wooden screens, and heavy studded door, re-creates a traditional *hutong* (alleyway).

Made in China ¥¥¥
Regional **Map** 4 E1
Grand Hyatt, 1 Chang'an Dong Jie
Tel *(010) 8518 1234, ext 3608*
This sophisticated and much-loved venue brings a modern sensibility to Chinese dining. The Peking duck is the undisputed star attraction, plus there is a superb wine list.

TRB Forbidden City ¥¥¥
Fusion **Map** 2 F5
95 Donghuamen Dajie
Tel *(010) 6401 6676*
A second helping of Beijing's lauded TRB restaurant, with a similar menu but better views, and close to the Forbidden City. Ask for a table that overlooks the moat and order one of the chef's multi-course tasting menus.

DK Choice

TRB Hutong ¥¥¥
International **Map** 2 D4
23 Shatan Houjie
Tel *(010) 8400 2232*
This restaurant is located in a building within the walls of a 600-year-old temple complex, most recently used as a factory producing TVs. All the dishes are good, though the classic French food with a Chinese twist is exceptional. The wine list is considered Beijing's best. Diners can order from both à la carte and set menus.

Hebei, Tianjin & Shanxi

BEIDAIHE: Bai Wei Jiaozi Cheng ¥
Regional
222 Gangchen Jie
Tel *(0335) 321 1727*
Outside the tourist zone, this is a clean, modern choice to try the local seafood and spicy *jiaozi* dumplings.

CHENGDE: Da Qing Hua ¥
Regional
19 Lizheng Lu
Tel *(0314) 2036 111*
Open all hours, this local chain specializes in noodles and dumplings – those stuffed with venison and carrot are a regional specialty.

CHENGDE: Milan Restaurant ¥
Italian
9 Wulie Lu
Tel *(0314) 2665 939*
Offering Italian fare for a Chinese palate, Milan is one of the only places in town with good pizza.

CHENGDE: Qianlong Dajiudian ¥
Regional
Xinhua Lu
Tel *(0314) 2072 2222*
This popular hangout offers a range of local favorites, such as venison – either served with ginger or as a stuffing in dumplings. The staff speak only Chinese, so make use of the picture menus available.

DATONG: Fenglin Ge ¥
Regional
Corner of Xiasipo Jie & Huayan Jie
Tel *(0352) 205 9699*
This restaurant is renowned for its excellent Shanxi dishes, which are enjoyed in beautifully decorated surroundings with a friendly service.

For more information on types of restaurant *see pp566–7*

DATONG: Tonghe Dafandian ¥
Regional
11 Zhanqian Jie
Tel *(0352) 7166 944*
Adjacent to the Hongqi Hotel, this is easily the best choice in town for inexpensive spicy Sichuanese and Hunanese cuisine. The Shanxi fried noodles are not to be missed.

PINGYAO: Coffee by Shrew ¥
Café
9 Chenghuangmiao Jie
Scrumptious brews, breakfast, and pastries are served in a charming setting with wooden interiors and bookshelves. Also serves a range of simple cocktails.

PINGYAO: Tianyuankui ¥
Regional
73 Nan Dajie
Tel *(0354) 568 0069*
Expect an old-world vibe and great service at this hotel restaurant. Order fine local dishes and chilled beer on an iPad.

TAIYUAN: Taiyuan Mianshiguan ¥
Regional
5 Jiefang Lu
Tel *(0351) 2022 230* **Closed** *Spring Festival*
This unassuming restaurant serves inexpensive classics such as *guo you rou* – succulent pork that is first boiled and then fried.

DK Choice

TIANJIN: Goubuli Baozi ¥
Regional
77 Shandong Jie
Tel *(022) 2730 2540*
This is the original venue of the Goubuli Baozi chain, where the renowned steamed-pork buns were first served over 150 years ago. Customers flock to this inexpensive, no-frills joint to feast on delicious, moreish snacks. Try the meatball dumplings and wash them down with one of the specialty teas.

TIANJIN: South Beauty ¥
Regional
1 Youyi Lu
Tel *(022) 2325 9327*
Spicy Sichuanese dishes are on offer here. The stone-grilled beef is considered a classic. Great atmosphere and friendly service.

TIANJIN: Twin Lotuses Vegetarian Club ¥
Vegetarian
68 Changde Dao
Tel *(022) 2331 8629*
Book ahead at this popular venue serving delectable Chinese food – both traditional and contemporary – that is prepared using only vegan ingredients.

Shandong & Henan

JINAN: Chongqing Xiao Tian ¥
Regional
162 Ying Xiong Shan Lu
Tel *(0531) 8298 1688*
Savor steaming bowls of broth and a variety of thinly sliced meats and vegetables, as well as noodles – tasty, warm, and filling.

JINAN: Yuchi Palace Restaurant ¥
Seafood
6 Luyou Lu
Tel *(0531) 8238 6666*
The main ingredient for your dish can be seen swimming in tanks and is caught only after an order is placed. Popular with locals.

JINAN: Biscotti Italian Restaurant ¥¥
Italian
Sofitel Jinan Silver Plaza, 66 Luoyuan Avenue
Tel *(0531) 8981 6288*
Come here for Italian classics and friendly service. There's a good weekend lunch, fine lasagna, and seafood spaghetti.

LUOYANG: Lao Luoyang Mianguan ¥
Regional
Corner of Qiyu Lu & Jiudu Lu
Tel *(0379) 6322 6636*
This popular pit stop serves hearty helpings of fried noodles, such as *zha jiang mian* (fried pork noodles in a soybean paste sauce).

LUOYANG: Zhen Bu Tong ¥
Regional
369 Zhong Zhou Dong Lu
Tel *(0379) 6395 2609*
Staff dress in period costume at this historic restaurant serving popular renditions of local dishes, such as meatballs decorated with peony flowers.

QINGDAO: Din Tai Fung ¥
Taiwanese
86 Aomen Lu, Shinan district
Tel *(0532) 6606 1309*
Part of an international chain, Din Tai Fung offers delicious Taiwanese dumplings, including the famous *xiaolongbao* (steamed bun).

QINGDAO: Harbor Seafood Restaurant ¥
Seafood
220–308 Guo Dao
Tel *(0532) 8098 8888*
Take advantage of this restaurant's harborside location and enjoy fresh seafood dishes. There is also a popular *dim sum* brunch on Sundays.

QINGDAO: Knuckles ¥
American
274–276 Wiyushan Jie
Tel *(0532) 8610 6581*
This is a pub-style venue with live music and good Western food, including great burgers, plus a lively atmosphere.

QINGDAO: Italiano Doc ¥¥¥
Italian
InterContinental Hotel, 98 Aomen Lu
Tel *(0532) 8589 0526*
The Neapolitan father-and-son team here create excellent pizzas, along with more elaborate, authentic dishes. There is also a good wine list.

The elegant and well-located Harbor Seafood Restaurant in Qingdao

Key to Price Guide *see p 572*

DK Choice

QINGDAO: Shang Palace ¥¥¥
Regional
1st Floor, Shangri-La Hotel, 9 Xiang Gang Zhong Lu
Tel *(0532) 8388 3838 (ext. 6459)*
A glamorous, upscale establishment located in one of Qingdao's finest hotels, Shang Palace serves beautifully prepared classic Huaiyang fare such as *char siu pork* (BBQ pork). However, the chef is not afraid to innovate and the menu features braised pork ribs with pine nuts in red wine sauce. The staff are dressed in traditional attire.

Shaanxi

XI'AN: Defachang Restaurant ¥
Regional
28 Pingan Market (Bell Tower Square)
Tel *(029) 8767 6615*
One of Xi'an's most famous restaurants. Diners have a choice of 100 different items that can be ordered from a picture menu.

XI'AN: Delhi Darbar Xi'an ¥
Indian
3 Datang Tongyifang, Yanta Xilu
Tel *(029) 8525 5157*
Guests looking to get a break from local cuisine should come to this long-standing Indian restaurant that serves good curries and naan bread. Frequented by expats.

XI'AN: First Noodle Under the Sun ¥
Regional
Hanguang Nan Lu
Tel *(029) 8728 6088*
This vibrant restaurant specializing in noodles is located near Xi'an's famous Great Goose Pagoda, and it is popular with both tourists and locals.

DK Choice

XI'AN: Haidilao Hot Pot ¥
Regional
63 Jiefeng Lu, south of Xinjie Jie
Tel *(029) 8739 0099*
Very popular hotpot joint specializing in beef. Expect a bustling atmosphere and long waits at mealtimes, but it's open around the clock.

XI'AN: Huimin Jie ¥
Regional
Huimin Jie
Xi'an's Muslim Street is a lively destination thanks to its bustling market stalls and street vendors selling *roujiamo* (Chinese burgers in pitta bread) and a variety of other snacks.

Opulent furnishings at the renowned Shang Palace, Qingdao

XI'AN: Tang Dynasty Music and Dance Show ¥¥
Regional
165 Wenyi Lu
Tel *(029) 8822 1873*
This is a great place for visitors to enjoy reasonable buffet food while watching the cultural performances held every night.

Shanghai

Baker and Spice ¥
Café
195 Anfu Lu, French Concession
Tel *(021) 5404 2733*
This chic artisanal bakery café (part of a chain in Shanghai) serves a fine selection of hand crafted breads, pastries and cakes, as well as great coffee and a range of breakfasts that really hit the spot.

Brasa Chicken ¥
International
450 Taixing Lu, near Xinzha Rd
Tel *(021) 6277 8166*
A no-frills, laid-back place, with a meat-oriented menu. One of the highlights is the delicious Peruvian-style rotisserie-cooked chicken. Food to take away and a delivery service are also available.

CH2 ¥
Café
1250 Huaihai Zhong Lu, near Changshu Lu
Tel *(021) 5404 7770*
This stylish venue is a chocoholic's dream. From an espresso with just the perfect mix of hot chocolate to the double-chocolate cupcakes, everything here hits the spot.

Hunan Fengwei Xiaochi ¥
Regional
1233 Beijing Xi Lu
Tel *(021) 6279 4513*
Come to this hole-in-the-wall place for a spicy feast of homely Hunan cuisine. There is no menu, so overcome the language barrier by pointing at what other diners are enjoying.

Jia Jia Tang Bao ¥
Regional
90 Huanghe Lu, near Fengyang Lu
Tel *(021) 6327 6878*
Jia Jia is one of the top contenders for Shanghai's best *xiaolongbao* dumplings – called *tang bao*, or pork soup dumplings, here. Payment is expected upfront at this tiny and popular place.

Kota's Kitchen ¥
Japanese
Lanfan Plaza, 1333 Huaihai Zhong Lu
Tel *(021) 6252 1717*
This Beatles-themed spot just south of the French Concession sees long lines of diners eager for its *yakitori* (skewered chicken), pork ramen, and *shochu* (a Japanese alcoholic drink).

My Kitchen ¥
Regional
1783 Huaihai Zhong Lu
Tel *(021) 6433 5834*
Intimate and earthy Taiwanese-run restaurant serving various regional specialties such as Hangzhou beef at a decent price.

Yuan Yuan ¥
Regional
4/F, Westgate Mall, 1038 Nanjing Xi Lu
Tel *(021) 6272 6972*
The efficient staff at this Shanghainese chain restaurant serve flavorful dishes in a smart setting. It is hugely popular, so book ahead.

For more information on types of restaurant *see pp566–7*

Blue Frog Bar & Grill ¥¥
American
131 Tianyueqiao Lu
Tel *(021) 3368 6117*
This well-run bar and restaurant chain serves classic American fare. The burgers are a specialty, and there is a happy hour every day with half-price drinks (4–8pm).

Crystal Jade ¥¥
Dim Sum
Xintiandi, South Block Plaza, 2/F, 123 Xingye Lu
Tel *(021) 6385 8752*
Hungry diners will find high-quality Cantonese *dim sum* at this well-known chain, which has several branches in the city. The *xiaolongbao* (steamed bun) dumplings vie with the prawn noodles for the best item on the menu.

Di Shui Dong ¥¥
Regional
56 Maoming Nan Lu
Tel *(021) 6253 2689*
Succulent Hunan food for spice-lovers. The sublime spare ribs are a must-try. Cool off your mouth with plum-based Suan Mei Tang. Popular with expats.

Din Tai Fung ¥¥
Taiwanese
2/F Building 6, Xintiandi South Block, Lane 123, Xinye Lu
Tel *(021) 6385 8378*
Din Tai Fung is a Taiwanese chain that serves unforgettable *xiaolongbao* (steamed bun) dumplings and other tasty steamed snacks. There is a children's play area, and the staff are friendly and helpful.

Element Fresh ¥¥
International
Shanghai Centre, 1376 Nanjing Xi Lu
Tel *(021) 6279 8682*
This casual place is one of 16 branches across Shanghai. It serves good Western options, such as salads, sandwiches, and pasta dishes. It is particularly popular for weekend brunch, when it gets quite crowded.

Haiku by Hatsune ¥¥
Japanese
28B Taojiang Lu
Tel *(021) 6445 0021*
A slick and stylish restaurant and sushi bar. The cream cheese and sushi rolls may be unusual, but they are delicious all the same. Prior booking recommended.

Hang Yuen Hin ¥¥
Dim Sum
290–292 Wanping Lu
Tel *(021) 6472 9778*
In a verdant park setting, this is one of Shanghai's best *dim sum* restaurants. It serves tasty shrimp dumplings with almond, and has an economic afternoon tea menu that includes congee.

Kommune Cafe ¥¥
Café
The Yard, 7 Lane 210, Taikang Lu
Tel *(021) 6466 2416*
Located in the trendy Tianzifang district, this revolutionary themed café serves plenty of Western comfort food, including substantial breakfasts.

Mammamia Pizzeria ¥¥
Italian
1333 Huaihai Zhong Lu, Xuhui, nr Changshu Road Metro
Tel *(021) 5081 0966*
A top-class bar and pizzeria with a relaxed, rustic ambience. The Neapolitan-style pizza is as authentic as it gets in Shanghai.

Mercato ¥¥
Italian
6th Floor, Three on the Bund
Tel *(021) 6321 9922*
Come to Mercato to savor excellent-value Italian food from chef Jean-Georges Vongerichten. With great views, fabulous service, and a relaxed smart-casual ambience, the restaurant is unsurprisingly popular, so it's wise to book ahead.

Ye Olde Station Restaurant ¥¥
Regional
201 Caoxi Bei Lu, near Nandan Lu
Tel *(021) 6427 2233*
Uniquely located in an ancient French monastery, this place draws history enthusiasts as diners get to enjoy Shanghai food in the railway carriage of former Empress Cixi. Try the shredded crab tofu. Book ahead.

Ye Shanghai ¥¥
Regional
338 Huang Pi Nan Rd, Xintiandi
Tel *(021) 6311 2323*
This upscale and appealingly decorated restaurant serves distinctive interpretations of classic Shanghainese dishes, as well as food from the nearby provinces of Zhejiang, Jiangsu, and Guangdong. The weekend *dim sum* brunch sets offer great value for money.

8 ½ Otto e Mezzo Bombana ¥¥¥
Italian
6th Floor, 169 Yuanmingyuan Lu
Tel *(021) 6087 2890*
This is a Michelin-starred Italian restaurant with a slinky bar near the Bund. The seasonal à la carte menu features dishes such as fresh poached Normandy blue lobster. The food and service are impeccable, and children are made welcome.

Elefante ¥¥¥
Spanish
20 Donghu Lu, near Huaihai Zhong Lu
Tel *(021) 5404 8085* **Closed** *Mon*
The extensive menu at Spanish chef El Willy's sleek and stylish restaurant could make choosing a difficult proposition. Menu highlights include a wide-ranging cheese platter, and a cheaper set brunch menu.

Jade on 36 ¥¥¥
French
Pudong Shangri-La, Level 36, Grand Tower, 33 Fu Cheng Lu, Pudong
Tel *(021) 6882 8888*
Highly exclusive and exquisite fine dining from chef Jeremy Biasiol is accompanied by sweeping views over the Bund at this elegant, glitzy restaurant on the 36th floor of the Shangri-La Hotel.

The ultra-fancy bar at 8½ Otto e Mezzo Bombana, Shanghai

Key to Price Guide *see p572*

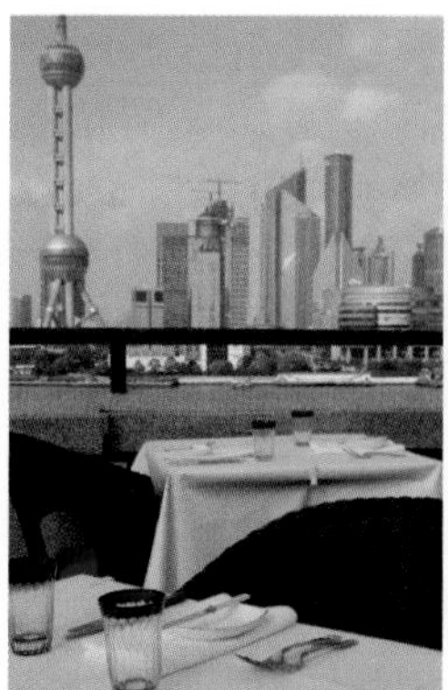

Tables with a fabulous view at M on the Bund, Shanghai

DK Choice

M on the Bund ¥¥¥
International
7/F, No. 5 the Bund (corner of Guangdong Lu)
Tel *(021) 6350 9988*
One of Shanghai's oldest Western restaurants, M on the Bund never disappoints with its sophisticated pan-European cuisine. The menu also features dishes from the Middle East and Africa and the chef uses fresh, local ingredients to prepare delectable food. Gear up for some stunning views too.

Tsukiji Aoasora Sandaime ¥¥¥
Japanese
191 Changle Lu
Tel *(021) 5466 1817*
Authentic Japanese cuisine, including delicious sushi, is served here, the sister restaurant of a famous Tokyo establishment. For a selection of the best dishes, order the sushi sets; otherwise, try the outstanding tuna nigiri.

Jiangsu & Anhui

NANJING: Bainian Lao Feng Xiaochi ¥
Street Food
122 Gongyuan Jie
Try the vast array of Huaiyang street food available at this night market, outside the Fuzi Miao.

NANJING: Finnegans Wake ¥
Pub/Restaurant
6 Xinanli Jie, off Zhongshan Nan Lu
Tel *(025) 5220 7362*
This Irish pub with an authentic atmosphere and drinks also serves tasty burgers and steaks.

NANJING: Nanjing Da Pai Dang, Deji Plaza ¥
Regional
18 Zhongshan Lu, near Xinjiekou Metro
Tel *(025) 8472 2777*
Traditional Nanjing food in fun and kitschy surroundings. There is usually a long line of university students outside.

NANJING: Bellini (by Mira) ¥¥
Italian
Wenfan Lu 9, Xianling City University
Tel *(025) 8579 1577*
A relatively inexpensive place offering sumptuous authentic Italian food; the lasagna is particularly good.

NANJING: South Beauty ¥¥
Regional
6 Gulouqu Zhongshan Beilu
Tel *(025) 8351 8850*
Minimalist in style, this place turns up the heat with spicy Sichuan classics, including *mapo doufu* (spicy tofu with minced pork).

NANJING: Plum Garden ¥¥¥
Regional
JinLing Hotel, Xin Jie Kou Square
Tel *(025) 8472 2888*
This restaurant specializes in exceptional Huaiyang-style cooking, and it is noted for its seafood and salty duck.

DK Choice

SUZHOU: The Bookworm ¥
International
77 Gunxiufang, Shiquan Lu
Tel *(0512) 6526 4720*
A branch of the all-in-one café, bar, and library where travelers can get a break from the spicy local fare. The wine list is extensive, and the excellent brunch menu includes dishes such as eggs Benedict and freshly squeezed juices.

SUZHOU: Songhelou Restaurant ¥
Regional
198 Shantang Jie
Tel *(0512) 6532 1398*
This is Suzhou's most famous restaurant. The sweet-and-sour squirrelfish is a must-order.

SUZHOU: Wang Si ¥
Regional
15 Taijian Nong, Guanqian Jie
Tel *(0512) 6522 7277*
Excellent tea and local dishes make Wang Si an increasingly popular spot. The delicious lotus root is highly recommended.

SUZHOU: Wumen Renjia ¥¥
Regional
31 Panru Xiang
Tel *(0512) 6728 8041*
The well-presented Suzhou food served here is as traditional as the Qing dynasty building in which the restaurant is housed.

SUZHOU: Paradox ¥¥¥
French
711 Shiquan Jie
Tel *(0512) 6572 5632*
If you fancy a change from Chinese food, this restaurant has a romantic ambience, a superb wine list, and well-presented food.

YANGZHOU: Republican Spring Restaurant ¥
Regional
79 GanQuan Lu
Tel *(0514) 8734 2551*
A local chain with superb noodle dishes. Worth it despite the gruff service and shared tables.

YANGZHOU: Ye Chun Cha She ¥
Teahouse
10 Fengle Jie
Tel *(0514) 8731 4650*
This famous teahouse is located in a traditional dark building with a garden outside. Try the delicious soup dumplings.

Dining with views at Jade on 36 in Shanghai

For more information on types of restaurant *see pp566–7*

Dining room with an open kitchen at Amanfayun – Steam House in Hangzhou

Zhejiang & Jiangxi

HANGZHOU: Green Tea ¥
Regional
83 Longjing Lu
Tel *(0571) 8788 8022*
The consistently high-quality fare and a frequently changing menu keep a clientele of both locals and visitors flocking to this place. Be sure to try the roast pork.

HANGZHOU: Weizhuang Zhiweiguan ¥
Regional
10–12 Yanggongti, Xihu Qu
Tel *(0571) 8797 0568*
With a superb location on the lake, this busy restaurant serves classic Hangzhou dishes, such as West Lake fish in vinegar sauce.

HANGZHOU: Amanfayun – Steam House ¥¥
Regional
22 Fayun Xiang, Xi Hu Jie
Tel *(0571) 8732 9999*
Located inside the Amanfayun Hotel, this casual restaurant focuses on *dim sum* and authentic local specialties. There is a terrace for alfresco dining.

HANGZHOU: Angelo's ¥¥
Italian
6 Lane 2, Baoshi Hill, off Baochu Lu
Tel *(0571) 8521 2100*
Classic New York City photos adorn the walls of this very modish chain restaurant offering authentic Italian fare from pizzas to deep-fried calamari.

HANGZHOU: La Pedrera ¥¥
Spanish
2 Hangda Lu, next to Dragon Hotel
Tel *(0571) 8899 5577*
This restaurant and tapas bar specializes in paella. Try the chorizo and chicken version, and wash it down with a Spanish beer or a glass of sangria.

HANGZHOU: 28 Hubin Road ¥¥¥
Regional
Hyatt Regency Hangzhou, Hubin Lu
Tel *(0571) 8779 1234*
It is difficult to say which is the bigger attraction here: the *dongpo* (pork belly) or the state-of-the-art wine cellar.

NANCHANG: Le Bistro 100 ¥
French/Italian
100 Rongmen Jie
Tel *(0791) 8610 0100*
When you need a break from local cuisine, this French bistro, which also serves pizza, does the job.

NANCHANG: Folk Restaurant ¥
Regional
342 XiMaZhuang
Tel *(0791) 8623 6820*
The crowd of hungry diners here reiterates the quality of its Jiangxi dishes, particularly the duck soup.

DK Choice

SHAOXING: Xian Xiang Jiu Dian ¥
Regional
179 Lu Xun Zhong Lu
Tel *(0575) 8511 6666*
The most famous self-service restaurant in Shaoxing specializes in delicacies such as crispy-skinned chicken and smoked red dates in rice wine and fermented tofu. The manager speaks superb English, and there is a helpful picture menu on the wall.

SHAOXING: Xiang Hui Lou ¥
Regional
244 Luxun Xi Lu
Tel *(0575) 8522 6577*
Use the picture menu to order local specialties such as beef and chili with Shaoxing vinegar. Nice wood decor.

WENZHOU: Corner Of Days (Tian Yijiao) ¥
Regional
9 Xueyuan Zhong Lu
Tel *(0577) 8815 8888*
The perfect place to try local snacks such as Zhuzang noodles, Dengzhao cake, and steamed buns. Watch as the chef prepares your dish in the open kitchen.

Hunan & Hubei

CHANGSHA: Crave Deli & Bar ¥
American
C31 Wanda Plaza, Xichang Jie
Tel *153 8803 4382*
Owned by a Canadian expat, this bar serves a range of decent burgers, sandwiches, and other simple Western comfort foods.

CHANGSHA: Huo Gong Dian ¥
Regional
127 Pozijie
Tel *(0731) 8581 4228*
The food – dishes from Hunan and other Chinese provinces – comes on carts, and diners can feast on a wide variety of small plates and snacks.

DK Choice

CHANGSHA: West Lake Restaurant (Xihu Lou) ¥
Regional
Hongshan Lu
Tel *(0731) 8425 8188*
One of the largest restaurants in the world, West Lake employs 300 chefs to cater for 5,000 seats. The menu includes exotic fare, such as snakes, as well as good renditions of classic dishes such as crispy fried pork and sweet-and-sour Mandarin fish. With live stage shows daily, this is an experience not to be missed.

Key to Price Guide *see p572*

CHANGSHA: Xuji Seafood Restaurant ¥
Seafood
88 Shuguang Bei Lu
Tel *(0731) 8415 1560*
Changsha's poshest dining experience, with fresh seafood that can be picked from the huge tanks lining the restaurant.

WUHAN: Charm/Wuhantiandi ¥
Taiwanese
1616 Zhongshan Dajie, Wuhantiandi No. 2 – 2 Building
Tel *(027) 8272 7606*
Charm specializes in tasty Taiwanese snacks, such as bubble tea and scallion pancakes. For the adventurous, there is stinky tofu.

WUHAN: Wuhan Changchunguan Sucaiguan ¥
Vegetarian
145 Wuluo Lu
Tel *(027) 8885 4229*
Adjacent to a Daoist temple, this charming Buddhist restaurant specializes in mock-meat dishes in which pressed tofu is used as a meat substitute.

WUHAN: Miaoyu Youxiang ¥¥
Regional
Huangli Lu
Tel *137 2037 2772*
Upscale local food is served in a beautiful garden pavilion. The place is very popular with locals at weekends.

WUHAN: Noi Mediterraneo ¥¥
Italian
A109 Huayuan Dajie, 308 Qingnian Lu
Tel *(027) 8581 5868*
This Italian-run restaurant serves excellent food – from the pizzas and calzones, to the lamb chops and risottos.

Fujian

FUZHOU: Ez Café ¥¥
International
Shangri-La Hotel, 9 Xin Quan Nan Lu
Tel *(0591) 8798 8566*
Visit at lunch for the well-stocked international buffet, and at dinner for the excellent sampling of both Asian and European dishes. Good desserts, too.

FUZHOU: Xinjinyue Restaurant ¥¥
Seafood
638 Fu Ma Lu
Tel *(0591) 8569 2333*
One of the city's fanciest restaurants, offering delicious regional delicacies and sashimi.

DK Choice

XIAMEN: Bellagio ¥
Taiwanese
16 Jianye Lu
Tel *(0592) 6577 333*
The Xiamen branch of an affordable and stylish chain of Taiwanese restaurants. Order the sweet-and-sour fish from the gigantic picture menu, and wash it down with a freshly made fruit *lassi* (yogurt drink) and peanut-butter ice cream.

XIAMEN: Prague Café ¥
Café
3/F, University City Mall, 47 Yanwu Lu
Tel *137 2088 4867* **Closed** *Tue*
Run by a Czech (hence the name), this popular café has a good line in sandwiches. English is spoken.

XIAMEN: Big Mouth Japanese Restaurant ¥¥
Japanese
123 Lian Qian Dong Lu
Tel *(0592) 5922 166*
A buffet-only restaurant with an array of fresh sashimi and udon-noodle dishes. Book ahead.

Guangdong & Hainan

GUANGZHOU: 1920 Restaurant and Bar ¥¥
German
4/F, 1, Jianshe Liu Ma Lu
Tel *(020) 8388 1142*
Come to the 1920 if you fancy a break from Cantonese food. This restaurant provides a vast selection of German beer, massive plates of cold cuts, schnitzels, and sausage platters.

DK Choice

GUANGZHOU: Bai Yun Xuan ¥¥
Regional
Baiyun Hotel, 367 Huanshi Dong Lu
Tel *(020) 8333 3998, ext 3271*
A local institution famous for its delicious *dim sum*, this hotel-restaurant fills up in the mornings, particularly Sundays, and stays that way for much of the day. The *shu mai* dumplings and steamed ribs in black-bean sauce are sublime.

GUANGZHOU: Dongjiang Hong Xing Seafood Restaurant ¥¥
Seafood
198 Yanjiang Zhong Lu
Tel *(020) 8318 4901*
Spread over five floors and with a seating capacity of 3,000, this lively restaurant offers a wide range of delicious seafood dishes. Do not to miss the *dim sum*.

GUANGZHOU: Peninsula Yuzhenxuan ¥¥
Regional
2–3/F, 1 Yuchang Jie, Ersha Dao
Tel *(020) 8732 0666*
This is a favorite haunt of those who want to see and be seen. The steamed frog's legs served on a lotus leaf are much talked about.

GUANGZHOU: Summer Palace ¥¥
Regional
1 Huizhan Dong Lu
Tel *(020) 8917 6498*
The award-winning chef here serves meticulously presented interpretations of classic Cantonese dishes. There are also *dim sum* and, unusually, a small range of desserts.

Informal dining space at Ez Café in Fuzhou

The beautifully decorated Shang Palace in Shenzhen

SANYA: Casa Mia ¥¥
Italian
88 Sanya Bay Rd
Tel *(0898) 8888 9828*
With a lovely location on the waterfront, this is the place to order platefuls of pasta and red wine for a taste of *la dolce vita*.

SANYA: Hai Ya Restaurant ¥¥
Regional
138 Xin Feng Lu
Tel *(0898) 8827 6962*
A world away from Sanya's fancier restaurants, this busy, noisy joint caters to those in search of Hainan chicken, the island's most famous dish.

SANYA: Fresh at Mandarin Oriental ¥¥¥
Seafood
12 Yuhai Lu
Tel *(0898) 8820 9999*
Tucked away in the luxurious Mandarin Oriental Hotel, this is the place for an expensive treat. Try the oysters and shimmering platters of fresh seafood.

SHENZHEN: Muslim Noodle House ¥
Regional
8 Taizi Rd
An unassuming shack that attracts large numbers of local diners looking for meaty and spicy fare with that extra something. Noodles are made fresh in front of the guests. Note that there are no restroom facilities.

SHENZHEN: Benjia Korean Restaurant ¥¥
Korean
8 Baishi Lu
Tel *(0755) 8654 1158*
Spread over two floors, this restaurant is always packed with Korean expats enjoying mouthwatering BBQ pork and beef served with pickled *kimchi* on the side.

SHENZHEN: Laurel Restaurant ¥¥
Regional
19 Nong Yuan Lu
Tel *(0755) 8317 1818*
Diners here enjoy the outdoor setting as the friendly staff bring out an extensive selection of Cantonese dishes. The Peking duck is divine.

DK Choice

SHENZHEN: Shang Palace ¥¥
Regional
Shangri-La Hotel, East Side, Railway Station, 1002 Jianshe Rd
Tel *(0755) 8396 1383*
With its magnificent decor and outstanding *dim sum*, this place is truly delightful. Enjoy creative combinations of tantalizing flavors such as crispy pork flamed with Chinese rose wine, and sliced roasted duck with mango. Shang Palace is definitely worth a visit.

Hong Kong & Macau

HONG KONG: Bep Vietnamese Kitchen ¥
Vietnamese **Map** 2 B3
L/G, 9–11 Staunton Street, Central
Tel *(852) 2522 7533*
This popular restaurant serving good-value Vietnamese fare takes pride in the freshness of its ingredients. The *pho* noodle soup is a specialty.

DK Choice

HONG KONG: Maxim's Palace ¥
Dim Sum **Map** 3 D3
2/F Low Block, City Hall, 5 Edinburgh Place, Central
Tel *(852) 2521 1303*
The place for a typical Hong Kong *dim sum* experience. Join the crowds of cheerful locals selecting their favorite fillings from service carts. From the BBQ pork buns to the stir-fried green vegetables in oyster sauce, the food is flawless, classic, and inexpensive. Great harbor views, too.

HONG KONG: Serenade Chinese Restaurant ¥
Dim Sum **Map** 1 C4
1–2/F, Hong Kong Cultural Centre, Salisbury Rd, Tsim Sha Tsui
Tel *(852) 2722 0932*
Apart from *dim sum*, this restaurant also serves shrimp wontons and Singapore noodles. Enjoy your meal while taking in views of the Victoria Harbour.

HONG KONG: Smrat Pure Veg ¥
Indian **Map** 1 B1
5/F, Block B, Chungking Mansion, 36–44 Nathan Rd, Tsim Sha Tsui
Tel *(852) 2369 5762*
Inexpensive and excellent vegetarian food makes a trek to this spot worthwhile. The menu is varied and extensive.

HONG KONG: Guru ¥¥
Indian **Map** 2 B3
G/F, 13 Elgin St, Central
Tel *(852) 2547 9998*
A small, charming restaurant decorated with vibrant Indian artworks, Guru serves food from all regions of the subcontinent.

Dine with a stunning view at Above and Beyond in Hong Kong

HONG KONG: 8 ½ Otto e Mezzo Bombana ¥¥¥
Italian **Map** 2 C3
Shop 202, Landmark Alexandra, 18 Chater Rd, Central
Tel *(852) 2537 8859*
This is the only Italian restaurant outside Italy with three Michelin stars. Chef Umberto Bombana has a penchant for truffles. Book well in advance.

HONG KONG: Above and Beyond ¥¥¥
Regional **Map** 1 C3
28F, Hotel Icon, 17 Science Museum Rd, Tsim Sha Tsui East
Tel *(852) 3400 1318*
Fine harbor views and spot-on renditions of Cantonese classics, such as roast pork belly and *char siu* (barbecued pork), have made this modern venue very popular.

HONG KONG: The Chairman ¥¥¥
Regional
18 Kau U Fong, Central
Tel *(852) 2555 2202*
Book at least a month in advance to enjoy the experimental contemporary Cantonese food prepared here – baked Coca-Cola braised-pork buns, for instance.

HONG KONG: Chiu Tang ¥¥¥
Regional **Map** 2 C3
Shop 222, The Galleria, 9 Queen's Rd, Central
Tel *(852) 2526 8798*
The beautiful 1930s Art Deco ambience provides the perfect backdrop for quality Cantonese cuisine and a variety of *dim sum*.

HONG KONG: Luk Yu Tea House & Restaurant ¥¥¥
Dim Sum **Map** 2 B3
24–26 Stanley St, Central
Tel *(852) 2523 5464*
This colonial-style teahouse has been a destination for travelers for 80 years. Expect old-fashioned service as well.

HONG KONG: Pierre ¥¥¥
French **Map** 2 C3
25/F, The Mandarin Oriental, 5 Connaught Rd, Central
Tel *(852) 2825 4001* **Closed** *Sun, public hols*
Order innovative French-Mediterranean fare prepared by a celebrity chef at this restaurant overlooking Victoria Harbour.

HONG KONG: RECH by Alain Ducasse ¥¥¥
French **Map** 1 C5
InterContinental, 18 Salisbury Rd, Tsim Sha Tsui
Tel *(852) 2313 2323* **Closed** *Mon*
The staff here do Alain Ducasse credit by producing superb eclectic food that lives up to his reputation. The breathtaking view of the harbor is a bonus.

HONG KONG: The Square ¥¥¥
Regional **Map** 2 C2
4/F, Exchange Square II, Central
Tel *(852) 2525 1163*
The award-winning authentic Cantonese cuisine has made this restaurant a popular destination for foodies. The platters of roast meats are a real treat.

HONG KONG: Super Star Seafood Restaurant ¥¥¥
Dim Sum **Map** 1 C3
3/F, Grand Centre, 8 Humphrey's Ave
Tel *(852) 2628 0698*
Head to this high-end place – one of several branches in Hong Kong – for its menu of appetizing crab dishes and *dim sum*.

DK Choice

HONG KONG: La Table de Patrick ¥¥¥
French **Map** 2 B3
6/F Cheung Hing Building, 37–43 Cochrane St, Central
Tel *(852) 2541 1401* **Closed** *Sun, public hols*
French fine dining in an intimate modern setting with an open kitchen. The chef changes his menu every month, but the restaurant's signature dishes, such as king prawns and baby artichoke tartare, and goat's cheese and beetroot ice cream, are always available.

HONG KONG: Tsui Hang Village Restaurant ¥¥¥
Regional **Map** 2 C3
2/F, 16–18 Queen's Rd, Central
Tel *(852) 2524 2012*
Famous for *char siu* (barbecued pork), this no-nonsense restaurant may not be a place to linger, but it is the perfect spot to grab a bite on the run.

HONG KONG: La Vache! ¥¥¥
French **Map** 2 B3
G/F, 48 Peel St, Central
Tel *(852) 2880 0248*
This busy French-style steakhouse is a big hit among Hong Kong's French expats and locals alike, who queue up here for the city's best steak-frites.

MACAU: A Lorcha ¥
Portuguese
289 Rua do Almirante Sergio
Tel *(853) 2831 3193* **Closed** *Tue*
A lively and long-established local institution that serves exceedingly well-prepared piri piri chicken and *feijoada*, the classic stew made with pork knuckle, sausage, and red beans. Reservations essential.

The glamorous setting at The Eight in Macau

MACAU: Lord Stow's Bakery ¥
Café
1 Rua Do Tassara, Coloane Town Square
Tel *(853) 2888 2534*
The classic egg tart you can see being sold all over Hong Kong was invented here. True fans still take the ferry to Macau to buy boxes of the original.

MACAU: The Eight ¥¥¥
Dim Sum
Grand Lisboa Hotel, 2nd Floor, Avenida de Lisboa
Tel *(853) 8803 7788*
Come to this Michelin-starred restaurant for a lavish dining experience. The Eight serves Cantonese and Huaiyang cuisine, plus delicious *dim sum* at lunch.

Sichuan & Chongqing

CHENGDU: The Bookworm ¥
International
2 Yujie Dong Jie
Tel *(028) 8552 0177*
All-in-one bookstore, library, bar, restaurant, and event space. This, the sister branch to the famous Beijing edition, is very popular for its warm atmosphere and good wine and food.

CHENGDU: Chen Mapo Doufu ¥
Regional
197 Xi Yulong Jie
Tel *(028) 8675 4512*
Established in 1862, this restaurant claims to be the originator of the *mapo doufu* – a hot, spicy mixture of beancurd and minced meat. There are free performances of Chinese zither music on the second floor.

For more information on types of restaurant *see pp566–7*

The modern and light-filled interior of The Temple Café in Chengdu

CHENGDU: Momi Café ¥
Café
Shop M020, Tai Koo Li Mall, 8 Zhongshamao Jie
Tel *(028) 8316 0501*
This modern café, teahouse, and patisserie also sells books, postcards, and little souvenirs designed and made in-house.

CHENGDU: Flair International ¥¥
International
269 Shuncheng Avenue
Tel *(028) 8358 8888*
Sushi, Asian tapas, and creative cocktails can be enjoyed in this sophisticated lounge-style restaurant that is built around an outdoor patio with views over the city.

CHENGDU: Impression of Chengdu ¥¥
Regional
Zhaixiangzi Alley 16, Qingyang district
Tel *(028) 8624 5678*
This restaurant is famous for its spicy Sichuan cusine. It also offers guests the cultural experience of a Sichuan Opera show every day at lunchtime.

CHENGDU: The Temple Café ¥¥
Café
81 Bitieshi Jie, Jinjiang district
Tel *(028) 6297 4191*
This modern café serving French bistro cuisine is attached to a hotel in a refurbished courtyard house. There are also tea, coffee, pastries and a breakfast buffet.

CHONGQING: Cuihe Kitchen ¥
Regional
5/F, Chongqing Times Square, 100 Zourong Lu
Tel *(023) 6373 3211*
Popular for providing well-presented Sichuanese and Chongqing cuisines at reasonable prices, Cuihe Kitchen also boasts a convenient location in the central Times Square mall.

CHONGQING: Dalong Hotpot ¥
Regional
290 Diantai Xiang Jie, Xiaolongkan
Tel *(139) 8372 6399*
The most famous hotpot restaurant in Chongqing sees long lines for tables almost every day. Beware of the spicy broth – it is exceedingly hot.

CHONGQING: Grandma's Kitchen ¥
American
5/F C Block, Shidai Tianjie, 38 Daping Zheng Jie
Tel *(023) 8908 1468*
A branch of a well-known Beijing chain that offers excellent service, Grandma's Kitchen attracts large crowds thanks to the big portions of burgers and sandwiches, which are served in a warm and homely atmosphere.

CHONGQING: Qiqi Hotpot ¥
Regional
2/F–3/F, Building B, 151 Zourong Lu
Tel *(023) 6379 9369*
Part of a well-established and popular hotpot chain in Chongqing, Qiqi offers a typical menu in bright and clean surroundings.

CHONGQING: Yuxin Sichuan Dish ¥
Regional
67 Nanbin Lu
Tel *(023) 6282 2088*
This local favorite on the south bank of the Yangtze River offers excellent views and spicy, authentic Sichuan cuisine.

CHONGQING: Origano Roma ¥¥
Italian
Shop 0203, Building N37, Starfest Liangjiang Centre, 6 Huangshan Dadao Zhong
Tel *(023) 6308 8318*
The Italian chef at this outpost of a Roman original prepares well-presented dishes in good portions. Staff speak English.

Yunnan

DALI: Bakery 88 ¥
Café
17 Renmin Lu
Tel *(0872) 2679 129*
Bakery 88 serves delicious cheesecakes, healthy breakfasts, and apple pie, as well as good coffee. Friendly service.

DALI: Cang Er Chun ¥
Regional
84 Renmin Lu
Tel *132 3872 9057*
An old and famous Yunnan restaurant located inside a stunning wooden building. Try the Crossing the Bridge noodles. Prior booking recommended.

DALI: The Good Panda Restaurant ¥
Regional
81 Renmin Lu
Tel *151 8722 2105*
Try food typical of the Bai minority, such as goat's cheese and ham with piquant pickles, in a stylish environment with traditional and rustic decor.

DALI: Zai Hui Shou ¥
Regional
198 Renmin Lu
Tel *133 6872 6980*
A small hole-in-the-wall joint with lots of reasonably priced and delicious options. Famous for its Yunnan rice noodles.

Key to Price Guide *see p572*

KUNMING: De Yi Ju ¥
Regional
No. JB3-6-1, Jinmabiji Square, Jinbi Lu
Tel *(0871) 6788 1789*
Housed in a former general's mansion, this three-story restaurant is the most famous place for Yunnan dishes such as the Crossing the Bridge noodles.

KUNMING: Salvador's Coffee House ¥¥
International
76 Wenhua Xiang, Wenlin Jie
Tel *(0871) 6536 3525*
This student hangout with a full Western menu is run by three Americans and a Japanese. The home-made bagels and ice cream are popular.

KUNMING: Wei Cai ¥¥
Regional
1 Cuihu Xi Lu
Tel *(0871) 6519 3999*
Enjoy contemporary Yunnan cuisine with a lakeside view. The chef serves seasonal delicacies.

DK Choice

LIJIANG: A Ma Yi Naxi Snacks ¥
Regional
Near Xiaoshiqiao Qiao, Wuyi Jie
Tel *(0888) 5309 588*
Try the cuisine of the Naxi minority in an alley in the old town. This place also serves *Lijiang baba*, a pancake made of wheat flour, ham, and scallion.

LIJIANG: Chattering Room ¥
Regional
Dashiqiao Bunongling, Wuyi St, Gucheng district
Tel *(0888) 5180 439*
Unfussy cuisine from the owner/chef, who is famous locally for her chatter and heartwarming personality. Vegetarian-friendly.

LIJIANG: Upstairs N's Kitchen ¥
Café
2/F, Jishan Alley 17, Xinyi Jie
Tel *(0888) 5120 060*
In the evening, this friendly café famous for its milkshakes and pizzas starts to have more of a pub vibe.

LIJIANG: Flower Private Home Cuisine ¥¥
Regional
At the end of Zhenxingxiang Alley, Wuyi Jie
Tel *(151) 2607 6718*
A cozy restaurant worth seeking out in a small alley. On the menu is classic Lijiang cuisine, plus several vegetarian options. The manager speaks English.

Guizhou & Guangxi

GUILIN: Chong Shan ¥
Regional
5 Yiren Lu
Tel *(0773) 282 6036*
The flagship of a famous rice-noodle chain, Chong Shan is very popular with locals, especially for breakfast. Try the scallion pancakes.

GUILIN: Chun Ji Roast Goose ¥
Regional
Zhongshan Hotel, 2 Zhongshan Zhong Lu
Tel *(0773) 2806 188*
Renowned for its signature goose dishes, this perennially popular restaurant also serves up excellent *dim sum*. Prior booking is recommended at weekends.

GUIYANG: Lao Kai Li ¥
Regional
23 Yanwu Jie
Tel *(0851) 8683 1902*
Local foodies come here for the must-order dish: fish in sour soup. It is always crowded, with people lining up to get a table.

YANGSHUO: Farmer's Restaurant ¥
Regional
Jiu Xian, near Yulong River
Tel *(0773) 8772 715*
Cheap, cheerful, and tourist-friendly, this restaurant offering delicious Guangxi cuisine is a must after rafting in the Yulong River. Try the famous beer fish.

YANGSHUO: Ganga Impression ¥
Indian
110B, Block D, Yangguang 100, Diecui Lu
Tel *(0773) 881 1456*
Tucked away in a little street in downtown Yangshuo, this small place is run by a friendly Indian who speaks good English. It attracts locals and visitors alike for its authenticity and good value.

Liaoning, Jilin & Heilongjiang

CHANGCHUN: Bao Jia ¥
Regional
Tongguang Lu
Tel *(0431) 8676 1285*
Bao Jia is famous for its authentically prepared Dongbei cuisine. The hearty portions are twice the size you'll find elsewhere. Efficient staff.

CHANGCHUN: Z-Space International ¥¥¥
Steakhouse
2632 Gongnongda Jie
Tel *(0431) 8564 5757*
A refined, high-end restaurant, Z-Space Steak House is the place where locals go for *foie gras* and caviar, followed by a large, succulent steak.

DALIAN: 68–86 Old Dalian Restaurant ¥
Seafood
3 Xinsheng Jie
Tel *(0411) 8265 7491*
A small dining room means that this unassuming place is packed every day, full of people eager to try its famous seafood dishes.

DALIAN: Brooklyn Restaurant & Bar ¥
American
184 Bulao Jie, Wanda Huafu Erqi
Tel *(0411) 8686 7426*
Unadulterated American-style menu, featuring popular classics in the form of big juicy burgers and pizzas. For dessert, the cheesecake will satisfy every sweet tooth, and you can wash it all down with your cocktail of choice.

The casual Upstairs N's Kitchen in Lijiang

For more information on types of restaurant *see pp566–7*

DALIAN: Wan Bao Haixianfang ¥¥
Seafood
108 Jiefang Lu
Tel *(0411) 3991 2888*
Dalian's best seafood restaurant offers elegant decor and professional staff – not to mention prices to match. The spicy crayfish are excellent.

DK Choice

HARBIN: Katusha Restaurant ¥
Russian
261 Zhongyang Jie
Tel *(138) 3614 8098*
Head to Harbin's most famous Russian restaurant if you are in the mood for typical Russian decor, service, and fare, such as chicken Kiev and hearty beef stroganoff. Even the bread and butter is Russian. Unsurprisingly, it also has a peerless vodka list. There is occasional live music.

HARBIN: Lao Chu Jia ¥
Regional
118 Wen Zheng Jie
Tel *(0451) 8647 5018*
At this reasonably priced and popular Dongbei restaurant, you can order local favorites, such as the sweet and sour *guo bao rou* pork, from menu tablets that display pictures of all the dishes.

HARBIN: Europa Restaurant ¥¥
European
22 Shidao Xi Jie
Tel *(0451) 8469 8887*
This is the place to visit for traditional European and Russian fare, such as hearty steaks and French casseroles. The meals here are accompanied by live classical music.

SHENYANG: Guan Dong Da Yuan ¥
Regional
112 Taibaishan Lu
Tel *(024) 8671 8222*
This restaurant stands out thanks to its innovative design, though the food is more traditional – hearty, filling, and simple.

SHENYANG: Laobian Zhongjie ¥
Regional
208 Zhongjie Jie
Tel *(024) 2486 5369*
This is the place to come for dumplings – they serve more than 40 varieties in a pleasant, spacious dining room.

Inner Mongolia & Ningxia

HOHHOT: Le Chef by Chef Henry ¥
Steakhouse
26 Xinhua Dong Lu
Tel *(0471) 328 5570*
Serving steaks, pasta, pizza, and other Western standbys, this friendly restaurant brings a dash of internationalism to Hohhot.

HOHHOT: Gerile Ama Milk Tea House ¥
Teahouse
2/F, Xinhua Square, 93 Xilin Bei Lu
Tel *(0471) 692 4755*
Enjoy authentic Mongolian tea, local dishes, and dairy desserts in a friendly atmosphere.

HOHHOT: Meng Gu Da Ying ¥
Regional
Inside the Inner Mongolia Race Course, 27 Hulun Bei Lu
Tel *(0471) 651 6868*
Set in yurts, this authentic place offers great Mongolian cuisine, such as pulled lamb and Mongolian milk tea.

YINCHUAN: Guo Qiang Shou Zhua ¥
Regional
408 Jiefang Xi Jie
Tel *(0951) 503 6220*
Give the cutlery a miss and dig into the great mutton dishes with your fingers at this typical Xinjiang restaurant, also known for its medicinal tea.

DK Choice

YINCHUAN: Ying Bin Lou ¥
Regional
11 Jiefang Xi Jie
Tel *(0951) 602 5950*
A famous Muslim restaurant popular for its home-made pomegranate ice cream in summer, and lamb hotpot in winter. No English is spoken, but there is a picture menu, and the staff are keen to help.

Gansu & Qinghai

DUNHUANG: Daji Lvrou Huangmian ¥
Regional
In the alley east of Jinshan Hotel, near Shazhou Hotel
Donkey meat with yellow noodles is the Dunhuang specialty on offer at this homey place.

DK Choice

DUNHUANG: Dun Lai Shun ¥
Regional
11 Mingshan Lu
Tel *(0937) 883 2203*
The city's best restaurant, Dun Lai Shun is cheap, yet stylish and welcoming. Dishes from all over China are served, as well as Xinjiang staples, such as roast mutton and spicy cucumber.

The popular Wan Bao Haixianfang seafood restaurant in Dalian, Liaoning

Key to Price Guide *see p 572*

Staff in traditional attire at Wordo Kitchen in Shigatse, Tibet

LANZHOU: Wu Mu Le ¥
Regional
2168 Beibinhe Xi Lu **Closed** *eves*
Be prepared to wait at this popular draw to try the city's most famous and tastiest noodles and beef dishes.

LANZHOU: Zhong Hua ¥
Regional
765 Nanchang Lu
Tel *(0931) 888 0555*
The flagship establishment of a well-known local chain of Muslim restaurants. Be sure to try the succulent roast mutton, which is best eaten using your fingers instead of cutlery.

XINING: Brahmaputra Indian Restaurant ¥
Indian
Cangmen Lu
Tel *(0971) 856 2973*
With English-speaking staff, authentic North Indian cuisine, and excellent coffee, this friendly restaurant is a good place for a break from local flavors.

XINING: Qinghai Tu Huoguo ¥
Regional
Intersection of Xiaoxin Jie and Yinma Jie
Qinghai-style hotpot is the perfect dish for the long winter, and the one served here is truly memorable. Beware of the spicy variety, though, as it is quite hot.

XINING: Shalihai Food City ¥
Regional
4 Bei Dajie
Tel *(0971) 823 4444*
This popular local chain specializes in mutton dishes. Try the stewed mutton in rice wine and deep-fried diced potatoes. No English is spoken here, so guests might have to do some pointing.

Xinjiang

KASHGAR: Orda ¥
Middle Eastern
169 Renmin Dong Lu
This authentic Xinjiang restaurant serves spicy kabobs accompanied by cooling bowls of yogurt. The Uighur waiting staff are quite friendly.

KASHGAR: Altun Orda ¥¥
Middle Eastern
Renmin Xi Lu
Tel *(0998) 258 3555*
Altun Orda is a very high-end and luxuriously furbished Xinjiang restaurant. The excellent pilaf is recommended. The staff speak some basic English.

TURPAN: Herembeg ¥
Regional
Shahezi Lu
Tel *(0995) 855 5111*
Part of a Xinjiang-wide chain, this restaurant serves a range of well-executed Uighur and Turkish dishes. There are other outlets in Kashgar and Ürümqi.

ÜRÜMQI: Miraj ¥
Regional
Yan'an Lu
Tel *(0991) 288 5522*
Do not miss this exotically decorated Uighur restaurant. Miraj is one of Ürümqi's premier fine-dining venues, serving spicy and tasty lamb kabobs.

ÜRÜMQI: Rendezvous Café ¥
International
960 Yan'an Lu
Tel *(0991) 255 5003*
Cakes, sandwiches, and burgers are the order of the day in this café that makes for a pleasant break from the hectic streets of Ürümqi. English-speaking staff.

Tibet

LHASA: Guangming Gangqiongtian Tea House ¥
Teahouse
Danjielin Lu
Tel *(0891) 6885 357*
A local favorite known for serving Tibetan sweet tea and noodles.

LHASA: House of Shambala ¥
Regional
7 Jiri Erxiang
Tel *(0891) 632 6695*
The menu at this atmospheric terrace restaurant atop a charming boutique hotel features tasty Tibetan specialties, plus international dishes.

DK Choice

LHASA: Lhasa Namaste Restaurant ¥
International
11 Lugu Wu Xiang
Tel *(0891) 6324 669*
This friendly place offers Indian, European, Chinese, Tibetan, and Nepali dishes, as well as burgers, ice creams, and cakes. A great place to meet travelers.

SHIGATSE: Third Eye Restaurant ¥
Regional
Zhufeng Lu
Tel *(0892) 883 8898*
A mix of well-executed dishes from Tibet and Nepal. Try the *thukpa* (noodle soup) or the tasty curries.

SHIGATSE: Wordo Kitchen ¥
Regional
8 Zhade Dong Lu
Tel *(0892) 8823 994*
Gorgeous decor and friendly staff await diners here. The food is traditional yet wholesome; try the roasted leg of lamb.

For more information on types of restaurant *see pp566–7*

SHOPS & MARKETS

China's rich artistic heritage is reflected in its stunning range of characteristic works of art – from stylized landscape paintings and calligraphy to delicate ceramic bowls and exquisitely carved bamboo. With the burgeoning of tourism and the official encouragement of enterprise, Chinese cities are alive with shops and markets selling an often bewildering array of trinkets and souvenirs. Even though the market is flooded with cheap imitations, many objects are still made by age-old techniques, and authentic items are not hard to find. Perhaps some of the most unique souvenirs are those produced by China's ethnic minorities, particularly their accomplished embroidery. The major cities have malls and department stores, which provide certificates of authenticity for items such as jewelry and semiprecious stones (although still no guarantee). Many large hotels also have souvenir shops, although these tend to stock over-priced, high-end items, such as silk and jade.

Opening Hours

Shops in Chinese cities are usually open from 8:30am until fairly late in the evening – around 8pm – while winter timings are generally 9am to 7pm. High street stores and malls tend to open from 10am to 10pm regardless of the season. They can be very busy in the evening once offices have closed. The opening and closing times of shops vary from place to place. Local food shops remain open for business from early in the morning until late at night; while markets selling fresh produce shut down early in the afternoon. Some shops remain closed on public holidays such as the three-day Chinese New Year (Spring Festival), National Day (October 1), and New Year's Day (January 1), although most malls remain open.

An array of calligraphy brushes for sale in a Beijing market

How to Pay

The Chinese currency is the *yuan renminbi* or "people's money" (shortened to RMB). One *yuan* is divided into 10 *jiao* or *mao*, each of which is divided even further into 10 *fen* (though these are rarely seen these days). International credit and debit cards are widely accepted in malls, shops, hotels, restaurants, and bars. Likewise, ATMs are widespread in every city, including at most major banks, such as Bank of China, ICBC, HSBC, China Construction Bank, and Bank of Communications. ATMs should display in both Chinese and English. The commission and exchange rates charged for ATM withdrawals depend on your bank, so it is worth checking before your visit.

Bank of China is the best place to exchange foreign currency or traveler's checks. Branches are also found at airports, and in larger hotels. Be sure to keep your exchange receipts, since you may need them to convert your spare *renminbi* into another currency before leaving the country *(see pp608–9)*.

Bustling Nanjing Road with its brightly colored billboards, Shanghai

Bargaining

Bargaining is a common practice in China, especially in street markets, night bazaars, and at souvenir stands. It is even worth trying in the smarter, more expensive hotels, modern shops, department stores, and government emporia. Stallholders are notorious for charging visitors three times the "real" price, and sometimes their starting price may be up to ten times the cost. Make a comparison of prices and be conscious of what others are paying, particularly local Chinese.

A busy street in Zhaoqing, Guangdong

International Stores

The consumer revolution in China has led to the influx of upmarket brand stores, shopping plazas, and fashion boutiques in every city, especially Beijing and Shanghai. Brands from Gucci and Prada to Gap, Zara, and Apple can now be found in the leading retail cities of Shanghai and Beijing, as well as the many malls in other Chinese cities.

As in most developed countries, there is heavy emphasis on high-end items such as electrical goods, designer fashion, perfumes, jewelry, and watches, while large stores, such as Carrefour, Marks & Spencer, IKEA, and Walmart, offer foods, souvenirs, and household goods at reasonable prices.

Shopping Malls

As in all fast-emerging Asian nations, mall shopping is a favored urban leisure pursuit. In most Chinese cities, glassy retail plazas dominate the downtown areas. They are usually built to a similar design and house a mix of upmarket brands, coffee shops, fast food outlets, and local eateries, with a giant supermarket in the basement. In the central business districts of the largest cities, upscale shopping malls are attached to luxury hotels. While the malls multiply, China's department store heritage is fast diminishing.

Markets

The best way to experience China's diversity and its many ethnic cultures is to visit the bustling local markets, especially in rural areas. Usually taking place on specific days of the week, they may also be daily or held to coincide with seasonal festivals. Some traders travel a circuit from market to market.

Selling carpets at a market in Linxia, Gansu

Traditionally, people from the surrounding countryside came into town on market days to buy or sell their farm produce. Nowadays, however, rural markets are expanding their scope, and it is not uncommon to see stalls selling a range of household items from toothbrushes to woks and cooking pots. While some markets still follow the lunar calendar, which is confusing for most visitors, many have shifted to a more regular schedule. Such markets are busiest between mid-morning and mid-afternoon. The variety of food, souvenirs, and domestic items on sale is astounding, but be prepared to bargain hard.

Antiques

Unless you're an expert, buying antiques in China is a rather risky proposition. Many Chinese cities have flourishing antiques markets, but most of the items on sale will undoubtedly be fake. However, as long as you don't mistake them for the real thing, it is fun to browse and bargain for cheap replicas. The state-run antique shops, like the Friendship Stores, are in decline – and never had any bargains anyway. Shops in the foyers of art galleries and museums also sell works of art such as scroll paintings, calligraphy, and attractive silk scarves. In China, objects dating to 1795 or earlier may not be legally exported, so make sure any antiques (of a later date) that you purchase carry a red wax seal permitting export. Always keep the receipts as they may be required at Customs.

A souvenir shop in Qingcheng Shan park near Chengdu

What to Buy in China

Market stalls and small shops sell interesting souvenirs in tourist centers throughout China. Traditionally styled items can be found just about everywhere, while many other crafts are regional. You can find beautifully intricate embroidery in the southwest, prayer wheels and flags in Tibet, carpets in Xinjiang, and ginseng in the northeast. When shopping in markets it is essential to bargain. Gift shops at factories usually have fixed, but inflated, prices.

A collection of Mao statuettes in many different poses

Calligraphy

A skill as revered as painting, calligraphy is an ancient Chinese art that is a fluid form of self-expression. Master calligraphers practice their art assiduously, and one of their works could be very expensive. Less costly examples of calligraphy are widely available.

Marble chops are traditionally used to imprint a calligrapher's seal on to a work. At many craft markets vendors create personalized chops by carving a character version of a person's name on the base.

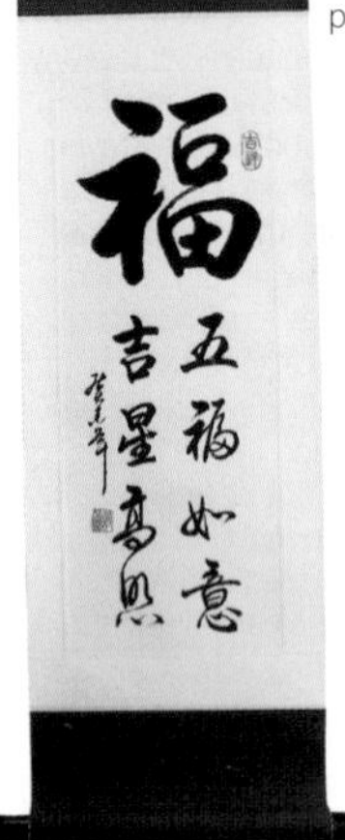

Scrolls painted with elegantly striking script make excellent souvenirs. Skilled calligraphers will paint chosen sayings in different styles or you can purchase pre-painted works.

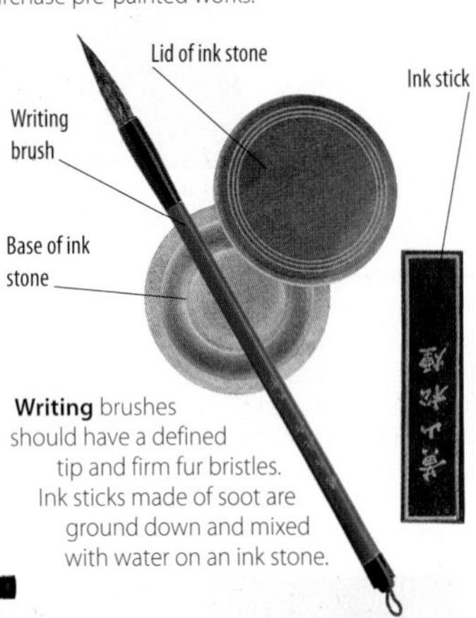

Writing brushes should have a defined tip and firm fur bristles. Ink sticks made of soot are ground down and mixed with water on an ink stone.

Painted on paper or silk with simple brushstrokes, painting is one of the most important traditional arts. Many paintings now have contemporary touches.

Ceramics

Chinese ceramics are known the world over. They have been mass produced for hundreds of years, with fired pots being passed through a line of artisans, each adding a layer to the glaze. Porcelain, a fine, translucent ceramic, was invented during the Sui dynasty, and high-quality pieces are still produced.

Jingdezhen in Jiangxi has been one of the main producers of porcelain since the 10th century *(see pp260–61)*. It still produces fine pieces, although some of the cheaper wares may be decorated by stencil.

Yixing ware, or purple sand pottery, from Ding Shan in Jiangsu *(see p224)*, is usually a dark reddish brown, but can also be green, buff, or gray.

Silk

Woven from the strands that make up a silkworm's cocoon, silk is also a Chinese invention *(see pp214–15)*. Clothes made of silk, such as ladies' *cheongsams*, are widely available, but be aware that silk sold in markets is likely to be rayon. Beautiful embroidery on silk is also available.

Silk embroidered coasters

Silk bags

Silk-covered cushions

Jade, a semiprecious stone, is associated with immortality. These pendants are green, but the gem can also be other colors, including brown and purple.

Other Traditional Handicrafts

Occasionally created by skilled craftsmen but often mass produced, Chinese handicrafts are almost always highly intricate and of vibrant color. The variety of goods on offer is staggering, from delicate miniature glass bottles to the bold graphics of Communist memorabilia.

The best paper cuts are made in a few minutes by a master craftsman with a pair of scissors. Most paper cuts are mass produced, with many simultaneously cut to a pattern.

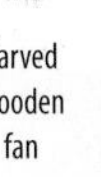

Lacquerware jewelry box

Decorative tassel

Cloisonné vases, boxes, and jars have been copper-enameled: copper is faced with pieces of colored enamel and fired, creating a shiny finish.

Glass snuff bottles were popularized during the Qing dynasty, when snuff usage was common. Using a hooked brush, artisans paint miniature scenes inside.

Carved wooden fan

Baoding balls are weighted and sometimes contain a chime. The two balls are maneuvered in one hand, strengthening grip and massaging the channels through which *qi* runs *(see p238)*.

Mao memorabilia is based on designs that existed during Mao's rule. Some is authentic, but most Communist souvenirs are produced for the tourist market.

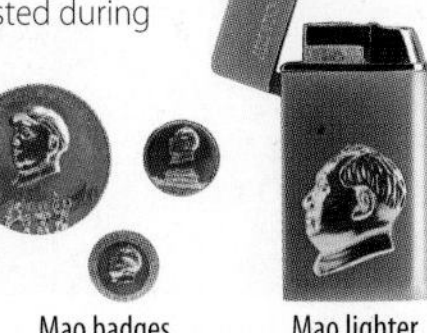

Mao badges

Mao lighter

Tea, often sold in colorful tin caddies, is available everywhere. *Tie guanyin* and other *oolong* teas of Fujian are very fine. *Pu'er* is a specialty of the southwest.

ENTERTAINMENT

The Chinese work hard, but they also take their leisure seriously, and have a range of traditional and modern entertainment. The vast tradition of performing arts reflects China's rich cultural heritage, and includes Chinese opera, theater, shadow puppetry, and the circus. Many types of dance and music derive from ethnic cultures, adding to the diversity of entertainment. China's increasing Westernization has meant that young people in particular enjoy the same leisure activities as their Western counterparts, including contemporary films and music concerts. Karaoke is hugely popular, and most towns and cities have numerous bars, where visitors can sing along to popular Chinese and Western songs, accompanied by the latest videos. The Internet has opened up avenues for online entertainment, with many people carrying smartphones, tablets, and laptops. Casino gambling is only permitted in the specially administered region of Macau, and horse-racing is popular in Hong Kong *(see p338)*.

Passing the time with a game of *xiangqi* on the sidewalks of Xi'an

Games

Playing games in public parks is an age-old Chinese custom, and though visitors may feel too inhibited to challenge locals to a game, they are great fun to watch. Some Chinese games date back thousands of years. The most well-known game is *mahjong*, which uses plastic tiles, originally made of bamboo or ivory. The rules are similar to rummy, with players trying to create identical, or consecutively numbered, sets. More advanced versions of the game have special tiles representing the four winds, four dragons, seasons, and flowers. When a game is in full swing, the quick movements of the participants make the tiles click and clatter – a popular translation of *mahjong* is "chattering sparrows."

Chinese checkers *(xiangqi)* is another popular game. Here, there are two opposing sets of round counters. The board is divided into squares by nine vertical and ten horizontal lines. The board game Go *(weiqi)* dates back more than 4,000 years. Also known as encirclement chess, it involves two opposing sides, each with a set of circular stones, struggling for territory.

Spectator Sports

The most popular sports at schools and colleges are basketball, badminton, and table tennis (ping pong), and the Chinese excel internationally in the latter two. Soccer is also played and followed with enthusiasm. The top European clubs have a strong fan base in China, and Chinese soccer players are now being recruited by them. Fitness centers and gyms are becoming increasingly popular in cities. Traditional martial arts such as *tai ji quan* are popular among the older generation, and people practice early in the morning in parks, squares, and gardens.

Traditional Forms of Theater

Beijing Opera *(jingju)* is a world-famous traditional art form unique to China *(see pp80–81)*. It is highly stylized and characters wear elaborate costumes with special makeup and masks. Performances usually take place on a simple stage with few props. Other regions have their own styles of opera.

The Chinese circus has a worldwide reputation for its highly trained gymnasts who perform breathtaking routines that showcase their unnerving flexibility. Displays of balance often involve household props, such as brooms, plates, and chairs, with one of the most

Actors in a Beijing Opera, performing in opulent costumes

popular tricks being performed by 20 or so acrobats piled precariously on a bicycle. These routines are often combined with acts involving caged and tame animals, but the current trend is toward a purer display of acrobatics.

Some forms of traditional dance still exist, especially among China's ethnic groups. Some relate to shamanistic or other religious rituals, and often involve the wearing of special masks.

Shadow Plays & Puppet Theater

Shadow plays *(piyingxi)* are popular, and usually involve the use of leather puppets with jointed limbs. These are manipulated close to a white sheet and lit from behind, throwing their shadows on to the sheet. The performance is accompanied by singing and music. Plays with wooden puppets *(mu'ouxi)* involve elaborate and colorfully dressed marionettes, glove puppets, or puppets on the end of rods.

Traditional Music

Chinese music can be traced back as far as the Shang era. Ancient sets of 65 bells from the 5th century BC have been unearthed. During the Tang dynasty, the traditional musical forms began to take root and music was also an important part of Confucian education.

Traditional instruments include strings, winds, and percussion. Stringed instruments played with the fingers, plectrum, or bow are the *erhu*, the harp-like *konghou*, and many-stringed zithers, such as the *zheng* and *guqin*. The lute-like *pipa* is one of the most important stringed instruments. The most common bamboo flutes are the vertical *(xiao)* and horizontal *(di)*. The *hulusu*, made from a gourd and bamboo, is popularly used in folk music. The *sheng*, one of the oldest Chinese instruments, has up to 17 bamboo pipes and a vibrating reed. Another ancient instrument is the earthenware *xun*. Dating back 8,000 years, and sometimes made of bone or ivory, it has a mouthpiece and a series of holes for varying the tones. Percussion instruments include gongs, chimes, drums, woodblocks, and xylophones.

Traditional shadow play performance using colorful puppets

A musician strums the lute-like *pipa*

Kite-Flying

Kite-flying is a major hobby in China, especially on public holidays when parks, gardens, and even city squares are crowded with displays of colorful and fantastically shaped kites. Birds and dragons are the most common kite designs.

Bars, Discos & Karaoke

Bars, nightclubs, and karaoke lounges have sprung up all over urban China. Some bars specialize in live bands, and these are very popular with expats, foreign visitors, and urban Chinese – be warned that drinks are expensive. Coffee bars are also increasingly popular with young people, although the older generation remain faithful to their traditional teahouses.

Rock & Pop Music

China's rock scene is young and rebellious, and only really emerged in the late 1980s, when it played a peripheral role at the Tian'an Men Square protests. Still not accepted by state-run radio stations, bands rely on the Internet and word of mouth. Chinese pop music is following in the same footsteps as the West, with young singers from TV talent shows like *Chinese Idol* and *Voice of China* making it big nationwide.

Canto-pop, Hong Kong's popular music tradition, has sugary lyrics of love and loss, sung in Cantonese. Many Canto-pop singers become hugely popular pin-ups, as have a new generation of Mando-pop stars, singing in Mandarin, from Taiwan and the mainland.

Cinema

China has traditionally produced many good films, based mainly on folk tales, love stories, or strong patriotic themes. Chinese cinema has also embraced international tastes, including those of both Hollywood and Bollywood, and movies such as Zhang Yimou's popular *Hero*, released in 2004, blended martial arts with impressive special effects. All cities show foreign movies, although they are often censored.

Delicate kites for sale catching the breeze from the Yangzi, Wuhan

SPORTS & SPECIALIST HOLIDAYS

As the Olympic host for 2008, Beijing was the showpiece city for a nation that celebrates sporting heroes with the fervor once reserved for political icons – soccer and basketball have become big spectator sports. The spending power and leisure interests of China's booming middle classes translate into more sporting choices for visitors too – there's skiing, golf, rock-climbing and more. Courses in martial arts can be found in most tourist centers, or head to the hallowed halls of the Shaolin Temple to find a master. Organized tours ply the major sights of the country, but for a really memorable experience book a trip that has a fascinating focus, whether photography, whitewater rafting, costume, or horse-trekking.

The Olympic Games

Infrastructure improvements and massive construction projects transformed Beijing in the run-up to 2008 Olympics. The city promised a "Green Olympics, Hi-tech Olympics, People's Olympics," so visitors enjoyed acres of parkland and futuristic stadiums. Half of the main Olympic Park area, at the apex of an extended imperial axis running north–south through the city, is being turned into woodland and lawns.

At the 2008 Olympics, 43 world records and 132 new Olympic records were set. China won 100 medals, 51 of them gold, and so the Games were declared a national success.

In 2010, the Asian Games took place in Guangzhou; in 2014, Nanjing hosted the Youth Olympics; and in 2015, Beijing's National Stadium hosted the World Athletics Championships.

Spectator Sports

Although ancient records describe a game of kick-ball with three players on each side, and paintings show a Song emperor juggling a ball with his feet, soccer is a fairly recent phenomenon here. The Chinese Professional Soccer League was established in 1994, and the **China Super League**, an elite group of teams, kicked off in 2004. The Super League has a huge fan base, but has run into problems with corruption and sponsorship. Basketball is also gaining in popularity, its profile boosted by Chinese NBA stars such as the towering Yao Ming. Beijing and Shanghai host the annual **NBA China Games** in August, featuring two of the top US basketball teams. In 2019, China hosts the FIBA World Cup.

The annual Rugby Sevens tournament in March is a massive – and very rowdy – event in Hong Kong, with international teams playing almost 70 games over three days. The **Hong Kong Rugby Football Union** plays regular fixtures during the rugby season, which runs from November through March.

Both Shanghai and Beijing host tennis tournaments – Shanghai has the **ATP Rolex Masters** and Beijing the **China Open**.

Shanghai's **Formula One Grand Prix** is held each year in April. Tickets are expensive, but 60 percent of the circuit is visible from the stands. The Macau Grand Prix is held each year in November.

For a Chinese flavor, track down the Minority Nationalities Traditional Sports Games. Ethnic groups play unusual sports from dragon-boat racing to elephant tug-of-war.

Golf

Despite initial Communist Party reluctance to embrace this elitist, land-hungry sport, golf's popularity is surging in China. Visiting golfers can enjoy over 500 courses nationwide. **Mission Hills** has 12 courses at its Shenzhen site, making it the largest golf facility in the world; while the course on Jade Dragon Snow Mountain near Lijiang, Yunnan, is one of the world's highest. Perhaps the most alluring is the beautiful **Spring City** course near Kunming. Most courses are open to the public, and prices are similar to those in Western countries.

Swimming

China has plenty of coastline but lacks the beach culture of its southeast Asian neighbors. However, Hainan Island is touted as China's Hawaii, and the resorts there are improving fast, while Beihai in Guangxi boasts a very long stretch of sand. Closer to the capital, enjoy

Horse trek up the steep sides of Tiger Leaping Gorge, Yunnan

Traversing the sand dunes of Mingsha Shan by camel, near Dunhuang, Gansu

Beidaihe, long the Communist Party's summer retreat, or the seashores of the lovely city of Qingdao.

Downhill Skiing

The best natural snow and ski resorts lie in Heilongjiang and Jilin provinces. **Yabuli**, about 100 miles (160 km) from Harbin, is one of the most established resorts, and **Club Med** has opened its first winter sports resort there. There are also several upscale ski resorts at Changbai Shan. In the Beijing suburbs there are at least 10 slopes, mostly with man-made snow, and Shanghai has one of the world's largest indoor facilities. Large feet may cause problems with equipment rentals, and watch your back – complete novices abound.

Choosing a Tour

A multitude of tour companies ferry groups of tourists through the top sights of China. If you are thinking of booking a tour, do your research carefully; it is essential to find one that suits you well. Beyond the obvious essentials of types of accommodation, transportation, the size of the group, and the itinerary, be sure to ask about the tipping policy, which can sometimes add a sizable unexpected cost to your trip. Also query the frequency of shopping stops, the bane of all organized trips in China. These detours (from which your guide may be earning a commission) can cut sightseeing time short and will become increasingly boring.

There's a wide choice of tour companies to travel with. **Abercrombie & Kent** is an established international group that has provided well-organized trips for decades. **Steppes Travel**, which is particularly strong on the Silk Routes and Tibet, provides suggested itineraries that it is happy to tailor for private tours, as well as several expert-led itineraries for groups. **Tibetan Connections** is run by Tibetans and offers a good range of adventurous tours across China's ethnically Tibetan regions. **Myths and Mountains** has some well thought-out itineraries that cover Yunnan and Tibet, and an interesting range of festival-focused trips. **Wild China** organizes tours nationwide, including trips to remote Tibetan monasteries in western Sichuan and through the dense jungle and rural hamlets of Xishuangbanna. **The Bespoke Travel Company** is an excellent resource for tours, excursions, and guided walks in and around Beijing and Shanghai. They also arrange hotel and car bookings and restaurant reservations.

Train-Spotting

With its extensive rail network, China has been a favorite destination of train lovers for years, particularly as it continued to run steam locomotives well after other nations discontinued their use. Several lines – often private railroads in industrial areas – still use steam, and their services are increasingly popular with domestic and international visitors. China now has a national super-high-speed rail network, which has revolutionized rail travel *(see pp616–17)*.

Boarding a traditional raft kept afloat by inflated sheep stomachs, Yellow River

Hot-air balloon floating amongst the karst peaks of Yangshuo, Guangxi

Cycling

Although the curse of the automobile threatens the bicycle kingdom, China remains a great place to saddle up. You will see more from a bike than a bus, and gain greater insight into the lives of the locals. A well-organized tour should provide alternative transport if you become exhausted or fall ill, and will have all the fix-it gear and able mechanics to deal with problem chains and derailers. Itineraries are set at different levels, from easy to challenging, and some companies provide bikes, while others ask that you bring your own wheels to keep costs down. For biking tours, consider specialist operators like **Bike China Adventures** who are based in Chengdu, **Red Spokes**, and **Cycle China**.

In rural areas, renting a bike for a day or two is the best way to see sights just outside of town and get a feel for countryside life. There are plenty of bike-hire shops in most places, and many hotels can also arrange bike rental. In cities, remember to park in designated areas (retain the token) and keep to cycle lanes where possible.

Martial Arts

China attracts thousands of martial arts enthusiasts hoping to find the roots of their practice. Many head for famous Shaolin Temple in Henan *(see p164)*, where Bodhidarma is said to have first taught the monks exercises that developed into *shaolin quan* during the 6th century. The temple is surrounded by kung fu schools that have courses that range from a week to six months or longer. The less well-known monastery on Wudang Shan in Hubei *(see p278)*, said to be the home of *tai ji quan*, also has schools of martial arts.

Most forms of kung fu taught in China are watered-down versions of the original martial forms, which have become popular and effective ways to keep fit. If you are looking for pure fighting technique, you may have more luck overseas, or possibly in Hong Kong. In Beijing, Shanghai, and other big cities, courses are advertized in listings magazines, but although there are plenty of sports institutes in China with classes, you may have difficulty finding an English-speaking instructor. Head to one of the traveler havens, such as Yangshuo, Dali, or Lijiang, and you are certain to find capable instruction in English. Of course, you can always try joining the leagues of kung fu practitioners at daybreak in the nation's parks, particularly if your interest is *tai ji quan*.

If you want to fight with more than your bare hands, paintballing is growing in popularity – try the listings magazines in the large cities. For those who really need to let off steam, anti-aircraft guns and AK-47s are available for renting at the firing range en route from Beijing to the Great Wall at Badaling.

Climbing

Most of China's sacred and scenic mountains, such as Tai Shan and Huang Shan, have steps, cable cars, and crowds all the way to the summit. Some of the mountains have less-used paths that make for pleasant hiking, but if you are a serious mountaineer, you will need to head to western China. The true roof of the world awaits in Tibet – topping Mount Everest will require patience and official approval, but treks to Everest base camp in the Rongbuk Valley are offered by several travel operators. Other spectacular climbs include Gongga Shan in Sichuan and also Muztaghata in Xinjiang (an easier climb and you can ski down), but, again, seek permission first.

More feasible is rock-climbing at Yangshuo in Guangxi, where the limestone crags that inspired poets down the centuries now inspire climbers up the peaks. Asia's fastest developing sport-climbing area combines a wide range

A class of soon-to-be kung fu masters, Shaolin Temple, Henan

Panda at the Breeding Center near Chengdu

of climbs with beautiful views, winding rivers, and great accommodations.

A few intrepid spelunkers have been exploring the extensive karst cave network of Guangxi. A small industry of caving tours has developed, although, for the most part, the itineraries are geared to the experienced spelunker.

Trekking & Camping

The fascinating southwest offers some of the best trekking possibilities in the country, such as exploring the jungle of Xishuangbanna or visiting remote Tibetan monasteries. Horse-riding trips are possible in Tian Shin in Xinjiang and the national parks of Sichuan. Check with specialist tour companies and the **Northwest Yunnan Ecotourism Association**.

Whitewater rafting trips are popular in the southwest and in Tibet. If you are thinking of signing up, check the company's credentials and past history, and ensure that high-quality helmets, lifejackets, and, if necessary, wetsuits are provided.

Camping independently in China is tricky, and not recommended. However, the lack of legal camping facilities may be about to change, because caravan culture has just reached China. RVing is still in its birthing stages and as the industry develops, trailer parks and camp grounds are certain to appear. Currently restrictions on foreign drivers mean that motorhoming is only possible through a specialist tour operator.

Spot a panda at the Wanglang Nature Reserve *(see p375)* or in Chengdu's Breeding Center *(see p366)*, where efforts are made to conserve the threatened species. Bird-watching tours head to Qinghai province for Bird Island on Qinghai Hu *(see p503)*, and to parks such as Zhalong National Reserve *(see p458)*, in the northeastern province of Heilongjiang, and Xixi Wetlands Park near Hangzhou, a natural sanctuary for birds and wildlife.

China's environment was savaged in the 20th century by political campaigns to move mountains with manpower; in the 21st, rampant economic growth threatens both bio-diversity and cultural diversity, and conservation efforts are growing to save China's unique wildlife and ways of life.

To support a responsible approach to tourism and the environment, consider tours and eco-lodges offered by organizations such as the Northwest Yunnan Ecotourism Association, based near Lijiang in Yunnan.

DIRECTORY

Sports

Basketball
W **nbachina.com**

Formula One
W **f1-shanghai.com**

Rugby
W **hkrugby.com**

Soccer
W **fa.org.cn**

Tennis
W **chinaopen.com.cn**
W **shanghairolexmasters.com**

Golf

Mission Hills
Various locations. Visit website for details.
W **missionhillschina.com**

Spring City
Tangchi, Yiliang County, Yunnan. **Tel** (0871) 6767 1188. W **springcityresort.com**

Downhill Skiing

Club Med
160 miles (260 km) from Harbin airport.
W **clubmed.com**

Yabuli
100 miles (160 km) east of Harbin, Heilongjiang.
Tel (0451) 5345 8888.
W **yabuliski.com**

Tour Companies

Abercrombie & Kent
W **abercrombiekent.com**
In the US:
Tel 1-800 554 7016.
In the UK:
Tel (01242) 854 260.

The Bespoke Travel Company
B510, 107 Dongsi Bei Dajie, Dongcheng District, Beijing.
Tel (010) 6400 0133.
W **bespoketravelcompany.com**

Myths and Mountains
976 Tee Court, Incline Village, Nevada, USA 89451.
Tel 1-800 670 6984.
W **mythsandmountains.com**

Steppes Travel
51 Castle St, Cirencester, Gloucestershire, UK GL7 1QD.
Tel (01285) 601 495.
W **steppestravel.co.uk**

Tibetan Connections
W **tibetanconnections.com**

Wild China
Room 803 Oriental Palace, 9 East Dongfang Road, North Dongganhuan Road, Chaoyang district, Beijing.
Tel (010) 6465 6602.
W **wildchina.com**

Cycle Tours

Bike China Adventures
2 Fangcao Street, Chengdu.
Tel 186 8402 8967 (China).
Tel 502 802 8585 (US).
W **bikechina.com**

Cycle China
W **cyclechina.com**

Red Spokes
W **redspokes.co.uk**

Ecotourism

Northwest Yunnan Ecotourism Association
Tel (0139) 8882 6672.
W **ecotourism.com.cn**

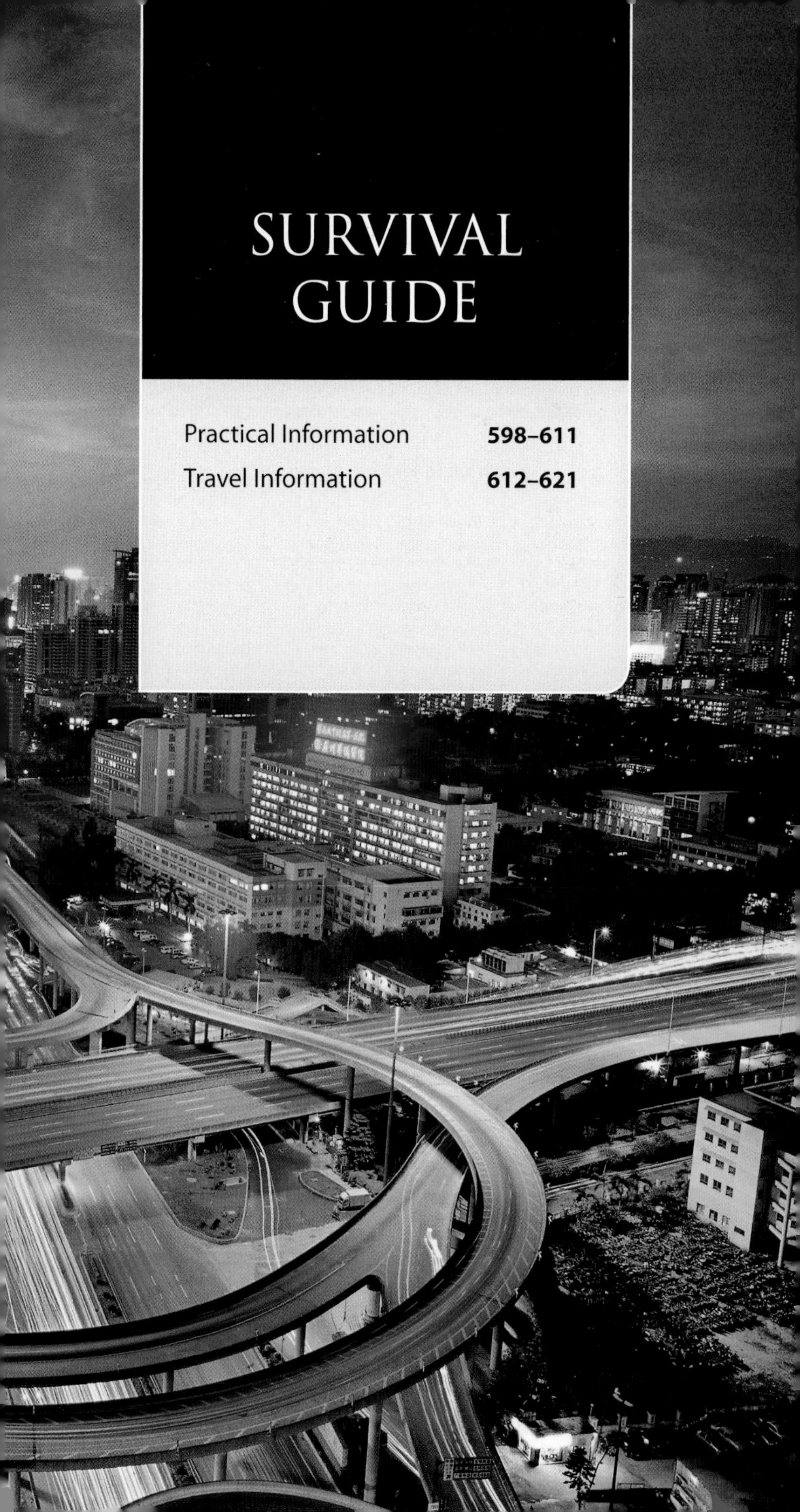

SURVIVAL GUIDE

PRACTICAL INFORMATION

China is going through an explosion in both international and domestic tourism. While there have been gradual improvements in the quality of tourist services, some of the remoter sights can still be difficult to reach independently, and most accessible sights get very crowded, especially during the summer season. Due to the absence of a nationwide non-profit network of tourist information centers, visitors often have to rely on hotels for guidance. In the larger cities the tourist infrastructure, including transportation, hotels, and restaurants, is on a par with international standards. The remoter areas, however, provide fairly basic accommodations and may not be equipped to cater to the needs of the international tourist. Communication also poses difficulties, as English is not spoken widely and its usage is generally restricted to major cities, tour groups, four- and five-star hotels, and restaurants catering to tourists.

When to Go

Spring and fall are the best months to travel to China. The peak tourist season, however, is June to September, best avoided if you don't like the heat – it is baking hot in north China, steamy in the Yangzi region, and sweltering in south China. Winter is fiercely cold in north China, particularly in the northeast. Winters in south China are more pleasant, especially on the perennially warm Hainan Island and in parts of Yunnan province. Climate and rainfall charts are found on *pages 54–5*. Planning a trip to coincide with the holiday and festival periods *(see pp48–53)* can lead to a fun and colorful trip experiencing China at its liveliest. However, tickets for air, train, and bus transport can be very difficult to acquire, as half of China will be traveling as well. Tourist sights are swamped with local sightseers, and most hotels and guesthouses raise their rates.

What to Take

In northern China, from November until March, you will require a down jacket, gloves, sweater, warm socks, thermal leggings, sturdy footwear, and lip balm. During the same season in the south, you still need a sweater and warm clothes, even as far south as Hong Kong. In summer, across most of China, you only need loose-fitting shirts or T-shirts, and thin trousers. Shorts will also do, though not many Chinese wear them. Bring a first-aid kit *(see p606)*, raincoat, sun hat, deodorant, pocket knife, flashlight, and some good reading material.

Advance Booking

The boom in domestic tourism means it is advisable to book ahead year-round, but especially during the peak holiday periods between May 1 and October 1, and the Chinese New Year.

Enjoying temperate weather at a tea garden in Chengdu

Booking in advance using the Internet can secure you good deals on accommodations. Unless traveling on short intercity routes, train tickets should be bought a few days before travel, as seats can be in short supply. Train tickets can be purchased up to 30 days in advance from stations and ticket offices and online. Bus tickets don't usually need to be booked in advance, but airplane tickets should be, especially during major holiday periods.

Visas & Passports

A passport, valid for at least six months, and a visa are necessary to enter the People's Republic of China. Most foreign nationals don't require a visa for entering Hong Kong and Macau but will need one if traveling on to mainland China. Chinese embassies and consulates around the world issue a standard single-entry, 30-day visa, although multiple-entry visas and 60-day visas can also be obtained, depending on the purpose of your visit. Visas cannot be issued at the border. When completing the visa application form, you must clearly specify what parts of China you plan to visit. Avoid mentioning Tibet or Xinjiang, even if you plan to visit these regions, as you may be questioned about your occupation and intent of visit – the list you provide is non-binding. Always carry your passport, as it is an essential document for checking into

◀ Night-time view of highway junction in Guangzhou

hotels and the Public Security Bureau (PSB) *(see p604)* may insist on seeing it. Photocopying the visa page and the personal information page will speed up replacement in case your passport is lost or stolen. Visa extensions are sometimes granted for 30 days by the foreign affairs branch of local PSBs throughout the country. Note that heavy fines are levied if you overstay your permitted period in China.

Travel Safety Advice

Visitors can get up-to-date travel safety information from the **UK Foreign and Commonwealth Office**, the **US Department of State**, and the **Australian Department of Foreign Affairs and Trade.**

Permits

Some areas of China – including Lushun (Liaoning), Xanadu (Inner Mongolia), and parts of Shennongjia (Hubei) – are either totally or partially off-limits, and may require a permit from the PSB. Check with the PSB before going to western Sichuan, where the rules of access are not fixed.

All travel to Tibet has to be arranged beforehand through a travel agency in China that will arrange a permit for you. If you want to travel outside of Lhasa, the agency will have to arrange a tour guide, private vehicle and driver, and any additional permits. The itinerary laid out in your entry permit is binding, and you will not be able to make changes unless it is an emergency.

Embassies and Consulates

Most countries have embassies in Beijing and consulates in Hong Kong, Shanghai, and Guangzhou, and to a lesser extent, in Chengdu, Chongqing, Qingdao, and Dalian. Consular offices can re-issue passports and assist in emergencies, such as theft, imprisonment, and hospitalization. Your hotel can put you in touch or try www.travelchinaguide.com.

Customs Information

When entering China, visitors are entitled to a duty-free allowance of 50 fluid ounces (1.5 liters) of wine or spirits, 400 cigarettes, and a certain amount of gold and silver. Foreign currency exceeding US$5,000, or its equivalent, must be declared. Items that are prohibited include fresh fruit, rare animals and plants, and arms and ammunition. Chinese law specifies limits on the export of certain items, such as herbal medicines. Also, objects pre-dating 1795 cannot be taken out of China, while antiques made after that date will need to have an official seal affixed. Although foreign visitors are largely left alone, it is not advisable to take in politically controversial literature, especially to sensitive areas such as Tibet, where there have been instances of books being confiscated.

Immunization

Ensure that all of your routine vaccinations, such as tetanus and polio, are up to date. It is also wise to get vaccinated against hepatitis A and B, and typhoid. Only visitors traveling from countries where yellow fever is endemic must provide proof of vaccination against the disease. Malaria medication is a good idea for those visiting rural areas, especially Yunnan and Hainan, as is a Japanese encephalitis vaccination. Try www.mdtravehealth.com for up-to-date travel-health information and advice on immunization.

Insurance

It is advisable to take out an insurance policy for medical emergencies as well as theft before leaving home, checking with your insurance company that it is entirely valid in China. The policy will cover the loss of baggage, tickets, and, to a certain extent, cash and checks. Insurance is also essential to cover any adventure activity or sport that you may undertake during your trip.

DIRECTORY

China International Travel Service (CITS)

W cits.net

Beijing
1 Dongdan Beidajie.
Tel (010) 6522 2991.

Dalian
Central Plaza Hotel,
145 Zhongshan Lu.
Tel (0411) 8368 7843.

Guangzhou
618 Jiefang Bei Lu.
Tel (020) 2201 3396.

Shanghai
1277 Beijing Xi Lu.
Tel (021) 6289 8899.

Suzhou
18 Dajing Xiang.
Tel (0512) 6515 9177.

Xi'an
48 Chang'an Bei Lu.
Tel (029) 6288 9999.

Travel Safety Advice

Australian Department of Foreign Affairs and Trade
W dfat.gov.au
W smartraveller.gov.au

UK Foreign and Commonwealth Office
W gov.uk/foreign-travel-advice

US Department of State
W travel.state.gov

Classic *tai hu* rock formations lining the shore in Yu Yuan (Jade Garden), Shanghai

Tourist Information

With the exception of the major cities, China has yet to recognize the value of professional Tourist Information Centers, either at home or abroad. Those that exist in Beijing and Shanghai are often under-funded, poorly staffed, and unreliable, although they are useful for obtaining free maps. The state-approved **China International Travel Service** (CITS) *(see p599)*, originally set up to cater to the needs of foreign visitors, today functions as any other local operator, offering nothing more than tours, tickets, and rented cars. A limited choice of government-run travel agencies abroad promote China tourism. However, they fail to offer professional and unbiased advice, instead steering customers toward group tours and standard hotels.

Admission Charges

Virtually every sight in China carries an admission fee. While many major museums are now free to enter, most temples and parks, smaller museums, palaces, historical monuments, sacred mountains, and wildlife reserves can only be entered after paying a fee. While temples charge anything from ¥5 to ¥80, prices of all other entry tickets vary. It is often hard to see where the money goes as many of China's temples and monuments appear severely neglected. Non-Chinese visitors occasionally have to pay a higher admission fee because of foreign visitor surcharges. Most sights, such as parks and temples, simply have a main ticket for entry *(men piao)*, but further tickets may need to be purchased for access to individual sights within the complex. Alternatively, a "through ticket" *(tao piao)* can be bought for access to all the sights. Occasionally there are further fees for storing bags. The sale of tickets often ceases half an hour or so before the sight closes for the day. Guides swarm around entrances to major sights and will latch onto you, even if you're not interested. It is wise to test their English first, as many just repeat fixed lines, parrot fashion, relating to the sight in question, and are unable to answer further queries.

Road sign in both Pinyin and Chinese characters

Holidays & Opening Hours

Even though New Year's Day (January 1) is a public holiday in China, the main holiday periods are during the Lunar New Year (Spring Festival) and October 1 (National Day) holidays (the May 1 Labor Day holiday is just a single day). Both holidays officially last three days, although most businesses and some banks remain shut for seven days. Accommodation prices rise as domestic tourism peaks. Tourist sights, however, remain open during these times.

Facade of the impressive Shaanxi History Museum, Xi'an

Language

The official language of China is *Putonghua* (literally "common tongue"), based on the dialect spoken in the northeast, and known outside China as Mandarin Chinese. Unlike other dialects, such as Cantonese, *Putonghua* doesn't specifically belong to any one region, and can be used throughout the country for communication between speakers of China's numerous dialects. Since the vast majority of Chinese people do not understand English, it is largely useless for communication outside of hotels. The tonal nature of *Putonghua* makes it difficult for English speakers to become accustomed to the language. Pinyin, a romanization system, helps in the recognition of sounds and has diacritical marks to indicate tone. A few basic phrases in *Putonghua* are listed on pages 656–60.

Facilities for the Disabled

If you are a wheelchair-user, China is not a recommended destination for you. With the exception of Hong Kong and, to some extent, Macau, China offers very basic facilities for the disabled, both in public transport and accommodations. Public buildings and places of interest are rarely fitted with ramps or rails, although this is slowly improving. Many of the pavements in urban areas are littered with obstacles and occasional potholes, and have high curbs, making wheelchair access troublesome.

The scarcity of safe crossing points on urban roads drives pedestrians onto overhead walkways; otherwise they have to join the crowds surging through the traffic. Rooms with services for disabled visitors are only available at the better hotels, although elevators are common in most hotels over three stories high.

Children with their parents enjoying a meal

Facilities for Children

The Chinese love children, and they are usually welcome everywhere in China. Even though baby-changing rooms are extremely rare, and very few restaurants have child seats, traveling with very young children can have its advantages as people will generally go out of their way to accommodate you in most places and situations. Supermarkets are well supplied with diapers, baby wipes, bottles, creams, medicine, clothing, infant milk formula, and baby food. However, the baby food is of a sweeter variety and nearly always heavily processed. The Chinese very rarely give pacifiers to their children, but you can find them in department stores in larger cities. Also bring a set of plastic cutlery for your child, as some restaurants and eating places only have chopsticks.

Photography

Everyone in urban China uses smartphone or digital cameras now, so film-developing stores are, as elsewhere, a novelty rather than the norm. While aged 35mm color print film is available almost everywhere, don't expect to find color slide or high-speed film outside of the large cities. Camera batteries are widely available in department stores in big cities, though it is best to bring your own supply. Many photo stores in Hong Kong, Macau, and mainland China provide transferring of images from a digital camera onto a disc.

Photographing people in China is generally not a problem, but it helps to first ask for their permission. Photography is rarely allowed within temple halls and museums, or at archeological sites, and signs indicate where photography is not permitted. In case you don't find a sign with such restrictions marked in English, it is advisable to ask around. Photographing politically sensitive images may cause offense, and it goes without saying that photography of military sites is banned. As far as the regulations go, photography from aircraft is banned, and so is taking photographs of airports, harbors, and railroads. However, barring the military installations, most of the other restrictions are seldom enforced.

If you are discreet and respectful, then you should encounter no problems.

Electricity

The electrical current in China is 220 volts. You will see a variety of plugs in China, including two flat prongs (the same as American plugs), or three flat prongs (the same as Australian ones). Outside Hong Kong, the British three square-pin arrangement is rare outside of smart hotels, so it is advisable to carry a travel conversion plug, readily available in most of the larger cities. A power-surge cable will protect laptops against voltage fluctuations, which are common in China. It is best to avoid cheap batteries, as they are very short-lived. Instead, buy a battery charger and rechargeable batteries, which can be easily found in most Chinese stores. Blackouts are not unheard of in China, so, given the erratic power cuts, it is wise to carry a flashlight.

Plugs with two and three prongs

Time & Calendar

Despite its extraordinary size, China occupies only one time zone, and there is no daylight saving time. Midday in Beijing is also midday in the farthest-flung parts of the country, including Lhasa and Ürümqi, which are along the same latitude as countries that are 2 and 3 hours behind China. China time is 8 hours ahead of Greenwich Mean Time (GMT), 2 hours behind Australian Eastern Standard Time, 15 hours ahead of US Pacific Standard Time, and 12 hours ahead of US Eastern Standard Time. The Western Gregorian Calendar is used for all official work in China, although the lunar calendar is still used for calculating the dates of festivals.

Measurements & Conversion Charts

The metric system is most commonly used in all parts of China.

Imperial to Metric
1 inch = 2.5 centimeters
1 foot = 30 centimeters
1 mile = 1.6 kilometers
1 ounce = 28 grams
1 pound = 454 grams
1 pint (US) = 0.473 liters
1 gallon (US) = 3.785 liters

Metric to Imperial
1 centimeter = 0.4 inches
1 meter = 3 feet 3 inches
1 kilometer = 0.6 miles
100 gram = 3.53 ounces
1 kilogram = 2.2 pounds
1 liter = 2.11 pints (US)

Etiquette

Despite rampant modernization, China remains a traditional society governed by strong family values. Although the cities and towns give the outward impression of Western modernity, their inhabitants retain a deep-seated and family-oriented conservatism. Confucian values promote respect for elders and those in positions of authority, and reinforce notions of conformity. Religious observance is also an important part of people's lives, but is largely separate from mainstream social behavior. The Chinese are, above all, welcoming and generous, and visitors are often amazed at their hospitality. If invited to someone's home, take a gift, such as French wine or chocolates, as a polite gesture.

Greeting People

Shaking hands is not customary in China, but Chinese men may shake your hand or expect their hand to be shaken by foreign visitors. Although the Chinese are not particularly tactile in their greetings, bodily contact is quite common between friends, even of the same sex. It is quite common to see young men and women walking arm in arm, or with their arm around another's shoulder. The usual Chinese greeting is *ni hao* ("how are you?") or *nimen hao* in its plural form, to which you reply *ni hao* or *nimen hao* – the polite form is *nin/ninmen hao*. Chinese people can be very direct, and will not blanch at asking you how much you earn, how old you are, or whether you are married. Such questions are seen as nothing more than taking a friendly interest in a new acquaintance. When proffering business cards, the Chinese do so politely, using the fingertips of both hands, and receive cards in the same manner. It is a good idea to take some business cards, with your particulars in Chinese on one side and in English on the reverse, as there will be many occasions to give them away.

Body Language

Once they reach the age of 30 or 40, the Chinese tend to dress conservatively, favoring dark and inconspicuous colors such as brown and black. In cities and towns, people wear jeans, T-shirts, and skirts, and many youngsters also dye their hair. Locals expect foreign visitors to dress and behave a little flamboyantly, so don't worry too much about what you wear, but try to avoid looking scruffy. It is also acceptable for both sexes to wear shorts in hot weather. On the beach, nudity and women sunbathing topless are rarely seen as Chinese beach culture is quite modest.

Advice for burning incense

Face

Reserved in manner and expression, the Chinese also harbor strong feelings of personal pride and respect. The maintenance of pride and the avoidance of shame is known as saving face. Loss of face *(mianzi)* creates great discomfort and embarrassment for the Chinese, so although you may often be frustrated by bureaucratic red-tape and delays, remember that arguing may make matters worse. Instead, try tackling difficult situations by being firm but polite, and use confrontation only as a last resort.

Places of Worship

Although there are no dress codes for Buddhist, Daoist, or Confucian temples, visitors to mosques should dress respectfully – avoid wearing shorts or short skirts and cover your upper arms. Buddhist, Daoist, and Confucian temples are relaxed about visitors wandering about, but do be considerate toward worshipers. Also, check whether you can take photographs within temple halls, as this is often not permitted. Taking photographs in courtyards, however, is usually not a problem. Most Buddhist and Daoist temples are active, and you should show respect toward the resident monks.

The courtyard of the Jade Buddha Temple in Shanghai

Dos & Don'ts

If invited out for dinner, expect to see the diners competing to pay the entire bill, rather than dividing it up between them. It is a good idea to join in the scramble for the bill, or at least make an attempt – your gesture will be appreciated, though almost certainly declined. The Chinese avoid talking about politics; it is best to follow suit.

Annoyances

The Chinese habit of staring, especially in smaller towns and rural areas, can be a little annoying. However, the intent is rarely hostile. Staring was common even in Beijing until the 1990s, and although it is rare in cities today, it helps to remember that China was closed to foreign nationals until the early 1980s.

Another annoyance that visitors face in smaller towns are the constant calls of "Hellooo!" or *laowai* ("foreigner"). It is best to either smile or ignore them, unless the person seems genuinely to be trying to make contact. In large cities, people often strike up conversation to practice their English. Sometimes, "art students" try and coerce you into visiting overpriced art galleries or cafés, which you should firmly decline to do.

Although line-ups are beginning to replace the usual mêlée at ticket offices, be prepared for a lot of pushing and shoving.

Since the outbreak of SARS in 2002 *(see p606)*, public health organizations have made considerable efforts to curb the habit of spitting. It is still widespread, however, especially in rural areas. Spitting is common on buses and trains, and it is not considered rude to spit in mid-conversation, so do not take offense.

Smoking & Alcohol

Smoking is now banned in public places in China, such as restaurants, hotels, train stations and theaters. However, as the world's largest producer and consumer of cigarettes *(xiangyan)*, these rules are difficult to enforce in China. Despite the appearance of no-smoking zones, many people choose to ignore them, and towns and cities remain shrouded in a haze of cigarette smoke. Many business owners resent banning their customers from smoking on their premises.

Bric-a-brac to be haggled over on display at a street market in Tianjin

Smoking is also banned on domestic flights and in train carriages. The Chinese are very generous when it comes to offering cigarettes; if you don't smoke, smile and say *"wo bu chou yan"*. They also enjoy drinking alcohol, and there is no taboo against moderate intoxication. The usual accompaniment during a meal is beer *(pijiu)*, or white spirit *(baijiu)*. People in cities are increasingly drinking wine, available in most large supermarkets. If someone raises a toast to you *(ganbei!)*, it is good form for you to toast the person back at a later stage.

A spirit consumed at business banquets

Bargaining

As a foreign national in China, it is essential to bargain *(jiangjia)*. You may often be overcharged – sometimes by large amounts – in markets and anywhere else where prices are not indicated. In some restaurants, the English menu has more expensive rates than the Chinese one. You may be able to bargain to reduce your hotel room rate, especially during the low season. When bargaining, there is no need to be aggressive. Instead, firmly state your price – which should never be unrealistic – and walk away if the vendor doesn't agree. Shopkeepers will often agree to the price once they realize they're losing a potential sale. The prices in large shops are usually fixed.

Tipping

Tipping is rare in China – there is no obligation to leave a tip *(xiaofei)* and people don't usually expect one. Some smarter restaurants, especially in Hong Kong, Macau, and the main Chinese cities, include a service charge on the bill.

Begging

China's imbalanced economic progress and huge population of rural poor have resulted in large numbers of beggars all over the country, especially in cities. Foreign visitors naturally attract their attention, and groups of children are often sent by their parents to extract money. The best strategy is to ignore them and walk away.

A beggar in Lhasa with colorful Buddhist regalia

Personal Security and Health

The Police Force in China is called the Public Security Bureau *(gong'anju)*, abbreviated to PSB. Foreign nationals are unlikely to encounter the PSB, unless extending their visa, applying for a permit to a restricted area, or reporting loss or theft. China is a bureaucratic police state, but foreign tourists are unlikely to encounter official corruption. Not all police stations *(paichusuo)* have English-speaking staff, so try to take along an interpreter if reporting a crime, although it is best to contact your embassy or consulate first for guidance. Throughout mainland China, call 110 for the police. Protect your valuables and important documents at all times, stay and eat in clean places, and drink only mineral water. For medical attention, it is better to opt for a private clinic rather than one of the many government hospitals.

Crowds in the busy shopping district of Causeway Bay, Hong Kong

General Precautions

Traveling in China is generally safe. Even though crime has burgeoned since the 1980s economic liberalization, with millions of unemployed migrants flocking to the cities, foreign visitors are unlikely to be the victims of crime, apart from petty theft. Tourists on buses and trains, particularly those in the hard-seat class *(see p617)* and on overnight journeys, are tempting targets for thieves. Guard your camera and valuables, wear a money belt at all times, and secure your luggage to the rack on overnight train journeys.

Hotels are, more or less, a lot more secure than dormitories, even though it is not unusual for things to go missing from hotel rooms. You could use the safes or storage areas that most hotels offer, but if you do so, insist on a receipt. If staying in a dormitory, never leave your essentials and important documents lying around, and be cautious about giving too many details to fellow travelers.

When walking in crowded streets, avoid wearing anything expensive or eye-catching, and keep your wallet in the bottom of your bag, but never in a backpack. Be discreet when taking out your wallet; it is best to carry only as much cash as you need for the day. Keep an eye on your belongings while visiting public washrooms, as quite a few travelers have had unpleasant experiences.

Keep cash, credit cards, passport, and visa documents in a money belt – ones that lie flat and are meant to be worn under clothing are best. Also, remember to make photocopies of the personal information and China visa pages of your passport and any other important documents and store them separately from the originals.

Security

Hosting the Olympic Games saw China upgrade security at airports, railway and metro stations, and at some sights, but it is rarely intrusive. At certain sights, you will be asked to deposit your bag before making a visit. Always carry your passport with you for identification.

Women Travelers

China is usually regarded as a very safe destination for women. In general, Chinese men are respectful toward women. That said, it is always worthwhile taking some commonsense precautions. Stay on your guard when visiting rural and far-flung areas if traveling alone. Always be aware of your surroundings and avoid wandering about alone in quiet and deserted places, especially after dark. Keep an eye on your drink if in a bar at night. It can be a good idea to join local tour groups or hire local guides, especially in more out-of-the-way places.

It is best to observe the clothing and behavior of local women, and adapt as closely as possible. It helps to dress modestly, especially in Muslim regions and rural areas.

If possible, avoid hotel dormitories and opt for single rooms in hotels located near the center of town on well-lit streets. To avert an undesirable encounter, carry a whistle or learn some basic self-defense moves.

Beijing PSB officer

Gay & Lesbian Travelers

The gay and lesbian scenes in China's main cities, in particular Shanghai, Beijing, and Hong Kong, are growing and diversifying, with clubs, bars, and venues increasing in number. However, China is still a highly conventional society, and homosexuality is largely disapproved of and misunderstood.

Homosexuality is legal, but there are no laws to protect gays, and police periodically crack down on meeting places. Even in cities, it is inadvisable for gays and lesbians to be open with their sexuality, despite the tactile relationship many Chinese have with friends of the same sex.

Hospitals & Medical Facilities

It is important to take out comprehensive medical insurance before arriving in China. China's state hospitals vary considerably in quality; better-equipped hospitals *(yiyuan)* can be found in the cities and large towns, but even at the best, communication can be problematic. Cities with large expatriate communities have private hospitals, where there are exclusive clinics with English-speaking staff to attend to non-Chinese visitors. Consider contacting your embassy for a list of approved hospitals. In general, medical services are reasonably cheap throughout China, but many hospitals may levy a certain amount of "foreigner surcharge" that could ensure better care. Whatever the type of institution, you will be expected to pay cash at the time of being admitted.

Pharmacies *(yaodian)*, identified by green crosses, are found all over China. Many of them stock both Western medicine *(xi yao)* and Chinese medicine *(zhong yao)*, and can treat you for minor injuries or ailments. Take adequate supplies of any prescription drugs you require, and also remember to take the chemical – not brand – name of all prescriptions, in case you need to restock. In large cities such as Beijing and Shanghai, prescriptions may not be required for a range of medicines, including antibiotics and sleeping pills.

Sign pointing the way to the facilities

Some large hotels have in-house clinics to help guests with diagnosis, medical assistance, and prescriptions. Large modern hotels may also be able to provide a Chinese speaker to accompany you to the hospital.

Distinctive green cross of a pharmacy

Those interested in traditional Chinese medicine *(see p238)* for treating chronic ailments can visit the traditional institutes attached to local hospitals and medical colleges. Some hotels, too, offer various traditional Chinese treatments.

Public Bathrooms

Public bathrooms are usually of the squat variety and range from squalid, filthy, and rarely cleaned, to pristine modern facilities watched over by an attendant. There is often little privacy – door-less cubicles, separated by low walls, are the norm. Toilet paper is a rarity, so carry your own supply. Toilet paper should be put in the receptacle, if provided, rather than down the toilet, as septic systems are often unable to handle paper products. You will sometimes be expected to pay a few *jiao* for using the facilities. Use hotel and fast-food restaurant bathrooms whenever you get the opportunity.

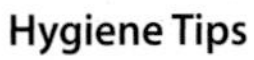

Hygiene Tips

The rigors of travel require a few extra hygiene considerations. Carry a small bar of soap or a bottle of hand sanitizer with you all the time. A packet of wet wipes always comes in handy.

Warts are easily picked up from poorly cleaned shower stalls. You will often find a pair of flip-flops under your hotel bed. These are meant to be worn in the shower, but you might consider packing a pair of your own.

DIRECTORY

In an Emergency

Tel Police 110.
Tel Fire 119.
Tel Ambulance 120.

Hospital and Medical Facilities

Beijing
Hong Kong International Medical Clinic, 9th floor, Office Tower, Hong Kong Macau Center, Swissotel, 2 Chaoyang Men Bei Dajie.
Tel (010) 6553 2288.
W hkclinic.com

International SOS, Suite 105, Wing 1, Kunsha Building, 16 Xin Yuan Li, Chaoyang. Clinic appts:
Tel (010) 6462 9112.
W internationalsos.com

Guangzhou
Can-Am International Medical Center, 5th floor, Garden Tower, Garden Hotel, 368 Huanshi Dong Lu. **Tel** (020) 8386 6988.
W canamhealthcare.com

Hong Kong
Queen Elizabeth Hospital, 30 Gascoigne Rd, Yau Ma Tei. **Tel** (0852) 3506 8888.

Shanghai
Parkway Health, 203/4 West Retail Plaza, Shanghai Center, 1376 Nanjing West Road.
Tel (021) 6445 5999.
W parkwayhealth.cn

Embassies in Beijing

Australia
21 Dongzhimen Wai Dajie.
Tel (010) 5140 4111.

Canada
19 Dongzhimen Wai Dajie.
Tel (010) 5139 4000.

Ireland
3 Ritan Dong Lu.
Tel (010) 8531 6200.

United Kingdom
11 Guanghua Lu.
Tel (010) 5192 4000.

USA
55 Anjia Lou Lu.
Tel (010) 8531 4000.

Travel Health

MASTA
Tel (0330) 100 4200 (UK).
W masta-travel-health.com

MD Travel Health
W mdtravelhealth.com

Sitting in the shade at the Botanical Gardens, Hangzhou, Zhejiang

Heat, Humidity & Pollution

During summer, it is hot all across China. If you're traveling during this time drink plenty of fluids to prevent dehydration, and increase your intake of salt to compensate its loss through sweating. Wear loose-fitting cotton clothing and sandals, remember to bring a sun hat and sunglasses, and use plenty of sunscreen. Most hotels, except the very cheapest, have rooms equipped with air-conditioning, and virtually all restaurants are air-conditioned as well. Prolonged exposure to the sun can cause heat stroke, a serious condition with high body temperature, severe headaches, and disorientation. To avoid heat rashes and fungal infections caused by humidity, wear clean, loose clothes made of natural fibers, and open sandals.

Many of China's cities, including Beijing, experience chronic levels of atmospheric pollution. This aggravates chest infections, and asthmatic travelers should always carry their own medication.

Cold & Hypothermia

Winter can be severe through most of north China. High-altitude travel in particular can expose you to extreme cold, and travelers to Tibet and other mountainous regions must be prepared for sudden changes in temperature. A waterproof and windproof layer is vital in cold conditions, as is adequate warm clothing, including thick socks, boots, jacket, gloves, and most importantly, a hat. The symptoms of hypothermia – shivering, dizziness, exhaustion, and irrational behavior – are brought on by prolonged exposure to the cold. Be aware of fingers and toes going white or numb, the first indications of frostbite, and rub them vigorously if they do.

A motorcyclist wrapped up against pollution

First-Aid Kit

Organize a basic first-aid kit, which should include: all personal medication, aspirin or painkillers for fevers and minor aches and pains, tablets for nausea and movement sickness, antiseptic cream for cuts and bites, an antifungal ointment, Band-Aids, gauze and tensor bandages, a pair of scissors, insect repellent, and tweezers. Also carry antihistamines for allergies, anti-diarrhea tablets, water purification tablets, disposable syringes, oral rehydration solution, and a thermometer. Taking a supply of antibiotics is a good idea but most of these items are readily available at Chinese pharmacies.

Stomach Upsets & Diarrhea

Usually caused by a change of diet, water, and climate, diarrhea is common among visitors. Chinese food, which can be quite oily and spicy, does require some getting used to for many people. If the change of diet is affecting you, stick to Western food and simple boiled food, such as plain rice, until the diarrhea subsides. Most importantly, drink lots of fluids, as diarrhea quickly leads to dehydration – oral rehydration solution (ORS) is an effective remedy. If you do not have any ORS, stir half a teaspoon of salt and three teaspoons of honey or sugar into a mug of boiled water.

To decrease your chances of stomach upset, avoid raw salads, cut fruit, cold cuts, roadside kabobs, fresh juice, and yogurt. It is important to avoid drinking tap water even in big cities, apart from Hong Kong. Drink boiled water, or bottled mineral water after checking that the seal is intact. Most international brands of carbonated drinks are widely available. Although street food can look tempting, it is safer to abstain unless it is hot and freshly cooked in front of you.

A good pharmacist can recommend standard diarrhea medication, such as Imodium, though if the attack is severe, it is best to consult a doctor. A popular and effective Chinese medicine for upset stomachs is *Huangliansu*.

SARS & Flu

In 2002, severe acute respiratory syndrome (SARS) spread throughout China and then to Toronto, Canada. China managed to contain the disease with a strict identification and quarantine program. Since then, there have only been minor, localized outbreaks of the disease. Another SARS outbreak is unlikely, but should one occur, do not travel to the affected area.

Bird flu, or avian influenza, is a serious problem in east Asia, but unlikely to affect travelers. Do not visit any poultry farms,

A food stall with a tempting but risky display

avoid birds at outdoor markets, and eat only poultry and eggs that have been thoroughly cooked.

In 2009, China underwent a mass vaccination program against swine flu (H1N1) for at-risk individuals (such as young children and pregnant women). The World Health Organisation (WHO) provides up-to-date information on serious diseases. If you develop symptoms of pneumonia or flu after your trip, see your physician immediately.

Sexually Transmitted & Other Infectious Diseases

After years of denial, Chinese authorities have begun to publicly admit to the alarming spread of HIV – the virus that causes Acquired Immune Deficiency Syndrome (AIDS) – via unprotected sex, drug use, and infected blood banks. Nonetheless, considerable ignorance about the disease and its prevention still exists in rural areas, and most prostitutes working in the cities are from rural China. Long-term visitors to China are screened for HIV infection.

Hepatitis B, also transmitted through contact with infected blood, is spread through sexual contact, unsterilized needles, tattoos, and shaves from roadside barbers. However, it can be prevented with a vaccine.

When visiting a clinic, ensure that the doctor opens a new syringe in front of you. You may even want to bring your own disposable syringe for the doctor to use. Any procedure using needles, such as tattooing or ear-piercing, is best avoided.

Water-Borne Diseases

Visitors must be on their guard against dysentery. Bacillary dysentery is accompanied by severe stomach pains, vomiting, and fever, whereas amoebic dysentery has similar symptoms but takes longer to manifest. Vaccination against Hepatitis A is advisable before leaving home, especially if you plan to visit rural areas. Other water-borne diseases, such as cholera and typhoid, can also be prevented with vaccines. Schistosomiasis (bilharzia), a disease caused by a water-borne parasitic worm found in south and central China, can be avoided by not swimming in fresh water. Drink bottled mineral water at all times, and avoid ice cubes.

Bottled mineral water

Rabies

The deadly rabies virus is spread via the bite of an infected animal. If you are bitten, clean the bite with an antiseptic solution and seek medical help at once. Treatment involves a course of injections. A rabies vaccine is only necessary if you are visiting high-risk areas for a long period and likely to come into contact with animals. Do not have this vaccine, unless advised by your doctor.

Insect-Borne Diseases

Mosquitos are rife during the summer in China. In the southern part of the country, mosquitos can carry a number of diseases. If you are visiting an area with a high risk of malaria, take preventive anti-malarial drugs before, during, and after your trip. In the UK, contact MASTA (Medical Advisory Services for Travellers Abroad) and check the MD Travel Health website *(see p605)* for information on malaria medication. Dengue fever and Japanese B encephalitis are also carried by mosquitos. To guard against mosquito bites, apply mosquito repellent and wear clothes that cover as much of your arms and legs as possible.

Altitude Sickness

A lack of sufficient oxygen at altitudes higher than 8,000 ft (2,500 m) can cause attacks of Acute Mountain Sickness (AMS) – severe headaches, dizziness, and loss of appetite. If these symptoms persist beyond 48 hours, you must descend to a lower altitude immediately and seek medical help. To avoid altitude sickness ascend slowly, drink plenty of fluids, and avoid alcohol and sedatives.

Trekking at high altitudes on Chomolungma (Mount Everest)

Banking & Local Currency

China provides a wide range of banking facilities and money exchange services, which are available in large cities, international airports, major banks, and top-end hotels. Always keep some cash to hand for transportation, restaurants, and purchases, as traveler's checks and credit cards cannot be used everywhere, especially in rural areas. ATMs that accept international cards are easy to find in all major cities. Foreign banks like HSBC and Standard Chartered are expanding their branch networks in major Chinese cities.

Banks & Banking Hours

The Bank of China has the most extensive network in the country. Several other major banks operate nationwide, including the Industrial and Commercial Bank of China (ICBC), the China Construction Bank, and China Merchants Bank. Banks are normally open 9am–4:30pm or 5pm Monday to Friday, but there are variations between places, and some banks are open on Saturdays. All banks remain closed for the first three days of the Chinese New Year, with reduced hours during other Chinese holidays.

ATMs

ATMs that accept foreign cards are common in all major cities of mainland China, plus Hong Kong and Macau, so can be relied upon for easy access to cash. In more remote areas of China, not all ATMs may accept international cards; visit your card issuer's website for locations that do. In cities, ATMs are located in banks, shopping malls, five-star hotels and airports. Some ATMs also dispense cash against credit cards. Cash withdrawn from ATMs is subject to the same exchange rate as credit cards, and there may be a limit to how much you can withdraw per day, so check with your bank for more information.

Hong Kong & Shanghai Banking Corporation (HSBC) ATMs

Changing Money

Chinese currency is not widely available internationally, though, increasingly, it can be exchanged in Asian airports and banks in major Asian cities, as well as Hong Kong and Macau. Within China, you can exchange currency at banks and international airports and most decent hotels will change money for guests. Most major currencies are accepted. All exchange operations are linked to the Bank of China, so rates vary little between them. Keep exchange receipts so that you can re-convert any surplus *renminbi* before leaving China. The Chinese "black market" for exchanging foreign currency offers only marginally better rates than banks. Dealing with the shady characters involved is not worth the hassle or risk, and you may end up with counterfeit *renminbi*.

Hong Kong dollars are convertible and available outside the country. They are accepted in Macau and most southern Special Economic Zones.

Credit Cards

Credit cards are widely accepted in upscale restaurants, hotels, and high-street stores, but always check before attempting to make a purchase that your foreign card is accepted. The accepted cards are MasterCard, Visa, Japan Credit Bureau (JCB), Diners Club, and American

DIRECTORY

Bank of China

Beijing
2 Chaoyang Men Nei Dajie. 1 Fuxing Men Nei Dajie, 100818.
W boc.cn

24-Hr ATMs
Arrivals Hall, Capital Airport. Corner of Sundongan Plaza, Wangfujing Dajie. Corner of Oriental Plaza, 1 Dongchang'an Jie.

Shanghai
39/F, Bank of China Tower, 200 Yincheng Zhong Lu, Pudong, 200120.

Hong Kong
1 Garden Road, Central
24–28 Carnarvon Road, Tsim Sha Tsui.

HSBC

Beijing
1/F, Fortune Financial Center, 5 Dongsanhuan Zhong Lu. **W hsbc.com.cn**

Shanghai
HSBC Tower, 8 Century Avenue, Pudong, 200120.

24-Hr ATMs
Shanghai Center, 1376 Nanjing Xi Lu.

Citibank

Beijing
1/F Tower 1, Bright Chang An Building, 7 Jianguomennei Dajie.
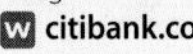
W citibank.com.cn

Shanghai
Citibank Tower, 33 Huayuan Shiqiao Lu, Pudong, 200120.

American Express

Beijing
Room 2101, China World Tower One, China World Trade Center, 1 Jianguo Men Wai Dajie, 100004.
W americanexpress.com.cn

Shanghai
Room 206, Retail Plaza, Shanghai Center, 200040.

Express. Air tickets can be bought by credit card from the Civil Aviation Administration of China (CAAC) offices, but train tickets have to be paid for in cash. Cash advances can be made on credit cards at the Bank of China.

Traveler's Checks

Traveler's checks are safer to carry than cash and offer a better exchange rate, but you will have to pay a commission. In addition, they are very hard to exchange; indeed, only the Bank of China will change them, and even then, they will do so reluctantly, as the process is complicated. Avoid bringing traveler's checks if at all possible. Keep the proof of purchase slips and a record of the serial numbers in case of loss or theft. Hold on to encashment slips, so you can convert spare *renminbi* to another currency before leaving the country.

Currency

China's currency is called *yuan renminbi*, literally "people's money". One *yuan* divides into 10 *jiao*, which divides into 10 almost worthless *fen*. In colloquial Chinese, *jiao* is called *mao*, and *yuan* is *kuai*. The most common coins include 1 *yuan*, 5 *jiao*, and 1 *jiao*, while the bills in circulation are 1, 2, and 5 *jiao*, and 1, 2, 5, 10, 20, 50, and 100 *yuan*. There are also some *fen* coins and notes, but this tiny denomination is rarely accepted. Try not to acquire too many damaged notes, as they may be difficult to get rid of. Counter-feiting is widespread, and shop-keepers regularly scrutinize large denominations. Hong Kong dollars divide into 100 cents, and Macanese *patacas* into 100 *avos*.

Banknotes

The more recently minted bills have Mao Zedong on one side and a well-known heritage sight on the other. The older bills depict the traditional dress of various ethnic minorities.

1-yuan note

5-yuan note

10-yuan note

20-yuan note

50-yuan note

100-yuan note

Coins

Except in some cities, like Guangzhou, where they are used for subway machines, coins are not widely circulated. There is a 1 yuan coin, some jiao *denominations, and tiny* fen.

5 jiao

1 jiao

1 yuan

Communications & Media

China has an efficient postal network with a variety of services, including registered post and express mail. Telecommunication systems are reasonably advanced and international telephone calls can be made from all but the cheapest hotels. The Internet is hugely popular, and cafés and bars with Wi-Fi access are widespread. The government, however, polices the internet, and websites that it considers controversial may be blocked. Foreign newspapers and magazines are sold in five-star hotel bookstores, and in some supermarkets and other bookshops.

Wheelchair-accessible phone booth, Beijing

International & Local Telephone Calls

Public telephones do exist in China but are rarely used in the cities – China has the largest number of cell phone users in the world. If you do use a public telephone, card phones that accept a wide variety of phonecards are available in large cities, and are the cheapest way of making calls. IC (Integrated Circuit) cards come in denominations of ¥20, ¥50, and ¥100. They are largely used for domestic calls. They can also be used for international calls, though the rates are not very good. IP (Internet Phone) cards come in denominations of ¥100 and offer the cheapest rates for international calls.

If you buy a local SIM card you can hook your GSM cell phone up to the Chinese system in minutes (North Americans need unlocked tri- or quad-band phones). Top-up cards are available on almost every street corner. Phones can also be purchased for modest prices (all have English menus) and there is a thriving second-hand market. Most international mobile networks have "roaming" partnerships with Chinese phone companies, but it is a good idea to check the call rates before you travel.

Internet

Personal computer ownership is widespread in China, though Internet cafés *(wangba)* can still be found in most towns. China is a very wired nation; most urbanites carry a smartphone and laptop or iPad. Many smart, modern cafés, coffee shops, and bars offer free Wi-Fi. Similarly, free broadband access for those with their own computers is commonplace in most hotels of a reasonable standard, as well as in the majority of youth hostels. Overseas websites and blogs are carefully monitored in China and often blocked. The government has been clamping down on the use of paid-for virtual private networks (VPNs), which had previously offered access to banned sites.

Postal Services

The postal service in China is, for the most part, reliable, and the domestic service is reasonably fast. It takes a day for mail to reach local destinations, two or more days to inland destinations, while the international postal service takes up to ten days for airmail and postcards overseas. Visitors can send mail by standard or registered post *(guahaoxin)*, while EMS (Express Mail Service) is a reliable way to send packages and documents abroad and within the country.

Main post offices are open seven days a week, from 8am to 8pm, while smaller ones usually close earlier or for lunch, and remain shut on the weekends. Large hotels usually have post desks.

Although it may help postal staff sort your letter if you write the country's name in Chinese characters, it isn't really necessary. Aerograms and packaging materials for parcels are available at post offices.

Reliable poste restante services are available all over China. You will need some form of identification – preferably your passport – to retrieve your mail. Envelopes should be addressed with the surname underlined and in capitals. Chinese addresses always start with

Accessing free Wi-Fi, which is widely available in many modern cafés

A choice of Chinese newspapers on display at a newsstand

the country, then the province, city, street, house number, and name of recipient. The postcode should be written at the top left.

Courier Services

Courier services are widely available, but less so in small towns and remote areas. While it is preferable to send large, bulky items by regular land, sea, or air cargo, important letters, documents, and smaller parcels are best sent through a courier agency. **UPS**, **Federal Express**, **DHL Worldwide Express**, and **China Post** are international courier agencies with a wide network.

Mail box, Beijing

Newspapers & Magazines

The *China Daily* is China's official English-language newspaper. Its reputation for being dry remains, but its scope and coverage has greatly improved. The state-run *Shanghai Daily* offers good coverage of events in the city. Most international newspapers and magazines can be found at tourist hotel stores and a small selection of supermarkets and other bookstores. Titles available include the *Inter-national Herald Tribune*, the *Financial Times*, *Time*, *Newsweek*, and *The Economist*. In Beijing, Shanghai, Tianjin, Guangzhou, and other large cities, look out for expat entertainment and culture magazines, which offer the best news on local events. The *Shanghai Daily* also covers entertainment, dining options, and cultural events.

TV & Radio

The state-run television network, Chinese Central Television (CCTV), has two English-language channels. CCTV9 has some interesting programs and gives a Chinese perspective on current affairs. Some English programs are also broadcast on CCTV4.

Cable and satellite television is available in most international chain hotels, and you will find BBC News 24 or CNN in many of them, too. Chinese programs range from historical costume dramas and tepid soaps to domestic travel, wildlife programs, war films, and news programs. As with all media, the State exercises control over what may be broadcast.

There is also a wide Chinese-language radio network, but only a few local English-language programs. You will need a shortwave radio to pick up the BBC World Service, Voice of America, and other international programs. The BBC has closed its Chinese-language World Service broadcasts. Some English broadcasts may be subject to disruption.

DIRECTORY

China Post
Tel 11185.
W ems.com.cn
W chinapost.com.cn

DHL Worldwide Express
Tel 95380 (nationwide).
W dhl.com

Federal Express
Tel 800 988 1888 (toll free nationwide). **W fedex.com.**

General Post Office
1 Beijing Zhan Qian Jie, Beijing.
100 Yan'an Dong Lu, Shanghai.
2 Connaught Place, Central, Hong Kong.

International Post Office
Jianguomen Bei Dajie, Beijing.
Sichuan Bei Lu, Shanghai.

UPS
Tel 800 820 8388 (toll free nationwide). **W ups.com**

Useful Dialing Codes & Numbers

- To call China from abroad, dial your international access code, China's country code (86), the area code omitting the first 0, followed by the local number.
- Neither Hong Kong nor Macau have area codes; they only have country codes – 852 and 853 respectively.
- To make an inter-city call, dial the area code of that city and the local number. For Beijing, dial 010; Shanghai 021; Guangzhou 020; Chongqing 023; Kunming 0871.
- To make a local call, omit the area code.
- To make an international call from China, dial 00, the country code, the area code omitting any initial 0, and the local number.
- Country codes: UK 44; France 33; USA and Canada 1; Australia 61; Ireland 353; New Zealand 64; South Africa 27; Japan 81.
- Dial 115 for international directory assistance.
- Dial 114 for local directory enquiries in Chinese; dial the area code followed by 114 for numbers in another town.

TRAVEL INFORMATION

Most visitors to China arrive by air, though overland routes exist with train links to neighboring Russia, Mongolia, Kazakhstan, and Vietnam, and a bus link to Pakistan. It is also possible to arrive by sea; there are regular ferries from Japan and South Korea. Traveling within the country – even to remote areas – is possible by air, train, road, and, on a few routes, by boat. China has a huge, rapidly expanding rail network, although tickets – especially for sleeping berths – can be rare during the holiday periods. The intercity high-speed rail network is extensive, and often a good substitute for flying. Bus travel is improving, with buses covering the entire country, including a number of "luxury" buses that offer reasonable comfort. Renting a car is not advised; the paperwork required to obtain a Chinese driving licence is extensive.

Arriving by Air

All major international airlines fly to China. **Air China**, the country's main international carrier, has quite basic service and facilities, but has a near-spotless safety record and its flights, to most of the world's major airports, are competitively priced. North American and European carriers such as **United Airlines**, **British Airways**, **Virgin Atlantic**, **Lufthansa**, **KLM**, and **Air France**, have regular, often direct, flights to some, or all, of China's three main – and most sophisticated – airports at Hong Kong, Shanghai, and Beijing. Flights to the other parts of the Far East, Australia, and New Zealand are offered, among others, by **Singapore Airlines**, **Japan Airlines**, **All Nippon Airways**, **Korean Air**, **Qantas**, **Cathay Pacific**, **Air New Zealand**. Cheaper flight options to China are also available via **Air China**, **China Eastern**, **Aeroflot** (via Moscow), **Malaysia Airlines** (via Kuala Lumpur), and **Air Asia**, **Jetstar**, **HK Express**, and **Tiger Airways** (from Southeast Asia).

State-of-the-art terminal at Beijing Airport

International Flights & Airports

China's three main international airports are at Hong Kong, Beijing, and Shanghai. The Chinese government is investing a considerable amount of money to provide its international airports with state-of-the-art features. Beijing Capital Airport has three impressive terminals – terminal three was designed by architect Norman Foster and opened in time for the 2008 Olympics. In 1999, Pudong Airport was built in Shanghai, making it the first city in China to have two international airports. Macau, too, has an international airport on Taipa Island, although most visitors arrive via boat from Hong Kong. Other international airports offering flights to overseas destinations include Changchun (Nagoya, Seoul, and Tokyo), Changsha (Seoul), Chengdu (Amsterdam, Bangkok, Frankfurt, Kathmandu, Singapore, and Tokyo), Chongqing (Nagoya, Seoul, and Singapore), Dalian (Hiroshima, Munich, Sendai, Seoul, and Tokyo), Guangzhou (Kuala Lumpur, Los Angeles, Sydney, Singapore, Paris, and other destinations), Guilin (Seoul and Bangkok), Haikou (Bangkok, Osaka, and Seoul), Hangzhou (Bangkok, Kuala Lumpur, Seoul, Tokyo, and Amsterdam), Harbin (Seoul, Khabarovsk, and Vladivostok), Kunming (Bangkok), Lhasa (Kathmandu), Nanjing (Bangkok, Seoul, Singapore, and Frankfurt), Qingdao (Osaka, Seoul, and Tokyo), Shenyang (Osaka and Seoul), Shenzhen (Bangkok, Manila, and Tokyo), Tianjin (Nagoya and Seoul), Xi'an (Nagoya, Pusan, Seoul, and Tokyo), Xiamen (Manila, Singapore, Osaka, and Tokyo), Ürümqi (Almaty, Bishkek, Islamabad, Moscow, and Novosibirsk), and Wuhan (Seoul).

Air Fares

Air fares vary according to the airline and the season. The peak season for international flights to China is between June and September, when prices are highest. Reasonably priced tickets are also hard to find during the holidays: Chinese New Year and the first week of October. While flying via another country is cheaper than flying direct, traveling by a Chinese airline such as Air China or China Eastern *(see p615)* will be cheaper than international airlines. Plenty of discount tickets are available for long-term travel, which are valid for 12 months with multiple stopovers and open dates. The best deals can usually be found online (try www.ctrip.com and www.elong.com). Numerous travel agencies across the world have websites, making it easy to compare prices. Tickets can be booked through ticket offices, travel agents, and hotels, but travel agents – especially those away from hotels and areas used by expats – tend to offer the best prices.

On Arrival

On the airplane, visitors are given a customs arrival form to complete, combining immigration, customs, and health information, which has to be submitted along with their passport at the airport immigration counter (between the plane and the arrivals hall).

International airports throughout China offer a limited range of facilities, but you will find foreign exchange counters, ATMs, public telephones, left-luggage services, restaurants (though rather overpriced), very limited shops, and toilets. Airport tourist information centers in China are of varying degrees of usefulness, and are often manned by staff who speak poor English.

Getting from the Airport

Airports are linked to the city by express train or by bus routes that make several stops in town. Avoid the overpriced taxi touts who try and force their services on foreign visitors. Instead, head for the taxi rank, where trips into town are charged by the meter. Four- and five-star hotels usually run shuttle buses to their hotels and the Civil Aviation Administration of China (CAAC) runs buses to their office in town.

Check-In

The check-in time for international flights is officially 2 hours before departure. Most passengers are allowed up to 44 lbs (20 kg) of baggage, while first-class passengers may be allowed up to 66 lbs (30 kg). One additional item of hand luggage weighing up to 11 lbs (5 kg) is also usually permitted. Baggage allowance depends on the destination, and travelers to North America are generally allowed more luggage. If you are carrying heavy luggage, check with your airline to make sure that your luggage is within the weight limit, as excess baggage charges can be very high.

AIR CHINA

Logo of China's national airline, Air China

Departure

Departure tax is included in the price of an airplane ticket and a fee is no longer payable at airports.

DIRECTORY

Airline Offices

Aeroflot W aeroflot.com

Air Asia W airasia.com

Air China
W airchina.com.cn

Air France
W airfrance.com.cn

Air New Zealand
W airnewzealand.com

All Nippon Airways
W ana.co.jp

British Airways
W britishairways.com

Cathay Pacific
W cathaypacific.com

China Eastern
W www.flychinaeastern.com

HK Express
W hkexpress.com

Japan Airlines
W jal.com

Jetstar W jetstar.com

KLM W klm.com

Korean Air
W koreanair.com

Lufthansa
W lufthansa.com

Malaysia Airlines
W malaysiaairlines.com

Qantas W qantas.com.au

Singapore Airlines
W singaporeair.com

Tiger Airways
W tigerair.com

United Airlines
W united.com

Virgin Atlantic
W virgin-atlantic.com

Airport	Telephone	Distance to City Center	Average Journey Time
Beijing Capital Airport	(010) 96158	16 miles (25 km) northeast	40 mins (taxi)
Hongqiao Airport (Shanghai)	(021) 96990	12 miles (19 km) west	30 mins (taxi)
Pudong Airport (Shanghai)	(021) 6834 5328	28 miles (45 km) east	45 mins (taxi)
Hong Kong International Airport	(0852) 2181 8888	20 miles (32 km) west	25 mins (train)
Macau International Airport	(0853) 2886 1111	3 miles (5 km) northwest	15 mins (taxi)

Domestic Air Travel

The arrival of cheap, high-speed train travel in China has led Chinese airlines to step up the competition in terms of both the cost and comfort of their services, especially on the popular Shanghai–Beijing route. The extensive domestic flight network involves numerous regional airlines flying to over 150 airports. The main cities of Beijing, Nanjing, Chengdu, Tianjin, Chongqing, Hong Kong, Shanghai, Dalian, Guangzhou, and Xi'an are particularly well connected to airports throughout the country. Domestic air tickets are straightforward to buy, so wait until you arrive in the country and then shop around for discounts. Flight cancellations and delays due to bad weather are common, especially in winter and on less-traveled routes in the more remote provinces, so remember to reconfirm your ticket and the time of your flight.

The domestic departure hall of Beijing Capital Airport

Domestic Airlines

A few private airlines operate from Hong Kong and Macau, but most other airlines in China are administered by the Civil Aviation Administration of China (CAAC). There are currently about ten domestic carriers operating in China. (The initials in parentheses are the airline code or flight-number prefix.) Some of the domestic airlines, such as **China Southern** (CZ), and **China Eastern** (MU), also fly international routes. You can buy domestic flights from these airlines overseas, but rates are far better when booked in China. Other domestic airlines include **Sichuan Airlines** (3U), **Shenzhen Airlines** (ZH), **Hainan Airlines** (HU), and **Xiamen Airlines** (MF).

The CAAC is driving service improvement throughout the industry, especially on board, and changes are noticeable from even just a few years ago. Unfortunately, frequent delays and cancellations still occur. Announcements are in both Chinese and English if there are foreign nationals on board. In-flight service can be brusque, and foreign visitors have felt neglected in the past, but service has improved greatly.

Air China's international flying safety record is good, and now almost all domestic airlines have fleets of new aircraft, which means safety records have improved further. Older aircraft are sometimes used in China's peripheral regions. Before you choose to book with a particular airline, you may wish to ask what kind of plane you will be boarding.

The baggage allowance is up to 44 lbs (20 kg) for economy class and up to 66 lbs (30 kg) for first and business class. You are also allowed up to 11 lbs (5 kg) of hand luggage, although airlines almost never weigh it. The charge for excess baggage is 1 percent of the full fare per 2.2 lbs (1 kg).

Domestic Airports

Air travel is becoming much more convenient in China, with new airports being built and old ones renovated and expanded. It has been made a national priority to upgrade all city airports, and state-of-the-art facilities are now available at Beijing Capital Airport, Shanghai's Pudong International Airport and Hongqiao Airport, Guangzhou Baiyun International Airport, and the Hong Kong International Airport at Chek Lap Kok. These modern airports easily compare with the best in the world. Airports in some major tourist cities, such as Xi'an, Hangzhou, Tianjin, Kunming, Chengdu, and Nanjing also offer up-to-date facilities. Many new airports are being built in cities across China, including a second one in Beijing (in Daxing district, in Hebei province). A number of airlines operate to and from Hong Kong and Macau, as well as from the mainland. These include the low-cost carrier **Spring Airlines**, Hong Kong-based **Cathay Dragon** (part of Cathay Pacific, *see p613*) and **HK Express**, and the Hainan Island-based operator Hainan Airlines.

Flight attendants aboard Sichuan Airlines en route to Chengdu

Getting to & from the Airport

The distance from airports to city centers varies considerably in China, so factor this into your journey time. Also, always allow time for unforeseen delays en route. In many large cities and towns, you can reach the airport or travel from the airport into town on a CAAC bus, which departs from and arrives at the CAAC office in town. In larger cities, such as Beijing, Shanghai, and Hong Kong, dedicated bus and train services run from town to the airport. Hong Kong, Shanghai and Beijing airports all have express train links to the city. Shanghai's Hongqiao and Pudong Airports are connected to the city's metro system (line 2). For faster travel to and from downtown, the high-speed Maglev train connects with Longyang Road metro station (also line 2), near the Pudong commercial/residential centre.

Taxis wait for passengers outside the arrivals hall. Make sure you head for the taxi rank and avoid the numerous touts who will try to direct you towards their own car. Insist on the driver using the meter. Drivers rarely speak English so have your destination written in Chinese characters or keep the phone number of your accommodation on hand so the driver can call for directions. If you have booked accommodation, check whether your hotel offers transport to and from the airport.

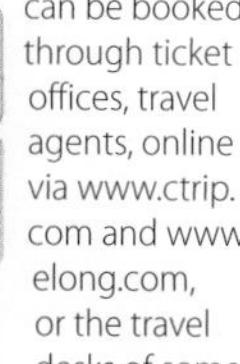

Road signs to the airport, Hong Kong

Check-In

For most domestic flights, the check-in time is at least an hour and a half before departure, although very few passengers arrive that early. Make sure all your bags are tagged, and do not pack sharp objects, such as scissors, tweezers, nail files, or knitting needles, in your hand luggage. The airport tax for domestic flights is usually ¥50, and is paid at the time of purchasing the ticket.

Tickets, Reservations & Cancellations

Each domestic airline has a booking office in most cities, as well as a reservation counter at each airport. Tickets can be booked through ticket offices, travel agents, online via www.ctrip.com and www.elong.com, or the travel desks of some of the better hotels – you should not be charged a booking fee. Travel agents and websites tend to offer the best discounts. Credit cards are accepted by many travel agents and CAAC offices. Visitors are required to show their passports when purchasing tickets. There is generally no shortage of tickets unless you are flying between Hong Kong and a mainland destination, except in the run up to and during the Chinese New Year, and the week-long holiday period after October 1, when it is advisable to book well ahead.

A combined international and domestic timetable is published by CAAC in both English and Chinese. These publications can be bought at most airline offices and CAAC outlets. Individual airlines also print their own timetables, which are available at booking offices throughout the country. Flight schedules are revised in April and October each year.

Ticket prices are calculated according to a one-way fare, and a return-ticket is simply double the single fare. Discounts on official fares are the norm, so it is best to check with travel agents for good deals. Business class tickets cost 25 percent more than economy, while first class tickets cost 60 percent more. Children over the age of 12 are charged adult fares, while there are special discounted fares for younger children and infants.

If you wish to return or change your air ticket, you can get a refund as long as you cancel at least 24 hours before departure, and return your ticket to the same agent who sold it to you. Even if you miss your flight, you are entitled to a refund of 50 percent of the full fare. You may be asked to buy travel insurance from your ticketing agent. However, this is generally not worthwhile, as the amount you can claim is very low.

DIRECTORY

CAAC Offices

Beijing
Tel (010) 8778 6114.
W **caac.gov.cn**

Airlines

China Eastern
Tel (010) 95530 (nationwide hotline).
W **en.ceair.com**

China Southern Airlines
Tel 400 669 5539 (nationwide hotline).
W **csair.com/en**

Hainan Airlines
Tel 0898 95339.
W **hainanairlines.com**

HK Express
Hong Kong
Tel (0852) 3902 0288.
Shanghai
Tel 4000 122 388 (nationwide in mainland China).
W **hkexpress.com**

Shenzhen Airlines
W **globalshenzenair.com**

Sichuan Airlines
Tel 4008 300 999.
W **scal.com.cn**

Spring Airlines
W **en.ch.com**

Xiamen Airlines
W **xiamenair.com**

Traveling by Train

China is a vast country and, for many travelers, train journeys are an excellent way to see the countryside and get to know the people. Trains are punctual, fast, and relatively safe, and are a reliable transport option. Since 2009, China has been rolling out an extensive network of high-speed "bullet" trains running on key intercity routes. Journey times are much shorter, but ticket prices are higher. Trains are usually crowded so it is advisable to either buy your ticket well in advance, or ask your hotel or travel agent to arrange your bookings.

The Rail Network

Since the cost of air travel is beyond the reach of many Chinese, traveling by train is the preferred alternative, especially over long distances. China has an efficient and extensive rail network that covers every province, including Hainan Island, connected to the mainland by a special train ferry, and mountainous Tibet, connected to Qinghai by a new railroad line. Hong Kong is also connected to mainland China by rail. Depending on which type of ticket you purchase, Chinese trains can be quite comfortable, and there are fast services running between most large towns and cities.

Trains & Timetables

Although trains in China are commendably punctual, trying to decipher a Chinese timetable is an impossible task, unless you can read Chinese. Timetables are published in April and October each year, and are available at train station ticket offices. A good online timetable can be found at www.travelchinaguide.com. Stations can be frustrating places, and

Platform food stall, Yinchuan train station

visitors will need patience to deal with them. Trying to locate English-speaking staff on platforms is difficult, even in large cities such as Beijing and Shanghai. Telephoning stations with enquiries is pointless unless you speak Chinese.

Each train is identified by a train number, written on the outside of each carriage, that indicates its route and destination. As a rule, incoming and outgoing trains running between two destinations are numbered sequentially. For example, train K79 travels from Shanghai to Kunming, while train K80 runs from Kunming to Shanghai.

Trains are of five types: those with numbers prefixed by the letter "T" or "K" are express *(te kuai)* or fast *(kuai)* trains, and those whose numbers have no prefix are ordinary *(pu kuai)* trains, with frequent stops. "G" indicates direct high-speed trains, while "D" is used for high-speed trains with stops. Express trains have carriages of all classes, and are the most modern and comfortable, with few stops and superior services. All long-distance trains are equipped with sleepers.

There is no smoking permitted within compartments, although most trains allow passengers to smoke in the corridors. Most trains have dining cars, and staff will continuously push trolleys through the carriages selling noodles, snacks, mineral water, coffee, and newspapers. The noise level in carriages is often very high, as music and announcements are regularly broadcast over the speakers. China's modern fleet of trains are much cleaner than the old ones and have air-conditioning. The older trains can be very dingy indeed; prepare yourself for sordid and filthy bathrooms.

Classes

Whereas high-speed trains have only two classes (economy and first), regular Chinese trains have four. The most luxurious class is **Soft Sleeper** *(ruan wo)*, with four comfortable berths per compartment. Offering more privacy, security, and cleanliness than less-expensive classes, soft sleeper tickets are

Grand Soviet-style Taiyuan train station

Modern glass-and-steel train station, Changzhou

comparatively pricey, and are not much cheaper than air tickets on certain routes.

For long journeys lasting over 6 hours, **Hard Sleeper** *(ying wo)* is the best way to travel. Consequently, these tickets are the hardest to procure, and you'll be lucky to get one on short notice. Hard sleeper can be an economical choice when traveling between cities overnight, as it saves the cost of a night in a hotel. Carriages consist of doorless compartments, each with six bunks. Tickets are of three types – upper berth *(shang pu)*, middle berth *(zhong pu)*, and lower berth *(xia pu)*, with a small price difference between each. The lowest berth is the most expensive, while the top one is the cheapest. Some people, however, prefer the middle one. The upper bunk has little headroom and is closest to the speakers. During the day, the lower bunk acts as seating and fills with fellow passengers. Pillows, sheets, and blankets are provided by the railways, as are two thermos flasks of boiling water, which you can replenish yourself from the massive boiler at the end of each carriage. Once aboard the train, the inspector will exchange your ticket for a token, and return the ticket at the end of the journey.

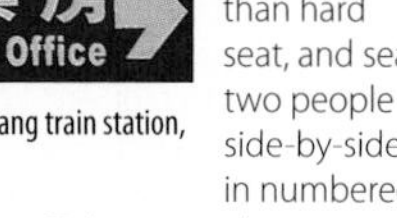

Booking office sign, Zhenjiang train station,

The cheapest class is **Hard Seat** *(ying zuo)*, which seats three people side-by-side on lightly cushioned seats. Although fine for short journeys, spending more than 4 hours in a hard-seat carriage can be quite unpleasant. Carriages are usually crowded and dirty, the speakers blare endlessly, lights remain on at night, and compartments are filled with smoke. It is possible to upgrade *(bu piao)* once aboard the train, if there is space available in the class of your choice. Note that hard-seat tickets bought on the same day are usually unreserved.

Available only on certain routes, **Soft Seat** *(ruan zuo)* carriages are much more comfortable and spacious than hard seat, and seat two people side-by-side in numbered seats. Tickets cost about as much as hard sleeper.

Train Tickets, Fares & Reservations

When buying tickets, it is wise to plan in advance. On most routes, it is advisable to buy tickets at least two or three days before you travel. Tickets are available as early as 30 days before departure. On short routes, you may be able to secure a ticket just before departure, but it is safest to buy ahead. Tickets on longer routes sell out, especially those for hard sleepers.

Train fares are calculated according to the class and the distance traveled. All tickets are one-way, so you will need to buy another ticket for the return journey, although return tickets are gradually being introduced for the high-speed intercity routes. Joining the crowds at station ticket counters can be very trying, so unless the station has a separate ticket office for foreign visitors, which is the case at Beijing train station, consider asking your hotel, tourist office, or travel agent to buy tickets for you. You must show your passport when buying train tickets, and the passport number will be printed on them. Don't buy black-market tickets, since you won't be allowed in the station unless the number on the ticket matches your passport.

Before boarding the train, visitors wait in a hall before filing past ticket-checkers to the platform. Retain your ticket as inspectors will ask to see it again, just before you reach your destination. Note that getting hold of tickets during the Chinese New Year (Spring Festival), and the May and October holiday periods can be very difficult, and it is inadvisable to travel during these times.

A uniformed guard minding a double-decker train, Dalian

Traveling by Bus & Ferry

China's extensive network of road transport connects most cities, as well as distant, rural areas. Bus travel is essential for reaching places that are not served by train. Tickets are both easier to procure and are cheaper than train tickets, and there is a wider choice of departure times, stops, and itineraries. The absence of a national operator, however, means that numerous competing businesses exist, coupled with minimal regulation. Furthermore, driving is often rash, vehicles are poorly maintained, and road conditions can be bad, especially in the more remote areas. A small network of passenger ferries serves ports along China's coastline and some of the inland waterways.

Long-Distance Buses

There are still many parts of China that are not accessible by train, making it necessary to make the long haul by road. In Fujian, where rail services exist but are infuriatingly indirect, bus travel makes a lot of sense. In Guizhou and Guangxi, the more interesting areas inhabited by ethnic minorities are only accessible by bus and the tropical area of Xishuangbanna in Yunnan is best explored by bus or taxi. You will also need to take a bus (unless you are flying) to reach western Sichuan. Numerous sights throughout China are off rail lines, and you will need to tackle the bus system at some point if you wish to go beyond the towns on the main train line.

Many smooth, wide highways now link some of the major cities, making some bus travel, particularly on the east coast, reasonably comfortable. In some cases, the bus is now a faster way to reach your destination than the train.

All cities and most large towns have at least one long-distance bus station *(changtu qiche zhan)* where state-run buses arrive and depart. Private bus firms may have set up a few of their own bus stations in town; often, one of these is located next to the train station. Other stations may be located on the edges of town – the North or East bus station will usually serve destinations to the north or east. Determining which of these stations serves the place you are trying to reach can be tricky, so you will need to ask around. Destinations are displayed in Chinese characters on the front of buses.

Long-distance buses vary enormously in quality, age, and comfort. You may find that several buses are running along the same route, so make sure you are sold a ticket for the fastest, most comfortable bus, or the cheapest, if you prefer. In general, long-haul bus journeys are taxing. Road conditions are often poor and road works are common, slowing the journey considerably. Drivers can be reckless and bus crashes are distressingly frequent. The noise level can be deafening, with music blaring and the driver leaning on the horn, so take earplugs. Most buses are choked with cigarette smoke.

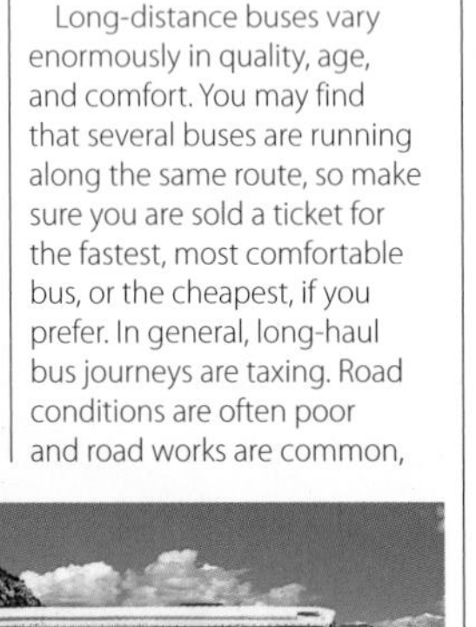

Bus stop, Hong Kong

Ordinary buses *(putong che)* are the cheapest and have basic, lightly padded seats. These buses stop often, so progress can be slow. They provide little space for baggage – there's no room under the seats and the luggage racks are minuscule. Suitcases and backpacks are usually stacked next to the driver, and you may be charged. **Sleeper buses** *(wopu che)* speed through the night making few stops, so reach their destination in good time. They usually have two tiers of bunks, or seats that recline almost flat. The older models can be quite dirty. Lower bunks *(xia pu)* cost more than the upper bunks *(shang pu)*, but are worth the extra cost as you are less likely to be thrown from your bed when the driver takes a corner at speed.

Shorter routes are served by rattling **minibuses** *(xiao ba)*, which depart only when every spare space has been filled by a paying passenger. Crammed to the roof, minibus trips can be quite uncomfortable.

Express buses *(kuai che)* are the best way to travel. Some are luxury *(hao hua)*, have air-conditioning, and enforce a no-smoking policy. Luggage is stowed in a hold, which is fairly safe, given the few stops that are made en route.

In certain parts of China – in Gansu and Sichuan, for instance – you may be required to purchase insurance from the People's Insurance Company of China (PICC) before being allowed on a bus. Usually, however, it is included in the price of the ticket. This insurance waives any responsibility of the

A basic long-distance bus *(putong che)* awaiting passengers, Qinghai

A ferry on the Huangpu River, sailing through Shanghai

government bus company should you be injured in a bus crash and it does not cover you in the event of an accident.

Bus Tickets & Fares

Traveling by road is not always cheaper than traveling by train. Tickets are sold at long-distance bus stations and, depending on the route, do occasionally sell out. Tickets for private buses and minibuses are either purchased on board the bus or from touts nearby. Main bus stations invariably have computerized ticket offices, and the queues are much shorter than those experienced at train stations.

Promotional river cruise sign outside tourist office

Ferries, Boats & Cruise Ships

A small network of coastal routes survives in China, and vessels still ply the Yangzi River, but the increased convenience of traveling by air, road, and rail has reduced the variety and frequency of sea- and river-ferry sailings in China.

The most popular river route is the trip along the Yangzi between Chongqing and Yichang, through the Three Gorges *(see pp358–60)*. An overnight ferry service for tourists runs along the Grand Canal between Suzhou and Hangzhou, and Wuxi and Hangzhou *(see p223)*. There are no regular passenger ferry services up the Yangzi River available to foreign visitors until Wuhan.

Popular coastal ferry routes include boats to Hainan Island from ports in the province of Guangdong (including Guangzhou) and Beihai in Guangxi. A large number of vessels ply between Hong Kong and Macau, many of which are high-speed and operate round the clock. Macau is also connected to ports in Guangdong, while Hong Kong is linked to Zhuhai and several ports on the Pearl River delta. Within Hong Kong, a medley of craft run to the outlying islands. There are now a few vessels connecting Hong Kong with the rest of China.

Because of the prohibitively long overland routes, ferries link the booming northeastern city of Dalian with Yantai and Tianjin. Yantai and Weihai on the eastern tip of Shandong peninsula are accessible from Shanghai, Dalian, and Tianjin. Note that ferry timetables may change frequently and services may have been added or terminated.

Several international sea routes link China to other countries. From Japan, Kobe is connected to both Tianjin and Shanghai on the east coast, while ferries also link Osaka with Shanghai. From South Korea, the port of Inchon is connected to the Chinese ports of Dalian, Weihai, Qingdao, Shanghai, and Tianjin.

Shanghai's two international terminals – at Wusongkou and the smaller Shanghai International Cruise Terminal – are seeing increasing numbers of cruise ships, with the fast-developing cruise industry forming a key part of the city's plan to become an international shipping center. Shanghai welcomes 500 cruise ships annually, bringing 1.2 million visitors to the city. Costa and Royal Caribbean already use the city as an Asian base port, and several other Asia-Pacific cruise routes – including to Russia, Taiwan, and Southeast Asia – are expected to open in the next few years. Cruise passengers arriving in Shanghai should now be able to shop in duty-free stores at the port.

Tourist boats docked on the vast Qinghai Lake

Transportation in Cities

Transportation options vary greatly between cities in China. Many of the largest metropolises have complex networks with subway systems that, in many cases, are in the process of being extensively expanded. In Beijing and Shanghai, the subway *(ditie)* is the best way to get around, while in Hong Kong, the transportation system is well-integrated, and subways, trains, and buses are all convenient options. In most cities, buses are slow and usually packed, but are very cheap. Taxis *(chuzu qiche)* are a necessity for most travelers and, despite the language barrier and misunderstandings with drivers, are the most convenient way to get around. Bicycles once ruled the roads of China's cities and although not as popular today, they are still one of the best ways to explore.

Beijing's Subway

The subway system in Beijing underwent major development in preparation for the 2008 Olympic Games. The system has been expanded and includes an express rail line which goes direct to Beijing Capital Airport.

The subway is a swift way to get around this spread-out city. The system is easy to use, although walks between lines at interchange stations can be long. The current ticketing system is based on the distance traveled, with fares varying from ¥3 to ¥10. Only the Airport Express is more expensive, costing ¥25 one-way. Buy your ticket at the ticket booth near the entrance, or from a vending machine.

Sign for Beijing subway

Shanghai's Subway

The rapidly expanding Shanghai subway system is clean and efficient, with the first line built in 1995. The 14 lines currently in operation are expected to increase to a total of 22 by 2020. Lines 1, 2, and 10 are most useful to the tourist, with line 2 connecting the city's two airports, Pudong and Honqqiao. Line 10 links several of the city's major sights. Fares range between ¥3 and ¥15, depending on the number of stops traveled. Check the map to determine your fare and then buy a ticket from the booth or machine. You can also buy ¥50 pre-paid tickets. Put your ticket into the slot at the barrier and the gates will open. Retrieve your ticket on the other side of the gate and hold on to it – you will need it at the destination exit.

The much-touted Maglev (magnetic levitation) runs between Pudong Airport and the Longyang Road metro station (on Line 2) and reaches speeds of 270 miles per hour (430 km/h). Check the times of departure.

Hong Kong's MTR

Integrated and efficient, Hong Kong has the best public transportation system in the country. The city is easy to get around using all of its forms of transport – MTR (subway and overground trains), buses, trams, and ferries – and most signage is in English. You can buy single tickets for your journeys, but each type of transit requires a separate ticket. Alternatively, you can buy an Octopus card, an electronic card that allows you to hop on and off most of the system. You can buy these for a minimum of HK$150 including a HK$50 deposit, which is refunded when you return the card. You can easily add credit at MTR stations, ferry piers, and convenience stores.

The Mass Transit Railway (MTR) currently has 12 lines, with two more under construction. The fare increases with the distance traveled, except on the Airport Express Line where a higher fee is charged. If you buy a single ticket, tap it on the turnstile sensor to open the gate. At the end of your journey, feed the ticket into the turnstile to exit the system. If you have an Octopus card, touch the card to the turnstile sensor at the start and end of your journey.

There are three overground MTR lines that cover destinations in the New Territories. East Rail was the original Kowloon–Canton railroad and heads north into mainland China. Do not go past Sheung Shui (the second-last stop), if you do not have the correct documentation to enter the mainland.

Buses & Trams

City bus networks are extensive and cheap. The buses *(gonggong qiche)*, however, are almost always overcrowded – so much so that you are unlikely to be able to see out of the windows. These conditions are perfect for thieves, so stay well-aware of your belongings. Consider using buses only for short straightforward journeys. Avoid them if you are trying to get from one end of town to the other – you are likely to get stuck in traffic.

Motor-rickshaw for hire, Harbin

Bicycles in Beijing – the traditional way to get around the city

Bus routes can be tricky to navigate, particularly as most routes and destinations are listed in Chinese only. Hong Kong has the most easy to use bus system, although traffic can be as bad here as anywhere else. Hong Kong also has an old tram line that runs from Kennedy Town to Causeway Bay on Hong Kong Island. Dalian has a few trams as well. Maps of bus and tram routes are widely available, especially in and around train stations.

Taxis

The best way to get about in cities that don't have subway systems is by taxi *(chuzu qiche)*. Taxis are found in large numbers in all Chinese cities – often congregating near train stations – and can be hailed easily in the street. Guests staying at hotels can also ask the reception desk to summon a taxi. When arriving at airports, avoid the touts who immediately surround you, and head instead to the taxi rank outside where you are less likely to be overcharged. Also, make sure the driver uses the meter *(biao)* or negotiate a flat rate in advance. Taxis rarely have rear seat belts *(anquan dai)*, so sit in front if you are traveling alone. Few taxi drivers speak English, so it is advisable to have your destination written down in Chinese, which the staff at your hotel will gladly do for you. Fares vary slightly from city to city, the most expensive being Beijing and Shanghai, but taxis generally offer both good value and convenience. In many cities, different models of cars will have different rates. Note that tipping the driver is not necessary.

Taxis can also be hired for the day – a convenient way to see sights just out of town. Agree on a price beforehand, and make sure your driver is clear on the extent of your itinerary. In Tibet, you may find that hiring a jeep and driver is the only way to get to some sights. It is customary to pay for the driver's lunch. In smaller towns, motorcycle rickshaws *(sanlun motuoche)* and bicycle rickshaws *(sanlun che)* are a convenient and entertaining way to get around town. Do not take these in major cities – they cost about the same as a taxi and frequently target tourists for substantial rip-offs. In some small towns, they are the only form of transport. Agree on the fare before climbing aboard.

A city taxi in Beijing

Motorcycle taxis are a very quick way to cover longer distances, although they are really only practical if you are traveling alone with little luggage. Insist on the driver providing you with a helmet.

Cycling

Hiring a bicycle is one of the best ways to explore towns and their environs. Bike lanes are common (although not always respected by drivers) and roadside repair stalls are everywhere. In Beijing, the bicycle is a major mode of transport. With its spread-out sights and flat terrain, bikes are a good way to traverse the city, but you may find the traffic intimidating. Hangzhou has the best bike hire system, with dozens of kiosks to hire official public bicycles from. Make sure that any bike you rent has a lock. Handy bike stands are found in big cities and have an attendant to watch the bikes for a nominal fee.

Road Names

Main streets, avenues, and thoroughfares are often divided into different sections based on the four cardinal points. For example, Zhongshan Lu (Zhongshan Road) may be divided into Zhongshan *Xi* Lu (West Road) and Zhongshan *Dong* Lu (East Road). Similarly, you may also see Zhongshan *Bei* Lu (North Road) and Zhongshan *Nan* Lu (South Road). Apart from *lu* (road), other key words are *jie* (street), and *hutong* and *xiang* (lane or historic alleyway). Road names in large cities such as Beijing may also display the Pinyin transliteration, but in smaller towns and remote destinations, only Chinese is used. A proposal to remove Pinyin from street signs in Shanghai doesn't seem to have caught on.

Taxis and buses on a busy street in the center of Macau

General Index

Page numbers in **bold** refer to main entries.

D

E

H

K

L

M

S

T

U

X

Acknowledgments

Dorling Kindersley would like to thank the following people whose contributions have made the preparation of this book possible.

Publishing Managers
Kate Poole, Scarlett O'Hara

Managing Editors
Vicki Ingle, Anna Streiffert

Publisher
Douglas Amrine

Production Co-ordinator
Linda Dare

Additional Contributors
Calum Macleod, Helen Glaister, Sarah Waldram, Martin Walters

Editorial Assistants
Katherine Haw, Alka Thakur

Cartographic Designer
Alok Pathak

Cartographic Proofreader
Tony Chambers

Artwork Reference
Other Shore Arts Inc.

Proofreader
Stewart Wild

Proofreader, Chinese
Jiewei Cheng

Indexer
Hilary Bird

Revisions and Relaunch Team
Emma Anacootee, Claire Baranowski, Sonal Bhatt, Tessa Bindloss, Gary Bowerman, Emma Brady, Tom Deas, Caroline Evans, Anna Freiberger, Lydia Halliday, Tim Hannigan, Rose Hudson, Helena Iveson, Joanna James, Sumita Khatwani, Olivia King, Priya Kukadia, Rahul Kumar, Maite Lantaron, David Leffmann, Neil Lockley, Shobhna Lyer, Carly Madden, Tanya Mahendru, Nicola Malone, Rosie Mayer, Peter Neville-Hadley, George Nimmo, Garima Pandey, Sangita Patel, Susie Peachey, Helen Peters, Marianne Petrou, Pollyanna Poulter, Rada Radojicic, Sands Publishing Solutions, Alice Saggers, Supriya Sahai, Avijit Sengupta, Rituraj Singh, Beverly Smart, Meredith Smith, Chirstine Stroyan, Josh Summers, Craig Turp, Stuti Tiwari, Janis Utton, Conrad Van Dyk, Ros Walford, Catherine Waring, Christine Watts, Jamin York, Gao Xing, Charles Young, Gui Zhiping

DTP
Shailesh Sharma, Vinod Harish

Digital Media Team
Nishi Bhasin, Manjari Rathi Hooda, Pramod Pant, Mahesh Singh

Additional Photography
Max Alexander, Geoff Brightling, Chen Chao © Rough Guides/Tim Draper, Andy Crawford, Gadi Farfour, Steve Gorton, Nigel Hicks, Colin Keates, Dave King, Stephen Lam, Ian O'Leary, Chester Ong, Jane Miller, Colin Sinclair, Hugh Thompson, Walia BPS, Paul Williams

Photography Permissions
The Publishers thank all the temples, monasteries, museums, hotels, restaurants, shops, and other sights for their assistance and kind permission to photograph their establishments.

Picture Credits
Key: a-above; b-below/bottom; c-centre; f-far; l-left; r-right; t-top.

Works of art have been reproduced with the permission of the following copyright holders:

Zhang San Feng from *The Explanation of Taijiquan Shi Yi* by Dong Yingjie scanned by Chip Ellis with thanks to Gordon Jolly 279cl.

123RF.com: 4045qd 153b; Tom Baker 201c; bassphoto 586bl, Manit Larpluechai 380cl; Yifeng 535br; Zhang Yongxin 591tc; **8 1/2 Otto e Mezzo BOMBANA Shanghai**: 576bl.

Agua: 572bc; **Akg-Images**: Archives CDA/St-Genes 260tr; Han Kan 214cl; Laurent Lacat 59tr; VISIOARS 468cl. **Alamy Images**: age fotostock 16tr, 223crb; ART Collection 44–45c; Pat Behnke 80br, 601tr; Beijing Eastphoto stockimages Co.,Ltd 126; Best View Stock 162–3; Peter Bowater 39cr; Jon Bower 313bc; China Span /Keren Su 358cla; Dallas & John Heaton 188; David Crausby 608c, 618cr; Nick Dawson 50bc; Delphotos 41bl; Dorling Kindersley ltd 381c; First Light/Ken Straiton 79tc; Eddie Gerald 467c; Granger Historical Picture Archive 203c; John Henshall 15b; Johnny Henshall 15tr; JTB MEDIA CREATION, Inc. 226cl; Lou Linwei 577br; Iain Masterton 25b, 611tl; MCLA Collection 214–15, 215cl; Colin Monteath 514br; Jake Norton 607br; Panorama Stock 109br, 134br, 138bc, 166, 294–5, 468br; /Ru Suichu 108br; /Zhang Zhenguang 212tr; Pixel 8 283bl; Prisma Bildagentur AG 16bl; Robert Harding World Imagery 159cla, 17t; Rochaphoto 511cra; David Sanger 470tr; Snap 2000 Images/David Robinson 95c; Valery Rizzo 48bl; Sergi Reboredo 195b; View Stock China 128cl, 159clb; Matthew Wellings 51b; Henry Westheim Photography 17br, 451tc; Ron Yue 52cr. **Amanfayun**: 554cr, 560tl, 578t.

Ancient Art & Architecture Collection: 481bc.
Ardea.com: Mary Clay 29crb; David Dixon 26crb, 350cl; Kenneth W. Fink 28bl; Nick Gordon 29cl; Pascal Goetgheluck 417cla; Joanna Van Grulsen 26clb, 26cb; C Clem Haagner 28clb; Keith & Liz Laid 350cra; Tom & Pat Leeson 27br; Adrian Warren 367cra; M. Watson 28cb, 29br, 409br.
The Art Archive: Bibliotheque Nationale de Paris 59cra, 223cra, 470–71, /Marc Charmet 34tr; British Library 32br, 34bl, 63tr; British Museum/Eileen Tweedy 80tr; Freer Gallery of Art 63cr, 286cla; Genius of China Exhibition 44tr, 57bc, 60bl, 470bl, 470cla; Musée Thomas Dobrée Nantes/ Dagli Orti 69tl; National Palace Museum of Taiwan 36cl; Palace Museum Beijing 438–9; Private Collection Paris/ Dagli Orti 141bc; School of Oriental & African Studies/Ellen Tweedy 428bl; William Sewell 269tr.

Steven Baigel: 537br.
Benoy Behl: 527bc.
Biblioteca Nazionale Centrale, Rome: 238cl.
Bibliothèque Nationale de France, Paris: 32tr, 42ca.
www.bridgeman.co.uk: 36cr, 37cra, 37cl, 42tr, 42cl, 43clb, 49tr, 268tr, 440bl, 68crb, 439bl; Bibliotheque des Arts Décoratifs, Paris 439br; Bibliothèque Municipal, Poitiers 215tr; Bibliothèque Nationale Paris 8–9, 34cl, 37tr, 68cb, 149br, 477cb; British Museum 491br; Giraudon 60br; James Gray (1757–1815) 439cr; Miss E. M. Gregson 351br; Hermitage 499cb; Illustrated London News 440cl; National Palace Museum, Taipei, Taiwan 477cra; Private Collection 215tl, 268cl; Société Asiatique, Collège de France, Paris 299cla; V & A Museum 438bl; Yu Zhiding (1647 – p.1709) *The Depiction of the Poet Wang Yuang* (1634–1711) watercolor 184tr (d).
British Library, London: 63tl. **© The British Museum**: 35tr, 44br, 44bc, 44clb, 45tr, 45bc, 45bl, 45br, 45cra, 62–3, 526bc.

China Stock: 59bl, 65c, 65bl, 70bl, 71cra, 262br, 300, 422br; Liu Liqun, 42cb, 42br, 359tl, 359cra, 409cra; Liu Xiaoyang 274ca.
Chinapix: 192tr; Zhang Chaoyin 538cl, 538bc.
China Span: Keren Su 185cl.
Christian MANGE: 584b.
Corbis: 69c, 72bl, 73tc, 92cla, 107tl; Archivio Iconografico, S.A. 439cra; Art on File 13cl; Asian Art & Archaeology Inc. 58cb, 60ca, 62bl,
64bc, 64tc, 470crb; Tiziana and Gianni Baldizzone 35cra, 550tc; Dave Bartruff 268bl, 565br, 568cla; Bettman 43ca, 71tl, 71br, 72tl, 165bl, 203br, 256bc, 263tl, 303crb, 303ca, 383br, 452br; Bohemian Nomad Picturemakers 565tl; Burstein Collection 36br, 56, 59clb, 61tc, 66bl, 214bc, 499br; China features, /Li Gang 25tr; Christie's Images 58tr; ChromoSohm INC/Joseph Sohm 112br; Pierre Colombel 491crb, 500tr, 500cla, 500cra, 500clb, 500bl, 500crb, 500br, 501tl, 501cla, 501clb, 501bl; Dean Conger 141cra, 249br, 511cl, 569c; The Cover Story 469tl; Design Pics/Keith Levit 552–3; EPA/Wu Hong 548bl; Ric Ergenbright 223bl; Macduff Everton 73bl, 73cr; Eye Ubiquitous/Bennett Dean 401tr, 544bl; /Julia Waterlow 34br, 468clb; Michele Falzone/ JAI 14bc; Free Agents Limited 42tr, 441cra; Christel Gerstenberg 214clb; Philip Gould 286tr; Franck Guiziou/ Hemis 132–3; Peter Guttman 517cra; Robert Harding World Imagery 14tr, /Jochen Schlenker 208; Historical Picture Archive 299cl, 439tr; Angelo Hornak 499bl; Dave G. Houser 49bl; Hulton Collection 249bl, 440cla, 547tr; Imaginechina 604bc; Hanan Isachar 30b; Robbie Jack 47bl; Wolfgang Kaehler 139bl, 160tr, 440tr, 440br, 440–41c, 441crb; Kelly-Mooney Photography 103tc; Christine Kolisch 536tr; Earl & Nazima Kowall 31tr, 39tl, 51tl, 460br, 461cr, 461cl, 461crb, 461br, 461bl, 519cl, 468bl, 569bc; Daniel Lainé 399crb; Charles & Josette Lenars 65tr, 151tl; Paul W. Liebhardt 413bl; Liu Liqun 22tc, 31br, 115tr, 199clb, 311tl, 359clb, 469bl; Chris Lisle 537cr; Craig Lovell 529br, 539br, 544tr; Ludovic Maisant 399clb; Lawrence Manning 269bl; Tom Nebbia 418bc; Papilio/John R. Jones 508tl; Louie Psihoyos 459bl; Carl & Ann Purcell 30tr, 37crb, 509br; Jose Fuste Raga 12br; Red link, 432–3; Reuters 38bl, 48br, 53tc, 275br, 564br, 614br; Roger Ressmeyer 100cr; David Samuel Robbins 539bl; Galen Rowell 518t, 528cla, 528–9, 528bc, 529cr, 537tc; Royal Ontario Museum 44bl, 45crb, 62ca, 66t, 260br, 261tl, 417cr; Royalty-Free 49bc; Sean Sexton Collection 203bl; Stapleton Collection 81tr; 30clb, 48cl, 241cla, 241br, 242cla, 243br, 274br, 362br, 412br, 412clb, 413br, 413tl, 413cr, 419tl, 468–9, 510cl, 514cl; Vince Streano 429bl; Keren Su 402, 448–9; Swim Ink 269tl; Wen Tao 542–3; Robert van der Hilst 187cl, 499cla; Viewstock/HeZhiFongi 276–7; Reza Webistan 519br; Nevada Weir 469cr, 513tl; Nick Wheeler 238br; Janet Wishnetsky 471br; Alison Wright 495clb, 518br; Michael S. Yamashita 185br, 215crb, 417br; Liang Zhuoming 508b; Xinhua Photo 459br.

CPA Media: 68t, 70tr, 203cl, 438cl, 439tl, 495c; David Henley 231cra, 235crb; Meng Qingbiao/Chinese Government (1961) 71crb; Oliver Hagreave 303cl; Oliver Hagreave/Bibliothèque Nationale Paris 66clb.

Dreamstime.com: Aakahunaa 470br; Addingwater 386–7; Andrius Aleksandravicius 192bl; Steve Allen 11tl, 520–21; Beijing Hetuchuangyi Images Co,. Ltd. 88tr; Bjmcse 2–3; Cao Hai 23; Chuyu 232tr, 257tl; Cqyoung 356tr; Cupertino 193tl; Inna Felker 90t; Lin Gang 5tr; Glowon-concept 13tr; Sam D\'cruz 320cl; Dk88888 134tl; Gringos4; Jianquing Gu 4crb; Hanshua 189b; Hungchungchih 117br; Hupeng 46tr; Wangkun Jia 233cl, 235bl; Mike K. 571br, 614tr; Vichaya Kiatyingangsulee 357cr; Liz Lee 356cl; Jianhua Liang 367cb; Liumangtiger 193t; Yiu Tung Lee 312; Liangwm 462–3; Lonestarforever 250–51; Xueguo Lu 148t; Denis Makarenko 47cr; Mengzhang 116br, 223clb; Jun Mu 290; Zhang Nan 344–5; Leung Cho Pan 280–81; Ricardo De Paula Ferreira 351cb; William Perry 442; Pindiyath100 13br; Ppy2010ha 353bl; Rodho 222tl; Shupian 20; Sophiejames 517tl; Starfield 188; Tab1962 201cla; Tempestz 21b; Tonyv3112 201bl Tvorecxtra 378; Wenling01 24t; Ivonne Wierink 215bc; Wingkit 354; Wxj651208 182b; Yongsky 230tr; Zhanghaobeibei 420cl; Zhaojiankang 244; Xishuiyuan 388tl, 457tl; Xi Zhang 74–5; Xiye 610brl; Xfdly3 410–11; Zhanglianxun 222bl.
DK Images: British Museum 43tl, 44cla, 225bl, /David Gower 214tr, /Alan Hills 225clb, 225cr, 238cra; Glasgow Museum/Ellen Howdon 527cra; Judith Miller Archive 260bl,

/Sloan's 260bl, 491bl; courtesy National Maritime Museum/David Spence 155bc, /James Stevenson 43crb; courtesy of Pitt Rivers Museum/ Geoff Brightling 42tl; private collection 519tc; courtesy of Science Museum 43bl, /Dave King 43bc; Yorkshire Museum/Harry Taylor 459crb.
Tim Draper: 427br.
Ray Dunning: 225c.

Fotoe: 36tr, 303cb; A Chun 358br; An Ge 27cr; Wang Yizhong 389clb; Wu Dongjun 412–13; Yang Xingbin 382tl; Ying Ge 358cra; Zhang Weiqing 36bl; **Fotolia**: choikh 324–5.
Getty Images: 619tl; AFP 48–9; Walter Bibikow 264; Luis Castaneda Inc. 84; Feargus Cooney/Lonely Planet Images 294–5; HAIBO BI 482; Robert Harding tr 472; Image Bank/Angelo Cavalli 612bl; Christian Kober/AWL Images 166; MelindaChan 492–3; National Geographic 58ca, /Louis Mazzatenta 459cra; Panorama Media 596–7; Photographer's Choice/John Warden 113tl; Photographer's Choice/Nikolay Zurek 269cl; David Silverman 369cr; Travel Ink 237tl; Berthold Trenkel 395tl; Feng Wei Photography 506; Huang Xin 300.
Grand Lisboa: 581tr; **Sally & Richard Greenhill**: S.A.C.U. 70cl, 71tr, 70br.

Nigel Hicks: 174–5, 284bc; 350clb, 350crb, 350bl, 350br, 377tc, 458br, 508c, 509tl, 510tr, 510bl, 512tl.
Hilton Worldwide: 574bl.
Hong Kong Tourism Board: 317tr, 326br, 331tc.
Hotel ICON: 580br.

Imagine China: 72crb, 115br, 128bl, 268–9; Adrian Bradshaw 459cla; Chen Shuyi 101br; Chen Yun 495br; CNS 81cr; Fan Chongzhi 287tl, 287tr, 287cra; Fang Zhonglin 198clb; Gong Weizhi 93cr; Guangyao 184cr; Hu Qingming 159br; Huang Jinguo 185cr; Huang Shaoyi 286br; Huang Yizhu 362cla; Jia Guorong 225crb; Jiang Chao 39cra; Jiang Guohong 46br; Jiang Ren 165cra; Jin Baoyuan 185tr; Kan Kan 36cb; Lang Congliu 235tc; Li Jiangsong 35br; Li Wei 260cla, 260crb, 287br; Liang Weijie 446tl, 446b; Lin Weijian 184bl, 192cl, 192cr; Ling Long 52br; Liu Jianming 382br; Liu ling 259br; Liu Liqun 270cl, 270bl, 360cla; Liu Quanju 52tl; Liu Zhaoming 478br, 478t; Long Hai 80bc, 81bcr, 195cra, 225br; Luoxiaoyun 460tl; Lu Baohe 299bc; Ma Kang 516tr; Olivia Savoure 516cla, 517br, 526tr; Shen Yu 184br, 204br, 610br; Shui Xiaojie 278br, 418car; Tang Jianwei 278tl; Wang Jianxin 81bcl, 366tl; Wang Mengxiang 430cr, 431br; Wu Changqing 110tr, 303cla; Wu Hong 47br, 91br; Xiong Yijun 29cr; Xu Ruikang 185tc; Yan Shi 151bc; Yang Xi 234cl, 287cr; Yin Zi 32–3; Yuan Yanwu 38–9; Yue Sheng 529tl; Zeng Yun 286clb; Zhan Xiadong 529tr; Zhang Fenquan 447br; Zhang Guosheng 97bl; Zhang Jie 303bl; Zhang Xing 287br; Zhang Xinmin_Xinjiang 509c, 512b, 509br; Zhang Yongzhe 215br; Zhou Kang 196tr; Zhu Xuesong 271tl, 271cr, 271br; Zhuge Ming 453bl, 528tr; Zou Xian 38br; Zuo Shan 389br.
Institute of History & Philology: Academia Sinica 32clb.
iStockphoto.com: Alantobey 515tl; LordRunar 89cr; MosayMay 323tc; Winhorse 587tl; Zorazhuang 178–9.

Jia Shanghai: 559tr.

Kobal Collection: Columbia 47tr; Tomson films 47tl.
www.kungfumagazine.com 2005: 165crb, 165clb.

David Leffman: 430tl.
Library of Congress, Washington, D.C.: 399bl.
Linden Centre, Dali: 555br, 562br.

Magnum: Rene Burri 262tr.
Mary Evans Picture Library: 39br, 495crb, 495cr; Kieou King 238c.

Nasa: 159cra.
National Trust Photographic Library: John Hammond 299cr.
Nature Picture Library: Bernard Castelein 26crb; G & H Denzau 27cl, 466b; Elio Delia Ferrera 409bl; Martha Holmes 28cl; Pete Oxford 26bc, 29bl; David Pike 409cla; Jose B. Ruiz 28crb, 28br; Warwick Sloss 28crb; Lynn Stone 26cra, 26bl; Solvin Zankl 29clb; Xi Zhinong 409crb.
National Geographic Image Collection: Doug Stern 174bc; Joseph Rock 396bc.
NHPA: 26cla; James Warwick 367br.
N's Kitchen, Lijiang: 583br.

OSF/Photolibrary.com: 27bl; Deni Bown 27clb; Irvine Cushing 27cb; Robert A. Lubeck 29crb; George Reszeter 29clb; Konrad Wothe 27clb.

Panos Pictures: 33cra.
The Peak: 319cr, 319tl.
Marianne Petrou: 526cl.
Photo12.Com: OIPS 115cl, 117cl; Panorama Stock 28cr, 104bl, 111tl, 112cl, 431t, 438br; Panorama Stock/Zhao Guangtian 470clb.
Photolibrary.com: Jiangshu Li 31cr; James Montgomery 14; Keren Su 49c, 50cl; Ming Li 430bl; Panorama 469br; Xin Li 469tr.
Popperfoto.com: 70–71c, 203cra.
Powerstock: Digital Vision Royalty Free 286–7.

By permission of **The Random House Group Ltd**: 269br.
Red Gate Gallery: 101tl.
The Red Mansion Ltd: Cang Xin "The Unification of Heaven and Men (Ice)" 46cla; Fang Lijun "Series 2 no 2" 46–7; Zhan Wang "Torso" 46clb.
Reuters: 359br; Jason Lee 117tr.
Robert Harding Picture Library: 205tr, 517bl; Nigel Blythe 516bc; Panorama Stock 67tc; A.C. Waltham 528bl.

Science & Society Picture Library: 33bl.
Shaanxi History Museum: 62br, 62clb, 172br, 173cra, 173crb.
Shanghai Museum: 196tl, 196cla, 196c, 196clb, 197cl, 197cr, 197tc.
Shangri-La International Hotel Management Ltd.: 554bl, 556tr, 556bl, 558br, 575tl, 579br, 580tl.
Silk Road Lodges: 563tr;
Sinopix Photo Agency: Lou Linwei 48tr, 174br.
Superstock: Stock Connection 220–21; TAO Images 472, 530; Yoshio Tomii 372–3.
The Swatch Art Peace Hotel: 193cla.

The Temple Café: 582t.
Temple Restaurant Beijing: 573tr.
Terracotta Army Museum: 174clb, 175tl, 175cra, 175br, 175cr.
Terra Galleria Photography: Quang Tuan Luong 368tr, 368cr, 369br, 369tc, 370tr.
Thames & Hudson Ltd: Photo Eileen Tweedy 34–5.
Tibet Images: Neville Hopwood 526c.
Tibet Heritage Fund: Andre Alexander 535tl; Yutaka Hirako 535cra.
Topfoto.co.uk: 262cla, 262clb; British Museum 37bc, 69bl; Sven Hedin Foundation 499cra; The Museum of East Asian Art/HIP 67cb.

The Upper House: 555tl, 561br.

Waldorf Astoria Shanghai on the Bund: 557c
The Wellcome Institute Library, London: 38cl.
Werner Forman Archive: 61cb; Forest of Stelae Museum, Xi'an 471cr; P'yongyang Gallery, North Korea 37cla; Peking Palace Museum 64crb; Private Collection 59br, 67c, 69br; Private Collection/Sotheby's 1986 63br; Tanzania National Museum 471bl; Victoria & Albert Museum 59br; Yang-Tzu-Shaw 60crb.

Wordo Kitchen: 585t.

Brian K.h. Yim: 327cl.

Front Endpaper - **Alamy Images**: Beijing Eastphoto stockimages Co.,Ltd Rtc; **Corbis**: Robert Harding World Imagery/Jochen Schlenker Lftl; Keren Su Lfbl; **Dreamstime.com**: Steve Allen Ltl; Gringos4 Rcr; Yiu Tung Lee Lbr; Jun Mu Rbr; William Perry Rtl; Starfield Lc; Wingkit Lbl; Zhaojiankang Lcl; **Fotolia**: Gary Lbc; **Getty Images**: AWL Images/Christian Kober Rtr; Walter Bibikow Lclb; HAIBO BI Lcr; Luis Castaneda Inc. Rcl; Feng Wei Photography Ltc; Huang Xin Rcrb; **Superstock**: TAO Images Ltr.

Cover Front and Spine – **Alamy Stock Photo:** Li Ding
Back Cover – **Dreamstime.com:** Rigamondis

Glossary

Architecture

cheng city; also means city wall
chorten or stupa, a Buddhist tower containing sacred objects
dian pavilion
dougong elaborate bracket attaching column to beam
ge storied pavilion
gompa Tibetan monastery
gong palace; usually denotes a Daoist temple
gulou drum tower
hutong alleyway
ling tomb
lou storied building
men city gate
miao temple, usually Confucian
mu tomb
nanmu cedar with much-valued straight trunk used for columns
paifang ornamental gateway
pailou ornamental gateway
qiao bridge
si temple, usually Buddhist
siheyuan courtyard house
Spirit Tower pavilion at entrance to an imperial tomb
Spirit Way straight road leading to an imperial tomb and lined with guardian statues
stele free-standing stone slab or pillar engraved with text
stupa a Buddhist tower containing sacred objects
ta pagoda
tang hall
yuan garden
zhonglou bell tower

Culture

celadon pottery with greenish glaze
cloisonné enameling, in which the enamel is raised and separated by fine pieces of wire
erhu two-stringed fiddle
huaju spoken theater
jingju Beijing Opera
lacquer wood glazed with sap from the lac tree which is carved before completely dry *(see p298)*
lusheng bamboo instrument with numerous pipes
model opera operas based on a proletarian heroic model, promoted by Mao's wife Jiang Qing during the Cultural Revolution
pipa lute-like instrument
porcelain translucent ceramic ware made from clay containing kaolin and feldspar, and fired at high temperatures *(see p260)*
sancai tri-glazed pottery, prevalent during Tang dynasty
sanxian three-stringed lute
sheng modern instrument based on the *lusheng* with 17 to 37 pipes
suona double-reeded wind instrument, similar to an oboe
taotie pattern on Shang bronze; possibly representing a mythical man-eating beast
xiao bamboo flute
xun rounded clay wind instrument
zheng many-stringed zither

History and Politics

cadre Communist party bureaucrat
canton a small territory where foreign traders were required to reside during 18th and 19th centuries
Communist Party ruling party in China since 1949
concession an area of land ceded to a foreign government
Cultural Revolution radical attempt to socialize China's culture, 1966–76 *(see pp70–71)*
Gang of Four high-profile group responsible for some of the Cultural Revolution's worst excesses *(see p71)*
Great Leap Forward Mao's disastrous policy to force the collectivism of agriculture (1958–60), resulting in widespread famine
Kuomintang (KMT) founded by Sun Yat-sen; fought the Communists for 25 years under Chiang Kai-shek; moved to Taiwan where it is still a major party
Legalism fascistic political philosophy dominant during the Qin dynasty based on the idea that man is undisciplined and must be controlled through fear
Little Red Book Mao's sayings compiled by Lin Biao, head of the PLA, in 1966 as a treatise for Red Guards and the PLA
Long March epic tactical retreat of the Communist Party from Nationalist forces in 1935 *(see p262)*
Nationalist Party the Kuomintang
People's Liberation Army (PLA) Communist military forces
Red Guard unruly movement approved by Mao during the Cultural Revolution to weed out counter-revolutionaries and destroy evidence of the past
soviet regional Communist base, e.g. Jiangxi Soviet
Special Administrative Region (SAR) regions, such as Hong Kong and Macau, provided with a high degree of autonomy and a capitalist economy
Special Economic Zone (SEZ) areas, such as Shenzhen, set aside in the 1980s for a capitalist test of a freer economy and to attract foreign investment
triad a secret society, especially one involved in organized crime

Natural Features

chi lake or pool
dao island
dong cave
feng peak
gongyuan park
gou gully
hai sea
haitan beach
he river
hu lake
jiang river
karst limestone landscape with irregular peaks, underground streams, caves, and sinkholes *(see pp418–19)*
pubu waterfall
shan mountain
shui water
shuiku reservoir
tan pool
xi stream
xia gorge

Religion and Philosophy

A-Ma Macau's Goddess of the Sea; see Tianhou
Amitabha Buddha Buddha of boundless light
Analects *(Lunyu)* major work compiled by Confucius's followers of his sayings
arhat or *luohan*; one of the Buddha's 18 disciples
Avalokitesvara bodhisattva of compassion
bagua eight trigrams ranged around a *yin-yang* symbol; a codification of *qi (see pp36–7)*
Bodhidarma Indian monk who traveled to China in the 6th century and started the Chan (Zen) sect of Buddhism
bodhisattva Buddhist deities who have postponed nirvana to help others
Bon indigenous animistic faith of Tibet *(see p526)*
Buddha the awakened one, originally the Indian Gautama Buddha; in Chinese and Tibetan schools the Buddha has numerous forms *(see pp36, 491, 526–7)*
Buddhism religion based on the teachings of the 6th-century BC Indian teacher Gautama Buddha

Chan School of Buddhism spread by Bodhidarma; popular in Japan as Zen Buddhism
Chenresig Tibetan name for bodhisattva Avalokitesvara
Confucius or Kong Fuzi (551–479 BC); developed the philosophy of Confucianism, which was then spread by his followers
Confucianism dominant philosophy prescribing a structured society based on filial relationships *(see p36)*
Dafo Great Buddha
Damo Chinese name for Bodhidarma
Dao in Daoism the way that permeates reality; a single cosmic force
Daode Jing Daoist *The Way and Power* classic attributed to Laozi
Daoism philosophy expounding non-action and living in harmony with the Dao or Way; became a pantheistic religion *(see p37)*
dharmapala protector deities of Tibetan Buddhism
Dipamkara in Tibetan Buddhism, the Past Buddha
Eight Immortals Daoist adepts each with a superhuman power
feng shui a form of geomancy that determines the flow of *qi* through a physical place *(see p37)*
fo a Buddha in Putonghua
Gelugpa Most powerful Tibetan Buddhist sect, headed by the Dalai Lama; also called the Yellow Hat sect
Guanyin bodhisattva of compassion in Chinese Buddhism
Guardian Kings four protective deities of the cardinal directions; often stationed at the entrance of a temple
Guru Rinpoche spreader of Buddhism through Tibet
Jampa the Future or Maitreya Buddha in the Tibetan pantheon
Jampelyang bodhisattva of wisdom in Tibetan Buddhism
Jowo Sakyamuni in Tibetan Buddhism, the Present Buddha
karma in Buddhism, the merit accrued by a person's actions, determining their destiny
kora circuits of holy sites made by Tibetan Buddhists to accrue merit
Laozi first Daoist, who may have lived during the 6th century BC and produced the *Daode Jing*
Laughing Buddha Milefo, the Future Buddha
Lunyu Confucian writings, the *Analects*
luohan or *arhat*; one of the Buddha's 18 disciples
Mahayana Greater Vehicle, dominant form of Buddhism in China and Japan with ritual and devotional practices, and worship of *bodhisattvas*
Maitreya the Future Buddha; the Buddha that has yet to come
mandala an esoteric diagram of circles and squares around a central focal point used as a meditation aid and forming an important part of Tibetan Buddhist iconography
Manjushri bodhisattva of wisdom
Marmedze the past or Gautama Buddha
Mazu Goddess of the Sea; see Tianhou
Milefo the Future or Maitreya Buddha represented as the plump Laughing Buddha
nirvana in Buddhism, having broken from the cycle of rebirth; attained via the extinction of desire and individual consciousness
Nyingma oldest Tibetan Buddhist sect founded by Guru Rinpoche
Padmasambhava Guru Rinpoche
Puxian bodhisattva of universal benevolence; rides an elephant
qi concept of vital force and cosmic energy *(see pp38–9)*
Sakyamuni the Historical Buddha; Gautama Buddha
sutra sacred Buddhist writing; a discourse of the Buddha
thangka Buddhist painting on silk; originally used as objects of meditation and portable teaching tools
Theravada (Hinayana, Lesser Vehicle) school of Buddhism practiced in Southeast Asia and India emphasizing the importance of an ascetic way of life
Tianhou Daoist Empress of Heaven and Goddess of the Sea, equal to Buddhist Guanyin *(see p155)*
Tinhau Tianhou in Hong Kong**trigram** one of the eight sets of three broken *(yin)* and unbroken *(yang)* lines combined in pairs to make hexagrams for divination using the *Yijing*
Wenshu bodhisattva of wisdom
yang masculine, sun, positive; interacts with the complementary opposing force of yin
Yijing classic ancient text, *The Book of Changes*, made up of oracles consulted for divination; source of Daoist and Confucian philosophies *(see p39)*
yin feminine, moon, negative; interacts with the complementary opposing force of *yang*

Miscellaneous

bei north
binguan tourist hotel
bowuguan museum
CAAC Civil Aviation Administration Authority
canting restaurant
Cantonese dialect of Chinese spoken in the south
cheongsam a tight-fitting dress with a high collar and slit skirt
CITS China International Travel Service; organization for international tourists, whose main interest is selling tours and tickets
CTS China Travel Service; organization similar to CITS
cun village
da big
dadao wide street or boulevard
dajie avenue (literally "big road")
dong east
fandian hotel or restaurant
fen smallest denomination; there are 100 *fen* to a *yuan*
ger round tent used by nomads of the steppe; a yurt
jiao there are 10 *fen* to one *jiao*; and 10 *jiao* to one *yuan*; also called *mao*
jie street
jiudian hotel
kuai colloquial word for *yuan*
laowai foreigner
lokbar traditional heavy wool Tibetan robe
lu road
mahjong popular rummy-like game played with small tiles
mao colloquial term for *jiao*
nan south
Pinyin a standardized system for transliterating Chinese characters into the roman alphabet
PRC People's Republic of China
PSB Public Security Bureau; branch of the police force that deals with foreigners
Putonghua Mandarin; the form of Chinese that is the official language of China
qigong martial art concentrating on the control of breath and *qi*
renminbi currency; literally "the people's money"
sheng province
shi city or municipality
tai ji quan (supreme ultimate fist) martial art made up of slow, flowing movements *(see p279)*
xi west
yuan China's currency; divided into 10 *jiao* and 100 *fen*; also called *kuai*
zhong middle

Phrase Book

The Chinese language belongs to the Sino-Tibetan family of languages and uses characters which are ideographic – a symbol is used to represent an idea or an object. Mandarin Chinese, known as Putonghua in mainland China, is fairly straightforward as each character is monosyllabic. Traditionally, Chinese is written in vertical columns from top right to bottom left, however the Western style is widely used. There are several romanization systems; the Pinyin system used here is the official system in mainland China. This phrase book gives the English word or phrase, followed by the Chinese script, then the Pinyin for pronunciation.

Guidelines for Pronunciation

Pronounce vowels as in these English words:

a	as in "father"
e	as in "lurch"
i	as in "see"
o	as in "solid"
u	as in "pooh"
ü	as the French u or German ü (place your lips to say oo and try to say ee)

Most of the consonants are pronounced as in English. As a rough guide, pronounce the following consonants as in these English words:

c	as ts in "hats"
q	as ch in "cheat"
x	as sh in "sheet"
z	as ds in "heads"
zh	as j in "Joe"

Mandarin Chinese is a tonal language with four tones, represented in Pinyin by one of the following marks ˉ ˊ ˇ ˋ above each vowel – the symbol shows whether the tone is flat, rising, falling and rising, or falling. The Chinese characters do not convey this information: tones are learnt when the character is learnt. Teaching tones is beyond the scope of this small phrasebook, but a language course book with a cassette or CD will help those who wish to take the language further.

Dialects

There are many Chinese dialects in use. It is hard to guess exactly how many, but they can be roughly classified into one of seven large groups (Mandarin, Cantonese, Hakka, Hui etc.), each group containing a large number of more minor dialects. Although all these dialects are quite different – Cantonese uses six tones instead of four – Mandarin or Putonghua, which is mainly based on the Beijing dialect, is the official language. Despite these differences all Chinese people are more or less able to use the same formal written language so they can understand each other's writing, if not each other's speech.

In an Emergency

Help!	请帮忙！	*Qing bangmang*
Stop!	停住！	*Ting zhu*
Call a doctor!	叫医生！	*Jiao yisheng*
Call an ambulance!	叫救护车！	*Jiao jiuhuche*
Call the police!	叫警察！	*Jiao jiingcha*
Fire!	火！	*Huo*
Where is the hospital/police station?	医院/警察分局在哪里?	*Yiyuan/jingcha fenju zai nali ?*

Communication Essentials

Hello	你好	*Nihao*
Goodbye	再见	*Zaijian*
Yes/no	是 / 不是	*shi/bushi*
… not …	不是	*bushi*
I'm from…	我是 … 人	*Wo shi … ren*
I understand	我明白	*Wo mingbai*
I don't know	我不知道	*Wo bu zhidao*
Thank you	谢谢你	*Xiexie ni*
Thank you very much	多谢	*Duo xie*
Thanks (casual)	谢谢	*Xiexie*
You're welcome	不用谢	*Bu yong xie*
No, thank you	不，谢谢你	*Bu, xiexie ni*
Please (offering)	请	*Qing*
Please (asking)	请问	*Qing wen*
I don't understand	我不明白	*Wo Bu mingbai*
Do you speak English?	你会讲英语吗?	*Ni hui jiang yingyu ma?*
I can't speak Chinese	我不会讲汉语	*Wo buhui jiang hanyu*
Please speak more slowly	请讲慢一点	*Qing jiang man yidian*
Sorry/Excuse me!	抱歉 / 对不起	*Baoqian/duibuqi*
Could you help me please? (not emergency)	你能帮助我吗?	*Ni neng bang zhu wo ma?*

Useful Phrases

My name is ….	我叫 …	*Wo jiao …*
How do you do, pleased to meet you	你好，很高兴见到你。	*Ni hao, hen gaoxing jiandao ni*
How are you?	你好吗?	*Ni hao ma?*
Good morning	早上好	*Zaoshang hao*
Good afternoon/ good day	下午好/你好	*Xiawu hao/ Ni hao*
Good evening	晚上好	*Wanshang hao*
Good night	晚安	*Wan an*
Goodbye	再见	*Zaijian*
Take care	保重	*Bao zhong*
Keep well (casual)	注意身体	*Zhuyi shenti*
The same to you	你也是	*Ni yeshi*
What is (this)?	（这）是什么?	*(zhe) shi shenme?*
How do you use this?	你怎样用这个东西?	*Ni zenyang yong zhege dongxi?*
Could I possibly have …? (very polite)	能不能请你给我 …?	*Neng buneng qing ni gei wo …*
Is there … here?	这儿有 … 吗?	*Zhe'r you … ma?*

Where can I get …?	我在哪里可以得到 …?	*Wo zai na li keyi de dao …?*
How much is it?	它要多少钱?	*Ta yao duoshao qian?*
What time is …?	… 什么时间?	*… shenme shijian*
Cheers! (toast)	干杯	*Ganbei*
Where is the restroom/toilet?	卫生间 / 洗手间在哪里?	*Weishengjian/ Xishoujian zai nali?*
Here's my business card.	这是我的名片。	*Zhe shi wo de mingpian.*

Useful Words

I	我	*wo*
woman	女人	*nüren*
man	男人	*nanren*
wife	妻子	*qizi*
husband	丈夫	*zhangfu*
daughter	女儿	*nü'er*
son	儿子	*er'zi*
child	小孩	*xiaohai*
children	儿童	*er'tong*
businessman/ woman	商人 / 女商人	*shangren/ nüshangren*
student	学生	*xuesheng*
Mr./Mrs./Ms. …	先生 / 太太 / 女士	*xiansheng/taitai/ nüshi*
big/small	大/小	*da/xiao*
hot/cold	热/凉	*re/liang*
cold (to touch)	冷	*leng*
warm	暖	*nuan*
good/not good/ bad	好 / 不好 / 坏	*hao/buhao/ huai*
enough	够了	*goule*
free (no charge)	免费	*mianfei*
here	这里	*zheli*
there	那里	*nali*
this	这个	*zhege*
that (nearby)	那	*na*
that (far away)	那个	*nage*
what?	什么?	*Shenme?*
when?	什么时候?	*Shenme shihou?*
why?	为什么?	*Wei shenme?*
where?	在哪里?	*Zai nali?*
who?	谁?	*Shui?*
which way?	哪个方向?	*Nage fangxiang?*

Signs

open	开	*kai*
closed	关	*guan*
entrance	入口	*rukou*
exit	出口	*chukou*
danger	危险	*weixian*
emergency exit	安全门	*anquanmen*
information	信息	*xinxi*
restroom/toilet (men) (women)	卫生间 / 洗手间（男士）（女士）	*Weishengjian/ Xishoujian (nanshi) (nüshi)*
occupied	占用	*zhanyong*
free (vacant)	空闲	*kongxian*
men	男士	*nanshi*
women	女士	*nüshi*

Money

Could you change this into? please.	请你把它换成 …, 好吗?	*Qing ni ba ta huancheng … hao ma?*
I'd like to cash these travelers' checks.	我想把旅行支票换成现金。	*Wo xiang ba lüxing zhipiao huancheng xianjjin.*
Do you take credit cards/travelers' checks?	你收信用卡 / 旅行支票吗?	*Ni shou xinyongka/ lüxing zhipiao ma?*
bank	银行	*yinhang*
cash	现金	*xianjin*
credit card	信用卡	*xinyongka*
currency exchange office	外汇兑换处	*waihui duihuanchu*
dollars	美元	*meiyuan*
pounds	英镑	*yingbang*
yuan	元	*yuan*

Keeping in Touch

Where is a telephone?	电话在哪里?	*Dianhua zai nali?*
May I use your phone?	我可以用你的电话吗?	*Wo keyi yong nide dianhua ma?*
Mobile phone	手机	*shouji*
sim card	卡	*sim ka*
Hello, this is …	你好，我是 …	*Nihao, wo shi*
I'd like to make an international call	我想打个国际长途电话。	*Wo xiang da ge guoji changtu dianhua.*
Where can I get online?	我可以在哪里上网?	*Wo keyi zai nali shangwang?*
airmail	航空	*hangkong*
e-mail	电子邮件	*dianzi youjian*
fax	传真	*chuanzhen*
internet	互联网	*hulianwang*
postcard	明信片	*mingxinpian*
post office	邮局	*youju*
stamp	邮票	*youpiao*
telephone booth	电话亭	*dianhua ting*
telephone card	电话卡	*dianhua ka*

Shopping

Where can I buy …?	我可以在哪里买到 …?	*Wo keyi zai nali maidao …?*
How much does this cost?	这要多少钱?	*Zhe yao duoshao qian?*
Too much!	太贵了！	*Tai gui le!*
I'm just looking	我只是看看。	*Wo zhishi kankan.*
Do you have …?	你有 … 吗?	*Ni you …… ma?*
May I try this on?	我可以试穿吗?	*Wo keyi shi chuan ma?*
My size?	我的尺寸?	*Wo de chicun?*
Please show me that.	请给我看看那个。	*Qing gei wo kankan na ge.*
Does it come in other colors?	有没有其它颜色?	*You meiyou qita yanse?*
black	黑色	*heise*
blue	蓝色	*lanse*
brown	棕色	*zongse*
green	绿色	*lüse*
purple	紫色	*zise*
red	红色	*hongse*
white	白色	*baise*
yellow	黄色	*huangse*
cheap/expensive	便宜 / 贵	*pianyi/gui*
audio equipment	音响设备	*yinxiang shebei*
bookstore	书店	*shudian*
boutique	时装商店	*shizhuangshang-dian*
clothes	衣服	*yifu*
department store	百货商店	*baihuo shangdian*
electrical store	电器商店	*dianqi shangdian*
fish market	鱼市	*yu shi*
folk crafts	民间工艺品	*minjian gongyipin*
ladies' wear	女式服装	*nüshi fuzhuang*
local specialty	地方特产	*difang techan*
market	市场	*shichang*
men's wear	男式服装	*nanshi fuzhuang*
newsstand	报摊	*baotan*
pharmacist	药剂师	*yaojishi*
picture postcard	图片明信片	*tupian mingxinpian*
sale	廉价出售	*lianjiachushou*
souvenir shop	纪念品店	*jinianpin dian*
supermarket	超市	*chaoshi*
travel agent	旅行社	*lüxing she*

Sightseeing

Where is …?	... 在哪里?	*… zai nali?*
How do I get to …?	我怎么到 ...?	*Wo zenme dao …?*
Is it far?	远不远?	*Yuan bu yuan?*
art gallery	美术馆	*meishu guan*
reservations desk	订票台	*dingpiao tai*
bridge	桥	*qiao*
city	城市	*chengshi*
city center	市中心	*shi zhongxin*
free entry	免费入场	*mianfei ruchang*
gardens	花园	*huayuan*
hot spring	温泉	*wen quan*
tourist information office	旅游信息处	*lüyou xinxi chu*
island	岛	*dao*
monastery	寺院	*siyuan*
mountain	山	*shan*
museum	博物馆	*bowuguan*
palace	宫殿	*gongdian*
park	公园	*gongyuan*
port	港口	*gangkou*
river	江，河	*jiang, he*
ruins	废墟	*feixu*
shopping area	购物区	*gouwu qu*
shrine	神殿	*shendian*
street	街	*jie*
temple	寺庙	*si/miao*
tour, travel	旅行	*lüxing*
town	镇	*zhen*
village	村	*cun*
province/county	省 / 县	*sheng/xian*
zoo	动物园	*dongwuyuan*
north	北	*bei*
south	南	*nan*
east	东	*dong*
west	西	*xi*
left/right	左 / 右	*zuo/you*
straight ahead	一直向前	*yizhi xiangqian*
between	在 ... 之间	*zai … zhijian*
near/far	近 / 远	*jin/yuan*
up/down	上 / 下	*shang/xia*
new	新	*xin*
old/former	旧	*jiu*
upper/lower	更高 / 更低	*genggao/gengdi*
middle/inner	中间	*zhongjian*
in	在 ... 里	*zai … li*
in front of	在 ... 前面	*zai … qianmian*

Getting around

airport	机场	*jichang*
bicycle	自行车	*zixingche*
rickshaw	人力车	*renliche*
I want to rent a bicycle	我想租一辆自行车。	*Wo xiang zu yiliang zixingche.*
Ordinary bus	公共汽车	*gonggong qiche*
Express bus	特快公共汽车	*tekuai gonggong qiche*
Minibus	面包车	*mianbaoche*
Main bus station	公共汽车总站	*gonggong qiche zong zhan*
Which bus goes to …?	哪一路公共汽车到 ... 去?	*Nayilu gonggong qiche dao … qu?*
When is the next bus?	下一辆公共汽车是什么时候?	*Xiayiliang gonggong qiche shi shenme shihou?*
Please tell me where to get off?	请告诉我在哪里下车?	*Qing gaosu wo zai nali xia che.*
car	小汽车	*xiaoqiche*
ferry	渡船	*duchuan*
ferry dock	渡口	*du kou*
baggage room	行李室	*xingli shi*
motorcycle	摩托车	*motuoche*
one-way ticket	单程票	*dancheng piao*
return ticket	往返票	*wangfan piao*
taxi	出租车	*chuzuche*
ticket	票	*piao*
ticket office	售票处	*shoupiao chu*
timetable	时刻表	*shikebiao*

Trains

What is the fare to …?	去 ... 的票价是多少?	*Qu … de piaojia shi duoshao?*
When does the train for … leave?	去 ... 的火车什么时候开车?	*Qu … de huoche shenme shihou kai?*
How long does it take to get to …?	去 ... 要多少时间?	*Qu … yao duoshao shijian?*
A ticket to …, please	买一张去 ... 的票。	*Mai yizhang qu … de piao*
Do I have to change?	我要不要换车?	*Wo yao buyao huanche?*
I'd like to reserve a seat, please	我想预定一个座位。	*Wo xiang yuding yige zuowei*
Which platform for the train to …?	去 ... 的火车在哪个站台?	*Qu … de huoche zai nage zhantai?*
Which station is this?	这是什么车站?	*Zhe shi shenme chezhan?*
Is this the right train for …?	这火车是不是去 ...?	*Zhe huoche shi bushi qu …?*
train station	火车站	*huoche zhan*
express train	直达快车	*zhida kuaiche*
fast train	快车	*kuai che*
ordinary train	普通列车	*putong lieche*
line	线路	*xianlu*
local train	地方列车	*difang lieche*
platform	站台	*zhantai*
reserved seat	预定座位	*yuding zuowei*
subway	地铁	*ditie*
train	火车	*huoche*
unreserved seat	未预定的座位	*wei yuding de zuowei*
hard seat	硬座	*yingzuo*
soft seat	软座	*ruanzuo*
hard sleeper	硬卧	*yingwo*
soft sleeper	软卧	*ruanwo*
upgrade ticket	升级车票	*shengji chepiao*

Accommodations

Do you have any vacancies?	你们有没有空房间?	*Nimen you meiyou kong fang jian?*
I have a reservation	我有预定的房间。	*Wo you yuding de fangjian*
I'd like a room with a bathroom	我想要一个有卫生间的套间。	*Wo xiang yao yige you weishengjian de taojian*
What is the charge per night?	每晚的收费是多少?	*Mei wan de shoufei shi duoshao?*
Are the taxes included in the price?	价格有没有包括税?	*Jiage you meiyou baokuo shui?*
Can I leave my luggage here for a little while?	我可以把行李放在这里一会儿吗?	*Wo keyi ba xingli fang zai zheli yihui 'er ma?*
Can I have a look at the room?	我可以看一看房间吗?	*Wo keyi kan yi kan fangjian ma?*
air-conditioning	空调	*Kongtiao*
bath	洗澡	*xizao*
check-out	退房	*tui fang*
deposit	定金	*dingjin*
double bed	双人床	*shuangren chuang*
hair drier	吹风机	*chuifeng ji*
hot (boiled) water	热（开）水	*re (kai) shui*
hotel (upscale)	饭店	*fangdian*
hotel (downscale)	旅馆	*lüguan*
hostel	招待所	*zhaodaisuo*
room	房间	*fangjian*
economy room	经济房	*jingji fang*
key	钥匙	*yaoshi*
front desk	前台	*qiantai*

single/twin room	单人／双人房	*danren/shuangren fang*
single beds	单人床	*danren chuang*
shower	淋浴	*linyu*
standard room	标准房间	*biaozhun fangjian*
deluxe suite	豪华套房	*haohua taofang*

Eating Out

A table for one/two/three, please	请给我一／两／三个人的桌子。	*Qing gei wo yi/liang/san ge ren de zhuozi*
May I see the menu?	请给我看看菜单。	*Qing gei wo kankan caidan*
Is there a set menu?	有没有套餐?	*You meiyou taocan?*
I'd like ….	我想要 ...	*Wo xiang yao …*
May I have one of those?	请给我这个。	*Qing gei wo zhege*
I am a vegetarian	我是素食者。	*Wo shi sushizhe.*
Waiter/waitress!	服务员!	*Fuwuyuan!*
What would you recommend?	你建议那几个?	*Ni tuijian na jige?*
How do you eat this?	这个怎么吃?	*Zhege zenme chi?*
May I have a fork/knife/spoon	请给我一把叉／刀／汤匙。	*Qing gei wo yiba cha/dao/tangshi*
May we have the check please.	请把帐单开给我们。	*Qing ba zhangdan kaigei women*
May we have some more …	请再给我们一些 ...	*Qing zai gei women yixie …*
The meal was very good, thank you	饭菜很好吃,谢谢。	*Fancai hen hao chi, xiexie*
assortment	混合餐	*hunhe can*
packed lunch	盒装午餐	*hezhuang wucan*
breakfast	早餐	*zaocan*
buffet	自助餐	*zizhucan*
chopsticks	筷子	*kuaizi*
delicious	好吃	*haochi*
dinner	晚餐	*wancan*
to drink	喝	*he*
a drink	一杯饮料	*yibei yinliao*
to eat	吃	*chi*
food	食品	*shipin*
full (stomach)	饱	*bao*
hot/cold	热／冷	*re/leng*
hungry	饿	*e*
lunch	午餐	*wucan*
set menu	套餐	*taocan*
spicy	酸辣	*suan la*
hot (spicy)	辣	*la*
sweet	甜	*tian*
mild	淡	*dan*
Western food	西餐	*xi can*

Places to eat

cafeteria/canteen	自助餐馆／餐厅	*zizhucanguan/canting*
coffee shop	咖啡店	*kafei dian*
Internet café	网吧	*wang ba*
local bar	当地酒吧	*dangdi jiuba*
noodle stall	面铺	*mianpu*
restaurant	餐馆	*canguan*
restaurant (upscale)	饭店	*fangdian*
tea garden	茶室	*chashi*
vegetarian restaurant	素菜馆	*sucai guan*

Food

apple	苹果	*pingguo*
bacon	咸肉	*xianrou*
bamboo shoots	笋	*sun*
beancurd	豆腐	*doufu*
bean sprouts	豆芽	*dou ya*
beans	豆	*dou*
beef	牛肉	*niurou*
beer	啤酒	*pijiu*
bread	面包	*mianbao*
butter	黄油	*huangyou*
cabbage	卷心菜	*juanxincai*
cake	蛋糕	*dangao*
chicken	鸡	*ji*
candies	糖果	*tangguo*
crab	蟹	*xie*
duck	鸭	*ya*
eel	鳗	*man*
egg	蛋	*dan*
eggplant	茄子	*qiezi*
fermented soybean paste	酱	*jiang*
fish	鱼	*yu*
fried egg	炒蛋	*chao dan*
fried tofu	油豆腐	*you doufu*
fruit	水果	*shuiguo*
fruit juice	果汁	*guo zhi*
ginger	姜	*jiang*
ham	火腿	*huotui*
hamburger	汉堡包	*hanbaobao*
haute cuisine	美味佳肴	*meiwei jiayao*
hors d'oeuvres	冷盆	*leng pen*
ice cream	冰淇淋	*bingqilin*
jam	果酱	*guojiang*
lobster	龙虾	*longxia*
mackerel	鲭鱼	*qingyu*
mandarin orange	柑橘	*gan ju*
meat	肉	*rou*
melon	瓜	*gua*
mountain vegetables	山地蔬菜	*shandi shucai*
noodles	面	*mian*
egg noodles	鸡蛋面	*jidan mian*
wheat flour noodles	面粉面	*mianfen mian*
rice flour noodles	米粉面	*mifen mian*
octopus	章鱼	*zhangyu*
omelet	煎蛋饼	*jiandanbing*
onion	洋葱	*yangcong*
oyster	牡蛎	*muli*
peach	桃子	*taozi*
pepper	胡椒粉，辣椒	*hujiaofen, lajiao*
pickles	泡菜	*paocai*
pork	猪肉	*zhurou*
potato	土豆	*tudou*
rice	米饭	*mifan*
rice crackers	爆米花饼干	*baomihua bing'gan*
rice wine	米酒	*mi jiu*
roast beef	烤牛肉	*kao niurou*
salad	色拉	*sela*
green salad	绿菜色拉	*lücai sela*
mixed salad	混拌色拉	*hunban sela*
salmon	鲑鱼,大马哈鱼	*guiyu, damahayu*
salt	盐	*yan*
sandwich	三明治	*sanmingzhi*
sausage	香肠	*xiangchang*
scallion	韭葱	*jiucong*
seaweed	海带	*haidai*
shrimp	虾	*xia*
snapper (fish)	笛鲷	*didiao*
soup	汤	*tang*
soy sauce	酱油	*jiangyou*
squid	鱿鱼	*youyu*
steak	牛排	*niupai*
sugar	糖	*tang*
toast	烤面包	*kao mianbao*
trout	鳟鱼	*zunyu*
vegetables	蔬菜	*shucai*
watermelon	西瓜	*xigua*
yoghurt	酸奶	*suannai*

Drinks

beer	啤酒	*pijiu*
black tea	红茶	*hong cha*
coffee (hot)	（热）咖啡	*(re) kafei*
black	不加牛奶	*bu jia niunai*
coffee with milk	加牛奶	*jia niunai*
filter	过滤	*guolü*
cappuccino	卡普契诺咖啡	*kapuqinuo kafei*
cola	可乐	*kele*
green tea	绿茶	*lü cha*
iced coffee	冰咖啡	*bing kafei*
lemon tea	柠檬茶	*ningmeng cha*
milk	牛奶	*niunai*
mineral water	矿泉水	*kuang quanshui*
orange juice	橙汁	*cheng zhi*
soya drink (milk)	豆浆	*dou jiang*
tea (Western-style)	茶（西式）	*cha (xi shi)*
tea with milk	加牛奶的茶	*jia niunai de cha*
water	水	*shui*
whiskey	威士忌	*weishiji*
wine	葡萄酒	*putaojiu*
yoghurt drink	酸奶饮料	*suannai yinliao*

Health

I don't feel well	我感觉不舒服。	*Wo ganjue bu shufu*
I have a pain in …	我 … 疼。	*Wo … teng.*
I'm allergic to …	我对 … 过敏。	*Wo dui … guomin*
acetaminophen (paracetamol)	扑热息痛	*purexitong*
aspirin	阿司匹林	*asipilin*
asthma	哮喘	*xiaochuan*
cold	感冒	*ganmao*
condom	避孕套	*biyuntao*
cough	咳嗽	*kesou*
dentist	牙医	*yayi*
diabetes	糖尿病	*tangniaobing*
diarrhea	腹泻	*fuxie*
doctor	医生	*yisheng*
fever	发烧	*fashao*
flu	流感	*liugan*
headache	头疼	*touteng*
hospital	医院	*yiyuan*
medicine	药品	*yaopin*
mosquito coil	蚊香	*wenxiang*
mosquito netting	蚊帐	*wenzhang*
traditional Chinese medicine	传统中医	*chuantong zhongyi*
pharmacy	药店	*yaodian*
prescription	处方	*chufang*
sanitary pads	卫生巾	*weishengjin*
stomach ache	胃痛	*weitong*
tissues	纸巾	*zhijin*
toothache	牙疼	*yateng*

Numbers

0	零	*ling*
1	一	*yi*
2	二	*er*
3	三	*san*
4	四	*si*
5	五	*wu*
6	六	*liu*
7	七	*qi*
8	八	*ba*
9	九	*jiu*
10	十	*shi*
11	十一	*shiyi*
12	十二	*shier*
20	二十	*ershi*
21	二十一	*ershi yi*
22	二十二	*ershi er*
30	三十	*sanshi*
40	四十	*sishi*
100	一百	*yi bai*
101	一百零一	*yi bai ling yi*
200	二百	*er bai*
300	三百	*san bai*
400	四百	*si bai*
500	五百	*wu bai*
600	六百	*liu bai*
700	七百	*qi bai*
800	八百	*ba bai*
900	九百	*jiu bai*
1,000	一千	*yi qian*
1,001	一千零一	*yi qian ling yi*
2,000	两千	*liang qian*
10,000	一万	*yi wan*
20,000	两万	*liang wan*
100,000	十万	*shi wan*
1,000,000	一百万	*yi bai wan*
123,456	十二万三千四百五十六	*shier wan san qian si bai wushi liu*

Time

Monday	星期一	*xingqiyi*
Tuesday	星期二	*xingqi'er*
Wednesday	星期三	*xingqisan*
Thursday	星期四	*xingqisi*
Friday	星期五	*xingqiwu*
Saturday	星期六	*xingqiliu*
Sunday	星期天	*xingqitian*
January	一月	*yiyue*
February	二月	*eryue*
March	三月	*sanyue*
April	四月	*siyue*
May	五月	*wuyue*
June	六月	*liuyue*
July	七月	*qiyue*
August	八月	*bayue*
September	九月	*jiuyue*
October	十月	*shiyue*
November	十一月	*shiyiyue*
December	十二月	*shi'eryue*
Spring	春	*chun*
Summer	夏	*xia*
fall/autumn	秋	*qiu*
winter	冬	*dong*
noon	中午	*zhongwu*
midnight	午夜	*wuye*
today	今天	*jintian*
yesterday	昨天	*zuotian*
tomorrow	明天	*mingtian*
this morning	今天上午	*jintian shangwu*
this afternoon	今天下午	*jintian xiawu*
this evening	今天晚上	*jintian wanshang*
for the whole day (continuous)	一整天	*yi zheng tian*
every day	每天	*mei tian*
month	月	*yue*
hour	小时	*xiaoshi*
time/hour (duration)	时间	*shijian*
minute	分钟	*fenzhong*
this year	今年	*jin nian*
last year	去年	*qu nian*
next year	明年	*ming nian*
one year	一年	*yi nian*
late	晚	*wan*
early	早	*zao*
soon	很快	*henkuai*
now	现在	*xianzai*

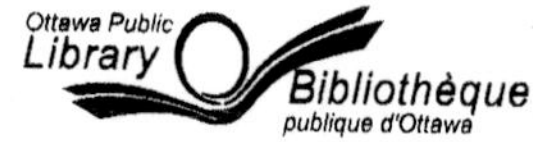
Ottawa Public
Library
Bibliothèque
publique d'Ottawa

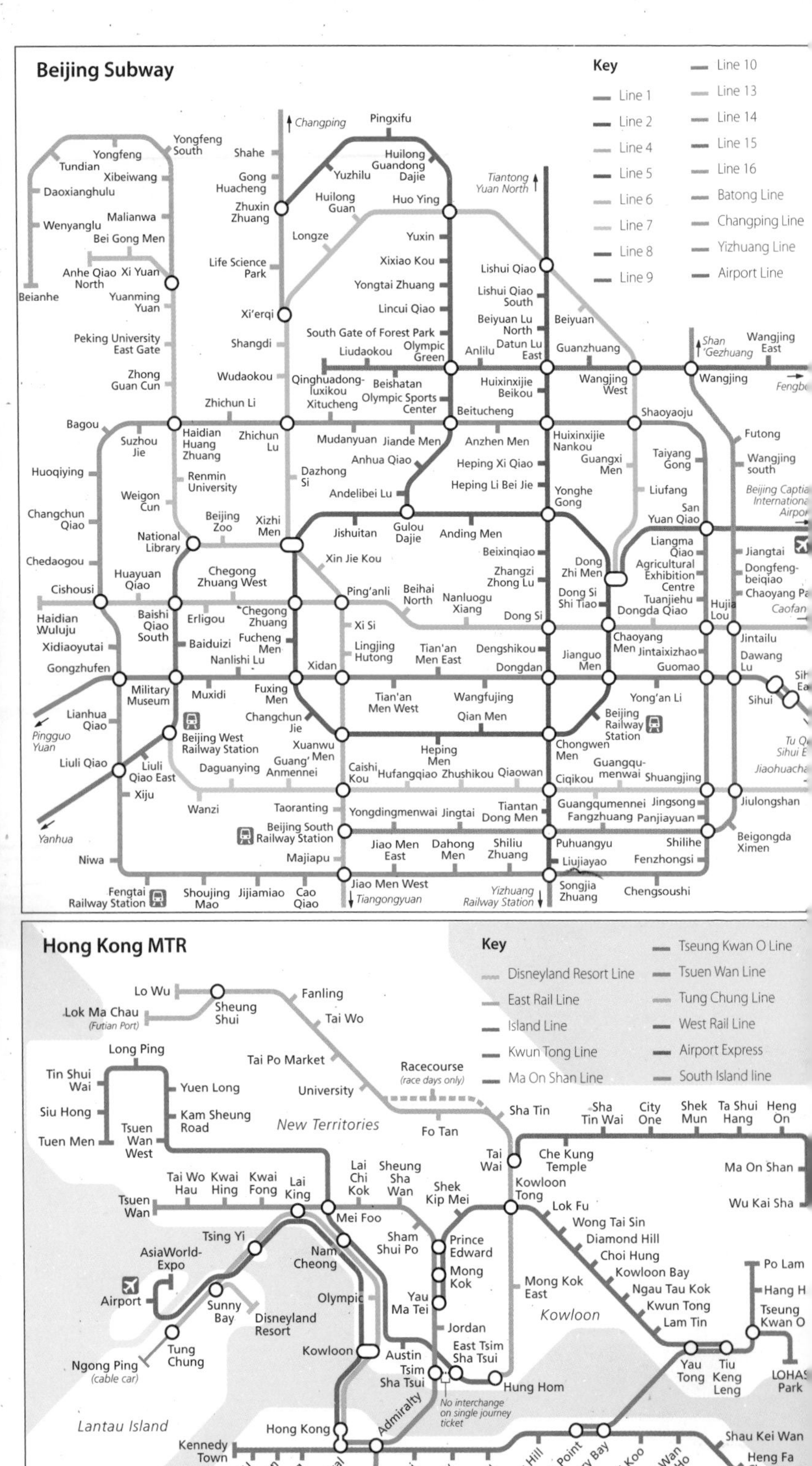

Beijing Subway
Key
Line 1
Line 2
Line 4
Line 5
Line 6
Line 7
Line 8
Line 9
Line 10
Line 13
Line 14
Line 15
Line 16
Batong Line
Changping Line
Yizhuang Line
Airport Line
Changping
Pingxifu
Yongfeng South
Yongfeng
Tundian
Xibeiwang
Daoxianghulu
Malianwa
Wenyanglu
Bei Gong Men
Anhe Qiao North
Xi Yuan
Beianhe
Yuanming Yuan
Peking University East Gate
Zhong Guan Cun
Shahe
Gong Huacheng
Zhuxin Zhuang
Life Science Park
Xi'erqi
Shangdi
Wudaokou
Huilong Guandong Dajie
Yuzhilu
Huilong Guan
Huo Ying
Longze
Yuxin
Xixiao Kou
Yongtai Zhuang
Lincui Qiao
South Gate of Forest Park
Liudaokou
Olympic Green
Tiantong Yuan North
Lishui Qiao
Lishui Qiao South
Beiyuan Lu North
Beiyuan
Anlilu
Datun Lu East
Guanzhuang
Shan 'Gezhuang
Wangjing East
Wangjing
Fengbo
Qinghuadong-luxikou
Beishatan
Xitucheng
Olympic Sports Center
Huixinxijie Beikou
Wangjing West
Zhichun Li
Beitucheng
Shaoyaoju
Bagou
Suzhou Jie
Haidian Huang Zhuang
Zhichun Lu
Mudanyuan
Jiande Men
Anzhen Men
Huixinxijie Nankou
Futong
Huoqiying
Renmin University
Dazhong Si
Anhua Qiao
Heping Xi Qiao
Guangxi Men
Taiyang Gong
Wangjing south
Weigon Cun
Andelibei Lu
Heping Li Bei Jie
Yonghe Gong
Liufang
Beijing Capital International Airport
Changchun Qiao
Beijing Zoo
Xizhi Men
Jishuitan
Gulou Dajie
Anding Men
San Yuan Qiao
National Library
Liangma Qiao
Jiangtai
Chedaogou
Xin Jie Kou
Beixinqiao
Dong Zhi Men
Agricultural Exhibition Centre
Dongfeng-beiqiao
Huayuan Qiao
Chegong Zhuang West
Zhangzi Zhong Lu
Chaoyang Pa
Cishousi
Ping'anli
Beihai North
Nanluogu Xiang
Dong Si Shi Tiao
Tuanjiehu
Hujia Lou
Caofang
Haidian Wuluju
Baishi Qiao South
Erligou
Chegong Zhuang
Dong Si
Dongda Qiao
Xidiaoyutai
Baiduizi
Fucheng Men
Xi Si
Chaoyang Men
Jintaixizhao
Jintailu
Lingjing Hutong
Tian'an Men East
Dengshikou
Jianguo Men
Dawang Lu
Gongzhufen
Nanlishi Lu
Xidan
Dongdan
Guomao
Military Museum
Muxidi
Fuxing Men
Tian'an Men West
Wangfujing
Yong'an Li
Sihui
Sihui East
Lianhua Qiao
Changchun Jie
Qian Men
Beijing Railway Station
Pingguo Yuan
Beijing West Railway Station
Xuanwu Men
Heping Men
Chongwen Men
Tu Qiao
Liuli Qiao
Liuli Qiao East
Daguanying
Guang' Anmennei
Caishi Kou
Hufangqiao
Zhushikou
Qiaowan
Ciqikou
Guangqu-menwai
Shuangjing
Jiaohuachang
Xiju
Wanzi
Taoranting
Yongdingmenwai
Jingtai
Tiantan Dong Men
Guangqumennei
Jingsong
Jiulongshan
Yanhua
Beijing South Railway Station
Fangzhuang
Panjiayuan
Jiao Men East
Dahong Men
Shiliu Zhuang
Puhuangyu
Shilihe
Beigongda Ximen
Niwa
Majiapu
Liujiayao
Fenzhongsi
Jiao Men West
Songjia Zhuang
Fengtai Railway Station
Shoujing Mao
Jijiamiao
Cao Qiao
Tiangongyuan
Yizhuang Railway Station
Chengsoushi
Hong Kong MTR
Key
Disneyland Resort Line
East Rail Line
Island Line
Kwun Tong Line
Ma On Shan Line
Tseung Kwan O Line
Tsuen Wan Line
Tung Chung Line
West Rail Line
Airport Express
South Island line
Lo Wu
Sheung Shui
Fanling
Lok Ma Chau (Futian Port)
Tai Wo
Long Ping
Tai Po Market
Racecourse (race days only)
Tin Shui Wai
Yuen Long
University
Siu Hong
Kam Sheung Road
Sha Tin
Sha Tin Wai
City One
Shek Mun
Ta Shui Hang
Heng On
Tuen Men
Tsuen Wan West
New Territories
Fo Tan
Tai Wai
Che Kung Temple
Ma On Shan
Tai Wo Hau
Kwai Hing
Kwai Fong
Lai King
Lai Chi Kok
Sheung Sha Wan
Shek Kip Mei
Kowloon Tong
Wu Kai Sha
Tsuen Wan
Mei Foo
Lok Fu
Wong Tai Sin
Tsing Yi
Sham Shui Po
Prince Edward
Diamond Hill
AsiaWorld-Expo
Nam Cheong
Choi Hung
Mong Kok
Kowloon Bay
Po Lam
Airport
Sunny Bay
Olympic
Yau Ma Tei
Mong Kok East
Ngau Tau Kok
Hang H
Disneyland Resort
Kwun Tong
Tseung Kwan O
Jordan
Kowloon
Lam Tin
Tung Chung
Kowloon
East Tsim Sha Tsui
Austin
Ngong Ping (cable car)
Tsim Sha Tsui
Hung Hom
Yau Tong
Tiu Keng Leng
LOHAS Park
No interchange on single journey ticket
Lantau Island
Hong Kong
Admiralty
Shau Kei Wan
Kennedy Town
Heng Fa Chuen
HKU
Sai Ying Pun
Sheung Wan
Central
Wan Chai
Causeway Bay
Tin Hau
Fortress Hill
North Point
Quarry Bay
Tai Koo
Sai Wan Ho
Chai Wan
South Horizons
Hong Kong Island